psychology

Important Dates in Psychology

Use this timeline to get a better understanding of key dates in the history of psychology.

360 Plato writes the *Theaetetus* examining theories of perception, knowledge, and truth.

350 Aristotle writes *De Anima* about the relationship of the soul to the body.

1848 Phineas Gage suffers brain damage and provides a famous case study of the effects of brain damage.

1859 Charles Darwin publishes the theory of natural selection, which influences the field of evolutionary psychology.

1884 James-Lange theory of emotion proposed.

1900 Freud publishes *The Interpretation of Dreams*.

1906 Ivan Pavlov publishes his findings on classical conditioning.

1906 Ramon y Cajal discovers that the nervous system is composed of individual cells.

1908 Yerkes-Dodson law proposed to explain relationship between performance and arousal.

1920 Francis Sumner becomes the first African American to receive a Ph.D. in psychology at Clark University.

1920 Watson and Rayner publish the "Little Albert" experiment.

1921 The first neurotransmitter, acetylcholine, is discovered.

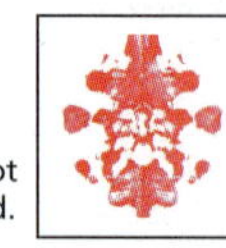

1921 The Rorschach Inkblot Test is developed.

1921 Allport proposes a trait theory of personality.

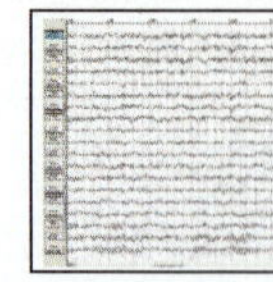

1929 Hans Berger introduces EEG method for studyi[ng] the human brain.

430 Hippocrates proposes that mental illnesses are caused by an imbalance of four major fluids in the human body.

1649 Descartes publishes *The Passion of the Soul*, outlining the pineal gland as the seat of the soul.

1860 Gustav Fechner is often credited with performing the first scientific experiments that would form the basis for experimentation in psychology.

1861 Broca's Area and its role in speech production is discovered.

1874 Wernicke's Area and its role in language comprehension is discovered.

1879 Wilhelm Wundt establishes the first laboratory of psychology in Leipzig, Germany.

1890 William James publishes his book, *Principles of Psychology*.

1892 American Psychological Association (APA) founded and G. Stanley Hall elected first president.

1894 Margaret Floy Washburn is the first woman to receive a Ph.D. in psychology at Cornell University.

1904 Spearman proposes a general factor of intelligence.

1905 Mary Whiton Calkins becomes the first female president of the APA.

1905 Freud proposes his psychosexual theory of personality development.

1905 The first widely used IQ test, the Binet-Simon, was created.

1911 Thorndike proposes the Law of Effect.

1912 Gestalt psychology first developed by Max Wertheimer.

1912 The intelligence quotient is developed by William Stern.

1913 Carl Jung develops his theory of the collective conscious.

1915 Freud first proposes the concept of defense mechanisms.

1930 Tolman and [...] demonstrate laten[t] learning in rats.

1930 Jean Piaget proposes four stag[es of] cognitive develop[ment]

1933 Sigmund [...] proposes the c[...] id, ego, and su[...]

1934 Lev Vy[...] proposes co[...] of zone of p[...] developmen[...]

1935 Hen[...] Murray cre[...] the Thema[...] Appercept[...] Test.

1935 Pref[...] lobotomy developed [...] Dr. Antoni[...] Moniz.

8 B.F. Skinner
oduces the
cept of operant
ditioning.

8
troconvulsive
k first used
human
ent.

9 Clark and
k classic study
rejudice
ducted.

1942 Carl Rogers develops client-centered therapy.

1942 The Minnesota Multiphasic Personality Inventory is created.

1950 Erik Erikson proposes his psychosocial stages of personality development.

1951 Soloman Asch's classic study on conformity conducted.

1952 The first edition of the *Diagnostic and Statistical Manual of Mental Disorders (DSM)* is published.

1952 Chlorpromazine first drug treatment introduced for the treatment of schizophrenia.

1961 Carl Rogers creates the concepts of ideal self, real self, conditional positive regard, and unconditional positive regard.

1961 Muzafer Sherif conducts the "Robber's Cave" study.

1967 Seligman demonstrates learned helplessness in dogs.

1967 Holmes and Rahe create the Social Readjustment Rating Scale.

1967 Beck proposes a cognitive theory for explaining depression.

1968 Roger Sperry demonstrates hemispheric specialization with split-brain patients.

1977 The stress-vulnerability model of schizophrenia proposed by Zubin and Spring.

1977 Thomas and Chess conduct studies of different types of infant temperament.

1978 Elizabeth Loftus puts into question the validity of eyewitness testimony with discovery of misinformation effect.

1979 Mary Ainsworth uses the Strange Situation experiment to study infant attachment styles.

1979 Thomas Bouchard begins the Minnesota study of twins reared apart to identify the influence of genetics and the environment on personality traits.

1994 Herrnstein and Murray publish *The Bell Curve*.

1995 Goleman proposes idea of emotional intelligence.

2000 Genetic researchers finish mapping human genome.

2002 Steven Pinker publishes *The Blank Slate* arguing the concept of *tabula rasa*.

2002 New Mexico is the first state to allow licensed psychologists to prescribe drug treatments for psychological disorders.

2004 Massachusetts first state in US to legalize same-sex marriage.

1940 **1960** **1970** **1990** **2010**

1948 Alfred Kinsey begins survey research on sexual behavior.

1953 The American Psychological Association publishes the first edition of *Ethical Standards in Psychology*.

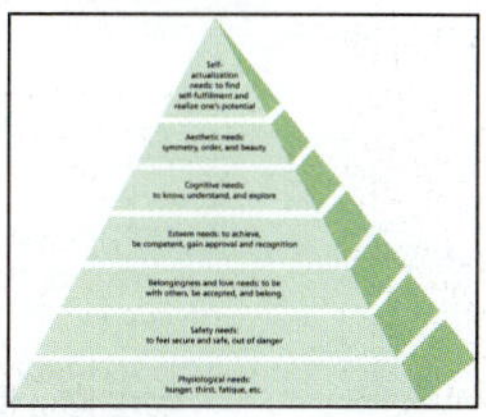

1954 Abraham Maslow proposes a hierarchy of needs to describe human motivation.

1955 Albert Ellis proposes rational emotive behavioral therapy.

1956 Hans Selye proposes the General Adaptation Syndrome to describe responses to stress.

1959 Festinger and Carlsmith publish their study on cognitive dissonance.

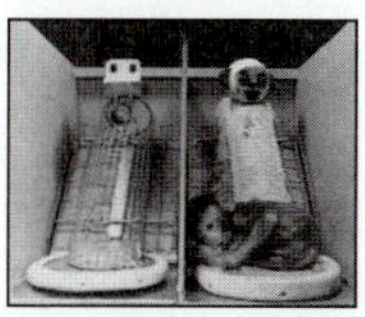

1959 Harlow and Zimmerman demonstrate the importance of contact comfort with their study on infant monkeys.

1962 Cognitive arousal theory of emotion proposed by Schachter and Singer.

1963 Albert Bandura's "Bobo doll" study is conducted.

1963 Stanley Milgram conducts his classic study on obedience.

1963 Lawrence Kohlberg creates his theory of moral development.

1966 Masters and Johnson introduce four stages of sexual response cycle.

1974 Friedman and Rosenman discover link between heart disease and Type-A personality.

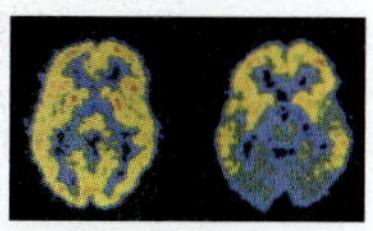

1974 The PET scan is first introduced as a brain imaging technique.

1981 David Wechsler begins to devise IQ tests for specific age groups.

1983 Gardner first proposes his theory of multiple intelligences.

1985 Robert Sternberg proposes the triarchic theory of intelligence.

1989 Albert Bandura proposes the concept of reciprocal determinism.

1996 McCrae and Costa propose the Big Five Personality dimensions.

1997 Elisabeth Kubler-Ross publishes *On Grief and Grieving*, exploring the process of grieving through expansion of her theory of the five stages of death from *On Death and Dying* (1969)

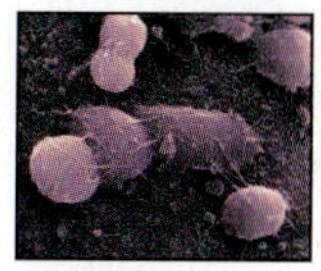

2004 Alexander Storch presents possibility of obtaining stem cells from adults to repair damaged neural tissue.

2005 FDA mandates black box warnings of increased suicide risk on antidepressants.

2008 Law passed requiring insurance companies to provide equal coverage for mental health services.

2009 US President Barack Obama lifts federal funding limits on scientific research involving human stem cells.

2013 DSM-V scheduled for publication.

PEARSON ALWAYS LEARNING

Saundra K. Ciccarelli • J. Noland White

Psychology

A Pearson Learning Solutions Edition
for Ivy Tech Community College
Based on the Third Edition

Taken from:
Psychology, Third Edition
by Saundra K. Ciccarelli and J. Noland White

Cover Art: Courtesy of PhotoDisc/Getty Images.

Taken from:

Psychology, Third Edition
by Saundra K. Ciccarelli and J. Noland White

Published by Prentice Hall
Upper Saddle River, New Jersey 07458

This special edition published in cooperation with Pearson Learning Solutions.

Pearson Learning Solutions, 501 Boylston Street, Suite 900, Boston, MA 02116
A Pearson Education Company
www.pearsoned.com

Printed in the United States of America

2 3 4 5 6 7 8 9 10 V303 16 15 14 13 12 11

000200010270761119

CT

PEARSON

ISBN 10: 1-256-16397-X
ISBN 13: 978-1-256-16397-8

brief contents

contents

psychology in action
secrets for surviving college and improving your grades I-2

1 

the science of psychology 2

2 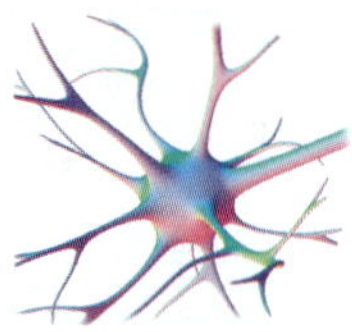

the biological perspective 44

3 sensation and perception 88

4 consciousness: sleep, dreams, hypnosis and drugs 128

5 learning 168

6 

7 

8 

development across the life span 296

9 

motivation and emotion 342

10 

sexuality and gender 376

11

stress and health 408

12

social psychology 446

13 

theories of personality 492

14 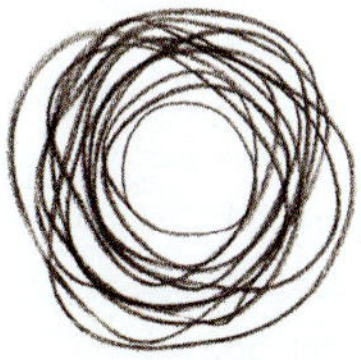

psychological disorders 530

15

psychological therapies 572

why do you need this new edition?

If you're wondering why you should buy this new third edition of *Psychology*, here are 10 good reasons!

1. Engaging online resources to help you succeed! MyPsychLab provides you with online study resources to help make your study time even more effective. MyPsychLab is improved with exciting resources, such as a concept mapping tool to help you personalize your notes and an experiments application that allows you to participate first-hand in psychological experiments. MyPsychLab: where you are always learning!

2. Get a better grade with the expanded and improved introductory chapter, *Psychology in Action: Secrets for Surviving College and Improving Your Grades.* It provides practical information on study methods as well as strategies for improving your memory.

3. A new Study Tip feature at the beginning of each chapter reminds you to refer back to *Psychology in Action* for helpful tips that will help you succeed in your course.

4. The Visual Concept Summaries at the end of every chapter are redesigned and improved to make your chapter review more effective.

5. New and expanded coverage throughout. Every chapter of the third edition has been updated with current and relevant research citations; instructors will include this new information on your exams.

6. Chapter 2, *The Biological Perspective,* is reorganized to improve its clarity. The section "Looking Inside the Living Brain," is expanded and reorganized to clearly present information on cutting-edge techniques psychologists use to study the brain.

7. Chapter 6, *Memory,* includes the latest information about the famous "patient H. M.," whose case helped revolutionized the scientific study of memory. Learn the amazing story of what happened to his brain after his death in 2008.

8. Chapter 14, *Psychological Disorders,* has been substantially restructured. Disorders such as eating disorders and PTSD, which were previously covered in other chapters, are now included here.

9. Chapter 15, *Psychological Therapies,* includes an extended section on effective therapy, with new discussions of which therapies are the most effective for a variety of disorders.

10. New and compelling topics for many of the book's feature essays will enrich your understanding of how psychology impacts our lives today. New topics include: "Beyond 'Smoke and Mirrors'—The Psychological Science and Neuroscience of Magic," "The Link Between Spanking and Aggression in Young Children," and "The Big Lie: Dr. Andrew Wakefield and the Vaccine Scandal."

the NEW MyPsychLab

Engage. Assess. Succeed.

The NEW MyPsychLab combines original online materials with powerful online assessment to engage students, assess their learning, and help them succeed. MyPsychLab ensures students are always learning and always improving.

new video

New, exclusive 30-minute video segments for every chapter take the viewer from the research laboratory to inside the brain to out on the street for real-world applications.

new experiments

A new experiment tool allows students to experience psychology. Students do experiments online to reinforce what they are learning in class and reading about in the book.

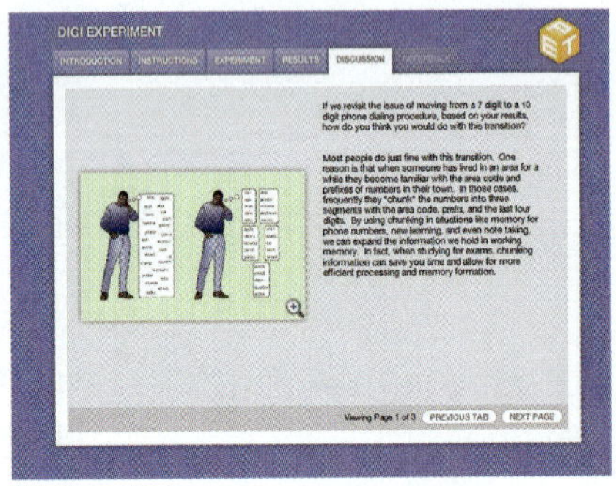

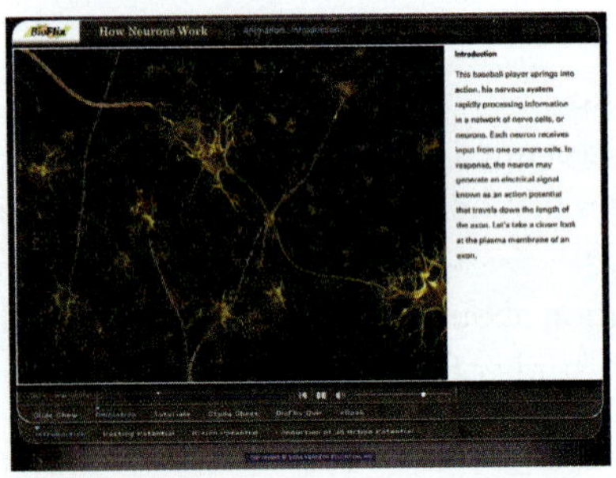

new BioFlix animations

Bring difficult-to-teach biological concepts to life with dramatic "zoom" sequences and 3D movement.

eText

The Pearson eText lets students access their textbook anytime, anywhere, in any way they want it, including listening to it online.

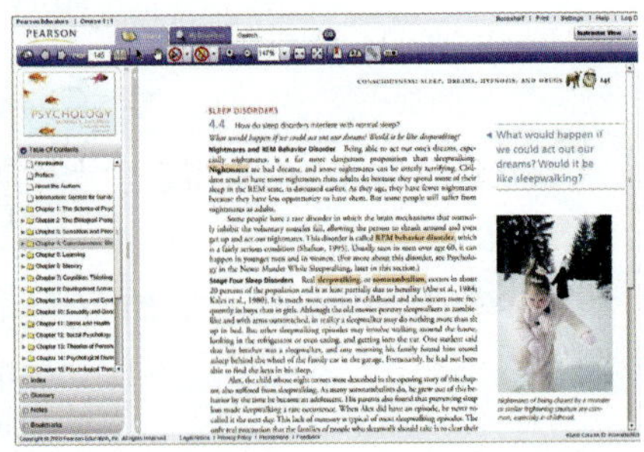

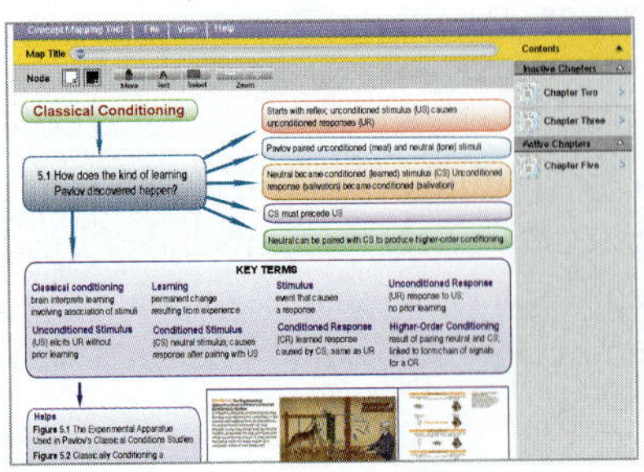

new concept mapping

A new concept mapping tool allows students to create their own graphic study aids or note-taking tools using preloaded content from each chapter. Concept maps can be saved, e-mailed, or printed.

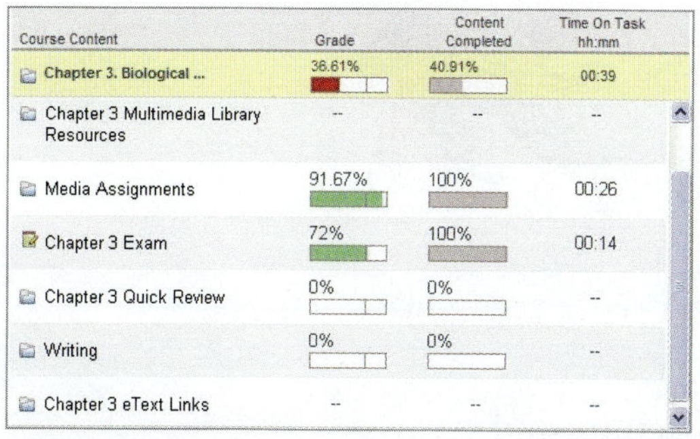

Course Content	Grade	Content Completed	Time On Task hh:mm
Chapter 3. Biological ...	36.61%	40.91%	00:39
Chapter 3 Multimedia Library Resources	--	--	--
Media Assignments	91.67%	100%	00:26
Chapter 3 Exam	72%	100%	00:14
Chapter 3 Quick Review	0%	0%	--
Writing	0%	0%	--
Chapter 3 eText Links	--	--	--

Overall, students are much better prepared for class than students in classes where I don't have a tool like MyPsychLab.

assessment

With powerful online assessment tied to every video, application, and chapter of the text, students can get immediate feedback. Instructors can see what their students know and what they don't know with just a few clicks. Instructors can then personalize MyPsychLab course materials to meet the needs of their students.

MyPsychLab allows us to take assessments and connect them to outcomes in accordance with APA guidelines.

new APA assessments

A unique bank of assessment items allows instructors to assess student progress against the American Psychological Association's Learning Goals and Outcomes. These assessments have been keyed to the APA's latest progressive Learning Outcomes (basic, developing, advanced) published in 2008.

In nine years of experience MyPsychLab has been completely reliable and has never gone down.

Proven Results

Instructors and students have been using MyPsychLab for nearly 10 years. To date, over 500,000 students have used MyPsychLab. During that time, three white papers on the efficacy of MyPsychLab were published. Both the white papers and user feedback show compelling results: MyPsychLab helps students succeed and improve their test scores. One of the key ways MyPsychLab improves student outcomes is by providing continuous assessment as part of the learning process. Over the years, both instructor and student feedback have guided numerous improvements, making MyPsychLab even more flexible and effective.

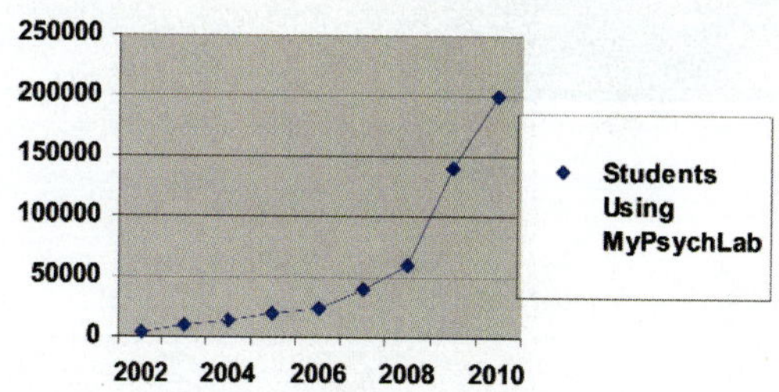

Faculty Advisor Program

Pearson is committed to helping instructors and students succeed with MyPsychLab. To that end, we offer a Psychology Faculty Advisor Program designed to provide peer-to-peer support for new users of MyPsychLab. Experienced Faculty Advisors help instructors understand how MyPsychLab can improve student performance. To learn more about the Faculty Advisor Program, please contact your local Pearson representative or one of the Faculty Advisors listed below:

Noland White at noland.white@gcsu.edu

Gabe Mydland at gabe.mydland@dsu.edu

Teresa Stalvey at stalveyt@nfcc.edu

MyPsychLab simplifies my life and allows me be more informative, knowledgeable, creative, and entertaining. The entertainment factor increases the number of students that sign up for my class.

presentation resources for instructors

Powerful and Exclusive

Instructors consistently tell us that making their classroom lectures and online instruction exciting and dynamic is a top priority in order to engage students and bring psychology to life. We have been listening and we have responded by creating state-of-the-art presentation resources, putting the most powerful presentation resources at your fingertips.

NEW! MyPsychLab video series (17 episodes)

This new video series offers instructors and students the most current and cutting-edge introductory psychology video content available anywhere. These exclusive videos take the viewer into today's research laboratories, inside the body and brain via breathtaking animations, and onto the street for real-world applications. Guided by the Design, Development and Review team, a diverse group of introductory psychology instructors, this comprehensive series features 17 half-hour episodes organized around the major topics covered in the introductory psychology course syllabus. For maximum flexibility, each half-hour episode features several brief clips that bring psychology to life:

- *The Big Picture* introduces the topic of the episode and provides the hook to draw students fully into the topic.
- *The Basics* uses the power of video to present foundational topics, especially those that students find difficult to understand.
- *Special Topics* delves deeper into high-interest and cutting-edge topics, showing research in action.
- *In the Real World* focuses on applications of psychological research.
- *What's in It for Me?* These clips show students the relevance of psychological research to their own lives.

Available in MyPsychLab and also on DVD to adopters of Pearson psychology textbooks (ISBN 0205035817).

NEW! ClassPrep available in MyPsychLab

Finding, sorting, organizing, and presenting your instructor resources is faster and easier than ever before with ClassPrep. This fully searchable database contains hundreds and hundreds of our best teacher resources, such as lecture launchers and discussion topics, in-class and out-of-class activities and assignments, handouts, as well as video clips, photos, illustrations, charts, graphs, and animations. Instructors can search or browse by topic, and it is easy to sort your results by type, such as photo, document, or animation. You can create personalized folders to organize and store what you like, or you can download resources. You can also upload your own content and present directly from ClassPrep.

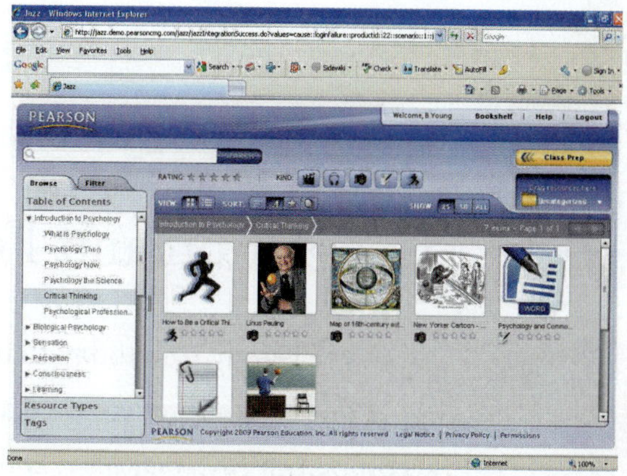

interactive PowerPoint slides

(ISBN 0205153496) These slides bring the powerful Ciccarelli/White design right into the classroom, drawing students into the lecture and providing wonderful interactive activities and rich visuals.

New with this edition, the Interactive PowerPoint Slides now offer embedded video clips, which allow instructors an easy and seamless way to show video content without leaving the slide presentation.

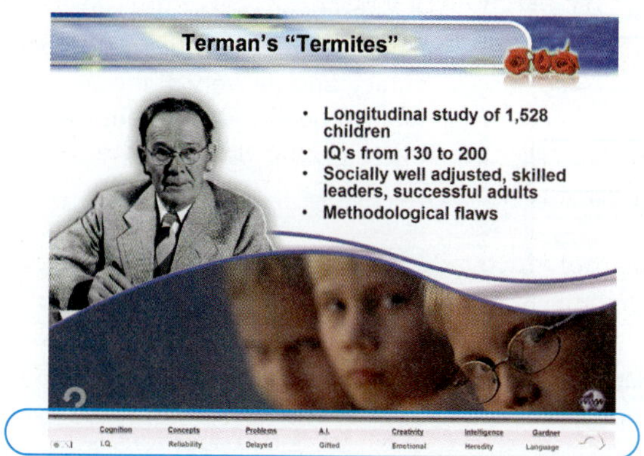

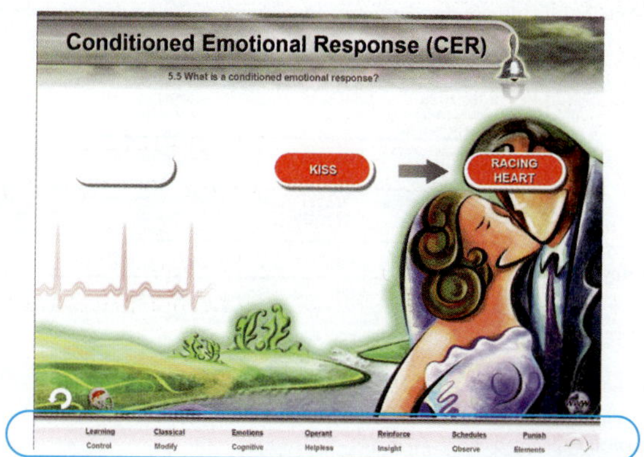

The slides are built around the text learning objectives and offer multiple pathways or links between content areas.

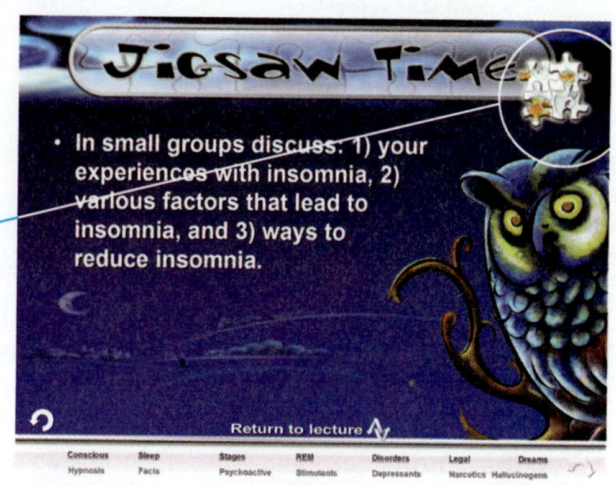

Icons integrated throughout the slides indicate interactive exercises, simulations, and activities that can be accessed directly from the slides.

teaching and learning package

Integration and Feedback

It is increasingly true today that as valuable as a good textbook is, it is still only one element of a comprehensive learning package. The teaching and learning package that accompanies *Psychology*, 3e, is the most comprehensive and integrated on the market. We have made every effort to provide high-quality instructor resources that will save you preparation time and will enhance the time you spend in the classroom. Noland White has overseen the development of each of the components of the teaching and assessment package, by working directly with the authors and reviewers to ensure consistency in quality and content.

The **Test Item File** (ISBN 020515350X) contains a primary test bank with over 3,200 questions. Each chapter includes a two-page Total Assessment Guide that categorizes all test items by learning objective and question type (factual, conceptual, or applied) in an easy-to-reference grid.

TOTAL ASSESSMENT GUIDE — Chapter 5 Learning

Learning Objective	Factual (Multiple Choice)	Conceptual (Multiple Choice)	Applied (Multiple Choice)	True/False Questions	Short Answer Questions	Essay Questions
5.1– What is learning?	1, 2	3, 4, 5		152		180
5.2– What is classical conditioning and who first studied it?	6, 7, 8, 9, 10, 11			153		
5.3– What are the important concepts in classical conditioning?	13, 14, 18, 19, 20		12, 15, 16, 17, 21, 22	154	167	181
5.4– What was Pavlov's classic experiment in conditioning?	23, 27, 28, 30, 31, 32, 33	24, 34	25, 26, 29	155, 156, 157	169, 173	179
5.5– What is a conditioned emotional response?	35, 42, 43, 44, 49, 50, 51, 53, 54	45, 47	36, 37, 38, 39, 40, 41, 46, 48, 52	158, 159	168, 172	177, 183
5.6– Why does classical conditioning work?		55, 56, 57, 58, 59	60	160	175	
5.7– What is operant conditioning and	63, 64, 65	61, 62, 66		161		178

The test item file has been thoroughly revised in response to feedback. It has also been analyzed line-by-line by a development editor and a copy editor to ensure clarity, accuracy, and delivery of the highest quality assessment tool.

Answer Key

1. a Explanation: Alterations due to a genetic blueprint w
examples of maturation.
(Page 166–167, Conceptual, LO 5.1)

2. b Explanation: The food acted as an unconditioned sti
automatically evoked the conditioned response. Foo
causes one to salivate. (Page 167, Applied, LO 5.3)

3. b Explanation: The UCS was a loud noise because it au
evoked a fear response.
(Page 167, Applied, LO 5.5)

4. b Explanation: Thorndike was known for his work wit
(Page 176, Factual, LO 5.7

Definitions of Learning

1. The process by which experience or practice results in a relatively permanent change in behavior or potential behavior is known as __________.
a. learning
b. intelligence formation
c. imprinting
d. cognition
Answer a % correct 89 a= 89 b= 2 c= 5 d= 4 r = .40

2. Learning is a process by which experience results in __________.
a. acquisition of motivation
b. relatively permanent behavior change
c. amplification of sensory stimuli
d. delayed genetic behavioral contributions
Answer b % correct 80 a= 10 b= 80 c= 10 d= 0 r = .23. Learning is a process by which

In addition to the high-quality test bank just described, a second bank of over 2,000 questions is available, which has been class-tested with item analysis available for each question.

An additional feature for the test bank, currently not found in any other introductory psychology text, is the inclusion of rationales for each correct answer and the key distracter in the multiple-choice questions. The rationales help instructors reviewing the content to further evaluate the questions they are choosing for their tests and give instructors the option to use the rationales as an answer key for their students. Feedback from current customers indicates this unique feature is very useful for ensuring quality and quick response to student queries.

The test bank comes with Pearson MyTest (ISBN 0205153453), a powerful assessment generation program that helps instructors easily create and print quizzes and exams. Questions and tests can be authored online, allowing instructors ultimate flexibility and the ability to efficiently manage assessments anytime, anywhere! Instructors can easily access existing questions and then edit, create, and store using simple drag-and-drop and Word-like controls. Data on each question provides information relevant to difficulty level and page number. In addition, each question maps to the text's major section and learning objective. For more information go to **www.PearsonMyTest.com**.

- **Instructor's Resource Manual**, (ISBN 020515347X), offers an exhaustive collection of resources in an easy-to-use format. For each chapter, you'll find activities, exercises, assignments, handouts, and demonstrations for in-class use, as well as useful guidelines for integrating the many Pearson media resources into your classroom and syllabus. The electronic format features click-and-view hotlinks that allow instructors to quickly review or print any resource from a particular chapter. This resource saves prep work and helps you maximize your classroom time.
- A student **Study Guide With Concept Notes** (ISBN 0205153461) includes a chapter summary and practice exams structured around the chapter learning objectives. An innovative study-hints section helps students with the most difficult-to-understand concepts from the chapter. Each chapter's concept summary is included. The Study Guide is perforated and three-hole-punched so students can pull out and use the pages they need.

Accessing All Resources

For a list of all student resources available with Ciccarelli/White, *Psychology*, 3e, go to **www.mypearsonstore.com** and enter the text ISBN 0205832571, and check out the "Everything That Goes With It" section under the photo of the book cover.

For access to all instructor resources for Ciccarelli/White, *Psychology*, 3e, simply go to **http://pearsonhighered.com/irc** and follow the directions to register (or log in if you already have a Pearson login name and password). Once you have registered and your status as an instructor is verified, you will be e-mailed a login name and password. Use your login name and password to access the catalogue. Click on the "online catalogue" link, click on "psychology" followed by "introductory psychology" and then the Ciccarelli/White, *Psychology*, 3e, text. Under the description of each supplement is a link that allows you to download and save the supplement to your desktop.

For technical support for any of your Pearson products, you and your students can contact **http://247.pearsoned.com**.

Note: The Ciccarelli/White, *Psychology*, 3e, textbook is available in paperback (ISBN 0205011357) or casebound (ISBN 0205832571).

learner-centered approach

Curiosity and Dialogue

In recent years there has been an increased focus on a more learner-centered approach in higher education. A learner-centered approach encourages dialogue and recognizes the importance of actively engaging students. The first edition of this textbook came about because we recognized the importance of motivating students to read. When we say "read," we mean *really* read the text, not just skim it looking for answers to some study-guide questions or trying to cram it all in the night before the exam. We set out to write in a style that draws the reader into an ongoing dialogue about psychology. We also want to see students inspired to use the study materials integrated with the text. Our goal is to awaken students' curiosity and energize their desire to learn more, and we are delighted with the feedback from students and instructors who have used our text and who tell us this approach is working.

chapter opening prologues

are designed to capture student interest immediately. Taken from a case study or recent event in the news, these openers engage students in the material from the very start of the chapter. The design truly captures the imagination of students and adds to the appeal of the chapter content.

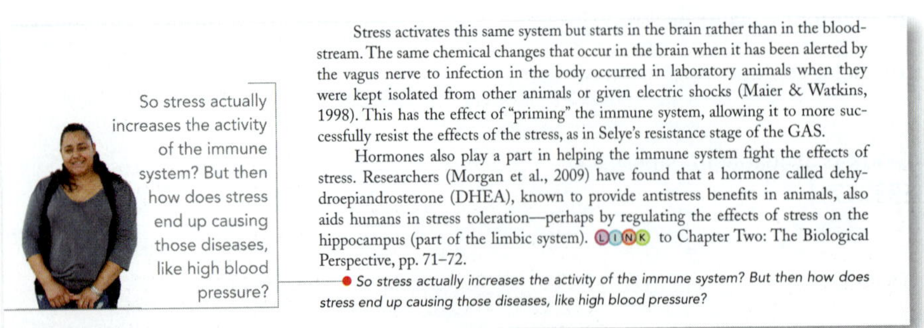

Stress activates this same system but starts in the brain rather than in the bloodstream. The same chemical changes that occur in the brain when it has been alerted by the vagus nerve to infection in the body occurred in laboratory animals when they were kept isolated from other animals or given electric shocks (Maier & Watkins, 1998). This has the effect of "priming" the immune system, allowing it to more successfully resist the effects of the stress, as in Selye's resistance stage of the GAS.

Hormones also play a part in helping the immune system fight the effects of stress. Researchers (Morgan et al., 2009) have found that a hormone called dehydroepiandrosterone (DHEA), known to provide antistress benefits in animals, also aids humans in stress toleration—perhaps by regulating the effects of stress on the hippocampus (part of the limbic system). LINK to Chapter Two: The Biological Perspective, pp. 71–72.

So stress actually increases the activity of the immune system? But then how does stress end up causing those diseases, like high blood pressure?

So stress actually increases the activity of the immune system? But then how does stress end up causing those diseases, like high blood pressure?

student voice questions

encourage students to stop, to clarify, and to think critically. Written by students for students, these questions create a dialogue between the text and the reader and encourage students to ask similar questions in the classroom or online. Cited by students and instructors alike as a truly unique and key feature, we highlight photographs of students who used the text in their introductory class and who provided questions, comments, and invaluable feedback on the book.

Some of his well-known followers were Alfred Adler, Carl Jung, and his own daughter, Anna Freud. Anna Freud began what became known as the ego movement in psychology, which produced one of the best known psychologists in the study of personality development, Erik Erikson. LINK to Chapter Eight: Development Across the Life Span, p. 317.

LINKS

One thing that is often difficult for students to do is make connections from topics in one chapter to topics in other chapters. Throughout each chapter, when one topic relates to another topic, a LINK symbol is shown that includes specific chapter and page numbers. The links refer to content covered within the same chapter or in earlier chapters—as well as in subsequent chapters—giving students a real sense of the connections throughout the text material.

MyPsychLab icons

indicate that students can find related video, podcasts, simulations, practice quizzes, and more in MyPsychLab to expand their learning. There are many more resources available in MyPsychLab than those highlighted in the book, but the icons draw attention to some of the most high-interest materials available at **www.mypsychlab.com**

Watch on **mypsychlab.com**

Listen on **mypsychlab.com**

Explore on **mypsychlab.com**

Simulate on **mypsychlab.com**

Study and Review on **mypsychlab.com**

Read on **mypsychlab.com**

Map the Concepts on **mypsychlab.com**

1.6 1.7 1.8 CONCEPT MAP

scientific method
- perceiving the question about some empirical event for which you would like an explanation; can be derived from the goal of description: What is happening here?
- forming a hypothesis, a tentative explanation about an event
- testing the hypothesis by collecting data, analyzing results
- drawing conclusions about investigation's success or failure to explain event
- reporting your results; share exactly what, why, and how you did it, which provides means for replication

Psychology: The Scientific Methodology
(psychology uses the scientific method to try to determine facts and reduce uncertainty)

descriptive data collection methods
- **naturalistic observation:** observe people or animals in natural environment
- **laboratory observation:** observe people or animals in laboratory setting
- **case studies:** individual is studied in greater detail, researchers try to learn everything they can about the individual
- **surveys:** ask questions about topic researchers are studying via telephone, Internet, or a questionnaire

can lead to formation of hypotheses that can later be tested

PRACTICE quiz How much do you remember? ANSWERS ON PAGE AK-1.

Pick the best answer.

1. In the scientific method, the first step is
   a. reporting your results.
   b. perceiving a question.
   c. drawing conclusions.
   d. testing the hypothesis
2. In a naturalistic observation, the phenomenon in which the behavior of the subjects being observed changes because they are being watched is called
   a. observer bias.
   b. participant observation.
   c. observer effect.
   d. representative sampling.
3. The use of ______________ helps to control for the effect of observer bias.
   a. blind observers
   b. a single trained observer
   c. randomly selected observers
   d. none of the above
4. The main disadvantage of a case study is that it is not
   a. easily done due to the large number of subjects.
   b. detailed enough for most research questions.
   c. generalizable to other similar conditions.
   d. biased.
5. Which of the following is the BEST example of a representative sample?
   a. You ask your fellow students to be participants in a study of adult memory.
   b. You ask people from your church to participate in a study of family values.
   c. You choose people shopping in an expensive store in the mall to respond to your survey.
   d. You choose people randomly from the telephone book to respond to your survey.

Brainstorming: Let's assume that you want to find out if telepathy really exists. Would any of the descriptive methods for studying behavior be a good method to use in examining this question? Why or why not?

concept maps and practice quizzes

are included in each chapter at the end of every major section. Concept mapping is a key study tool for students, and its use is encouraged in the American Psychological Association assessment guidelines. The section-level maps help make connections and encourage students to stop, review, and reinforce their learning before moving on. Practice quizzes to further help students think critically and apply their understanding are included with each map.

test yourself

sample exams are found at the end of every chapter. Both the quizzes and the end-of-chapter tests are in multiple-choice format to replicate the experience most students have with graded assessments. Answers to all practice quizzes and end-of-chapter tests are in an **Answer Key** found in the back of the book.

test YOURSELF ANSWERS ON PAGE AK-2

Study and Review on **mypsychlab.com** Ready for your test? More quizzes and a customized study plan **www.mypsychlab.com**

Pick the best answer.

1. The approach to motivation that forced psychologists to consider the hereditary factors in motivation was the ________ approach.
   a. arousal c. instinct
   b. drive-reduction d. incentive
2. The need for money is an example of a(n) ________ drive.
   a. primary c. innate
   b. acquired d. instinctive
3. Jocelyn needs to be the one whose ideas are always used and craves prestige among others. She drives an expensive car and wears nothing but the most expensive clothes. Jocelyn is high in the need for ________.
   a. achievement. c. power.
   b. affiliation. d. attention.
4. People who are always looking for a challenge may be high in the need for ________.
   a. achievement. c. power.
   b. affiliation. d. attention.
5. Evidence from a study with 2-year-olds who were given an opportunity to explore a black box with a hole in it suggests that sensation seeking may be ________.
   a. learned. c. acquired over time.
   b. abnormal. d. innate.
6. Gene is trying to choose a snack. There is a bowl of fruit on the table, but there's also a candy bar that he bought yesterday. The fact that Gene feels drawn to choose the candy bar instead of the fruit is an example of the power of ________.
   a. needs. c. incentives.
   b. drives. d. arousal.
7. According to Maslow, a person who wants to become self-actualized must first satisfy ________.
   a. higher needs before other more primary needs.
   b. primary needs such as food and safety.
   c. needs for creativity, justice, and the appreciation of beauty.
   d. needs for achievement, affiliation, and power.
8. Shontia works at a day-care center. The pay is low and the hours are long, but she loves being around children and has no desire to look for a higher paying job. Shontia's motivation appears to be ________.
   a. intrinsic. c. selfish.
   b. extrinsic. d. external.
9. When we eat, the pancreas releases ________, which lowers
11. The rate at which your body burns energy when at rest is called the ________.
   a. basal metabolic rate. c. basal set point.
   b. weight set point. d. weight metabolic rate.
12. According to Rodin, externals are people who may produce insulin in response to anticipating food as a result of ________.
   a. genetic tendencies. c. classical conditioning.
   b. biological sensitivity. d. operant conditioning.
13. If there is a history of obesity in a family, each family member has ________ of becoming obese compared to people without such a family history.
   a. the same risk c. five times the risk
   b. double or triple the risk d. less risk
14. Leptin is a ________ involved in appetite control.
   a. hormone c. organ
   b. fatty tissue d. neurotransmitter
15. Your heart is racing, your breathing is rapid, and your mouth is dry. What emotion are you experiencing?
   a. anger
   b. fear
   c. happiness
   d. It is not always possible to distinguish one emotion from another by physiological reactions only.
16. Dora is experiencing positive emotions while Milly is experiencing negative emotions. If researchers are examining EEG recordings of their brains, where are they most likely to see increases in activity?
   a. in Dora's left frontal lobe c. in their thalamic regions
   b. in Milly's right frontal lobe d. both a and b are correct.
17. The ________ is a brain structure that allows us to quickly and unconsciously respond to potentially dangerous stimuli before we are completely conscious of the threat.
   a. thalamus c. prefrontal cortex
   b. hippocampus d. amygdala
18. In Schachter and Singer's classic study, participants were physically aroused by ________.
   a. exposure to a "happy" man.
   b. exposure to an "angry" man.
   c. receiving epinephrine.
   d. watching an exciting film.
19. The theory of emotion that owes a lot to Darwin's work is the ________ theory.
   a. James-Lange c. Schachter-Singer

concept summaries
at the end of each chapter provide students with a graphic summary of content covered in the chapter. By pulling together the content in this highly visual manner, students can better understand the connections and grasp how the chapter material fits together.

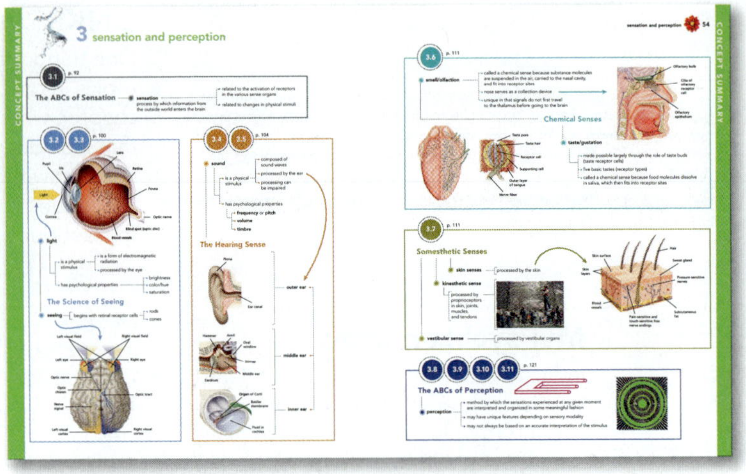

classic studies in psychology

The Angry/Happy Man

In 1962, Stanley Schachter and Jerome Singer designed an experiment to test their theory that emotions are determined by an interaction between the physiological state of arousal and the label, or cognitive interpretation, that a person places on the arousal. Male student volunteers were told that they were going to answer a questionnaire about their reactions to a new vitamin called Suproxin. In reality, they were all injected with a drug called epinephrine, which causes physical arousal in the form of increased heart rate, rapid breathing, and a reddened face—all responses that happen during a strong emotional reaction.

psychology in the news

Cartoon Characters Influence Children's Food and Taste Preferences

Since the 1970s, rates of obesity have doubled for American preschoolers and more than tripled for children ages 6 to 11; these alarming statistics, not surprisingly, are of concern to parents and health-care professionals alike. Each year, food and beverage companies spend more than $1.6 billion targeting young consumers through television, the Internet, video games, and movie- or television-character licensing agreements (Roberto et al., 2010).

Many parents are all too familiar with the allure of cartoon and movie characters on

issues in psychology

The Big Lie: Dr. Andrew Wakefield and the Vaccine Scandal

In 1998, British Dr. Andrew Wakefield (a gastroenterologist and certainly not an autism expert, nor even a pediatrician) published the results of two studies that seemed to link the MMR (measles, mumps, and rubella) vaccine to autism and bowel disease in children (Wakefield et al., 1998). The studies were quickly denounced as inadequate and dangerous by autism specialists and others: There were only 12 children considered in the research, hardly a large enough participant group from which to draw valid conclusions; there were no

other features of each chapter
are special sections covering interesting topics related to the chapter material, especially topics of diversity and cultural interest. These are not set off from the text in boxes, and the authors refer to these features in the chapter content, making it more likely that students will read the enriching material. The test bank, practice quizzes, and the tests at the end of each chapter include questions on this material, further encouraging students to read these features. Each section ends with **Questions for Further Study** that encourage students to think critically about the content they have just read.

162 CHAPTER 4

Individuals sometimes awaken with the very real feeling that they have been visited by aliens, or a ghost, demon or even an angel. The more logical explanation is that they have been startled awake from either a hypnogogic and hypnopompic hallucination experienced at some point as they were sleeping.

Applying Psychology to Everyday Life: Thinking Critically About Ghosts, Aliens, and Other Things That Go Bump in the Night

4.10 What are hypnogogic and hypnopompic hallucinations?

Down through the ages, people have been visited by ghosts, spirits, and other sorts of mystical or mysterious visitors—or so they have believed. In more modern times, ghostly visitations have often given way to aliens, who may perform some sort of medical examination or who may abduct the person, only to return them to their beds. And it is to their beds that they are usually returned, and such visitations typically are experienced when the person is in bed. Is there a simpler, more parsimonious explanation for these experiences?

As mentioned earlier in this chapter, a type of hallucination can occur just as a person is entering Stage 1 sleep, called a *hypnogogic hallucination* (Ohayon et al., 1996; Siegel & West, 1975) If you remember that people in Stage 1 sleep, when awakened, will deny having been asleep, a simple explanation for so-called supernatural visitations does present itself. Hypnogogic hallucinations are not dreamlike in nature. Instead, they feel very real to the person experiencing them (who does not think he or she is asleep, remember). Most common are the auditory hallucinations, in which a person might hear a voice calling out the person's name, not all that unusual and probably not remembered most of the time.

Imagine for a moment, though, that your hypnogogic hallucination is that of some person whom you know to be dead or ill, or a strange and frightening image, perhaps with equally strange and frightening sound effects. That you will remember, especially since you are likely to wake up right after *and be completely convinced that you were awake at the time of the hallucination.* Combine this experience with the natural tendency many people have to want to believe that there is life after death or that there are other sentient life forms visiting our planet, and *voilà!*—a ghost/spirit/alien has appeared.

Sometimes people have a similar experience in the middle of the night. They awaken to find that they are paralyzed and that something—ghost, demon, alien—is standing over them and perhaps doing strange things to their helpless bodies. When a hallucination happens just as a person is in the between-state of being in REM sleep (in which the voluntary muscles are paralyzed) and not-yet-fully-awake, it is called a *hypnopompic hallucination* and is once again a much simpler explanation of visits by aliens or spirits during the night than any supernatural explanation. Such visitations are not as rare as you might think, but once again, it is only the spectacular, frightening, or unusual ones that will be remembered (Cheyne, 2003; Greeley, 1987; Ohayon et al., 1996).

learning outcomes and assessment

Goals and Standards

In recent years many psychology departments have been focusing on core competencies and how methods of assessment can better enhance students' learning. In response, the American Psychological Association (APA) established ten recommended goals for the undergraduate psychology major. Specific learning outcomes were established for each of the ten goals and suggestions were made on how best to tie assessment practices to these goals. In 2008, the APA identified a progression of learning outcomes for the goals associated directly with the discipline of psychology moving from basic (retention and comprehension), to developing (application and analysis), to advanced (evaluation and creation). In writing this text, we have used the APA goals and assessment recommendations as guidelines for structuring content and integrating the teaching and homework materials. For details on the APA learning goals and assessment guidelines, please see **www.apa.org/**.

Based on APA recommendations, each chapter is structured around detailed **learning objectives**. All of the instructor and student resources are also organized around these objectives, making the text and resources a fully integrated system of study. The flexibility of these resources allows instructors to choose which learning objectives are important in their courses as well as which content they want their students to focus on.

learning objectives

- **5.1** What does the term *learning* really mean?
- **5.2** How was classical conditioning first studied, and what are the important elements and characteristics of classical conditioning?
- **5.3** What is a conditioned emotional response, and how do cognitive psychologists explain classical conditioning?
- **5.4** How does operant conditioning occur, and what were the contributions of Thorndike and Skinner?
- **5.5** What are the important concepts in operant conditioning?
- **5.6** What are the schedules of reinforcement?
- **5.7** How does punishment differ from reinforcement?
- **5.8** What are some of the problems with using punishment?
- **5.9** How do operant stimuli control behavior, and what are some other concepts that can enhance or limit operant conditioning?
- **5.10** What is behavior modification, and how can behavioral techniques be used to modify involuntary biological responses?
- **5.11** How do latent learning, learned helplessness, and insight relate to cognitive learning theory?
- **5.12** What occurs in observational learning, and what are the findings from Bandura's classic Bobo doll study and the four elements of observational learning?
- **5.13** What is a real-world example of the use of conditioning?

APA UNDERGRADUATE LEARNING GOALS AND OUTCOMES | **CICCARELLI CONTENT**

1 Knowledge Base of Psychology

Demonstrate familiarity with the major concepts, theoretical perspectives, empirical findings, and historical trends in psychology.

1.1 Characterize the nature of psychology as a discipline.

1.2 Demonstrate knowledge and understanding representing appropriate breadth and depth in selected content areas of psychology: theory and research representing general domains, the history of psychology, relevant levels of analysis, overarching themes, and relevant ethical issues.

1.3 Use the concepts, language, and major theories of the discipline to account for psychological phenomena.

1.4 Explain major perspectives of psychology (e.g., behavioral, biological, cognitive, evolutionary, humanistic, psychodynamic, and sociocultural).

Ch 1: 1.1–1.5
Ch 2: 2.1–2.11
Ch 3: 3.1–3.11
Ch 4: 4.1–4.8
Ch 5: 5.1–5.7, 5.9–5.12
Ch 6: 6.1–6.13
Ch 7: 7.1, 7.3, 7.6–7.9
Ch 8: 8.2–8.5, 8.7–8.11
Ch 9: 9.1–9.9
Ch 10: 10.1–10.6
Ch 11: 11.1–11.3, 11.7–11.10, 11.13
Ch 12: 12.1–12.12
Ch 13: 13.1–13.8
Ch 14: 14.1–14.10
Ch 15: 15.1–15.10
Major concepts all reinforced with student study guide materials, online homework tools, and instructor's teaching and assessment package

2 Research Methods in Psychology

Understand and apply basic research methods in psychology, including research design, data analysis, and interpretation.

2.1 Describe the basic characteristics of the science of psychology.

2.2 Explain different research methods used by psychologists.
- **a.** Describe how various research designs address different types of questions and hypotheses.
- **b.** Articulate strengths and limitations of various research designs.
- **c.** Distinguish the nature of designs that permit causal inferences from those that do not.

2.3 Evaluate the appropriateness of conclusions derived from psychological research.
- **a.** Interpret basic statistical results.
- **b.** Distinguish between statistical significance and practical significance.
- **c.** Describe effect size and confidence intervals.
- **d.** Evaluate the validity of conclusions presented in research reports.

2.4 Design and conduct basic studies to address psychological questions using appropriate research methods.
- **a.** Locate and use relevant databases, research, and theory to plan, conduct, and interpret results of research studies.
- **b.** Formulate testable research hypotheses, based on operational definitions of variables.
- **c.** Select and apply appropriate methods to maximize internal and external validity and reduce the plausibility of alternative explanations.
- **d.** Collect, analyze, interpret, and report data using appropriate statistical strategies to address different types of research questions and hypotheses.
- **e.** Recognize that theoretical and sociocultural contexts as well as personal biases may shape research questions, design, data collection, analysis, and interpretation.

2.5 Follow the APA Code of Ethics in the treatment of human and nonhuman participants in the design, data collection, interpretation, and reporting of psychological research.

2.6 Generalize research conclusions appropriately based on the parameters of particular research methods.
- **a.** Exercise caution in predicting behavior based on limitations of single studies.
- **b.** Recognize the limitations of applying normative conclusions to individuals.
- **c.** Acknowledge that research results may have unanticipated societal consequences.
- **d.** Recognize that individual differences and sociocultural contexts may influence the applicability of research findings.

Ch 1: 1.6–1.12
Ch 2: 2.6 and Classic Studies in Psychology: Through the Looking Glass: Spatial Neglect
Ch 4: Psychology in the News: Murder While Sleepwalking
Ch 5: 5.12 and Classic Studies: Biological Constraints of Operant Conditioning
Ch 6: Classic Studies: Elizabeth Loftus and Eyewitnesses and Applying Psychology to Everyday Life: Alzheimer's Disease
Ch 7: 7.2, 7.4–7.5 and Classic Studies: Terman's Termites
Ch 8: 8.1, 8.6, 8.10 and Classic Studies: The Visual Cliff and Classic Studies: Harlow and Contact Comfort
Ch 9: Classic Studies: The Angry/Happy Man
Ch 10: 10.7 and Classic Studies: Masters and Johnson's Observational Study of the Human Sexual Response
Ch 12: Classic Studies: Brown Eyes, Blue Eyes
Ch 13: 13.9 and Classic Studies: Geert Hofstede's Four Dimensions of Cultural Personality
Ch 15: Psychology in the News: Mental Health on Campus
Appendix A: Statistics A.1–A.6
Appendix B: Applied Psychology B.7
Methodology reinforced with student study guide materials, online homework tools, and instructor's teaching and assessment package

APA UNDERGRADUATE LEARNING GOALS AND OUTCOMES	CICCARELLI CONTENT

3 Critical Thinking Skills in Psychology

Respect and use critical and creative thinking, skeptical inquiry, and, when possible, the scientific approach to solving problems related to behavior and mental processes.

APA Outcomes	Ciccarelli Content
3.1 Use critical thinking effectively. **3.2** Engage in creative thinking. **3.3** Use reasoning to recognize, develop, defend, and criticize arguments and other persuasive appeals. **3.4** Approach problems effectively.	**Ch 1:** 1.13–1.14 and Applying Psychology to Everyday Life: Thinking Critically About Critical Thinking **Ch 3:** Applying Psychology to Everyday Life: Beyond "Smoke and Mirrors"—The Psychological Science and Neuroscience of Magic **Ch 4:** 4.8–4.10, Applying Psychology to Everyday Life: Thinking Critically About Ghosts, Aliens, and Other Things That Go Bump in the Night **Ch 5:** 5.8, 5.12 **Ch 7:** 7.10–7.11 and Psychology in the News: Neuropsychology Sheds Light on Head Injuries **Ch 8:** 8.2, 8.10 and Current Issues: The Big Lie: Dr. Andrew Wakefield and the Vaccine Scandal **Ch 9:** 9.5–9.6 **Ch 10:** Issues in Psychology: Sex Differences in the Brain **Ch 11:** 11.2 and 11.8 and Issues in Psychology: Health Psychology and Stress **Ch 12:** 12.8, 12.12–12.13 Applying Psychology: Anatomy of a Cult **Ch 13:** 13.8–13.9 Applying Psychology to Everyday Life: The Biological Basis of the Big Five **Ch 14:** 14.1 and Issues in Psychology: Abnormality Versus Insanity **Ch 15:** 15.5, 15.7–15.8, 15.11 and Applying Psychology to Everyday Life: Virtual Realities Critical thinking skills reinforced with student study guide materials, online homework tools, and instructor's teaching and assessment package

4 Application of Psychology

Understand and apply psychological principles to personal, social, and organizational issues.

APA Outcomes	Ciccarelli Content
4.1 Describe major applied areas of psychology (e.g., clinical, counseling, industrial/organizational, school, health). **4.2** Identify appropriate applications of psychology in solving problems. **4.3** Articulate how psychological principles can be used to explain social issues and inform public policy. **4.4** Apply psychological concepts, theories, and research findings as these relate to everyday life. **4.5** Recognize that ethically complex situations can develop in the application of psychological principles.	**Ch 1:** 1.5, 1.12, 1.14, study skills **Ch 2:** Psychology in the News: Stem Cells: Fact or Fiction—Focus on the Brain, but Check Your Sources! and Applying Psychology to Everyday Life: Paying Attention to the Causes of Attention Deficit/Hyperactivity Disorder **Ch 4:** Psychology in the News: Murder While Sleepwalking and 4.10, Applying Psychology to Everyday Life: Thinking Critically About Ghosts, Aliens, and Other Things That Go Bump in the Night **Ch 5:** 5.12 and Applying Psychology to Everyday Life: Can You Really Toilet Train Your Cat? **Ch 6:** 6.12–6.13 **Ch 7:** 7.11 and Applying Psychology to Everyday Life: Mental and Physical Exercises Combine for Better Cognitive Health **Ch 8:** 8.10 and 8.11 and Applying Psychology to Everyday Life: Cross-Cultural Views on Death **Ch 9:** Psychology in the News: Cartoon Characters Influence Children's Food and Taste Preferences and Applying Psychology to Everyday Life: When Motivation Is Not Enough **Ch 10:** 10.6–10.9 and Applying Psychology to Everyday Life: The AIDS Epidemic in Russia **Ch 11:** 11.2, 11.6–11.9 and Applying Psychology to Everyday Life: Exercising for Mental Health **Ch 12:** 12.13 and Applying Psychology to Everyday Life: Anatomy of a Cult **Ch 13:** 13.8–13.9 and Applying Psychology to Everyday Life: The Biological Basis of the Big Five **Ch 14:** 14.10 and Applying Psychology to Everyday Life: Taking the Worry Out of Exams **Ch 15:** 15.1, 15.5, 15.7, 15.9, 15.11 **Appendix B:** Applied Psychology Applications reinforced with student study guide materials, online homework tools, and instructor's teaching and assessment package

APA UNDERGRADUATE LEARNING GOALS AND OUTCOMES	CICCARELLI CONTENT

5 Values in Psychology

Value empirical evidence, tolerate ambiguity, act ethically, and reflect other values that are the underpinnings of psychology as a science.

5.1 Recognize the necessity for ethical behavior in all aspects of the science and practice of psychology. **5.2** Demonstrate reasonable skepticism and intellectual curiosity by asking questions about causes of behavior. **5.3** Seek and evaluate scientific evidence for psychological claims. **5.4** Tolerate ambiguity and realize that psychological explanations are often complex and tentative. **5.5** Recognize and respect human diversity and understand that psychological explanations may vary across populations and contexts. **5.6** Assess and justify their engagement with respect to civic, social, and global responsibilities. **5.7** Understand the limitations of their psychological knowledge and skills.	**Ch 1:** 1.12–1.14 **Ch 4:** 4.8–4.9 **Ch 8:** 8.2, 8.4 **Ch 9:** 9.5–9.6 and Psychology in the News: Cartoon Characters Influence Children's Food and Taste Preferences **Ch 10:** 10.2–10.8 and Issues in Psychology: Sex Differences in the Brain **Ch 11:** 11.8–11.9 **Ch 12:** 12.4, 12.7–12.9, 12.11–12.12 and Classic Studies: Brown Eyes, Blue Eyes **Ch 13:** 13.8 **Ch 14:** 14.1 **Ch 15:** 15.11 Values reinforced with content in student study guide and instructor's teaching and assessment package

6 Information and Technological Literacy

Demonstrate information competence and the ability to use computers and other technology for many purposes.

6.1 Demonstrate information competence at each stage in the following process: formulating a researchable topic, choosing relevant and evaluating relevant resources, and reading and accurately summarizing scientific literature that can be supported by database search strategies. **6.2** Use appropriate software to produce understandable reports of the psychological literature, methods, and statistical and qualitative analyses in APA or other appropriate style, including graphic representations of data. **6.3** Use information and technology ethically and responsibly. **6.4** Demonstrate basic computer skills, proper etiquette, and security safeguards.	**Ch 1:** 1.6–1.11 **Ch 2:** 2.6 and Psychology in the News: Fact or Fiction—Focus on the Brain, but Check Your Sources! and Classic Studies in Psychology: Through the Looking Glass: Spatial Neglect **Ch 5:** Classic Studies: Biological Constraints of Operant Conditioning **Ch 6:** Classic Studies: Elizabeth Loftus and Eyewitnesses and Applying Psychology to Everyday Life: Alzheimer's Disease **Ch 7:** Classic Studies: Terman's Termites **Ch 8:** Classic Studies: The Visual Cliff and Classic Studies: Harlow and Contact Comfort **Ch 9:** Classic Studies: The Angry/Happy Man **Ch 10:** 10.7 and Classic Studies: Masters and Johnson's Observational Study of the Human Sexual Response **Ch 12:** 12.2–12.5, 12.8–12.13 and Classic Studies: Brown Eyes, Blue Eyes **Ch 13:** Classic Studies: Geert Hofstede's Four Dimensions of Cultural Personality **Ch 15:** 15.11 **Appendix A:** Statistics **Study Guide Chapter 1:** summary section on the scientific method, and study hints examples 2, 3, and 4; information and technological literacy reinforced with student study guide materials, online homework tools, and instructor's teaching and assessment package

7 Communication Skills

Communicate effectively in a variety of formats.

7.1 Demonstrate effective writing skills in various formats (e.g., essays, correspondence, technical papers, note taking) and for various purposes (e.g., informing, defending, explaining, persuading, arguing, teaching). **7.2** Demonstrate effective oral communication skills in various formats (e.g., group discussion, debate, lecture) and for various purposes (e.g., informing, defending, explaining, persuading, arguing, teaching). **7.3** Exhibit quantitative literacy. Demonstrate effective interpersonal communication skills. **7.4** Exhibit the ability to collaborate effectively.	Ciccarelli Student Voice questions Narrative of the text—like a dialogue between author and reader Test bank essay question Instructor's Resource Manual—see student assignments, lecture launchers, and classroom activities sections Ciccarelli online homework and assessment tools

APA UNDERGRADUATE LEARNING GOALS AND OUTCOMES	CICCARELLI CONTENT

8 Sociocultural and International Awareness

Recognize, understand, and respect the complexity of sociocultural and international diversity.

8.1 Interact effectively and sensitively with people from diverse backgrounds and cultural perspectives. **8.2** Examine the sociocultural and international contexts that influence individual differences. **8.3** Explain how individual differences influence beliefs, values, and interactions with others and vice versa. **8.4** Understand how privilege, power, and oppression may affect prejudice, discrimination, and inequity. Recognize prejudicial attitudes and discriminatory behaviors that might exist in themselves and others.	**Ch 1:** 1.13, 1.14 **Ch 7:** 7.10–7.11 **Ch 9:** 9.5, 9.6 **Ch 10:** 10.2–10.8 and Issues in Psychology: Sex Differences in the Brain **Ch 11:** 11.5–11.6, 11.15–11.16 **Ch 12:** 12.1, 12.3–12.5, 12.7–12.9, 12.12–12.13 and Classic Studies: Brown Eyes, Blue Eyes **Ch 13:** 13.8 **Ch 14:** 14.1 and Issues in Psychology: Abnormality Versus Insanity **Ch 15:** 15.8 Diversity issues also covered in student study guide materials, online homework tools, and instructor's teaching and assessment package

9 Personal Development

Develop insight into their own and others' behavior and mental processes and apply effective strategies for self-management and self-improvement.

9.1 Reflect on their experiences and find meaning in them. **9.2** Apply psychological principles to promote personal development. **9.3** Enact self-management strategies that maximize healthy outcomes. **9.4** Display high standards of personal integrity with others.	**Psychology in Action** study skills material. **Ch 1:** Study skills section **Ch 7:** Applying Psychology to Everyday Life: Mental and Physical Exercises Combine for Better Cognitive Health **Ch 9:** Applying Psychology to Everyday Life: When Motivation Is Not Enough **Ch 10:** 10.7–10.9 and Applying Psychology to Everyday Life: The AIDS Epidemic in Russia **Ch 11:** 11.4, 11.12, 11.14, 11.17 and Applying Psychology to Everyday Life: Exercising for Mental Health **Ch 12:** 12.4–12.5, 12.7, 12.9, 12.12–12.13 **Ch 13:** Applying Psychology to Everyday Life: The Biological Basis of the Big Five **Ch 14:** Applying Psychology to Everyday Life: Taking the Worry Out of Exams **Ch 15:** Psychology in the News: Mental Health on Campus **Appendix B:** Applied Psychology **Study Guide:** Study Challenge sections

10 Career Planning and Development

Pursue realistic ideas about how to implement their psychological knowledge, skills, and values in occupational pursuits in a variety of settings.

10.1 Apply knowledge of psychology (e.g., decision strategies, life span processes, psychological assessment, types of psychological careers) to formulating career choices. **10.2** Identify the types of academic experience and performance in psychology and the liberal arts that will facilitate entry into the workforce, post-baccalaureate education, or both. **10.3** Describe preferred career paths based on accurate self-assessment of abilities, achievement, motivation, and work habits. **10.4** Identify and develop skills and experiences relevant to achieving selected career goals. **10.5** Demonstrate an understanding of the importance of lifelong learning and personal flexibility to sustain personal and professional development as the nature of work evolves.	**Ch 1:** 1.5 **Appendix A:** Statistic A.7 **Appendix B:** Applied Psychology B.1–B.6 Career planning content also found in student study guide materials, online homework tools, and instructor's teaching and assessment package

development story

Insight and Collaboration

The creation of this text and package is the result of the most extensive development investment in a text that this discipline has ever experienced. For the first edition and second edition, over 1,000 instructors and students contributed to decisions regarding issues such as organization, content coverage, pedagogical innovation, and writing style through feedback from reviews and focus groups. The third edition continues to carry the benefit of this input, and has been even further improved based on specific feedback from reviewers of the second edition, including expert reviewers for each major topic area who provided feedback on the currency and accuracy of the research. A full-time development editor analyzed this feedback on the previous edition and worked with the authors, editing the prose line-by-line for clarity. Student reviewers who had used the second edition in their introductory psychology class provided valuable input by evaluating the writing style and in-text learning tools; you will see some of these student reviewers in the photos included with the Student Voice questions. We are grateful to all who provided feedback on changes for the third edition text, as well as changes to the design—which we hope you find as inviting as we do!

INSTRUCTORS

Alabama

Clarissa Arms-Chavez, Auburn University
Lisa D. Hager, Spring Hill College
Royce Simpson, Spring Hill College

Alaska

Gwen Lupfer-Johnson, University of Alaska, Anchorage

Arizona

Olga Carranza, Pima Community College–Desert Vista
Mike Todd, Paradise Valley Community College
Deborah Van Marche, Glendale Community College

California

Patricia Alexander, Long Beach City College
Stacy Bacigalupi, Mt. San Antonio College
Ronald Barrett, Loyola Marymount University
John Billimek, California State University–Long Beach
Jessica Cail, Long Beach City College
David Campbell, Humboldt State University
Linda Chaparro, Oxnard College
Kimberley Duff, Cerritos College
Vera Dunwoody, Chaffey College
Mark Eastman, Diablo Valley College
Michael Feiler, Merritt College
Gaithri Fernando, California State University, Los Angeles
Maria Fitzpatrick, Chaffey College
Lenore Frigo, Shasta College
David Gard, San Francisco State University
Gregg Gold, Humboldt State University
Mark Harmon, Reedley College–Clovis Center
Ann Hennessey, Los Angeles Pierce College
Melissa Holmes, San Joaquin Delta College
Karin Hu, City College of San Francisco
Senqi Hu, Humboldt State University
Lori Hubbard-Welsh, California State University–Chico
Steve Isonio, Golden West Community College
J.R. Jones, Cuyamaca College
Inna Kanevsky, San Diego Mesa College
Fred Leavitt, California State University, East Bay
Randy Martinez, Cypress College
Terry Maul, San Bernardino Valley College
Lee Merchant, Modesto Junior College
Arthur Olguin, Santa Barbara City College
Fernando Ortiz, Santa Ana Community College
Jeff Pedroza, Santa Ana College
Michelle Pilati, Rio Hondo College
Scott Reed, California State University–Chico
Angela Sadowski, Chaffey College
Harry Saterfield, Foothill College
Cindy Selby, California State University–Chico
Alan Spivey, Shasta College
Mark Stewart, American River College
Joan Thomas-Spiegel, Los Angeles Harbor College
Inger Thompson, Glendale Community College

Herkie Williams, El Camino College–Compton Center
Dean Yoshizumi, Sierra College

Colorado

Layton Curl, Metropolitan State College
Karla Gingerich, Colorado State University
Jan Hickman, Westwood College
Misty Hull, Pikes Peak Community College
Diane Martichuski, University of Colorado at Boulder
Lisa Routh, Pikes Peak Community College
Frank Vattano, Colorado State University

Connecticut

Marlene Adelman, Norwalk Community College
Carrie Bulger, Quinnipiac University
Moises Salinas, Central Connecticut State University
Lawrence Venuk, Naugatuck Valley Community College

Florida

Lise Abrams, University of Florida
Melissa Acevedo, Valencia Community College–West
Diane Ashe, Valencia Community College
Kathleen Bey, Palm Beach Community College–Central
Gary Bothe, Pensacola Junior College
Carol Connor, Florida State University
Kelvin Faison, Pasco Hernando Community College
Bethany Fleck, University of Tampa
Jodi Grace, St. Thomas University
Peter Gram, Pensacola Junior College
Joe Grisham, Indian River Community College
Marlene Grooms, Miami Dade College–Homestead Campus
Gregory Harris, Polk Community College
Sheryl Hartman, Miami Dade Community College
Debra Hollister, Valencia Community College
James Jakubow, Florida Atlantic University
Carrie Lane, Florida State University
Manuel Mares, Florida National College
Glenn J. Musgrove, Broward Community College–Central Campus
Jeanne O'Kon, Tallahassee Community College
Jennifer P. Peluso, Florida Atlantic University
Jeanine Plowman, Florida State University
Lawrence Siegel, Palm Beach Community College–South
Wayne Stein, Brevard Community College–Melbourne
Patricia Stephenson, Miami Dade Community College
Richard Townsend, Miami Dade Community College
Barbara Van Horn, Indian River Community College
Steven Zombory, Palm Beach Atlantic University

Georgia

Sheree Barron, Georgia College & State University
Deb Briihl, Valdosta State University
Kristen Diliberto-Macaluso, Berry College
Dan Fawaz, Georgia Perimeter College
Deborah Garfin, Georgia State University
Adam Goodie, University of Georgia
Amy Hackney, Georgia Southern University
Charles Huffman, Georgia Southwestern State University
Jeff Knighton, Gordon College
John Lindsay, Georgia College
Antoinette Miller, Clayton State University
Amy Skinner, Gordon College

Hawaii

Robert Dotson, Honolulu Community College

Idaho

Randy Simonson, College of Southern Idaho

Illinois

Elizabeth Arnott-Hill, Chicago State University
Jason Barker, University of Illinois, Springfield
Rachel Berry, Southeastern Illinois College
Paula J. Biedenharm, Aurora University
Martha Bonne, Joliet Junior College
Lorelei Carvajal, Triton College
David Das, Elgin Community College
Alice Eagly, Northwestern University
Joseph Ferrari, DePaul University
Renae Franiuk, Aurora University
Pablo Gomez, DePaul University
Gary Greenberg, University of Illinois
Christine Grela, McHenry County College
Susan Harris-Mitchell, College of DuPage
Suzanne Hester, Oakton Community College
Lisa Hollis-Sawyer, Northeastern Illinois University
Charmaine Jake-Matthews, Prairie State College
Lynnel Kiely, Harold Washington College
Shari Larson, College of Lake County
Karen Owens, College of Lake County
Deborah Podwika, Kankakee Community College
Eric Rogers, College of Lake County
Ada Wainwright, College of DuPage
Joan Warmbold-Boggs, Oakton Community College

Indiana

Cathy Alsman, Ivy Tech Community College–Terre Haute
Deborah Caudell, Indiana University
Dan Dickman, Ivy Tech Community College of Indiana
Patricia Kemerer, Ivy Tech Community College–Fort Wayne
John Krantz, Hanover College
Darrell Rudmann, Indiana East University
Don Shull, Ivy Tech Community College–Evansville
Deb Stipp-Evans, Ivy Tech Community College–Gary
Colin William, Ivy Tech Community College–Lafayette
Martin Wolfger, Ivy Tech Community College of Indiana

Iowa

Tim Boffeli, Clarke College
Lee Skeens, Southeastern Community College
Susan Troy, Northeast Iowa Community College
Robert West, Iowa State University

Kansas

Deborah Allen, Fort Scott Community College
Diane Kappen, Johnson County Community College
Rupert Klein, Kansas State University
John Sanders, Garden City Community College
Joe Slobko, Garden City Community College

Kentucky

Dan Collins, Morehead State University
Sabra Jacobs, Big Sandy Community and Technical College–Prestonburg
Cecile Marczinski, Northern Kentucky University

Louisiana

Brett Heintz, Delgado Community College
Mike Majors, Delgado Community College–City Park
Jack Palmer, University of Louisiana–Monroe
Mary Boone Treuting, Louisiana State University–Alexandria
Carrie Wyland, Tulane University

Maryland

Patrick Allen, College of Southern Maryland
Katherine Helfrich, Frederick Community College

Cynthia Koenig, St. Mary's College of Maryland
Misty Kolchakian, Anne Arundel Community College

Massachusetts
Marcelle Bartolo-Abela, Holyoke Community and Baypath Colleges
Shirley Cassarra, Bunker Hill Community College
Pamela Ludemann, Framingham State College
Christopher Overtree, University of Massachusetts, Amherst
Chitra Ranganathan, Framingham State College
Doe West, Boston University

Michigan
Joseph Cesario, Michigan State University
Gregory Cutler, Bay de Noc Community College
Michael Drissman, Macomb Community College–South
Mary Eberly, Oakland University
Cassandra George-Sturges, Washtenaw Community College
Terri Heck, Macomb Community College–South
Tracy Juliao, University of Michigan
Patricia Lanzon, Henry Ford Community College
Theresa Lee, University of Michigan
Shawn Talbot, Kellogg Community College
Michael Vargo, Grand Rapids Community College
Amber Vesotski, Alpena Community College
Edie Woods, Macomb Community College

Minnesota
Dawn Albertson, Minnesota State University–Mankato
Tawnda Bickford, Hennepin Technical College
Ivonne Tjoe Fat, Rochester Community and Technical College
Joan Ostrove, Macalester College

Mississippi
Collin Billingsley, Northeast Mississippi Community College
Shaila Khan, Tougaloo Community College
Randy Vinzant, Jones County Junior College

Missouri
Michele Breault, Truman State University
John Gambon, Ozarks Technical College
Matthew Westra, Metropolitan Community College–Longview

Montana
Linda Eagleheart, University of Montana

Nebraska
Patrick Dolan, Drew University
Jean Mandernach, University of Nebraska, Kearney
Keith Matthews, Northeast Community College
James Thomas, University of Nebraska–Omaha

New Hampshire
Mark Henn, University of New Hampshire

New Jersey
Fred Bonato, Saint Peter's College
Deborah Fish Ragin, Montclair State University
Joan Rafter, Hudson County Community College
John Ramirez, Middlesex County College
Darla Silverman, Sussex County Community College
Jonathon Springer, Kean University
John Suler, Rider University
Jordan Vosmik, Drew University
Anthony Zoccolillo, DeVry University

New Mexico
Katherine Demitrakis, Albuquerque Tech–Vocational Institute
Andrea Ericksen, San Juan College
Sarah Erickson, University of New Mexico
Jim Johnson, Central New Mexico Community College
Marisa McLeod, Santa Fe Community College
Brian Parry, Mesa State College
Ron Salazar, San Juan College

New York
Thomas Cleland, Cornell University
Julia Daniels, Westchester Community College
Miles Groth, Wagner College
Melvyn King, SUNY–Cortland
Joe Lao, Teachers College, Columbia University
Michael Magee, Brooklyn College
Martha Mendez-Baldwin, Manhattan College
George Meyer, Suffolk County Community College–Ammerman
William Price, North Country Community College
Billa Reiss, St. John's University
Tim Servoss, Canisius College

North Carolina
Beth Barton, Coastal Carolina Community College and University of North Carolina–Wilmington
Pam Bradley, Sandhills Community College
Kathy Foster, Surry Community College
Donnell Griffin, Davidson County Community College
Amy Holmes, Davidson County Community College
Shirley Kuhn, Pitt Community College
Julie Lee, Cape Fear Community College
Joseph Lowman, University of North Carolina, Chapel Hill
Michele Mathis, Cape Fear Community College
Mark Mitchell, Johnston Community College
Micha Pitzen, Coastal Carolina Community College
John Schulte, Cape Fear Community College
Stephanie Williford, Coastal Carolina Community College

North Dakota
Dorothy Renner, Dickinson State University

Ohio
Leslie Angel, Sinclair Community College
Ronald Craig, Cincinnati State College
Lorry Cology, Owens Community College
Chris Cunningham, Bowling Green State University
Diane Feibel, University of Cincinnati, Raymond Walters College
Carolyn Kaufman, Columbus State Community College
Elaine McLeskey, Belmont Technical College
Keith Syrja, Owens Community College
Courtney Ward, Southwestern College

Oklahoma
James Hunsicker, Southwestern Oklahoma State University
Mike Knight, University of Central Oklahoma
Jerrie Scott, Rose State College

Oregon
Barbara DeFilippo, Lane Community College
Aurora Sherman, Oregon State University

Pennsylvania
Joseph Hardy, Harrisburg Area Community College
Daniel Klaus, Community College of Beaver County
Sonya Lott-Harrison, Community College of Philadelphia
Barbara Radigan, Community College of Allegheny County
Cathy Sigmund, Geneva College
Peter Zubritzky, Community College of Beaver County

Rhode Island
Thomas Malloy, Rhode Island College

South Carolina
Dan Bellack, Trident Technical College
Eurnestine Brown, Winthrop University
Devin Byrd, University of South Carolina–Aiken
William House, University of South Carolina–Aiken
Laura May, University of South Carolina–Aiken
Nancy Simpson, Trident Technical College

South Dakota
Gabe Mydland, Dakota State University

Tennessee
Erskine Ausbrooks, Dyersburg State Community College
Merida Grant, Vanderbilt University
Vivian Grooms, Jackson State Community College
Colin Key, University of Tennessee
Michelle Merwin, University of Tennessee–Martin
Aubrey Shoemaker, Walters State Community College

Texas
Amber Bush Amspoker, University of Houston
Tim Barth, Texas Christian University
Dr. Joyce Bateman-Jones, Central Texas College
Robert Benefield, East Texas Baptist University
Diane Boudreaux-Kraft, Houston Community College–Southwest
Patrick Carroll, University of Texas–Austin
Monica Castator, Navarro College
Dr. Ili Castillo, Houston Community College–Northwest
Natalie Ceballos, Texas State University
Jane Cirillo, Houston Community College–Southeast
Wanda Clark, South Plains College
Perry Collins, Wayland Baptist University
Mary Cordell, Hill College–Hillsboro
Michael Devoley, Lonestar College–Montgomery
Wendy Domjan, University of Texas–Austin
Dawn Eaton, San Jacinto College–South
Daniel Fox, Sam Houston State University
James Francis, San Jacinto College–South
Perry Fuchs, University of Texas–Arlington
Michael Garza, Brookhaven Community College
Robert C. Gates, Cisco Junior College
Jerry Green, Tarrant County College–Northwest
Brooke Hall, Lamar State College
Richard Harland, West Texas A&M University
Rose Hattoh, Austin Community College–South Austin
Laura Hebert, Angelina College
Helen Just, St. Edward's University
Judith Keith, Tarrant County Community College–Northeast
Shirin Khosropour, Austin Community College
Richard Kirk, Texas State Technical College
Nicole Korzetz, Lee College
Irv Lichtman, Houston Community College–Northeast
Nancey Lobb, Alvin Community College
Don Lucas, Northwest Vista College
Ronnie Naramore, Angelina College
Lynn New, East Texas Baptist University
Annette Nolte, Tarrant County College–Northwest
Jane Ogden, East Texas Baptist University
Julie Penley, El Paso Community College
Jean Raniseski, Alvin Community College
Cynthia Reed, Tarrant County College–Northeast
Eric Reittinger, Texas A&M University
Karen Saenz, Houston Community College–Southeast
David Shepard, South Texas Community College
Sangeeta Singg, Angelo State University
Lynn Skaggs, Central Texas College
Peggy Skinner, South Plains College
Christopher L. Smith, Tyler Junior College
Jeanne Spaulding, Houston Community College–Northwest
Genevieve Stevens, Houston Community College–Central
Donna Thompson, Midland College
Cheryl Willard, Lee College
Tom Wood, Sam Houston State University
Melissa Wright, Victoria College
Andrea Zabel, Midland College
Clare Zaborowski, San Jacinto College–Central

Utah
Leigh Shaw, Weber State University
David Yells, Utah Valley State College

Virginia
Jeffrey Clark, Virginia Union University
Rosalyn King, Northern Virginia Community College–Loudoun
Molly Lynch, NOVA–Manassas
Bethany Marcus, ECPI College of Technology
James O'Brien, Tidewater Community College
Theresa Tuttle, ECPI College of Technology
Patti Williams, Tidewater Community College

Washington
Pamela Costa, Tacoma Community College
Craig Cowden, Tacoma Community College
Brian Smith, Seattle Central Community College
Connie Veldink, Everett Community College

West Virginia
Chris LeGrow, Marshall University

Wisconsin
Andrew Berns, Milwaukee Area Technical College
Regan Gurung, University of Wisconsin–Green Bay
Kathleen Kavanaugh, Milwaukee Area Technical College
Bart Van Voorhis, University of Wisconsin–La Crosse
Carmen Wilson-Van Voorhis, University of Wisconsin–La Crosse

Wyoming
Scott Freng, University of Wyoming

Supplements Review Conference Participants
Cathy Alsman, Ivy Tech Community College–Terre Haute
Derek Borman, Mesa Community College
Brenda Fonseca, Mesa Community College
John Gambon, Ozarks Technical Community College
Debra Hollister, Valencia Community College
Jason Spiegelman, Community College of Baltimore County
Fred Whitford, Montana State University

Text Focus Group
John Creech, Collin County Community College
Vera Dunwoody, Chaffey College
Dan Fawaz, Georgia Perimeter College
Dan Grangaard, Austin Community College
Wayne Hall, San Jacinto College–Central
Susan Hornstein, Southern Methodist University
Shirin Khosropor, Austin Community College
Irv Lichtman, Houston Community College
Michael McCoy, Cape Fear Community College
Wendy Mills, San Jacinto College–North
Annette Nolte, Tarrant County College
Laura Overstreet, Tarrant County College
Gloria Scheff, Broward Community College
Nancy Simpson, Trident Technical College

Joe Tinnin, Richland College
Andrea Zabel, Midland College

Reviewer Conference Participants
Dan Bellack, Trident Technical College
Jane Cirillo, Houston Community College Southeast
Vera Dunwoody, Chaffey College
Perry Fuchs, University of Texas, Arlington
Amy Hackney, Georgia Southern University
Jennifer Peluso, Florida Atlantic University
Cynthia Reed, Tarrant County College–Northeast
Stephanie Williford, Coastal Carolina Community College

Supplements Focus Groups
Kristin Anderson, Houston Community College–Southwest
Susan Anderson, University of South Alabama
Melissa Avecedo, Valencia Community College
Mike Barber, Lake City Community College
Kathy Bey, Palm Beach Community College
Jack Chuang, San Jacinto College–Central
Jane Cirillo, Houston Community College–Southeast
Wanda Clark, South Plains College
Perry Collins, Wayland Baptist University
Jacqueline Cuevas, Midwestern State University
Barbara DeFilippo, Lane Community College
Ann Ewing, Mesa Community College
Brenda Fonesca, Mesa Community College
Dan Grangaard, Austin Community College
Sheryl Hartman, Miami Dade College
Karen Hoblit, Victoria College
Debra Hollister, Valencia Community College
Shirin Khospour, Austin Community College
Irv Lichtman, Houston Community College–Northeast
Jerry Marshall, Green River Community College
Marisa McLeod, Santa Fe Community College
Fred Miller, Portland Community College
Jennifer Peluso, Florida Atlantic University
Skip Pollock, Mesa Community College
Genevieve Stevens, Houston Community College–Central
Larry Symon, Western Washington University
Richard Townsend, Miami Dade College
Madeline Wright, Houston Community College–Central
Charles Verschoor, Miami Dade Community College
Andrea Zabel, Midland College
Clare Zaborowski, San Jacinto College–South

STUDENT REVIEWERS

Claudia Adu-Amankwah
Joseph Alfonso
Jasmine Anderson
Evan Aruny
Russell Lee Asher
Brenda Atwell
Lesli Baumer
Elizabeth Belt
Jessica Benz
Jennifer Bieda
Samantha Boggs
Deandre Bravo
Shayla Brooks
Arielle Brooks
Latifah Brown
Nyssa Bryant
Nicholas Cadestin
Penny Callahan
Mariah Carvalho
Omar G. Castillo
Jeanne Chandler
Brittaney Cherry
Ty Childers
Brooke Clevenger
Denise Cole
Zack Cole
Ashlee Coleman
Shawnetta Craet
Heather Darter
Devonah Davis
Monica Delks
Savittri Deonarine
Krystal Desai
Sandy DeSousa
Jacquelin D'Meara
Michael Durocher
Nicholas Echeverri
Kevin Eichelman
Lauren Finch
Joseph Ford II
Reuben Frane
Ying Furey-King
Chad Gabbard
David Gans
Ashlie Garcia
Brandy Gomber
Roberto Gonzales
Jennifer Gonzalez
Jeremy K. Gordon
Jennifer Grexon
Drew Heimlich
Joanna Heintze
Penny Henry
Giselle A. Hernandez
Lamar Holmes
Doris Hyculiak
Matt Ireland
Heesoo Jang
Amelia Javoszuli
Raymonde Jean-Charles
Amy Jones
Matt Jurgensen
Andrea Kaiser
Ihola Kayoise
Habib Khan
Kristina Kupilik
Corinne Laberdee
Elizabeth Lavin
Toni Lee
Jenifer Leiniz
Brenda Limpus
Jerry L. Litton
Andrew Lox
Coranda Lyken
Amanda Martin
Katrina Mathews
Marcus McGriff
Karyn Meekins
Sandra Molinares
Allie Morgan
Sandy Nath
Mykhaylo Neumerzhylskyy
Phil Nufrio
Christine Osorio
Nick Pace
Eric Palm
John Park
Travis Power
Rick Pritchett
Gabrielle Quinones
Ikeyshia Reynolds
Mollie Ried
Zuley Rigo
John Rinehart
Yiovana Rivera
Carol Ruert
Diana Sabatino
Sarah Sahli
Ed Salavarria Jr.
Nicki Schmelzer
Robin Shawner
Eric Sieck
Jessica Sigler
Timothy Paul Singh
Jennifer Smith
Paige Snyder
Abe Sodowsky
Edwin Stagmer
Liz Stanton
David Stewart
Daniel Sweney
Tracy Tackett
Dustin Tanasescu
Jessie Tarlton
William Joseph Tatum
Jacob Terhaar
Monique Trausch
Liem Ung
Surmaliz Valentin
Donna Walker
Kyron Walker
Dana Ward-Dalton
Jessica White
Sharon Williams
Caitlin Williams
Julia Williams
Shamita Williams
Kellie Wolfe
Gil Wright
Mercedes Yount

acknowledgments

It seems like only yesterday that my longtime friend and Prentice Hall superstar, Cindy Sullivan, talked me into writing a textbook. We were in a wonderful little restaurant in Panama City, Florida, along with two other Prentice Hall people. Maybe it was the smell of the salt air wafting onto the veranda where we were having lunch. Maybe it was the crab cakes or possibly the key lime pie. Maybe it was the wine, but something made me say yes. Cindy, thank you for believing in me and gently prodding me into this whole endeavor. (Okay, maybe it was more like a giant shove.) My husband, Joe Ciccarelli, and my young adult offspring, Al and Liz, deserve thanks for putting up with my working at odd hours of the day and night.

Yolanda de Rooy, Craig Campanella, Amber Mackey, and Paige Clunie of the editorial team supported and advised me, and all of these lovely people put a tremendous amount of support behind this third edition—thank you all so much. I have to thank Jessica Mosher, the editor who never quits—and apparently sleeps very little—and somehow manages to have a life squeezed into the spare moments between trips to visit schools. Special thanks to Jeanette Koskinas, Brandy Dawson, and Shauna Fishweicher for a fantastic marketing campaign. Thanks also to Rochelle Diogenes for moral support and great guidance behind the scenes.

Anne DeMarinis is the designer extraordinaire who, for three editions now, has pulled all of this together to create what, I modestly think, is one of the most visually appealing textbooks to ever grace a student's desk. I also owe special thanks to Maria Piper, who coordinated the art program and kept her cool through many rounds of corrections, as well as the other members of the production team: Sherry Lewis (not *that* one), Nancy Wells, and a special thanks to Harriet Tellem, a bastion of production know-how and good sense, who kept us all on track (not an easy job!).

Thank you to all of my supplement authors who waited patiently for the final, final versions of this edition so that they could finish revising all of their work.

Special thanks to Joanne Tinsley, our development editor, presented with the difficult task of following in the shoes of Susanna Lesan (who had the unmitigated gall to retire, of all things). Joanne, thanks for putting up with us pesky, know-it-all authors.

And, of course, I can't forget Noland White, my coauthor, pal, and Grand High Expert, who helped in many ways to make this edition soar to new heights. His extensive revisions and additions to the neurophysiological information in this edition, not to mention his revisions of half of the chapters and all of the chapter maps, have made this edition a real standout. Thank you from the bottom of my heart, Buddy!

Sandy Ciccarelli
Gulf Coast Community College
Panama City, Florida
sciccarelli@gulfcoast.edu

I would like to personally thank:

My wife and best friend, Leah, and our wonderful children, Sierra, Alexis, and Landon, thank you for your love and patience. I would not be able to do any of this without you;

My lead author and collaborator, Sandy Ciccarelli, for making all of this possible in the first place—and for your assistance, advice, and continuing to be the best mentor that I could ever hope to work with!

My students, for your inspiration and encouragement, along with those student and faculty users and reviewers of this text whom I have not met, for your very useful comments and suggestions;

My friends and colleagues in the Department of Psychological Science at Georgia College, for your encouragement, frequent discussions, and feedback, with special thanks to Lee Gillis, John Lindsay, Walt Isaac, and Greg Jarvie for your individual input and support along the way on this edition;

Jessica Mosher, for your enthusiasm, vision, support, and for being such a wonderful person;

Amber Mackey and Joanne Tinsley for stepping in and providing oversight and direction during the revision process;

Everyone who has worked so hard on updating and revising the supplements, including Jason Spiegelman, Fred Whitford, Diane Ash, Deb Hollister, Natalie Ceballos, and Marcus Dickson.

Harriet Tellem, Rebecca Dunn, Anne DeMarinis, Maria Piper, Paige Clunie, Jeanette Koskinas, Stephen Frail, Paul DeLuca, Jackie Moya, Kerri Hart-Morris, Marne Evans, Maggie Fenton, Debra Nichols, and all of the other Pearson and associated staff, for your part in making all of this such a great experience.

Noland White
Georgia College
Milledgeville, Georgia
noland.white@gcsu.edu

about the authors

SAUNDRA K. CICCARELLI is a Professor of Psychology at Gulf Coast Community College in Panama City, Florida. She received her Ph.D. in Developmental Psychology from George Peabody College of Vanderbilt University, Nashville, Tennessee. She is a member of the American Psychological Association and the Association for Psychological Science. Originally interested in a career as a researcher in the development of language and intelligence in developmentally delayed children and adolescents, Dr. Ciccarelli had publications in the *American Journal of Mental Deficiency* while still at Peabody. However, she discovered a love of teaching early on in her career. This led her to the position at Gulf Coast Community College, where she has been teaching Introductory Psychology and Human Development for over 29 years. Her students love her enthusiasm for the field of psychology and the many anecdotes and examples she uses to bring psychology to life for them. Before writing this text, Dr. Ciccarelli authored numerous ancillary materials for several introductory psychology and human development texts.

J. NOLAND WHITE is an Associate Professor of Psychology at Georgia College, Georgia's Public Liberal Arts University, located in Milledgeville. He received both his B.S. and M.S. in Psychology from Georgia College and joined the faculty there in 2001 after receiving his Ph.D. in Counseling Psychology from the University of Tennessee. As a licensed psychologist, Dr. White also works as a consultant in a variety of settings, including adult mental health, developmental disabilities, and juvenile justice. Back on campus, he has an active lab and with his students he is currently investigating the psychophysiological characteristics and neuropsychological performance of adults with and without ADHD. Outside of the lab, Dr. White is engaged in collaborative research examining the effectiveness of incorporating technology in and out of the college classroom to facilitate student learning. He also serves as a mentor for other faculty wanting to expand their use of technology with their classes. In April 2008 he was a recipient of the Georgia College Excellence in Teaching Award.

psychology in action

secrets for surviving college and improving your grades

CHAPTER OUTLINE

- Study Methods: Different Strokes for Different Folks
- Reading Textbooks: Textbooks Are Not Meatloaf
- How to Take Notes: Printing Out PowerPoint Slides Is Not Taking Notes
- Studying for Exams: Cramming Is Not an Option
- Writing Papers: Planning Makes Perfect
- APPLYING PSYCHOLOGY TO EVERYDAY LIFE: Strategies for Improving Your Memory

Pamela was struggling in her introductory psychology class. She would read the assigned chapters in the text, but what she read just didn't seem to "stick," no matter how hard she tried or how many times she read it. The funny thing was that she understood nearly all of what the professor was saying in class, but found it hard to listen *and* try to take notes that made any kind of sense. Her test grades were mediocre C's even though, once the teacher went over the exam, she understood exactly what she had done wrong. Feeling depressed and overwhelmed, she finally went to the instructor to ask for advice.

Her professor listened carefully to Pamela's tale of woe, then suggested that Pamela go to the college's counseling center to seek advice about alternate ways in which she could study. Upon hearing Pamela's problems, the guidance counselor suggested buying a digital recorder for class, so that Pamela would be able to listen to the lecture without having to worry about taking notes at the same time. It was also suggested that Pamela try a technique for reading the text chapters that includes reciting what she has just read aloud—something called the "SQ3R" method. After following the counselor's suggestions, Pamela's grades have gone from C's to A's, not just in her psychology class but in all of her classes. Now she knows how to tailor her study habits to fit her own learning preferences, and it has made all the difference in the world.

Why study how to study?

Pamela's story is not uncommon. Many students find that they need to study in different ways, and also to use the old "listen and write notes" technique. This chapter will detail some helpful study tips as well as provide you with some good information you can use to improve your reading, writing, and memory skills.

learning objectives

PIA.1 What are some different methods of studying?

PIA.2 How should you go about reading a textbook so that you get the most out of your reading efforts?

PIA.3 What are the best ways to take notes in class and while reading the text?

PIA.4 How should you approach studying for exams, and why do different kinds of test questions require different study approaches?

PIA.5 What are the key steps in writing papers for college?

PIA.6 How can you improve your memory for facts and concepts?

warning

Reading the following material may lead to higher grades and lower anxiety

I want to make better grades, But sometimes it seems that no matter how hard I study, the test questions turn out to be hard and confusing and I end up not doing very well. Is there some trick to getting good grades?

I want to make better grades, But sometimes it seems that no matter how hard I study, the test questions turn out to be hard and confusing and I end up not doing very well. Is there some trick to getting good grades?

Many students would probably say that their grades are not what they want them to be. They may make the effort, but they still don't seem to be able to achieve the higher grades that they wish they could earn. A big part of the problem is that despite many different educational experiences, students are rarely taught how to study. Many students entering college have developed a system of taking notes, reading the textbook, and reviewing for exams that may have worked pretty well in the past; but what worked in grade school and high school may not work in college, where the expectations from teachers are higher and the workload is far greater. Students should know five things in order to do their absolute best in any college course:

- How to identify which study methods work best for them and for different kinds of materials.
- How to read a textbook and take notes that are understandable and memorable the *first* time.
- How to listen and take useful notes during lectures.
- How to study efficiently for exams.
- How to write good term papers.

This introduction presents various techniques and information aimed at maximizing knowledge and skills in each of these five areas.

Study Methods: Different Strokes for Different Folks

PIA.1 What are some different methods of studying?

Most college students, at one point or another in their educational experiences, have probably run into the concept of a *learning style,* but what exactly is it? In general, a learning style is the particular way in which a person takes in, or absorbs, information (Dunn et al., 1989, 2001; Felder & Spurlin, 2005). Educators and others who use this concept believe that people take in information in several ways: through the eyes, by reading text or looking at charts, diagrams, and maps; through the ears, by listening, talking things out, and discussing things with others; and through the sense of touch and the movement of the body, by touching things, writing things down, drawing pictures and diagrams, and learning by doing (Barsch, 1996).

For quite some time now, many educators and psychologists have believed that accommodating their teaching methods to each student's learning style is a key element of good instruction: You find out what the learning style is and then adjust your method of teaching to that style. To adapt their teaching, educators began to supplement a straight lecture approach by adding visual elements such as slide presentations or videos, for example. This is not a bad thing, of course: The more varied the presentation, the more likely students are to pay attention. But trying to tailor one lecture to all of the various learning styles? Not so practical (Coffield et al., 2004; Willingham, 2005). Research strongly suggests that a strong and varied teaching style will yield better student success regardless of any differences in students' learning styles (Geake, 2008; Zhang, 2006).

Teachers often use multiple methods to present a point, but trying to cover all learning methods in one lecture would not be practical.

In a fascinating article in *Psychological Science in the Public Interest,* a journal published by the Association for Psychological Science (Pashler et al., 2009), researchers did an extensive literature review of learning-style studies and discovered several key points:

1. Students definitely have preferences about how information is presented to them.
2. Students do seem to have different capabilities when it comes to processing different kinds of information.
3. No real evidence exists that tailoring the presentation of information to different learning styles has any effect on a student's ability to learn the information (Pashler et al., 2009).

What? What was that last bit? There was *no real evidence* that tailoring the instructional method to the student's learning style makes any difference in the student's ability to learn that material. While some learning-styles theorists are critical of the researchers' conclusions (Braio et al., 1997; Drysdale et al., 2001; Ford & Chen, 2001; Glenn, 2009), others go so far as to say that the implication that a student can have only one or two learning styles is a disservice to the student (Henry, 2007). Instead of trying to limit a student's study methods to just one or two modalities (which simply isn't going to happen very often in the world outside academia), wouldn't it be better to help students learn several different styles of studying? We learn many different kinds of things during our lives, and one method of learning probably isn't going to work for everyone. So instead of focusing on different learning styles, this *Psychology in Action* introduction will focus on different *study methods*—take the opportunity to try them out and find which methods work best for you. Table 1 lists just some of the ways in which you can study. All of the methods listed in this table are good for students who wish to improve both their understanding of a subject and their grades on tests. See if you can think of some other ways in which you might prefer to practice the various study methods.

Some students find it helpful to hear the content in addition to reading it. This is especially true when learning a new language. This woman is listening to an audio recording from her textbook as she follows along and looks at the figures and photos.

No matter what the study method, students must read the textbook to be successful in the course. (While that might seem obvious to some, many students today seem to think that just taking notes on lectures or slide presentations will be enough.) The next section deals with how to read textbooks for understanding rather than just to "get through" the material. **Read** on **mypsychlab.com**

Read the handbook *What Every Student Should Know about Study Skills* in the library on **mypsychlab.com**

Reading Textbooks: Textbooks Are Not Meatloaf

PIA.2 How should you go about reading a textbook so that you get the most out of your reading efforts?

Students make two common mistakes in regard to reading a textbook. The first mistake is simple: Many students don't bother to read the textbook *before* going to the lecture that will

Table 1
Multiple Study Methods

VERBAL METHODS	VISUAL METHODS	AUDITORY METHODS	ACTION METHODS
Use flash cards to identify main points or key terms.	Make flash cards with pictures or diagrams to aid recall of key concepts.	Join or form a study group or find a study partner so that you can discuss concepts and ideas.	Sit near the front of the classroom and take notes by jotting down key terms and making pictures or charts to help you remember what you are hearing.
Write out or recite key information in whole sentences or phrases in your own words.	Make charts and diagrams and sum up information in tables.	While studying, speak out loud or into a digital recorder that you can play back later.	While studying, walk back and forth as you read out loud.
When looking at diagrams, write out a description.	Use different colors of highlighter for different sections of information in text or notes.	Make speeches.	Study with a friend.
Use "sticky" notes to remind yourself of key terms and information, and put them in the notebook or text or on a mirror that you use frequently.	Visualize charts, diagrams, and figures.	Record the lectures (with permission). Take notes on the lecture sparingly, using the recording to fill in parts that you might have missed.	While exercising, listen to recordings you have made of important information.
Practice spelling words or repeating facts to be remembered.	Trace letters and words to remember key facts.	Read notes or text material into a digital recorder or get study materials recorded and play back while driving or doing other chores.	Write out key concepts on a large board or poster.
Rewrite things from memory.	Redraw things from memory.	When learning something new, state or explain the information in your own words out loud or to a study partner.	Make flash cards, using different colors and diagrams, and lay them out on a large surface. Practice putting them in order.
		Use musical rhythms as memory aids, or put information to a rhyme or a tune.	Make a three-dimensional model.
			Spend extra time in the lab.
			Go to outside areas such as a museum or historical site to gain information.

cover that material. Trying to get anything out of a lecture without having read the material first is like trying to find a new, unfamiliar place without using a map or any kind of directions. It's easy to get lost. This is especially true because of the assumption that most instructors make when planning their lectures: They take for granted that the students have already read the assignment. The instructors then use the lecture to go into detail about the information the students supposedly got from the reading. If the students have not done the reading, the instructor's lecture isn't going to make a whole lot of sense.

The second mistake that most students make when reading textbook material is to try to read it the same way they would read a novel: They start at the first page and read continuously. With a novel, it's easy to do this because the plot is usually interesting and people want to know what happens next, so they keep reading. It isn't necessary to remember every little detail—all they need to remember are the main plot points. One could say that a novel is like meatloaf—some meaty parts with lots of filler. Meatloaf can be eaten quickly, without even chewing for very long.

With a textbook, the material may be interesting but not in the same way that a novel is interesting. A textbook is a big, thick steak—all meat, no filler. Just as a steak has to be chewed to be enjoyed and to be useful to the body, textbook material has to be "chewed" with the mind. You have to read slowly, paying attention to every morsel of meaning.

So how do you do that? Probably one of the best-known reading methods is called SQ3R, first used by F. P. Robinson in a 1946 book called Effective Study. The letters S-Q-R-R-R stand for:

SURVEY Look at the chapter you've been assigned to read.

- Take a look at the outline at the beginning of the chapter or any opening questions, learning objectives, or other material the author has chosen to provide as a preview to the chapter.
- Flip through the chapter and read the headings of each section, and look at the tables, figures, graphs, and cartoons to get an idea of the kinds of things that you will be learning.
- Finally, quickly read through the chapter summary if there is one.

It might sound like it takes too much time to do this, but you should just be skimming at this point—a couple of minutes is all it should take. Why do this at all? Surveying the chapter, or "previewing" it, as some experts call it, helps you form a framework in your head around which you can organize the information in the chapter when you read it in detail. Organization is one of the main ways to improve your memory for information. LINK to Chapter Six: Memory, p. 226. Think of it this way: As mentioned earlier, if you are going to drive to a new place, it's helpful to have a road map to give you an idea of what's up ahead. Surveying the chapter is like setting yourself up with a "road map" for the material covered in the chapter.

Before reading any chapter in a text, survey the chapter by reading the outline and the section headings.

QUESTION After previewing the chapter, read the heading for the first section. *Just* the first section! Try to think of a question based on this heading that the section should answer as you read. For example, in Chapter One there's a section titled "Pavlov, Watson, and the Dawn of Behaviorism." You could ask yourself, "What did Pavlov and Watson do for psychology?" or "What is behaviorism?" Some textbooks even include questions at the start of many sections. In this text, a list of learning objectives for the key concepts in the chapter is presented in the form of questions that can be used with the SQ3R method. There are also student questions that can serve the same purpose. These questions, which are based on the author's years of hearing and answering similar questions from students in the classroom, will be in gray type in the margin, often with the picture of a typical student who is asking the question. Now when you read the section, you aren't *just* reading—you're reading to *find an answer*. That makes the material much easier to remember later on.

As you read, take notes. Write down key terms and try to summarize the main points of each paragraph and section in the chapter. These notes will be useful when you later review the chapter material.

READ Now read the section, looking for the answer to your questions. As you read, take notes by making an outline of the main points and terms in the section. This is another area where some students make a big mistake. They assume that using a highlighter to mark words and phrases is as good as writing notes. One of the author's former students is conducting research on the difference between highlighting and note taking, and her preliminary findings are clear: Students who wrote their own notes during the reading of a text or while listening to a lecture scored significantly higher on their exam grades than students who merely used a highlighter on the text (Boyd & Peeler, 2004). Highlighting requires no real mental effort (no "chewing," in other words), but writing the words down yourself requires you to read the words in depth and to understand them. When we study cognition, you'll learn more about the value of processing information in depth. LINK to Chapter Seven: Cognition: Thinking, Intelligence, and Language, p. 215.

RECITE It may sound silly, but reciting out loud what you can remember from the section you've just read is another good way to process the information more deeply and completely. How many times have you thought you understood something, only to find that when you tried to explain it to someone, you didn't understand it at all? Recitation forces you to put the information in your own words—just as writing it in notes does. Writing it down accesses your visual memory; saying it out loud gives you an auditory memory for the same information. If you have ever learned something well by teaching it to someone else, you already know the value of recitation. If you feel self-conscious about talking to yourself, talk into a digital recorder—and it's a great way to review later while traveling in the car.

Now repeat the Question, Read, and Recite instructions for each section, taking a few minutes' break after every two or three sections. Why take a break? There's a process that has to take place in your brain when you are trying to form a permanent memory for information, and that process takes a little time. When you take a break every 10 to 20 minutes, you are giving your brain the time to accomplish this process. A break will help you avoid a common problem in reading texts—finding yourself reading the same sentence over and over again because your brain is too overloaded from trying to remember what you just read.

RECALL/REVIEW Finally, you've finished reading the entire chapter. If you've used the guidelines listed previously, you'll only have to read the chapter as thoroughly this one time, instead of having to read it over and over throughout the semester and just before exams. Once you've read the chapter, take a few minutes to try to remember as much of what you learned while reading it as you can. A good way to do this is to take any practice quizzes that might be available, either in your text or in a student workbook that goes with the text. Many publishers have Web sites for their textbooks that have practice quizzes available online. If there are no quizzes, read the chapter summary in detail, making sure that you understand everything in it. If there's anything that's confusing, go back to that section in the chapter and read again until you understand it.

Some educators and researchers now add a fourth R: *Reflect*. To reflect means to try to think critically about what you have read by trying to tie the concepts into what you already know, thinking about how you can use the information in your own life, and deciding which of the topics you've covered interests you enough to look for more information on that topic (Richardson & Morgan, 1997). For example, if you have learned about the genetic basis for depression, you might better understand why that disorder seems to run in your best friend's family. LINK to Chapter Fourteen: Psychological Disorders, pp. 548-549.

After reading a chapter section, take time to reflect on what the information means and how it might relate to real-world situations.

Reading textbooks in this way means that, when it comes time for the final exam, all you will have to do is carefully review your notes to be ready for the exam—you won't have to read the entire textbook all over again. What a time-saver! Recent research suggests that the most important steps in this method are the three R's: Read, Recite, and Review. In two experiments with college students, researchers found that when compared with other study methods such as rereading and note-taking study strategies, the 3R strategy produced superior recall of the material (McDaniel et al., 2009).

How to Take Notes: Printing Out PowerPoint Slides Is Not Taking Notes

PIA.3 What are the best ways to take notes in class and while reading the text?

Remember the study showing that highlighting is not as effective as note taking (Boyd & Peeler, 2004)? One of this researcher's earliest studies was a comparison of students who took notes by hand while listening to a lecture with PowerPoint slides and students who printed out the PowerPoint slides and merely used a highlighter to stress certain ideas on the printout. Students taking notes by hand scored an average of one letter grade higher on exams than did the students who used a highlighter on the printouts. PowerPoint slides are not meant to be notes at all; they are merely talking points that help the instructor follow a particular sequence in lecturing. Typically, the instructor will have more to say about each point on the slide, and that is the information students should be listening to and writing down. In Table 1, the suggestions to use highlighters of different colors are not meant to replace taking notes but instead to supplement the notes you do take.

TAKING NOTES WHILE READING THE TEXT

How should you take notes? As stated earlier, you should try to take notes while reading the chapter by writing down the main points and the vocabulary terms *in your own words* as much as possible. This forces you to think about what you are reading. The more you think about it, the more likely it is that the concepts will become a part of your permanent memory. LINK to Chapter Six: Memory, p. 223.

TAKING NOTES DURING THE LECTURE

Taking notes while listening to the lecture is a slightly different procedure. First, you should have your notes from your earlier reading in front of you, and it helps to leave plenty of space between lines to add notes from the lecture. As mentioned in the section on how to read a textbook, a major mistake made by many students is to come to the lecture without having read the material first. This is an EXTREMELY BAD IDEA. In case that didn't sink in the first time, let me repeat it: **Extremely Bad Idea.** If you come to the lecture totally unprepared, you will have no idea what is important enough to write down and what is just the instructor's asides and commentary. Reading the material first gives you a good idea of exactly what is important in the lecture and reduces the amount of notes you must take.

If you are like Pamela in the opening introduction, ask your instructor if you can bring a digital recorder to class to record the lecture. You will then be able to listen during the class and use the recording to take notes from later. Some students may prefer to jot down diagrams, charts, and other visual aids along with their written notes. When you have good notes taken while reading the text and from the lectures, you will also have ready-made study aids for preparing to take exams. The next section deals with the best ways to study for exams.

Here are two things that instructors love to see: attentive looks and note taking during the lecture. And for the student who learns better just listening, a small digital recorder (used with permission) can help for later review of the lecture. How should these students have prepared before coming to this class?

PRACTICE quiz How much do you remember?

ANSWERS ON PAGE AK-1.

Pick the best answer.

1. Which of the following statements is NOT one of the conclusions drawn in the Pashler et al. 2009 study of learning styles?
   - **a.** People have preferences about the way information is presented to them.
   - **b.** People have different capabilities when processing different kinds of information.
   - **c.** There is definite evidence that tailoring the information presentation to different learning styles has a profound effect on student learning.
   - **d.** All of the above are true of the Pashler study.
2. Which of the following statements is TRUE?
   - **a.** You should approach reading a textbook in the same way that you would a novel.
   - **b.** Never take notes while reading—do it at least 2 days later.
   - **c.** Read the text assignment *before* going to the lecture.
   - **d.** Try not to look ahead in the chapter before starting your reading.
3. It is helpful to _________ when taking notes.
   - **a.** use your own words as much as possible
   - **b.** write down every word on any PowerPoint slides
   - **c.** use a highlighter and the text rather than write your own
   - **d.** use the exact wording of the instructor or slides

Brainstorming: What are some reasons that thinking about material to be learned in your own words would lead to stronger, longer lasting memories?

Studying For Exams: Cramming Is Not an Option

PIA.4 How should you approach studying for exams, and why do different kinds of test questions require different study approaches?

There is a right way to study for a test, believe it or not. Here are some good things to remember when preparing for an exam, whether it's a quiz, a unit test, a midterm, or a final (Carter et al., 2002; Reynolds, 2002):

Could this be you? The scattered materials, the frantic phone call to a friend or professor, the tense and worried facial expression are all hallmarks of that hallowed yet useless student tradition, cramming. Don't let this happen to you.

- **Timing is everything.** One of the worst things that students can do is to wait until the last minute to study for an exam. Remember the analogy about "chewing" the steak? (Just as a steak has to be chewed to be enjoyed and to be useful to the body, textbook material has to be "chewed" with the mind.) The same concept applies to preparing for an exam: You have to give yourself enough time. If you've read your text material and taken good notes as discussed in the previous sections, you'll be able to save a lot of time in studying for the exam, but you still need to give yourself ample time to go over all of those notes. One helpful thing to do is to make a study schedule in which you plan out (at least a week before the exam) the hours of the day during which you intend to study and the topics you will cover in those hours. Always give yourself more time than you think you will need, just in case something comes up at the last minute to throw off your schedule: unexpected company, car trouble, or other unforeseen events that might require you to forgo studying for one night.
- **Find out as much as you can about the type of test and the material it will cover.** The type of test can affect the way in which you want to study the material. An objective test, for example, such as multiple-choice or true/false, is usually fairly close to the text material, so you'll want to be very familiar with the wording of concepts and definitions in the text, although this is not a suggestion to memorize a lot of material.

  These kinds of tests can include one of three types of questions:
- **Factual:** Questions that ask you to remember a specific fact from the text material. For example, "Who built the first psychological laboratory?" requires that you recognize a person's name. (The answer is Wilhelm Wundt.)
- **Applied:** Questions that ask you to use, or apply, information presented in the text. For example, consider the following question from Chapter Five, Learning:

  One-year-old Ben learned to say the word "duck" when his mother showed him a duck in their backyard. That evening he sees a cartoon with a rooster in it and says, "Duck!," pointing to the rooster. Ben is exhibiting __________.
  a. generalization.
  b. discrimination.
  c. spontaneous recovery.
  d. shaping.

  This question requires you to take a concept (in this case, generalization) and apply it to a real-world example.
- **Conceptual:** Questions that demand that you think about the ideas or concepts presented in the text and demonstrate that you understand them by answering questions like the following: "Freud is to __________ as Watson is to __________." (The answers could vary, but a good set would be "the unconscious" and "observable behavior.")

Notice that although memorizing facts might help on the first type of question, it isn't going to help at all on the last two. Memorization doesn't always help on factual questions either, because the questions are sometimes worded quite differently from the text. It is far better to understand the information rather than be able to "spit it back" without understanding it. "Spitting it back" is memorization; understanding it is true learning. LINK to Chapter Six: Memory, p. 216. There are different levels of analysis for information you are trying to learn, and the higher the level of analysis, the more likely you are to remember (Anderson et al., 2001; Bloom, 1956). *Factual questions* are the lowest level of analysis: knowledge. *Applied questions* are a higher level and are often preferred by instructors for that reason—it's hard to successfully apply information if you don't really understand it. *Conceptual questions* are a kind of analysis, a level higher than either of the other two. Not only do you have to understand the concept, you have to understand it well enough to compare and contrast it with other concepts. They might be harder questions to answer, but in the long run, you will get more "bang for your buck" in terms of true learning.

Subjective tests, such as essay tests and short-answer exams, require that you not only are able to recall and understand the information from the course but also that you are able to organize it in your own words. To study for a subjective test means that you need to be familiar with the material *and* that you need to be able to write it down. Make outlines of your notes. Rewrite both reading and lecture notes and make flash cards, charts, and drawings. Practice putting the flash cards in order. Talk out loud or study with someone else and discuss the possible questions that could be on an essay test. You may find that only a few of these methods work best for you, but the more ways in which you try to study, the better you will be able to retrieve the information when you need it. It may sound like a big investment of your time, but most students vastly underestimate how long it takes to study—and fail to recognize that many of these techniques are doable when first reading the textbook assignment and preparing for the classroom lecture. DON'T CRAM!

You might also look at old tests (if the instructor has made them available) to see what kinds of questions are usually asked. If this is not possible, make sure that you pay close attention to the kinds of questions asked on the first exam so that you will know how to prepare for future tests. Write out your own test questions as if you were the instructor. Not only does this force you to think about the material the way it will appear on the test, it also provides a great review tool. Other helpful advice:

- **Use SQ3R.** You can use the same method that you used to read the text material to go over your notes. Skim through your notes to get an overview of the material that will be on the test. Try to think of possible test questions that the instructor might include on an exam. Reread your notes, referring back to the text if necessary. Recite the main ideas and definitions of terms, either out loud, into a digital recorder, or to a friend or study group. Review by summarizing sections of material or by making an outline or flash cards that you can use in studying important concepts.
- **Use the concept maps if provided.** When surveying the chapter, make sure you look over any concept maps. (In this text, they are provided at the end of each major section of the chapters, just before the practice quizzes in most cases, and also at the end of each chapter). **Concept maps** are a visual organization of the key concepts, terms, and definitions that are found in each section and are an excellent way to "see" how various concepts are linked together (Carnot et al., 2001; Novak, 1995; Wu et al., 2004). They are also a great way to review the chapter once you have finished reading it, just to check for understanding—if the concept maps don't make sense, then you've

concept map an organized visual representation of knowledge consisting of concepts and their relationships to other concepts.

Many students studying for exams ignore one of the most valuable resources to which they have access: the instructor. Most instructors are happy to answer questions or schedule time for students who are having difficulty understanding the material.

Holding your eyes open is not going to help you study when you are this tired. Sleep has been shown to improve memory and performance on tests, so get a good night's sleep before every exam.

missed something and need to go back over the relevant section. You can also make your own concept maps as you take notes on the chapter. A guide to making concept maps, examples from your text, and a tool for creating them can be found on mypsychlab.

- **Take advantage of all the publisher's test materials.** Practice does help, and most textbooks come with a study guide or a Web site (such as **www.mypsychlab.com** for this text, see pp. xii–xiii). Those materials should have practice quizzes available—take them. The more types of quiz questions you try to answer, the more successful you will be at interpreting the questions on the actual exam. You'll also get a very good idea of the areas that you need to go back and review again.
- **Make use of the resources.** If you find that you are having difficulty with certain concepts, go to the instructor well in advance of the exam for help. (This is another good reason to manage your study time so that you aren't trying to do everything in a few hours the night before the exam.) There are help centers on most college and university campuses with people who can help you learn to study, organize your notes, or tutor you in the subject area.
- **Don't forget your physical needs.** Studies have shown that not getting enough sleep is bad for memory and learning processes (Stickgold et al., 2001; Vecsey et al., 2009). Try to stop studying an hour or so before going to bed at a reasonable time to give your body time to relax and unwind. Get a full night's sleep if possible. Do not take sleep-inducing medications or drink alcohol, as these substances prevent normal stages of sleep, including the stage that seems to be the most useful for memory and learning (Davis et al., 2003). Do eat breakfast; hunger is harmful to memory and mental performance. A breakfast heavy on protein and light on carbohydrates is the best for concentration and recall (Benton & Parker, 1998; Dani et al., 2005; Pollitt & Matthews, 1998; Stubbs et al., 1996).
- **Use your test time wisely.** When taking the test, don't allow yourself to get stuck on one question that you can't seem to answer. If an answer isn't clear, skip that question and go on to others. After finishing all of the questions that you can answer easily, go back to the ones you have skipped and try to answer them again. This accomplishes several things: You get to experience success in answering the questions that you can answer, which makes you feel more confident and relaxed; other questions on the test might act as memory cues for the exact information you need for one of those questions you skipped; and once you are more relaxed, you may find that the answers to those seemingly impossible questions are now clear because anxiety is no longer blocking them. This is a way of reducing stress by dealing directly with the problem, one of many ways of dealing effectively with stress. LINK to Chapter Eleven: Stress and Health, p. 436.

The next section gives some helpful information about another form of assessment: the term paper.

Writing Papers: Planning Makes Perfect

PIA.5 What are the key steps in writing papers for college?

Several steps are involved in writing a paper, whether it be a short paper or a long one. You should begin all of these steps well in advance of the due date for the paper (not the night before):

1. **Choose a topic.** The first step is to choose a topic for your paper. In some cases, the instructor may have a list of acceptable subjects, which makes your

job easier. If that is not the case, don't be afraid to go to your instructor during office hours and talk about some possible topics. Try to choose a topic that interests you, one that you would like to learn more about. The most common mistake students make is to choose subject matter that is too broad. For example, the topic "autism" could fill a book. A narrower focus might discuss a single form of autism in detail. Again, your instructor can help you narrow down your topic choices.

2. **Do the research.** Find as many sources as you can that have information about your topic. Don't limit yourself to encyclopedias or textbooks. Go to your school library and ask the librarian to point you in the direction of some good scientific journals that would have useful information on the subject. Be very careful about using the Internet to do research: Not everything on the Internet is correct or written by true experts—avoid other students' papers and "encyclopedia" Web sites that can be written and updated by darn near anyone. **Explore** on **mypsychlab.com**
3. **Take notes.** While reading about your topic, use note cards to remember key points. On the back of the note card (a 3 × 5 card), write the reference that will go along with the reading. (You might also start a document on the computer and type your references into the document as you read, but that only works if you have your computer with you while you are reading.) References for psychology papers are usually going to be in APA (American Psychological Association) style, which can be found at **www.apastyle.org**. Write your notes about the reading on the front of the note card. Some people prefer two note cards, one for the notes and one for the reference, so that they can sort them separately. Remember, taking notes helps you avoid **plagiarism**, the copying of someone else's ideas or exact words (or a close imitation of the words) and presenting them as your own. Note taking also helps you avoid using too many direct quotes—papers are supposed to be in *your* words, not someone else's, even if you give them credit.
4. **Decide on the thesis.** The thesis is the central message of your paper—the message you want to communicate to your audience—which may be your instructor, your classmates, or both, depending on the nature of the assignment. Some papers are persuasive, which means the author is trying to convince the reader of a particular point of view, such as "Autism is not caused by immunizations." Some papers are informative, providing information about a topic to an audience that may have no prior knowledge, such as "Several forms of autism have been identified." **Read** on **mypsychlab.com**
5. **Write an outline.** Using your notes from all your readings, create an outline of your paper—a kind of "road map" of how the paper will go. Start with an introduction (e.g., a brief definition and discussion of what autism is). Then decide what the body of the paper should be. If your paper is about a specific type of autism, for example, your outline might include sections about the possible causes of that type. The last section of your outline should be some kind of conclusion. For example, you might have recommendations about how parents of a child with autism can best help that child to develop as fully as possible.
6. **Write a first draft.** Write your paper using the outline and your notes as guides. If using APA style, place citations with all of your statements and assertions. Failure to use citations (which point to the particular reference work from which your information came) is also a common mistake that many students make. It is very important that you avoid plagiarism, as discussed in tip 3.

Instructors are a good source of suggestions for paper topics—they know the kind of information they want to be reading and grading in the wee hours of the night.

Explore the research process and find reliable sources in Research Navigator on **mypsychlab.com**

Read the handbook *What Every Student Should Know about Avoiding Plagiarism* in the library on **mypsychlab.com**

plagiarism the copying of someone else's exact words (or a close imitation of the words) and presenting them as your own.

In earlier times, people actually had to write or type their first, second, and sometimes third drafts on real paper. The advent of computers with word-processing programs that allow simple editing and revision have no doubt saved a lot of trees from the paper mill. This also means there is no good excuse for failing to write a first draft and for proofreading one's work.

When you use a source, you are supposed to explain the information that you are using in your own words *and* cite the source, as in the following example:

In one study comparing both identical and fraternal twins, researchers found that stressful life events of the kind listed in the SRRS were excellent predictors of the onset of episodes of major depression (Kendler & Prescott, 1999).

Your paper's reference section would have the following citation: Kendler, K. S., & Prescott, C. A. (1999). A population-based twin study of lifetime major depression in men and women. *Archives of General Psychiatry, 56*(1): 39–44. [Author's note: the number in front of the parentheses is the volume of the journal, the one inside is the issue number, and the last numbers are the page numbers of that article.]

7. **Let it sit.** Take a few days (if you have been good about starting the paper on time) to let the paper sit without reading it. Then go back over and mark places that don't sound right and need more explanation, a citation, or any other changes. This is much easier to do after a few days away from the paper; the need to reword will be more obvious.
8. **Write the revised draft.** Some people do more than one draft, while others do only a first draft and a final. In any case, revise the draft carefully, making sure to check your citations—and your spelling!

PRACTICE quiz How much do you remember? ANSWERS ON PAGE AK-1.

Pick the best answer.

1. When studying for an exam, you should ______________.
   a. wait until just before the scheduled exam, so that the information will be fresh in your mind.
   b. study all night long before the exam—you can sleep after the test.
   c. memorize as much of the information as possible.
   d. tailor your studying to the type of test questions that will be on the exam, making sure that you are understanding the concepts in your own words.
2. When writing a paper, a "road map" of how the paper will go is provided by ______________
   a. your detailed notes on your readings.
   b. the first draft of the paper.
   c. an outline of the paper's major sections.
   d. letting the paper "sit" for a while after writing the first draft.

Brainstorming: Given the research about protein and learning, can you think of a reason why attention-deficit/hyperactivity disorder might be on the rise in schoolchildren? What other reasons might there be for this increase?

Applying Psychology to Everyday Life: Strategies for Improving Your Memory

PIA.6 How can you improve your memory for facts and concepts?

Everyone needs a little memory help now and then. Even memory experts use strategies to help them perform their unusual feats of remembering. These strategies may be unique to that individual, but there are many memory "tricks" that are quite simple and available for anyone to learn and use. A memory trick or strategy to help people remember is called a **mnemonic** from the Greek word for memory. Here are a few of the more popular mnemonics, some of which may sound familiar:

- **Linking.** Make a list in which items to be remembered are linked in some way. If trying to remember a list of the planets in the solar system, for example, a person could string the names of the planets together like this: *Mercury* was the messenger god, who carried lots of love notes to *Venus*, the beautiful goddess who sprang from the *Earth's* sea. She was married to *Mars*, her brother, which didn't please her father *Jupiter* or his father *Saturn*, and his uncle *Uranus*

mnemonic a strategy or trick for aiding memory.

complained to the sea god, *Neptune*. That sounds like a lot, but once linked in this way, the names of the planets are easy to recall in proper order.

- **The peg-word method.** In this method, it is necessary to first memorize a series of "peg" words, numbered words that can be used as keys for remembering items associated with them. A typical series of peg words is:

  One is a bun

  Two is a shoe

  Three is a tree

  Four is a door

  Five is a hive

  Six is bricks

  Seven is heaven

  Eight is a gate

  Nine is a line

  Ten is a hen

  To use this method, each item to be remembered (e.g., on a grocery list) is associated with a peg word and made into an image. If the items to be remembered are cheese, milk, eggs, bread, and sugar, the series of images might be a bun with a big wedge of cheese in it, a shoe with milk pouring out of it, a tree with eggs hanging from it, a door made of a slice of bread, and a hive with little bags of sugar flying around it instead of bees. The images are bizarre, and that actually helps cement the memory. When retrieving the list, all the person has to do is recite, "One is a bun, cheese. Two is a shoe, milk . . ." and so on, and the images will pop up readily.
- **The method of loci (LOW-kee or LOW-si).** This method, often credited to the ancient Romans and sometimes called the Roman Room Method, was actually invented by the Greeks. In both cultures, orators and speech makers used this method to keep track of the points they wanted to make in their speeches, which were often quite long and involved. There were no cue cards or teleprompters, so they had to rely on memory alone. In this method, the person pictures a very familiar room or series of rooms in a house or other building. Each point of the speech is then made into an image and "placed" mentally in the room at certain locations. For example, if the first point was about military spending, the image might be a soldier standing in the doorway of the house throwing money out into the street. Each point would have its place, and all the person would need to do to retrieve the memories would be to take a "mental walk" around the house.
- **Verbal/rhythmic organization.** How do you spell relief? If when spelling a word with an *ie* or an *ei* in it, you resort to the old rhyme "I before E except after C, or when sounded as A as in neighbor or weigh," you have made use of a verbal/rhythmic organization mnemonic. "Thirty days hath September, April, June, and November . . ." is another example of this technique. Setting information into a rhyme aids memory because it uses verbal cues, rhyming words, and the rhythm of the poem itself to aid retrieval. Sometimes this method is accomplished through making a sentence by using the first letters of each word to be remembered and making them into new words that form a sentence. The colors of the rainbow are ROY G. BIV (red, orange, yellow, green, blue, indigo, and violet). The notes on the musical staff are "Every Good Boy Does Fine." There are countless examples of this technique.

- **Put it to music (a version of the rhythmic method).** Some people have had success with making up little songs, using familiar tunes, to remember specific information. The best example of this? The alphabet song.

This *Psychology in Action* introduction has covered several different ways to help you get more out of your psychology class as well as all of your other college course work. If you follow the advice given in this chapter for reading, taking notes, studying, writing papers, and improving your memory, you will find that making good grades will be easier than ever before and that you will actually remember a great deal of what you've studied long after the last final exam is over.

Questions for Further Discussion

1. The use of images appears to help form better memories. How might imagery be linked to the earliest kinds of memories we have?
2. What are some mnemonics that you or people you know have used? Which method do you think those personal mnemonics represent?

Other Resources

There are some excellent books and Web resources available for help in maximizing your studying. Three excellent books are the following:

Carter, C., Bishop, J., & Kravits, S. (2011). *Keys to effective learning: Study skills and habits for success* (6th ed.) Upper Saddle River, NJ: Prentice Hall.

Carter, C., Bishop, J., Kravits, S., & Block, J. (2009). *Keys to success: Building analytical, creative, and practical skills* (6th ed.).Upper Saddle River, NJ: Prentice Hall.

Sellers, D., Dochen, C. W., & Hodges, R. W. (2011). *Academic transformation: The road to college success* (2nd ed.) Upper Saddle River, NJ: Prentice Hall.

Web Sites

The Virginia Polytechnic Institute and State University has a good online site at www.ucc.vt.edu/stdyhlp.html

Another good source created by Joe Landsberger is the Web site Study Guides and Strategies, available at www.studygs.net

A good resource for the background behind concept maps and how to use them is at cmap.ihmc.us/Publications/ResearchPapers/TheoryCmaps/TheoryUnderlying ConceptMaps.htm.

psychology in action summary

Listen on **mypsychlab.com** Listen to an audio file of your chapter **www.mypsychlab.com**

Study Methods: Different Strokes for Different Folks

PIA.1 What are some different methods of studying?

- While students may have preferred methods of learning, research has shown that using multiple methods to study is probably more useful than trying to learn in any one particular style.

Reading Textbooks: Textbooks Are Not Meatloaf

PIA.2 How should you go about reading a textbook so that you get the most out of your reading efforts?

- Textbooks must be read in a different way from novels or popular books.
- The SQ3R method is an excellent way to approach reading a textbook: survey, question, read, recite, review.

How to Take Notes: Printing Out PowerPoint Slides Is Not Taking Notes

PIA.3 **What are the best ways to take notes in class and while reading the text?**

- Notes should be in your own words and written or typed, not highlighted in the text or on handouts.
- When taking notes from a lecture, you should be prepared by having the notes from your reading in front of you; some people may benefit from recording the lecture and taking notes afterward.

Studying For Exams: Cramming Is Not an Option

PIA.4 **How should you approach studying for exams, and why do different kinds of test questions require different study approaches?**

- Don't wait until the last minute to study.
- Find out about the types of questions on the exam.
- Use concept maps, the SQ3R method, publisher's practice-test materials.
- Get plenty of sleep and eat breakfast, preferably something with protein.

Writing Papers: Planning Makes Perfect

PIA.5 **What are the key steps in writing papers for college?**

- Key steps in writing a research paper are to choose a topic, read about the topic, take notes on your reading, decide upon the central message of your paper, write an outline, a first draft, and allow the paper to sit for a few days before going back and writing the final draft.

Applying Psychology to Everyday Life: Strategies for Improving Your Memory

PIA.6 **How can you improve your memory for facts and concepts?**

- There are memory strategies called mnemonics, including methods that use imagery, rhymes, linking, and even music to improve memory.

test YOURSELF

ANSWERS ON PAGE AK-1.

Study and Review on **mypsychlab.com** Ready for your test? More quizzes and a customized study plan **www.mypsychlab.com**

Pick the best answer.

1. Which of the following statements IS one of the conclusions drawn in the Pashler et al. 2009 study of learning styles?
   a. People do not have preferences about the way information is presented to them.
   b. People do not have different capabilities when processing different kinds of information.
   c. There is little evidence that tailoring the information presentation to different learning styles has a profound effect on student learning.
   d. There is no such thing as having a learning style.

2. Which of the following statements is FALSE?
   a. Textbooks can be read as easily as a novel if you are a good reader.
   b. Take notes while reading, putting the concepts into your own words.
   c. Read the text assignment *before* going to the lecture.
   d. Take a survey of the chapter's headings, figures, and outlines before reading in depth.

3. In the Boyd and Peeler (2004) study, highlighting ___________.
   a. produced better memory than relying on your own notes.
   b. led to the same quality of memory as traditional note taking.
   c. was associated with GPAs a full letter-grade below those of students who took notes by writing during the lecture.
   d. produced results no different than taking notes during the lecture.

4. When studying for an exam, you should NOT ___________.
   a. wait until just before the scheduled exam, so that the information will be fresh in your mind.
   b. get a good night's sleep.
   c. try to understand the information in your own words.
   d. tailor your studying to the type of test questions that will be on the exam.

5. When writing a paper, the thesis is/are ___________.
   a. your detailed notes from your readings.
   b. the central message of your paper.
   c. an outline of the paper's major sections.
   d. the topic you choose at the beginning of the process.

CONCEPT SUMMARY

psychology in action

secrets for surviving college and improving your grades

PIA.1

Study Methods

- **verbal methods** see and say
  - rewrite or recite key information in your own words
- **visual methods** use your eyes
  - use different colors of highlighter for different ideas in your notes
  - draw diagrams and summary tables of information from memory
- **auditory methods** use your hearing
  - study with a partner and discuss concepts and ideas; take turns explaining concepts to each other
  - talk out loud while studying or into an audio recorder

- **action methods** use movement
  - use exercise and movement while studying
    - walk around while reading out loud from your materials
    - write out and diagram key concepts on a poster or white board
  - create your own models or go on your own "field trips" to gather information

PIA.2

Reading Textbooks

- **reading for learning** is not the same as reading for pleasure
- **break up your reading sessions** so you have time to process and understand the information
- **reading, reciting, and reviewing** is very effective
  - SQ3R

PIA.3

How to Take Notes

- **takes notes and write information in your own words**
- **read your textbook and take notes before class** so you can focus on the lecture—in the lecture, only take notes on the most important ideas

PIA.4 Studying for Exams

- **spacing out studying sessions** (distributed practice) is more effective than cramming (massed practice); start early!

- **knowing what kind test questions to expect** can help guide your study efforts
- **use effective time-management strategies** both when studying and while preparing for exams
- **don't forget to take care of yourself** by getting enough sleep, proper nutrition, and exercise

PIA.5 Writing Papers

- **quality papers require timely preparation, research, planning, and outlining** write an initial draft followed by a revised draft
  - **don't forget to proofread** for spelling and grammar

PIA.6 Strategies for Improving Your Memory

- **memory strategies (mnemonics)** can be helpful for some types of information
  - linking
  - peg-word method
  - method of loci
  - verbal or rhythmic organization
    - put it to music

- **MyPsychLab** is an online resource that can help make your study time more effective
  - **study tools** on MyPsychLab
    - extra quizzing
    - concept mapping tool
    - videos
    - and more

PEARSON mypsychlab

- **icons** throughout this book direct you to additional content on MyPsychLab
  - Watch
  - Listen
  - Explore
  - Simulate
  - Study and Review
  - Read
  - Map the Concepts

psychology

1 the science of psychology

CHAPTER OUTLINE

WHAT CAN PSYCHOLOGY DO FOR ME?

Have you ever wondered . . .

. . . why birds of a feather flock together, but opposites so often attract?

. . . how you can remember some things easily and at other times forget what you really need to remember?

. . . what dreams might mean and why we need to sleep at all?

. . . how a person's culture might affect personality?

. . . if ESP really exists?

. . . why you find some people attractive but not others?

. . . why some people become serial killers?

. . . how prejudice forms?

. . . what scores on an IQ test really mean?

. . . how the salesperson managed to talk you into buying more than you wanted to buy?

. . . how different men and women really are?

. . . why buying lottery tickets can be so addictive?

. . . why people tend to get sick right before final exam week?

. . . why identical twins aren't so identical when it comes to their personalities?

If you've ever been curious about any of these questions, this book is for you. Psychologists study all of these things and more. If you've puzzled about it, thought about doing it, or actually done it, chances are psychology has an explanation for it.

Why study psychology?

Psychology not only helps you understand why people (and animals) do the things they do, but it also helps you better understand yourself and your reactions to others. Psychology can help you comprehend how your brain and body are connected, how to improve your learning abilities and memory, and how to deal with the stresses of life, both ordinary and extraordinary. In studying psychology, an understanding of the methods psychologists use is crucial because research can be flawed, and knowing how research should be done can bring those flaws to light. And finally, psychology and its research methods promote critical thinking, which can be used to evaluate not just research but also claims of all kinds, including those of advertisers and politicians.

learning objectives

Study Help Note: For each section of every chapter in this text there are numbered learning objectives. These objectives represent the key concepts that students should be able to recognize, discuss, analyze, and use after reading the chapter. They appear at the beginning of each chapter, at the beginning of each relevant section in the chapter, and in the chapter summary. Learning objectives are also linked to the practice quizzes and concept maps in the chapter.

These are your learning objectives for this chapter:

1.1 What defines psychology as a field of study, and what are psychology's four primary goals?

1.2 How did structuralism and functionalism differ, and who were the important people in those early fields?

1.3 What were the basic ideas and who were the important people behind the early approaches known as Gestalt, psychoanalysis, and behaviorism?

1.4 What are the basic ideas behind the seven modern perspectives, and what were the important contributions of Skinner, Maslow, and Rogers?

1.5 How does a psychologist differ from a psychiatrist, and what are the other types of professionals who work in the various areas of psychology?

1.6 Why is psychology considered a science, and what are the steps in using the scientific method?

1.7 How are naturalistic and laboratory settings used to describe behavior, and what are some of the advantages and disadvantages associated with these settings?

1.8 How are case studies and surveys used to describe behavior, and what are some drawbacks to each of these methods?

1.9 What is the correlational technique, and what does it tell researchers about relationships?

1.10 How are operational definitions, independent and dependent variables, experimental and control groups, and random assignment used in designing an experiment?

1.11 How do the placebo and experimenter effects cause problems in an experiment, and how can single-blind and double-blind studies control for these effects?

1.12 What are the basic elements of a real-world experiment?

1.13 What are some ethical concerns that can occur when conducting research with people and animals?

1.14 What are the basic principles of critical thinking, and how can critical thinking be useful in everyday life?

study tip

As you are reading this chapter, remember to use the SQ3R method discussed on pages I-5–I-8 in *Psychology in Action*. Breaking your reading into small sections will help you get more out of every chapter.

What Is Psychology?

THE FIELD OF PSYCHOLOGY

Some people believe psychology is just the study of people and what motivates their behavior. Psychologists do study people, but they study animals as well. And to better understand what motivates behavior, psychologists study not only what people and animals do, but also what happens in their bodies and in their brains as they do it.

1.1 What defines psychology as a field of study, and what are psychology's four primary goals?

Psychology is the scientific study of behavior and mental processes. *Behavior* includes all of our outward or overt actions and reactions, such as talking, facial expressions, and movement. The term *mental processes* refers to all the internal, covert activity of our minds, such as thinking, feeling, and remembering. Why "scientific"? To study behavior and mental processes in both animals and humans, researchers must observe them. Whenever a human being observes anyone or anything, there's always a possibility that the observer will see only what he or she *expects* to see. Psychologists don't want to let these possible biases* cause them to make faulty observations. They want to be precise, and to measure as carefully as they can—so they use the *scientific method* to study psychology.

PSYCHOLOGY'S GOALS

Every science has the common goal of learning how things work. The goals specifically aimed at uncovering the mysteries of human and animal behavior are description, explanation, prediction, and control.

psychology the scientific study of behavior and mental processes.

*biases: personal judgments based on beliefs rather than facts.

In this an environment that you would want to work in? Some researchers have wondered if your answer might be influenced by your gender.

DESCRIPTION: WHAT IS HAPPENING? The first step in understanding anything is to describe it. *Description* involves observing a behavior and noting everything about it: what is happening, where it happens, to whom it happens, and under what circumstances it seems to happen.

For example, a psychologist might wonder why so many computer scientists seem to be male. She makes further observations and notes that many "non-techies" stereotypically perceive the life and environment of a computer scientist as someone who lives and breathes at the computer, surrounds himself with computer games, junk food, and science-fiction gadgets—characteristics that add up to a very masculine ambiance.

That's what *seems* to be happening. The psychologist's observations are a starting place for the next goal: Why do females seem to avoid going into this environment?

EXPLANATION: WHY IS IT HAPPENING? Based on her observations, the psychologist might try to come up with a tentative explanation, such as "women feel they do not belong in such stereotypically masculine surroundings." In other words, she is trying to understand or find an *explanation* for the lower proportion of women in this field. Finding explanations for behavior is a very important step in the process of forming theories of behavior. A *theory* is a general explanation of a set of observations or facts. The goal of description provides the observations, and the goal of explanation helps to build the theory.

The preceding example comes from a real experiment conducted by psychologist Sapna Cheryan and colleagues (Cheryan et al., 2009). Professor Cheryan (who teaches psychology at the University of Washington in Seattle), set up four experiments with more than 250 female and male student participants who were not studying computer science. In the first experiment, students came into a small classroom that had one of two sets of objects: either Star Trek® posters, video-game boxes, and Coke™ cans, or nature posters, art, a dictionary, and coffee mugs (among other things). Told to ignore the objects because they were sharing the room with another class, the students spent several minutes in the classroom. While still sitting in the classroom, they were asked to fill out a questionnaire asking about their attitude toward computer science. While the attitudes of male students were not different between the two environments, women exposed to the stereotypically masculine setup were less interested in computer science than those who were exposed to the nonstereotypical environment. The three other similar experiments yielded the same results.

PREDICTION: WHEN WILL IT HAPPEN AGAIN? Determining what will happen in the future is a *prediction*. In the Cheryan et al. study, the prediction is clear: If we want more women to go into computer science, we must do something to change either the environment or the perception of the environment typically associated with this field. This is the purpose of the last of the four goals of psychology: changing or modifying behavior.

CONTROL: HOW CAN IT BE CHANGED? The focus of control, or the modification of some behavior, is to change a behavior from an undesirable one (such as women avoiding a certain academic major) to a desirable one (such as more equality in career choices).

Professor Cheryan suggests that changing the image of computer science may help increase the number of women choosing to go into this field. Not all psychological investigations will try to meet all four of these goals. In some cases, the main focus might be on description and prediction, as it would be for a personality theorist who wants to know what people are like (description) and what they might do in certain situations (prediction). Some psychologists are interested in both description and explanation, as is the case with experimental psychologists who design research to find explanations for observed (described) behavior. Therapists may be more interested in controlling or influencing behavior and mental processes, although the other three goals would be important in achieving this objective.

Although these goals have not really changed over the years, in the time since psychology's beginnings, the methods of achieving them certainly have changed. In the next section, we'll take a look at the early pioneers in psychology.

How long has psychology been around?

Psychology Then: The History of Psychology

IN THE BEGINNING: WUNDT, INTROSPECTION, AND THE LABORATORY

How long has psychology been around?

Psychology is a relatively new field in the realm of the sciences, only about 130 years old. It's not that no one thought about why people and animals do the things they do before then; on the contrary, there were philosophers,* medical doctors, and physiologists** who thought about little else—particularly with regard to people. Aristotle, who lived from 384–322 B.C., wrote about the relationship of the soul to the body (with the two being aspects of the same underlying structure) in *De Anima* as well as other works (Durrant, 1993; Everson, 1995). Plato (427–347 B.C.), Aristotle's teacher, felt the soul could exist separately from the body, a view that has become known as *dualism* (Jackson, 2001). René Descartes, a seventeenth-century French philosopher and mathematician, agreed with Plato and believed that the pineal gland (a small organ at the base of the brain involved in sleep) was the seat of the soul (Kenny, 1968, 1994). LINK to Chapter Four: Consciousness, p. 130. Philosophers tried to understand or explain the human mind and its connection to the physical body, while medical doctors and physiologists wondered about the physical connection between the body and the brain. For example, physician and physicist Gustav Fechner is often credited with performing some of the first scientific experiments that would form a basis for experimentation in psychology with his studies of perception (Fechner, 1860), and physician Hermann von Helmholtz (von Helmholtz, 1852, 1863) performed groundbreaking experiments in visual and auditory perception. LINK to Chapter Three: Sensation and Perception, pp. 91, 97. **Explore** on **mypsychlab.com**

Explore a time line of important dates in psychology on **mypsychlab.com**

1.2 **How did structuralism and functionalism differ, and who were the important people in those early fields?**

It really all started to come together in a laboratory in Leipzig, Germany, in 1879. It was here that Wilhelm Wundt (VILL-helm Voont, 1832–1920), a physiologist, attempted to apply scientific principles to the study of the human mind. In his laboratory, students from around the world were taught to study the structure of the human mind. Wundt believed that the mind was made up of thoughts, experiences, emotions, and other basic elements. In order to inspect these nonphysical elements, students had to learn to think objectively about their own thoughts—after all, they could hardly read someone else's mind. Wundt called this process **objective introspection**, the process of objectively examining and measuring one's own thoughts and mental activities (Rieber & Robinson, 2001). For example, Wundt might place an object, such as a rock, into a student's hand and have the student tell him everything that he was feeling as a result of having the rock in his hand—all the sensations stimulated by the

objective introspection the process of examining and measuring one's own thoughts and mental activities.

*philosophers: people who seek wisdom and knowledge through thinking and discussion.

**physiologists: scientists who study the physical workings of the body and its systems.

rock. (Objectivity* was—and is—important because scientists need to remain unbiased. Observations need to be clear and precise, but unaffected by the individual observer's beliefs and values.)

This was really the first attempt by anyone to bring objectivity and measurement to the concept of psychology. This attention to objectivity, together with the establishment of the first true experimental laboratory in psychology, is why Wundt is known as the father of psychology.

German physiologist Wilhelm Wundt participates in an experiment in his laboratory as students look on.

TITCHENER AND STRUCTURALISM IN AMERICA

One of Wundt's students was Edward Titchener (1867–1927), an Englishman who eventually took Wundt's ideas to Cornell University in Ithaca, New York. Titchener expanded on Wundt's original ideas, calling his new viewpoint **structuralism** because the focus of study was the structure of the mind. He believed that every experience could be broken down into its individual emotions and sensations (Brennan, 2002). Although Titchener agreed with Wundt that consciousness, the state of being aware of external events, could be broken down into its basic elements, Titchener also believed that objective introspection could be used on thoughts as well as on physical sensations. For example, Titchener might have asked his students to introspect about things that are blue rather than actually giving them a blue object and asking for reactions to it. Such an exercise might have led to something like the following: "What is blue? There are blue things, like the sky or a bird's feathers. Blue is cool and restful, blue is calm . . ." and so on.

In 1894, one of Titchener's students at Cornell University became famous for becoming the first woman to receive a Ph.D. in psychology (Goodman, 1980; Guthrie, 2004). Her name was Margaret F. Washburn, and she was Titchener's only graduate student for that year. In 1908 she published a book on animal behavior that was considered an important work in that era of psychology, *The Animal Mind* (Washburn, 1908).

Structuralism was a dominant force in the early days of psychology, but it eventually died out in the early 1900s, as the structuralists were busily fighting among themselves over just which key elements of experience were the most important. A competing view arose not long after Wundt's laboratory was established, shortly before structuralism came to America.

Structuralists would be interested in all of the memories and sensations this woman is experiencing as she smells the rose.

WILLIAM JAMES AND FUNCTIONALISM

Harvard University was the first school in America to offer classes in psychology in the late 1870s. These classes were taught by one of Harvard's most illustrious instructors, William James (1842–1910). James began teaching anatomy and physiology, but as his interest in psychology developed, he began teaching it almost exclusively (Brennan, 2002). His comprehensive textbook on the subject, *Principles of Psychology*, is so brilliantly written that copies are still in print (James, 1890, 2002).

Unlike Wundt and Titchener, James was more interested in the importance of consciousness to everyday life rather than just its analysis. He believed that the scientific study of consciousness itself was not yet possible. Conscious ideas are constantly flowing in an ever-changing stream, and once you start thinking about what you were just thinking about, what you were thinking about is no longer what you *were* thinking about—it's what you *are* thinking about—and . . . excuse me, I'm a little dizzy. I think you get the picture, anyway.

structuralism early perspective in psychology associated with Wilhelm Wundt and Edward Titchener, in which the focus of study is the structure or basic elements of the mind.

*objectivity: expressing or dealing with facts or conditions as they really are without allowing the influence of personal feelings, prejudices, or interpretations.

Mary Whiton Calkins, despite being denied a Ph.D. degree by Harvard because she was a woman, became the first female president of the American Psychological Association and had a successful career as a professor and researcher. Source: Archives of the History of American Psychology–The University of Akron

Instead, James focused on how the mind allows people to *function* in the real world—how people work, play, and adapt to their surroundings, a viewpoint he called **functionalism**. (He was heavily influenced by Charles Darwin's ideas about *natural selection*, in which physical traits that help an animal adapt to its environment and survive are passed on to its offspring.) If physical traits could aid in survival, why couldn't behavioral traits do the same? Animals and people whose behavior helped them to survive would pass those traits on to their offspring, perhaps by teaching or even by some mechanism of heredity.* (Remember that this was early in the days of trying to understand how heredity worked.) For example, a behavior such as avoiding the eyes of others in an elevator can be seen as a way of protecting one's personal space—a kind of territorial protection that may have its roots in the primitive need to protect one's home and source of food and water from intruders (Manusov & Patterson, 2006) or as a way of avoiding what might seem like a challenge to another person (Brown et al., 2005; Jehn et al., 1999).

It is interesting to note that one of James's early students was Mary Whiton Calkins, who completed every course and requirement for earning a Ph.D. but was denied that degree by Harvard University because she was a woman. She was allowed to take those classes as a guest only. Calkins eventually established a psychological laboratory at Wellesley College. Her work was some of the earliest research in the area of human memory and the psychology of the self. In 1905, she became the first female president of the American Psychological Association (Furumoto, 1979, 1991; Zedler, 1995). Unlike Washburn, Calkins never earned the elusive Ph.D. degree despite a successful career as a professor and researcher (Guthrie, 2004).

This is a good place to point out that women were not the only minority to make contributions in the early days of psychology. In 1920, for example, Francis Cecil Sumner became the first African American to earn a Ph.D. in psychology at Clark University. He eventually became the chair of the psychology department at Howard University and is assumed by many to be the father of African American psychology (Guthrie, 2004). Kenneth and Mamie Clark worked to show the negative effects of school segregation on African American children (Lal, 2002). Hispanic psychologist Jorge Sanchez conducted research in the area of intelligence testing, focusing on the cultural biases in such tests. Since those early days, psychology has seen an increase in the contributions of all minorities, although the percentages are still small when compared to the population at large. For a summary of the contributions of African Americans to the early days of psychology, see the following section, *Issues in Psychology: Psychology's African American Roots.*

Is functionalism still an important point of view in psychology?

Is functionalism still an important point of view in psychology?

In the new field of psychology, functionalism offered an alternative viewpoint to the structuralists. But like so many of psychology's early ideas, it is no longer a major perspective. Instead, one can find elements of functionalism in the modern fields of *educational psychology* (studying the application of psychological concepts to education) and *industrial/organizational psychology* (studying the application of psychological concepts to businesses, organizations, and industry), as well as other areas in psychology. LINK to Appendix B: Applied Psychology, B-7–B-8. Functionalism also played a part in the development of one of the more modern perspectives, evolutionary psychology, discussed later in this chapter.

functionalism early perspective in psychology associated with William James, in which the focus of study is how the mind allows people to adapt, live, work, and play.

*heredity: the transmission of traits and characteristics from parent to offspring through the actions of genes.

issues in psychology

Psychology's African American Roots

Even the Rat Was White is an excellent and thought-provoking book. Written by the late Dr. Robert V. Guthrie in 1976 and recently republished (Guthrie, 2004), it is an enlightening summary of the history of African Americans in the field of psychology. It is a book every psychologist and would-be psychologist should read. The contributions to early psychology of African American psychologists have often been ignored in textbooks. Dr. Guthrie (who died from cancer in 2005 at the age of 75) includes in his text a detailed listing of the important African American psychologists and their contributions to the relatively new field of psychology. The following is a brief summary of just a few of these often neglected scholars and their work.

- Dr. Charles Henry Thompson (1896–1980) was the first African American to receive a doctorate in educational psychology in 1925 from the University of Chicago. For 30 years he was the editor of the *Journal of Negro Education.*
- Dr. Albert Sidney Beckham (1897–1964) received his Ph.D. in psychology in 1930 from New York University. He was senior assistant psychologist at the National Committee for Mental Hygiene at the Illinois Institute for Juvenile Research in the early 1930s; he also counseled many Black youths in his role as the psychologist at DuSable High School in Chicago. He, like Thompson, had many publications of his research in the areas of intelligence and social concerns of the African American youth of his time.
- Dr. Robert Prentiss Daniel (1902–1968) earned his Ph.D. in educational psychology from Columbia University in 1932. At one time the Director of the Division of Educational Psychology and Philosophy at Virginia Union University, he became president of Shaw University in North Carolina and finally the president of Virginia State College.
- Dr. Inez Beverly Prosser (1897–1934) earned her Ph.D. in educational psychology from the University of Cincinnati in 1933 and was the first African American woman to earn this degree. Her promising teaching career met a tragic end when she died in an automobile accident only 1 year after earning her doctorate.
- Dr. Howard Hale Long (1888–1948) received his Ed.D. in educational psychology from Harvard University in 1933. After teaching psychology and doing research in educational psychology for many years, Dr. Long became Dean of Administration at Wilberforce State College in Ohio.
- Dr. Ruth Howard (1900–1997) is known as the first African American woman to earn the Ph.D. in psychology (not educational psychology) in 1934 from the University of Minnesota. She served with her husband, Dr. Albert Beckham, as codirector for the Center for Psychological Services and also maintained a private practice in clinical psychology.

These few African American pioneers in the field of psychology represent only a fraction of all those who made important contributions to psychology's early days.

Francis Cecil Sumner, the first African American to receive a Ph.D. in psychology, went on to chair the psychology department at Howard University and is considered by many to be the father of African American psychology.

Figure 1.1 A Gestalt Perception
The eye tends to "fill in" the blanks here and sees both of these figures as circles rather than as a series of dots or a broken line.

Gestalt psychology early perspective in psychology focusing on perception and sensation, particularly the perception of patterns and whole figures.

GESTALT PSYCHOLOGY: THE WHOLE IS GREATER THAN THE SUM OF ITS PARTS

Meanwhile, back in Germany, other psychologists were attacking the concepts of psychology in yet another way. Max Wertheimer (VERT-hi-mer), like James, objected to the structuralist point of view, but for different reasons. Wertheimer believed that psychological events such as perceiving* and sensing** could not be broken down into any smaller elements and still be properly understood. For example, you can take a compact disc player apart, but then you no longer have a CD player—you have a pile of unconnected bits and pieces. Or, just as a melody is made up of individual notes that can only be understood if the notes are in the correct relationship to one another, so perception can only be understood as a whole, entire event. Hence, the familiar slogan, "The whole is greater than the sum of its parts." The Gestalt psychologists believed that people naturally seek out patterns ("wholes") in the sensory information available to them. See Figure 1.1 for an example of Gestalt perceptual patterns.

1.3 What were the basic ideas and who were the important people behind the early approaches known as Gestalt, psychoanalysis, and behaviorism?

Wertheimer and others devoted their efforts to studying sensation and perception in this new perspective, **Gestalt psychology**. *Gestalt* (Gesh-TALT) is a German word meaning "an organized whole" or "configuration," which fit well with the focus on studying whole patterns rather than small pieces of them. Today, Gestalt ideas are part of the study of *cognitive psychology*, a field focusing not only on perception but also on learning, memory, thought processes, and problem solving; the basic Gestalt principles of perception are still taught within this newer field (Ash, 1998; Kohler, 1992; Wertheimer, 1982). LINK to Chapter Three: Sensation and Perception, pp. xxx–xxx. The Gestalt approach has also been influential in psychological therapy, becoming the basis for a therapeutic technique called *Gestalt therapy*. LINK to Chapter Fifteen: Psychological Therapies, pp. 579–580.

What about Freud? Everybody talks about him when they talk about psychology. Are his ideas still in use?

SIGMUND FREUD'S THEORY OF PSYCHOANALYSIS

It should be clear by now that psychology didn't start in one place and at one particular time. People of several different viewpoints were trying to promote their own perspective on the study of the human mind and behavior in different places all over the world. Up to now, this chapter has focused on the physiologists who became interested in psychology, with a focus on understanding consciousness but little else. The medical profession took a whole different approach to psychology.

What about Freud? Everybody talks about him when they talk about psychology. Are his ideas still in use?

Sigmund Freud had become a noted physician in Austria while the structuralists were arguing, the functionalists were specializing, and the Gestaltists were looking at the big picture. Freud was a neurologist, a medical doctor who specializes in disorders of the nervous system; he and his colleagues had long sought a way to understand the patients who were coming to them for help.

Freud's patients suffered from nervous disorders for which he and other doctors could find no physical cause. Therefore, it was thought, the cause must be in the mind, and that is where Freud began to explore. He proposed that there is an *unconscious* (unaware) mind into which we push, or *repress*, all of our threatening urges and desires. He believed that these repressed urges, in trying to surface, created the nervous disorders in his patients (Freud et al., 1990). LINK to Chapter Thirteen: Theories of Personality, p. 495.

Freud stressed the importance of early childhood experiences, believing that personality was formed in the first 6 years of life; if there were significant problems, those problems must have begun in the early years.

Psychoanalyst Sigmund Freud walks with his daughter Anna, also a psychoanalyst.

*perceiving: becoming aware of something through the senses.
**sensing: seeing, hearing, feeling, tasting, or smelling something.

psychoanalysis the theory and therapy based on the work of Sigmund Freud.

behaviorism the science of behavior that focuses on observable behavior only.

Some of his well-known followers were Alfred Adler, Carl Jung, and his own daughter, Anna Freud. Anna Freud began what became known as the ego movement in psychology, which produced one of the best known psychologists in the study of personality development, Erik Erikson. LINK to Chapter Eight: Development Across the Life Span, p. 322.

Freud's ideas are still influential today, although in a somewhat modified form. He had a number of followers in addition to those already named, many of whom became famous by altering Freud's theory to fit their own viewpoints, but his basic ideas are still discussed and debated. LINK to Chapter Thirteen: Theories of Personality, pp. 500–502.

Physiologist Ivan Pavlov uses a dog to demonstrate the conditioned reflex to students at the Russian Military Medical Academy.

While some might think that Sigmund Freud was the first person to deal with people suffering from various mental disorders, the truth is that mental illness has a fairly long (and not very pretty) history. For more on the history of mental illness, see the LINK to Chapter Fourteen: Psychological Disorders, pp. 532–533.

Freudian **psychoanalysis**, the theory and therapy based on Freud's ideas, has been the basis of much modern *psychotherapy* (a process in which a trained psychological professional helps a person gain insight into and change his or her behavior), but another major and competing viewpoint has actually been more influential in the field of psychology as a whole.

PAVLOV, WATSON, AND THE DAWN OF BEHAVIORISM

Ivan Pavlov, like Freud, was not a psychologist. He was a Russian physiologist who showed that a *reflex* (an involuntary reaction) could be caused to occur in response to a formerly unrelated stimulus. While working with dogs, Pavlov observed that the salivation reflex (which is normally produced by actually having food in one's mouth), could be caused to occur in response to a totally new stimulus, in this case, the sound of a ticking metronome. At the onset of his experiment, Pavlov would turn on the metronome, give the dogs food, and they would salivate. After several repetitions, the dogs would salivate to the sound of the metronome *before* the food was presented—a learned (or "conditioned") reflexive response (Klein & Mowrer, 1989). This process was called *conditioning*. LINK to Chapter Five: Learning, p. 171.

By the early 1900s, psychologist John B. Watson had tired of the arguing among the structuralists; he challenged the functionalist viewpoint, as well as psychoanalysis, with his own "science of behavior," or **behaviorism** (Watson, 1924). Watson wanted to bring psychology back to a focus on scientific inquiry, and he felt that the only way to do that was to ignore the whole consciousness issue and focus only on *observable behavior*—something that could be directly seen and measured. He had read of Pavlov's work and thought that conditioning could form the basis of his new perspective of behaviorism.

American psychologist John Watson is known as the father of behaviorism. Behaviorism focuses only on observable behavior.

OF BABIES AND RATS Watson was certainly aware of Freud's work and his views on unconscious repression. Freud believed that all behavior stems from unconscious motivation, whereas Watson believed that all behavior is learned. Freud had stated that a *phobia*, an irrational fear, is really a symptom of an underlying, repressed conflict and cannot be "cured" without years of psychoanalysis to uncover and understand the repressed material.

Watson believed that phobias are learned through the process of conditioning and set out to prove it. He took a baby, known as "Little Albert," and taught him to fear a white rat by making a loud, scary noise every time the infant saw the rat, until finally, just seeing the rat caused the infant to cry and become fearful (Watson & Rayner, 1920). Even though "Little Albert" was not afraid of the rat at the start, the experiment worked very well—in fact, he later appeared to be afraid of other fuzzy things including a rabbit, a dog, and a sealskin coat. **Watch** on **mypsychlab.com**

Watch classic footage of Watson and "Little Albert" on **mypsychlab.com**

This sounds really bizarre—what does scaring a baby have to do with the science of psychology?

This sounds really bizarre—what does scaring a baby have to do with the science of psychology?

Watson wanted to prove that all behavior was a result of a stimulus–response relationship such as that described by Pavlov. Because Freud and his ideas about unconscious motivation were becoming a dominant force, Watson felt the need to show the world that a much simpler explanation could be found. Although scaring a baby sounds a little cruel, he felt that the advancement of the science of behavior was worth the baby's relatively brief discomfort. One of Watson's graduate students later decided to repeat Watson and Rayner's study but added training that would "cancel out" the phobic reaction of the baby to the white rat.

Mary Cover Jones, one of the early pioneers of behavior therapy, earned her master's degree under the supervision of John Watson. She had a long and distinguished career, including the publication in 1952 of the first educational television course in child development.

One of those students was Mary Cover Jones, who completed her master's degree in 1920 under Watson's supervision (Rutherford, 2000). She duplicated the "Little Albert" study with another child, "Little Peter," successfully conditioning Peter to be afraid of a white rabbit (Jones, 1924). She then began a process of *counterconditioning*, in which Peter was exposed to the white rabbit from a distance while eating a food that he really liked. The pleasure of the food outweighed the fear of the far-away rabbit. Day by day, the situation was repeated with the rabbit being brought closer each time, until Peter was no longer afraid of the rabbit. Jones went on to become one of the early pioneers of behavior therapy. She was also a key figure in the Oakland Growth Study, a study of 200 fifth- and sixth-grade children that followed their development from the beginning of puberty to the end of adolescence. It is her work that is often cited when textbook authors talk about the benefits and problems associated with early and late maturation in puberty. She and her husband, Harold Jones, published the first educational television course in child development in 1952 (Rutherford, 2000).

Behaviorism is still a major perspective in psychology today. It has also influenced the development of other perspectives, such as *cognitive psychology*.

1.1 1.2 1.3 CONCEPT MAP

- **it has methods for studying phenomena**
- **it has four primary goals**
  - **describe**
  - **explain**
  - **predict**
  - **control**

What Is Psychology?

(is the scientific study of behavior and mental processes)

- A relatively new science that formally began in 1879 when Wilhelm Wundt ("father of psychology") established the first psychological laboratory in Leipzig, Germany
  - studied nonphysical structure (i.e., thought, experiences, emotions, etc.) of the human mind
  - used objective introspection to study processes that were the result of physical sensations
  - first attempt to bring objectivity and measurement to psychology
- was a student of Wundt's
- **Structuralism** founded by Edward Titchener
  - expanded Wundt's original ideas; believed every experience could be broken down into individual emotions and sensations
  - applied introspection method to thoughts as well as physical sensations
- **Functionalism** founded by William James
  - influenced by Darwin's ideas about natural selection—focused on how the mind allows people to function in the real world
  - interested in how behavioral traits could aid in survival
  - influenced development of evolutionary psychology
  - has elements in educational psychology and industrial/organizational psychology

Psychology Then: The History of Psychology

(has roots in several disciplines, including philosophy, medicine, and physiology, and has developed through several perspectives)

Psychology Then: The History of Psychology (continued)

- **Gestalt psychology** founded by Max Wertheimer — did not believe that psychological events could be broken down into smaller elements; could only be understood as a whole, entire event; has influenced field of cognitive psychology and a form of psychological therapy, Gestalt therapy
- **Psychoanalysis** ideas put forth by Sigmund Freud — stressed importance of early life experiences, the role of the unconscious, and development through stages
- **Behaviorism** associated with work of John B. Watson, who was greatly influenced by Ivan Pavlov's work in conditioning/learning — wanted to bring focus back on scientific inquiry and believed only way to do so was to focus on observable behavior and ignore "consciousness" issue; early work examined phobias

PRACTICE quiz How much do you remember? ANSWERS ON PAGE AK-1.

Study Help Note: These practice quizzes are spaced throughout each chapter to give you an opportunity to check your understanding of the material in each section and to provide practice for exams.

Pick the best answer.

1. In the definition of psychology, *behavior* means
   - a. internal, covert processes.
   - b. mental processes.
   - c. outward or overt actions and reactions.
   - d. only human behavior.
2. Dr. Edwards designs a special behavior program for helping children diagnosed with autism to learn to communicate with others. Dr. Edwards is most interested in the goal of
   - a. description.
   - b. explanation.
   - c. prediction.
   - d. control.
3. Cheryan et al. (2009) tested for the reason why there are so few women in the computer science field. This study most clearly illustrates the goal of
   - a. description.
   - b. explanation.
   - c. prediction.
   - d. control.
4. Which of the following early psychologists would have been most likely to agree with the statement, "The study of the mind should focus on how it allows us to adapt to our surroundings"?
   - a. Wilhelm Wundt
   - b. William James
   - c. John Watson
   - d. Sigmund Freud
5. Which early perspective would have been LEAST likely to agree with the structuralists?
   - a. introspectionism
   - b. functionalism
   - c. psychoanalysis
   - d. Gestalt
6. Who was the first woman president of the American Psychological Association?
   - a. Mary Whiton Calkins
   - b. Mary Cover Jones
   - c. Margaret Washburn
   - d. Ruth Howard
7. Who among the early African American psychologists eventually became president of two universities?
   - a. Dr. Ruth Howard
   - b. Dr. Robert Prentiss Daniel
   - c. Dr. Inez Beverly Prosser
   - d. Dr. Albert Sidney Beckham

Brainstorming: Would it be possible to do a study such as Watson and Rayner's "Little Albert" research today? Why or why not? What might justify such a study today?

Psychology Now: Modern Perspectives

1.4 What are the basic ideas behind the seven modern perspectives, and what were the important contributions of Skinner, Maslow, and Rogers?

Even in the twenty-first century, there isn't one single perspective that is used to explain all human behavior and mental processes. There are actually seven modern perspectives, with two of those being holdovers from the early days of the field.

PSYCHODYNAMIC PERSPECTIVE

Freud's theory is still used by many professionals in therapy situations. It is far less common today than it was a few decades ago, however, and even those who use his techniques modify them for contemporary use. In the more modern **psychodynamic perspective**, the focus may still include the unconscious mind and

psychodynamic perspective modern version of psychoanalysis that is more focused on the development of a sense of self and the discovery of motivations behind a person's behavior other than sexual motivations.

its influence over conscious behavior and on early childhood experiences, but with less of an emphasis on sex and sexual motivations and more emphasis on the development of a sense of self, social and interpersonal relationships, and the discovery of other motivations behind a person's behavior. LINK to Chapter Thirteen: Theories of Personality, pp. 500–502. Some modern psychodynamic practitioners have even begun to recommend that the link between neurobiology (the study of the brain and nervous system) and psychodynamic concepts should be more fully explored (Glucksman, 2006).

Behaviorist B. F. Skinner puts a rat through its paces. What challenges might arise from applying information gained from studies with animals to human behavior?

BEHAVIORAL PERSPECTIVE

Like modern psychodynamic perspectives, behaviorism is still also very influential. When its primary supporter, John B. Watson, moved on to greener pastures in the world of advertising, B. F. Skinner became the new leader of the field.

Skinner not only continued research in classical conditioning, but he also developed a theory called *operant conditioning*, to explain how voluntary behavior is learned (Skinner, 1938). In this theory, *behavioral* responses that are followed by pleasurable consequences are strengthened, or *reinforced.* For example, a child who cries and is rewarded by getting his mother's attention will cry again in the future. Skinner's work is discussed later in more depth. LINK to Chapter Five: Learning, pp. 180–181. In addition to the psychodynamic and behavioral perspectives, there are five newer perspectives that have developed within the last 50 years.

HUMANISTIC PERSPECTIVE

Often called the "third force" in psychology, humanism was really a reaction to both psychoanalytic theory and behaviorism. If you were a psychologist in the early to mid-1900s, you were either a psychoanalyst or a behaviorist—there weren't any other major viewpoints to rival those two.

In contrast to the psychoanalytic focus on sexual development and behaviorism's focus on external forces in guiding personality development, some professionals began to develop a perspective that would allow them to focus on people's ability to direct their own lives. Humanists held the view that people have *free will*, the freedom to choose their own destiny, and strive for *self-actualization,* the achievement of one's full potential. Two of the earliest and most famous founders of this view were Abraham Maslow (1908–1970) and Carl Rogers (1902–1987). Today, humanism exists as a form of psychotherapy aimed at self-understanding and self-improvement. LINK to Chapter Fifteen: Psychological Therapies, pp. 578–580.

COGNITIVE PERSPECTIVE

Cognitive psychology, which focuses on how people think, remember, store, and use information, became a major force in the field in the 1960s. It wasn't a new idea, as the Gestalt psychologists had themselves supported the study of mental processes of learning. The development of computers (which just happened to make ideal models of human thinking), the work of Piaget with children, Chomsky's analysis of Skinner's views of language, and discoveries in biological psychology all stimulated an interest in studying the processes of thought. The **cognitive perspective** with its focus on memory, intelligence, perception, thought processes, problem solving, language, and learning has become a major force in psychology. LINK to Chapter Seven: Cognition: Thinking, Intelligence, and Language, pp. 252–291.

cognitive perspective modern perspective that focuses on memory, intelligence, perception, problem solving, and learning.

Within the cognitive perspective, the relatively new field of **cognitive neuroscience** includes the study of the physical workings of the brain and nervous system when engaged in memory, thinking, and other cognitive processes. Cognitive neuroscientists use tools for imaging the structure and activity of the living brain, such as magnetic resonance imaging (MRI), functional magnetic resonance imaging (fMRI) and positron emission tomography (PET). LINK to Chapter Two: The Biological Perspective, pp. 67-68. The continually developing field of brain imaging is important in the study of cognitive processes.

SOCIOCULTURAL PERSPECTIVE

Another modern perspective in psychology is the **sociocultural perspective**, which actually combines two areas of study: *social psychology*, which is the study of groups, social roles, and rules of social actions and relationships; and *cultural psychology*, which is the study of cultural norms,* values, and expectations. These two areas are related in that they are both about the effect that people have on one another, either individually or in a larger group such as a culture (Peplau & Taylor, 1997). LINK to Chapter Twelve: Social Psychology, pp. 446–485. Russian psychologist Lev Vygotsky (1978) also used sociocultural concepts in forming his sociocultural theory of children's cognitive development. LINK to Chapter Eight: Development Across the Life Span, p. 315.

The sociocultural perspective is important because it reminds people that the way they and others behave (or even think) is influenced not only by whether they are alone, with friends, in a crowd, or part of a group but also by the social norms, fads, class differences, and ethnic identity concerns of the particular culture in which they live. *Cross-cultural research* also fits within this perspective. In cross-cultural research, the contrasts and comparisons of a behavior or issue are studied in at least two or more cultures. This type of research can help illustrate the different influences of environment (culture and training) when compared to the influence of heredity (genetics, or the influence of genes on behavior).

For example, in a classic study covered in Chapter Twelve: Social Psychology (pp. xxx, xxx–xxx), researchers Darley and Latané (1968) found that the presence of other people actually *lessened* the chances that a person in trouble would receive help. The phenomenon is called the "bystander effect" and it is believed to be the result of *diffusion of responsibility*, which is the tendency to feel that someone else is responsible for taking action when others are present. But would this effect appear in other cultures? Shorey (2001), in his discussion of the brutal beating death of a Somali prisoner in a Canadian military facility while bystanders looked on without acting, suggests that it just might. But is Canadian culture too similar to our own to lead us to this conclusion? Would another culture very different from Western culture show the same effect? This is exactly the kind of question that the sociocultural perspective asks and attempts to answer, using cross-cultural research.

BIOPSYCHOLOGICAL PERSPECTIVE

Biopsychology, or the study of the biological bases of behavior and mental processes, isn't really as new a perspective as one might think. Also known as physiological psychology, biological psychology, psychobiology, and behavioral neuroscience, biopsychology is part of the larger field of *neuroscience*: study of the physical structure, function, and development of the nervous system. Also, the previously discussed field of cognitive neuroscience often overlaps with biopsychology.

In the **biopsychological perspective**, human and animal behavior is seen as a direct result of events in the body. Hormones, heredity, brain chemicals, tumors, and

*norms: standards or expected behavior.

cognitive neuroscience study of the physical changes in the brain and nervous system during thinking.

sociocultural perspective perspective that focuses on the relationship between social behavior and culture.

biopsychological perspective perspective that attributes human and animal behavior to biological events occurring in the body, such as genetic influences, hormones, and the activity of the nervous system.

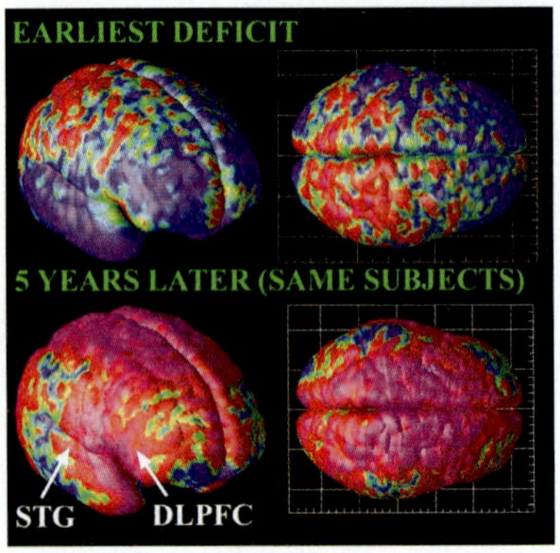

These scans highlight gray matter loss in the brains of individuals with very early-onset, adolescent schizophrenia over a five-year period, highlighting one focus of the biological perspective.

diseases are some of the biological causes of behavior and mental events. LINK to Chapter Two: The Biological Perspective, pp. 44–82. Some of the topics researched by biopsychologists include sleep, emotions, aggression, sexual behavior, and learning and memory—as well as disorders. While disorders may have multiple causes (family issues, stress, or trauma, for example), research in biopsychology points clearly to biological factors as one of those causes.

For example, evidence continues to mount for a genetic cause for *schizophrenia*, a mental disorder involving delusions (false beliefs), hallucinations (false sensory impressions), and extremely distorted thinking (Brzustowicz et al., 2004; Maziade et al., 1997; Pogue-Geile & Yokley, 2010). LINK to Chapter Fourteen: Psychological Disorders, pp. 556–560. Other research suggests that human sexual orientation may be related to the developing baby's exposure in the womb to testosterone (G. Brown et al., 2002) as well as the birth order of male children (Puts et al., 2006). The Puts, Jordan, and Breedlove (2006) study suggests that the more older brothers a male child has, the more likely he is to have a homosexual orientation. LINK to Chapter Ten: Sexuality and Gender, p. 396. Still another example of research in this field is Escandon, Al-Hammadi, and Galvin's (2010) study finding a possible link between the tendency to lose one's train of thought in later adulthood—staring into space, unexplained excessive daytime sleepiness, and disorganized thinking, for example—and the development of Alzheimer's disease. LINK to Chapter Six: Memory, p. 246.

EVOLUTIONARY PERSPECTIVE

The **evolutionary perspective** focuses on the biological bases for universal mental characteristics that all humans share. It seeks to explain general mental strategies and traits, such as why we lie, how attractiveness influences mate selection, why fear of snakes is so common, or why people universally like music and dancing. This approach may also overlap with biopsychology.

In this perspective, the mind is seen as a set of information-processing machines, designed by the same process of natural selection that Darwin (1859) first theorized, allowing human beings to solve the problems faced in the early days of human evolution—the problems of the early hunters and gatherers. For example, *evolutionary psychologists* (psychologists who study the evolutionary origins of human behavior) would view the human behavior of not eating substances that have a bitter taste (such as poisonous plants) as an adaptive* behavior that evolved as early humans came into contact with such bitter plants. Those who ate the bitter plants would die, while those who spit them out survived to pass on their "I-don't-like-this-taste" genes to their offspring, who would pass on the genes to *their* offspring, and so on, until after a long period of time there is an entire population of humans that naturally avoids bitter-tasting substances.

That explains why people don't like bitter stuff, like the white part of an orange peel, but that's really a physical thing. How would the evolutionary perspective help us understand something psychological like relationships?

That explains why people don't like bitter stuff, like the white part of an orange peel, but that's really a physical thing. How would the evolutionary perspective help us understand something psychological like relationships?

Relationships between men and women are one of the many areas in which evolutionary psychologists conduct research. For example, in one study researchers surveyed young adults about their relationships with the opposite sex, asking the participants how likely they would be to forgive either a sexual infidelity or an emotional one (Shackelford et al., 2002). Evolutionary theory would predict that men would find it more difficult to forgive a woman who had sex with someone else than a

evolutionary perspective perspective that focuses on the biological bases of universal mental characteristics that all humans share.

*adaptive: having the quality of adjusting to the circumstances or need; in the sense used here, a behavior that aids in survival.

woman who was only emotionally involved with someone because the man wants to be sure that the children the woman bears are his (Geary, 2000, in press). Why put all that effort into providing for children who could be another man's offspring? Women, on the other hand, should find it harder to forgive an emotional infidelity, as they are always sure that their children are their own, but (in evolutionary terms, mind you) they need the emotional loyalty of the men to provide for those children (Buss et al., 1992; Daly et al., 1982; Edlund et al., 2006). The results support the prediction: Men find it harder to forgive a partner's sexual straying and are more likely to break up with the woman than if the infidelity is purely emotional; for women, the opposite results were found. Other research concerning mating has found that women seem to use a man's kissing ability to determine his worthiness as a potential mate (Hughes et al., 2007; Walter, 2008).

Psychologists with an evolutionary perspective would be interested in how this couple selected each other as partners.

Psychological Professionals and Areas of Specialization

Psychology is a large field, and the many professionals working within it have different training, different focuses, and may have different goals from the typical psychologist.

1.5 How does a psychologist differ from a psychiatrist, and what are the other types of professionals who work in the various areas of psychology?

A **psychologist** has no medical training but has a doctorate degree. Psychologists undergo intense academic training, learning about many different areas of psychology before choosing a specialization. Because the focus of their careers can vary so widely, psychologists work in many different vocational* settings. Figure 1.2a shows the types

psychologist a professional with an academic degree and specialized training in one or more areas of psychology.

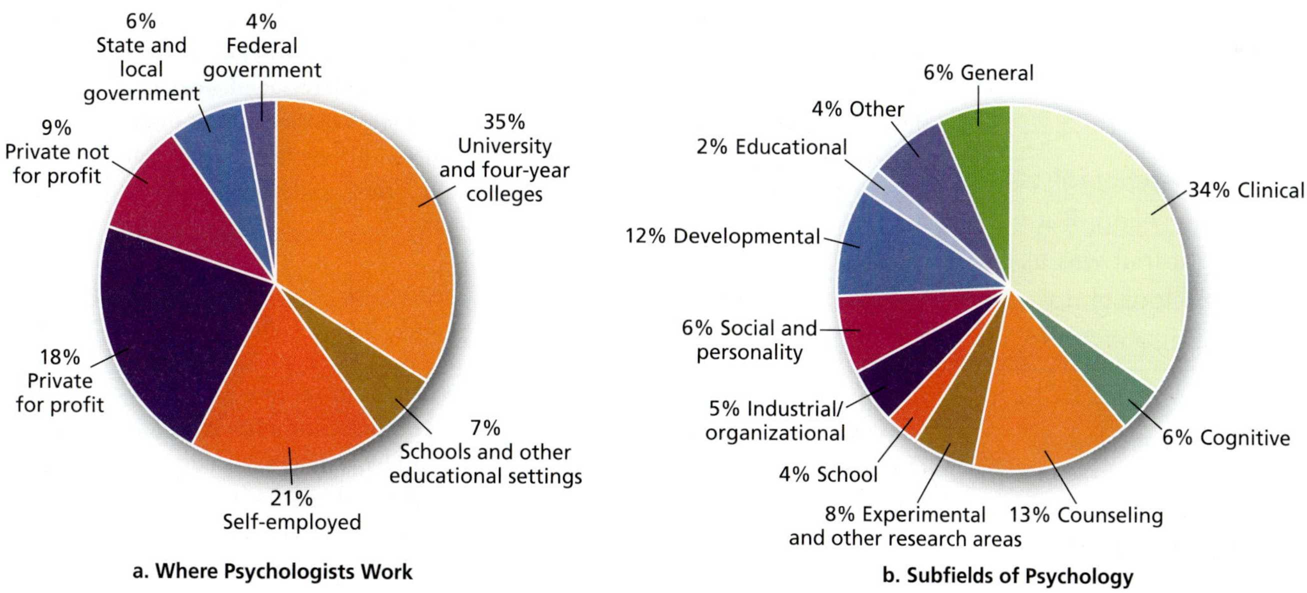

Figure 1.2 Work Settings and Subfields of Psychology

(a) There are many different work settings for psychologists. Although not obvious from the chart, many psychologists work in more than one setting. For example, a clinical psychologist may work in a hospital setting and teach at a university or college. (Tsapogas et al., 2006) (b) This pie chart shows the specialty areas of psychologists who recently received their doctorates. (Hoffer et al., 2007)

*vocational: having to do with a job or career.

Psychiatric social workers help many kinds and ages of people. The woman on the right might be going through a divorce, dealing with the loss of a spouse, or even recovering from drug abuse.

of settings in which psychologists work. Remember, not all psychologists are trained to do counseling! Psychologists in the counseling specialization must also be licensed to practice in their states. Read on **mypsychlab.com**

Read and learn more about psychological professionals on **mypsychlab.com**

In contrast, a **psychiatrist** has a medical (M.D. or D.O.) degree and is a medical doctor who has specialized in the diagnosis and treatment (including the prescription of medications) of psychological disorders. A **psychiatric social worker** is trained in the area of social work and usually possesses a master's degree in that discipline. These professionals focus more on the environmental conditions that can have an impact on mental disorders, such as poverty, overcrowding, stress, and drug abuse.

You said not all psychologists do counseling. But I thought that was all that psychologists do—what else is there?

AREAS OF SPECIALIZATION

You said not all psychologists do counseling. But I thought that was all that psychologists do—what else is there?

Although many psychologists do participate in delivering therapy to people who need help, there is a nearly equal number of psychologists who do other tasks: researching, teaching, designing equipment and workplaces, and developing educational methods, for example. Also, not every psychologist is interested in the same area of human—or animal—behavior and most psychologists work in several different areas of interest, as shown in Figure 1.2b, "Subfields of Psychology."

There are many other areas of specialization: Psychology can be used in fields such as health; sports performance; legal issues; business concerns; and even in the design of equipment, tools, and furniture. For a more detailed look at some of thes areas in which psychological principles can be applied and a listing of careers that can benefit from a degree in psychology, see LINK to Appendix B: Applied Psychology, B-1–B-13.

psychiatrist a medical doctor who has specialized in the diagnosis and treatment of psychological disorders.

psychiatric social worker a social worker with some training in therapy methods who focuses on the environmental conditions that can have an impact on mental disorders, such as poverty, overcrowding, stress, and drug abuse.

CONCEPT MAP

1.4 1.5

- **Psychodynamic** based on Freud's theory — focuses on the role of the unconscious mind and its influence on conscious behavior, early childhood experiences, development of sense of self, and other motivations
- **Behavioral** based on early work of Watson and later B. F. Skinner — focuses on how behavioral responses are learned through classical or operant conditioning
- **Humanistic** two pioneers are Carl Rogers and Abraham Maslow — focuses on human potential, free will, and possibility of self-actualization
- **Cognitive** has roots in Gestalt psychology — focuses on memory, intelligence, perception, thought processes, problem solving, language, and learning

Psychology Now: Modern Perspectives

(no one single perspective is used to explain all human behavior and processes)

- **Sociocultural** — focuses on the behavior of individuals as the result of the presence (real or imagined) of other individuals, as part of groups, or as part of a larger culture
- **Biopsychological** — focuses on influences of hormones, brain structures and chemicals, disease, etc.; human and animal behavior is seen as a direct result of events in the body
- **Evolutionary** — focuses on the biological bases for universal mental characteristics, such as why we lie, how attractiveness influences mate selection, the universality of fear, and why we enjoy things like music and dance

Psychological Professionals and Areas of Specialization

(people working in the field of psychology have a variety of training experiences and different focuses)

psychologist
- has a doctorate degree (Ph.D., Psy.D., or Ed.D.) and works with either humans or animals in a variety of settings based on the area of specialization
- must be licensed to practice independently; typically does not prescribe medications but can go through specialized training to do so in a few states

psychiatrist
- medical doctor (M.D. or D.O.) that specializes in diagnosis and treatment of psychological disorders; can prescribe medication

psychiatric social worker
- has training in area of social work (M.S.W.) and often has a professional license to practice (L.C.S.W.)

PRACTICE quiz How much do you remember?

ANSWERS ON PAGE AK-1.

Pick the best answer.

1. Which of the following pairs represents the oldest of today's psychological perspectives?
   a. humanism and behaviorism
   b. behaviorism and psychodynamics
   c. psychodynamics and evolutionary psychology
   d. cognitive psychology and sociocultural psychology
2. Which perspective is known as the "third force" in psychology?
   a. psychoanalysis
   b. behaviorism
   c. cognitive psychology
   d. humanism
3. Wesley was behaving oddly and showing signs of memory problems and odd behavior. Doctors found that an earlier fall had created fluid pressure on his brain, causing the odd symptoms. Which of the following perspectives BEST explains Wesley's disordered behavior?
   a. psychodynamics
   b. cognitive psychology
   c. behaviorism
   d. biopsychology

(continued)

4. Which perspective would a researcher be taking if she were studying the way children learn through reinforcement of their actions?
   a. psychoanalysis
   b. cognitive psychology
   c. behaviorism
   d. evolutionary perspective
5. Which of the following professionals in psychology focuses more on the environmental conditions that affect mental disorders?
   a. psychiatrist
   b. psychoanalyst
   c. psychiatric social worker
   d. psychologist
6. Dr. Roaden works in a school system, dealing directly with children who have emotional, academic, and behavioral problems. Dr. Roaden is most likely which type of psychologist?
   a. personality
   b. developmental
   c. school
   d. comparative

Brainstorming: Do you believe that violence is a part of human nature? Is violent behavior something that can someday be removed from human behavior or, at the very least, be controlled? Think about this question from each of the perspectives discussed in this chapter.

Psychology: The Scientific Methodology

WHY PSYCHOLOGISTS USE THE SCIENTIFIC METHOD

Have you ever played the "airport game"? You sit at the airport (bus terminal, doctor's office, or any other place where people come and go and you have a long wait) and try to guess what people do for a living based only on their appearance. Although it's a fun game, the guesses are rarely correct. People's guesses also sometimes reveal the biases that they may have about certain physical appearances: men with long hair are musicians, people wearing suits are executives, and so on. On the other hand, psychology is about trying to determine facts and reduce uncertainty.

The scientific method can be used to determine if children who watch violence on television are more likely to be aggressive than those who do not.

1.6 Why is psychology considered a science, and what are the steps in using the scientific method?

In psychology, researchers want to see only what is really there, not what their biases might lead them to see. This can be achieved using the **scientific method**, a system for reducing bias and error in the measurement of data. The scientific method is a way to accomplish the goals of psychology as discussed earlier: description, explanation, prediction, and control.

The first step in any investigation is to have a question to investigate, right? So the first step in the scientific method is this:

1. **Perceiving the Question:** You notice something interesting happening in your surroundings for which you would like to have an explanation. An example might be that you've noticed that your children seem to get a little more aggressive with each other after watching a particularly violent children's cartoon program on Saturday morning. You wonder if the violence in the cartoon could be creating the aggressive behavior in your children. This step is derived from the goal of *description*: What is happening here?

   Once you have a question, you want an answer. The next logical step is to form a tentative* answer or explanation for the behavior you have seen. This tentative explanation is known as a **hypothesis**.
2. **Forming a Hypothesis:** Based on your initial observations of what's going on in your surroundings, you form an educated guess about the explanation for your observations, putting it into the form of a statement that can be tested in some way. Going back to the previous example, you might say, "Children who watch violent cartoons will become more aggressive." (Forming a hypothesis based on observations is related to the goals of *description* and *explanation*.)

scientific method system of gathering data so that bias and error in measurement are reduced.

hypothesis tentative explanation of a phenomenon based on observations.

*tentative: something that is not fully worked out or completed as yet.

The next step is testing the hypothesis. People have a tendency to notice only things that agree with their view of the world, a kind of selective perception called *confirmation bias*. LINK to Chapter Seven: Cognition, p. 262. For example, if a person is convinced that all men with long hair smoke cigarettes, that person will tend to notice only those long-haired men who are smoking and ignore all the long-haired men who don't smoke. The scientific method is designed to overcome the tendency to look at only the information that confirms people's biases by forcing them to actively seek out information that might *contradict* their biases (or hypotheses). So when you test your hypothesis, you are trying to determine if the factor you suspect has an effect and that the results weren't due to luck or chance. That's why psychologists keep doing research over and over—to get more evidence that hypotheses are "supported."

3. **Testing the Hypothesis**: The method you use to test your hypothesis will depend on exactly what kind of answer you think you might get. You could make more detailed observations or do a survey in which you ask questions of a large number of people, or you might design an experiment in which you would deliberately change one thing to see if it causes changes in the behavior you are observing. In the example, the best method would probably be an experiment in which you select a group of children, show half of them a cartoon with violence and half of them a cartoon with no violence, and then find some way of measuring aggressive behavior in the two groups.

   What do you do with the results of your testing? Of course, testing the hypothesis is all about the goal of getting an *explanation* for behavior, which leads to the next step.

4. **Drawing Conclusions**: Once you know the results of your hypothesis testing, you will find that either your hypothesis was supported—which means that your experiment worked, and that your measurements supported your initial observations—or that they weren't supported, which means that you need to go back to square one and think of another possible explanation for what you have observed. (Could it be that Saturday mornings make children a little more aggressive? Or Saturday breakfasts?)

   The results of any method of hypothesis testing won't be just the raw numbers or measurements. Any data that come from your testing procedure will be analyzed with some kind of statistical method that helps to organize and refine the data. LINK to Appendix A: Statistics, A-1–A-12. Drawing conclusions can be related to the goal of *prediction*: If your hypothesis is supported, you can make educated guesses about future, similar scenarios.

5. **Report Your Results**: You have come to some conclusion about your investigation's success or failure, and you want to let other researchers know what you have found.

   Why tell anyone what happened if it failed?

   Just because one experiment or study did not find support for the hypothesis does not necessarily mean that the hypothesis is incorrect. Your study could have been poorly designed, or there might have been factors out of your control that interfered with the study. But other researchers are asking the same kinds of questions that you might have asked. They need to know what has already been found out about the answers to those questions so that they can continue investigating and adding more knowledge about the answers to those questions. Even if your own investigation didn't go as planned, your report will tell other researchers what *not* to do in the future. So the final step in any scientific investigation is reporting the results.

Why tell anyone what happened if it failed?

At this point, you would want to write up exactly what you did, why you did it, how you did it, and what you found. If others can **replicate** your research (meaning, do exactly the same study over again and get the same results), it gives much more support to your findings. This allows others to predict behavior based on your findings and to use the results of those findings to modify or *control* behavior, the last goal in psychology.

This might be a good place to make a distinction between questions that can be scientifically or empirically studied and those that cannot. For example, "What is the meaning of life?" is not a question that can be studied using the scientific or empirical method. Empirical questions are those that can be tested through direct observation or experience. For example, "Has life ever existed on Mars?" is a question that scientists are trying to answer through measurements, experimentation, soil samples, and other methods. Eventually they will be able to say with some degree of confidence that life could have existed or could not have existed. That is an empirical question, because it can be supported or disproved by gathering real evidence. The meaning of life, however, is a question of belief for each person. One does not need proof to *believe*, but scientists need proof (in the form of objectively gathered evidence) to *know*.

In psychology, researchers try to find the answers to empirical questions. Questions that involve beliefs and values are best left to philosophy and religion.

DESCRIPTIVE METHODS

1.7 How are naturalistic and laboratory settings used to describe behavior, and what are some of the advantages and disadvantages associated with these settings?

There are a number of different ways to investigate the answers to research questions, and which one researchers use depends on the kind of question they want to answer. If they only want to gather information about what has happened or what is happening, they would select a method that gives them a detailed description.

This researcher is studying the behavior of a group of lemurs. Is this naturalistic observation? Why or why not?

NATURALISTIC OBSERVATION Sometimes all a researcher needs to know is what is happening to a group of animals or people. The best way to look at the behavior of animals or people is to watch them behave in their normal environment. That's why animal researchers go to where the animals live and watch them eat, play, mate, and sleep in their own natural surroundings. With people, researchers might want to observe them in their workplaces, homes, or on playgrounds. For example, if someone wanted to know how adolescents behave with members of the opposite sex in a social setting, that researcher might go to the mall on a weekend night.

What is the advantage of naturalistic observation? It allows researchers to get a realistic picture of how behavior occurs because they are actually watching that behavior in its natural setting. In a more controlled arranged environment, like a laboratory, they might get behavior that is contrived or artificial rather than genuine. Of course, there are precautions that must be taken. An observer should have a checklist of well-defined and specific behavior to record, perhaps using a special handheld computer to log each piece of data. In many cases, animals or people who know they are being watched will not behave normally—a process called the **observer effect**—so, often the observer must remain hidden from view. When researching humans, remaining hidden often a difficult thing to do. In the earlier example of the mall setting with the teenagers, a researcher might find that pretending to read a book is a good disguise, especially if one wears glasses to hide the movement of the eyes. Using such a scenario, researchers would be able to observe what goes on between the teens without them knowing that they were being watched. In other cases, researchers might use one-way

replicate in research, repeating a study or experiment to see if the same results will be obtained in an effort to demonstrate reliability of results.

observer effect tendency of people or animals to behave differently from normal when they know they are being observed.

mirrors, or they might actually become participants in a group, a technique called **participant observation**.

Are there disadvantages to this method? Unfortunately, yes. One of the disadvantages of naturalistic observation is the possibility of **observer bias**. That happens when the person doing the observing has a particular opinion about what he or she expects to see. If that is the case, sometimes that person recognizes only those actions that support the preconceived expectation and ignores actions that coincide with it. One way to avoid observer bias is to use *blind observers*: People who do not know what the research question is and, therefore, have no preconceived notions about what they "should" see. It's also a good idea to have more than one observer, so that the various observations can be compared.

The researcher in the foreground is watching the children through a one-way mirror to get a description of their behavior. Observations such as these are just one of many ways that psychologists have of investigating behavior. Why is it important for the researcher to be behind a one-way mirror?

Another disadvantage is that each naturalistic setting is unique and unlike any other. Observations that are made at one time in one setting may not hold true for another time, even if the setting is similar, because the conditions are not going to be identical time after time—researchers don't have that kind of control over the natural world. For example, famed gorilla researcher Diane Fossey had to battle poachers who set traps for the animals in the area of her observations (Mowat, 1988). The presence and activities of the poachers affected the normal behavior of the gorillas she was trying to observe.

LABORATORY OBSERVATION Sometimes observing behavior in animals or people is just not practical in a natural setting. For example, a researcher might want to observe the reactions of infants to a mirror image of themselves, and to record the reactions with a camera mounted behind a one-way mirror. That kind of equipment might be difficult to set up in a natural setting. In a laboratory observation, the researcher would bring the infant to the equipment, controlling the number of infants and their ages, as well as everything else that goes on in the laboratory.

As mentioned previously, laboratory settings have the disadvantage of being an artificial situation that might result in artificial behavior—both animals and people often react differently in the laboratory than they would in the real world. The main advantage of this method is the degree of control that it gives to the observer.

Both naturalistic and laboratory observations can lead to the formation of hypotheses that can later be tested.

After a gunpowder explosion, Phineas Gage ended up with a steel rod in his head. A model of Gage's head is shown next to his actual skull. Visible above the left side of his mouth is the entry point of the steel rod, and the exit point is at the top of the skull.

1.8 How are case studies and surveys used to describe behavior, and what are some drawbacks to each of these methods?

CASE STUDIES Another descriptive technique is called the **case study**, in which one individual is studied in great detail. In a case study, researchers try to learn everything they can about that individual. For example, Sigmund Freud based his entire theory of psychoanalysis on case studies of his patients in which he gathered information about their childhoods and relationships with others from the very beginning of their lives to the present. LINK to Chapter Thirteen: Theories of Personality, p. 495.

The advantage of the case study is the tremendous amount of detail it provides. It may also be the only way to get certain kinds of information. For example, one famous case study was the story of Phineas Gage, who, in an accident, had a large metal rod driven through his head and suffered a major personality change as a result (Damasio et al., 1994). Researchers couldn't study that with naturalistic observation and an experiment is out of the question. Imagine anyone responding to an ad in the newspaper that read:

> *Wanted: 50 people willing to suffer nonfatal brain damage for scientific study of the brain. Will pay all medical expenses.*

participant observation a naturalistic observation in which the observer becomes a participant in the group being observed.

observer bias tendency of observers to see what they expect to see.

case study study of one individual in great detail.

It's pretty certain that anyone who actually answered such an ad might already be suffering from some rather extensive brain damage. Case studies are also good ways to study things that are rare, such as dissociative identity disorder. LINK to Chapter Fourteen: Psychological Disorders, p. 554.

The disadvantage of the case study is that researchers can't really apply the results to other similar people. In other words, they can't assume that if another person had the same kind of experiences growing up that he or she would turn out just like the person in their case study. People are unique and have too many complicating factors in their lives to be that predictable. So what researchers find in one case won't necessarily apply or generalize to others. Another weakness of this method is that case studies are a form of detailed observation and are vulnerable to bias on the part of the person conducting the case study, just as observer bias can occur in naturalistic or laboratory observation. **Read** on **mypsychlab.com**

Read and learn more about the fascinating Phineas Gage case study on **mypsychlab.com**

SURVEYS Sometimes what psychologists want to know about is pretty personal—like what people do in their sexual relationships, for example. (I'm pretty sure naturalistic observation of human sexual behavior could end in an arrest!) The only way to find out about very private (covert) behavior is to ask questions.

In the survey method, researchers will ask a series of questions about the topic they are studying. Surveys can be conducted in person in the form of interviews or on the telephone, the Internet, or with a questionnaire. The questions used in interviews or on the telephone can vary, but usually the questions in a survey are all the same for everyone answering the survey. In this way, researchers can ask lots of questions and survey literally hundreds of people.

That is the big advantage of surveys, aside from their ability to get at private information. Researchers can get a tremendous amount of data on a very large group of people. Of course, there are disadvantages. For one, researchers have to be very careful about the group of people they survey. If they want to find out what college freshmen think about politics, for example, they can't really ask every single college freshman in the entire United States. But they can select a **representative sample** from that group. They could randomly* select a certain number of college freshmen from several different colleges across the United States, for example. Why randomly? Because the sample has to be *representative* of the **population**, which is the entire group in which the researcher is interested. If researchers selected only freshmen from Ivy League schools, for example, they would certainly get different opinions on politics than they might get from small community colleges. But if they take a lot of colleges and select their *participants* (people who are part of the study) randomly, they will be more certain of getting answers that a broad selection of college students would typically give.

"Next question: I believe that life is a constant striving for balance, requiring frequent tradeoffs between morality and necessity, within a cyclic pattern of joy and sadness, forging a trail of bittersweet memories until one slips, inevitably, into the jaws of death. Agree or disagree?"

That brings up the other major disadvantage of the survey technique: People aren't always going to give researchers accurate answers. The fact is, people tend to misremember things, distort the truth, and may lie outright—even if the survey is an anonymous** questionnaire. Remembering is not a very accurate process sometimes, especially when people think that they might not come off sounding very desirable or socially appropriate. Some people deliberately give the answer they think is more socially correct rather than their true opinion, so that no one gets offended, in a process called *courtesy bias*. Researchers must take their survey results with a big grain of salt†—they may not be as accurate as they would like them to be.

representative sample randomly selected sample of subjects from a larger population of subjects.

population the entire group of people or animals in which the researcher is interested.

*randomly: in this sense, selected so that each member of the group has an equal chance of being chosen.

**anonymous: not named or identified.

†grain of salt: a phrase meaning to be skeptical; to doubt the truth or accuracy of something.

Both the wording of survey questions and the order in which they appear can affect the outcome. It is difficult to find a wording that will be understood in exactly the same way by all those who read the question. For example, questions can be worded in a way that the desired answer becomes obvious (often resulting in courtesy bias–type answers), or a question that appears at the end of a survey might be answered quite differently if it appears at the beginning.

1.6 1.7 1.8

CONCEPT MAP

scientific method
- perceiving the question about some empirical event for which you would like an explanation; can be derived from the goal of description: What is happening here?
- forming a hypothesis, a tentative explanation about an event
- testing the hypothesis by collecting data, analyzing results
- drawing conclusions about investigation's success or failure to explain event
- reporting your results; share exactly what, why, and how you did it, which provides means for replication

Psychology: The Scientific Methodology

(psychology uses the scientific method to try to determine facts and reduce uncertainty)

descriptive data collection methods
- **naturalistic observation:** observe people or animals in natural environment
- **laboratory observation:** observe people or animals in laboratory setting
- **case studies:** individual is studied in greater detail, researchers try to learn everything they can about the individual
- **surveys:** ask questions about topic researchers are studying via telephone, Internet, or a questionnaire

(naturalistic and laboratory observation) can lead to formation of hypotheses that can later be tested

PRACTICE quiz How much do you remember?

ANSWERS ON PAGE AK-1.

Pick the best answer.

1. In the scientific method, the first step is
   a. reporting your results.
   b. perceiving a question.
   c. drawing conclusions.
   d. testing the hypothesis
2. In a naturalistic observation, the phenomenon in which the behavior of the subjects being observed changes because they are being watched is called
   a. observer bias.
   b. participant observation.
   c. observer effect.
   d. representative sampling.
3. The use of ______________ helps to control for the effect of observer bias.
   a. blind observers
   b. a single trained observer
   c. randomly selected observers
   d. none of the above
4. The main disadvantage of a case study is that it is not
   a. easily done due to the large number of subjects.
   b. detailed enough for most research questions.
   c. generalizable to other similar conditions.
   d. biased.
5. Which of the following is the BEST example of a representative sample?
   a. You ask your fellow students to be participants in a study of adult memory.
   b. You ask people from your church to participate in a study of family values.
   c. You choose people shopping in an expensive store in the mall to respond to your survey.
   d. You choose people randomly from the telephone book to respond to your survey.

Brainstorming: Let's assume that you want to find out if telepathy really exists. Would any of the descriptive methods for studying behavior be a good method to use in examining this question? Why or why not?

FINDING RELATIONSHIPS

The methods discussed so far only provide descriptions of behavior. There are really only two methods that allow researchers to know more than just a description of what has happened: correlations and experiments. Correlation is actually a statistical technique, a particular way of organizing numerical information so that it is easier to look for patterns in the information. This method will be discussed here rather than in the statistics appendix found at the back of this text because correlation, like the experiment, is about finding relationships. In fact, the data from the descriptive methods just discussed are often analyzed using the correlational technique.

1.9 What is the correlational technique, and what does it tell researchers about relationships?

CORRELATIONS A **correlation** is a measure of the relationship between two or more variables. A *variable* is anything that can change or vary—scores on a test, temperature in a room, gender, and so on. For example, researchers might be curious to know whether or not cigarette smoking is connected to life expectancy—the number of years a person can be expected to live. Obviously, the scientists can't hang around people who smoke and wait to see when those people die. The only way (short of performing a very unethical and lengthy experiment) to find out if smoking behavior and life expectancy are related to each other is to use the medical records of people who have already died. (For privacy's sake, the personal information such as names and social security numbers would be removed, with only the facts such as age, gender, weight, and so on available to researchers.) Researchers would look for two facts from each record: the number of cigarettes the person smoked per day and the age of the person at death.

Now the researcher has two sets of numbers for each person in the study that go into a mathematical formula, LINK to Appendix A: Statistics, A-10–A-11, to produce a number called the **correlation coefficient**. The correlation coefficient represents two things: the direction of the relationship and its strength.

Direction? How can a mathematical relationship have a direction?

Direction? How can a mathematical relationship have a direction?

Whenever researchers talk about two variables being related to each other, what they really mean is that knowing the value of one variable allows them to predict the value of the other variable. For example, if researchers found that smoking and life expectancy are indeed related, they should be able to predict how long someone might live if they know how many cigarettes a person smokes in a day. But which way does that prediction work? If a person smokes a lot of cigarettes, does that mean that he or she will live a longer life or a shorter one? Does life expectancy go up or down as smoking increases? That's what is meant by the *direction* of the relationship.

In terms of the correlation coefficient (represented by the small letter *r*), the number researchers get from the formula will either be a positive number or a negative number. If positive, the two variables increase in the same direction—as one goes up, the other goes up; as one decreases, the other also decreases. If negative, the two variables have an inverse* relationship. As one increases, the other decreases. If researchers find that the more cigarettes a person smoked, the younger that person was when he or she died, it would mean that the correlation between the two variables is negative. (As smoking goes up, life expectancy goes down—an inverse relationship.)

The strength of the relationship between the variables will be determined by the actual number itself. That number will always range between +1.00 and −1.00. The reason that it cannot be greater than +1.00 or less than −1.00 has to do with the

correlation a measure of the relationship between two variables.

correlation coefficient a number derived from the formula for measuring a correlation and indicating the strength and direction of a correlation.

*inverse: opposite in order.

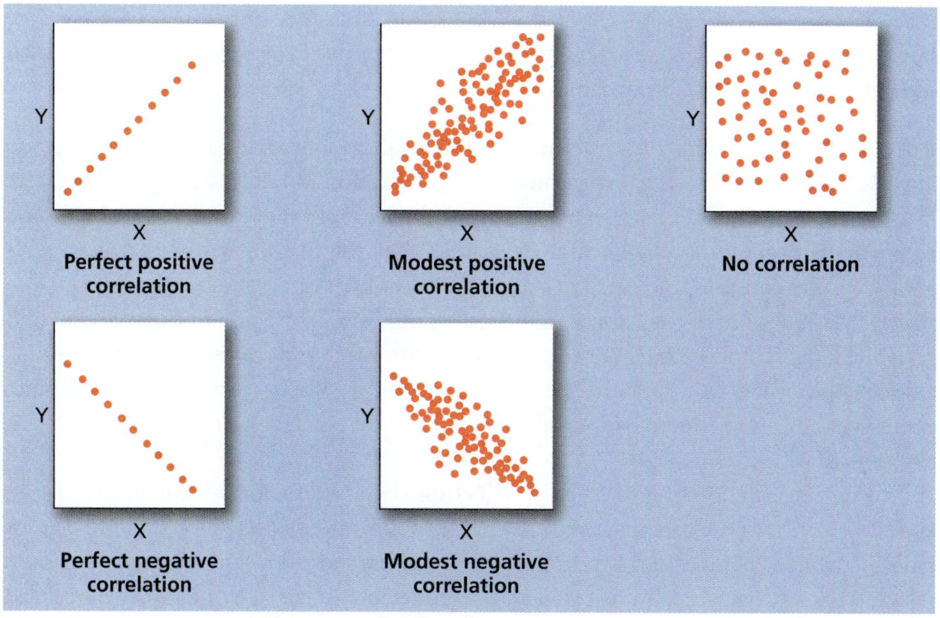

Figure 1.3 Five Scatterplots

These scatterplots show direction and strength of correlation. It should be noted that perfect correlations, whether positive or negative, rarely occur in the real world.

formula and an imaginary line on a graph around which the data points gather, a graph called a scatterplot (see Figure 1.3). If the relationship is a strong one, the number will be closer to +1.00 or to −1.00 A correlation of +.89 for example, would be a very strong positive correlation. That might represent the relationship between scores on the SAT and an IQ test, for example. A correlation of −.89 would be equally strong but negative. That would be more like the correlation researchers would probably find between smoking cigarettes and the age at which a person dies.

Notice that the closer the number is to zero, the weaker the relationship becomes. Researchers would probably find that the correlation coefficient for the relationship between people's weight and the number of freckles they have is pretty close to zero, for example.

Go back to the cigarette thing—if we found that the correlation between cigarette smoking and life expectancy was high, does that mean that smoking causes your life expectancy to be shortened?

Go back to the cigarette thing—if we found that the correlation between cigarette smoking and life expectancy was high, does that mean that smoking causes your life expectancy to be shortened?

Not exactly. The biggest error that people make concerning correlation is to assume that it means one variable is the cause of the other. Remember that *correlation does not prove causation.* Although adverse health effects from cigarette smoking account for approximately 438,000 deaths each year in the United States alone, correlation by itself cannot be used to prove causation (Centers for Disease Control and Prevention, 2009). Just because two variables are related to each other, researchers cannot assume that one of them causes the other one to occur. They could both be related to some other variable that is the cause of both. For example, cigarette smoking and life expectancy could be linked only because people who smoke may be less likely to take care of their health by eating right and exercising, whereas people who don't smoke may tend to eat healthier foods and exercise more than smokers do.

To sum up, a correlation will tell researchers if there is a relationship between the variables, how strong the relationship is, and in what direction the relationship goes. If researchers know the value of one variable, they can predict the value of the other. If they know someone's IQ score, for example, they can predict approximately what score that person should get on the SAT—not the

experiment a deliberate manipulation of a variable to see if corresponding changes in behavior result, allowing the determination of cause-and-effect relationships.

operational definition definition of a variable of interest that allows it to be directly measured.

exact score, just a reasonable estimate. Also, even though correlation does not prove causation, it can provide a starting point for examining causal relationships with another type of study, the experiment.

THE EXPERIMENT The only method that will allow researchers to determine the cause of a behavior is the **experiment**. In an experiment, researchers deliberately manipulate (change in some purposeful way) the variable they think is causing some behavior while holding all the other variables that might interfere with the experiment's results constant and unchanging. That way, if they get changes in behavior (an effect, in other words), they know that those changes must be due to the manipulated variable. For example, remember the discussion of the steps in the scientific method. It talked about how to study the effects of watching violent cartoons on children's aggressive behavior. The most logical way to study that particular relationship is by an experiment.

First, researchers might start by selecting the children they want to use in the experiment. The best method to do that is through random selection of a sample of children from a "population" determined by the researchers—just as a sample would be selected for a survey. Ideally, researchers would decide on the age of child they wanted to study—say, children who are 3 to 4 years old. Then researchers would go to various day care centers and randomly select a certain number of children of that age. Of course, that wouldn't include the children who don't go to a day care center. Another way to get a sample in the age range might be to ask several pediatricians to send out letters to parents of children of that age and then randomly select the sample from those children whose parents responded positively.

1.10 How are operational definitions, independent and dependent variables, experimental and control groups, and random assignment used in designing an experiment?

The Variables Another important step is to decide on the variable the researchers want to manipulate (which would be the one they think causes changes in behavior) and the variable they want to measure to see if there are any changes (this would be the effect on behavior of the manipulation). Often deciding on the variables in the experiment comes before selection of the participants or subjects.

The act of hitting each other with toy swords could be part of an operational definition of aggressive behavior.

In the example of aggression and children's cartoons, the variable that researchers think causes changes in aggressive behavior is the violence in the cartoons. Researchers would want to manipulate that in some way, and in order to do that they have to define the term *violent cartoon*. They would have to find or create a cartoon that contains violence. Then they would show that cartoon to the participants and try to measure their aggressive behavior afterwards. In measuring the aggressive behavior, the researchers would have to define exactly what they mean by "aggressive behavior" so that it can be measured. This definition is called an **operational definition** because it specifically names the operations (steps or procedures) that the experimenter must use to control or measure the variables in the experiment. An operational definition of aggressive behavior might be a checklist of very specific actions such as hitting, pushing, and so on that an observer can mark off as the children do the items on the list. If the observers were just told to look for "aggressive behavior," the researchers would probably get half a dozen or more different interpretations of what aggressive behavior is.

The name for the variable that is manipulated in any experiment is the **independent variable** because it is *independent* of anything the participants do. The participants in the study do not get to choose or vary the independent variable, and their behavior does not affect this variable at all. In the preceding example, the independent variable would be the presence or absence of violence in the cartoons.

The response of the participants to the manipulation of the independent variable *is* a dependent relationship, so the response of the participants that is measured is known as the **dependent variable.** Their behavior, if the hypothesis is correct, should *depend* on whether or not they were exposed to the independent variable, and in the example, the dependent variable would be the measure of aggressive behavior in the children. The dependent variable is always the thing (response of subjects or result of some action) that is measured to see just how the independent variable may have affected it. **Simulate** on **mypsychlab.com**

Simulate to distinguish independent and dependent variables on **mypsychlab.com**

The Groups *If researchers do all of this and find that the children's behavior is aggressive, can they say that the aggressive behavior was caused by the violence in the cartoon?*

If researchers do all of this and find that the children's behavior is aggressive, can they say that the aggressive behavior was caused by the violence in the cartoon?

No, what has been described so far is not enough. The researchers may find that the children who watch the violent cartoon are aggressive, but how would they know if their aggressive behavior was caused by the cartoon or was just the natural aggressive level of those particular children or the result of the particular time of day they were observed? Those sorts of *confounding variables* (variables that interfere with each other and their possible effects on some other variable of interest) are the kind researchers have to control for in some way. For example, if most children in this experiment just happened to be from a fairly aggressive family background, any effects the violent cartoon in the experiment might have had on the children's behavior could be confused (confounded) with the possible effects of the family background. The researchers wouldn't know if the children were being aggressive because they watched the cartoon or because they liked to play aggressively anyway.

The best way to control for confounding variables is to have two groups of participants: those who watch the violent cartoon, and those who watch a nonviolent cartoon for the same length of time. Then the researchers would measure the aggressive behavior in both groups. If the aggressive behavior is significantly greater in the group that watched the violent cartoon (statistically speaking), then researchers can say that in this experiment, violent cartoon watching caused greater aggressive behavior.

The group that is exposed to the independent variable (the violent cartoon in the example) is called the **experimental group**, because it is the group that receives the experimental manipulation. The other group that gets either no treatment or some kind of treatment that should have no effect (like the group that watches the nonviolent cartoon in the example) is called the **control group** because it is used to *control* for the possibility that other factors might be causing the effect that is being examined. If researchers were to find that both the group that watched the violent cartoon and the group that watched the nonviolent cartoon were equally aggressive, they would have to assume that the violent content did not influence their behavior at all.

The Importance of Randomization As mentioned previously, random selection is the best way to choose the participants for any study. Participants must then be assigned to either the experimental group or the control group. Not surprisingly, **random assignment** of participants to one or the other condition is the best way to ensure control over other interfering, or *extraneous*, variables. Random assignment means that each participant has an equal chance of being assigned to each condition. If researchers simply looked at the children and put all of the children from one day care center or one pediatrician's recommendations into the experimental group and the

independent variable variable in an experiment that is manipulated by the experimenter.

dependent variable variable in an experiment that represents the measurable response or behavior of the subjects in the experiment.

experimental group subjects in an experiment who are subjected to the independent variable.

control group subjects in an experiment who are not subjected to the independent variable and who may receive a placebo treatment.

random assignment process of assigning subjects to the experimental or control groups randomly, so that each subject has an equal chance of being in either group.

same for the control group, they would run the risk of biasing their research. Some day care centers may have more naturally aggressive children, for example, or some pediatricians may have a particular client base in which the children are very passive. So researchers want to take the entire participant group and assign each person randomly to one or the other of the groups in the study. Sometimes this is as simple as picking names out of a hat.

1.11 **How do the placebo and experimenter effects cause problems in an experiment, and how can single-blind and double-blind studies control for these effects?**

Experimental Hazards: The Placebo Effect and the Experimenter Effect There are a few other problems that might arise in any experiment, even with the use of control groups and random assignment. These problems are especially likely when studying people instead of animals, because people are often influenced by their own thoughts or biases about what's going on in an experiment. For example, say there is a new drug that is supposed to improve memory in people who are in the very early stages of *Alzheimer's disease* (a form of mental deterioration that occurs in some people as they grow old). LINK to Chapter Six: Memory, p. 246. Researchers would want to test the drug to see if it really is effective in helping to improve memory, so they would get a sample of people who are in the early stages of the disease, divide them into two groups, give one group the drug, and then test for improvement. They would probably have to do a test of memory both before and after the administration of the drug to be able to measure improvement.

Let me see if I've got this straight. The group that gets the drug would be the experimental group, and the one that doesn't is the control group, right?

Let me see if I've got this straight. The group that gets the drug would be the experimental group, and the one that doesn't is the control group, right?

Right, and getting or not getting the drug is the independent variable, whereas the measure of memory improvement is the dependent variable. But there's still a problem with doing it this way. What if the researchers do find that the drug group had greater memory improvement than the group that received nothing? Can they really say that the drug itself caused the improvement? Or is it possible that the participants who received the drug *knew* that they were supposed to improve in memory and, therefore, made a major effort to do so? The improvement may have had more to do with participants' *belief* in the drug than the drug itself, a phenomenon* known as the **placebo effect**: The expectations and biases of the participants in a study can influence their behavior. In medical research, the control group is often given a harmless substitute for the real drug, such as a sugar pill or an injection of salt water, and this substitute (which has no medical effect) is called the *placebo*. If there is a placebo effect, the control group will show changes in the dependent variable even though the participants in that group received only a placebo.

Another way that expectations about the outcome of the experiment can influence the results, even when the participants are animals rather than people, is called the **experimenter effect**. It has to do with the expectations of the experimenter, not the participants. As discussed earlier in the section about naturalistic observations, sometimes observers are biased—they see what they expect to see. Observer bias can also happen in an experiment. When the researcher is measuring the dependent variable, it's possible that he or she could give the participants clues about how they are supposed to respond—through the use of body language, tone of voice, or even eye contact. Although not deliberate, it does happen. It could go something like this in the memory drug example mentioned earlier: You, the Alzheimer's patient, are in the

This elderly woman has Alzheimer's disease, which causes a severe loss of recent memory. If she were given a drug to improve her memory, the researcher could not be certain that any improvement shown was caused by the drug rather than by the elderly woman's belief that the drug would work. The expectations of any person in an experimental study can affect the outcome of the study, a phenomenon known as the placebo effect.

placebo effect the phenomenon in which the expectations of the participants in a study can influence their behavior.

experimenter effect tendency of the experimenter's expectations for a study to unintentionally influence the results of the study.

*phenomenon: an observable fact or event.

experimenter's office to take your second memory test after trying the drug. The experimenter seems to pay a lot of attention to you and to every answer that you give in the test, so you get the feeling that you are supposed to have improved a lot. So you try harder, and any improvement you show may be caused only by your own increased effort, not by the drug. That's an example of the experimenter effect in action: The behavior of the experimenter caused the participant to change his or her response pattern.

Single-Blind and Double-Blind Studies Fortunately, there are ways to control for these effects. The classic way is to avoid the placebo effect is to give the control group an actual placebo—some kind of treatment that doesn't affect behavior at all. In the drug experiment, the placebo would have to be some kind of sugar pill or saline (salt) solution that looks like and is administered just like the actual drug. The participants in both the experimental and the control groups would not know whether or not they got the real drug or the placebo. That way, if their expectations have any effect at all on the outcome of the experiment, the experimenter will be able to tell by looking at the results for the control group and comparing them to the experimental group. Even if the control group improves a little, the drug group should improve significantly more if the drug is working. This is called a **single-blind study** because the participants are "blind" to the treatment they receive.

For a long time, that was the only type of experiment researchers carried out in psychology. But researchers Robert Rosenthal and Lenore Jacobson reported in their 1968 book, *Pygmalion in the Classroom*, that when teachers were told that some students had a high potential for success and others a low potential, the students showed significant gains or decreases in their performance on standardized tests depending on which "potential" they were supposed to have (Rosenthal & Jacobson, 1968). Actually, the students had been selected randomly and were randomly assigned to one of the two groups, "high" or "low." Their performances on the tests were affected by the attitudes of the teachers concerning their potential. This study and similar ones after it highlighted the need for the experimenter be "blind" as well as the participants in research. So in a **double-blind study** neither the participants nor the person or persons measuring the dependent variable know who got what. That's why every element in a double-blind experiment gets coded in some way, so that only after all the measurements have been taken can anyone determine who was in the experimental group and who was in the control group.

Other Experimental Designs In the field of developmental psychology, researchers are always looking for the ways in which a person's age influences his or her behavior. The problem is that age is a variable that cannot be randomly controlled. In a regular experiment, for example, participants can be randomly assigned to the various conditions: drug or placebo, special instructions or no special instructions, and so on. But participants cannot be randomly assigned to different age groups. It would be like saying, "Okay, these people are now going to be 20, and these others will be 30."

To get around this problem, researchers use alternative designs (called *quasi-experimental designs*) that are not considered true experiments because of the inability to randomly assign participants to the experimental and control groups (Gribbons & Herman, 1997). These designs are discussed more fully in Chapter Eight. LINK to Chapter Eight: Development Across the Life Span, pp. 298–299.

For a good example of a typical experiment, read the following section about stereotypes, athletes, and test grades.

single-blind study study in which the subjects do not know if they are in the experimental or the control group.

double-blind study study in which neither the experimenter nor the subjects know if the subjects are in the experimental or control group.

issues in psychology

Stereotypes, Athletes, and College Test Performance

1.12 What are the basic elements of a real-world experiment?

It seems that many people have a negative stereotype of college athletes—that they are graded and promoted on the basis of their ability on the athletic field and not on the basis of classroom performance. Evidence does exist for poorer performance on academic tests of athletes when compared to nonathletes in college (National Collegiate Athletic Association, 2002; Purdy et al., 1982; Upthegrove et al., 1999). If you are an athlete, can that negative stereotype actually have a negative impact on your test performance? Wesleyan University researchers Matthew Jameson, Robert Diehl, and Henry Danso have some evidence that such stereotypes can have just that kind of negative impact (Jameson et al., 2007).

Could knowing that other people might think your success in school is due to your athletic ability and not to your intelligence make you perform poorly on an academic test?

In their experiment, 72 male college athletes from the sports teams of the university were given an intellectual test. Half of the athletes answered a brief questionnaire before taking the test, whereas the other half received the same questionnaire after taking the test. The questionnaire asked three questions, with the third question being, "Rate your likelihood of being accepted to the university without the aid of athletic recruiting." This item was designed to bring the negative stereotype of athletes ("dumb jocks") to the forefront of students' minds, creating a "high threat" for that stereotype. This difference in threat level between the two groups before taking the intellectual test represents the *independent variable* in this experiment.

The results? Those students who answered the "high threat" question *before* the intellectual test (the *experimental* group) scored significantly lower on that test (the measurement of the *dependent* variable) than those who answered the question *after* the test (the *control* group). The researchers also found a correlation between the students' exposure to the "high threat" stereotype condition and accuracy on the intellectual test: The more students believed that they got into college primarily because of their ability in sports (based on their rating of that third question), the worse they performed on the subsequent test. Jameson and colleagues concluded that obvious negative stereotypes in higher education may be an important cause underlying the tendency of college athletes to underperform in academics.

Questions for Further Discussion

1. In this experiment, what might be some extraneous variables affecting the students' test performance?
2. What might educators do to try to prevent the effect of the "dumb jock" negative stereotype on college athletes?

Ethics of Psychological Research

The study that Dr. Watson did with "Little Albert" and the white rat seems pretty cruel, when you think about it. Do researchers today do that kind of study?

The study that Dr. Watson did with "Little Albert" and the white rat seems pretty cruel, when you think about it. Do researchers today do that kind of study?

Actually, as the field and scope of psychology began to grow and more research with people was being done, psychologists began to realize that some protections had to be put in place. No one wanted to be thought of as a "mad scientist," and if studies were permitted that could actually harm people, the field of psychology might die out pretty quickly. LINK to Chapter Five: Learning, p. 177; Chapter Twelve: Social Psychology, pp. 453–455. Scientists in other areas of research were also realizing that ethical treatment of the participants in studies had to be ensured in some way. Ethical treatment, of course, means that people who volunteer for a study will be able to expect that no physical or psychological harm should come to them.

1.13 What are some ethical concerns that can occur when conducting research with people and animals?

Universities and colleges (where most psychological research is carried out) usually have *institutional review boards*, groups of psychologists or other professionals who look over each proposed study and judge it according to its safety and consideration for the research participants. These review boards look at all aspects of the projected study, from the written materials that explain the research to the potential subjects to the equipment that may be used in the study itself.

THE GUIDELINES FOR DOING RESEARCH WITH PEOPLE

There are quite a few ethical concerns when dealing with human subjects in an experiment or other type of study. Here is a list of some of the most common ethical guidelines:

1. **Rights and well-being of participants must be weighed against the study's value to science.** In other words, people come first, research second.
2. **Participants must be allowed to make an informed decision about participation.** This means that researchers have to explain the study to the people they want to include before they do anything to them or with them—even children—and it has to be in terms that the participants can understand. If researchers are using infants or children, their parents have to be informed and give their consent, a legal term known as *informed consent*. Even in single- or double-blind studies, it is necessary to tell the participants that they may be members of either the experimental or the

"He says he wants a lawyer."

control group—they just won't find out which group they were actually in until after the experiment is concluded.

3. **Deception must be justified.** In some cases, it is necessary to deceive the participants because the study wouldn't work any other way. The participants have to be told after the study exactly why the deception was important. This is called *debriefing*.
4. **Participants may withdraw from the study at any time.** The participants must be allowed to drop out for any reason. For example, sometimes people get bored with the study, decide they don't have the time, or don't like what they have to do. Children participating in studies often decide to stop "playing" (play is a common part of studies of children). Researchers have to release them, even if it means having to get more participants.
5. **Participants must be protected from risks or told explicitly of risks.** For example, if researchers are using any kind of electrical equipment, care must be taken to ensure that no participant will experience a physical shock from faulty electrical equipment.
6. **Investigators must debrief participants, telling the true nature of the study and expectations of results.** This is important in all types of studies but particularly in those involving a deception.
7. **Data must remain confidential.** Freud recognized the importance of confidentiality, referring to his patients in his books and articles with false names. Likewise, psychologists and other researchers today tend to report only group results rather than results for a single individual, so that no one could possibly be recognized.
8. **If for any reason a study results in undesirable consequences for the participant, the researcher is responsible for detecting and removing, or correcting, these consequences.** Sometimes people react in unexpected ways to the manipulations in an experiment, despite the researcher's best efforts to prevent any negative impact upon participants. If this happens, the researcher must find some way of helping the participant overcome that impact (American Psychological Association, 2002).

Psychologists also study animals to find out about behavior, often drawing comparisons between what the animals do and what people might do under similar conditions.

But why not just study people in the first place?

But why not just study people in the first place?

Some research questions are extremely important but difficult or impossible to answer by using human participants. Animals live shorter lives, so looking at long-term effects becomes much easier. Animals are also easier to control—the scientist can control diet, living arrangements, and even genetic relatedness. The white laboratory rat has become a recognized species different from ordinary rats, bred with its own kind for many decades until each white rat is essentially a little genetic "twin" of all the others. Animals also engage in much simpler behavior than humans do, making it easier to see the effects of manipulations. But the biggest reason that researchers use animals in some research is that animals can be used in ways that researchers could never use people. For example, it took a long time for scientists to prove that the tars and other harmful substances in tobacco cause cancer because they had to do correlational studies with people and experiments only with animals. There's the catch—researchers can do many things to animals that they can't do to people. That might seem cruel at first, but when you think that without animal research there would be no vaccines for deadly diseases, no insulin treatments for diabetics, no transplants, and so on, then the value of the research and its benefits to humankind far outweigh the hazards to which the research animals are exposed.

There are also ethical considerations when dealing with animals in research, just as there are with humans. With animals, though, the focus is on avoiding exposing them to any *unnecessary* pain or suffering. So if surgery is part of the study, it is done under anesthesia. If the research animal must die for the effects of some drug or other treatment to be examined in a necropsy (autopsy performed on an animal), the death must be accomplished humanely. Animals are used in only about 7 percent of all psychological studies (Committee on Animal Research and Ethics, 2004).

1.9 1.10 1.11 1.12 1.13

CONCEPT MAP

Finding Relationships

(different ways to find out more than just descriptions of behavior)

- **correlation**
  - is a measure of relationship between two or more variables (anything that can change or vary)
  - produces a value called the *correlation coefficient* that represents both direction and strength of relationship
  - does not prove causation—variables can be related but you can not assume that one of them causes the other to occur
- **experiments** the only research method that will allow researchers to determine the cause of a behavior by deliberately manipulating some variable and measuring changes in the variable of interest
  - **operational definition** specifically names the steps or procedures used to control or measure the variable in the experiment
    - independent variable is the variable that is manipulated, it is independent of anything participants do
    - dependent variable is the measure used to evaluate the manipulation of the independent variable
  - **groups**
    - **experimental:** gets the independent variable or experimental manipulation
    - **control:** receives no treatment or treatment that should not have an effect
    - random assignment to conditions is the best way to assure control over extraneous variables or confounding variables, variables that interfere with each other, and/or on the variable of interest
  - **hazards**
    - **placebo effect:** beliefs or expectations about a study can influence their behavior
    - **experimenter effect:** experimenter's biases can affect or influence participants' behavior
    - can be controlled through single-blind (participant "blind" to treatment/condition) and double-blind studies where the experimenter measuring the dependent variable does not know the treatment/condition associated with the data

Ethics of Psychological Research

(psychological scientists have a primary goal of protecting the health and welfare of their animal or human participants)

- **guidelines for research with humans**
  - rights and well-being of participants must be weighed against the study's value to science
  - participants must be allowed to make an informed decision about participating (informed consent)
  - deception must be justified
  - participants may withdraw from the study at any time
  - participants must be protected from risks or told explicitly of risks
  - investigator must debrief participants, telling the true nature of the study and expectations of results
  - data must remain confidential
- **research with animals**
  - any animal research is also covered by ethical considerations; primary focus is on avoiding any unnecessary pain or suffering
  - why use animals?
    - some research questions are important but can be difficult or dangerous to answer with human participants
    - animals are easier to control
    - animals have shorter lives; easier to study long-term effects

(continued)

PRACTICE quiz How much do you remember? ANSWERS ON PAGE AK-1.

Pick the best answer.

1. It's common knowledge that the more you study, the higher your grade will be. What kind of correlation is this relationship?
   - **a.** positive
   - **b.** negative
   - **c.** zero
   - **d.** causal
2. Which of the following would indicate the strongest relationship between two variables?
   - **a.** +1.04
   - **b.** –0.89
   - **c.** +0.75
   - **d.** +0.54
3. In an experiment to test the effects of alcohol on memory, the experimenter gives vodka mixed in orange juice to one group of subjects and orange juice with no vodka to the other group. She then measures the memory skills of both groups by means of a memory test. In this study, the independent variable would be
   - **a.** scores on the memory test.
   - **b.** the presence or absence of vodka in the orange juice.
   - **c.** intelligence.
   - **d.** a placebo.
4. In that same experiment, the control group is the one that gets
   - **a.** only one drink of orange juice with vodka.
   - **b.** a fake test of memory.
   - **c.** only something to eat.
   - **d.** the orange juice without vodka.
5. In a __________ study, neither the experimenter nor the participants know who is in the control group and who is in the experimental group.
   - **a.** placebo
   - **b.** single-blind
   - **c.** double-blind
   - **d.** triple-blind
6. In the "dumb jock" stereotype threat experiment, what was the dependent variable?
   - **a.** the degree of stereotype threat
   - **b.** the testing room
   - **c.** the scores on the intellectual test
   - **d.** the intelligence level of the athletes
7. Which of the following is NOT one of the common ethical rules?
   - **a.** Participants have to give informed consent.
   - **b.** Deception cannot be used in any studies with human beings.
   - **c.** The rights and well-being of the participants must come first.
   - **d.** Data must remain confidential.
8. We use animals in research because
   - **a.** animals have simple behavior that makes it easy to see changes.
   - **b.** animals don't live as long as humans and are easier to control.
   - **c.** we can do things to animals that we can't do to people.
   - **d.** all of the above are true.

Applying Psychology to Everyday Life: Thinking Critically About Critical Thinking

What good is all this focus on science and research going to do for me? I live in the real world, not a laboratory.

What good is all this focus on science and research going to do for me? I live in the real world, not a laboratory.

The real world is full of opportunities for scientific thinking. Think about all the commercials on television for miracle weight loss, hair restoration, or herbal remedies for arthritis, depression, and a whole host of physical and mental problems. Wouldn't it be nice to know how many of these claims people should believe? Wouldn't you like to know how to evaluate statements like these and possibly save yourself some time, effort, and money? That's exactly the kind of "real-world" problem that critical thinking can help sort out. **Listen** on **mypsychlab.com**

Listen to the Psychology in the News podcast on critical thinking **mypsychlab.com**

THE CRITERIA FOR CRITICAL THINKING

1.14 What are the basic principles of critical thinking, and how can critical thinking be useful in everyday life?

According to Beyer (1995), **critical thinking** means making reasoned judgments. The word *reasoned* means that people's judgments should be logical and well thought out. Critical thinking also includes the ability to ask and seek answers for critical questions at the right time (Browne & Keeley, 2009). (A relevant example of a critical question might be, "Is someone paying you to do this research, and is this a conflict of interest?" or "Do you have any good evidence for your assertions, or are you just giving your opinion?")

critical thinking making reasoned judgments about claims.

While the word *critical* is often viewed as meaning "negative," that is not the use of this term here. Instead, it's more related to the word *criteria,** as in thinking that meets certain high criteria or standards (Nosich, 2008). There are four basic criteria for critical thinking that people should remember when faced with statements about the world around them (Browne & Keeley, 2009; Gill, 1991; Shore, 1990):

1. **There are very few "truths" that do not need to be subjected to testing.** Although people may accept religious beliefs and personal values on faith, everything else in life needs to have supporting evidence. Questions that can be investigated empirically should be examined using established scientific methods. One shouldn't accept anything at face value but should always ask, "How do you know that? What is the evidence? Can you be more specific in your terms?" (These are more examples of those important questions to ask when thinking critically.) For example, many people still believe that astrology, the study of the supposed influence of the stars and planets on the birth of an infant, can be used to make predictions about that infant's personality and life events as he or she grows. But scientific investigations have shown us, time after time, that astrology is without any basis in truth or scientific fact (Ben-Shakhar et al., 1986; Bunge, 1984; Dean et al., 1992; Dean & Kelly, 2000; Hines, 2003; Kelly, 1980; Wiseman, 2007).
2. **All evidence is not equal in quality.** One of the most important, often overlooked steps in critical thinking is evaluating how evidence is gathered before deciding that it provides good support for some idea. For example, there are poorly done experiments, incorrect assumptions based on correlations rather than experiments, studies that could not be replicated, and studies in which there was either no control group or no attempt made to control for placebo effects or experimenter effects. There are also studies that have been deliberately manipulated to produce the findings that the researcher (or whoever is paying the researcher) would prefer—some people are more motivated by money than by the search for the truth, sad but oh, so true. As a critical thinker you should be aware that the more wild the claim, the better the evidence should be: for example, I have not yet seen any evidence that convinces me of alien visitations or abductions! **Read** on **mypsychlab.com**
3. **Just because someone is considered to be an authority or to have a lot of expertise does not make everything that person claims automatically true.** One should always ask to see the evidence rather than just take some expert's word for anything. How good is the evidence? Are there other alternative explanations? Is the alternative explanation simpler? If there are two explanations for some phenomenon and both account for the phenomenon equally well, the *simplest* explanation is *more often* the best one—a rule of thumb known as *the law of parsimony.*) For example, let's look at crop circles, those geometric patterns of flattened crop stalks that have at times been discovered in farmers' fields. Two possible explanations for crop circles exist: either they are made by aliens in space ships—as is the claim by many alleged experts—or they are made by human beings as a hoax. Which explanation is simpler? Obviously, the hoax rationalization is the simplest, and it turned out to be correct for the crop circles that appeared in England in the late 1970s and 1980s: David Bower and Doug Chorley, two British men, confessed to creating the crop circles as a prank, thought up in a barroom and meant to make fun of people who believe in alien visitations (Nickell, 1995; M. Ridley, 2002; Schnabel, 1994).

Read and learn more about the pseudoscience on **mypsychlab.com**

Many people believe that crop circles are created by alien visitors, despite clear evidence that crop circles are hoaxes created by ordinary people.

*criteria: standards on which a judgment or decision may be based.

4. **Critical thinking requires an open mind.** Although it is good to be a little skeptical, people should not close their minds to things that are truly possible. At the same time, it's good for people to have open minds but not so open that they are gullible* and apt to believe anything. Critical thinking requires a delicate balance between skepticism and willingness to consider possibilities—even possibilities that contradict previous judgments or beliefs. For example, scientists have yet to find any convincing evidence that there was once life on Mars. That doesn't mean that scientists totally dismiss the idea, just that there is no convincing evidence *yet*. I don't believe that there are Martians on Mars, but if I were shown convincing evidence, I would have to be willing to change my thinking—as difficult as that might be.

Questions for Further Discussion

1. How might critical thinking be applied to the issue of global climate change?
2. Why do you think some people (even very smart people) sometimes avoid thinking critically about issues such as politics, the existence of ESP, or the supernatural?

---

*gullible: easily fooled or cheated.

1.14 CONCEPT MAP

- scientific thinking can be applied to many real-world situations

Thinking Critically About Critical Thinking

- four basic criteria for making reasoned judgments
  - there are very few "truths" in the world that do not need to be subjected to testing
  - all evidence is not equal in quality
  - just because someone is considered to be an authority or to have a lot of expertise does not make everything that person claims automatically true
  - critical thinking requires an open mind

chapter summary

Listen on **mypsychlab.com** Listen to an audio file of your chapter **www.mypsychlab.com**

What Is Psychology?

1.1 What defines psychology as a field of study, and what are psychology's four primary goals?

- Psychology is the scientific study of behavior and mental processes.
- The four goals of psychology are description, explanation, prediction, and control.

Psychology Then: The History of Psychology

1.2 How did structuralism and functionalism differ, and who were the important people in those early fields?

- In 1879 psychology began as a science of its own in Germany with the establishment of Wundt's psychology laboratory. He developed the technique of objective introspection.
- Titchener, a student of Wundt, brought psychology in the form of structuralism to America. Structuralism died out in the early twentieth century. Margaret F. Washburn, Titchener's student, was the first woman to receive a Ph.D. in psychology in 1894 and published *The Animal Mind*.
- William James proposed a countering point of view called functionalism, that stressed the way the mind allows us to adapt.
- Many of psychology's early pioneers were minorities such as the African Americans who, despite prejudice and racism, made important contributions to the study of human and animal behavior.
- Functionalism influenced the modern fields of educational psychology, evolutionary psychology, and industrial/organizational psychology.

ISSUES IN PSYCHOLOGY: Psychology's African American Roots

1.3 **What were the basic ideas and who were the important people behind the early approaches known as Gestalt, psychoanalysis, and behaviorism?**

- Wertheimer and others studied sensation and perception, calling the new perspective Gestalt (an organized whole) psychology.
- Freud proposed that the unconscious mind controls much of our conscious behavior in his theory of psychoanalysis.
- Watson proposed a science of behavior called behaviorism, which focused only on the study of observable stimuli and responses.
- Watson and Rayner demonstrated that a phobia could be learned by conditioning a baby to be afraid of a white rat.
- Mary Cover Jones, one of Watson's more famous students in behaviorism and child development, later demonstrated that a learned phobia could be counterconditioned.

Psychology Now: Modern Perspectives

1.4 **What are the basic ideas behind the seven modern perspectives, and what were the important contributions of Skinner, Maslow, and Rogers?**

- Modern Freudians such as Anna Freud, Jung, and Adler changed the emphasis in Freud's original theory into a kind of neo-Freudianism.
- Skinner's operant conditioning of voluntary behavior became a major force in the twentieth century. He introduced the concept of reinforcement to behaviorism.
- Humanism, which focuses on free will and the human potential for growth, was developed by Maslow and Rogers, among others, as a reaction to the deterministic nature of behaviorism and psychoanalysis.
- Cognitive psychology is the study of learning, memory, language, and problem solving, and includes the field of cognitive neuroscience
- Biopsychology emerged as the study of the biological bases of behavior, such as hormones, heredity, chemicals in the nervous system, structural defects in the brain, and the effects of phsycial diseases
- The principles of evolution and the knowledge we currently have about evolution are used in this perspective to look at the way the mind works and why it works as it does. Behavior is seen as having an adaptive or survival value.

Psychological Professionals and Areas of Specialization

1.5 **How does a psychologist differ from a psychiatrist, and what are the other types of professionals who work in the various areas of psychology?**

- Psychologists have academic degrees and can do counseling, teaching, and research and may specialize in any one of a large number of areas within psychology.
- There are many different areas of specialization in psychology, including clinical, counseling, developmental, social, and personality as areas of work or study.
- Psychiatrists are medical doctors who provide diagnosis and therapy for persons with mental disorders.
- Psychiatric social workers are social workers with special training in the influences of the environment on mental illness.

Psychology: The Scientific Methodology

1.6 **Why is psychology considered a science, and what are the steps in using the scientific method?**

- The scientific method is a way to determine facts and control the possibilities of error and bias when observing behavior. The five steps are perceiving the question, forming a hypothesis, testing the hypothesis, drawing conclusions, and reporting the results.

1.7 **How are naturalistic and laboratory settings used to describe behavior, and what are some of the advantages and disadvantages associated with these settings?**

- Naturalistic observations involve watching animals or people in their natural environments but have the disadvantage of lack of control.
- Laboratory observations involve watching animals or people in an artificial but controlled situation, such as a laboratory.

1.8 **How are case studies and surveys used to describe behavior, and what are some drawbacks to each of these methods?**

- Case studies are detailed investigations of one subject, whereas surveys involve asking standardized questions of large groups of people that represent a sample of the population of interest.
- Information gained from case studies cannot be applied to other cases. People responding to surveys may not always tell the truth or remember information correctly.

1.9 **What is the correlational technique, and what does it tell researchers about relationships?**

- Correlation is a statistical technique that allows researchers to discover and predict relationships between variables of interest.
- Positive correlations exist when increases in one variable are matched by increases in the other variable, whereas negative correlations exist when increases in one variable are matched by decreases in the other variable.
- Correlations cannot be used to prove cause-and-effect relationships.

1.10 **How are operational definitions, independent and dependent variables, experimental and control groups, and random assignment used in designing an experiment?**

- Experiments are tightly controlled manipulations of variables that allow researchers to determine cause-and-effect relationships.
- The independent variable in an experiment is the variable that is deliberately manipulated by the experimenter to see if related changes occur in the behavior or responses of the participants and is given to the experimental group.
- The dependent variable in an experiment is the measured behavior or responses of the participants.
- The control group receives either a placebo treatment or nothing.
- Random assignment of participants to experimental groups helps to control for individual differences both within and between the groups that might otherwise interfere with the experiment's outcome.

1.11 **How do the placebo and experimenter effects cause problems in an experiment, and how can single-blind and double-blind studies control for these effects?**

- Experiments in which the subjects do not know if they are in the experimental or control groups are single-blind studies, whereas experiments in which neither the experimenters nor the subjects know this information are called double-blind studies.

ISSUES IN PSYCHOLOGY: Stereotypes, Athletes, and College Test Performance

1.12 What are some basic elements of a real-world experiment?

- An experiment studying the effect of negative stereotypes on text performance of athletes (Jameson et al., 2007) found that exposure to negative stereotypes prior to taking a test resulted in poorer performance by athletes than the performance of athletes whose exposure came after the test.

Ethics of Psychological Research

1.13 What are some ethical concerns that can occur when conducting research with people and animals?

- Ethical guidelines for doing research with human beings include the protection of rights and well-being of participants, informed consent, justification when deception is used, the right of participants to withdraw at any time, protection of participants from physical or psychological harm, confidentiality, and debriefing of participants at the end of the study. Researchers are also responsible for correcting any undesirable consequences that may result from the study.
- Animals in psychological research make useful models because they are easier to control than humans, they have simpler behavior, and they can be used in ways that are not permissible with humans.

Applying Psychology to Everyday Life: Thinking Critically About Critical Thinking

1.14 What are the basic principles of critical thinking, and how can critical thinking be useful in everyday life?

- Critical thinking is the ability to make reasoned judgments. The four basic criteria of critical thinking are that there are few concepts that do not need to be tested, evidence can vary in quality, claims by experts and authorities do not automatically make something true, and keeping an open mind is important.

test YOURSELF

ANSWERS ON PAGE AK-1.

Study and Review on mypsychlab.com Ready for your test? More quizzes and a customized study plan. **www.mypsychlab.com**

Study Help Note: These longer quizzes appear at the end of every chapter and cover all the major learning objectives that you should know after reading the chapter. These quizzes also provide practice for exams. The answers to each Test Yourself section can be found in the Answer Key at the back of the book.

Pick the best answer.

1. In the definition of psychology, the term *mental processes* means
   a. internal, covert processes.
   b. outward behavior.
   c. overt actions and reactions.
   d. only animal behavior.
2. A psychologist is interested in finding out why identical twins have different personalities. This psychologist is most interested in the goal of
   a. description.
   b. explanation.
   c. prediction.
   d. control.
3. Psychologists who give potential employees tests that determine what kind of job those employees might best fit are interested in the goal of
   a. description.
   b. explanation.
   c. prediction.
   d. control.
4. Which early theorist developed his perspective on psychology by basing it on Darwin's "survival of the fittest" doctrine?
   a. Wilhelm Wundt
   b. William James
   c. John Watson
   d. Sigmund Freud
5. "The whole is greater than the sum of its parts" is a statement associated with the perspective of
   a. introspectionism.
   b. functionalism.
   c. psychoanalysis.
   d. Gestalt psychology.
6. __________ was (were) the focus of Watson's behaviorism.
   a. Conscious experiences
   b. Gestalt perceptions
   c. The unconscious mind
   d. Observable experiences
7. Who is most associated with the technique of introspection?
   a. Wundt
   b. James
   c. Watson
   d. Wertheimer
8. Who was denied a Ph.D. despite completing all the requirements for earning the degree?
   a. Mary Whiton Calkins
   b. Mary Cover Jones
   c. Margaret Washburn
   d. Eleanor Gibson
9. Which perspective focuses on free will and self-actualization?
   a. psychoanalysis
   b. behaviorism
   c. cognitive psychology
   d. humanism
10. Jenna suffers from a nervous tic of washing her hands repeatedly and being unable to resist washing them again and again. Which perspective would explain Jenna's hand-washing behavior as a result of repressed conflicts?
    a. psychodynamic perspective
    b. cognitive psychology
    c. behaviorism
    d. biopsychology
11. Which perspective looks at perception, learning, and memory?
    a. psychoanalysis
    b. behaviorism
    c. cognitive psychology
    d. evolutionary perspective
12. Which perspective emphasizes the biological bases for shared, universal mental characteristics?
    a. psychoanalysis
    b. behaviorism
    c. cognitive psychology
    d. evolutionary perspective
13. Which of the following professionals in psychology has the broadest area of interests and functions?
    a. psychiatrist
    b. psychoanalyst
    c. psychiatric social worker
    d. psychologist
14. A person who has suffered a major stroke and is now experiencing severe personality problems because of the damage would best be advised to see a
    a. psychiatrist.
    b. psychoanalyst.
    c. psychiatric social worker.
    d. psychologist.

15. Which of the following specialties in psychology provides diagnosis and treatment for less serious mental problems such as adjustment disorders?
a. developmental
b. counseling
c. personality
d. experimental

16. In the scientific method, forming an educated guess is called
a. reporting your results.
b. perceiving a question.
c. drawing conclusions.
d. forming a hypothesis.

17. The main advantage of laboratory observation is
a. the degree of control it allows the observer.
b. the degree of participation it allows the observer.
c. the observer effect.
d. the opportunity for representative sampling.

18. Harlan wanted to write realistically about street gangs, so he pretended to be a teenager and joined a real gang. This is most similar to the method of
a. laboratory observation.
b. the observer effect.
c. the case study.
d. participant observation.

19. The main advantage of a case study is
a. the ease of generalizing the results to others.
b. being able to determine cause and effect.
c. the amount of detail it provides about an individual.
d. the large number of people that can be studied at one time.

20. The entire group that a researcher is interested in is called a
a. sample.
b. population.
c. subject pool.
d. survey.

21. Professor Jones surveyed her six classes and found that students who slept less than 5 hours the night before an exam received lower exam scores than those students who slept 7 hours or more. What kind of correlation is this relationship between hours of sleep and scores?
a. positive
b. negative
c. zero
d. causal

22. Drinking orange juice is negatively correlated with the risk of cancer. Based on this information, which of the following statements is TRUE?
a. The more orange juice you drink, the higher your risk of cancer.
b. The more orange juice you drink, the lower your risk of cancer.
c. The less orange juice you drink, the lower your risk of cancer.
d. Drinking orange juice causes people to be cancer free.

23. A researcher designs an experiment to test the effects of playing video games on memory. What would be the dependent variable?
a. scores on a memory test
b. playing video games
c. number of hours spent playing video games
d. the type of video game played

24. In that same experiment, the experimental group would
a. not play the video games.
b. take the memory test while the control group would not.
c. not take the memory test while the control group would.
d. play the video games.

25. In the stereotypes and athletes study, what was the independent variable?
a. the test scores
b. the room in which the test was given
c. the control group
d. the difference in threat level

26. In a __________ study, only the experimenter knows who is in the control group and who is in the experimental group.
a. placebo
b. single-blind
c. double-blind
d. triple-blind

27. Double-blind studies control for
a. the placebo effect.
b. the experimenter effect.
c. the placebo effect and the experimenter effect.
d. extrinsic motivation.

28. Dr. Silverberg conducted a study in which she tests infants for memory ability. Before she can begin her study, she must obtain
a. permission from the infants.
b. permission from the parents.
c. informed consent from the parents.
d. confidential information from the parents.

29. Several years ago two scientists announced that they had achieved "cold fusion" in the laboratory, but further studies failed to replicate their findings and later other scientists found that the original two scientists had used sloppy methods. This highlights which of the following critical thinking principles?
a. Few "truths" do not need to be tested.
b. All evidence is not equal in quality.
c. Authority or expertise does not make the claims of the authority or expert true.
d. Critical thinking requires an open mind.

30. A famous newscaster advertises a new magnetic mattress for controlling pain. If Nathaniel decides to order the mattress because he believes that such a well-known personality should know if it works or not, he has made an error in which of the following?
a. Few "truths" do not need to be tested.
b. All evidence is not equal in quality.
c. Authority or expertise does not make the claims of the authority or expert true.
d. Critical thinking requires an open mind.

31. Critical thinking means making judgments based on
a. emotional issues.
b. keeping a closed mind.
c. reason and logical evaluation.
d. authority and expertise.

1 the science of psychology

1.1 What Is Psychology?

p. 12

(is the scientific study of behavior and mental processes)

- it has methods for studying phenomena
- it has four primary goals
  - describe
  - explain
  - predict
  - control

1.2 1.3 Psychology Then: The History of Psychology

pp. 12–13

(has roots in several disciplines, including philosophy, medicine, and physiology, and has developed through several perspectives)

- A relatively new science that formally began in 1879 when Wilhelm Wundt ("father of psychology") established the first psychological laboratory in Leipzig, Germany

- **Structuralism** founded by Edward Titchener (was a student of Wundt's)
- **Functionalism** founded by William James
- **Gestalt psychology** founded by Max Wertheimer
- **Psychoanalysis** ideas put forth by Sigmund Freud

- **Behaviorism** associated with work of John B. Watson, who was greatly influenced by Ivan Pavlov's work in conditioning/learning

1.4 Psychology Now: Modern Perspectives

p. 19

(no one single perspective is used to explain all human behavior and processes)

- **Psychodynamic** based on Freud's theory
  - **Behavioral** based on early work of Watson and later B. F. Skinner
  - **Humanistic** two pioneers are Carl Rogers and Abraham Maslow
  - **Cognitive** has roots in Gestalt psychology

  - **Sociocultural**
  - **Biopsychological**
  - **Evolutionary**

1.5 Psychological Professionals and Areas of Specialization

p. 19

(people working in the field of psychology have a variety of training experiences and different focuses)

- psychologist
- psychiatrist
- psychiatric social worker

1.6 1.7 1.8 p. 25

Psychology: The Scientific Methodology

(psychology uses the scientific method to try to determine facts and reduce uncertainty)

- **scientific method**
  - perceiving the question
  - forming a hypothesis
  - testing the hypothesis
  - drawing conclusions
  - reporting your results
- **descriptive data collection methods**
  - **naturalistic observation**
  - **laboratory observation**
  - **case studies**
  - **surveys**

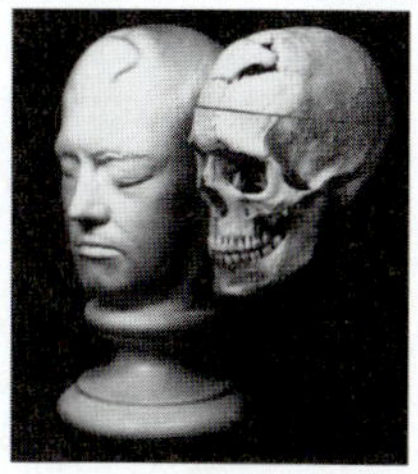

1.9 1.10 1.11 1.12 p. 35

Finding Relationships

(different ways to find out more than just descriptions of behavior)

- **correlation**
  - is a measure of relationship between two or more variables
  - produces a value called the *correlation coefficient*
  - does not prove causation
- **experiments** the only research method that will allow researchers to determine the cause of a behavior by deliberately manipulating some variable and measuring changes in the variable of interest
  - **operational definition** specifically names the steps or procedures used to control or measure the variable in the experiment
  - **groups** include both experimental and control
  - **hazards** may include the placebo effect, experimenter effects, and extraneous variables

1.13 p. 35

Ethics of Psychological Research

(psychological scientists have a primary goal of protecting the health and welfare of their animal or human participants)

- **guidelines for research with humans**
  - rights and well-being of participants must be weighed against the study's value to science
  - participants must be allowed to make an informed decision about participating (informed consent)
  - deception must be justified
  - participants may withdraw from the study at any time
  - participants must be protected from risks or told explicitly of risks
  - investigator must debrief participants, telling the true nature of the study and expectations of results
  - data must remain confidential
- **research with animals**

"He says he wants a lawyer."

1.14 p. 38

Thinking Critically About Critical Thinking

- **scientific thinking can be applied to many real-world situations**
- **four basic criteria for making reasoned judgments**
  - there are very few "truths" in the world that do not need to be subjected to testing
  - all evidence is not equal in quality
  - just because someone is considered to be an authority or to have a lot of expertise does not make everything that person claims automatically true
  - critical thinking requires an open mind

2 the biological perspective

CHAPTER OUTLINE

ASSISTING THE BRAIN

Team Hoyt is composed of Rick Hoyt and his father Dick Hoyt. Together, they have competed in over 1,000 races including six Ironman® competitions. The Ironman® competition consists of a 2.4-mile swim, a 112-mile bike ride, and a 26.2-mile run. Impressive as that is, what makes their accomplishments even more spectacular is that they approach each race a bit differently than any other competitors. For the swimming stage of a triathlon, Dick pulls Rick in a boat that is attached to a bungee cord, then he peddles Rick on a special two-seater bicycle for the biking segment. The third leg of the race is completed with Dick pushing Rick across the finish line in a customized running chair.

Rick was born with spastic quadriplegia and cerebral palsy as the result of oxygen deprivation to his brain during birth. Dick and Judy Hoyt discovered that although Rick could not walk or talk, he had a bright mind behind those bright eyes, and they worked hard to teach him the alphabet and basic words. In 1972, with a specially designed computer, Rick was able to communicate with his parents and others by tapping his head against a head piece attached to his wheelchair when specific letters of the alphabet were highlighted on a computer screen. Using this device, he eventually entered and graduated from high school and later from Boston University with a degree in Special Education.

Current research to help individuals with brain injuries or neurological conditions has moved far beyond the then-amazing but relatively simple computer that assisted Rick. Some of the most promising areas are in brain–computer interfaces (BCI) that use the brain's electrical activity to communicate with others. New developments in "hybrid" brain–computer interfaces use different sources of brain information, or even an external device (Pfurtscheller et al., 2010). It is possible that in the future, brain activity will enable individuals to control such assistive devices as prosthetic limbs or wheelchairs.

In this chapter, you will learn about the nervous system (which includes the brain) and some of the techniques used in brain research—research that may one day improve the quality of life for individuals like Rick and those with similar challenges.

Why study the nervous system and the glands?

How could we possibly understand any of our behavior, thoughts, or actions without knowing something about the incredible organs that allow us to act, think, and react? If we can understand how the brain, the nerves, and the glands interact to control feelings, thoughts, and behavior, we can begin to truly understand the complex organism called a human being.

learning objectives

2.1 What are the nervous system, neurons, and nerves, and how do they relate to one another?

2.2 How do neurons use neurotransmitters to communicate with each other and with the body?

2.3 How do the brain and spinal cord interact?

2.4 How do the somatic and autonomic nervous systems allow people and animals to interact with their surroundings and control the body's automatic functions?

2.5 How do the hormones released by glands interact with the nervous system and affect behavior?

2.6 How do psychologists study the brain and how it works?

2.7 What are the different structures of the bottom part of the brain and what do they do?

2.8 What are the structures of the brain that control emotion, learning, memory, and motivation?

2.9 What parts of the cortex control the different senses and the movement of the body?

2.10 What parts of the cortex are responsible for higher forms of thought, such as language?

2.11 How does the left side of the brain differ from the right side?

study tip

As you are reading this chapter, refer to page I-14 in *Psychology in Action* for some helpful memory strategies to use when learning the terminology in this chapter.

An Overview of the Nervous System

2.1 What are the nervous system, neurons, and nerves, and how do they relate to one another?

This chapter will explore a complex system of cells, chemicals, and organs that work together to produce behavior, thoughts, and actions. The first part of this complex arrangement is the **nervous system**, a network of cells that carries information to and from all parts of the body. Before beginning the discussion of the cells that make up the nervous system, take a look at Figure 2.1 and maybe tag it for easy reference to keep the big picture in mind as you read this chapter. This figure shows the organization of the various parts of the nervous system and will help in understanding how all the different parts work together in controlling the way people and animals think, act, and feel.

nervous system an extensive network of specialized cells that carries information to and from all parts of the body.

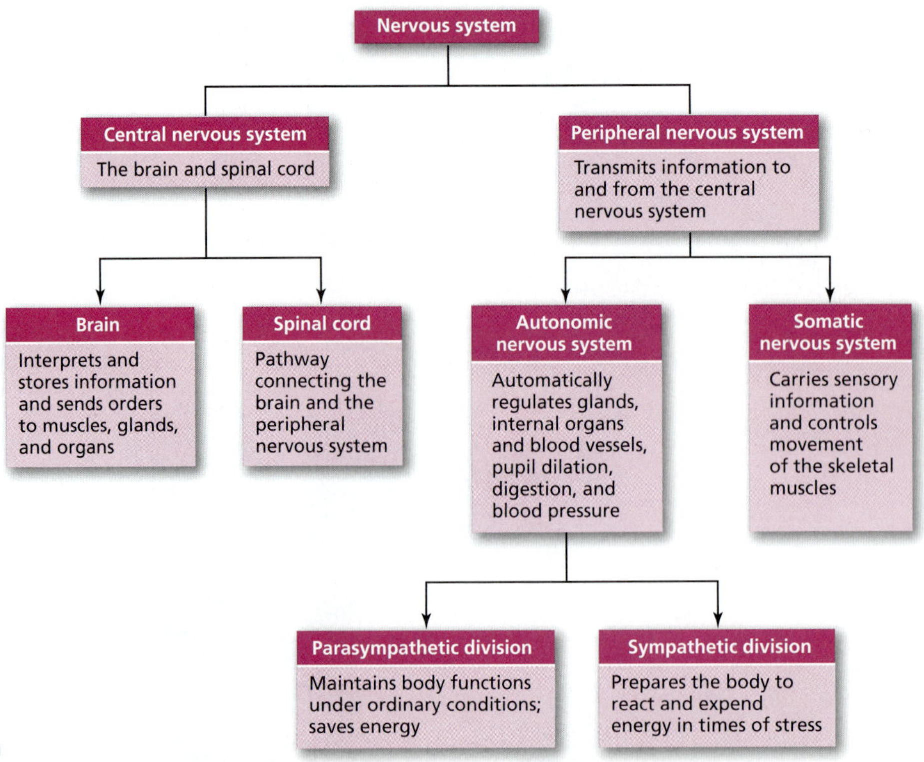

Figure 2.1 An Overview of the Nervous System

Neurons and Nerves: Building the Network

The field of **neuroscience** is a branch of the life sciences that deals with the structure and functioning of the brain and the neurons, nerves, and nervous tissue that form the nervous system. It was Santiago Ramón y Cajal, a doctor studying slides of brain tissue, who in 1887 first theorized that the nervous system was made up of individual cells (Ramón y Cajal, translation, 1995). In this discipline, the focus is on neural function in the central and peripheral nervous systems at the molecular, cellular, circuit, and behavioral levels. **Biological psychology**, or **behavioral neuroscience**, is the branch of neuroscience that focuses on the biological bases of psychological processes, behavior, and learning. Read on mypsychlab.com

neuroscience a branch of the life sciences that deals with the structure and function of neurons, nerves, and nervous tissue.

biological psychology or **behavioral neuroscience** branch of neuroscience that focuses on the biological bases of psychological processes, behavior, and learning.

neuron the basic cell that makes up the nervous system and that receives and sends messages within that system.

dendrites branchlike structures that receive messages from other neurons.

soma the cell body of the neuron responsible for maintaining the life of the cell.

axon tubelike structure that carries the neural message to other cells.

Read and learn more about Cajal's influence and discoveries on **mypsychlab.com**

STRUCTURE OF THE NEURON: THE NERVOUS SYSTEM'S BUILDING BLOCK

Although the entire body is composed of cells, each type of cell has a special purpose and function and, therefore, a special structure. For example, skin cells are flat, but muscle cells are long and stretchy. Most cells have three things in common: a nucleus, a cell body, and a cell membrane holding it all together. The **neuron** is the specialized cell in the nervous system that receives and sends messages within that system. Neurons are one of the messengers of the body, and that means that they have a very special structure.

The parts of the neuron that receive messages from other cells are called the **dendrites**. The name *dendrite* means "branch," and this structure does indeed look like the branches of a tree. The dendrites are attached to the cell body, or **soma**, which is the part of the cell that contains the nucleus and keeps the entire cell alive and functioning. The **axon** (from the Greek for "axis") is a fiber attached to the soma, and its job is to carry messages out to other cells. (See Figure 2.2.)

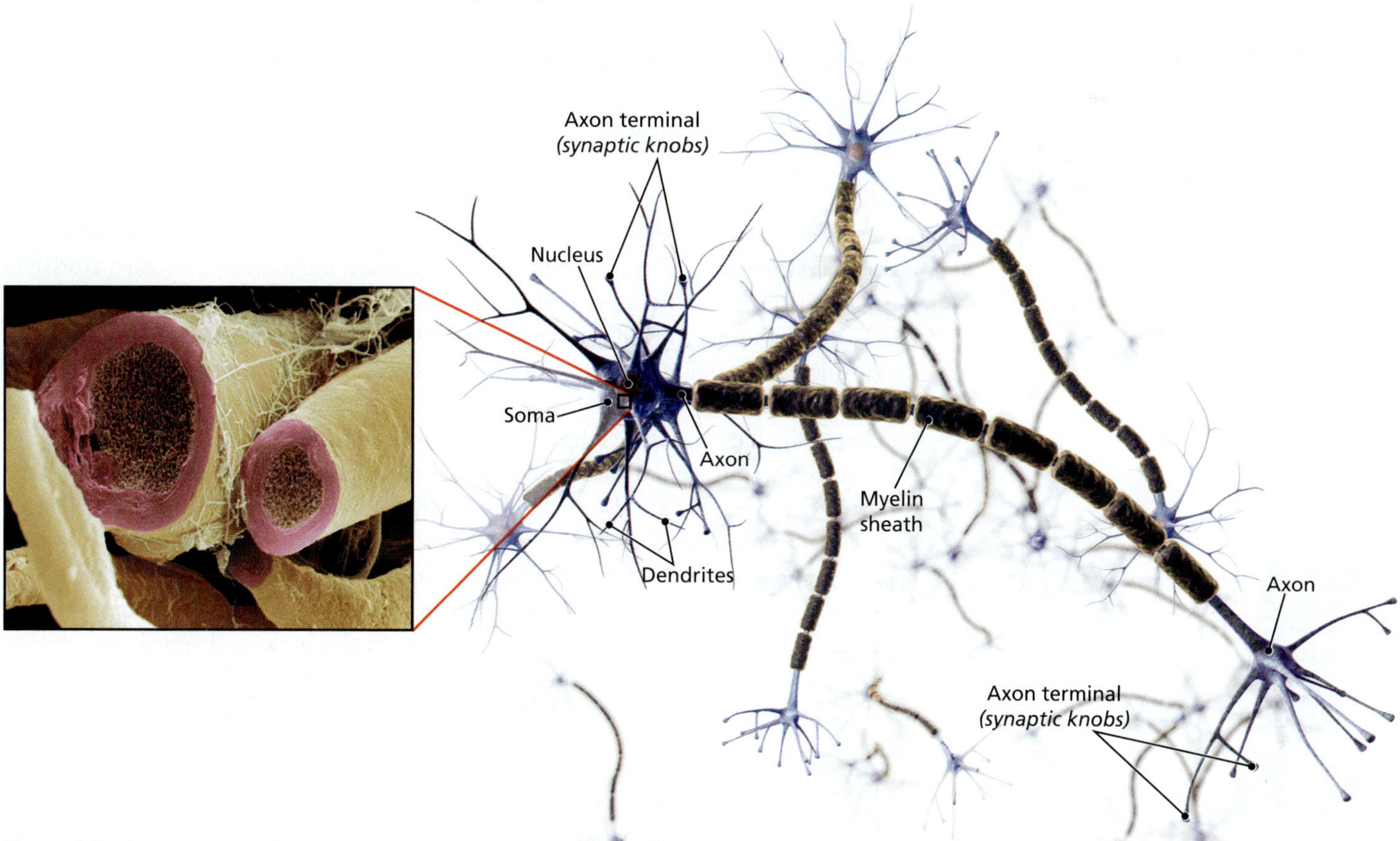

Figure 2.2 The Structure of the Neuron

The electronmicrograph on the left shows myelinated axons.

glial cells cells that provide support for the neurons to grow on and around, deliver nutrients to neurons, produce myelin to coat axons, clean up waste products and dead neurons, influence information processing, and, during prenatal development, influence the generation of new neurons.

myelin fatty substances produced by certain glial cells that coat the axons of neurons to insulate, protect, and speed up the neural impulse.

nerves bundles of axons coated in myelin that travel together through the body.

Neurons make up only 10 percent of the cells in the brain. The other 90 percent of the brain is composed of **glial cells** that serve as a sort of structure on which the neurons develop and work and that hold the neurons in place. For example, during early brain development, radial glial cells (extending from inner to outer areas like the spokes of a wheel) help guide migrating neurons to form the outer layers of the brain. There are several different types of glial cells that perform various functions, such as getting nutrients to the neurons, cleaning up the remains of neurons that have died, communicating with neurons and other glial cells, and providing insulation for neurons. Recent research has found that some types of glial cells affect both the functioning and structure of neurons and specific types also have properties similar to stem cells, which allow them to develop into new neurons, both during prenatal development and in adult mammals (Bullock et al., 2005; Kriegstein & Alvarez-Buylla, 2009).

Two special types of glial cells, called *oligodendrocytes* and *Schwann cells*, generate a layer of fatty substances called **myelin**. Oligodendrocytes produce myelin for the neurons in the brain and spinal cord (the central nervous system); Schwann cells produce myelin for the neurons of the body (the peripheral nervous system). Myelin wraps around the shaft of the axons, forming a protective sheath. It's really the axons that do the bulk of the traveling through the body, with the somas clumped together near the spinal cord. So the axons of those various neurons can travel together throughout the body and never touch each other directly. It's similar to the concept of a telephone cable. Within the cable are lots of copper wires coated in plastic; the plastic serves the same insulating purpose for the wires as the myelin sheath does for the axons. Bundled all together, they form a cable that is much stronger and less vulnerable to breakage than any wire alone would be. It works the same way in the nervous system: Bundles of myelin-coated axons travel together in "cables" called **nerves**.

The myelin sheath is a very important part of the neuron. It not only insulates the neuron, but it also offers protection from damage and speeds up the neural message traveling down the axon. As shown in Figure 2.2, sections of myelin bump up next to each other on the axon, similar to the way sausages are linked together. The places where the myelin seems to bump are actually small spaces on the axon called nodes, which are not covered in myelin. When the electrical impulse that is the neural message travels down an axon coated with myelin, it "jumps" between the myelin sheath sections to the places where the axon is accessible at the nodes. That makes the message go much faster down the coated axon than it would down an uncoated axon of a neuron in the brain. In the disease called *multiple sclerosis* (MS), the myelin sheath is destroyed (possibly by the individual's own immune system), which leads to diminished or complete loss of neural functioning in those damaged cells. Early symptoms of MS may include fatigue, changes in vision, balance problems, and numbness, tingling, or muscle weakness in the arms or legs.

In addition to the myelin sheath produced by the Schwann cells, axons of neurons found in the body are also coated with a thin membrane called the *neurilemma*, or Schwann's membrane. This membrane, which surrounds the axon and the myelin sheath, serves as a tunnel through which damaged nerve fibers can repair themselves. That's why a severed toe might actually regain some function and feeling if sewn back on in time. Unfortunately, axons of the neurons in the brain and spinal cord do not have this coating and are, therefore, more likely to be permanently damaged.

Exactly how does this "electrical message" work inside the cell?

Exactly how does this "electrical message" work inside the cell?

GENERATING THE MESSAGE WITHIN THE NEURON: THE NEURAL IMPULSE

A neuron that's at rest—not currently firing a neural impulse or message—is actually electrically charged. Inside the cell is a semiliquid (jelly-like) solution in which there are charged particles, or *ions*. A semiliquid solution also surrounds the outside of the cell and contains ions, too. Although both positive and negative ions are located inside and outside of the cell, the relative charge of ions inside the cell is mostly negative, and the relative charge of ions outside the cell is mostly positive (due to both **diffusion** and electrostatic pressure). The cell membrane itself is *semipermeable*. This means some substances that are outside the cell can enter through tiny protein openings, or *channels*, in the membrane, while other substances in the cell can go outside. Many of these channels are gated—they open or close based on the electrical potential of the membrane—more about that in a minute. Inside the cell is a concentration of both smaller positively charged potassium ions and larger negatively charged protein ions. The negatively charged protein ions, however, are so big that they can't get out, which leaves the inside of the cell primarily negative when at rest. Outside the cell are lots of positively charged sodium ions and negatively charged chloride ions, but they are unable to enter the cell membrane when the cell is at rest because the ion channels that would allow them in are closed. But because the outside sodium ions are positive and the inside ions are negative, and because opposite electrical charges attract each other, the sodium ions will cluster around the membrane. This difference in charges creates an electrical potential.

Think of the ions inside the cell as a baseball game inside a stadium (the cell walls). The sodium ions outside the cell are all the fans in the area, and they want to get inside to see the game. When the cell is resting (the electrical potential is in a state called the **resting potential**, because the cell is at rest), the fans are stuck outside. The sodium ions cannot enter when the cell is at rest, because even though the cell membrane has all these channels, the *particular channels* for the big sodium ions aren't open yet. But when the cell receives a strong enough stimulation from another cell (meaning that the dendrites are activated), the cell membrane opens up those particular channels, one after the other, all down its surface, allowing the sodium ions (the "fans") to rush into the cell. That causes the inside of the cell to become mostly positive and the outside of the cell to become mostly negative, because many of the positive sodium ions are now inside the cell—at the point where the first ion channel opened. This electrical charge reversal will start at the part of the axon closest to the soma (the first ion channel) and then proceed down the axon in a kind of chain reaction. (Picture a long hallway with many doors in which the first door opens, then the second, and so on all the way down the hall.) This electrical charge reversal is known as the **action potential** because the electrical potential is now in action rather than at rest. Each action potential sequence takes about one-thousandth of a second, so the neural message travels very fast—from 2 miles per hour in the slowest, shortest neurons to 270 miles per hour in other neurons. (See Figure 2.3.) **Explore** on **mypsychlab.com**

Explore neurons and neurotransmitters on **mypsychlab.com**

Now the action potential is traveling down the axon. When it gets to the end of the axon, something else happens: the message will get transmitted to another cell (that step will be discussed momentarily). Meanwhile, what is happening to the parts of the cell that the action potential has already left behind? How does the cell get the "fans" back outside? Remember, the action potential means that the cell is now positive inside and negative outside at the point where the channel opened. Several things happen to return the cell to its resting state. First, the sodium ion channels close immediately after the action potential has passed, allowing no more "fans" (sodium ions) to enter. The cell membrane also literally pumps the positive sodium ions back outside the cell, kicking the "fans" out until the next action potential opens the ion channels again. This pumping process is a little slow, so another type of ion gets into the act. Small, positively charged potassium ions inside the neuron move rapidly out of the cell after the action potential passes, helping to more quickly restore the inside of the cell to a negative charge. Now the cell becomes negative inside and positive outside, and the neuron is capable of "firing off" another message. Once the sodium pumps finish pumping out the sodium ions, the neuron can be said to have returned to its full resting potential, poised and ready to do it all again.

diffusion process of molecules moving from areas of high concentration to areas of low concentration.

resting potential the state of the neuron when not firing a neural impulse.

action potential the release of the neural impulse consisting of a reversal of the electrical charge within the axon.

Figure 2.3 The Neural Impulse Action Potential

In the graph below, voltage readings are shown at a given place on the neuron over a period of 20 or 30 milliseconds (thousandths of a second). At first the cell is resting; it then reaches threshold and an action potential is triggered. After a brief hyperpolarization period, the cell returns to its resting potential.

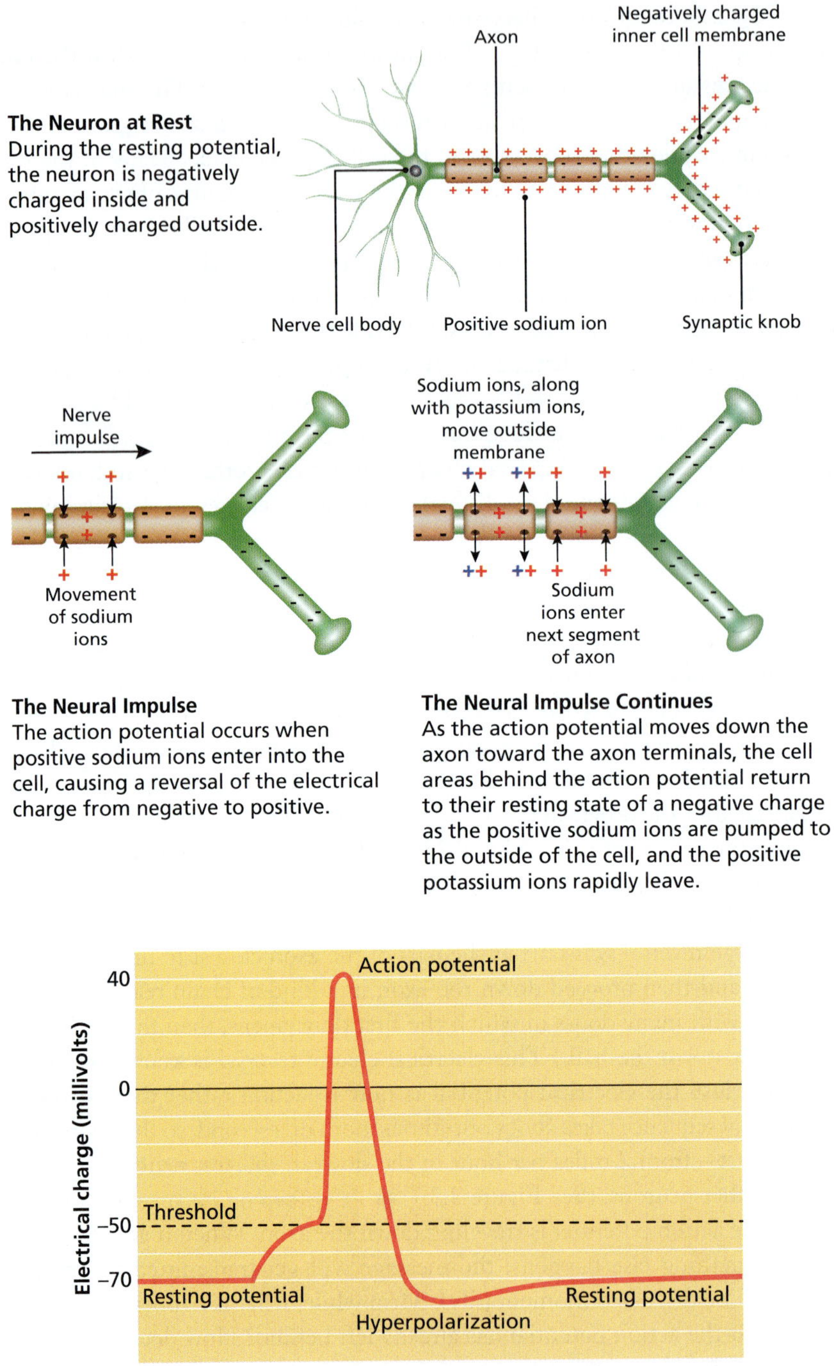

To sum all that up, when the cell is stimulated, the first ion channel opens and the electrical charge *at that ion channel* is reversed. Then the next channel opens and *that* charge is reversed, but in the meantime the *first* ion channel has been closed and the charge is returning to what it was when it was at rest. The action potential is the *sequence* of ion channels opening all down the length of the cell.

So if the stimulus that originally causes the neuron to fire is very strong, will the neuron fire more strongly than it would if the stimulus were weak?

So if the stimulus that originally causes the neuron to fire is very strong, will the neuron fire more strongly than it would if the stimulus were weak?

Neurons actually have a threshold for firing, and all it takes is a stimulus that is just strong enough to get past that threshold to make the neuron fire. Here's a simple version of how this works: Each neuron is receiving many signals from other neurons.

Some of these signals are meant to cause the neuron to fire, whereas others are meant to prevent the neuron from firing. The neuron constantly adds together the effects of the "fire" messages and subtracts the "don't fire" messages, and if the fire messages are great enough, the threshold is crossed and the neuron fires. When a neuron does fire, it fires in an **all-or-none** fashion. That is, neurons are either firing at full strength or not firing at all—there's no such thing as "partial" firing of a neuron. It would be like turning on a light switch—it's either on or it's off. Once the switch is turned to the on position, the light will come on. When it's turned to the off position, the light is off.

So, what's the difference between strong stimulation and weak stimulation? A strong message will cause the neuron to fire repeatedly (as if someone flicked the light switch on and off as quickly as possible), and it will also cause more neurons to fire (as if there were a lot of lights going on and off instead of just one).

Now that we know how the message travels within the axon of the cell, what is that "something else" that happens when the action potential reaches the end of the axon?

Now that we know how the message travels within the axon of the cell, what is that "something else" that happens when the action potential reaches the end of the axon?

SENDING THE MESSAGE TO OTHER CELLS: THE SYNAPSE

2.2 How do neurons use neurotransmitters to communicate with each other and with the body?

Look once again at Figure 2.2 on page 47. The end of the axon fans out into several shorter fibers that have swellings or little knobs on the ends called **synaptic knobs** or **axon terminals** (may also be called *terminal buttons*). Figure 2.4 shows this knob enlarged to giant scale. Notice that the synaptic knob is not empty. It has a number of little saclike structures in it called **synaptic vesicles**. The word *vesicle* is Latin and means a "little blister" or "fluid-filled sac."

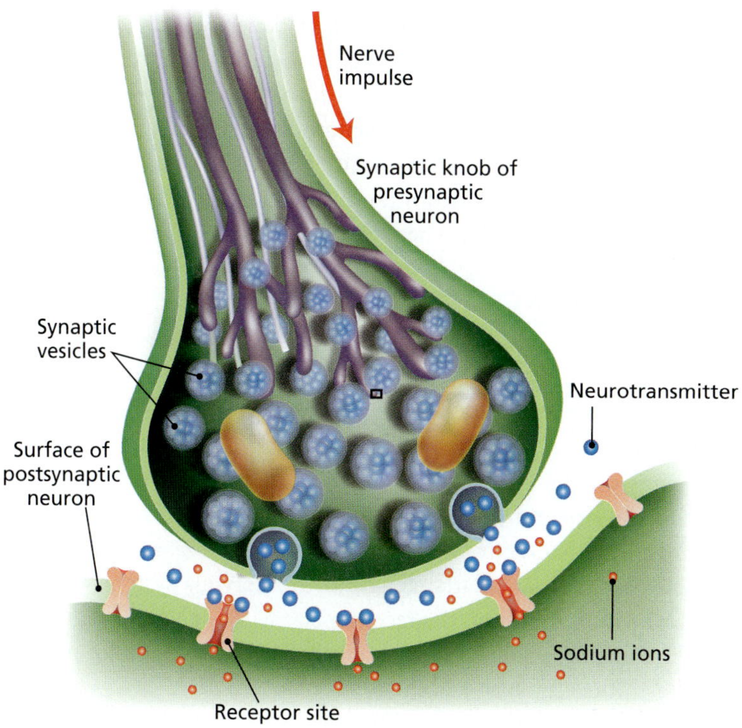

Figure 2.4 The Synapse

The nerve impulse reaches the synaptic knobs, triggering the release of neurotransmitters from the synaptic vesicles. The molecules of neurotransmitter cross the synaptic gap to fit into the receptor sites that fit the shape of the molecule, opening the ion channel and allowing sodium ions to rush in.

all-or-none referring to the fact that a neuron either fires completely or does not fire at all.

synaptic knob rounded areas on the end of the axon terminals.

axon terminals branches at the end of the axon.

synaptic vesicles saclike structures found inside the synaptic knob containing chemicals.

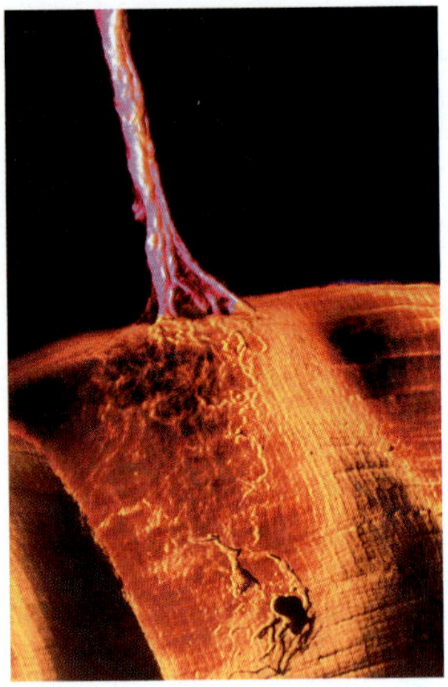

This electromicrograph shows a motor neuron making contact with muscle fibers.

Inside the synaptic vesicles are chemicals suspended in fluid, which are molecules of substances called **neurotransmitters**. The name is simple enough—they are inside a neuron and they are going to transmit a message. (There are neurons that contain only one primary neurotransmitter but there are also some neurons that contain more than one neurotransmitter.) Next to the synaptic knob is the dendrite of another neuron (see Figure 2.4). Between them is a fluid-filled space called the **synapse** or the **synaptic gap**. Instead of an electrical charge, the vesicles at the end of the axon (also called the presynaptic membrane) contain the molecules of neurotransmitters, and the surface of the dendrite next to the axon (the postsynaptic membrane) contains ion channels that have **receptor sites**, proteins that allow only particular molecules of a certain shape to fit into it, just as only a particular key will fit into a keyhole.

How do the neurotransmitters get across the gap? Recall the action potential making its way down the axon after the neuron has been stimulated. When that action potential, or electrical charge, reaches the synaptic vesicles, the synaptic vesicles release their neurotransmitters into the synaptic gap. The molecules then float across the synapse and many of them fit themselves into the receptor sites, opening the ion channels and allowing sodium to rush in, activating the next cell. It is this very activation that stimulates, or releases, the action potential in that cell. It is important to understand that the "next cell" may be a neuron, but it may also be a cell on a muscle or a gland. Muscles and glands have special cells with receptor sites on them, just like on the dendrite of a neuron.

So far, we've been talking about the synapse as if neurotransmitters always cause the next cell to fire its action potential (or, in the case of a muscle or gland, to contract or start secreting its chemicals). But the neurons must have a way to be turned *off* as well as on. Otherwise, when a person burns a finger, the pain signals from those neurons would not stop until the burn was completely healed. Muscles are told to contract or relax, and glands are told to secrete or stop secreting their chemicals. The neurotransmitters found at various synapses around the nervous system can either turn cells on (called an *excitatory* effect) or turn cells off (called an *inhibitory* effect), depending on exactly what synapse is being affected. Although some people refer to neurotransmitters that turn cells on as *excitatory* neurotransmitters and the ones that turn cells off as *inhibitory* neurotransmitters, it's really more correct to refer to **excitatory synapses** and **inhibitory synapses**. In other words, it's not the neurotransmitter itself that is excitatory or inhibitory, but rather it is the effect of that neurotransmitter that is either excitatory or inhibitory at the receptor sites of a particular synapse.

NEUROTRANSMITTERS: MESSENGERS OF THE NETWORK

There are at least 100 identified neurotransmitters (Snyder, 2002) and possibly many more exist. The first neurotransmitter to be identified was named *acetylcholine*. It is found at the synapses between neurons and muscle cells. Acetylcholine stimulates the skeletal muscles to contract but actually slows contractions in the heart muscle. If acetylcholine receptor sites on the muscle cells are blocked in some way, then the acetylcholine can't get to the site and the muscle will be incapable of contracting—paralyzed, in other words. This is exactly what happens when *curare*, a drug used by South American Indians on their blow darts, gets into the nervous system. Curare's molecules are just similar enough to fit into the receptor site without actually stimulating the cell, making curare an **antagonist** (a chemical substance that blocks or reduces the effects of a neurotransmitter) for acetylcholine.

What would happen if the neurons released too much acetylcholine? The bite of a black widow spider does just that. Its venom stimulates the release of excessive amounts of acetylcholine and causes convulsions and possible death. Black widow spider venom is an **agonist** (a chemical substance that mimics or enhances the effects of a neurotransmitter) for acetylcholine.

neurotransmitter chemical found in the synaptic vesicles that, when released, has an effect on the next cell.

synapse (synaptic gap) microscopic fluid-filled space between the synaptic knob of one cell and the dendrites or surface of the next cell.

receptor sites 3-dimensional proteins on the surface of the dendrites or certain cells of the muscles and glands, which are shaped to fit only certain neurotransmitters.

excitatory synapse synapse at which a neurotransmitter causes the receiving cell to fire.

inhibitory synapse synapse at which a neurotransmitter causes the receiving cell to stop firing.

antagonists chemical substances that block or reduce a cell's response to the action of other chemicals or neurotransmitters.

agonists chemical substances that mimic or enhance the effects of a neurotransmitter on the receptor sites of the next cell, increasing or decreasing the activity of that cell.

Acetylcholine also plays a key role in memory, arousal, and attention. For example, acetylcholine is found in the hippocampus, an area of the brain that is responsible for forming new memories, and low levels of acetylcholine have been associated with Alzheimer's disease, the most common type of dementia. LINK to Chapter Six: Memory, pp. 246–247. We will focus more on agonists and antagonists later in the chapter.

Although acetylcholine was the first neurotransmitter found to have an excitatory effect at the synapse, the nervous system's major excitatory neurotransmitter is *glutamate.* Like acetylcholine, glutamate plays an important role in learning and memory, and may also be involved in the development of the nervous system and in synaptic plasticity (the ability of the brain to change connections among its neurons). However, an excess of glutamate results in overactivation and neuronal damage, and may be associated with the cell death that occurs in head injury or Alzheimer's disease (Julien et al., 2008).

The venom of the black widow spider causes a flood of acetylcholine to be released into the body's muscle system, causing convulsions.

Another neurotransmitter is *GABA*, or *γ-aminobutyric acid* (spoken as *gamma-aminobutyric acid).* Whereas glutamate is the major neurotransmitter with an excitatory effect, GABA is the most common neurotransmitter producing inhibition in the brain. GABA can help to calm anxiety, for example, by binding to the same receptor sites that are affected by tranquilizing drugs and alcohol. In fact, the effect of alcohol is to enhance the effect of GABA, which causes the general inhibition of the nervous system associated with getting drunk. This makes alcohol an agonist for GABA. LINK to Chapter Four: Consciousness, p. 155.

Serotonin is a neurotransmitter originating in the lower part of the brain that can have either an excitatory or inhibitory effect, depending on the particular synapses being affected. It is associated with sleep, mood, and appetite. For example, low levels of serotonin activity have been linked to depression. LINK to Chapter Fourteen: Psychological Disorders, p. 548.

Dopamine is found in the brain and, like serotonin, can have different effects depending on the exact location of its activity. If too little dopamine is released in a certain area of the brain, the result is Parkinson's disease—the disease currently being battled by former boxing champ Muhammad Ali and actor Michael J. Fox (Ahlskog, 2003). If too much dopamine is released in other areas, the result is a cluster of symptoms that may be part of schizophrenia (Akil et al., 2003). LINK to Chapter Fourteen: Psychological Disorders, pp. 558-560. (See Table 2.1 for a list of some neurotransmitters and their functions.)

Table 2.1

Some Neurotransmitters and Their Functions

NEUROTRANSMITTERS	FUNCTIONS
Acetylcholine	Excitatory or inhibitory; involved in arousal, attention, memory, and controls muscle contractions
Serotonin	Excitatory or inhibitory; involved in mood, sleep, and appetite
GABA (gamma-aminobutyric acid)	Major inhibitory neurotransmitter; involved in sleep and inhibits movement
Glutamate	Major excitatory neurotransmitter; involved in learning, memory formation, nervous system development, and synaptic plasticity
Norepinephrine	Mainly excitatory; involved in arousal and mood
Dopamine	Excitatory or inhibitory; involved in control of movement and sensations of pleasure
Endorphins	Inhibitory neural regulators; involved in pain relief

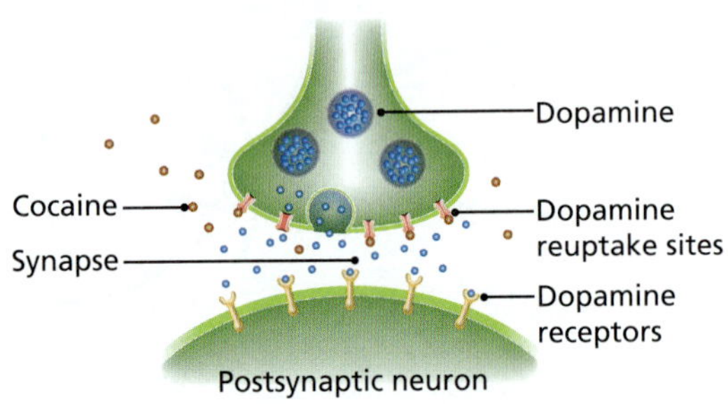

Figure 2.5 Reuptake of Dopamine
Dopamine is removed from the synapse by reuptake sites. Cocaine acts by blocking dopamine reuptake sites, allowing dopamine to remain active in the synapse longer.

Some neurotransmitters directly control the release of other neurotransmitters. These special neurotransmitters are called *neural regulators* or *neural peptides* (Agnati et al., 1992), and *endorphins*—pain-controlling chemicals in the body—are transmitters that you may have heard about. When a person is hurt, a neurotransmitter that signals pain is released. When the brain gets this message, it triggers the release of endorphins. The endorphins bind to receptors that open the ion channels on the axon. This causes the cell to be unable to fire its pain signal and the pain sensations eventually lessen. For example, you might bump your elbow and experience a lot of pain right at first, but the pain will quickly subside to a much lower level. Sports players may injure themselves during an event and yet not feel the pain until after the competition is over, when the endorphin levels go down.

The name *endorphin* comes from the term *endogenous morphine*. (*Endogenous* means "native to the area"—in this case, native to the body.) Scientists studying the nervous system found receptor sites that fit morphine molecules perfectly and decided that there must be a natural substance in the body that has the same effect as morphine. Endorphins are the reason that heroin and the other drugs derived from opium are so addictive—when people take morphine or heroin, their bodies neglect to produce endorphins. When the drug wears off, they are left with no protection against pain at all, and *everything* hurts. This pain is one reason why most people want more heroin, creating an addictive cycle of abuse. LINK to Chapter Four: Consciousness, p. 157.

If the neurotransmitters are out there in the synaptic gap and in the receptor sites, what happens to them when they aren't needed anymore?

If the neurotransmitters are out there in the synaptic gap and in the receptor sites, what happens to them when they aren't needed anymore?

CLEANING UP THE SYNAPSE: REUPTAKE AND ENZYMES

The neurotransmitters have to get out of the receptor sites before the next stimulation can occur. Some just drift away through the process of diffusion but most will end up back in the synaptic vesicles in a process called **reuptake**. (Think of a little suction tube, sucking the chemicals back into the vesicles.) That way, the synapse is cleared for the next release of neurotransmitters. Some drugs, like cocaine, affect the nervous system by blocking the reuptake process. See Figure 2.5 for a visual representation of how dopamine is affected by cocaine.

There is one neurotransmitter that is not taken back into the vesicles, however. Because acetylcholine is responsible for muscle activity, and muscle activity needs to happen rapidly and continue happening, it's not possible to wait around for the "sucking up" process to occur. Instead, an enzyme* specifically designed to break apart acetylcholine clears the synaptic gap very quickly (a process called **enzymatic degradation**.) There are enzymes that break down other neurotransmitters as well.

I think I understand the synapse and neurotransmitters now, but how do I relate that to the real world?

I think I understand the synapse and neurotransmitters now, but how do I relate that to the real world?

Knowing how and why drugs affect us can help us understand why a doctor might prescribe a particular drug or why certain drugs are dangerous and should be avoided. Because the chemical molecules of various drugs, if similar enough in shape to the neurotransmitters, can fit into the receptor sites on the receiving neurons just like the neurotransmitters do, drugs can act as agonists or antagonists. Drugs acting as agonists, for example, can mimic or enhance the effects of neurotransmitters on the receptor sites of the next cell. This can result in an increase or decrease in the activity of the receiving cell, depending on what the effect of the original neurotransmitter (excitatory or inhibitory) was going to be. So if the original neurotransmitter was excitatory, the effect of the agonist will be to increase that excitation. If it was inhibitory, the effect of the agonist will be to increase that inhibition. Another deciding factor is the nervous system location of the neurons that use a specific neurotransmitter.

reuptake process by which neurotransmitters are taken back into the synaptic vesicles.

enzymatic degradation process by which structure of neurotransmitter is altered so it can no longer act on a receptor.

*enzyme: a complex protein that is manufactured by cells.

For example, some antianxiety medications, such as diazepam (Valium®), are classified as benzodiazepines (LINK to Chapter Fifteen: Psychological Therapies, p. 597) and are agonists for GABA, the primary inhibitory neurotransmitter in the brain. Areas of the brain that play a role in controlling anxiety, agitation, and fear include the amygdala, orbitofrontal cortex, and the insula (Julien et al., 2008; Naqvi et al., 2006). By increasing the inhibitory (calming) action of GABA, the benzodiazepines directly calm these specific brain areas (Julien et al., 2008; Preston et al., 2008).

Other drugs act as antagonists, blocking or reducing a cell's response to the action of other chemicals or neurotransmitters. Although an antagonist might sound like it has only an inhibitory effect, it is important to remember that if the neurotransmitter that the antagonist affects is inhibitory itself, the result will actually be an *increase* in the activity of the cell that would normally have been inhibited; the antagonist *blocks* the inhibitory effect.

Lastly, some drugs yield their agonistic or antagonistic effects by impacting the amount of neurotransmitter in the synapse. They do so by interfering with the regular reuptake or enzymatic degradation process. Remember that the neurotransmitter serotonin helps regulate and adjust people's moods, but in some people the normal process of adjustment is not working properly. In one theory of depression, serotonin is either not produced or not released in great enough amounts, so it can't fully activate the receptors on the next neuron, leaving the person in a state of depression. Some of the drugs used to treat depression are called SSRIs (selective serotonin reuptake inhibitors). SSRIs block the reuptake of serotonin, leaving more serotonin available in the synapse to bond with the receptor sites. Eventually, this elevates mood and lifts the depression.

This section covered the neuron and how neurons communicate. The next section looks at the bigger picture—the nervous system itself.

study tip

For this part of the section, if you focus your attention on the general ideas about agonistic and antagonistic effects, the brain areas will soon make more sense to you. You may also want to revisit this information after reading the sections on brain anatomy.

2.1 2.2 CONCEPT MAP

- The nervous system is a network of cells that carries information to and from all parts of the body; **neuroscience** is the field of study that deals with the structure of the brain and components of the nervous system

Neurons and Nerves

- **brain is comprised of neurons and glial cells**
  - **glial cells:** provide physical and metabolic support to neurons; communicate with other cells; specific types have stem cell-like properties
    - **oligodendrocytes:** produce myelin in the central nervous system
    - **Schwann cells:** produce myelin in the peripheral nervous system
      - myelin insulates axons and speeds up transmission of neural message
  - **neurons:** specialized cells in nervous system; send and receive messages within that system
    - have specialized components
      - **dendrites**
      - **soma**
      - **axon** — axon terminals/synaptic knobs
    - have an electrical charge at rest—the resting potential
      - made possible by balance between ions in and outside of the cell
      - membrane is semipermeable; inside is negatively charged as compared to outside
      - change in the electrical charge can result in an action potential; cell fires; inside becomes positive relative to outside
        - fires in an all-or-none fashion
        - cell firing is dependent on sum of excitatory and inhibitory messages received by the cell
    - are affected by neurotransmitters (see Table 2.1); chemicals that have an effect on neurons
    - are separated by a gap called the synapse; when nerve impulse reaches synaptic knobs, neurotransmitter is released into synaptic space
      - neurotransmitters (NTs) move across synapse and activate ion channel receptor sites on adjacent cells; some NTs are agonistic/excitatory, others are antagonistic/inhibitory
      - neurotransmitter action stopped by exiting synapse; neurotransmitters end back up in the releasing cell through reuptake or broken down by enzymes

(continued)

PRACTICE quiz How much do you remember? ANSWERS ON PAGE AK-1.

Pick the best answer.

1. Which part of the neuron receives messages from other cells?
   a. axon
   b. dendrite
   c. soma
   d. myelin
2. Which one of the following is NOT a function of the myelin sheath?
   a. insulates the axon
   b. speeds up the neural message
   c. protects the nerve fiber from damage
   d. aids in reuptake
3. When a neuron's action potential occurs, _________ ions are rushing into the axon through openings on the membrane.
   a. sodium
   b. potassium
   c. chloride
   d. oxygen
4. When the action potential reaches the end of the axon terminals, it causes the release of _________.
   a. an electrical spark that sets off the next neuron.
   b. positively charged ions that excite the next cell.
   c. negatively charged ions that inhibit the next cell.
   d. neurotransmitters that excite or inhibit the next cell.
5. Receiving neurons have special _________ that fit the shape of certain molecules.
   a. synaptic vesicles
   b. gaps
   c. receptor sites
   d. branches
6. Which of the following is associated with sleep, mood, and appetite?
   a. acetylcholine
   b. GABA
   c. serotonin
   d. endorphin

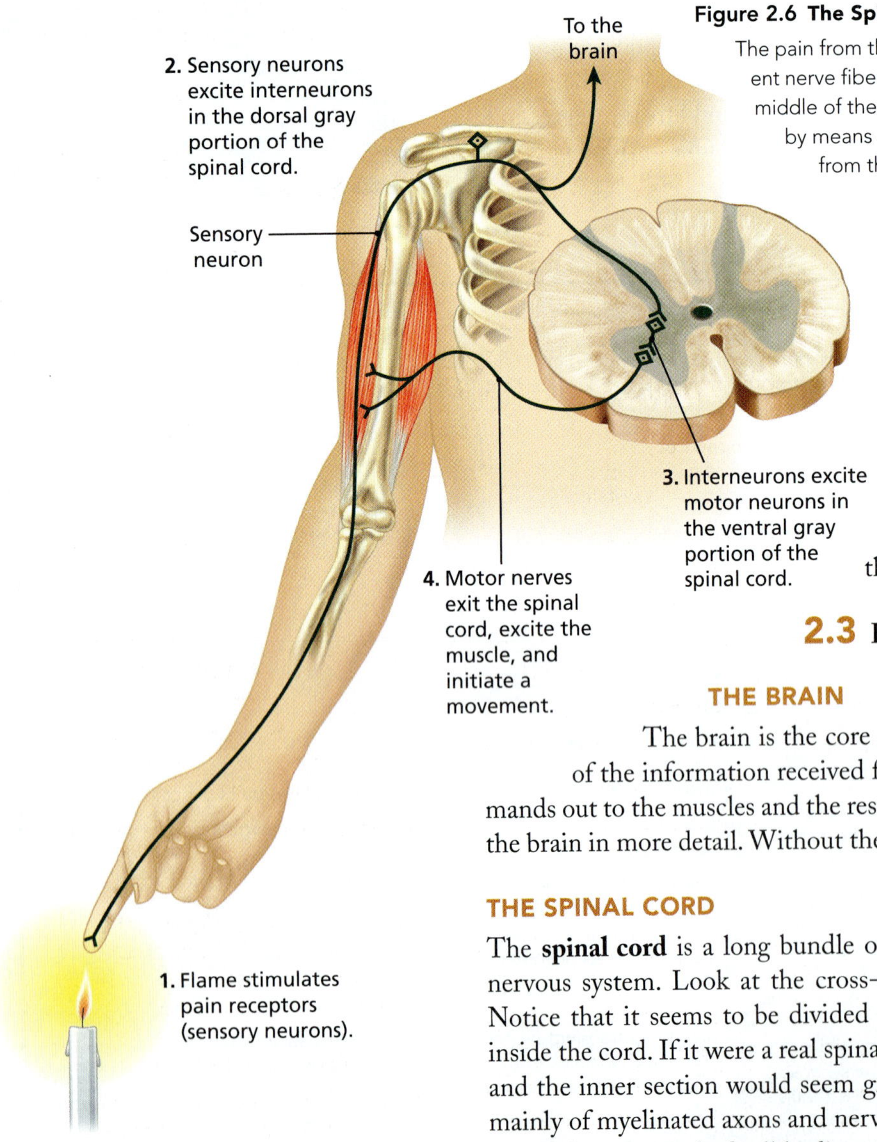

Figure 2.6 The Spinal Cord Reflex
The pain from the burning heat of the candle flame stimulates the afferent nerve fibers, which carry the message up to the interneurons in the middle of the spinal cord. The interneurons then send a message out by means of the efferent nerve fibers, causing the hand to jerk away from the flame.

The Central Nervous System: The "Central Processing Unit"

The **central nervous system (CNS)** is composed of the brain and the spinal cord. Both the brain and the spinal cord are composed of neurons and glial cells that control the life-sustaining functions of the body as well as all thought, emotion, and behavior.

2.3 How do the brain and spinal cord interact?

THE BRAIN

The brain is the core of the nervous system, the part that makes sense of the information received from the senses, makes decisions, and sends commands out to the muscles and the rest of the body. Later parts of this chapter will cover the brain in more detail. Without the spinal cord, however, the brain would be useless.

THE SPINAL CORD

The **spinal cord** is a long bundle of neurons that serves two vital functions for the nervous system. Look at the cross-sectional view of the spinal cord in Figure 2.6. Notice that it seems to be divided into two areas, one around the outside and one inside the cord. If it were a real spinal cord, the outer section would appear to be white and the inner section would seem gray. That's because the outer section is composed mainly of myelinated axons and nerves, which appear white, whereas the inner section is mainly composed of cell bodies of neurons, which appear gray. The purpose of the outer section is to carry messages from the body up to the brain and from the brain down to the body. It is simply a message "pipeline."

THE REFLEX ARC: THREE TYPES OF NEURONS The inside section, which is made up of cell bodies separated by glial cells, is actually a primitive sort of "brain." This part of the spinal cord is responsible for certain reflexes—very fast, lifesaving reflexes. To understand how the spinal cord reflexes work, it is important to know there are three basic types of neurons: **afferent (sensory) neurons** that carry messages from the senses to the spinal cord, **efferent (motor) neurons** that carry messages from the spinal cord to the muscles and glands, and **interneurons** that connect the afferent neurons to the motor neurons (and make up the inside of the spinal cord and much of the brain itself). (See Figure 2.6.) Touch a flame or a hot stove with your finger, for example, and an afferent neuron will send the pain message up to the spinal column where it enters into the central area of the spinal cord. The interneuron in that central area will then receive the message and send out a response along an efferent neuron, causing your finger to pull back. This all happens very quickly. If the pain message had to go all the way up to the brain before a response could be made, the response time would be greatly increased and more damage would be done to your finger. So having this kind of **reflex arc** controlled by the spinal cord alone allows for very fast response times. (A good way to avoid mixing up the terms *afferent* and *efferent* is to remember "afferent neurons access the spinal cord, efferent neurons exit." The pain message does eventually get to the brain, where other motor responses may be triggered, like saying "Ouch!" and putting the finger in your mouth. **Simulate** on **mypsychlab.com**

The look on this young woman's face clearly indicates that she has experienced pain in her finger. Pain is a warning signal that something is wrong, in this case that touching the thorns on the stem of the rose was a bad idea. What might be some of the problems encountered by a person who could feel no pain at all?

Simulate the nerve impulse in afferent and efferent neurons on **mypsychlab.com**

psychology in the news

Fact or Fiction: Focus on the Brain, but Check Your Sources!

As stressed in Chapter One, critical thinking is a valuable skill and one that is very useful in the study of psychology. One of the basic points highlighted was that not all evidence is equal in quality. LINK to Chapter One: The Science of Psychology, p. 37. Have you ever heard a claim about the brain that you were not sure was true?

Whether you get your news from blogs or Web sites, listen to podcasts, or watch the local or national news on your television, computer, or smartphone, you have probably read/heard/seen a segment that addresses some aspect of the human brain. Some recent, and not-so-recent brain-related news items have included:

"Older brains can't make new cells"
"Listening to classical music makes you smarter—also known as *The Mozart Effect*"
"Autism is caused by childhood vaccinations"
"People only use 10 percent of their brain"

Items adapted from Neuromyth Busters: Eight Myths About the Brain, Society for Neuroscience. Available at *www.sfn.org/skins/main/pdf/neuromyth_busters/neuromyth_busters.pdf*

Do any of the above "headlines" look familiar? Given the inherent interest in many of these topics and the number of people who reportedly "know" these facts, they have often been considered the truth. But in fact, all of the above items have been found to be false or have not been supported by conclusive, scientific evidence. So how do you go about evaluating brain-related news the next time it flashes across the headlines or shows up on your news feed?

central nervous system (CNS) part of the nervous system consisting of the brain and spinal cord.

spinal cord a long bundle of neurons that carries messages between the body and the brain and is responsible for very fast, lifesaving reflexes.

afferent (sensory) neuron a neuron that carries information from the senses to the central nervous system.

efferent (motor) neuron a neuron that carries messages from the central nervous system to the muscles of the body.

interneuron a neuron found in the center of the spinal cord that receives information from the afferent neurons and sends commands to the muscles through the efferent neurons. Interneurons also make up the bulk of the neurons in the brain.

reflex arc the connection of the afferent neurons to the interneurons to the efferent neurons, resulting in a reflex action.

neuroplasticity the ability within the brain to constantly change both the structure and function of many cells in response to experience or trauma.

Some of the best sources are the original research studies, assuming the researchers collected data in an unbiased manner and followed established research methods. LINK *to* Chapter One: The Science of Psychology, pp. 20-31. Findings that are published in peer-reviewed journals (where research is reviewed by other experts in that area) are especially helpful, as are edited books with contributions by experts in the associated field. The challenge for students early in their psychological studies is that it is not so easy to fully understand the methods, statistics, or terminology used in the studies.

For students, aside from your textbooks and professors, other good resources are the educational materials provided by professional organizations. For psychology in general, the American Psychological Association (APA) and the Association for Psychological Science (APS) are two great sources of information. In addition to various peer-reviewed journals and other educational publications, they both have informative Web sites.

For information more specifically related to the brain and neuroscience, one of the best sources of research and educational material is the Society for Neuroscience (SfN). The four misconceptions mentioned earlier are based on eight myths about the brain that are covered in one of their educational publications *Neuromyth Busters: Eight Myths About the Brain* and is available from their Web site, *www.sfn.org/skins/main/pdf/neuromyth_busters/neuromyth_busters.pdf*

So the next time you see a news item about the brain, check your sources and remain mindful that some sources are certainly more helpful than others.

Useful Web sites:

American Psychological Association (APA)—*www.apa.org*

Association for Psychological Science (APS)—*www.psychologicalscience.org*

Society for Neuroscience (SfN)—*www.sfn.org/home.aspx*

Questions for Further Discussion

1. How might your personal experience with a brain-related disorder (e.g., grandparent with Alzheimer's disease) affect your ability to critically evaluate a claim related to the disorder (e.g., "Cure for Alzheimer's Found!")?
2. As a student in psychological science, how would you explain the need for replicability in research to a family member that is not as familiar with the scientific method?

If the spinal cord is such an important link between the body and the brain, what happens if it is damaged?

If the spinal cord is such an important link between the body and the brain, what happens if it is damaged?

Damage to the central nervous system was once thought to be permanent. Neurons in the brain and spinal cord were not seen as capable of repairing themselves. When people recovered from a stroke, for example, it was assumed that healthy brain cells took over the function of the damaged ones. Scientists have known for a while now that some forms of central nervous system damage can be repaired by the body's systems, and in recent years great strides have been made in repairing spinal cord damage. The brain actually exhibits a great deal of **neuroplasticity**, the ability to constantly change both the structure and function of many cells in the brain in response to experience and even trauma (Neville & Bavelier, 2000; Rossini et al., 2007; Sanders et al., 2008.) Scientists have been able to *implant* nerve fibers from outside the spinal cord onto a damaged area and then "coax" the damaged spinal nerves to grow through these "tunnels" of implanted fibers (Cheng et al., 1996). The first human trials have already begun (Blits & Bunge, 2006; Bunge & Pearse, 2003). It is also now known that the brain can change itself quite a bit by adapting neurons to serve new functions when old neurons die or are damaged. Dendrites grow and new synapses are formed in at least some areas of the brain, as people learn new things throughout life (Abraham & Williams, 2003).

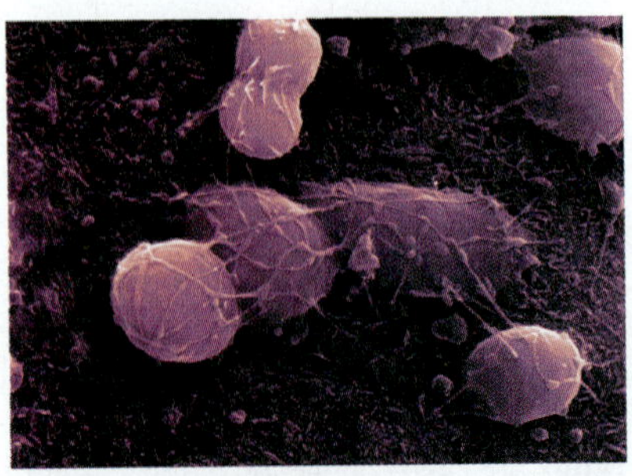

This electronmicrograph shows a stem cell in the process of becoming a neuron.

Researchers are constantly looking for new ways to repair the brain. One avenue of research has involved scientists investigating the possibility of transplanting **stem cells** to repair damaged or diseased brain tissue. Stem cells can become other cells, such as blood cells, nerve cells, and brain cells (National Institutes of Health, 2007) and may offer promise for addressing diseases such as Parkinson's and Alzheimer's, or the repair of damaged spinal cords or brain tissue (see Figure 2.7). If stem cells can be implanted into areas that have been damaged, the newly developed neurons may assume the roles that the original (now damaged) neurons can no longer perform. **Listen** on **mypsychlab.com**

Listen to the Psychology in the News podcast and learn more about stem cell in **mypsychlab.com**

The Peripheral Nervous System: Nerves on the Edge

Okay, that takes care of the central nervous system, except for the detail on the brain. How does the central nervous system communicate with the rest of the body?

Okay, that takes care of the central nervous system, except for the detail on the brain. How does the central nervous system communicate with the rest of the body?

The term *peripheral* refers to things that are not in the center or that are on the edges of the center. The **peripheral nervous system** or **PNS** (see Figure 2.7 and also Figure 2.1, p. 46) is made up of all the nerves and neurons that are not contained in the brain and spinal cord. It is this system that allows the brain and spinal cord to communicate with the sensory systems of the eyes, ears, skin, and mouth and allows the brain and spinal cord to control the muscles and glands of the body. The PNS can be divided into two major systems, the **somatic nervous system** and the **autonomic nervous system (ANS)**.

2.4 **How do the somatic and autonomic nervous systems allow people and animals to interact with their surroundings and control the body's automatic functions?**

THE SOMATIC NERVOUS SYSTEM

One of the parts of a neuron is the soma, or cell body (the word *soma* means "body"). The somatic nervous system is made up of the **sensory pathway**, which comprises all the nerves carrying messages from the senses to the central nervous system (those nerves containing afferent neurons), and the **motor pathway**, which is all of the nerves carrying messages from the central nervous system to the voluntary, or skeletal,* muscles of the body—muscles that allow people to move their bodies (those nerves composed of efferent neurons). When people are walking, raising their hands in class, smelling a flower, or directing their gaze toward the person they are talking to or to look at a pretty picture, they are using the somatic nervous system. (As seen in the discussion of spinal

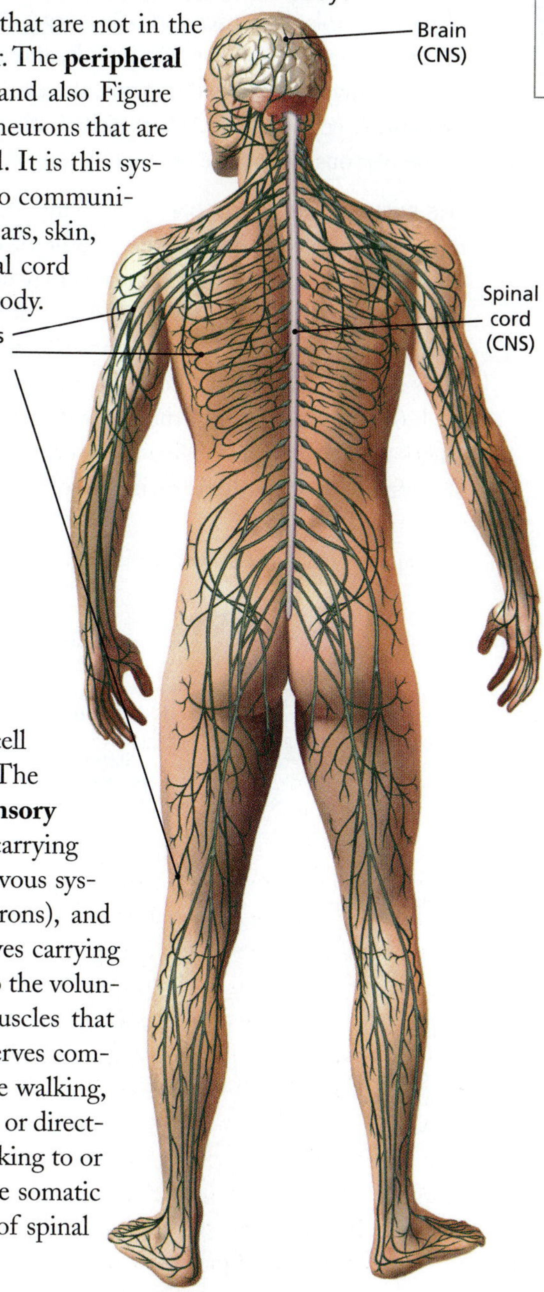

Figure 2.7 The Peripheral Nervous System

*skeletal: having to do with the bones of the body, or skeleton.

stem cells special cells found in all the tissues of the body that are capable of becoming other cell types when those cells need to be replaced due to damage or wear and tear.

peripheral nervous system (PNS) all nerves and neurons that are not contained in the brain and spinal cord but that run through the body itself.

somatic nervous system division of the PNS consisting of nerves that carry information from the senses to the CNS and from the CNS to the voluntary muscles of the body.

autonomic nervous system (ANS) division of the PNS consisting of nerves that control all of the involuntary muscles, organs, and glands.

sensory pathway nerves coming from the sensory organs to the CNS consisting of afferent neurons.

motor pathway nerves coming from the CNS to the voluntary muscles, consisting of efferent neurons.

cord reflexes, although these muscles are called the "voluntary muscles," they can move involuntarily when a reflex response occurs. They are called "voluntary" because they *can* be moved at will but are not limited to only that kind of movement.)

Involuntary* muscles, such as the heart, stomach, and intestines, together with glands such as the adrenal glands and the pancreas are all controlled by clumps of neurons located on or near the spinal column. (The words *on* or *near* are used quite deliberately here. The neurons *inside* the spinal column are part of the central nervous system, not the peripheral nervous system.) These large groups of neurons near the spinal column make up the *autonomic nervous system.*

These young soccer players are using their senses and voluntary muscles controlled by the somatic division of the peripheral nervous system. What part of the autonomic nervous system are these girls also using at this time?

sympathetic division (fight-or-flight system) part of the ANS that is responsible for reacting to stressful events and bodily arousal.

parasympathetic division part of the ANS that restores the body to normal functioning after arousal and is responsible for the day-to-day functioning of the organs and glands.

THE AUTONOMIC NERVOUS SYSTEM

The word *autonomic* suggests that the functions of this system are more or less automatic, which is basically correct. Whereas the somatic division of the peripheral nervous system controls the senses and voluntary muscles, the autonomic division controls everything else in the body—organs, glands, and involuntary muscles. The autonomic nervous system is divided into two systems, the **sympathetic division** and the **parasympathetic division.** (See Figure 2.8.) (For a schematic representation of how all the various sections of the nervous system are organized, look back at Figure 2.1 on page 46.)

THE SYMPATHETIC DIVISION The sympathetic division of the autonomic nervous system is primarily located on the middle of the spinal column—running from near the top of the ribcage to the waist area. It may help to think of the name in these terms: The *sympathetic* division is in *sympathy* with one's emotions. In fact, the sympathetic division is usually called the "fight-or-flight system" because it allows people and animals to deal with all kinds of stressful events. LINK to Chapter Eleven: Stress and Health, p. 420. Emotions during these events might be anger (hence, the term *fight*) or fear (that's the "flight" part, obviously) or even extreme joy or excitement. Yes, even joy can be stressful. The sympathetic division's job is to get the body ready to deal with the stress.

*involuntary: not under deliberate control.

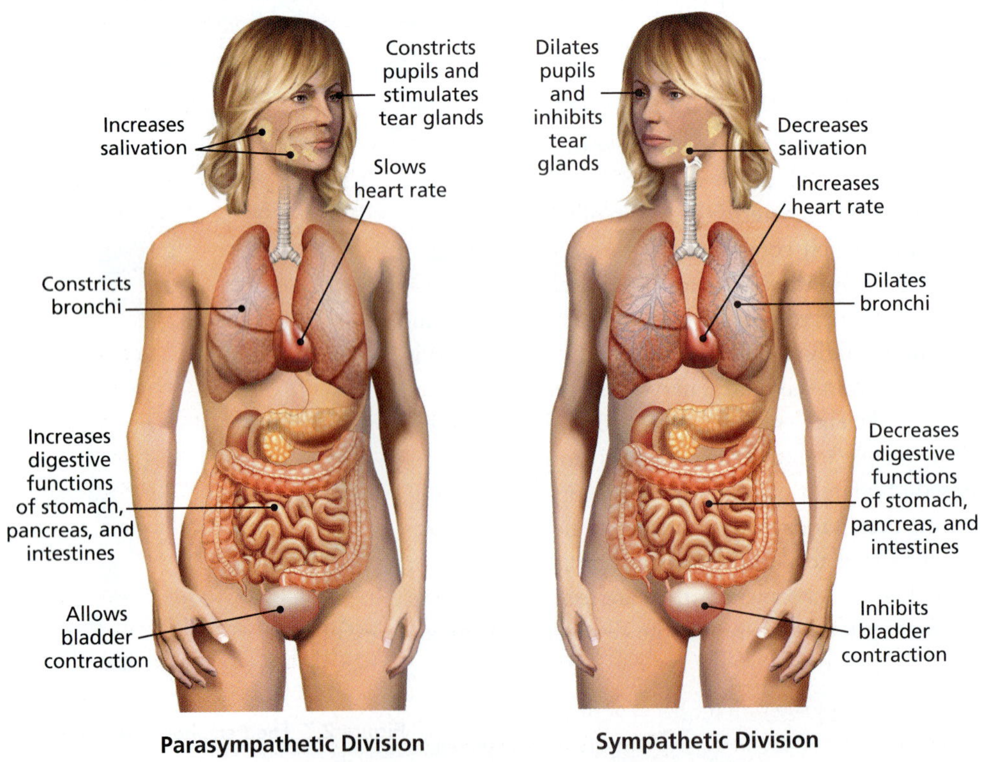

Figure 2.8 Functions of the Parasympathetic and Sympathetic Divisions of the Nervous System

What are the specific ways in which this division readies the body to react? (See Figure 2.8.) The pupils seem to get bigger, perhaps to let in more light and, therefore, more information. The heart starts pumping faster and harder, drawing blood away from nonessential organs such as the skin (so at first the person may turn pale) and sometimes even away from the brain itself (so the person might actually faint). Blood needs lots of oxygen before it goes to the muscles, so the lungs work overtime, too (the person may begin to breathe faster). One set of glands in particular receives special instructions. The adrenal glands will be stimulated to release certain stress-related chemicals (members of a class of chemicals released by glands called *hormones*) into the bloodstream. These stress hormones will travel to all parts of the body, but they will only affect certain target organs. Just as a neurotransmitter fits into a receptor site on a cell, the molecules of the stress hormones fit into receptor sites at the various target organs—notably, the heart, muscles, and lungs. This further stimulates these organs to work harder. (There are other hormones for other functions that have nothing to do with stress. For more about hormones and glands, see the section that follows, Distant Connections: The Endocrine Glands.) But not every organ or system will be stimulated by the activation of the sympathetic division. Digestion of food and excretion* of waste are not necessary functions when dealing with stressful situations, so these systems tend to be shut down or inhibited. Saliva, which is part of digestion, dries right up (ever try whistling when you're scared?). Food that was in the stomach sits there like a lump. Usually, the urge to go to the bathroom will be suppressed, but if the person is really scared the bladder or bowels may actually empty (this is why people who die under extreme stress, such as hanging or electrocution, will release their urine and waste). The sympathetic division is also going to demand that the body burn a tremendous amount of fuel, or blood sugar.

Now, all this bodily arousal is going on during a stressful situation. If the stress ends, the activity of the sympathetic division will be replaced by the activation of the parasympathetic division. If the stress goes on too long or is too intense, the person might actually collapse (as a deer might do when being chased by another animal). This collapse occurs because the parasympathetic division overresponds in its inhibition of the sympathetic activity. The heart slows, blood vessels open up, blood pressure in the brain drops, and fainting can be the result.

Snowboarder Shaun White of the U.S.A. 2010 Olympics Team won the gold medal in the halfpipe competition in Vancouver. What part of the autonomic nervous system is likely to be working as Shaun flies through the air, as in this picture?

THE PARASYMPATHETIC DIVISION If the sympathetic division can be called the fight-or-flight system, the parasympathetic division might be called the "eat-drink-and-rest" system. The neurons of this division are located at the top and bottom of the spinal column, on either side of the sympathetic division neurons (*para* means "beyond" or "next to" and in this sense refers to the neurons located on either side of the sympathetic division neurons).

In looking at Figure 2.8, it might seem as if the parasympathetic division does pretty much the opposite of the sympathetic division, but it's a little more complex than that. The parasympathetic division's job is to restore the body to normal functioning after a stressful situation ends. It slows the heart and breathing, constricts the pupils, and reactivates digestion and excretion. Signals to the adrenal glands stop because the parasympathetic division isn't connected to the adrenal glands. In a sense, the parasympathetic division allows the body to put back all the energy it burned—which is why people are often very hungry *after* the stress is all over. Simulate on mypsychlab.com

Simulate the autonomic nervous system on **mypsychlab.com**

The parasympathetic division does more than just react to the activity of the sympathetic division. It is the parasympathetic division that is responsible for most of the ordinary, day-to-day bodily functioning, such as regular heartbeat and normal

*excretion: in this sense, the act of eliminating waste products from the body.

breathing and digestion. People spend the greater part of their 24-hour day eating, sleeping, digesting, and excreting. So it is the parasympathetic division that is typically active. At any given moment, then, one or the other of these divisions, sympathetic or parasympathetic, will determine whether people are aroused or relaxed.

Distant Connections: The Endocrine Glands

How do the glands fit into all of this? Aren't there more glands than just the adrenal glands? How do they affect our behavior?

Earlier we addressed neurons and the neurotransmitters and how they release into the synapse to communicate with postsynaptic neurons. This type of chemical communication is fairly specific, primarily affecting neurons in the immediate vicinity of the originating neuron, and also very fast (almost immediate). Other structures also use chemical communication but do so at a different rate and act in a more far-reaching manner. For example, glands are organs in the body that secrete chemicals. Some glands, such as salivary glands and sweat glands, secrete their chemicals directly onto the body's tissues through tiny tubes, or ducts. This kind of gland affects the functioning of the body but doesn't really affect behavior. Other glands, called **endocrine glands**, have no ducts and secrete their chemicals directly into the bloodstream (see Figure 2.9). The chemicals secreted by this type of gland are called **hormones**. As mentioned earlier in the chapter when talking about the sympathetic division of the autonomic nervous system, these hormones flow into the bloodstream, which carries them to their target organs. The molecules of these hormones then fit into receptor

endocrine glands glands that secrete chemicals called hormones directly into the bloodstream.

hormones chemicals released into the bloodstream by endocrine glands.

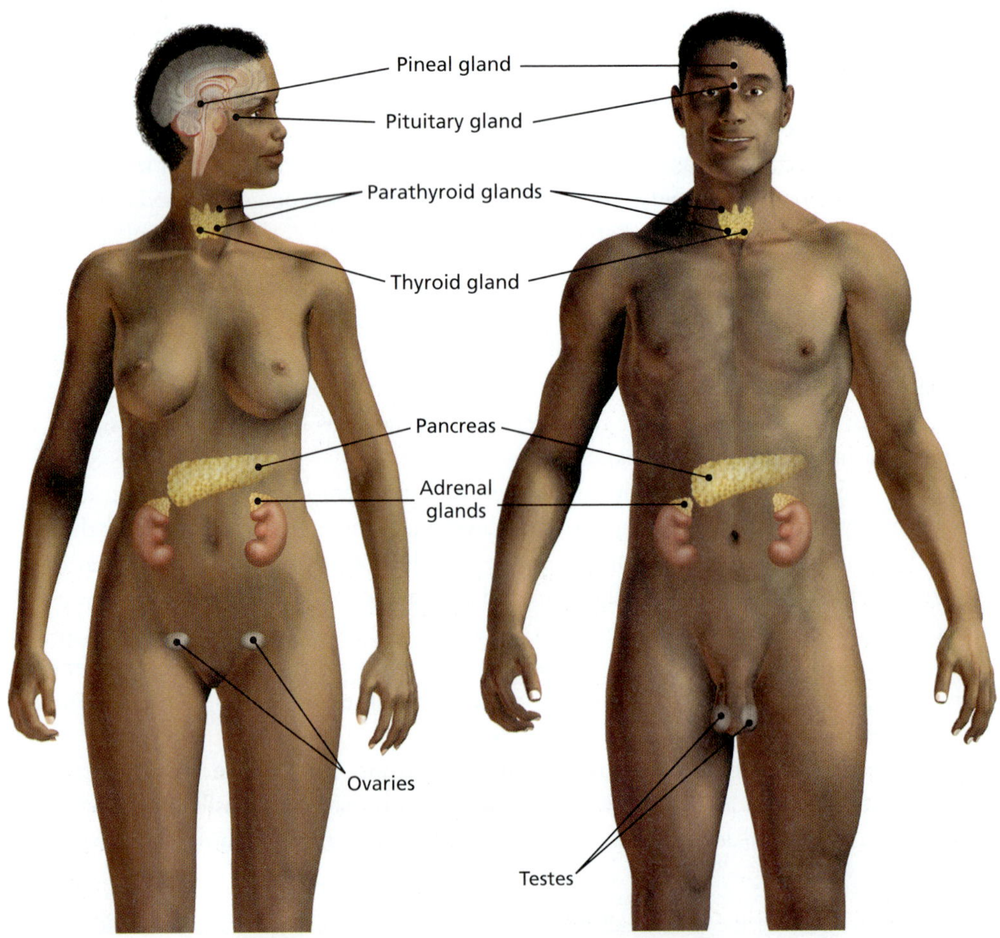

Figure 2.9 The Endocrine Glands
The endocrine glands secrete hormones directly into the bloodstream, which carries them to organs in the body, such as the heart, pancreas, and sex organs.

sites on those organs to fulfill their function, affecting behavior as they do so. As compared to synaptic communication, endocrine communication is generally slower due to the time it takes hormones to travel to target organs and the behaviors and responses they affect may not occur until hours, weeks, or years later.

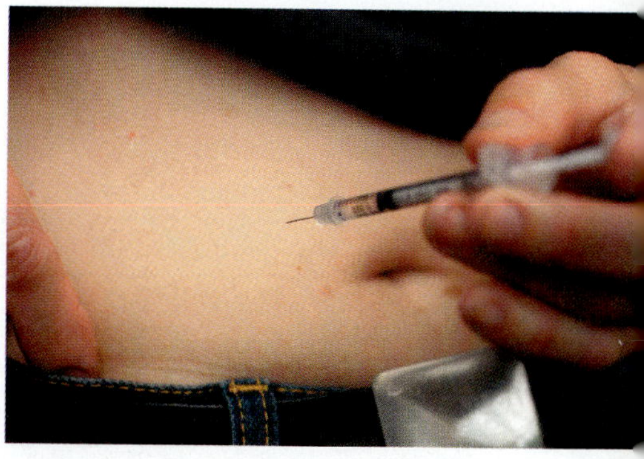

When the pancreas does not secrete enough insulin, the result is diabetes. Many diabetic people must give themselves insulin shots to supply enough of the hormone.

2.5 How do the hormones released by glands interact with the nervous system and affect behavior?

The hormones affect behavior and emotions by stimulating muscles, organs, or other glands of the body. Some theories of emotion state that the surge in certain hormones actually triggers the emotional reaction (Izard, 1988; Zajonc, 1980, 1984). LINK to Chapter Nine: Motivation and Emotion, p. 365. Some of the hormones produced by endocrine glands also influence the activity of the brain, producing excitatory or inhibitory effects (Mai et al., 1987).

THE PITUITARY: MASTER OF THE HORMONAL UNIVERSE

The **pituitary gland** is located in the brain itself, just below the hypothalamus. The hypothalamus (see p. xxx) controls the glandular system by influencing the pituitary. That is because the pituitary gland is the *master gland*, the one that controls or influences all of the other endocrine glands. One part of the pituitary controls things associated with pregnancy, such as production of milk for nursing infants and the onset of labor, as well as the levels of salt and water in the body. Another part of the pituitary secretes several hormones that influence the activity of the other glands. One of these hormones is a *growth hormone* that controls and regulates the increase in size as children grow from infancy to adulthood. There are also hormones that stimulate the gonads (ovaries and testes) to release female or male sex hormones, which in turn influence the development and functioning of the reproductive organs, development of secondary sex characteristics in puberty, and reproductive behavior in general. LINK to Chapter Ten: Sexuality and Gender, p. 378.

As the master gland, the pituitary forms a very important part of a feedback system, one that includes the hypothalamus and the organs targeted by the various hormones. The balance of hormones in the entire endocrine system is maintained by feedback from each of these "players" to the others. **Explore** on **mypsychlab.com**

Explore the endocrine glands on **mypsychlab.com**

THE PINEAL GLAND

The **pineal gland** is also located in the brain, near the back, directly above the brain stem. It plays an important role in several biological rhythms. The pineal gland secretes a hormone called *melatonin*, which helps tracks day length (and seasons). In some animals, this influences seasonal behaviors such as breeding and molting. In humans, melatonin levels are more influential in regulating the sleep–wake cycle. LINK to Chapter Four: Consciousness, p. 132.

THE THYROID GLAND

The **thyroid gland** is located inside the neck and secretes hormones that regulate growth and metabolism. One of these, a hormone called *thyroxin,* regulates metabolism (how fast the body burns its available energy). As related to growth, the thyroid plays a crucial role in body and brain development.

PANCREAS

The **pancreas** controls the level of blood sugar in the body by secreting *insulin* and *glucagons*. If the pancreas secretes too little insulin, it results in *diabetes*. If it secretes too much insulin, it results in *hypoglycemia*, or low blood sugar, which causes a person to feel hungry all the time and often become overweight as a result. LINK to Chapter Nine: Motivation and Emotion, p. 355.

pituitary gland gland located in the brain that secretes human growth hormone and influences all other hormone-secreting glands (also known as the master gland).

pineal gland endocrine gland located near the base of the cerebrum; secretes melatonin.

thyroid gland endocrine gland found in the neck; regulates metabolism.

pancreas endocrine gland; controls the levels of sugar in the blood.

THE GONADS

The **gonads** are the sex glands, including the **ovaries** in the female and the **testes** in the male. They secrete hormones that regulate sexual behavior and reproduction. They do not control all sexual behavior, though. In a very real sense, the brain itself is the master of the sexual system—human sexual behavior is not controlled totally by instincts and the actions of the glands as in some parts of the animal world but it is also affected by psychological factors such as attractiveness. LINK to Chapter Ten: Sexuality and Gender, p. 378.

THE ADRENAL GLANDS

Everyone has two **adrenal glands,** one on top of each kidney. The origin of the name is simple enough; *renal* comes from a Latin word meaning "kidney" and *ad* is Latin for "to," so *adrenal* means "to or on the kidney." Each adrenal gland is actually divided into two sections, the *adrenal medulla* and the *adrenal cortex*. It is the adrenal medulla that releases epinephrine and norepinephrine, when people are under stress, and aids in sympathetic arousal.

The adrenal cortex produces over 30 different hormones called *corticoids* (also called steroids) that regulate salt intake, help initiate* and control stress reactions, and also provides a source of sex hormones in addition to those provided by the gonads. One of the most important of these adrenal hormones is *cortisol*, released when the body experiences stress, both physical stress (such as illness, surgery, or extreme heat or cold) and psychological stress (such as an emotional upset). LINK to Chapter Eleven: Stress and Health, p. 408. Cortisol is important in the release of glucose into the bloodstream during stress, providing energy for the brain itself, and the release of fatty acids from the fat cells that provide the muscles with energy.

gonads sex glands; secrete hormones that regulate sexual development and behavior as well as reproduction.

ovaries the female gonads.

testes the male gonads.

adrenal glands endocrine glands located on top of each kidney that secrete over 30 different hormones to deal with stress, regulate salt intake, and provide a secondary source of sex hormones affecting the sexual changes that occur during adolescence.

---

*initiate: begin or start.

2.3 2.4 2.5 **CONCEPT MAP**

The Central Nervous System (comprised of the brain and spinal cord)

- **brain** — true core of nervous system: takes information from senses, processes it, makes decisions, sends commands to rest of body
- **spinal cord** — long bundle of neurons that carries information to and away from the brain; helps control pain response
  - spinal cord reflexes involve several different neurons (sensory neurons, interneurons, and motor neurons)
  - spinal reflexes enable fast, often lifesaving, actions that do not require conscious thought

The Peripheral Nervous System (comprised of the nerves and neurons not contained in the brain and spinal cord; allows the brain and spinal cord to communicate with the sensory systems and to control the muscles and glands of the body; divided into somatic and autonomic nervous systems)

- **somatic nervous system** controls the voluntary muscles of the body; involves the sensory pathway (sensory neurons carrying information to spinal cord and/or brain) and the motor pathway (nerves that carry information to voluntary skeletal muscles)
- **autonomic nervous system** controls automatic functions of the body (organs, glands, involuntary muscles)
  - **sympathetic division:** "fight-or-flight" functions—reacts to stressful events and bodily arousal
  - **parasympathetic division:** "eat-drink-and-rest" functions—restores body to normal functioning after arousal and is responsible for day-to-day functioning of glands and organs

glands are organs in the body that secrete chemicals; some affect functioning of the body but not behavior; others have widespread influence on the body and behavior

Distant Connections: The Endocrine Glands

endocrine glands secrete chemicals called *hormones* into bloodstream; affect behavior and emotions by influencing the activity of the brain and by controlling muscles and organs such as the heart, pancreas, and sex organs

- **pituitary gland**
- **pineal gland**
- **thyroid gland**
- **pancreas**
- **gonads**
- **adrenal glands**

PRACTICE quiz How much do you remember?

ANSWERS ON PAGE AK-1.

Pick the best answer.

1. If you burn your finger, your immediate reaction will probably involve all BUT which of the following?
   a. the brain **c.** afferent neurons
   b. the spinal cord **d.** efferent neurons
2. If you are typing on the computer keyboard, the sensation of your fingers touching the keys is most likely communicated by _________.
   a. the autonomic nervous system.
   b. motor pathway neurons.
   c. sensory pathway neurons.
   d. autonomic neurons.
3. The neurons of the motor pathway control _________.
   a. stress reactions. **c.** involuntary muscles.
   b. organs and glands. **d.** voluntary muscles.
4. What type of cell can become other types of cells in the body?
   a. blood cells **c.** neurons
   b. stem cells **d.** basal cells
5. Which of the following is NOT a function of the sympathetic division?
   a. increasing digestive activity to supply fuel for the body
   b. dilating the pupils of the eyes
   c. increasing the heart rate
   d. increasing the activity of the lungs
6. Which of the following would be active if you are sleeping?
   a. sympathetic division
   b. parasympathetic division
   c. somatic division
   d. motor division
7. Andrew never really grew to be very tall. The doctor told his parents that Andrew's _________ gland did not secrete enough growth hormone, causing his small stature.
   a. pituitary **c.** thyroid
   b. adrenal **d.** pancreas
8. If the pancreas secretes too little insulin, it causes _________.
   a. diabetes. **c.** hypothyroidism.
   b. hypoglycemia. **d.** virilism.

Looking Inside the Living Brain

2.6 How do psychologists study the brain and how it works?

Scientists can't be sure what brain tissue really looks like when it's inside the skull of a living person—nor can they be certain that it looks identical to that of a brain sitting on a dissecting table. How can scientists find out what the various parts of the brain do?

LESIONING STUDIES

One way to get some idea of the functions that various areas of the brain control is to study animals or people with damage in those areas. In animals, that may mean researchers will deliberately damage a part of the brain, after which, they test the animal to see what has happened to its abilities. In such an experiment, once the test animal is anesthetized and given medication for pain, a thin wire, which is insulated everywhere but at its tip, is surgically inserted into the brain. An electrical current strong enough to kill off the target neurons is sent through the tip of the wire. This procedure is called **deep lesioning**. (When cells are destroyed on the surface of the brain or just below it, the process is sometimes called *shallow lesioning.*)

deep lesioning insertion of a thin, insulated wire into the brain through which an electrical current is sent that destroys the brain cells at the tip of the wire.

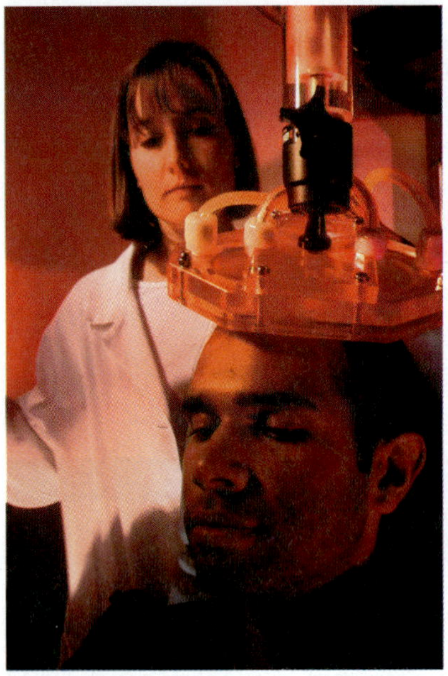

A doctor at the National Institute of Mental Health in Bethesda, Maryland, uses an electromagnet as part of an experimental treatment for depression. This treatment, called Repetitive Transcranial Magnetic Stimulation (rTMS) excites neurons in the brain, triggering activity.

It should be obvious that researchers cannot destroy areas of brains in living human beings. One method they can use is to study and test people who already have brain damage. However, this is not an ideal way to study the brain. No two case studies of humans are likely to present damage in exactly the same area of the brain, nor would the cases involve exactly the same amount of damage.

BRAIN STIMULATION

In contrast to lesioning, a less harmful way to study the brain is to temporarily disrupt or enhance the normal functioning of specific brain areas through electrical stimulation, and then study the resulting changes in behavior or cognition. The procedure of stimulating a specific area of the brain is much the same as in lesioning, but the much milder current in this research does no damage to the neurons. It does cause the neurons to react as if they had received a message. This is called *electrical stimulation of the brain*, or *ESB*. It has become an important technique in psychology, as its use in animals (and humans under very special circumstances such as testing before surgery to address seizure disorders) has informed us in many areas of investigation, including new directions for therapy.

INVASIVE TECHNIQUES: STIMULATING FROM THE INSIDE A specific type of ESB called *deep brain stimulation (DBS)* has been shown to be very helpful in some disorders in humans. In this procedure, neurosurgeons place electrodes in specific deep-brain areas and then route the electrode wires to a pacemaker-like device called an impulse generator that is surgically implanted under the collar bone. The impulse generator then sends impulses to the implanted electrodes, stimulating the specific brain areas of interest. Deep brain stimulation has been widely used as a treatment for Parkinson's disease and may play an important role in the treatment of seizure disorder, chronic pain, and possibly some psychiatric disorders (Fisher et al., 2010; Rabins et al., 2009; Weaver et al., 2009) among other areas. Techniques such as DBS are typically only used after all other less intrusive treatments have been shown to be ineffective or whose side effects have been deemed undesirable.

NONINVASIVE TECHNIQUE: STIMULATING FROM THE OUTSIDE There are also noninvasive techniques for stimulating the brain that contribute to research and our knowledge of the brain in a variety of areas. In *repetitive transcranial magnetic stimulation* (rTMS), magnetic pulses are applied to the cortex using special copper wire coils that are positioned over the head. The resulting magnetic fields stimulate neurons in the targeted area of the cortex. Another procedure called *transcranial direct current stimulation* (tDCS) uses scalp electrodes to pass very low amplitude direct currents to the brain to change the excitability of cortical neurons directly below the electrodes. Both rTMS and tDCS are being evaluated as research tools in studies of cognition such as memory retrieval and decision making (Boggio et al., 2010; Boggio, Fregni et al., 2009) and as possible treatment options for a variety of psychological disorders including posttraumatic stress disorder (PTSD) and depression, and physical disorders due to suffering a stroke (Boggio, Rocha et al., 2009; Nitsche, Boggio, Fregni, & Pascual-Leone, 2009; J. A. Williams, Pascual-Leone, & Fregni, 2010).

Note: tDCS is NOT the same as electroconvulsive therapy, which uses much higher levels of current through the entire brain resulting in a grand mal seizure and changes in the brain chemistry associated with depression. LINK to Chapter Fifteen: Psychological Therapies, p. 599.

All of these methods of stimulation yield important information about the brain and behavior, but they do not allow us to see what is going on inside the brain. Instead, various neuroimaging techniques can do this, either by directly imaging the brain's structure (the different parts) or its function (how the parts work). These methods also vary in their degree of spatial resolution (ability to see fine detail) and temporal resolution (ability to time lock a recorded event.)

MAPPING STRUCTURE

COMPUTED TOMOGRAPHY (CT) Scientists have several ways to look inside the human brain without causing harm to the person. One way is to take a series of X-rays of the brain, aided by a computer. This is accomplished during a CT scan (**computed tomography** involves mapping "slices" of the brain by computer). CT scans can show stroke damage, tumors, injuries, and abnormal brain structure. (See Figure 2.10a and 2.10b.) CT scans are also useful for imaging possible skull fractures and are the imaging method of choice when there is metal in the body (e.g., a bullet or surgical clips.)

MAGNETIC RESONANCE IMAGING (MRI) As useful as a CT scan can be for imaging the skull, it doesn't show very small details within the brain. The relatively newer technique of **magnetic resonance imaging**, or **MRI**, provides much more detail (see Figure 2.10c and 2.10d), even allowing doctors to see the effects of very small strokes. The person getting an MRI scan is placed inside a machine that generates a powerful magnetic field to align hydrogen atoms in the brain tissues (these normally spin in a random fashion); then radio pulses are used to make the atoms spin at a particular frequency and direction. The time it takes for the atoms to return to their normal spin allows a computer to create a three-dimensional image of the brain and display "slices" of that image on a screen.

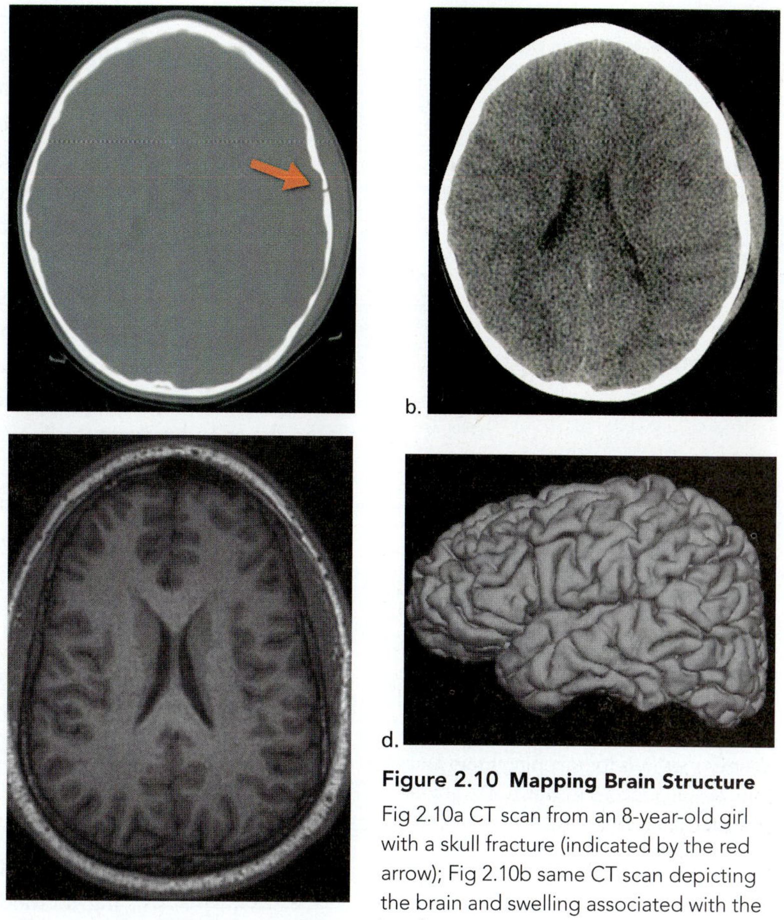

a. b. c. d.

Figure 2.10 Mapping Brain Structure
Fig 2.10a CT scan from an 8-year-old girl with a skull fracture (indicated by the red arrow); Fig 2.10b same CT scan depicting the brain and swelling associated with the head injury. Contrast the brain detail of Fig 2.10b with the MRI scan in Fig 2.10c (different, adult individual). Note the scans are in the horizontal plane, separating the brain into upper and lower portions. Fig 2.10d uses the same MRI data to provide an estimate of what the left external surface of the brain looks like. Fig 2.10a, b, & c images created with OsiriX software; 2.10d cortical reconstruction was performed with the Freesurfer image analysis suite. CT and MRI data courtesy of N. White.

Using MRI as a basis, several techniques have been developed that allow us to study other aspects of the brain. *MRI spectroscopy* allows researchers to estimate the concentration of specific chemicals and neurotransmitters in the brain. Another fascinating technique is called *DTI*, or *diffusion tensor imaging*. The brain has two distinct color regions, *gray matter*, the outer areas consisting largely of neurons with unmyelinated axons, and *white matter*, the fiber tracts consisting of myelinated axons (the myelin is responsible for the lighter color). DTI uses MRI technology to provide a way to measure connectivity in the brain by imaging these white matter tracts. DTI has been used to investigate many disorders and conditions including multiple sclerosis, dementia, and schizophrenia (Assaf & Pasternak, 2008; Bremmer, 2005; Ulmer, Parsons, Moseley, & Gabrieli, 2006; Voineskos et al., 2010). **Watch** on **mypsychlab.com**

Watch a video on brain scans on **mypsychlab.com**

MAPPING FUNCTION

THE ELECTROENCEPHALOGRAM (EEG). As important as imaging brain structure is, it is sometimes important to know how different brain areas function. A fairly harmless way to study the activity of the living brain is to record the electrical activity of the cortex just below the skull using a device called an **electroencephalograph**. The first **electroencephalogram (EEG)** recording in humans was accomplished in 1924 by Hans Berger (Niedermeyer, 2005). Recording the EEG involves using small metal disk or sponge-like electrodes placed directly on the scalp, and a special solution to help conduct the electrical signals from the cortex just below. These electrodes are connected to an amplifier and then to a computer to view the information. The resulting electrical output forms waves that indicate many things, such as stages of sleep, seizures, and even

computed tomography (CT) brain-imaging method using computer-controlled X-rays of the brain.

magnetic resonance imaging (MRI) brain-imaging method using radio waves and magnetic fields of the body to produce detailed images of the brain.

electroencephalograph machine designed to record the electroencephalogram.

electroencephalogram (EEG) a recording of the electrical activity of large groups of cortical neurons just below the skull, most often using scalp electrodes.

the presence of tumors. The EEG can also be used to help determine which areas of the brain are active during various mental tasks that involve memory and attention.

EEG activity can be classified according to appearance and frequency. Very fast, irregular waves called *beta waves* indicate waking activity. Slightly more regular and slower waves called *alpha waves* are a sign of relaxation (seen in bottom two lines in Figure 2.11a), *theta waves* are associated with drowsiness and sleep, and much slower, larger waves called *delta waves* indicate deep sleep. (These waveforms are covered in more detail in Chapter Four) LINK to Chapter Four: Consciousness, p. 135.

Another common EEG-based technique focuses on *event-related potentials*, or *ERPs*. In ERP studies, multiple presentations of a stimulus are measured during an EEG and then averaged to remove variations in the ongoing brain activity that is normally recorded during the EEG. The result is a measurement of the response of the brain related to the stimulus event itself, or an event-related potential. ERPs allow the study of different stages of cognitive processing. For example, one recent study has investigated differences in brain processing associated with the recognition of facial expression of emotion in individuals with and without schizophrenia (Lee, Kim, Kim, & Bae, 2010); in another study, ERPs are being studied as a possible method of lie detection (Rosenfeld et al., 2008).

While the EEG alone does not allow for the direct identification of areas of brain activation, a closely related technique does. *Magnetoencephalography* (MEG) uses devices that are very sensitive to magnetic fields called superconducting quantum interference devices which are contained in a helmet-like device that is placed over the individual's head. MEG has many applications and is currently being used to differentiate dementia disorders and to explore cognitive processes in autism (M. A. Williams & Sachdev, 2010). **Read** on **mypsychlab.com**

positron emission tomography (PET) brain-imaging method in which a radioactive sugar is injected into the subject and a computer compiles a color-coded image of the activity of the brain.

single photon emission computed tomography (SPECT) neuroimaging method that is similar to PET but uses a different radioactive tracer and can be used to examine brain blood flow.

Read and learn more about EEG and related techniques on **mypsychlab.com**

POSITRON EMISSION TOMOGRAPHY (PET) The functional neuroimaging methods discussed so far rely on the electrical activity of the brain. Other techniques make use of other indicators of brain activity, including energy consumption or changes in blood oxygen levels (if areas of the brain are active, they are likely using fuel and oxygen.) In **positron emission tomography (PET)**, the person is injected with a radioactive glucose (a kind of sugar). The computer detects the activity of the brain cells by looking at which cells are using up the radioactive glucose and projecting the image of that activity onto a monitor. The computer uses colors to indicate different levels of brain activity, with lighter colors indicating greater activity. (See Figure 2.11b.) With this method, researchers can actually have the person perform different tasks while the computer shows what his or her brain is doing during the task. A related technique is **single photon emission computed tomography (SPECT)**, which measures brain blood flow and uses more easily used radioactive tracers than those used for PET (Bremmer, 2005).

Figure 2.11 Mapping Brain Function

Various methods for mapping brain function. An EEG record is shown in 2.11a, a PET scan image in 2.11b, and an image from an fMRI study in 2.11c.

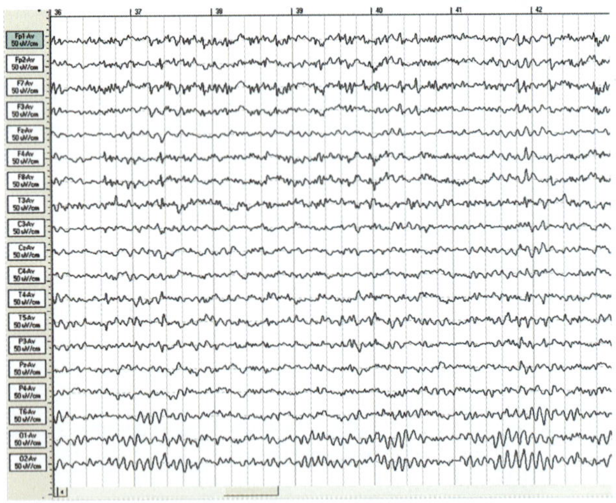

a.

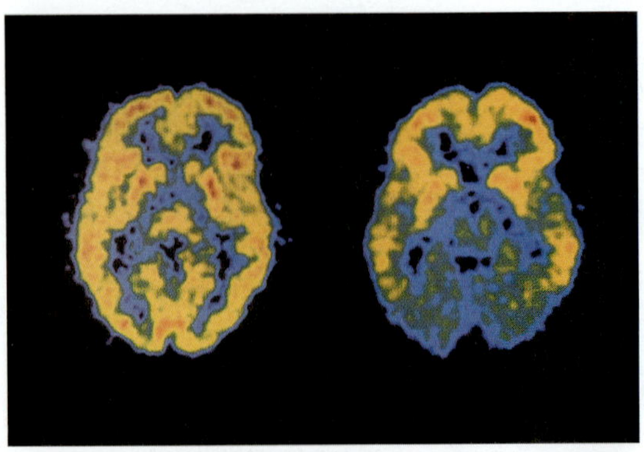

b.

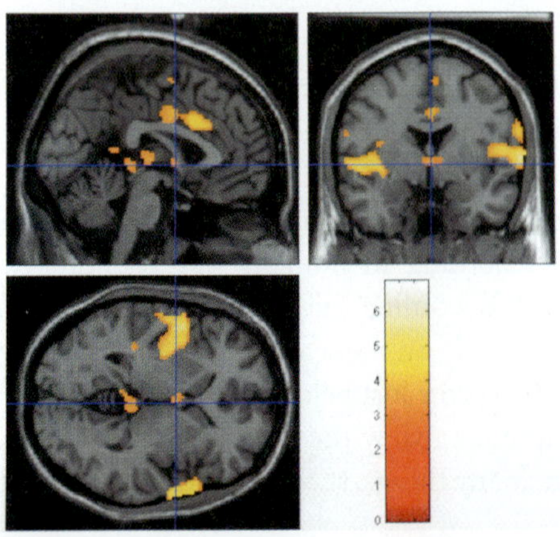

c.

FUNCTIONAL MRI (FMRI) Although traditional MRI scans only show structure, there is a technique called **functional MRI (fMRI)** in which the computer tracks changes in the oxygen levels of the blood (see Figure 2.11c). By superimposing this picture of where the oxygen goes in the brain over the picture of the brain's structure, researchers can identify what areas of the brain are active. By combining such images taken over a period of time, a sort of "movie" of the brain's functioning can be made (Lin et al., 2007). Functional MRIs can give more detail, tend to be clearer than PET scans, and are an incredibly useful tool for research into the workings of the brain. For example, fMRI has been used to demonstrate that older adults with a genetic risk for Alzheimer's disease show greater activation in brain areas associated with semantic knowledge and word retrieval when compared to older adults without that genetic risk. This finding may one day help clinicians and researchers identify individuals at risk for Alzheimer's much earlier in the disease process (Wierenga et al., 2010).

Okay, now I understand a little more about how we look inside the brain. What exactly IS inside the brain?

functional magnetic resonance imaging (fMRI) MRI-based brain-imaging method that allows for functional examination of brain areas through changes in brain oxygenation.

medulla the first large swelling at the top of the spinal cord, forming the lowest part of the brain, which is responsible for life-sustaining functions such as breathing, swallowing, and heart rate.

Okay, now I understand a little more about how we look inside the brain. What exactly IS inside the brain?

From the Bottom Up: The Structures of the Brain

Now it's time to look at the various structures of the brain, starting from the bottom and working up to the top. (**Note:** This text won't be discussing every single part of the brain, only major areas of interest to psychologists as explorers of behavior. Many areas also have multiple roles, but a full understanding of the brain is not possible within one chapter of an introductory psychology text.)

2.7 What are the different structures of the bottom part of the brain and what do they do?

THE HINDBRAIN

MEDULLA The **medulla** is located at the top of the spinal column. In Figure 2.12, it is the first "swelling" at the top of the spinal cord, just at the very bottom of the brain.

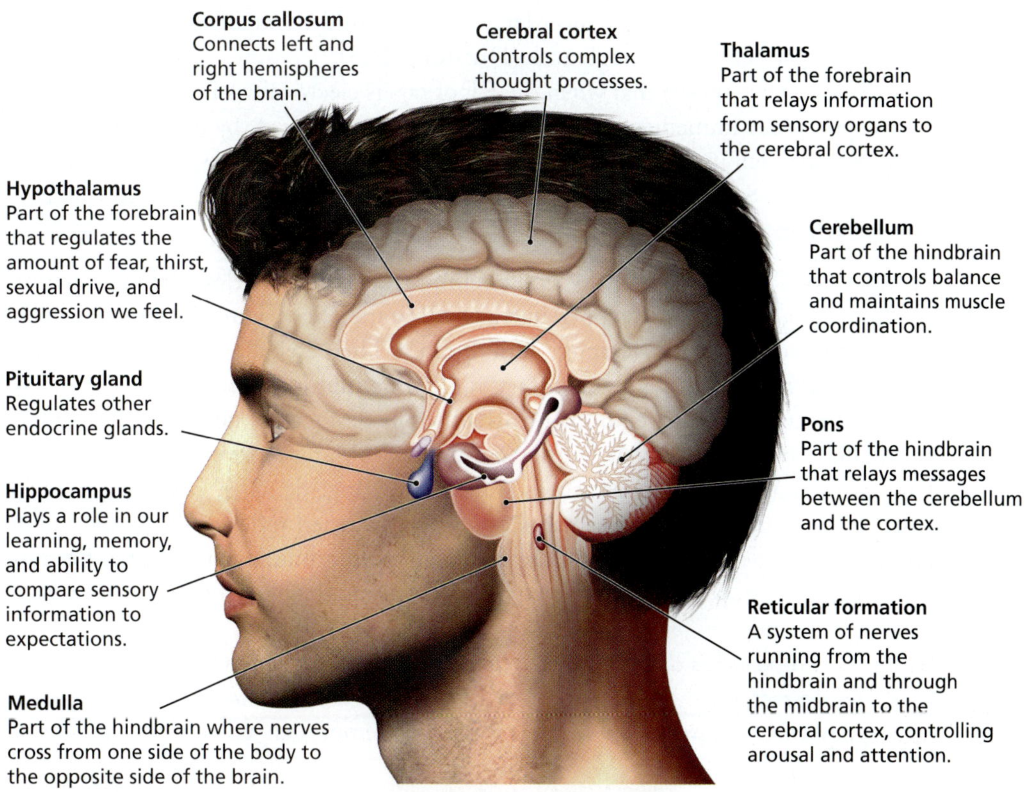

Figure 2.12 The Major Structures of the Human Brain

This pitcher must count on his cerebellum to help him balance and coordinate the many fine motor commands that allow him to pitch the baseball accurately and swiftly. What other kinds of professions depend heavily on the activity of the cerebellum?

This is the part of the brain that a person would least want to have damaged, as it controls life-sustaining functions such as heartbeat, breathing, and swallowing. It is in the medulla that the sensory nerves coming from the left and right sides of the body crossover, so that sensory information from the left side of the body goes to the right side of the brain and vice versa.

PONS The **pons** is the larger "swelling" just above the medulla. This term means "bridge," and the pons is indeed the bridge between the lower parts of the brain and the upper sections. As in the medulla, there is a crossover of nerves, but in this case it is the motor nerves carrying messages from the brain to the body. This allows the pons to coordinate the movements of the left and right sides of the body. (It will be useful to remember these nerve crossovers when reading about the functions of the left and right sides of the brain in a later part of this chapter.) The pons also influences sleep, dreaming, and arousal. The role that the pons plays in sleep and dreams will be discussed in more detail in Chapter Four. LINK to Chapter Four: Consciousness, p. 144.

THE RETICULAR FORMATION The **reticular formation (RF)** is an area of neurons running through the middle of the medulla and the pons and slightly beyond. These neurons are responsible for people's ability to generally attend to certain kinds of information in their surroundings. Basically, the RF allows people to ignore constant, unchanging information (such as the noise of an air conditioner) and become alert to changes in information (for example, if the air conditioner stopped, most people would notice immediately).

The reticular formation is also the part of the brain that helps keep people alert and aroused. One part of the RF is called the *reticular activating system (RAS)*, and it stimulates the upper part of the brain, keeping people awake and alert. When a person is driving and someone suddenly pulls out in front of the vehicle, it is the RAS that brings that driver to full attention. It is also the system that lets a mother hear her baby cry in the night, even though she might sleep through other noises. The RAS has also been suggested by brain-scanning studies as a possible area involved in attention-deficit/hyperactivity disorder, in which children or adults have difficulty maintaining attention to a single task (Durston, 2003).

Studies have shown that when the RF of rats is electrically stimulated while they are sleeping, they immediately awaken. If the RF is destroyed (by deep lesioning, for example), they fall into a sleeplike coma from which they never awaken (Moruzzi & Magoun, 1949; Steriade & McCarley, 1990). The RF is also implicated in comas in humans (Plum & Posner, 1985).

pons the larger swelling above the medulla that connects the top of the brain to the bottom and that plays a part in sleep, dreaming, left–right body coordination, and arousal.

reticular formation (RF) an area of neurons running through the middle of the medulla and the pons and slightly beyond that is responsible for general attention, alertness, and arousal.

cerebellum part of the lower brain located behind the pons that controls and coordinates involuntary, rapid, fine motor movement.

CEREBELLUM At the base of the skull, behind the pons and below the main part of the brain, is a structure that looks like a small brain. (See Figure 2.12 on page 69.) This is the **cerebellum** (meaning "little brain"). The cerebellum is the part of the lower brain that controls all involuntary, rapid, fine motor movement. People can sit upright because the cerebellum controls all the little muscles needed to keep them from falling out of their chair. It also coordinates voluntary movements that have to happen in rapid succession, such as walking, skating, dancing, playing a musical instrument, and even the movements of speech. Learned reflexes, skills, and habits are also stored here, which allows them to become more or less automatic. Because of the cerebellum, people don't have to consciously think about their posture, muscle tone, and balance.

So if your cerebellum is damaged, you might be very uncoordinated?

So if your cerebellum is damaged, you might be very uncoordinated?

Yes. In fact, this happens in a disease called *spinocerebellar degeneration* where the first symptoms of cerebellum deterioration are tremors, an unsteady walk, slurred speech, dizziness, and muscle weakness. The person suffering from this disease will eventually be unable to walk, stand, or even get a spoon to his or her own mouth (Schöls et al., 1998). These symptoms are similar to what one might see in a person who is suffering from alcohol intoxication.

limbic system a group of several brain structures located under the cortex and involved in learning, emotion, memory, and motivation.

thalamus part of the limbic system located in the center of the brain, this structure relays sensory information from the lower part of the brain to the proper areas of the cortex and processes some sensory information before sending it to its proper area.

2.8 What are the structures of the brain that control emotion, learning, memory, and motivation?

STRUCTURES UNDER THE CORTEX

The cortex, which is discussed in detail later in this chapter, is the outer wrinkled covering of the brain. But there are a number of important structures located just under the cortex and above the brain stem. Each of these structures plays a part in our behavior. (See Figure 2.13.)

LIMBIC SYSTEM The **limbic system** (the word *limbic* means "marginal" and these structures are found in the inner margin of the upper brain) includes the thalamus, hypothalamus, hippocampus, amygdala, and the cingulate cortex. In general, the limbic system is involved in emotions, motivation, memory, and learning. Simulate on mypsychlab.com

Simulate the limbic system on mypsychlab.com

Thalamus The **thalamus** ("inner chamber") is in some ways similar to a triage* nurse. This somewhat round structure in the center of the brain acts as a kind of relay station for incoming sensory information. Like a nurse, the thalamus might perform some processing of that sensory information before sending it on to the part of the cortex that deals with that kind of sensation—hearing, sight, touch, or taste. Damage to the thalamus might result in the loss or partial loss of any or all of those sensations. LINK to Chapter Three: Sensation and Perception, p. 108.

* triage: a process for sorting injured people into groups based on their need for, or likely benefit from, immediate medical treatment.

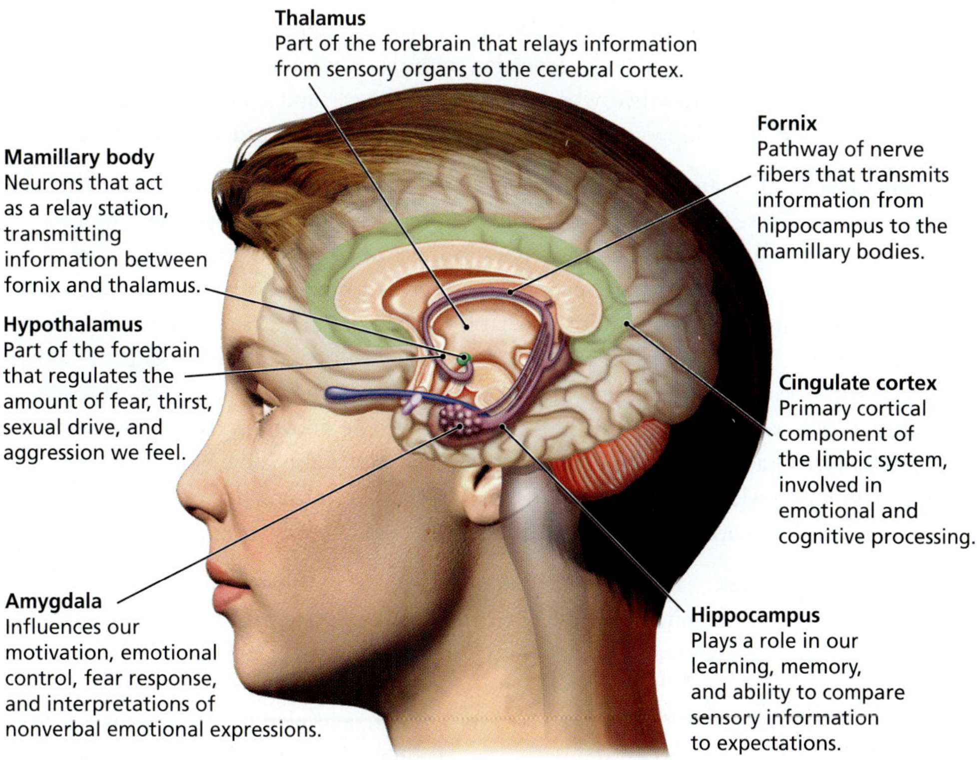

Figure 2.13 The Limbic System

This young woman's thirst is regulated by her hypothalamus.

The sense of smell is unique in that signals from the neurons in the sinus cavity go directly into special parts of the brain called **olfactory bulbs**, just under the front part of the brain. Smell is the only sense that does not have to first pass through the thalamus.

olfactory bulbs two bulb-like projections just under the front of the brain that receive information from the receptors in the nose.

hypothalamus small structure in the brain located below the thalamus and directly above the pituitary gland, responsible for motivational behavior such as sleep, hunger, thirst, and sex.

hippocampus curved structure located within each temporal lobe, responsible for the formation of long-term memories and the storage of memory for location of objects.

amygdala brain structure located near the hippocampus, responsible for fear responses and memory of fear.

HYPOTHALAMUS A very small but extremely powerful part of the brain is located just below and in front of the thalamus (see Figure 2.13). The **hypothalamus** ("below the inner chamber") regulates body temperature, thirst, hunger, sleeping and waking, sexual activity, and emotions. It sits right above the pituitary gland. The hypothalamus controls the pituitary, so the ultimate regulation of hormones lies with the hypothalamus.

HIPPOCAMPUS The **hippocampus** is the Greek word for "seahorse" and it was given to this structure of the brain because the first scientists who dissected the brain thought it looked like a seahorse. Research has shown that the hippocampus is instrumental in forming long-term (permanent) declarative memories that are then stored elsewhere in the brain (Bigler et al., 1996). As mentioned earlier, acetylcholine, the neurotransmitter involved in muscle control, is also involved in the memory function of the hippocampus. People who have Alzheimer's disease, for example, have much lower levels of acetylcholine in that structure than is normal and the drugs given to these people boost the levels of acetylcholine. The hippocampus is located within the temporal lobes on each side of the brain, and electrical stimulation of the temporal lobe may produce memory-like or dreamlike experiences.

The hippocampus may be very close to the area of the brain where the memories for locations of objects are stored as well. Researchers have found that the right parahippocampal gyrus, located alongside the right hippocampus, is more active when a person is planning a travel route (Maguire et al., 1998), which might explain why elderly people who develop memory problems associated with deterioration of the hippocampus also tend to forget where they live, where they parked the car, and similar location problems. Deterioration in the hippocampal area may spread to or affect other nearby areas.

AMYGDALA The **amygdala** ("almond") is an area of the brain located near the hippocampus. These two structures seem to be responsible for fear responses and memory of fear. Information from the senses goes to the amygdala before the upper part of the brain is even involved, so that people can respond to danger very quickly, sometimes before they are consciously aware of what is happening. In 1939 researchers found that monkeys with large amounts of their temporal lobes removed—including the amygdala—were completely unafraid of snakes and humans, both normally fear-provoking stimuli (Klüver & Bucy, 1939). This effect came to be known as the *Klüver-Bucy syndrome.* Rats that have damaged amygdala structures will also show no fear when placed next to a cat (Maren & Fanselow, 1996). Case studies of human with damage to the amygdala also show a link to decreased fear response (Adophs et al., 2005).

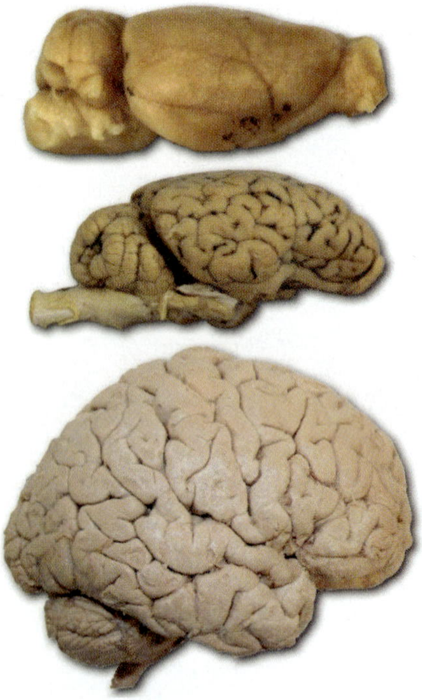

From top to bottom, a rat brain, sheep brain, and human brain (not to scale!). Note the differences in the amount of corticalization, or wrinkling, of the cortex between these three brains. Greater amounts of corticalization are associated with increases in size and complexity. Images are courtesy of Dr. Walter Isaac.

CINGULATE CORTEX The cingulate cortex is the limbic structure that is actually found in the cortex. It is found right above the corpus callosum (see page xx) in the frontal and parietal lobes (see pages xx and xx) and plays an important role in both emotional and cognitive processing. It has been shown to be active during a variety of cognitive tasks such as selective attention, written word recognition, and working memory (Cabeza & Nyberg, 2000) and has been implicated in a variety of psychological and mental disorders including attention-deficit/hyperactivity disorder (Bush et al., 1999; Bush et al.,

2008), schizophrenia, major depressive disorder, and bipolar disorder (Fornito et al., 2009; Maletic et al., 2007). The next section further explores the cortex and its functions.

cortex outermost covering of the brain consisting of densely packed neurons, responsible for higher thought processes and interpretation of sensory input.

THE CORTEX

As stated earlier, the **cortex** ("rind" or outer covering) is the outermost part of the brain, which is the part of the brain most people picture when they think of what the brain looks like. It is made up of tightly packed neurons and actually is only about one-tenth of an inch thick on average (Fischl et al., 2001; MacDonald et al., 2000; Zilles, 1990). The cortex is very recognizable surface anatomy because it is full of wrinkles.

Why is the cortex so wrinkled?

Why is the cortex so wrinkled?

The wrinkling of the cortex allows a much larger area of cortical cells to exist in the small space inside the skull. If the cortex were to be taken out, ironed flat, and measured, it would be about 2 to 3 square feet. (The owner of the cortex would also be dead, but that's fairly obvious, right?) As the brain develops before birth, it forms a smooth outer covering on all the other brain structures. This will be the cortex, which will get more and more wrinkled as the brain increases in size and complexity. This increase in wrinkling is called "corticalization." (See images on previous page.)

CONCEPT MAP 2.6 2.7 2.8

Looking Inside the Living Brain

(methods for studying the structures and/or activity of the living brain)

- **older methods**
  - often relied on dissection techniques after death
  - unable to directly observe function
- **lesioning studies**
  - study animals or humans with brain damage; damage may by accident, injury, or in animals, deliberate
  - brain areas can be studied according to the location of lesions (injured or destroyed areas) or through electrical stimulation (invasive or noninvasive)
- **mapping structure**
  - **computed tomography (CT)** — based on X-ray technology; good for imaging brain structure, especially when there is metal in the body
  - **magnetic resonance imaging (MRI)** — superior spatial resolution for structure
- **mapping function**
  - **the electroencephalogram (EEG)**
    - has good temporal but relatively poor spatial resolution; records the electrical activity of the brain through the use of scalp electrodes; both spontaneous activity and event-related potentials (ERP) can be studied
    - activity can be classified according to frequency and morphology; traditional bands include delta, theta, alpha, and beta
  - **positron emission tomography (PET)** — used for imaging function; involves injection of a radioactive tracer that binds to glucose, records activity of cells that use radioactive glucose
  - **functional MRI (fMRI)** — image brain function through tracking changes in blood oxygen levels; increase in oxygen levels associated with increased functioning

From the Bottom Up: The Structures of the Brain

- **the hindbrain**
  - **medulla**
  - **pons**
  - **reticular formation**
  - **cerebellum**
- **structures under the cortex**
  - **thalamus**
  - **hypothalamus**
  - **hippocampus**
  - **amygdala**

(continued)

PRACTICE quiz How much do you remember? ANSWERS ON PAGE AK-1.

Pick the best answer.

1. Which of the following techniques uses a radioactive sugar to look at the functioning of the brain?
   a. EEG
   b. CT
   c. MRI
   d. PET
2. Which brain structure is most responsible for our balance, posture, and muscle tone?
   a. medulla
   b. cerebellum
   c. reticular formation
   d. pons
3. Which brain structure would most likely result in death if damaged?
   a. medulla
   b. cerebellum
   c. reticular formation
   d. pons
4. If you were to develop a rare condition in which signals from your eyes were sent to the area of the brain that processes sound and signals from the ears were sent to the area of the brain that processes vision, which part of the brain would most likely be damaged?
   a. hippocampus
   b. hypothalamus
   c. thalamus
   d. amygdala
5. If you have problems storing away new memories, the damage is most likely in the _________ area of the brain.
   a. hippocampus
   b. hypothalamus
   c. cerebellum
   d. amygdala

cerebral hemispheres the two sections of the cortex on the left and right sides of the brain.

corpus callosum thick band of neurons that connects the right and left cerebral hemispheres.

occipital lobe section of the brain located at the rear and bottom of each cerebral hemisphere containing the visual centers of the brain.

2.9 What parts of the cortex control the different senses and the movement of the body?

THE LOBES AND THEIR SPECIALTIES The cortex is divided into two sections called the **cerebral hemispheres**, which are connected by a thick, tough band of neural fibers (axons) called the **corpus callosum** (literally meaning "hard bodies," as calluses on the feet are hard). (See Figure 2.12 on page 69.) The corpus callosum allows the left and right hemispheres to communicate with each other. Each hemisphere can be roughly divided into four sections by looking at the deeper wrinkles, or fissures, in its surface (see Figure 2.14).

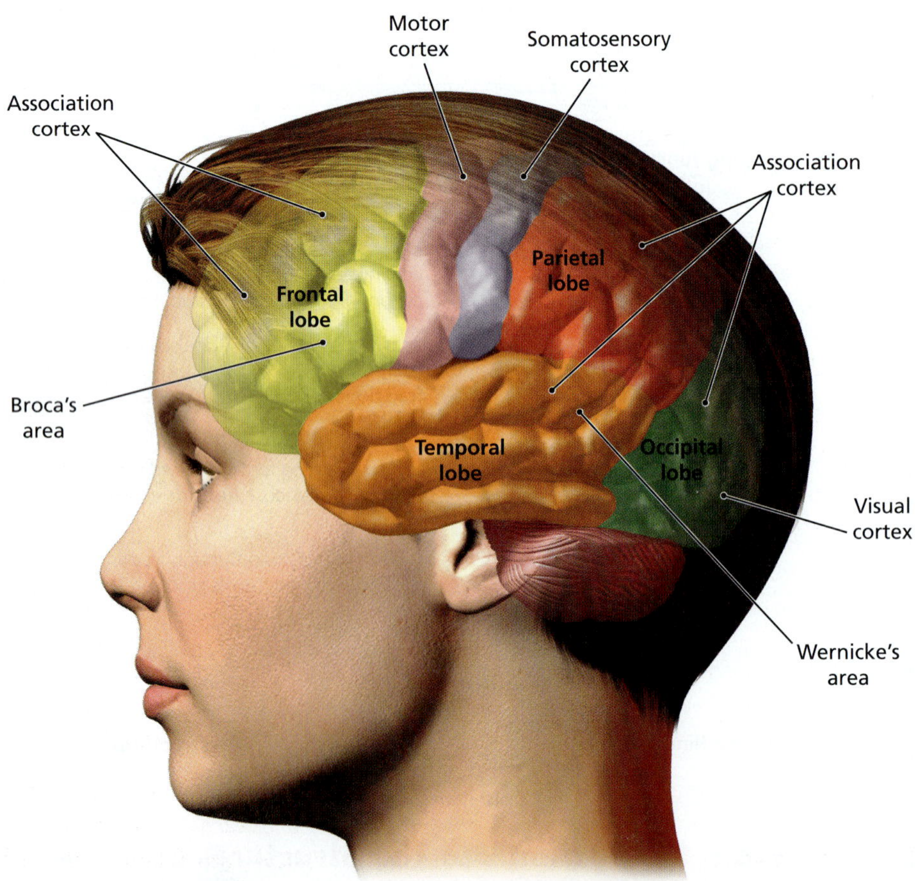

Figure 2.14 The Lobes of the Brain: Occipital, Parietal, Temporal, and Frontal

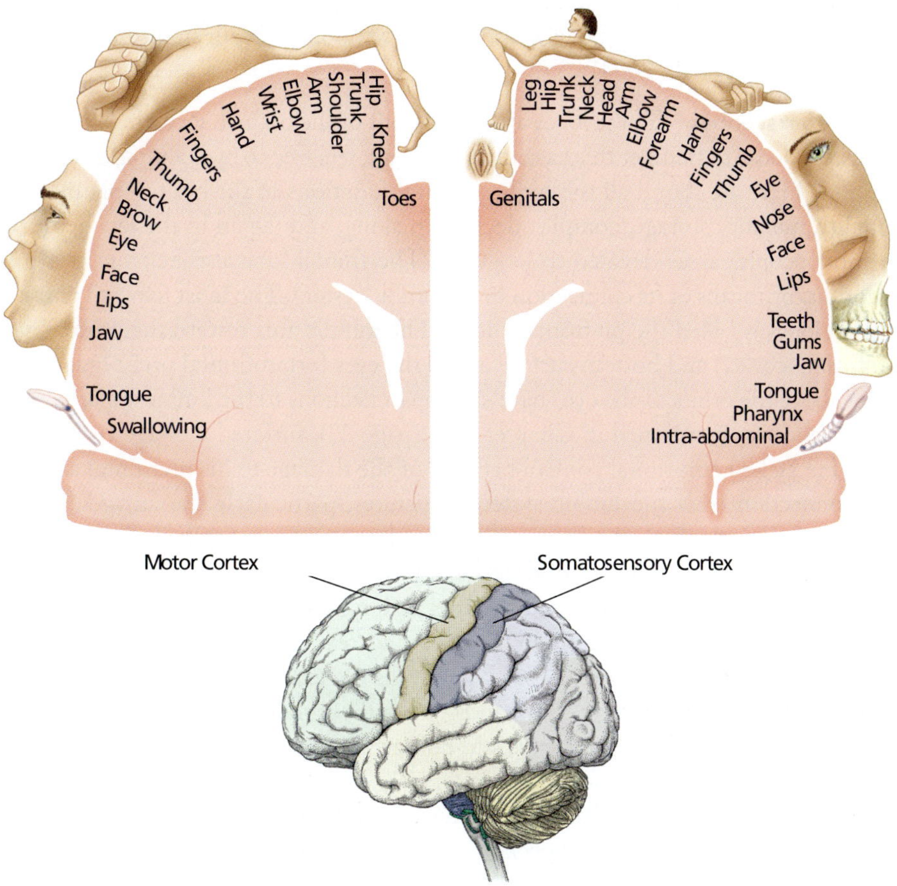

Figure 2.15 The Motor and Somatosensory Cortex

The motor cortex in the frontal lobe controls the voluntary muscles of the body. Cells at the top of the motor cortex control muscles at the bottom of the body, whereas cells at the bottom of the motor cortex control muscles at the top of the body. Body parts are drawn larger or smaller according to the number of cortical cells devoted to that body part. For example, the hand has many small muscles and requires a larger area of cortical cells to control it. The somatosensory cortex, located in the parietal lobe just behind the motor cortex, is organized in much the same manner and receives information about the sense of touch and body position.

parietal lobes sections of the brain located at the top and back of each cerebral hemisphere containing the centers for touch, taste, and temperature sensations.

somatosensory cortex area of neurons running down the front of the parietal lobes responsible for processing information from the skin and internal body receptors for touch, temperature, body position, and possibly taste.

temporal lobes areas of the cortex located just behind the temples containing the neurons responsible for the sense of hearing and meaningful speech.

Occipital Lobes At the base of the cortex, toward the back of the brain is an area called the **occipital lobe** (the term *occipital* refers to the rear of the head). This area processes visual information from the eyes in the *primary visual cortex*. The *visual association cortex*, also in this lobe, is the part of the brain that helps identify and make sense of the visual information from the eyes. The famed neurologist Oliver Sacks once had a patient who had a tumor in his right occipital lobe area. He could still see objects and even describe them in physical terms, but he could not identify them by sight alone. When given a rose, the man began to describe it as a "red inflorescence" of some type with a green tubular projection. Only when he held it under his nose (stimulating the sense of smell) did he recognize it as a rose (Sacks, 1990). Each area of the cortex has these association areas that help people make sense of sensory information.

Parietal Lobes The **parietal lobes** (*parietal* means "wall") are at the top and back of the brain, just under the parietal bone in the skull. This area contains the **somatosensory cortex**, an area of neurons (see Figure 2.15) running down the front of the parietal lobes on either side of the brain. This area processes information from the skin and internal body receptors for touch, temperature, and body position. The somatosensory cortex is laid out in a rather interesting way—the cells at the top of the brain receive information from the bottom of the body, and as one moves down the area, the signals come from higher and higher in the body. It's almost as if a little upside-down person were laid out along this area of cells. (See Figure 2.15.)

This boxer must rely on his parietal lobes to sense where his body is in relation to the floor of the ring and the other boxer, his occipital lobes to see his target, and his frontal lobes to guide his hand and arm into the punch.

Temporal Lobes The beginning of the **temporal lobes** (*temporal* means "of or near the temples") are found just behind the temples of the head. These lobes contain the *primary auditory cortex* and the *auditory association area*. Also found in the left

As this boy imitates the motions his father goes through while shaving, certain areas of his brain are more active than others, areas that control the motions of shaving. But even if the boy were only *watching* his father, those same neural areas would be active—the neurons in the boy's brain would *mirror* the actions of the father he is observing.

temporal lobe is an area that in most people is particularly involved with language. The sense of taste also seems to be processed in the temporal lobe, deep inside a fold of the cortex (Fresquet et al., 2004).

Frontal Lobes These lobes are at the front of the brain, hence, the name **frontal lobes.** (It doesn't often get this easy in psychology; feel free to take a moment to appreciate it.) Here are found all the higher mental functions of the brain—planning, personality, memory storage, complex decision making, and (again in the left hemisphere in most people) areas devoted to language. The frontal lobe also helps in controlling emotions by means of its connection to the limbic system. The most forward part of the frontal lobes is called the prefrontal cortex. The middle area toward the center (medial prefrontal cortex) and bottom surface above the eyes (orbitofrontal prefrontal cortex—right above the orbits of the eye) have strong connections to the limbic system. Phineas Gage, who was mentioned in Chapter One (page 23), suffered damage to his frontal lobe. He lacked emotional control because of the damage to his prefrontal cortex and the connection with the limbic system structures, particularly the amygdala. People with damage to the frontal lobe may also experience problems with performing mental tasks, such as getting stuck on one step in a process or on one wrong answer in a test and repeating it over and over again (Goel & Grafman, 1995).

The frontal lobes also contain the **motor cortex**, a band of neurons located at the back of each lobe. (See Figure 2.14.) These cells control the movements of the body's voluntary muscles by sending commands out to the somatic division of the peripheral nervous system. The motor cortex is laid out just like the somatosensory cortex, which is right next door in the parietal lobes.

This area of the brain has been the focus of a great deal of recent research, specifically as related to the role of a special type of neuron. These neurons are called **mirror neurons**, which fire when an animal performs an action—but they also fire when an animal observes that same action being performed by another. Previous brain-imaging studies in humans suggested that we, too, have mirror neurons in this area of the brain (Buccino et al., 2001; Buccino et al., 2004; Iacoboni et al., 1999). However, recent single-cell and multi-cell recordings in humans have demonstrated that neurons with mirroring functions are not only found in motor regions but also in parts of the brain involved in vision and memory, suggesting such neurons provide much more information than previously thought about our own actions as compared to the actions of others (Mukamel et. al., 2010). These new findings may have particular relevance for better understanding or treating specific clinical conditions that are believed to involve a faulty mirror system in the brain such as autism (Oberman & Ramachandran, 2007; Rizzolatti et al., 2009). LINK to Chapter Eight, Development Across the Life Span, p. 317.

You've mentioned association cortex a few times. Do the other lobes of the brain contain association cortex as well?

● *You've mentioned association cortex a few times. Do the other lobes of the brain contain association cortex as well?*

THE ASSOCIATION AREAS OF THE CORTEX

2.10 What parts of the cortex are responsible for higher forms of thought, such as language?

Association areas are made up of neurons in the cortex that are devoted to making connections between the sensory information coming into the brain and stored memories, images, and knowledge. In other words, association areas help people make sense of the incoming sensory input. Although the association areas in the occipital and temporal lobes have already been mentioned, much of the brain's association cortex is in the frontal lobes. Some special association areas are worth talking about in more detail.

frontal lobes areas of the cortex located in the front and top of the brain, responsible for higher mental processes and decision making as well as the production of fluent speech.

motor cortex section of the frontal lobe located at the back, responsible for sending motor commands to the muscles of the somatic nervous system.

mirror neurons neurons that fire when an animal or person performs an action and also when an animal or person observes that same action being performed by another.

association areas areas within each lobe of the cortex responsible for the coordination and interpretation of information, as well as higher mental processing.

BROCA'S AREA In the left frontal lobe of most people is an area of the brain devoted to the production of speech. (In a small portion of the population, this area is in the right frontal lobe.) More specifically, this area allows a person to speak smoothly and fluently. It is called *Broca's area* after nineteenth-century neurologist Paul Broca, who first studied people with damage to this area (Leonard, 1997). Damage to Broca's area causes a person to be unable to get words out in a smooth, connected fashion. People with this condition may know exactly what they want to say and understand what they hear others say, but they cannot control the actual production of their own words. Speech is halting and words are often mispronounced, such as saying "cot" instead of "clock" or "non" instead of "nine." Some words may be left out entirely, such as "the" or "for." This is called **Broca's aphasia**. *Aphasia* refers to an inability to use or understand either written or spoken language (Goodglass et al., 2001). (Stuttering is a somewhat different problem in getting words *started*, rather than mispronouncing them or leaving them out, but may also be related to Broca's area.)

WERNICKE'S AREA In the left temporal lobe (again, in most people) is an area called *Wernicke's area*, named after the physiologist and Broca's contemporary, Carl Wernicke, who first studied problems arising from damage in this location. This area of the brain appears to be involved in understanding the meaning of words (Goodglass et al., 2001). A person with **Wernicke's aphasia** would be able to speak fluently and pronounce words correctly, but the words would be the wrong ones entirely. For example, Elsie suffered a stroke to the temporal lobe, damaging this area of the brain. As the ER nurse inflated a blood pressure cuff, Elsie said, "Oh, that's so Saturday hard." Elsie *thought* she was making sense. She also had trouble understanding what the people around her were saying to her. In another instance, Ernest suffered a stroke at the age of 80 and also showed signs of Wernicke's aphasia. For example, he asked his wife to get him some milk out of the air conditioner. Right idea, wrong word.

As this woman brushes the right side of her hair, is she really "seeing" the left side? If she has spatial neglect, the answer is "no." While her eyes work just fine, her damaged right hemisphere refuses to notice the left side of her visual field.

classic studies in psychology

Through the Looking Glass—Spatial Neglect

Dr. V. S. Ramachandran reported in his fascinating book, *Phantoms in the Brain* (Ramachandran & Blakeslee, 1998), the case of a woman with an odd set of symptoms. When Ellen's son came to visit her, he was shocked and puzzled by his formerly neat and fastidious* mother's appearance. The woman who had always taken pride in her looks, who always had her hair perfectly done and her nails perfectly manicured, looked messy and totally odd. Her hair was uncombed on the left side. Her green shawl was hanging neatly over her right shoulder but hanging onto the floor on the left. Her lipstick was neatly applied to the right side of her lips, and *only to the right side—the left side of her face was completely bare of makeup!* Yet her eyeliner, mascara, and rouge were all neatly applied to the right side of her face.

What was wrong? The son called the doctor and was told that his mother's stroke had left her with a condition called **spatial neglect**, in which a person with damage to the right parietal and occipital lobes of the cortex will ignore everything in the left visual field. Damage to areas of the frontal and temporal lobes may also play a part along with the parietal damage. Spatial neglect can affect the left hemisphere, but this condition occurs less frequently and in a much milder form than right-hemisphere neglect (Heilman et al., 1993; Corbetta et al., 2005; Springer & Deutsch, 1998).

*fastidious: having demanding standards, difficult to please.

Broca's aphasia condition resulting from damage to Broca's area, causing the affected person to be unable to speak fluently, to mispronounce words, and to speak haltingly.

Wernicke's aphasia condition resulting from damage to Wernicke's area, causing the affected person to be unable to understand or produce meaningful language.

spatial neglect condition produced by damage to the association areas of the right hemisphere resulting in an inability to recognize objects or body parts in the left visual field.

cerebrum the upper part of the brain consisting of the two hemispheres and the structures that connect them.

When the doctor examined this woman, he tried to get her to notice her left side by holding up a mirror (remember, she was not blind—she just would not notice anything on her left side unless her attention was specifically called to it). She responded correctly when asked what the mirror was and she was able to describe her appearance correctly, but when an assistant held a pen just within the woman's reach, reflected in the mirror on her left side, she tried to reach *through the mirror* to get the pen with her good right hand. When the doctor told her that he wanted her to grab the real object and not the image of it in the mirror, she told him that the pen was *behind* the mirror and even tried to reach around to get it.

Clearly, persons suffering from spatial neglect can no longer perceive the world in the same way as other people do. For these people, the left sides of objects, bodies, and spaces are somewhere "through the looking glass."

Questions for Further Discussion

1. If a person with spatial neglect only eats the food on the right side of the plate, what could caregivers do to help that person get enough to eat?
2. What other odd things might a person with spatial neglect do that a person with normal functioning would not? What other things might a person with spatial neglect fail to do?

I've heard that some people are right-brained and some are left-brained. Are the two sides of the brain really that different?

THE CEREBRAL HEMISPHERES: ARE YOU IN YOUR RIGHT MIND?

I've heard that some people are right-brained and some are left-brained. Are the two sides of the brain really that different?

Most people tend to think of the two cerebral hemispheres as identical twins. Both sides have the same four lobes and are arranged in much the same way. But language seems to be confined to only the left hemisphere in about 90 percent of the population (Toga & Thompson, 2003). What other special tasks do the two halves of the **cerebrum** (the upper part of the brain consisting of the two hemispheres and the structures connecting them) engage in, and how do researchers know about such functions? **Simulate** on **mypsychlab.com**

Simulate the cerebrum on **mypsychlab.com**

2.11 How does the left side of the brain differ from the right side?

SPLIT-BRAIN RESEARCH Roger Sperry was a pioneer in the field of hemisphere specialization. He won a Nobel Prize for his work in demonstrating that the left and right hemispheres of the brain specialize in different activities and functions (Sperry, 1968). In looking for a way to cure epilepsy (severe muscle spasms or seizures resulting from brain damage), Sperry cut through the corpus callosum, the thick band of neural fibers that joins the two hemispheres. In early research with animals, this technique worked and seemed to have no side effects. The first people to have this procedure done also experienced relief from their severe epileptic symptoms, but testing found that (in a sense) they now had two brains in one body.

The special testing involves sending messages to only one side of the brain, which is now possible because the connecting tissue, the corpus callosum, has been cut. Figure 2.16 shows what happens with a typical split-brain patient. **Simulate** on **mypsychlab.com**

Simulate split-brain experiments on **mypsychlab.com**

In a split-brain patient, if a picture of a ball is flashed to the right side of the screen, the image of the ball will be sent to the left occipital lobe. The person will be able to say that he or she sees a ball. If a picture of a hammer is flashed to the left side of the screen, the person will not be able to *verbally* identify the object or be able to state with any certainty that something was seen. But if the left *hand* (controlled

Table 2.2

Specialization of the Two Hemispheres

LEFT HEMISPHERE	RIGHT HEMISPHERE
Controls the right hand	Controls the left hand
Spoken language	Nonverbal
Written language	Visual–spatial perception
Mathematical calculations	Music and artistic processing
Logical thought processes	Emotional thought and recognition
Analysis of detail	Processes the whole
Reading	Pattern recognition
	Facial recognition

by the right hemisphere) is used, the person can point to the hammer he or she "didn't see." The right occipital lobe clearly saw the hammer, but the person could not *verbalize* that fact (Sperry, 1968). By doing studies such as these, researchers have found that the left hemisphere specializes in language, speech, handwriting, calculation (math), sense of time and rhythm (which is mathematical in nature), and basically any kind of thought requiring analysis. The right hemisphere appears to specialize in more global (widespread) processing involving perception, visualization, spatial perception, recognition of patterns, faces, emotions, melodies, and expression of emotions. It also comprehends simple language but does not produce speech.

Springer and Deutsch (1998) found that, in general, the left hemisphere processes information in a sequence and is good at breaking things down into smaller parts, or performing analysis. The right hemisphere, by contrast, processes information all at once and simultaneously, a more global or holistic* style of processing. Remember the discussion in Chapter One of the early days of psychology, the structuralists, and the Gestalt psychologists? One could almost say that the left hemisphere of the brain is a structuralist who wants to break everything down into its smallest parts, and the right side of the brain is a Gestaltist, who wants to study only the whole. (See Table 2.2.)

So there really are left-brained and right-brained people?

Actually, unless one is a split-brain patient, the two sides of the brain are always working together as an integrated whole. For example, the right side might recognize someone's face, while the left side struggles to recall the person's name. People aren't really left- or right-brained, they are "whole-brained." Michael Gazzaniga was one of Roger Sperry's students, collaborator, and is a long-time researcher in the area of brain asymmetry and cognitive neuroscience. Gazzaniga's continuing work in brain lateralization has led to insights of the integrated mind, and he continues to work in related areas including human consciousness, perception, and neuroethics (Gazzaniga, 2006, 2009).

The separate functions of the left and right sides of the brain are often confused with handedness, or the tendency to use one hand for most fine motor skills. While most right-handed people also have their left hemisphere in control of their other fine motor

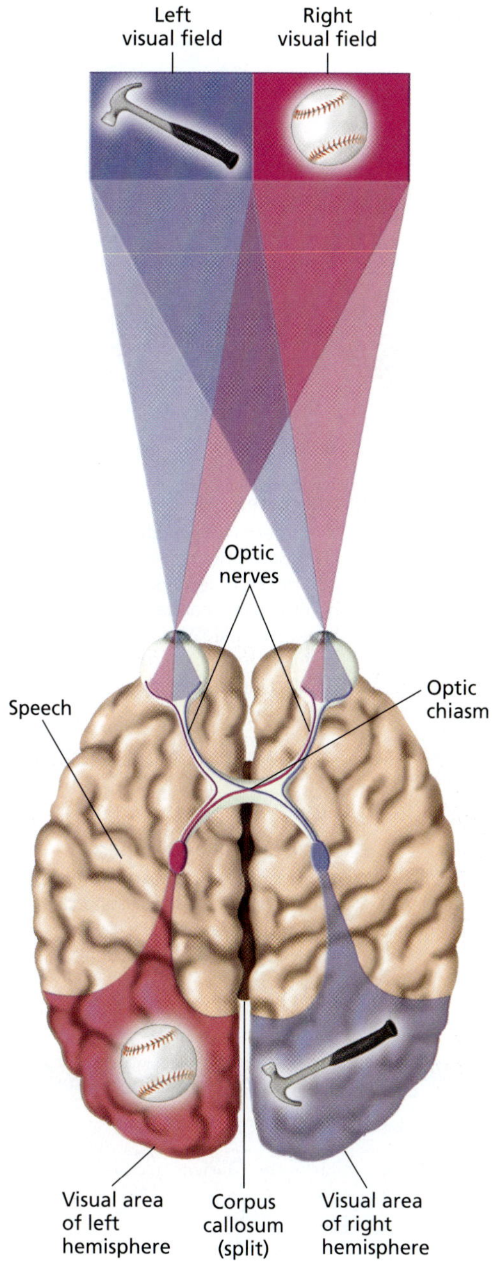

Figure 2.16 The Split-Brain Experiment
Roger Sperry created this experiment to demonstrate the specialization of the left and right hemispheres of the brain.

So there really are left-brained and right-brained people?

*holistic: relating to or concerned with complete systems or wholes.

skills, such as speech, a few right-handers actually have their language functions in the right hemisphere, in spite of the dominance of the left hemisphere for controlling the right hand. Among left-handed people, there are also many who, although right-brain dominant for motor control, still have their language functions on the left side of the brain. Why? Unfortunately, there are far too many theories of why we use one hand over the other for us to cover in the scope of this text. **Read** on **mypsychlab.com**

Read and learn more about right and left handedness on **mypsychlab.com**

2.9 2.10 2.11

CONCEPT MAP

The Structures of the Brain (continued)

- **the cortex**
  the outermost, wrinkled layer of the brain; comprised of left and right hemispheres, connected by corpus callosum; each hemisphere can be further divided into four lobes
  - **frontal lobes**
  - **temporal lobes**
  - **parietal lobes**
  - **occipital lobes**
- **the association areas of the cortex**
  devoted to making connections between incoming sensory information and stored memories, images, and knowledge; damage to right association areas can result in spatial neglect where person fails to recognize the left side of the visual field
  - **Broca's area:** found in left frontal lobe; devoted to speech production; damage to this area can result in Broca's aphasia
  - **Wernicke's area:** found in the left temporal lobe; plays a role in understanding the meaning of words
- **the cerebral hemispheres**
  some brain functions governed by one hemisphere more than the other; differences found due to work of various researchers (e.g., split-brain studies by both Sperry and Gazzaniga; work of Springer & Deutsch)
  - **left hemisphere** specializes in tasks that involve sequence and analysis (language, speech, handwriting, math)
  - **right hemisphere** processes information in a more global sense (perception; visualization; spatial perception; recognition of patterns, faces, and emotional expression)

PRACTICE quiz How much do you remember?

ANSWERS ON PAGE AK-1.

Pick the best answer.

1. In which of the following lobes of the cortex would you find the primary auditory area?
   a. frontal
   b. temporal
   c. occipital
   d. parietal
2. The higher mental functions, such as thinking and problem solving, are found in the __________ lobe.
   a. frontal
   b. parietal
   c. temporal
   d. corpus
3. In an old *Twilight Zone* episode, a man wakes up one morning to find that people around him are using words that make no sense to him, and they also don't seem to understand him. His wife tells him that their son forgot his dinosaur today, and when he looks puzzled, she holds up the son's lunchbox and repeats, "You know, his dinosaur." This man's predicament is most like which of the following disorders?
   a. Wernicke's aphasia
   b. Broca's aphasia
   c. apraxia
   d. spatial neglect
4. When Dr. Ramachandran's spatial neglect patient was asked to reach for the pen, she __________.
   a. reached to the wrong side of the mirror.
   b. said she couldn't see the pen.
   c. tried to reach through the mirror.
   d. successfully grabbed the pen.
5. If you are a split-brain patient, which of the following would be TRUE?
   a. Objects in your left visual field would be easily named.
   b. Objects in your left visual field are invisible.
   c. Objects in your right visual field would be easily named.
   d. Objects in your right visual field are invisible.

Applying Psychology to Everyday Life: Paying Attention to the Causes of Attention-Deficit/Hyperactivity Disorder

Attention-deficit/hyperactivity disorder (ADHD) is a developmental disorder involving behavioral and cognitive aspects of inattention, impulsivity, and hyperactivity. Previously referred to as attention deficit disorder (ADD), there are currently three diagnostic categories for this disorder in the *Diagnostic and Statistical Manual of Mental Disorders* (*DSM-IV-TR*). These include ADHD predominantly hyperactive type, ADHD predominantly inattentive type, and ADHD combined type (American Psychiatric Association, 2000). Although ADHD is most commonly diagnosed in children, the disorder tends to persist into adolescence and adulthood. Inattention and impulsivity are often reported in adults, whereas symptoms of hyperactivity tend to decline with age. The ADHD-related problems in adults can range from strained relations with family, friends, or a significant other to problems with substance abuse, traffic accidents, or job stability (Barkley, Murphy, & Fischer, 2008).

The brain areas involved in the behavioral and cognitive characteristics of ADHD are typically divided into those responsible for regulating attention and cognitive control and those responsible for alertness and motivation (Nigg, 2010). Cortical and subcortical brain areas involved, and found to be smaller in neuroimaging studies of ADHD, are the prefrontal cortex (primarily on the right side), basal ganglia (subcortical structures involved in response control), cerebellum, and corpus callosum (Nigg, 2006).

Since ADHD involves a variety of behaviors and cognitive aspects, research has often looked for specific markers that may lead to the actual causes of the disorder. These markers may be biological, cognitive, or behavioral measures (Nigg, 2010). To assess individual markers, researchers may combine neuroimaging and electrophysiological studies of individuals with ADHD while at rest or while they perform specific cognitive tasks (like various tests of attention). Some studies use EEG or ERPs (Clarke et al., 2007; Loo et al., 2009; van der Stelt et al., 2010) whereas others use MRI, fMRI, or PET (Bush et al., 2008; Volkow et al., 2007).

As Nigg points out, much of the research over the past 10 years has focused on the cognitive markers for ADHD, such as attention problems, that may or may not be combined with neuroimaging. More recent research suggests that some aspects of attention are actually normal in individuals with ADHD. The aspect of attention with which individuals with ADHD do have problems is vigilance (being able to "watch out" for something important). Another cognitive area that appears to be impaired is being able to effectively control one's own cognitive processes such as staying on task, maintaining effort, or engaging in self-control (Nigg, 2010).

These recent findings have prompted researchers to reexamine the causes of ADHD and have highlighted the likelihood of more than one cause and more than one brain route to ADHD. Current research is looking at a variety of areas including environmental factors such as low-level lead exposure, genetic influences, the role of heredity and familial factors, and personality factors (Nigg, 2010). Granted, some of these areas of investigation are not completely new and have been examined before, but the possibility of multiple causes and interactions between these causes has not been examined as closely as it is at present in ADHD research.

Questions for Further Discussion

1. How might a psychology professional help parents or teachers understand the neuroimaging techniques and brain areas associated with ADHD?
2. If a college student has ADHD, what aspects of their school or personal lives might be impacted by problems with vigilance or cognitive control?

chapter summary

Listen on **mypsychlab.com** Listen to an audio file of your chapter **www.mypsychlab.com**

An Overview of the Nervous System

2.1 What are the nervous system, neurons, and nerves, and how do they relate to one another?

- The nervous system is a complex network of cells that carries information to and from all parts of the body.

Neurons and Nerves: Building the Network

2.2 How do neurons use neurotransmitters to communicate with each other and with the body?

- The brain is made up of two types of cells, neurons and glial cells.
- Neurons have dendrites, which receive input, a soma or cell body, and axons that carry the neural message to other cells.
- Glial cells separate, support, and insulate the neurons from each other and make up 90 percent of the brain.
- Myelin insulates and protects the axons of neurons that travel in the body. These axons bundle together in "cables" called nerves. Myelin also speeds up the neural message.
- Neurons in the peripheral nervous system are also coated with neurilemma, which allows the nerves to repair themselves.
- A neuron contains charged particles called ions. When at rest, the neuron is negatively charged on the inside and positively charged on the outside. When stimulated, this reverses the charge by allowing positive sodium ions to enter the cell. This is the action potential.
- Neurons fire in an all-or-nothing manner. It is the speed and number of neurons firing that tell researchers the strength of the stimulus.
- Synaptic vesicles in the end of the axon terminal release neurotransmitter chemicals into the synapse, or gap, between one cell and the next. The neurotransmitter molecules fit into receptor sites on the next cell, stimulating or inhibiting that cell's firing. Neurotransmitters may be either excitatory or inhibitory.
- The first known neurotransmitter was acetylcholine. It stimulates muscles, helps in memory formation, and plays a role in arousal and attention. Curare is a poison that blocks its effect.
- GABA is the major inhibitory neurotransmitter; high amounts of GABA are released when drinking alcohol.
- Serotonin is associated with sleep, mood, and appetite.
- Dopamine is associated with Parkinson's disease and schizophrenia.
- Endorphins are neural regulators that control our pain response.
- Most neurotransmitters are taken back into the synaptic vesicles in a process called reuptake.
- Acetylcholine is cleared out of the synapse by enzymes that break up the molecules.

The Central Nervous System: The "Central Processing Unit"

2.3 How do the brain and spinal cord interact?

- The central nervous system consists of the brain and the spinal cord.
- The spinal cord serves two functions. The outer part of the cord transmits messages to and from the brain, whereas the inner part controls lifesaving reflexes such as the pain response.
- Spinal cord reflexes involve afferent neurons, interneurons, and efferent neurons, forming a simple reflex arc.
- Great strides are being made in spinal cord repair and the growth of new neurons in the central nervous system.

PSYCHOLOGY IN THE NEWS: Fact or Fiction: Focus on the Brain, but Check Your Sources!

- Information about the brain and brain research comes from a variety of sources but sources such as peer-reviewed journals and publications from professional associations offer the most reliable information.

The Peripheral Nervous System: Nerves on the Edge

- The peripheral nervous system is all the neurons and nerves that are not part of the brain and spinal cord and that extend throughout the body.
- There are two systems within the peripheral nervous system, the somatic nervous system and the autonomic nervous system.

2.4 How do the somatic and autonomic nervous systems allow people and animals to interact with their surroundings and control the body's automatic functions?

- The somatic nervous system contains the sensory pathway, or neurons carrying messages to the central nervous system, and the motor pathway, or neurons carrying messages from the central nervous system to the voluntary muscles.
- The autonomic nervous system consists of the parasympathetic division and the sympathetic division. The sympathetic division is our fight-or-flight system, reacting to stress, whereas the parasympathetic division restores and maintains normal day-to-day functioning of the organs.

Distant Connections: The Endocrine Glands

2.5 How do the hormones released by glands interact with the nervous system and affect behavior?

- Endocrine glands secrete chemicals called hormones directly into the bloodstream, influencing the activity of the muscles and organs.

- The pituitary gland is found in the brain just below the hypothalamus. It has two parts, the anterior and the posterior. It controls the levels of salt and water in the system and, in women, the onset of labor and lactation, as well as secreting growth hormone and influencing the activity of the other glands.
- The pineal gland is also located in the brain. It secretes melatonin, a hormone that regulates the sleep–wake cycle, in response to changes in light.
- The thyroid gland is located inside the neck. It controls metabolism (the burning of energy) by secreting thyroxin.
- The pancreas controls the level of sugar in the blood by secreting insulin and glucagons. Too much insulin produces hypoglycemia, whereas too little causes diabetes.
- The gonads are the ovaries in women and testes in men. They secrete hormones to regulate sexual growth, activity, and reproduction.
- The adrenal glands, one on top of each kidney, control the stress reaction through the adrenal medulla's secretion of epinephrine and norepinephrine. The adrenal cortex secretes over 30 different corticoids (hormones) controlling salt intake, stress, and sexual development.

Looking Inside the Living Brain

2.6 How do psychologists study the brain and how it works?

- We can study the brain by using deep lesioning to destroy certain areas of the brain in laboratory animals or by electrically stimulating those areas (ESB).
- We can use case studies of human brain damage to learn about the brain's functions but cannot easily generalize from one case to another.
- rTMS and tDCS are noninvasive methods for stimulating the brain.
- Different neuroimaging methods allows scientists to investigate the structure or the function of the living brain
- The electroencephalograph allows researchers to look at the electroencephalogram (EEG), or electrical activity of the surface of the brain, through the use of electrodes placed on the scalp that are then amplified and viewed using a computer. ERPs allow researchers to look at the timing and progression of cognitive processes.
- CT scans are computer-aided X-rays of the brain and show the skull and brain structure.
- MRI scans use a magnetic field, radio pulses, and a computer to give researchers an even more detailed look at the structure of the brain.
- fMRI allows researchers to look at the activity of the brain over a time period.
- PET scans use a radioactive sugar injected into the bloodstream to track the activity of brain cells, which is enhanced and color-coded by a computer. SPECT allows for the imaging of brain blood flow.

From the Bottom Up: The Structures of the Brain

2.7 What are the different structures of the bottom part of the brain and what do they do?

- The medulla is at the very bottom of the brain and at the top of the spinal column. It controls life-sustaining functions such as breathing and swallowing. The nerves from each side of the body also cross over in this structure to opposite sides.
- The pons is above the medulla and acts as a bridge between the lower part of the brain and the upper part. It influences sleep, dreaming, arousal, and coordination of movement on the left and right sides of the body.
- The reticular formation runs through the medulla and the pons and controls our general level of attention and arousal.
- The cerebellum is found at the base and back of the brain and coordinates fine, rapid motor movement, learned reflexes, posture, and muscle tone.

2.8 What are the structures of the brain that control emotion, learning, memory, and motivation?

- The thalamus is the switching station that sends sensory information to the proper areas of the cortex.
- The hypothalamus controls hunger, thirst, sleep, sexual behavior, sleeping and waking, and emotions. It also controls the pituitary gland.
- The limbic system consists of the thalamus, hypothalamus, hippocampus, amygdala, and the fornix.
- The hippocampus is the part of the brain responsible for storing memories and remembering locations of objects.
- The amygdala controls our fear responses and memory of fearful stimuli.

2.9 What parts of the cortex control the different senses and the movement of the body?

- The cortex is the outer covering of the cerebrum and consists of a tightly packed layer of neurons about one tenth of an inch in thickness. Its wrinkles, or corticalization, allow for greater cortical area and are associated with greater brain complexity.
- The cortex is divided into two cerebral hemispheres connected by a thick band of neural fibers called the corpus callosum.
- The occipital lobes at the back and base of each hemisphere process vision and contain the primary visual cortex.
- The parietal lobes at the top and back of the cortex contain the somatosensory area, which processes our sense of touch, temperature, and body position. Taste is also processed in this lobe.
- The temporal lobes contain the primary auditory area and are also involved in understanding language.
- The frontal lobes contain the motor cortex, which controls the voluntary muscles, and are also where all the higher mental functions occur, such as planning, language, and complex decision making.

2.10 What parts of the cortex are responsible for higher forms of thought, such as language?

- Association areas of the cortex are found in all the lobes but particularly in the frontal lobes. These areas help people make sense of the information they receive from the lower areas of the brain.
- A region called Broca's area in the left frontal lobe is responsible for producing fluent, understandable speech. If damaged, the person has Broca's aphasia in which words will be halting and pronounced incorrectly.
- An area called Wernicke's area in the left temporal lobe is responsible for the understanding of language. If damaged, the person has Wernicke's aphasia in which speech is fluent but nonsensical. The wrong words are used.

CLASSIC STUDIES IN PSYCHOLOGY: Through the Looking Glass—Spatial Neglect

- Spatial neglect comes from damage to the association areas on one side of the cortex, usually the right side. A person with this condition will ignore information from the opposite side of the body or the opposite visual field.

2.11 How does the left side of the brain differ from the right side?

- Studies with split-brain patients, in which the corpus callosum has been severed to correct epilepsy, reveal that the left side of the brain seems to control language, writing, logical thought, analysis, and mathematical abilities. The left side also processes information sequentially.
- The right side of the brain processes information globally and controls emotional expression, spatial perception, recognition of faces, patterns, melodies, and emotions. Information presented only to the left hemisphere can be verbalized but information only sent to the right cannot.

Applying Psychology to Everyday Life: Paying Attention to the Causes of Attention-Deficit/Hyperactivity Disorder

- ADHD may be caused by the interaction of variety of factors and often persists into adulthood.

test YOURSELF

ANSWERS ON PAGE AK-1.

Study and Review on mypsychlab.com Ready for your test? More quizzes and a customized study plan **www.mypsychlab.com**

Pick the best answer.

1. In the structure of the neuron, the _________ sends information to other cells.
   a. axon
   b. dendrite
   c. soma
   d. myelin
2. Which type of cell makes up 10 percent of the brain?
   a. glial cells
   b. neurons
   c. stem cells
   d. afferent cells
3. Damaged nerve fibers in the body can sometimes repair themselves because they are coated with _________, which forms a protective tunnel around the nerve fibers.
   a. glial
   b. soma
   c. myelin
   d. neurilemma
4. When a neuron is in the resting potential state, where are there more sodium ions?
   a. inside the cell
   b. outside the cell
   c. inside the soma
   d. in the synapse
5. How does one neuron communicate with another neuron?
   a. An electrical spark jumps over the gap between cells.
   b. Charged particles leap from one cell to the next.
   c. Chemicals in the end of one neuron float across the gap to fit into holes on the next neuron.
   d. The end of one neuron extends to touch the other neuron.
6. Which neurotransmitter is associated with the control of the pain response?
   a. acetylcholine
   b. GABA
   c. serotonin
   d. endorphin
7. Which of the following is the correct path of a reflex arc?
   a. efferent neuron to interneuron to afferent neuron
   b. efferent neuron to afferent neuron to interneuron
   c. afferent neuron to interneuron to efferent neuron
   d. afferent neuron to efferent neuron to the brain
8. Voluntary muscles are controlled by the _________ nervous system.
   a. somatic
   b. autonomic
   c. sympathetic
   d. parasympathetic
9. Your heart races. You begin to breathe faster. Your pupils enlarge and your appetite is gone. Your _________ division has just been activated.
   a. sympathetic
   b. parasympathetic
   c. autonomic
   d. somatic
10. The _________ division controls ordinary, day-to-day bodily functions.
    a. sympathetic
    b. parasympathetic
    c. central
    d. somatic
11. Heather is beautifully proportioned, but at 18 years of age she is still no taller than the average 10-year-old. Heather most likely had a problem in her _________ gland(s) while she was growing up.
    a. pituitary
    b. adrenal
    c. thyroid
    d. pineal
12. The action of hormones in the bloodstream is most similar to which of the following?
    a. the action of sodium ions in the action potential
    b. the action of myelin surrounding the axons
    c. the action of glial cells in the brain
    d. the action of neurotransmitters in the synapse
13. Melatonin is secreted by the _________ gland(s).
    a. pituitary
    b. adrenal
    c. thyroid
    d. pineal
14. Which of the following techniques for imaging the brain would *not* be advisable for a person with a metal plate in his or her head?
    a. EEG
    b. CT
    c. MRI
    d. PET
15. Which technique of studying the brain involves recording the electrical activity of large groups of cortical neurons?
    a. EEG
    b. deep lesioning
    c. ESB
    d. MRI
16. Maria suffered a stroke that damaged a part of her brain. She fell into a sleeplike coma and could not be awakened. If we know that the area of damage is somewhere in the brain stem, which structure is most likely damaged?
    a. medulla
    b. pons
    c. reticular formation
    d. cerebellum
17. Alexis is learning several new routines in her gymnastics class. After enough practice, her _________ will play an important role in helping her to perform the routines correctly and smoothly.
    a. medulla
    b. pons
    c. reticular formation
    d. cerebellum

18. Which sensory information does NOT have to be first sent to the thalamus before going to the cortex?
    a. auditory (hearing)
    b. olfactory (smell)
    c. gustatory (taste)
    d. visual (vision)

19. Which part of the brain is the link between the brain and the glandular system?
    a. hippocampus
    b. thalamus
    c. hypothalamus
    d. amygdala

20. Jeff is undergoing brain surgery to remove a tumor. The surgeon applies electrical stimulation to various areas around the tumor, causing Jeff to report tingling sensations in various areas of his skin. The tumor is most likely in which lobe of Jeff's brain?
    a. frontal
    b. temporal
    c. occipital
    d. parietal

21. George had a small stroke that resulted in a partial paralysis of his left side. The damaged area is most likely in his __________ lobe.
    a. right frontal
    b. left frontal
    c. right parietal
    d. left temporal

22. Linda is recovering from damage to her brain. Her main symptom is a speech problem; instead of saying, "I am going to PT (physical therapy) at nine o'clock" she says, "I go . . . PT . . . non o'cot." Linda's problem is __________.
    a. spatial neglect.
    b. visual agnosia.
    c. Broca's aphasia.
    d. Wernicke's aphasia.

23. In the split-brain operation, the __________ is severed, which is the primary communication pathway between the two hemispheres.
    a. cingulate cortex
    b. corpus callosum
    c. caudate
    d. cerebellum

24. Recognizing the face of someone you run into at the mall is a function of the __________ hemisphere; being able to retrieve that person's name from memory is a function of the __________ hemisphere.
    a. left; right
    b. right; left
    c. right; right
    d. left; left

2 the biological perspective

2.1 2.2 p. 55

Neurons and Nerves

(the brain is comprised of glial cells and neurons)

- have an electrical charge at rest—the resting potential (see Fig. 2.3, p. 50)
- are affected by neurotransmitters (see Table 2.1, p. 53)
- are separated by a gap called the synapse

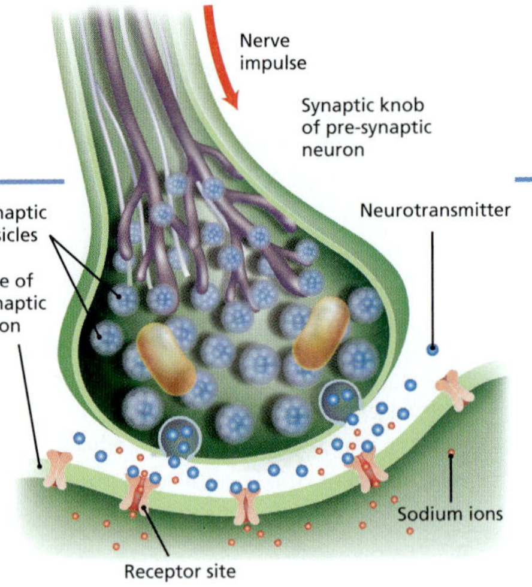

- **neurons** specialized cells in nervous system — have specialized components
- **glial cells** provide physical and metabolic support to neurons

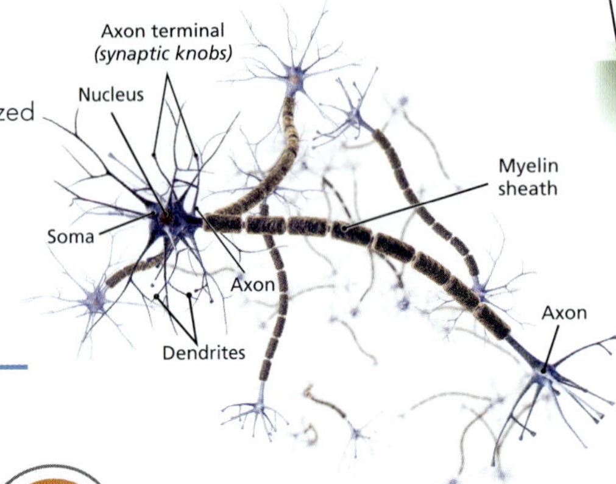

2.3 p. 64

The Central Nervous System

(comprised of the brain and spinal cord)

- **brain** true core of nervous system: takes information from senses, processes it, makes decisions, sends commands to rest of body
- **spinal cord** long bundle of neurons that carries information to and away from the brain; helps control pain response

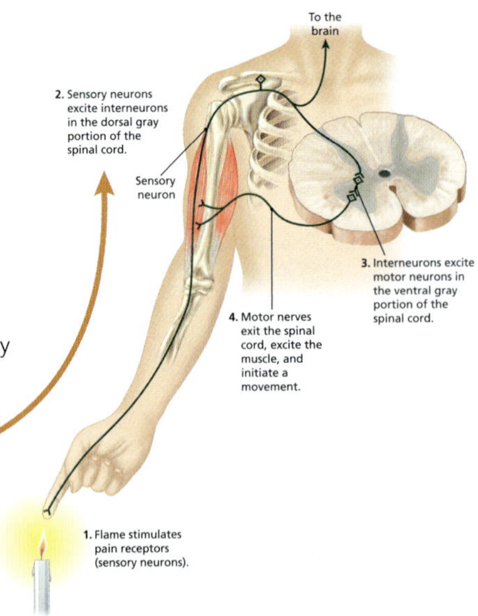

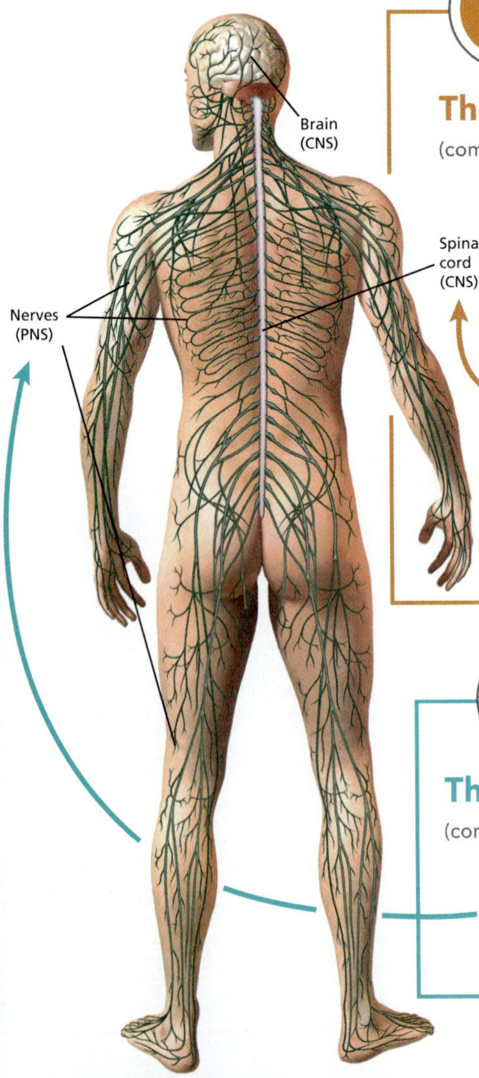

2.4 p. 64

The Peripheral Nervous System

(comprised of the nerves and neurons not contained in the brain and spinal cord)

- **somatic nervous system** controls the voluntary muscles of the body
- **autonomic nervous system** controls automatic functions of the body

2.5 p. 65

Distant Connections: The Endocrine Glands

- **glands**
  organs in the body that secrete chemicals
- **endocrine glands**
  secrete chemicals called *hormones* into bloodstream
  - **pituitary gland**
  - **pineal gland**
  - **thyroid gland**
  - **pancreas**
  - **gonads**
  - **adrenal glands**

2.6 p. 73

Looking Inside the Living Brain

(methods for studying the structures and/or activity of the living brain)

- **mapping structure**

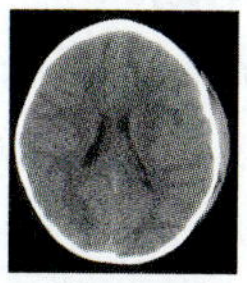

computed tomography (CT)

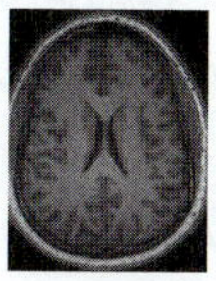

magnetic resonance imaging (MRI)

- **mapping function**

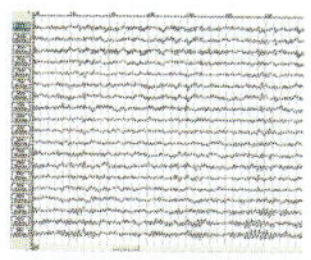

electroencephalogram (EEG)

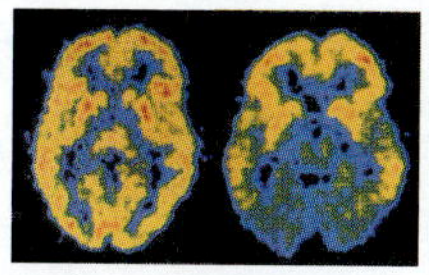

positron emission tomography (PET)

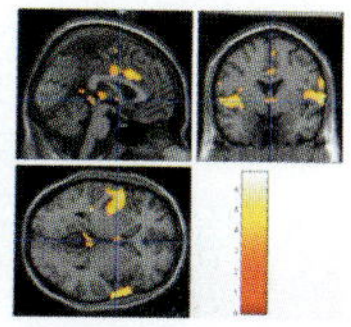

fMRI

2.7 **2.8** p. 73 **2.9** **2.10** **2.11** p. 80

The Structures of the Brain

- **the hindbrain**
  - **medulla**
  - **pons**
  - **reticular formation**
  - **cerebellum**
- **structures under the cortex**
  - **thalamus**
  - **hypothalamus**
  - **hippocampus**
  - **amygdala**
- **the cortex**
  the outermost, wrinkled layer of the brain
  - **frontal lobes**
  - **temporal lobes**
  - **parietal lobes**
  - **occipital lobes**
- **the cerebral hemispheres**
  some brain functions governed by one hemisphere more than the other

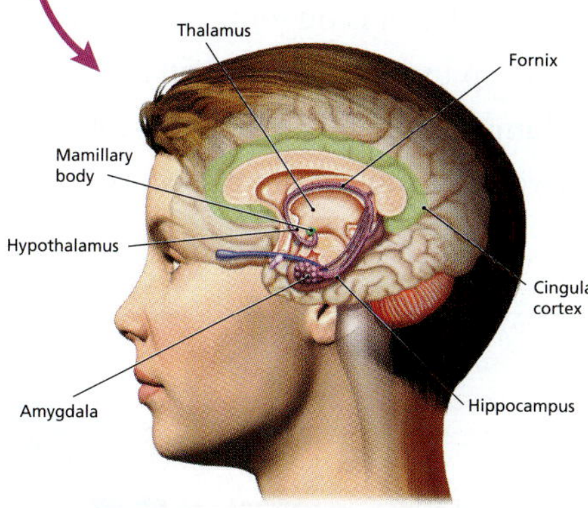

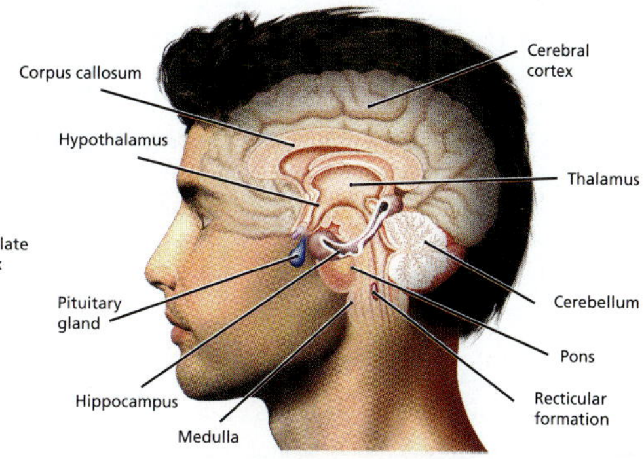

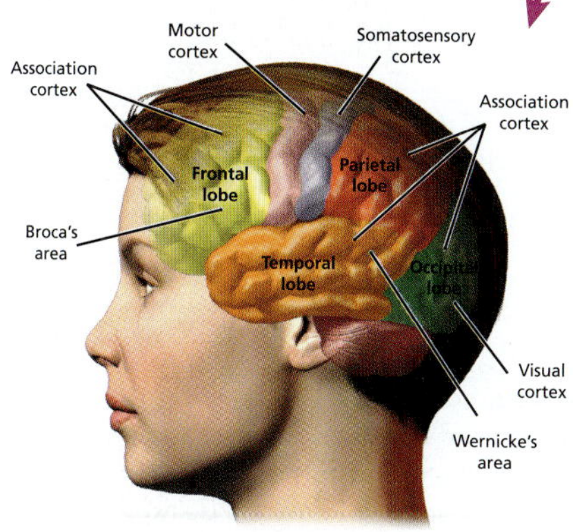

3 sensation and perception

SEEING SOUNDS AND HEARING COLORS: SYNESTHESIA

"There was a piece of music by a group called Uman. The first note was grey and it was like a band of grey with a slight curve to it, and it was a gradient—light grey going to dark grey—it had gold specks on it. The background was black but it was being broken up by other colours, moving shapes of fuchsia and there was a small sound like a click, almost like a drumbeat, something being struck, and as it was struck, a black shape appeared, and the shapes appeared from left to right, going horizontally across the bottom of this—like a movie screen that I was watching. And the shapes were so exquisite, so simple, so pure and so beautiful, I wanted somehow to be able to capture them, but they were moving too quickly and I couldn't remember them all."
—Carol Steen (1996), New York artist and synesthete, quoted from ABC Radio National Transcripts, Health Report with Robin Hughes

Ms. Steen is a most unusual artist because she is able to perceive a world where sounds have colors and shapes, an ability she often turns into unusual and beautiful sculptures. A *synesthete* is a person with **synesthesia**, which literally means "joined sensation." People with this condition are rare—about 1 in 25,000. In the synesthete, the signals that come from the sensory organs, such as the eyes or the ears, go to places in the brain where they weren't originally meant to be, causing those signals to be interpreted as more than one sensation. A fusion of sound and sight is most common, but touch, taste, and even smell can enter into the mix (Cytowic, 1989).

Although research on the physical causes of synesthesia is ongoing, some studies suggest that areas of the left side of the brain deep inside the temporal lobe and nearby in the parietal lobe may be responsible (Ramachandran & Hubbard, 2003; Rouw & Scholte, 2007). LINK to Chapter Two: The Biological Perspective, pp. 75–76.

synesthesia disorder in which the signals from the various sensory organs are processed in the wrong cortical areas, resulting in the sense information being interpreted as more than one sensation.

Why study sensation and perception?

Without sensations to tell us what is outside our own mental world, we would live entirely in our own minds, separate from one another and unable to find food or any other basics that sustain life. Sensations are the mind's window to the world that exists around us. Without perception, we would be unable to understand what all those sensations mean—perception is the process of interpreting the sensations we experience so that we can act upon them.

learning objectives

3.1 How does sensation travel through the central nervous system, and why are some sensations ignored?

3.2 What is light, and how does it travel through the various parts of the eye?

3.3 How do the eyes see, and how do the eyes see different colors?

3.4 What is sound, and how does it travel through the various parts of the ear?

3.5 Why are some people unable to hear, and how can their hearing be improved?

3.6 How do the senses of taste and smell work, and how are they alike?

3.7 What allows people to experience the sense of touch, pain, motion, and balance?

3.8 What are perception and perceptual constancies?

3.9 What are the Gestalt principles of perception?

3.10 What is depth perception and what kind of cues are important for it to occur?

3.11 What are visual illusions and how can they and other factors influence and alter perception?

study tip

As you are reading this chapter, remember to use the SQ3R method discussed on pages I-7–I-8 in *Psychology in Action*. Breaking your reading into small sections will help you get more out of every chapter.

How do we get information from the outside world into our brains?

The ABCs of Sensation

How do we get information from the outside world into our brains?

Information about the world has to have a way to get into the brain, where it can be used to determine actions and responses. The way into the brain is through the sensory organs and the process of sensation.

WHAT IS SENSATION?

3.1 **How does sensation travel through the central nervous system, and why are some sensations ignored?**

Sensation occurs when special receptors in the sense organs—the eyes, ears, nose, skin, and taste buds—are activated, allowing various forms of outside stimuli to become neural signals in the brain. (This process of converting outside stimuli, such as light, into neural activity is called **transduction**.) Let's take a closer look at these special receptors.

SENSORY RECEPTORS The *sensory receptors* are specialized forms of neurons, the cells that make up the nervous system. Instead of receiving neurotransmitters from other cells, these receptor cells are stimulated by different kinds of energy—for example, the receptors in the eyes are stimulated by light, whereas the receptors in the ears are activated by vibrations. Touch receptors are stimulated by pressure or temperature, and the receptors for taste and smell are triggered by chemical substances.

SENSORY THRESHOLDS

Ernst Weber (1795–1878) did studies trying to determine the smallest difference between two weights that could be detected. His research led to the formulation known as Weber's law of **just noticeable differences (jnd,** or the **difference threshold**). A jnd is the smallest difference between two stimuli that is detectable 50 percent of the time, and Weber's law simply means that whatever the difference between stimuli might be, it is always a *constant*. If to notice a difference the amount of sugar a person would need to add to a cup of coffee that is already sweetened with 5 teaspoons is 1 teaspoon, then the percentage of change needed to detect a just noticeable difference is one-fifth, or 20 percent. So if the coffee has 10 teaspoons of sugar in it, the person would have to add another 20 percent, or 2 teaspoons, to be able to taste the difference half of the time. Most people would not

sensation the process that occurs when special receptors in the sense organs are activated, allowing various forms of outside stimuli to become neural signals in the brain.

transduction the process of converting outside stimuli, such as light, into neural activity.

just noticeable difference (jnd or the **difference threshold)** the smallest difference between two stimuli that is detectable 50 percent of the time.

typically drink a cup of coffee with 10 teaspoons of sugar in it, let alone 12 teaspoons, but you get the point.

Gustav Fechner (1801–1887) expanded on Weber's work by studying something he called the **absolute threshold** (Fechner, 1860). An absolute threshold is the lowest level of stimulation that a person can consciously detect 50 percent of the time the stimulation is present. (Remember, the jnd is detecting a difference *between two* stimuli.) For example, assuming a very quiet room and normal hearing, how far away can someone sit and you might still hear the tick of their analog watch on half of the trials? For some examples of absolute thresholds for various senses, see Table 3.1.

absolute threshold the lowest level of stimulation that a person can consciously detect 50 percent of the time the stimulation is present.

I've heard about people being influenced by stuff in movies and on television, things that are just below the level of conscious awareness. Is that true?

I've heard about people being influenced by stuff in movies and on television, things that are just below the level of conscious awareness. Is that true?

Stimuli that are below the level of conscious awareness are called *subliminal stimuli.* (The word *limin* means "threshold," so *sublimin* means "below the threshold.") These stimuli are just strong enough to activate the sensory receptors but not strong enough for people to be consciously aware of them. Many people believe that these stimuli act upon the unconscious mind, influencing behavior in a process called *subliminal perception.*

At one time, many people believed that a market researcher named James Vicary had demonstrated the power of subliminal perception in advertising. It was five years before Vicary finally admitted that he had never conducted a real study (Merikle, 2000; Pratkanis, 1992). Furthermore, many researchers have gathered scientific evidence that subliminal perception does not work in advertising (Bargh et al., 1996; Broyles, 2006; Moore, 1988; Pratkanis & Greenwald, 1988; Trappey, 1996; Vokey & Read, 1985).

This is not to say that subliminal perception does not exist—there is a growing body of evidence that we process some stimuli without conscious awareness, especially stimuli that are fearful or threatening (LeDoux & Phelps, 2008; Öhman, 2008). In this effort, researchers have used *event-related potentials* (ERPs) and functional magnetic resonance imaging (fMRI) to verify the existence of subliminal perception and associated learning in the laboratory (Babiloni et al., 2010; Bernat et al., 2001; Fazel-Rezai & Peters, 2005; Sabatini et al., 2009). However, as in about every other case where subliminal perception has reportedly occurred, these studies use stimuli that are *supraliminal*—"above the threshold"—and detectable by our sensory systems. However, they are below the level of conscious perception and participants are not aware or conscious that they have been exposed to the stimuli due to masking or manipulation of attention. Furthermore,

In some parts of the USA, "coffee regular" refers to coffee with two creams and two sugars. How much more sugar would you need to add to taste a difference?

This young woman does not feel the piercings on her ear and nose because sensory adaptation allows her to ignore a constant, unchanging stimulation from the metal rings. What else is she wearing that would cause sensory adaptation?

Table 3.1
Examples of Absolute Thresholds

SENSE	THRESHOLD
Sight	A candle flame at 30 miles on a clear, dark night
Hearing	The tick of a watch 20 feet away in a quiet room
Smell	One drop of perfume diffused throughout a three-room apartment
Taste	1 teaspoon of sugar in 2 gallons of water
Touch	A bee's wing falling on the cheek from 1 centimeter above

the stimuli typically influence automatic reactions (such as an increase in facial tension) rather than direct voluntary behaviors (such as going to buy something suggested by advertising).

The real world is full of complex motives that are not as easily influenced as one might think (Pratkanis, 1992). Even the so-called hidden pictures that some artists airbrush into the art in advertisements aren't truly subliminal—if someone points one out, it can be seen easily enough.

HABITUATION AND SENSORY ADAPTATION

In Chapter Two it was stated that the lower centers of the brain filter sensory stimulation and "ignore" or prevent conscious attention to stimuli that do not change. The brain is only interested in changes in information. That's why people don't really "hear" the noise of the air conditioner unless it suddenly cuts off or the noise made in some classrooms unless it gets very quiet. Although they actually are *hearing* it, they aren't paying attention to it. This is called **habituation**, and it is the way the brain deals with unchanging information from the environment. LINK to Chapter Two: The Biological Perspective, p. 70.

Sometimes I can smell the odor of the garbage can in the kitchen when I first come home, but after a while the smell seems to go away—is this also habituation?

Sometimes I can smell the odor of the garbage can in the kitchen when I first come home, but after a while the smell seems to go away—is this also habituation?

Although different from habituation, **sensory adaptation** is another process by which constant, unchanging information from the sensory receptors is effectively ignored. In habituation, the sensory receptors are still responding to stimulation but the lower centers of the brain are not sending the signals from those receptors to the cortex. The process of sensory adaptation differs because the receptor cells *themselves* become less responsive to an unchanging stimulus—garbage odors included—and the receptors no longer send signals to the brain.

For example, when you eat, the food that you put in your mouth tastes strong at first, but as you keep eating the same thing, the taste does fade somewhat, doesn't it? Smell, taste, and touch are all subject to sensory adaptation.

You might think, then, that if you stare at something long enough, it would also disappear, but the eyes are a little different. Even though the sensory receptors in the back of the eyes adapt to and become less responsive to a constant visual stimulus, under ordinary circumstances the eyes are never entirely still. There's a constant movement of the eyes, tiny little vibrations called "microsaccades" or "saccadic movements" that people don't consciously notice. These movements keep the eyes from adapting to what they see. (That's a good thing, because otherwise many students would no doubt go blind from staring off into space.)

habituation tendency of the brain to stop attending to constant, unchanging information.

sensory adaptation tendency of sensory receptor cells to become less responsive to a stimulus that is unchanging.

3.1 CONCEPT MAP

The ABCs of Sensation

- **sensation** process by which information from the outside world enters the brain
  - related to the activation of receptors in the various sense organs
  - related to changes in physical stimuli
    - detected by sensory receptors
    - sometimes "ignored" through sensory adaptation or cognitive habituation

PRACTICE quiz How much do you remember? ANSWERS ON PAGE AK-1.

Pick the best answer.

1. The smallest difference between two stimuli that can be detected 50 percent of the time it is present is called _________.
   a. absolute threshold.
   b. just noticeable difference.
   c. sensation.
   d. sensory adaptation.
2. When receptor cells for the senses are activated, the process called _________ has begun.
   a. perception
   b. sublimination
   c. adaptation
   d. sensation
3. You have a piece of candy that you are holding in your mouth. After a while, the candy doesn't taste as strong as it did when you first tasted it. What has happened?
   a. sensory adaptation
   b. subliminal perception
   c. habituation
   d. perceptual defense
4. While driving down the road looking for the new restaurant you want to try out, not hearing the clicking of the turn signal you forgot to turn off until one of your friends point it out is likely due to _________:
   a. accommodation
   b. adaptation
   c. sublimation
   d. habituation

The Science of Seeing

I've heard that light is waves, but I've also heard that light is made of particles—which is it?

Light is a complicated phenomenon. Although scientists have long argued over the nature of light, they finally have agreed that light has the properties of both waves and particles. The following section gives a brief history of how scientists have tried to "shed light" on the mystery of light.

I've heard that light is waves, but I've also heard that light is made of particles—which is it?

PERCEPTUAL PROPERTIES OF LIGHT: CATCHING THE WAVES

3.2 What is light, and how does it travel through the various parts of the eye?

It was Albert Einstein who first proposed that light is actually tiny "packets" of waves. These "wave packets" are called *photons* and have specific wavelengths associated with them (Lehnert, 2007; van der Merwe & Garuccio, 1994).

When people experience the physical properties of light, they are not really aware of its dual, wavelike and particle-like, nature. With regard to its psychological properties, there are three aspects to our perception of light: *brightness, color*, and *saturation.*

Brightness is determined by the amplitude of the wave—how high or how low the wave actually is. The higher the wave, the brighter the light appears to be. Low waves are dimmer. *Color*, or hue, is largely determined by the length of the wave. Long wavelengths (measured in nanometers) are found at the red end of the *visible spectrum* (the portion of the whole spectrum of light that is visible to the human eye; see Figure 3.1), whereas shorter wavelengths are found at the blue end. (Note that when combining different colors, light behaves differently than pigments or paint. We will look at this distinction when we examine perception of color).

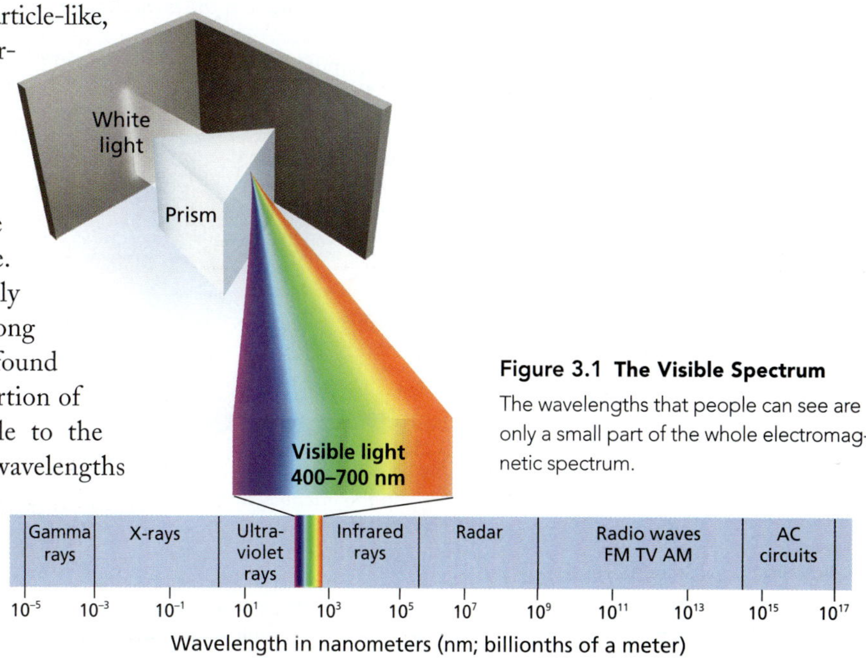

Figure 3.1 The Visible Spectrum
The wavelengths that people can see are only a small part of the whole electromagnetic spectrum.

Saturation refers to the purity of the color people perceive: A highly saturated red, for example, would contain only red wavelengths, whereas a less-saturated red might contain a mixture of wavelengths. For example, when a child is using the red paint from a set of poster paints, the paint on the paper will look like a pure red, but if the child mixes in some white paint, the paint will look pink. The hue is still red but it will be less of a saturated red because of the presence of white wavelengths. Mixing in black or gray would also lessen the saturation.

THE STRUCTURE OF THE EYE

Simulate the structures of the eye on **mypsychlab.com**

The best way to talk about how the eye processes light is to talk about what happens to an image being viewed as the photons of light from that image travel through the eye. Refer to Figure 3.2 to follow the path of the image. **Simulate** on **mypsychlab.com**

FROM FRONT TO BACK: THE PARTS OF THE EYE Light enters the eye directly from a source (such as the sun) or indirectly by reflecting off of an object. To see clearly, a single point of light from a source or reflected from an object must travel through the structures of the eye and end up on the retina as a single point. Light bends as it passes through substances of different densities, through a process known as refraction. For example, have you ever looked at a drinking straw in a glass of water through the side of the glass? It appears that the straw bends, or is broken, at the surface of the water. That optical illusion is due to the refraction of light. The structures of the eye play a vital role in both collecting and focusing of light so we can see clearly.

The surface of the eye is covered in a clear membrane called the *cornea*. The cornea not only protects the eye but also is the structure that focuses most of the light coming into the eye. The cornea has a fixed curvature, like a camera that has no option to adjust the focus. However, this curvature can be changed somewhat through vision-improving techniques that change the shape of the cornea. For example, ophthalmologists can use both *photoreactive keratectomy (PRK)* and *laser-assisted in situ keratomileusis (LASIK)* procedures to remove small portions of the cornea, changing its curvature, and thus the focus in the eye.

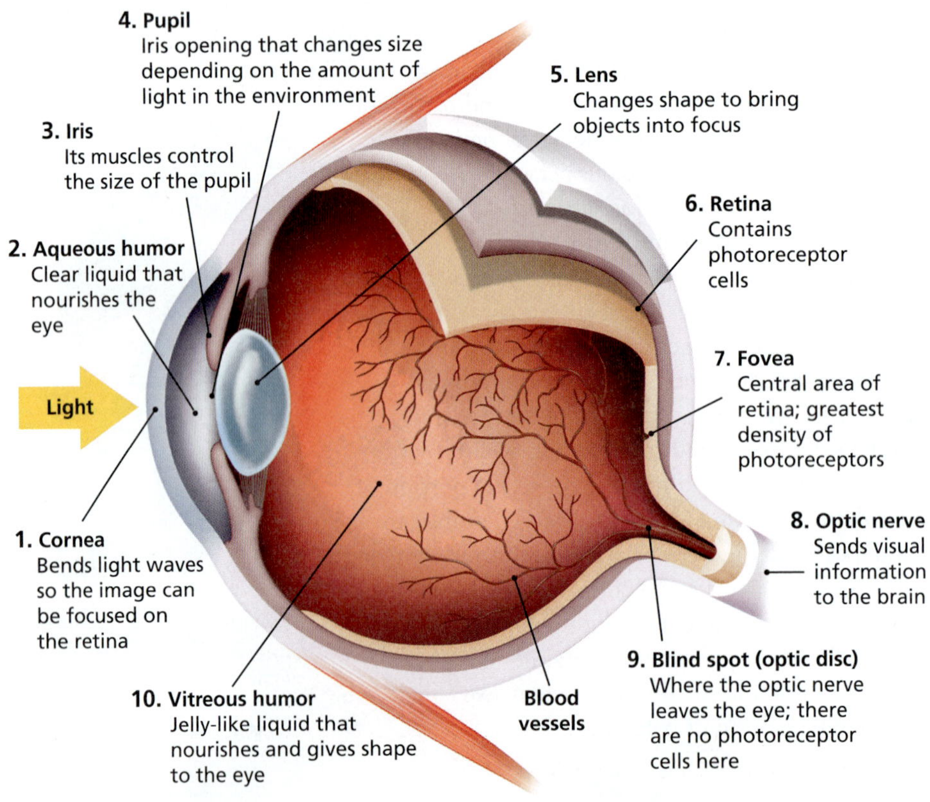

Figure 3.2 Structure of the Eye

Light enters the eye through the cornea and pupil. The iris controls the size of the pupil. From the pupil, light passes through the lens to the retina, where it is transformed into nerve impulses. The nerve impulses travel to the brain along the optic nerve.

The next visual layer is a clear, watery fluid called the *aqueous humor*. This fluid is continually replenished and supplies nourishment to the eye. The light from the visual image then enters the interior of the eye through a hole, called the *pupil*, in a round muscle called the *iris* (the colored part of the eye). The iris can change the size of the pupil, letting more or less light into the eye. That also helps focus the image; people try to do the same thing by squinting.

Behind the iris, suspended by muscles, is another clear structure called the *lens*. The flexible lens finishes the focusing process begun by the cornea. In a process called **visual accommodation**, the lens changes its shape from thick to thin, enabling it to focus on objects that are close or far away. The variation in thickness allows the lens to project a sharp image on the retina. People lose this ability as the lens hardens through aging (a disorder called *presbyopia*). Although people try to compensate* for their inability to focus on things that are close to them, eventually they usually need bifocals because their arms just aren't long enough anymore.

Once past the lens, light passes through a large, open space filled with a clear, jelly-like fluid called the *vitreous humor*. This fluid, like the aqueous humor, also nourishes the eye and gives it shape.

RETINA, RODS, AND CONES The final stop for light within the eye is the *retina*, a light-sensitive area at the back of the eye containing three layers: ganglion cells, bipolar cells, and the **rods** and **cones**, special cells (*photoreceptors*) that respond to the various light waves. (See Figures 3.3a and b.) The rods and the cones are the business end of the retina—the part that actually receives the photons of light and turns them into neural signals to the brain, sending them first to the *bipolar cells* (a type of interneuron; called bipolar or "two-ended" because they have a single dendrite at one end and a single axon on the other; LINK to Chapter Two: The Biological Perspective, p. 57) and then to the retinal *ganglion cells* whose axons form the optic nerve. (See Figure 3.3a.)

visual accommodation the change in the thickness of the lens as the eye focuses on objects that are far away or close.

rods visual sensory receptors found at the back of the retina, responsible for non-color sensitivity to low levels of light.

cones visual sensory receptors found at the back of the retina, responsible for color vision and sharpness of vision.

This photo illustrates an optical illusion caused by the refraction of light. The straw is not really broken although it appears that way.

a. b. c.

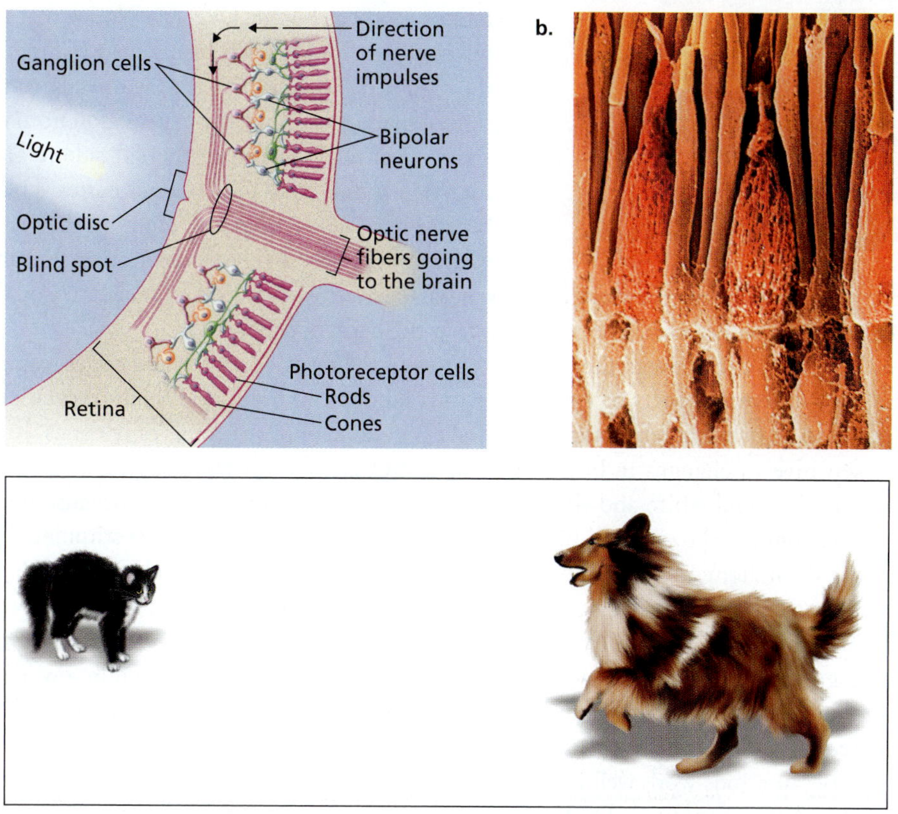

Figure 3.3 The Parts of the Retina

(a) Light passes through ganglion and bipolar cells until it reaches and stimulates the rods and cones. Nerve impulses from the rods and cones travel along a nerve pathway to the brain. (b) On the right of the figure is a photomicrograph of the long, thin rods and the shorter, thicker cones; the rods outnumber the cones by a ratio of about 20 to 1. (c) The blind spot demonstration. Hold the book in front of you. Close your right eye and stare at the picture of the dog with your left eye. Slowly bring the book closer to your face. The picture of the cat will disappear at some point because the light from the picture of the cat is falling on your blind spot.

*compensate: to correct for an error or defect.

blind spot area in the retina where the axons of the three layers of retinal cells exit the eye to form the optic nerve, insensitive to light.

dark adaptation the recovery of the eye's sensitivity to visual stimuli in darkness after exposure to bright lights.

THE BLIND SPOT The eyes don't adapt to constant stimuli under normal circumstances because of saccadic movements. But if people stare with one eye at one spot long enough, objects that slowly cross their visual field may at one point disappear briefly because there is a "hole" in the retina—the place where all the axons of those ganglion cells leave the retina to become the optic nerve. There are no rods or cones here, so this is referred to as the **blind spot**. You can demonstrate the blind spot for yourself by following the directions in Figure 3.3c.

HOW THE EYE WORKS

3.3 How do the eyes see, and how do the eyes see different colors?

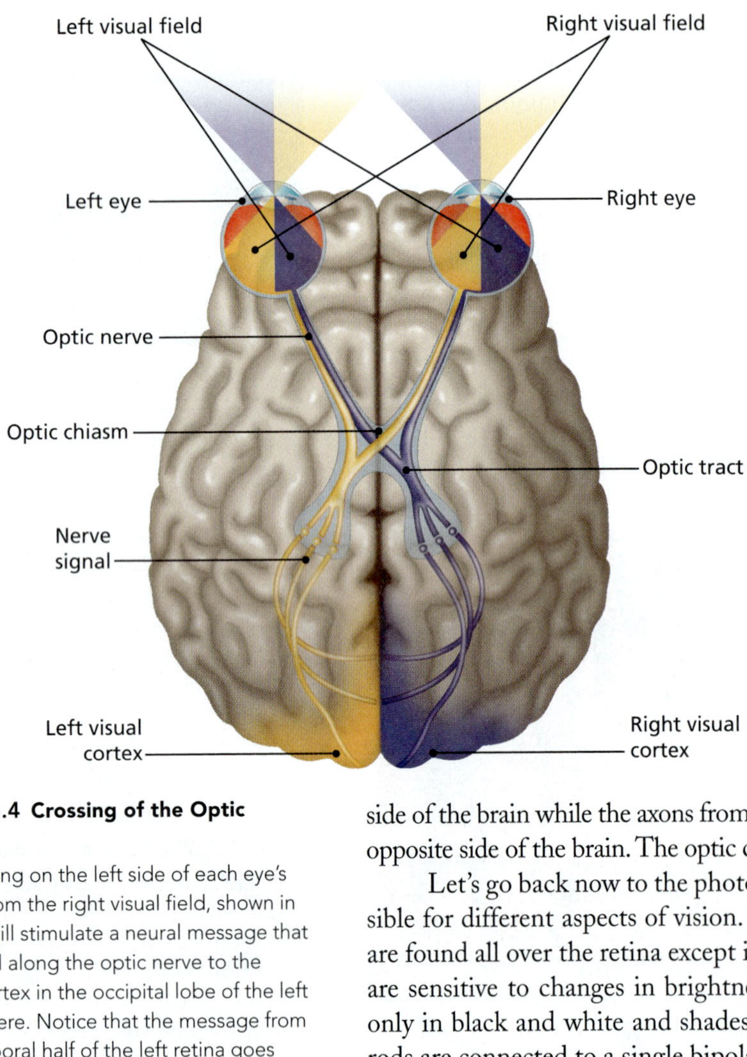

Figure 3.4 Crossing of the Optic Nerve

Light falling on the left side of each eye's retina (from the right visual field, shown in yellow) will stimulate a neural message that will travel along the optic nerve to the visual cortex in the occipital lobe of the left hemisphere. Notice that the message from the temporal half of the left retina goes directly to the left occipital lobe, while the message from the nasal half of the right retina crosses over to the left hemisphere (the optic chiasm is the point of crossover). The optic nerve tissue from both eyes joins together to form the left optic tract before going on to the left occipital lobe. For the left visual field (shown in blue), the messages from both right sides of the retinas will travel along the right optic tract to the right visual cortex in the same manner.

THROUGH THE EYES TO THE BRAIN You may want to first look at Figure 3.4 for a moment before reading this section. Light entering the eyes can be separated into the left and right visual fields. Light from the right visual field falls on the left side of each eye's retina; light from the left visual field falls on the right side of each retina. Light travels in a straight line through the cornea and lens; resulting in the image projected on the retina actually being upside down and reversed from left to right as compared to the visual fields. Thank goodness our brains can compensate for this!

The areas of the retina can be divided into halves, with the halves toward the temples of the head referred to as the temporal retinas and the halves toward the center, or nose, called the nasal retinas. Look at Figure 3.4 again. Notice that the information from the left visual field (falling on the right side of each retina) goes directly to the right visual cortex, while the information from the right visual field (falling on the left side of each retina) goes directly to the left visual cortex. This is because the axons from the temporal halves of each retina project to the visual cortex on the same side of the brain while the axons from the nasal halves cross over to the visual cortex on the opposite side of the brain. The optic chiasm is the point of crossover.

Let's go back now to the photoreceptors in the retina, the rods and cones responsible for different aspects of vision. The rods (about 120 million of them in each eye) are found all over the retina except in the very center, which contains only cones. Rods are sensitive to changes in brightness but not to changes in wavelength, so they see only in black and white and shades of gray. They can be very sensitive because many rods are connected to a single bipolar cell, so that if even only one rod is stimulated by a photon of light, the brain perceives the whole area of those rods as stimulated (because the brain is receiving the message from the single bipolar cell). But because the brain doesn't know exactly what part of the area (which rod) is actually sending the message, the visual acuity (sharpness) is quite low. That's why things seen in low levels of light, such as twilight or a dimly lit room, are fuzzy and grayish. Because rods are located on the periphery of the retina, they are also responsible for peripheral vision.

Because rods work well in low levels of light, they are also the cells that allow the eyes to adapt to low light. **Dark adaptation** occurs as the eye recovers its ability to see when going from a brightly lit state to a dark state. (The light-sensitive pigments that allow us to see are able to regenerate or "recharge" in the dark.) The brighter the light was, the longer it takes the rods to adapt to the new lower levels of light (Bartlett, 1965). This is why the bright headlights of an oncoming car can leave a person less able to see for a while after that car has passed. Fortunately, this is usually a temporary condition because the bright light was on so briefly and the rods readapt to the dark night relatively quickly. Full dark adaptation, which occurs when going from more constant light to darkness such as turning out one's bedroom lights, takes about 30 minutes. As people get older this process takes longer, causing many older persons to be less able to see at night and in darkened rooms (Klaver et al., 1998). This age-related change can cause *night blindness*, in which a person has difficulty seeing well enough to drive at night or get around in a darkened room or house. Some research indicates that taking supplements such as vitamin A can reverse or relieve this symptom in some cases (Jacobsen et al., 1995).

While this deer may see quite well when using its rods at night, the bright headlights of a car will activate the cones. The cones will adapt rather quickly, but it takes time for the deer's pupil to contract, leaving the deer blinded by the light until then.

When going from a darkened room to one that is brightly lit, the opposite process occurs. The cones have to adapt to the increased level of light, and they accomplish this **light adaptation** much more quickly than the rods adapt to darkness—it takes a few seconds at most (Hood, 1998). There are 6 million cones in each eye; of these, 50,000 have a private line to the optic nerve (one bipolar cell for each cone). This means that the cones are the receptors for visual acuity. Cones are located all over the retina but are more concentrated at its very center where there are no rods (the area called the *fovea*). Cones also need a lot more light to function than the rods do, so cones work best in bright light, which is also when people see things most clearly. Cones are also sensitive to different wavelengths of light, so they are responsible for color vision.

PERCEPTION OF COLOR

Earlier you said the cones are used in color vision. There are so many colors in the world—are there cones that detect each color? Or do all cones detect all colors?

Earlier you said the cones are used in color vision. There are so many colors in the world—are there cones that detect each color? Or do all cones detect all colors?

Although experts in the visual system have been studying color and its nature for many years, at this point in time there is an ongoing theoretical discussion about the role the cones play in the sensation of color.

THEORIES OF COLOR VISION Two theories about how people see colors were originally proposed in the 1800s. The first is called the **trichromatic** ("three colors") **theory**. First proposed by Thomas Young in 1802 and later modified by Hermann von Helmholtz in 1852, this theory proposed three types of cones: red cones, blue cones, and green cones, one for each of the three primary colors of light.

In trichromatic theory, the three types of cones combine to form different colors much as these three colored lights combine.

Most people probably think that the primary colors are red, yellow, and blue, but these are the primary colors when talking about *painting*—not when talking about *light*. Paints *reflect* light, and the way reflected light mixes is different from the way direct light mixes. For example, if an artist were to blend red, yellow, and blue paints together, the result would be a mess—a black mess. The mixing of paint (reflected light) is subtractive, removing more light as you mix in more colors. As all of the colors are mixed, the more light waves are absorbed and we see black. But if the artist were to blend a red, green, and blue light together by focusing lights of those three colors on one common spot, the result would be white, not black. The mixing of direct light is additive, resulting in lighter colors, more light, and when mixing red, blue, and green, we see white, the reflection of the entire visual spectrum.

In the trichromatic theory, different shades of colors correspond to different amounts of light received by each of these three types of cones. These cones then fire their message to the brain's vision centers. It is the combination of cones and the rate at which they are firing that determine the color that will be seen. For example, if the red and green cones are firing in response to a stimulus at fast enough rates, the color the person sees is yellow. If the red and blue cones are firing fast enough, the result is magenta. If the blue and green cones are firing fast enough, a kind of cyan color (blue-green) appears.

light adaptation the recovery of the eye's sensitivity to visual stimuli in light after exposure to darkness.

trichromatic theory theory of color vision that proposes three types of cones: red, blue, and green.

Figure 3.5 Color Afterimage

Stare at the white dot in the center of this oddly colored flag for about 30 seconds. Now look at a white piece of paper or a white wall. Notice that the colors are now the normal, expected colors of the American flag. They are also the primary colors that are opposites of the colors in the picture and provide evidence for the opponent-process theory of color vision.

Brown and Wald (1964) identified three types of cones in the retina, each sensitive to a range of wavelengths, measured in nanometers (nm), and a peak sensitivity that roughly corresponds to three different colors (although hues/colors can vary depending on brightness and saturation). The peak wavelength of light the cones seem to be most sensitive to turns out to be just a little different from Young and von Helmholtz's original three corresponding colors: Short wavelength cones detect what we see as blue-violet (about 420 nm), medium wavelength cones detect what we see as green (about 530 nm), and long wavelength cones detect what we see as green-yellow (about 560 nm). Interestingly, none of the cones identified by Brown and Wald have a peak sensitivity to light where most of us see red (around 630 nm). Keep in mind though, each cone responds to light across a range of wavelengths, not just its wavelength of peak sensitivity. Depending on the intensity of the light, both the medium and long wavelength cones respond to light that appears red.

THE AFTERIMAGE The trichromatic theory would, at first glance, seem to be more than adequate to explain how people perceive color. But there's an interesting phenomenon that this theory cannot explain. If a person stares at a picture of the American flag for a little while—say, a minute—and then looks away to a blank white wall or sheet of paper, that person will see an afterimage of the flag. **Afterimages** occur when a visual sensation persists for a brief time even after the original stimulus is removed. The person would also notice rather quickly that the colors of the flag in the afterimage are all wrong—green for red, black for white, and yellow for blue. If you follow the directions for Figure 3.5, in which the flag is yellow, green, and black, you should see a flag with the usual red, white, and blue.

Hey, now the afterimage of the flag has normal colors! Why does this happen?

The phenomenon of the color afterimage is explained by the second theory of color perception, called the **opponent-process theory** (De Valois & De Valois, 1993; Hurvich & Jameson, 1957), based on an idea first suggested by Edwald Hering in 1874 (Finger, 1994). In opponent-process theory, there are four primary colors: red, green, blue, and yellow. The colors are arranged in pairs, red with green and blue with yellow. If one member of a pair is strongly stimulated, the other member is inhibited and cannot be working—so there are no reddish-greens or bluish-yellows.

So how can this kind of pairing cause a color afterimage? From the level of the bipolar and ganglion cells in the retina, all the way through the thalamus, and on to the visual cortical areas in the brain, some neurons (or groups of neurons) are stimulated by light from one part of the visual spectrum and inhibited by light from a different part of the spectrum. For example, let's say we have a red-green ganglion cell in the retina whose baseline activity is rather weak when we expose it to white light. However, the cell's activity is increased by red light, so we experience the color red. If we stimulate the cell with red light for a long enough period of time, the cell becomes fatigued. If we then swap out the red light with white light, the now-tired cell responds even less than the original baseline. Now we experience the color green, because green is associated with a decrease in the responsiveness of this cell.

So which theory is the right one? Both theories play a part in color vision. Trichromatic theory can explain what is happening with the raw stimuli, the actual detection of various wavelengths of light. Opponent-process theory can explain afterimages and other aspects of visual perception that occur after the initial detection of light from our environment. In addition to the retinal bipolar and ganglion cells, opponent-process cells are contained inside the thalamus in an area called the lateral

Hey, now the afterimage of the flag has normal colors! Why does this happen?

afterimages images that occur when a visual sensation persists for a brief time even after the original stimulus is removed.

opponent-process theory theory of color vision that proposes visual neurons (or groups of neurons) are stimulated by light of one color and inhibited by light of another color.

geniculate nucleus (LGN). The LGN is part of the pathway that visual information takes to the occipital lobe. It is when the cones in the retina send signals through the retinal bipolar and ganglion cells that we see the red versus green pairings and blue versus yellow pairings. Together with the retinal cells, the cells in the LGN appear to be the ones responsible for opponent-processing of color vision and the afterimage effect.

So which theory accounts for color blindness? I've heard that there are two kinds of color blindness, when you can't tell red from green and when you can't tell blue from yellow.

So which theory accounts for color blindness? I've heard that there are two kinds of color blindness, when you can't tell red from green and when you can't tell blue from yellow.

COLOR BLINDNESS From the mention of red-green and yellow-blue color blindness, one might think that the opponent-process theory explains this problem. But in reality "color blindness" is caused by defective cones in the retina of the eye and as a more general term, *color-deficient vision* is more accurate, as most people with "color blindness" have two type of cones working and can see many colors.

There are really three kinds of color-deficient vision. In a very rare type, *monochrome color blindness*, people either have no cones or have cones that are not working at all. Essentially, if they have cones, they only have one type and, therefore, everything looks the same to the brain—shades of gray. The other types of color-deficient vision, or *dichromatic vision*, are caused by the same kind of problem—having one cone that does not work properly. *Protanopia* (red-green color deficiency) is due to the lack of functioning red cones and *deuteranopia* (another type of red-green color deficiency) results from the lack of functioning green cones. In both of these, the individual confuses reds and greens, seeing the world primarily in blues, yellows, and shades of gray. A lack of functioning blue cones is much less common and called *tritanopia* (blue-yellow color deficiency). These individuals see the world primarily in reds, greens, and shades of gray. To get an idea of what a test for color-deficient vision is like, look at Figure 3.6.

Why are most of the people with color-deficient vision men?

Why are most of the people with color-deficient vision men?

Color-deficient vision involving one set of cones is inherited in a pattern known as *sex-linked inheritance*. The gene for color-deficient vision is *recessive*. To inherit a recessive trait, you normally need two of the genes, one from each parent. LINK to Chapter Eight: Development Across the Life Span, p. 301. But the gene for color-deficient vision is attached to a particular chromosome (a package of genes) that helps to determine the sex of a person. Men have one X chromosome and one smaller Y chromosome (named for their shapes), whereas women have two X chromosomes. The smaller Y has fewer genes than the larger X, and one of the genes missing is the one that would suppress the gene for color-deficient vision. For a woman to have color-deficient vision, she must inherit two recessive genes, one from each parent, but a man only needs to inherit *one* recessive gene—the one passed on to him on his mother's X chromosome. His odds are greater; therefore, more males than females have color-deficient vision. **Read** on **mypsychlab.com**

Read and learn more about color blindness on **mypsychlab.com**

Figure 3.6 The Ishihara Color Test

In the circle on the left, the number 8 is visible only to those with normal color vision. In the circle on the right, people with normal vision will see the number 96, while those with red-green color blindness will see nothing but a circle of dots.

3.2 3.3

CONCEPT MAP

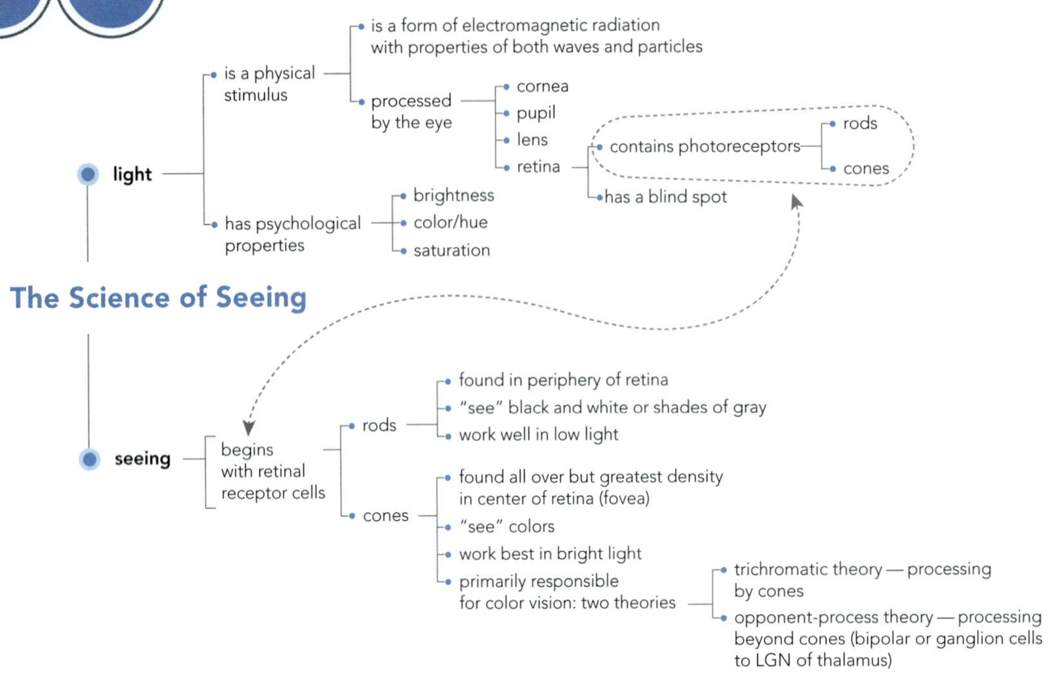

PRACTICE quiz How much do you remember? ANSWERS ON PAGE AK-1.

Pick the best answer.

1. Which of the following terms refers to the perceived effect of the amplitude of light waves?
   - **a.** color
   - **b.** brightness
   - **c.** saturation
   - **d.** hue
2. Which of the following represents the correct path of light through the eye?
   - **a.** iris, cornea, lens, retina
   - **b.** cornea, vitreous humor, iris, lens, aqueous humor, retina
   - **c.** cornea, pupil, lens, vitreous humor, retina
   - **d.** cornea, lens, pupil, iris, retina
3. If you wanted to locate a dimly lit star better at night, what should you do?
   - **a.** Look directly at it because the cones will focus better at night.
   - **b.** Look off to the side, using the cones in the periphery of the retina.
   - **c.** Look directly at it because the rods can see sharply at night.
   - **d.** Look off to the side, using the rods in the periphery of the retina.
4. Which theory of color vision best accounts for afterimages?
   - **a.** trichromatic theory
   - **b.** opponent-process theory
   - **c.** both a and b
   - **d.** neither a nor b
5. Which statement about color-deficient vision is TRUE?
   - **a.** There are more men with color-deficient vision than women.
   - **b.** All people with color-deficient vision see only in black and white.
   - **c.** Some people with color-deficient vision see only in blue.
   - **d.** Some people with color-deficient vision see only in blue and red.

If light works like waves, then do sound waves have similar properties?

The Hearing Sense: Can You Hear Me Now?

If light works like waves, then do sound waves have similar properties?

The properties of sound are indeed similar to those of light, as both senses rely on waves. But the similarity ends there, as the physical properties of sound are different from those of light.

PERCEPTION OF SOUND: GOOD VIBRATIONS

3.4 What is sound, and how does it travel through the various parts of the ear?

Sound waves do not come in little packets the way light comes in photons. Sound waves are simply the vibrations of the molecules of air that surround us. Sound waves do have the same properties of light waves though—wavelength, amplitude, and

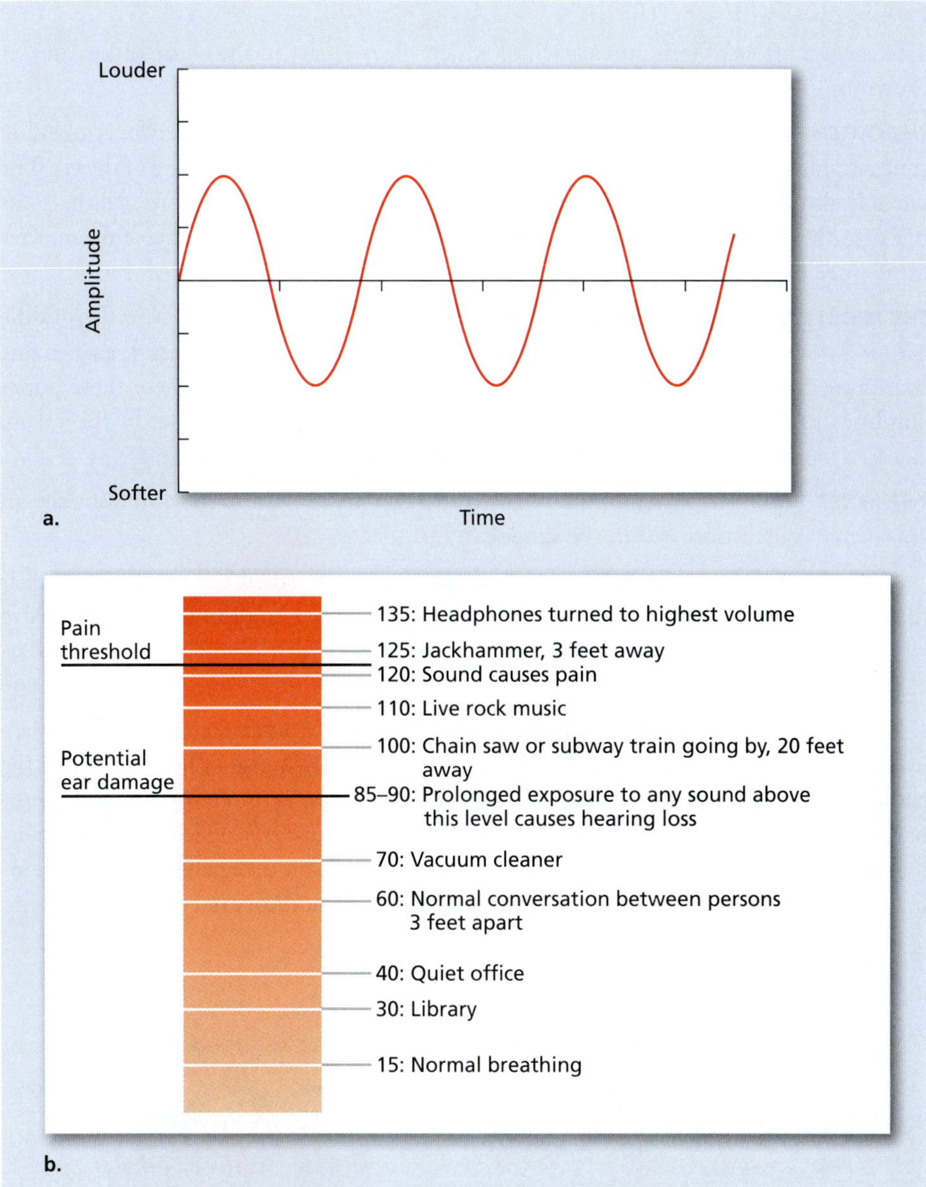

Figure 3.7 Sound Waves and Decibels

(a) A typical sound wave. The higher the wave, the louder the sound; the lower the wave, the softer the sound. If the waves are close together in time (high frequency), the pitch will be perceived as a high pitch. Waves that are farther apart (low frequency) will be perceived as having a lower pitch. (b) Decibels of various stimuli. A *decibel* is a unit of measure for loudness. Psychologists study the effects that noise has on stress, learning, performance, aggression, and psychological and physical well-being.

purity. Wavelengths are interpreted by the brain as the frequency or *pitch* (high, medium, or low). Amplitude is interpreted as *volume*, how soft or loud a sound is. (See Figure 3.7.) Finally, what would correspond to saturation or purity in light is called *timbre* in sound, a richness in the tone of the sound. And just as people rarely see pure colors in the world around us, they also seldom hear pure sounds. The everyday noises that surround people do not allow them to hear many pure tones.

Just as a person's vision is limited by the visible spectrum of light, a person is also limited in the range of frequencies he or she can hear. Frequency is measured in cycles (waves) per second, or **hertz (Hz)**. Human limits are between 20 and 20,000 Hz, with the most sensitivity from about 2000 to 4000 Hz, very important for conversational speech. (In comparison, dogs can hear between 50 and 60,000 Hz, and dolphins can hear up to 200,000 Hz.) To hear the higher and lower frequencies of a piece of music on a CD, for example, a person would need to increase the amplitude or volume—which explains why some people like to "crank it up."

"And only you can hear this whistle?"

hertz (Hz) cycles or waves per second, a measurement of frequency.

pinna the visible part of the ear.

auditory canal short tunnel that runs from the pinna to the eardrum.

cochlea snail-shaped structure of the inner ear that is filled with fluid.

auditory nerve bundle of axons from the hair cells in the inner ear.

Explore the structures of the ear on **mypsychlab.com**

THE STRUCTURE OF THE EAR: FOLLOW THE VIBES

The ear is a series of structures, each of which plays a part in the sense of hearing, as shown in Figure 3.8.

THE OUTER EAR The **pinna** is the visible, external part of the ear that serves as a kind of concentrator, funneling* the sound waves from the outside into the structure of the ear. The pinna is also the entrance to the **auditory canal** (or ear canal), the short tunnel that runs down to the *tympanic membrane*, or eardrum. When sound waves hit the eardrum, they cause three tiny bones in the middle ear to vibrate. **Explore** on **mypsychlab.com**

THE MIDDLE EAR: HAMMER, ANVIL, AND STIRRUP The three tiny bones in the middle ear are known as the hammer (*malleus*), anvil (*incus*), and stirrup (*stapes*), each name stemming from the shape of the respective bone. The vibration of these three bones amplifies the vibrations from the eardrum. The stirrup, the last bone in the chain, causes a membrane covering the opening of the inner ear to vibrate.

THE INNER EAR This membrane is called the *oval window*, and its vibrations set off another chain reaction within the inner ear.

Cochlea The inner ear is a snail-shaped structure called the **cochlea**, which is filled with fluid. When the oval window vibrates, it causes the fluid in the cochlea to vibrate. This fluid surrounds a membrane running through the middle of the cochlea called the *basilar membrane*.

Basilar Membrane and the Organ of Corti The *basilar membrane* is the resting place of the *organ of Corti*, which contains the receptor cells for the sense of hearing. When the basilar membrane vibrates, it vibrates the organ of Corti, causing it to brush against a membrane above it. On the organ of Corti are special cells called *hair cells*, which are the receptors for sound. When these auditory receptors or hair cells are bent up against the other membrane, it causes them to send a neural message through the **auditory nerve** (which contains

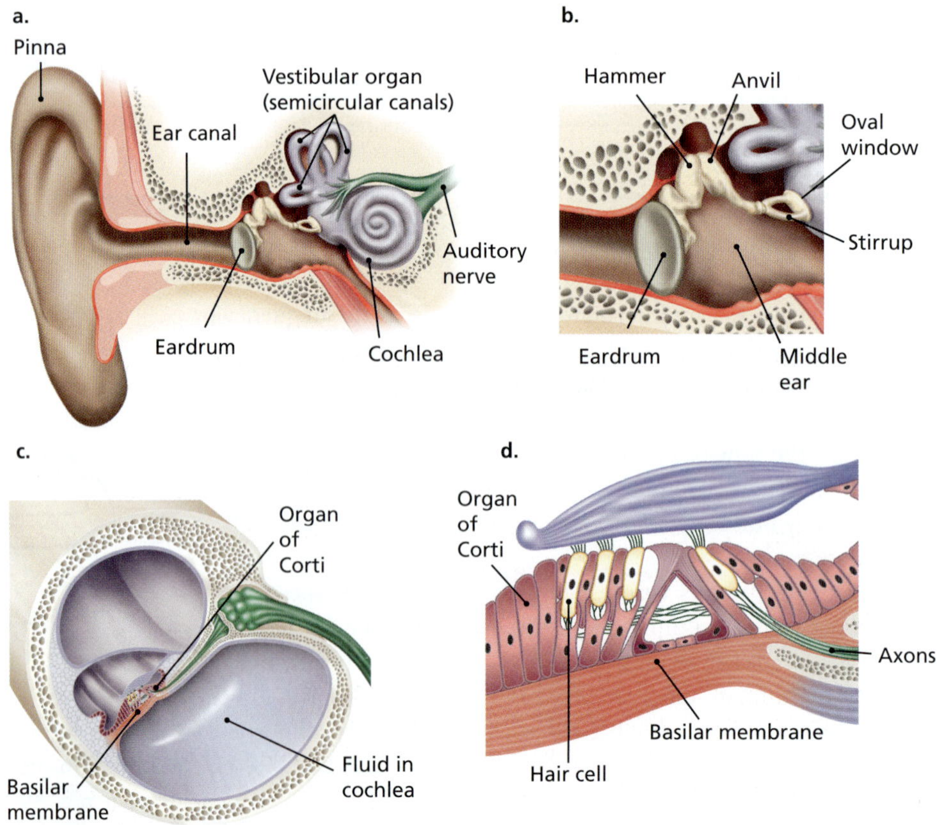

Figure 3.8 The Structure of the Ear
(a) This drawing shows the entire ear, beginning with the outer ear (pinna, ear canal, and eardrum). The vestibular organ includes the semicircular canals and the otolith organs (inside the round structures just above the cochlea). (b) The middle ear. Sound waves entering through the ear canal cause the eardrum to vibrate, which causes each of the three bones of the middle ear to vibrate, amplifying the sound. The stirrup rests on the oval window, which transmits its vibration to the fluid in the inner ear. (c) The inner ear. Large spaces are filled with fluid (shown in purple) that vibrates as the oval window vibrates. A thin membrane suspended in this fluid is called the basilar membrane, which contains the organ of Corti, the structure composed of the hairlike cells that send signals to the auditory cortex of the brain by way of the auditory nerve. (d) A close-up view of the basilar membrane (in dark pink) with the hair cells of the organ of Corti (in lighter pink). Notice the axons (small green lines) leaving the hair cells to form the auditory nerve.

*funneling: moving to a focal point.

the axons of all the receptor neurons) and into the brain, where the auditory cortex will interpret the sounds (the transformation of the vibrations of sound into neural messages is transduction). The louder the sound in the outside world, the stronger the vibrations that stimulate more of those hair cells—which the brain interprets as loudness.

I think I have it straight—but all of that just explains how soft and loud sounds get to the brain from the outside. How do we hear different kinds of sounds, like high pitches and low pitches?

I think I have it straight—but all of that just explains how soft and loud sounds get to the brain from the outside. How do we hear different kinds of sounds, like high pitches and low pitches?

PERCEIVING PITCH

Pitch refers to how high or low a sound is. For example, the bass tones in the music pounding through the wall of your apartment from the neighbors next door is a low pitch, whereas the scream of a 2-year-old child is a very high pitch. *Very* high. There are three primary theories about how the brain receives information about pitch.

The oldest of the three theories, **place theory**, is based on an idea proposed in 1863 by Hermann von Helmholtz and elaborated on and modified by Georg von Békésy, beginning with experiments first published in 1928 (Békésy, 1960). In this theory, the pitch a person hears depends on where the hair cells that are stimulated are located on the organ of Corti. For example, if the person is hearing a high-pitched sound, all of the hair cells near the oval window will be stimulated, but if the sound is low pitched, all of the hair cells that are stimulated will be located farther away on the organ of Corti.

Frequency theory, developed by Ernest Rutherford in 1886, states that pitch is related to how fast the basilar membrane vibrates. The faster this membrane vibrates, the higher the pitch; the slower it vibrates, the lower the pitch. (In this theory, all of the auditory neurons would be firing at the same time.)

So which of these first two theories is right? It turns out that both are right—up to a point. For place-theory research to be accurate, the basilar membrane has to vibrate unevenly—which it does when the frequency of the sound is *above* 1000 Hz. For the frequency theory to be correct, the neurons associated with the hair cells would have to fire as fast as the basilar membrane vibrates. This only works up to 1000 Hz, because neurons don't appear to fire at exactly the same time and rate when frequencies are faster than 1000 times per second.

The frequency theory works for low pitches, and place theory works for moderate to high pitches. Is there another explanation? Yes, and it is a third theory, developed by Ernest Wever and Charles Bray, called the **volley principle** (Wever, 1949; Wever & Bray, 1930), which appears to account for pitches from about 400 Hz up to about 4000. In this explanation, groups of auditory neurons take turns firing in a process called *volleying*. If a person hears a tone of about 3000 Hz, it means that three groups of neurons have taken turns sending the message to the brain—the first group for the first 1000 Hz, the second group for the next 1000 Hz, and so on.

TYPES OF HEARING IMPAIRMENTS

Hearing impairment is the term used to refer to difficulties in hearing. A person can be partially hearing impaired or totally hearing impaired, and the treatment for hearing loss will vary according to the reason for the impairment.

3.5 Why are some people unable to hear, and how can their hearing be improved?

CONDUCTION HEARING IMPAIRMENT *Conduction hearing impairment* means that sound vibrations cannot be passed from the eardrum to the cochlea. The cause might be a damaged eardrum or damage to the bones of the middle ear (usually from an infection). In this kind of impairment, hearing aids may be of some use in restoring hearing.

NERVE HEARING IMPAIRMENT In *nerve hearing impairment*, the problem lies either in the inner ear or in the auditory pathways and cortical areas of the brain. Normal aging causes

pitch psychological experience of sound that corresponds to the frequency of the sound waves; higher frequencies are perceived as higher pitches.

place theory theory of pitch that states that different pitches are experienced by the stimulation of hair cells in different locations on the organ of Corti.

frequency theory theory of pitch that states that pitch is related to the speed of vibrations in the basilar membrane.

volley principle theory of pitch that states that frequencies from about 400 Hz to 4000 Hz cause the hair cells (auditory neurons) to fire in a volley pattern, or take turns in firing.

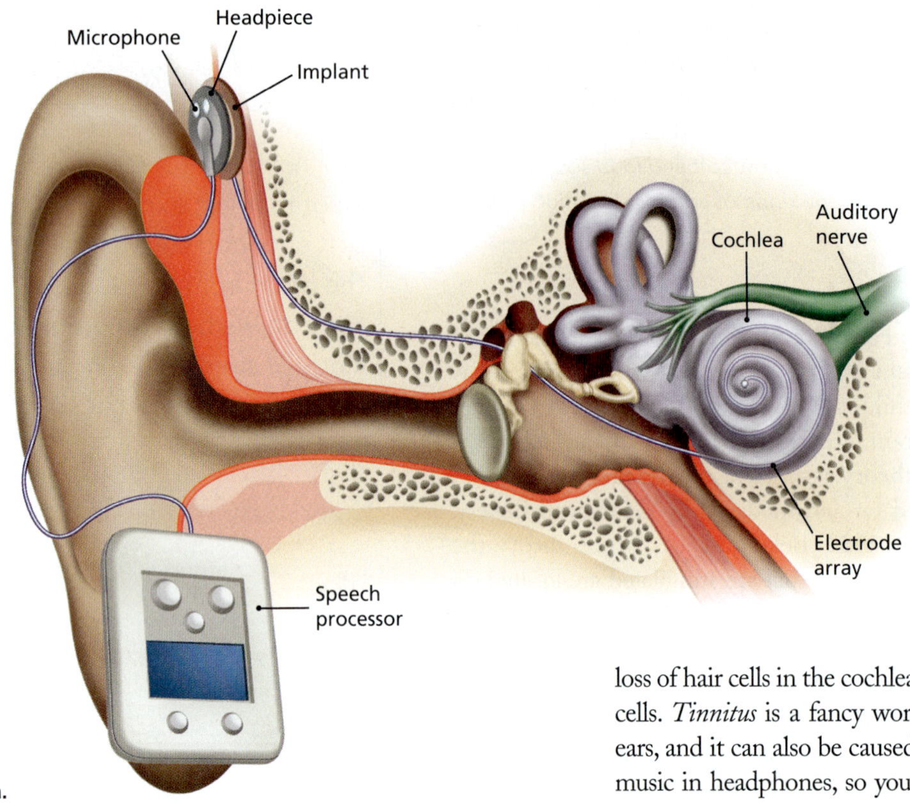

a.

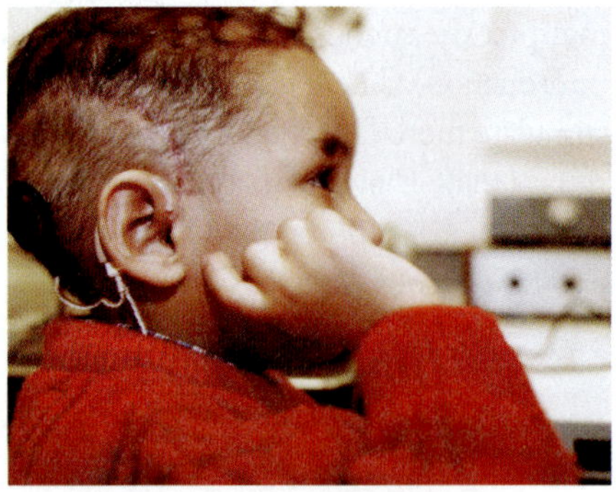

b.

Figure 3.9 Cochlear Implant

(a) In a cochlear implant, a microphone implanted just behind the ear picks up sound from the surrounding environment. A speech processor, attached to the implant and worn outside the body, selects and arranges the sound picked up by the microphone. The implant itself is a transmitter and receiver, converting the signals from the speech processor into electrical impulses that are collected by the electrode array in the cochlea and then sent to the brain. (b) This child is able to hear with the help of a cochlear implant. Hearing spoken language during the early years of a child's life helps in the development of the child's own speech.

Listen to the Psychology in the News podcast on cochlear implants on **mypsychlab.com**

loss of hair cells in the cochlea, and exposure to loud noises can damage hair cells. *Tinnitus* is a fancy word for an extremely annoying ringing in one's ears, and it can also be caused by infections or loud noises—including loud music in headphones, so you might want to turn down that music player!

Because the damage is to the nerves or the brain, nerve hearing impairment cannot be helped with ordinary hearing aids, which are basically sound amplifiers. A technique for restoring some hearing to those with nerve hearing impairment makes use of an electronic device called a *cochlear implant*. This device sends signals from a microphone worn behind the ear to a sound processor worn on the belt or in a pocket, which then translates those signals into electrical stimuli that are sent to a series of electrodes implanted directly into the cochlea, allowing transduction to take place and stimulating the auditory nerve. (See Figure 3.9.) The brain then processes the electrode information as sound. **Listen** on **mypsychlab.com**

CONCEPT MAP 3.4 3.5

The Hearing Sense

- **sound**
  - is a physical stimulus
    - composed of sound waves
      - have wavelengths and wavelike properties that can be measured
      - result of vibrations of air molecules
    - processed by the ear
      - **outer ear**
      - **middle ear**
      - **inner ear**
    - processing can be impaired
  - has psychological properties
    - **frequency** or **pitch** — shorter wavelengths = more waves per second = higher frequencies — theories of pitch perception
      - place theory
      - frequency theory
      - volley theory
    - **volume** — larger wave amplitudes associated with louder volume
    - **timbre** — increase in number of sounds results in greater richness

PRACTICE quiz How much do you remember? ANSWERS ON PAGE AK-1.

Pick the best answer.

1. Which of the following properties of sound would be the most similar to the color or hue of light?
   a. pitch
   b. loudness
   c. purity
   d. timbre
2. The eardrum is also called the ________.
   a. pinna.
   b. oval window.
   c. tympanic membrane.
   d. cochlea.
3. The ________ theory best explains how we hear sounds above 4000 Hz.
   a. place
   b. frequency
   c. volley
   d. adaptive
4. If the bones of the middle ear begin to deteriorate, you will develop ________ hearing impairment.
   a. nerve
   b. stimulation
   c. brain pathway
   d. conduction

Chemical Senses: It Tastes Good and Smells Even Better

3.6 How do the senses of taste and smell work, and how are they alike?

The sense of taste (taste in food, not taste in clothing or friends) and the sense of smell are very closely related. Have you ever noticed that when your nose is all stopped up, your sense of taste is affected, too? That's because the sense of taste is really a combination of taste and smell. Without the input from the nose, there are actually only four, and possibly five, kinds of taste sensors in the mouth.

GUSTATION: HOW WE TASTE THE WORLD

TASTE BUDS *Taste buds* are the common name for the taste receptor cells, special kinds of neurons found in the mouth that are responsible for the sense of taste, or **gustation**. Most taste buds are located on the tongue, but there are a few on the roof of the mouth, the cheeks, and under the tongue as well. How sensitive people are to various tastes depends on how many taste buds they have; some people have only around 500, whereas others have 20 times that number. The latter are called "supertasters" and need far less seasoning in their food than those with fewer taste buds (Bartoshuk, 1993).

So taste buds are those little bumps I can see when I look closely at my tongue?

So taste buds are those little bumps I can see when I look closely at my tongue?

No, those "bumps" are called *papillae*, and the taste buds line the walls of these papillae. (See Figure 3.10.)

Each taste bud has about 20 receptors that are very similar to the receptor sites on receiving neurons at the synapse. LINK to Chapter Two: The Biological Perspective, p. 52. In fact, the receptors on taste buds work exactly like receptor sites on neurons—they receive molecules of various substances that fit into the receptor like a key into a lock. Taste is often called a chemical sense because it works with the molecules of foods people eat in the same way the neural receptors work with neurotransmitters. When the molecules (dissolved in saliva) fit into the receptors, a signal is fired to the brain, which then interprets the taste sensation.

What happens to the taste buds when I burn my tongue? Do they repair themselves? I know when I have burned my tongue, I can't taste much for a while, but the taste comes back.

What happens to the taste buds when I burn my tongue? Do they repair themselves? I know when I have burned my tongue, I can't taste much for a while, but the taste comes back.

In general, the taste receptors get such a workout that they have to be replaced every 10 to 14 days (McLaughlin & Margolskee, 1994). And when the tongue is burned, the damaged cells no longer work. As time goes on, those cells get replaced and the taste sense comes back.

THE FIVE BASIC TASTES In 1916 a German psychologist named Hans Henning proposed that there are four primary tastes: sweet, sour, salty, and bitter. Lindemann (1996) supported the idea that there is a fifth kind of taste receptor that

gustation the sensation of a taste.

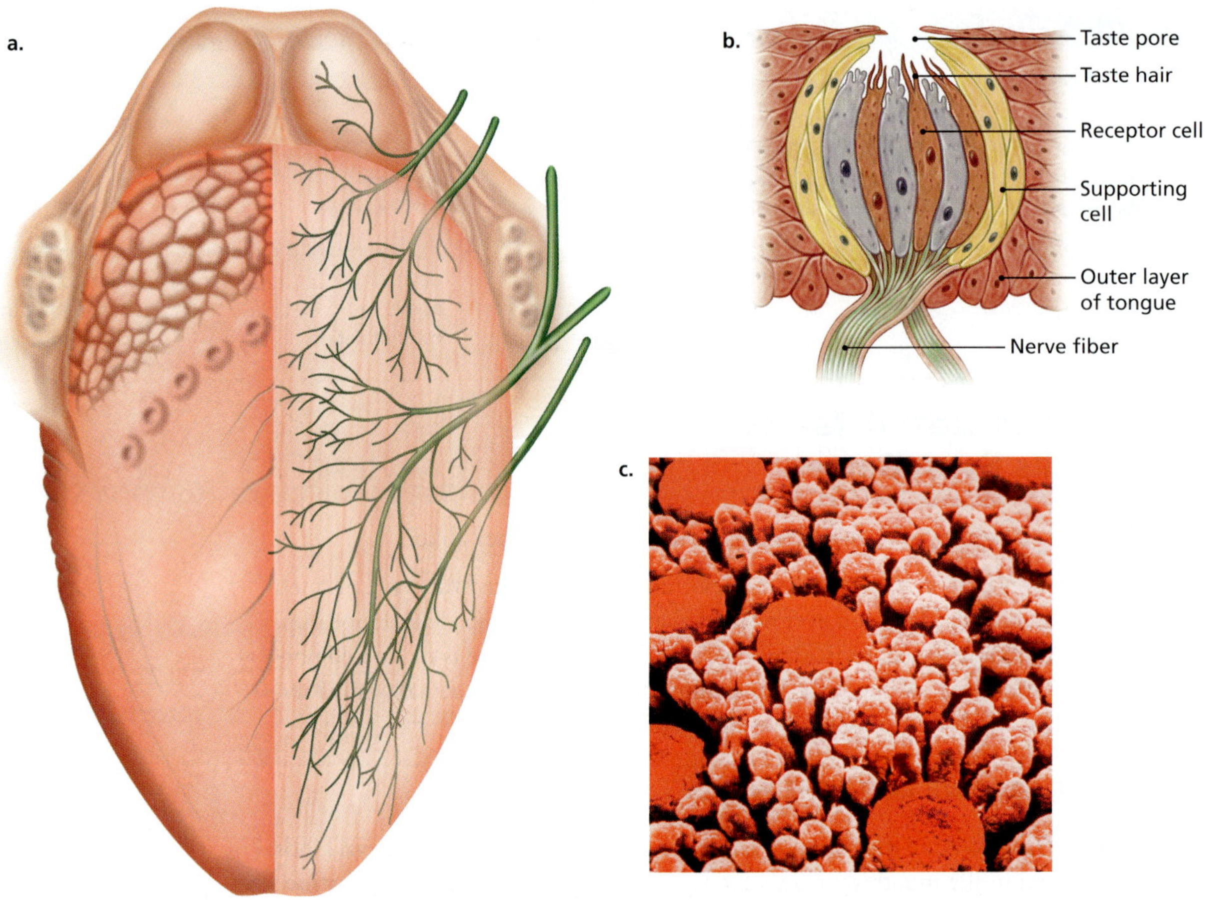

Figure 3.10 The Tongue and Taste Buds—A Crosscut View of the Tongue

(a) The right side of this drawing shows the nerves in the tongue's deep tissue. (b) The taste bud is located inside the papillae and is composed of small cells that send signals to the brain when stimulated by molecules of food. (c) Microphotograph of the surface of the tongue, showing two different sizes of papillae. The taste buds are located under the surface of the larger red papillae, whereas the smaller and more numerous papillae form a touch-sensitive rough surface that helps in chewing and moving food around the mouth.

detects a pleasant "brothy" taste associated with foods like chicken soup, tuna, kelp, cheese, and soy products, among others. Lindemann proposed that this fifth taste be called *umami*, a Japanese word first coined in 1908 by Dr. Kikunae Ikeda of Tokyo Imperial University to describe the taste. Dr. Ikeda had succeeded in isolating the substance in kelp that generated the sensation of umami—glutamate (Beyreuther et al., 2007). LINK to Chapter Two: The Biological Perspective, p. 53. Glutamate exists not only in the foods listed earlier, but is also present in human breast milk and is the reason that the seasoning MSG—monosodium *glutamate*—adds a pleasant flavor to foods.

The five taste sensations work together, along with the sense of smell and the texture, temperature, and "heat" of foods, to produce thousands of taste sensations. Although researchers used to believe that certain tastes were located on certain places on the tongue, it is now known that all of the taste sensations are processed all over the tongue (Bartoshuk, 1993).

Just as individuals and groups can vary on their food preferences, they can also vary on level of perceived sweetness. For example, obese individuals have been found to experience less sweetness than individuals who are not obese; foods that are both sweet and high in fat tend to be especially attractive to individuals who are obese (Bartoshuk et al., 2006). Such differences (as well as genetic variations like the supertasters) complicate direct comparison of food preferences. One possible solution is to have individuals rate taste in terms of an unrelated "standard" sensory experience of known intensity, such as the brightness of a light or loudness of a sound or preference in terms of all pleasurable experiences, and not just taste (Bartoshuk et al., 2005; Snyder & Bartoshuk, 2009).

Turning our attention back to how things taste for us as individuals, have you ever noticed that when you have a cold, food tastes very bland? Everything becomes bland or muted because you can taste only sweet, salty, bitter, sour, and umami—and because your nose is stuffed up with a cold, you don't get all the enhanced variations of those tastes that come from the sense of smell.

olfaction (olfactory sense) the sensation of smell.

THE SENSE OF SCENTS: OLFACTION

Like the sense of taste, the sense of smell is a chemical sense. The ability to smell odors is called **olfaction,** or the **olfactory sense**.

The outer part of the nose serves the same purpose for odors that the pinna and ear canal serve for sounds: Both are merely ways to collect the sensory information and get it to the part of the body that will translate it into neural signals.

The part of the olfactory system that transduces odors—turns odors into signals the brain can understand—is located at the top of the nasal passages. This area of olfactory receptor cells is only about an inch square in each cavity yet contains about 10 million olfactory receptors. (See Figure 3.11.)

OLFACTORY RECEPTOR CELLS The *olfactory receptor cells* each have about a half dozen to a dozen little "hairs," called *cilia*, that project into the cavity. Like taste buds, there are receptor sites on these hair cells that send signals to the brain when stimulated by the molecules of substances that are in the air moving past them.

Wait a minute—you mean that when I can smell something like a skunk, there are little particles of skunk odor IN my nose?

Wait a minute—you mean that when I can smell something like a skunk, there are little particles of skunk odor IN my nose?

Yes. When a person is sniffing something, the sniffing serves to move molecules of whatever the person is trying to smell into the nose and into the nasal cavities. That's okay when it's the smell of baking bread, apple pie, flowers, and the like, but when it's skunk, rotten eggs, dead animals—well, try not to think about it too much.

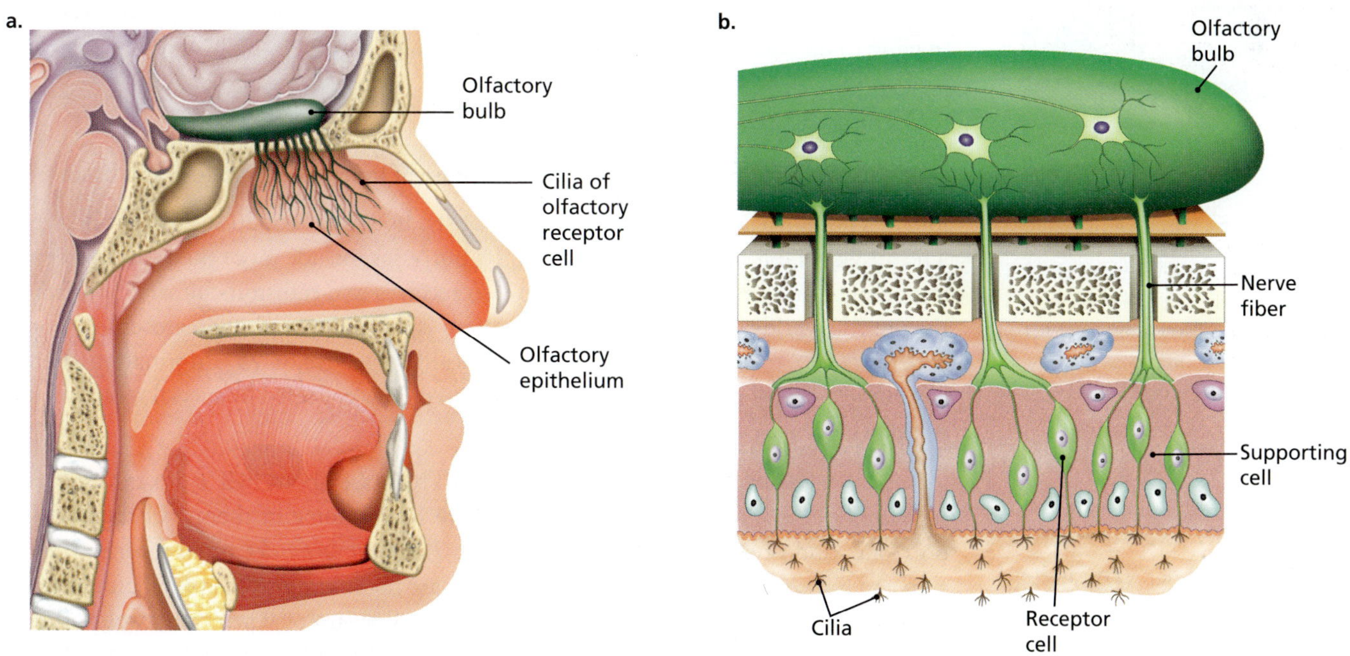

Figure 3.11 The Olfactory Receptors

(a) A cross section of the nose and mouth. This drawing shows the nerve fibers inside the nasal cavity that carry information about smell directly to the olfactory bulb just under the frontal lobe of the brain (shown in green). (b) A diagram of the cells in the nose that process smell. The olfactory bulb is on top. Notice the cilia, tiny hairlike cells that project into the nasal cavity. These are the receptors for the sense of smell.

olfactory bulbs areas of the brain located just above the sinus cavity and just below the frontal lobes that receive information from the olfactory receptor cells.

somesthetic senses the body senses consisting of the skin senses, the kinesthetic sense, and the vestibular senses.

skin senses the sensations of touch, pressure, temperature, and pain.

kinesthetic sense sense of the location of body parts in relation to the ground and each other.

vestibular senses the sensations of movement, balance, and body position.

Olfactory receptors are like taste buds in another way, too. Olfactory receptors also have to be replaced as they naturally die off, about every 5 to 8 weeks. Unlike the taste buds, there are way more than five types of olfactory receptors—in fact, there are at least 1,000 of them.

You might remember from Chapter Two that signals from the olfactory receptors in the nasal cavity do not follow the same path as the signals from all the other senses. Vision, hearing, taste, and touch all pass through the thalamus and then on to the area of the cortex that processes that particular sensory information. But the sense of smell has its own special place in the brain—the olfactory bulbs, which are actually part of the brain.

THE OLFACTORY BULBS The **olfactory bulbs** are located right on top of the sinus cavity on each side of the brain directly beneath the frontal lobes. (Refer back to Figure 3.11.) The olfactory receptors send their neural signals directly up to these bulbs, bypassing the thalamus, the relay center for all other sensory information. The olfactory information is then sent from the olfactory bulbs to higher cortical areas, including the primary olfactory cortex (the *piriform cortex*), the orbitofrontal cortex, and the amygdala (remember from Chapter Two that the orbitofrontal cortex and amygdala play important roles in emotion). LINK to Chapter Two: The Biological Perspective, pp. 72 and 76.

Her sense of touch is allowing this blind girl to "read" a Braille book with her fingers. The fingertips are extremely sensitive to fine differences in texture, allowing her to distinguish between small dots representing the different letters of the alphabet.

Somesthetic Senses: What the Body Knows

So far, this chapter has covered vision, hearing, taste, and smell. That leaves touch. What is thought of as the sense of touch is really several sensations, originating in several different places in—and on—the body. It's really more accurate to refer to these as the body senses, or **somesthetic senses**. The first part of that word, *soma*, means "body," as mentioned in Chapter Two. The second part, *esthetic*, means "feeling," hence, the name. There are three somesthetic sense systems, the **skin senses** (having to do with touch, pressure, temperature, and pain), the **kinesthetic sense** (having to do with the location of body parts in relation to each other), and the **vestibular senses** (having to do with movement and body position).

PERCEPTION OF TOUCH, PRESSURE, AND TEMPERATURE

3.7 What allows people to experience the sense of touch, pain, motion, and balance?

Here's a good trivia question: What organ of the body is about 20 square feet in size? The answer is the skin. Skin is an organ. Its purposes include more than simply keeping bodily fluids in and germs out; skin also receives and transmits information from the outside world to the central nervous system (specifically, to the somatosensory cortex). LINK to Chapter Two: The Biological Perspective, p. 75. Information about light touch, deeper pressure, hot, cold, and even pain is collected by special receptors in the skin's layers.

TYPES OF SENSORY RECEPTORS IN THE SKIN There are about half a dozen different receptors in the layers of the skin. (See Figure 3.12.) Some of them will respond to only one kind of sensation. For example, the *Pacinian corpuscles* are just beneath the skin and respond to changes in pressure. There are nerve endings that wrap around the ends of the hair follicles, a fact people may be well aware of when they tweeze their eyebrows, or when someone pulls their hair. These nerve endings are sensitive to both pain and touch. There are *free nerve endings* just beneath the uppermost layer of the skin that respond to changes in temperature and to pressure—and to pain.

How exactly does pain work? Why is it that sometimes I feel pain deep inside? Are there pain receptors there, too?

How exactly does pain work? Why is it that sometimes I feel pain deep inside? Are there pain receptors there, too?

Yes, there are pain nerve fibers in the internal organs as well as receptors for pressure. How else would people have a stomachache or intestinal* pain—or get that full feeling of pressure when they've eaten too much or their bladder is full?

There are actually different types of pain. There are receptors that detect pain (and pressure) in the organs, a type of pain called *visceral pain*. Pain sensations in the skin, muscles, tendons, and joints are carried on large nerve fibers and are called *somatic pain*. Somatic pain is the body's warning system that something is being, or is about to be, damaged and tends to be sharp and fast. Another type of somatic pain is carried on small nerve fibers and is slower and more of a general ache. This somatic pain acts as a kind of reminder system, keeping people from further injury by reminding them that the body has already been damaged. For example, if you hit your thumb with a hammer, the immediate pain sensation is of the first kind—sharp, fast, and bright. But later the bruised tissue simply aches, letting you know to take it easy on that thumb.

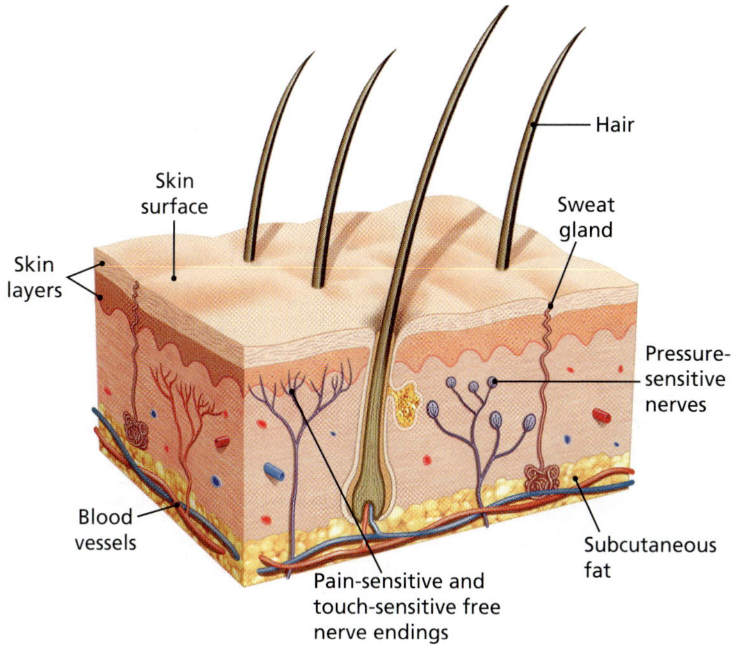

Figure 3.12 Cross Section of the Skin and Its Receptors

The skin is composed of several types of cells that process pain, pressure, and temperature. Some of these cells are wrapped around the ends of the hairs on the skin and are sensitive to touch on the hair itself, whereas others are located near the surface, and still others just under the top layer of tissue.

People may not like pain, but its function as a warning system is vitally important. There are people who are born without the ability to feel pain, rare conditions called *congenital analgesia* and *congenital insensitivity to pain with anhidrosis (CIPA)*. Children with these disorders cannot feel pain when they cut or scrape themselves, leading to an increased risk of infection when the cut goes untreated (Mogil, 1999). They fear nothing—which can be a horrifying trial for the parents and teachers of such a child. These disorders affect the neural pathways that carry pain, heat, and cold sensations. (Those with CIPA have an additional disruption in the body's heat–cold sensing perspiration system [anhidrosis], so that the person is unable to cool off the body by sweating.)

A condition called *phantom limb pain* occurs when a person who has had an arm or leg removed sometimes "feels" pain in the missing limb (Nikolajsen & Jensen, 2001; Woodhouse, 2005). As many as 50 to 80 percent of people who have had amputations experience various sensations: burning, shooting pains, or pins-and-needles sensations where the amputated limb used to be. Once believed to be a psychological problem, some now believe that it is caused by the traumatic injury to the nerves during amputation (Ephraim et al., 2005).

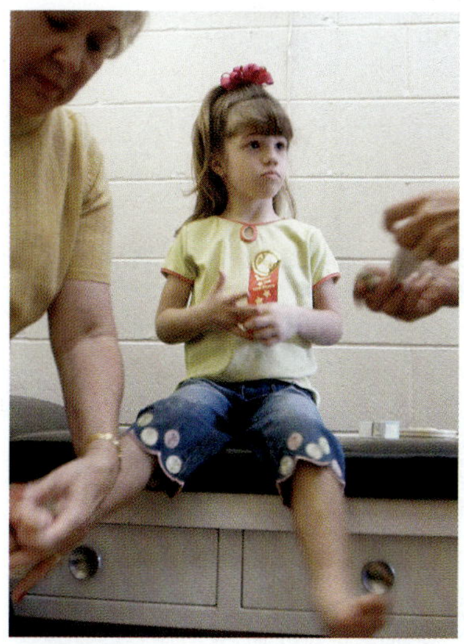

Congenital insensitivity to pain with anhidrosis (CIPA) is a rare genetic disorder that makes 5-year-old Ashlyn unable to feel pain. She must be examined carefully for scrapes and cuts after recess at school because she cannot feel when she hurts herself, putting her at risk for infection. What are some of the problems that Ashlyn and her parents may face as she grows older?

PAIN: GATE-CONTROL THEORY

The best current explanation for how the sensation of pain works is called *gate-control theory*, first proposed by Melzack and Wall (1965) and later refined and expanded (Melzack & Wall, 1996). In this theory, the pain signals must pass through a "gate" located in the spinal cord. The activity of the gate can be closed by nonpain signals coming into the spinal cord from the body and by signals coming from the brain. The gate is not a physical structure but instead represents the relative balance in neural activity of cells in the spinal cord that receive information from the body and then send information to the brain.

Stimulation of the pain receptor cells releases a chemical called *substance P* (for "pain," naturally). Substance P released into the spinal cord activates other neurons that send their messages through spinal gates (opened by the pain signal). From the

*intestinal: having to do with the tubes in the body that digest food and process waste material.

spinal cord, the message goes to the brain, activating cells in the thalamus, somatosensory cortex, areas of the frontal lobes, and the limbic system. The brain then interprets the pain information and sends signals that either open the spinal gates farther, causing a greater experience of pain, or close them, dampening the pain. Of course, this decision by the brain is influenced by the psychological aspects of the pain-causing stimulus. Anxiety, fear, and helplessness intensify pain, whereas laughter, distraction, and a sense of control can diminish it. (This is why people might bruise themselves and not know it if they were concentrating on something else.) Pain can also be affected by competing signals from other skin senses, which is why rubbing a sore spot can reduce the feeling of pain.

I've always heard that women are able to stand more pain than men. Is that true?

Those same psychological aspects can also influence the release of the *endorphins*, the body's natural version of morphine. LINK to Chapter Two: The Biological Perspective, p. 54. Endorphins can inhibit the transmission of pain signals in the brain, and in the spinal cord they can inhibit the release of substance.

I've always heard that women are able to stand more pain than men. Is that true?

On the contrary, research has shown that women apparently feel pain more intensely than do men, and they also report pain more often than men do (Chesterton et al., 2003; Faucett et al., 1994; Norrbrink et al., 2003). Men have been shown to cope better with many kinds of pain, possibly because men are often found to have a stronger belief than women that they can (or should) control their pain by their own efforts (Jackson et al., 2002).

THE KINESTHETIC SENSE

Special receptors located in the muscles, tendons, and joints are part of the body's sense of movement and position in space—the movement and location of the arms, legs, and so forth in relation to one another. This sense is called *kinesthesia*, from the Greek words *kinein* ("to move") and *aesthesis* ("sensation"). When you close your eyes and raise your hand above your head, you know where your hand is because these special receptors, called proprioceptors, tell you about joint movement or the muscles stretching or contracting.

If you have ever gotten sick from traveling in a moving vehicle, you might be tempted to blame these proprioceptors. Actually, it's not the proprioceptors in the body that make people get sick. The culprits are special structures in the ear that tell us about the position of the body in relation to the ground and movement of the head that make up the *vestibular sense*—the sense of balance.

This tightrope-walking violinist is performing an amazing feat of coordination and muscular control. He must not only use his vestibular organs to help maintain his balance, but also his kinesthetic sense to be aware of exactly where each foot is in relation to the rope.

THE VESTIBULAR SENSE

The name of this particular sense comes from a Latin word that means "entrance" or "chamber." The structures for this sense are located in the innermost chamber of the ear. There are two kinds of vestibular organs, the otolith organs and the semicircular canals.

The *otolith organs* are tiny sacs found just above the cochlea. These sacs contain a gelatin-like fluid within which tiny crystals are suspended (much like pieces of fruit in a bowl of Jello®). The head moves and the crystals cause the fluid to vibrate, setting off some tiny hairlike receptors on the inner surface of the sac, telling the person that he or she is moving forward, backward, sideways, or up and down. (It's pretty much the way the cochlea works but with movement being the stimulus instead of sound vibrations.)

The *semicircular canals* are three somewhat circular tubes that are also filled with fluid that will stimulate hairlike receptors when rotated. Having three tubes allows one to be located in each of the three planes of motion. Remember learning in geometry class about the *x*-, *y*-, and *z*-axes? Those are the three planes through which the body can rotate, and when it does, it sets off the receptors in these canals. When you spin around and then stop, the fluid in the horizontal canal is still rotating and will make you feel dizzy because your body is telling you that you are still moving, but your eyes are telling you that you have stopped.

MOTION SICKNESS This disagreement between what the eyes say and what the body says is pretty much what causes *motion sickness*, the tendency to get nauseated when in a moving vehicle, especially one with an irregular movement. Normally, the vestibular sense coordinates with the other senses. But for some people, the information from the eyes may conflict a little too much with the vestibular organs, and dizziness, nausea, and disorientation are the result. This explanation of motion sickness is known as **sensory conflict theory** (Oman, 1990; Reason & Brand, 1975). The dizziness is the most likely cause of the nausea. Many poisons make a person dizzy, and the most evolutionarily adaptive thing to do is to expel the poison. Even without any poison in a case of motion sickness, the nausea occurs anyway (Treisman, 1977).

One way some people overcome motion sickness is to focus on a distant point or object. This provides visual information to the person about how he or she is moving, bringing the sensory input into agreement with the visual input. This is also how ballerinas and ice skaters manage not to get sick when turning rapidly and repeatedly—they focus their eyes at least once on some fixed object every so many turns.

Astronauts, who travel in low gravity conditions, can get a related condition called space motion sickness (SMS). This affects about 60 percent of those who travel in space, typically for about the first week of space travel. After that time of adjustment, the astronauts are able to adapt and the symptoms diminish. Repeated exposure to some environment that causes motion sickness—whether it is space, a car, a train, or some other vehicle—is actually one of the best ways to overcome the symptoms (Hu & Stern, 1999).

sensory conflict theory an explanation of motion sickness in which the information from the eyes conflicts with the information from the vestibular senses, resulting in dizziness, nausea, and other physical discomfort.

3.6 3.7 CONCEPT MAP

Chemical Senses

- **smell/olfaction**
  - called a chemical sense because substance molecules are suspended in the air, carried to the nasal cavity, and fit into receptor sites
  - nose serves as a collection device
  - unique in that signals do not first travel to the thalamus before going to the brain
- **taste/gustation**
  - made possible largely through the role of taste buds (taste receptor cells)
  - five basic tastes (receptor types)
    - **sweet**
    - **sour**
    - **salty**
    - **bitter**
    - **unami**
  - called a chemical sense because food molecules dissolve in saliva, which then fits into receptor sites

Somesthetic Senses

- **skin senses** — processed by the skin
  - is an organ—receives and transmits information from the outside world to the somatosensory cortex of the brain
  - sensitive to touch, pressure, temperature — **pain**
- **kinesthetic sense** — processed by proprioceptors in skin, joints, muscles, and tendons
- **vestibular sense** — processed by vestibular organs
  - convey information about movement and body position
  - found in the inner ear
    - **otolith organs**
    - **semicircular canals**
  - responsible for motion sickness

(continued)

PRACTICE quiz How much do you remember? ANSWERS ON PAGE AK-1.

Pick the best answer.

1. The receptors on our taste buds work most like _________.
   a. receptors in the ears.
   b. receptors in the eyes.
   c. receptor sites on neurons.
   d. receptors in the skin.
2. Which of the following statements about olfactory receptors is FALSE?
   a. Olfactory receptors are replaced every few years.
   b. There are at least 1,000 types of olfactory receptors.
   c. Signals from the receptors go directly to the olfactory bulbs in the brain.
   d. Olfactory receptors have hairlike projections called cilia.
3. After some time has passed, you can no longer smell the odor of wet paint that you noticed when you first entered your classroom. Which is the most likely reason for this?
   a. The smell has gone away.
   b. You've adapted to the smell, even though it's still there.
   c. Your nose fell asleep.
   d. You fell asleep.
4. Pain sensations in the skin, muscles, tendons, and joints that are carried on large nerve fibers are called _________.
   a. visceral pain.
   b. somatic pain.
   c. referred pain.
   d. indigenous pain.
5. In gate-control theory, substance P _________.
   a. opens the spinal gates for pain.
   b. closes the spinal gates for pain.
   c. is unrelated to pain.
   d. is similar in function to endorphins.
6. A bowl of gelatin with fruit in it will wiggle more than if it contained no fruit. This is most similar to the way the _________ work.
   a. semicircular canals
   b. proprioceptors
   c. otolith organs
   d. both a and b

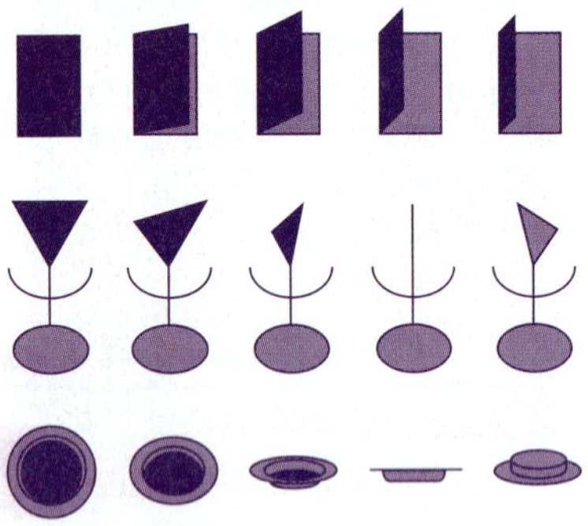

Figure 3.13 Shape Constancy
Three examples of shape constancy are shown here. The opening door is actually many different shapes, yet we still see it as basically a rectangular door. We do the same thing with a triangle and a circle—and, although when we look at them from different angles they cast differently shaped images on our retina, we experience them as a triangle and a circle because of shape constancy.

perception the method by which the sensations experienced at any given moment are interpreted and organized in some meaningful fashion.

size constancy the tendency to interpret an object as always being the same actual size, regardless of its distance.

shape constancy the tendency to interpret the shape of an object as being constant, even when its shape changes on the retina.

brightness constancy the tendency to perceive the apparent brightness of an object as the same even when the light conditions change.

The ABCs of Perception

3.8 What are perception and perceptual constancies?

Perception is the method by which the brain takes all the sensations people experience at any given moment and allows them to be interpreted in some meaningful fashion. Perception has some individuality to it. For example two people might be looking at a cloud and while one thinks it's shaped like a horse, the other thinks it's more like a cow. They both *see* the same cloud, but they *perceive* that cloud differently. As individual as perception might be, some similarities exist in how people perceive the world around them, as the following section will discuss.

THE CONSTANCIES: SIZE, SHAPE, AND BRIGHTNESS

One form of perceptual constancy* is **size constancy** the tendency to interpret an object as always being the same size, regardless of its distance from the viewer (or the size of the image it casts on the retina). So if an object that is normally perceived to be about 6 feet tall appears very small on the retina, it will be interpreted as being very far away.

Another perceptual constancy is the tendency to interpret the shape of an object as constant, even when it changes on the retina. This **shape constancy** is why a person still perceives a coin as a circle even if it is held at an angle that makes it appear to be an oval on the retina. Dinner plates on a table are also seen as round, even though from the angle of viewing they are oval. (See Figure 3.13.)

A third form of perceptual constancy is **brightness constancy**, the tendency to perceive the apparent brightness of an object as the same even when the light conditions change. If a person is wearing black pants and a white shirt, for example, in broad daylight the shirt will appear to be much brighter than the pants. But if the sun is covered by thick clouds, even though the pants and shirt have less light to reflect than previously, the shirt will still appear to be just as much brighter than the pants as before—because the different amount of light reflected from each piece of clothing is still the same difference as before (Zeki, 2001).

*constancy: something that remains the same, the property of remaining stable and unchanging.

THE GESTALT PRINCIPLES

Remember the discussion of the Gestalt theorists in Chapter One? Their original focus on human perception can still be seen in certain basic principles today, including the basic principles of the Gestalt tendency to group objects and perceive whole shapes.

3.9 What are the Gestalt principles of perception?

FIGURE–GROUND RELATIONSHIPS Take a look at the drawing of the cube in Figure 3.14. Which face of the cube is in the front? Look again—do the planes and corners of the cube seem to shift as you look at it?

This is called the "Necker cube." It has been around officially since 1832, when a Swiss scientist who was studying the structure of crystals first drew it in his published papers. The problem with this cube is that there are conflicting sets of depth cues, so the viewer is never really sure which plane or edge is in the back and which is in the front—the visual presentation of the cube seems to keep reversing its planes and edges.

A similar illusion can be seen in Figure 3.15. In this picture, the viewer can switch perception back and forth from two faces looking at each other to the outline of a goblet in the middle. Which is the figure in front and which is the background?

Figure–ground relationships refer to the tendency to perceive objects or figures as existing on a background. People seem to have a preference for picking out figures from backgrounds even as early as birth. The illusions in Figures 3.14 and 3.15 are **reversible figures**, in which the figure and the ground seem to switch back and forth.

PROXIMITY Another very simple rule of perception is the tendency to perceive objects that are close to one another as part of the same grouping, a principle called **proximity**, or "nearness." (See Figure 3.16.)

SIMILARITY **Similarity** refers to the tendency to perceive things that look similar as being part of the same group. When members of a sports team wear uniforms that are all the same color, it allows people viewing the game to perceive them as one group even when they are scattered around the field or court.

CLOSURE **Closure** is the tendency to complete figures that are incomplete. A talented artist can give the impression of an entire face with just a few cleverly placed strokes of the pen or brush—the viewers fill in the details.

CONTINUITY The principle of **continuity** is easier to see than it is to explain in words. It refers to the tendency to perceive things as simply as possible with a continuous pattern rather than with a complex, broken-up pattern. Look at Figure 3.16 for an example of continuity. Isn't it much easier to see the figure on the left as two wavy lines crossing each other than as the little sections in the diagrams to the right?

CONTIGUITY **Contiguity** isn't shown in Figure 3.16 because it involves not just nearness in space but nearness in time also. Basically, contiguity is the tendency to perceive two things that happen close together in time as being related. Usually the first occurring event is seen as causing the second event. Ventriloquists* make vocalizations without appearing to move their own mouths but move their dummy's mouth instead. The tendency to believe that the dummy is doing the talking is due largely to contiguity.

*ventriloquist: an entertainer who, through the use of misdirection and skill, makes other objects, such as a dummy, appear to talk.

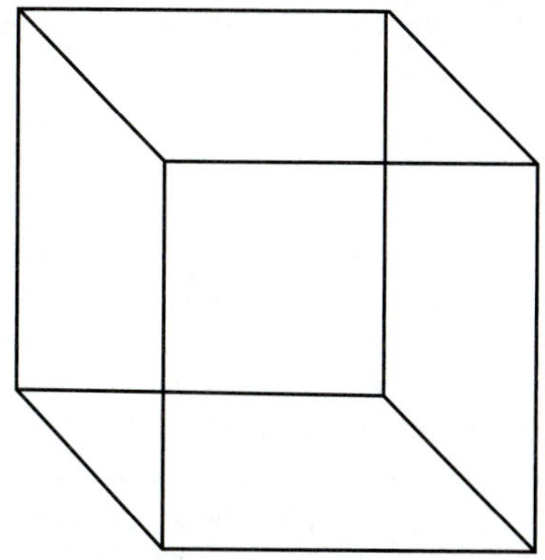

Figure 3.14 The Necker Cube
This is an example of a reversible figure. It can also be described as an ambiguous figure, since it is not clear which pattern should predominate.

Figure 3.15 Figure–Ground Illusion
What do you see when you look at this picture? Is it a wine goblet? Or two faces looking at each other? This is an example in which the figure and the ground seem to "switch" each time you look at the picture.

figure–ground the tendency to perceive objects, or figures, as existing on a background.

reversible figures visual illusions in which the figure and ground can be reversed.

proximity the tendency to perceive objects that are close to each other as part of the same grouping.

similarity the tendency to perceive things that look similar to each other as being part of the same group.

closure the tendency to complete figures that are incomplete.

continuity the tendency to perceive things as simply as possible with a continuous pattern rather than with a complex, broken-up pattern.

contiguity the tendency to perceive two things that happen close together in time as being related.

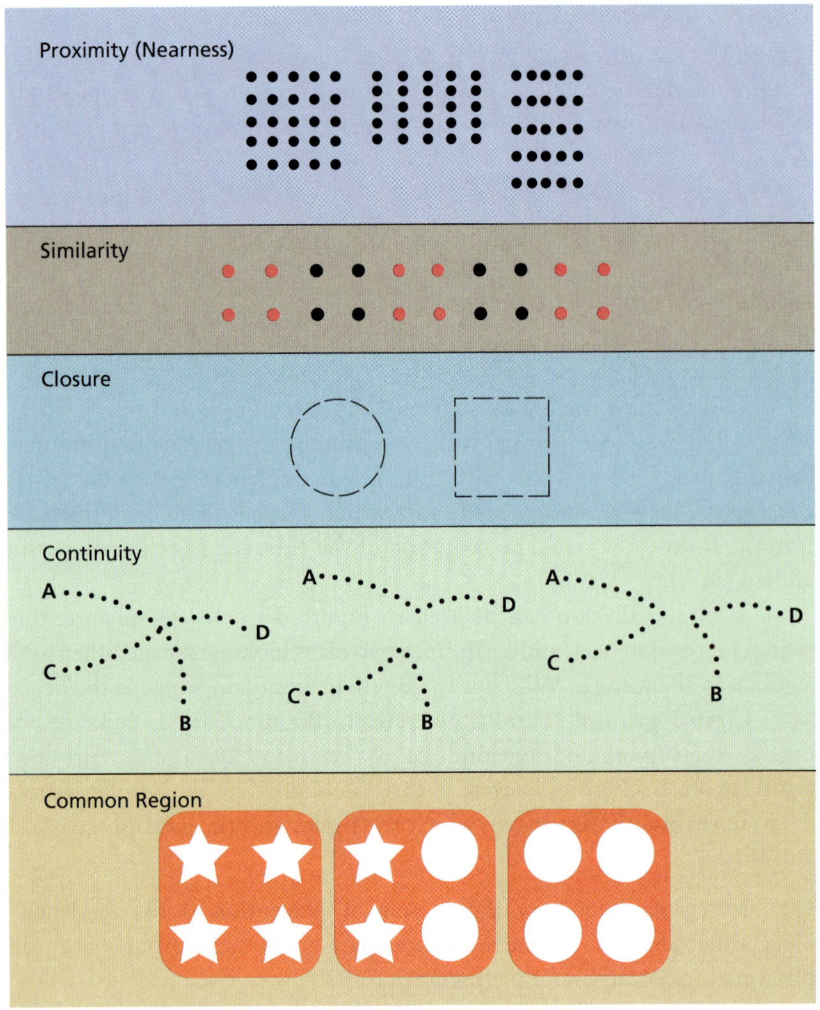

Figure 3.16 Gestalt Principles of Grouping

The Gestalt principles of grouping are shown here. These are the human tendency to organize isolated stimuli into groups on the basis of five characteristics: proximity, similarity, closure, continuity, and common region.

Proximity: The dots on the left can be seen as horizontal or vertical rows—neither organization dominates. But just by changing the proximity of certain dots, as in the other two examples, we experience the dots as vertical columns (middle) or horizontal rows (right).

Similarity: The similarity of color here makes you perceive these dots as forming black squares and color squares rather than two rows of black and colored dots.

Closure: Even though the lines are broken, we still see these figures as a circle and a square—an example of how we tend to "close" or "fill in" missing parts from what we know of the whole.

Continuity: Because of continuity, we are much more likely to see the figure on the left as being made up of two lines, A to B and C to D, than we are to see it as a figure made up of lines A to D and C to B or A to C and B to D.

Common Region: Similarity would suggest that people see two groups, stars and circles. But the colored backgrounds define a visible common region, and the tendency is to perceive three different groups.

There is one other principle of perceptual grouping that was not one of the original principles. It was added to the list (and can be seen at the bottom of Figure 3.16) by Stephen Palmer (Palmer, 1992). In *common region*, the tendency is to perceive objects that are in a common area or region as being in a group. In Figure 3.16, people could perceive the stars as one group and the circles as another on the basis of similarity. But the colored backgrounds so visibly define common regions that people instead perceive three groups—one of which has both stars and circles in it. **Listen** on **mypsychlab.com**

Listen to a podcast on Gestalt principles of perception on **mypsychlab.com**

DEPTH PERCEPTION

3.10 What is depth perception and what kind of cues are important for it to occur?

The capability to see the world in three dimensions is called **depth perception**. It's a handy ability because without it you would have a hard time judging how far away objects are. How early in life do humans develop depth perception? It seems to develop very early in infancy, if it is not actually present at birth. People who have had sight restored have almost no ability to perceive depth if they were blind from birth. Depth perception, like the constancies, seems to be present in infants at a very young age. LINK to Chapter Eight: Development Across the Life Span, pp. 310-311.

depth perception the ability to perceive the world in three dimensions.

a.

c.

b.

d.

Figure 3.17 Examples of Pictorial Depth Cues

(a) Both the lines of the trees and the sides of the road appear to come together or converge in the distance. This is an example of *linear perspective.* (b) Notice how the larger pebbles in the foreground seem to give way to smaller and smaller pebbles near the middle of the picture. *Texture gradient* causes the viewer to assume that as the texture of the pebbles gets finer, the pebbles are getting farther away. (c) In *aerial* or *atmospheric perspective,* the farther away something is the hazier it appears because of fine particles in the air between the viewer and the object. Notice that the road and farmhouse in the foreground are in sharp focus while the mountain ranges are hazy and indistinct. (d) The depth cue of *relative size* appears in this photograph. Notice that the flowers in the distance appear much smaller than those in the foreground. Relative size causes smaller objects to be perceived as farther away from the viewer.

Various cues exist for perceiving depth in the world. Some require the use of only one eye (**monocular cues**) and some are a result of the slightly different visual patterns that exist when the visual fields* of both eyes are used (**binocular cues**).

MONOCULAR CUES Monocular cues are often referred to as **pictorial depth cues** because artists can use these cues to give the illusion of depth to paintings and drawings. Examples of these cues are discussed next and can be seen in Figure 3.17.

1. **Linear perspective:** When looking down a long interstate highway, the two sides of the highway appear to merge together in the distance. This tendency for lines that are actually parallel to *seem* to converge** on each other is called **linear perspective**. It works in pictures because people assume that in the picture, as in real life, the converging lines indicate that the "ends" of the lines are a great distance away from where the people are as they view them.
2. **Relative size:** The principle of size constancy is at work in **relative size**, when objects that people expect to be of a certain size appear to be small and are, therefore, assumed to be much farther away. Movie makers use this principle to make their small models seem gigantic but off in the distance.

*visual field: the entire area of space visible at a given instant without moving the eyes.

**converge: come together.

monocular cues (pictorial depth cues) cues for perceiving depth based on one eye only.

binocular cues cues for perceiving depth based on both eyes.

linear perspective the tendency for parallel lines to appear to converge on each other.

relative size perception that occurs when objects that a person expects to be of a certain size appear to be small and are, therefore, assumed to be much farther away.

overlap (interposition) the assumption that an object that appears to be blocking part of another object is in front of the second object and closer to the viewer.

aerial (atmospheric) perspective the haziness that surrounds objects that are farther away from the viewer, causing the distance to be perceived as greater.

texture gradient the tendency for textured surfaces to appear to become smaller and finer as distance from the viewer increases.

motion parallax the perception of motion of objects in which close objects appear to move more quickly than objects that are farther away.

accommodation as a monocular cue, the brain's use of information about the changing thickness of the lens of the eye in response to looking at objects that are close or far away.

convergence the rotation of the two eyes in their sockets to focus on a single object, resulting in greater convergence for closer objects and lesser convergence if objects are distant.

3. **Overlap:** If one object seems to be blocking another object, people assume that the blocked object is behind the first one and, therefore, farther away. This cue is also known as **interposition**.
4. **Aerial (atmospheric) perspective:** The farther away an object is, the hazier the object will appear to be due to tiny particles of dust, dirt, and other pollutants in the air, a perceptual cue called **aerial (atmospheric) perspective.** This is why distant mountains often look fuzzy, and buildings far in the distance are blurrier than those that are close.
5. **Texture gradient:** If there are any large expanses of pebbles, rocks, or patterned roads (such as a cobblestone street) nearby, go take a look at them one day. The pebbles or bricks that are close to you are very distinctly textured, but as you look farther off into the distance, their texture becomes smaller and finer. **Texture gradient** is another trick used by artists to give the illusion of depth in a painting.
6. **Motion parallax:** The next time you're in a car, notice how the objects outside the car window seem to zip by very fast when they are close to the car, and objects in the distance, such as mountains, seem to move more slowly. This discrepancy in motion of near and far objects is called **motion parallax.**
7. **Accommodation:** A monocular cue that is not one of the pictorial cues, **accommodation** makes use of something that happens inside the eye. The lens of the human eye is flexible and held in place by a series of muscles. The discussion of the eye earlier in this chapter mentioned the process of visual accommodation as the tendency of the lens to change its shape, or thickness, in response to objects near or far away. The brain can use this information about accommodation as a cue for distance. Accommodation is also called a "muscular cue."

BINOCULAR CUES As the name suggests, these cues require the use of two eyes.

1. **Convergence:** Another muscular cue, **convergence**, refers to the rotation of the two eyes in their sockets to focus on a single object. If the object is close, the convergence is pretty great (almost as great as crossing the eyes). If the object is far, the convergence is much less. Hold your finger up in front of your nose, and then move it away and back again. That feeling you get in the muscles of your eyes is convergence. (See Figure 3.18, left.)

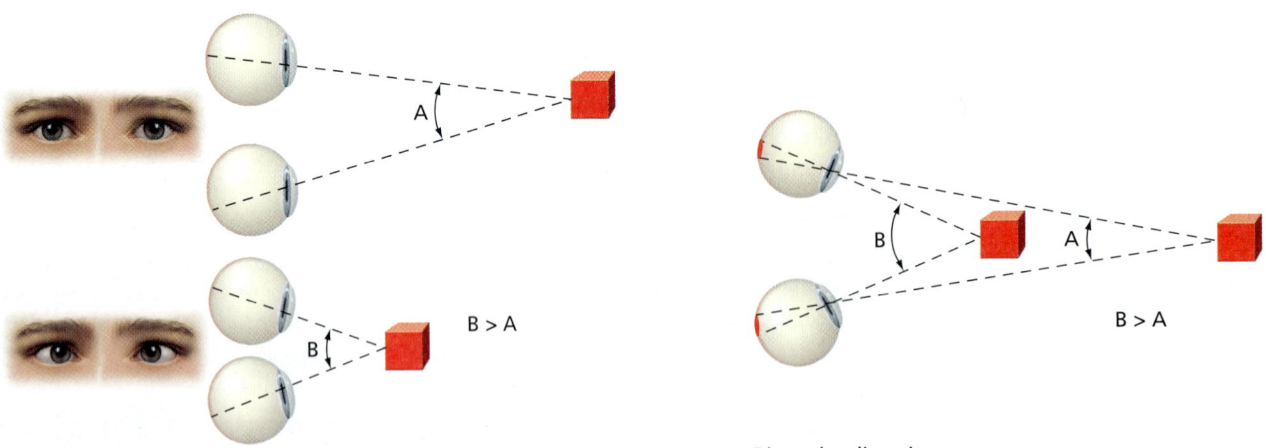

Convergence

Binocular disparity

Figure 3.18 Binocular Cues to Depth Perception

(left) Convergence is a depth cue that involves the muscles of the eyes. When objects are far away, the eye muscles are more relaxed; when objects are close, the eye muscles move together, or converge. (right) Binocular disparity. Because your eyes are separated by several centimeters, each eye sees a slightly different image of the object in front of you. In A, the object is far enough away that the difference is small. In B, while the object is closer, there is a greater difference between what each eye sees. The brain interprets this difference as the distance of the object.

2. **Binocular disparity: Binocular disparity** is a scientific way of saying that because the eyes are a few inches apart, they don't see exactly the same image. The brain interprets the images on the retina to determine distance from the eyes. If the two images are very different, the object must be pretty close. If they are almost identical, the object is far enough away to make the retinal disparity very small. You can demonstrate this cue for yourself by holding an object in front of your nose. Close one eye, note where the object is, and then open that eye and close the other. There should be quite a difference in views. But if you do the same thing with an object that is across the room, the image doesn't seem to "jump" or move nearly as much, if at all. (See Figure 3.18, right.)

binocular disparity the difference in images between the two eyes, which is greater for objects that are close and smaller for distant objects.

In spite of all the cues for perception that exist, even the most sophisticated perceiver can still fail to perceive the world as it actually is, as the next section demonstrates.

PERCEPTUAL ILLUSIONS

You've mentioned the word illusion *several times. Exactly what are illusions, and why is it so easy to be fooled by them?*

You've mentioned the word *illusion* several times. Exactly what are illusions, and why is it so easy to be fooled by them?

An *illusion* is a perception that does not correspond to reality: People *think* they see something when the reality is quite different. Another way of thinking of illusions is as visual stimuli that "fool" the eye. (Illusions are not hallucinations: an illusion is a distorted perception of something that is really there, but a hallucination originates in the brain, not in reality.)

3.11 What are visual illusions and how can they and other factors influence and alter perception?

Research involving illusions can be very useful for both psychologists and neuroscientists. These studies often provide valuable information about how the sensory receptors and sense organs work and how humans interpret sensory input.

Sometimes illusions are based on early sensory processes, subsequent processing, or higher level assumptions made by the brain's visual system (Eagleman, 2001; Macknik et al., 2008).

We've already discussed one visual illusion, color afterimages, which are due to opponent-processes in the retina or lateral geniculate nucleus (LGN) of the thalamus after light information has been detected by the rods and cones. Another postdetection, but still rather early, process has been offered for yet another illusion.

THE HERMANN GRID Look at the matrix of squares in Figure 3.19. Notice anything interesting as you look at different parts of the figure, particularly at the intersections of the white lines? You probably see gray blobs or diamonds that fade away or disappear completely when you try to look directly at them. This is the Hermann grid.

Figure 3.19 The Hermann Grid

Look at this matrix of squares. Do you notice anything interesting at the white intersections? What happens if you focus your vision directly on one of the intersections?

One explanation for this illusion is attributed to the responses of neurons in the primary visual cortex that respond best to bars of light of a specific orientation (Schiller & Carvey, 2005). Such neurons are called "simple cells" and were first discovered by David Hubel and Torsten Wiesel (Hubel & Wiesel, 1959). Hubel and Wiesel were later awarded the Nobel Prize for extensive work in the visual system. Other research into the Hermann grid illusion has documented that straight edges are necessary for

a. b.

Figure 3.20 The Müller-Lyer Illusion

(a) Which line is longer? In industrialized Western countries, people generally see the lines in part (a) in situations similar to those in part (b). According to one theory, people have become accustomed to seeing right angles in their environment and assume that the short, slanted lines are forming a right angle to the vertical line. They make that assumption because they are accustomed to seeing corners, such as the ones depicted in the house interiors shown on the right in part (b). Consequently, in part (a), they tend to perceive the line on the right as slightly longer than the line on the left.

this illusion to occur, as the illusion disappears when the edges of the grid lines are slightly curved, like a sine wave, and further suggests that the illusion may be due to a unique function of how our visual system processes information (Geier et al., 2008).

MÜLLER-LYER ILLUSION One of the most famous visual illusions, the **Müller-Lyer illusion**, is shown in Figure 3.20. The distortion happens when the viewer tries to determine if the two lines are exactly the same length. They are identical, but one line looks longer than the other. (It's always the line with the angles on the end facing outward.) Why is this illusion so powerful? The explanation is that most people live in a world with lots of buildings. Buildings have corners. When a person is outside a building, the corner of the building is close to that person, while the walls seem to be moving away (like the line with the angles facing inward). When the person is inside a building, the corner of the room seems to move away from the viewer while the walls are coming closer (like the line with the angles facing outward). In their minds, people "pull" the inward-facing angles toward them like the outside corners of a building, and they make the outward-facing angles "stretch" away from them like the inside corners of the room (Enns & Coren, 1995; Gregory, 1990).

Segall and colleagues (Segall et al., 1966) found that people in Western cultures, having carpentered buildings with lots of straight lines and corners (Segall and colleagues refer to this as a "carpentered world"), are far more susceptible to this illusion than people from non-Western cultures (having round huts with few corners—an "uncarpentered world"). Gregory (1990) found that Zulus, for example, rarely see this illusion. They live in round huts arranged in circles, use curved tools and toys, and experience few straight lines and corners in their world.

The moon illusion. When this moon is high in the night sky, it will still be the same size to the eye as it is now. Nevertheless, it is perceived to be much larger when on the horizon. In the sky, there are no objects for comparison, but on the horizon, objects such as this tree are seen as being in front of a very large moon.

THE MOON ILLUSION Another common illusion is the *moon illusion*, in which the moon on the horizon* appears to be much larger than the moon in the sky (Plug & Ross, 1994). One explanation for this is that the moon high in the sky is all alone, with no cues for depth surrounding it. But on the horizon, the moon appears behind trees and houses, cues for depth that make the horizon seem very far away. The moon is seen as being behind these objects and, therefore, farther away from the viewer. Because people know that objects that are farther away from them yet still appear large are very large indeed, they "magnify" the moon in their minds—a misapplication of the principle of size constancy. This explanation of the moon illusion is called the *apparent distance hypothesis*. This explanation goes back to the second century A.D., first written about by the Greek-Egyptian astronomer Ptolemy and later further developed by an eleventh-century Arab astronomer, Al-Hazan (Ross & Ross, 1976).

Müller-Lyer illusion illusion of line length that is distorted by inward-turning or outward-turning corners on the ends of the lines, causing lines of equal length to appear to be different.

*horizon: the place where the earth apparently meets the sky.

ILLUSIONS OF MOTION Sometimes people perceive an object as moving when it is actually still. One example of this takes place as part of a famous experiment in conformity called the *autokinetic effect*. In this effect, a small, stationary light in a darkened room will appear to move or drift because there are no surrounding cues to indicate that the light is *not* moving. Another is the *stroboscopic motion* seen in motion pictures, in which a rapid series of still pictures will seem to be in motion. Many a student has discovered that drawing little figures on the edges of a notebook and then flipping the pages quickly will also produce this same illusion of movement.

Another movement illusion related to stroboscopic motion is the *phi phenomenon*, in which lights turned on in sequence appear to move. For example, if a light is turned on in a darkened room and then turned off, and then another light a short distance away is flashed on and off, it will appear to be one light moving across that distance. This principle is used to suggest motion in many theater marquee signs, flashing arrows indicating direction that have a series of lights going on and off in a sequence, and even in strings of decorative lighting, such as the "chasing" lights seen on houses at holiday times.

What about seeing motion in static images? There are several examples, both classic and modern, of illusory movement or apparent motion being perceived in a static image. The debate about the causes for such illusions, whether they begin in the eyes or the brain, has been going on for at least 200 years (Troncoso et al., 2008).

Look at Figure 3.21. What do you see?

The "Rotating Snakes" illusion is one of many motion-illusion images designed by Dr. Akiyoshi Kitaoka. There have been a variety of explanations for this type of motion illusion, ranging from factors that depend on the image's luminance and/or the color arrangement, or possibly slight differences in the time it takes the brain to process this information. When fMRI and equipment used to track eye movements was used to investigate participants' perception of the illusion, researchers found that there was an increase in brain activity in a visual area sensitive to motion. However,

Figure 3.21 "Rotating Snakes"

Notice anything as you move your eyes over this image? The image is not moving; seeing the "snakes" rotate is due at least in part to movements of your eyes.

Created by and courtesy of Dr. Akiyoshi Kitaoka, Ritsumeikan University.

Figure 3.22 "Reinterpretation of Enigma"

As in Figure 3.21, the motion you see in this static image is because of movements of your eyes, this time due more to tiny movements called *microsaccades*.
Created by and courtesy of Jorge Otero-Millan, Martinez-Conde Laboratory, Barrow Neurological Institute.

this activity was greatest when accompanied by guided eye movements, suggesting eye movements play a significant role in the perception of the illusion (Kuriki et al., 2008).

Eye movements have also been found to be a primary cause for the illusory motion seen in images based on a 1981 painting by Isia Levant, *The Enigma*. Look at the center of Figure 3.22, notice anything within the green rings? Many people will see the rings start to "sparkle" or the rings rotating. Why does this occur? By using special eye-tracking equipment that allowed them to record even the smallest of eye movement, researchers found that tiny eye movements called *microsaccades*, discussed earlier in the chapter, are directly linked to the perception of motion in *Enigma* and are at least one possible cause of the illusion (Troncoso et al., 2008).

These two studies highlight some of the advances researchers have made in examining questions related to visual perception. For more information about the study of visual illusions as used in magic, and the study of such illusions from a neuroscientific perspective, see the Applying Psychology section at the end of the chapter.

The Ames Room illusion.

Simulate the concept of perceptual expectancy with an activity on ambiguous figures on **mypsychlab.com**

OTHER FACTORS THAT INFLUENCE PERCEPTION

Human perception of the world is obviously influenced by things such as culture and misinterpretations of cues. Following are other factors that cause people to alter their perceptions.

PERCEPTUAL SETS AND EXPECTANCIES People often misunderstand what is said to them because they were expecting to hear something else. People's tendency to perceive things a certain way because their previous experiences or expectations influence them is called **perceptual set** or **perceptual expectancy**. Although expectancies can be useful in interpreting certain stimuli, they can also lead people down the wrong path. For example, look at Figure 3.23. The drawing in the middle is a little hard to identify. People who look at these five drawings and start with the drawing on the far left (which is clearly a man's face) tend to see the middle drawing as a man's face. But people who begin looking from the far right (where the drawing is a kneeling woman with one arm over her chest and one touching her knee) see the middle picture as a woman. What you see depends on what you expect to see. Simulate on **mypsychlab.com**

The way in which people *interpret* what they perceive can also influence their perception. For example, people can try to understand what they perceive by using information they already have (as is the case of perceptual expectancy). But if there is no existing information that relates to the new information, they can look at each feature of what they perceive and try to put it all together into one whole.

Anyone who has ever worked on a jigsaw puzzle knows that it's a lot easier to put it together if there is a picture of the finished puzzle to refer to as a guide. It also helps to have worked the puzzle before—people who have done that already know what it's going to look like when it's finished. In the field of perception, this is known as **top-down processing**—the use of preexisting knowledge to organize individual features into a unified whole. This is also a form of perceptual expectancy.

perceptual set (perceptual expectancy) the tendency to perceive things a certain way because previous experiences or expectations influence those perceptions.

top-down processing the use of preexisting knowledge to organize individual features into a unified whole.

If the puzzle is one the person has never worked before or if that person has lost the top of the box with the picture on it, he or she would have to start with a small section, put it together, and keep building up the sections until the recognizable picture appears. This analysis of smaller features and building up to a complete perception is

Figure 3.23 Perceptual Set

Look at the drawing in the middle. What do you see? Now look at the drawings on each end. Would you have interpreted the middle drawing differently if you had looked at the drawing of the man's face or the sitting woman first?

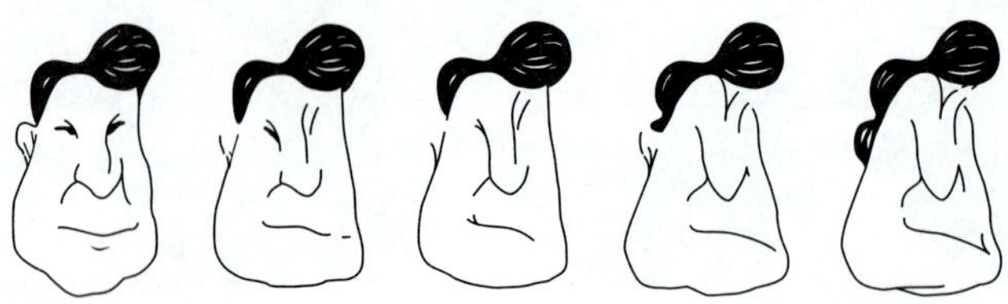

called **bottom-up processing** (Cave & Kim, 1999). In this case, there is no expectancy to help organize the perception, making bottom-up processing more difficult in some respects. Fortunately, the two types of processing are often used together in perceiving the surrounding world.

Would people of different cultures perceive objects differently because of different expectancies? Some research suggests that this is true. For example, take a look at Figure 3.24. This figure is often called the "devil's trident." Europeans and North Americans insist on making this figure three dimensional, so they have trouble looking at it—the figure is impossible if it is perceived in three dimensions. But people in less technologically oriented cultures have little difficulty with seeing or even reproducing this figure, because they see it as a two-dimensional drawing, quite literally a collection of lines and circles rather than a solid object (Deregowski, 1969). By contrast, if you give Europeans and North Americans the task of reproducing a drawing of an upside-down face, their drawings tend to be more accurate because the upside-down face has become a "collection of lines and circles." That is, they draw what they actually see in terms of light and shadow rather than what they "think" is there three dimensionally. **Explore** on **mypsychlab.com**

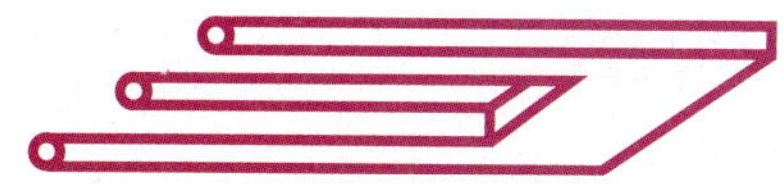

Figure 3.24 The Devil's Trident

At first glance, this seems to be an ordinary three-pronged figure. But a closer look reveals that the three prongs cannot be real as drawn. Follow the lines of the top prong to see what goes wrong.

bottom-up processing the analysis of the smaller features to build up to a complete perception.

Explore top down processing on **mypsychlab.com**

3.8 3.9 3.10 3.11 CONCEPT MAP

The ABCs of Perception

perception
- method by which the sensations experienced at any given moment are interpreted and organized in some meaningful fashion — has a subjective nature; no two people perceive the world in the exact same way
- may have unique features depending on sensory modality — e.g., vision — **depth perception**
  - ability to perceive the world in three dimensions
  - made possible by differential information from the eyes
- may not always be based on an accurate interpretation of the stimulus — **perceptual illusions**
  - an illusion is a perception that does not correspond to physical reality
  - can be caused by default mode of sensory or brain processing and perceptual sets or expectancies

PRACTICE quiz How much do you remember?

ANSWERS ON PAGE AK-1.

Pick the best answer.

1. The tendency to perceive a quarter as being round even when it is viewed at an angle is called _________.
   - a. size constancy.
   - b. shape constancy.
   - c. brightness constancy.
   - d. color constancy.
2. A reversible figure, such as the Necker cube, makes use of which principle of perception?
   - a. shape constancy
   - b. expectancy
   - c. figure–ground relationships
   - d. depth perception
3. Which of the following is NOT a monocular cue for depth?
   - a. convergence
   - b. linear perspective
   - c. overlap
   - d. texture gradient
4. An illusion _________.
   - a. is the same thing as a hallucination.
   - b. exists only in the brain cells of the viewer.
   - c. is a distorted perception of an actual stimulus.
   - d. corresponds directly to reality.
5. Ned found a decaying carcass lying on the beach one day. Looking at the size of the body (which had decomposed quite a bit), Ned decided that it was the body of a sea monster, something like the Loch Ness monster in Scotland. If we know that Ned loves to read about weird, mythical animals, we might expect that he has made an error of perception due to _________.
   - a. perceptual set.
   - b. perceptual defense.
   - c. bottom-up processing.
   - d. cognitive convergence.
6. The first time Joe had to put together a child's bicycle, it took a long time. But several bicycles later, he's a whiz at constructing them. His improved speed and skill can be attributed to _________.
   - a. bottom-up processing.
   - b. top-down processing.
   - c. perceptual expectancy.
   - d. perceptual set.

Applying Psychology to Everyday Life: Beyond "Smoke and Mirrors"—The Psychological Science and Neuroscience of Magic

Penn & Teller have performed together for over 30 years and have joined neuroscientists in the effort to gain insights into the brain mechanisms behind magical illusions.

Many people enjoy watching magic acts in person or on television. Perhaps you have been amazed by a Mindfreak® performed by Criss Angel or the performance and edgy antics of Penn & Teller. If you are one of those people, you likely witnessed a performance that included many various illusions. And like many of us, you probably wondered at some point in the performance, "How did they do that?!" Did you think the tricks were due to some type of special device (such as a fake thumb tip for hiding a scarf), or perhaps they were accomplished with "smoke and mirrors," or maybe the magician distracted the audience with one movement while actually doing something else to pull off the illusion? Magicians use many techniques to take advantage of, or manipulate, our actual level of awareness of what is happening right in front of us or perhaps to manipulate our attention.

Though magic is not a new topic of interest in psychology, there has been renewed interest in recent years, especially in the neuroscientific study of magic. This view suggests that researchers can work alongside magicians so we may be able to gain a better understanding of various cognitive and perceptual processes by not only examining the sensory or physical mechanics behind magic tricks, or even the psychological explanations, but to look further by examining what is happening in the brain (Macknik & Martinez-Conde, 2009).

Dr. Stephen L. Macknik and Dr. Susanna Martinez-Conde of the Barrow Neurological Institute are two neuroscientists who have teamed up with professional magicians to study their techniques and tricks in the effort to better understand the brain mechanisms underlying the illusions and how that information can be used by researchers in the laboratory. They have identified several types of illusions that can be used alone or in combination with others to serve as a basis for various magic tricks; two of these are visual illusions and cognitive illusions (Macknik et al., 2008).

As discussed earlier in the chapter, visual illusions occur when our individual perception does not match a physical stimulus. These illusions are caused by organizational or processing biases in the brain. Furthermore, our brain activity from the perception does not directly match the brain activity associated with the physical stimulus (Macknik et al., 2008). One example Dr. Macknik and Dr. Martinez-Conde point out is similar to a trick you may have performed yourself in grade school. Did you ever take a pencil or pen, grasp it in the middle, and then shake or wiggle it up and down? If you did it correctly, the pen or pencil would appear to bend or be made of rubber. Magicians use this illusion when they "bend" solid objects, such as spoons. So what is the brain explanation? We have special neurons in the visual cortex that are sensitive to both motion and edges called *end-stopped neurons*. These neurons respond differently if an object is bouncing or moving up and down quickly, causing us to perceive a solid spoon or pencil as if it is bending.

Another effect or trick that is based on the functioning of our visual system is when a magician makes an object disappear, such as a ball vanishing into the air or perhaps the outfit of an assistant changing suddenly. By showing the audience the target object, such as the ball or outfit, and then removing it very quickly from the visual field, the *persistence of vision* effect will make it appear that the object is still there. This is due to a response in vision neurons called the after-discharge, which will create an afterimage that lasts for up to 100 milliseconds after a stimulus is removed (Macknik et al., 2008). Again, you may have performed a similar trick if you have ever taken a lit sparkler or flashlight and twirled it around quickly to make a trail of light in the dark. Read on mypsychlab.com

Read and learn more about the science of magic on mypsychlab.com

Questions for Further Discussion

1. The examples highlighted in this discussion are based on visual illusions; can you think of a magic trick or performance that may have been based on an illusion in a different sensory modality?
2. Of the neuroimaging methods covered in Chapter Two, which methods might be best for examining the brain activity of someone who is watching a magic performance? Why?

chapter summary

Listen on **mypsychlab.com** Listen to an audio file of your chapter **www.mypsychlab.com**

The ABCs of Sensation

3.1 How does sensation travel through the central nervous system, and why are some sensations ignored?

- Sensation is the activation of receptors located in the eyes, ears, skin, nasal cavities, and tongue.
- Sensory receptors are specialized forms of neurons that are activated by different stimuli such as light and sound.
- A just noticeable difference is the point at which a stimulus is detectable half the time it is present.
- Weber's law of just noticeable differences states that the just noticeable difference between two stimuli is always a constant.
- Absolute thresholds are the smallest amount of energy needed for conscious detection of a stimulus at least half the time it is present.
- Subliminal stimuli are stimuli presented just below the level of conscious awareness and subliminal perception has been demonstrated in the laboratory. It has not been shown to be effective in advertising.
- Habituation occurs when the brain ignores a constant stimulus.
- Sensory adaptation occurs when the sensory receptors stop responding to a constant stimulus.

The Science of Seeing

3.2 What is light, and how does it travel through the various parts of the eye?

- Brightness corresponds to the amplitude of light waves, whereas color corresponds to the length of the light waves.
- Saturation is the psychological interpretation of wavelengths that are all the same (highly saturated) or varying (less saturated).
- Light enters the eye and is focused through the cornea, passes through the aqueous humor, and then through the hole in the iris muscle called the pupil.
- The lens also focuses the light on the retina, where it passes through ganglion and bipolar cells to stimulate the rods and cones.

3.3 How do the eyes see, and how do the eyes see different colors?

- Rods detect changes in brightness but do not see color and function best in low levels of light. They do not respond to different colors and are found everywhere in the retina except the center, or fovea.
- Cones are sensitive to colors and work best in bright light. They are responsible for the sharpness of visual information and are found in the fovea.
- Trichromatic theory of color perception assumes three types of cones: red, green, and blue. All colors would be perceived as combinations of these three.
- Opponent-process theory of color perception assumes four primary colors of red, green, blue, and yellow. Colors are arranged in pairs, and when one member of a pair is activated, the other is not.
- Color blindness is a total lack of color perception whereas color-deficient vision refers to color perception that is limited primarily to yellows and blues or reds and greens only.

The Hearing Sense: Can You Hear Me Now?

3.4 What is sound, and how does it travel through the various parts of the ear?

- Sound has three aspects: pitch (frequency), loudness, and timbre (purity).
- Sound enters the ear through the visible outer structure, or pinna, and travels to the eardrum and then to the small bones of the middle ear.
- The bone called the stirrup rests on the oval window, causing the cochlea and basilar membrane to vibrate with sound.
- The organ of Corti on the basilar membrane contains the auditory receptors, which send signals to the brain about sound qualities as they vibrate.
- Place theory states that the location of the hair cells on the organ of Corti correspond to different pitches of sound. This can explain pitch above 1000 Hz.
- Frequency theory states that the speed with which the basilar membrane vibrates corresponds to different pitches of sound. This can explain pitch below 1000 Hz.
- The volley principle states that neurons take turns firing for sounds above 400 Hz and below 4000 Hz.

3.5 Why are some people unable to hear, and how can their hearing be improved?

- Conduction hearing impairment is caused by damage to the outer or middle ear structures, whereas nerve hearing impairment is caused by damage to the inner ear or auditory pathways in the brain.

Chemical Senses: It Tastes Good and Smells Even Better

3.6 How do the senses of taste and smell work, and how are they alike?

- Gustation is the sense of taste. Taste buds in the tongue receive molecules of substances, which fit into receptor sites.
- The five basic types of taste are sweet, sour, salty, bitter, and umami (brothy).
- Olfaction is the sense of smell. The olfactory receptors in the upper part of the nasal passages receive molecules of substances and create neural signals that then go to the olfactory bulbs under the frontal lobes.

Somesthetic Senses: What the Body Knows

- The somesthetic senses include the skin senses and the vestibular senses.

3.7 What allows people to experience the sense of touch, pain, motion, and balance?

- Pacinian corpuscles respond to pressure, certain nerve endings around hair follicles respond to pain and pressure, and free nerve endings respond to pain, pressure, and temperature.
- The gate-control theory of pain states that when receptors sensitive to pain are stimulated, a neurotransmitter called substance P is released into the spinal cord, activating other pain receptors by opening "gates" in the spinal column and sending the message to the brain.
- The kinesthetic senses allow the brain to know the position and movement of the body through the activity of special receptors responsive to movement of the joints and limbs.
- The vestibular sense also contributes to the body's sense of spatial orientation and movement through the activity of the otolith organs (up-and-down movement) and the semicircular canals (movement through arcs).
- Motion sickness is explained by sensory conflict theory, in which information from the eyes conflicts with information from the vestibular sense, causing nausea.

The ABCs of Perception

3.8 What are perception and perceptual constancies?

- Perception is the interpretation and organization of sensations.
- Size constancy is the tendency to perceive objects as always being the same size, no matter how close or far away they are.
- Shape constancy is the tendency to perceive objects as remaining the same shape even when the shape of the object changes on the retina of the eye.
- Brightness constancy is the tendency to perceive objects as a certain level of brightness, even when the light changes.

3.9 What are the Gestalt principles of perception?

- The Gestalt psychologists developed several principles of perception that involve interpreting patterns in visual stimuli. The principles are figure–ground relationships, closure, similarity, continuity, contiguity, and common region.

3.10 What is depth perception, and what kind of cues are important for it to occur?

- Depth perception is the ability to see in three dimensions.
- Monocular cues for depth perception include linear perspective, relative size, overlap, aerial (atmospheric) perspective, texture gradient, motion parallax, and accommodation.
- Binocular cues for depth perception include convergence and binocular overlap.

3.11 What are visual illusions and how can they and other factors influence and alter perception?

- Illusions are perceptions that do not correspond to reality or are distortions of visual stimuli.
- Perceptual set or expectancy refers to the tendency to perceive objects and situations in a particular way because of prior experiences.
- Top-down processing involves the use of preexisting knowledge to organize individual features into a unified whole.
- Bottom-up processing involves the analysis of smaller features, building up to a complete perception.

Applying Psychology to Everyday Life: Beyond "Smoke and Mirrors"—The Psychological Science and Neuroscience of Magic

- Magicians take advantage of some well-known properties of our visual system to accomplish a variety of magic tricks.
- By collaborating with magicians, psychologists and neuroscientists can learn more about magic and the brain processes responsible for our perception of magic tricks.

test YOURSELF

ANSWERS ON PAGE AK-1.

Study and Review on **mypsychlab.com** Ready for your test? More quizzes and a customized plan. **www.mypsychlab.com**

Pick the best answer.

1. You find that you have to add 1 teaspoon of sugar to a cup of coffee that already has 5 teaspoons of sugar in it to notice the difference in sweetness. If you have a cup of coffee with 10 teaspoons of sugar in it, how many teaspoons would you have to add to notice the difference in sweetness at least half the time?
   a. 1 **c.** 4
   b. 2 **d.** 5
2. The process by which the brain stops attending to constant, unchanging information is called:
   a. adaptation **c.** habituation
   b. sensation **d.** accomodation
3. Which of the following terms refers to the psychological effect of the length of light waves?
   a. color **c.** pitch
   b. brightness **d.** amplitude

4. Which of the following is responsible for controlling how much light enters the eye?
   a. cornea
   b. lens
   c. retina
   d. iris

5. Which type of retinal cell forms the optic nerve?
   a. rods
   b. cones
   c. ganglion cells
   d. bipolar cells

6. Which type of retinal cell plays a role in color vision?
   a. rods
   b. cones
   c. ganglion cells
   d. bipolar cells

7. Which set of colors are the primary colors when mixing light?
   a. red, yellow, and blue
   b. red, blue, and green
   c. blue, green, and yellow
   d. red, green, and yellow

8. Which of the following properties of sound would be the most similar to the brightness of light?
   a. pitch
   b. loudness
   c. purity
   d. timbre

9. The thin membrane stretched over the opening to the inner ear is the _________.
   a. pinna.
   b. oval window.
   c. tympanic membrane.
   d. cochlea.

10. The _________ theory appears to account for how we hear sounds between 400 and 4000 Hz.
    a. wave
    b. frequency
    c. volley
    d. adaptive

11. If a severe ear infection damages the bones of the middle ear, you may develop _________ hearing impairment.
    a. nerve
    b. stimulation
    c. brain pathway
    d. conduction

12. The sense of taste is closely related to the sense of _________.
    a. sight.
    b. hearing.
    c. smell.
    d. touch.

13. The "bumps" on the tongue that are visible to the eye are the _________.
    a. taste buds.
    b. papillae.
    c. taste receptors.
    d. olfactory receptors.

14. The olfactory receptor cells are located in the _________.
    a. tops of the nasal passages.
    b. auditory passages.
    c. roof of the mouth.
    d. lining of the outer nose.

15. Which of the following statements about olfactory receptors is TRUE?
    a. Olfactory receptors are replaced every 5 to 8 weeks.
    b. There are fewer than 50 types of olfactory receptors.
    c. Signals from the receptors go through the brain stem and then to the cortex.
    d. Olfactory receptors respond to pressure.

16. In the spinal cord, _________ inhibit(s) the release of substance P.
    a. hormones
    b. serotonin
    c. norepinephrine
    d. endorphins

17. We know when we are moving up and down in an elevator because of the movement of tiny crystals in the _________.
    a. outer ear.
    b. inner ear.
    c. otolith organs.
    d. middle ear.

18. Ellis turns around and around in a circle. When he stops, he feels like his head is still spinning. What is responsible for this sensation?
    a. semicircular canals
    b. proprioceptors
    c. otolith organs
    d. otolith crystals

19. An old comedy routine on television had a character who would line up the heads of people who were very far away from him between his fingers. Then he would pinch his fingers together and say gleefully, "I'm crushing your head, I'm crushing your head." The comedian was playing around with which perceptual constancy?
    a. size constancy
    b. shape constancy
    c. brightness constancy
    d. color constancy

20. Which Gestalt principle is at work when a ventriloquist moves the dummy's mouth while doing the talking, making it seem like the dummy is talking?
    a. closure
    b. similarity
    c. contiguity
    d. continuity

21. Which of the following is occurring when looking down a set of railroad tracks, they appear to merge together in the distance?
    a. convergence
    b. linear perspective
    c. overlap
    d. texture gradient

22. The Müller-Lyer illusion exists in cultures in which there are _________.
    a. more men than women.
    b. more women than men.
    c. lots of trees.
    d. buildings with lots of corners.

23. Allison opened her new jigsaw puzzle but soon realized that the puzzle pieces inside had nothing to do with the picture on the box. With no picture to go by, she realized she would have to use _________.
    a. bottom-up processing.
    b. top-down processing.
    c. perceptual expectancy.
    d. perceptual set.

24. Juan just attended a terrific magic show. In one of the tricks, the magician made a ball disappear that had just been in plain sight. Which aspect of our visual system likely allowed the magician to accomplish this illusion?
    a. lateral inhibition
    b. microsaccades of the eyes
    c. persistence of vision
    d. achromatopsia

3 sensation and perception

3.1 p. 92

The ABCs of Sensation

- **sensation**
  process by which information from the outside world enters the brain
  - related to the activation of receptors in the various sense organs
  - related to changes in physical stimuli

3.2 3.3 p. 100

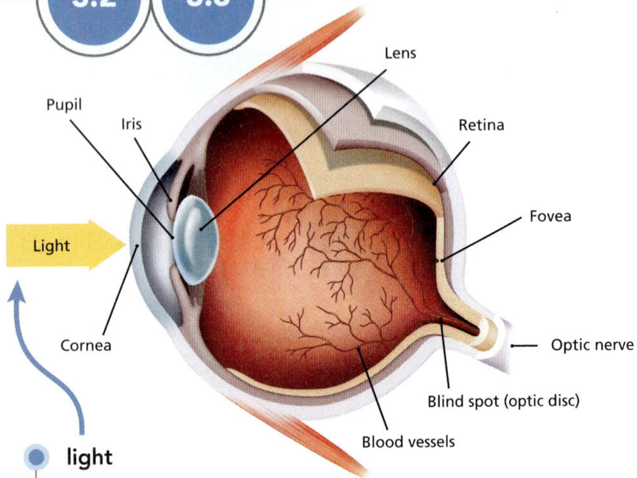

- **light**
  - is a physical stimulus
    - is a form of electromagnetic radiation
    - processed by the eye
  - has psychological properties
    - brightness
    - color/hue
    - saturation

The Science of Seeing

- **seeing**
  - begins with retinal receptor cells
    - rods
    - cones

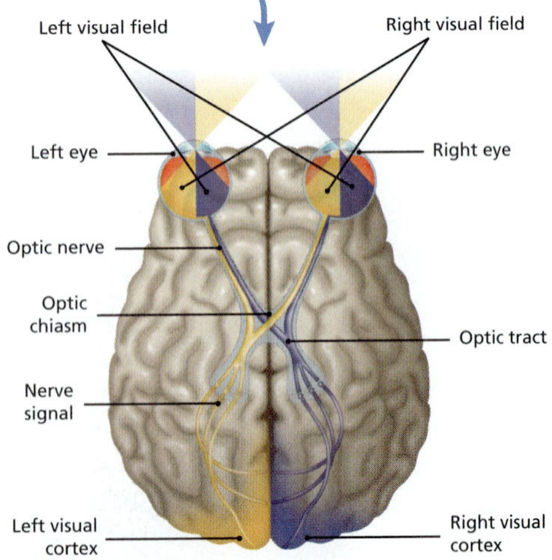

3.4 3.5 p. 104

- **sound**
  - is a physical stimulus
    - composed of sound waves
    - processed by the ear
    - processing can be impaired
  - has psychological properties
    - **frequency** or **pitch**
    - **volume**
    - **timbre**

The Hearing Sense

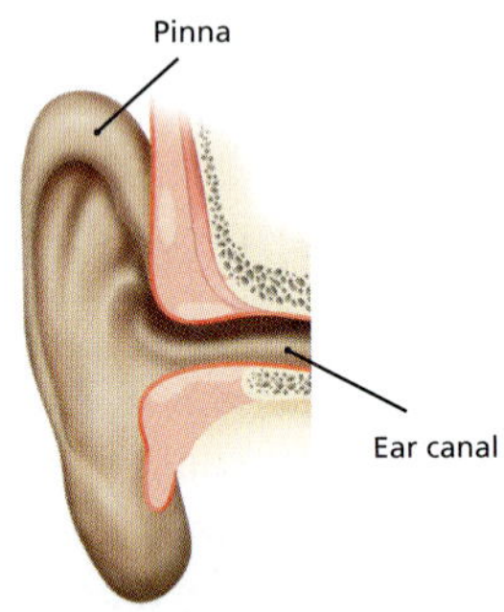

outer ear

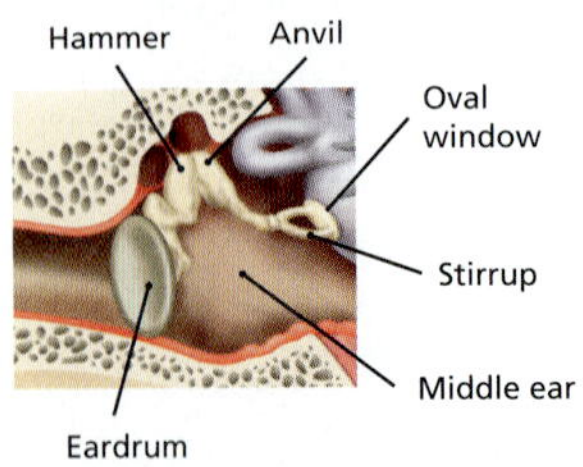

middle ear

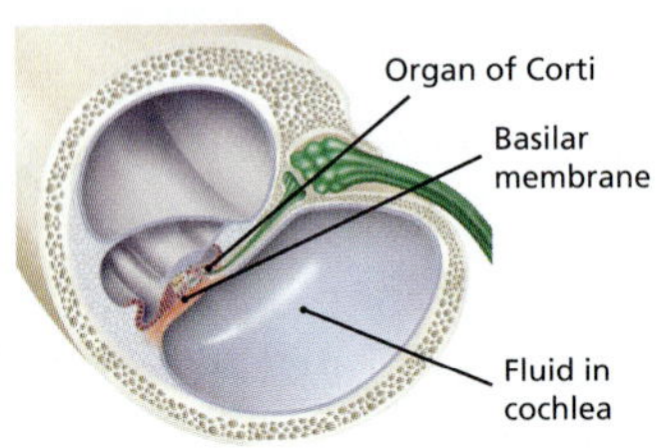

inner ear

3.6 p. 111

Chemical Senses

- **smell/olfaction**
  - called a chemical sense because substance molecules are suspended in the air, carried to the nasal cavity, and fit into receptor sites
  - nose serves as a collection device
  - unique in that signals do not first travel to the thalamus before going to the brain

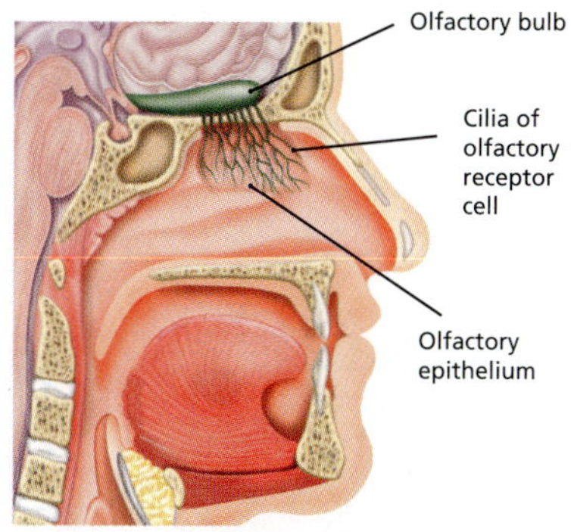

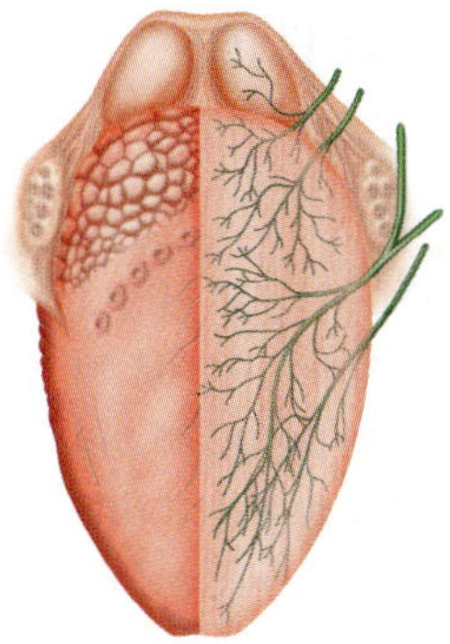

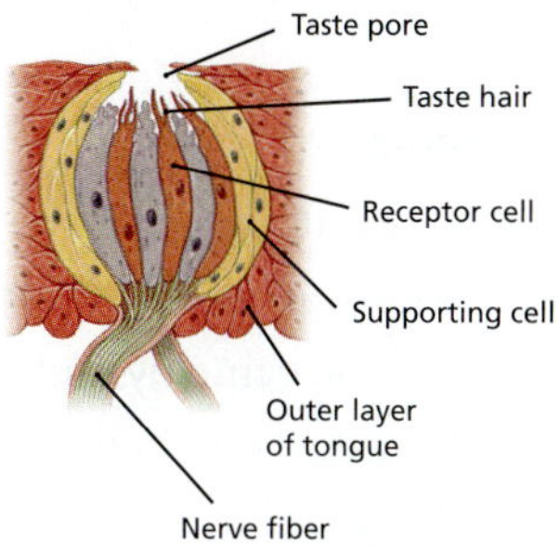

- **taste/gustation**
  - made possible largely through the role of taste buds (taste receptor cells)
  - five basic tastes (receptor types)
  - called a chemical sense because food molecules dissolve in saliva, which then fits into receptor sites

3.7 p. 111

Somesthetic Senses

- **skin senses** — processed by the skin

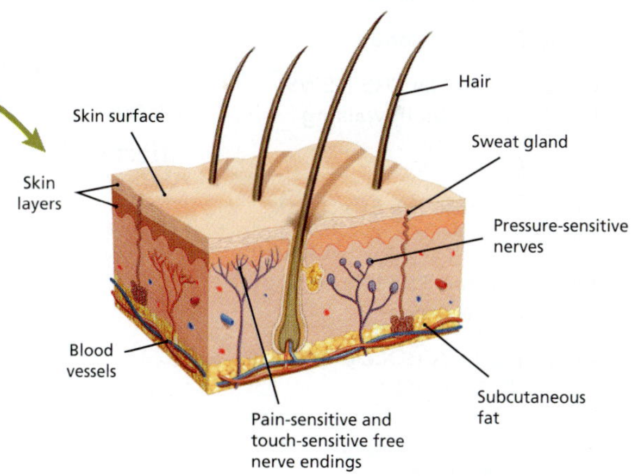

- **kinesthetic sense** — processed by proprioceptors in skin, joints, muscles, and tendons

- **vestibular sense** — processed by vestibular organs

3.8 3.9 3.10 3.11 p. 121

The ABCs of Perception

- **perception**
  - method by which the sensations experienced at any given moment are interpreted and organized in some meaningful fashion
  - may have unique features depending on sensory modality
  - may not always be based on an accurate interpretation of the stimulus

4 consciousness

sleep, dreams, hypnosis, and drugs

WHAT DO YOU MEAN, IT'S ALL OVER?

While the doctor and nurses assured Latashia that she would not feel any discomfort or even remember anything about her colonoscopy, she wasn't so sure. As she lay on the gurney, the nurse came by and said, "I'm going to put the medication in your IV now." Latashia watched as the nurse inserted the hypodermic needle into the IV tubing and then walked away. She waited for some kind of "sleepy" feeling, but nothing seemed to be happening.

In what Latashia estimated to be about 5 minutes later, the nurse returned and asked if she wanted some juice to drink. Surprised that she was being offered something, Latashia said, "Can I have something to drink before the procedure?" The nurse just smiled and pointed to the clock on the wall. "Honey, the procedure was over nearly an hour ago." The drug Latashia received had completely erased her memories of the last 2 hours! How could a drug have such a powerful affect on her awareness? Read on!

CHAPTER OUTLINE

- What Is Consciousness?
- Altered States: Sleep
- PSYCHOLOGY IN THE NEWS: Murder While Sleepwalking
- Dreams
- Altered States: The Effects of Hypnosis
- Altered States: The Influence of Psychoactive Drugs
- APPLYING PSYCHOLOGY TO EVERYDAY LIFE: Thinking Critically About Ghosts, Aliens, and Other Things that Go Bump in the Night

Why study consciousness?

In a very real sense, to understand consciousness is to understand what it means to be who we are. Waking, sleeping, dreaming, daydreaming, and other forms of conscious awareness make up the better part of the human experience. Human consciousness can be affected by drugs, and by all accounts, the use of drugs is on the rise. In the United States, drugs are prescribed for many health and psychological conditions, including the treatment of children. It is also common for people to use drugs to enhance their cognitive performance. Unfortunately, as you'll see in the upcoming discussion, drug use has also found its way into the realm of "recreation" for many Americans. Because of the pervasive use of drugs in our culture, both beneficial and negative, it seems obvious that we need to understand how drugs affect our awareness and behavior in everyday life.

learning objectives

4.1 What does it mean to be conscious, and are there different levels of consciousness?

4.2 Why do people need to sleep, and how does sleep work?

4.3 What are the different stages of sleep, including the stage of dreaming and its importance?

4.4 How do sleep disorders interfere with normal sleep?

4.5 Why do people dream, and what do they dream about?

4.6 How does hypnosis affect consciousness?

4.7 What is the difference between a physical dependence and a psychological dependence on a drug?

4.8 How do stimulants and depressants affect consciousness and what are the dangers associated with taking them, particularly alcohol?

4.9 What are some of the effects and dangers of using narcotics and hallucinogens, including marijuana?

4.10 What are hypnogogic and hypnopompic hallucinations?

study tip

As you are reading this chapter, take a look back at page I-12 in *Psychology in Action* for some useful information about how sleep affects your ability to remember what you study.

What Is Consciousness?

4.1 What does it mean to be conscious, and are there different levels of consciousness?

What exactly is meant by the term *consciousness*? I've heard it a lot, but I'm not sure that I know everything it means.

What exactly is meant by the term consciousness? *I've heard it a lot, but I'm not sure that I know everything it means.*

Consciousness is one of those terms that most people think they understand until someone asks them to define it. Various sorts of scientists, psychologists, neuroscientists, philosophers, and even computer scientists (who have been trying to develop an artificial intelligence for some time now), have tried to define consciousness, and so there are several definitions—one for nearly every field in which consciousness is studied. Philosopher Daniel Dennett, in his 1991 book *Consciousness Explained,* asserts that (contrary to the opinion of William James in his 1894 text) there is no single stream of consciousness but rather multiple "channels," each of which is handling its own tasks (Dennett, 1991). All of these channels operate in parallel, a kind of chaos of consciousness. People must somehow organize all this conscious experience, and that organization is influenced by their particular social groups and culture.

Do animals experience consciousness in the same way as people? That is a question too complex to answer fully here, but many researchers into animal behavior, language, and cognition have some reason to propose that there is a kind of consciousness in at least some animals, although its organization would naturally not be the same as human consciousness (Block, 2005; Browne, 2004; Hurley & Nudds, 2006; Koch & Mormann, 2010). In their chapter on neurobiology and consciousness, Dr. Christof Koch and Dr. Florian Mormann (Koch & Mormann, 2010, p. 1225) state that "there is little reason to doubt that other mammals share conscious feelings . . . with humans." Chapter Seven in this text includes a discussion of animal language that touches on some of these issues. LINK to Chapter Seven: Cognition, pp. 288–289.

So where does that leave us in the search for a working definition of consciousness?

DEFINITION OF CONSCIOUSNESS

So where does that leave us in the search for a working definition of consciousness?

For our purposes, a more useful definition of consciousness might be the following: **Consciousness** is your awareness of everything that is going on around you and inside your own head at any given moment, which you use to organize your behavior (Farthing, 1992), including your thoughts, sensations, and feelings. In a cognitive neuroscience view, consciousness is generated by a set of action potentials in the communication among neurons just sufficient to produce a specific perception, memory, or experience in our awareness (Crick & Koch, 1990, 2003; Koch & Mormann, 2010). In other words, your eyes see a dog, the neurons along the optic pathway to the occipital lobe's visual cortex are activated, and the visual association cortex is activated

consciousness a person's awareness of everything that is going on around him or her at any given moment, which is used to organize behavior.

to identify the external stimulus as a "dog." Bam!—consciousness! LINK to Chapter Two: The Biological Perspective, p. 75.

Much of people's time awake is spent in a state called **waking consciousness** in which their thoughts, feelings, and sensations are clear and organized, and they feel alert. But there are many times in daily activities and in life when people experience states of consciousness that differ from this organized waking state. These variations are called "altered states of consciousness."

The driver of this car has several competing demands on his attention: working his cell phone, listening to the passenger read to him, and driving his car. If he manages to get himself and his passenger safely to their destination—and by multitasking while driving he is certainly endangering both of their lives, and others as well—it's possible that he won't even remember the trip; he may be driving in an altered state of consciousness.

ALTERED STATES OF CONSCIOUSNESS

An **altered state of consciousness** occurs when there is a shift in the quality or pattern of your mental activity. Thoughts may become fuzzy and disorganized and you may feel less alert, or your thoughts may take bizarre turns, as they so often do in dreams. Sometimes being in an altered state may mean being in a state of *increased* alertness, as when under the influence of a stimulant. You may also divide your conscious awareness, as when you drive to work or school and then wonder how you got there—one level of conscious awareness was driving, while the other was thinking about the day ahead, perhaps. This altered state of divided consciousness can be a dangerous thing, as many people who try to drive and talk on a cell phone at the same time have discovered. Driving and carrying on a phone conversation are both processes that should demand focused attention, and it is simply not possible to do both at once in a safe and efficient manner. Studies have shown that driving while talking on a cell phone, even a hands-free phone, puts a person at the same degree of risk as driving under the influence of alcohol (Alm & Nilsson, 1995; Briem & Hedman, 1995; Strayer & Drews, 2007; Strayer & Johnston, 2001; Strayer et al., 2006). Texting while driving is more than risky—it can be murderous (Eastern Virginia Medical School, 2009).

There are many forms of altered states of consciousness. For example, daydreaming, being hypnotized, or achieving a meditative state are usually considered to be altered states. LINK to Chapter Eleven: Stress and Health, pp. 437–438. Being under the influence of certain drugs such as caffeine, tobacco, or alcohol are definitely examples of altered states. In recent years, there has been a definite rise in the use of stimulants and memory-enhancing drugs to boost cognitive performance in adults—drugs that would ordinarily be prescribed for children and adolescents with Attention-Deficit/Hyperactivity Disorder, but are now used by college students and older adults who do not have a disorder, but who feel that the drugs give them an "edge" (Szalavitz, 2009). But the most common altered state people experience is the one they spend about a third of their lives in on a nightly basis—sleep.

Sleep, according to Webb (1992), is the "gentle tyrant." As this picture shows, when the urge to sleep comes upon a person, it can be very difficult to resist—no matter where that person is at the time. Can you think of a time or place when you fell asleep without meaning to do so? Why do you think it happened?

Altered States: Sleep

Have you ever wondered why people have to sleep? They could get so much more work done if they didn't have to sleep, and they would have more time to play and do creative things.

THE BIOLOGY OF SLEEP

4.2 Why do people need to sleep, and how does sleep work?

Sleep was once referred to as "the gentle tyrant" (Webb, 1992). People can try to stay awake, and sometimes they may go for a while without sleep, but eventually they *must* sleep. One reason for this fact is that sleep is one of the human body's *biological rhythms*, natural cycles of activity that the body must go through. Some biological rhythms are monthly, like the cycle of a woman's menstruation, whereas others are far shorter—the beat of the heart is a biological rhythm. But many biological rhythms take place on a daily basis, like the rise and fall of blood pressure and body temperature

waking consciousness state in which thoughts, feelings, and sensations are clear, organized, and the person feels alert.

altered state of consciousness state in which there is a shift in the quality or pattern of mental activity as compared to waking consciousness.

or the production of certain body chemicals (Moore-Ede et al., 1982). The most obvious of these is the sleep–wake cycle (Baehr et al., 2000).

THE RHYTHMS OF LIFE: CIRCADIAN RHYTHMS The sleep–wake cycle is a **circadian rhythm**. The term actually comes from two Latin words, *circa* ("about") and *diem* ("day"). So a circadian rhythm is a cycle that takes "about a day" to complete.

For most people, this means that they will experience several hours of sleep at least once during every 24-hour period. The sleep–wake cycle is ultimately controlled by the brain, specifically by an area within the *hypothalamus*, the tiny section of the brain that influences the glandular system. LINK to Chapter Two: The Biological Perspective, p. 72.

There was a big fuss over something called melatonin a few years ago—isn't melatonin supposed to make people sleep?

There was a big fuss over something called melatonin a few years ago—isn't melatonin supposed to make people sleep?

THE ROLE OF THE HYPOTHALAMUS: THE MIGHTY MITE A lot of people were buying supplements of *melatonin* (a hormone normally secreted by the pineal gland) several years ago, hoping to sleep better and perhaps even slow the effects of aging (Folkard et al., 1993; Herxheimer & Petrie, 2001; Young, 1996). The release of melatonin is influenced by a structure deep within the hypothalamus in an area called the *suprachiasmatic* (SOO-prah-ki-AS-ma-tik) *nucleus*, the internal clock that tells people when to wake up and when to fall asleep (Quintero et al., 2003; Yamaguchi et al., 2003; Zisapel, 2001). The suprachiasmatic nucleus, or SCN, is sensitive to changes in light. As daylight fades, the SCN tells the pineal gland (located in the base of the brain) to secrete melatonin (Bondarenko, 2004; Delagrange & Guardiola-Lemaitre, 1997). As melatonin accumulates, a person will feel sleepy. As the light coming into the eyes increases (as it does in the morning), the SCN tells the pineal gland to stop secreting melatonin, allowing the body to awaken.

Melatonin supplements are often used to treat a condition called *jet lag*, in which the body's circadian rhythm has been disrupted by traveling to another time zone. It may help people who suffer from sleep problems due to shift work. Shift-work sleep problems, often attributed to the custom of having workers change shifts against their natural circadian rhythms (e.g., from a day shift to a night shift, and then back again to an evening shift), have been linked to increased accident rates, increased absence from work due to illness, and lowered productivity rates (Folkard et al., 1993; Folkard & Tucker, 2003; Folkard et al., 2005). In addition to melatonin supplements, it has been found that gradually changing the shifts that workers take according to the natural cycle of the day (e.g., from day shift to evening shift to night shift, rather than from night shift directly back to day shift) has significantly reduced the problems (Czeisler et al., 1982; Folkard et al., 2006).

Melatonin is not the whole story, of course. There is ongoing discussion and research into the role of the neurotransmitter serotonin in the regulation of sleep (Joiner et al., 2006; Veasey, 2003; Yuan et al., 2005). As the day goes by, serotonin levels in the nervous system increase and seem to be associated with sleepiness. This correlation would explain why, at the end of the day, it is very hard for people to stay awake past their usual bedtime. The serotonin level may be high enough at that time to produce an intense feeling of sleepiness.

Body temperature plays a part in inducing sleep, too. The suprachiasmatic nucleus, as part of the hypothalamus, controls body temperature. The higher the body temperature, the more alert people are; the lower the temperature, the sleepier they are. When people are asleep at night, their body temperature is at its lowest level. Be careful: The research on the effects of serotonin and body temperature on sleep is correlational, which means that it cannot yet be assumed that these two factors actually *cause* sleep to occur. LINK to Chapter One: The Science of Psychology, pp. 26–27.

In studies in which volunteers spend several days without access to information about day or night, their sleep–wake cycles lengthened (Czeisler, 1995; Czeisler et al., 1980). The daily activities of their bodies—such as sleeping, waking, waste production, blood pressure rise and fall, and so on—took place over a period of 25 hours rather

circadian rhythm a cycle of bodily rhythm that occurs over a 24-hour period.

than 24 hours. Based on this research, it appears that the suprachiasmatic nucleus may be responsible for resetting the body's biological "clock" to a 24-hour cycle every day.

In the same studies, body temperature dropped consistently even in the absence of light (Czeisler et al., 1980). As body temperature dropped, sleep began, giving further support to the importance of body temperature in the regulation of sleep.

THE PRICE OF NOT SLEEPING Although people can do without sleep for a while, they cannot do without it altogether. In one experiment, rats were placed on moving treadmills over water. They couldn't sleep normally because they would then fall into the water and be awakened, but they did drift repeatedly into **microsleeps**, or brief sidesteps into sleep lasting only seconds (Goleman, 1982; Konowal et al., 1999). People can have microsleeps, too, and if this happens while they are driving a car or a truck, it's obviously bad news (Dinges, 1995; Lyznicki et al., 1998; Thomas et al., 1998). Microsleep periods are no doubt responsible for a lot of car accidents that occur when drivers have had very little sleep.

What will losing out on one night's sleep do to a person? For most people, a missed night of sleep will result in concentration problems and the inability to do simple tasks that normally would take no thought at all, such as loading a CD into a player. More complex tasks, such as math problems, suffer less than these simple tasks because people *know* they must concentrate on a complex task (Chee & Choo, 2004; Lim et al., 2007).

Even so, **sleep deprivation**, or loss of sleep, is a serious problem, which many people have without realizing it. People stay up too late at night during the week, get up before they've really rested to go to work or school, and then try to pay off the "sleep debt" on the weekend. All of that disrupts the normal sleep–wake cycle and isn't good for anyone's health. Students, for example, may stay up all night to study for an important test the next day. In doing so, they will lose more information than they gain, as a good night's sleep is important for memory and the ability to think well. LINK to Psychology in Action, p. I-12. Some typical symptoms of sleep deprivation include trembling hands, inattention, staring off into space, droopy eyelids, and general discomfort (Naitoh et al., 1989), as well as emotional symptoms such as irritability and even depression. LINK to Chapter Fourteen: Psychological Disorders, p. 546.

Just how serious is missing a few nights' sleep? Sleep researchers conducted a study in which healthy adults between the ages of 21 and 38 were randomly placed in one of four restricted sleep conditions (Van Dongen et al., 2003). Participants began the experiment with at least 3 days of regular sleep and then were allowed to get only 4 hours, 6 hours, or 8 hours (this was the control group) of sleep each day for 14 days. A fourth group of participants was totally deprived of sleep (by being kept awake by the researchers) for 3 days in a row. Measurements of the participants' cognitive abilities and physical alertness were taken every 2 hours during the scheduled "awake" times. The results showed that even in the 6-hour sleep condition, participants' abilities to function mentally and physically were as negatively affected as if they had been entirely deprived of sleep for 2 nights. All participants in the sleep-deprived and no-sleep conditions were seriously impaired in their functioning and were relatively unaware of the seriousness of the impairment. That the participants did not seem to be aware of their problems in functioning may account for the impression many people have that a few nights of poor sleep are not that serious. The results of this study seem to indicate that even moderate sleep loss is a serious problem.

Okay, so we obviously need to sleep. But what does it do for us? Why do we have to sleep at all?

The Adaptive Theory of Sleep Sleep is a product of evolution (Webb, 1992) according to the **adaptive theory** of sleep. It proposes that animals and humans evolved different sleep patterns to avoid being present during their predators' normal hunting times, which typically would be at night. For example, if a human or a prey animal (one a predator will eat) is out and about at night, they are more at risk of

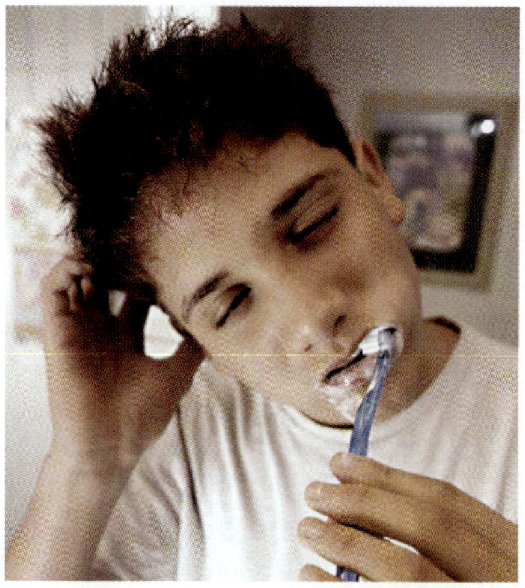

Contrary to popular belief, sleep deprivation often affects younger people more than it does older people, who need less sleep. Does this young man look well rested and able to successfully complete the task of brushing his teeth?

In one study, researchers found that air-traffic controllers, such as those pictured here, were significantly more impaired in performance after working an 8-hour midnight shift as compared to a day or evening shift of equal length (Heslegrave & Rhodes, 1997).

Okay, so we obviously need to sleep. But what does it do for us? Why do we have to sleep at all?

microsleeps brief sidesteps into sleep lasting only a few seconds.

sleep deprivation any significant loss of sleep, resulting in problems in concentration and irritability.

adaptive theory theory of sleep proposing that animals and humans evolved sleep patterns to avoid predators by sleeping when predators are most active.

restorative theory theory of sleep proposing that sleep is necessary to the physical health of the body and serves to replenish chemicals and repair cellular damage.

rapid eye movement (REM) sleep stage of sleep in which the eyes move rapidly under the eyelids and the person is typically experiencing a dream.

non-REM (NREM) sleep any of the stages of sleep that do not include REM.

These lionesses are predators and have no need to sleep at night to protect themselves. They sleep and hunt on and off during the day in perfect safety, while the animals that the lionesses prey upon sleep at night in the safety of trees, dens, or other shelter—often in very short naps.

being eaten. However, if during active hunting hours the prey is in a safe place sleeping and conserving energy, it is more likely to remain unharmed. If this theory is true, then one would expect prey animals to sleep mostly at night and for shorter periods of time than predator animals; you would also expect that predators could sleep in the daytime—virtually as much as they want. This seems to be the case for predators like lions that have very few natural predators themselves. Lions will sleep nearly 15 hours a day, whereas animals such as gazelles that are lions' prey sleep a mere 4 hours a day, usually in short naps. Nocturnal animals such as the opossum can afford to sleep during the day and be active at night (when their food sources are available), because they are protected from predators by sleeping high up in trees.

The Restorative Theory of Sleep The other major theory of why organisms sleep is called **restorative theory**, which states that sleep is necessary to the physical health of the body. During sleep, chemicals that were used up during the day's activities are replenished and cellular damage is repaired (Adam, 1980; Moldofsky, 1995). There is evidence that most bodily growth and repair occur during the deepest stages of sleep, when enzymes responsible for these functions are secreted in higher amounts (Saper et al., 2001).

Which of these theories is correct? The answer is that both are probably needed to understand why sleep occurs the way it does. Adaptive theory explains why people sleep *when* they do, and restorative theory explains why people *need* to sleep.

How Much Sleep Do People Need? How much sleep is enough sleep? The answer varies from person to person because of each person's age and possibly inherited sleep needs (Feroah et al., 2004), but most young adults need about 7 to 9 hours of sleep each 24-hour period in order to function well. (See Figure 4.1.) Some people are short sleepers, needing only 4 or 5 hours, whereas others are long sleepers and require more than 9 hours of sleep (McCann & Stewin, 1988). As we age, we seem to sleep less during each night until the average length of sleep approaches only 6 hours.

THE STAGES OF SLEEP

So are there different kinds of sleep? Do you go from being awake to being asleep and dreaming—is it instant?

So are there different kinds of sleep? Do you go from being awake to being asleep and dreaming—is it instant?

There are actually two kinds of sleep: **REM (rapid eye movement) sleep** and **non-REM (NREM) sleep**. REM sleep is a relatively active type of sleep when most of a person's dreaming takes place, whereas non-REM sleep is a much deeper, more restful kind of sleep. In REM sleep, the voluntary muscles are inhibited, meaning that the person in REM sleep moves very little, whereas in non-REM sleep the person's body is free to move around (including kicking one's bed partner!). There are also several different stages of sleep that

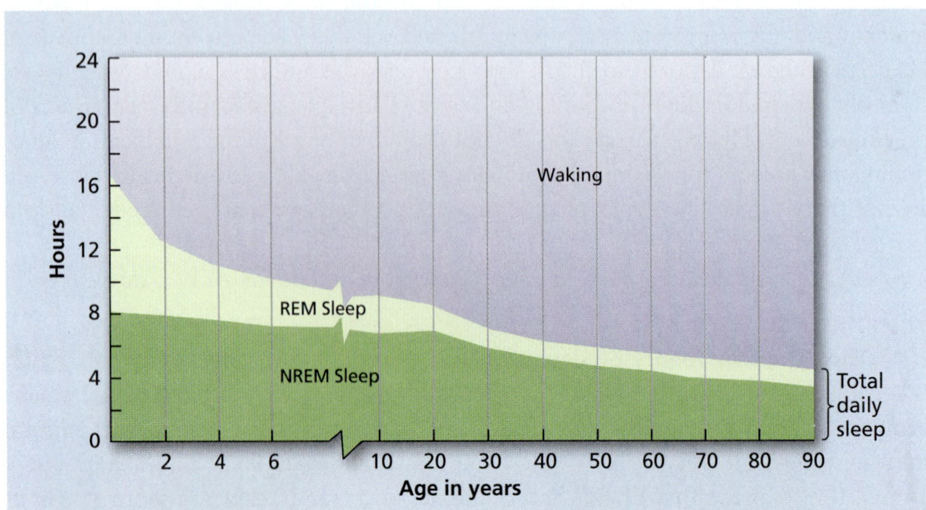

Figure 4.1 Sleep Patterns of Infants and Adults

Infants need far more sleep than older children and adults. Both REM sleep and NREM sleep decrease dramatically in the first 10 years of life, with the greatest decrease in REM sleep. Nearly 50 percent of an infant's sleep is REM, compared to only about 20 percent for a normal, healthy adult. (Roffwarg, 1966) people go through each night in which REM sleep and non-REM sleep occur. A machine called an electroencephalograph allows scientists to record the brain-wave activity as a person passes through the various stages of sleep and to determine what type of sleep the person has entered (Aserinsky & Kleitman, 1953). See Figure 4.2 for a look at what happens in each stage of sleep.

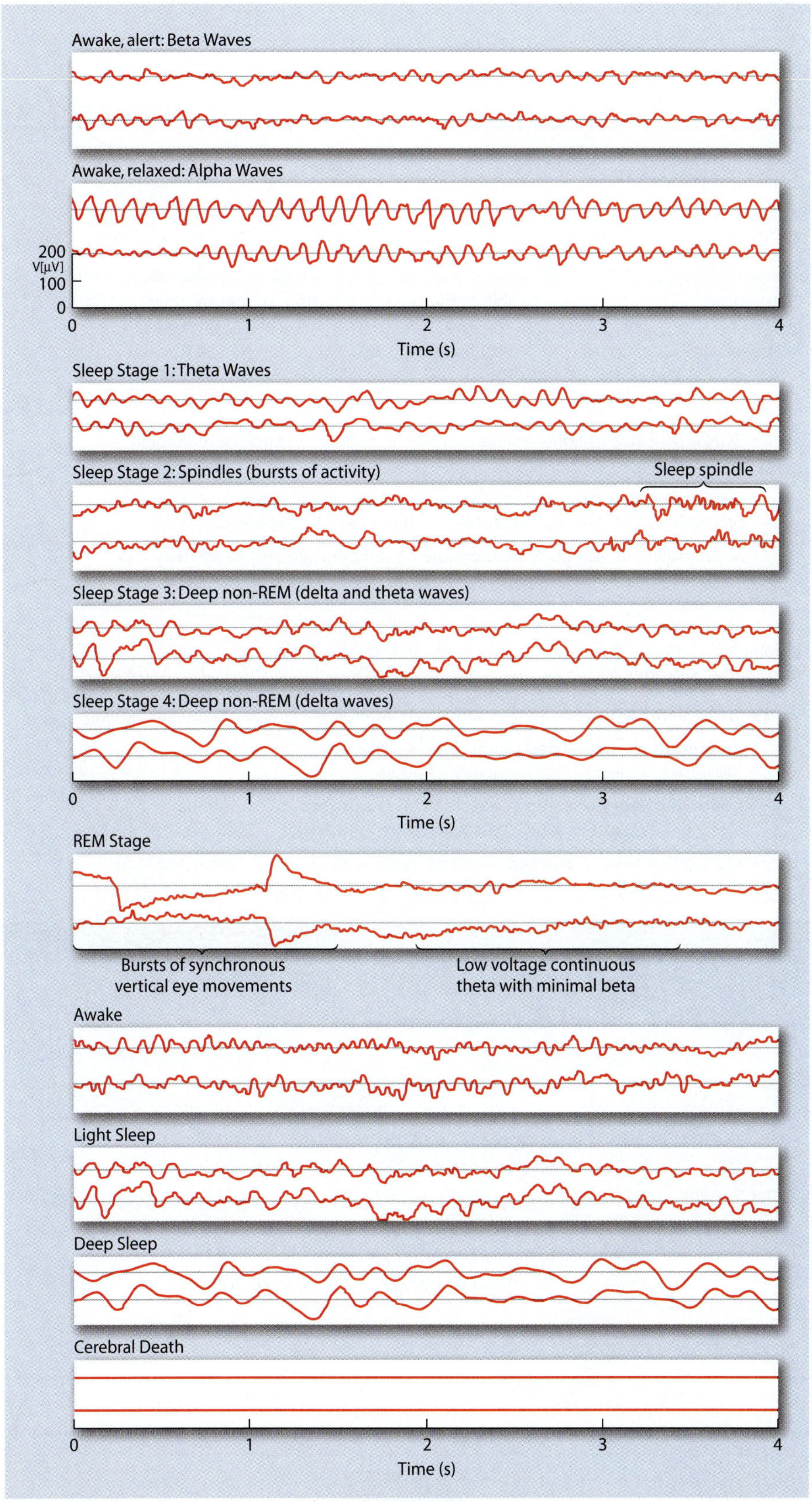

Figure 4.2 Brain Activity During Sleep

The EEG reflects brain activity during both waking and sleep. This activity varies according to level of alertness while awake (top two segments) and the stage of sleep (middle segments). Sleep Stages 3 and 4 are indicated by the presence of delta activity, which is much slower and accounts for the larger, slower waves on these graphs. [NOTE: The American Academy of Sleep Medicine (Iber et al., 2007) has recently published updated guidelines for the scoring of sleep activity and one major change has been to combine NREM stages 3 and 4 into a single stage, now indicated by N3.] REM has activity that resembles alert wakefulness but has relatively no muscle activity except rapid eye movement. The bottom segments illustrate how EEG activity differs between wakefulness, light and deep sleep, and lastly what it looks like when brain activity has ceased in cerebral death. EEG data and images in this figure are courtesy of Dr. Leslie Sherlin.

beta waves smaller and faster brain waves, typically indicating mental activity.

alpha waves brain waves that indicate a state of relaxation or light sleep.

theta waves brain waves indicating the early stages of sleep.

A person who is wide awake and mentally active will show a brain-wave pattern on the electroencephalogram (EEG) called **beta waves.** Beta waves are very small and very fast. As the person relaxes and gets drowsy, slightly larger and slower **alpha waves** appear. The alpha waves are eventually replaced by even slower and larger **theta waves.**

4.1 4.2 CONCEPT MAP

What Is Consciousness?

- people's awareness of everything that is going on around them at any given moment (thoughts, sensations, and feelings); much of the day is spent in waking consciousness where these are clear and organized
- altered states of consciousness occur when there is a shift in the quality or pattern of mental activity as compared to waking consciousness; alertness, thought content, and focus can vary greatly

Altered States—Sleep

(sleep is one of the body's daily [circadian] biological rhythms; sleep–wake cycle controlled by the brain including the hypothalamus and the neurotransmitter serotonin)

- hypothalamus contains the suprachiasmatic nucleus (SCN)
  - SCN is sensitive to light—influences pineal gland's secretion of melatonin (↑ melatonin = ↑ sleepiness)
  - light through eyes relayed to SCN; SCN signals pineal gland to stop producing melatonin (↓ melatonin = ↑ alertness / ↓ sleepiness)
  - SCN also influences body temperature (↓ temperature = ↑ sleepiness)
- people can live without sleep for a while, can't live without it altogether
  - **sleep deprivation** can lead to serious changes in body and mental functioning
  - **amount of sleep needed** ranges from 4–10 hours; most people need 7–9 hours every 24 hours
  - **adaptive theory of sleep** suggests sleep is a product of evolution; sleep has evolved to avoid the active time of predators
  - **restorative theory of sleep** suggests sleep is vital to the physical health of the body; body growth and repair occur during the deepest stages of sleep

PRACTICE quiz How much do you remember?

ANSWERS ON PAGE AK-1.

Pick the best answer.

1. When our mental activity undergoes a change in quality or pattern, this is called a(n) __________.
   a. waking consciousness.
   b. altered state of consciousness.
   c. transient state of consciousness.
   d. hallucination.
2. The sleep–wake cycle is a(n) __________ rhythm, normally occurring every 24 hours.
   a. annual c. circadian
   b. monthly d. nocturnal
3. The suprachiasmatic nucleus instructs the __________ gland to release __________.
   a. pineal; melatonin. c. pituitary; melatonin.
   b. pineal; serotonin. d. pituitary; serotonin.
4. Which of the following does NOT have a role in determining when we sleep?
   a. light and dark information c. digestion
   b. body temperature d. serotonin
5. Which theory of why we sleep explains why we sleep *when* we do?
   a. restorative theory c. reactive theory
   b. adaptive theory d. REM theory

4.3 What are the different stages of sleep, including the stage of dreaming and its importance?

delta waves long, slow waves that indicate the deepest stage of sleep.

NON-REM STAGE 1: LIGHT SLEEP As theta wave activity increases and alpha wave activity fades away, people are said to be entering Stage 1 sleep, or light sleep. Several rather interesting things can happen in this non-REM stage of sleep. If people are awakened at this point, they will probably not believe that they were actually asleep. They may also experience vivid visual events called *hypnogogic images* or *hallucinations* (Mavromatis, 1987; Mavromatis & Richardson, 1984). (The Greek word *hypnos* means "sleep.") Many researchers now believe that peoples' experiences of ghostly visits, alien abductions, and near-death experiences may be most easily explained by these hallucinations (Moody & Perry, 1993). For more about hypnogogic experiences and the role they may play in "hauntings," see the Applying Psychology section at the end of this chapter.

A much more common occurrence is called the *hypnic jerk* (Mahowald & Schenck, 1996; Oswald, 1959). Have you ever been drifting off to sleep when your knees, legs, or sometimes your whole body gives a big "jerk"? Although experts have no solid proof of why this occurs, many believe that it has something to do with the possibility that our ancestors slept in trees: The relaxation of the muscles as one drifts into sleep causes a "falling" sensation, at which point the body jerks awake to prevent the "fall" from the hypothetical tree (Coolidge, 2006; Sagan, 1977).

NON-REM STAGE 2: SLEEP SPINDLES As people drift further into sleep, the body temperature continues to drop. Heart rate slows, breathing becomes more shallow and irregular, and the EEG will show the first signs of *sleep spindles*, brief bursts of activity lasting only a second or two. Theta waves still predominate in this stage, but if people are awakened during this stage, they will be aware of having been asleep.

NON-REM STAGE 3 AND STAGE 4: DELTA WAVES ROLL IN In the third stage of sleep, the slowest and largest waves make their appearance. These waves are called **delta waves**. In Stage 3, delta waves make up only about 20 to 50 percent of the brain-wave pattern.

Once delta waves account for more than 50 percent of total brain activity, the person is said to have entered Stage 4 sleep, the deepest stage of sleep. It is during this stage that growth hormones (often abbreviated as GH) are released from the pituitary gland and reach their peak. The body is at its lowest level of functioning. Eventually, the delta waves become the dominant brain activity for this stage of sleep. See Figure 4.3 to show movement through the sleep stages throughout one night.

People in deep sleep are very hard to awaken. If something does wake them, they may be very confused and disoriented at first. It is not unusual for people to wake up in this kind of disoriented state only to hear the crack of thunder and realize

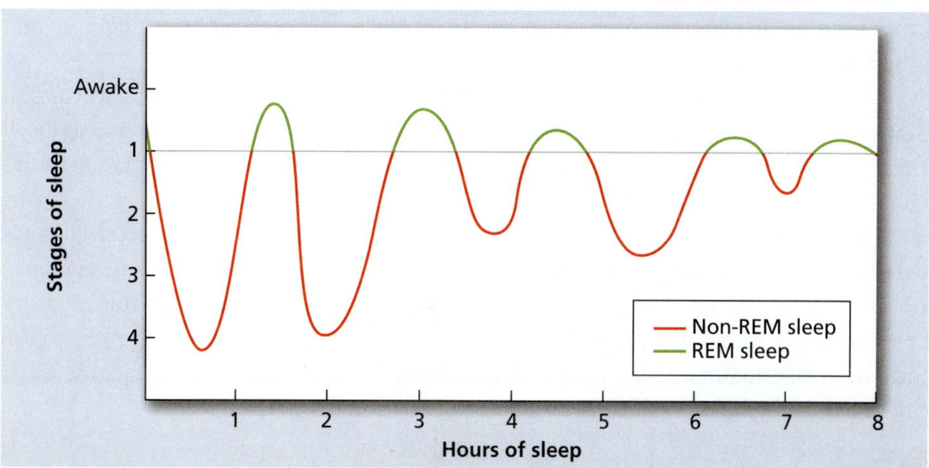

Figure 4.3 A Typical Night's Sleep
The graph shows the typical progression through the night of Stages 1–4 and REM sleep. Stages 1–4 are indicated on the *y*-axis, and REM stages are represented by the green curves on the graph. The REM periods occur about every 90 minutes throughout the night (Dement, 1974).

that a storm has come up. Children are even harder to wake up when in this state than are adults. As mentioned earlier, deep sleep is the time when body growth occurs. This may explain why children in periods of rapid growth need to sleep more and also helps to explain why children who are experiencing disrupted sleep (as is the case in situations of domestic violence) suffer delays in growth (Gilmore & Skuse, 1999; Swanson, 1994).

The fact that children do sleep so deeply may explain why certain sleep disorders are more common in childhood. Indeed, many sleep disorders are more common in boys than in girls because boys sleep more deeply than do girls due to high levels of the male hormone testosterone (Miyatake et al., 1980; Thiedke, 2001). Simulate on mypsychlab.com

Simulate the stages of sleep on mypsychlab.com

WHAT HAPPENS IN REM SLEEP?

After spending some time in Stage 4, the sleeping person will go back up through Stage 3, Stage 2, and then into a stage in which body temperature increases to near-waking levels, the eyes move rapidly under the eyelids, the heart beats much faster, and brain waves resemble beta waves—the kind of brain activity that usually signals wakefulness. The person is still asleep but in the stage known as rapid eye movement sleep (REM).

When a person in REM sleep is awakened, he or she almost always reports being in a dream state (Shafton, 1995). REM sleep is, therefore, associated with dreaming, and 90 percent of dreams actually take place in REM sleep. People do have dreams in the other non-REM stages, but REM dreams tend to be more vivid, more detailed, longer, and more bizarre than the dreams of NREM sleep. NREM dreams tend to be more like thoughts about daily occurrences and far shorter than REM dreams (Foulkes & Schmidt, 1983; Takeuchi et al., 2003). Fortunately, the body is unable to act upon these dreams under normal conditions because the voluntary muscles are paralyzed during REM sleep, a condition known as **REM paralysis**. (This is why you sometimes have a dream in which you are trying to run or move, and can't—you are partially aware of REM paralysis.)

THE NEED FOR REM SLEEP Why two kinds of sleep? And why would REM sleep ever be considered restful when the body is almost awake and the brain is so active? REM sleep seems to serve a different purpose than does NREM, or deep sleep. After a very physically demanding day, people tend to spend more time in NREM deep sleep than is usual. But an emotionally stressful day leads to increased time in REM sleep (Horne & Staff, 1983). Perhaps the dreams people have in REM sleep are a way of dealing with the stresses and tensions of the day, whereas physical activity would demand more time for recovery of the body in NREM sleep. Also, if deprived of REM sleep (as would occur with the use of sleeping pills or other depressant drugs), a person will experience greatly increased amounts of REM sleep the next night, a phenomenon called **REM rebound** (Vogel, 1975, 1993).

An early study of REM sleep deprivation (Dement, 1960) seemed to suggest that people deprived of REM sleep would become paranoid, seemingly mentally ill from lack of this one stage of sleep. This is called the *REM myth* because later studies failed to reliably produce the same results (Dement et al., 1969).

Other early research attempted to link REM sleep with the physical changes that occur during storing a memory for what one has recently learned, but the evidence today suggests that no one particular stage of sleep is the "one" in which this memory process occurs; rather, the evidence is mounting for sleep in general as necessary to the formation of memory (Ellenbogen et al., 2006; Maquet et al., 2003; Siegel, 2001; Stickgold et al., 2001; Walker, 2005).

REM paralysis the inability of the voluntary muscles to move during REM sleep.

REM rebound increased amounts of REM sleep after being deprived of REM sleep on earlier nights.

REM sleep in early infancy differs from adult REM sleep in several ways: Babies spend nearly 50 percent of their sleep in REM as compared to adults' 20 percent, the brain-wave patterns on EEG recordings are not exactly the same in infant REM when compared to adult REM recordings, and infants can and do move around quite a bit during REM sleep (Carskadon & Dement, 2005; Davis et al., 2004; Sheldon, 2002; Tucker et al., 2006). These differences can be explained: When infants are engaged in REM sleep, they are not dreaming but rather forming new connections between neurons (Carskadon & Dement, 2005; Davis et al., 2004; Sheldon, 2002). The infant brain is highly plastic, and much of brain growth and development takes place during REM sleep. LINK to Chapter Two: The Biological Perspective, p. 58. As the infant's brain nears its adult size by age 5 or 6, the proportion of REM sleep has also decreased to a more adultlike ratio of REM to non-REM. For infants, to sleep is perchance to grow synapses.

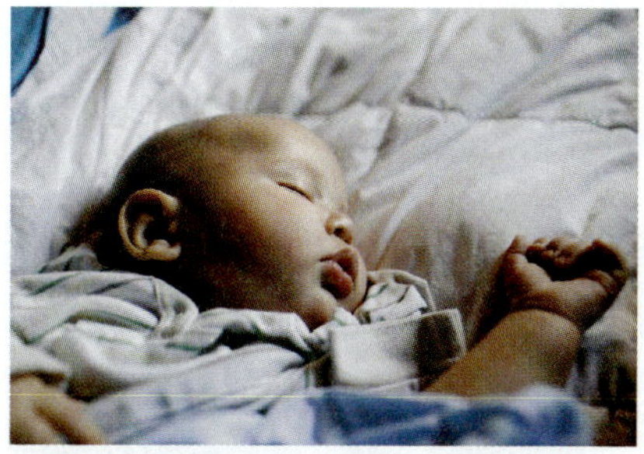

While this infant is sleeping, her REM sleep (occurring about half of the time she is asleep) allows her brain to make new neural connections.

SLEEP DISORDERS

4.4 How do sleep disorders interfere with normal sleep?

What would happen if we could act out our dreams? Would it be like sleepwalking?

What would happen if we could act out our dreams? Would it be like sleepwalking?

NIGHTMARES AND REM BEHAVIOR DISORDER Being able to act out one's dreams, especially nightmares, is a far more dangerous proposition than sleepwalking. **Nightmares** are bad dreams, and some nightmares can be utterly terrifying. Children tend to have more nightmares than adults do because they spend more of their sleep in the REM state, as discussed earlier. As they age, they have fewer nightmares because they have less opportunity to have them. But some people still suffer from nightmares as adults.

Some people have a rare disorder in which the brain mechanisms that normally inhibit the voluntary muscles fail, allowing the person to thrash around and even get up and act out nightmares. This disorder is called **REM behavior disorder**, which is a fairly serious condition (Shafton, 1995). Usually seen in men over age 60, it can happen in younger men and in women. For more about this disorder, read the following Psychology in the News.

Nightmares of being chased by a monster or a similar frightening creature are common, especially in childhood.

psychology in the news

Murder While Sleepwalking

According to a compilation of information by Dr. Lawrence Martin, Associate Professor at Case Western Reserve University and specialist in pulmonary* and sleep medicine, at least 20 cases of "murder while *sleepwalking*" have been recorded. The term *sleepwalking* as used in these cases most likely refers to the very real condition called REM behavior disorder rather than ordinary sleepwalking. Use of this disorder as a defense in a murder trial has sometimes been successful. Here are short descriptions of four cases and their outcomes.

Case One: In 1987, Kenneth Parks, a 23-year-old man from Toronto, Canada, got up early in the morning, got in his car, and drove 23 kilometers (about 14 miles) to the home of his wife's parents. He stabbed his mother-in-law to death, attacked his father-in-law, and then drove to the police. Once there, he told them that he thought he had killed some people. Parks had no motive and had been suffering from severe insomnia. He did have a history of sleepwalking and his defense team, which included sleep experts and psychiatrists, concluded that he was indeed unaware of his actions at the time of the crime. He was acquitted (Denno, 2002; Martin, 2004).

*pulmonary: having to do with the lungs.

nightmares bad dreams occurring during REM sleep.

REM behavior disorder a rare disorder in which the mechanism that blocks the movement of the voluntary muscles fails, allowing the person to thrash around and even get up and act out nightmares.

Scott Falater testifies at his trial for the murder of his wife, which he claims he committed while he was sleepwalking.

Case Two: Scott Falater, 43 years old, was accused of murdering his wife in 1997. A neighbor, looking over a fence, witnessed Scott holding his wife's head under water in the swimming pool. He called the police, who found a bloody pool and the body of Yamila Falater with 44 stab wounds.

Falater had performed a series of very deliberate and time-consuming actions in cleaning up after the murder. But Falater claimed to be sleepwalking during all of these actions. Although sleep experts for the defense stated that Falater's story was possible, the prosecution pointed to marital troubles as motive. Most damaging to his case was the witness who stated that 3 weeks before the murder, Falater had been discussing the case of Kenneth Parks and Parks's acquittal for murder based on a sleepwalking defense. The jury found Falater guilty of murder in the first degree and he was given a life sentence (Martin, 2004; Tresniowski, 1999).

Case Three: In July of 2008 Brian Thomas of South Wales in Great Britain, a devoted husband and father of two children, killed his wife while dreaming of intruders breaking into their camper. Thomas had a history of sleepwalking and normally slept apart from his wife. Experts found that he suffered from night terrors, and he was acquitted of her murder by reason of temporary insanity (Morris, 2009).

Questions for Further Discussion

1. Should sleepwalking be a valid defense for a crime as serious as murder? What about other kinds of crimes?
2. What kind of evidence should be required to convince a jury that a crime was committed while sleepwalking?

"Wait! Don't! It can be dangerous to wake them."

STAGE 4 SLEEP DISORDERS Real **sleepwalking**, or **somnambulism**, occurs in about 20 percent of the population and is at least partially due to heredity (Abe et al., 1984; Kales et al., 1980). It is much more common in childhood and also occurs more frequently in boys than in girls. Although the old movies portray sleepwalkers as zombie-like and with arms outstretched, in reality a sleepwalker may do nothing more than sit up in bed. But other sleepwalking episodes may involve walking around the house, looking in the refrigerator or even eating, and getting into the car. Most sleepwalkers typically do not remember the episode the next day. One student said that her brother was a sleepwalker, and one morning his family found him sound asleep behind the wheel of the family car in the garage. Fortunately, he had not been able to find the keys in his sleep.

Many somnambulists grow out of their sleepwalking by the time they become adolescents. Many parents have found that preventing sleep loss makes sleepwalking a rare occurrence. The only real precaution that the families of people who sleepwalk should take is to clear their floors of obstacles and to put not-easy-to-reach locks on the doors. And although it is typically not dangerous to wake sleepwalkers, they may strike out before awakening.

NIGHT TERRORS A rare disorder, **night terrors** are more likely in children and also likely to disappear as the child grows older (Garland & Smith, 1991). A night terror is essentially a state of panic experienced while sound asleep. People may sit up, scream, run around the room, or flail at some unseen attacker. It is also not uncommon for people to feel unable to breathe while they are in this state. Considering that people suffering a night-terror episode are in a deep stage of sleep and breathing shallowly, one can understand why breathing would seem difficult when they are suddenly active. Most people do not remember what happened during a night-terror episode, although a few people can remember vividly the images and terror they experienced.

sleepwalking (somnambulism) occurring during deep sleep, an episode of moving around or walking around in one's sleep.

night terrors relatively rare disorder in which the person experiences extreme fear and screams or runs around during deep sleep without waking fully.

But that sounds like the description of a nightmare—what's the difference?

But that sounds like the description of a nightmare—what's the difference?

Some very real differences exist between night terrors and nightmares. Nightmares are usually vividly remembered immediately upon waking. A person who has had a nightmare, unlike a person experiencing a night terror, will actually be able to awaken and immediately talk about the bad dream. Perhaps the most telling difference is that nightmares occur during REM sleep rather than deep non-REM sleep, which is the domain of night terrors, which means that people don't move around in a nightmare as they do in a night terror experience.

A number of other problems can occur during sleep in addition to sleepwalking, nightmares, and REM behavior disorder.

INSOMNIA Most people think that **insomnia** is the inability to sleep. Although that is the literal meaning of the term, in reality insomnia is the inability to get to sleep, stay asleep, or get a good quality of sleep (Kryger, Lavie, & Rosen, 1999). There are many causes of insomnia, both psychological and physiological. Some of the psychological causes are worrying, trying too hard to sleep, or having anxiety. Some of the physiological causes are too much caffeine, indigestion, or aches and pain. **Listen** on **mypsychlab.com**

Listen to the Psychology in the News podcast about sleep deprivation and obesity on **mypsychlab.com**

There are several steps people can take to help them sleep. Obvious ones are taking no caffeinated drinks or foods that cause indigestion before bedtime, taking medication for pain, and dealing with anxieties in the daytime rather than facing them at night. That last bit of advice is easy to say but not always easy to do. Here are some other helpful hints (Kupfer & Reynolds, 1997; National Sleep Foundation, 2009):

1. Go to bed only when you are sleepy. If you lie in bed for 20 minutes and are still awake, get up and do something like reading or other light activity (avoid watching TV or being in front of a computer screen) until you feel sleepy, and then go back to bed.
2. Don't do anything in your bed but sleep. Your bed should be a cue for sleeping, not for studying or watching television. Using the bed as a cue for sleeping is a kind of learning called *classical conditioning,* or the pairing of cues and automatic responses. LINK to Chapter Five: Learning, p. 171.
3. Don't try too hard to get to sleep, and especially do not look at the clock and calculate how much sleep you aren't getting. That just increases the tension and makes it harder to sleep.
4. Keep to a regular schedule. Go to bed at the same time and get up at the same time, even on days that you don't have to go to work or class.
5. Don't take sleeping pills or drink alcohol or other types of drugs that slow down the nervous system (see the category Depressants later in this chapter). These drugs force you into deep sleep and do not allow you to get any REM or lighter stages of sleep. When you try to sleep without these drugs the next night, you will experience REM rebound, which will cause you to feel tired and sleepy the next day. REM rebound is one way to experience the form of insomnia in which a person sleeps but sleeps poorly.

Tossing and turning can be a sign of someone who has trouble getting to sleep, staying asleep, or getting enough sleep—all signs of insomnia. If this woman does suffer from insomnia, how might she feel when she wakes up in the morning?

If none of these things seems to be working, there are sleep clinics and sleep experts who can help people with insomnia. The American Academy of Sleep Medicine has an excellent Web site at **www.aasmnet.org** that provides links to locate sleep clinics in any area. One treatment that seems to have more success than any kind of sleep medication is the use of cognitive-behavior therapy, a type of therapy in which both rational thinking and controlled behavior are stressed (Bastien et al., 2004; Irwin et al., 2006; Morin et al., 2006). LINK to Chapter Fifteen: Psychological Therapies, pp. 585–586.

SLEEP APNEA Gerald was a snorer. Actually, that's an understatement. Gerald could give a jet engine some serious competition. Snoring is fairly common, occurring when the breathing passages (nose and throat) get blocked. Most people snore only when they have

insomnia the inability to get to sleep, stay asleep, or get a good quality of sleep.

sleep apnea disorder in which the person stops breathing for nearly half a minute or more.

narcolepsy sleep disorder in which a person falls immediately into REM sleep during the day without warning.

a cold or some other occasional problem, but some people snore every night and quite loudly, like Gerald. It is this type of snoring that is often associated with a condition called **sleep apnea**, in which the person stops breathing for nearly half a minute or more. When breathing stops, there will be a sudden silence, followed shortly by a gasping sound as the person struggles to get air into the lungs. Many people do not wake up while this is happening, but they do not get a good, restful night's sleep because of the apnea.

Apnea is a serious problem. Not only does it disturb nightly sleep, making the person excessively sleepy in the daytime, but also it can cause heart problems (Flemons, 2002). If a person suspects the presence of apnea, a visit to a physician is the first step in identifying the disorder and deciding on a treatment. With mild apnea, treatment may be a device worn on the nose at night to open the nostrils and prevent blockage. Obesity is a primary cause of apnea, especially in men, so another solution might be to lose excess weight. There are also sprays that are supposed to shrink the tissues lining the throat (much as a nasal decongestant spray shrinks the tissues of the nasal passages). Some people sleep with a device that delivers a continuous stream of air under mild pressure, called a *continuous positive airway pressure (CPAP) device*. Others undergo a simple surgery in which the *uvula* (the little flap that hangs down at the back of the throat) and some of the soft tissues surrounding it are removed.

Some very young infants also experience a kind of apnea due to immaturity of the brain stem. These infants are typically placed on monitors that sound an alarm when breathing stops, allowing caregivers to help the infant begin breathing again. Although sleep apnea in infants is often associated with sudden infant death syndrome, or SIDS, it is not necessarily caused by it: Many infants who die of SIDS were never diagnosed with sleep apnea (Blackmon et al., 2003). Read on mypsychlab.com

Read and learn more more about SIDS on mypsychlab.com

"On your application it says you have narcolepsy. What is that?"

NARCOLEPSY A disorder affecting 1 in every 2,000 persons, **narcolepsy** is a kind of "sleep seizure." In narcolepsy, the person may slip suddenly into REM sleep during the day (especially when the person experiences strong emotions). Another symptom is excessive daytime sleepiness that results in the person falling asleep throughout the day at inappropriate times and in inappropriate places (Overeem et al., 2001). These sleep attacks may occur many times and without warning, making the operation of a car or other machinery very dangerous for the *narcoleptic* (person who suffers from narcolepsy). The sudden REM attacks are especially dangerous because of the symptom of *cataplexy*, or a sudden loss of muscle tone. This REM paralysis may cause injuries if the person is standing when the attack occurs. The same hypnogogic images that may accompany Stage 1 sleep may also occur in the narcoleptic person. Table 4.1 has a more detailed list of known, treatable sleep disorders.

Table 4.1
Sleep Disorders

NAME OF DISORDER	PRIMARY SYMPTOMS
Somnambulism	Sitting, walking, or performing complex behavior while asleep
Night terrors	Extreme fear, agitation, screaming while asleep
Restless leg syndrome	Uncomfortable sensations in legs causing movement and loss of sleep
Nocturnal leg cramps	Painful cramps in calf or foot muscles
Hypersomnia	Excessive daytime sleepiness
Circadian rhythm disorders	Disturbances of the sleep–wake cycle such as jet lag and shift work
Enuresis	Urinating while asleep in bed

CONCEPT MAP

4.3 4.4

Altered States—Sleep: Stages and Disorders

- consist of both REM (rapid eye movement) and non-REM stages; REM is relatively active whereas non-REM is much deeper and restful; stages defined by level of brain activity as measured by the EEG (beta, alpha, theta, delta waves); sleep cycle is made up of various stages repeated 4–5 times a night
  - **non-REM Stage 1:** while awake, primarily beta activity, more alpha as one relaxes, onset of sleep in Stage 1 is associated with alpha being replaced by theta
  - **non-REM Stage 2:** EEG sleep spindles appear; theta activity is predominant; body temperature continues to drop, heart rate and breathing slow
  - **non-REM Stages 3 and 4:** delta activity makes up 20–50% of EEG activity in Stage 3; over 50% indicates Stage 4; body is at lowest level of functioning and people are hard to awaken; sleep disorders such as sleepwalking and night terrors occur in Stage 4
  - **REM sleep:** dreaming occurs; eyes move rapidly under the eyelids and EEG indicates presence of beta, but body is typically still, due to sleep paralysis; REM behavior disorder occurs when body is not still or acts out dreams, usually seen in men over age 60
- sleep disorders include a variety of problems that can interfere with sleep
  - **insomnia** is the inability to get to sleep, stay asleep, or get good quality sleep
  - **sleep apnea** consists of loud snoring and stopped breathing
  - **narcolepsy** consists of sudden onset of REM sleep during otherwise waking hours

PRACTICE quiz How much do you remember? ANSWERS ON PAGE AK-1

Pick the best answer.

1. In which stage(s) of sleep is a person hardest to wake?
   a. Stage 1 **c.** Stages 3 and 4
   b. Stage 2 **d.** REM
2. Which of the following is NOT a characteristic of REM sleep?
   a. paralysis of voluntary muscles
   b. increased heart rate
   c. slower, deeper breathing
   d. increased body temperature
3. Acting out your nightmares is a rare condition called ________.
   a. sleep apnea. **c.** narcolepsy.
   b. night terrors. **d.** REM behavior disorder.
4. In which disorder does breathing stop for nearly half a minute or more?
   a. sleep apnea **c.** sleepwalking
   b. night terrors **d.** narcolepsy
5. Which of the following is bad advice for someone suffering from insomnia?
   a. Do not watch TV or read in bed.
   b. Avoid coffee, tea, and other caffeine-containing products before bed.
   c. Do not study or work in bed.
   d. Lie in bed until you fall asleep, even if it takes several hours.
6. Nightmares occur in ________ sleep, whereas night terrors occur in ________ sleep.
   a. Stage 1; Stage 2 **c.** Stage 4; Stage 1
   b. REM; NREM **d.** NREM; REM

Brainstorming: Do you think that sleepwalking is an adequate defense for someone who has harmed or killed another person? Should a person who has done harm while sleepwalking be forced by the courts to take preventive actions, such as installing special locks on bedroom doors? How might this affect the person's safety, such as in a fire?

Dreams

4.5 Why do people dream, and what do they dream about?

Dreams have long been a source of curiosity. People of ancient times tried to find meaning in dreams. Some viewed dreams as prophecy, some as messages from the spirits. But the real inquiry into the process of dreaming began with the publication of Freud's *The Interpretation of Dreams* (1900).

FREUD'S INTERPRETATION: DREAMS AS WISH FULFILLMENT

Sigmund Freud (1856–1939) believed that the problems of his patients stemmed from conflicts and events that had been buried in their unconscious minds since childhood. These early traumas were seen as the cause of behavior problems in adulthood, in

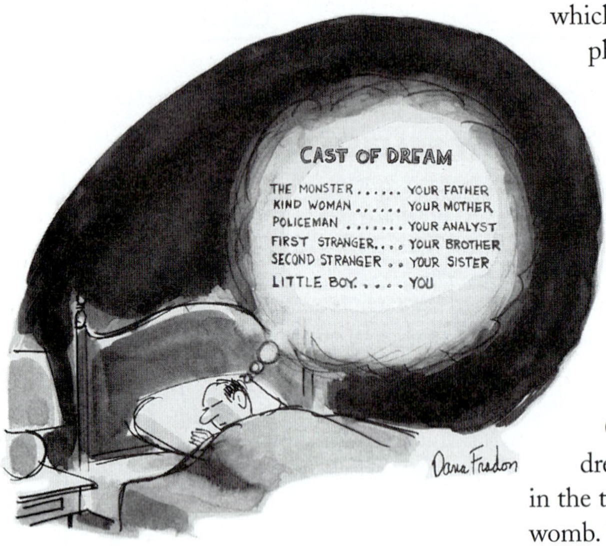

which his patients suffered from symptoms such as a type of paralysis that had no physical basis or repetitive, ritualistic* hand washing. One of the ways Freud devised to get at these early memories was to examine the dreams of his patients, believing that conflicts, events, and desires of the past would be represented in symbolic** form in the dreams. LINK to Chapter Thirteen: Theories of Personality, p. 503.

MANIFEST CONTENT The *manifest content* of a dream is the actual dream itself. For example, if Chad has a dream in which he is trying to climb out of a bathtub, the manifest content of the dream is exactly that—he's trying to climb out of a bathtub.

LATENT CONTENT But, of course, Freud would no doubt find more meaning in Chad's dream than is at first evident. He believed that the true meaning of a dream was hidden, or *latent*, and only expressed in symbols. In the dream, the water in the tub might symbolize the waters of birth, and the tub itself might be his mother's womb. Using a Freudian interpretation, Chad may be dreaming about being born.

Seems like quite a stretch. Wouldn't there be lots of other possible interpretations?

Seems like quite a stretch. Wouldn't there be lots of other possible interpretations?

Yes, and today many professionals are no longer as fond of Freud's dream analysis as they once were. But there are still some people who insist that dreams have symbolic meaning. For example, dreaming about being naked in a public place is very common, and most dream analyzers interpret that to mean feeling open and exposed, an expression of childhood innocence, or even a desire for sex. Exactly how the dream is interpreted depends on the other features of the dream and what is happening in the person's waking life.

The development of techniques for looking at the structure and activity of the brain (see LINK to Chapter Two: The Biological Perspective, pp. 67–69) has led to an explanation of why people dream that is more concrete than that of Freud.

THE ACTIVATION-SYNTHESIS HYPOTHESIS

Using brain-imaging techniques such as a PET scan (see Chapter Two), researchers have found evidence that dreams are products of activity in the pons (Hobson, 1988; Hobson & McCarley, 1977; Hobson et al., 2000). This lower area inhibits the neurotransmitters that would allow movement of the voluntary muscles while sending random signals to the areas of the cortex that interpret vision, hearing, and so on (see Figure 4.4).

When signals from the pons bombard† the cortex during waking consciousness, the association areas of the cortex interpret those signals as seeing, hearing, and so on. Because those signals come from the real world, this process results in an experience of reality. But when people are asleep, the signals from the brain stem are random and not necessarily attached to actual external stimuli, yet the brain must somehow interpret these random signals. It *synthesizes* (puts together) an explanation of the cortex's activation from memories and other stored information.

In this theory, called the **activation-synthesis hypothesis**, a dream is merely another kind of thinking that occurs when people sleep. It is less realistic because it comes not from the outside world of reality but from within people's memories and experiences of the past. The frontal lobes, which people normally use in daytime thinking, are more or less shut down during dreaming, which may also account for the unrealistic and often bizarre nature of dreams (Macquet & Franck, 1996).

Dreams are often filled with unrealistic and imaginative events and images. A common dream is that of flying, What do you think flying might represent in a dream?

*ritualistic: referring to an action done in a particular manner each time it is repeated, according to some specific pattern.

**symbolic: having the quality of representing something other than itself.

†bombard: to attack or press.

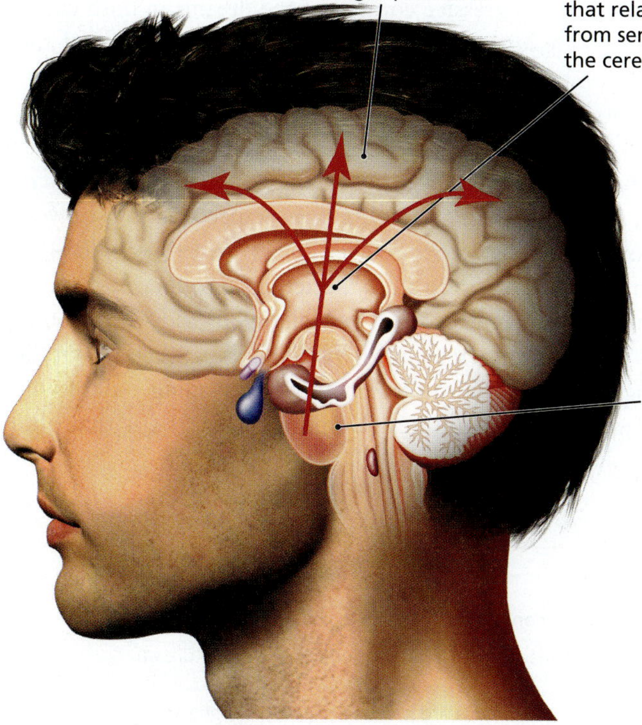

Figure 4.4 The Brain and Activation-Synthesis Theory

According to the activation-synthesis theory of dreaming, the pons in the brainstem sends random signals to the upper part of the brain during REM sleep. These random signals pass through the thalamus, which sends the signals to the proper sensory areas of the cortex. Once in the cortex, the association areas of the cortex respond to the random activation of these cortical cells by synthesizing (making up) a story, or dream, using bits and pieces of life experiences and memories.

My dreams can be really weird, but sometimes they seem pretty ordinary or even seem to mean something. Can dreams be more meaningful?

My dreams can be really weird, but sometimes they seem pretty ordinary or even seem to mean something. Can dreams be more meaningful?

There are dream experts who suggest that dreams may have more meaning than Hobson and McCarley originally theorized. A survey questioning subjects about their dream content, for example, concluded that much of the content of dreams is meaningful, consistent over time, and fits in with past or present emotional concerns rather than being bizarre, meaningless, and random (Domhoff, 1996, 2005).

Hobson and colleagues have reworked the activation-synthesis hypothesis to reflect concerns about dream meaning, calling it the **activation-information-mode model**, or **AIM** (Hobson et al., 2000). In this newer version, information that is accessed during waking hours can have an influence on the synthesis of dreams. In other words, when the brain is "making up" a dream to explain its own activation, it uses meaningful bits and pieces of the person's experiences from the previous day or the last few days rather than just random items from memory.

WHAT DO PEOPLE DREAM ABOUT?

Calvin Hall collected over 10,000 dreams and concluded that most dreams reflect the events that occur in everyday life (Hall, 1966). Although most people dream in color, people who grew up in the era of black and white television sometimes have dreams in black and white. There are gender differences, although whether those differences are caused by hormonal/genetic influences, sociocultural influences, or a combination of influences remains to be seen. In his book *Finding Meaning in Dreams*, Dr. William Domhoff (1996) concluded that across many cultures, men more often dream of other males whereas women tend to dream about males and females equally. Men across various cultures also tend to have more physical aggression in their dreams than do women, and women are more often the victims of such aggression in their own dreams. Domhoff also concluded that where there are differences in the content of

activation-synthesis hypothesis premise that states that dreams are created by the higher centers of the cortex to explain the activation by the brain stem of cortical cells during REM sleep periods.

activation-information-mode model (AIM) revised version of the activation-synthesis explanation of dreams in which information that is accessed during waking hours can have an influence on the synthesis of dreams.

dreams across cultures, the differences make sense in light of the culture's "personality." For example, American culture is considered fairly aggressive when compared to the culture of the Netherlands, and the aggressive content of the dreams in both cultures reflects this difference: There were lower levels of aggression in the dreams of those from the Netherlands when compared to the Americans' dream content.

Girls and women tend to dream about people they know, personal appearance concerns, and what issues related to family and home. Boys and men tend to have more male characters in their dreams, which are also typically in outdoor or unfamiliar settings and may involve weapons, tools, cars, and roads. Men also report more sexual dreams, usually with unknown and attractive partners (Domhoff, 1996; Foulkes, 1982; Van de Castle, 1994).

In dreams people run, jump, talk, and do all of the actions that they do in normal daily life. Nearly 50 percent of the dreams recorded by Hall (1966) had sexual content, although later research has found lower percentages (Van de Castle, 1994). Then there are dreams of flying, falling, and of trying to do something and failing—all of which are very common dreams, even in other cultures (Domhoff, 1996). So is that often-recounted dream of being naked in public!

CONCEPT MAP 4.5

Dreams

- **Why do we dream?**
  - **Freud's interpretation:** wish fulfillment—conflicts, events, and desires represented in symbolic form in dreams
    - **manifest content:** actual dream itself
    - **latent content:** hidden or symbolic meaning of dream
  - **activation-synthesis hypothesis**
    - dreams are product of random signals (activation), with brain forming explanation of signals based on memories and other information (synthesis)
    - activation-information-mode model (AIM) suggests that information access during waking hours can influence the synthesis of dreams
- **What do people dream about?**
  - typically about events that occur in everyday life; most in color; content influenced by gender and culture

PRACTICE quiz How much do you remember?

ANSWERS ON PAGE AK-1.

Pick the best answer.

1. In Freud's theory, the symbolic content of dreams is called ______.
   a. manifest content.
   b. latent content.
   c. symbolic content.
   d. hidden content.
2. Which dream theory states that dreams are simply the brain's way of explaining random neural activity while sleeping?
   a. Freudian dream theory
   b. dreams for survival theory
   c. activation-synthesis hypothesis
   d. Hall's dreams as reflections of everyday life
3. According to Hobson and McCarley, the ______ area of the brain sends signals to the ______, creating what we interpret as dreams.
   a. cerebellum; forebrain
   b. forebrain; cerebellum
   c. cortex; pons
   d. pons; cortex
4. The ______ lobes "shut down" during dreaming, explaining the often bizarre nature of dreams.
   a. frontal
   b. temporal
   c. occipital
   d. parietal
5. Shelia once had a dream in which she was trying to reach something important but couldn't. The harder she tried, the less she could move—it was like moving in molasses. This is most likely explained by ______.
   a. anxiety.
   b. REM paralysis.
   c. Stage 4 paralysis.
   d. a night terror.

Brainstorming Keep a notepad near your bed for the next few nights. When you wake up, immediately write down any dream that you experienced. After you've recorded a few dreams, think about how the events in the dream relate to your life. Are things included that were happening the day before the dream occurred? Were there memories? Were some of the elements of the dream repetitions from past dreams? Which dream theory seems to fit your dreams best?

Altered States: The Effects of Hypnosis

hypnosis state of consciousness in which the person is especially susceptible to suggestion.

Hypnosis is a state of consciousness in which a person is especially susceptible to suggestion. Although a lot of misunderstandings exist about hypnosis, it can be a useful tool when properly managed. **Watch** on **mypsychlab.com**

Watch a video about hypnosis on **mypsychlab.com**

STEPS IN HYPNOTIC INDUCTION

4.6 How does hypnosis affect consciousness?

There are several key steps in inducing hypnosis. According to Druckman and Bjork (1994), although every hypnotist may have a different style or use different words, these four steps are always present:

1. The hypnotist tells the person to focus on what is being said.
2. The person is told to relax and feel tired.
3. The hypnotist tells the person to "let go" and accept suggestions easily.
4. The person is told to use vivid imagination.

The real key to hypnosis seems to be a heightened state of suggestibility.* People can be hypnotized when active and alert, but only if they are willing to be hypnotized. Only 80 percent of all people can be hypnotized, and only 40 percent are good hypnotic subjects. People who fantasize a lot, who daydream and have vivid imaginations, as well as people who get "really into" whatever task they are doing are more susceptible** to hypnosis than others (Silva & Kirsch, 1992).

A test of *hypnotic susceptibility*, or the degree to which a person is a good hypnotic subject, often makes use of a series of ordered suggestions. The more suggestions in the ordered list the person responds to, the more susceptible that person is. (See Table 4.2 for an example of a susceptibility scale developed at Stanford University.)

FACT OR MYTH: WHAT CAN HYPNOSIS REALLY DO?

Is it true that people can be hypnotized into doing things that they would never do under normal conditions?

Is it true that people can be hypnotized into doing things that they would never do under normal conditions?

Books, movies, and television programs have often misrepresented the effects of hypnosis. Although the popular view is that the hypnotized person is acting involuntarily, the fact is that the hypnotized person is really the one in control. In fact, the hypnotist may only be a guide into a more relaxed state, while the subject actually hypnotizes himself or herself (Kirsch & Lynn, 1995). So relax, you won't be committing any immoral acts or doing anything really objectionable under hypnosis because you are really the one in control. People cannot be hypnotized against their will. The tendency to act as though their

Table 4.2

Sample Items from the Stanford Hypnotic Susceptibility Scale: Form A (SHSS:A)

1. Postural sway	**5.** Finger lock	**9.** Hallucination (fly)
2. Eye closure	**6.** Arm rigidity (left arm)	**10.** Eye catalepsy
3. Hand lowering (left)	**7.** Hands moving together	**11.** Posthypnotic (changes chairs)
4. Immobilization (right arm)	**8.** Verbal inhibition (name)	**12.** Amnesia

Source: Hilgard, E. (1965). *Hypnotic Susceptibility*. New York: Harcourt, Brace & World.

*suggestibility: being readily influenced.

**susceptible: easily affected emotionally.

Table 4.3

Facts About Hypnosis

HYPNOSIS CAN:	HYPNOSIS CANNOT:
Create amnesia for whatever happens during the hypnotic session, at least for a brief time (Bowers & Woody, 1996).	Give people superhuman strength. (People may use their full strength under hypnosis, but it is no more than they had before hypnosis.)
Relieve pain by allowing a person to remove conscious attention from the pain (Holroyd, 1996).	Reliably enhance memory. (There's an increased risk of false-memory retrieval because of the suggestible state hypnosis creates.)
Alter sensory perceptions. (Smell, hearing, vision, time sense, and the ability to see visual illusions can all be affected by hypnosis.)	Regress people back to childhood. (Although people may act like children, they do and say things children would not.)
Help people relax in situations that normally would cause them stress, such as flying on an airplane (Muhlberger et al., 2001).	Regress people to some "past life." There is no scientific evidence for past-life regression (Lilienfeld et al., 2004).

behavior is automatic and out of their control is called the *basic suggestion effect* (Kihlstrom, 1985); it gives people an excuse to do things they might not otherwise do because the burden of responsibility for their actions falls on the hypnotist.

Hypnosis is also a controversial tool when used in therapy to help people "recover" what are thought to be repressed memories. For a more detailed discussion of the problems in using hypnosis for memory retrieval, LINK to Chapter Six: Memory, pp. 236–238. For a concise look at what hypnosis can and cannot do, see Table 4.3.

In general, hypnosis is a handy way to help people relax and/or to control pain. These subjective experiences are very much under people's mental influence. Actual physical behavior is harder to change, and that is why hypnosis is not as effective at changing eating habits or helping people to stop smoking (Druckman & Bjork, 1994). Hypnosis is sometimes used in psychological therapy to help people cope with anxiety or deal with cravings for food or drugs. **Read** on **mypsychlab.com**

Read and learn more about hypnosis and research by Elizabeth Bowman on **mypsychlab.com**

THEORIES OF HYPNOSIS

There are two views of why hypnosis works. One emphasizes the role of *dissociation*, or a splitting of conscious awareness, whereas the other involves a kind of social role-playing.

Stage hypnotists often make use of people's willingness to believe that something ordinary is extraordinary. This woman was hypnotized and suspended between two chairs after the person supporting her middle stepped away. The hypnotist led the audience to believe that she could not do this unless hypnotized, but in reality anyone can do this while fully conscious.

HYPNOSIS AS DISSOCIATION: THE HIDDEN OBSERVER Ernest Hilgard (1991; Hilgard & Hilgard, 1994) believed that hypnosis worked only on the immediate conscious mind of a person, while a part of that person's mind (a "hidden observer") remained aware of all that was going on. It's the same kind of dissociation that takes place when people drive somewhere familiar and then wonder how they got there. One part of the mind, the conscious part, is thinking about dinner or a date or something else, while the other part is doing the actual driving. When people arrive at their destination, they don't really remember the actual trip. In the same way, Hilgard believes that there is a hidden part of the mind that is very much aware of the hypnotic subject's activities and sensations, even though the "hypnotized" part of the mind is blissfully unaware of these same things.

In one study (Miller & Bowers, 1993), subjects were hypnotized and told to put their arms in ice water, although they were instructed to feel no pain. There had to be pain—most people can't even get an ice cube out of the

*dissociate: break a connection with something.

freezer without *some* pain—but subjects reported no pain at all. The subjects who were successful at denying the pain also reported that they imagined being at the beach or in some other place that allowed them to dissociate* from the pain.

HYPNOSIS AS SOCIAL ROLE-PLAYING: THE SOCIAL-COGNITIVE EXPLANATION The other theory of why hypnosis works began with an experiment in which participants who were *not* hypnotized were instructed to behave as if they were (Sarbin & Coe, 1972). These participants had no trouble copying many actions previously thought to require a hypnotic state, such as being rigidly suspended between two chairs. The researchers also found that participants who were not familiar with hypnosis, and had no idea what the "role" of a hypnotic subject was supposed to be, could not be hypnotized.

Add to those findings the later findings of Kirsch (2000) that expectancies of the hypnotized person play a big part in how the person responds and what the person does under hypnosis. The **social-cognitive theory of hypnosis** assumes that people who are hypnotized are not in an altered state but are merely playing the role expected of them in the situation. They might believe that they are hypnotized, but in fact it is all a very good performance, so good that even the "participants" are unaware that they are role-playing. Social roles are very powerful influences on behavior, as anyone who has ever worn a uniform can understand—the uniform stands for a particular role that becomes very easy to play (Zimbardo, 1970; Zimbardo et al., 2000). LINK to Chapter Twelve: Social Psychology, pp. 479–480.

social-cognitive theory of hypnosis theory that assumes that people who are hypnotized are not in an altered state but are merely playing the role expected of them in the situation.

4.6 CONCEPT MAP

Altered States: Hypnosis

(state of consciousness during which person is more susceptible to suggestion)

- can be assessed by scale of hypnotic susceptibility
- induction typically involves relaxed focus and "permission to let go"; person being hypnotized is in control and cannot be hypnotized against his or her will
- can be used in therapy—helps people deal with pain, anxiety, or cravings (e.g., food, drug)
- theories
  - **dissociation:** one part of the mind is aware of actions/activities taking place, while the "hypnotized" part is not
  - **social-cognitive theory** suggests that people assume roles based on expectations for a given situation

PRACTICE quiz How much do you remember

ANSWERS ON PAGE AK-1.

Pick the best answer.

1. Which of the following is NOT one of the steps in inducing hypnosis?
   a. putting the person to sleep
   b. telling the person to relax
   c. telling the person to use vivid imagination
   d. telling the person to "let go"
2. The tendency to act as though your behavior is out of your control and involuntary is called (the) __________.
   a. hypnosis effect.
   b. basic involuntary effect.
   c. basic suggestion effect.
   d. none of the above.
3. Hypnosis has been successfully used to __________.
   a. give a person superhuman strength.
   b. recall memories accurately and completely.
   c. reduce sensations of pain.
   d. regress a person back to infancy.
4. In the __________ theory of hypnosis, a part of the person's mind is not hypnotized and is fully aware of the proceedings.
   a. social-cognitive
   b. dissociative
   c. role-playing
   d. expectancy

psychoactive drugs drugs that alter thinking, perception, and memory.

physical dependence condition occurring when a person's body becomes unable to function normally without a particular drug.

withdrawal physical symptoms that can include nausea, pain, tremors, crankiness, and high blood pressure, resulting from a lack of an addictive drug in the body systems.

Simulate psychoactive drugs on **mypsychlab.com**

Altered States: The Influence of Psychoactive Drugs

Whereas some people seek altered states of consciousness in sleep, daydreaming, meditation, or even hypnosis, others try to take a shortcut. They use **psychoactive drugs** that alter thinking, perception, memory, or some combination of those abilities. Many of the drugs discussed in the following sections are very useful and were originally developed to help people. Some allow sedation so that surgeries and procedures that would otherwise be impossible can be performed, whereas others help people deal with the pain of injuries or disease. Still others may be used in helping to control various conditions such as sleep disorders or attention deficits in children and adults.

The usefulness of these drugs must not blind us to the dangers of misusing or abusing them. When taken for pleasure, to get "high" or to dull psychological pain, or when taken without the supervision of a qualified medical professional, these drugs can pose serious risks to one's health and may even cause death. One danger of such drugs is their potential to create either a physical or psychological dependence, both of which can lead to a lifelong pattern of abuse as well as the risk of taking increasingly larger doses, leading to one of the clearest dangers of dependence: a drug overdose. Drug overdoses do not happen only with illegal drugs; even certain additives in so-called natural supplements can have a deadly effect. For example, in January 2003, Steve Bechler, a prospective pitcher for the Baltimore Orioles, died after taking three Ephedra pills on an empty stomach (Shekelle et al., 2003). Ephedra is a substance derived from a shrub found in desert areas and has been used in supplements that claim to promote weight loss. **Simulate** on **mypsychlab.com**

PHYSICAL DEPENDENCE

4.7 What is the difference between a physical dependence and a psychological dependence on a drug?

Drugs that people can become physically dependent on cause the user's body to crave the drug (Abadinsky, 1989; Fleming & Barry, 1992; Pratt, 1991). After using the drug for some period of time, the body becomes unable to function normally without the drug and the person is said to be dependent or addicted, a condition commonly called **physical dependence**.

DRUG TOLERANCE One sign of physical dependence is the development of a *drug tolerance* (Pratt, 1991). As the person continues to use the drug, larger and larger doses of the drug are needed to achieve the same initial effects of the drug.

WITHDRAWAL Another sign of a physical dependence is that the user experiences symptoms of **withdrawal** when deprived of the drug. Depending on the drug, these symptoms can range from headaches, nausea, and irritability to severe pain, cramping, shaking, and dangerously elevated blood pressure. These physical sensations occur because the body is trying to adjust to the absence of the drug. Many users will take more of the drug to alleviate the symptoms of withdrawal, which makes the entire situation worse. This is actually an example of *negative reinforcement*, the tendency to continue a behavior that leads to the removal of or escape from unpleasant circumstances or sensations. Negative reinforcement is a very powerful motivating factor, and scores of drug-dependent users exist as living proof of that power. LINK to Chapter Five: Learning, pp. 182–183.

But not all drugs produce physical dependence, right? For example, some people say that you can't get physically dependent on marijuana. If that's true, why is it so hard for some people to quit smoking pot?

But not all drugs produce physical dependence, right? For example, some people say that you can't get physically dependent on marijuana. If that's true, why is it so hard for some people to quit smoking pot?

PSYCHOLOGICAL DEPENDENCE

Not all drugs cause physical dependence; some cause **psychological dependence**, or the belief that the drug is needed to continue a feeling of emotional or psychological well-being, which is a very powerful factor in continued drug use. The body may not need or crave the drug, and people may not experience the symptoms of physical withdrawal or tolerance, but they will continue to use the drug because they *think* they need it. In this case, it is the rewarding properties of using the drug that cause a dependency to develop. This is an example of *positive reinforcement*, or the tendency of a behavior to strengthen when followed by pleasurable consequences. LINK to Chapter Five: Learning, pp. 182–183. Negative reinforcement is also at work here, as taking the drug will lower levels of anxiety.

Although not all drugs produce physical dependence, *any* drug can become a focus of psychological dependence. Indeed, because there is no withdrawal to go through or to recover from, psychological dependencies can last forever. Some people who gave up smoking marijuana decades ago still say that the craving returns every now and then (Roffman et al., 1988).

The effect of a particular drug depends on the category to which it belongs and the particular neurotransmitter the drug affects. LINK to Chapter Two: The Biological Perspective, pp. 52–54. In this current chapter we will describe several of the major drug categories, including **stimulants** (drugs that increase the functioning of the nervous system), **depressants** (drugs that decrease the functioning of the nervous system), **narcotics** (painkilling depressant drugs derived from the opium poppy), and **hallucinogenics** (drugs that alter perceptions and may cause hallucinations).

One of the dangers of psychoactive drugs is that they may lead to physical or psychological dependence. Cocaine is a powerful and addictive stimulant and can be sniffed in through the nose or injected, as the man in this photograph is doing.

STIMULANTS: UP, UP, AND AWAY

Stimulants are a class of drugs that cause either the sympathetic division or the central nervous system (or both) to increase levels of functioning, at least temporarily. In simple terms, stimulants "speed up" the nervous system—the heart may beat faster or the brain may work faster, for example. Many of these drugs are called "uppers" for this reason.

4.8 How do stimulants and depressants affect consciousness and what are the dangers associated with taking them, particularly alcohol?

AMPHETAMINES **Amphetamines** are stimulants that are synthesized (made) in laboratories rather than being found in nature. Among the amphetamines are drugs like Benzedrine, Methedrine, and Dexedrine. Some truck drivers use amphetamines to stay awake while driving long hours, and many doctors used to prescribe these drugs as diet pills for overweight people. A related compound, *methamphetamine*, is sometimes used to treat attention-deficit hyperactivity disorder or narcolepsy. "Crystal meth" is a crystalline form that can be smoked and is used by "recreational" drug users, people who do not need drugs but instead use them to gain some form of pleasure.

Like other stimulants, amphetamines cause the sympathetic nervous system to go into overdrive. LINK to Chapter Two: The Biological Perspective, p. 60. Stimulants won't give people any extra energy, but they will cause people to burn up whatever energy reserves they do have. They also depress the appetite, which is another function of the sympathetic division. When the energy reserves are exhausted, or the drug wears off, a "crash" is inevitable.

When the inevitable "crash" or depression comes, the tendency is to take more pills to get back "up." This is why people who take amphetamines often develop a physical dependency on the drug and quickly develop a tolerance. The person taking these pills finds that it takes more and more pills to get the same stimulant effect. Doses can easily become toxic and deadly. Nausea, vomiting, high blood pressure, and strokes are possible, as is a state called "amphetamine psychosis." This condition causes

psychological dependence the feeling that a drug is needed to continue a feeling of emotional or psychological well-being.

stimulants drugs that increase the functioning of the nervous system.

depressants drugs that decrease the functioning of the nervous system.

narcotics a class of opium-related drugs that suppress the sensation of pain by binding to and stimulating the nervous system's natural receptor sites for endorphins.

hallucinogenics drugs including hallucinogens and marijuana that produce hallucinations or increased feelings of relaxation and intoxication.

amphetamines stimulants that are synthesized (made) in laboratories rather than being found in nature.

addicts to become delusional (losing contact with what is real) and paranoid. They think people are out to "get" them. Violence is a likely outcome, both against the self and others (Kratofil et al., 1996).

Of course, amphetamines are also used to treat narcolepsy, the sleep disorder discussed earlier in this chapter. They are still used as diet pills, but only on a short-term basis and under strict medical supervision. The diet aids people buy over the counter usually contain another relatively mild stimulant, caffeine.

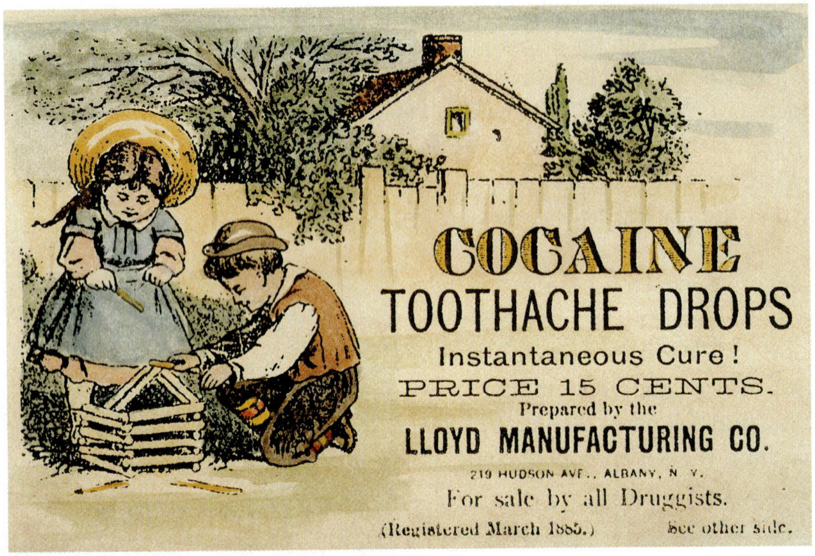

Far from being illegal, cocaine was once used in many health drinks and medications, such as this toothache medicine used in the late 1800s.

COCAINE Unlike amphetamines, **cocaine** is a natural drug found in coca plant leaves. It produces feelings of euphoria (a feeling of great happiness), energy, power, and pleasure. It also deadens pain and suppresses the appetite. It was used rather liberally by both doctors and dentists (who used it in numbing the mouth prior to extracting a tooth, for example) near the end of the nineteenth century and the beginning of the twentieth century, until the deadly effects of its addictive qualities became known. Many patent medicines contained minute traces of cocaine, including the now famous Coca-Cola™ (this popular soft drink was originally marketed as a nerve tonic). The good news is that even in 1902, there wasn't enough cocaine in a bottle of cola to affect even a fly, and by 1929, all traces of cocaine were removed (Allen, 1994).

Cocaine is a highly dangerous drug, not just for its addictive properties. Some people have convulsions and may even die when using cocaine for the first time (Lacayo, 1995). It can have devastating effects on the children born to mothers who use cocaine and has been associated with increased risk of learning disabilities, delayed language development, and an inability to cope adequately with stress, among other symptoms (Cone-Wesson, 2005; Eiden et al., 2009; Kable et al., 2008; Morrow et al., 2006). Laboratory animals have been known to press a lever to give themselves cocaine rather than eating or drinking, even to the point of starvation and death (Iwamoto & Martin, 1988; Ward et al., 1996).

What are the signs of physical dependency? Although cocaine users do not go through the same kind of physical withdrawal symptoms that users of heroin, alcohol, and other physically addictive drugs go through, users will experience a severe mood swing into depression (the "crash"), followed by extreme tiredness, nervousness, an inability to feel pleasure, and paranoia. The brain is the part of the body that develops the craving for cocaine because of chemical changes caused by the drug (Hurley, 1989). Three basic signs characterize physical dependency:

- **Compulsive use.** If cocaine is available, the dependent person has to use it. He or she can't say no to it.
- **Loss of control.** Those dependent upon cocaine can't stop using it when it's available until it's all gone or until they have exhausted themselves to the point where they can no longer function.
- **Disregard for the consequences of use.** Cocaine addicts will lie, cheat, steal, lose their jobs, damage or break up relationships, and use rent money to buy cocaine—nothing else matters to them but the drug. (This does not mean that before their dependency they were bad people—it is the drug's powerful addictive properties influencing their subsequent behavior, both physical and psychological dependencies.)

cocaine a natural drug derived from the leaves of the coca plant.

As addictive as cocaine is, there is one other stimulant that is usually described as even more addictive. Most experts in addiction seem to agree that although crack cocaine (a less pure, cheaper version found on the streets) produces addiction in nearly three fourths of the people who use it, nicotine produces addiction in 99 percent of the people who use it (Benowitz, 1988; Centers for Disease Control and Prevention [CDC], 1992; Franklin, 1990; Henningfield et al., 1991; Hilts, 1998; Perrine, 1997).

Hasn't nicotine just been the victim of a lot of bad press? After all, it's legal, unlike cocaine and heroin.

Hasn't nicotine just been the victim of a lot of bad press? After all, it's legal, unlike cocaine and heroin.

NICOTINE Every year, nearly 430,000 people in the United States die from illnesses related to smoking. That's more people than those who die from accidents in motor vehicles, alcohol, cocaine, heroin and other drug abuse, AIDS, suicide, and homicide *combined* (CDC, 2008). Remember, cocaine, heroin, morphine, and many other currently controlled substances or illegal drugs once used to be legal. One has to wonder what would have been the fate of these drugs if as many people had been making money off of them at that time as do those who farm, manufacture, and distribute tobacco products today.

Nicotine is a relatively mild but nevertheless toxic stimulant, producing a slight "rush" or sense of arousal as it raises blood pressure and accelerates the heart, as well as providing a rush of sugar into the bloodstream by stimulating the release of adrenalin (Rezvani & Levin, 2001). As is the case with many stimulants, it also has a relaxing effect on most people and seems to reduce stress (Pormerleau & Pormerleau, 1994).

Nicotine is highly addictive, and many smokers will go to great lengths to be able to smoke—including smoking right next to the "No Smoking" sign.

Although fewer Americans are smoking (down to about 25 percent from over 40 percent in the 1960s), women and teenagers are actually smoking more than before (CDC, 2008). This is alarming news when one considers the toxic nature of nicotine: In the 1920s and 1930s it was used as an insecticide and is considered to be highly toxic and fast acting (Gosselin et al., 1984). Although the amount of nicotine in a cigarette is low, first-time smokers often experience nausea as a result of the toxic effects after just a few puffs.

Quitting is a good idea but hard to accomplish for many people. Although there are a lucky few who can quit "cold turkey" without ever smoking again, the majority of people who quit will start smoking again, even after having quit for years.

Why is it so difficult to quit using tobacco products? Aside from the powerfully addictive nature of nicotine, the physical withdrawal symptoms can be as bad as those resulting from alcohol, cocaine, or heroin abuse (Epping-Jordan et al., 1998). People don't think about nicotine as being as bad as cocaine or heroin because nicotine is legal and easily obtainable, but in terms of its addictive power, it is *more powerful* than heroin or alcohol (Henningfield et al., 1990).

Effective "stop smoking" methods involve both education and behavior change. They might include initial or ongoing contact with a psychologist, physician, or other health-care provider. Social or programmatic support also helps, such as defining a quit date with a group of others, receiving counseling, or contacting a phone or chat-based counselor. Specific medications help users deal with cravings for nicotine. There are nicotine-containing gums, lozenges and patches (worn on the skin to deliver a measured dose of nicotine). Such nicotine replacement therapies deliver nicotine in a much safer and controlled manner, allowing the user to reduce cravings and the severity of nicotine withdrawal symptoms until quitting completely. Lastly, the combined strategies of counseling and medication work better than either alone (Fiore, et al., 2008).

CAFFEINE Although many people will never use amphetamines or take cocaine, and others will never smoke or will quit successfully, there is one stimulant that almost everyone uses, with many using it every day. This, of course, is **caffeine**, the stimulant found in coffee, tea, most sodas, chocolate, and even many over-the-counter drugs.

nicotine the active ingredient in tobacco.

caffeine a mild stimulant found in coffee, tea, and several other plant-based substances.

Sleep deprivation causes this man to struggle to wake up. Caffeine can help with alertness but may worsen his sleep deprivation when he tries to get a decent night's sleep tonight.

Caffeine is another natural substance, like cocaine and nicotine, and is found in coffee beans, tea leaves, cocoa nuts, and at least 60 other types of plants (Braun, 1996). It is a mild stimulant, helps maintain alertness, and can increase the effectiveness of some pain relievers such as aspirin. Caffeine is often added to pain relievers for that reason and is the key ingredient in medications meant to keep people awake.

Contrary to popular belief, coffee does not help induce sobriety. All one would get is a wide-awake drunk. Coffee is fairly acidic, too, and acids are not what the stomach of a person with a hangover needs. (And since the subject has come up, drinking more alcohol or "hair of the dog that bit you" just increases the problem later on—the best cure for a hangover is lots of water to put back all the fluids that alcohol takes out of the body and sleep.)

For a comparison of amounts of caffeine in some beverages, see Table 4.4.

DOWN IN THE VALLEY: DEPRESSANTS

Another class of psychoactive drugs is *depressants*, drugs that slow the central nervous system.

BARBITURATES OR THE MAJOR TRANQUILIZERS Commonly known as the *major tranquilizers* (drugs that have a strong depressant effect) or sleeping pills, **barbiturates** are drugs that have a sedative (sleep-inducing) effect. The effects, depending on dosage levels, range from mild sedation or sleepiness to unconsciousness or coma. Overdoses can lead to death as breathing and heart action are stopped. Barbiturates are highly addictive and users can quickly develop a tolerance. Withdrawal can be as serious as convulsions, which are life threatening (Olin, 1993).

Another danger of barbiturate use is the combination of one of these drugs with alcohol, another kind of depressant drug. A person who takes a dose of barbiturates that is not deadly in and of itself may die from the interaction of that dose with alcohol. This is called a *drug interaction* and is a major contributor to many unfortunate deaths.

Actor Heath Ledger died on January 22, 2010, from an accidental drug interaction. Six different types of depressant drugs were found in his system. He was 28.

Table 4.4
Average Caffeine Content of Some Beverages

PRODUCT (8 OZ EXCEPT AS NOTED)	CAFFEINE (MILLIGRAMS)
Brewed coffee	60–120
Decaffeinated coffee	2–4
Espresso/cappuccino (1 oz)	30–50
Tea brewed 1 minute	9–33
Tea brewed 3 minutes	20–46
Tea brewed 5 minutes	20–50
Iced tea (8 oz/12 oz)	15–24/22–36
Hot cocoa	3–32
Milk chocolate (1 oz)	1–15
Dark chocolate (1 oz)	5–35
Jolt soda (8 oz/12 oz)	47/71
Mountain Dew (8 oz/12 oz)	36/54
Coca-Cola (8 oz/12 oz)	31/46
Pepsi (8 oz/12 oz)	24/36

Source: Barone and Roberts (1996).

barbiturates depressant drugs that have a sedative effect.

BENZODIAZEPINES OR THE MINOR TRANQUILIZERS One common group of *minor tranquilizers* (drugs having a relatively mild depressant effect) are called **benzodiazepines**. These drugs are used to lower anxiety and reduce stress. They are considered safer than barbiturates and are now the drugs of choice to treat sleep problems, nervousness, and anxiety. Some of the most common are Valium, Xanax, Halcion, Ativan, and Librium.

Even these minor tranquilizers can be addictive, and large doses can be dangerous, as can an interaction with alcohol or other drugs. Rohypnol is a benzodiazepine tranquilizer that has become famous as the "date rape" drug. Unsuspecting victims drink something that has been doctored with this drug, which causes them to be unaware of their actions, although still able to respond to directions or commands, similar to the drug used on Latashia in this chapter's opening story. Rape or some other form of sexual assault can then be carried out without fear that the victim will remember it or be able to report it (Armstrong, 1997; Gable, 2004).

ALCOHOL

The most commonly used and abused depressant is **alcohol**, the chemical resulting from fermentation or distillation of various kinds of vegetable matter. Anywhere from 10 to 20 million people in the United States suffer from alcoholism. Aside from the obvious health risks to the liver, brain, and heart, alcohol is associated with loss of work time, loss of a job, and loss of economic stability.

SIGNS OF ALCOHOL ABUSE Many people are alcoholics but deny the fact. LINK to Chapter Thirteen: Theories of Personality, p. 498. They believe that getting drunk, especially in college, is a ritual of adulthood. Many college students and even older adults engage in binge drinking (drinking four or five drinks within a limited amount of time, such as at "happy hour"). Binge drinking quickly leads to being drunk, and drunkenness is a major sign of alcoholism. Some other danger signs are feeling guilty about drinking, drinking in the morning, drinking to recover from drinking, drinking alone, being sensitive about how much one drinks when others mention it, drinking so much that one does and says things one later regrets, drinking enough to have blackouts or memory loss, drinking too fast, lying about drinking, and drinking enough to pass out.

The dangers of abusing alcohol cannot be stressed enough. According to the National Center for Health Statistics (National Center for Health Statistics [NCHS], 2007), the number of alcohol-induced deaths in 2003 was 20,687. This figure does *not* include deaths due to accidents and homicides, that may be related to abuse of alcohol—only those deaths that are caused by the body's inability to handle the alcohol. Of these deaths, 12,360 were attributed to liver disease caused by alcoholism. The National Institute on Alcoholism and Alcohol Abuse (National Institute on Alcoholism and Alcohol Abuse [NIAAA], 2007) has statistics from 2001 to 2002 showing that the rate of psychiatric disorders, including alcohol and other drug abuse as well as depression and anxiety disorders, increases from about 2.5 percent for a light drinker to 13.2 percent for a moderate drinker and around 17.1 percent for a heavy drinker. Alcohol was involved in nearly 22.5 percent of the fatal traffic crashes for drivers under 21 years old and 24.8 percent of the fatal crashes for those over 21 (NIAAA, 2007).

There are numerous disorders that can be caused by alcoholism in addition to liver disease. *Korsakoff's syndrome* is a form of dementia brought about by a severe vitamin B1 deficiency, caused by the alcoholic's tendency to drink rather than eat (Manzo et al., 1994). Pregnant women should not drink at all, as alcohol can damage the growing embryo, causing a condition of mental retardation and physical deformity known as fetal alcohol syndrome. LINK to Chapter Eight: Development Across the Life Span, p. 306. Increased risk of loss of bone density (known as osteoporosis) and heart disease has also been linked to alcoholism (Abbott et al., 1994). These are just a few of the many health problems that alcohol can cause.

Although many young adults see drinking as a rite of passage into adulthood, few may understand the dangers of "binge" drinking, or drinking four to five drinks within a limited amount of time. Inhibitions are lowered and poor decisions may be made, such as driving while intoxicated. Binge drinking, a popular activity on some college campuses, can also lead to alcoholism.

benzodiazepines drugs that lower anxiety and reduce stress.

alcohol the chemical resulting from fermentation or distillation of various kinds of vegetable matter.

I have friends who insist that alcohol is a stimulant because they feel more uninhibited when they drink, so why is it considered a depressant?

If you are concerned about your own drinking or are worried about a friend or loved one, there is a free and very simple online assessment at this site on the Internet: **www.alcoholscreening.org**.

● *I have friends who insist that alcohol is a stimulant because they feel more uninhibited when they drink, so why is it considered a depressant?*

Alcohol is often confused with stimulants. Many people think this is because alcohol makes a person feel "up" and euphoric (happy). Actually, alcohol is a depressant that gives the illusion of stimulation, because the very first thing alcohol depresses is a person's natural inhibitions, or the "don'ts" of behavior. Inhibitions are all the social rules people have learned that allow them to get along with others and function in society. Inhibitions also keep people from taking off all their clothes and dancing on the table at a crowded bar—inhibitions are a good thing.

Many people are unaware of exactly what constitutes a "drink." Table 4.5 explains this and shows the effects of various numbers of drinks on behavior. Alcohol, as stated in Chapter Two, indirectly stimulates the release of a neurotransmitter

Table 4.5

Blood Alcohol Level and Behavior Associated With Amounts of Alcohol

A drink is a drink. Each contains half an ounce of alcohol.
So a drink is. . .

- 1 can of beer (12 oz 4–5% alcohol)
- 1 glass of wine (4 oz 12% alcohol)
- 1 shot of most liquors (1 oz 40–50% alcohol)

At times "a drink" is really the equivalent of more than just one drink, like when you order a drink with more than one shot of alcohol in it, or you do a shot followed by a beer.

AVERAGE NUMBER OF DRINKS	BLOOD ALCOHOL LEVEL	BEHAVIOR
1–2 drinks	.05%	Feeling of well-being Release of inhibitions Judgment impaired Coordination and level of alertness lowered Increased risk of collision while driving
3–5 drinks	.10%	Reaction time significantly slowed Muscle control and speech impaired Limited night and side vision Loss of self-control Crash risk greatly increased
6–7 drinks	.15%	Consistent and major increases in reaction time
8–10 drinks	.20%	Loss of equilibrium and technical skills Sensory and motor capabilities depressed Double vision and legal blindness (20/200) Unfit to drive for up to 10 hours
10–14 drinks	.20% and .25%	Staggering and severe motor disturbances
10–14 drinks	.30%	Not aware of surroundings
10–14 drinks	.35%	Surgical anesthesia Lethal dosage for a small percentage of people
14–20 drinks	.40%	Lethal dosage for about 50% of people Severe circulatory/respiratory depression Alcohol poisoning/overdose

Source: Adapted from the *Moderate Drinking Skills Study Guide*. (2004). Eau-Claire, WI: University of Wisconsin.

called GABA, the brain's major depressant (Brick, 2003). GABA slows down or stops neural activity. As more GABA is released, the brain's functioning actually becomes more and more inhibited, depressed, or slowed down. The areas of the brain that are first affected by alcohol are unfortunately the areas that control social inhibitions, so alcohol (due to its simulation of GABA) has the effect of depressing the inhibitions. As the effects continue, motor skills, reaction time, and speech are all affected.

Some people might be surprised that only one drink can have a fairly strong effect. People who are not usually drinkers will feel the effects of alcohol much more quickly than those who have built up a tolerance. Women also feel the effects sooner, as their bodies process alcohol differently than men's bodies do. (Women are typically smaller, too, so alcohol has a quicker impact on women.) **Watch** on **mypsychlab.com**

Watch videos on alcohol and the brain as well as alcoholism on **mypsychlab.com**

NARCOTICS: I FEEL YOUR PAIN

4.9 What are some of the effects and dangers of using narcotics and hallucinogens, including marijuana?

Narcotics are a class of drugs that suppress the sensation of pain by binding to and stimulating the nervous system's natural receptor sites for endorphins, the neurotransmitters that naturally deaden pain sensations (Olin, 1993). Because they also slow down the action of the nervous system, drug interactions with alcohol and other depressants are possible—and deadly. All narcotics are a derivative of a particular plant-based substance—opium.

OPIUM **Opium**, made from the opium poppy, has pain-relieving and euphoria-inducing properties that have been known for at least 2,000 years. It was commonly used by ladies of the Victorian era in a form called *laudanum* and was still prescribed as *paregoric* for teething infants in the middle of the twentieth century. (Your own parents or grandparents may have been given paregoric as infants.) It was not until 1803 that opium was developed for use as a medication by a German physician. The new form—morphine—was hailed as "God's own medicine" (Hodgson, 2001).

MORPHINE **Morphine** was created by dissolving opium in an acid and then neutralizing the acid with ammonia. Morphine was thought to be a wonder drug, although its addictive qualities soon became a major concern to physicians and their patients. Morphine is still used today but in carefully controlled doses and for short periods of time.

HEROIN Ironically, **heroin** was first hailed as the new wonder drug—a derivative of morphine that did not have many of the disagreeable side effects of morphine. The theory was that heroin was a purer form of the drug, and that the impurities in morphine were the substances creating the harmful side effects. It did not take long, however, for doctors and others to realize that heroin was even more powerfully addictive than morphine or opium. Although usage as a medicine ceased, it is still used by many people.

Why are morphine and heroin so addictive?

Why are morphine and heroin so addictive?

Think back to Chapter Two, which discussed the roles of endorphins in relieving pain. Opium and its derivatives, morphine and heroin, duplicate the action of endorphins so well that the nervous system slows or stops its production of the neurotransmitter. When the drug wears off, there is no protection against any kind of pain, causing the severe symptoms of withdrawal associated with these drugs. The addict who tries to quit using the drug feels such pain that the urge to use again becomes unbearable.

Methadone is a synthetic opioid but does not produce the euphoric "high" of morphine or heroin. It is used to control heroin dependency and can be taken only once a day to control the withdrawal symptoms that would otherwise follow when stopping heroin use (Kahan & Sutton, 1998). Two other drugs, buprenorphine and naltrexone, are also used to treat opiate addictions (Kakko et al., 2003; Ward et al., 1999). Eventually, as the

opium substance derived from the opium poppy from which all narcotic drugs are derived.

morphine narcotic drug derived from opium, used to treat severe pain.

heroin narcotic drug derived from opium that is extremely addictive.

addicted person is weaned from these drugs, the natural endorphin system starts to function more normally. This means that one does not have to take these other drugs forever.

The "high" of drug use, whether it comes from an opiate derivative, a stimulant, or a depressant such as alcohol, often takes place in certain surroundings, with certain other people, and perhaps even using certain objects, such as the tiny spoons used by cocaine addicts. These people, settings, and objects can become cues that are associated with the drug high. When the cues are present, it may be even harder to resist using the drug because the body and mind have become conditioned, or trained, to associate drug use with the cues. This is a form of *classical conditioning.* LINK to Chapter Five: Learning, pp. 171–173. This learned behavioral effect has led to nondrug treatments that make use of behavioral therapies such as *contingency-management therapy* (an operant conditioning strategy), in which patients earn vouchers for negative drug tests (Tusel et al., 1994). The vouchers can be exchanged for healthier, more desirable items like food. These behavioral therapies can include residential and outpatient approaches. LINK to Chapter Fifteen: Psychological Therapies, p. 584. *Cognitive-behavioral interventions* work to change the way people think about the stresses in their lives and react to those stressors, working toward more effective coping without resorting to heroin.

HALLUCINOGENS: HIGHER AND HIGHER

Hallucinogens actually cause the brain to alter its interpretation of sensations (Olin, 1993) and can produce sensory distortions very similar to *synesthesia* (LINK to Chapter Three: Sensation and Perception, p. 88), in which sensations cross over each other—colors have sound, sounds have smells, and so on. False sensory perceptions, called *hallucinations*, are often experienced, especially with the more powerful hallucinogens. There are two basic types—those that are created in a laboratory and those that are from natural sources.

MANUFACTURED HIGHS There are several drugs that were developed in the laboratory instead of being found in nature. Perhaps because these drugs are manufactured, they are often more potent than drugs found in the natural world. **Read** on **mypsychlab.com**

Read and learn more about other dangerous synthetic drugs on **mypsychlab.com**

LSD **LSD**, or **lysergic acid diethylamide**, is synthesized from a grain fungus called *ergot*. Ergot fungus commonly grows on rye grain but can be found on other grains as well. First manufactured in 1938, LSD is one of the most potent, or powerful, hallucinogens (Johnston et al., 2007; Lee & Shlain, 1986). It takes only a very tiny drop of LSD to achieve a "high."

People who take LSD usually do so to get that high feeling. Some people feel that LSD helps them expand their consciousness or awareness of the world around them. Colors seem more intense, sounds more beautiful, and so on. But the experience is not always a pleasant one, just as dreams are not always filled with positive emotions. "Bad trips" are quite common, and there is no way to control what kind of "trip" the brain is going to decide to take.

One of the greater dangers in using LSD is the effect it has on a person's ability to perceive reality. Real dangers and hazards in the world may go unnoticed by a person "lost" in an LSD fantasy, and people under the influence of this drug may make poor decisions, such as trying to drive while high.

PCP Another synthesized drug was found to be so dangerous that it remains useful only in veterinary medicine as a tranquilizer. The drug is **PCP** (which stands for *p*henyl *c*yclohexyl *p*iperidine, a name which is often contracted as *phencyclidine*) and can have many different effects. Depending on the dosage, it can be a hallucinogen, stimulant, depressant, or an analgesic (painkilling) drug. As with LSD, users of PCP can experience hallucinations, distorted sensations, and very unpleasant effects. PCP can also lead to acts of violence against others or suicide (Brecher 1988; Cami et al.,

hallucinogens drugs that cause false sensory messages, altering the perception of reality.

LSD (lysergic acid diethylamide) powerful synthetic hallucinogen.

PCP synthesized drug now used as an animal tranquilizer that can cause stimulant, depressant, narcotic, or hallucinogenic effects.

2000; Johnston et al., 2007). Users may even physically injure themselves unintentionally because PCP causes them to feel no warning signal of pain.

MDMA (Ecstasy) The last synthetic drug we will address here is technically an amphetamine but it is capable of producing hallucinations as well. In fact, both **MDMA** (a "designer drug" known on the streets as **Ecstasy** or simply **X**) and PCP are now classified as **stimulatory hallucinogenics**, drugs that produce a mixture of psychomotor stimulant and hallucinogenic effects (National Institute on Drug Abuse, 2006; Shuglin, 1986). Although many users of MDMA believe that it is relatively harmless, the fact is that it—like many other substances—can be deadly when misused. MDMA is a common drug at "raves" or all-night dance parties. One of the properties of this drug is to dehydrate the body and raise body temperature, so it is very important that someone taking this drug drink enough water. But excessive drinking of water can also lead to coma and death, as excess fluid can disrupt the salt content of body tissue, making it impossible for all body parts to function properly. Nightclubs that sponsor raves usually pass out or sell bottled water to offset the dehydration, but in the midst of having fun it is easy for a person to forget to drink enough—or to drink far too much. Adding to the risk is the possibility that Ecstasy users are also consuming alcohol, and that interaction increases the dehydration and rise in body temperature (Leccese et al., 2000).

Many of these young people enjoying themselves at a rave may be using MDMA, or Ecstasy. The dehydrating effect of the drug, together with the intense dancing and physical activity at raves like this one, can have a deadly effect on the user.

NONMANUFACTURED HIGHS A number of substances found in nature can produce hallucinogenic effects. Although some people might refer to these substances as "natural" highs, they are still drugs and still potentially dangerous, especially when used in conjunction with driving a vehicle or performing some other task that requires a clear head and focused attention.

Mescaline **Mescaline** comes from the buttons found on the peyote cactus and has long been a part of many Native American religious and spiritual rituals. The duration of its hallucinogenic effects can last longer than those of LSD (Aghajanian & Marek, 1999; Johnston et al., 2007). Native Americans have used mescaline in combination with sitting in a hut or other enclosed space while water is poured over very hot rocks. This sauna effect, together with the drug, may produce sensations of being out of one's own body or talking with spirits, which is the purpose of these rituals (Lyvers, 2003).

Psilocybin **Psilocybin** (si-luh-SIGH-bun) is another naturally occurring hallucinogen, contained in a certain kind of mushroom, often referred to as "magic mushrooms." Like mescaline, it has also been used in similar rituals by several native cultures (Aghajanian & Marek, 1999; Griffiths et al., 2006).

Is using mescaline or psilocybin addictive?

Neither mescaline nor psilocybin has been shown to create physical dependency, but as with any psychoactive drug, psychological dependency is possible (Lyvers, 2003). Eating psilocybin has been linked, however, to a psychiatric disorder called hallucinogen-persisting perception disorder (HPPD), as has the next drug: marijuana (Espiard et al., 2005).

MARIJUANA

One of the best known and most commonly abused of the hallucinogenic drugs, **marijuana** (also called "pot" or "weed") comes from the leaves and flowers of the hemp plant called *Cannabis sativa*. (*Hashish* is the concentrated substance made by scraping the resin from these leaves, and both marijuana and hashish contain *cannabinoids*.) The most psychoactive cannabinoid, and the active ingredient in marijuana, is *tetrahydrocannabinol* (THC). Marijuana is best known for its ability to produce a feeling of well-being, mild intoxication, and mild sensory distortions or hallucinations.

The effects of marijuana are relatively mild compared to the other hallucinogens. In fact, an inexperienced user who doesn't know what to expect upon smoking that first marijuana cigarette may feel nothing at all. Most people do report a feeling of mild euphoria and relaxation, along with an altered time sense and mild visual distortions. Higher doses can lead to hallucinations, delusions, and the all-too-common paranoia. Most studies of

MDMA (Ecstasy or X) designer drug that can have both stimulant and hallucinatory effects.

stimulatory hallucinogenics drugs that produce a mixture of psychomotor stimulant and hallucinogenic effects.

mescaline natural hallucinogen derived from the peyote cactus buttons.

psilocybin natural hallucinogen found in certain mushrooms.

marijuana mild hallucinogen (also known as "pot" or "weed") derived from the leaves and flowers of a particular type of hemp plant.

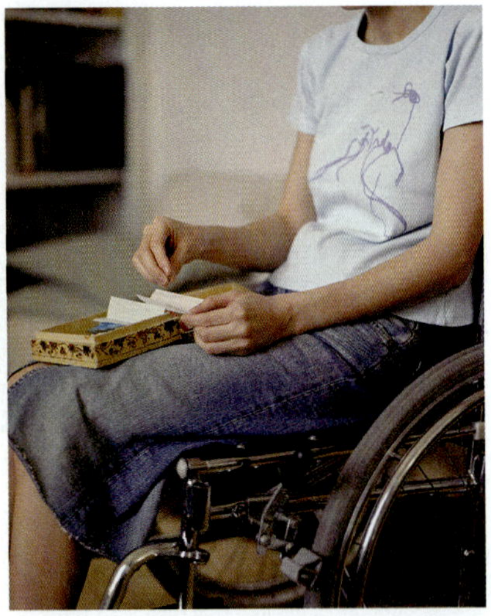
This woman is preparing a cannabis (marijuana) cigarette. Cannabis is reported to relieve pain in cases of multiple sclerosis and chronic pain from nerve damage. Such use is controversial as cannabis is classified as an illegal drug in some countries.

marijuana's effects have concluded that while marijuana can create a powerful psychological dependency, it does not produce physical dependency or physical withdrawal symptoms. However, after alcohol and nicotine, cannabis dependence is the most common form of drug dependence in the United States, Canada, and Australia (Hall & Degenhardt, 2009).

Even at mild doses, it is not safe to operate heavy machinery or drive a car while under the influence of marijuana because it negatively affects reaction time and perception of surroundings; the drug reduces a person's ability to make the split-second decisions that driving a car or other equipment requires. Information processing in general, attention, and memory, are all likely to be impaired in a person who has used marijuana.

Marijuana is most commonly smoked like tobacco, but some people have been known to eat it baked into brownies or other foods. This is a kind of double duty for the doctored food, as marijuana stimulates the appetite.

Although no one has ever been known to die from an overdose of marijuana, smoking it is not a healthy habit. Research linking marijuana smoking and lung cancer is not definitive due to the fact that many studies have not been able to control for confounding variables, such as cigarette smoking, alcohol use, or other risk factors (Hall & Degenhardt, 2009). LINK to Chapter One: The Science of Psychology, p. 29. Aside from those previously mentioned, probable adverse effects from chronic nonmedical marijuana use also include increased risk of motor vehicle crashes, chronic bronchitis or other lung problems, and cardiovascular disease. In adolescents who are regular users, psychosocial development, educational attainment, and mental health can be negatively impacted (Hall & Degenhardt, 2009). With regard to the possible mental health problems, there especially appears to be an increased risk for psychotic symptoms and disorders later in life for adolescents who are regular and heavier users (Hall & Degenhardt, 2009; Moore et al., 2007).

Table 4.6 summarizes the various types of drugs, their common names, and their effects on human behavior.

Table 4.6
How Drugs Affect Consciousness

DRUG CLASSIFICATION	COMMON NAME	MAIN EFFECT	ADVERSE EFFECTS
Depressants			
Alcohol	Beer, wine, spirits	Relaxation	Alcoholism, health problems, depression, increased risk of accidents, death
Barbiturates (tranquilizers)	Nembutal, Seconal		Addiction, brain damage, death
Benzodiazepines (minor tranquilizers)	Valium, Xanax, Halcion, Ativan, Rohypnol		Lower risk of overdose and addiction when taken alone
Stimulants			
Amphetamines	Methamphetamine, speed, Ritalin, Dexedrine	Stimulation, excitement	Risk of addiction, stroke, fatal heart problems, psychosis
Cocaine	Cocaine, crack		Risk of addiction, stroke, fatal heart problems, psychosis
Nicotine	Tobacco		Addiction, cancer
Caffeine	Coffee, tea		Addiction, high blood pressure
Narcotics (Opiates)	Morphine, heroin	Euphoria	Addiction, death
Hallucinogens	Marijuana, hashish, LSD, Ecstasy	Distorted consciousness, altered perception	Possible permanent memory problems bad "trips," suicide, overdose, and death

4.7 4.8 4.9

CONCEPT MAP

Altered States: Psychoactive Drugs

(drugs that alter thinking, perception, or memory)

- **Why do some people continue to use or become addicted to psychoactive drugs?**
  - **physical dependence:** user's body needs a drug to function; drug tolerance and withdrawal are warning signs/symptoms
  - **psychological dependence:** user believes drug is needed to function
- **types**
  - **stimulants**
    increase functioning of nervous system
    - **amphetamines**
    - **cocaine**
    - **nicotine**
    - **caffeine**
  - **depressants**
    have sedative effect
    - **barbiturates**
      major tranquilizers
    - **benzodiazepines**
      minor tranquilizers—Valium, Xanax, Halcion, Ativan, Librium, Rohypnol
    - **alcohol**
  - **narcotics**
    euphoria-producing and pain-relieving drugs derived from opium
    - **morphine**
    - **heroin**
    - **methadone**
      does not produce euphoria; used to treat heroin addiction
  - **hallucinogens**
    alter brain's interpretation of sensations
    - **manufactured**
      - **LSD**
      - **PCP**
      - **MDMA (Ectasy)**
    - **nonmanufactured**
      - **mescaline**
      - **psilocybin**
      - **marijuana**

PRACTICE quiz How much do you remember?

ANSWERS ON PAGE AK-1.

Pick the best answer.

1. What are two signs of physical dependency?
   a. drug tolerance and psychological cravings
   b. psychological cravings and withdrawal
   c. drug tolerance and withdrawal
   d. psychological cravings and nausea
2. Larger and larger doses of amphetamines can lead to a severe mental disturbance and paranoia called _______.
   a. amphetamine neurosis. **c.** amphetaminism.
   b. amphetamine psychosis. **d.** amphetamine toxicity.
3. Which of the following is NOT one of the three signs of cocaine abuse?
   a. withdrawal **c.** loss of control
   b. compulsive use **d.** disregard for consequences
4. Caffeine replaced _________ in patent medicines and over-the-counter preparations in the early 1900s.
   a. cocaine **c.** opium
   b. morphine **d.** nicotine
5. The "date rape" drug, Rohypnol, is one of the _________.
   a. major tranquilizers. **c.** minor tranquilizers.
   b. barbiturates. **d.** opiates.
6. Several of her friends suspect that Marnie is using some sort of drug. She is very thin, stays awake for long periods of time, and is often jittery, nervous, and somewhat paranoid. If Marnie is using a drug, it is likely to be _________.
   a. alcohol. **c.** sleeping pills.
   b. an amphetamine. **d.** benzodiazapine.
7. All narcotics are derived from _________.
   a. cannabis. **c.** mescaline.
   b. opium. **d.** morphine.
8. This drug was at first hailed as the new wonder drug because the impurities that supposedly caused many of the addictive and unpleasant side effects of the previous version had been removed. In fact, _________ was even more addictive and deadly.
   a. laudanum **c.** morphine
   b. heroin **d.** ergot
9. Which of the following hallucinogens is NOT a synthetically created drug?
   a. psylocybin **c.** PCP
   b. LSD **d.** MDMA
10. Of the following, which comes from the peyote cactus?
    a. mescaline **c.** marijuana
    b. psilocybin **d.** ergot
11. Which of the following have been correlated with long-term marijuana use?
    a. breathing problems **c.** mental health issues
    b. cardiovascular disease **d.** all of the above
12. Which of the following statements about marijuana is TRUE?
    a. Marijuana is not physically addictive.
    b. It is safe to drive under the influence of pot.
    c. Marijuana is healthier than tobacco.
    d. Short-term memory is enhanced by smoking marijuana.

Individuals sometimes awaken with the very real feeling that they have been visited by aliens, or a ghost, demon or even an angel. The more logical explanation is that they have been startled awake from either a hypnogogic and hypnopompic hallucination experienced at some point as they were sleeping.

Applying Psychology to Everyday Life: Thinking Critically About Ghosts, Aliens, and Other Things That Go Bump in the Night

4.10 What are hypnogogic and hypnopompic hallucinations?

Down through the ages, people have been visited by ghosts, spirits, and other sorts of mystical or mysterious visitors—or so they have believed. In more modern times, ghostly visitations have often given way to aliens, who may perform some sort of medical examination or who may abduct the person, only to return them to their beds. And it is to their beds that they are usually returned, and such visitations typically are experienced when the person is in bed. Is there a simpler, more parsimonious explanation for these experiences?

As mentioned earlier in this chapter, a type of hallucination can occur just as a person is entering Stage 1 sleep, called a *hypnogogic hallucination* (Ohayon et al., 1996; Siegel & West, 1975). If you remember that people in Stage 1 sleep, when awakened, will deny having been asleep, a simple explanation for so-called supernatural visitations does present itself. Hypnogogic hallucinations are not dreamlike in nature. Instead, they feel very real to the person experiencing them (who does not think he or she is asleep, remember). Most common are the auditory hallucinations, in which a person might hear a voice calling out the person's name, not all that unusual and probably not remembered most of the time.

Imagine for a moment, though, that your hypnogogic hallucination is that of some person whom you know to be dead or ill, or a strange and frightening image, perhaps with equally strange and frightening sound effects. That you will remember, especially since you are likely to wake up right after *and be completely convinced that you were awake at the time of the hallucination.* Combine this experience with the natural tendency many people have to want to believe that there is life after death or that there are other sentient life forms visiting our planet, and *voilà!*—a ghost/spirit/alien has appeared.

Sometimes people have a similar experience in the middle of the night. They awaken to find that they are paralyzed and that something—ghost, demon, alien—is standing over them and perhaps doing strange things to their helpless bodies. When a hallucination happens just as a person is in the between-state of being in REM sleep (in which the voluntary muscles are paralyzed) and not yet fully awake, it is called a *hypnopompic hallucination* and is once again a much simpler explanation of visits by aliens or spirits during the night than any supernatural explanation. Such visitations are not as rare as you might think, but once again, it is only the spectacular, frightening, or unusual ones that will be remembered (Cheyne, 2003; Greeley, 1987; Ohayon et al., 1996).

Questions for Further Discussion

1. Have you ever had one of these experiences? Can you now understand how that experience might have been one that you would remember?
2. Talk to friends or family about their similar experiences, looking for the simpler explanation.

chapter summary

Listen on **mypsychlab.com** Listen to an audio file of your chapter **www.mypsychlab.com**

What Is Consciousness?

4.1 What does it mean to be conscious, and are there different levels of consciousness?

- Consciousness is a person's awareness of everything that is going on at any given moment. Most waking hours are spent in waking consciousness.
- Altered states of consciousness are shifts in the quality or pattern of mental activity.

Altered States: Sleep

4.2 Why do people need to sleep, and how does sleep work?

- Sleep is a circadian rhythm, lasting 24 hours, and is a product of the activity of the hypothalamus, the hormone melatonin, the neurotransmitter serotonin, and body temperature.
- Adaptive theory states that sleep evolved as a way to conserve energy and keep animals safe from predators that hunt at night.
- Restorative theory states that sleep provides the body with an opportunity to restore chemicals that have been depleted during the day as well as the growth and repair of cell tissue.
- The average amount of sleep needed by most adults is about 7 to 9 hours within each 24-hour period.

4.3 What are the different stages of sleep, including the stage of dreaming and its importance?

- Stage 1 sleep is light sleep.
- Stage 2 sleep is indicated by the presence of sleep spindles, bursts of activity on the EEG.
- Stage 3 is highlighted by the first appearance of delta waves, the slowest and largest waves, whereas Stage 4 is predominantly delta waves, and the body is at its lowest level of functioning.
- REM sleep occurs four or five times a night, replacing Stage 1 after a full cycle through Stages 1 through 4 and then back to Stage 1. It is accompanied by paralysis of the voluntary muscles but rapid movement of the eyes.

4.4 How do sleep disorders interfere with normal sleep?

- Sleepwalking and sleeptalking occur in Stage 4 sleep.
- Voluntary muscles are paralyzed during REM sleep.
- Nightmares and a rare disorder called REM behavior disorder occur during REM sleep.

PSYCHOLOGY IN THE NEWS: Murder While Sleepwalking

- Sleepwalking has been used as a defense in numerous cases of murder. In many of these cases, the defendant has been acquitted because of the sleepwalking defense.

- Night terrors are attacks of extreme fear that the victim has while sound asleep.
- Nightmares are bad or unpleasant dreams that occur during REM sleep.
- REM behavior disorder is a rare condition in which REM paralysis fails and the person moves violently while dreaming, often acting out the elements of the dream.
- Insomnia is an inability to get to sleep, stay asleep, or get enough sleep.
- Sleep apnea occurs when a person stops breathing for nearly half a minute or more.
- Narcolepsy is a genetic disorder in which the person suddenly and without warning collapses into REM sleep.

Dreams

4.5 Why do people dream, and what do they dream about?

- Manifest content of a dream is the actual dream and its events. Latent content of a dream is the symbolic content, according to Freud.
- Without outside sensory information to explain the activation of the brain cells in the cortex by the pons area, the association areas of the cortex synthesize a story, or dream, to explain that activation in the activation-synthesis hypothesis.
- A revision of activation-synthesis theory, the activation-information-mode model (AIM) states that information experienced during waking hours can influence the synthesis of dreams.

Altered States: The Effects of Hypnosis

4.6 How does hypnosis affect consciousness?

- Hypnosis is a state of consciousness in which a person is especially susceptible to suggestion.
- The hypnotist will tell the person to relax and feel tired, to focus on what is being said, to let go of inhibitions and accept suggestions, and to use vivid imagination.
- Hypnosis cannot give increased strength, reliably enhance memory, or regress people to an earlier age or an earlier life, but it can produce amnesia, reduce pain, and alter sensory impressions.
- Hilgard believed that a person under hypnosis is in a state of dissociation, in which one part of consciousness is hypnotized and susceptible to suggestion, while another part is aware of everything that occurs.
- Other theorists believe that the hypnotized subject is merely playing a social role—that of the hypnotized person. This is called the social-cognitive theory of hypnosis.

Altered States: The Influence of Psychoactive Drugs

4.7 What is the difference between a physical dependence and a psychological dependence on a drug?

- Drugs that are physically addictive cause the user's body to crave the drug. When deprived of the drug, the user will go through physical withdrawal.
- Drug tolerance occurs as the user's body becomes conditioned to the level of the drug. After a time, the user must take more and more of the drug to get the same effect.
- In psychological dependence, the user believes that he or she needs the drug to function well and maintain a sense of well-being. Any drug can produce psychological dependence.

4.8 How do stimulants and depressants affect consciousness and what are the dangers associated with taking them, particularly alcohol?

- Stimulants are drugs that increase the activity of the nervous system, particularly the sympathetic division and the central nervous system.
- Amphetamines are synthetic drugs such as Benzedrine or Dexedrine. They help people stay awake and reduce appetite but are highly physically addictive.
- Cocaine is highly addictive and can cause convulsions and death in some first-time users.
- Nicotine is a mild stimulant and is very physically addictive.
- Caffeine is the most commonly used stimulant, found in coffee, tea, chocolate, and many sodas.
- Barbiturates, also known as major tranquilizers, have a sedative effect and are used as sleeping pills.
- The minor tranquilizers are benzodiazepines such as Valium or Xanax.
- Alcohol is the most commonly used and abused depressant.
- Alcohol can interact with other depressants.
- Excessive use of alcohol can lead to alcoholism, health problems, loss of control, and death.

4.9 What are some of the effects and dangers of using narcotics and hallucinogens, including marijuana?

- Narcotics are pain-relieving drugs of the depressant class that are derived from the opium poppy.
- Opium is the earliest form of this drug and is highly addictive because it directly stimulates receptor sites for endorphins. This causes natural production of endorphins to decrease.
- Morphine is a more refined version of opium but is highly addictive.
- Heroin was believed to be a purer form of morphine and, therefore, less addictive but in fact is even more powerfully addictive.
- Methadone has the ability to control the symptoms of heroin or morphine withdrawal without the euphoria, or "high," of heroin or morphine.
- Hallucinogens are stimulants that alter the brain's interpretation of sensations, creating hallucinations. Three synthetically created hallucinogens are LSD, PCP, and MDMA.
- Three naturally occurring hallucinogens are mescaline, psilocybin, and marijuana.
- Marijuana is a mild hallucinogen, producing a mild euphoria and feelings of relaxation in its users. Larger doses can lead to hallucinations and paranoia. It contains substances that may be carcinogenic and impairs learning and memory.

Applying Psychology to Everyday Life: Thinking Critically About Ghosts, Aliens, and Other Things That Go Bump in the Night

4.10 What are hypnogogic and hypnopompic hallucinations?

- Vivid, realistic hallucinations that occur in Stage 1 sleep are called hypnogogic hallucinations and are often misinterpreted as ghosts or other supernatural visitations.
- Similar hallucinations that occur when awakening from REM sleep are called hypnopompic hallucinations.

test YOURSELF

ANSWERS ON PAGE AK-1.

Study and Review on **mypsychlab.com** Ready for your test? More quizzes and a customized study plan **www.mypsychlab.com**

Pick the best answer.

1. Most of our time awake is spent in a state called _________, in which our thoughts, feelings, and sensations are clear and organized, and we feel alert.
   a. altered state of consciousness
   b. waking consciousness
   c. unconsciousness
   d. working consciousness
2. Which of the following situations is NOT an altered state of consciousness?
   a. You are daydreaming.
   b. You have been drinking beer.
   c. You are concentrating on a math test.
   d. You are asleep.
3. Which of the following is NOT an example of a circadian rhythm?
   a. menstrual cycle
   b. sleep–wake cycle
   c. blood pressure changes
   d. body temperature changes
4. When light begins to fade at the end of the day, the suprachiasmatic nucleus in the _________ signals the pineal gland to release _________.
   a. hippocampus; melatonin.
   b. hippocampus; serotonin.
   c. hypothalamus; melatonin.
   d. hypothalamus; serotonin.
5. Which of the following was NOT listed as one of the factors involved in the ability to go to sleep?
   a. body mass
   b. body temperature
   c. serotonin levels
   d. melatonin levels
6. The symptoms of sleep deprivation include all but which of the following?
   a. trembling hands
   b. inability to concentrate
   c. feeling of general discomfort
   d. hypnic jerk
7. You hear about an accident that took place at 3:00 A.M. The car was traveling along and then seemed to drift into the opposing lane of traffic, hitting an oncoming car head on. Given the early morning time, you suspect that the driver of the car that drifted over the center line most likely experienced a _________.
   a. lapse in judgment.
   b. microsleep episode.
   c. hypnogogic episode.
   d. hypnopompic episode.
8. It might be best to say that adaptive theory explains _________, whereas restorative theory explains _________.
   a. why we *need* to sleep; *when* we sleep.
   b. *where* we sleep; why we *need* to sleep.
   c. why we *need* to sleep; *where* we sleep.
   d. *when* we sleep; why we *need* to sleep.

9. What is the first stage of sleep in which, if awakened, you will realize that you were asleep?
a. Stage 1
b. Stage 2
c. Stage 3
d. Stage 4

10. In which stage of sleep do night terrors occur?
a. Stage 1
b. Stage 2
c. Stage 3
d. Stage 4

11. Sleepwalking _________.
a. is partly hereditary.
b. occurs more frequently in girls than in boys.
c. occurs in about 50 percent of the population.
d. lasts well into late adulthood in most people.

12. Night terrors _________.
a. are the same thing as nightmares.
b. are always vividly remembered afterward.
c. are more common in children.
d. take place in one of the lighter stages of sleep.

13. Which of the following statements about REM sleep is FALSE?
a. The eyes move rapidly back and forth under the eyelids.
b. Most people report that they were dreaming if awakened.
c. The body is aroused and brain waves resemble waking beta waves.
d. Lack of REM sleep produces psychological disorders.

14. If you are in REM sleep but are able to move around and act out your dreams, you may have a rare condition called _________.
a. REM behavior disorder.
b. somnambulism.
c. nightmare disorder.
d. narcolepsy.

15. If you suddenly and without warning slip into REM sleep during the day, often falling down as you do so, you may have the condition called _________.
a. sleep apnea.
b. insomnia.
c. narcolepsy.
d. epilepsy.

16. A sleep disorder that may require the use of a machine to force air gently into the nasal passages is called _________.
a. sleep apnea.
b. insomnia.
c. narcolepsy.
d. cataplexy.

17. Randall tells his therapist that he had a dream about riding on a train that went through a tunnel. The therapist tells Randall that his dream was most likely about sexual intercourse, as the tunnel represents a woman's vagina. Randall's therapist is using the _________ theory of dreams to explain Randall's dream.
a. activation-synthesis
b. dreams-for-survival
c. Hobson/McCarley
d. Freudian

18. Hypnosis has been shown to do all of the following BUT _________.
a. induce amnesia for what happens during the hypnotic state.
b. provide pain relief without medication.
c. alter sensory perceptions.
d. regress people back to their early childhood experiences.

19. Jackie used Ecstasy while she was in college, but now that she has a government job she has avoided using any recreational drugs. Although she had no problem quitting, she still finds that every now and then she gets a strong craving to use Ecstasy again. Her craving is most likely the result of _________.
a. psychological dependence.
b. physical dependency.
c. withdrawal.
d. none of the above.

20. Which of the following is NOT a naturally occurring substance?
a. nicotine
b. amphetamine
c. caffeine
d. cocaine

21. Which of the following is NOT a depressant?
a. alcohol
b. valium
c. PCP
d. barbiturate

22. Alcohol actually _________ the release of GABA, a neurotransmitter that inhibits many brain functions.
a. depresses
b. decreases
c. stimulates
d. prevents

23. _________ was originally thought to be a more pure form of morphine, with fewer side effects.
a. Heroin
b. Laudanum
c. Paregoric
d. Methadone

24. "Magic mushrooms" are the source of _________.
a. marijuana.
b. psilocybin.
c. mescaline.
d. Ecstasy.

25. High doses of marijuana can lead to _________.
a. death.
b. hallucinations and delusions.
c. extreme arousal.
d. none of the above.

4 consciousness

sleep, dreams, hypnosis, and drugs

4.2 p. 136

Altered States—Sleep

(sleep is one of the body's daily [circadian] biological rhythms; sleep–wake cycle controlled by the brain including the hypothalamus and the neurotransmitter serotonin)

- hypothalamus contains the suprachiasmatic nucleus (SCN)
  - SCN is sensitive to light—influences pineal gland's secretion of melatonin (↑ melatonin = ↑ sleepiness)
  - light through eyes relayed to SCN; SCN signals pineal gland to stop producing melatonin (↓ melatonin = ↑ alertness / ↓ sleepiness)
  - SCN also influences body temperature (↓ temperature = ↑ sleepiness)
- people can live without sleep for a while, can't live without it altogether
  - **sleep deprivation** can lead to serious changes in body and mental functioning
  - **amount of sleep needed** ranges from 4–10 hours; most people need 7–9 hours every 24 hours
  - **adaptive theory of sleep** suggests sleep is a product of evolution; sleep has evolved to avoid the active time of predators
  - **restorative theory of sleep** suggests sleep is vital to the physical health of the body; body growth and repair occur during the deepest stages of sleep

4.3 **4.4** p. 143

Altered States—Sleep: Stages and Disorders

- consist of both REM (rapid eye movement) and non-REM stages
  - **non-REM Stage 1**
  - **non-REM Stage 2**
  - **non-REM Stages 3 and 4**
  - **REM sleep**

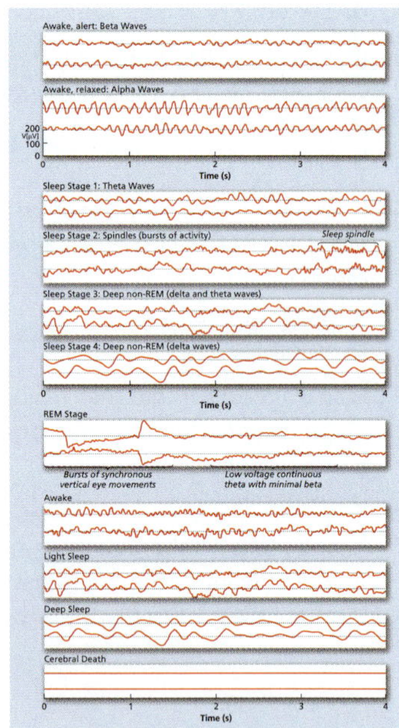

- sleep disorders include a variety of problems that can interfere with sleep
  - **insomnia**
  - **sleep apnea**
  - **narcolepsy**

"On your application it says you have narcolepsy. What is that?"

Table 4.1
Sleep Disorders

NAME OF DISORDER	PRIMARY SYMPTOMS
Somnambulism	Sitting, walking, or performing complex behavior while asleep
Night terrors	Extreme fear, agitation, screaming while asleep
Restless leg syndrome	Uncomfortable sensations in legs causing movement and loss of sleep
Nocturnal leg cramps	Painful cramps in calf or foot muscles
Hypersomnia	Excessive daytime sleepiness
Circadian rhythm disorders	Disturbances of the sleep–wake cycle such as jet lag and shift work
Enuresis	Urinating while asleep in bed

4.5 p. 146

Dreams

- **Why do we dream?**
  - **Freud's interpretation:** wish fulfillment—conflicts, events, and desires represented in symbolic form in dreams
  - **activation-synthesis hypothesis**
- **What do people dream about?**
  - typically about events that occur in everyday life; most in color; content influenced by gender and culture

4.6 p. 149

Altered States: Hypnosis

(state of consciousness during which person is more susceptible to suggestion)

- can be assessed by scale of hypnotic susceptibility
- induction typically involves relaxed focus and "permission to let go"; person being hypnotized is in control and cannot be hypnotized against his or her will
- can be used in therapy—helps people deal with pain, anxiety, or cravings (e.g., food, drug)
- theories
  - **dissociation:** one part of the mind is aware of actions/activities taking place, while the "hypnotized" part is not
  - **social-cognitive theory** suggests that people assume roles based on expectations for a given situation

Table 4.3
Facts About Hypnosis

HYPNOSIS CAN:	HYPNOSIS CANNOT:
Create amnesia for whatever happens during the hypnotic session, at least for a brief time (Bowers & Woody, 1996).	Give people superhuman strength. (People may use their full strength under hypnosis, but it is no more than they had before hypnosis.)
Relieve pain by allowing a person to remove conscious attention from the pain (Holroyd, 1996).	Reliably enhance memory. (There's an increased risk of false memory because retrieval of the suggestible state hypnosis creates.)
Alter sensory perceptions. (Smell, hearing, vision, time sense, and the ability to see visual illusions can all be affected by hypnosis.)	Regress people back to childhood. (Although people may *act* like children, they do and say things children would not.)
Help people relax in situations that normally would cause them stress, such as flying on an airplane (Muhlberger et al., 2001).	Regress people to some "past life." There is no scientific evidence for past-life regression (Lilienfeld et al., 2004).

4.7 4.8 4.9 p. 161

- **Why do some people continue to use or become addicted to psychoactive drugs?**
  - **physical dependence:** user's body needs a drug to function; drug tolerance and withdrawal are warning signs/symptoms
  - **psychological dependence:** user believes drug is needed to function

Altered States: Psychoactive Drugs

(drugs that alter thinking, perception, or memory)

"Nowadays, Hal is ninety-nine per cent caffeine-free."

- types
  - **stimulants** increase functioning of nervous system
    - **amphetamines**
    - **cocaine**
    - **nicotine**
    - **caffeine**
  - **depressants** have sedative effect
    - **barbiturates** major tranquilizers
    - **benzodiazepines** minor tranquilizers—Valium, Xanax, Halcion, Ativan, Librium, Rohypnol
    - **alcohol**
  - **narcotics** euphoria-producing and pain-relieving drugs derived from opium
    - **morphine**
    - **heroin**
    - **methadone** does not produce euphoria; used to treat heroin addiction
  - **hallucinogens** alter brain's interpretation of sensations
    - **manufactured**
      - **LSD**
      - **PCP**
      - **MDMA (Ectasy)**
    - **nonmanufactured**
      - **mescaline**
      - **psilocybin**
      - **marijuana**

5 learning

WHY CLOWNS CAN BE SCARY

Angelica was only 5 years old when her parents took her to the circus. While she enjoyed seeing the animals and acrobats, she was not sure about the clowns. One clown, attempting to amuse the little girl, suddenly jumped in front of her and laughed loudly while making what was supposed to be a funny face. The sudden movement and noise, together with the unfamiliar clown makeup, scared Angelica badly.

Small wonder, then, that Angelica began to show fear in the presence of any clown, including the clown pictures on the walls of what used to be her favorite fast-food restaurant! Angelica's fear of clowns was a result of a special type of learning called *classical conditioning*. In this type of learning, objects or situations (such as a scary clown at the circus) can become associated or linked with other kinds of situations (such as the restaurant clown). Once the association is made, similar objects or situations can cause the same response (e.g., fear) that the earlier situation caused.

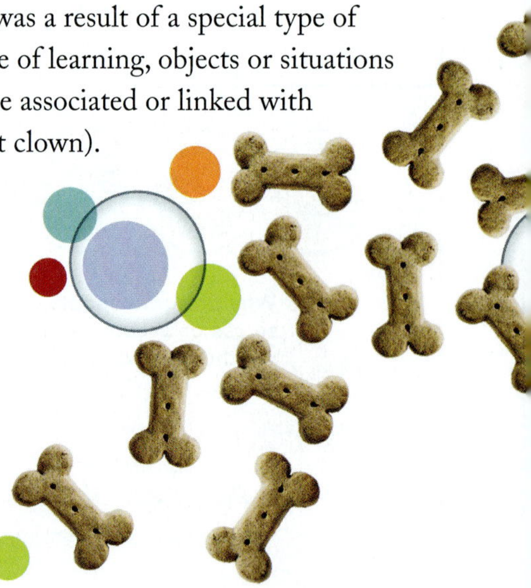

CHAPTER OUTLINE

Why study learning?

If we had not been able to learn, we would have died out as a species long ago. Learning is the process that allows us to adapt to the changing conditions of the world around us. We can alter our actions until we find the behavior that leads us to survival and rewards, and we can eliminate actions that have been unsuccessful in the past. Without learning, there would be no buildings, no agriculture, no lifesaving medicines, and no human civilization.

learning objectives

5.1 What does the term *learning* really mean?

5.2 How was classical conditioning first studied, and what are the important elements and characteristics of classical conditioning?

5.3 What is a conditioned emotional response, and how do cognitive psychologists explain classical conditioning?

5.4 How does operant conditioning occur, and what were the contributions of Thorndike and Skinner?

5.5 What are the important concepts in operant conditioning?

5.6 What are the schedules of reinforcement?

5.7 How does punishment differ from reinforcement?

5.8 What are some of the problems with using punishment?

5.9 How do operant stimuli control behavior, and what are some other concepts that can enhance or limit operant conditioning?

5.10 What is behavior modification, and how can behavioral techniques be used to modify involuntary biological responses?

5.11 How do latent learning, learned helplessness, and insight relate to cognitive learning theory?

5.12 What occurs in observational learning, and what are the findings from Bandura's classic Bobo doll study and the four elements of observational learning?

5.13 What is a real-world example of the use of conditioning?

study tip

As you are reading this chapter, take a look back at page I-12 in *Psychology in Action* for some useful information about how practice and the use of small successes can influence learning and performance.

Definition of Learning

5.1 What does the term *learning* really mean?

The term *learning* is one of those concepts whose meaning is crystal clear until one has to put it in actual words. "Learning is when you learn something." "Learning is learning how to do something." A more useful definition is as follows: *Learning* is any relatively permanent change in behavior brought about by experience or practice.

What does "relatively permanent" mean? And how does experience change what we do?

What does "relatively permanent" mean? And how does experience change what we do?

The "relatively permanent" part of the definition refers to the fact that when people learn anything, some part of their brain is physically changed to record what they've learned (Goldstein, 2005; Loftus & Loftus, 1980). This is actually a process of memory, for without the ability to remember what happens, people cannot learn anything. Although there is no conclusive proof as yet, research suggests that once people learn something, it may be present somewhere in memory in physical form (Barsalou, 1992; Smolen et al., 2008). They may be unable to "get" to it, but it's there. LINK to Chapter Six: Memory, p. 222.

As for the inclusion of experience or practice in the definition of learning, think about the last time you did something that caused you a lot of pain. Did you do it again? Probably not. You didn't want to experience that pain again, so you changed your behavior to avoid the painful consequence.* This is how children learn not to touch hot stoves. Remember Angelica in the chapter opener? Her reaction to clowns, such as the one in the fast-food restaurant, changed to fear after her experience with the circus clown. In contrast, if a person does something resulting in a very pleasurable experience, that person is more likely to do that same thing again. This is another change in behavior and is explained by the law of effect (see page 180).

Not all change is accomplished through learning. Changes like an increase in height or the size of the brain are another kind of change controlled by a genetic blueprint. This kind of change is called *maturation*, and is due to biology, not experience. For example, children learn to walk *when* they do because their nervous systems, muscle strength, and sense of balance have reached the point where walking is possible for

An instantaneous learning experience.

*consequence: an end result of some action.

them—all factors controlled by maturation, not by how much practice those children have had in trying to walk. No amount of experience or practice will help that child walk before maturation makes it possible—in spite of what some eager parents might wish.

It Makes Your Mouth Water: Classical Conditioning

5.2 How was classical conditioning first studied, and what are the important elements and characteristics of classical conditioning?

In the early 1900s, research scientists were unhappy with psychology's focus on mental activity. LINK to Chapter One: The Science of Psychology, pp. 11–12. Many were looking for a way to bring some kind of objectivity and scientific research to the field. It was a Russian *physiologist* (a person who studies the workings of the body) named Ivan Pavlov (1849–1936) who pioneered the empirical study of the basic principles of a particular kind of learning (Pavlov, 1906, 1926).

Studying the digestive system in his dogs, Pavlov had built a device that would accurately measure the amount of saliva produced by the dogs when they were fed a measured amount of food. Normally, when food is placed in the mouth of any animal, the salivary glands automatically start releasing saliva to help with chewing and digestion. This is a normal **reflex**—an unlearned, involuntary response that is not under personal control or choice—one of many that occur in both animals and humans. The food causes a particular reaction, the salivation. A *stimulus* can be defined as any object, event, or experience that causes a *response*, the reaction of an organism. In the case of Pavlov's dogs, the food is the stimulus and salivation is the response

PAVLOV AND THE SALIVATING DOGS

Pavlov soon discovered that his dogs began salivating when they weren't supposed to be salivating. Some dogs would start salivating when they saw the lab assistant bringing their food, others when they heard the clatter of the food bowl from the kitchen, and still others when it was the time of day they were usually fed. Switching his focus, Pavlov spent the rest of his career studying what eventually he termed **classical conditioning**, learning to elicit* an involuntary reflex response to a stimulus other than the original, natural stimulus that normally produces the reflex.

Dr. Ivan Pavlov and students working in his laboratory. Pavlov, a Russian physiologist, was the first to study and write about the basic principles of classical conditioning.

ELEMENTS OF CLASSICAL CONDITIONING

Pavlov eventually identified several key elements that must be present and experienced in a particular way for conditioning to take place.

UNCONDITIONED STIMULUS The original, naturally occurring stimulus mentioned in the preceding paragraph is called the **unconditioned stimulus (UCS)**. The term *unconditioned* means "unlearned." This is the stimulus that ordinarily leads to the reflex response. In the case of Pavlov's dogs, the food is the unconditioned stimulus.

UNCONDITIONED RESPONSE The reflex response to the unconditioned stimulus is called the **unconditioned response (UCR)** for much the same reason. It is unlearned and occurs because of genetic "wiring" in the nervous system. For example, in Pavlov's experiment, the salivation to the food is the UCR (unconditioned response).

CONDITIONED STIMULUS Pavlov determined that almost any kind of stimulus could become associated with the unconditioned stimulus (UCS) if it is paired with the UCS often enough. In his original study, the sight of the food dish itself became a stimulus for salivation *before* the food was given to the dogs. Every time they got food (to which they reflexively salivated), they saw the dish. At this point, the dish was called a **neutral stimulus (NS)** because it had no effect on salivation. After

*elicit: to draw forth.

reflex an involuntary response, one that is not under personal control or choice.

classical conditioning learning to make an involuntary (reflex) response to a stimulus other than the original, natural stimulus that normally produces the reflex.

unconditioned stimulus (UCS) a naturally occurring stimulus that leads to an involuntary (reflex) response.

unconditioned response (UCR) an involuntary (reflex) response to a naturally occurring or unconditioned stimulus.

neutral stimulus (NS) stimulus that has no effect on the desired response.

being paired with the food so many times, the dish came to produce the same salivation response, although a somewhat weaker one, as did the food itself. When a previously neutral stimulus, through repeated pairing with the unconditioned stimulus, begins to cause the same kind of reflexive response, learning has occurred. The neutral stimulus can now be called a **conditioned stimulus (CS)**. (*Unconditioned* means "unlearned," and, as mentioned earlier, *conditioned* means "learned.")

CONDITIONED RESPONSE The response that is given to the CS (conditioned stimulus) is not usually quite as strong as the original unconditioned response (UCR), but it is essentially the same response. However, because it comes as a response to the conditioned stimulus (CS), it is called the **conditioned response (CR)**.

Classical conditioning in the real world. These children are, no doubt, salivating to the sound of the ice cream truck's bell, much as Pavlov's dogs were conditioned to respond to a metronome. What other kinds of stimuli might make a person salivate?

PUTTING IT ALL TOGETHER: PAVLOV'S CANINE CLASSIC, OR TICK TOCK TICK TOCK

Pavlov did a classic experiment in which he paired the ticking sound of a metronome (a simple device that produces a rhythmic ticking sound) with the presentation of food to see if the dogs would eventually salivate at the sound of the metronome (Pavlov, 1927). Since the metronome's ticking did not normally produce salivation, it was the neutral stimulus (NS) before any conditioning took place. The repeated pairing of the NS and the UCS (unconditioned stimulus) is usually called *acquisition*, because the organism is in the process of acquiring learning. Figure 5.1 is a chart of how each element of the conditioning relationship worked in Pavlov's experiment.

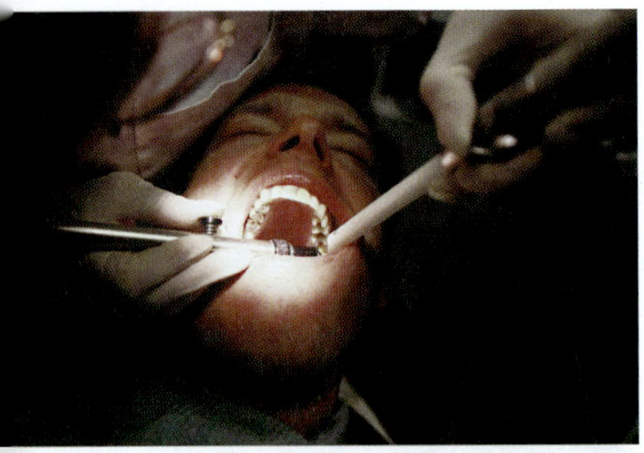

Could this be you? The anxiety that many people feel while in the dentist's office is a conditioned response, with the dentist's chair and the smells of the office acting as conditioned stimuli.

Notice that the responses, CR (conditioned response) and UCR (unconditioned response), are very similar—salivation. They differ not only in strength but also in the stimulus to which they are the response. An *unconditioned* stimulus (UCS) is always followed by an *unconditioned* response (UCR), and a *conditioned* stimulus (CS) is always followed by a *conditioned* response (CR).

Is this rocket science? No, not really. Classical conditioning is actually one of the simplest forms of learning. It's so simple that it happens to people all the time without them even being aware of it. Does your mouth water when you merely *see* an advertisement for your favorite food on television? Do you feel anxious every time you hear the high-pitched whine of the dentist's drill? These are both examples of classical conditioning. Over the course of many visits to the dentist, for example, the body comes to associate that sound (CS) with the anxiety or fear (UCR) the person has felt while receiving a painful dental treatment (UCS), and so the sound produces a feeling of anxiety (CR) whether that person is in the chair or just in the outer waiting area. **Simulate** on **mypsychlab.com**

Simulate Pavlov's classical conditioning experiment on **mypsychlab.com**

Pavlov and his fellow researchers did many experiments with the dogs. In addition to the metronome, whistles, tuning forks, various visual stimuli, and bells were used (Thomas, 1994). Although classical conditioning happens quite easily, Pavlov and his other researchers formulated a few basic principles about the process (although we will see that there are a few exceptions to some of these principles):

1. The CS must come *before* the UCS. If Pavlov sounded the metronome just after he gave the dogs the food, they did not become conditioned (Rescorla, 1988).
2. The CS and UCS must come very close together in time—ideally, no more than 5 seconds apart. When Pavlov tried to stretch the time between the potential CS and the UCS to several minutes, no association or link between the two was made. Too much could happen in the longer interval of time to interfere with conditioning (Pavlov, 1926; Wasserman & Miller, 1997). Recent studies have found that the interstimulus interval (ISI, or the time between the CS and UCS) can vary depending on the nature of the conditioning task and even the organism being conditioned. In these studies, shorter ISIs (less than 500 milleseconds) have been found to be ideal for conditioning (Polewan et al., 2006).

conditioned stimulus (CS) stimulus that becomes able to produce a learned reflex response by being paired with the original unconditioned stimulus.

conditioned response (CR) learned reflex response to a conditioned stimulus.

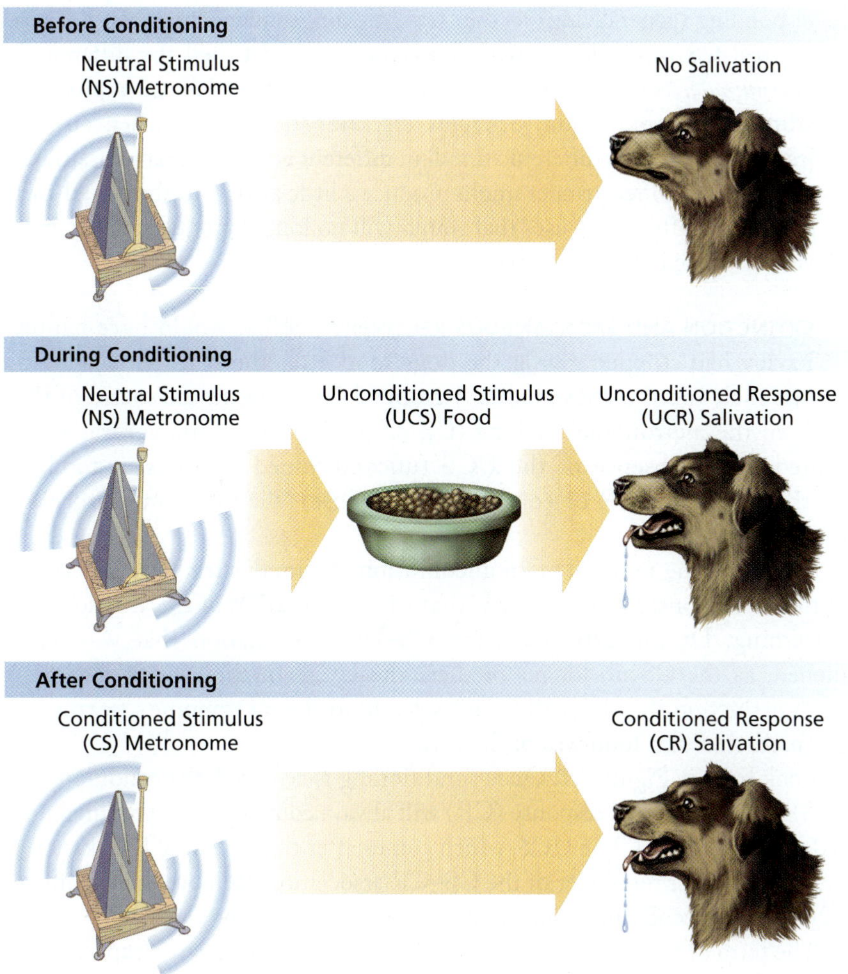

Figure 5.1 Classical Conditioning

Before conditioning takes place, the sound of the metronome does not cause salivation and is a neutral stimulus, or NS. During conditioning, the sound of the metronome occurs just before the presentation of the food, the UCS. The food causes salivation, the UCR. When conditioning has occurred after several pairings of the metronome with the food, the metronome will begin to elicit a salivation response from the dog without any food. This is learning, and the sound of the metronome is now a CS and the salivation to the bell is the CR.

3. The neutral stimulus must be paired with the UCS several times, often many times, before conditioning can take place (Pavlov, 1926).
4. The CS is usually some stimulus that is distinctive* or stands out from other competing stimuli. The metronome, for example, was a sound that was not normally present in the laboratory and, therefore, distinct (Pavlov, 1927; Rescorla, 1988).

That seems simple enough. But I wonder—would Pavlov's dogs salivate to other ticking sounds?

That seems simple enough. But I wonder—would Pavlov's dogs salivate to other ticking sounds?

STIMULUS GENERALIZATION AND DISCRIMINATION Pavlov did find that similar sounds would produce a similar conditioned response from his dogs. He and other researchers found that the strength of the response to similar sounds was not as strong as it was to the original one, but the more similar the other sound was to the original sound (be it a metronome or any other kind of sound), the more similar the strength of the response was (Siegel, 1969). (See Figure 5.2.) The tendency to respond to a stimulus that is similar to the original conditioned stimulus is called **stimulus generalization**. For example, a person who reacts with anxiety to the sound of a dentist's drill might react with some slight anxiety to a similar-sounding machine, such as an electric coffee grinder.

Of course, Pavlov did not give the dogs any food after the similar ticking sound. They only got food following the correct CS. It didn't take long for the dogs to stop

stimulus generalization the tendency to respond to a stimulus that is only similar to the original conditioned stimulus with the conditioned response.

*distinctive: separate, having a different quality from something else.

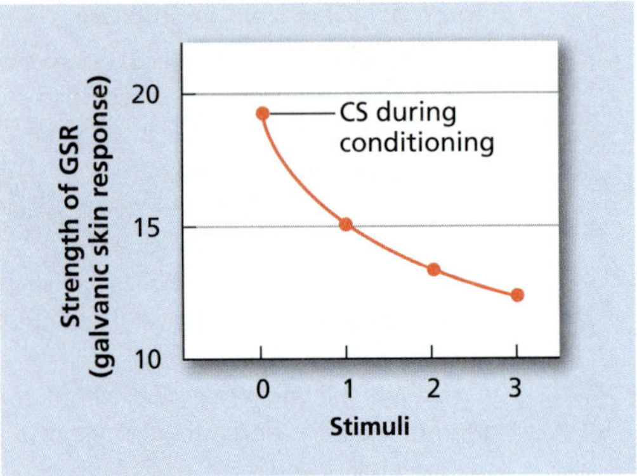

Figure 5.2 Strength of the Generalized Response

An example of stimulus generalization. The UCS was an electric shock and the UCR was the galvanic skin response (GSR), a measure associated with anxiety. The subjects had been conditioned originally to a CS tone (0) of a given frequency. When tested with the original tone, and with tones 1, 2, and 3 of differing frequencies, a clear generalization effect appeared. The closer the frequency of the test tone to the frequency of tone 0, the greater was the magnitude of the galvanic skin response to the tone (Hovland, 1937).

responding (generalizing) to the "fake" ticking sounds altogether. Because only the real CS was followed with food, they learned to tell the difference, or to *discriminate*, between the fake ticking and the CS ticking, a process called **stimulus discrimination**. Stimulus discrimination occurs when an organism learns to respond to different stimuli in different ways. For example, although the sound of the coffee grinder might produce a little anxiety in the dental-drill-hating person, after a few uses that sound will no longer produce anxiety because it isn't associated with dental pain.

EXTINCTION AND SPONTANEOUS RECOVERY What would have happened if Pavlov had stopped giving the dogs food after the real CS? Pavlov did try just that, and the dogs gradually stopped salivating to the sound of the ticking. When the metronome's ticking (CS or conditioned stimulus) was repeatedly presented in the absence of the UCS (unconditioned stimulus or food, in this case), the salivation (CR or conditioned response) "died out" in a process called **extinction**.

Why does the removal of an unconditioned stimulus lead to extinction of the conditioned response? One theory is that the presentation of the CS alone leads to new learning. During extinction, the CS–UCS association that was learned is weakened, as the CS no longer predicts the UCS. In the case of Pavlov's dogs, through extinction they learned to not salivate to the metronome's ticking, as it no longer predicted that food was on its way.

Look back at Figure 5.1. Once conditioning is acquired, the conditioned stimulus (CS) and conditioned response (CR) will always come *before* the original unconditioned stimulus (UCS). The UCS, which comes after the CS and CR link, now serves as a strengthener, or reinforcer of the CS–CR association. Remove that reinforcer, and the CR it strengthens will weaken and disappear—at least for a while.

The term *extinction* is a little unfortunate in that it seems to mean that the original conditioned response is totally gone, dead, never coming back, just like the dinosaurs. Remember the definition of learning is any relatively *permanent* change in behavior. The fact is that once people learn something, it's almost impossible to "unlearn" it. People can learn new things that replace it or lose their way to it in memory, but it's still there. In the case of classical conditioning, this is easily demonstrated.

After extinguishing the conditioned salivation response in his dogs, Pavlov waited a few weeks, putting the conditioned stimulus (e.g., the metronome) away. There were no more training sessions and the dogs were not exposed to the metronome's ticking in that time at all. But when Pavlov took the metronome back out and set it ticking, the dogs all began to salivate, although it was a fairly weak response and didn't last very long. This brief recovery of the conditioned response proves that the CR is "still in there" somewhere (remember, learning is *relatively permanent*). It is just suppressed or inhibited by the lack of an association with the unconditioned stimulus of food (which is no longer reinforcing or strengthening the CR). As time passes, this inhibition weakens, especially if the original conditioned stimulus has not been present for a while. In **spontaneous recovery** the conditioned response can briefly reappear when the original CS returns, although the response is usually weak and short lived. See Figure 5.3 for a graph showing both extinction and spontaneous recovery. People experience classical conditioning in many ways. People who are allergic to cats sometimes sneeze when they see a *picture* of a cat. Remember the discussion of how to treat insomnia in Chapter Four (page 139)? One of the recommendations was to avoid reading, working, watching television, or eating in bed. The bed should only be used for sleeping and will eventually become a conditioned stimulus (CS) for sleeping.

stimulus discrimination the tendency to stop making a generalized response to a stimulus that is similar to the original conditioned stimulus because the similar stimulus is never paired with the unconditioned stimulus.

extinction the disappearance or weakening of a learned response following the removal or absence of the unconditioned stimulus (in classical conditioning) or the removal of a reinforcer (in operant conditioning).

spontaneous recovery the reappearance of a learned response after extinction has occurred.

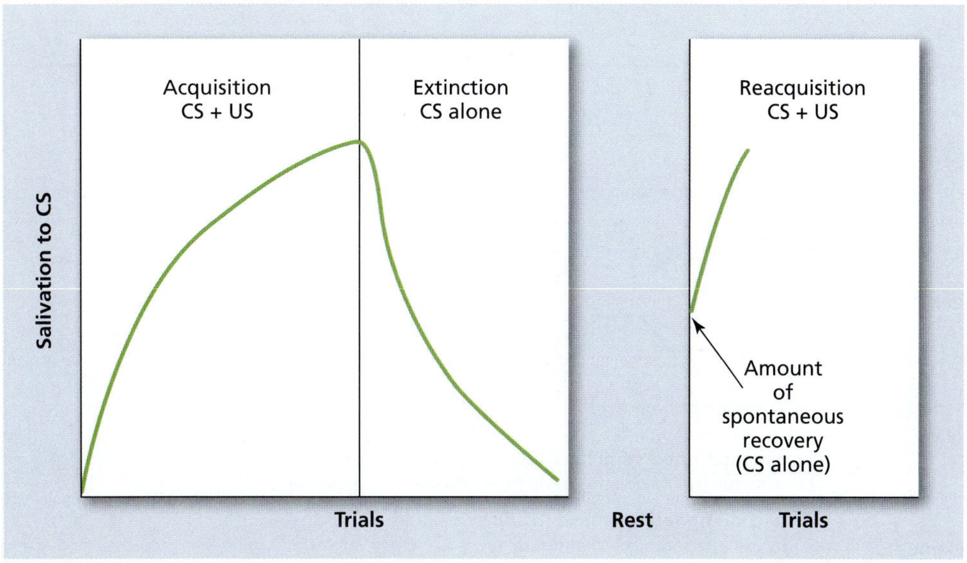

Figure 5.3 Extinction and Spontaneous Recovery

This graph shows the acquisition, extinction, spontaneous recovery, and reacquisition of a conditioned salivary response. Typically, the measure of conditioning is the number of drops of saliva elicited by the CS on each trial. Note that on the day following extinction, the first presentation of the CS elicits quite a large response.

HIGHER-ORDER CONDITIONING Another concept in classical conditioning is **higher-order conditioning** (see Figure 5.4). This occurs when a strong conditioned stimulus is paired with a neutral stimulus. The strong CS can actually play the part of a UCS, and the previously neutral stimulus becomes a *second* conditioned stimulus. Explore on mypsychlab.com

Explore higher-order conditioning on **mypsychlab.com**

For example, let's revisit the point when Pavlov has conditioned his dogs to salivate at the sound of the metronome. What would happen if just before Pavlov turned on the metronome, he snapped his fingers? The sequence would now be "snap-ticking-salivation," or "NS–CS–CR" ("neutral stimulus/conditioned stimulus/conditioned response"). If this happens enough times, the finger snap will eventually also produce a salivation response. The finger snap becomes associated with the ticking through the same process that the ticking became associated with the food originally and is now another conditioned stimulus. Of course, the food (UCS) would have to be presented every now and then to maintain the original conditioned response to the metronome's ticking. Without the UCS, the higher-order conditioning would be difficult to maintain and would gradually fade away.

higher-order conditioning occurs when a strong conditioned stimulus is paired with a neutral stimulus, causing the neutral stimulus to become a second conditioned stimulus.

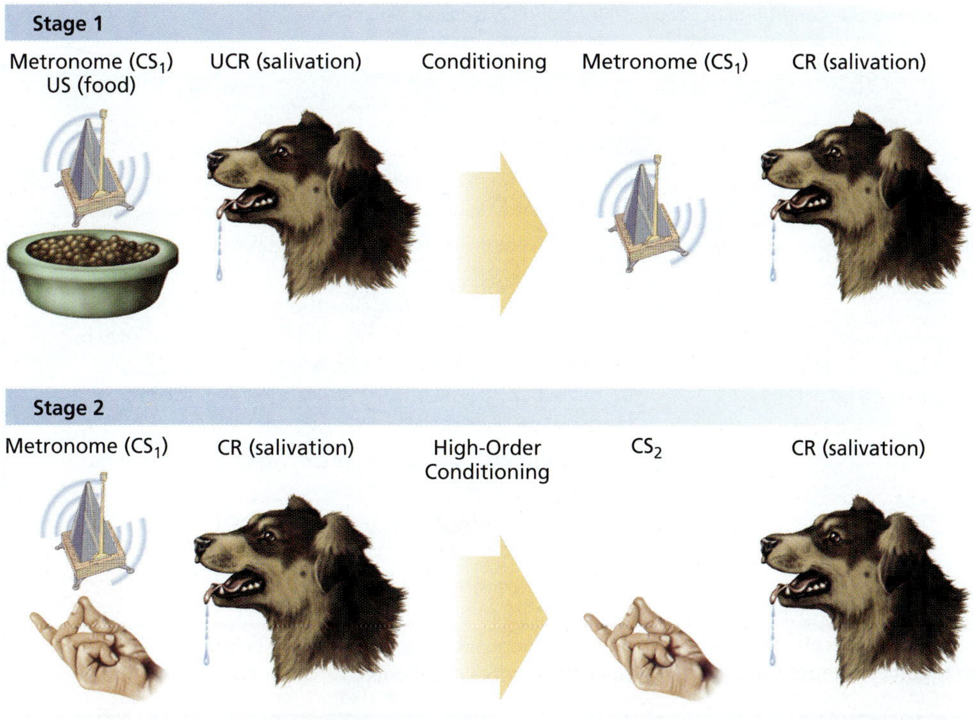

Figure 5.4 Higher-Order Conditioning

In Stage 1, a strong salivation response is conditioned to occur to the sound of the metronome (CS_1). In Stage 2, finger snapping (CS_2) is repeatedly paired with the ticking of the metronome (CS_1) until the dog begins to salivate to the finger snapping alone. This is called "higher-order conditioning," because one CS is used to create another, "higher" CS.

5.1 5.2

CONCEPT MAP

Definition of Learning

(any relatively permanent change in behavior brought about by experience or practice)

- "relatively permanent" aspect of learning refers to learning being associated with physical changes in the brain
- although physical changes may be present we may not always be able to "get" to the information

- **discovered by Ivan Pavlov** worked with salivating dogs — focused on observable, measurable behavior
  - **several key elements must be present and experienced**
    - **unconditioned stimulus (UCS):** original, naturally occurring stimulus that ordinarily leads to an involuntary response
    - **unconditioned response (UCR):** involuntary response to the unconditioned stimulus
    - **conditioned stimulus (CS):** previously neutral stimulus that begins to cause the same kind of involuntary response when paired repeatedly with the UCS
    - **conditioned response (CR):** response that is given to the CS

Classical Conditioning

(learning to make an involuntary response to a stimulus other than the original, natural stimulus that normally produces it)

- **basic principles for classical conditioning to occur**
  - CS must come before the UCS
  - CS and UCS must come very close together in time (< 5 sec)
  - CS must be paired with the UCS many times
  - CS must be distinct from other competing stimuli
- **key features**
  - **stimulus generalization:** response to a stimulus that is similar to the original CS
  - **stimulus discrimination:** response to different stimuli in different ways
  - **extinction:** presentation of the CS in the absence of the UCS leads to reduction in the CR
  - **spontaneous recovery:** reappearance of a previously extinguished CR
  - **higher-order conditioning:** occurs when strong CS is paired with new neutral stimulus; new previously neutral stimulus becomes a second CS

PRACTICE quiz How much do you remember?

ANSWERS ON PAGE AK-1.

Pick the best answer.

1. Which of the following statements about learning is NOT TRUE?
   a. Learning is another word for maturation.
   b. Learning is relatively permanent.
   c. Learning involves changes in behavior.
   d. Learning involves experiences.
2. Ed noticed that whenever he used his electric can opener, his cat would come into the kitchen and act hungry—drooling and mewing pitiably. He reasoned that because he used the can opener to open the cat's food, the sound of the can opener had become a(n) __________.
   a. unconditioned stimulus.
   b. conditioned stimulus.
   c. unconditioned response.
   d. conditioned response.
3. Which of the following statements about conditioning is FALSE, according to Pavlov?
   a. The CS and UCS must come close together in time.
   b. The CS must come immediately after the UCS.
   c. The neutral stimulus and UCS must be paired several times before conditioning takes place.
   d. The CS is usually some rather distinctive stimulus.
4. The prologue is about Angelica's fear of clowns as a child. The fact that she was not only afraid of the circus clown but also other types of clowns is an example of __________.
   a. extinction.
   b. spontaneous recovery.
   c. stimulus discrimination.
   d. stimulus generalization.
5. A conditioned response that briefly reappears after it has been extinguished is called __________.
   a. spontaneous recovery.
   b. higher-order conditioning.
   c. extinction.
   d. stimulus generalization.
6. The use of a strong CS to create a second CS is called __________.
   a. spontaneous recovery.
   b. higher-order conditioning.
   c. extinction.
   d. stimulus generalization.

CONDITIONED EMOTIONAL RESPONSES: RATS!

Later scientists took Pavlov's concepts and expanded them to explain not only animal behavior but also human behavior. One of the earliest of these studies showed that even an emotional response could be conditioned.

5.3 What is a conditioned emotional response, and how do cognitive psychologists explain classical conditioning?

WATSON AND "LITTLE ALBERT" In the first chapter of this text, John B. Watson's classic experiment with "Little Albert" and the white rat was discussed. This study was a demonstration of the classical conditioning of a phobia—an irrational fear response (Watson & Rayner, 1920).

Figure 5.5 Conditioning of "Little Albert"

After "Little Albert" had been conditioned to fear a white rat, he also demonstrated fear to a rabbit, a dog, and a sealskin coat (although it remains uncertain if stimulus generalization actually occurred as this fear was to a single rabbit, a single dog, etc.). Can you think of any emotional reactions you experience that might be classically conditioned emotional responses?

Watson paired the presentation of the white rat to the baby with a loud, scary noise. Although the baby was not initially afraid of the rat, he was naturally afraid of the loud noise and started to cry. After only seven pairings of the noise with the rat, every time the baby saw the rat, he started to cry. In conditioning terms, the loud noise was the UCS, the fear of the noise the UCR, the white rat became the CS, and the fear of the rat (the phobia) was the CR. (See Figure 5.5.) (It should be pointed out that Watson didn't really "torture" the baby—Albert's fright was temporary. Still, no ethics committee today would approve an experiment in which an infant experiences psychological distress like this.)

The learning of phobias is a very good example of a certain type of classical conditioning, the **conditioned emotional response (CER)**. Conditioned emotional responses are some of the easiest forms of classical conditioning to accomplish and our lives are full of them. It's easy to think of fears people might have that are conditioned or learned: a child's fear of the dentist's chair, a puppy's fear of a rolled-up newspaper, or the fear of dogs that is often shown by a person who has been attacked by a dog in the past. But other emotions can be conditioned, too.

What kind of conditioning could be happening to the children who are waiting to get their vaccination?

The next time you watch television, watch the commercials closely. Advertisers often use certain objects or certain types of people in their ads to generate a specific emotional response in viewers, hoping that the emotional response will become associated with their product. Sexy models, cute little babies, and adorable puppies are some of the examples of stimuli the advertising world uses to tug at our heartstrings, so to speak.

It is even possible to become classically conditioned by simply watching someone else respond to a stimulus in a process called **vicarious conditioning** (Bandura & Rosenthal, 1966; Hygge & Öhman, 1976; Jones & Menzies, 1995). Many years ago, children received vaccination shots in school. The nurse lined up the children, and one by one they had to go forward to get a needle in the arm. When some children received their shots, they cried quite a bit. By the time the nurse got near the end of the line of children, they were all crying—many of them before she ever touched needle to skin. They had learned their fear response from watching the reactions of the other children. **Watch** on **mypsychlab.com**

Watch classic footage of Little Albert on **mypsychlab.com**

OTHER CONDITIONED RESPONSES IN HUMANS

Are there any foods that you just can't eat anymore because of a bad experience with them? Believe it or not, your reaction to that food is a kind of classical conditioning.

Many experiments have shown that laboratory rats will develop a **conditioned taste aversion** for any liquid or food they swallow up to 6 hours before becoming nauseated. Researchers (Garcia et al., 1989; Garcia & Koelling, 1966) found that rats that were given a sweetened liquid and then injected with a drug or exposed to radiation* that caused nausea would not touch the liquid again. In a similar manner, alcoholics who are given a drug to make them violently nauseated

*radiation: beams of energy.

conditioned emotional response (CER) emotional response that has become classically conditioned to occur to learned stimuli, such as a fear of dogs or the emotional reaction that occurs when seeing an attractive person.

vicarious conditioning classical conditioning of a reflex response or emotion by watching the reaction of another person.

conditioned taste aversion development of a nausea or aversive response to a particular taste because that taste was followed by a nausea reaction, occurring after only one association.

Conditioned taste aversions in nature. This moth is not poisonous to birds, but the monarch butterfly whose coloring the moth imitates is quite poisonous. Birds find their food by vision and will not eat anything that resembles the monarch.

But I thought that it took several pairings of these stimuli to bring about conditioning. How can classical conditioning happen so fast?

when they drink alcohol may learn to avoid drinking any alcoholic beverage. The chemotherapy drugs that cancer patients receive also can create severe nausea, which causes those people to develop a taste aversion for any food they have eaten before going in for the chemotherapy treatment (Berteretche et al., 2004).

But I thought that it took several pairings of these stimuli to bring about conditioning. How can classical conditioning happen so fast?

BIOLOGICAL PREPAREDNESS Pavlov's basic principles included two that seem to be violated by taste aversions: (1) The pairing of the CS and UCS should be timed very close together, and (2) it should take several pairings of CS with UCS to achieve conditioning. Yet one instance of nausea can create a taste aversion for something you might have eaten the previous day. Conditioned taste aversions, along with phobic reactions and a few other responses, are an example of something called **biological preparedness**. Most mammals find their food by smell and taste and will learn to avoid any food that smells or tastes like something they ate just before becoming ill. It's a survival mechanism, because if they kept on eating a "bad" food, they might die. The mammalian* body seems to be prepared to associate smell and taste with getting sick (Garcia & Koelling, 1966; Seligman, 1970). Although most conditioning requires repeated pairings of CS with UCS, when the response is nausea, one pairing may be all that is necessary. Taste aversion conditioning is so effective that it has even been used by renowned psychologist Dr. John Garcia and colleagues as a tool to stop coyotes from killing ranchers' sheep and also to stop the ranchers from wiping out the coyote population entirely (Gustavson et al., 1976). Garcia and his fellow researchers laced sheep meat with lithium chloride and left it for the coyotes to find. The coyotes ate the drugged meat, got extremely sick, and avoided eating sheep for quite some time afterwards. The coyotes got to live and the ranchers got to keep their sheep. Note also that the nausea does not have to occur immediately—we and other organisms seem prepared to associate new or different tastes with nausea, even if those new and different tastes happened hours ago.

It's interesting to note that birds, which find their food by sight, will avoid any object or insect that simply *looks* like the one that made them sick. There is a certain species of moth with coloring that mimics the monarch butterfly. That particular butterfly is poisonous to birds, but the moth isn't. The moth's mimicry causes birds to avoid eating it, even though it is quite edible. Whereas mammals are biologically prepared to associate taste with illness, birds are biologically prepared to associate visual characteristics with illness (Shapiro et al., 1980).

As for phobias, fear is a reflex emotional response that has ties to survival—we need to remember what the fear-inducing stimuli are so we can safely avoid them in future. It shouldn't take more than one snake bite to learn to avoid snakes! Nausea and fear are both examples of reflexes that help organisms survive to reproduce and pass on their genetic material, so the innate tendency to make quick and strong associations between stimuli and these reflexes has evolutionary importance.

WHY DOES CLASSICAL CONDITIONING WORK?

There are two ways to explain how one stimulus comes to "stand in" for another. One is the original explanation given by Pavlov, and the other is based on a cognitive explanation. Pavlov believed that the conditioned stimulus, through its association close in time with the unconditioned stimulus, came to activate the same place in the animal's brain that was originally activated by the unconditioned stimulus. He called this process **stimulus substitution**. But if a mere association in time is all that is needed, why would conditioning *fail to happen* when the CS is presented immediately *after* the UCS?

biological preparedness referring to the tendency of animals to learn certain associations, such as taste and nausea, with only one or few pairings due to the survival value of the learning.

stimulus substitution original theory in which Pavlov stated that classical conditioning occurred because the conditioned stimulus became a substitute for the unconditioned stimulus by being paired closely together.

*mammalian: having to do with mammals (animals with fur or hair that feed their young with milk from milk glands).

Robert Rescorla (1988) found that the CS has to provide some kind of information about the coming of the UCS in order to achieve conditioning. In other words, the CS must predict that the UCS is coming. In one study, Rescorla exposed one group of rats to a tone, and just after the tone's onset and while the tone was still able to be heard, an electric shock was administered for some of the tone presentations. Soon the rats became agitated* and reacted in fear by shivering and squealing at the onset of the tone, a kind of conditioned emotional response. But with a second group of rats, Rescorla again sounded a tone but administered the electric shock only *after* the tone *stopped*, not while the tone was being heard. That group of rats responded with fear to the *stopping* of the tone (Rescorla, 1968).

The tone for the second group of rats provided a different kind of information than the tone in the first instance. For the first group, the tone means the shock is coming, whereas for the second group, the tone means there is no shock while the tone is on. It was the particular *expectancy* created by pairing the tone or absence of tone with the shock that determined the particular response of the rats. Because this explanation involves the mental activity of consciously expecting something to occur, it is an example of an explanation for classical conditioning called the **cognitive perspective**.

cognitive perspective modern theory in which classical conditioning is seen to occur because the conditioned stimulus provides information or an expectancy about the coming of the unconditioned stimulus.

*agitated: excited, upset.

5.3 CONCEPT MAP

- **other features**
  - **conditioned emotional responses:** emotional responses that have become classically conditioned to occur in response to learned stimuli; based on work of John B. Watson; helps explain development of phobias
  - **conditioned taste aversion** is one situation where classical conditioning can occur quickly without repeated pairings
    - some associations are relatively quick and easy to learn due to survival value for organism (biological preparedness)
  - **vicarious conditioning** can occur by simply watching someone else respond to a stimulus

Classical Conditioning (continued)

(learning to make an involuntary response to a stimulus other than the original, natural stimulus that normally produces it)

- **Why does it work?**
  - **Pavlov**—stimulus substitution occurs where the CS comes to activate the same part of the brain that was originally activated by the UCS
  - **cognitive perspective**—organism consciously expects something to occur; CS provides information about the coming of the UCS (based on work of Rescorla)

PRACTICE quiz How much do you remember?

ANSWERS ON PAGE AK-1.

Pick the best answer.

1. In Watson's experiment with "Little Albert," the unconditioned stimulus was.
   a. the white rat.
   b. the loud noise.
   c. the fear of the rat.
   d. the fear of the noise.
2. Often, people with certain types of cancer must take chemotherapy treatments. The drugs used in these treatments are powerful and usually cause strong nausea reactions. If Cindy had scrambled eggs for breakfast and then took a chemotherapy treatment later that same morning, what might we predict based on conditioned taste aversion research?
   a. Cindy will probably develop a strong liking for scrambled eggs.
   b. Cindy will probably be able to eat scrambled eggs with no nausea at all.
   c. Cindy will probably get nauseated the next time she tries to eat scrambled eggs.
   d. None of the above is likely.

(continued)

3. Your pet parakeet eats some cooked spaghetti noodles. Later the poor bird gets very ill. What would the research on biological preparedness predict?
   a. The parakeet will probably not eat shell macaroni because it smells similar to spaghetti.
   b. The parakeet will probably not eat shell macaroni because it tastes similar to spaghetti.
   c. The parakeet will probably not eat linguini noodles because they are long and thin and look similar to spaghetti.
   d. The parakeet will eat spaghetti again.

4. The fact that the CS must come immediately *before* the UCS, and not after, is a problem for the _________ theory of why classical conditioning works.
   a. stimulus substitution
   b. cognitive perspective
   c. cognitive substitution
   d. stimulus perspective

5. Rescorla found that the CS must _________ the UCS for conditioning to take place.
   a. replace
   b. come after
   c. come at the same time as
   d. predict

So far, all learning seems to involve reflex behavior, but I know that I am more than just reflexes. People do things on purpose, so is that kind of behavior also learned?

So far, all learning seems to involve reflex behavior, but I know that I am more than just reflexes. People do things on purpose, so is that kind of behavior also learned?

What's in It for Me? Operant Conditioning

5.4 How does operant conditioning occur, and what were the contributions of Thorndike and Skinner?

There are two kinds of behavior that all organisms are capable of doing: involuntary (reflexive) and voluntary. If Inez blinks her eyes because a gnat flies close to them, that's a reflex and totally involuntary. But if she then swats at the gnat to frighten it, that's a voluntary choice. She *had* to blink, but she *chose* to swat.

Classical conditioning is the kind of learning that occurs with reflexive, involuntary behavior. The kind of learning that applies to voluntary behavior is called **operant conditioning**, which is both different from and similar to classical conditioning.

operant conditioning the learning of voluntary behavior through the effects of pleasant and unpleasant consequences to responses.

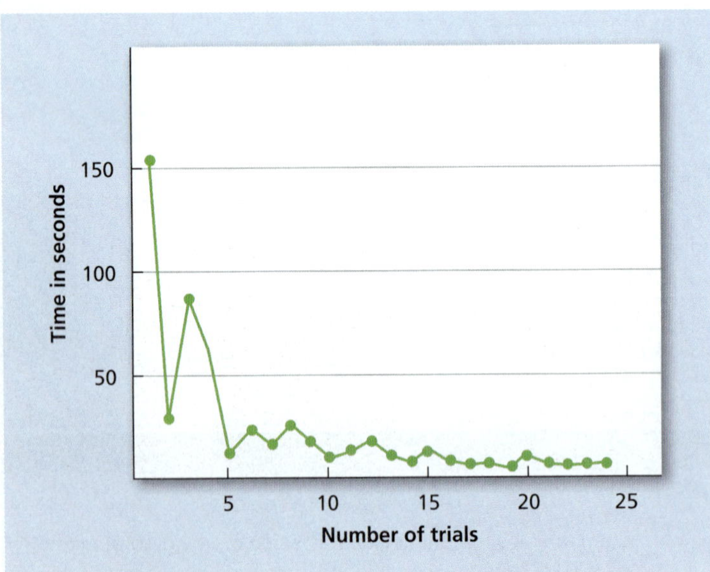

Figure 5.6 Graph of the Time to Learn in Thorndike's Experiment

This is one of the earliest "learning curves" in the history of the experimental study of conditioning. The time required by one of Thorndike's cats to escape from the puzzle box gradually decreased with trials but with obvious reversals.

FRUSTRATING CATS: THORNDIKE'S PUZZLE BOX AND THE LAW OF EFFECT

Edward L. Thorndike (1874–1949) was one of the first researchers to explore and attempt to outline the laws of learning voluntary responses, although the field was not yet called operant conditioning. Thorndike placed a hungry cat inside a "puzzle box" from which the only escape was to press a lever located on the floor of the box. Thorndike placed a dish of food *outside* the box, so the hungry cat is highly motivated to get out. Thorndike observed that the cat would move around the box, pushing and rubbing up against the walls in an effort to escape. Eventually, the cat would accidentally push the lever, opening the door. Upon escaping, the cat was fed from a dish placed just outside the box. The lever is the stimulus, the pushing of the lever is the response, and the consequence is both escape (good) and food (even better).

The cat did not learn to push the lever and escape right away. After a number of trials (and many errors) in a box like this one, the cat took less and less time to push the lever that would open the door (see Figure 5.6). It's important not to assume that the cat had "figured out" the connection between the lever and freedom—Thorndike kept moving the lever to a different position, and the cat had to learn the whole process over again. The cat would simply continue to rub and push in the same general area that led to food and freedom the last time, each time getting out and fed a little more quickly.

Based on this research, Thorndike developed the **law of effect**: If an action is followed by a pleasurable consequence, it will tend to be repeated. If an action is followed by an unpleasant consequence, it will tend not to be repeated (Thorndike, 1911). This is the basic principle behind learning voluntary behavior. In the case of the cat in the box, pushing the lever was followed by a pleasurable consequence (getting out and getting fed), so pushing the lever became a repeated response.

So did Thorndike call this operant conditioning?

No, but Thorndike's important and groundbreaking work began the study of what would eventually become *operant conditioning*.

law of effect law stating that if an action is followed by a pleasurable consequence, it will tend to be repeated, and if followed by an unpleasant consequence, it will tend not to be repeated.

operant any behavior that is voluntary.

reinforcement any event or stimulus, that when following a response, increases the probability that the response will occur again.

So did Thorndike call this operant conditioning?

B. F. SKINNER: THE BEHAVIORIST'S BEHAVIORIST

B. F. Skinner (1904–1990) was the behaviorist who assumed leadership of the field after John Watson. He was even more determined than Watson that psychologists should study only measurable, observable behavior. In addition to his knowledge of Pavlovian classical conditioning, Skinner found in the work of Thorndike a way to explain all behavior as the product of learning. He even gave the learning of voluntary behavior a special name: *operant conditioning* (Skinner, 1938). Voluntary behavior is what people and animals do to *operate* in the world. When people perform a voluntary action, it is to get something they want or to avoid something they don't want, right? So voluntary behavior, for Skinner, is **operant** behavior, and the learning of such behavior is operant conditioning.

The heart of operant conditioning is the effect of consequences on behavior. Thinking back to the section on classical conditioning, learning a reflex really depends on what comes *before* the response—the unconditioned stimulus and what will become the conditioned stimulus. These two stimuli are the *antecedent* stimuli (antecedent means something that comes before another thing). But in operant conditioning, learning depends on what happens *after* the response—the consequence. In a way, operant conditioning could be summed up as this: "If I do this, what's in it for me?" **Simulate** on **mypsychlab.com**

Simulate operant conditioning on **mypsychlab.com**

THE CONCEPT OF REINFORCEMENT

5.5 What are the important concepts in operant conditioning?

"What's in it for me?" represents the concept of **reinforcement**, one of Skinner's major contributions to behaviorism. The word itself means "to strengthen," and Skinner defined reinforcement as anything that, when following a response, causes that response to be more likely to happen again. Typically, this means that reinforcement is a consequence that is in some way pleasurable to the organism, which relates back to Thorndike's law of effect. The "pleasurable consequence" is what's "in it" for the organism. (Keep in mind that a pleasurable consequence might be something like getting food when hungry or a paycheck when you need money, but it might also mean *avoiding* a tiresome chore, like doing the dishes or taking out the garbage. I'll do almost anything to get out of doing the dishes, myself!)

Going back to Thorndike's puzzle-box research, what was in it for the cat? We can see that the escape from the box and the food that the cat received after getting out are both *reinforcement* of the lever-pushing response. Every time the cat got out of the box, it got reinforced for doing so. In Skinner's view, this reinforcement is the reason that the cat learned anything at all. In operant conditioning, reinforcement is the key to learning.

Skinner had his own research device called a "Skinner box" or "operant conditioning chamber" (see Figure 5.7). His early research often involved placing a rat into one of these chambers and training it to push down on a bar to get food.

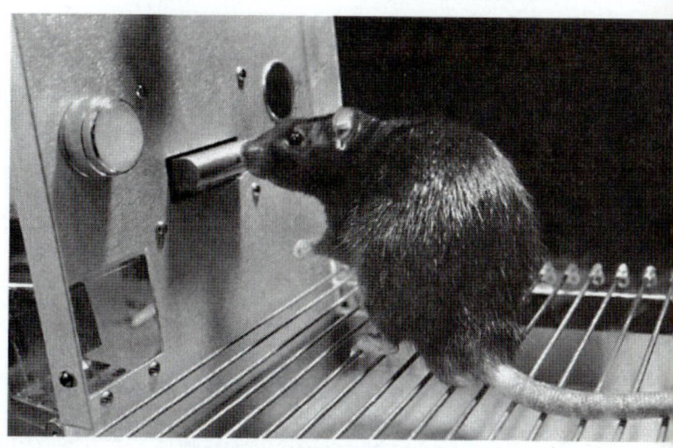

Figure 5.7 A Typical Skinner Box
This rat is learning to press the bar in the wall of the cage in order to get food (delivered a few pellets at a time in the food trough on lower left). In some cases, the light on the top left might be turned on to indicate that pressing the bar will lead to food or to warn of an impending shock delivered by the grate on the floor of the cage.

PRIMARY AND SECONDARY REINFORCERS The events or items that can be used to reinforce behavior are not all alike. Let's say that a friend of yours asks you to help her move some books from the trunk of her car to her apartment on the second floor. She offers you a choice of $25 or a candy bar. Unless you've suffered recent brain damage,

reinforcers any events or objects that, when following a response, increase the likelihood of that response occurring again.

primary reinforcer any reinforcer that is naturally reinforcing by meeting a basic biological need, such as hunger, thirst, or touch.

secondary reinforcer any reinforcer that becomes reinforcing after being paired with a primary reinforcer, such as praise, tokens, or gold stars.

positive reinforcement the reinforcement of a response by the addition or experiencing of a pleasurable stimulus.

you'll most likely choose the money, right? With $25, you could buy more than one candy bar. (At today's prices, you might even be able to afford three.)

Now pretend that your friend offers the same deal to a 3-year-old child who lives downstairs for carrying up some of the paperback books: $25 or a candy bar. Which reward will the child more likely choose? Most children at that age have no real idea of the value of money, so the child will probably choose the candy bar. The money and the candy bar represent two basic kinds of **reinforcers**, items or events that when following a response will strengthen it. The reinforcing properties of money must be learned, but candy gives immediate reward in the form of taste and satisfying hunger.

A reinforcer such as a candy bar that fulfills a basic need like hunger is called a **primary reinforcer**. Examples would be any kind of food (hunger drive), liquid (thirst drive), or touch (pleasure drive). Infants, toddlers, preschool-age children, and animals can be easily reinforced by using primary reinforcers. (It's not a good idea, however, to start thinking of reinforcers as rewards—freedom from pain is also a basic need, so pain itself can be a primary reinforcer when it is *removed*. Removal of a painful stimulus fills a basic need just as eating food when hungry fills the hunger need.)

A **secondary reinforcer** such as money, however, gets its reinforcing properties from being associated with primary reinforcers in the past. A child who is given money to spend soon realizes that the ugly green paper can be traded for candy and treats—primary reinforcers—and so money becomes reinforcing in and of itself. If a person praises a puppy while petting him (touch, a primary reinforcer), the praise alone will eventually make the puppy squirm with delight.

That sounds very familiar. Isn't this related to classical conditioning?

That sounds very familiar. Isn't this related to classical conditioning?

Secondary reinforcers do indeed get their reinforcing power from the process of classical conditioning. After all, the pleasure people feel when they eat, drink, or get a back rub is an automatic response, and any automatic response can be classically conditioned to occur to a new stimulus. In the case of money, the candy is a UCS for pleasure (the UCR) and the money is present just before the candy is obtained. The money becomes a CS for pleasure, and people certainly do feel pleasure when they have a lot of that green stuff, don't they?

In the case of the puppy, the petting is the UCS, the pleasure at being touched and petted is the UCR. The praise, or more specifically the tone of voice, becomes the CS for pleasure. Although classical and operant conditioning often "work together," as in the creation of secondary reinforcers, they are two different processes. Table 5.1 presents a brief look at how the two types of conditioning differ from each other.

POSITIVE AND NEGATIVE REINFORCEMENT Reinforcers can also differ in the way they are used. Most people have no trouble at all understanding that following a response with some kind of pleasurable consequence (like a reward) will lead to an increase in the likelihood of that response being repeated. This is called **positive reinforcement**, the reinforce-

Table 5.1

Comparing Two Kinds of Conditioning

OPERANT CONDITIONING	CLASSICAL CONDITIONING
End result is an increase in the rate of an already occurring response.	End result is the creation of a new response to a stimulus that did not normally produce that response.
Responses are voluntary, emitted by the organism.	Responses are involuntary and reflexive, elicited by a stimulus.
Consequences are important in forming an association.	Antecedent stimuli are important in forming an association.
Reinforcement should be immediate.	CS must occur immediately before the UCS.
An expectancy develops for reinforcement to follow a correct response.	An expectancy develops for UCS to follow CS.

ment of a response by the *addition* or experience of a pleasurable consequence, such as a reward or a pat on the back. But many people have trouble understanding that the opposite is also true: Following a response with *the removal or escape* from something *unpleasant* will also increase the likelihood of that response being repeated—a process called **negative reinforcement**. Remember the idea that pain can be a reinforcer if it is removed? If a person's behavior gets pain to stop, the person is much more likely to do that same thing again—which is part of the reason people can get addicted to painkilling medication. (We'll discuss the concepts of positive and negative reinforcement in more detail later on.)

We've discussed what reinforcement is and how it affects the behavior that follows the reinforcement. In the next section we'll discuss the different ways in which reinforcement can be administered as well as the difference between reinforcement and punishment. We'll also look at the role of the stimuli that come *before* the behavior that is to be reinforced and a few other operant conditioning concepts. **Listen** on **mypsychlab.com**

negative reinforcement the reinforcement of a response by the removal, escape from, or avoidance of an unpleasant stimulus.

Listen to the podcast on positive reinforcement on **mypsychlab.com**

5.4 5.5

CONCEPT MAP

focused on observable, measurable behavior

Thorndike was among the first to study learning of voluntary responses — developed law of effect—action followed by pleasurable consequence will tend to be repeated; action followed by unpleasant consequence will tend not to be repeated

Skinner led field of behaviorism after Watson — coined term *operant conditioning*—voluntary behavior that people and animals do to operate in the world

Operant Conditioning
(learning to make voluntary responses through the effects of positive or negative consequences)

reinforcement any event or stimulus, that when following a response increases the probability that the response will occur again

- **primary reinforcers:** satisfy basic biological needs (e.g., hunger, thirst, touch)
- **secondary reinforcers:** gain reinforcing properties through previous association with primary reinforcers
- **positive reinforcement:** addition, or experiencing of, a pleasurable stimulus
- **negative reinforcement:** removal, escape, or avoidance of unpleasant stimulus

PRACTICE quiz How much do you remember? ANSWERS ON PAGE AK-1.

Pick the best answer.

1. In Thorndike's puzzle-box experiments, the cats were rewarded by _______.
   a. getting out of the box.
   b. getting food.
   c. being petted and praised.
   d. both a and b.
2. _______ is an example of a primary reinforcer, whereas _______ is an example of a secondary reinforcer.
   a. A candy bar; a gold star
   b. A gold star; money
   c. Food; a drink
   d. A gold star; candy
3. Carmen hates to clean up after dinner. One night she volunteers to bathe the baby before cleaning up. When she finishes with the baby and returns to the kitchen, her husband has cleaned everything up for her. Which of the following statements is most *likely* TRUE?
   a. Carmen will start cleaning up the kitchen before she bathes the baby.
   b. Carmen's husband has positively reinforced her for bathing the baby.
   c. Carmen's husband has negatively reinforced her for bathing the baby.
   d. Carmen will never bathe the baby again.
4. Bennie is afraid of snakes. He won't even look at pictures of them but turns the page or closes the book instead. When he sees a picture of a snake, his anxiety goes up, but when he avoids looking at the picture, his anxiety goes down. It is *most* correct to say that Bennie's avoidance behavior is being __________.
   a. punished because he feels anxious after doing so.
   b. punished because he will never get better.
   c. positively reinforced because he is rewarded by his anxiety going down.
   d. negatively reinforced because he is rewarded by his anxiety going down.

Brainstorming: What type of reinforcement worked best for you when you were in grade school? Positive or negative? Did this change in high school?

SCHEDULES OF REINFORCEMENT: WHY THE ONE-ARMED BANDIT IS SO SEDUCTIVE

The timing of reinforcement can make a tremendous difference in the speed at which learning occurs and the strength of the learned response. However, Skinner (1956) found that reinforcing every response was not necessarily the best schedule of reinforcement for long-lasting learning.

5.6 What are the schedules of reinforcement?

"Remember, every time he gives you a pellet, reinforce that behavior by pulling the lever."

THE PARTIAL REINFORCEMENT EFFECT Consider the following scenario: Alicia's mother agrees to give her a quarter every night she remembers to put her dirty clothes in the clothes hamper. Bianca's mother agrees to give her a dollar at the end of the week, but only if she has put her clothes in the hamper every night. Alicia learns to put her clothes in the hamper more quickly than does Bianca because responses that are reinforced each time they occur are more easily and quickly learned. After a time, the mothers stop giving the girls the money. Which child is more likely to stop putting her clothes in the hamper?

The answer might surprise you. It is more likely that Alicia, who has expected to get a reinforcer (the quarter) after *every single response*, will stop putting her clothes in the hamper. As soon as the reinforcers stop for her, the behavior is no longer reinforced and is likely to extinguish. In contrast, Bianca has expected to get a reinforcer only after *seven correct responses*. When the reinforcers stop for her, she might continue to put the clothes in the hamper for several more days or even another whole week, hoping that the reinforcer will eventually come anyway. Bianca may have learned more slowly than Alicia, but once she learned the connection between putting her clothes in the hamper and getting that dollar, she is less likely to stop doing it—even when her mother fails to give the dollar as expected.

Bianca's behavior illustrates the **partial reinforcement effect** (Skinner, 1956): A response that is reinforced after some, but not all, correct responses will be more resistant to extinction than a response that receives **continuous reinforcement** (a reinforcer for each and every correct response). Although it may be easier to teach a new behavior using continuous reinforcement, partially reinforced behavior is not only more difficult to suppress but also more like real life. Imagine being paid for every hamburger you make or every report you turn in. In the real world, people tend to receive partial reinforcement rather than continuous reinforcement for their work.

Partial reinforcement can be accomplished according to different patterns or schedules. For example, it might be a certain interval of time that's important, such as an office safe that can only be opened at a certain time of day. It wouldn't matter how many times one tried to open the safe if the effort didn't come at the right *time*. On the other hand, it might be the number of responses that is important, as it would be if one had to sell a certain number of raffle tickets in order to get a prize. When the timing of the response is more important, it is called an *interval schedule*. When it is the number of responses that is important, the schedule is called a *ratio schedule* because a certain number of responses is required for each reinforcer (e.g., 50 raffle tickets for each prize). The other way in which schedules of reinforcement can differ is in whether the number of responses or interval of time is *fixed* (the same in each case) or *variable* (a different number or interval is required in each case). So it is possible to have a fixed interval schedule, a variable interval schedule, a fixed ratio schedule, and a variable ratio schedule (Skinner, 1961).

FIXED INTERVAL SCHEDULE OF REINFORCEMENT If you receive a paycheck once a week, you are familiar with what is called a **fixed interval schedule of reinforcement**, in which a reinforcer is received *after* a certain, fixed interval of time has passed. If Professor Conner were teaching a rat to press a lever to get food pellets, she might require it to push the lever *at least once* within a 2 minute time span to get

partial reinforcement effect the tendency for a response that is reinforced after some, but not all, correct responses to be very resistant to extinction.

continuous reinforcement the reinforcement of each and every correct response.

fixed interval schedule of reinforcement schedule of reinforcement in which the interval of time that must pass before reinforcement becomes possible is always the same.

a pellet. It wouldn't matter how many times the rat pushed the bar press; the rat would only get a pellet at the end of the 2 minute interval if it had pressed the bar at least once. It is the *first* correct response that gets reinforced at the end of the interval.

As shown in the graph in the upper left corner of Figure 5.8, a fixed interval schedule of reinforcement does not produce a fast rate of responding (notice that the line doesn't go "up" as fast as the fixed ratio line in the graph on the upper right). Since it only matters that at least *one* response is made *during* the specific interval of time, speed is not that important. Eventually, the rat will start pushing the lever only as the interval of time nears its end, causing the *scalloping* effect you see in the graph. The response rate goes up just before the reinforcer and then drops off immediately after, until it is almost time for the next food pellet. This is similar to the way in which factory workers speed up production just before payday and slow down just after payday (Critchfield et al., 2003).

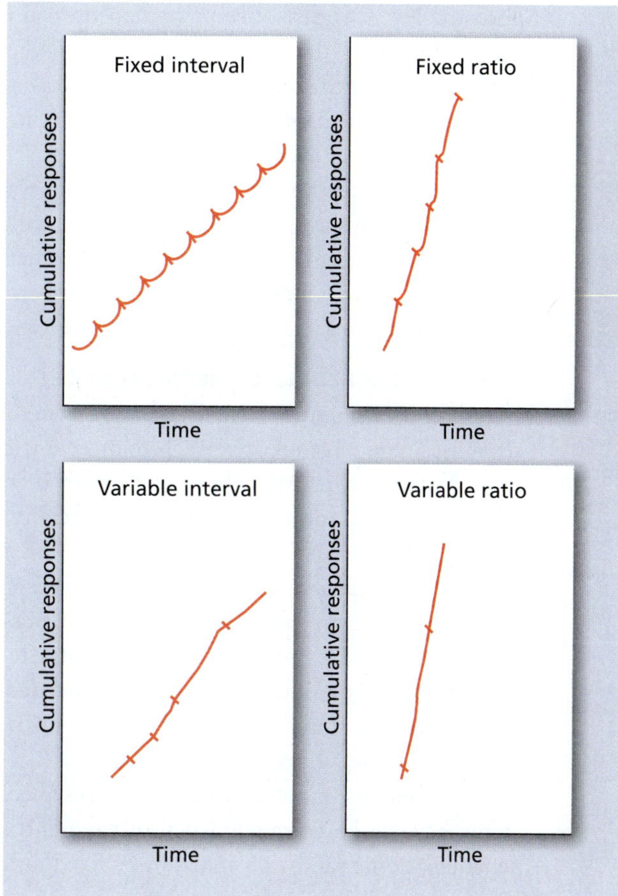

Figure 5.8 Schedules of Reinforcement

These four graphs show the typical pattern of responding for both fixed and variable interval and ratio schedules of reinforcement. The responses are cumulative, which means new responses are added to those that come before, and all graphs begin after the learned pattern is well established. Slash marks mean that a reinforcement has been given. In both the fixed interval and fixed ratio graphs, there is a pause after each reinforcement as the learner briefly "rests." The "scalloped" shape of the fixed interval curve is a typical indicator of this pause, as is the stair-step shape of the fixed ratio curve. In the variable interval and ratio schedules, no such pause occurs, because the reinforcements are unpredictable. Notice that both fixed and variable interval schedules are slower (less steep) than the two ratio schedules because of the need to respond as quickly as possible in the ratio schedules.

Paychecks aren't the only kind of fixed schedule that people experience. When do you study the hardest? Isn't it right before a test? If you know when the test is to be given, that's like having a fixed interval of time that is predictable, and you can save your greatest studying efforts until closer to the exam. (Some students save *all* of their studying for the night before the exam, which is not the best strategy.) Another example of a fixed interval schedule would be the way that many people floss and brush their teeth most rigorously* for a few days before their next dental exam—especially those who have not been flossing until just before their appointment! In this case, they are probably hoping for negative reinforcement. The cleaner they get their teeth before the appointment, the less time they might have to spend in that chair.

So if a scheduled test is a fixed interval, then would a pop quiz be a variable interval schedule?

So if a scheduled test is a fixed interval, then would a pop quiz be a variable interval schedule?

VARIABLE INTERVAL SCHEDULE OF REINFORCEMENT Pop quizzes are unpredictable. Students don't know exactly what day they might be given a pop quiz, so the best strategy is to study a little every night just in case there is a quiz the next day. Pop quizzes are good examples of a **variable interval schedule of reinforcement**, where the interval of time after which the individual must respond in order to receive a reinforcer (in this case, a good grade on the quiz) changes from one time to the next. In a more basic example, a rat might receive a food pellet when it pushes a lever, every 5 minutes on average. Sometimes the interval might be 2 minutes, sometimes 10, but the rat must

variable interval schedule of reinforcement schedule of reinforcement in which the interval of time that must pass before reinforcement becomes possible is different for each trial or event.

*rigorously: strictly, consistently.

When people go fishing, they never know how long they may have to dangle the bait in the water before snagging a fish. This is an example of a variable interval schedule of reinforcement and explains why some people, such as this father and son, are reluctant to pack up and go home.

push the lever at least once *after* that interval to get the pellet. Because the rat can't predict how long the interval is going to be, it pushes the bar more or less continuously, producing the smooth graph in the lower left corner of Figure 5.8. Once again, speed is not important, so the rate of responding is slow but steady.

Another example of a variable interval schedule might be the kind of fishing in which people put the pole in the water and wait—and wait—and—wait, until a fish takes the bait, if they are lucky. They only have to put the pole in once, but they might refrain from taking it out for fear that just when they do, the biggest fish in the world would swim by. Dialing a busy phone number is also this kind of schedule, as people don't know *when* the call will go through, so they keep dialing and dialing.

FIXED RATIO SCHEDULE OF REINFORCEMENT In ratio schedules, it is the number of responses that counts. In a **fixed ratio schedule of reinforcement**, the number of responses required to receive each reinforcer will always be the same number.

Notice two things about the graph in the upper right corner of Figure 5.8. The rate of responding is very fast, especially when compared to the fixed interval schedule on the left, and there are little "breaks" in the response pattern immediately after a reinforcer is given. The rapid response rate occurs because the rat wants to get to the next reinforcer just as fast as possible, and the number of lever pushes counts. The pauses or breaks come right after a reinforcer, because the rat knows "about how many" lever pushes will be needed to get to the next reinforcer because it's always the same. Fixed schedules—both ratio and interval—are predictable, which allows rest breaks.

In human terms, anyone who does piecework, in which a certain number of items have to be completed before payment is given, is reinforced on a fixed ratio schedule. Some sandwich shops use a fixed ratio schedule of reinforcement with their customers by giving out punch cards that get punched one time for each sandwich purchased. When the card has 10 punches, for example, the customer might get a free sandwich.

In Figure 5.8 the graph on the lower right is also very fast, but it's so much smoother, like the variable interval graph on the left. Why are they similar?

In Figure 5.8 the graph on the lower right is also very fast, but it's so much smoother, like the variable interval graph on the left. Why are they similar?

VARIABLE RATIO SCHEDULE OF REINFORCEMENT A **variable ratio schedule of reinforcement** is one in which the number of responses changes from one trial to the next. In the rat example, the rat might be expected to push the bar an *average* of 20 times to get reinforcement. That means that sometimes the rat would push the lever only 10 times before a reinforcer comes, but at other times it might take 30 lever pushes or more.

The graph at the lower right of Figure 5.8 shows a line that is just as rapid a response rate as the fixed ratio schedule because the *number* of responses still matters. But the graph is much smoother because the rat is taking no rest breaks. It can't afford to do so because it *doesn't know* how many times it may have to push that lever to get the next food pellet. It pushes as fast as it can and eats while pushing. It is the *unpredictability* of the variable schedule that makes the responses more or less continuous—just as in a variable interval schedule. Simulate on **mypsychlab.com**

In human terms, people who shove money into the one-armed bandit, or slot machine, are being reinforced on a variable ratio schedule of reinforcement (they hope). They put their coins in (response), but they don't know how many times they will have to do this before reinforcement (the jackpot) comes. People who do this tend to sit there until they either win or run out of money. They don't dare stop because the "next one" might hit that jackpot. Buying lottery tickets is much the same thing, as is any kind of gambling. People don't know how many tickets they will have to buy, and they're afraid that if they don't buy the next one, that will be the ticket that would have won, so they keep buying and buying.

Simulate the schedules of reinforcement on **mypsychlab.com**

fixed ratio schedule of reinforcement schedule of reinforcement in which the number of responses required for reinforcement is always the same.

variable ratio schedule of reinforcement schedule of reinforcement in which the number of responses required for reinforcement is different for each trial or event.

Regardless of the schedule of reinforcement one uses, two additional factors contribute to making reinforcement of a behavior as effective as possible. The first factor is *timing*: In general, a reinforcer should be given as immediately as possible *after* the desired behavior. Delaying reinforcement tends not to work well, especially when dealing with animals and small children. (For older children and adults who can think about future reinforcements, such as saving up one's money to buy a highly desired item, some delayed reinforcement can work—for them, just saving the money is reinforcing as they think about their future purchase.) The second factor in effective reinforcement is to reinforce *only* the desired behavior. This should be obvious, but we all slip up at times; for example, many parents make the mistake of giving a child who has not done some chore the promised treat anyway, which completely undermines the child's learning of that chore or task. And who hasn't given a treat to a pet that has not really done the trick?

So I think I get reinforcement now, but what about punishment? How does punishment fit into the big picture?

Slot machines provide reinforcement in the form of money on a variable ratio schedule, making the use of these machines very addictive for many people. People don't want to stop for fear the next pull of the lever will be that "magic" one that produces a jackpot.

So I think I get reinforcement now, but what about punishment? How does punishment fit into the big picture?

THE ROLE OF PUNISHMENT IN OPERANT CONDITIONING

Let's go back to the discussion of positive and negative reinforcement. These strategies are important for *increasing* the likelihood that the targeted behavior will occur again. But what about behavior that we do not want to reoccur?

5.7 How does punishment differ from reinforcement?

People experience two kinds of things as consequences in the world: things they like (food, money, candy, sex, praise, and so on) and things they don't like (spankings, being yelled at, and experiencing any kind of pain, to name a few). In addition, people experience these two kinds of consequences in one of two ways: Either people experience them directly (such as getting money for working or getting yelled at for misbehaving) or they don't experience them, such as losing an allowance for misbehaving or avoiding a scolding by lying about misbehavior. These four consequences are named and described in Table 5.2.

First, take a look at the left column of Table 5.2, the one labeled "Reinforcement." Getting money for working is an example of *positive reinforcement*, the reinforcement of a response by the *addition* or experience of a *pleasurable* consequence, as mentioned earlier. That one everyone understands. But what about avoiding a penalty by turning one's income tax return in on time? That is an example of *negative reinforcement*, the reinforcement of a response by the *removal or escape* from an *unpleasant* consequence. Because the behavior (submitting the return before the deadline) results in *avoiding* an unpleasant

Table 5.2
Four Ways to Modify Behavior

	REINFORCEMENT	PUNISHMENT
Positive (Adding)	Something valued or desirable	Something unpleasant
	Positive Reinforcement Example: getting a gold star for good behavior in school	*Punishment by Application* Example: getting a spanking for disobeying
Negative (Removing/Avoiding)	Something unpleasant	Something valued or desirable
	Negative Reinforcement Example: avoiding a ticket by stopping at a red light	*Punishment by Removal* Example: losing a privilege such as going out with friends

punishment any event or object that, when following a response, makes that response less likely to happen again.

punishment by application the punishment of a response by the addition or experiencing of an unpleasant stimulus.

punishment by removal the punishment of a response by the removal of a pleasurable stimulus.

stimulus (a penalty), the likelihood that the person will behave that way again (turn it in on time in the future) is *increased*—just as positive reinforcement will increase a behavior's likelihood. Examples are the best way to figure out the difference between these two types of reinforcement, so try to figure out which of the following examples would be positive reinforcement and which would be negative reinforcement:

1. Arnie's father nags him to wash his car. Arnie hates being nagged, so he washes the car so his father will stop nagging.
2. Trey learns that talking in a funny voice gets him lots of attention from his classmates, so now he talks that way often.
3. Allen is a server at a restaurant and always tries to smile and be pleasant because that seems to lead to bigger tips.
4. An Li turns her report in to her teacher on the day it is due because papers get marked down a letter grade for every day they are late.

Here are the answers:

1. Arnie is being negatively reinforced for washing his car because the nagging (unpleasant stimulus) stops when he does so.
2. Trey is getting positive reinforcement in the form of his classmates' attention.
3. Allen's smiling and pleasantness are positively reinforced by the customers' tips.
4. An Li is avoiding an unpleasant stimulus (the marked-down grade) by turning in her paper on time, which is an example of negative reinforcement.

I'm confused—I thought taking something away was a kind of punishment?

I'm confused—I thought taking something away was a kind of punishment?

TWO KINDS OF PUNISHMENT People get confused because "negative" sounds like it ought to be something bad, like a kind of punishment. **Punishment** is actually the opposite of reinforcement. It is any event or stimulus that, when following a response, causes that response to be less likely to happen again. Punishment *weakens* responses, whereas reinforcement (no matter whether it is positive or negative) *strengthens* responses. There are two ways in which punishment can happen, just as there are two ways in which reinforcement can happen.

Now take a look at the right column of Table 5.2, labeled "Punishment." **Punishment by application** occurs when something unpleasant (such as a spanking, scolding, or other unpleasant stimulus) is added to the situation or *applied*. This is the kind of punishment that most people think of when they hear the word *punishment*. This is also the kind of punishment that many child development specialists strongly recommend parents avoid using with their children because it can easily escalate into abuse (Dubowitz & Bennett, 2007; Saunders & Goddard, 1998; Straus, 2000; Straus & Stewart, 1999; Straus & Yodanis, 1994; Trocmé et al., 2001). A spanking might be *physically* harmless if it is only two or three swats with a hand, but if done in anger or with a belt or other instrument, it becomes abuse, both physical and emotional.

This young man's father is applying punishment by removal as he takes the car keys away from his son.

Punishment by removal, on the other hand, is the kind of punishment most often confused with negative reinforcement. In this type of punishment, behavior is punished by the removal of something pleasurable or desired after the behavior occurs. "Grounding" a teenager is removing the freedom to do what the teenager wants to do and is an example of this kind of punishment. Other examples would be placing a child in time-out (removing the attention of the others in the room), fining someone for disobeying the law (removing money), and punishing aggressive behavior by taking away television privileges. This type of punishment is typically far more acceptable to child development specialists because it involves no physical aggression and avoids many of the problems caused by more aggressive punishments.

Table 5.3

Negative Reinforcement Versus Punishment by Removal

EXAMPLE OF NEGATIVE REINFORCEMENT	EXAMPLE OF PUNISHMENT BY REMOVAL
Stopping at a red light to avoid getting in an accident.	Losing the privilege of driving because you got into too many accidents.
Mailing an income tax return by April 15 to avoid paying a penalty.	Having to lose some of your money to pay the penalty for late tax filing.
Obeying a parent before the parent reaches the count of "three" to avoid getting a scolding.	Being "grounded" (losing your freedom) because of disobedience.

The confusion over the difference between negative reinforcement and punishment by removal makes it worth examining the difference just a bit more. Negative reinforcement occurs when a response is followed by the *removal* of an *unpleasant* stimulus. If something unpleasant has just gone away as a consequence of that response, wouldn't that response tend to happen again and again? If the response increases, the consequence has to be a kind of *reinforcement*. The problem is that the name sounds like it should be some kind of punishment because of the word *negative*, and that's exactly the problem that many people experience when they are trying to understand negative reinforcement. Many people get negative reinforcement mixed up with punishment by removal, in which a *pleasant* thing is removed (like having your driver's license taken away because you caused a bad accident). Because something is removed (taken away) in both cases, it's easy to think that they will both have the effect of punishment, or weakening a response. The difference between them lies in *what* is taken away: In the case of negative reinforcement, it is an *unpleasant* thing; in the case of punishment by removal, it is a *pleasant* or desirable thing. For a head-to-head comparison of negative reinforcement and this particular type of punishment by removal, see Table 5.3.

5.8 What are some of the problems with using punishment?

PROBLEMS WITH PUNISHMENT Although punishment can be effective in reducing or weakening a behavior, it has several drawbacks. The job of punishment is much harder than that of reinforcement. In using reinforcement, all one has to do is strengthen a response that is already there. But punishment is used to weaken a response, and getting rid of a response that is already well established is not that easy. (Ask any parent or pet owner.) Many times punishment only serves to temporarily suppress or inhibit a behavior until enough time has passed. For example, punishing a child's bad behavior doesn't always eliminate the behavior completely. As time goes on, the punishment is forgotten, and the "bad" behavior may occur again in a kind of spontaneous recovery of the old (and probably pleasurable for the child) behavior.

Look back at Table 5.2 under the "Punishment" column. Punishment by application can be quite severe, and severe punishment does do one thing well: It stops the behavior immediately (Bucher & Lovaas, 1967; Carr & Lovass, 1983). It may not stop it permanently, but it does stop it. In a situation in which a child might be doing something dangerous or self-injurious, this kind of punishment is sometimes more acceptable (Duker & Seys, 1995). For example, if a child starts to run into a busy street, the parent might scream at the child to stop and then administer several rather severe swats to the child's rear. If this is not usual behavior on the part of the parent, the child will most likely never run into the street again.

Other than situations of immediately stopping dangerous behavior, severe punishment has too many drawbacks to be really useful. It should also be discouraged because of its potential for leading to abuse (Dubowitz & Bennett, 2007; Gershoff, 2000; Millan et al., 1999; Trocmé et al., 2001):

- Severe punishment may cause the child (or animal) to avoid the punisher instead of the behavior being punished, so the child (or animal) learns the wrong response.
- Severe punishment may encourage lying to avoid the punishment (a kind of negative reinforcement)—again, not the response that is desired.
- Severe punishment creates fear and anxiety, emotional responses that do not promote learning (Baumrind, 1997; Gershoff, 2000; Gershoff, 2002). If the point is to teach something, this kind of consequence isn't going to help.
- Hitting provides a successful model for aggression (Gershoff, 2000; Milner, 1992).

That last point is worth a bit more discussion. In using an aggressive type of punishment, such as spanking, the adult is actually modeling (presenting a behavior to be imitated by the child). After all, the adult is using aggression to get what the adult wants from the child. Children sometimes become more likely to use aggression to get what they want when they receive this kind of punishment (Bryan & Freed, 1982; Larzelere, 1986), and the adult has lost an opportunity to model a more appropriate way to deal with parent–child disagreements. Since aggressive punishment does tend to stop the undesirable behavior, at least for a while, the parent who is punishing actually experiences a kind of negative reinforcement: "When I spank, the unpleasant behavior goes away." This may increase the tendency to use aggressive punishment over other forms of discipline and could even lead to child abuse (Dubowitz & Bennett, 2007). Finally, some children are so desperate for attention from their parents that they will actually misbehave on purpose. The punishment is a form of attention, and these children will take whatever attention they can get, even negative attention.

Punishment by removal is less objectionable to many parents and educators and is the only kind of punishment that is permitted in many public schools. But this kind of punishment also has its drawbacks—it teaches the child what *not* to do but not what the child should do. Both punishment by removal and punishment by application are usually only temporary in their effect on behavior. After some time has passed, the behavior will most likely return as the memory of the punishment gets weaker, allowing spontaneous recovery.

If punishment doesn't work very well, what can a parent do to keep a child from behaving badly?

If punishment doesn't work very well, what can a parent do to keep a child from behaving badly?

HOW TO MAKE PUNISHMENT MORE EFFECTIVE The way to make punishment more effective involves remembering a few simple rules:

1. **Punishment should immediately follow the behavior it is meant to punish.** If the punishment comes long after the behavior, it will not be associated with that behavior. (This is also true of reinforcement.)
2. **Punishment should be consistent.** This actually means two things. First, if the parent says that a certain punishment will follow a certain behavior, then the parent must make sure to follow through and do what he or she promised to do. Second, punishment for a particular behavior should stay at the same intensity or increase slightly but never decrease. For example, if a child is scolded for jumping on the bed the first time, the second time this behavior happens the child should also be punished by scolding or by a stronger penalty, such as removal of a favorite toy. But if the first misbehavior is punished by spanking and the second by only a scolding, the child learns to "gamble" with the possible punishment.

3. **Punishment of the wrong behavior should be paired, whenever possible, with reinforcement of the right behavior.** Instead of yelling at a 2-year-old for eating with her fingers, the parent should pull her hand gently out of her plate while saying something such as, "No, we do not eat with our fingers. We eat with our fork," and then placing the fork in the child's hand and praising her for using it. "See, you are doing such a good job with your fork. I'm so proud of you." Pairing punishment (the mild correction of pulling her hand away while saying "No, we do not eat with our fingers") with reinforcement allows parents (and others) to use a much milder punishment and still be effective. It also teaches the desired behavior rather than just suppressing the undesired one.

The following section discusses some very recent research on the problems that can be generated by a particular form of punishment by application: spanking.

issues in psychology

The Link Between Spanking and Aggression in Young Children

To spank or not to spank has been a controversial issue for many years now. Child development experts have typically advised parents to use other methods of disciplining their children, citing the possibility of encouraging child abuse as well as the role spanking plays in the modeling of aggression. Now the results of a new study suggest that there is a significantly increased risk of higher levels of aggression at age 5 when spanking is used at age 3 (C. Taylor et al., 2010).

While older studies have found similar results, the study by Dr. Catherine Taylor and her colleagues, Drs. Jennifer Manganello, Shawna Lee, and Janet Rice, differs from those earlier studies in that possible maternal risk factors such as neglect, the mother's use of drugs, and maternal psychological problems were measured and controlled.

In this study, 2,461 mothers participated in reporting their use of spanking at age 3 as well as their children's aggressive behavior at age 3 and then 2 years later at age 5. Factors such as child maltreatment by the mothers, psychological maltreatment, neglect, aggression from the mother's intimate partner, victimization, stress, depression, substance abuse, and the mother's consideration of abortion were also assessed. The Taylor study found that when mothers stated that they spanked their 3-year-olds more than twice in the previous month, those same children at 5 years of age were much more likely to be more aggressive (bullying, for example) when compared to children of mothers who spanked less than twice or not at all when their children were 3. This result held even when the individual differences between the natural aggression levels of the 3-year-olds and the other possible confounding factors were taken into account.

The conclusion seems to be that sparing the rod may spare the child (and those around the child) from an unpleasant personality trait. **Read** on **mypsychlab.com**

Read and learn more about the controversy surrounding spanking on **mypsychlab.com**

Questions for Further Discussion

1. How did your own parents discipline you, and do you think that it affected you in a positive or negative way?
2. Why might this finding exist: Why would spanking at age 3 lead to higher aggression in that same child at age 5?

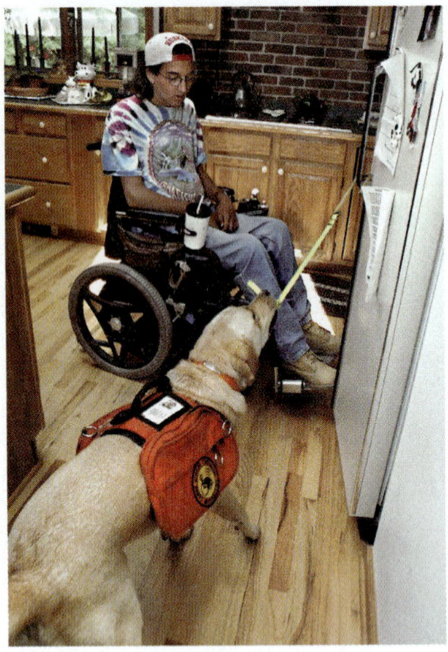

This dog has been trained to help its physically challenged owner. Operant conditioning principles can be used to train animals to do many useful tasks, including opening the refrigerator.

STIMULUS CONTROL: SLOW DOWN, IT'S THE COPS

5.9 How do operant stimuli control behavior, and what are some other concepts that can enhance or limit operant conditioning?

You see a police car in your rearview mirror and automatically slow down, even if you weren't speeding. The traffic light turns red, so you stop. When you want to get into a store, you head for the door and push or pull on the handle. All of these things—slowing down, stopping, using the door handle—are learned. But how do you know what learned response to make, and when? The police car, the stoplight, and the door handle are all cues, or stimuli, which tell you what behavior will get you what you want.

A **discriminative stimulus** is any stimulus that provides an organism with a cue for making a certain response in order to obtain reinforcement—specific cues would lead to specific responses, and discriminating between the cues leads to success. For example, a police car is a discriminative stimulus for slowing down and a red stoplight is a cue for stopping because both of these actions are usually followed by negative reinforcement—people don't get a ticket or don't get hit by another vehicle. A doorknob is a cue for where to grab the door in order to successfully open it. In fact, if a door has a knob, people always turn it, but if it has a handle, people usually pull it, right? The two kinds of opening devices each bring forth a different response from people, and their reward is opening the door.

OTHER CONCEPTS IN OPERANT CONDITIONING

Operant conditioning is more than just the reinforcement of simple responses. For example, have you ever tried to teach a pet to do a trick? Yes, it was really hard.

How do the circus trainers get their animals to do all those complicated tricks?

How do the circus trainers get their animals to do all those complicated tricks?

SHAPING When you see an animal in a circus or in a show at a zoo perform tricks, you are seeing the result of apply the rules of conditioning—both classical and operant—to animals. But the more complex tricks are a process in operant conditioning called **shaping**, in which small steps toward some ultimate goal are reinforced until the goal itself is reached.

For example, if Jody wanted to train his dog to jump through a hoop, he would have to start with some behavior that the dog is already capable of doing on its own. Then he would gradually "mold" that starting behavior into the jump—something the dog is capable of doing but not likely to do on its own. Jody would have to start with the hoop on the ground in front of Rover's face and then call the dog through the hoop, using the treat as bait. After Rover steps through the hoop (as the shortest way to the treat), Jody should give Rover the treat (positive reinforcement). Then he could raise the hoop just a little, reward him for walking through it again, raise the hoop, reward him . . . until Rover is jumping through the hoop to get the treat. The goal is achieved by reinforcing each **successive approximation** (small steps one after the other that get closer and closer to the goal). This process is shaping (Skinner, 1974). Through pairing of a sound such as a whistle or clicker with the primary reinforcer of food, animal trainers can use the sound as a secondary reinforcer and avoid having an overfed learner.

discriminative stimulus any stimulus, such as a stop sign or a doorknob, that provides the organism with a cue for making a certain response in order to obtain reinforcement.

shaping the reinforcement of simple steps in behavior that lead to a desired, more complex behavior.

successive approximations small steps in behavior, one after the other, that lead to a particular goal behavior.

EXTINCTION, GENERALIZATION, AND SPONTANEOUS RECOVERY IN OPERANT CONDITIONING *Extinction* in classical conditioning involves the removal of the UCS, the unconditioned stimulus that eventually acts as a reinforcer of the CS–CR bond. It should come as no surprise, then, that extinction in operant conditioning involves the removal of the reinforcement. Have you ever seen a child throw a temper tantrum in the checkout line because the little one wanted some candy or toy? Many exasperated* parents will cave in and give the child the treat, positively reinforcing the tantrum. The parent is also being negatively reinforced for giving in, because the obnoxious** behavior stops. The only way to get the tantrum behavior to stop is to remove the reinforcement, which means no candy, no treat, and if possible, no attention from the parent. (Not only is this hard enough to do while enduring the tantrum but also the tantrum behavior may actually get worse before it extinguishes!)

Just as in classical conditioning, operantly conditioned responses also can be generalized to stimuli that are only *similar* to the original stimulus. For example, what parent has not experienced that wonderful moment when Baby, who is just learning to label objects and people, says "Dada" in response to the presence of her father and is reinforced by his delight and attention to her. But in the beginning, Baby may cause Dad to cringe when she generalizes her "Dada" response to any man. As other men fail to reinforce her for this response, she'll learn to discriminate among them and her father and only call her father "Dada." In this way, the man who is actually her father becomes a discriminative stimulus just like the stoplight or the doorknob mentioned earlier.

Spontaneous recovery (in classical conditioning, the recurrence of a conditioned response after extinction) will also happen with operant responses. Remember the hoop-jumping dog? Anyone who has ever trained animals to do several different tricks will say that when first learning a new trick, most animals will try to get reinforcers by performing their *old* tricks. Rover might very well have tried to roll over, speak, and shake paws to get that treat before finally walking through the hoop.

While animals can learn many types of behavior through the use of operant conditioning, it seems that not every animal can be taught *anything*—see the following section on biological constraints for more on this topic.

One way to deal with a child's temper tantrum is to ignore it. The lack of reinforcement for the tantrum behavior will eventually result in extinction.

*exasperated: irritated or annoyed.

**obnoxious: highly offensive or undesirable.

classic studies in psychology

Biological Constraints on Operant Conditioning

Raccoons are fairly intelligent animals and are sometimes used in learning experiments. In a typical experiment, a behaviorist would use shaping and reinforcement to teach a raccoon a trick. The goal might be to get the raccoon to pick up several coins and drop them into a metal container, for which the raccoon would be rewarded with food. The behaviorist starts by reinforcing the raccoon for picking up a single coin. Then the metal container is introduced and the raccoon is now required to drop the coin into the slot on the container in order to get reinforcement.

It is at this point that operant conditioning seems to fail. Instead of dropping the coin in the slot, the raccoon puts the coin in and out of the slot and rubs it against the inside of the container, then holds it firmly for a few seconds before finally letting it go. When the requirement is upped to two coins, the raccoon spends several minutes rubbing them against each other and dipping them into the container, without actually dropping them in. In spite of the fact that this dipping and rubbing behavior is not reinforced, it gets worse and worse until conditioning becomes impossible.

Keller and Marian Breland, in their attempt to train a raccoon, found that this problem was not limited to the raccoon (Breland & Breland, 1961). They ran into a similar difficulty with a pig that was being trained to pick up a total of five large wooden coins and put them

Raccoons commonly dunk their food in and out of water before eating. This "washing" behavior is controlled by instinct and difficult to change even using operant techniques.

into a "piggy bank." Although at first successful, the pig became slower and slower at the task over a period of weeks, dropping the coin, rooting (pushing) it around with its nose, picking it up, dropping it again, and rooting some more. This behavior became so persistent that the pig actually did not get enough to eat for the day.

The Brelands concluded that the raccoon and the pig were reverting* to behavior that was instinctual for them. Instinctual behavior is genetically determined and not under the influence of learning. Apparently, even though the animals were at first able to learn the tricks, as the coins became more and more associated with food, the animals began to drift back into the instinctual patterns of behavior that they used with real food. Raccoons rub their food between their paws and dip it in and out of water. Pigs root and throw their food around before eating it. The Brelands called this tendency to revert to genetically controlled patterns **instinctive drift**.

In their 1961 paper describing these and other examples of instinctive drift, the Brelands (both trained by Skinner himself) determined that three assumptions in which most Skinnerian behaviorists believed were not actually true. The three false assumptions:

1. The animal comes to the laboratory a *tabula rasa*, or "blank slate," and can, therefore, be taught anything with the right conditioning.
2. Differences between species of animals are insignificant.
3. All responses are equally able to be conditioned to any stimulus.

As became quickly obvious in their studies with these animals, each animal comes into the world (and the laboratory) with certain genetically determined instinctive patterns of behavior already in place. These instincts differ from species to species, with the result that there are some responses that simply cannot be trained into an animal regardless of conditioning.

Questions for Further Discussion

1. What other kinds of limitations do animals have in learning?
2. What kinds of behavior might people do that would be resistant to conditioning?
3. How can these research findings about animal behavior be generalized to human behavior?

*reverting: to go back in action, thought, speech, and so on.

USING OPERANT CONDITIONING: BEHAVIOR MODIFICATION

5.10 What is behavior modification, and how can behavioral techniques be used to modify involuntary biological responses?

Operant conditioning principles such as reinforcement and the process of shaping have been used for many years to change undesirable behavior and create desirable responses in animals and humans—particularly in schoolchildren. The term **behavior modification** refers to the application of operant conditioning (and sometimes classical conditioning) to bring about such changes. People might recall their grade school teacher offering gold stars or some other incentive* as a reward for reading a certain number of books or giving a reward like a wooden stick that could be traded in for a treat.

For example, if a teacher wants to use behavior modification to help a child learn to be more attentive during the teacher's lectures, the teacher may do the following:

1. Select a target behavior, such as making eye contact with the teacher.
2. Choose a reinforcer. This may be a gold star applied to the child's chart on the wall, for example.

*incentive: something that encourages a particular action.

instinctive drift tendency for an animal's behavior to revert to genetically controlled patterns.

behavior modification the use of operant conditioning techniques to bring about desired changes in behavior.

3. Put the plan in action. Every time the child makes eye contact, the teacher gives the child a gold star. Inappropriate behavior (such as looking out of the window) is not reinforced with gold stars.
4. At the end of the day, the teacher gives the child a special treat or reward for having a certain number of gold stars. This special reward is decided on ahead of time and discussed with the child.

Both gold stars and wooden sticks can be considered *tokens*, secondary reinforcers that can be traded in for other kinds of reinforcers. The use of tokens to modify behavior is called a **token economy**. LINK to Chapter Fifteen: Psychological Therapies, p. 584. In the example, the child is collecting gold stars to "buy" the special treat at the end of the day. When one thinks about it, the system of money is very much a token economy. People are rewarded for working for money, which they then trade for food, shelter, and so on.

Another tool that behaviorists can use to modify behavior is the process of *time-out*. Time-out is a form of mild punishment by removal in which a misbehaving animal, child, or adult is placed in a special area away from the attention of others. Essentially, the organism is being "removed" from any possibility of positive reinforcement in the form of attention. When used with children, a time-out should be limited to 1 minute for each year of age with a maximum time-out of 10 minutes (longer than that and the child can forget why the time-out occurred).

Applied behavior analysis (ABA), is the modern term for a form of behavior modification that uses both analysis of current behavior and behavioral techniques to address a socially relevant issue. An example is using the shaping process to mold a desired behavior or response and has been used with a variety of populations including individuals with *autism*. Autism is a disorder in which the person has great difficulty in communicating with others, often refusing to look at another person. LINK to Chapter Eight: Development Across the Life Span, p. 317. This specific application can be said to have begun with the work of Lovaas (1964) and his associates, although the basic general techniques are those first outlined by Skinner. Lovaas used small pieces of candy as reinforcers to teach social skills and language to children with autism. People who are autistic may also fail to learn to speak at all, and they normally do not like to be touched.

In ABA, skills are broken down to their simplest steps and then taught to the child through a system of reinforcement. Prompts (such as moving a child's face back to look at the teacher or the task) are given as needed when the child is learning a skill or refuses to cooperate. As the child begins to master a skill and receives reinforcement in the form of treats or praise, the prompts are gradually withdrawn until the child can do the skill independently. Applied behavior analysis is a growing field with many colleges and universities offering degrees at both the undergraduate and graduate levels. A person graduating from one of these programs may act as a consultant* to schools or other institutions, or may set up a private practice. Typical uses for ABA are treating with children with disorders, training animals, and developing effective teaching methods for children and adults of all levels of mental abilities (Baer et al., 1968).

Other techniques for modifying responses have been developed so that even biological responses that are normally considered involuntary such as blood pressure, muscle tension, and hyperactivity can be brought under conscious control. For nearly 60 years, scientists have known how to use feedback from person's biological information (such as heart rate) to create a state of relaxation (Margolin & Kubic, 1944). **Biofeedback** is the traditional term used to describe this kind of biological feedback of information, and through its use many problems can be relieved or controlled.

*consultant: someone who offers expert advice or services.

token economy type of behavior modification in which desired behavior is rewarded with tokens.

applied behavior analysis (ABA) modern term for a form of functional analysis and behavior modification that uses a variety of behavioral techniques to mold a desired behavior or response.

biofeedback using feedback about biological conditions to bring involuntary responses, such as blood pressure and relaxation, under voluntary control.

neurofeedback form of biofeedback using brain-scanning devices to provide feedback about brain activity in an effort to modify behavior.

A relatively newer biofeedback technique called **neurofeedback** involves trying to change brain-wave activity. LINK to Chapter Two: The Biological Perspective p. 68. Although this technique uses the latest in technology, the basic principles behind it are much older. Traditionally, to record brain-wave activity, a person would have to be connected to a stand-alone *electroencephalograph*, a machine that amplifies and records the brain's electrical activity. In today's modern age, biofeedback and neurofeedback amplifers are often connected to a computer that records and analyzes the physiological activity of the brain. Neurofeedback applications can also be used with functional magnetic resonance imaging (fMRI). Neurofeedback can be integrated with video-game–like programs that individuals can use to learn how to produce brain waves or specific types of brain activity associated with specific cognitive or behavioral states (e.g., increased attention, staying focused, relaxed awareness). Individuals learn to make these changes through the principles of operant conditioning. Playing a video game to help solve problems like anxiety or attention problems? It sounds like a child's dream world. **Read** on **mypsychlab.com**

Read and learn more about neurofeedback on **mypsychlab.com**

5.6 5.7 5.8 5.9 5.10

CONCEPT MAP

Operant Conditioning (continued)

(learning to make voluntary responses through the effects of positive or negative consequences)

- **schedules of reinforcement**
  - **timing of reinforcement** influences speed of learning, strength of learned response, and subsequent behavior pattern
  - **continuous reinforcement:** provision of reinforcer for each and every correct response
    - easier to establish new responses but more sensitive to extinction
  - **partial reinforcement:** reinforcing behavior after some but not all correct responses
    - leads to a response that is resistant to extinction
    - schedule can be specified by the pattern/ratio of responses or by time/interval
    - both ratio and interval schedules can be either fixed or variable
- **punishment** is any event or stimulus that, when following a response, decreases the probability that the response will occur again
  - opposite of reinforcement, which increases the probability that the response will occur again
  - punishment by application—something unpleasant is added to the situation
  - punishment by removal—something pleasurable is removed
  - to work—must be immediate, consistent, and paired with reinforcement of actual behavior desired
- **other features**
  - stimuli must be discriminative; specific cues lead to specific responses
  - some behaviors can be established through shaping, reinforcing small steps, or each successive approximation, toward the ultimate goal
  - as in classical conditioning, extinction, generalization, and spontaneous recovery can occur
  - instinctive drift, or the tendency to revert to genetically controlled patterns of behavior, can serve as a biological constraint on operant conditioning
- **behavior modification**
  - application of operant conditioning principles (sometimes classical conditioning) to change undesirable behaviors and create desirable behaviors in both humans and animals
  - token economies, time-out, applied behavior analysis, biofeedback, and neurofeedback use these principles

PRACTICE quiz How much do you remember?

ANSWERS ON PAGE AK-1.

Pick the best answer.

1. In a popular television series, Desmond lived in a bunker underground on a mysterious island. He had one task: When the alarm sounds, type in a series of numbers on the computer and push enter. Desmond was being reinforced for doing so by avoiding some terrible disaster that would occur if he did *not* type in the numbers at the right time—every 108 minutes. What kind of schedule of reinforcement was Desmond on?
   a. fixed interval
   b. fixed ratio
   c. variable interval
   d. variable ratio

2. Joe was trying to get tickets to a concert and called the ticket outlet only to find that the phone line was busy. He dialed again—busy—and then again and again, sometimes waiting a minute, sometimes a few minutes, not knowing how much time would go by before his call would go through. What schedule of reinforcement is evident here?
   a. fixed interval
   b. fixed ratio
   c. variable interval
   d. variable ratio

3. Jessica's mother was upset to find that Jessica had used her crayons to draw flowers on her bedroom wall. Her mother took the crayons away from her and made Jessica wash the drawings off the wall. Which of the following statements is TRUE?
   a. Having her crayons taken away was a form of punishment by removal.
   b. Being made to wash off the drawings was a form of punishment by application.
   c. Having her crayons taken away was a form of negative reinforcement.
   d. Both a and b are true.
4. Which of the following is NOT a problem with punishment?
   a. The effect of punishment is often temporary.
   b. Severe punishment creates fear and anxiety.
   c. Mild punishment can be paired with reinforcement of the correct behavior.
   d. Aggressive punishment can model aggressive behavior for the child.
5. Elizabeth's parents want her to put her clothes in the hamper. At first, they praise her for putting the clothes together in one pile. Then they praise her for getting the clothes on the same side of the room as the hamper. When she gets the clothes on top of the hamper, she gets praise. Finally, her parents praise her when she puts her clothes in the hamper. This is an example of _________.
   a. negative reinforcement.
   b. punishment.
   c. extinction.
   d. shaping.
6. Professor Elliot told his students that if his door was open, it meant that he was available to them and would gladly answer any questions they might have. But if his door was pushed almost completely shut, it meant that he was busy and would prefer not to answer questions at that time. Professor Elliot's door being open was a _________ for _________.
   a. discriminative stimulus; asking questions.
   b. discriminative stimulus; not asking questions.
   c. discriminative response; asking questions.
   d. discriminative response; not asking questions.
7. Ella is teaching her parrot a new word. Every time the parrot says a sound that is close to the new word, she gives it a treat. But the parrot keeps repeating other words it has learned in the past, trying to get a treat that way. The parrot is exhibiting _________.
   a. generalization.
   b. extinction.
   c. spontaneous recovery.
   d. discrimination.
8. Applied behavior analysis involves _________.
   a. the process of shaping and other behavioral techniques.
   b. is useful only for teaching autistic children.
   c. is different from behavior modification.
   d. cannot be used with animals.

Brainstorming: How did your parents discipline you when you were a child? What type of reinforcement or punishment did they use most often?

Cognitive Learning Theory

5.11 How do latent learning, learned helplessness, and insight relate to cognitive learning theory?

In the early days of behaviorism, the focus of Watson, Skinner, and many of their followers was on observable, measurable behavior. Anything that might be occurring inside a person or animal's head during learning was considered to be of no interest to the behaviorist because it could not be seen or directly measured. Other psychologists, however, were still interested in the mind's influence over behavior. Gestalt psychologists, for instance, were studying the way that the human mind tried to force a pattern on stimuli in the world around the person. LINK to Chapter One: The Science of Psychology, p. 10. This continued interest in the mind was followed, in the 1950s and 1960s, by the comparison of the human mind to the workings of those fascinating "thinking machines," computers. Soon after, interest in *cognition*, the mental events that take place inside a person's mind while behaving, began to dominate experimental psychology. Many behavioral psychologists could no longer ignore the thoughts, feelings, and expectations that clearly existed in the mind and that seemed to influence observable behavior and eventually began to develop a cognitive learning theory to supplement the more traditional theories of learning (Kendler, 1985). Three important figures often cited as key theorists in the early days of the development of cognitive learning theory were the Gestalt psychologists Edward Tolman and Wolfgang Köhler, and modern psychologist Martin Seligman.

"Bathroom? Sure, it's just down that hall to the left, jog right, left, another left, straight past two more lefts, then right, and it's at the end of the third corridor on your right."

TOLMAN'S MAZE-RUNNING RATS: LATENT LEARNING

One of Gestalt psychologist Edward Tolman's best-known experiments in learning involved teaching three groups of rats the same maze, one at a time (Tolman & Honzik, 1930). In the first group, each rat was placed in the maze and reinforced

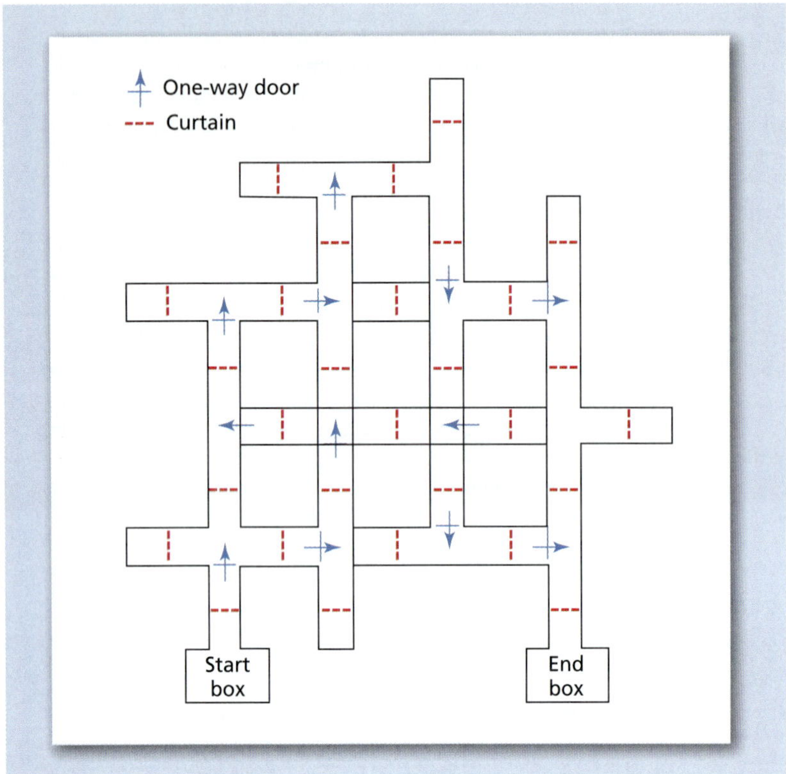

Figure 5.9 A Typical Maze

This is an example of a maze such as the one used in Tolman's experiments in latent learning. A rat is placed in the start box. The trial is over when the rat gets to the end box.

with food for making its way out the other side. The rat was then placed back in the maze, reinforced upon completing the maze again, and so on until the rat could successfully solve the maze with no errors (see Figure 5.9).

The second group of rats was treated exactly like the first, except that they never received any reinforcement upon exiting the maze. They were simply put back in again and again, until the 10th day of the experiment. On that day, the rats in the second group began to receive reinforcement for getting out of the maze. The third group of rats, serving as a control group, was also not reinforced and was not given reinforcement for the entire duration of the experiment.

A strict Skinnerian behaviorist would predict that only the first group of rats would learn the maze successfully because learning depends on reinforcing consequences. At first, this seemed to be the case. The first group of rats did indeed solve the maze after a certain number of trials, whereas the second and third groups seemed to wander aimlessly around the maze until accidentally finding their way out.

On the 10th day, however, something happened that would be difficult to explain using only Skinner's basic principles. The second group of rats, upon receiving the reinforcement for the first time, *should* have then taken as long as the first group to solve the maze. Instead, they began to solve the maze almost immediately (see Figure 5.10).

Tolman concluded that the rats in the second group, while wandering around in the first 9 days of the experiment, had indeed learned where all the blind alleys, wrong turns, and correct paths were and stored this knowledge away as a kind of "mental map," or *cognitive map* of the physical layout of the maze. The rats in the second group had learned and stored that learning away mentally but had not *demonstrated* this learning because there was no reason to do so. The cognitive map had remained hidden, or latent, until the rats had a reason to demonstrate their knowledge by getting to the food. Tolman called this **latent learning**. The idea that learning could happen without reinforcement, and then later affect behavior, was not something traditional operant conditioning could explain.

KÖHLER'S SMART CHIMP: INSIGHT LEARNING

Another exploration of the cognitive elements of learning came about almost by accident. Wolfgang Köhler (1887–1967) was a Gestalt psychologist who became marooned* on an island in the Canaries (a series of islands off the coast of North Africa) when World War I broke out. Stuck at the primate research lab that had first drawn him to the island, he turned to studies of animal learning.

In one of his more famous studies (Köhler, 1925), he set up a problem for one of the chimpanzees. Sultan the chimp was faced with the problem of how to get to a banana that was placed just out of his reach outside his cage. Sultan solved this

latent learning learning that remains hidden until its application becomes useful.

*marooned: in this sense, being placed on an island from which escape is impossible.

problem relatively easily, first trying to reach through the bars with his arm, then using a stick that was lying in the cage to rake the banana into the cage. As chimpanzees are natural tool users, this behavior is not surprising and is still nothing more than simple trial-and-error learning.

But then the problem was made more difficult. The banana was placed just out of reach of Sultan's extended arm with the stick in his hand. At this point there were two sticks lying around in the cage, which could be fitted together to make a single pole that would be long enough to reach the banana. Sultan first tried one stick, then the other (simple trial and error). After about an hour of trying, Sultan seemed to have a sudden flash of inspiration. He pushed one stick out of the cage as far as it would go toward the banana and then pushed the other stick behind the first one. Of course, when he tried to draw the sticks back, only the one in his hand came. He jumped up and down and was very excited, and when Köhler gave him the second stick, he sat on the floor of the cage and looked at them carefully. He then fitted one stick into the other and retrieved his banana. Köhler called Sultan's rapid "perception of relationships" **insight** and determined that insight could not be gained through trial-and-error learning alone (Köhler, 1925). Although Thorndike and other early learning theorists believed that animals could not demonstrate insight, Köhler's work seems to demonstrate that insight requires a sudden "coming together" of all the elements of a problem in a kind of "aha" moment that is not predicted by traditional animal learning studies. LINK to Chapter Seven: Cognition, pp. 260–261. More recent research has also found support for the concept of animal insight (Heinrich, 2000; Heyes, 1998; Zentall, 2000), but there is still controversy over how to interpret the results of those studies (Wynne, 1999).

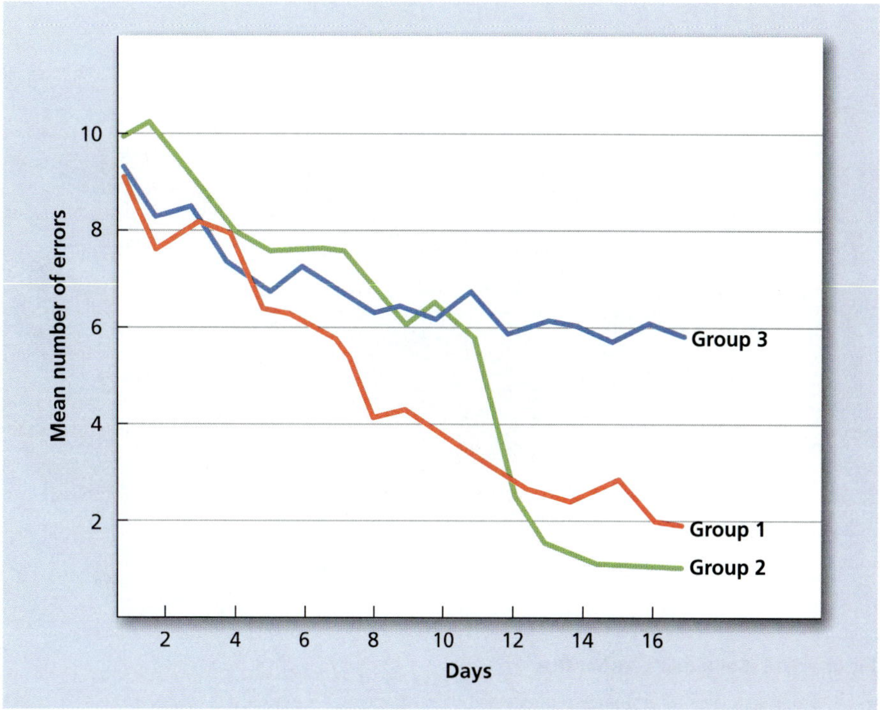

Figure 5.10 Learning Curves for Three Groups of Rats

In the results of the classic study of latent learning, Group 1 was rewarded on each day, while Group 2 was rewarded for the first time on Day 11. Group 3 was never rewarded. Note the immediate change in the behavior of Group 2 on Day 12 (Tolman & Honzik, 1930).

Another of Köhler's chimpanzees, Grande, has just solved the problem of how to get to the banana by stacking boxes. Does this meet the criteria for insight, or was it simple trial-and-error learning?

insight the sudden perception of relationships among various parts of a problem, allowing the solution to the problem to come quickly.

learned helplessness the tendency to fail to act to escape from a situation because of a history of repeated failures in the past.

SELIGMAN'S DEPRESSED DOGS: LEARNED HELPLESSNESS

Martin Seligman is now famous for founding the field of *positive psychology*, a new way of looking at the entire concept of mental health and therapy. But in the mid- to late 1960s learning theorist Seligman (1975) and his colleagues were doing classical conditioning experiments on dogs. They accidentally discovered an unexpected phenomenon, which Seligman called **learned helplessness**, the tendency to fail to act to escape from a situation because of a history of repeated failures in the past. Their original intention was to study escape and avoidance learning. Seligman and colleagues presented a tone followed by a harmless but painful electric shock to one group of dogs (Overmier & Seligman, 1967; Seligman & Maier, 1967). The dogs in this group were harnessed so that they could not escape the shock. The researchers assumed that the dogs would learn to fear the sound of the tone and later try to escape from the tone before being shocked.

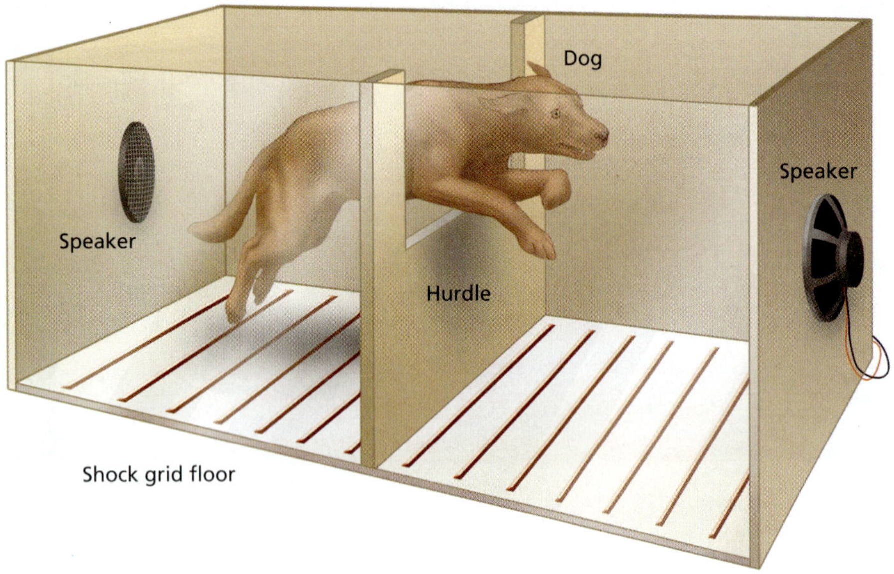

Figure 5.11 Seligman's Apparatus

In Seligman's studies of learned helplessness, dogs were placed in a two-sided box. Dogs that had no prior experience with being unable to escape a shock would quickly jump over the hurdle in the center of the box to land on the "safe" side. Dogs that had previously learned that escape was impossible would stay on the side of the box in which the shock occurred, not even trying to go over the hurdle.

These dogs, along with another group of dogs that had not been conditioned to fear the tone, were placed into a special box consisting of a low fence that divided the box into two compartments. The dogs, which were now unharnessed, could easily see over the fence and jump over if they wished—which is precisely what the dogs that had not been conditioned did as soon as the shock occurred (see Figure 5.11). Imagine the researchers' surprise when, instead of jumping over the fence when the tone sounded, the previously conditioned dogs just sat there. In fact, these dogs showed distress but didn't try to jump over the fence *even when the shock itself began*.

Why would the conditioned dogs refuse to move when shocked? The dogs that had been harnessed while being conditioned had apparently learned in the original tone/shock situation that there was nothing they could do to escape the shock. So when placed in a situation in which escape was possible, the dogs still did nothing because they had learned to be "helpless." They believed they could not escape, so they did not try.

More recently, Seligman's colleague and co-researcher in those early studies, Steven F. Maier, has revisited the phenomenon of learned helplessness from a neuroscientific approach, and this work has provided some new insights. Maier and others have investigated the brain mechanisms underlying this phenomenon, focusing on an area of the brain stem that releases serotonin and can play a role in activating the amygdala (which plays an important role in fear and anxiety) but also participates in decreasing activity in brain areas responsible for the "fight-or-flight" response. This combination of increased fear/anxiety with non-escape or freezing is the very behavior associated with learned helplessness. This part of the brain stem (the dorsal raphe nucleus) is a much older part of the brain and not able to determine what type of stressors are controllable. Their research suggests that a higher-level area, a part of the frontal lobe called the *ventromedial prefrontal cortex* (vmPFC), is able to help determine what is controllable. In turn, the vmPFC inhibits the brain stem area and calms the amygdala's response, allowing an animal to effectively respond to a stressor and exhibit control (Amat et al., 2005; Maier et al., 2006; Maier & Watkins, 2005). In other words, it is possible that the dogs in the early studies, rather than learning to be helpless were *not* learning how to relax and take control of the situation. Maier and colleagues suggest that both training and input from the vmPFC are necessary for animals to learn how to take control (Maier et al., 2006).

I know some people who seem to act just like those dogs—they live in a horrible situation but won't leave. Is this the same thing?

I know some people who seem to act just like those dogs—they live in a horrible situation but won't leave. Is this the same thing?

Seligman extended the concept of learned helplessness to explain some behaviors characteristic of *depression*. Depressed people seem to lack normal emotions and become somewhat apathetic, often staying in unpleasant work environments or bad marriages or relationships rather than trying to escape or better their situation. Seligman proposed that this depressive behavior is a form of learned helplessness. Depressed people may have learned in the past that they seem to have no control over what happens to them (Alloy &

Clements, 1998). A sense of powerlessness and hopelessness is common to depressed people, and certainly this would seem to apply to Seligman's dogs as well. Maier's recent work also has implications here, especially the focus on the components necessary for learning how to relax and exhibit control: input from the vmPFC, and training (repeated exposures to stressors). This combination provides a mechanism for not only understanding resilience*, but also for possibly helping people foster resilience and avoid anxiety or mood disorders such as posttraumatic stress disorder (PTSD) or depression (Maier et al., 2006). LINK to Chapter Eleven: Stress and Health, pp. 541–547.

Think about how learned helplessness might apply to other situations. There are many students who feel that they are bad at math because they have had problems with it in the past. Is it possible that this belief could make them not try as hard or study as much as they should? Is this kind of thinking also an example of learned helplessness or is it possible that these students have simply not had enough experiences of success or control?

Cognitive learning is also an important part of a fairly well-known form of learning, often simplified as "monkey see, monkey do." Let's take a look at learning through watching the actions of others.

observational learning learning new behavior by watching a model perform that behavior.

Observational Learning

5.12 What occurs in observational learning, and what are the findings from Bandura's classic Bobo doll study and the four elements of observational learning?

Observational learning is the learning of new behavior through watching the actions of a model (someone else who is doing that behavior). Sometimes that behavior is desirable, and sometimes it is not, as the next section describes.

BANDURA AND THE BOBO DOLL

Albert Bandura's classic study in observational learning involved having a preschool child in a room in which the experimenter and a model interacted with toys in the room in front of the child (Bandura et al., 1961). In one condition, the model interacted with the toys in a nonaggressive manner, completely ignoring the presence of a "Bobo" doll (a punch-bag doll in the shape of a clown). In another condition, the model became very aggressive with the doll, kicking it and yelling at it, throwing it in the air and hitting it with a hammer. **Watch** on **mypsychlab.com**

Watch footage from Bandura's Bobo doll experiment on **mypsychlab.com**

When each child was left alone in the room and had the opportunity to play with the toys, a camera filming through a one-way mirror caught the children who were exposed to the aggressive model beating up on the Bobo doll, in exact imitation of the model. (See Figure 5.12.) The children who saw the model ignore the doll did

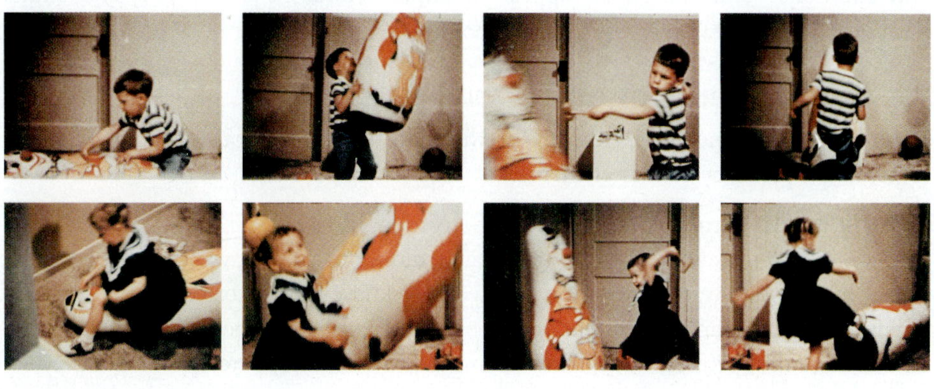

Figure 5.12 Bandura's Bobo Doll Experiment

In Albert Bandura's famous Bobo doll experiment, the doll was used to demonstrate the impact of observing an adult model performing aggressive behavior on the later aggressive behavior of children. The children in these photos are imitating the adult model's behavior even though they believe they are alone and are not being watched.

*resilience: the ability to recover quickly from change and/or stress.

Ah, but would that child have imitated the model if the model had been punished? Wouldn't the consequences of the model's behavior make a difference?

not act aggressively toward the toy. Obviously, the aggressive children had learned their aggressive actions from merely watching the model—with no reinforcement necessary. The fact that learning can take place without actual performance (a kind of latent learning) is called **learning/performance distinction**.

Ah, but would that child have imitated the model if the model had been punished? Wouldn't the consequences of the model's behavior make a difference?

In later studies, Bandura showed a film of a model beating up the Bobo doll. In one condition, the children saw the model rewarded afterward. In another, the model was punished. When placed in the room with toys, the children in the first group beat up the doll, but the children in the second group did not. But, when Bandura told the children in the second group that he would give them a reward if they could show him what the model in the film did, each child duplicated the model's actions. Both groups had learned from watching the model, but only the children watching the successful (rewarded) model imitated the aggression with no prompting (Bandura, 1965). Apparently, consequences do matter in motivating a child (or an adult) to imitate a particular model. The tendency for some movies and television programs to make "heroes" out of violent, aggressive "bad guys" is particularly disturbing in light of these findings. In fact, Bandura began this research to investigate possible links between children's exposure to violence on television and aggressive behavior toward others.

In a recent nationwide study of youth in the United States, it was found that young people ages 8 to 18 spend on average almost 7.5 hours per day involved in media consumption (television, computers, video games, music, cell phones, print, and movies), 7 days a week. Furthermore, given the prevalence of media multitasking (using more than one media device at a time), they are packing in approximately 10 hours and 45 minutes of media during those 7.5 hours! (Rideout et al., 2010). While not all media consumption is of violent media, it is quite easy to imagine that some of that media is of a violent nature.

Correlational research stretching over nearly 2 decades suggests that a link exists between viewing violent television and an increased level of aggression in children (Bushman & Huesmann, 2001; Huesmann & Eron, 1986). LINK to Chapter One: The Science of Psychology, pp. 26–27. While correlations do not prove that viewing violence on TV is the *cause* of increased violence, one cannot help but be curious as to the effects, especially given the continuing rise of media consumption in young people, coupled with the multiple ways young people interact with media. As such there has been an ongoing debate as to the validity of the links between aggression and exposure to media violence (primarily focusing on television, movies, video games, and music). Although still a topic of debate for some, there appears to be a strong body of evidence that exposure to media violence does have immediate and long-term effects, increasing the likelihood of aggressive verbal and physical behavior and aggressive thoughts and emotions—and the effects appear to impact children, adolescents, and adults (Anderson et al., 2003). **Simulate** on **mypsychlab.com**

Simulate Bandura's study on observational learning on **mypsychlab.com**

THE FOUR ELEMENTS OF OBSERVATIONAL LEARNING

Bandura (1986) concluded, from his studies and others, that observational learning required the presence of four elements.

ATTENTION To learn anything through observation, the learner must first pay *attention* to the model. For example, a person at a fancy dinner party who wants to know which utensil to use has to watch the person who seems to know what is correct. Certain characteristics of models can make attention more likely. For example, people pay more attention to those they perceive as similar to them, and to those they perceive as attractive.

MEMORY The learner must also be able to retain the *memory* of what was done, such as remembering the steps in preparing a dish that was first seen on a cooking show.

learning/performance distinction referring to the observation that learning can take place without actual performance of the learned behavior.

IMITATION The learner must be capable of reproducing, or *imitating*, the actions of the model. A 2-year-old might be able to watch someone tie shoelaces and might even remember most of the steps, but the 2-year-old's chubby little fingers will not have the dexterity* necessary for actually tying the laces. A person with extremely weak ankles might be able to watch and remember how some ballet move was accomplished but will not be able to reproduce it. The mirror neurons discussed in Chapter Two may be willing, but the flesh is weak. LINK to Chapter Two: The Biological Perspective, p. 76.

MOTIVATION Finally, the learner must have the desire or *motivation* to perform the action. That person at the fancy dinner, for example, might not care which fork or which knife is the "proper" one to use. Also, if a person expects a reward because one has been given in the past, or has been promised a future reward (like the children in the second group of Bandura's study), or has witnessed a model getting a reward (like the children in the first group), that person will be much more likely to imitate the observed behavior. Successful models are powerful figures for imitation, but rarely would we be motivated to imitate someone who fails or is punished.

(An easy way to remember the four elements of modeling is to remember the letters AMIM, which stand for the first letters of each of the four elements. This is a good example of using a strategy to improve memory. LINK to Introduction: Psychology in Action, pp. I-14–I-16.)

*dexterity: skill and ease in using the hands.

5.11 5.12 CONCEPT MAP

Cognitive Learning Theory

(focuses on role of cognition, or thought processes, on learning)

- **Tolman** worked with rats in a maze
  - suggested animals form a cognitive map of the physical layout of the maze
  - performance not due to reinforcement
  - **latent learning:** learning occurs but behavior not manifested until organism has reason to demonstrate it
- **Köhler** worked with chimpanzees; set up a problem situation
  - chimp first exhibited trial-and-error approach
  - later appeared to experience a sudden insight into solving the problem (retrieving a banana)
- **Seligman** originally studied escape and avoidance learning in dogs
  - discovered that the animals did nothing in a specific situation
  - **learned helplessness:** tendency to fail to act to escape from a situation because of a past history of repeated failures; or according to recent work by Maier, possibly due to not learning how to relax and take control accompanied by activation of key brain structures

Observational Learning

(the learning of a new behavior through the observation of a model; typically associated with classic work of Bandura and "Bobo doll" study)

- **key elements for learner**
  - pay attention to the model
  - able to remember what was done
  - capable of reproducing, or imitating, the actions of the model
  - have the desire or motivation to perform the action
- **children observing** an adult model's aggressive or nonaggressive behaviors tended to later act in the same manner they saw modeled; no reinforcement was necessary
  - later research suggested that potential consequences can influence motivation to imitate a particular model

(continued)

PRACTICE quiz How much do you remember? ANSWERS ON PAGE AK-1.

Pick the best answer.

1. Cognition refers to _________.
   a. behavior that is observable and external.
   b. behavior that is directly measurable.
   c. the mental events that take place while a person is behaving.
   d. memories.
2. In Tolman's maze study, the fact that the group of rats receiving reinforcement only after day 10 of the study solved the maze far more quickly than did the rats who had been reinforced from the first day can be interpreted to mean that these particular rats _________.
   a. were much smarter than the other rats.
   b. had already learned the maze in the first 9 days.
   c. had the opportunity to cheat by watching the other rats.
   d. were very hungry and, therefore, learned much more quickly.
3. Seligman found many similarities between his "helpless" dogs and people suffering from _________.
   a. aggressive behavior syndrome.
   b. mental illness.
   c. schizophrenia.
   d. depression.
4. Köhler determined that Sultan's two-stick solution to the banana problem was an example of insight because it was _________.
   a. the result of trial-and-error learning.
   b. sudden and rapid.
   c. arrived at after a long time period.
   d. intelligent.
5. In Bandura's study with the Bobo doll, the children in the group that saw the model punished did not imitate the model at first. They would only imitate the model if given a reward for doing so. The fact that these children had obviously learned the behavior without actually performing it is an example of _________.
   a. latent learning.
   b. operant conditioning.
   c. classical conditioning.
   d. insight learning.
6. Miranda wanted to make a casserole she saw on a TV food show. She bought the ingredients, put them together, baked it, and served it at dinner that night. To her horror, it tasted awful. She realized that she had left out a key ingredient and vowed next time to write everything down as she watched the show. Miranda's dinner disaster was an example of failing at which of Bandura's four elements of observational learning?
   a. attention
   b. memory
   c. imitation
   d. motivation

Brainstorming: Do you think that watching violence on television increases violence and aggression in viewers? Why or why not?

Applying Psychology to Everyday Life: Can You Really Toilet Train Your Cat?

5.13 What is a real-world example of the use of conditioning?

(This article has been excerpted with permission of the author and cat-trainer extraordinaire, Karawynn Long. Karawynn Long is a published writer and Web designer who lives in Seattle with her family. Sadly, since this article was written, her cat, Misha has passed away. Ms. Long can be reached at her Web site **www.karawynn.net/mishacat/toilet.html**. The italicized words in brackets are the author's "editorial" comments.)

There have been more books and articles about toilet-training cats than you'd think. In the summer of 1989, when Misha was a small kitten with big ears and enough meow for five cats, I searched out and read a half-dozen of them. And then tried it myself, and discovered there were a couple of things they all failed to mention . . . here's what worked for me and Misha.

The central idea is that the transition from litter box to toilet should be accomplished in a series of stages. [*This is shaping.*] You make a small change and then give your cat time to adjust before you make another small change. If at any time Felix gives the whole thing up and goes on the rug instead, you're pushing him too far too fast; back up a stage or two and try again, more slowly.

READY? FIRST START BY TRAINING YOURSELF . . .

The very most important thing to remember is: Lid Up, Seat Down. Post a note on the back of the door or the lid of the toilet if you think you (or your housemates or guests) might forget. And if you are accustomed to closing the bathroom door when it's empty, you'll have to break that habit too. [*In operant conditioning, this is part of "preparing the training arena."*]

Begin by moving the cat's current litter box from wherever it is to one side of the toilet. Make sure he knows where it is and uses it. Rest (this means doing nothing for a period of between a day and a week, depending on how flappable your cat is). Next put something—a stack of newspapers, a phone book, a cardboard box—under the litter box to raise it, say, about an inch. (Magazines are too slick; you don't want the litter box sliding around and making your cat feel insecure. Tape the litter box down if you need to.) Rest. Get another box or phone book and raise it a little higher. Rest. Continue this process until the bottom of the litter box is level with the top of the toilet seat. (For Misha I raised it about two inches per day.) [*Notice that this is the step-by-step process typically used in shaping.*]

At the beginning of this process, your cat could just step into the litter box; later he began jumping up into it, until at some point he probably started jumping up onto the toilet seat first and stepping into the box from there. Lift the seat on your toilet and measure the inside diameter of the top of the bowl at its widest point. Venture forth and buy a metal mixing bowl of that diameter. Do not (I discovered this the hard way) substitute a plastic bowl. A plastic bowl will not support the cat's weight and will bend, dropping into the toilet bowl and spilling litter everywhere, not to mention startling the cat.

Misha's first attempt without the box. He scored two out of a possible four.

Now you move the litter box over so that it's sitting directly over the toilet seat. (If your cat has shown reluctance over previous changes, you might want to split this into two stages, moving it halfway onto the seat and then fully over.) Take away the stack of phone books or whatever you used. Rest. [*Again, notice that everything has to be done in small steps. This is the heart of the shaping process—requiring too large a step will stop the process.*]

Here's the cool part. Take away the litter box entirely. (Ta da!) Nestle the metal mixing bowl inside the toilet bowl and lower the seat. Fill the bowl with about two inches of litter (all of this is much easier if you have the tiny granules of litter that can be scooped out and flushed).

Naturally, any humans using the toilet at this point will want to remove the metal bowl prior to their own use and replace it afterward. The next week or two the whole process is likely to be something of an annoyance; if you begin to think it's not worth it, just remember that you will never have to clean a litter box again.

Watch your cat using the bathroom in the metal bowl. Count the number of feet he gets up on the toilet seat (as opposed to down in the bowl of litter). The higher the number, the luckier you are and the easier your job is going to be . . .

. . . because next you have to teach him proper squatting posture. Catch him beginning to use the toilet as much of the time as possible and show him where his feet are supposed to go. Just lift them right out of the bowl and place them on the seat (front legs in the middle, hind legs on the outside). If he starts out with three or, heaven forbid, all four feet in the bowl, just get the front two feet out first. Praise him all over the place every time he completes the activity in this position. [*The praise is the positive reinforcement, and should be done with each successful step.*]

(Misha is very doglike in that he craves approval and praise. If your cat is indifferent to this sort of thing, you can also reward him with small food treats and wean him from them later when the toilet behavior has "set." Just keep the treats as small and infrequent as possible—half a Pounce™ or similar treat per occasion should be plenty.) [*If treats are too frequent, it will make it difficult to phase out the reinforcer after the behavior is well learned.*]

When he is regularly using the toilet with his front feet out (and some cats naturally start from this position), begin lifting a hind foot out and placing it on the seat outside the front paws. Your cat will probably find this awkward at first and try to replace the foot in the litter. Be persistent. Move that foot four times in a row if you have to, until it stays there. Praise and/or treat.

Repeat with the other hind foot, until your cat learns to balance in that squat. Once he's getting all four feet regularly on the seat, it's all easy from here.

Misha demonstrates proper squatting posture. Note the look of firm concentration.

Which is fortunate, because the last bit is also the most unpleasant. I suggest that you postpone this stage until you have at least a weekend, and preferably several days, when you (or another responsible party) will be at home most of the time. I skipped through this part in about two days; I only hope that your cat allows you to move along that fast.

Begin reducing the litter in the bowl. Go as fast as he'll feel comfortable with, because as the litter decreases, the odor increases. You'll want to be home at this point so that you can praise him and dump out the contents of the bowl immediately after he's finished, to minimize both the smell and the possibility that your cat, in a confused attempt to minimize the smell on his own, tries to cover it up with litter that no longer exists and ends up tracking unpleasantness into the rest of the house.

By the time you're down to a token teaspoonful of litter in the bottom of the bowl, your next-door neighbors will probably be aware of the precise instant your cat has used the toilet. This is as bad as it gets. The next time you rinse out the metal bowl, put a little bit of water in the bottom. Increase the water level each time, just as you decreased the litter level. Remember—if at any point Felix looks nervous enough about the change to give the whole thing up and take his business to the corner behind the door, back up a step or two and try the thing again more slowly. [*Shaping takes a lot of patience, depending on the behavior being shaped and the learning ability of the animal—or person.*]

Once the water in the mixing bowl is a couple of inches deep and your cat is comfortable with the whole thing, you get to perform the last bit of magic. Take the mixing bowl away, leaving the bare toilet. (Lid Up, Seat Down.)

VOILÀ! YOUR CAT IS NOW TOILET TRAINED

Some useful books on using operant conditioning to toilet train cats:

Brotman, E. (2001). *How to Toilet Train Your Cat: The Education of Mango.* Sherman Oaks, CA: Bird Brain Press.

DeCarlo, P. (2008). *Kick litter: Nine-step program for recovering litter addicts.* Coeur d'Alene, Idaho: CDA Press.

Kunkel, P., & Mead K. P. (1991). *How to Toilet Train Your Cat: 21 Days to a Litter-Free Home.* New York: Workman Publishing.

Questions for Further Discussion

1. Why would this technique probably not work with a dog?
2. Are there any safety concerns with teaching a cat in this way?
3. Are there any other difficulties that might arise when doing this training?

chapter summary

Listen on **mypsychlab.com** Listen to an audio file of your chapter **www.mypsychlab.com**

Definition of Learning

5.1 What does the term *learning* really mean?

- Learning is any relatively permanent change in behavior brought about by experience or practice and is different from maturation, which is genetically controlled.

It Makes Your Mouth Water: Classical Conditioning

5.2 How was classical conditioning first studied, and what are the important elements and characteristics of classical conditioning?

- Pavlov accidentally discovered the phenomenon in which one stimulus can, through pairing with another stimulus, come to produce a similar response. He called this "classical conditioning."
- The unconditioned stimulus (UCS) is the stimulus that is naturally occurring and produces the reflex, or involuntary unconditioned response (UCR). Both are called "unconditioned" because they are not learned.
- The conditioned stimulus (CS) begins as a neutral stimulus, but when paired with the unconditioned stimulus eventually begins to elicit the reflex on its own. The reflex response to the conditioned stimulus is called the "conditioned response" (CR), and both stimulus and response are learned.
- Pavlov paired a sound with the presentation of food to dogs and discovered several principles for classical conditioning: The neutral stimulus (NS) and UCS must be paired several times and the CS must precede the UCS by only a few seconds.

- Other important aspects of classical conditioning include stimulus generalization, stimulus discrimination, extinction, spontaneous recovery, and higher-order conditioning.

5.3 **What is a conditioned emotional response, and how do cognitive psychologists explain classical conditioning?**

- Watson was able to demonstrate that an emotional disorder called a phobia could be learned through classical conditioning by exposing a baby to a white rat and a loud noise, producing conditioned fear of the rat in the baby.
- Conditioned taste aversions occur when an organism becomes nauseated some time after eating a certain food, which then becomes aversive to the organism.
- Some kinds of conditioned responses are more easily learned than others because of biological preparedness.
- Pavlov believed that the NS became a substitute for the UCS through association in time.
- The cognitive perspective asserts that the CS has to provide some kind of information or expectancy about the coming of the UCS in order for conditioning to occur.

What's in It for Me? Operant Conditioning

5.4 **How does operant conditioning occur, and what were the contributions of Thorndike and Skinner?**

- Thorndike developed the law of effect: A response followed by a pleasurable consequence will be repeated, but a response followed by an unpleasant consequence will not be repeated.
- B. F. Skinner named the learning of voluntary responses "operant conditioning" because voluntary responses are what we use to operate in the world around us.

5.5 **What are the important concepts in operant conditioning?**

- Skinner developed the concept of reinforcement, the process of strengthening a response by following it with a pleasurable, rewarding consequence.
- A primary reinforcer is something such as food or water that satisfies a basic, natural drive, whereas a secondary reinforcer is something that becomes reinforcing only after being paired with a primary reinforcer.
- In positive reinforcement, a response is followed by the presentation of a pleasurable stimulus, whereas in negative reinforcement, a response is followed by the removal or avoidance of an unpleasant stimulus.
- Shaping is the reinforcement of successive approximations to some final goal, allowing behavior to be molded from simple behavior already present in the organism.
- Extinction, generalization and discrimination, and spontaneous recovery also occur in operant conditioning.

5.6 **What are the schedules of reinforcement?**

- Continuous reinforcement occurs when each and every correct response is followed by a reinforcer.
- Partial reinforcement, in which only some correct responses are followed by reinforcement, is much more resistant to extinction. This is called the partial reinforcement effect.
- In a fixed ratio schedule of reinforcement, a certain number of responses is required before reinforcement is given.
- In a variable ratio schedule of reinforcement, a varying number of responses is required to obtain reinforcement.
- In a fixed interval schedule of reinforcement, at least one correct response must be made within a set interval of time to obtain reinforcement.
- In a variable interval schedule of reinforcement, reinforcement follows the first correct response made after an interval of time that changes for each reinforcement opportunity.

5.7 **How does punishment differ from reinforcement?**

- Punishment is any event or stimulus that, when following a response, makes that response less likely to happen again.
- In punishment by application, a response is followed by the application or experiencing of an unpleasant stimulus, such as a spanking.
- In punishment by removal, a response is followed by the removal of some pleasurable stimulus, such as taking away a child's toy for misbehavior.

5.8 **What are some of the problems with using punishment?**

- A person who uses aggressive punishment, such as spanking, can act as a model for aggressive behavior. This will increase aggressive behavior in the one being punished, which is an undesirable response.
- Punishment of both kinds normally has only a temporary effect on behavior.
- Punishment can be made more effective by making it immediate and consistent and by pairing punishment of the undesirable behavior with reinforcement of the desirable one.

ISSUES IN PSYCHOLOGY: The Link Between Spanking and Aggression in Young Children

A recent study has found that children who were spanked at age 3 are more likely to be aggressive at age 5 than children who were not spanked.

5.9 **How do operant stimuli control behavior, and what are some other concepts that can enhance or limit operant conditioning?**

- Discriminative stimuli are cues, such as a flashing light on a police car or a sign on a door that says "Open," which provide information about what response to make in order to obtain reinforcement.
- Shaping, extinction, generalization and discrimination, and spontaneous recovery are other concepts in operant conditioning.

CLASSIC STUDIES IN PSYCHOLOGY: Biological Constraints on Operant Conditioning

- Instinctive behavior in animals is resistant to conditioning or modification. Although an animal may change its behavior at first through conditioning, the behavior will revert to the instinctual pattern in a process called "instinctive drift."

5.10 **What is behavior modification, and how can behavioral techniques be used to modify involuntary biological responses?**

- Operant conditioning can be used in many settings on both animals and people to change, or modify, behavior. This use is termed *behavior modification* and includes the use of reinforcement and shaping to alter behavior.
- Token economies are a type of behavior modification in which secondary reinforcers, or tokens, are used.
- Applied behavior analysis (ABA) is the modern version of behavior modification and makes use of functional analysis and behavioral techniques to change human behavior.

- Neurofeedback is a modified version of biofeedback in which the person is typically connected to an electroencephalograph, a machine that records the brain's electrical activity.

Cognitive Learning Theory

5.11 How do latent learning, learned helplessness, and insight relate to cognitive learning theory?

- Cognitive learning theory states that learning requires cognition, or the influence of an organism's thought processes.
- Tolman found that rats that were allowed to wander in a maze but were not reinforced still showed evidence of having learned the maze once reinforcement became possible. He termed this hidden learning *latent learning*, a form of cognitive learning.
- Seligman found that dogs that had been placed in an inescapable situation failed to try to escape when it became possible to do so, remaining in the painful situation as if helpless to leave. Seligman called this phenomenon "learned helplessness" and found parallels between learned helplessness and depression.
- Köhler found evidence of insight, the sudden perception of the relationships among elements of a problem, in chimpanzees.

Observational Learning

5.12 What occurs in observational learning, and what are the findings from Bandura's classic Bobo doll study and the four elements of observational learning?

- Observational learning is acquired by watching others perform, or model, certain actions.
- Bandura's famous Bobo doll experiment demonstrated that young children will imitate the aggressive actions of a model even when there is no reinforcement for doing so.
- Bandura determined that four elements needed to be present for observational learning to occur: attention, memory, imitation, and motivation.

Applying Psychology to Everyday Life: Can You Really Toilet Train Your Cat?

5.13 What is a real-world example of the use of conditioning?

- Writer Karawynn Long used shaping, reinforcement, and classical conditioning to train her cat to use the toilet in her bathroom instead of a litter box.

test YOURSELF

ANSWERS ON PAGE AK-1.

Study and Review on **mypsychlab.com** Ready for your test? More quizzes and a customized study plan **www.mypsychlab.com**

Pick the best answer.

1. Learning is __________.
   a. any temporary change in behavior.
   b. a change in behavior due to maturation.
   c. any relatively permanent change in behavior brought about by experience.
   d. any permanent change in behavior due to maturation.

2. In your college dorm, any time you take a shower, someone always flushes the toilet and causes the water in your shower to turn icy cold, making you cringe. After several episodes like this, you find that you tend to cringe whenever you hear a toilet flush, no matter where you are. In this example, what is the conditioned stimulus?
   a. the cold water
   b. the sound of the flushing
   c. the cringing reaction
   d. the sight of a toilet

3. A child has been classically conditioned to fear a white rat. If the child also shows fear when shown a white rabbit, this is called __________.
   a. stimulus generalization.
   b. stimulus discrimination.
   c. spontaneous recovery.
   d. extinction.

4. You move out of your dorm into an apartment shared with three other people. Unlike the shower in the dorm, this shower does not turn cold when the toilet is flushed, and you eventually stop cringing every time you hear the flushing sound. What has occurred?
   a. stimulus generalization
   b. stimulus discrimination
   c. spontaneous recovery
   d. extinction

5. When one conditioned stimulus is used to create another, this is called __________.
   a. spontaneous recovery.
   b. extinction.
   c. higher-order conditioning.
   d. shaping.

6. Tenia ate out with some friends and had fried oysters. The next morning she was nauseated and sick for much of the day. The next time she saw someone eating fried oysters, she felt queasy and quickly looked away. Her queasiness at the sight of the fried oysters was probably due to __________.
   a. higher-order conditioning.
   b. a conditioned taste aversion.
   c. stimulus substitution.
   d. stimulus generalization.

7. The fact that some kinds of stimuli (like a taste) are more easily and quickly connected to a response (like nausea) is explained by the concept of __________.
   a. biological preparedness.
   b. psychological preparedness.
   c. instinctive drift.
   d. stimulus substitution.

8. The key to the cognitive perspective of classical conditioning is that the presentation of the conditioned stimulus must __________.
   a. provide information about the coming of the unconditioned response.
   b. provide information about the coming of the unconditioned stimulus.
   c. provide information about the coming of the conditioned response.
   d. act as a substitute for the unconditioned stimulus.

9. In classical conditioning, the __________ are important in learning, but in operant conditioning, it is the __________ that determine whether learning will occur.
   a. antecedents; consequences
   b. consequences; antecedents
   c. rewards; punishments
   d. punishments; rewards

10. Who added the concept of reinforcement to learning theory?
    a. Watson
    b. Thorndike
    c. Skinner
    d. Pavlov

11. Which of the following is an example of a secondary reinforcer?
   a. a candy bar
   b. a glass of water
   c. petting a dog
   d. praising a child

12. Joaquin's parents have given his 2-year-old daughter, Marie, a very noisy jack-in-the-box toy for her birthday. Marie loves to turn the crank and make the puppet pop up, over and over and over. Desperate to have some peace and quiet, Joaquin gives Marie a popsicle, which distracts her and produces the quiet he was craving. But when the popsicle is finished, Marie goes back to the toy, cranking and cranking. Joaquin tries another popsicle. What kind of reinforcement process is taking place in this situation?
   a. Marie is being positively reinforced for playing with the toy by receiving the treat.
   b. Joaquin is being positively reinforced for giving her the treat by the quiet that follows.
   c. Joaquin is being negatively reinforced for giving her the treat by the absence of the noise.
   d. Both a and c are correct.

13. Sherry wants her dog to "heel" on command. At first she gives the dog a treat for coming to her when she speaks the command, "Heel!" Then she only rewards the dog when it stands at her side when she gives the command and, finally, rewards the dog only when it is at her side and facing front. Sherry is using __________.
   a. higher-order conditioning.
   b. biological readiness.
   c. shaping.
   d. generalization.

14. One-year-old Ben learned to say the word *duck* when his mother showed him a duck in their backyard. That evening he sees a cartoon with a rooster in it and says "duck," pointing to the rooster. Ben is exhibiting __________.
   a. generalization.
   b. discrimination.
   c. spontaneous recovery.
   d. shaping.

15. For every 10 boxes of cookies that Lisa sells, her scout troop gets a dollar. Lisa is being reinforced on what schedule?
   a. fixed ratio
   b. fixed interval
   c. variable ratio
   d. variable interval

16. Dennis buys a lottery ticket every Saturday, using the same set of numbers. Although he has only won $25 on one occasion, he keeps buying the tickets. In fact, he's a little afraid that if he doesn't buy a ticket, that would be the one that would win really big. The fact that Dennis seems addicted to buying lottery tickets is a common characteristic of which schedule of reinforcement?
   a. fixed ratio
   b. fixed interval
   c. variable ratio
   d. variable interval

17. Sandy had learned that if her mother was smiling at her when she came into the kitchen, it meant that Sandy would probably be given a treat to eat if she asked nicely. But if her mother was frowning, she would not give Sandy anything and instead would shoo her away. Sandy's mother's facial expression was serving as a __________.
   a. conditioned stimulus.
   b. discriminative stimulus.
   c. positive reinforcer.
   d. negative reinforcer.

18. Liz failed her math test, so her parents told her that she could not play video games for a month. Her parents are using __________.
   a. positive reinforcement.
   b. negative reinforcement.
   c. punishment by removal.
   d. punishment by application.

19. To make punishment more effective, it should be __________.
   a. very intense.
   b. applied every other time the bad behavior occurs.
   c. an aggressive type, such as spanking.
   d. paired with reinforcement of the correct behavior.

20. In applied behavior analysis, __________.
   a. skills are broken down into their smallest steps and then reinforced.
   b. punishment by application is often used to control behavior.
   c. researchers develop new theories of learning rather than actually solving problems.
   d. the basic form of learning used is classical conditioning.

21. Jody has had repeated failures at asking guys out on dates. Finally, she gives up. One day at the office a really nice guy seems interested in her, but she refuses to even approach him. What concept might explain her reluctance?
   a. latent learning
   b. learned helplessness
   c. insight learning
   d. observational learning

22. Jared's father is ill and cannot prepare his famous chili recipe, which Jared has watched his father make many times. When his father tells Jared that he must cook the chili, he panics at first. But then Jared finds that he knows how to put the recipe together anyway. His ability to prepare the recipe is an example of __________.
   a. latent learning.
   b. learned helplessness.
   c. insight learning.
   d. discovery learning.

23. Archimedes was told by the king to find a way to prove that a gold crown was really gold. While in his bath, he noticed the water that his body displaced out of the tub and shouted, "Eureka!" which means "I have found it!" If the crown was really gold, it should displace the same amount of water as an equal amount of real gold. This is a famous example of __________.
   a. latent learning.
   b. learned helplessness.
   c. insight.
   d. observational learning.

24. Jared realized that he had learned how to prepare his father's famous chili recipe by watching his father in the kitchen for many years. This kind of learning is called __________.
   a. discovery learning.
   b. helplessness learning.
   c. insight learning.
   d. observational learning.

25. Barry would really like to learn to do ballroom dancing, but he has a severe limp in his left leg. Although he watches ballroom dancing on television and can remember all the moves and dips, he will be very unlikely to be able to learn to dance this way because he is missing a key element of observational learning. What is it?
   a. attention
   b. memory
   c. imitation
   d. motivation

5 learning

5.1 p. 176

Definition of Learning

(any relatively permanent change in behavior brought about by experience or practice)

- "relatively permanent" aspect of learning refers to learning being associated with physical changes in the brain
- although physical changes may be present we may not always be able to "get" to the information

5.2 p. 176

Classical Conditioning

(learning to make an involuntary response to a stimulus other than the original, natural stimulus that normally produces it)

- **discovered by Ivan Pavlov** worked with salivating dogs — focused on observable, measurable behavior
- **several key elements must be present and experienced**
  - **unconditioned stimulus (UCS)**
  - **unconditioned response (UCR)**
  - **conditioned stimulus (CS)**
  - **conditioned response (CR)**

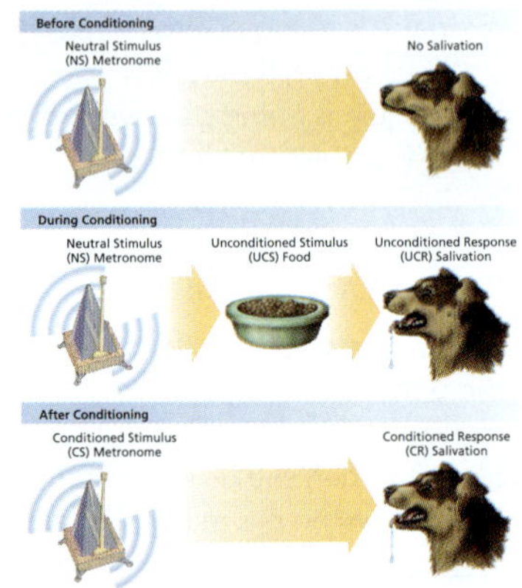

- **basic principles for classical conditioning to occur**
  - CS must come before the UCS
  - CS and UCS must come very close together in time (< 5 sec)
  - CS must be paired with the UCS many times
  - CS must be distinct from other competing stimuli
- **key features**
  - **stimulus generalization**
  - **stimulus discrimination**
  - **extinction**
  - **spontaneous recovery**
  - **higher-order conditioning**

5.3 p. 179

Classical Conditioning (continued)

(learning to make an involuntary response to a stimulus other than the original, natural stimulus that normally produces it)

- **other features**
  - **conditioned emotional responses**

  - **conditioned taste aversion**

  - **vicarious conditioning**
- **Why does it work?**
  - **Pavlov**
  - **cognitive perspective**

5.4 5.5 p. 183

Operant Conditioning

(learning to make voluntary responses through the effects of positive or negative consequences)

- **Thorndike** was among the first to study learning of voluntary responses — developed law of effect
- **Skinner** led field of behaviorism after Watson — coined term *operant conditioning*

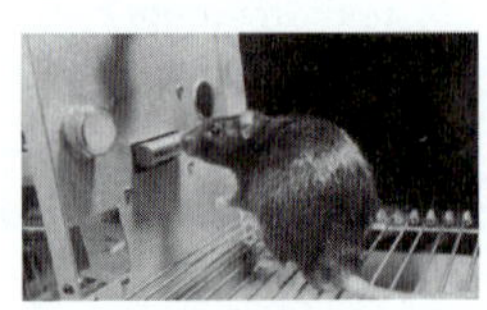

"Remember, every time he gives you a pellet, reinforce that behavior by pulling the lever."

- **reinforcement** any event or stimulus, that when following a response increases the probability that the response will occur again
  - **primary reinforcers**
  - **secondary reinforcers**
  - **positive reinforcement**
  - **negative reinforcement**

5.6 5.7 5.8 5.9 5.10 p. 196

Operant Conditioning (continued)

(learning to make voluntary responses through the effects of positive or negative consequences)

punishment is any event or stimulus that, when following a response, decreases the probability that the response will occur again

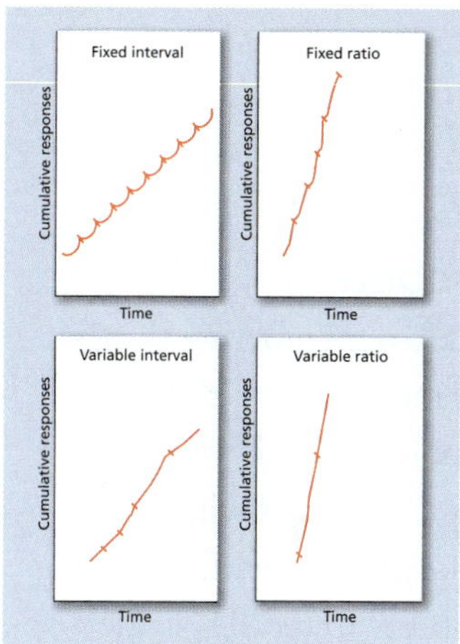

- **schedules of reinforcement**
  - **timing of reinforcement**
  - **continuous reinforcement**
  - **partial reinforcement**

Table 5.2
Four Ways to Modify Behavior

	REINFORCEMENT	PUNISHMENT
Positive (Adding)	Something valued or desirable	Something unpleasant
	Positive Reinforcement Example: getting a gold star for good behavior in school	*Punishment by Application* Example: getting a spanking for disobeying
Negative (Removing/Avoiding)	Something unpleasant	Something valued or desirable
	Negative Reinforcement Example: avoiding a ticket by stopping at a red light	*Punishment by Removal* Example: losing a privilege such as going out with friends

- **other features**
- **behavior modification**

5.11 p. 203

Cognitive Learning Theory

(focuses on role of cognition, or thought processes, on learning)

- **Tolman**
  worked with rats in a maze
- **Köhler**
  worked with chimpanzees; set up a problem situation
- **Seligman**
  originally studied escape and avoidance learning in dogs

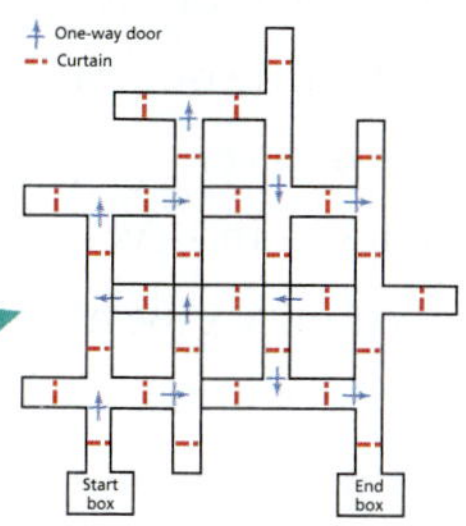

"Bathroom? Sure, it's just down the hall to the left, jog right, left, another left, straight past two more lefts, then right, and it's at the end of the third corridor on your right."

5.12 p. 203

Observational Learning

(the learning of a new behavior through the observation of a model; typically associated with classic work of Bandura and "Bobo doll" study)

- **key elements for learner**
  - pay attention to the model
  - able to remember what was done
  - capable of reproducing, or imitating, the actions of the model
  - have the desire or motivation to perform the action

- **children observing**
  an adult model's aggressive or nonaggressive behaviors tended to later act in the same manner they saw modeled; no reinforcement was necessary
  - later research suggested that potential consequences can influence motivation to imitate a particular model

6 memory

CHAPTER OUTLINE

UNFORGETTABLE: BRAD WILLIAMS, THE "HUMAN GOOGLE"

Most of us, at some point in our busy lives, have trouble remembering things. This is especially true of the events of the past—how much do you really remember about your own childhood? What if you could remember nearly every day of your life? This rare ability is possessed by individuals with a syndrome called *hyperthymesia* (hī-pər-thī-mē-sē-uh). A person with hyperthymesia not only has an astonishing and rare ability to recall specific events from his or her personal past (called *autobiographical memory*) but also spends an unusually large amount of time thinking about that personal past (Parker et al., 2006). To date there are only a few people with hyperthymesia who are being studied by memory researchers.

Brad Williams is one of those few. Known as the "Human Google," Brad can recall almost any news event or personal event he himself has experienced, particularly specific dates—and even the weather on those dates. Brad Williams is otherwise a pretty ordinary guy, likeable and possessed of a good sense of humor. A radio broadcaster in the city of La Crosse, Wisconsin, Brad is involved in the local theater group (he never forgets his lines) and is well known to his listening audience as the man with the amazing memory. Callers try to stump him by asking him trivia questions—as long as the questions are about anything but sports, a subject Brad does not follow (Edwards & Williams, 2010).

When the neuroscientists at The Center from the Neurobiology of Learning and Memory at the University of California at Irvine began to study Brad, his brother, Eric Williams, began filming a documentary about Brad and his extraordinary abilities. Titled *Unforgettable*, the 88-minute documentary chronicles Brad's childhood through his moments of fame as a guest on talk shows as he demonstrates his amazing ability.

If you'd like to know more about Brad and hyperthymesia, you can reach Eric Williams at **www.unforgettabledoc.com**.

Why study memory?

Without memory, how would we be able to learn anything? The ability to learn is the key to our very survival, and we cannot learn unless we can remember what happened the last time a particular situation arose. Why study forgetting? If we can learn about the ways in which we forget information, we can apply that learning so that unintended forgetting occurs less frequently.

learning objectives

6.1 What are the three processes of memory and the different models of how memory works?

6.2 How does sensory memory work?

6.3 What is short-term memory, and how does it differ from working memory?

6.4 How is long-term memory different from other types of memory?

6.5 What are the various types of long-term memory, and how is information stored in long-term memory organized?

6.6 What kinds of cues help people remember?

6.7 How do the retrieval processes of recall and recognition differ, and how reliable are our memories of events?

6.8 How are long-term memories formed, and how can this process lead to inaccuracies in memory?

6.9 What is false-memory syndrome?

6.10 Why do we forget?

6.11 How and where are memories formed in the brain?

6.12 How does amnesia occur?

6.13 What are the facts about Alzheimer's disease?

study tip

As you are reading this chapter, take a look back at pages I-14–I-16 in *Psychology in Action* for some useful memory strategies.

Three Processes of Memory

6.1 What are the three processes of memory and the different models of how memory works?

Is memory a place or a process? The answer to that question is not simple. In reading through this chapter, it will become clear that memory is a process but that it also has a "place" in the brain as well. Perhaps the best definition of **memory** is an active system that receives information from the senses, puts that information into a usable form, organizes it as it stores it away, and then retrieves the information from storage (adapted from Baddeley, 1996, 2003).

Although there are several different models of how memory works, all of them involve the same three processes: getting the information into the memory system, storing it there, and getting it back out.

It sounds like memory encoding works just like the senses—is there a difference?

PUTTING IT IN: ENCODING

The first process in the memory system is to get sensory information (sight, sound, etc.) into a form that the brain can use. This is called **encoding**. Encoding is the set of mental operations that people perform on sensory information to convert that information into a form that is usable in the brain's storage systems. For example, when people hear a sound, their ears turn the vibrations in the air into neural messages from the auditory nerve (*transduction*), which make it possible for the brain to interpret that sound. LINK to Chapter Three: Sensation and Perception, p. 90.

It sounds like memory encoding works just like the senses—is there a difference?

Encoding is not limited to turning sensory information into signals for the brain. Encoding is accomplished differently in each of three different storage systems of memory. In one system, encoding may involve rehearsing information over and over to keep it in memory, whereas in another system, encoding involves elaborating on the meaning of the information—but let's elaborate on that later.

KEEPING IT IN: STORAGE

The next step in memory is to hold on to the information for some period of time in a process called **storage**. The period of time will actually be of different lengths, depending on the system of memory being used. For example, in one system of

memory an active system that receives information from the senses, puts that information into a usable form, and organizes it as it stores it away, and then retrieves the information from storage.

encoding the set of mental operations that people perform on sensory information to convert that information into a form that is usable in the brain's storage systems.

storage holding onto information for some period of time.

memory, people hold on to information just long enough to work with it, about 20 seconds or so. In another system of memory, people hold on to information more or less permanently.

GETTING IT OUT: RETRIEVAL

The biggest problem many people have is **retrieval**, that is, getting the information they know they have out of storage. Have you ever handed in an essay test and *then* remembered several other things you could have said? Retrieval problems are discussed thoroughly in a later section of this chapter.

Brad Williams, the man with the amazing memory described in the opening pages of this chapter, is seen here with famous neuroscientist Dr. Oliver Sacks.

Models of Memory

Exactly how does memory work? When the storage process occurs, where does that information go and why? Memory experts have proposed several different ways of looking at memory. The model that many researchers feel is the most comprehensive* and has perhaps been the most influential over the last several decades is the **information-processing model**. This approach focuses on the way information is handled, or processed, through three different systems of memory. The processes of encoding, storage, and retrieval are seen as part of this model.

While it is common to refer to the three systems of the information-processing model as *stages* of memory, that term seems to imply a sequence of events. While many aspects of memory formation may follow a series of steps or stages, there are those who see memory as a simultaneous** process, with the creation and storage of memories taking place across a series of mental networks "stretched" across the brain (McClelland & Rumelhart, 1988; Plaut & McClelland, 2010; Rumelhart et al., 1986). This simultaneous processing allows people to retrieve many different aspects of a memory all at once, facilitating much faster reactions and decisions—something Brad Williams in our opening story seems to be very good at. This model of memory, derived from work in the development of artificial intelligence (AI), is called the **parallel distributed processing (PDP) model**. In the AI world, PDP is related to *connectionism* (the use of artificial neural networks to explain the mental abilities of humans (Bechtel & Abrahamsen, 2002; Clark, 1991; Marcus, 2001; Schapiro & McClelland, 2009).

retrieval getting information that is in storage into a form that can be used.

information-processing model model of memory that assumes the processing of information for memory storage is similar to the way a computer processes memory in a series of three stages.

parallel distributed processing (PDP) model a model of memory in which memory processes are proposed to take place at the same time over a large network of neural connections.

levels-of-processing model model of memory that assumes information that is more "deeply processed," or processed according to its meaning rather than just the sound or physical characteristics of the word or words, will be remembered more efficiently and for a longer period of time.

The information-processing model assumes that the length of time that a memory will be remembered depends on the stage of memory in which it is stored. Other researchers have proposed that a memory's duration depends on the depth (i.e., the effort made to understand the meaning) to which the information is processed or encoded (Cermak & Craik, 1979; Craik & Lockhart, 1972). If the word *BALL* is flashed on a screen, for example, and people are asked to report whether the word was in capital letters or lowercase, the word itself does not have to be processed very much at all—only its visual characteristics need enter into conscious attention. But if those people were to be asked to use that word in a sentence, they would have to think about what a ball is and how it can be used. They would have to process its meaning, which requires more mental effort than processing just its "looks." This model of memory is called the **levels-of-processing model**. Numerous experiments have shown that thinking about the meaning of something is a deeper level of processing and results in longer retention of the word (Cermak & Craik, 1979; Craik & Tulving, 1975; Paul et al., 2005; Watson et al., 1999).

So which model is right?

So which model is right?

*comprehensive: all inclusive, covering everything.

**simultaneous: all at the same time.

Figure 6.1 Three-Stage Process of Memory

Information enters through the sensory system, briefly registering in sensory memory. Selective attention filters the information into short-term memory, where it is held while attention (rehearsal) continues. If the information receives enough rehearsal (maintenance or elaborative), it will enter and be stored in long-term memory

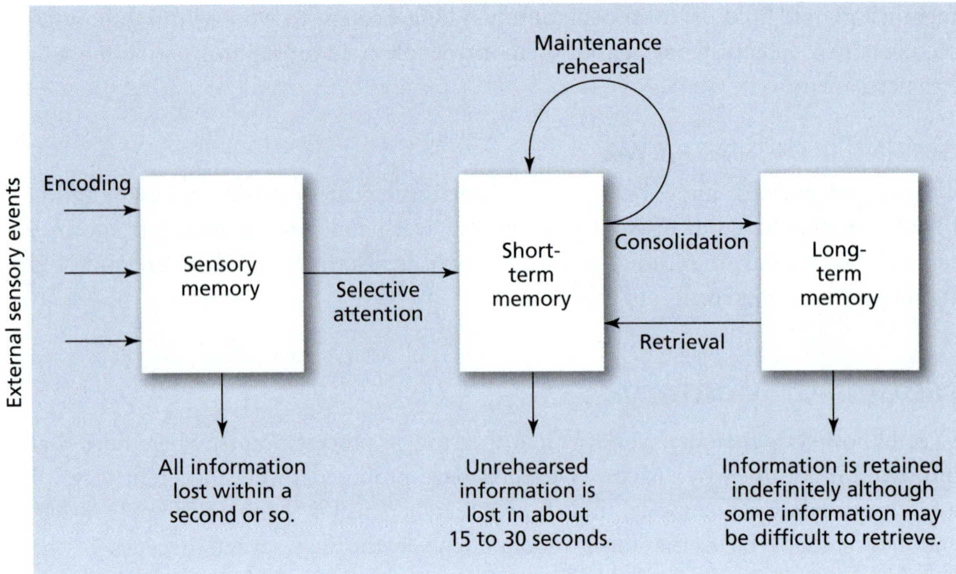

"Which model is right?" is not the correct question. The correct question is, *Which model explains the findings of researchers about how memory works?* The answer to that question is that all of these models can be used to explain some, if not all, research findings. Each of these views of the workings of memory can be seen as speaking to different aspects of memory. For example, the information-processing model provides a "big picture" view of how the various memory systems relate to each other—how the "memory machine" works. The PDP model is less about the mechanics of memory and more about the connections and timing of memory processes. The depth to which information is processed can be seen to address the strength of those parallel connections within each of the three memory systems, with strength and duration of the memory increasing as the level of processing deepens. Although the information-processing model of memory (see Figure 6.1) may take center stage for now, as you read this chapter, it is important to remember the concepts of the levels at which information is processed and the way that those processes may take place.

6.1 CONCEPT MAP

Three Processes of Memory

- an active system that receives, organizes, stores, and retrieves information
- three basic steps
  - **encoding**
  - **storage**
  - **retrieval**

Models of Memory

- **information-processing model** — focuses on the way information is processed through different stages of memory
- **levels-of-processing model**
  - focuses on the depth of processing associated with specific information
  - deeper processing associated with longer retention
- **parallel distributed processing (PDP) model** — focuses on simultaneous processing of information across multiple neural networks

PRACTICE quiz How much do you remember? ANSWERS ON PAGE AK-1.

Pick the best answer.

1. Eldon has just finished his essay test and handed it in. As he walks out of the classroom, he realizes that there were a few more things he should have included in the essay. Eldon's problem is in the memory process of _________.
   a. encoding.
   b. storage.
   c. retrieval.
   d. retention.
2. When Edie studies her psychology terms, she tries to tie each concept in to something she already knows. She thinks about the meaning of the concept rather than just saying the words over and over. Which model of memory would best explain Edie's approach to encoding memories?
   a. levels-of-processing model
   b. parallel distributed processing model
   c. information-processing model
   d. three-stage model
3. Long ago (in the dark ages of television), when a television set was turned off it took a while for the last image that was on the screen to fade away. This is most like _________.
   a. iconic memory.
   b. echoic memory.
   c. short-term memory.
   d. long-term memory.
4. Which type of memory is used to keep the flow of conversations going by allowing a person to remember what was just said?
   a. iconic memory
   b. echoic memory
   c. short-term memory
   d. long-term memory

The Information-Processing Model: Three Memory Systems

The link between cognitive psychology and information-processing theory was discussed briefly in Chapter One. Information-processing theory, which looks at how memory and other thought processes work, bases its model for human thought on the way that a computer functions (Massaro & Cowan, 1993). Data are encoded in a manner that the computer can understand and use. The computer stores that information on a disc, hard drive, or—these days—a memory stick, and then the data are retrieved out of storage as needed. It was also information-processing theorists who first proposed that there are three stages or types of memory systems (see Figure 6.1): sensory memory, short-term memory, and long-term memory (Atkinson & Shiffrin, 1968). **Simulate** on **mypsychlab.com**

Simulate the information-processing model on **mypsychlab.com**

SENSORY MEMORY: WHY DO PEOPLE DO DOUBLE TAKES?

6.2 How does sensory memory work?

Sensory memory is the first stage of memory, the point at which information enters the nervous system through the sensory systems—eyes, ears, and so on. Think of it as a door that is open for a brief time. Looking through the door, one can see many people and objects, but only some of them will actually make it through the door itself. Sensory memory is a kind of door onto the world.

Information is encoded into sensory memory as neural messages in the nervous system. As long as those neural messages are traveling through the system, it can be said that people have a "memory" for that information that can be accessed if needed. For example, image that Elaina is driving down the street, looking at the people and cars on either side of her vehicle. All of a sudden she thinks, "What? Was that man wearing any pants?" and she looks back to check. How did she know to look back? Her eyes had already moved past the possible pants-less person, but some part of her brain must have just processed what she saw (most likely it was the reticular formation, which notices new and important information). This is called a "double take" and can only be explained by the presence, however brief, of a memory for what she saw.

There are two kinds of sensory memory that have been studied extensively. They are the iconic (visual) and echoic (hearing) sensory memories. These and other

sensory memory the very first stage of memory, the point at which information enters the nervous system through the sensory systems.

Rows of Letters	Tone Signaling Which Row to Report
LHTY	High tone
EPNR	Medium tone
SBAX	Low tone

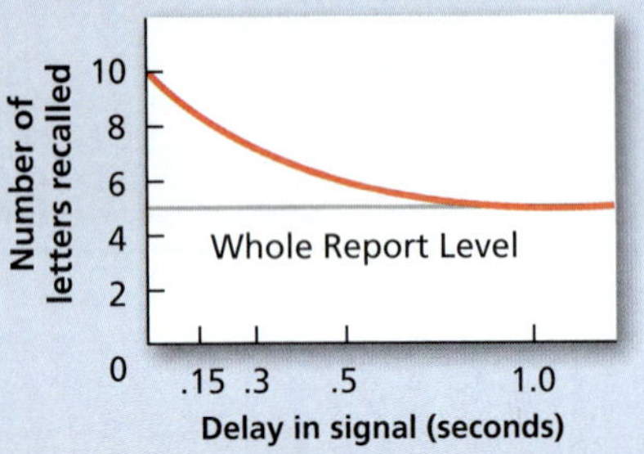

Figure 6.2 Iconic Memory Test

Sample grid of letters for Sperling's test of iconic memory. To determine if the entire grid existed in iconic memory, Sperling sounded a tone associated with each row after the grid's presentation. Participants were able to recall the letters in the row for which they heard the tone. The graph shows the decrease in the number of letters recalled as the delay in presenting the tone increased.

iconic memory visual sensory memory, lasting only a fraction of a second.

eidetic imagery the ability to access a visual memory for 30 seconds or more.

types of memories—as well as several of the experiments that have added a great deal of information to the understanding of memory—will be discussed in the sections that follow.

ICONIC SENSORY MEMORY The example of seeing the possibly pants-less person is an example of how visual sensory memory, or **iconic memory**, works. *Icon* is the Greek word for "image." Iconic memory was studied in several classic experiments by George Sperling (1960).

Capacity of Iconic Memory Sperling had found in his early studies that if he presented a row of letters using a machine that allowed very fast presentation, his subjects could only remember about four or five of the letters, no matter how many had been presented.

Sperling became convinced that this method was an inaccurate measure of the capacity of iconic memory because the human tendency to read from top to bottom took long enough that the letters on the bottom of the grid may have faded from memory by the time the person had "read" the letters at the top. He developed a method called the *partial report method*, in which he showed a grid of letters similar to those in Figure 6.2, but immediately sounded a high, medium, or low tone just after the grid was shown. Subjects were told to read off the top row of letters if they heard the high tone, the middle row for the medium tone, or the lowest row for the low tone. As they didn't hear the tone until after the grid went away, they couldn't look at just one row in advance (see Figure 6.2).

Using this method, Sperling found that subjects could accurately report any of the three rows. This meant that the entire grid was in iconic memory and available to the subjects. The capacity of iconic memory is everything that can be seen at one time.

Duration of Iconic Memory Sperling also found that if he delayed the tone for a brief period of time, after about a second, subjects could no longer recall letters from the grid any better than they had during the whole report procedure. The iconic information had completely faded out of sensory memory in that brief time.

In real life, information that has just entered iconic memory will be pushed out very quickly by new information, a process called *masking* (Cowan, 1988). Research suggests that after only a quarter of a second, old information is replaced by new information.

Although it is rare, some people do have what is properly called **eidetic imagery**, or the ability to access a visual sensory memory over a long period of time. Although the popular term *photographic memory* is often used to mean this rare ability, some people claiming to have photographic memory actually mean that they have an extremely good memory. Having a very good memory and having eidetic imagery ability are two very different things. People with eidetic imagery ability might be able to look quickly at a page in a book, then by focusing on a blank wall or piece of paper, "read" the words from the image that still lingers in their sensory memory. Although it might sound like a great ability to have while in college, it actually provides little advantage when taking tests, because it's just like having an open-book test. If a student can't *understand* what's written on the pages, having the book open is useless. It is unknown why some people have this ability, but it is more common in children and tends to diminish by adolescence or young adulthood (Haber, 1979; Leask et al., 1969; Stromeyer & Psotka, 1971).

Pablo Picasso was one of the most creative artists of his time. Here he is seen drawing an abstract of a woman in the air with a flashlight, using multiple exposures of the camera. What does his ability to "hold" the light image in his head long enough to complete the abstract tell us about his visual memory?

If iconic memory lasts such a brief time, what use is it to us?

If iconic memory lasts such a brief time, what use is it to us?

Function of Iconic Memory Iconic memory actually serves a very important function in the visual system. Chapter Three discussed the way the eyes make tiny little movements called *saccades* that keep vision from adapting to a constant visual stimulus, so that what is stared at steadily doesn't slowly disappear. Iconic memory helps the visual system to view surroundings as continuous and stable in spite of these saccadic movements. It also allows enough time for the brain stem to decide if the information is important enough to be brought into consciousness—like the possibly pants-less person.

ECHOIC SENSORY MEMORY Another type of sensory memory is **echoic memory**, or the brief memory of something a person has heard. A good example of echoic memory is the "What?" phenomenon. You might be reading or concentrating on the television, and your parent, roommate, or friend walks up and says something to you. You sit there for a second or 2, and then say "What? Oh—yes, I'm ready to eat now," or whatever comment is appropriate. You didn't really process the statement from the other person as he or she said it. You heard it, but your brain didn't interpret it immediately. Instead, it took several seconds for you to realize that (1) something was said, (2) it may have been important, and (3) you'd better try to remember what it was. If you realize all this within about 4 seconds (the duration of echoic memory), you will more than likely be able to "hear" an echo of the statement in your head, a kind of "instant replay."

Echoic memory's capacity is limited to what can be heard at any one moment and is smaller than the capacity of iconic memory, although it lasts longer—about 2 to 4 seconds (Schweickert, 1993).

Echoic memory is very useful when a person wants to have meaningful conversations with others. It allows the person to remember what someone said just long enough to recognize the meaning of a phrase. As with iconic memory, it also allows people to hold on to incoming auditory information long enough for the lower brain centers to determine whether or not processing by higher brain centers is needed. It is echoic memory that allows a musician to tune a musical instrument, for example. The memory of the tuning fork's tone lingers in echoic memory long enough for the person doing the tuning to match that tone on the instrument.

Once these piano strings have been attached to the tuning pins, the piano can be tuned. Tuning a piano requires the use of echoic sensory memory. What other occupations might find a good echoic memory to be an asset?

What happens if the lower brain centers send the information on to the higher centers?

What happens if the lower brain centers send the information on to the higher centers?

SHORT-TERM AND WORKING MEMORY

6.3 What is short-term memory, and how does it differ from working memory?

If an incoming sensory message is important enough to enter consciousness, that message will move from sensory memory to the next stage of memory, called **short-term memory (STM)**, through the process of **selective attention**, the ability to focus on only one stimulus from among all sensory input (Broadbent, 1958). In Dr. Donald E. Broadbent's original filter theory, a kind of "bottleneck" occurs between sensory memory and short-term memory. Only a stimulus that is "important" enough (determined by a kind of "pre-analysis" accomplished by the attention centers in the brain stem) will be passed on to be analyzed for meaning in STM. Other stimuli are filtered out and will not reach consciousness. When a person is thinking actively about information, that information is said to be conscious and is also in STM. LINK to Chapter Four: Consciousness, p. 128.

short-term memory (STM) the memory system in which information is held for brief periods of time while being used.

selective attention the ability to focus on only one stimulus from among all sensory input.

echoic memory the brief memory of something a person has just heard.

Each person at this gathering is involved in a conversation with others, with dozens of such conversations going on at the same time all around. Yet if a person in another conversation says the name of one of the people in the crowd, that person in the crowd will be able to selectively attend to his or her name. This is known as the "cocktail party effect."

It is somewhat difficult to use Broadbent's selective-attention filter to explain the "cocktail-party effect" that has been long established in studies of perception and attention (Bronkhorst & Adelbert, 2000; Cherry, 1953; Handel, 1989). If you've ever been at a party where there's a lot of noise and several conversations going on in the background but you are still able to notice when someone says your name, you have experienced this effect. In this kind of a situation, the areas of the brain that are involved in selective attention had to be working—even though you were not consciously aware of it. Then, when that important bit of information (your name) "appeared," those areas somehow filtered the information into your conscious awareness—in spite of the fact that you were not paying conscious attention to the other background noise (Hopfinger et al., 2000; Stuss et al., 2002).

Dr. Anne M. Treisman (Treisman, 2006; Triesman & Gelade, 1980) proposed that selective attention operates in a two-stage filtering process: In the first stage, incoming stimuli in sensory memory are filtered on the basis of simple physical characteristics. This is very similar to Broadbent's original idea. However, the filtering in this case is not an "all-or-nothing" event as in Broadbent's theory, it either moves to STM or is lost—but rather, it is a lessening (*attenuation*) of the "signal strength" of those unattended sensory stimuli when compared to attended stimuli. The second stage involves the processing of only the stimuli that meet a certain threshold of importance. Since the attenuated stimuli are present at this second stage, something as subjectively important as one's own name may be able to be "plucked" out of the attenuated incoming stimuli. Even when deeply asleep, when the selective attention filter is not working at its peak level, it still functions: A mother awakens, hearing her infant's soft cries but sleeps through the nightly noises that come from the nearby train that passes by every night (LaBerge, 1980). The train sound may be louder but is not important (i.e., has been attenuated), whereas the baby's cry is most certainly important. The threshold of meaning for the baby's cry has been lowered, while that of the predictable, yet louder, train has been raised.

What happens when information does pass through the selective attention filter and into short-term memory? Short-term memory tends to be encoded primarily in auditory (sound) form. That simply means that people tend to "talk" inside their own heads. Although some images are certainly stored in STM in a kind of visual "sketchpad" (Baddeley, 1986), auditory storage accounts for much of short-term encoding. Even a dancer planning out moves in her head will not only visualize the moves but also be very likely to verbally describe the moves in her head as she plans. An artist planning a painting certainly has visual information in STM but may also keep up an internal dialogue that is primarily auditory. Research in which participants were asked to recall numbers and letters showed that errors were nearly always made with numbers or letters that *sounded like* the target but not with those that *looked like* the target word or number (Acheson et al., 2010; Conrad & Hull, 1964).

Some memory theorists use the term *working memory* as another way of referring to short-term memory. This usage is not entirely correct: Short-term memory has traditionally been thought of as a thing or a place into which information is put. **Working memory** is more correctly thought of as an active system that processes the information present in short-term memory. Working memory is thought to consist of three interrelated systems: a central executive (a kind of "CEO" or "Big Boss") that controls and coordinates the other two systems, the visual "sketchpad" of sorts that was mentioned earlier, and a kind of auditory

working memory an active system that processes the information in short-term memory.

"recorder" (Baddeley, 1986; Baddeley & Hitch, 1974; Baddeley & Larsen, 2007; Engle & Kane, 2004). The central executive acts as interpreter for both the visual and auditory information, and the visual and auditory information is itself contained in short-term memory. For example, when a person is reading a book, the sketchpad will contain images of the people and events of the particular passage being read, while the recorder "plays" the dialogue in the person's head. The central executive helps interpret the information from both systems and pulls it all together. In a sense, then, short-term memory can be seen as being a part of the working memory system (Acheson et al., 2010; Bayliss et al., 2005; Colom et al., 2006; Kail & Hall, 2001).

As an example, let's say you run into someone familiar at the mall. You pull that person's name (perhaps with a little difficulty) from your more permanent memory and visualize that name along with the memory of the last time you saw the person, almost as if you were viewing it on a screen. At the same time, you will hear the name in your head. The central executive pulls these different types of information together and you are able to successfully greet good old Bob. *Where* you see and hear this is in short-term memory; the *process* that allows this to happen and coordinates it all is working memory.

6 8 2 5

5 7 2 1 4

3 5 9 7 2 1

9 2 5 4 6 3 8

2 8 3 7 1 5 6 9

7 3 2 4 9 6 8 5 1

6 5 4 7 8 9 3 2 1 7

Figure 6.3 Digit-Span Test

Instructions for the digit-span test: Listen carefully as the instructor reads each string of numbers out loud. As soon as each string is ended (the instructor may say "go"), write down the numbers in the exact order in which they were given.

CAPACITY: THE MAGICAL NUMBER SEVEN, OR FIVE, OR FOUR George Miller (1956) wanted to know how much information humans can hold in short-term memory at any one time (or how many "files" will fit on the "desk"). He reviewed several memory studies, including some using a memory test called the *digit-span test*, in which a series of numbers is read to subjects in the study who are then asked to recall the numbers in order. Each series gets longer and longer, until the subjects cannot recall any of the numbers in order (see Figure 6.3). **Simulate** on **mypsychlab.com**

Simulate the digit-span test on **mypsychlab.com**

What you will discover is that most everyone you test will get past the first two sequences of numbers, but some people will make errors on the six-digit span, about half of the people you test will slip up on the seven-digit span, and very few will be able to get past the nine-digit span without errors. This led Miller to conclude that the capacity of STM is about seven items or pieces of information, plus or minus two items, or from five to nine bits of information. Miller called this the magical number seven, plus or minus two. Since Miller's review of those early studies and subsequent conclusion about the capacity of STM being about seven items, research methods have improved, as has our knowledge and understanding of memory processes. Current research suggests younger adults can hold 3 to 5 items of information at a time if a strategy of some type is not being used. When the information is the form of longer, similar-sounding, or unfamiliar words, however, that capacity reduces until it is only about four items (Cowan, 2001; Cowan et al., 2005; Palva et al., 2010).

Working memory is an important area of research and has implications for understanding not only intelligence but also learning and attention disorders such as attention deficit/hyperactivity disorder, and various dementia-related memory problems (Alloway et al., 2009; Kensinger et al., 2003; Martinussen et al., 2005). Researchers have recently trained mice to improve their working memory and found that the mice become more intelligent with improved working memory (e.g., Light et al., 2010).

This woman must hold the phone number she is reading in short-term memory long enough to dial it on the phone next to her.

Chunking There is a way to "fool" STM into holding more information than is usual. (Think of it as "stacking" related files on the desk.) If the bits of information are combined into meaningful units, or chunks, more information can be held in STM. If someone were to recode the last sequence of numbers as "654-789-3217," for example, instead of 10 separate bits of information, there would only be three "chunks" that read like a phone number. This process of recoding or reorganizing the information is called *chunking*. Chances are that anyone who can easily remember more than eight or nine digits in the digit-span test is probably recoding the numbers into chunks.

WHY DO YOU THINK THEY CALL IT "SHORT TERM"? How long is the "short" of short-term memory? Research has shown that short-term memory lasts from about 12 to 30 seconds without rehearsal (Atkinson & Shiffrin, 1968; J. Brown, 1958; Peterson & Peterson, 1959). After that, the memory seems to rapidly "decay" or disappear. In fact, the findings of one recent study with mice suggest that in order to form new memories, old memories must be "erased" by the formation of newly formed neurons (Kitamura et al., 2009). The hippocampus only has so much storage room, and while many of the memories formed there will be transferred to more permanent storage in other areas of the brain, some memories, without rehearsal, will decay as new neurons (and newer memories) are added to the already existing neural circuits.

What do you mean by rehearsal? How long can short-term memories last if rehearsal is a factor?

What do you mean by rehearsal? How long can short-term memories last if rehearsal is a factor?

Most people realize that saying something they want to remember over and over again in their heads can help them remember it longer. (Isn't that what most of us do when we want to remember a phone number—we keep repeating it just long enough to allow us to dial?) This is a process called **maintenance rehearsal**. With maintenance rehearsal, a person is simply continuing to pay attention to the information to be held in memory, and since attention is how that information got into STM in the first place, it works quite well (Atkinson & Shiffrin, 1968; Rundus, 1971). With this type of rehearsal, information will stay in short-term memory until rehearsal stops. When rehearsal stops, the memory rapidly decays and is forgotten. If anything interferes with maintenance rehearsal, memories are also likely to be lost. For example, if someone is trying to count a stack of dollar bills by reciting each number out loud while counting, and someone else asks that person the time and interferes with the counting process, the person who is counting will probably forget what the last number was and have to start all over again. Short-term memory helps people keep track of things like counting.

Interference in STM can also happen if the amount of information to be held in STM exceeds its capacity (about five to nine "bits" of information, remember). Information already in STM may be "pushed out" to make room for newer information. This is why it might be possible to remember the first few names of people you meet at a party, but as more names are added, they displace the older names. A better way to remember a person's name is to associate the name with something about the person's appearance, a process that may help move the name from STM into more permanent storage. This more permanent storage is long-term memory, which is the topic of the next section.

It is very important for this pharmacist to count out the number of pills in the prescription accurately. Short-term memory allows her to remember the last number she counted, but if she is interrupted, she will have to start all over again. Short-term memory is very susceptible to interference.

maintenance rehearsal practice of saying some information to be remembered over and over in one's head in order to maintain it in short-term memory.

long-term memory (LTM) the system of memory into which all the information is placed to be kept more or less permanently.

LONG-TERM MEMORY

6.4 How is long-term memory different from other types of memory?

The third stage of memory is **long-term memory (LTM)**, the system into which all the information is placed to be kept more or less permanently. In terms of capacity, LTM seems to be unlimited for all practical purposes (Bahrick, 1984; Barnyard & Grayson, 1996). Think about it: Would there ever really come a time when you could not fit one more piece of information into your head? When you could learn nothing more? If humans lived much longer lives, there might be a finite end to the capacity of LTM stores. But in practical terms, there is always room for more information (in spite of what some students may believe).

As for duration,* the name *long term* says it all. There is a relatively permanent physical change in the brain itself when a memory is formed. That means that many of the memories people have stored away for a long, long time—even since childhood—may still be there. That does not mean that people can always retrieve those memories. The memories may be *available* but not *accessible*, meaning that they are still there, but for various reasons (discussed later under the topic of forgetting) people cannot "get to" them. It's like knowing that there is a certain item on the back of the top shelf of the kitchen cabinet but having no ladder or step stool to reach it. The item is there (available), but you can't get to it (not accessible).

"Long term" also does not mean that *all* memories are stored forever; our personal memories are too numerous to be permanently retained, for example. Nor do we store every single thing that has ever happened to us. We only store long-lasting memories of events and concepts that are meaningful to us.

I once memorized a poem by repeating it over and over—that's maintenance rehearsal, right? Since I still remember most of the poem, it must be in long-term memory. Is maintenance rehearsal a good way to get information into long-term memory?

I once memorized a poem by repeating it over and over—that's maintenance rehearsal, right? Since I still remember most of the poem, it must be in long-term memory. Is maintenance rehearsal a good way to get information into long-term memory?

Information that is rehearsed long enough may actually find its way into long-term memory. After all, it's how most people learned their Social Security number and the letters of the alphabet (although people cheated a little on the latter by putting the alphabet to music, which makes it easier to retrieve). Most people tend to learn poems and the multiplication tables by maintenance rehearsal, otherwise known as rote learning. *Rote* is like "rotating" the information in one's head, saying it over and over again. But maintenance rehearsal is not the most efficient way of putting information into long-term storage, because to get the information back out, one has to remember it almost exactly as it went in. Try this: What is the 15th letter of the alphabet? Did you have to recite or sing through the alphabet song to get to that letter?

Although many long-term memories are encoded as images (think of the *Mona Lisa*), sounds, smells, or tastes (Cowan, 1988), in general, LTM is encoded in meaningful form, a kind of mental storehouse of the meanings of words, concepts, and all the events that people want to keep in mind. Even the images, sounds, smells, and tastes involved in these events have some sort of meaning attached to them that gives them enough importance to be stored long term. If STM can be thought of as a working "surface" or desk, then LTM can be thought of as a huge series of filing cabinets behind the desk, in which files are stored in an organized fashion, according to meaning. Files have to be placed into the cabinets in a certain organized fashion to be useful—how could anyone ever remember any kind of information quickly if the files were not in some order? The best way to encode information into LTM in an organized fashion is to make it meaningful through *elaborative rehearsal.*

ELABORATIVE REHEARSAL **Elaborative rehearsal** is a way of transferring information from STM into LTM by making that information meaningful in some way (Postman, 1975). The easiest way to do this is to connect new information with something that is already well known (Craik & Lockhart, 1972; Postman, 1975). For example, the French word *maison* means "house." A person could try to memorize that (using maintenance

elaborative rehearsal a method of transferring information from STM into LTM by making that information meaningful in some way.

*duration: how long something lasts.

These students are rehearsing for a concert. They will use maintenance rehearsal (repeating the musical passages over and over) until they can play their parts perfectly. The movements of their fingers upon the strings of their instruments will be stored in long-term memory. How is this kind of long-term memory different from something like the memorized lines of one's part in a play?

rehearsal) by saying over and over, "*Maison* means house, *maison* means house." But it would be much easier and more efficient if that person simply thought, "*Maison* sounds like masons, and masons build houses." That makes the meaning of the word tie in with something the person already knows (masons, who lay stone or bricks to build houses) and helps in remembering the French term.

As discussed in the beginning of this chapter, Craik and Lockhart (1972) theorized that information that is more "deeply processed," or processed according to its meaning rather than just the sound or physical characteristics of the word or words, will be remembered more efficiently and for a longer period of time. As the levels-of-processing approach predicts, elaborative rehearsal is a deeper kind of processing than maintenance rehearsal and so leads to better long-term storage (Craik & Tulving, 1975).

I can remember a lot of stuff from my childhood. Some of it is stuff I learned in school and some of it is more personal, like the first day of school. Are these two different kinds of long-term memories?

I can remember a lot of stuff from my childhood. Some of it is stuff I learned in school and some of it is more personal, like the first day of school. Are these two different kinds of long-term memories?

TYPES OF LONG-TERM INFORMATION

6.5 **What are the various types of long-term memory, and how is information stored in long-term memory organized?**

Long-term memories include general facts and knowledge, personal facts, and even skills that can be performed. Memory for skills is called *procedural (nondeclarative) memory* because it usually involves a series of steps or procedures; memory for facts is called *declarative memory* because facts are things that are known and can be declared (stated outright). These two types of long-term memory are quite different, as the following sections will explain.

Procedural (Nondeclarative) LTM Memories for skills that people know how to do, like tying shoes and riding a bicycle, are a kind of LTM called **procedural (nondeclarative) memory**. Procedural memories also include emotional associations, habits, and simple conditioned reflexes that may or may not be in conscious awareness, which are often very strong memories. LINK to Chapter Five: Learning, p. 170. Referring back to Chapter Two, the amygdala is the most probable location for emotional associations, such as fear, and the cerebellum in the hindbrain is responsible for storage of memories of conditioned responses, skills, and habits (Dębiec et al., 2010; Squire et al., 1993).

Evidence that separate areas of the brain control procedural memory comes from studies of people with damage to the hippocampus area of the brain. This damage causes them to have **anterograde amnesia**, in which new long-term declarative memories cannot be formed. (This disorder is fairly accurately represented by the character of Lenny in the 2000 motion picture *Memento*.) One of the more famous anterograde amnesia patients, H. M., is discussed in detail later in this chapter on page 243.

In one study (Cohen et al., 1985), patients with this disorder were taught how to solve a particular puzzle called the Tower of Hanoi (see Figure 6.4). Although the patients were able to learn the sequence of moves necessary to solve the puzzle, when brought back into the testing room at a later time, they could not remember ever having seen the puzzle before—or, for that matter, the examiner. Each trial was like the first one ever for these patients, as they were unable to store the long-term memory of having been in the room or having previously met the examiner. Yet they were able to solve the puzzle even while claiming that they had never seen it before. Their procedural memories for how to solve the puzzle were evidently formed and stored in a part of the brain separate from the part controlling the memories they could no longer form.

procedural (nondeclarative) memory type of long-term memory including memory for skills, procedures, habits, and conditioned responses. These memories are not conscious but are implied to exist because they affect conscious behavior.

anterograde amnesia loss of memory from the point of injury or trauma forward, or the inability to form new long-term memories.

The patients in this study had the kind of memory problems that people with Alzheimer's disease have. Yet even people with Alzheimer's disease do not forget how to walk, talk, fasten clothing, or even tie shoes (although they do lose motor ability because the brain eventually fails to send the proper signals). These are all procedural, nondeclarative memories. They may not be able to tell someone who asks that they know how to do these things, but they can still do them. Alzheimer's disease affects the hippocampus and the frontal cortex (involved in decision making and planning) and eventually affects other areas of the brain after it has progressed nearly to the end (Kanne et al., 1998). In fact, it would be rare to find someone who has lost procedural memory. Literally, these are the kind of memories people "never forget."

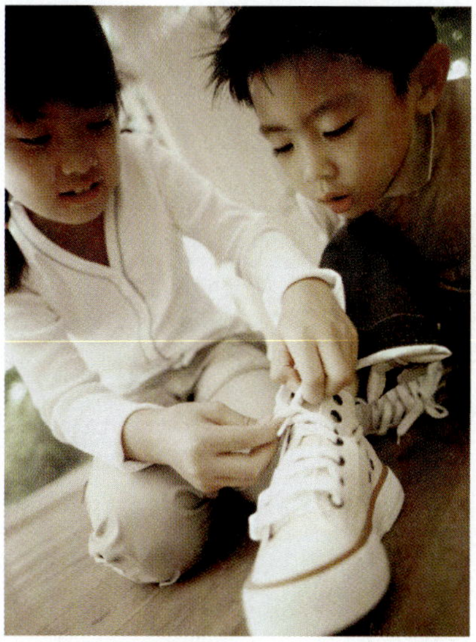

Procedural knowledge, such as tying one's shoes, often must be learned by doing, as it is difficult to put into words. Once this child learns how to tie shoes, the knowledge will always be there to retrieve.

Procedural memory is similar to the concept of **implicit memory** because memories for these skills, habits, and learned reflexes are not easily retrieved into conscious awareness (i.e., nondeclarative). The fact that people have the knowledge of how to tie their shoes, for example, is *implied* by the fact that they can actually tie them. But have you ever tried to tell someone how to tie shoes without using your hands to show them? The subjects in the Tower of Hanoi study provide a good example of implicit memory, as they could solve the puzzle but had no conscious knowledge of how to do so. Such knowledge is in people's memories because they use this information, but they are often not consciously aware of this knowledge (Roediger, 1990). Although procedural memories are very often implicit, not all implicit memories are necessarily procedural. A memory from one's early childhood of being frightened by a dog, for example, may not be a conscious memory in later childhood but may still be the cause of that older child's fear of dogs. Conscious memories for events in childhood, on the other hand, are usually considered to be a different kind of long-term memory called declarative memory.

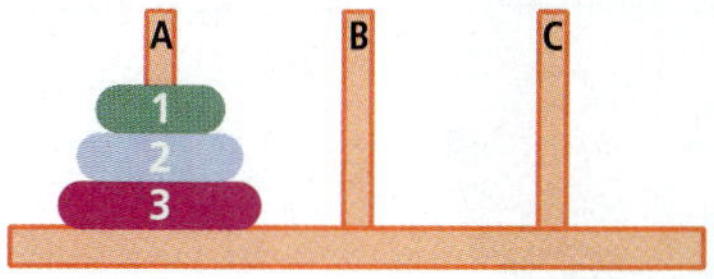

Figure 6.4 Tower of Hanoi

The Tower of Hanoi is a puzzle that is solved in a series of steps by moving one disk at a time. The goal is to move all of the disks from peg A to peg C; the rules are that a larger disk can not be moved on top of a smaller one and a disk can not be moved if there are other disks on top of it. Amnesia patients were able to learn the procedure for solving the puzzle but could not remember that they knew how to solve it.

Declarative LTM Procedural memory is about the things that people can *do*, but **declarative memory** is about all the things that people can *know*—the facts and information that make up knowledge. People know things such as the names of the planets in the solar system, that adding 2 and 2 makes 4, and that a noun is the name of a person, place, or thing. These are general facts, but people also know about the things that have happened to them personally. For example, I know what I ate for breakfast this morning and what I saw on the way to work, but I don't know what you had for breakfast or what you might have seen. There are two types of declarative long-term memories, *semantic* and *episodic* (Nyberg & Tulving, 1996).

One type of declarative memory is general knowledge that anyone has the ability to know. Most of this information is what is learned in school or by reading. This kind of LTM is called **semantic memory**. The word *semantic* refers to meaning, so this kind of knowledge is the awareness of the meanings of words, concepts, and terms as well as names of objects, math skills, and so on. This is also the type of knowledge that is used on game shows such as *Jeopardy* and *Who Wants to Be a Millionaire?* Semantic memories, like procedural memories, are relatively permanent. But it is possible to "lose the way" to this kind of memory, as discussed later in the section on forgetting.

The other kind of factual memory is the personal knowledge that each person has of his or her daily life and personal history, a kind of autobiographical* memory. Memories of what has happened to people each day, certain birthdays, anniversaries that were particularly special, childhood events, and so on are called **episodic memory**, because they represent episodes from their lives. Unlike procedural and semantic

implicit memory memory that is not easily brought into conscious awareness, such as procedural memory.

declarative memory type of long-term memory containing information that is conscious and known.

semantic memory type of declarative memory containing general knowledge, such as knowledge of language and information learned in formal education.

episodic memory type of declarative memory containing personal information not readily available to others, such as daily activities and events.

*autobiographical: the story of a person's life as told by that person.

explicit memory memory that is consciously known, such as declarative memory.

long-term memories, episodic memories tend to be updated and revised more or less constantly. You can probably remember what you had for breakfast today, but what you had for breakfast 2 years ago on this date is most likely a mystery. Episodic memories that are especially *meaningful*, such as the memory of the first day of school or your first date, are more likely to be kept in LTM (although these memories may not be as exact as people sometimes assume they are). The updating process is a kind of survival mechanism, because although semantic and procedural memories are useful and necessary on an ongoing basis, no one really needs to remember every little detail of every day. As becomes obvious later, the ability to forget some kinds of information is very necessary.

Episodic and semantic memories are examples of declarative or **explicit memory**, memories that are easily made conscious and brought from long-term storage into short-term memory. The knowledge of semantic memories such as word meanings, science concepts, and so on can be brought out of the "filing cabinet" and placed on the "desk" where that knowledge becomes *explicit*, or obvious. The same is often true of personal, episodic memories.

But sometimes I can't remember all the names of the planets or what I had for breakfast yesterday. Doesn't that make these memories implicit instead of explicit?

But sometimes I can't remember all the names of the planets or what I had for breakfast yesterday. Doesn't that make these memories implicit instead of explicit?

The difference between implicit memories, such as how to balance on a bicycle, and explicit memories, such as naming all the planets, is that it is impossible or extremely difficult to bring implicit memories into consciousness. Explicit memories can be forgotten but always have the potential to be made conscious. When someone reminds you of what you had for breakfast the day before, for example, you will remember that you had that knowledge all along—it was just temporarily "mislaid." For a look at the connections among all these types of LTM, see Figure 6.5.

LONG-TERM MEMORY ORGANIZATION As stated before, LTM has to be fairly well organized for retrieval to be so quick. Can you remember the name of your first-grade teacher? If you can, how long did it take you to pull that name out of LTM and pull it into STM? It probably took hardly any time at all.

Research suggests that long-term memory is organized in terms of related meanings and concepts (Collins & Loftus, 1975; Collins & Quillian, 1969). In their original study, Collins and Quillian (1969) had subjects respond "true" or "false" as quickly as possible to sentences such as "a canary is a bird" and "a canary is an animal." Looking at Figure 6.6, it is apparent that information exists in a kind

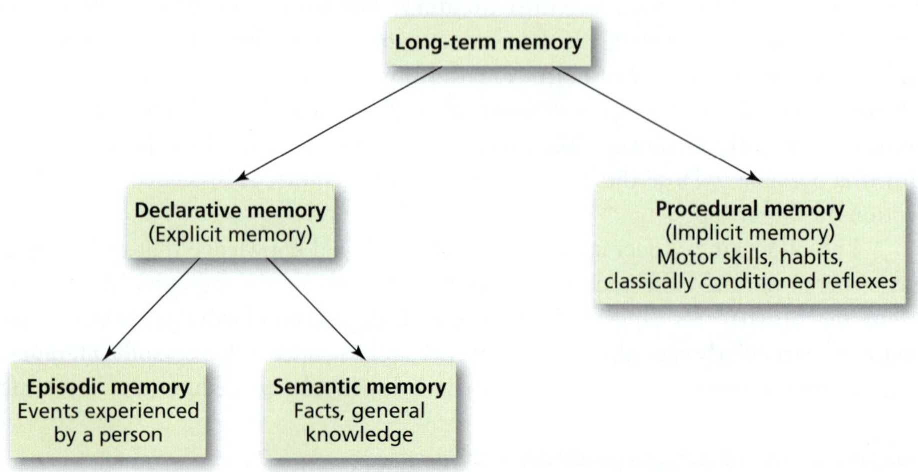

Figure 6.5 Types of Long-Term Memories
Long-term memory can be divided into declarative memories, which are factual and typically conscious (explicit) memories, and nondeclarative memories, which are skills, habits, and conditioned responses that are typically unconscious (implicit). Declarative memories are further divided into episodic memories (personal experiences) and semantic memories (general knowledge).

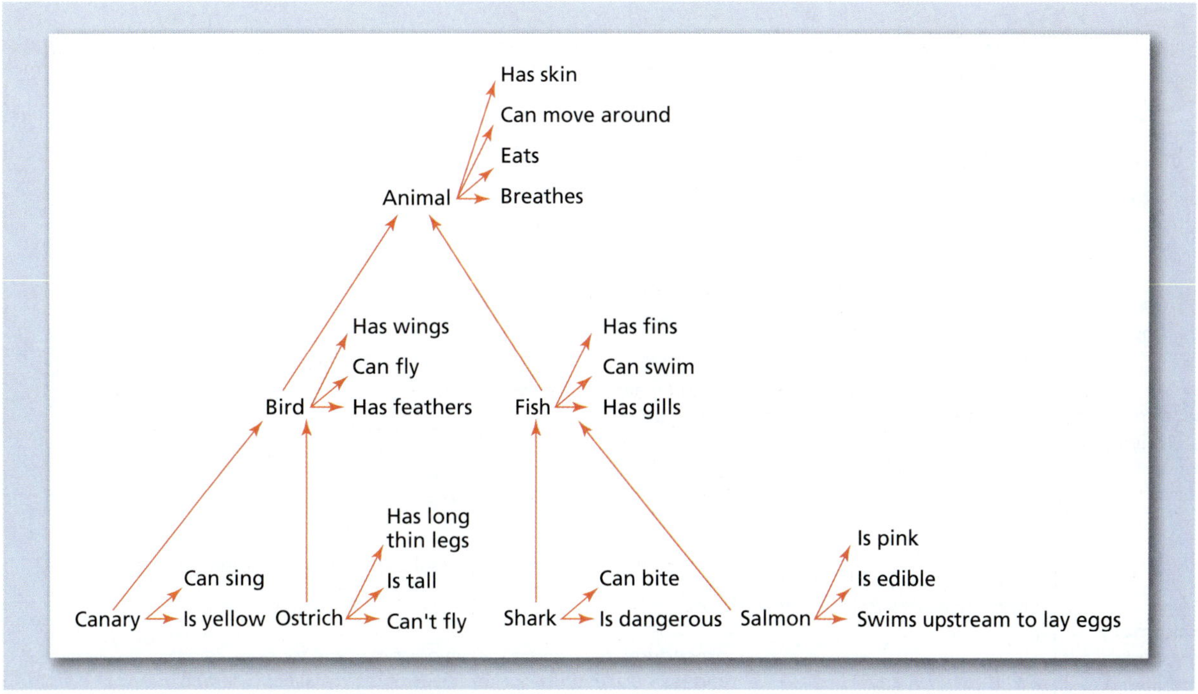

Figure 6.6 An Example of a Semantic Network

In the semantic network model of memory, concepts that are related in meaning are thought to be stored physically near each other in the brain. In this example, canary and ostrich are stored near the concept node for "bird," whereas shark and salmon are stored near "fish." But the fact that a canary is yellow is stored directly with that concept.

of network, with nodes (focal points) of related information linked to each other in a kind of hierarchy.* To verify the statement "a canary is a bird" requires moving to only one node, but "a canary is an animal" would require moving through two nodes and should take longer. This was exactly the result of the 1969 study, leading the researchers to develop the **semantic network model**, which assumes that information is stored in the brain in a connected fashion with concepts that are related to each other stored physically closer to each other than concepts that are not highly related (Collins & Quillian, 1969).

The parallel distributed processing model (Rumelhart et al., 1986) discussed earlier in this chapter can be used to explain how rapidly the different points on the networks can be accessed. Although the access of nodes within a particular category (for example, *birds*) may take place in a serial fashion, explaining the different response times in the Collins and Quillian (1969) study, access across the entire network may take place in a parallel fashion, allowing several different concepts to be targeted at the same time (for example, one might be able to think about *birds*, *cats*, and *trees* simultaneously).

Perhaps the best way to think of how information is organized in LTM is to think about the Internet. A person might go to one Web site and from that site link to many other related sites. Each related site has its own specific information but is also linked to many other related sites, and a person can have more than one site open at the same time. This may be very similar to the way in which the mind organizes the information stored in LTM.

semantic network model model of memory organization that assumes information is stored in the brain in a connected fashion, with concepts that are related stored physically closer to each other than concepts that are not highly related.

*hierarchy: a ranked and ordered list or series.

6.2 6.3 6.4 6.5

CONCEPT MAP

The Information-Processing Model

(proposes three stages that vary both in duration and capacity; information must be processed effectively at earlier stages before long-term storage occurs)

- **sensory memory** capacity limited, duration <1 sec to 4 sec
  - **iconic** (visual)
  - **echoic** (auditory)
- **short-term and working memory** capacity limited (3–5 items), duration 12–30 secs without rehearsal
  - chunking and maintenance rehearsal can be used to increase capacity and duration, respectively
  - maintenance rehearsal differs from elaborative rehearsal
- **long-term memory** capacity seemingly unlimited, duration relatively permanent
  - associated with physical changes in the brain; hippocampus and cortex involved in consolidation of information from short-term to long-term memory
    - elaborative rehearsal can lead to better long-term storage
  - different types, based on information stored; different brain areas associated with each
    - **procedural** (nondeclarative): implicit memory for skills, habits, and learned responses; likely involves amygdala and cerebellum
    - **declarative:** explicit memory for facts and information; involves widespread cortical areas
      - **semantic:** general knowledge/meaning
      - **episodic:** episodes/events from one's life
  - organized in terms of related meanings and concepts
    - **semantic network model** can explain how information is stored in connected fashion
    - **parallel distributed processing model** can be used to explain speed at which different points can be accessed

PRACTICE quiz How much do you remember?

ANSWERS ON PAGE AK-1.

Pick the best answer.

1. Fethia learned her multiplication facts by repeating them over and over until she had them memorized. Fethia was using what kind of rehearsal?

a. repetitive **c.** elaborative
b. imagery **d.** maintenance

2. Of the following, which is the most similar to the concept of long-term memory?

a. a revolving door **c.** a desk top
b. a filing cabinet **d.** a computer keyboard

3. Long-term memories are encoded in terms of _________.

a. sounds.
b. visual images.
c. meanings of words and concepts.
d. all of the above.

4. Which type of LTM is seldom, if ever, lost by people with Alzheimer's disease?

a. procedural **c.** episodic
b. semantic **d.** both b and c

5. In the game show *Who Wants to Be a Millionaire?* contestants are asked a series of questions of general information, although of increasing difficulty. The type of memory needed to access the answers to these kinds of questions is _________.

a. procedural. **c.** episodic.
b. semantic. **d.** working.

6. The Internet, with its series of links from one site to many others, is a good analogy for the organization of _________.

a. short-term memory. **c.** long-term memory.
b. episodic memory. **d.** procedural memory.

Brainstorming: In thinking about a typical day, how do you use each type of memory: procedural, episodic, and semantic?

Getting It Out: Retrieval of Long-Term Memories

My problem isn't so much getting information into *my head; it's finding it later that's tough.*

Oddly enough, most people's problems with getting information stored in LTM back out again has to do with *how* they put that information *into* LTM.

My problem isn't so much getting information *into* my head; it's finding it later that's tough.

RETRIEVAL CUES

6.6 What kinds of cues help people remember?

Remember the previous discussion about maintenance rehearsal versus elaborative rehearsal? One of the main reasons that maintenance rehearsal is not a very good way to get information into LTM is that saying something over and over gives only one kind of **retrieval cue** (a stimulus for remembering), the sound of the word or phrase. When people try to remember a piece of information by thinking of what it means and how it fits in with what they already know, they are giving themselves cues for meaning in addition to sound. The more cues stored with a piece of information, the easier the retrieval of that information will be (Roediger, 2000; Roediger & Guynn, 1996). LINK to Psychology in Action, pp. I-14–I-16.

When this bride and groom dance together later on in their marriage, they will be able to recall this moment at their wedding and the happiness they felt at that time. State-dependent learning makes it easier for people to recall information stored while in a particular emotional state (such as the happiness of this couple) if the recall occurs in a similar emotional state.

ENCODING SPECIFICITY AND STATE-DEPENDENT LEARNING: CONTEXT AND MOOD EFFECTS ON MEMORY RETRIEVAL Although most people would assume that cues for retrieval would have to be directly related to the concepts being studied, the fact is that almost anything in one's surroundings is capable of becoming a cue. If you usually watch a particular television show while eating peanuts, for example, the next time you eat peanuts you might find yourself thinking of the show you were watching. This connection between surroundings and remembered information is called *encoding specificity.*

Have you ever had to take a test in a different classroom than the one in which you learned the material being tested? Do you think that your performance on that test was hurt by being in a different physical context? Researchers have found strong evidence for the concept of **encoding specificity**, the tendency for memory of any kind of information to be improved if the physical surroundings available when the memory is first formed are also available when the memory is being retrieved (Reder et al., 1974; Tulving & Thomson, 1973; Vaidya et al., 2002). For example, encoding specificity would predict that the best place to take one's chemistry test is in the same room in which you learned the material. Also, it's very common to walk into a room and know that there was something you wanted, but in order to remember it, you have to go back to the room you started in to use your surroundings as a cue for remembering.

In one study, researchers had students who were learning to scuba dive in a pool also learn lists of words while they were either out of the pool or in the pool under the water (Godden & Baddeley, 1975). Subjects were then asked to remember the two lists in each of the two conditions. Words that were learned while out of the pool were remembered significantly better when the subjects were out of the pool, and words that were learned underwater were more easily retrieved if the subjects were underwater while trying to remember (see Figure 6.7).

retrieval cue a stimulus for remembering.

encoding specificity the tendency for memory of information to be improved if related information (such as surroundings or physiological state) that is available when the memory is first formed is also available when the memory is being retrieved.

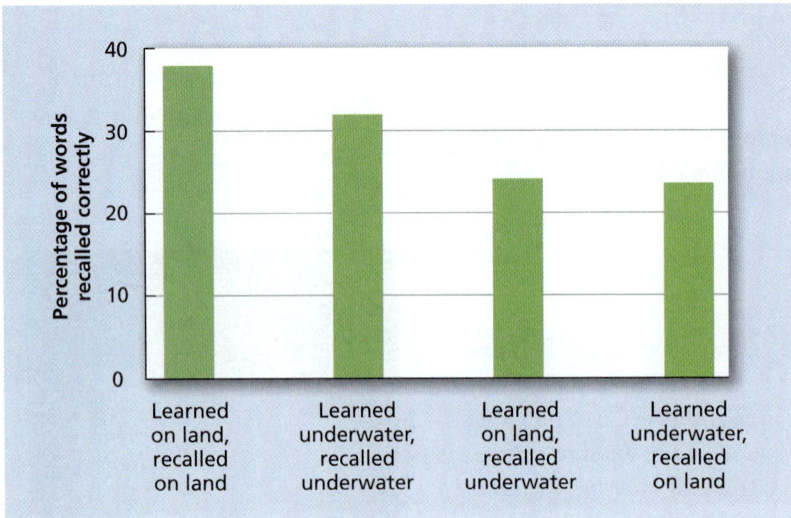

Figure 6.7 Recall of Target Words in Two Contexts

The retrieval of words learned while underwater was higher when the retrieval also took place underwater. Similarly, words learned while out of the water (on land) were retrieved at a higher rate out of the water. Reproduced with permission from the *British Journal of Psychology*, © The British Psychology Society.

Physical surroundings at the time of encoding a memory are not the only kinds of cues that can help in retrieval. In *state-dependent learning*, memories formed during a particular physiological or psychological state will be easier to remember while in a similar state. For example, when you are fighting with someone, it's much easier to remember all of the bad things that person has done than to remember the good times. In one study (Eich & Metcalfe, 1989), researchers had subjects try to remember words that they had read while listening to music. Subjects read one list of words while listening to sad music (influencing their mood to be sad) and another list of words while listening to happy music. When it came time to recall the lists, the researchers again manipulated the mood of the subjects. The words that were read while subjects were in a happy mood were remembered better if the manipulated mood was also happy but far less well if the mood was sad. The reverse was also true.

6.7 How do the retrieval processes of recall and recognition differ, and how reliable are our memories of events?

Why do multiple-choice tests seem so much easier than essay tests?

There are two kinds of retrieval of memories, *recall* and *recognition*. It is the difference between these two retrieval methods that makes some kinds of exams seem harder than others. In **recall**, memories are retrieved with few or no external cues, such as filling in the blanks on an application form. **Recognition**, on the other hand, involves looking at or hearing information and matching it to what is already in memory. A word-search puzzle, in which the words are already written down in the grid and simply need to be circled, is an example of recognition. The following section takes a closer look at these two important processes.

Why do multiple-choice tests seem so much easier than essay tests?

RECALL: HMM . . . LET ME THINK

When someone is asked a question such as "Where were you born?" the question acts as the cue for retrieval of the answer. This is an example of recall, as are essay question, short-answer, and fill-in-the-blank tests that are used to measure a person's memory for information (Borges et al., 1977; Gillund & Shiffrin, 1984; Raaijmakers & Shiffrin, 1992).

RETRIEVAL FAILURE: IT'S RIGHT ON THE TIP OF MY TONGUE Whenever people find themselves struggling for an answer, recall has failed (at least temporarily). Sometimes the answer seems so very close to the surface of conscious thought that it feels like it's "on the tip of the tongue." (If people could just get their tongues out there far enough, they could read it.) This is sometimes called the *tip of the tongue (TOT)* phenomenon (Brown & McNeill, 1966; Burke et al., 1991). Although people may be able to say how long the word is or name letters that start or even end the word, they cannot retrieve the sound or actual spelling of the word to allow it to be pulled into the auditory "recorder" of STM so that it can be fully retrieved.

How can a person overcome TOT? The best solution is the one "everyone" seems to know: Forget about it. When you "forget about it," the brain apparently continues to work on retrieval. Some time later (perhaps when you run across a similar-sounding word in your surroundings), the word or name will just "pop out." This can make for interesting conversations, because when that particular word does "pop out," it usually has little to do with the current conversation.

recall type of memory retrieval in which the information to be retrieved must be "pulled" from memory with very few external cues.

recognition the ability to match a piece of information or a stimulus to a stored image or fact.

serial position effect tendency of information at the beginning and end of a body of information to be remembered more accurately than information in the middle of the body of information.

THE SERIAL POSITION EFFECT Another interesting feature of recall is that it is often subject to a kind of "prejudice" of memory retrieval, in which information at the beginning and the end of a list, such as a poem or song, tends to be remembered more easily and accurately. This is called the **serial position effect** (Murdock, 1962).

A good demonstration of this phenomenon involves instructing people to listen to and try to remember words that are read to them that are spaced about 4 or 5 seconds apart. People typically use maintenance rehearsal by repeating each word in their heads. They are then asked to write as many of the words down as they can remember. If the frequency of recall for each word in the list is graphed, it will nearly always look like the graph in Figure 6.8.

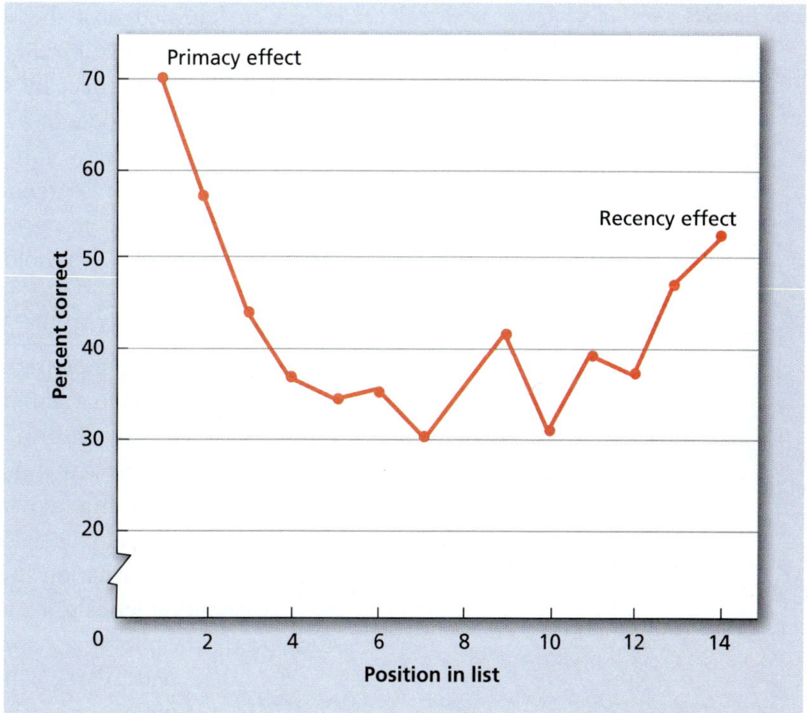

Figure 6.8 Serial Position Effect

In the serial position effect, information at the beginning of a list will be recalled at a higher rate than information in the middle of the list (primacy effect), because the beginning information receives more rehearsal and may enter LTM. Information at the end of a list is also retrieved at a higher rate (recency effect), because the end of the list is still in STM, with no information coming after it to interfere with retrieval.

Words at the very beginning of the list tend to be remembered better than those in the middle of the list. This effect is called the **primacy effect** and is due to the fact that the first few words, when the listener has nothing already in STM to interfere with their rehearsal, will receive far more rehearsal time than the words in the middle, which are constantly being replaced by the next word on the list (Craik, 1970; Murdock, 1962). In fact, the first words may actually move into LTM if they are rehearsed long enough, because rote memorization, although not the best way to remember something, can lead to long-term storage.

At the end of the graph there is another increase in recall. This is the **recency effect**; it is usually attributed to the fact that the last word or two was *just heard* and is still in short-term memory for easy retrieval, with no new words entering to push the most recent word or words out of memory (Bjork & Whitten, 1974; Murdock, 1962). The serial position effect works with many different kinds of information. In fact, business schools often teach their students that they should try not to be "in the middle" for job interviews. Going first or last in the interview process is much more likely to make a person's interview more memorable.

These people are waiting to audition for a play. The person who auditioned first and the one who auditioned last have the greatest chance of being remembered when the time comes for the director to choose. The serial position effect will cause the impression made by the actors who come in the "middle" to be less memorable.

The serial position effect is often used to demonstrate that there are indeed two memory systems, STM and LTM. Memory researchers point to the primacy effect as a result of LTM storage and the recency effect as a result of STM. But the serial position effect can also apply to LTM exclusively (Baddeley & Hitch, 1974; Roediger & Crowder, 1976). Think about the presidents of the United States. How many of them can you remember? Everyone remembers Washington because he was *first*. After Washington, though, it becomes a struggle for many people to remember who came next. Even if a person can get the first several, the middle presidents are almost impossible to remember. But everyone remembers who is president right now and who was president before him, and so on, up until about the time of childhood (Roediger & Crowder, 1976). In this case, the primacy effect is most likely caused by Washington's importance in history, whereas the recency effect is more likely an effect of the importance of recent events. (Lincoln is the exception to the rule, as most people always remember him because of his importance during the Civil War.)

primacy effect tendency to remember information at the beginning of a body of information better than the information that follows.

recency effect tendency to remember information at the end of a body of information better than the information at the beginning of it.

false positive error of recognition in which people think that they recognize some stimulus that is not actually in memory.

Can knowledge of the serial position effect be of help to students trying to remember the information they need for their classes? Yes—students can take advantage of the recency effect by skimming back over their notes just before an exam. Knowing that the middle of a list of information is more likely to be forgotten means that students should pay more attention to that middle, and breaking the study sessions up into smaller segments helps reduce the amount of "middle to muddle." (Students can also use *mnemonic strategies* to help offset this memory problem, as well as others. LINK to Psychology in Action, p. I-14.)

RECOGNITION: HEY, DON'T I KNOW YOU FROM SOMEWHERE?

The other form of memory retrieval is *recognition*, the ability to match a piece of information or a stimulus to a stored image or fact (Borges et al., 1977; Gillund & Shiffrin, 1984; Raaijmakers & Shiffrin, 1992). Recognition is usually much easier than recall because the cue is the actual object, word, sound, and so on, that one is simply trying to detect as familiar and known. Examples of tests that use recognition are multiple-choice, matching, and true–false tests. The answer is right there and simply has to be matched to the information already in memory.

Recognition tends to be very accurate for images, especially human faces. In one study, over 2,500 photographs were shown to participants at the rate of one every 10 seconds. Participants were then shown pairs of photographs in which one member of each pair was one of the previously seen photographs. Accuracy for identifying the previous photos was between 85 to 95 percent (Standing et al., 1970).

FALSE POSITIVES Recognition isn't foolproof, however. Sometimes there is just enough similarity between a stimulus that is not already in memory and one that is in memory so that a **false positive** occurs (Muter, 1978). A false positive occurs when a person thinks that he or she has recognized (or even recalled) something or someone but in fact does not have that something or someone in memory.

False positives can become disastrous in certain situations. In one case, in a series of armed robberies in Delaware, word had leaked out that the suspect sought by police might be a priest. When police put Father Bernard Pagano in a lineup for witnesses to identify, he was the only one in the lineup wearing a priest's collar. Seven eyewitnesses identified him as the man who had robbed them. Fortunately for Father Pagano, the real robber confessed to the crimes halfway through Pagano's trial (Loftus, 1987). Eyewitness recognition can be especially prone to false positives, although most people seem to think that "seeing is believing." For more about the problems with eyewitnesses, see the following Classic Studies in Psychology.

classic studies in psychology

Elizabeth Loftus and Eyewitnesses

Elizabeth Loftus is a Distinguished Professor of Social Ecology, a Professor of Law, and a Professor of Cognitive Science at the University of California in Irvine. For over 30 years, Dr. Loftus has been one of the world's leading researchers in the area of memory. Her focus has been on the accuracy of recall of memories—or rather, the inaccuracies of memory retrieval. She has been an expert witness or consultant in hundreds of trials, including that of Ted Bundy, the serial killer who eventually was executed in Florida (Neimark, 1996).

Loftus and many others have demonstrated time and again that memory is not an unchanging, stable process but rather is a constantly changing one. People continually update and revise their memories of events without being aware that they are doing so, and they incorporate information gained after the actual event, whether correct or incorrect.

Here is a summary of one of Loftus's classic studies concerning the ways in which eyewitness testimony can be influenced by information given after the event in question (Loftus, 1975).

In this experiment, Loftus showed subjects a 3-minute video clip taken from the movie *Diary of a Student Revolution.* In this clip, eight demonstrators run into a classroom and eventually leave after interrupting the professor's lecture in a noisy confrontation. At the end of the video, two questionnaires were distributed containing one key question and 90 "filler" questions. The key question for half of the subjects was, "Was the leader of the four demonstrators who entered the classroom a male?" The other half were asked, "Was the leader of the twelve demonstrators who entered the classroom a male?" One week later, a new set of questions was given to all subjects in which the key question was, "How many demonstrators did you see entering the classroom?" Subjects who were previously asked the question incorrectly giving the number as "four" stated an average recall of 6.4 people, whereas those who were asked the question incorrectly giving the number as "twelve" recalled an average of 8.9 people. Loftus concluded that subjects were trying to compromise the memory of what they had actually seen—eight demonstrators—with later information. This study, along with the Father Pagano story and many others, clearly demonstrates the heart of Loftus's research: What people see and hear about an event after the fact can easily affect the accuracy of their memories of that event.

Dr. Elizabeth Loftus is an internationally known expert on the accuracy of eyewitness testimony. She is often called on to testify in court cases.

Questions for Further Discussion

1. How might police officers taking statements about a crime avoid getting inaccurate information from eyewitnesses?
2. How might Loftus's research apply to situations in which a therapist is trying to help a client recover memories that may have been repressed? What should that therapist avoid doing?

AUTOMATIC ENCODING: FLASHBULB MEMORIES

Although some long-term memories need extensive maintenance rehearsal or effortful encoding in the form of elaborative rehearsal to enter from STM into LTM, many other kinds of long-term memories seem to enter permanent storage with little or no effort at all, in a kind of **automatic encoding** (Kvavilashvili et al., 2009; Mandler, 1967; Schneider et al., 1984). People unconsciously notice and seem able to remember a lot of things, such as the passage of time, knowledge of physical space, and frequency of events. For example, a person might make no effort to remember how many times cars have passed down the street but when asked can give an answer of "often," "more than usual," or "hardly any."

A special kind of automatic encoding takes place when an unexpected event or episode in a person's life has strong emotional associations, such as fear, horror, or joy. Memories of highly emotional events can often seem vivid and detailed, as if the person's mind took a "flash picture" of the moment in time. These kinds of memories are called **flashbulb memories** (Neisser, 1982; Neisser & Harsch, 1992; Winningham et al., 2000).

automatic encoding tendency of certain kinds of information to enter long-term memory with little or no effortful encoding.

flashbulb memories type of automatic encoding that occurs because an unexpected event has strong emotional associations for the person remembering it.

Fans of entertainer Michael Jackson may remember the moment they heard of his death on June 25, 2009. Events like this are so emotional for many people that the memories for the event are stored automatically, as if the mind had taken a "flash" picture of that moment in time. Such "flashbulb" memories seem to be very accurate but are actually no more accurate than any other memory.

Many people share certain flashbulb memories. People of the "baby boomer" generation remember exactly where they were when the news came that President John F. Kennedy had been shot. Younger generations may remember the explosions of the space shuttles *Challenger* and *Columbia* and certainly remember the horrific events of September 11, 2001, and the disastrous Hurricane Katrina. But personal flashbulb memories also exist. These memories tend to be major emotional events, such as the first date, an embarrassing event, or a particularly memorable birthday party.

Why do flashbulb memories seem so vivid and exact? The answer lies in the emotions felt at the time of the event. Emotional reactions stimulate the release of hormones that have been shown to enhance the formation of long-term memories (Dolcos et al., 2005; McEwen, 2000; McGaugh, 2004; Sharot et al., 2004). But is this kind of memory really all that accurate? Although some researchers have found evidence for a high degree of accuracy in flashbulb memories of *major events*, such as the election of President Barack Obama in November 2008 or the death of pop legend Michael Jackson in June 2009, others have found that while flashbulb memories are often convincingly real, they are just as subject to decay and alterations over time as other kinds of memories (Neisser & Harsch, 1992). Apparently, no memories are completely accurate after the passage of time. The next section will discuss some of the reasons for faulty memories.

CONCEPT MAP

6.6 6.7

Retrieval of Long-Term Memories

- **getting it out**
  - **retrieval cues** — more cues stored with a piece of information, the easier the retrieval
  - **encoding specificity** — improved memory for information if physical surroundings are similar to those when the memory was first formed
  - **state-dependent learning** — improved memory for information if physiological or psychological state is similar to that when the memory was first formed
- **recall vs. recognition**
  - **recall:** few or no external cues required
    - **retrieval failure:** (e.g., "tip of the tongue")
    - **serial position effect:** memory improved for items at beginning (primacy) and end (recency) of a list
  - **recognition:** match incoming sensory information (e.g., see or hear) to what is already in memory — false positives can occur (e.g., eyewitness testimony)
- **automatic encoding** — strong emotional associations can lead to vivid and detailed "flashbulb" memories

PRACTICE quiz How much do you remember? ANSWERS ON PAGE AK-1.

Pick the best answer.

1. The best place to take your math exam to ensure good retrieval of math concepts is in ________.
   a. the math classroom.
   b. an auditorium, to prevent cheating.
   c. the English classroom.
   d. the special testing room used for all exams.

2. Sarah can remember names of the first two people she was introduced to at Ted's party, and she can remember the name of the last person she met, but the names of the dozen or so people in between are gone. This is an example of the ________.
   a. encoding specificity effect.
   b. serial position effect.
   c. tip-of-the-tongue effect.
   d. redintegrative effect.

3. This quiz question, as well as the other quiz questions, makes use of which form of retrieval of memories?
   a. rehearsal
   b. relearning
   c. recall
   d. recognition
4. Which of the following statements about Loftus's classic study is TRUE?
   a. All of the subjects were able to correctly recall the number of demonstrators.
   b. Subjects given a question stating that there were four demonstrators remembered only three demonstrators.
   c. Subjects given a question stating that there were twelve demonstrators remembered eight demonstrators.
   d. Subjects either increased or decreased the number of demonstrators in an attempt to compromise their memory with the later false information.
5. Which of the following statements about flashbulb memories is FALSE?
   a. They may be formed by the hormones released at emotional moments.
   b. They are vivid and detailed.
   c. They are unusually accurate.
   d. They can be personal or concern world events.

The Reconstructive Nature of Long-Term Memory Retrieval: How Reliable Are Memories?

I think my memory is pretty good, but my brother and I often have arguments about things that happened when we were kids. Why don't we have the same exact memories? We were both there!

I think my memory is pretty good, but my brother and I often have arguments about things that happened when we were kids. Why don't we have the same exact memories? We were both there!

People tend to assume that their memories are accurate when, in fact, memories are revised, edited, and altered on an almost continuous basis. The reason for the changes that occur in memory has to do with the way in which memories are formed as well as how they are retrieved.

CONSTRUCTIVE PROCESSING OF MEMORIES

6.8 How are long-term memories formed, and how can this process lead to inaccuracies in memory?

Many people have the idea that when they recall a memory, they are recalling it as if it were an "instant replay." As new memories are created in LTM, old memories can get "lost," but they are more likely to be changed or altered in some way (Baddeley, 1988). In reality, memories (including those very vivid flashbulb memories) are never quite accurate, and the more time that passes, the more inaccuracies creep in. Psychologist John Kihlstrom, when talking about the early twentieth-century memory schema theorist Sir Frederic Bartlett's (1932) book on the constructive nature of memory, says that ". . . remembering is more like making up a story than it is like reading one printed in a book. For Bartlett, every memory is a blend of knowledge and inference. Remembering is problem-solving activity, where the problem is to give a coherent account of some past event, and the memory is the solution to that problem" (Kihlstrom, 2002, p. 3).

Elizabeth Loftus, along with other researchers (Hyman, 1993; Hyman & Loftus, 1998, 2002), has provided ample evidence for the **constructive processing** view of memory retrieval. In this view, memories are literally "built," or reconstructed, from the information stored away during encoding. Each time a memory is retrieved, it may be altered or revised in some way to include new information, or to exclude details that may be left out of the new reconstruction.

An example of how memories are reconstructed occurs when people, upon learning the details of a particular event, revise their memories to reflect their feeling that they "knew it all along." They will discard any incorrect information they actually had and replace it with more accurate information gained after the fact. This tendency of people to falsely believe that they would have accurately predicted an outcome without

constructive processing referring to the retrieval of memories in which those memories are altered, revised, or influenced by newer information.

These men may engage in "Monday morning quarterbacking" as they apply hindsight to their memories of this game. Their memories of the game may be altered by information they get afterward from the television, newspapers, or their friends.

having been told about it in advance is called **hindsight bias** (Bahrick et al., 1996; Hoffrage et al., 2000). People who have ever done some "Monday morning quarterbacking" by saying that they knew all along who would win the game have fallen victim to hindsight bias.

MEMORY RETRIEVAL PROBLEMS

Some people may say that they have "total recall." What they usually mean is that they feel that their memories are more accurate than those of other people. As should be obvious by now, true total recall is not a very likely ability for anyone to have. Here are some reasons why people have trouble recalling information accurately.

THE MISINFORMATION EFFECT Police investigators sometimes try to keep eye witnesses to crimes or accidents from talking with each other. The reason is that if one person tells the other about something she has seen, the other person may later "remember" that same detail, even though he did not actually see it at the time. Such false memories are created by a person being exposed to information after the event. That misleading information can become part of the actual memory, affecting its accuracy (Loftus et al., 1978). This is called the **misinformation effect**. Loftus, in addition to her studies concerning eyewitness testimony, has also done several similar studies that demonstrate the misinformation effect. In one study, subjects viewed a slide presentation of a traffic accident. The actual slide presentation contained a stop sign, but in a written summary of the presentation, the sign was referred to as a yield sign. Subjects who were given this misleading information after viewing the slides were far less accurate in their memories for the kind of sign present than were subjects given no such information. One of the interesting points made by this study is that information that comes not only after the original event but also in an entirely different format (i.e., written instead of visual) can cause memories of the event to be incorrectly reconstructed.

RELIABILITY OF MEMORY RETRIEVAL

6.9 What is false-memory syndrome?

If memory gets edited and changed when individuals are in a state of waking consciousness, alert and making an effort to retrieve information, how much more might memory be changed when individuals are being influenced by others or in an altered state of conscious, such as hypnosis? *False-memory syndrome* refers to the creation of inaccurate or false memories through the suggestion of others, often while the person is under hypnosis (Hochman, 1994). Simulate on **mypsychlab.com**

Simulate the creation of false memories on **mypsychlab.com**

For example, research has shown that, although hypnosis may make it easier to recall some real memories, it also makes it easier to create false memories. Hypnosis also has been found to increase the confidence people have in their memories, regardless of whether those memories are real or false (Bowman, 1996). False memories have been accidentally created by therapists' suggestions during hypnotic therapy sessions. LINK to Chapter Four: Consciousness, pp. 145–146. For more information on false-memory syndrome, visit the Web site at **www.fmsfonline.org**.

Some recent evidence suggests that false memories are created in the brain in much the same way as real memories are formed, especially when visual images are involved (Gonsalves et al., 2004). Researchers, using MRI scans, looked at brain activity of individuals who were looking at real visual images and then were asked to imagine looking at visual images. They found that these same individuals were often unable

hindsight bias the tendency to falsely believe, through revision of older memories to include newer information, that one could have correctly predicted the outcome of an event.

misinformation effect the tendency of misleading information presented after an event to alter the memories of the event itself.

to later distinguish between the images they had really seen and the imagined images when asked to remember which images were real or imagined. This might explain why asking people if they saw a particular person at a crime scene (causing them to imagine the image of that person) might affect the memories those people have of the crime when questioned some time later—the person they were asked to think about may be falsely remembered as having been present. Clearly, memories obtained through hypnosis should not be considered accurate without solid evidence from other sources.

But I've heard about people who under hypnosis remember being abused as children. Aren't those memories sometimes real?

But I've heard about people who under hypnosis remember being abused as children. Aren't those memories sometimes real?

The fact that some people recover false memories under certain conditions does not mean that child molestation does not really happen; nor does it mean that a person who was molested might not push that unwanted memory away from conscious thought. Molestation is a sad fact, with one conservative estimate stating that nearly 20 percent of all females and 7 percent of all males have experienced molestation during childhood (Abel & Osborn, 1992). There are also many therapists and psychological professionals who are quite skilled at helping clients remember events of the past without suggesting possible false memories, and they find that clients do remember information and events that were true and able to be verified but were previously unavailable to the client (Dalenberg, 1996). False-memory syndrome is not only harmful to the persons directly involved but also makes it much more difficult for genuine victims of molestation to be believed when they do recover their memories of the painful traumas of childhood.

So can we trust any of our memories at all? There is evidence to suggest that false memories cannot be created for just any kind of memory content. The *memories* must at least be plausible, according to the research of cognitive psychologist and memory expert Kathy Pezdek, who with her colleagues has done several studies demonstrating the resistance of children to the creation of implausible false memories (Hyman et al., 1998; Pezdek et al., 1997; Pezdek & Hodge, 1999).

In the 1999 study, Pezdek and Hodge asked children to read five different summaries of childhood events. Two of these events were false, but only one of the two false events was plausible (e.g., getting lost). Although the children all were told that all of the events happened to them as small children, the results indicated that the plausible false events were significantly more likely to be "remembered" as false memories than were the implausible false events (e.g., getting a rectal enema). A second experiment (Pezdek & Hodge, 1999) found similar results: Children were significantly less likely to form a false memory for an implausible false event than for a plausible false event.

As this girl observes the activity below, she is storing some of the things she sees into memory while ignoring others. If she were to witness a crime, how would investigators know if her memories of the events were accurate or not? Would hypnotizing her to help her remember be effective? Why or why not?

The idea that only plausible events can become false memories runs contrary to the earlier work of Loftus and colleagues and to research concerning some very implausible false memories that have been successfully implanted, such as a memory for satanic rituals and alien abductions (Mack, 1994). Loftus and colleagues (Mazzoni et al., 2001) conducted several experiments in which they found that implausible events could be made more plausible by having the experimenters provide false feedback to the participants, who read articles telling of the implausible events as if they had actually happened to other people. The false feedback involved telling the participants that their responses to a questionnaire about fears were typical of people who had been through one of the false events (much as a well-meaning therapist might suggest to a client that certain anxieties and feelings are typical of someone who has been abused). These manipulations were so successful that participants not only developed false memories for the events but also even contradicted their own earlier statements in which they denied having these experiences in childhood. The researchers concluded that there are two steps that must occur before people will be likely to interpret their thoughts and fantasies about false events as true memories:

1. The event must be made to seem as plausible as possible.
2. Individuals are given information that helps them believe that the event could have happened to them personally.

The personality of the individual reporting such a memory also matters, it seems. In one study, people who claimed to have been abducted by aliens (an implausible event) were compared to a control group with no such memories on a measure of false-memory recall and false recognition. Those who reported recovered memories of alien abduction were far more likely to recall or recognize items that were false than were the controls (Clancy et al., 2002). Other variables that predicted a higher false recall and recognition response were susceptibility to hypnosis, symptoms of depression, and the tendency to exhibit odd behavior and unusual beliefs (such as past-life regression or the healing ability of crystals).

6.8 6.9

CONCEPT MAP

The Reconstructive Nature of Long-Term Memory

- **constructive processing of memories**
  - memories are rarely completely accurate and become less accurate over time
  - Loftus and others have suggested that memory retrieval is a constructive process; memories are "built" at time of retrieval
- **memory retrieval problems**
  - **misinformation effect:** incorporation of inaccurate information into actual memory
  - **reliability of memory retrieval:** false memories can result from change in both waking, conscious states and in altered states (e.g., hypnosis)
    - influenced by plausibility of event and individual receiving collaborative feedback that makes it easier to believe

PRACTICE quiz How much do you remember?

ANSWERS ON PAGE AK-1.

Pick the best answer.

1. The phenomenon of hindsight bias is an example of the __________ of long-term memory retrieval.
   a. instant-replay view
   b. constructive-processing view
   c. levels-of-processing view
   d. misinformation effect
2. In Loftus's 1978 study, subjects viewed a slide presentation of an accident. Later, some of the subjects were asked a question about a yield sign when the actual slides contained pictures of a stop sign. When these same subjects were later asked about what kind of sign was at the accident, they were very likely to be confused in this situation. This is an example of the __________.
   a. instant-replay effect.
   b. constructive-processing effect.
   c. levels-of-processing effect.
   d. misinformation effect.
3. Which of the following statements about memory retrieval while under hypnosis is TRUE?
   a. These memories are more accurate than other kinds of memories.
   b. People recalling memories under hypnosis are more confident in their memories, regardless of accuracy.
   c. Hypnosis makes it harder to recall memories in general.
   d. Age regression through hypnosis can increase the accuracy of recall of early childhood memories.
4. Pezdek and colleagues found that for a person to interpret thoughts and fantasies about false events as true memories __________.
   a. the event must seem as plausible as possible.
   b. the person must believe in repression.
   c. there is very little information provided about the event.
   d. they only need to hear about the event once.

Brainstorming: Think about the last time you argued with a family member about something that happened when you were younger. How might hindsight bias have played a part in your differing memories of the event?

What Were We Talking About? Forgetting

Why do we forget things? And why do we forget some things but not others?

Why do we forget things? And why do we forget some things but not others?

6.10 Why do we forget?

Brad Williams, the Human Google of the opening story, seems to have a fairly normal life despite his unusual memory abilities. But the same has not been true of other people with not only the ability to remember nearly everything, but also the inability to *forget*. That is exactly the problem experienced in the case of A. R. Luria's (1968) famous *mnemonist*, Mr. S. (A mnemonist is a memory expert or someone with exceptional memory ability.) Mr. S. was a performing mnemonist, astonishing his audiences with lists of numbers that he memorized in minutes. But Mr. S. found that he *was unable to forget* the lists. He also could not easily separate important memories from trivial ones, and each time he looked at an object or read a word, images stimulated by that object or word would flood his mind. He eventually invented a way to "forget" things—by writing them on a piece of paper and then burning the paper (Luria, 1968).

The ability to forget seems necessary to one's sanity if the experience of Mr. S. is any indicator. But how fast do people forget things? Are there some things that are harder or easier to forget?

EBBINGHAUS AND THE FORGETTING CURVE

Hermann Ebbinghaus (1913) was one of the first researchers to study forgetting. Because he did not want any verbal associations to aid him in remembering, he created several lists of "nonsense syllables," pronounceable but meaningless (such as GEX and WOL). He memorized a list, waited a specific amount of time, and then tried to retrieve the list, graphing his results each time. The result has become a familiar graph: the **curve of forgetting**. This graph clearly shows that forgetting happens quickly within the first hour after learning the lists and then tapers off gradually. (See Figure 6.9.) In other words, forgetting is greatest just after learning. This curve can be applied to other types of information as well. Although meaningful material is forgotten much more slowly and much less completely, the pattern obtained when testing for forgetting is similar (Conway et al., 1992).

DISTRIBUTED PRACTICE In his early studies, Ebbinghaus (1885) found that it is also important not to try to "cram" information you want to remember into your brain. Research has found that spacing out one's study sessions, or **distributed practice**, will produce far better retrieval of information studied in this way than

curve of forgetting a graph showing a distinct pattern in which forgetting is very fast within the first hour after learning a list and then tapers off gradually.

distributed practice spacing the study of material to be remembered by including breaks between study periods.

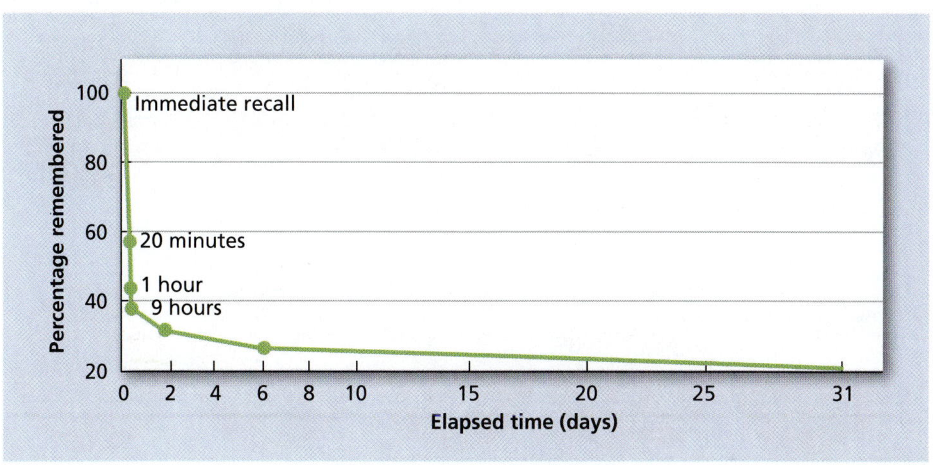

Figure 6.9 Curve of Forgetting
Ebbinghaus found that his recall of words from his memorized word lists was greatest immediately after learning the list but rapidly decreased within the first hour. After the first hour, forgetting leveled off.

encoding failure failure to process information into memory.

memory trace physical change in the brain that occurs when a memory is formed.

decay loss of memory due to the passage of time, during which the memory trace is not used.

disuse another name for decay, assuming that memories that are not used will eventually decay and disappear.

does *massed practice*, or the attempt to study a body of material all at once. For example, studying your psychology material for 3 hours may make you feel that you've done some really hard work, and you have. Unfortunately, you won't remember as much of what you studied as you would if you had shorter study times of 30 minutes to an hour followed by short breaks (Cepeda et al., 2006; Dempster & Farris, 1990; Donovan & Radosevich, 1999; Simon & Bjork, 2001). LINK to Psychology in Action, p. I-8.

ENCODING FAILURE

There are several reasons why people forget things. One of the simplest is that some things never get encoded in the first place. Your friend, for example, may have said something to you as he walked out the door, and you may have heard him, but if you weren't paying attention to what he said, it would not get past sensory memory. This isn't forgetting so much as it is **encoding failure**, the failure to process information into memory. Researchers (Nickerson & Adams, 1979) developed a test of encoding failure using images of pennies. Look at Figure 6.10. Which view of a penny is the correct one? People see pennies nearly every day, but how many people actually look at what's on the penny and try to remember it?

The fact that this woman can remember the things shown in the pictures even after many years makes it unlikely that the memory trace decay theory can explain all forgetting in long-term memory.

MEMORY TRACE DECAY THEORY

One of the older theories of forgetting involves the concept of a **memory trace**. A memory trace is some physical change in the brain, perhaps in a neuron or in the activity between neurons, which occurs when a memory is formed (Brown, 1958; Peterson & Peterson, 1959). Over time, if these traces are not used, they may **decay**, fading into nothing. It would be similar to what happens when a number of people walk across a particular patch of grass, causing a path to appear in which the grass is trampled down and perhaps turning brown. But if people stop using the path, the grass grows back and the path disappears.

Forgetting in sensory memory and short-term memory seems easy to explain as decay: Information that is not brought to attention in sensory memory or continuously rehearsed in STM will fade away. But is decay a good explanation for forgetting from long-term memory? When referring to LTM, decay theory is usually called **disuse**, and the phrase "use it or lose it" takes on great meaning (Bjork & Bjork, 1992). Although the fading of information from LTM through disuse sounds logical, there are many times when people can recall memories they had assumed were long forgotten. There must be other factors involved in the forgetting of long-term memories.

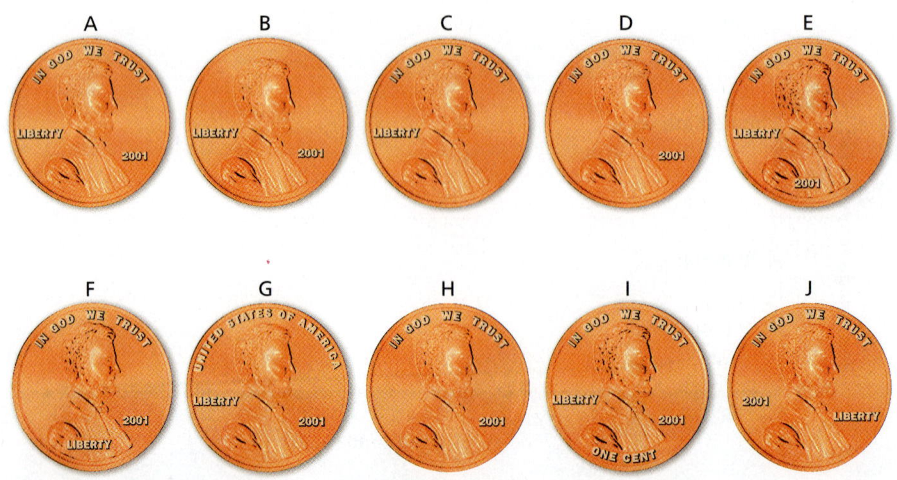

Figure 6.10 Which Penny Is Real?
Most people do not really look at the face of a penny. Which of these pennies represents an actual penny? The answer can be found on the next page.

INTERFERENCE THEORY

A possible explanation of LTM forgetting is that although most long-term memories may be stored more or less permanently in the brain, those memories may not always be accessible to attempted retrieval because other information interferes (Anderson & Neely, 1995). (And even memories that are accessible are subject to constructive processing, which can lead to inaccurate recall.) An analogy might be this: The can of paint that Phillip wants may very well be on some shelf in his storeroom, but there's so much other junk in its way that he can't see it and can't get to it. In the case of LTM, interference can come from two different "directions."

proactive interference memory problem that occurs when older information prevents or interferes with the learning or retrieval of newer information.

retroactive interference memory problem that occurs when newer information prevents or interferes with the retrieval of older information.

PROACTIVE INTERFERENCE Have you ever switched from driving a car with the gearshift on the wheel to one with the gearshift on the floor of the car? If the answer is yes, you probably found that you had some trouble when you first got into the new car. You may have grabbed at the wheel instead of reaching to the gearshift on the floor. The reason you reached for the gearshift in the "old" place is called **proactive interference**: the tendency for older or previously learned material to interfere with the learning (and subsequent retrieval) of new material. (See Figure 6.11.)

Another example of proactive interference often occurs when someone gets a new cell phone number. People in this situation often find themselves remembering their old cell phone number or some of its digits instead of the new cell phone number when they are trying to give the new number to friends.

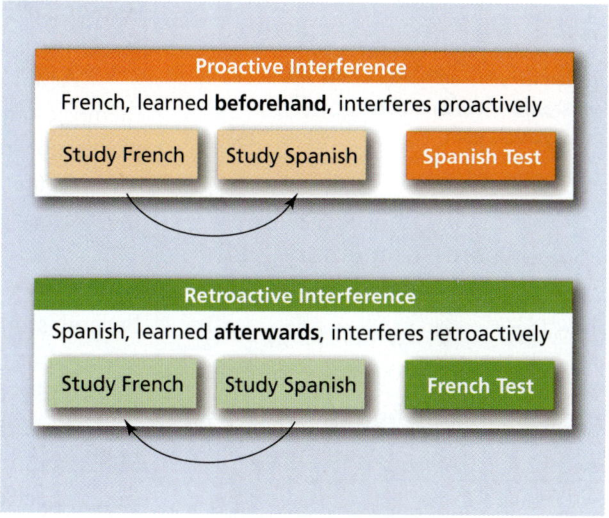

Figure 6.11 Proactive and Retroactive Interference

If a student were to study for a French exam and then a Spanish exam, interference could occur in two directions. When taking the Spanish exam, the French information studied first may proactively interfere with the learning of the new Spanish information. But when taking the French exam, the more recently studied Spanish information may retroactively interfere with the retrieval of the French information.

RETROACTIVE INTERFERENCE When newer information interferes with the retrieval of older information, this is called **retroactive interference**. (See Figure 6.11.) What happens when you change back from the car with the gearshift on the floor to the older car with the gearshift on the wheel? You'll probably reach down to the floor at least once or twice because the newer skill retroactively interferes with remembering the old way of doing it.

How might interference work in each of the following cases?

1. Moving from the United States to England, where people drive on the left instead of the right side of the road.
2. Trying to program your old DVR after having the new one for a year.
3. Moving from one operating system to a different one, such as from Windows to Mac.

The different ways that forgetting occurs are summarized in Table 6.1.

The answer to **Figure 6.10** on page 240 is A.

Table 6.1

Reasons for Forgetting

REASON	DESCRIPTION
Encoding Failure	The information is not attended to and fails to be encoded.
Decay or Disuse	Information that is not accessed decays from the storage system over time.
Proactive Interference	Older information already in memory interferes with the learning of newer information.
Retroactive Interference	Newer information interferes with the retrieval of older information.

Neuroscience of Memory

6.11 How and where are memories formed in the brain?

Researchers have evidence that specific areas of the brain may be the places in which memories are physically formed and that these areas are different for different types of memory. For example, procedural memories seem to be stored in the cerebellum (Boyd & Winstein, 2004; Daum & Schugens, 1996). Research involving PET scanning techniques strongly suggest that short-term memories are stored in the prefrontal cortex (the very front of the frontal lobe) and the temporal lobe (Goldman-Rakic, 1998; Rao et al., 1997). Memories of fear seem to be stored in the amygdala (Dębiec et al., 2010). Read on **mypsychlab.com**

Read and learn more about how researchers are mapping where memories are stored in the brain on **mypsychlab.com**

As for semantic and episodic long-term memories, evidence suggests that these memories are also stored in the frontal and temporal lobes but not in exactly the same places, nor in the same location, as short-term memories (Weis et al., 2004).

All that explains is the "where" of memory. Did scientists ever find out the "what" or the exact physical change that happens in the brain when memories are stored?

All that explains is the "where" of memory. Did scientists ever find out the "what" or the exact physical change that happens in the brain when memories are stored?

NEURAL ACTIVITY, STRUCTURE, AND PROTEINS IN MEMORY FORMATION

Several studies have offered evidence that memory is not simply one physical change but many: changes in the number of receptor sites, changes in the sensitivity of the synapse through repeated stimulation (called *long-term potentiation*), and changes in the dendrites and specifically in the proteins within the neurons (Alkon, 1989; Kandel & Schwartz, 1982; Squire & Kandel, 1999). Researchers have identified a specific protein in mammals, 4E-BP2, which seems to control the production of new nervous-system proteins (Bidinosti et al., 2010). Protein molecules are necessary for all cellular activity—including the very important one of strengthening the connections and communications between neurons. The mammalian brain modifies 4E-BP2 in a certain way, affecting its normal function. This alteration and the other changes that take place as a memory is forming are called **consolidation**. Consolidation may take only a few minutes for some memories, such as learning a new friend's name, but may take years for others, such as learning a new language (Dudai, 2004).

THE HIPPOCAMPUS AND MEMORY

In the discussion of the *hippocampus* (a part of the limbic system) in Chapter Two (page 72), it was identified as the part of the brain that is responsible for the formation of new long-term memories. One of the clearest pieces of evidence of this function comes from the study of a man known as H. M. (Milner et al., 1968).

H. M. was 16 when he began to suffer from severe epileptic seizures. Eleven years later, H. M.'s hippocampi and adjacent medial temporal lobe structures were removed in an experimental operation that the surgeon hoped would stop his seizures. The last thing H. M. could remember was being rolled on the gurney to the operating room, and from then on his ability to form new declarative memories was profoundly impaired. The hippocampus was not the source of his problem (his seizures were reduced but not eliminated), but it was apparently the source of his ability to consolidate and store any new factual information he encountered, because without either hippocampus, he was completely unable to remember new events or facts. Consolidation had become impossible. He had a magazine that he carried around, reading and rereading the stories, because each time he did so the stories were completely new to him. As with most amnesic patients of this type (although H. M.'s case was quite

consolidation the changes that take place in the structure and functioning of neurons when a memory is formed.

severe), his procedural memory was still intact. It was only new declarative memory—both semantic and episodic—that was lost. H. M., who can now be revealed as Henry Gustav Molaison, died in December, 2008, at the age of 82. His experience and his brain will continue to educate students and neuroscientists as he agreed many years ago that his brain would be donated for further scientific study upon his death. It has now been cut into 2401 slices, each about the width of a human hair, in preparation for further study. You can read more about H.M.'s contributions to science at Suzanne Corkin's web site: http://web.mit.edu/bnl/publications.htm and about the H.M. postmortem project at the web site of the The Brain Observatory, housed at the University of California San Diego, http://thebrainobservatory.ucsd.edu (Carey, 2009).

Henry Gustav Molaison.

WHEN MEMORY FAILS: ORGANIC AMNESIA

6.12 How does amnesia occur?

From movies and TV, many people are familiar with the concept of repression, a type of psychologically motivated forgetting in which a person supposedly cannot remember a traumatic event. LINK to Chapter Fourteen: Psychological Disorders, p. 553. But what about an inability to remember brought about by some physical cause? There are two forms of severe loss of memory disorders caused by problems in the functioning of the memory areas of the brain. These problems can result from concussions, brain injuries brought about by trauma, alcoholism (Korsakoff's syndrome), or disorders of the aging brain.

RETROGRADE AMNESIA If the hippocampus is that important to the formation of declarative memories, what would happen if it got temporarily "disconnected"? People who are in accidents in which they received a head injury often are unable to recall the accident itself. Sometimes they cannot remember the last several hours or even days before the accident. This type of amnesia (literally, "without memory") is called **retrograde amnesia**, which is loss of memory from the point of injury backwards (Hodges, 1994). What apparently happens in this kind of memory loss is that the consolidation process, which was busy making the physical changes to allow new memories to be stored, gets disrupted and loses everything that was not already nearly "finished."

Think about this: You are working on your computer, trying to finish a history paper that is due tomorrow. Your computer saves the document every 10 minutes, but you are working so furiously that you've written a lot in the last 10 minutes. Then the power goes out—horrors! When the power comes back on, you find that while all the files you had already saved to your disc are still intact,* your history paper is missing that last 10 minutes' worth of work. This is similar to what happens when someone's consolidation process is disrupted. All memories that were in the process of being stored—but are not yet permanent—are lost.

One of the therapies for severe depression is *ECT*, or *electroconvulsive therapy*. LINK to Chapter Fifteen: Psychological Therapies, p. 599. In one study with depressed patients who were being treated with ECT (Squire et al., 1975), participants were tested for their memory of certain television programs both before and after the treatment. Before treatment, recent programs were recalled in more detail and more often than older ones. But after treatment, these patients seemed to forget the *last 3*

retrograde amnesia loss of memory from the point of some injury or trauma backwards, or loss of memory for the past.

*intact: whole or complete.

Major league baseball outfielder Johnny Damon (seen here colliding with player Damian Jackson) suffered a concussion after this injury. Concussions such as this can "wipe out" whatever was in the process of being consolidated into long-term memory. Which type of amnesia would you expect Johnny Damon to have—retrograde or anterograde?

years of programs, remembering only the older ones. Not only does this indicate that memories are lost when consolidation is interrupted (as it is by the seizure caused by the treatment) but also that consolidation may take not just days or months but sometimes years to be completed.

ANTEROGRADE AMNESIA Concussions can also cause a more temporary version of the kind of amnesia experienced by H. M. This kind of amnesia is called *anterograde amnesia*, or the loss of memories from the point of injury or illness forward (Squire & Slater, 1978). People with this kind of amnesia, like H. M., have difficulty remembering anything new. This is also the kind of amnesia most often seen in people with *senile dementia*, a mental disorder in which severe forgetfulness, mental confusion, and mood swings are the primary symptoms. (Dementia patients also may suffer from retrograde amnesia in addition to anterograde amnesia.) If retrograde amnesia is like losing a document in the computer because of a power loss, anterograde amnesia is like discovering that your hard drive has become defective—you can read data that are already on the hard drive, but you can't store any new information. As long as you are looking at the data in your open computer window (i.e., attending to it), you can access it, but as soon as you close that window (stop thinking about it), the information is lost, because it was never transferred to the hard drive (long-term memory).

This is the reason that elderly people with a dementia such as Alzheimer's disease will sometimes take several doses of medicine because they cannot remember having already taken a dose. It also makes for some very repetitive conversations, such as being told the same story or being asked the same question numerous times in the space of a 20-minute conversation. For more about Alzheimer's disease, see Applying Psychology to Everyday Life on page 246.

I've tried to remember things from when I was a baby, but I don't seem to be able to recall much. Is this some kind of amnesia, too?

I've tried to remember things from when I was a baby, but I don't seem to be able to recall much. Is this some kind of amnesia, too?

INFANTILE AMNESIA What is the earliest memory you have? Chances are you cannot remember much that happened to you before age 3. When a person does claim to "remember" some event from infancy, a little investigation usually reveals that the "memory" is really based on what family members have told the person about that event and is not a genuine memory at all. This type of "manufactured" memory often has the quality of watching yourself in the memory as if it were a movie and you were an actor. In a genuine memory, you would remember the event through your own eyes—as if you were the camera.

Why can't people remember events from the first 2 or 3 years of life? One explanation of **infantile amnesia** involves the type of memory that exists in the first few years of life, when a child is still considered an infant. Early memories tend to be implicit and, as stated earlier in this chapter, implicit memories are difficult to bring to consciousness. Explicit memory, which is the more verbal and conscious form of memory, does not really develop until after about age 2, when the hippocampus is more fully developed and language skills blossom (Carver & Bauer, 2001).

Katherine Nelson (1993) also gives credit to the social relationships that small children have with others. As children are able to talk about shared memories with adults, they begin to develop their **autobiographical memory**, or the memory for events and facts related to one's personal life story.

infantile amnesia the inability to retrieve memories from much before age 3.

autobiographical memory the memory for events and facts related to one's personal life story.

CONCEPT MAP

6.10 6.11 6.12

Forgetting

(originally studied by Ebbinghaus in 1913, research produced forgetting curve)

- **distributed practice** produces far better retrieval than massed practice (cramming)
- **encoding failure** nonattended information is not encoded into memory
- **memory trace decay** over time, if not used, neuronal connections can weaken or decay
- **interference** other information interferes with accurate retrieval
  - **proactive:** previously learned
  - **retroactive:** newly acquired

Neuroscience of Memory

- different brain areas are associated with different types of memory
  - **procedural memories:** cerebellum
  - **short-term memories:** prefrontal cortex and temporal lobes
  - **semantic and episodic long-term memories:** frontal and temporal lobes (different locations than short-term memories)
- several physical changes in brain are associated with memory formation (consolidation)
  - changes at receptor (long-term potentiation)
  - changes in dendrites
- **hippocampus** plays a vital role in the formation of new declarative long-term memories
- **amnesia**
  - **organic amnesia:** caused by problems in brain function associated with brain trauma, disease, or aging
    - **retrograde**
    - **anterograde** — patient H. M. is a classic case study
  - **infantile amnesia:** memories before age 3 are likely implicit, not explicit

PRACTICE quiz How much do you remember?

ANSWERS ON PAGE AK-1.

Pick the best answer.

1. Salvatore was introduced to a number of new people on his first day at his new job. According to Ebbinghaus, when should Salvatore expect to have forgotten the greatest number of the names he has just learned?
a. within the first hour after learning the names
b. within the first day after learning the names
c. near the end of the first week on the job
d. near the middle of the first week on the job

2. When a person "forgets" what someone has just said because he wasn't paying attention to the speaker at all, it is an example of the _________ explanation of forgetting.
a. interference **c.** encoding failure
b. memory trace **d.** repression

3. Edna took sociology in the fall semester and is now taking psychology. Some of the concepts are similar, and Edna finds that she sometimes has trouble recalling some of the major sociology theorists. She keeps getting them confused with psychology theorists. Edna's problem is most likely due to _________.
a. encoding failure. **c.** proactive interference.
b. retroactive interference. **d.** none of the above.

4. Brian went from the United States, where he grew up, to England. The first week he was there he had a terrible time remembering to drive on the left side of the road. His problem was most likely due to _________.
a. encoding failure. **c.** proactive interference.
b. retroactive interference. **d.** none of the above.

5. Katherine is trying to hold the names of the students she just met in her psychology class in her short-term memory. According to studies, these short-term memories will be stored in what part of the brain?
a. cerebellum **c.** amygdala
b. hippocampus **d.** prefrontal lobes

6. Research suggests that memory formation is a function of _________.
a. changes in the number of receptor sites.
b. changes in the sensitivity of the synapse.
c. changes in the dendrites and proteins within neurons.
d. all of the above.

7. The role of the _________ in the formation of new long-term declarative memories was first made apparent in the case of H. M., a famous case study in amnesia.
a. hippocampus **c.** frontal lobes
b. amygdala **d.** cerebellum

8. T. J. was in a car accident and suffered a concussion. After he recovered, he found that he could not remember the accident itself or the events of the morning leading up to the accident. T. J. had which kind of amnesia?
a. retrograde **c.** Alzheimer's disease
b. anterograde **d.** infantile amnesia

Brainstorming: Why do you think that amnesia (no matter what type it is) seems to affect mainly episodic-type memories?

Applying Psychology to Everyday Life: Alzheimer's Disease

6.13 What are the facts about Alzheimer's disease?

Nearly 5.3 million Americans of all ages have Alzheimer's disease (Alzheimer's Association, 2010). It is the most common type of dementia found in adults and the elderly, accounting for nearly 60 to 80 percent of all cases of dementia. It is estimated that 1 out of 8 people over the age of 65 has Alzheimer's disease. It has also become the third leading cause of death in late adulthood, with only heart disease and cancer responsible for more deaths (Alzheimer's Association, 2010; Antuono et al., 2001). **Watch** on **mypsychlab.com**

Watch footage about Alzheimer's and dementia on **mypsychlab.com**

With Alzheimer's disease the primary memory problem, at least in the beginning, is anterograde amnesia. Memory loss may be rather mild at first but becomes more severe over time, causing the person to become more and more forgetful about everyday tasks. (For example, the mother of one of the authors of your text would introduce her daughter to all of the nurses and workers at the nursing home where the mother lived—on every visit). Eventually more dangerous forgetting occurs, such as taking extra doses of medication or leaving something cooking on the stove unattended. As Alzheimer's disease progresses, memories of the past seem to begin "erasing" as retrograde amnesia also takes hold. It is a costly disease to care for, and caregivers often face severe emotional and financial burdens in caring for a loved one who is slowly becoming a stranger.

What causes Alzheimer's disease is not completely understood. While it is normal for the brain to begin to form beta-amyloid protein deposits (plaques) and for strands of the protein tau to become twisted ("tangles"), people who suffer from Alzheimer's disease are found to have far more of these physical signs of an aging brain. One of the neurotransmitters involved in the formation of memories in the hippocampus is acetylcholine, and the neurons that produce this chemical break down in the early stages of the disease. While one early-onset form of Alzheimer's appears to be genetic and involves several different genetic variations, this seems to be the case for fewer than 5 percent of the total cases of the disease (Alzheimer's Association, 2010; Bertram & Tanzi, 2005). The sad truth is that there is not one cause, but many, and even those who do NOT have Alzheimer's disease are not safe from other forms of dementia, such as dementia caused by strokes, dehydration, medications, and so on.

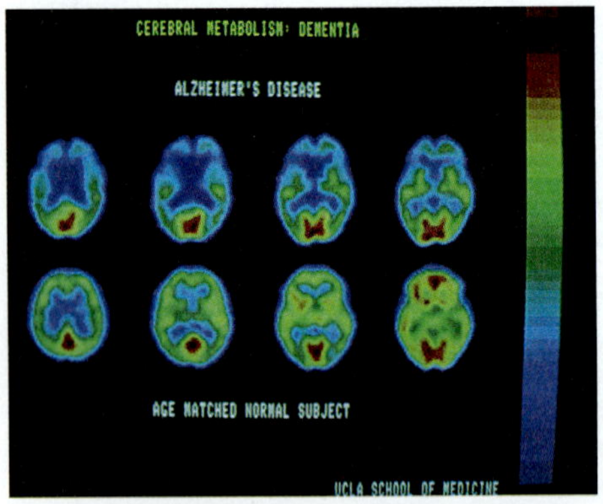

To track the cell death that occurs in Alzheimer's disease, researchers used MRI technology to scan both patients with Alzheimer's disease and normal, elderly subjects. Using supercomputers, the UCLA team created color-coded maps that revealed the degenerative sequence of the disease through novel brain-mapping methods. The wave of gray matter loss was strongly related to the progressive decline in cognitive functioning that is a key feature of the disease. Other researchers have used PET scans, as in the image above, to illustrate differences in brain activity between individuals with and without Alzheimer's disease.

Treatments can slow but not halt or reverse the course of the disease. Five drugs are currently approved for treatment, but as yet only slow down the symptoms for an average of 6 to 12 months. Many experimental therapies are in human trials, but it will be a while before any are known to be successful and are put into practice. What is known is that the risk factors for Alzheimer's (and many other forms of dementia) are something that can be managed: high cholesterol, high blood pressure, smoking, obesity, Type II diabetes, and lack of exercise all contribute (Alzheimer's Association, 2010; Sweat, 2010). Keeping the brain mentally active is also a way to help prolong good cognitive health. One recent study's findings indicate that continued everyday learning stimulates brain-derived neurotrophic factors (BDNF) a key protein involved in the formation of memories (L. Y. Chen et al., 2010).

Questions for Further Discussion

1. People are now living much longer than their ancestors, and it is no longer unusual to hear of people who are well over 100 years of age. How might this extension of life expectancy be related to an increased rate of Alzheimer's disease?
2. What kinds of social programs or interventions could help people who are taking care of a relative with Alzheimer's disease?

chapter summary

((•• Listen on mypsychlab.com Listen to an audio file of your chapter www.mypsychlab.com

Three Processes of Memory

6.1 What are the three processes of memory and the different models of how memory works?

- Memory can be defined as an active system that receives information from the senses, organizes and alters it as it stores it away, and then retrieves the information from storage.
- The three processes are encoding, storage, and retrieval.

Models of Memory

- In the levels-of-processing model of memory, information that gets more deeply processed is more likely to be remembered.
- In the parallel distributed processing model of memory, information is simultaneously stored across an interconnected neural network that stretches across the brain.

The Information-Processing Model: Three Memory Systems

6.2 How does sensory memory work?

- Iconic memory is the visual sensory memory, in which an afterimage or icon will be held in neural form for about one-fourth to one-half second.
- Echoic memory is the auditory form of sensory memory and takes the form of an echo that lasts for up to 4 seconds.

6.3 What is short-term memory, and how does it differ from working memory?

- Short-term memory is where information is held while it is conscious and being used. It holds about seven plus or minus two chunks of information and lasts about 30 seconds without rehearsal.
- STM can be lost through failure to rehearse, decay, interference by similar information, and the intrusion of new information into the STM system, which pushes older information out.

6.4 How is long-term memory different from other types of memory?

- Long-term memory is the system in which memories that are to be kept more or less permanently are stored and is unlimited in capacity and relatively permanent in duration.
- Information that is more deeply processed, or processed according to meaning, will be retained and retrieved more efficiently.

6.5 What are the various types of long-term memory, and how is information stored in long-term memory organized?

- Procedural memories are memories for skills, habits, and conditioned responses. Declarative memories are memories for general facts and personal experiences and include both semantic memories and episodic memories.
- Implicit memories are difficult to bring into conscious awareness, whereas explicit memories are those that a person is aware of possessing.
- LTM is organized in the form of semantic networks, or nodes of related information spreading out from a central piece of knowledge.

Getting It Out: Retrieval of Long-Term Memories

6.6 What kinds of cues help people remember?

- Retrieval cues are words, meanings, sounds, and other stimuli that are encoded at the same time as a new memory.
- Encoding specificity occurs when physical surroundings become encoded as retrieval cues for specific memories.
- State-dependent learning occurs when physiological or psychological states become encoded as retrieval cues for memories formed while in those states.

6.7 How do the retrieval processes of recall and recognition differ, and how reliable are our memories of events?

- Recall is a type of memory retrieval in which the information to be retrieved must be "pulled" out of memory with few or no cues, whereas recognition involves matching information with stored images or facts.
- The serial position effect, or primacy or recency effect, occurs when the first items and the last items in a list of information are recalled more efficiently than items in the middle of the list.

CLASSIC STUDIES IN PSYCHOLOGY: Elizabeth Loftus and Eyewitnesses

- Loftus and others have found that people constantly update and revise their memories of events. Part of this revision may include adding information acquired later to a previous memory. That later information may also be in error, further contaminating the earlier memory.
- Automatic encoding of some kinds of information requires very little effort to place information into long-term memory.
- Memory for particularly emotional or traumatic events can lead to the formation of flashbulb memories, memories that seem as vivid and detailed as if the person were looking at a snapshot of the event but that are no more accurate than any other memories.

The Reconstructive Nature of Long-Term Memory Retrieval: How Reliable Are Memories?

6.8 How are long-term memories formed, and how can this process lead to inaccuracies in memory?

- Memories are reconstructed from the various bits and pieces of information that have been stored away in different places at the time of encoding in a process called constructive processing.
- Hindsight bias occurs when people falsely believe that they knew the outcome of some event because they have included knowledge of the event's true outcome into their memories of the event itself.
- The misinformation effect refers to the tendency of people who are asked misleading questions or given misleading information to incorporate that information into their memories for a particular event.

6.9 What is false-memory syndrome?

- Rather than improving memory retrieval, hypnosis makes the creation of false memories more likely.
- False-memory syndrome is the creation of false or inaccurate memories through suggestion, especially while hypnotized.

- Pezdek and colleagues assert that false memories are more likely to be formed for plausible false events than for implausible ones.

What Were We Talking About? Forgetting

6.10 Why do we forget?

- Ebbinghaus found that information is mostly lost within 1 hour after learning and then gradually fades away. This is known as the curve of forgetting.
- Some "forgetting" is actually a failure to encode information.
- Memory trace decay theory assumes the presence of a physical memory trace that decays with disuse over time.
- Forgetting in LTM is most likely due to proactive or retroactive interference.

Neuroscience of Memory

- Evidence suggests that procedural memories are stored in the cerebellum, whereas short-term memories are stored in the prefrontal and temporal lobes of the cortex.
- Semantic and episodic memories may be stored in the frontal and temporal lobes as well but in different locations than short-term memory, whereas memory for fear of objects is most likely stored in the amygdala.

6.11 How and where are memories formed in the brain?

- Consolidation consists of the physical changes in neurons that take place during the formation of a memory.
- The hippocampus appears to be responsible for the storage of new long-term memories. If it is removed, the ability to store anything new is completely lost.

6.12 How does amnesia occur?

- In retrograde amnesia, memory for the past (prior to the injury) is lost, which can be a loss of only minutes or a loss of several years.
- ECT, or electroconvulsive therapy, can disrupt consolidation and cause retrograde amnesia.
- In anterograde amnesia, memory for anything new becomes impossible, although old memories may still be retrievable.
- Most people cannot remember events that occurred before age 2 or 3. This is called infantile amnesia and is most likely due to the implicit nature of infant memory.

Applying Psychology to Everyday Life: Alzheimer's Disease

6.13 What are the facts about Alzheimer's disease?

- The primary memory difficulty in Alzheimer's disease is anterograde amnesia, although retrograde amnesia can also occur as the disease progresses.
- Alzheimer's disease has multiple causes, many of which are not yet identified.
- There are various drugs in use or in development for use in slowing or stopping the progression of Alzheimer's disease.
- Exercising the brain and tending to the health of the cardiovascular system can help put off or prevent various forms of dementia, including Alzheimer's disease.

test YOURSELF

ANSWERS ON PAGE AK-1.

Study and Review on **mypsychlab.com** Ready for your test? More quizzes and a customized study plan **www.mypsychlab.com**

Pick the best answer.

1. Memory can best be described as _________.
   a. a series of storage bins or boxes.
   b. a process of storage.
   c. an active system that encodes, stores, and retrieves information.
   d. a series of passive data files.
2. In the _________ model of memory, memories are simultaneously created and stored across a mental network.
   a. levels-of-processing
   b. parallel distributed processing
   c. transfer-appropriate processing
   d. information-processing
3. Roberta looked up from her book, realizing that Joaquin had just said something to her. What was it? Oh, yes, he had just asked her if she wanted to go out to dinner. Roberta's ability to retrieve what Joaquin said is due to her _________.
   a. iconic sensory memory.
   b. echoic sensory memory.
   c. short-term memory.
   d. tactile sensory memory.
4. Although Sperling found evidence that iconic memory lasts about half a second, in reality information gets pushed out rather quickly by newer information. Evidence suggests that iconic memory really lasts about _________ of a second.
   a. three quarters
   b. half
   c. one quarter
   d. one tenth
5. The duration of echoic memory is _________ than iconic memory, but its capacity is probably _________.
   a. shorter; larger.
   b. longer; smaller.
   c. longer; about the same.
   d. shorter; about the same.
6. When Greg tried to remember the name of his employer's wife, he had trouble getting the right name. At first he thought it might be Sandy or Candy but finally realized that it was Mandy. Greg's confusion is evidence that short-term memories are primarily encoded in _________ form.
   a. acoustic
   b. visual
   c. tactile
   d. optical
7. Although the capacity of short-term memory is limited, more items can be held in this kind of storage through the process of _________.
   a. chunking.
   b. decoding.
   c. rote rehearsal.
   d. data compression.

8. The best method for encoding long-term memories is probably to use __________.
   a. maintenance rehearsal.
   b. rote rehearsal.
   c. elaborative rehearsal.
   d. sleep learning.

9. The levels-of-processing concept of Craik and Lockhart would suggest that which of the following questions would lead to better memory of the word *frog*?
   a. Does it rhyme with *blog*?
   b. Is it in capital letters?
   c. Is it written in cursive?
   d. Would it be found in a pond?

10. Which type of long-term memory is revised and updated more or less constantly?
    a. procedural
    b. declarative
    c. semantic
    d. episodic

11. Knowledge that we gain from school textbooks is called __________ memory.
    a. procedural
    b. declarative
    c. semantic
    d. episodic

12. The semantic network model of memory would suggest that which of the following questions would take longest to answer?
    a. Is a collie a dog?
    b. Is a collie a mammal?
    c. Is a collie an animal?
    d. There would be no difference in answering times.

13. The research of Eich and Metcalf would suggest that if you were really angry when you were learning Spanish, you should be __________ when taking the final exam for best retrieval.
    a. really calm
    b. unemotional
    c. angry
    d. depressed

14. Which of the following is NOT an example of a test using recall?
    a. short answer
    b. essay
    c. fill in the blanks
    d. true–false

15. The serial position effect predicts that the information that will be remembered best from a list will come at the __________ of the list.
    a. beginning
    b. end
    c. middle
    d. beginning and the end

16. Melanie was having a difficult time describing the man who took her purse in the mall parking lot. The officer showed her some pictures of people who had been involved in similar crimes, and she was quickly able to point out the right man. Melanie's situation is a reminder that in comparing recognition to recall, recognition tends to be __________.
    a. easier.
    b. slower.
    c. more difficult.
    d. less accurate.

17. Is eyewitness testimony usually accurate?
    a. Yes, because seeing is believing.
    b. No, because eyewitnesses are not usually honest.
    c. Yes, because eyewitnesses are very confident about their testimony.
    d. No, because there is a great possibility of a false-positive identification.

18. The passage of time and frequency of events are examples of knowledge that is often subject to __________.
    a. encoding specificity.
    b. automatic encoding.
    c. flashbulb memories.
    d. eidetic imagery.

19. When retrieving a long-term memory, bits and pieces of information are gathered from various areas and put back together in a process called __________.
    a. consolidation.
    b. redintegration.
    c. constructive processing.
    d. automatic processing.

20. Ebbinghaus found that information is forgotten __________.
    a. more rapidly as time goes by.
    b. gradually at first, then increasing in speed of forgetting.
    c. quickly at first, then tapering off gradually.
    d. most quickly 1 day after learning.

21. A problem with using decay or disuse theory to explain forgetting from long-term memory is that __________.
    a. older people can still remember things from their early years.
    b. there is no physical change in the brain when forming long-term memories.
    c. older memories always get lost, whereas newer memories always remain.
    d. older people cannot remember events in their childhood.

22. You started out by using WordPerfect and then moved to Microsoft Word because your company demanded that all documents be in Word. If you have trouble with Word, it is most likely due to __________.
    a. proactive interference.
    b. retroactive interference.
    c. anterograde interference.
    d. consolidation problems.

23. The earliest and main type of memory problem that people with dementia, including Alzheimer's disease, typically have is called __________.
    a. psychogenic amnesia.
    b. retrograde amnesia.
    c. retroactive amnesia.
    d. anterograde amnesia.

24. One theory that explains infantile amnesia states that these memories are __________.
    a. never fully stored and, therefore, not available.
    b. explicit and not retrievable consciously.
    c. implicit and not retrievable consciously.
    d. repressed.

6 memory

6.1 p. 216

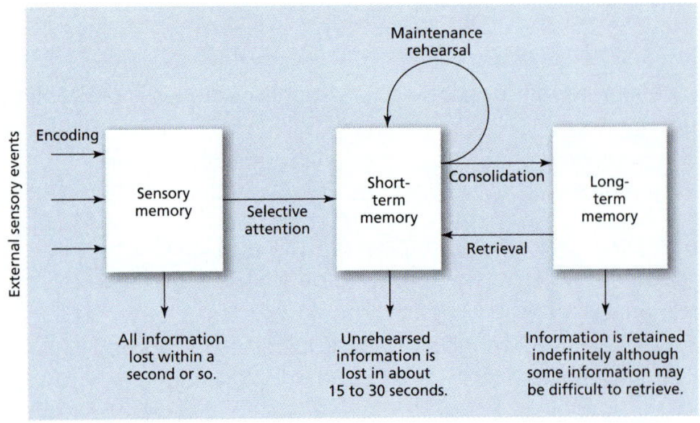

- an active system that receives, organizes, stores, and retrieves information

Three Processes of Memory

- three basic steps
  - **encoding**
  - **storage**
  - **retrieval**

Models of Memory

- **information-processing model** — focuses on the way information is processed through different stages of memory
- **parallel distributed processing (PDP) model** — focuses on simultaneous processing of information across multiple neural networks
- **levels-of-processing model**
  - focuses on the depth of processing associated with specific information
  - deeper processing associated with longer retention

6.2 6.3 6.4 6.5 p. 228

The Information-Processing Model

(proposes three stages that vary both in duration and capacity; information must be processed effectively at earlier stages before long-term storage occurs)

- **sensory memory** capacity limited, duration <1 sec to 4 sec
  - **iconic** (visual)
  - **echoic** (auditory)
- **short-term and working memory** capacity limited (3–5 items), duration 12–30 secs without rehearsal
  - chunking and maintenance rehearsal can be used to increase capacity and duration, respectively
- **long-term memory** capacity seemingly unlimited, duration relatively permanent
  - associated with physical changes in the brain; hippocampus and cortex involved in consolidation of information from short-term to long-term memory
  - different types, based on information stored; different brain areas associated with each
  - organized in terms of related meanings and concepts
    - **semantic network model**
    - **parallel distributed processing model**

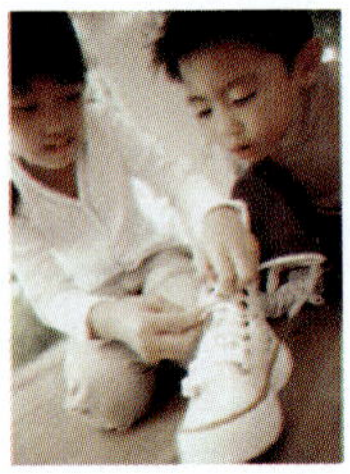

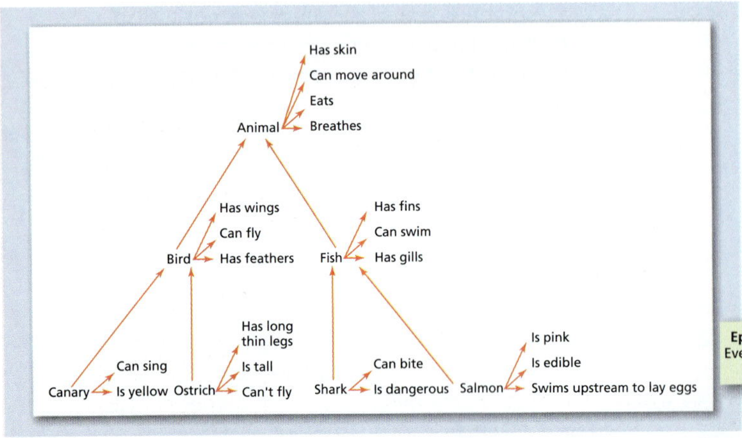

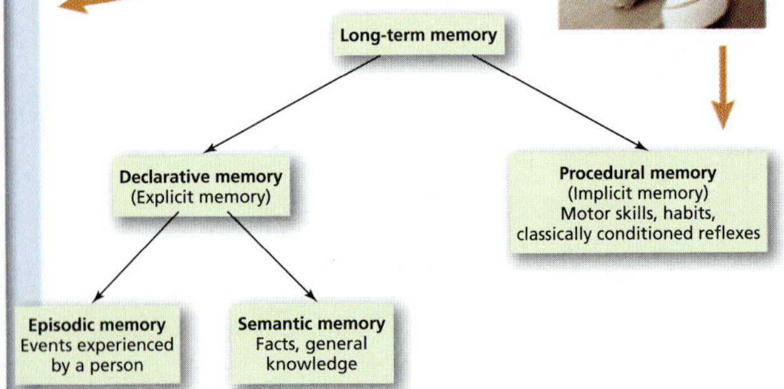

6.6 6.7 p. 234

Retrieval of Long-Term Memories

- **getting it out**
  - **retrieval cues**
  - **encoding specificity**
  - **state-dependent learning**
- **recall vs. recognition**
  - **recall:** few or no external cues required
  - **recognition:** match incoming sensory information (e.g., see or hear) to what is already in memory
- **automatic encoding**
  - strong emotional associations can lead to vivid and detailed "flashbulb" memories

6.8 6.9 p. 238

The Reconstructive Nature of Long-Term Memory

- **constructive processing of memories**
  - memories are rarely completely accurate and become less accurate over time
  - Loftus and others have suggested that memory retrieval is a constructive process; memories are "built" at time of retrieval
- **memory retrieval problems**
  - **misinformation effect**
  - **reliability of memory retrieval**

6.10 p. 245

Forgetting

(originally studied by Ebbinghaus in 1913, research produced forgetting curve)

- **distributed practice** produces far better retrieval than massed practice (cramming)
- **encoding failure** nonattended information is not encoded into memory
- **memory trace decay** over time, if not used, neuronal connections can weaken or decay
- **interference** other information interferes with accurate retrieval

Table 6.1

Reasons for Forgetting

REASONS	DESCRIPTION
Encoding Failure	The information is not attended to and fails to be encoded.
Decay or Disuse	Information that is not accessed decays from the storage system over time.
Proactive Interference	Older information already in memory interferes with the retrieval of newer information.
Retroactive Interference	Newer information interferes with the retrieval of older information.

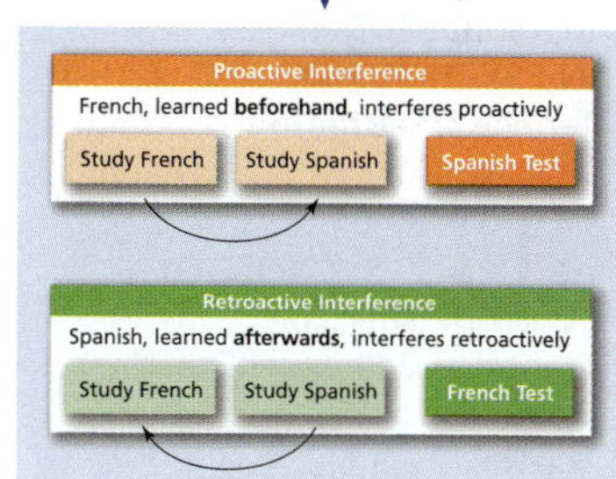

6.11 6.12 p. 245

Neuroscience of Memory

- **amnesia**
  - **organic amnesia**
  - **infantile amnesia**
- different brain areas are associated with different types of memory
  - **procedural memories**
  - **short-term memories**
  - **semantic and episodic long-term memories**
- several physical changes in brain are associated with memory formation (consolidation)
  - changes at receptor (long-term potentiation)
  - changes in dendrites
- **hippocampus** plays a vital role in the formation of new declarative long-term memories

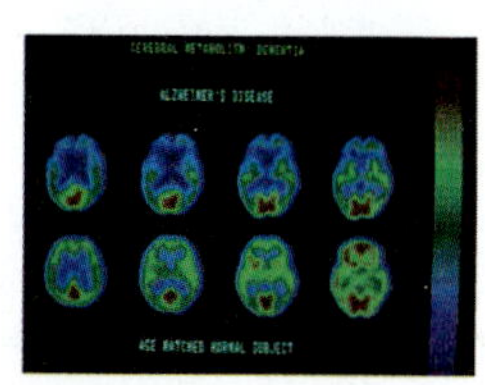

7

cognition

thinking, intelligence, and language

CHAPTER OUTLINE

- How People Think
- Intelligence
- PSYCHOLOGY IN THE NEWS: Neuropsychology Sheds Light on Head Injuries
- CLASSIC STUDIES IN PSYCHOLOGY: Terman's "Termites"
- Language
- APPLYING PSYCHOLOGY TO EVERYDAY LIFE: Mental and Physical Exercises Combine for Better Cognitive Health

THE LIFE OF ALEX

On September 6, 2007, Alex the African gray parrot died. Alex was not an ordinary pet; he was made famous by the groundbreaking work of Dr. Irene Pepperberg and her colleagues in cognition and communication research. Although most people know that parrots can learn to mimic words and sounds made by humans—and even machines—Alex could use language in a very different way. He could identify over 50 different objects, seven colors, and five shapes by naming them out loud. Alex could even count up to six objects, do very simple addition, and appeared to show some limited knowledge of "zero." (Pepperberg, 2006). He could verbally identify which of two objects was the bigger or the smaller, sort over 100 objects into categories, and say whether two objects were the same kind of object or different objects—hardly simple imitation.

But does this constitute a real use of language? Is Alex the parrot really thinking much like a very young child would think about these objects? Many cognitive theorists seem to think so (Pepperberg, 2005, 2007), although some caution against interpreting Alex's behavior in human terms and motivations (Premack, 2004). The researchers taught Alex by modeling competitive behavior—for example, one researcher might offer another a toy if he could correctly name it, and the second researcher would be "rewarded" by getting to play with the toy. Through modeling and shaping of Alex's words, the parrot was able to learn concepts similar to that of a very young child. Since Alex's death, Pepperberg and her colleagues have continued to work with their two other African gray parrots, Griffin and Arthur (affectionately known as "Wart") and are even teaching the parrots to "surf the Web" after a fashion by linking simple actions to different recorded sites on a television monitor.

As reported, Alex's last words to Pepperberg were, "You be good, see you tomorrow. I love you."

Why study the nature of thought?

To fully understand how we do any of the things we do (such as learning, remembering, and behaving), we need to understand how we think. How do we organize our thoughts? How do we communicate those thoughts to others? What do we mean by intelligence? Why are some people able to learn so much faster than others?

learning objectives

7.1 How are mental images and concepts involved in the process of thinking?

7.2 What are the methods people use to solve problems and make decisions?

7.3 Why does problem solving sometimes fail, and what is meant by creative thinking?

7.4 How do psychologists define intelligence, and how do various theories of intelligence differ?

7.5 How is intelligence measured and how are intelligence tests constructed?

7.6 What is intellectual disability and what are its causes?

7.7 What defines giftedness, and does being intellectually gifted guarantee success in life?

7.8 What is the influence of heredity and environment on the development of intelligence?

7.9 How is language defined, and what are its different elements and structure?

7.10 Does language influence the way people think, and are animals capable of learning language?

7.11 What are some ways to improve thinking?

study tip

As you are reading this chapter, remember to use the SQ3R method discussed on pages I-7–I-8 in *Psychology in Action*. Breaking your reading into small sections will help you get more out of every chapter.

How People Think

What does it mean to think? People are thinking all the time and talking about thinking as well: "What do you think?" "Let me think about that." "I don't think so." So, what does it mean to think? **Thinking**, or **cognition** (from a Latin word meaning "to know"), can be defined as mental activity that goes on in the brain when a person is processing information—organizing it, understanding it, and communicating it to others. Thinking includes memory, but it is much more. When people think, they are not only aware of the information in the brain but also are making decisions about it, comparing it to other information, and using it to solve problems.

Thinking also includes more than just a kind of verbal "stream of consciousness." When people think, they often have images as well as words in their minds.

7.1 How are mental images and concepts involved in the process of thinking?

MENTAL IMAGERY

As stated in Chapter Six, short-term memories are encoded in the form of sounds and also as visual images, forming a mental picture of the world. Thus, **mental images** (representations that stand in for objects or events and have a picturelike quality) are one of several tools used in the thought process.

Here's an interesting demonstration of the use of mental images. Get several people together and ask them to tell you *as fast as they can* how many windows are in the place where they live. Usually you'll find that the first people to shout out an answer have fewer windows in their houses than the ones who take longer to respond. You'll also notice that most of them look up, as if looking at some image that only they can see. If asked, they'll say that to determine the number of windows, they pictured where they live and simply counted windows as they "walked through" the image they created in their mind.

So more windows means more time to count them in your head? I guess mentally "walking" through a bigger house in your head would take longer than "walking" through a smaller one.

So more windows means more time to count them in your head? I guess mentally "walking" through a bigger house in your head would take longer than "walking" through a smaller one.

That's what researchers think, too. They have found that it does take longer to view a mental image that is larger or covers more distance than a smaller, more compact one (Kosslyn et al., 2001; Ochsner & Kosslyn, 1994). In one study (Kosslyn et al., 1978), participants were asked to look at a map of an imaginary island (see Figure 7.1). On this map were several landmarks, such as a hut, a lake, and a grassy area. After viewing the map and memorizing it, participants were asked to imagine a specific place on the island, such as the hut, and then to "look" for another place, like the lake. When they mentally "reached" the second place, they pushed a button that recorded reaction time. The

thinking (cognition) mental activity that goes on in the brain when a person is organizing and attempting to understand information and communicating information to others.

mental images mental representations that stand for objects or events and have a picturelike quality.

greater the physical distance on the map between the two locations, the longer it took participants to scan the image for the second location. The participants were apparently looking at their mental image and scanning it just as if it were a real, physical map.

Mental imagery is something people use every day. It helps them remember where they parked the car, find furniture that fits in their apartment, and relax by creating daydreams. It allows people to find their way home and to other places by using their learned "mental maps" of how to get to familiar locations. LINK to Chapter Five: Learning, p. 198. As discussed in the introduction to this text, mental imagery is also a very useful tool for remembering other ideas and concepts, such as remembering your grocery list by linking the items on it to a series of standard images (Paivio, 1971, 1986; Thomas, 2001). LINK to Psychology in Action, p. I-15.

People are even able to mentally rotate, or turn, images (Shepherd & Metzler, 1971). Kosslyn (1983) asked participants questions such as the following: "Do frogs have lips and a stubby tail?" He found that most participants reported visualizing a frog, starting with the face ("no lips"), then mentally rotating the image so it was facing away from them, and then "zooming in" to look for the stubby tail ("yes, there it is"). A very important aspect of the research on mental rotation is that we tend to engage *mental* images in our mind much like we engage or interact with *physical* objects. When we rotate an object in our minds (or in other ways interact with or manipulate mental images), it is not instantaneous—it takes time, just as it would if we were rotating a physical object with our hands.

In the brain, creating a mental image is almost the opposite of seeing an actual image. With an actual image, the information goes from the eyes to the visual cortex of the occipital lobe and is processed, or interpreted, by other areas of the cortex that compare the new information to information already in memory. LINK to Chapter Two: The Biological Perspective, p. 75. In creating a mental image, areas of the cortex associated with stored knowledge send information to the visual cortex, where the image is perceived in the "mind's eye" (Kosslyn et al., 1993; Sparing et al., 2002). PET scans show areas of the visual cortex being activated during the process of forming an image, providing evidence for the role of the visual cortex in mental imagery (Kosslyn et al., 1993, 1999, 2001).

Through the use of functional magnetic resonance imagery (fMRI), researchers have been able to see the overlap that occurs in brain areas activated during visual mental imagery tasks as compared to actual tasks involving visual perception (Ganis et al., 2004). During both types of tasks, activity was present in the frontal cortex (cognitive control), temporal lobes (memory), parietal lobes (attention and spatial memory), and occipital lobes (visual processing). However, the amount of activity in these areas differed between the two types of tasks. For example, activity in the visual cortex was stronger during perception than in imagery, suggesting sensory input activates this area more strongly than memory input. And an important finding overall, those areas activated during visual imagery were a subset of those activated during visual perception, with the greatest similarity in the frontal and parietal regions rather than the temporal and occipital regions. What does this mean? Simply that there is commonality between the processes of visual imagery and visual perception but it *is not* a complete overlap, and, as the authors point out, the greater overlap *was not* in the temporal and occipital regions (memory and vision functions) that might be assumed to be the most likely areas of overlap given the visual nature of the tasks (Ganis et al., 2004).

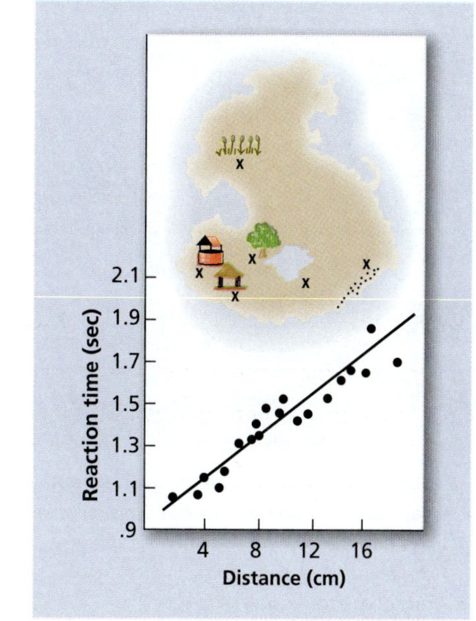

Figure 7.1 Kosslyn's Fictional Island

In Kosslyn's 1978 study, participants were asked to push a button when they had imagined themselves moving from one place on the island to another. As the graph below the picture shows, participants took longer times to complete the task when the locations on the image were farther apart.

Source: Kosslyn et al. (1978).

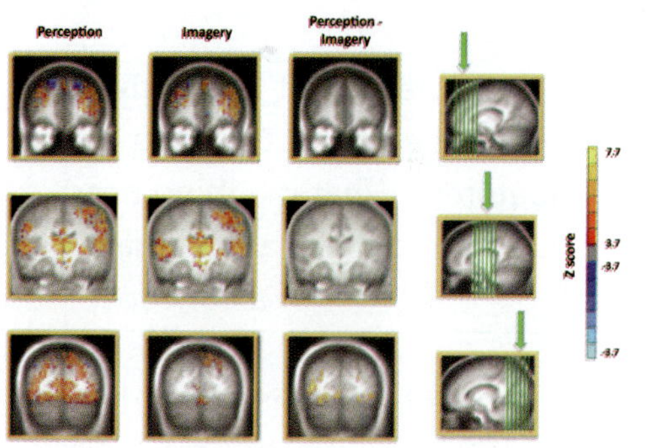

In the fMRI images above, the areas of the brain activated during perception and imagery showed a great deal of overlap but were not identical. Adapted from Ganis, G., Thompson, W. L., & Kosslyn, S. M. (2004). Images courtesy of, and used with permission from, Dr. Giorgio Ganis and Elsevier.

Images are not the only way we think, are they?

CONCEPTS

Images are not the only way we think, are they?

Mental images are only one form of mental representation. Another aspect of thought processes is the use of concepts. **Concepts** are ideas that represent a class or

concepts ideas that represent a class or category of objects, events, or activities.

Both of these animals are dogs. They both have fur, four legs, a tail—but the similarities end there. With so many variations in the animals we call "dogs," what is the prototype for "dog"?

category of objects, events, or activities. People use concepts to think about objects or events without having to think about all the specific examples of the category. For example, a person can think about "fruit" without thinking about every kind of fruit there is in the world, which would take far more effort and time. This ability to think in terms of concepts allows us to communicate with each other: If I mention a bird to you, you know what I am referring to, even if we aren't actually thinking of the same *type* of bird.

Concepts not only contain the important features of the objects or events people want to think about, but also they allow the identification of new objects and events that may fit the concept. For example, dogs come in all shapes, sizes, colors, and lengths of fur. Yet most people have no trouble recognizing dogs as dogs, even though they may never before have seen that particular breed of dog. Friends of the author have a dog called a briard, which is a kind of sheepdog. In spite of the fact that this dog is easily the size of a small pony, the author had no trouble recognizing it as a dog, albeit a huge and extremely shaggy one.

Concepts can represent many different levels of objects or events. Concepts can be of a very general form, such as "fruit," called a **superordinate concept**. The concept "apple" is more specific but can still be a **basic level type**. "Pear," "orange," and "watermelon" would also be basic level. A "Granny Smith apple" would be a **subordinate concept**, or one that is the most specific example (Mandler, 2000, 2003; Rosch et al., 1976). As discussed in Chapter Six, concepts are thought to form a network of associations based on these levels. (See Figure 6.6, on page 227.)

Concepts can have very strict definitions, such as the concept of a square as a shape with four equal sides. Concepts defined by specific rules or features are called **formal concepts** and are quite rigid. To be a square, for example, an object must be a two-dimensional figure with four equal sides and four angles adding up to 360 degrees. If an object has those features, it is not only a square, but also it cannot be anything BUT a square. Science and mathematics are full of formal concepts: Acid, limestone, asteroid, and wavelength are a few scientific formal concepts; in geometry, there are triangles, squares, rectangles, polygons, and lines. In psychology, there are double-blind experiments, sleep stages, and conditioned stimuli, to name a few. Each of these concepts must fit very specific features to be considered true examples.

But what about things that don't easily fit the rules or features? What if a thing has some, but not all, features of a concept?

But what about things that don't easily fit the rules or features? What if a thing has some, but not all, features of a concept?

In everyday life, people are surrounded by objects, events, and activities that are not as clearly defined as the concepts of science and mathematics. What is a vehicle? Cars and trucks leap immediately to mind, but what about a bobsled? How about a raft? Those last two objects aren't quite as easy to classify as vehicles immediately, but they fit some of the rules for "vehicle." These are examples of **natural concepts**, concepts people form not as a result of the application of a strict set of rules, but rather as the result of their experiences with these concepts in the real world (Ahn, 1998; Barton & Komatsu, 1989; Gelman, 1988; Rosch, 1973). Whereas formal concepts are well defined, natural concepts are "fuzzy" (Hampton, 1998). Is a whale a fish or a mammal? Is a platypus a mammal or a bird? People may know that whales are technically mammals, but whales also share a lot of fish-defining characteristics. Mammals have fur; birds lay eggs and have beaks. The duck-billed platypus has and does all three (has fur, lays eggs, and has a beak), yet it is classified as a mammal, not a bird.

Natural concepts are important in helping people understand their surroundings in a less structured manner than the formal concepts that are taught in school, and they form the basis for interpreting those surroundings and the events that may occur in everyday life.

PROTOTYPES When someone says "fruit," what's the first image that comes to mind? More than likely, it's a specific kind of fruit like an apple, pear, or orange. It's less likely that someone's first impulse will be to say "guava" or "papaya," or even "banana," unless

superordinate concept the most general form of a type of concept, such as "animal" or "fruit"; superordinate refers to highest in status or standing.

basic level type an example of a type of concept around which other similar concepts are organized, such as "dog," "cat," or "pear."

subordinate concept the most specific category of a concept, such as one's pet dog or a pear in one's hand; subordinate refers to lowest in status or standing.

formal concepts concepts that are defined by specific rules or features.

natural concepts concepts people form as a result of their experiences in the real world.

that person comes from a tropical area. In the United States, apples are a good example of a **prototype**, a concept that closely matches the defining characteristics of the concept (Mervis & Rosch, 1981; Rosch, 1977). Fruit is sweet, grows on trees, has seeds, and is usually round—all very applelike qualities. Coconuts are sweet and they also grow on trees, but many people in the Northern Hemisphere have never actually seen a coconut tree. They have more likely seen countless apple trees. So people who do have very different experiences with fruit, for instance, will have different prototypes, which are the most basic examples of concepts.

What about people who live in a tropical area? Would their prototype for fruit be different? And would people's prototypes be different in different cultures?

More than likely, prototypes develop according to the exposure a person has to objects in that category. So someone who grew up in an area where there are many coconut trees might think of coconuts as more prototypical than apples, whereas someone growing up in the northwestern United States would more likely see apples as a prototypical fruit (Aitchison, 1992). Research suggests that what a person knows about a particular type of object does affect the person's prototype for the category (Lynch et al., 2000; Shafto & Coley, 2003). For example, if describing the prototype of a tree, experts tend to describe the ideal characteristics (e.g., height, spread) rather than choosing one specific type of tree, while individuals who are not that knowledgeable about trees tend to pick a tree that is found where they live as the prototypical tree (such as an oak tree). For nonexperts, familiarity is important in selecting a prototype, while for experts, central characteristics more representative of trees in general are the standard (Lynch et al., 2000).

Culture also matters in the formation of prototypes. Research on concept prototypes across various cultures found greater differences and variations in prototypes between cultures that were dissimilar, such as Taiwan and American, than between cultures that are more similar, such as Hispanic Americans and non–Hispanic Americans living in Florida (Lin et al., 1990; Lin & Schwanenflugel, 1995; Schwanenflugel & Rey, 1986).

How do prototypes affect thinking? People tend to look at potential examples of a concept and compare them to the prototype to see how well they match—which is why it takes most people much longer to think about olives and tomatoes as fruit because they aren't sweet, one of the major characteristics of the prototype of fruit (Rosch & Mervis, 1975). Table 7.1 presents some prototypical American examples of the concepts "vehicle" and "fruit" as well as less typical examples.

A duck-billed platypus is classified as a mammal yet shares features with birds, such as webbed feet and a bill, and it also lays eggs. The platypus is an example of a "fuzzy" natural concept. Courtesy of Dave Watts, Nature Picture Library.

What about people who live in a tropical area? Would their prototype for fruit be different? And would people's prototypes vary in other cultures?

Table 7.1

From Prototypes to Atypical Examples (Most Typical to Least Typical)

VEHICLES	FRUITS
Car	Orange
Bus	Apple
Train	Peach
Bicycle	Grape
Airplane	Strawberry
Boat	Grapefruit
Wheelchair	Watermelon
Sled	Date
Skates	Tomato
Elevator	Olive

Source: Adapted from Rosch & Mervis (1975), p. 576.

prototype an example of a concept that closely matches the defining characteristics of a concept.

No matter what type, concepts are one of the ways people deal with all the information that bombards* their senses every day and allows them to organize their perceptions of the world around them. This organization may take the form of *schemas*, mental generalizations about objects, places, events, and people (for example, one's schema for "library" would no doubt include books and bookshelves), or *scripts*, a kind of schema that involves a familiar sequence of activities (for example, "going to a movie" would include traveling there, getting the ticket, buying snacks, finding the right theater, etc.). Concepts not only help people think, but also they are an important tool in *problem solving*, a type of thinking that people engage in every day and in many different situations.

Problem solving is certainly a big part of any college student's life. Is there any one "best" way to go about solving a problem?

PROBLEM SOLVING AND DECISION MAKING

Problem solving is certainly a big part of any college student's life. Is there any one "best" way to go about solving a problem?

Think about it as you read on and solve the following: Put a coin in a bottle and then cork the opening. How can you get the coin out of the bottle without pulling out the cork or breaking the bottle? (For the solution, see page 260.)

As stated earlier, images and concepts are mental tools that can be used to solve problems. For the preceding problem, you are probably trying to create an image of the bottle with a coin in it. **Problem solving** occurs when a goal must be reached by thinking and behaving in certain ways. Problems range from figuring out how to cut a recipe in half to understanding complex mathematical proofs to deciding what to major in at college. There are several different ways in which people can think in order to solve problems.

These children try one piece after another until finding the piece that fits. This is an example of trial-and-error learning.

7.2 What are the methods people use to solve problems and make decisions,?

TRIAL AND ERROR (MECHANICAL SOLUTIONS) One method is to use **trial and error**, also known as a **mechanical solution**. Trial and error refers to trying one solution after another until finding one that works. For example, if Shelana has forgotten the PIN for her online banking Web site, she can try one combination after another until she finds the one that works, if she has only a few such PINs that she normally uses. Mechanical solutions can also involve solving by *rote*, or a learned set of rules. This is how word problems were solved in grade school, for example. One type of rote solution is to use an algorithm.

ALGORITHMS **Algorithms** are specific, step-by-step procedures for solving certain types of problems. Algorithms will always result in a correct solution, if there is a correct solution to be found, and you have enough time to find it. Mathematical formulas are algorithms. When librarians organize books on bookshelves, they also use an algorithm: Place books in alphabetical order within each category, for example. Many puzzles, like a Rubik's Cube®, have a set of steps that, if followed exactly, will always result in solving the puzzle. But algorithms aren't always practical to use. For example, if Shelana didn't have a clue what those four numbers might be, she *might* be able to figure out her forgotten PIN by trying *all possible combinations* of four digits, 0 through 9. She would eventually find the right four-digit combination—but it might take years! Computers, however, can run searches like this one very quickly, so the systematic search algorithm is a useful part of some computer programs.

HEURISTICS Unfortunately, humans aren't as fast as computers and need some other way to narrow down the possible solutions to only a few. One way to do this is to use a

problem solving process of cognition that occurs when a goal must be reached by thinking and behaving in certain ways.

trial and error (mechanical solution) problem-solving method in which one possible solution after another is tried until a successful one is found.

algorithms very specific, step-by-step procedures for solving certain types of problems.

*bombards: attacks again and again.

heuristic. A **heuristic**, or "rule of thumb," is a simple rule that is intended to apply to many situations. Whereas an algorithm is very specific and will always lead to a solution, a heuristic is an educated guess based on prior experiences that helps narrow down the possible solutions for a problem. For example, if a student is typing a paper in a word-processing program and wants to know how to format the page, he or she could try to read an entire manual on the word-processing program. That would take a while. Instead, the student could type "format" into the help feature's search program or click on the word *Format* on the toolbar. Doing either action greatly reduces the amount of information the student will have to look at to get an answer. Using the help feature or clicking on the appropriate toolbar word will also work for similar problems.

Will using a rule of thumb always work, like algorithms do? Using a heuristic is faster than using an algorithm in many cases, but unlike algorithms, heuristics will *not* always lead to the correct solution. What you gain in speed is sometimes lost in accuracy. For example, a **representative heuristic** is used for categorizing objects and simply assumes that any object (or person) that shares characteristics with the members of a particular category is also a member of that category. This is a handy tool when it comes to classifying plants but doesn't work as well when applied to people. Are all people with dark skin from Africa? Does everyone with red hair also have a bad temper? Are all blue-eyed blondes from Sweden? See the point? The representative heuristic can be used—or misused—to create and sustain stereotypes (Kahneman & Tversky, 1973; Kahneman et al., 1982).

Another heuristic that can have undesired outcomes is the **availability heuristic**, which is based on our estimation of the frequency or likelihood of an event based on how easy it is to recall relevant information from memory or how easy it is for us to think of related examples (Tversky & Kahneman, 1973). Imagine, for example, that after you have already read this entire textbook (it could happen!) you are asked to estimate how many words in the book start with the letter *K* and how many have the letter *K* as the third letter in the word. Which place do you think is more frequent, the first letter or as the third letter? Next, what do you think the ratio of the more frequent placement is to the less frequent placement? What is easier to think of, words that begin with the letter *K* or words that have *K* as the third letter? Tversky & Kahneman (1973) asked this same question of 152 participants for five consonants (*K, N, L, R, V*) that appear more frequently in the third position as compared to the first in a typical text. Sixty-nine percent of the participants indicated that the first position was the more frequent placement and the median estimated ratio was 2:1, and for the letter *K*—there are typically twice as many words with *K* as the third letter as compared to the first. Can you think of an example where you may have used the availability heuristic and it did not work in your favor?

A useful heuristic that *does* work much of the time is to *work backward from the goal.* For example, if you want to know the shortest way to get to the new coffee shop in town, you already know the goal, which is finding the coffee shop. There are probably several ways to get there from your house, and some are shorter than others. Assuming you have the address of the store, for many the best way to determine the shortest route is to look up the location of the store on an Internet map, a GPS, or a smart phone, and compare the different routes by the means of travel (walking versus driving). People actually used to do this with a physical map and compare the routes manually! Think about it, does technology, help or hinder some aspects of problem solving? What are, if any, the benefits to using technology for solving some problems as compared to actively engaging in problem solving as a mental challenge?

One rule of thumb, or heuristic, involves breaking down a goal into subgoals. This woman is consulting the map to see which of several possible paths she needs to take to get to her goal destination.

Smartphones and other portable devices provide tools for easy navigation. How might the use or overuse of these tools affect our ability to navigate when we do not have access to them?

heuristic an educated guess based on prior experiences that helps narrow down the possible solutions for a problem. Also known as a "rule of thumb."

representative heuristic assumption that any object (or person) sharing characteristics with the members of a particular category is also a member of that category.

availability heuristic estimating the frequency or likelihood of an event based on how easy it is to recall relevant information from memory or how easy it is for us to think of related examples.

What if my problem is writing a term paper? Starting at the end isn't going to help me much!

What if my problem is writing a term paper? Starting at the end isn't going to help me much!

Sometimes it's better to break a goal down into *subgoals*, so that as each subgoal is achieved, the final solution is that much closer. Writing a term paper, for example, can seem overwhelming until it is broken down into steps: Choose a topic, research the topic, organize what has been gathered, write one section at a time, and so on. Other examples of heuristics include making diagrams to help organize the information concerning the problem or testing possible solutions to the problem one by one and eliminating those that do not work.

Another kind of heuristic is **means–end analysis**, in which a person determines the difference between the current situation and the goal and then tries to reduce that difference by various means (methods). For example, Katrina wanted a certain kind of invitation for her wedding, but buying it premade was very expensive and well over her budget. She ordered one sample of the invitation and examined it carefully. It had a pocket inside that held the response cards for people to send back to Katrina, a decorative seashell tied onto the outside of the card with fancy ribbon, and a small box instead of an envelope. Her goal was to make 200 of these invitations by hand. Her subgoals were to find the paper, take the invitation carefully apart to see how to put one together, buy the little shells, find and buy the right size boxes for mailing, and assemble the invitations. What might have seemed an impossible task became doable once it was broken down into smaller subgoals.

INSIGHT

Sometimes I have to find answers to problems one step at a time, but in other cases the answer seems to just "pop" into my head all of a sudden. Why do some answers come so easily to mind?

Sometimes I have to find answers to problems one step at a time, but in other cases the answer seems to just "pop" into my head all of a sudden. Why do some answers come so easily to mind?

When the solution to a problem seems to come suddenly to mind, it is called insight. Chapter Five (page 198) contained a discussion of Köhler's (1925) work with Sultan the chimpanzee, which demonstrated that even some animals can solve problems by means of a sudden insight. In humans, insight often takes the form of an "aha!" moment—the solution seems to come in a flash. A person may realize that this problem is similar to another one that he or she already knows how to solve or might see that an object can be used for a different purpose than its original one, like using a dime as a screwdriver.

Remember the problem of the bottle discussed earlier in this chapter? The task was to get the coin out of the bottle without removing the cork or breaking the bottle. The answer is simple: *Push the cork into the bottle and shake out the coin. Aha!*

Insight is not really a magical process, although it can seem like magic. What usually happens is that the mind simply reorganizes a problem, sometimes while the person is thinking about something else (Durso et al., 1994).

Here's a problem that can be solved with insight: Marsha and Marjorie were born on the same day of the same month of the same year to the same mother and the same father yet they are not twins. How is that possible? Think about it and then look for the answer on p. 262.

In summary, thinking is a complex process involving the use of mental imagery and various types of concepts to organize the events of daily life. Problem solving is a special type of thinking that involves the use of many tools, such as trial-and-error thinking, algorithms, and heuristics, to solve different types of problems.

means–end analysis heuristic in which the difference between the starting situation and the goal is determined and then steps are taken to reduce that difference.

7.1 7.2

CONCEPT MAP

How People Think

thinking (cognition) refers to mental activities that occur in the brain when processing, organizing, understanding, or communicating information to others

- **mental imagery**
  - mental images are representations for objects or events used in mental activities
  - mental images are interacted with in similar ways as physical objects (e.g., scanning a map or rotating an object)
  - mental images are processed in the brain slightly differently than actual objects
    - as opposed to seeing actual image (eyes → visual cortex → other cortical areas), cortical areas associated with stored knowledge send info to visual cortex
- **concepts**
  - are ideas that represent a class or category of objects, events, or activities
  - are used to interact and organize information without having to think about or process every specific example of the category
  - can represent different levels of objects or events
    - **superordinate** (e.g., fruit)
    - **basic level** (e.g., apple)
    - **subordinate** (e.g., Granny Smith apple)
  - can be well-defined based on strict criteria (formal), or fuzzy, based on personal experience (natural)
  - are represented by prototypes, best examples of the defining characteristics
    - vary according to personal experience, knowledge, and culture
  - are an important tool in problem solving
- **problem solving and decision making**
  - thinking and behaving in certain ways to reach a goal
  - can involve different strategies, logical methods (convergent thinking)
    - **trial and error**
      - trying one solution after another until one works
    - **algorithms**
      - specific, step-by-step procedures for solving certain problems
      - always result in correct solution if there is one
    - **heuristics**
      - simple rules intended to apply to many situations
      - educated guesses based on prior experience
      - generally faster than algorithms but will not always lead to correct solution
  - **insight**
    - "aha!" moments when solution seems to appear in a flash
    - usually based on reorganization of information

PRACTICE quiz How much do you remember? ANSWERS ON PAGE AK-1.

Pick the best answer.

1. Mental images __________.
   - **a.** represent abstract ideas.
   - **b.** have a picturelike quality.
   - **c.** consist entirely of unconscious information.
   - **d.** are always prototypes.
2. Knowing that the definition of psychology is the scientific study of behavior and mental processes is an example of a __________.
   - **a.** prototypical concept.
   - **b.** natural concept.
   - **c.** formal concept.
   - **d.** mental image.
3. A "rule of thumb" is another name for a __________.
   - **a.** heuristic.
   - **b.** algorithm.
   - **c.** trial-and-error solution.
   - **d.** means–end analysis.
4. What type of problem-solving strategy would be best to use when solving a problem in algebra class?
   - **a.** heuristic
   - **b.** algorithm
   - **c.** trial-and-error solution
   - **d.** means–end analysis
5. Miguel was struggling with the answer to one of the questions on his psychology midterm. Seeing that the answer was not going to come easily, he went on to answer some of the other easier questions. Then, suddenly, the answer to the problematic question just seemed to "pop" into his head. Miguel's experience is an example of __________.
   - **a.** means–end analysis.
   - **b.** a heuristic.
   - **c.** an algorithm.
   - **d.** insight.

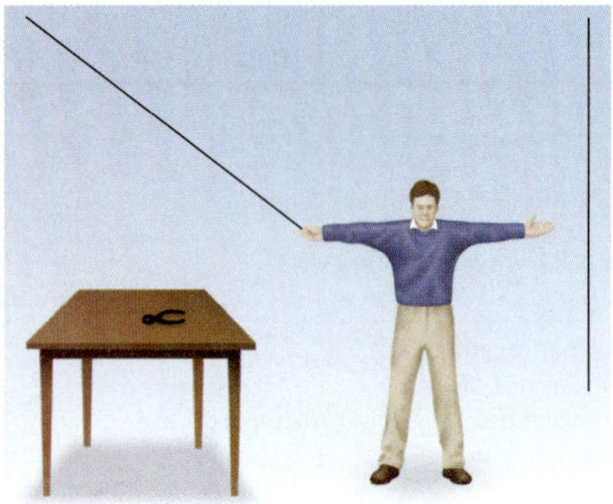

Figure 7.2 The String Problem
How do you tie the two strings together if you cannot reach them both at the same time?

Explore the two-string problem and confirmation bias on **mypsychlab.com**

Answer to insight problem on page 260: *Marsha and Marjorie are two of a set of triplets. Gotcha!*

Figure 7.3 The Dot Problem
Can you draw four straight lines so that they pass through all nine dots *without lifting your pencil from the page and without touching any dot more than once?*

functional fixedness a block to problem solving that comes from thinking about objects in terms of only their typical functions.

mental set the tendency for people to persist in using problem-solving patterns that have worked for them in the past.

confirmation bias the tendency to search for evidence that fits one's beliefs while ignoring any evidence that does not fit those beliefs.

PROBLEMS WITH PROBLEM SOLVING

7.3 Why does problem solving sometimes fail, and what is meant by creative thinking?

Using insight to solve a problem is not always foolproof. Sometimes a solution to a problem remains just "out of reach" because the elements of the problem are not arranged properly or because people get stuck in certain ways of thinking that act as barriers to solving problems. Such ways of thinking occur more or less automatically, influencing attempts to solve problems without any conscious awareness of that influence. Here's a classic example:

Two strings are hanging from a ceiling but are too far apart to allow a person to hold one and walk to the other. (See Figure 7.2.) Nearby is a table with a pair of pliers on it. The goal is to tie the two pieces of string together. How? For the solution to this problem, read on.

People can become aware of automatic tendencies to try to solve problems in ways that are not going to lead to solutions and in becoming aware can abandon the "old" ways for more appropriate problem-solving methods. Three of the most common barriers* to successful problem solving are functional fixedness, mental sets, and confirmation bias. Explore on **mypsychlab.com**

FUNCTIONAL FIXEDNESS One problem-solving difficulty involves thinking about objects only in terms of their typical uses, which is a phenomenon called **functional fixedness** (literally, "fixed on the function"). Have you ever searched high and low for a screwdriver to fix something around the house? All the while there are several objects close at hand that could be used to tighten a screw: a butter knife, a key, or even a dime in your pocket. Because the tendency is to think of those objects in terms of cooking, unlocking, and spending, we sometimes ignore the less obvious possible uses. The string problem introduced before is an example of functional fixedness. The pair of pliers is often seen as useless until the person realizes it can be used as a weight. (See page 264.)

Alton Brown, renowned chef and star of the Food Network's *Good Eats* cooking show, is a big fan of what he calls "multitaskers," kitchen items that can be used for more than one purpose. For example, a cigar-cutter can become a tool for cutting carrots, green onions, and garlic. Obviously, Chef Brown is not a frequent victim of functional fixedness.

MENTAL SETS Functional fixedness is actually a kind of **mental set**, which is defined as the tendency for people to persist in using problem-solving patterns that have worked for them in the past. Solutions that have worked in the past tend to be the ones people try first, and people are often hesitant or even unable to think of other possibilities. Look at Figure 7.3 and see if you can solve the dot problem.

People are taught from the earliest grades to stay within the lines, right? That tried-and-true method will not help in solving the dot problem. The solution involves drawing the lines beyond the actual dots, as seen in the solution on page 264.

CONFIRMATION BIAS Another barrier to logical thinking, called **confirmation bias**, is the tendency to search for evidence that fits one's beliefs while ignoring any evidence to the contrary. This is similar to a mental set, except that what is "set" is a belief rather than a method of solving problems. Believers in ESP tend to remember the few studies that seem to support their beliefs and psychic predictions that worked out while at the same time "forgetting" the cases in which studies found no proof or psychics made predictions that failed to come true. They remember only that which confirms their bias toward a belief in the existence of ESP. Another example, people who believe that they are good multitaskers and can safely drive a

*barrier: something that blocks one's path; an obstacle preventing a solution.

motor vehicle while talking or texting on their cell phones may tend to remember their own personal experiences, which may not include any vehicle accidents or "near-misses" (that they are aware of). While it might be tempting to think of one's self as a "supertasker," recent research suggests otherwise. When tested on driving simulators while having to perform successfully on two attention-demanding tasks, over 97 percent of individuals are unable to do so without significant impacts on their performance. During the dual-task condition, only 2.5 percent of individuals were able to perform without problems (Watson & Strayer, 2010). This specific example can be quite dangerous as it is estimated that at least 28 percent of all traffic crashes are caused by drivers using their cell phone and or texting (National Safety Council, 2010). [Note that the availability heuristic and representative heuristic could also come into play here and when misapplied, are often barriers to effective problem solving or the cause of errors in reasoning.]

The driver of this train was texting from his cell phone immediately before this crash that killed 25 people and injured more than 130 others.

CREATIVITY

So far, we've only talked about logic and pretty straightforward thinking. How do people come up with totally new ideas, things no one has thought of before?

So far, we've only talked about logic and pretty straightforward thinking. How do people come up with totally new ideas, things no one has thought of before?

Not every problem can be answered by using information already at hand and the rules of logic in applying that information. Sometimes a problem requires coming up with entirely new ways of looking at the problem or unusual, inventive solutions. This kind of thinking is called **creativity**: solving problems by combining ideas or behavior in new ways (Csikszentmihalyi, 1996; pronounced chĭck-sĕnt-mē-HĪ-ē).

DIVERGENT AND CONVERGENT THINKING The logical method for problem solving that has been discussed so far is based on a type of thinking called **convergent thinking**. In convergent thinking, a problem is seen as having only one answer and all lines of thinking will eventually lead to (converge on) that single answer by using previous knowledge and logic (Ciardiello, 1998). For example, the question "In what ways are a pencil and a pen alike?" can be answered by listing the features that the two items have in common: Both can be used to write, have similar shapes, and so on, in a simple comparison process. Convergent thinking works well for routine problem solving but may be of little use when a more creative solution is needed.

Divergent thinking is the reverse of convergent thinking. Here a person starts at one point and comes up with many different, or divergent, ideas or possibilities based on that point (Finke, 1995). For example, if someone were to ask the question, "What is a pencil used for?" the convergent answer would be "to write." But if the question is put this way: "How many different uses can you think of for a pencil?" the answers multiply: "writing, poking holes, a weight for the tail of a kite, a weapon." Divergent thinking has been attributed not only to creativity but also to intelligence (Guilford, 1967). **Explore** on **mypsychlab.com**

Explore problem-solving and creativity on **mypsychlab.com**

What are the characteristics of a creative, divergent thinker? Theorists in the field of creative thinking have found through examining the habits of highly creative people that the most productive periods of divergent thinking for those people tend to occur when they are doing some task or activity that is more or less automatic, such as walking or swimming (Csikszentmihalyi, 1996; Gardner, 1993a; Goleman, 1995). These automatic tasks take up some attention processes, leaving the remainder to devote to creative thinking. The fact that all of one's attention is not focused on the problem is actually a benefit, because divergent thinkers often make links and connections at a level of consciousness just below alert awareness, so that ideas can flow freely without being censored* by the higher mental processes (Goleman,

creativity the process of solving problems by combining ideas or behavior in new ways.

convergent thinking type of thinking in which a problem is seen as having only one answer, and all lines of thinking will eventually lead to that single answer, using previous knowledge and logic.

divergent thinking type of thinking in which a person starts from one point and comes up with many different ideas or possibilities based on that point.

*censored: blocked from conscious awareness as unacceptable thoughts.

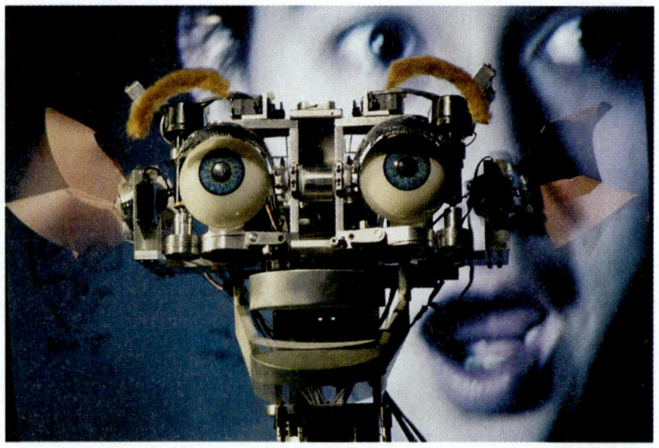

Cynthia Breazeal is a researcher at the Artificial Intelligence Lab at MIT. Here she is pictured with the robot she designed called Kismet. Designed to help with the study of infant emotional expressions, Kismet can display several "moods" on its face as emotional expressions. This is divergent thinking at its best—a "baby" that won't cry, wet, or demand to be fed.

1995). In other words, having part of one's attention devoted to walking, for example, allows the rest of the mind to "sneak up on" more creative solutions and ideas.

Divergent thinkers will obviously be less prone to some of the barriers to problem solving, such as functional fixedness. For example, what would most people do if it suddenly started to rain while they are stuck in their office with no umbrella? How many people would think of using a see-through vinyl tote bag as a makeshift umbrella?

Creative, divergent thinking is often a neglected topic in the education of young people. Although some people are naturally more creative, it is possible to develop one's creative ability. The ability to be creative is important—coming up with topics for a research paper, for example, is something that many students have trouble doing. Cross-cultural research (Basadur et al., 2002; Colligan, 1983) has found that divergent thinking and problem-solving skills cannot be easily taught in the Japanese or Omaha Native American cultures, for example. In these cultures, creativity in many areas is not normally prized and the preference is to hold to well-established, cultural traditions, such as traditional dances that have not varied for centuries. See Table 7.2 for some ways to become a more divergent thinker.

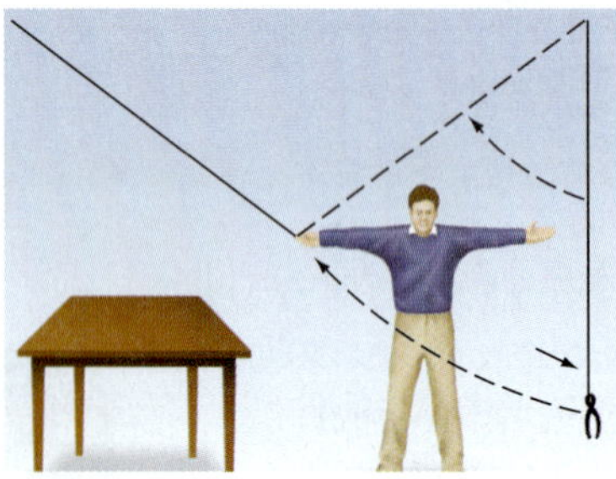

Solution to the String Problem
The solution to the string problem is to use the pliers as a pendulum to swing the second string closer to you.

Many people have the idea that creative people are also a little different from other people. There are artists and musicians, for example, who actually encourage others to see them as eccentric. But the fact is that creative people are actually pretty normal. According to Csikszentmihalyi (1997),

1. Creative people usually have a broad range of knowledge about a lot of subjects and are good at using mental imagery.
2. Creative people aren't afraid to be different—they are more open to new experiences than many people, and they tend to have more vivid dreams and daydreams than others do.
3. Creative people value their independence.
4. Creative people are often unconventional in their work, but not otherwise.

Solution to the Dot Problem
When people try to solve this problem, a mental set causes them to think of the dots as representing a box, and they try to draw the line while staying in the box. The only way to connect all nine dots without lifting the pencil from the paper is to draw the lines so they extend out of the box of dots—literally "thinking outside the box."

Table 7.2

Stimulating Divergent Thinking

Brainstorming	Generate as many ideas as possible in a short period of time, without judging each idea's merits until all ideas are recorded.
Keeping a Journal	Carry a journal to write down ideas as they occur or a recorder to capture those same ideas and thoughts.
Freewriting	Write down or record everything that comes to mind about a topic without revising or proofreading until all of the information is written or recorded in some way. Organize it later.
Mind or Subject Mapping	Start with a central idea and draw a "map" with lines from the center to other related ideas, forming a visual representation of the concepts and their connections.

7.3

CONCEPT MAP

problems with problem solving
- solutions to problems are not always apparent
- problems can be caused by three common barriers
  - **functional fixedness:** only thinking about objects in terms of their typical uses
  - **mental set:** a tendency to persist in using problem-solving patterns that have worked in the past
  - **confirmation bias:** a tendency to search for evidence that fits your beliefs while ignoring evidence to the contrary

Problem Solving and Decision Making

creativity
- consists of new ways of combining ideas or behavior
- typically the result of divergent thinking
  - less prone to common barriers of problem solving
  - can be stimulated (see Table 7.2)

PRACTICE quiz How much do you remember? ANSWERS ON PAGE AK-1.

Pick the best answer.

1. Al goes out one frosty morning to find that his car is covered with a layer of thick frost. He needs to get to work and looks for his ice scraper. Unable to find it, he thinks a moment, goes into the house, and returns with a hard plastic spatula from the kitchen. In using the spatula as a makeshift ice scraper, Al has overcome __________.
   a. functional fixedness.
   b. confirmation bias.
   c. creativity bias.
   d. confirmation fixedness.
2. Randall believes that aliens crashed in the western United States in the 1950s. When looking for information about this on the Internet, he ignores any sites that are skeptical of his belief and only visits and talks with his friends about the sites that support his belief. This is an example of __________.
   a. functional fixedness.
   b. confirmation bias.
   c. creativity bias.
   d. confirmation fixedness.
3. When a problem is seen as having only one answer, with all lines of thinking leading to that answer, this is known as __________ thinking.
   a. divergent
   b. creative
   c. convergent
   d. mental-set
4. Which of the following statements about creative people is TRUE?
   a. They are not very good at mental imagery.
   b. They are not afraid to be different.
   c. They value their dependence on others.
   d. They are often very conventional in their work.

Intelligence

Think back to Alex the parrot in the opening story. Whether you accept Alex's verbal abilities as true language or not, one thing is clear: Alex was one smart bird. But what do we mean when we say that? Is "smart" in a bird the same thing we mean when we say a human is smart? What exactly do we mean by the term *intelligence?*

In many ways, Alex was one smart bird. What are some of the ways psychologists might agree that Alex was "smart"?

DEFINITION

7.4 How do psychologists define intelligence, and how do various theories of intelligence differ?

Is intelligence merely a score on some test, or is it practical knowledge of how to get along in the world? Is it making good grades or being a financial success or a social success? Ask a dozen people and you will probably get a dozen different answers. Psychologists have come up with a workable definition that combines many of the ideas just mentioned: They define **intelligence** as the ability to learn from one's experiences, acquire knowledge, and use resources effectively in adapting to new situations or solving

intelligence the ability to learn from one's experiences, acquire knowledge, and use resources effectively in adapting to new situations or solving problems.

g factor the ability to reason and solve problems, or general intelligence.

s factor the ability to excel in certain areas, or specific intelligence.

This child is displaying only one of the many forms that intelligence can take, according to Gardner's multiple intelligences theory.

problems (Sternberg & Kaufman, 1998; Wechsler, 1975). These are the characteristics that individuals need in order to survive in their culture.

THEORIES OF INTELLIGENCE

Although we have defined intelligence in a general way, there are differing opinions of the specific knowledge and abilities that make up the concept of intelligence. In the following section we will discuss three theories that offer different explanations of the nature and number of intelligence-related abilities.

SPEARMAN'S G FACTOR Charles Spearman (1904) saw intelligence as two different abilities. The ability to reason and solve problems was labeled **g factor** for *general intelligence*, whereas task-specific abilities in certain areas such as music, business, or art are labeled **s factor** for *specific intelligence*. A traditional IQ test would most likely measure g factor, but Spearman believed that superiority in one type of intelligence predicts superiority overall. Although his early research found some support for specific intelligences, other researchers (Guilford, 1967; Thurstone, 1938) felt that Spearman had oversimplified the concept of intelligence. Intelligence began to be viewed as composed of numerous factors. In fact, Guilford (1967) proposed that there were 120 types of intelligence.

GARDNER'S MULTIPLE INTELLIGENCES One of the later theorists to propose the existence of several kinds of intelligence is Howard Gardner (1993b, 1999a). Although many people use the terms *reason*, *logic*, and *knowledge* as if they are the same ability, Gardner believes that they are different aspects of intelligence, along with several other abilities. He originally listed seven different kinds of intelligence but later added an eighth type and then a ninth (Gardner, 1998, 1999b). The nine types of intelligence are described in Table 7.3.

Table 7.3
Gardner's Nine Intelligences

TYPE OF INTELLIGENCE	DESCRIPTION	SAMPLE OCCUPATION
Verbal/linguistic	Ability to use language	Writers, speakers
Musical	Ability to compose and/or perform music	Musicians, even those who do not read musical notes but can perform and compose
Logical/mathematical	Ability to think logically and to solve mathematical problems	Scientists, engineers
Visual/spatial	Ability to understand how objects are oriented in space	Pilots, astronauts, artists, navigators
Movement	Ability to control one's body motions	Dancers, athletes
Interpersonal	Sensitivity to others and understanding motivation of others	Psychologists, managers
Intrapersonal	Understanding of one's emotions and how they guide actions	Various people-oriented careers
Naturalist	Ability to recognize the patterns found in nature	Farmers, landscapers, biologists, botanists
Existentialist	Ability to see the "big picture" of the human world by asking questions about life, death, and the ultimate reality of human existence	Various careers, philosophical thinkers

The idea of multiple intelligences has great appeal, especially for educators. However, some argue that there are few scientific studies providing evidence for the concept of multiple intelligences (Waterhouse, 2006a, 2006b), while others claim that the evidence does exist (Gardner & Moran, 2006). Some critics propose that such intelligences are no more than different abilities and that those abilities are not necessarily the same thing as what is typically meant by *intelligence* (E. Hunt, 2001).

STERNBERG'S TRIARCHIC THEORY Robert Sternberg (1988, 1997b) has theorized that there are three kinds of intelligence. Called the **triarchic theory of intelligence** (*triarchic* means three), this theory is similar to Aristotle's theory that intelligence is composed of theoretical, productive, and practical aspects.

In Sternberg's theory, the three aspects are *analytical, creative*, and *practical intelligence*. **Analytical intelligence** refers to the ability to break problems down into component parts, or analysis, for problem solving. This is the type of intelligence that is measured by intelligence tests and academic achievement tests, or "book smarts" as some people like to call it. **Creative intelligence** is the ability to deal with new and different concepts and to come up with new ways of solving problems (divergent thinking, in other words); it also refers to the ability to automatically process certain aspects of information, which frees up cognitive resources to deal with novelty (Sternberg, 2005). **Practical intelligence** is best described as "street smarts," or the ability to use information to get along in life. People with a high degree of practical intelligence know how to be tactful, how to manipulate situations to their advantage, and how to use inside information to increase their odds of success. **Watch** on **mypsychlab.com**

How might these three types of intelligence be illustrated? All three might come into play when planning and completing an experiment. For example:

- *Analytical:* Being able to run a statistical analysis on data from the experiment.
- *Creative:* Being able to design the experiment in the first place.
- *Practical:* Being able to get funding for the experiment from donors.

Practical intelligence has become a topic of much interest and research. Sternberg (1996, 1997a, b) has found that practical intelligence predicts success in life but has a surprisingly low relationship to academic (analytical) intelligence. In fact, the higher one's degree of practical intelligence, the less likely that person is to succeed in a university or other academic setting.

Sternberg's practical intelligence is a form of "street smarts" that includes the ability to adapt to one's environment and solve practical problems. These girls are giving their younger brother a drink of water by using a folded leaf as an impromptu cup.

Watch Robert Sternberg discussing intelligence on **mypsychlab.com**

MEASURING INTELLIGENCE

7.5 How is intelligence measured and how are intelligence tests constructed?

The history of intelligence testing spans the twentieth century and has at times been marked by controversies and misuse. A full history of how intelligence testing developed would take at least an entire chapter, so this section will discuss only some of the better known forms of testing and how they came to be.

It doesn't sound like intelligence would be easy to measure on a test—how do IQ tests work, anyway?

It doesn't sound like intelligence would be easy to measure on a test—how do IQ tests work, anyway?

The measurement of intelligence by some kind of test is a concept that is less than a century old. It began when educators in France realized that some students needed more help with learning than others did. They thought that if a way could be found to identify these students more in need, they could be given a different kind of education than the more capable students.

BINET'S MENTAL ABILITY TEST In those early days, a French psychologist named Alfred Binet was asked by the French Ministry of Education to design a formal test of intelligence that would help identify children who were unable to learn as quickly or as

triarchic theory of intelligence Sternberg's theory that there are three kinds of intelligence: analytical, creative, and practical.

analytical intelligence the ability to break problems down into component parts, or analysis, for problem solving.

creative intelligence the ability to deal with new and different concepts and to come up with new ways of solving problems.

practical intelligence the ability to use information to get along in life and become successful.

intelligence quotient (IQ) a number representing a measure of intelligence, resulting from the division of one's mental age by one's chronological age and then multiplying that quotient by 100.

Watch classic footage on mental age testing with Alfred Binet on **mypsychlab.com**

well as others, so that they could be given remedial education. Eventually, he and colleague Théodore Simon came up with a test that not only distinguished between fast and slow learners but also between children of different age groups as well (Binet & Simon, 1916). They noticed that the fast learners seemed to give answers to questions that older children might give, whereas the slow learners gave answers that were more typical of a younger child. Binet decided that the key element to be tested was a child's *mental age*, or the average age at which children could successfully answer a particular level of questions. **Watch** on **mypsychlab.com**

STANFORD-BINET AND IQ Lewis Terman (1916), a researcher at Stanford University, adopted German psychologist William Stern's method for comparing mental age and *chronological age* (number of years since birth) for use with the translated and revised Binet test. Stern's (1912) formula was to divide the mental age (MA) by the chronological age (CA) and multiply the result by 100 to get rid of any decimal points. The resulting score is called an **intelligence quotient**, or **IQ.** (A *quotient* is a number that results from dividing one number by another.)

$$IQ = MA/CA \times 100$$

For example, if a child who is 10 years old takes the test and scores a mental age of 15 (is able to answer the level of questions typical of a 15-year-old), the IQ would look like this:

$$IQ = 15/10 \times 100 = 150$$

The quotient has the advantage of allowing testers to compare the intelligence levels of people of different age groups. Today, the *Stanford-Binet Intelligence Scales, Fifth Edition* (*SB5*) (Roid, 2003) uses age-group comparison norms, like the Wechsler tests (see next page), and is often used by educators to make decisions about the placement of students into special educational programs, both for those with disabilities and for those with exceptionalities. Many children are given this test in the second grade, or age 7 or 8. The SB5 yields an overall estimate of intelligence, verbal and nonverbal domain scores, all comprised of five primary areas of cognitive ability—fluid reasoning, knowledge, quantitative processing, visual–spatial processing, and working memory (Roid, 2003). See Table 7.4 for descriptions of some items similar to those from the SB5.

Table 7.4

Paraphrased Sample Items from the Stanford-Binet Intelligence Test

AGE*	TYPE OF ITEM	PARAPHRASED SAMPLE ITEM
2	Board with three differently shaped holes	Child can place correct shape into matching hole on board.
4	Building block bridge	Child can build a simple bridge out of blocks after being shown a model.
7	Similarities	Child can answer such questions as "In what way are a ship and a car alike?"
9	Digit reversal	Child can repeat four digits backwards.
Average adult	Vocabulary	Child can define 20 words from a list.

*Age at which item typically is successfully completed.

Source: Roid, G. H. (2003).

THE WECHSLER TESTS Although the original Stanford-Binet Test is now in its fifth edition and includes different questions for people of different age groups, it is not the only IQ test that is popular today. David Wechsler (Wechsler, 2002, 2003, 2008) was the first to devise a series of tests designed for specific age groups. Originally dissatisfied with the fact that the Stanford-Binet was designed for children but being administered to adults, he developed an IQ test specifically for adults. He later designed tests specifically for older school-age children and preschool children, as well as those in the early grades. The Wechlser Adult Intelligence Scale (WAIS-IV), Wechsler Intelligence Scale for Children (WISC-IV), and the Wechsler Preschool and Primary Scale of Intelligence (WPPSI-III) are the three versions of this test, and in the United States these tests are now used more frequently than the Stanford-Binet. In earlier editions, another way these tests differed from the Stanford-Binet was by having both a verbal and performance (nonverbal) scale, as well as providing an overall score of intelligence (the original Stanford-Binet was composed predominantly of verbal items). While still using both verbal and nonverbal items, the WISC-IV and WAIS-IV organizes items into four index scales, that provide an overall score of intelligence and index scores related to four specific cognitive domains—verbal comprehension, perceptual reasoning, working memory, and processing speed. Table 7.5 has sample items for each of the four index scales from the WAIS-IV.

Table 7.5

Simulated Sample Items From the Wechsler Adult Intelligence Scale (WAIS-IV)

	SIMULATED SAMPLE TEST ITEMS
Verbal Comprehension Index	
Similarities	In what way are a circle and a triangle alike? In what way are a saw and a hammer alike?
Vocabulary	What is a hippopotamus? What does "resemble" mean?
Information	What is steam made of? What is pepper? Who wrote *Tom Sawyer*?
Perceptual Reasoning Index	
Block Design	After looking at a pattern or design, try to arrange small cubes in the same pattern.
Matrix Reasoning	After looking at an incomplete matrix pattern or series, select an option that completes the matrix or series.
Visual Puzzles	Look at a completed puzzle and select three components from a set of options that would re-create the puzzle, all within a specified time limit.
Working Memory Index	
Digit Span	Recall lists of numbers, some lists forward and some lists in reverse order, and recall a mixed list of numbers in correct ascending order.
Arithmetic	Three women divided 18 golf balls equally among themselves. How many golf balls did each person receive? If two buttons cost $.15, what will be the cost of a dozen buttons?
Processing Speed Index	
Symbol Search	Visually scan a group of symbols to identify specific target symbols, within a specified time limit.
Coding	Learn a different symbol for specific numbers and then fill in the blank under the number with the correct symbol. (This test is timed.)

Simulated items and descriptions similar to those in the *Wechsler Adult Intelligence Scale—Fourth Edition* (2008).

reliability the tendency of a test to produce the same scores again and again each time it is given to the same people.

validity the degree to which a test actually measures what it's supposed to measure.

TEST CONSTRUCTION: GOOD TEST, BAD TEST? All tests are not equally good tests. Some tests may fail to give the same results on different occasions for the same person when that person has not changed—making the test useless. These would be considered unreliable tests. **Reliability** of a test refers to the test producing consistent results each time it is given to the same individual or group of people. For example, if Nicholas takes a personality test today and then again in a month or so, the results should be very similar if the personality test is reliable. Other tests might be easy to use and even reliable, but if they don't actually measure what they are supposed to measure, they are also useless. These tests are thought of as "invalid" (untrue) tests. **Validity** is the degree to which a test actually measures what it's supposed to measure. Another aspect of validity is the extent that an obtained score accurately reflects the intended skill or outcome in real-life situations, or *ecological validity*, not just validity for the testing or assessment situation. For example, we hope that someone who passes his or her test for a driver's license will also be able to safely operate a motor vehicle when they are actually on the road. When evaluating a test, consider what a specific test score means and to what, or to whom, it is compared.

Take the hypothetical example of Professor Stumpwater, who—for reasons best known only to him—believes that intelligence is related to a person's golf scores. Let's say that he develops an adult intelligence test based on golf scores. What do we need to look at to determine if his test is a good one?

Standardization of Tests First of all, we would want to look at how he tried to standardize his test. *Standardization* refers to the process of giving the test to a large group of people that represents the kind of people for whom the test is designed. One aspect of standardization is in the establishment of consistent and standard methods of test administration. All test subjects would take the test under the same conditions. In the professor's case, this would mean that he would have his sample members to play the same number of rounds of golf on the same course under the same weather conditions, and so on. Another aspect addresses the comparison group whose scores will be used to compare individual tests results. Standardization groups are chosen randomly from the population for whom the test is intended and, like all samples, must be representative of that population. LINK to Appendix A: Statistics. If a test is designed for children, for example, then a large sample of randomly selected children would be given the test.

Norms The scores from the standardization group would be called the *norms*, the standards against which all others who take the test would be compared. Most tests of intelligence follow a *normal curve*, or a distribution in which the scores are the most frequent around the *mean*, or average, and become less and less frequent the further from the mean they occur (see Figure 7.4). LINK to Appendix A: Statistics.

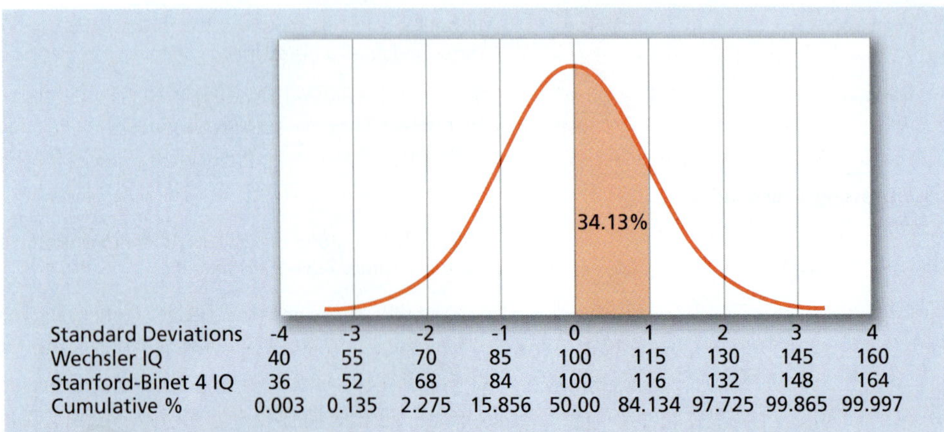

Figure 7.4 The Normal Curve

The percentages under each section of the normal curve represent the percentage of scores falling within that section for each *standard deviation (SD)* from the mean. Scores on intelligence tests are typically represented by the normal curve. The dotted vertical lines each represent one standard deviation from the mean, which is always set at 100. For example, an IQ of 115 on the Wechsler represents one standard deviation above the mean, and the area under the curve indicates that 34.13 percent of the population falls between 100 and 115 on this test. LINK to Appendix A: Statistics. Note: The figure shows the mean and standard deviation for the Stanford-Binet Fourth Edition (Stanford-Binet 4). The Stanford-Binet Fifth Edition was published in 2003 and now has a mean of 100 and a standard deviation of 15 for composite scores.

On the Wechsler IQ test, the percentages under each section of the normal curve represent the percentage of scores falling within that section for each *standard deviation (SD)* from the mean on the test. The standard deviation is the average variation of scores from the mean. LINK to Appendix A: Statistics.

In the case of the professor's golf test, he might find that a certain golf score is the average, which he would interpret as average intelligence. People who scored extremely well on the golf test would be compared to the average, as well as people with unusually poor scores.

The normal curve allows IQ scores to be more accurately estimated. The old IQ scoring method using the simple formula devised by Stern produces raw ratio IQ scores that start to become meaningless as the person's chronological age passes 16 years. (Once a person becomes an adult, the idea of questions that are geared for a particular age group loses its power. For example, what kind of differences would there be between questions designed for a 30-year-old versus a 40-year-old?) Test designers replaced the old ratio IQ of the earlier versions of IQ tests with **deviation IQ scores**, which are based on the normal curve distribution (Eysenck, 1994): IQ is assumed to be normally distributed with a mean IQ of 100 and a typical standard deviation of about 15 (the standard deviation can vary according to the particular test). An IQ of 130, for example, would be two standard deviations above the mean, whereas an IQ of 70 would be two standard deviations below the mean, and in each case the person's score is being compared to the population's average score. Simulate on mypsychlab.com

Simulate using the normal curve on **mypsychlab.com**

With respect to validity and reliability, the professor's test fares poorly. If the results of the professor's test were compared with other established intelligence tests, there would probably be no relationship at all. Golf scores have nothing to do with intelligence, so the test is not a valid, or true, measure of intelligence.

On the other hand, his test might work well for some people and poorly for others on the question of reliability. Some people who are good and regular golfers tend to score about the same for each game that they play, so for them, the golf score IQ would be fairly reliable. But others, especially those who do not play golf or play infrequently, would have widely varying scores from game to game. For those people, the test would be very unreliable, and if a test is unreliable for some, it's not a good test.

A test can fail in validity but still be reliable. If for some reason Professor Stumpwater chose to use height as a measure of intelligence, an adult's score on Stumpwater's "test" would always be the same, as height does not change by very much after the late teens. But the opposite is not true. If a test is unreliable, how can it accurately measure what it is supposed to measure? For example, adult intelligence remains fairly constant. If a test meant to measure that intelligence gave different scores at different times, it's obviously not a valid measure of intelligence.

Just because an IQ test gives the same score every time a person takes it doesn't mean that the score is actually measuring real intelligence, right?

Just because an IQ test gives the same score every time a person takes it doesn't mean that the score is actually measuring real intelligence, right?

That's right—think about the definition of intelligence for a moment: the ability to learn from one's experiences, acquire knowledge, and use resources effectively in adapting to new situations or solving problems. How can anyone define what "effective use of resources" might be? Does everyone have access to the same resources? Is everyone's "world" necessarily perceived as being the same? Intelligence tests are useful measuring devices but should not necessarily be assumed to be measures of all types of intelligent behavior, or even good measures for all groups of people, as the next section discusses.

IQ TESTS AND CULTURAL BIAS The problem with trying to measure intelligence with a test that is based on an understanding of the world and its resources is that not everyone comes from the same "world." People raised in a different culture, or even a

deviation IQ scores a type of intelligence measure that assumes that IQ is normally distributed around a mean of 100 with a standard deviation of about 15.

How might these two women, apparently from different cultures, come to an agreement on what best defines intelligence?

different economic situation, from the one in which the designer of an IQ test is raised are not likely to perform well on such a test—not to mention the difficulties of taking a test that is written in an unfamiliar language or dialect. In the early days of immigration, people from non-English-speaking countries would score very poorly on intelligence tests, in some cases being denied entry to the United States on the basis of such tests (Allen, 2006).

It is very difficult to design an intelligence test that is completely free of *cultural bias*, a term referring to the tendency of IQ tests to reflect, in language, dialect, and content, the culture of the person or persons who designed the test. A person who comes from the same culture (or even socioeconomic background) as the test designer may have an unfair advantage over a person who is from a different cultural or socioeconomic background (Helms, 1992). If people raised in an Asian culture are given a test designed within a traditional Western culture, many items on the test might make no sense to them. For example, one kind of question might be: Which one of the five is least like the other four?

DOG—CAR—CAT—BIRD—FISH

The answer is supposed to be "car," which is the only one of the five that is not alive. But a Japanese child, living in a culture that relies on the sea for so much of its food and culture, might choose "fish," because none of the others are found in the ocean. That child's test score would be lower but not because the child is not intelligent.

In 1971, Adrian Dove designed an intelligence test to highlight the problem of cultural bias. Dove, an African American sociologist, created the Dove Counterbalance General Intelligence Test (later known as the Chitling Test) in an attempt to demonstrate that a significant language/dialect barrier exists among children of different backgrounds. Look at Table 7.6 and take a sample of the test. **Watch** on **mypsychlab.com**

Watch Robert Guthrie discuss intelligence tests and cultural biases on **mypsychlab.com**

A person who is not from the African American culture of the southeastern United States will probably score very poorly on this test. African American people from different geographical regions don't always do well on this test either. The point is simply this: Tests such as these are created by people who are from a particular

Table 7.6

Sample of the Dove Counterbalance General Intelligence Test

1. A "handkerchief head" is:
   a. a cool cat,
   b. a porter,
   c. an Uncle Tom,
   d. a hoddi,
   e. a preacher.

2. Cheap chitlings (not the kind you purchase at a frozen food counter) will taste rubbery unless they are cooked long enough. How soon can you quit cooking them to eat and enjoy them?
   a. 45 minutes,
   b. 2 hours,
   c. 24 hours,
   d. 1 week (on a low flame),
   e. 1 hour.

3. What are the "Dixie Hummingbirds"?
   a. part of the KKK,
   b. a swamp disease,
   c. a modern gospel group,
   d. a Mississippi Negro paramilitary group,
   e. deacons.

4. "Money don't get everything it's true"
   a. but I don't have none and I'm so blue,
   b. but what it don't get I can't use,
   c. so make do with what you've got,
   d. but I don't know that and neither do you.

The answers are as follows:

1. c. 2. c. 3. c. 4. b.

Source: Dove, A. (1971).

culture and background. Test questions and answers that the creators might think are common knowledge may relate to their own experiences and not to people of other cultures, backgrounds, or socioeconomic levels.

Attempts have been made to create intelligence tests that are as free of cultural influences as is humanly possible. Many test designers have come to the conclusion that it may be impossible to create a test that is completely free of cultural bias (Carpenter et al., 1990). Instead, they are striving to create tests that are at least *culturally fair*. These tests use questions that do not create a disadvantage for people whose culture differs from that of the majority. Many items on a "culture-fair" test require the use of nonverbal abilities, such as rotating objects, rather than items about verbal knowledge that might be culturally specific.

If intelligence tests are so flawed, why do people still use them?

The one thing that IQ tests do well is predict academic success for those who score at the higher and lower ends of the normal curve. (For those who score in the average range of IQ, the predictive value is less clear.) The kinds of tests students are given in school are often similar to intelligence tests, and so people who do well on IQ tests typically do well on other kinds of academically oriented tests as well, such as the Scholastic Assessment Test (SAT), the American College Test (ACT), the Graduate Record Exam (GRE), and actual college examinations. These achievement tests are very similar to IQ tests but are administered to groups of people rather than to individuals.

Intelligence testing also plays an important role in neuropsychology, where specially trained psychologists use intelligence tests and other forms of cognitive and behavioral testing to assess neurobehavioral disorders in which cognition and behavior are impaired as the result of brain injury or brain malfunction (National Academy of Neuropsychology, 2001). As part of their profession, neuropsychologists use intelligence testing in diagnosis (e.g., head injury, learning disabilities, neuropsychological disorders), tracking progress of individuals with such disorders, and in monitoring possible recovery. For more on neuropsychological assessment, see the next special section. **Read** on **mypsychlab.com**

Read and learn more about intelligence tests and testing on **mypsychlab.com**

psychology in the news

Neuropsychology Sheds Light on Head Injuries

Many of the topics in this chapter are related to the interests of cognitive psychologists, cognitive neuroscientists, and neuropsychologists alike, but here we will expand on the work of clinical neuropsychologists (LINK to Appendix B, p. B-6), who often work with individuals who have traumatic brain injury (TBI). Unlike a broken limb or other bodily injury that might result in a temporary loss of function, many traumatic brain injuries not only have immediate effects but can also be permanent, impacting the day-to-day functioning of both individuals and their loved ones for the rest of their lives. Depending on the area or areas of the brain injured and the severity of the trauma, some possible outcomes might include difficulty thinking, speech disturbances, memory problems, reduced attention span, headaches, sleep disturbances, frustration, mood swings, and personality changes. Not only do these outcomes negatively impact formal tests of intelligence, the deficits from such injuries may also affect thinking, problem solving, and cognition in general.

Mild traumatic brain injury, or concussion, is an impairment of brain function for minutes to hours following a head injury. Concussions may include a loss of consciousness for up to 30 minutes, "seeing stars," headache, dizziness, and sometimes nausea or vomiting (Blumenfeld, 2002; Ruff et al., 2009). Amnesia for the events immediately before or after the accident is also a primary symptom and more likely to be anterograde in nature.

LINK to Chapter Six: Memory, p. 224. With regard to concussions and other levels of traumatic brain injury, athletes and military personnel have been of particular interest to neuropsychologists, as they have been a vehicle for new findings about different types of injuries and the effects of repeated injury, on long-term outcomes.

Athletics In high school athletes, concussions account for approximately 9 percent of all high school sports-related injuries; a recent survey of 15 college-level sports over a 16-year period found the rate of concussions has increased significantly (Gessel et al., 2007; Hootman et al., 2007). Cheerleading also has its share of head injuries as concussions are among the five most-common injuries reported in a sample of 412 cheerleading teams ranging from elementary school to college (Shields & Smith, 2009).

The effects of repeated concussions and the long-term effects of head injuries in general are of particular interest to neuropsychologists and other health professionals because the potential issues (memory problems, changes in personality, etc.) may not be evident until many years later. American football is one sport in which athletes may have extended playing careers. The possibility of an increased risk for depression, dementia, or other neurological risks for these athletes after they have quit playing has spawned ongoing research with professional football players (Guskiewicz et al., 2007; G. Miller, 2009). Former players who had three or more concussions were 3 times more likely to have significant memory problems and 5 times more likely to be diagnosed with mild cognitive impairment, often a precursor to Alzheimer's disease. Additional research suggests that some players develop high concentrations of the protein tau (LINK to Chapter Six: Memory, page 246), that has also been associated with Alzheimer's disease (Guskiewicz et al., 2005; McKee et al., 2009).

Military Historically, many military conflicts have been associated with a "signature wound," which is an injury that is suffered by a substantial number of veterans from that particular war. The wound may be physical or psychological in nature. For instance, "shell shock" is often associated with many veterans of World War I. For the Vietnam War, post-traumatic stress disorder is the pervasive injury that comes to mind. In the ongoing conflicts in Iraq and Afghanistan, the signature wound may be traumatic brain injury (TBI) (E. Jones et al., 2007; Okie, 2005). The degree of brain injuries being sustained range from mild to moderate to severe, and over 50 percent are considered to be moderate to severe (Okie, 2005). In some studies, more than 15 percent of soldiers returning from Iraq report experiencing a mild traumatic brain injury, most likely the result of high intensity combat or a blast mechanism (Hoge et al., 2008). Many of these blast injuries are caused by IEDs, or "improvised explosive devices." The prevalence of IEDs is currently greater in Iraq than it is in Afghanistan, with troops in Iraq being approximately 1.7 times more likely to be hospitalized with traumatic brain injury. Unfortunately, it is a trend that appears to be increasing (Wojcik et al., 2010). The pervasiveness of IEDs in Iraq has generated new areas of research with the goal of improving the lives of the injured by understanding the unique outcomes and consequences associated with this particular type of head injury as it appears to impact the brain in ways not seen in other types of head injury.

To learn more about traumatic brain injury:

National Institute of Neurological Disorders and Stroke **www.ninds.nih.gov/disorders/tbi/tbi.htm**

To learn more about blast injuries:

Centers for Disease Control and Prevention
www.bt.cdc.gov/masscasualties/explosions.asp

Questions for Further Thought

1. Do you know someone with a TBI? How has the injury affected their life?
2. Who do you think has a better chance of recovery from a TBI, a child or and adult? Why?

7.4 7.5

CONCEPT MAP

Intelligence

(the ability to learn from one's experiences, acquire knowledge, and use resources effectively)

- **theories**
  - **Spearman's g factor:** intelligence comprises two different abilities
    - **g factor:** general intelligence
    - **s factor:** specific intelligence
  - **Gardner's multiple intelligences:** overall intelligence comprises nine different types
    - (see Table 7.3)
  - **Sternberg's triarchic theory:** intelligence comprises three different aspects
    - **analytical**
    - **creative**
    - **practical**

Measuring Intelligence

- first formal test created by Alfred Binet and Theodore Simon to help identify French students who needed more help with learning
- **tests**
  - **Binet's Mental Ability Test**
    - key element to be tested was child's mental age
  - **Stanford-Binet**
    - **Terman** (researcher at Stanford) translated and revised Binet's test
    - first test to adopt intelligence quotient (IQ): IQ = mental age/chronological age × 100
      - now uses age-group comparison norms as the Wechsler does
    - uses a variety of verbal and nonverbal subtests to provide an overall estimate of intelligence and scores related to five areas of cognition (see Table 7.4)
  - **Wechsler Tests**
    - uses a variety of verbal and performance subtests to provide an overall score of intelligence and index scores related to four specific cognitive domains (see Table 7.5)
- **test construction**
  - good tests are both valid and reliable
  - standardized administration, scoring, and comparison against norms
  - intelligence is assumed to follow a normal curve
  - is challenging
    - different definitions of intelligence and multiple ways to assess them
    - difficult to design tests that are completely free of cultural bias

PRACTICE quiz How much do you remember?

ANSWERS ON PAGE AK-1.

Pick the best answer.

1. According to Spearman, a traditional IQ test would most likely measure __________.
   a. practical intelligence.
   b. specific intelligence.
   c. general intelligence.
   d. emotional intelligence.
2. In Gardner's view, astronauts, navigators, and artists would be high in __________ intelligence.
   a. verbal/linguistic
   b. visual–spatial
   c. interpersonal
   d. intrapersonal
3. Sternberg has found that __________ intelligence is a good predictor of success in life but has a low relationship to __________ intelligence.
   a. practical; academic
   b. practical; creative
   c. academic; practical
   d. academic; creative
4. Using the Stanford-Binet IQ formula, what IQ would a person have whose mental age is 10 and whose chronological age is 15?
   a. 150
   b. 1.50
   c. 0.67
   d. 67
5. Lia is 10 years old. The intelligence test that would most likely be used to determine her IQ is the __________.
   a. WAIS-IV.
   b. WISC-IV.
   c. WPPSI-III.
   d. Dove Test.
6. Professor Beckett designed an IQ test. To standardize this test, the professor should be careful to do which of the following?
   a. Use only a small sample to prevent possible cheating on the test.
   b. Select the people in the sample from the population of people for whom the test is designed.
   c. Select only university professors to take the test so that they can critique the questions on the test.
   d. Test each member of the sample under different conditions.
7. __________ would be the problem in a test that provides a consistent score for some people each time it is administered but yields different scores for other people.
   a. Reliability
   b. Validity
   c. Standardization
   d. Normalization

Brainstorming: Do you think a person's IQ can change? Why or why not?

INDIVIDUAL DIFFERENCES IN INTELLIGENCE

Another use of IQ tests is to identify people who differ from those of average intelligence by a great degree. Although one such group is composed of those who are sometimes called "geniuses" (who fall at the extreme high end of the normal curve for intelligence), the other group is made up of people who, for various reasons, are considered intellectually delayed and whose IQ scores fall well below the mean on the normal curve.

INTELLECTUAL DISABILITY

7.6 **What is intellectual disability and what are its causes?**

Intellectual disability (formerly *mental retardation*) is defined in several ways. First, the person's IQ score must fall below 70, or two standard deviations below the mean on the normal curve. Second, the person's *adaptive behavior* (skills that allow people to live independently, such as being able to work at a job, communicate well with others, and grooming skills such as being able to get dressed, eat, and bathe with little or no help) is severely below a level appropriate for the person's age. Finally, these limitations must be present before the age of 18 years. Intellectual disability occurs in about 3 percent of the population (American Psychiatric Association, 2000). Although the older term *mental retardation* is still sometimes used to refer to the condition of intellectual disability, individuals with this condition may more commonly be referred to as *developmentally delayed*, meaning that their behavioral and cognitive skills exist at an earlier developmental stage than the skills of others who are the same chronological age (Smith & Mitchell, 2001).

So how would a professional go about deciding whether or not a child has an intellectual disability? Is the IQ test the primary method?

So how would a professional go about deciding whether or not a child has an intellectual disability? Is the IQ test the primary method?

A diagnosis of intellectual disability is based not only on IQ tests scores but also on the strengths and weaknesses of the person in adaptive functioning and the onset of impairments in intellectual functioning and adaptive behavior is before 18 years of age (American Psychiatric Association, 2000). Recent recommendations from the American Association on Intellectual and Developmental Disabilities (AAIDD) also require deficits in more than one area, that is, not only in intellectual functioning but also in adaptive behavior that may be conceptual, social, or practical in nature (AAIDD, 2009; Schalock et al., 2010).

Classifications Intellectual disability can vary from mild to extremely severe. Even with their flaws, IQ test scores are still used to classify the various levels of delay, as can be seen in Table 7.7.

Causes What causes intellectual disability? Unhealthy living conditions can affect brain development. Examples of such conditions are lead poisoning from eating paint chips (Lanphear et al., 2000), exposure to PCBs (Darvill et al., 2000), prenatal exposure to mercury (Grandjean et al., 1997), as well as other toxicants (Ericksson et al., 2001; Eskenazi et al., 1999; Schroeder, 2000), poor nutrition resulting in inadequate development of the brain, or a lack of mental stimulation in one's surroundings during the formative years of infancy and childhood (Shah, 1991). Such environmental conditions are said to produce *familial retardation* (Schroeder, 2000), a delay related to living in poverty conditions and one that usually produces relatively mild intellectual disability.

The three most common biological causes of intellectual disability are Down syndrome (LINK to Chapter Eight: Development Across the Life Span, p. 302), fetal alcohol syndrome, and fragile X syndrome. *Fetal alcohol syndrome* is a condition that results from exposing a developing embryo to alcohol, and intelligence levels can

intellectual disability condition in which a person's behavioral and cognitive skills exist at an earlier developmental stage than the skills of others who are the same chronological age; may also be referred to as developmentally delayed. This condition was formerly known as mental retardation.

Table 7.7

Classifications of Intellectual Disability

CLASSIFICATION	RANGE OF IQ SCORES	ADAPTIVE LIMITATIONS	PERCENTAGE OF INTELLECTUALLY DISABLED POPULATION
Mild	55–70	Can reach 6th-grade skill level. Capable, with training, of living independently and being self-supporting. (This category makes up the vast majority of those with intellectual disabilities.)	90%
Moderate	40–55	Can reach 2nd-grade skill level. Can work and live in sheltered environments with supervision.	6%
Severe	25–40	Can learn to talk and perform basic self-care but needs constant supervision.	3%
Profound	Below 25	Very limited ability to learn, may only be able to learn very simple tasks; poor language skills and limited self-care.	1%

Source: Table based on classifications of mental retardation in *DSM-IV-TR* (American Psychiatric Association, 2000).

range from below average to levels associated with intellectual disability (Olson & Burgess, 1997). In *fragile X syndrome*, a male has a defect in a gene on the X chromosome of the 23rd pair, leading to a deficiency in a protein needed for brain development. Depending on the severity of the damage to this gene, symptoms of fragile X syndrome can range from mild to severe or profound intellectual disability (Dykens et al., 1994; Valverde et al., 2007).

There are many other causes of intellectual disability (Murphy et al., 1998). Lack of oxygen at birth, damage to the fetus in the womb from diseases, infections, or drug use by the mother, and even diseases and accidents during childhood can lead to intellectual disability.

One thing should always be remembered: Intellectual disability affects a person's intellectual capabilities and adaptive behaviors. Individuals with an intellectual disability are just as responsive to love and affection as anyone else and need to be loved and to have friends just as all people do. Intelligence is only one characteristic; warmth, friendliness, caring, and compassion also count for a great deal and should not be underrated.

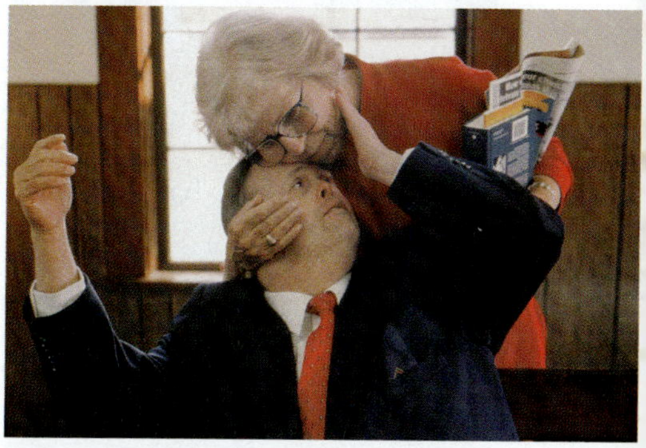

This middle-aged man, named Jack, lives in a small town in Arkansas and serves as a deacon in the local church. He is loved and respected and leads what, for him, is a full and happy life. Jack also has Down syndrome but he has managed to find his place in the world.

GIFTEDNESS

7.7 What defines giftedness, and does being intellectually gifted guarantee success in life?

At the other end of the intelligence scale* are those who fall on the upper end of the normal curve (see Figure 7.4, p. 270) above an IQ of 130 (about 2 percent of the population). The term applied to these individuals is **gifted**, and if their IQ falls above 140 to 145 (less than half of 1 percent of the population), they are often referred to as highly advanced or *geniuses*.

gifted the 2 percent of the population falling on the upper end of the normal curve and typically possessing an IQ of 130 or above.

*scale: a graded series of tests or performances used in rating individual intelligence or achievement.

I've heard that geniuses are sometimes a little "nutty" and odd. Are geniuses, especially the really high-IQ ones, "not playing with a full deck," as the saying goes?

I've heard that geniuses are sometimes a little "nutty" and odd. Are geniuses, especially the really high-IQ ones, "not playing with a full deck," as the saying goes?

People have long held many false beliefs about people who are very, very intelligent. One common phrase around the turn of the twentieth century was "early ripe, early rot," which meant that people expected young geniuses to lose their genius early in life (Shurkin, 1992). Other beliefs were that gifted people are weird and socially awkward, physically weak, and more likely to suffer from mental illnesses. From these beliefs comes the "mad scientist" of the cinema (think "Dr. Evil" of *Austin Powers*) and the "evil geniuses" of literature—Dr. Frankenstein, Dr. Jekyll, and Superman's archenemy,* Lex Luthor, to name a few.

Stanford University psychologist Lewis Terman is pictured at his desk in 1942. Terman spent a good portion of his career researching children with high IQ scores and was the first to use the term *gifted* to describe these children.

These beliefs were shattered by a groundbreaking study that was initiated in 1921 by Lewis M. Terman, the same individual responsible for the development of the Stanford-Binet (page 268). Terman (1925) selected 1,528 children to participate in a longitudinal study. LINK to Chapter Eight: Development Across the Life Span, p. 298. These children, 857 boys and 671 girls, had IQs (as measured by the Stanford-Binet) ranging from 130 to 200. The early findings of this major study (Terman & Oden, 1947) demonstrated that the gifted were socially well adjusted and often skilled leaders. They were also above average in height, weight, and physical attractiveness, putting an end to the myth of the weakling genius. Terman was able to demonstrate not only that his gifted children were *not* more susceptible to mental illness than the general population, but he was also able to show that they were actually more resistant to mental illnesses than these of average intelligence. Only those with the highest IQs (180 and above) were found to have some social and behavioral adjustment problems *as children* (Janos, 1987).

Terman's "Termites," as they came to be called, were also typically successful as adults. They earned more academic degrees and had higher occupational and financial success than their average peers (at least, the men in the study had occupational success—women at this time did not typically have careers outside the home). Researchers Zuo and Cramond (2001) examined some of Terman's gifted people to see if their identity formation as adolescents was related to later occupational success. LINK to Chapter Eight: Development Across the Life Span, pp. 327–328. They found that most of the more successful "Termites" had in fact successfully achieved a consistent sense of self, whereas those who were less successful had not done so. For more on Terman's famous study, see Classic Studies in Psychology.

*archenemy: a main enemy; the most important enemy.

classic studies in psychology

Terman's "Termites"

Terman's (1925) longitudinal study is still going on today, although many of his original subjects have passed away and those who remain are in their 90s. Terman himself died in 1956, but several other researchers (including Robert Sears, one of the original "Termites") have kept track of the remaining "Termites" over the years (Holahan & Sears, 1996).

As adults, the "Termites" were relatively successful, with a median income in the 1950s of $10,556, compared to the national median at that time of $5,800 a year. Most of them graduated from college, many earning advanced degrees. Their occupations included doctors, lawyers, business executives, university professors, scientists, and even one famous science fiction writer and an Oscar-winning director (Edward Dmytryk, director of *The Caine Mutiny* in 1954, among others).

By 2000, only about 200 "Termites" were still living. Although the study was marred by several flaws, it still remains one of the most important and rich sources of data on an entire generation. Terman's study was actually the first truly longitudinal study (LINK to Chapter Eight: Development Across the Life Span, p. 298) ever to be accomplished, and scientists have gotten data about the effects of phenomena such as World War II and the influence of personality traits on how long one lives from the questionnaires filled out by the participants over the years.

Terman and Oden (1959) compared the 100 most successful men in the group to the 100 least successful by defining "successful" as holding jobs that related to or used their intellectual skills. The more successful men earned more money, had careers with more prestige, and were healthier and less likely to be divorced or alcoholics than the less successful men. The IQ scores were relatively equal between the two groups, so the differences in success in life had to be caused by some other factor or factors. Terman and Oden found that the successful adults were different from the others in three ways: They were more goal oriented, more persistent in pursuing those goals, and were more self-confident than the less successful "Termites."

What were the flaws in this study? Terman acquired his participants by getting recommendations from teachers and principals, not through random selection, so that there was room for bias in the pool of participants from the start. It is quite possible that the teachers and principals were less likely, especially in 1921, to recommend students who were "troublemakers" or different from the majority. Consequently, Terman's original group consisted of almost entirely White, urban, and middle-class children, with the majority (857 out of 1,528) being male. There were only 2 African Americans, 6 Japanese Americans, and 1 Native American.

Another flaw is the way Terman interfered in the lives of his "children." In any good research study, the investigator should avoid becoming personally involved in the lives of the participants in the study to reduce the possibility of biasing the results. Terman seemed to find it nearly impossible to remain objective (Leslie, 2000). He became like a surrogate father to many of them, even going so far as to write a letter urging authorities to give Edward Dmytryk every consideration as they tried to determine whether 14-year-old runaway Edward was indeed being abused by his father or just telling a tall tale. Terman's letter did the trick, and Edward went to a good foster home and grew up to become a famous Hollywood director of 23 films. In another incident, one of Terman's Japanese American participants and family were in danger of being sent to an internment camp (essentially a prison camp) during World War II. They wrote to Terman and he again wrote a letter, this time to the government, vouching for the family's loyalty and arguing that they should not be interned. They were not interned. These are just two of the many ways in which Terman not only observed his participants but also influenced the course of their lives above and beyond their own intelligence levels.

Flawed as it may have been, Terman's groundbreaking study did accomplish his original goal of putting to rest the myths that existed about genius in the early part of the twentieth century. Gifted children and adults are no more prone to mental illnesses or odd behavior than any other group, and they also have their share of failures as well as successes. Genius is obviously not the only factor that influences success in life—personality and experiences are strong factors as well. For example, the homes of the children in the top 2 percent of Terman's group had an average of 450 books in their libraries, a sign that the parents of these children valued books and learning, and these parents were also more likely to be teachers, professionals, doctors, and lawyers. The experiences of these gifted children growing up would have been vastly different from those in homes with less emphasis on reading and lower occupational levels for the parents.

Questions for Further Discussion

1. In Terman and Oden's 1959 study of the successful and unsuccessful "Termites," what might be the problems associated with the definition of "successful" in the study?
2. Thinking back to the discussion of research ethics in Chapter One (pages 33–35), what ethical violations may Terman have committed while involved in this study?
3. If gifted children thrive when growing up in more economically sound and educationally focused environments, what should the educational system strive to do to nourish the gifted? Should the government get involved in programs for the gifted?

A book by Joan Freeman called *Gifted Children Grown Up* (Freeman, 2001) describes the results of a similar longitudinal study of 210 gifted and nongifted children in Great Britain. One of the more interesting findings from this study is that gifted children who are "pushed" to achieve at younger and younger ages, sitting for exams long before their peers would do so, often grow up to be disappointed, somewhat unhappy adults. Freeman points to differing life conditions for the gifted as a major factor in their success, adjustment, and well-being: Some lived in poverty and some in wealth, for example. Yet another longitudinal study (Torrance, 1993) found that in both gifted students and gifted adults there is more to success in life than intelligence and high academic achievement. In that study, liking one's work, having a sense of purpose in life, a high energy level, and persistence were also very important factors. If the picture of the genius as mentally unstable is a myth, so, too, is the belief that being gifted will always lead to success, as even Terman found in his original study.

EMOTIONAL INTELLIGENCE What about people who have a lot of "book smarts" but not much common sense? There are some people like that, who never seem to get ahead in life, in spite of having all that so-called intelligence. It is true that not everyone who is intellectually able is going to be a success in life (Mehrabian, 2000). Sometimes the people who are most successful are those who didn't do all that well in the regular academic setting.

One of the early explanations for why some people who do poorly in school succeed in life and why some who do well in school don't do so well in the "real" world was that success relies on a certain degree of **emotional intelligence**, the awareness of and ability to manage one's own emotions as well as the ability to be self-motivated, to feel what others feel, and to be socially skilled (Persaud, 2001).

emotional intelligence the awareness of and ability to manage one's own emotions as well as the ability to be self-motivated, able to feel what others feel, and socially skilled.

The concept of emotional intelligence was first introduced by Salovey and Mayer (1990) and later expanded upon by Goleman (1995). Goleman proposed that emotional intelligence is a more powerful influence on success in life than more traditional views of intelligence. One who is emotionally intelligent possesses self-control of emotions such as anger, impulsiveness, and anxiety. Empathy, the ability to understand what others feel, is also a component, as are an awareness of one's own emotions, sensitivity, persistence even in the face of frustrations, and the ability to motivate oneself (Salovey & Mayer, 1990).

That all sounds very nice, but how can anything like this be measured?

That all sounds very nice, but how can anything like this be measured?

Is there research to support this idea? In one study, researchers asked 321 participants to read passages written by nonparticipants and try to guess what the nonparticipants were feeling while they were writing (Mayer & Geher, 1996). The assumption was that people who were good at connecting thoughts to feelings would also have a high degree of empathy and emotional intelligence. The participants who more correctly judged the writers' emotional experiences (assessed by both how well each participant's emotional judgments agreed with a group consensus and the nonparticipant's actual report of feelings) also scored higher on the empathy measure and lower on the defensiveness measure. These same participants also had higher SAT scores (self-reported), leading Mayer and colleagues to conclude not only that emotional intelligence is a valid and measurable concept but also that general intelligence and emotional intelligence may be related: Those who are high in emotional intelligence are also smarter in the traditional sense (Mayer et al., 2000).

Emotional intelligence includes empathy, which is the ability to feel what others are feeling. This doctor is not only able to listen to her patient's problems but also is able to show by her facial expression, body language, and gestures that she understands how the patient feels.

Although his own work and that of his colleagues provide empirical support for the concept of emotional intelligence, Mayer (1999) has criticized the presentation of emotional intelligence in popular magazines and best-selling (but nonscientific) books by stating in an online article for the American Psychological Association,

> *. . . the popular literature's implication—that highly emotionally intelligent people possess an unqualified advantage in life—appears overly enthusiastic at present and unsubstantiated by reasonable scientific standards.*

THE NATURE/NURTURE CONTROVERSY REGARDING INTELLIGENCE: GENETIC INFLUENCES

7.8 What is the influence of heredity and environment on the development of intelligence?

Are people born with all of the "smarts" they will ever have, or does experience and learning count for something in the development of intellect? The influence of nature (heredity or genes) and nurture (environment) on personality traits has long been debated in the field of human development, and intelligence is one of the traits that has been examined closely. LINK to Chapter Eight: Development Across the Life Span, p. 299.

TWIN STUDIES The problem with trying to separate the role of genes from that of environment is that controlled, perfect experiments are neither practical nor ethical. Instead, researchers find out what they can from *natural experiments*, circumstances existing in nature that can be examined to understand some phenomenon. *Twin studies* are an example of such circumstances.

Identical twins are those who originally came from one fertilized egg and, therefore, share the same genetic inheritance. Any differences between them on a certain trait, then, should be caused by environmental factors. Fraternal twins come from two

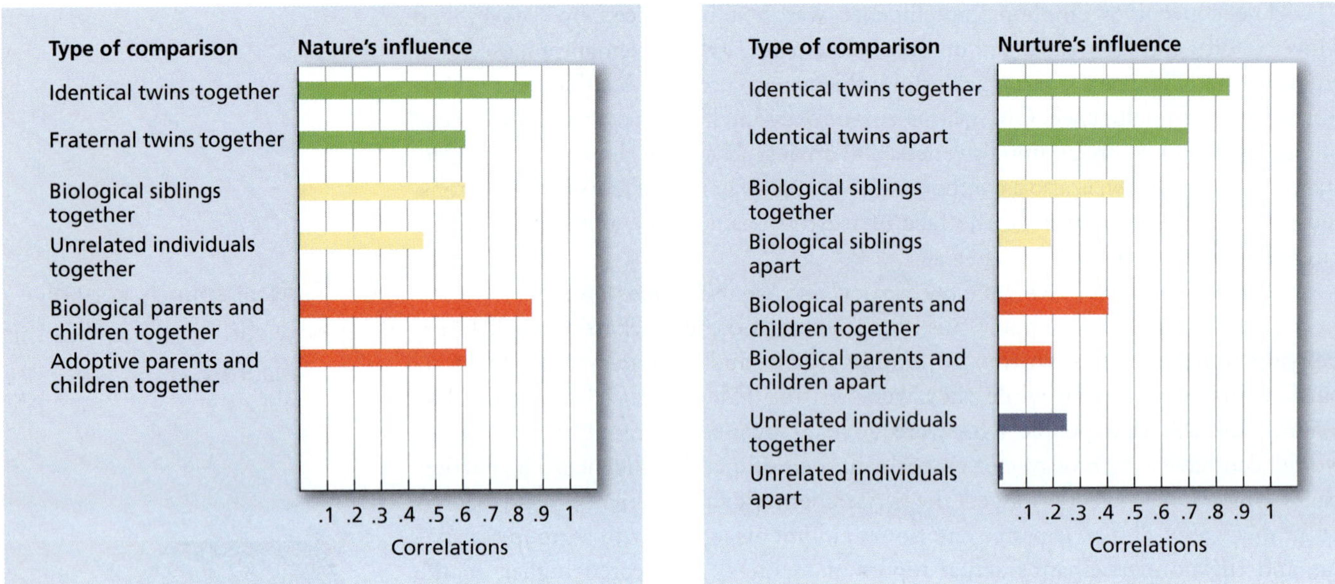

Figure 7.5 Correlations Between IQ Scores of Persons With Various Relationships

In the graph on the left, the degree of genetic relatedness seems to determine the agreement (correlation) between IQ scores of the various comparisons. For example, identical twins, who share 100 percent of their genes, are more similar in IQ than fraternal twins, who share only about 50 percent of their genes, even when raised in the same environment. In the graph on the right, identical twins are still more similar to each other in IQ than are other types of comparisons, but being raised in the same environment increases the similarity considerably.

different eggs, each fertilized by a different sperm, and share only the amount of genetic material that any two siblings would share. LINK to Chapter Eight: Development Across the Life Span, p. 304. By comparing the IQs of these two types of twins reared together (similar environments) and reared apart (different environments), as well as persons of other degrees of relatedness, researchers can get a general, if not exact, idea of how much influence heredity has over the trait of intelligence (see Figure 7.5). As can be easily seen from the chart, the greater the degree of genetic relatedness, the stronger the correlation is between the IQ scores of those persons. The fact that genetically identical twins show a correlation of 0.86 means that the environment must play a part in determining some aspects of intelligence as measured by IQ tests. If heredity alone were responsible, the correlation between genetically identical twins should be 1.00. At this time, researchers have determined that the estimated *heritability* (proportion of change in IQ within a population that is caused by hereditary factors) for intelligence is about 0.50 or 50 percent (Plomin & DeFries, 1998; Plomin & Spinath, 2004). Furthermore, the impact of genetic factors increases with increasing age, but the set of genes or genetic factors remain the same. The effects of the same set of genes becomes larger with increasing age (Posthuma et al., 2009).

Wait a minute—if identical twins have a correlation of 0.86, wouldn't that mean that intelligence is 86 percent inherited?

Wait a minute—if identical twins have a correlation of 0.86, wouldn't that mean that intelligence is 86 percent inherited?

Although the correlation between identical twins is higher than the estimated heritability of 0.50, that similarity is not entirely due to the twin's genetic similarity. Twins who are raised in the same household obviously share very similar environments as well. Even twins who are reared apart are usually placed in homes that are similar in socioeconomic and ethnic background—more similar than one might think. So when twins who are genetically similar are raised in similar environments, their IQ scores are also going to be similar. However, similar environmental influences become less important over time (where genetic influences increase over time) accounting for only about 20 percent of the variance in intelligence by age 11 or 12 (Posthuma et al., 2009). In turn, environmental influences tend not to be a factor by adolescence and with the increasing impact of genetic factors, it has been suggested that the heritability of intelligence might be as high as .91 or 91 percent by the age of 65 (Posthuma et al., 2009).

One of the things that people need to understand about heritability is that estimates of heritability apply only to changes in IQ within a *group* of people, *not to the individual people themselves*. Each individual is far too different in experiences, education, and other nongenetic factors to predict exactly how a particular set of genes will interact with those factors in that one person. Only differences among people *in general* can be investigated for the influence of genes (Dickens & Flynn, 2001). Genes always interact with environmental factors, and in some cases extreme environments can modify even very heritable traits, as would happen in the case of a severely malnourished child's growth pattern.

THE BELL CURVE AND MISINTERPRETATION OF STATISTICS One of the other factors that has been examined for possible heritable differences in performance on IQ tests is the concept of race. (The term *race* is used in most of these investigations as a way to group people with common skin colors or facial features, and one should always be mindful of how suspect that kind of classification is. Cultural background, educational experiences, and socioeconomic factors typically have far more to do with similarities in group performances than does the color of one's skin.) In 1994, Herrnstein and Murray published the controversial book *The Bell Curve*, in which they cite large amounts of statistical studies (never published in scientific journals prior to the book) that led them to make the claim that IQ is largely inherited. These authors go further by also implying that people from lower economic levels are poor because they are unintelligent.

In their book, Herrnstein and Murray made several statistical errors and ignored the effects of environment and culture. First, they assumed that IQ tests actually do measure intelligence. As discussed earlier, IQ tests are not free of cultural or socioeconomic bias. So all they really found was a correlation between race and *IQ*, not race and *intelligence*. Second, they assumed that intelligence itself is very heavily influenced by genetics, with a heritability factor of about 0.80. The current estimate of the heritability of intelligence is about 0.50 (Plomin & DeFries, 1998).

Herrnstein and Murray also failed to understand that heritability only applies to differences that can be found *within* a group of people as opposed to those *between* groups of people or individuals (Gould, 1981). Heritability estimates can only be made truly from a group that was exposed to a similar environment.

Although *The Bell Curve* stated that Japanese Americans are genetically superior in intelligence, the book's authors overlook the influence of cultural values. Many Japanese American parents put much time and effort into helping their children with schoolwork.

One of their findings was that Japanese Americans are at the top of the IQ ladder, a finding that they attribute to racial and genetic characteristics. They seem to ignore the cultural influence of intense focus on education and achievement by Japanese American parents (Neisser et al., 1996). Scientists (Beardsley, 1995; Kamin, 1995) have concluded that, despite the claims of *The Bell Curve*, there is no real scientific evidence for genetic differences in intelligence *between* different racial groups. A series of studies, using blood-group testing for racial grouping (different racial groups have different rates of certain blood groups, allowing a statistical estimation of ancestry), found no significant relationship between ethnicity and IQ (Neisser et al., 1996).

7.6 7.7 7.8

CONCEPT MAP

Intelligence

- **individual differences** IQ tests can be used to identify individuals who differ significantly from those of average intelligence
  - **giftedness**
    - **criteria**
      - IQ > 130 (2 SD above mean)
      - IQ > 140 are called geniuses
    - **characteristics**
      - typically grow up to be well-adjusted adults EXCEPT when "pushed" to achieve at younger and younger ages
      - extreme geniuses may experience social and behavioral adjustment issues as children
  - **intellectual disability/developmental delay**
    - **criteria**
      - IQ < 70 (2 SD below mean)
      - adaptive skills significantly below age-appropriate level
      - limitations present before age 18
    - **classifications**
      - **mild**
      - **moderate**
      - **severe**
      - **profound**
    - **causal factors**
      - **environmental**
        - lead
        - mercury
      - **biological**
        - Down syndrome
        - fetal alcohol syndrome
        - fragile X syndrome
  - **emotional intelligence**
    - awareness of and ability to manage one's own emotions, self-motivation, empathy, and social skills
    - may be related to traditional intelligence but data is still being collected
- **nature vs. nurture**
  - identical twins reared together show a correlation of .86 between their IQs — correlation is not 1.00, so environment also has to play a part
  - heritability estimates apply *within* groups of people, not *between* groups, not to individuals, and only in a general sense — current heritability estimate is about .50

PRACTICE quiz How much do you remember?

ANSWERS ON PAGE AK-1.

Pick the best answer.

1. Blake is 35 years old, but his cognitive abilities have never gone beyond the level of a second-grade child. Blake would be classified with an intellectual disability and __________ developmentally delayed.
   a. mildly
   b. moderately
   c. severely
   d. profoundly

2. A male with a defective chromosome leading to severe protein deficiency and poor brain development probably suffers from __________.
   a. Down syndrome.
   b. fetal alcohol syndrome.
   c. hydrocephaly.
   d. fragile X syndrome.

3. Elizabeth was tested while in grade school and was found to have an IQ of 134. Elizabeth's intelligence level can be labeled as __________.
   a. average.
   b. somewhat above normal.
   c. gifted.
   d. genius.

4. Which of the following statements about the successful "Termites" in the Terman and Oden (1959) study is NOT TRUE?
   a. The successful men earned more money.
   b. The successful men were more likely to be divorced.
   c. The unsuccessful men were less healthy.
   d. The unsuccessful men held jobs of lower prestige.

5. All of the following are considered errors by the authors of *The Bell Curve* EXCEPT:
   a. The authors assumed that IQ tests are good measures of intelligence.
   b. The authors found a correlation between race and IQ, not race and intelligence.
   c. The authors assumed that intelligence was heavily influenced by genetics.
   d. The authors assumed that heritability applied only to differences within groups of people.

Language

7.9 How is language defined, and what are its different elements and structure?

Language is a system for combining symbols (such as words) so that an infinite* number of meaningful statements can be made for the purpose of communicating with others. Language allows people not only to communicate with one another but also to represent their own internal mental activity. In other words, language is a very important part of how people think.

THE LEVELS OF LANGUAGE ANALYSIS

The structures of languages all over the world share common characteristics. Languages involve word order, word meanings, the rules for making words into other words, the sounds that exist within a language, the rules for practical communication with others, and the meanings of sentences and phrases.

GRAMMAR **Grammar** is the system of rules governing the structure and use of a language. According to famed linguist Noam Chomsky (Chomsky, 2006; Chomsky et al., 2002), humans have an innate ability to understand and produce language through a device he calls the *language acquisition device,* or *LAD.* While humans may learn the *specific* language (English, Spanish, Mandarin, etc.) through the processes of imitation, reinforcement, and shaping, LINK to Chapter Five: Learning, p. 192, the complexities of the grammar of a language are, according to Chomsky, to some degree "wired in" to the developing brain. The LAD "listens" to the language input of the infant's world and then begins to produce language sounds and eventually words and sentences in a pattern found across cultures. This pattern is discussed in greater detail in the next chapter. LINK to Chapter Eight: Development Across the Life Span, pp. 316–317. Grammar includes rules for the order of words known as syntax, morphology (the study of the formation of words), phonemes (the basic sounds of language), and pragmatics (the practical social expectations and uses of language).

SYNTAX **Syntax** is a system of rules for combining words and phrases to form grammatically correct sentences. Syntax is quite important, as just a simple mix-up can cause sentences to be completely misunderstood. For example, "John kidnapped the boy" has a different meaning from "John, the kidnapped boy," although all four words are the same (Lasnik, 1990). Another example of the importance of syntax can be found in the lobby of a Moscow hotel across from a monastery: "You are welcome to visit the cemetery where famous composers, artists, and writers are buried daily except Thursday." So if people want to watch famous composers, artists, and writers being buried, they should not go to this monastery on Thursday.

MORPHEMES **Morphemes** are the smallest units of meaning within a language. For example, the word *playing* consists of two morphemes, *play* and *ing*. Morphemes themselves are governed by **semantics**, rules for determining the meaning of words and sentences. Sentences, for example, can have the same semantic meaning while having different syntax: "Johnny hit the ball" and "the ball was hit by Johnny."

PHONEMES **Phonemes** are the basic units of sound in a language. The *a* in the word *car* is a very different phoneme from the *a* in the word *day*, even though it is the same letter of the alphabet. The difference is in how we say the sound of the *a* in each word. Phonemes are more than just the different ways in which we pronounce single letters,

*infinite: unlimited, without end.

language a system for combining symbols (such as words) so that an unlimited number of meaningful statements can be made for the purpose of communicating with others.

grammar the system of rules governing the structure and use of a language.

syntax the system of rules for combining words and phrases to form grammatically correct sentences.

morphemes the smallest units of meaning within a language.

semantics the rules for determining the meaning of words and sentences.

phonemes the basic units of sound in language.

Pragmatics involves the practical aspects of communicating. This young mother is talking and then pausing for the infant's response. In this way, the infant is learning about taking turns, an important aspect of language development. What kinds of games do adults play with infants that also aid the development of language?

too. *Th*, *sh*, and *au* are also phonemes. Phonemes for different languages are also different, and one of the biggest problems for people who are trying to learn another language is the inability to both hear and pronounce the phonemes of that other language. Although infants are born with the ability to recognize all phonemes (Werker & Lalonde, 1988), after about 9 months, that ability has deteriorated and the infant recognizes only the phonemes of the language to which the infant is exposed (Boyson-Bardies et al., 1989).

PRAGMATICS The **pragmatics** of language has to do with the practical aspects of communicating with others, or the social "niceties" of language. Simply put, pragmatics involves knowing things like how to take turns in a conversation, the use of gestures to emphasize a point or indicate a need for more information, and the different ways in which one speaks to different people (Yule, 1996). For example, adults speak to small children differently than they do to other adults by using simpler words. Both adults and children use higher pitched voices and many repeated phrases when talking to infants, such child-directed speech plays an important role in the development of language in children. Part of the pragmatics of language includes knowing just what rhythm and emphasis to use when communicating with others, called *intonation*. When speaking to infants, adults and children are changing the inflection when they use the higher pitch and stress certain words differently than others. Some languages, such as Japanese, are highly sensitive to intonation, meaning that changing the stress or pitch of certain words or syllables of a particular word can change its meaning entirely (Beckman & Pierrehumbert, 1986). For example, the Japanese name "Yoshiko" should be pronounced with the accent or stress on the first syllable: YO-she-koh. This pronunciation of the name means "woman-child." But if the stress is placed on the second syllable (yo-SHE-ko), the name means "woman who urinates."

THE RELATIONSHIP BETWEEN LANGUAGE AND THOUGHT

7.10 Does language influence the way people think, and are animals capable of learning language?

As with the controversy of nature versus nurture, researchers have long debated the relationship between language and thought. Does language actually influence thought, or does thinking influence language?

Two very influential developmental psychologists, Jean Piaget and Lev Vygotsky, often debated the relationship of language and thought (Duncan, 1995). Piaget (1926, 1962) theorized that concepts preceded and aided the development of language. For example, a child would have to have a concept or mental schema for "mother" before being able to learn the word "mama." In a sense, concepts become the "pegs" upon which words are "hung." Piaget also noticed that preschool children seemed to spend a great deal of time talking to themselves—even when playing with another child. Each child would be talking about something totally unrelated to the speech of the other, in a process Piaget called *collective monologue*. Piaget believed that this kind of nonsocial speech was very egocentric (from the child's point of view only, with no regard for the listener), and that as the child became more socially involved and less egocentric, these nonsocial speech patterns would reduce.

Vygotsky, however, believed almost the opposite. He theorized that language actually helped develop concepts and that language could also help the child learn to control behavior—including social behavior (Vygotsky, 1962, 1978, 1987). For Vygotsky, the word helped form the concept: Once a child had learned the word "mama," the various elements of "mama-ness"—*warm, soft, food, safety,* and so on—could come together around that word. Vygotsky also believed that the "egocentric" speech of the

pragmatics aspects of language involving the practical ways of communicating with others, or the social "niceties" of language.

preschool child was actually a way for the child to form thoughts and control actions. This "private speech" was a way for children to plan their behavior and organize actions so that their goals could be obtained. Since socializing with other children would demand much more self-control and behavioral regulation on the part of the preschool child, Vygotsky believed that private speech would actually *increase* as children became more socially active in the preschool years. This was, of course, the opposite of Piaget's assumption, and the evidence seems to bear out Vygotsky's view: Children, especially bright children, do tend to use more private speech when learning how to socialize with other children or when working on a difficult task (Berk, 1992; Berk & Spuhl, 1995; Bivens & Berk, 1990).

LINGUISTIC RELATIVITY HYPOTHESIS The hypothesis that language shapes and influences thoughts was accepted by many theorists, with a few notable exceptions, such as Piaget. One of the best-known versions of this view is the Sapir-Whorf hypothesis (named for the two theorists who developed it, Edward Sapir and his student, Benjamin Lee Whorf). This hypothesis assumes that the thought processes and concepts within any culture are determined by the words of the culture (Sapir, 1921; Whorf, 1956). It has come to be known as the **linguistic relativity hypothesis**, meaning that thought processes and concepts are controlled by (relative to) language. That is, the words people use determine much of the way in which they think about the world around them.

One of the most famous examples used by Whorf to support this idea was that of the Inuits, Native Americans living in the Arctic. Supposedly, the Inuits have many more words for *snow* than do people in other cultures. One estimate was 23 different words, whereas other estimates have ranged in the hundreds. Unfortunately, this anecdotal evidence has turned out to be false, being more myth than reality (Pullum, 1991). In fact, English speakers also have many different words for snow (sleet, slush, powder, dusting, and yellow, to name a few).

Is there evidence for the linguistic relativity hypothesis? Neither Sapir nor Whorf provided any scientific studies that would support their proposition. There have been numerous studies by other researchers, however. For example, in one study researchers assumed that a language's color names would influence the ability of the people who grew up with that language to distinguish among and perceive colors. The study found that basic color terms did directly influence color recognition memory (Lucy & Shweder, 1979). But an earlier series of studies of the perception of colors (Rosch-Heider, 1972; Rosch-Heider & Olivier, 1972) had already found just the opposite effect: Members of the Dani tribe, who have only two names for colors, were no different in their ability to perceive all of the colors than were the English speakers in the study. More recent studies (Davies et al., 1998a, 1998b; Laws et al., 1995; Pinker & Bloom, 1990) support Rosch-Heider's findings and the idea of a **cognitive universalism** (concepts are universal and influence the development of language) rather than linguistic relativity.

Other research suggests that although the linguistic relativity hypothesis may not work for fine perceptual discriminations such as those in the Rosch-Heider studies, it may be an appropriate explanation for concepts of a higher level. In one study, researchers showed pictures of two animals to preschool children (Gelman & Markman, 1986). The pictures were of a flamingo and a bat. The children were told that the flamingo feeds its baby mashed-up food but the bat feeds its baby milk. Then they were shown a picture of a blackbird (which looked more like the bat than the flamingo). Half of the children were told that the blackbird was a bird, while the other children were not. When asked how the blackbird fed its baby, the children who had been given the bird label were more likely to say that it fed its baby mashed-up food than were the children who were not given the label, indicating that the preschoolers were making inferences about feeding habits based on category membership rather

linguistic relativity hypothesis the theory that thought processes and concepts are controlled by language.

cognitive universalism theory that concepts are universal and influence the development of language.

than perceptual similarity—the word *bird* helped the children who were given that label to place the blackbird in its proper higher level category.

Research continues in the investigation of relationships between language and thought, and appears to support linguistic relativity and how language can shape our thoughts about space, time, colors, and objects (Boroditsky, 2001, 2009). However, researchers do not always agree, and for some studies that offer support, there are others that reinterpret the data, fail to replicate, or offer critiques of the original studies so findings are sometimes still in question (J. Y. Chen, 2007; January & Kako, 2007).

Psychologists cannot deny the influence of language on problem solving, cognition, and memory. Sometimes a problem can simply be worded differently to have the solution become obvious, and memory (LINK to Chapter Six: Memory, pp. 226–227) is certainly stored in terms of the semantics of language. Language can definitely influence the perception of others as well—"computer geek" and "software engineer" might be used to describe the same person, but one phrase is obviously less flattering and the image brought to mind is different for the two terms. In the end, trying to determine whether language influences thoughts or thoughts influence language may be like trying to determine which came first, the chicken or the egg.

ANIMAL STUDIES IN LANGUAGE

I've heard that chimpanzees can be taught to use sign language. Is this for real, or are the chimps just performing tricks like the animals in the circus or the zoo?

I've heard that chimpanzees can be taught to use sign language. Is this for real, or are the chimps just performing tricks like the animals in the circus or the zoo?

There are really two questions about animals and language. The first is "can animals communicate?" and the second is "can animals use language?" The answer to the first question is a definite "yes." Animals communicate in many ways. They use sounds such as the rattle of a rattlesnake or the warning growl of an angry dog. There are also physical behaviors, such as the "dance" of honeybees that tells the other bees where a source of pollen is (Gould & Gould, 1994). But the answer to the second question is more complicated, because language is defined as the use of symbols, and symbols are things that stand for something else. Words are symbols, and gestures can be symbols. But the gestures used by animals are instinctual, meaning they are controlled by the animal's genetic makeup. The honeybee doing the "dance" is controlled completely by instinct, as is the growling dog. In human language, symbols are used quite deliberately and voluntarily, not by instinct, and abstract symbols have no meaning until people assign meaning to them. (Although Chomsky's innate language acquisition device might lead some to think that language for humans is instinctual, it should be noted that the infant's production of speech sounds becomes quite deliberate within a short period of time.)

Kanzi looks at the keyboard used in teaching language to chimpanzees. Kanzi's language abilities were learned through watching researchers train his mother rather than directly—much as a human infant learns through listening to the speech of adults.

Can animals be taught to use symbols that are abstract? There have been attempts to teach animals (primates and dolphins) how to use sign language (as animals lack the vocal structure to form spoken words), but many of these attempts were simply not "good science." The most successful of these experiments (which is not without its critics as well) has been with Kanzi, a bonobo chimpanzee trained to press abstract symbols on a computer keyboard (Savage-Rumbaugh & Lewin, 1994). Kanzi actually was not the original subject of the study—his mother, Matata, was the chimp being trained. She did not learn many of the symbols, but Kanzi watched his mother use the keyboard and appeared to learn how to use the symbols through that observation. At last count, Kanzi could understand about 150 spoken English words. Trainers who speak to him are not in his view, so he is not responding to physical cues or symbols. He has managed to follow correctly complex instructions up to the level of a 2-year-old child (Savage-Rumbaugh et al., 1998). The most recent studies with Kanzi have him making sounds that seem to have consistent meaning across different situations (Tagliatatela et al., 2003). Nearly 100 videotaped hours of Kanzi engaged in day-to-day activities were analyzed for these sounds. The researchers were able to identify four sounds that seemed to represent banana, grapes, juice, and the word *yes*. (However, remember that four sounds do not come close to making an entire language.)

Other studies, with dolphins (Herman et al., 1993) and with parrots such as Alex in the opening story (Pepperberg, 1998, 2007), have also met with some success. Is it real language? The answer seems to be a qualified "yes." The qualification is that none of the animals that have achieved success so far can compare to the level of language development of a 3-year-old human child (Pinker, 1995). However, linguists still debate whether these animals are truly learning language if they are not also learning how to use syntax—combining words into grammatically correct sentences as well as being able to understand the differences between sentences such as "The girl kissed the boy" and "The boy kissed the girl." As yet, there is no conclusive evidence that any of the animals trained in language have been able to master syntax (Demers, 1988; Johnson, 1995; Pinker, 1995). **Read** on **mypsychlab.com**

Read and learn more about animal studies and language on **mypsychlab.com**

7.9 7.10

CONCEPT MAP

Language

- **levels of language analysis** language structures worldwide share common characteristics
  - **grammar**
    - system of rules governing structure and use of language
    - according to Chomsky, humans have an innate ability, language acquisition device (LAD) to understand and produce language
  - **syntax**
    - rules for combining words and phrases
  - **morphemes**
    - smallest units of meaning within a language
    - **governed by semantics:** rules for determining the meaning of words and sentences
  - **phonemes**
    - basic units of sound in a language
  - **pragmatics**
    - social "niceties" or practical aspects of communicating with others
      - taking turns
      - use of gestures
      - different ways of speaking to different people
- **the relationship between language and thought**
  - does language influence thought or does thinking influence language?
    - relationship has been debated
    - Piaget believed that concepts preceded, and aided, language development
    - Vgotsky believed that language helps develop concepts and helps the child learn to control behavior
  - linguistic relativity hypothesis
    - words people use determine the way they think about the world; originally proposed by Sapir and Whorf; may apply more to higher level concepts
    - suggests that some concepts are universal and influence the development of language
  - animal studies in language
    - all animals can communicate, their use of language is still under investigation
    - some success (chimpanzees, parrots, dolphins), may approach level of 3-year-old human, no conclusive evidence of syntax mastery

PRACTICE quiz How much do you remember?

ANSWERS ON PAGE AK-1.

Pick the best answer.

1. The system of rules for combining words and phrases to make meaningful sentences is called __________.
   a. grammar.
   b. phonics.
   c. syntax.
   d. morphology.
2. Grammar includes all but which of the following aspects of language?
   a. tone
   b. sounds
   c. order
   d. meaning
3. The sounds of the letters *b*, *z*, *c*, and *d* are examples of __________.
   a. morphemes.
   b. phonemes.
   c. semantics.
   d. syntax.
4. The Dani have only two words for color yet can distinguish between many different colors. This finding supports the language theory of __________.
   a. Sapir and Whorf.
   b. Lucy and Shweder.
   c. Pullum.
   d. Rosch.
5. The quality of language produced by animals cannot yet compare to the level achieved by a __________ human.
   a. 1-year-old
   b. 2-year-old
   c. 3-year-old
   d. 5-year-old

Applying Psychology to Everyday Life: Mental and Physical Exercises Combine for Better Cognitive Health

7.11 What are some ways to improve thinking?

You may have heard the saying "use it or lose it" and likely think of it in terms of maintaining physical fitness. But it is not limited to that; in many regards, the saying applies as well to our ability to maintain cognitive fitness. However, just as there is a difference between physical activity and physical exercise, there is a difference in mental *activity* and mental *exercise*.

Quite a few computerized brain-training programs and devices have hit the market in the last few years. In addition, a lot of attention in the media has focused on the benefits of specific computer-based brain exercises you can do to improve your cognitive fitness. While some are more scientifically grounded and offer the possibility of real benefits, many more appear to be riding the current wave of interest and may not be useful. For some individuals, practicing certain mental skills through cognitive exercises appears to help with those same skills when tested later. In general, however, research has not identified any benefits that transfer to untrained areas (A. M. Owen et al., 2010). Just as being physically active in general will not make you an Olympic athlete, to tune up your cognitive fitness you have to perform proper, focused cognitive exercises.

Wait a minute! You just said most skills don't transfer. That's correct, some do not, but just as in physical training, if you select the proper foundational exercises, you can benefit higher level cognitive functions. For example, impaired verbal working memory is one of the cognitive dysfunctions in schizophrenia. Deficits in early auditory processing are also present and have negative implications for both verbal learning and memory, and for understanding the semantics and emotional content of speech (M. Fisher et al., 2009). Imagine the difficulty you would have if you could not follow a conversation with another person because you could not remember what they just said or because you could not comprehend the meaning or the emotions they were expressing in their speech.

In a recent study, it was found that for a group of individuals with schizophrenia, computerized cognitive exercises that placed increasing demands on auditory perception (a foundational skill) were beneficial (M. Fisher et al., 2009). Those same individuals later demonstrated significant progress in verbal working memory and global cognition tasks (higher level skills). Although the cognitive exercise group originally received daily training for 10 weeks, when some participants were studied 6 months later, the researchers found that some of the gains were still evident and that gains overall were positively correlated with improved quality of life at the 6-month assessment point (Fisher et al., 2009). The authors acknowledged that some of the positive effects might have been due to the number of hours of training and the amount of repetition (the authors noted that each exercise was practiced for thousands of trials!). Furthermore, approximately 16 hours were devoted to tasks that had word stimuli or a learning/memory component while over 30 hours were spent performing tasks that focused on auditory perception, which also engaged working memory.

The noting of the auditory perception tasks involving *working memory* (LINK to Chapter Six, Memory, pp. 220–221) in the M. Fisher et al. (2009) study is very interesting, especially in light of recent research suggesting challenging, adaptive training in working memory appears to improve *fluid intelligence* in young adults (Jaeggi et al., 2008). Fluid intelligence is the ability to adapt and deal with new problems or challenges the first time you encounter them, without having to depend on knowledge you already possess.

What else can you do more generally to benefit your cognitive health? Exercise! And this time, we are referring to physical exercise. Physical activity and specifically aerobic fitness has repeatedly been demonstrated to be associated with improved cognitive function across the life span. A physically active lifestyle and greater aerobic fitness has been implicated with better executive control and memory processes in preadolescent children (Chaddock et al., 2010; Hillman et al., 2009), better educational outcomes later in life and improved affect and visuospatial memory in young adults (Åberg et al., 2009; Stroth et al., 2009), increased hippocampal volume (associated with better memory) in elderly adults (Erickson et al., 2009), and as a useful intervention in a group of individuals at high risk of cognitive decline or impairment, especially for females in the group (Baker et al., 2010).

At least one possible benefit of regular aerobic activity is promoting or maintaining functional connectivity among key brain areas of the frontal, temporal, and parietal lobes (Voss et al., 2010). The increases in oxygen and blood flow to the brain play key roles. Other benefits include increased levels of mood-related neurotransmitters including serotonin, norepinephrine, and dopamine, along with neurogenesis in specific brain areas including the hippocampus (Ratey & Hagerman, 2008). In another study, 3 months of aerobic activity and increased fitness were associated with small increases in the size of the hippocampus and improved memory in individuals with schizophrenia. Interestingly, controls without schizophrenia in this research *also* showed increases in their hippocampi associated with increases in aerobic fitness (Pajonk et al., 2010).

So instead of "use it or lose it," perhaps a better saying to keep in mind is "what is good for the heart or body is also good for the mind." If you want to learn more, an interesting overview of research related to exercise and brain health can be found in the book, *Spark: The Revolutionary New Science of Exercise and the Brain,* by John Ratey and Eric Hagerman (2008).

Questions for Further Discussion

1. Aside from those involving working memory, what other kinds of focused mental exercises might help to keep the brain fit?
2. Should doctors suggest aerobic exercise for their patients interested in maintaining or improving their cognitive functions? What about psychologists working with individuals who have mood or anxiety disorders, or clients with attention problems?
3. Based on this information, what might the implications be for schools that are reducing or eliminating their physical education requirements? What about college students who may experience a decrease in physical activity as compared to when they were in high school?

chapter summary

Listen on **mypsychlab.com** Listen to an audio file of your chapter **www.mypsychlab.com**

How People Think

- Thinking (cognition) is mental activity that occurs in the brain when information is being organized, stored, communicated, or processed.

7.1 How are mental images and concepts involved in the process of thinking?

- Mental images represent objects or events and have a picturelike quality.
- Concepts are ideas that represent a class or category of events, objects, or activities.
- Prototypes are examples of a concept that more closely match the defining characteristics of that concept.

7.2 What are the methods people use to solve problems and make decisions?

- Problem solving consists of thinking and behaving in certain ways to reach a goal.
- Mechanical solutions include trial-and-error learning and rote solutions.
- Algorithms are a type of rote solution in which one follows step-by-step procedures for solving certain types of problems.
- A heuristic or "rule of thumb" is a strategy that narrows down the possible solutions for a problem.
- Insight is the sudden perception of a solution to a problem.

7.3 Why does problem solving sometimes fail, and what is meant by creative thinking?

- Functional fixedness is the tendency to perceive objects as having only the use for which they were originally intended and, therefore, failing to see them as possible tools for solving other problems.
- Confirmation bias is the tendency to search for evidence that confirms one's beliefs, ignoring any evidence to the contrary.

- Divergent thinking involves coming up with as many different answers as possible. This is a kind of creativity (combining ideas or behavior in new ways).
- Creative people are usually good at mental imagery and have knowledge on a wide range of topics, are unafraid to be different, value their independence, and are often unconventional in their work but not in other areas.

Intelligence

7.4 How do psychologists define intelligence, and how do various theories of intelligence differ?

- Intelligence is the ability to understand the world, think rationally or logically, and use resources effectively when faced with challenges or problems.
- Spearman proposed general intelligence, or g factor, as the ability to reason and solve problems, whereas specific intelligence, or s factor, includes task-specific abilities in certain areas such as music, business, or art.
- Gardner proposed nine different types of intelligence, ranging from verbal, linguistic, and mathematical to interpersonal and intrapersonal intelligence.
- Sternberg proposed three types of intelligence: analytical, creative, and practical.
- Emotional intelligence is viewed as a powerful influence on success in life.

7.5 How is intelligence measured and how are intelligence tests constructed?

- The Stanford-Binet Intelligence Test yields an IQ score that was once determined by dividing the mental age of the person by the chronological age and multiplying that quotient by 100 but now involves comparing a person's score to a standardized norm.
- The Wechsler Intelligence Tests yield four index scores derived from both verbal and nonverbal subtests and an overall score of intelligence
- Standardization, validity, and reliability are all important factors in the construction of an intelligence test.
- Deviation IQs are based on the normal curve, defining different levels of intelligence based on the deviation of scores from a common mean.
- IQ tests are often criticized for being culturally biased.

PSYCHOLOGY IN THE NEWS: Neuropsychology Sheds Light on Head Injuries

- Neuropsychologists play an important role in the care of individuals with traumatic brain injury and other conditions where brain functioning has been negatively impacted.
- Concussion, or mild traumatic brain injury, affects the lives of many athletes and military personnel.

7.6 What is intellectual disability and what are its causes?

- Intellectual disability or developmental delay is a condition in which IQ falls below 70 and adaptive behavior is severely deficient for a person of a particular chronological age.
- The four levels of delay are mild (55–70 IQ), moderate (40–55 IQ), severe (25–40 IQ), and profound (below 25 IQ).
- Causes of intellectual disability include deprived environments as well as chromosome and genetic disorders and dietary deficiencies.

7.7 What defines giftedness, and does being intellectually gifted guarantee success in life?

- Gifted persons are defined as those having IQ scores at the upper end of the normal curve (130 or above).

CLASSIC STUDIES IN PSYCHOLOGY: Terman's "Termites"

- Terman conducted a longitudinal study that demonstrated that gifted children grow up to be successful adults for the most part.
- Terman's study has been criticized for a lack of objectivity because Terman became too involved in the lives of several of his participants, even to the point of intervening on their behalf.

7.8 What is the influence of heredity and environment on the development of intelligence?

- Stronger correlations are found between IQ scores as genetic relatedness increases. Heritability of IQ is estimated at 0.50.
- In 1994, Herrnstein and Murray published *The Bell Curve* in which they made widely criticized claims about the heritability of intelligence.

Language

7.9 How is language defined, and what are its different elements and structure?

- Language is a system for combining symbols so that an infinite number of meaningful statements can be created and communicated to others.
- Grammar is the system of rules by which language is governed and includes the rules for using phonemes, morphemes, and syntax. Pragmatics refers to practical aspects of language.

7.10 Does language influence the way people think, and are animals capable of learning language?

- Sapir and Whorf originally proposed that language controls and helps the development of thought processes and concepts, an idea that is known as the linguistic relativity hypothesis.
- Other researchers have found evidence that concepts are universal and directly influence the development of language, called the cognitive universalism viewpoint.
- Studies with chimpanzees, parrots, and dolphins have been somewhat successful in demonstrating that animals can develop a basic kind of language, including some abstract ideas.
- Controversy exists over the lack of evidence that animals can learn syntax, which some feel means that animals are not truly learning and using language.

Applying Psychology to Everyday Life: Mental and Physical Exercises Combine for Better Cognitive Health

7.11 What are some ways to improve thinking?

- Both specific mental exercises (such as those involving working memory) and physical exercise promoting aerobic fitness are important for optimal cognitive functioning.

test YOURSELF

ANSWERS ON PAGE AK-1.

Study and Review on **mypsychlab.com** Ready for your test? More quizzes and a customized study plan **www.mypsychlab.com**

Pick the best answer.

1. Mental activity that goes on in the brain when a person is processing information is called _________.
a. mentation. **b.** a concept. **c.** thinking. **d.** mental imagery.

2. Research suggests we interact with _________ images _________ the way interact with physical objects.
a. mental; differently than **b.** mental; similarly to **c.** prototypical; differently than **d.** prototypical; similarly to

3. On a popular quiz show, contestants are asked to match the audience in naming certain items. One contestant, when asked to "name a type of vehicle," replied "elevator!" The audience groaned, because they knew that the contestant was pretty far off the mark. The contestant should have picked a vehicle that was closer to a ________ for vehicles to match the audience's response.
a. formal concept **b.** natural concept **c.** fuzzy concept **d.** prototype

4. Algorithms are a type of _________.
a. mechanical solution. **b.** heuristic. **c.** rule of thumb. **d.** means–end analysis.

5. The _________ heuristic can be used to create and maintain stereotypes.
a. availability **b.** representative **c.** insight **d.** means–end analysis

6. When people persist in trying to solve a problem the same way they have always gone about solving problems, they have developed _________.
a. a mental set. **b.** functional fixedness. **c.** confirmation bias. **d.** transformation bias.

7. Which of the following questions would be more likely to produce divergent thinking?
a. "What is a coffee cup?"
b. "How do you spell *coffee cup*?"
c. "How many uses can you think of for a coffee cup?"
d. "What does a coffee cup look like?"

8. Which of the following is NOT part of the traditional definition of intelligence?
a. ability to adapt
b. ability to solve problems
c. ability to be creative
d. ability to use resources effectively

9. In Terman's study of gifted children, social and behavioral problems were found only in those _________.
a. with IQs of 150 or higher.
b. with IQs of 180 or higher.
c. with IQs of 180 or higher in adulthood.
d. with IQs of 180 or higher in childhood.

10. According to Sternberg, "street smarts" is another way of talking about which kind of intelligence?
a. analytical **b.** creative **c.** practical **d.** emotional

11. Which type of intelligence, according to Sternberg, would most likely be measured by traditional intelligence tests?
a. analytical **b.** creative **c.** practical **d.** emotional

12. Goleman has proposed that _________ intelligence is a more powerful influence on success in life than other forms of intelligence.
a. analytical **b.** creative **c.** practical **d.** emotional

13. Keneisha is only 11 years old, but she can answer questions that most 15-year-olds can answer. Fifteen is Keneisha's _________.
a. chronological age. **b.** mental age. **c.** IQ. **d.** standard age.

14. Which of the following makes the Wechsler tests different from the Stanford-Binet?
a. The Wechsler tests are administered to individuals.
b. The Wechsler is designed only for children.
c. The Stanford-Binet is designed only for adults.
d. Different Wechsler tests are available for different age groups.

15. A test that gives similar scores for a person each time the person takes it is considered to be a _________ test.
a. reliable **b.** valid **c.** standardized **d.** creative

16. When a test allows a person from one particular background to have an unfair advantage over persons from other backgrounds, it is called_________.
a. culturally free. **b.** culturally fair. **c.** culturally biased. **d.** unreliable.

17. Marcos' mother drank heavily while pregnant with him and he has been diagnosed with mild intellectual disability. Marcos most likely suffers from_________.
a. Down syndrome. **b.** fetal alcohol syndrome. **c.** fragile X syndrome. **d.** cretinism.

18. The current estimate of heritability of intelligence is_________.
a. 0.90. **b.** 0.86. **c.** 0.50. **d.** 0.34.

19. The basic units of sound are called _________.
a. morphemes. **b.** phonemes. **c.** semantics. **d.** syntax.

20. The linguistic relativity hypothesis states that _________.
a. language shapes thoughts.
b. thoughts shape language.
c. language and thought develop independently.
d. language and thought influence each other.

21. Research has supported the role of _________ in the maintenance of mental fitness and improved cognitive function.
a. visual activity
b. specific mental exercises such as those involving working memory
c. higher levels of aerobic fitness
d. b and c

22. Traumatic brain injuries can have a negative impact on which of the following?
a. problem solving **b.** memory **c.** attention **d.** all of the above

7 cognition

thinking, intelligence, and language

7.1 **7.2** p. 261

- **mental imagery**
  - mental images are representations for objects or events used in mental activities
  - mental images are interacted with in similar ways as physical objects (e.g., scanning a map or rotating an object)
  - mental images are processed in the brain slightly differently than actual objects

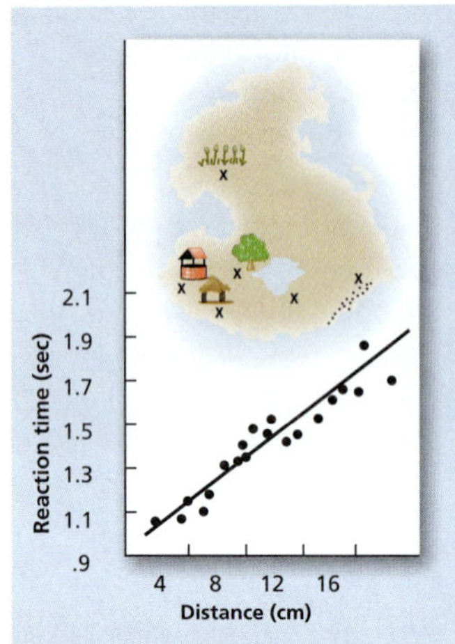

How People Think

thinking (cognition) refers to mental activities that occur in the brain when processing, organizing, understanding, or communicating information to others

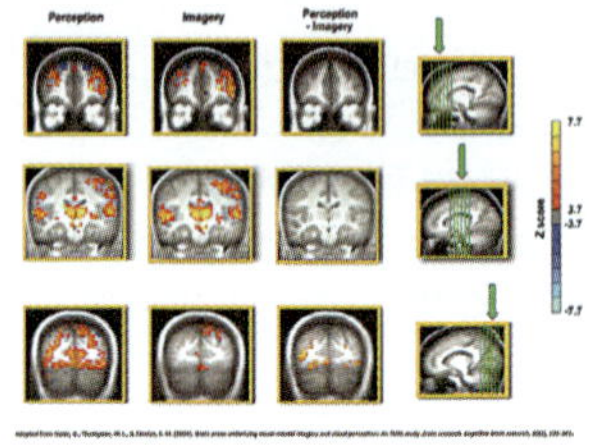

- **concepts**
  - are ideas that represent a class or category of objects, events, or activities
  - are used to interact and organize information without having to think about or process every specific example of the category
  - can represent different levels of objects or events
  - can be well-defined based on strict criteria (formal), or fuzzy, based on personal experience (natural)
  - are represented by prototypes, best examples of the defining characteristics
  - are an important tool in problem solving

- **problem solving and decision making**
  - thinking and behaving in certain ways to reach a goal
  - can involve different strategies, logical methods (convergent thinking)
    - **trial and error**
    - **algorithms**
    - **heuristics**
  - **insight**
    - "aha!" moments when solution seems to appear in a flash
    - usually based on reorganization of information

7.3 p. 265

- **problems with problem solving**
  - solutions to problems are not always apparent
  - problems can be caused by three common barriers

Problem Solving and Decision Making

- **creativity**
  - consists of new ways of combining ideas or behavior
  - typically the result of divergent thinking

7.4 7.5 p. 275

Intelligence

(the ability to learn from one's experiences, acquire knowledge, and use resources effectively)

- **theories**
  - **Spearman's g factor:** intelligence comprises two different abilities
  - **Gardner's multiple intelligences:** overall intelligence comprises nine different types
  - **Sternberg's triarchic theory:** intelligence comprises three different aspects

- first formal test created by Alfred Binet and Theodore Simon to help identify French students who needed more help with learning

Measuring Intelligence

- **tests**
  - **Binet's Mental Ability Test**
  - **Stanford-Binet**
  - **Wechsler Tests**
- **test construction**
  - good tests are both valid and reliable
  - standardized administration, scoring, and comparison against norms
  - intelligence is assumed to follow a normal curve
  - is challenging (e.g., different definitions, ways to assess, culture bias)

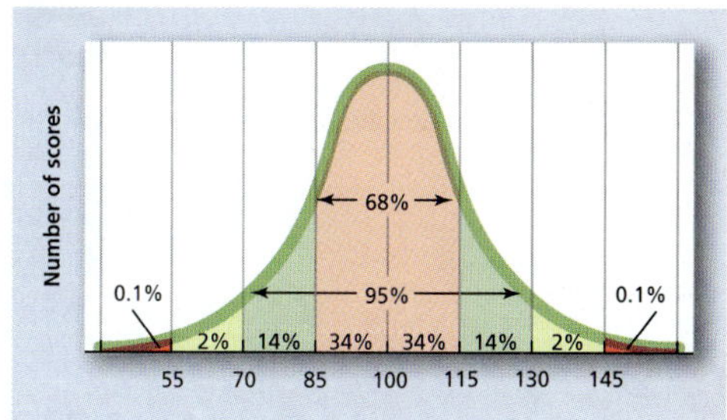

7.6 7.7 7.8 p. 284

- **individual differences**
  IQ tests can be used to identify individuals who differ significantly from those of average intelligence
  - **giftedness**
    - criteria
    - characteristics
  - **intellectual disability/developmental delay**
    - criteria
    - classifications
    - causal factors
  - **emotional intelligence**

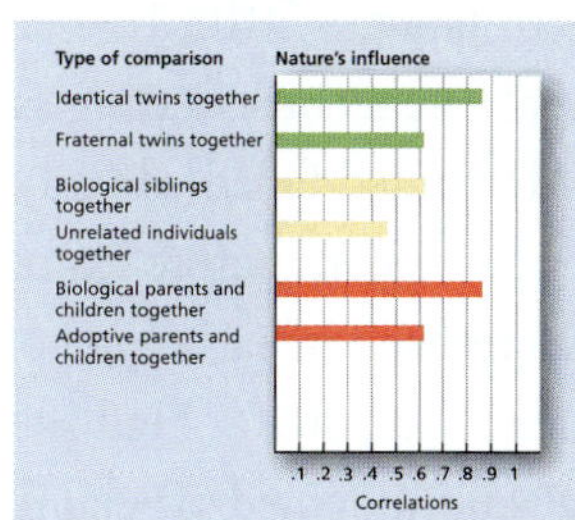

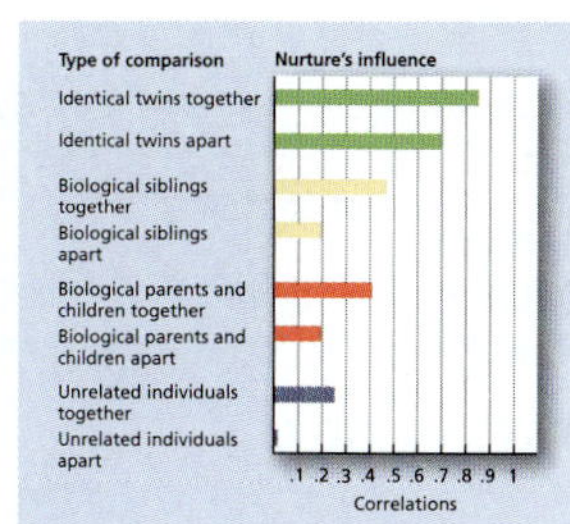

Intelligence

- **nature vs. nurture**
  - identical twins reared together show a correlation of .86 between their IQs
  - heritability estimates apply *within* groups of people, not *between* groups, not to individuals, and only in a general sense

7.9 7.10 p. 289

Language

- **levels of language analysis**
  language structures worldwide share common characteristics
  - **grammar**
  - **syntax**
  - **morphemes**
  - **phonemes**
  - **pragmatics**
- **the relationship between language and thought**
  - does language influence thought or does thinking influence language?
  - linguistic relativity hypothesis
  - animal studies in language

8 development across the life span

CHAPTER OUTLINE

NOT YOUR AVERAGE 16-YEAR-OLDS

At a time when many teenage girls are dating or shopping at the mall with friends, Jessica Watson was on a mission to become the youngest individual to sail nonstop and unassisted around the world. The 16-year old left Sydney, Australia, on October 18, 2009. Seven months later, she sailed back into Sydney on May 15, 2010, unofficially breaking the previous record, set by then 17-year-old Michael Perham (Marks, 2010; Munoz, 2010). Watson's record will remain unrecognized for two reasons: Some experts claimed that she did not sail far enough north of the equator to complete the "sail around the world, and the World Speed Sailing Record Council has now done away with its "youngest" category.

In January 2010, 16-year-old Abby Sunderland launched her own attempt to break the record. Setting sail from California, her bid to sail around the world solo and unaided failed when her mast broke, forcing the teenager to send up two emergency beacons before losing contact with her American-based back-up team. She was rescued in early June of 2010 and flew back to her home in California 2 weeks later (Tran, 2010). Had she succeeded, Abby, like Jessica before her, would probably have been denied official recognition by the World Speed Sailing Record Council, because the council wants to discourage what it considers dangerous and foolhardy attempts by those who are too young. Many people have commented in articles about these two teenage girls and others like them, questioning the wisdom of the teens' parents for allowing them to undertake such a dangerous voyage.

Adolescence is one among many stages of life, and while this chapter will cover several of the common features of human development in all of those stages, the stories of Jessica Watson and Abby Sunderland and their parents should be a reminder that each of us is an individual, with different motivations, goals, and desires. As you learn about the developing person in this chapter, keep in mind that the stages and ages discussed herein are generalities only. Like Jessica and Abby, each individual charts his or her own destiny.

Why study human development?

Beginning to understanding how we come to be the people we are is a critical step in understanding ourselves as we are today, and who we may become as we grow older. From the moment of conception, each of us is headed down a pathway of change, influenced by our biology, environment, and social interactions, to a final destination that is the same for all of us. The twists and turns of the pathway are what make each of us unique individuals. In this chapter, we'll look at the influences that help determine our developmental pathway through life.

learning objectives

8.1 What are some of the special research methods used to study development?

8.2 What is the relationship between heredity and environmental factors in determining development?

8.3 How do chromosomes, genes, and DNA determine a person's characteristics or disorders, and what causes multiple births?

8.4 What happens during the germinal, embryonic, and fetal periods of pregnancy and what are some hazards in prenatal development?

8.5 What kind of physical changes take place in infancy and childhood?

8.6 What are two ways of looking at cognitive development, and how does language develop?

8.7 How do infants and children develop personalities and form relationships with others, and what are Erikson's stages of psychosocial development for children?

8.8 What are the physical, cognitive, and personality changes that occur in adolescence, including concepts of morality and Erikson's search for identity?

8.9 What are the physical, cognitive, and personality changes that occur during adulthood and aging, including Erikson's last three psychosocial stages, and patterns of parenting?

8.10 How do psychologists explain why aging occurs, and what are the stages of death and dying?

8.11 What are some cross-cultural differences in views of death and dying?

study tip

As you are reading this chapter, take a look back at pages I-5–I-8 in *Psychology in Action* for some ways to get more out of this chapter as you read through it.

Issues in Studying Human Development

What is development? In the context of life, **human development** is the scientific study of the changes that occur in people as they age, from conception until death. This chapter will touch on almost all of the topics covered in the other chapters of this text, such as personality, cognition, biological processes, and social interactions. But here, all of those topics will be studied in the context of changes that occur as a result of the process of human development.

RESEARCH DESIGNS

8.1 What are some of the special research methods used to study development?

As briefly discussed in Chapter One, research in human development is affected by the problem of age. In any experiment, the participants who are exposed to the independent variable (the variable in an experiment that is deliberately manipulated by the experimenter) should be randomly assigned to the different experimental conditions. The problem in developmental research is that the age of the people in the study should always be an independent variable, but people cannot be randomly assigned to different age-groups.

There are some special designs that are used in researching age-related changes: the **longitudinal design**, in which one group of people is followed and assessed at different times as the group ages; the **cross-sectional design**, in which several different age-groups are studied at one time; and the **cross-sequential design**, which is a combination of the longitudinal and cross-sectional designs (Baltes et al., 1988).

The longitudinal design has the advantage of looking at real age-related changes as those changes occur in the same individuals. Disadvantages of this method are the lengthy amount of time, money, and effort involved in following participants over the years, as well as the loss of participants when they move away, lose interest, or die. The cross-sectional design has the advantages of being quick, relatively inexpensive, and easier to accomplish than the longitudinal design. Its main disadvantage is that the study no longer compares an individual to that same individual as he or she ages; instead, individuals of different ages are being compared to one

human development the scientific study of the changes that occur in people as they age from conception until death.

longitudinal design research design in which one participant or group of participants is studied over a long period of time.

cross-sectional design research design in which several different participant age-groups are studied at one particular point in time.

cross-sequential design research design in which participants are first studied by means of a cross-sectional design but are also followed and assessed longitudinally.

Table 8.1

A Comparison of Three Developmental Research Designs

CROSS-SECTIONAL DESIGN		
Different participants of various ages are compared at one point in time to determine age-related *differences.*	**Group One:** 20-year-old participants **Group Two:** 40-year-old participants **Group Three:** 60-year-old participants	Research done in 2011
LONGITUDINAL DESIGN		
The **same** participants are studied at various ages to determine age-related *changes.*	**Study One:** 20-year-old participants **Study Two:** Same participants at 40 years old **Study Three:** Same participants are now 60 years old	Research done in 1971 Research done in 1991 Research done in 2011
CROSS-SEQUENTIAL DESIGN		
Different participants of various ages are compared at several points in time, to determine both age-related *differences* and age-related *changes.*	**Study One:** *Group One*: 20-year-old participants *Group Two*: 40-year-old participants	Research done in 2011
	Study Two: *Group One*: Participants will be 25 years old *Group Two*: Participants will be 45 years old	Research to be done in 2016

another. Differences between age-groups are often a problem in developmental research. For example, if comparing the IQ scores of 30-year-olds to 80-year-olds to see how aging affects intelligence, questions arise concerning the differing educational experiences and opportunities those two age-groups have had that might affect IQ scores, in addition to any effects of aging. Table 8.1 shows a comparison between examples of a longitudinal design, a cross-sectional design, and a cross-sequential design.

In studying human development, developmental psychologists have outlined many theories of how these age-related changes occur. There are some areas of controversy, however, and one of these is the issue of nature versus nurture.

NATURE VERSUS NURTURE

8.2 What is the relationship between heredity and environmental factors in determining development?

Nature refers to heredity, the influence of inherited characteristics on personality, physical growth, intellectual growth, and social interactions. **Nurture** refers to the influence of the environment on all of those same things and includes parenting styles, physical surroundings, economic factors, and anything that can have an influence on development that does not come from within the person.

So, is a person like Hitler born that way, or did something happen to make him the person he was?

So, is a person like Hitler born that way, or did something happen to make him the person he was?

How much of a person's personality and behavior is determined by nature and how much is determined by nurture? This is a key question, and the answer is quite complicated. It is also quite important: Are people like Hitler or the infamous serial killer Ted Bundy the result of bad genes, bad parenting, or life-altering experiences in childhood? How much of Stephen Hawking's genius is due to his genetic inheritance? What part did the parenting choices of his family play? Or are his cognitive abilities the unique combination of both hereditary and environmental influences? After many years of scientific research, most developmental psychologists now agree

nature the influence of our inherited characteristics on our personality, physical growth, intellectual growth, and social interactions.

nurture the influence of the environment on personality, physical growth, intellectual growth, and social interactions.

Genetic researchers work with samples of DNA to examine the basic building blocks of life.

that the last possibility is the most likely explanation for most of human development: All that people are and all that people become is the product of an interaction between nature and nurture (Insel & Wang, 2010; Ridley, 1999; Sternberg & Grigorenko, 2006). This does not mean that the nature versus nurture controversy no longer exists; for example, intelligence is still a "hot topic" with regard to how much is inherited and how much is learned. Researchers and theorists assume a large genetic influence (Bouchard & Segal, 1985; Herrnstein & Murray, 1994; Jensen, 1969; Johnson et al., 2007; Kristensen & Bjerkedal, 2007) whereas many believe that culture, economics, nutrition in early childhood, and educational opportunities have a greater impact (Gardner et al., 1996; Gould, 1996; Rose et al., 1984; Wahlsten, 1997).

Behavioral genetics is a relatively new field in the investigation of the origins of behavior in which researchers try to determine how much of behavior is the result of genetic inheritance and how much is due to a person's experiences. For more on behavioral genetics and links to other sites, go to **www.ornl.gov/sci/techresources/Human_Genome/elsi/behavior.shtml**.

The Basic Building Blocks of Development

Any study of the human life span must begin with looking at the complex material contained in the cells of the body that carries the instructions for life itself. After discussing the basic building blocks of life, we will discuss how the processes of conception and the development of the infant within the womb take place.

CHROMOSOMES, GENES, AND DNA

8.3 How do chromosomes, genes, and DNA determine a person's characteristics or disorders, and what causes multiple births?

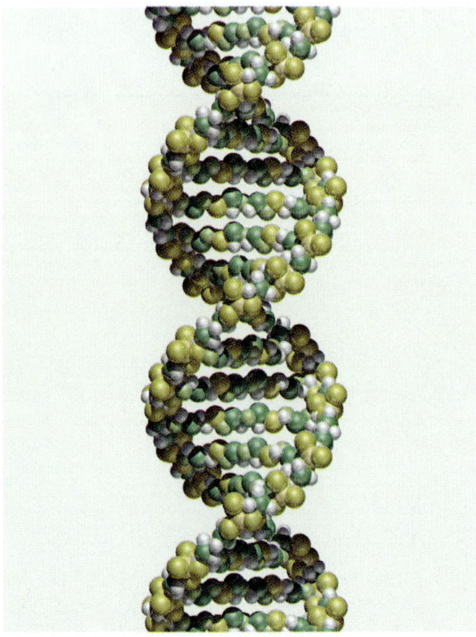

Figure 8.1 DNA Molecule

In this model of a DNA molecule, the two strands making up the sides of the "twisted ladder" are composed of sugars and phosphates. The "rungs" of the ladder that link the two strands are amines. Amines contain the genetic codes for building the proteins that make up organic life.

Genetics is the science of heredity. Understanding how genes transmit human characteristics and traits involves defining a few basic terms.

DNA (deoxyribonucleic acid) is a very special kind of molecule (the smallest particle of a substance that still has all the properties of that substance). DNA consists of two very long sugar–phosphate strands, each linked together by certain chemical elements called *amines* or *bases* arranged in a particular pattern. (See Figure 8.1 for a representation of DNA.) The amines are organic structures that contain the genetic codes for building the proteins that make up organic life (hair coloring, muscle, and skin, for example) and that control the life of each cell. Each section of DNA containing a certain sequence (ordering) of these amines is called a **gene**. These genes are located on rod-shaped structures called **chromosomes**, which are found in the nucleus of a cell.

Humans have a total of 46 chromosomes in each cell of their bodies (with the exception of the egg and the sperm). Twenty-three of these chromosomes come from the mother's egg and the other 23 from the father's sperm. Most characteristics are determined by 22 such pairs, called the *autosomes*. The last pair determines the sex of the person. The two chromosomes of this pair are called the *sex chromosomes*. Two X-shaped chromosomes indicate a female while an X and a Y indicate a male.

genetics the science of inherited traits.

DNA (deoxyribonucleic acid) special molecule that contains the genetic material of the organism.

gene section of DNA having the same arrangement of chemical elements.

chromosome tightly wound strand of genetic material or DNA.

DOMINANT AND RECESSIVE GENES

The 46 chromosomes can be arranged in pairs, with one member of each pair coming from the mother and the other member from the father. Let's consider just one of these pairs for the moment.

© Thaves. Reprinted by permission.

In this particular pair of chromosomes, assume that there is a gene for hair color on each chromosome. The observable color of the person's hair will be determined by those two genes, one gene from each parent. If both genes are for brown hair, the person will obviously have brown hair, right? And if both are for blond hair, the person's hair will be blond.

But what if one gene is for brown hair and the other is for blond hair?

But what if one gene is for brown hair and the other is for blond hair?

The answer lies in the nature of each gene. Some genes that are more active in influencing the trait are called **dominant**. A dominant gene will always be expressed in the observable trait, in this case, hair color. A person with a dominant gene for brown hair color will have brown hair, no matter what the other gene is, because brown is the most dominant of all the hair colors.

Some genes are less active in influencing the trait and will only be expressed in the observable trait if they are paired with another less active gene. These genes tend to recede, or fade, into the background when paired with a more dominant gene, so they are called **recessive**. Blond is most recessive hair color and it will only show up as a trait if that person receives a blond-hair-color gene from each parent.

What about red hair? And how come some people have a mixed hair color, like strawberry blond?

What about red hair? And how come some people have a mixed hair color, like a strawberry blond?

In reality, the patterns of genetic transmission of traits are usually more complicated. Almost all traits are controlled by more than one pair of genes in a process called *polygenic inheritance*. (*Polygenic* means "many genes.") Sometimes certain kinds of genes tend to group themselves with certain other genes, like the genes for blond hair and blue eyes. Other genes are so equally dominant or equally recessive that they combine their traits in the organism. For example, genes for blond hair and red hair are recessive. When a child inherits one of each from his or her parents, instead of one or the other controlling the child's hair color, they may blend together to form a strawberry-blond mix. Figure 8.2 illustrates a typical pattern of inheritance for dominant and recessive genes. **Explore** on **mypsychlab.com**

Explore dominant and recessive traits on **mypsychlab.com**

GENETIC AND CHROMOSOME PROBLEMS

Several genetic disorders are carried by recessive genes. Diseases carried by recessive genes are inherited when a child inherits two recessive genes, one from each parent. Examples of disorders inherited in this manner are cystic fibrosis (a disease of the respiratory and digestive tracts), sickle-cell anemia (a blood disorder), Tay-Sachs disorder (a fatal neurological disorder), and phenylketonuria (PKU), in which an infant is born without the ability to break down phenylalanine, an amino acid controlling coloring of the skin and hair. If levels of phenylalanine build up, brain damage can occur; if untreated, it can result in severe intellectual disabilities.

dominant referring to a gene that actively controls the expression of a trait.

recessive referring to a gene that only influences the expression of a trait when paired with an identical gene.

Figure 8.2 Dominant and Recessive Genes and PKU

This figure shows the variation of parents carrying one or two recessive genes and the result of this in their offspring.

(a) If only one parent carries the PKU gene, their children might be carriers, but will not have PKU.

(b) Only if both parents are carriers of PKU will a child have the 1 in 4 possibility of having PKU.

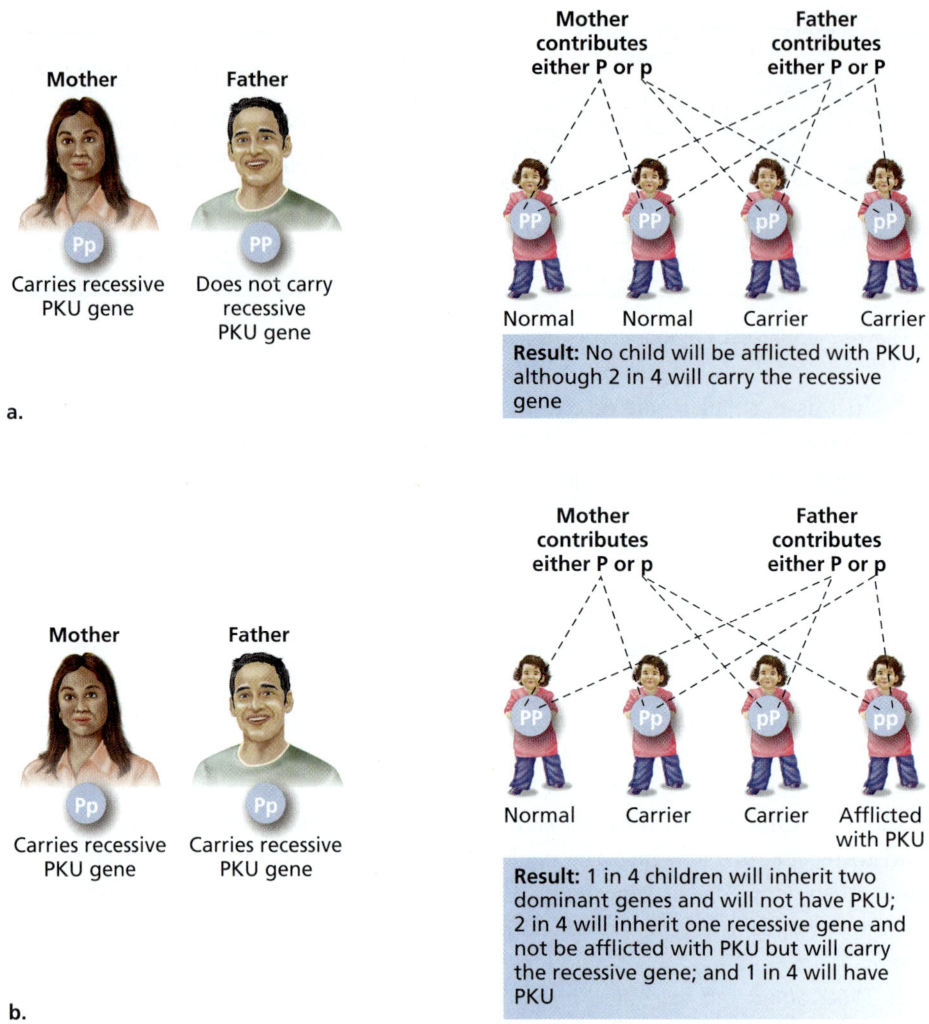

Sometimes the chromosome itself is the problem. Although each egg and each sperm are only supposed to have 23 chromosomes, in the creation of these cells a chromosome can end up in the wrong cell, leaving one cell with only 22 and the other with 24. If either of these cells survives to "mate," the missing or extra chromosome can cause mild to severe problems in development (American Academy of Pediatrics, 1995; Barnes & Carey, 2002; Centers for Disease Control, 2009; Gardner & Sutherland, 1996).

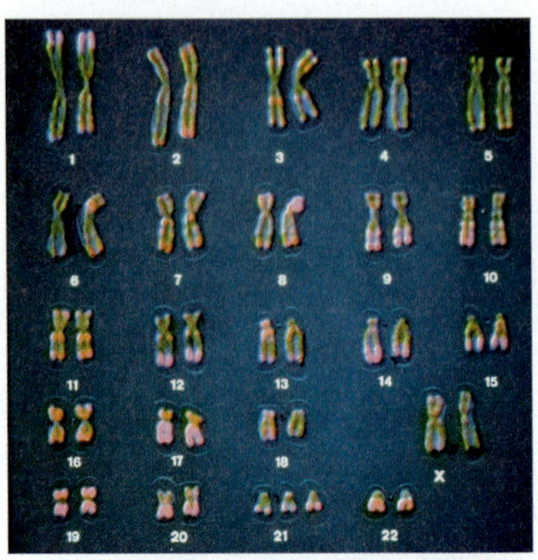

Down syndrome is a form of intellectual disability caused by an extra chromosome 21.

Examples of chromosome disorders include *Down syndrome*, a disorder in which there is an extra chromosome in what would normally be the 21st pair. Symptoms commonly include the physical characteristics of almond-shaped, wide-set eyes, as well as intellectual disability (Barnes & Carey, 2002; Hernandez & Fisher, 1996). Other chromosome disorders occur when there is an extra sex chromosome in the 23rd pair, such as *Klinefelter's syndrome*, in which the 23rd set of sex chromosomes is XXY, with the extra X producing a male with reduced masculine characteristics, enlarged breasts, obesity, and excessive height (Bock, 1993); and *Turner's syndrome*, in which the 23rd pair is actually missing an X, so that the result is a lone X chromosome (Ranke & Saenger, 2001). These females tend to be very short, infertile, and sexually underdeveloped (American Academy of Pediatrics, 1995; Rovet, 1993).

8.1 8.2 8.3

CONCEPT MAP

Issues in Studying Human Development

(scientific study of changes that occur in people as they age)

- **research designs**
  - **longitudinal:** one group of people is followed and assessed at different times as they age
  - **cross-sectional:** several different age-groups are studied at one time
  - **cross-sequential:** combination of longitudinal and cross-sectional
- **nature vs. nurture debate**
  - **nature** refers to heredity and the influence of inherited characteristics on personality, growth, intellect, social skills, etc.; behavioral genetics is relatively new field that attempts to identify genetic basis of behavior
  - **nurture** refers to influence of the environment on inherited traits including parenting styles, socioeconomic status, physical surroundings, etc.
  - most developmental psychologists agree that the most likely explanation for most human development is based on the interaction between nature and nurture
- **basic building blocks of development**
  - **genetics** is the science of heredity
  - **DNA (deoxyribonucleic acid):** contains genetic codes and chromosomes
    - aside from egg and sperm, humans have 46 chromosomes in each cell of the body
    - individual gets 23 chromosomes from mother's egg and 23 from father's sperm
    - most characteristics are determined by 22 such pairs (autosomes); the last pair determines sex of the person (sex chromosomes)
  - both dominant and recessive genes determine physical and behavioral traits
    - specific physical and behavioral traits are dependent upon pairing of genes; more active genes are dominant, others are recessive (see Figure 8.2)
    - most traits are polygenetic
  - genetic and chromosome problems can cause a variety of disorders
    - genetic disorders carried by recessive genes are expressed when a child gets two recessive genes
    - issue may also occur if chromosomes having an extra or a missing pair

PRACTICE quiz How much do you remember?

ANSWERS ON PAGE AK-2.

Pick the best answer.

1. In a _________ design, several different age-groups of participants are studied at one time.
   - a. longitudinal
   - b. cross-sectional
   - c. cross-sequential
   - d. cross-longitudinal
2. In the analogy of the twisted ladder, the sequence of amines would be represented by the _________ of the ladder.
   - a. sides
   - b. length
   - c. rungs
   - d. wood
3. Brandon has blue eyes, even though both his mother and father have brown eyes. What do we know about Brandon's parents?
   - a. At least one of his parents has a recessive blue-eye-color gene.
   - b. Each of his parents must have one recessive blue-eye-color gene.
   - c. Each of his parents must have one dominant blue-eye-color gene.
   - d. Neither of his parents has a blue-eye-color gene.
4. Which of the following is a disorder caused by having an extra chromosome?
   - a. Tay-Sachs
   - b. PKU
   - c. cystic fibrosis
   - d. Down syndrome
5. The fertilized egg cell is called a _________.
   - a. zygote.
   - b. ovum.
   - c. sperm.
   - d. blastocyst.

Prenatal Development

From conception to the actual birth of the baby is a period of approximately 9 months, during which a single cell becomes a complete infant. It is also during this time that many things can have a positive or negative influence on the developing infant.

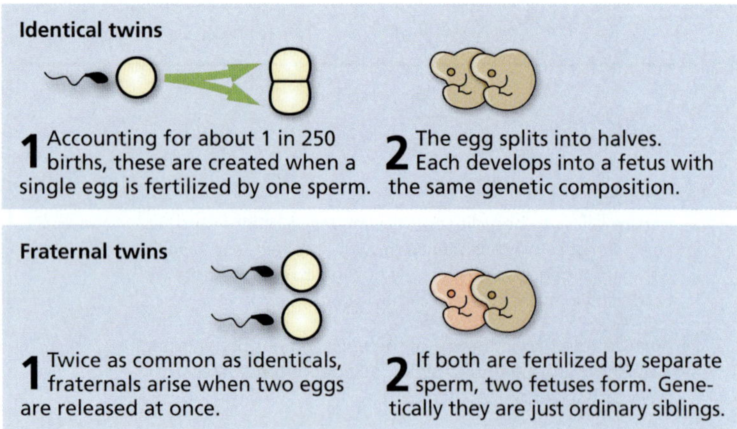

Figure 8.3 Monozygotic and Dizygotic Twins

Because identical twins come from one fertilized egg (zygote), they are called monozygotic. Fraternal twins, who come from two different fertilized eggs, are called dizygotic.

FERTILIZATION, THE ZYGOTE, AND TWINNING

When an egg (also called an **ovum**) and a sperm unite in the process of **fertilization**, the resulting single cell will have a total of 46 chromosomes and is called a **zygote**. Normally, the zygote will begin to divide, first into two cells, then four, then eight, and so on, with each new cell also having 46 chromosomes, because the DNA molecules produce duplicates, or copies, of themselves before each division. (This division process is called *mitosis*.) Eventually, the mass of cells becomes a baby. Sometimes this division process doesn't work exactly this way, and twins or multiples are the result.

There are actually two kinds of twins. Twins who are commonly referred to as "identical" are **monozygotic twins**, meaning that the two babies come from one (mono) fertilized egg (zygote). Early in the division process, the mass of cells splits completely—no one knows exactly why—into two separate masses, each of which will develop into a separate infant. The infants will be the same sex and have identical features because they each possess the same set of 46 chromosomes. The other type of twin is more an accident of timing and is more common in women who are older and who are from certain ethnic groups (Allen & Parisi, 1990; Bonnelykke, 1990; Imaizumi, 1998). A woman's body may either release more than one egg at a time or release an egg in a later ovulation period after a woman has already conceived once. If two eggs are fertilized, the woman may give birth to fraternal or **dizygotic twins** (two zygotes), or possibly triplets or some other multiple number of babies (Bryan & Hallett, 2001). This is also more likely to happen to women who are taking fertility drugs to help them get pregnant. (See Figure 8.3.)

For developmental psychologists, twins provide an important way to look at the contribution of nature and nurture to human development. Researchers may seek out identical twins who have been separated at birth, looking at all the ways those twins are alike in spite of being raised in different environments. (It should be noted that the environments in which children are raised within a particular culture are not necessarily that much different, so twin studies are not a perfect method.) LINK to Chapter Thirteen: Theories of Personality, p. 514. **Read** on **mypsychlab.com**

Read and learn more about mitosis and meiosis on **mypsychlab.com**

Sometimes in the twinning process, the mass of cells does not completely split apart. When this occurs, *conjoined twins* will result, and they will be joined at the point where the two cell masses remained "stuck." This joining may involve only soft tissues or may involve the sharing of certain body parts, like in the case of Abby and Brittany, who are discussed in the Psychology in the News section that follows.

ovum the female sex cell, or egg.

fertilization the union of the ovum and sperm.

zygote cell resulting from the uniting of the ovum and sperm.

monozygotic twins identical twins formed when one zygote splits into two separate masses of cells, each of which develops into a separate embryo.

dizygotic twins often called fraternal twins, occurring when two individual eggs get fertilized by separate sperm, resulting in two zygotes in the uterus at the same time.

psychology in the news

Abby and Brittany Hensel, Together for Life

Brittany loves milk. Her twin sister, Abigail (Abby), despises milk and would rather drink orange juice. Abby likes blue, Brittany likes pink. Abby likes oyster crackers in her soup but Brittany hates them. Brittany likes a full-course meal, Abby prefers pasta. Both are good with academics: Abby prefers math and Brittany prefers to do the reading. They are currently in college, turning 19 in March 2011.

Abby and Brittany Hensel sound like many other siblings, each with separate likes and dislikes as well as different interests. But Abby and Brittany are not separate and can never truly be separate, for they share one lower body. No more than four sets of surviving conjoined twins in recorded history have this condition, called *dicephaly*. In the case of Abby and Brittany, each girl has her own heart, stomach and pair of lungs. Their spines are joined at the pelvis, and below the waist they have only one set of organs. Each controls one arm and one leg on one side of the body, yet they somehow manage to move as one (Kaveny, 2001; Miller & Doman, 1996).

The girls play sports, swim, and put on makeup just like any other girls their age. Yet every action they undertake has to be a miracle of coordination, and they do it without even seeming to think about it. If Brittany coughs, *Abby's* hand may reflexively go up to cover Brittany's mouth. When Brittany is sick, she can't take the medicine for it (her stomach is sensitive) but Abby can take it for her (her stomach isn't sensitive). They are healthy and seem to be both happy and well adjusted, surrounded by a loving mother, father, younger brother, and sister.

Abby and Brittany Hensel are conjoined twins who share one body from the waist down but are two distinctly different individuals.

Questions for Further Discussion

1. What kinds of difficulties might Abby and Brittany have as college students?
2. How might being conjoined affect career decisions?
3. How can conjoined twins have different personalities?

THE GERMINAL PERIOD

8.4 What happens during the germinal, embryonic, and fetal periods of pregnancy and what are some hazards in prenatal development?

Once fertilization has taken place, the zygote begins dividing and moving down to the *uterus*, the muscular organ that will contain and protect the developing infant. This process takes about a week, followed by about a week during which the mass of cells, now forming a hollow ball, firmly attaches itself to the wall of the uterus. This 2-week period is called the **germinal period** of pregnancy. The *placenta* also begins to form during this period. The placenta is a specialized organ that provides nourishment and filters away the developing baby's waste products. The *umbilical cord* also begins to develop at this time, connecting the organism to the placenta.

How does a mass of cells become a baby, with eyes, nose, hands, feet, and so on? How do all those different things come from the same original single cell?

How does a mass of cells become a baby, with eyes, nose, hands, feet, and so on? How do all those different things come from the same original single cell?

During the germinal period, the cells begin to differentiate, or develop into specialized cells, in preparation for becoming all the various kinds of cells that make up the human body—skin cells, heart cells, and so on. Perhaps the most important of these cells are the *stem cells*, which stay in a somewhat immature state until needed to produce more cells. Researchers are looking into ways to use stem cells found in the umbilical cord to grow new organs and tissues for transplant or to repair neurological damage (Chen & Ende, 2000; Holden & Vogel, 2002; Lu & Ende, 1997). LINK to Chapter Two: The Biological Perspective, p. 59.

germinal period first 2 weeks after fertilization, during which the zygote moves down to the uterus and begins to implant in the lining.

THE EMBRYONIC PERIOD

Once firmly attached to the uterus, the developing organism is called an **embryo**. The **embryonic period** will last from 2 weeks after conception to 8 weeks, and during this time the cells will continue to specialize and become the various organs and structures of a human infant. By the end of 8 weeks after conception, the embryo is about 1-inch long and has primitive eyes, nose, lips, teeth, and little arms and legs, as well as a beating heart. Although no organ is fully developed or completely functional at this time, nearly all are "there."

embryo name for the developing organism from 2 weeks to 8 weeks after fertilization.

embryonic period the period from 2 to 8 weeks after fertilization, during which the major organs and structures of the organism develop.

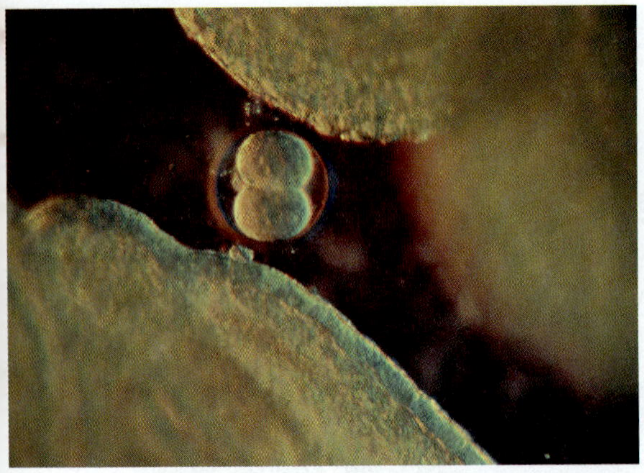
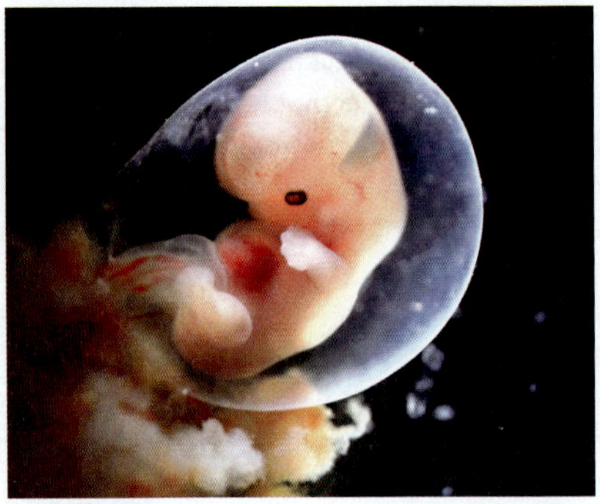
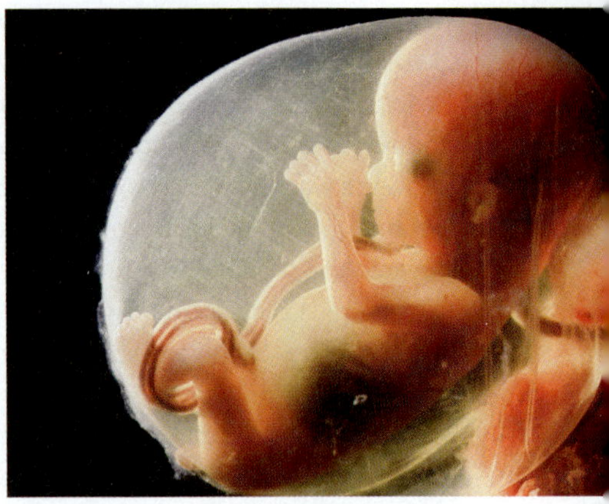

The three periods of pregnancy are the germinal period, lasting about 2 weeks, the embryonic period, from about 2 to 8 weeks, and the fetal period, which lasts from 8 weeks until the end of pregnancy.

CRITICAL PERIODS As soon as the embryo begins to receive nourishment from the mother through the placenta, it becomes vulnerable to hazards such as diseases of the mother, drugs, and other toxins that can pass from the mother through the placenta to the developing infant. (Because the developing organism in the germinal stage is not yet connected to the mother's system, the organism is not usually vulnerable to outside influences in that stage.) It is during the embryonic period that we most clearly see **critical periods**, times during which some environmental influences can have an impact—often devastating—on the development of the infant. The structural development of the arms and legs, for example, is only affected during the time that these limbs are developing ($3\frac{1}{2}$ to 8 weeks), whereas the heart's structure is most affected very early in this period ($2\frac{1}{2}$ to $6\frac{1}{2}$ weeks). Other physical and structural problems can occur with the central nervous system (2 to 5 weeks), eyes ($3\frac{1}{2}$ to $8\frac{1}{2}$ weeks), and the teeth and roof of the mouth (about 7 to 12 weeks).

critical periods times during which certain environmental influences can have an impact on the development of the infant.

teratogen any factor that can cause a birth defect.

PRENATAL HAZARDS: TERATOGENS Any substance such as a drug, chemical, virus, or other factor that can cause a birth defect is called a **teratogen**. Table 8.2 shows some common teratogens and their possible negative effects on the developing embryo.

Table 8.2
Common Teratogens

TERATOGENIC AGENT	EFFECT ON DEVELOPMENT
Rubella	Blindness, deafness, heart defects, brain damage
Marijuana	Irritability, nervousness, tremors; infant is easily disturbed, startled
Cocaine	Decreased height, low birth weight, respiratory problems, seizures, learning difficulties; infant is difficult to soothe
Alcohol	Fetal alcohol syndrome (intellectual disability, delayed growth, facial malformation), learning difficulties, smaller than normal head
Nicotine	Miscarriage, low birth weight, stillbirth, short stature, intellectual disability, learning disabilities
Mercury	Intellectual disability, blindness
Syphilis	Intellectual disability, deafness, meningitis
Caffeine	Miscarriage, low birth weight
Radiation	Higher incidence of cancers, physical deformities
High Water Temperatures	Increased chance of neural tube defects

Source: Shepard, T. H. (2001).

THE FETAL PERIOD: GROW, BABY, GROW

The **fetal period** is the time from about 8 weeks after conception until the birth of the child (now called a **fetus**) and is a period of tremendous growth. The fetus's length increases by about 20 times and its weight increases from about 1 ounce at 2 months to an average of a little over 7 pounds at birth. The organs, while accomplishing most of their differentiation in the embryonic period, continue to develop and become functional. At this time, teratogens will more likely affect the physical functioning (physiology) of the organs rather than their structure. The functioning of the central nervous system, for example, is vulnerable throughout the fetal period, as are the eyes and the external sexual organs.

Muscles begin to contract in the 3rd month. In the 4th month, the mother will begin to feel this movement as a tiny "flutter" or "quickening" at first, and by the 5th month, the flutter will become a "kick." The last few months continue the development of fat and the growth of the body, until about the end of the 38th week. At that time, the fetus is pushed out of the mother's body in the process of labor and childbirth and becomes a baby. Babies born before 38 weeks are called *preterm* and may need life support to survive. This is especially true if the baby weighs less than $5\frac{1}{2}$ pounds at birth.

The most likely time for a *miscarriage*, or *spontaneous abortion*, is in the first 3 months, as the organs are forming and first becoming functional (Katz, 2007; Speroff et al., 1999). Some 15 to 20 percent of all pregnancies end in miscarriage, many so early that the mother may not have even known she was pregnant (Hill, 1998; Medical Economics Staff, 1994). When a miscarriage occurs, it is most likely caused by a genetic defect in the way the embryo or fetus is developing that will not allow the infant to survive. In other words, there isn't anything that the mother did wrong or that could have been done to prevent the miscarriage.

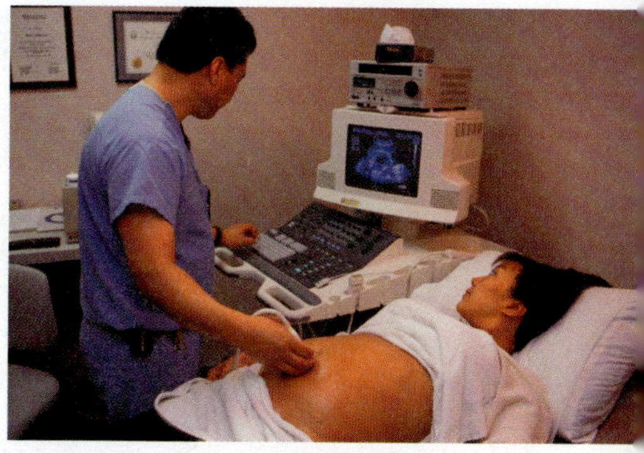

This pregnant woman is getting a sonogram. Sonograms allow doctors to see any physical deformities and make accurate measurements of gestational age without risk to the mother or the fetus.

fetal period the time from about 8 weeks after conception until the birth of the baby.

fetus name for the developing organism from 8 weeks after fertilization to the birth of the baby.

8.4 CONCEPT MAP

- from conception to birth of the baby is approximately 9 months in humans

Prenatal Development

zygote and twinning
- egg and sperm unite through process of fertilization, resulting in a single cell (zygote) that has 46 chromosomes
- through mitosis, zygote begins to divide, into two cells, then four, etc., until baby is formed
- alterations in mitosis can result in twins or multiples

germinal period (2-week period following fertilization)
- zygote continues dividing and moving toward the uterus; the placenta and umbilical cord also develop during this time
- cell differentiation is the process that results in specialized cells for all of the various parts of the body

embryonic period (2 weeks after conception to 8 weeks)
- once attached to the uterus, developing organism is called an embryo
- cell specialization continues to occur, resulting in the preliminary versions of various organs
- embryo is vulnerable to hazards such as diseases and substances ingested by the mother as it receives nourishment through the placenta

fetal period (from about 8 weeks to birth)
- developing organism now called a fetus; time of tremendous growth and development
- organs continue to develop and become fully functional
- muscles begin to contract during the 3rd month, mother can start to feel "flutters" by 4th month, kicks felt by 5 months
- full-term birth occurs around end of 38th week
- miscarriages (spontaneous abortions) are most likely to occur in the first three months

(continued)

PRACTICE quiz How much do you remember? ANSWERS ON PAGE AK-2.

Pick the best answer.

1. Which of the following statements about Abby and Brittany Hensel is FALSE?
   a. They are able to coordinate their actions.
   b. They are remarkably healthy.
   c. They could have been successfully separated.
   d. They are 1 of only 4 sets of living dicephalic twins.
2. The first 2 weeks of pregnancy are called the _________ period.
   a. fetal
   b. embryonic
   c. placental
   d. germinal
3. Which of the following does NOT happen in the germinal period?
   a. dividing mass of cells travels to the uterus
   b. developing organs can be affected by toxins passing through the placenta
   c. mass of cells form a hollow ball
   d. cells begins to differentiate
4. The period of pregnancy that contains the clearest examples of critical periods is the _________ period.
   a. germinal
   b. embryonic
   c. fetal
   d. gestational
5. Intellectual disability and blindness are possible outcomes of the effects of _________ on the developing baby.
   a. alcohol
   b. caffeine
   c. cocaine
   d. mercury

What can babies do? Aren't they pretty much unaware of what's going on around them at first?

Infancy and Childhood Development

What can babies do? Aren't they pretty much unaware of what's going on around them at first?

Surprisingly, babies can do a lot more than researchers used to believe they could. A lot of the early research on infants just after birth was done on babies who were still very drowsy from the general anesthesia that was administered to their mothers during the labor process. Drowsy babies don't tend to respond well, as one might imagine. In the next few sections, it becomes obvious that infants accomplish a great deal throughout infancy, even in the first few days of life on the "outside."

PHYSICAL DEVELOPMENT

8.5 What kind of physical changes take place in infancy and childhood?

Immediately after birth, several things start to happen. The respiratory system begins to function, filling the lungs with air and putting oxygen into the blood. The blood now circulates only within the infant's system because the umbilical cord has been cut. Body temperature is now regulated by the infant's own activity and body fat (which acts as insulation), rather than by the amniotic fluid. The digestive system probably takes the longest to adjust to life outside the womb. This is another reason for the baby's excess body fat. It provides fuel until the infant is able to take in enough nourishment on its own. That is why most babies lose a little weight in the first week after birth.

REFLEXES Babies come into this world able to interact with it. Infants have a set of *innate* (existing from birth) involuntary* behavior patterns called *reflexes*. Until a baby is capable of learning more complex means of interaction, reflexes help the infant to survive. Figure 8.4 shows five infant reflexes. Pediatricians use these and other reflexes to determine whether or not a newborn's nervous system is working properly. **Watch** on **mypsychlab.com**

Watch video footage on newborn reflexes on **mypsychlab.com**

*involuntary: in this sense, not under conscious, deliberate control.

a. b. c.

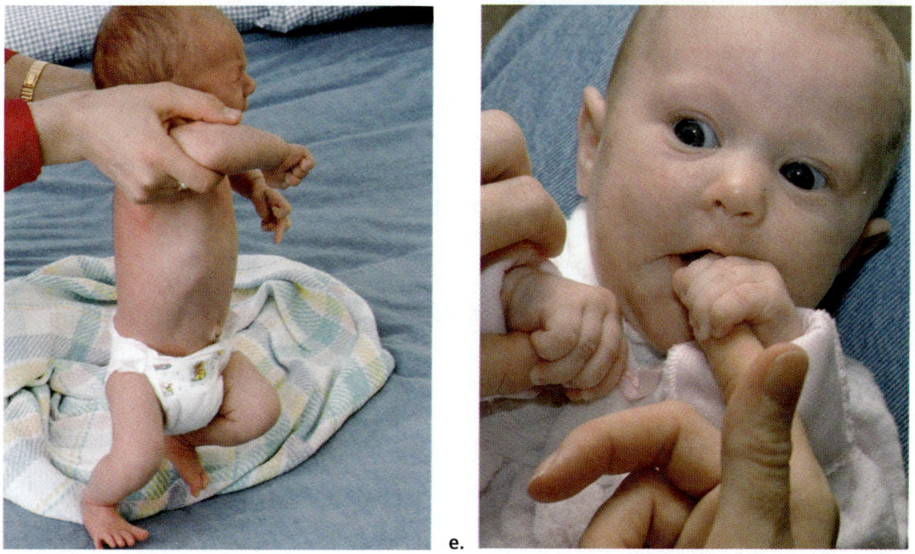

d. e.

Figure 8.4 Five Infant Reflexes

Shown here are (a) grasping reflex; (b) startle reflex (also known as the Moro reflex); (c) rooting reflex (when you touch a baby's cheek it will turn toward your hand, open its mouth, and search for the nipple); (d) stepping reflex; and (e) sucking reflex. These infant reflexes can be used to check the health of an infant's nervous system. If a reflex is absent or abnormal, it may indicate brain damage or some other neurological problem.

BABY, CAN YOU SEE ME? BABY, CAN YOU HEAR ME? SENSORY DEVELOPMENT

I've heard that babies can't see or hear very much at birth. Is that true?

I've heard that babies can't see or hear very much at birth. Is that true?

Although most infant sensory abilities are fairly well developed at birth, some require a bit more time to reach "full power." The sense of touch is the most well developed, which makes perfect sense when one realizes how much skin-to-womb contact the baby has had in the last months of pregnancy. The sense of smell is also highly developed. Breast-fed babies can actually tell the difference between their own mother's milk scent and another woman's milk scent within a few days after birth.

Taste is also nearly fully developed. At birth, infants show a preference for sweets (and human breast milk is very sweet) and by 4 months have developed a preference for salty tastes (which may come from exposure to the salty taste of their mother's skin). Sour and bitter, two other taste sensations, produce spitting up and the making of horrible faces (Ganchrow et al., 1983).

Hearing is functional before birth but may take a little while to reach its full potential after the baby is born. The fluids of the womb first must clear out of the auditory canals completely. From birth, newborns seem most responsive to high pitches, as in a woman's voice, and low pitches, as in a male's voice.

The least functional sense at birth is vision. As stated in Chapter Three, the eye is quite a complex organ. LINK to Chapter Three: Sensation and Perception, pp. 94–96. The rods, which see in black and white and have little visual acuity, are fairly well developed at birth, but the cones, which see color and provide sharpness of vision, will take about another 6 months to fully develop. So, the newborn has relatively poor color perception when compared to sharply contrasting lights and darks until about 2 months of age (Adams, 1987) and has fairly "fuzzy" vision, much as a nearsighted person would have. The lens of the newborn stays fixed until the muscles that hold it in place mature. Until then the newborn is unable to shift what little focus it has from close to far. Thus, newborns actually have a fixed distance for clear vision of about 7 to 10 inches, which is the distance from the baby's face to the mother's face while nursing (Slater, 2000).

Newborns also have visual preferences at birth, as discovered by researchers using measures of the time that infants spent looking at certain visual stimuli (Fantz, 1961). They found that infants prefer to look at complex patterns rather than simple ones, three dimensions rather than two, and that the most preferred visual stimulus was a human face. The fact that infants prefer human voices and human faces (DeCasper & Fifer, 1980; DeCasper & Spence, 1986; Fantz, 1964; Maurer & Young, 1983) makes it easier for them to form relationships with their caregivers and to develop language later on. Infants' preference for seeing things in three dimensions suggests that they possess depth perception. The following classic experiment provided evidence for that assumption. **Explore** on **mypsychlab.com**

Explore infants' perceptual and cognitive milestones on **mypsychlab.com**

classic studies in psychology

The Visual Cliff

Eleanor Gibson and her fellow researcher, Michael Walk, wondered if infants could perceive the world in three dimensions and so they devised a way to test babies for depth perception (Gibson & Walk, 1960). They built a special table (see Figure 8.5) that had a big drop on one side. The surface of the table on both the top and the drop to the floor were covered in a patterned tablecloth, so that the different size of the patterns would be a cue for depth (remember, in size constancy, if something looks smaller, people assume it is farther away from them). The whole table was then covered by a clear-glass top, so that a baby could safely be placed on or crawl across the "deep" side.

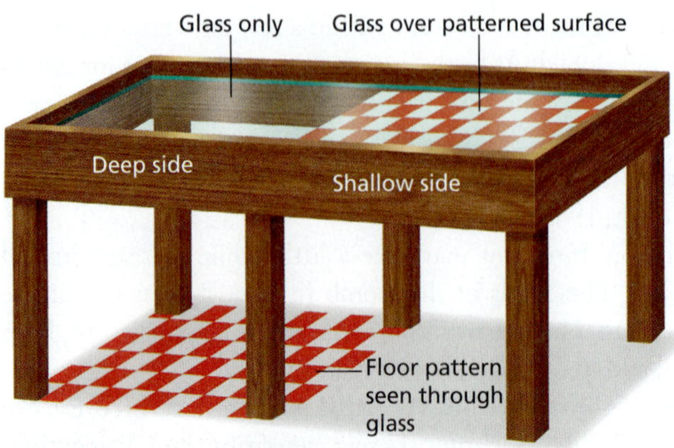

Figure 8.5 The Visual Cliff Experiment
In the visual cliff experiment, the table has both a shallow and a "deep" side, with glass covering the entire table. When an infant looks down at the deep-appearing side, the squares in the design on the floor look smaller than the ones on the shallow side, forming a visual cue for depth. Notice that this little girl seems to be very reluctant to cross over the deep-appearing side of the table, gesturing to be picked up, instead.

The infants tested in this study ranged from 6 months to 14 months in age. They were placed on the middle of the table and then encouraged (usually by their mothers) to crawl over either the shallow side or the deep side. Most babies—81 percent—refused to crawl over the deep side, even though they could touch it with their hands and feel that it was solid. They were upset and seemed fearful when encouraged to crawl across. Gibson and Walk interpreted this as a very early sign of the concept of depth perception.

Questions for Further Discussion

1. Does the fact that 19 percent of the infants did crawl over the deep side of the visual cliff necessarily mean that those infants could not perceive the depth?
2. What other factors might explain the willingness of the 19 percent to crawl over the deep side?
3. Are there any ethical concerns in this experiment?
4. Ducks aren't bothered by the visual cliff at all—why might that be?

FROM CRAWLING TO A BLUR OF MOTION: MOTOR DEVELOPMENT Infants manage a tremendous amount of development in motor skills from birth to about 2 years of age. Figure 8.6 shows some of the major physical milestones of infancy. When looking at the age ranges listed, remember that even these ranges are averages based on large samples of infants. An infant may reach these milestones earlier or later than the average and still be considered to be developing normally.

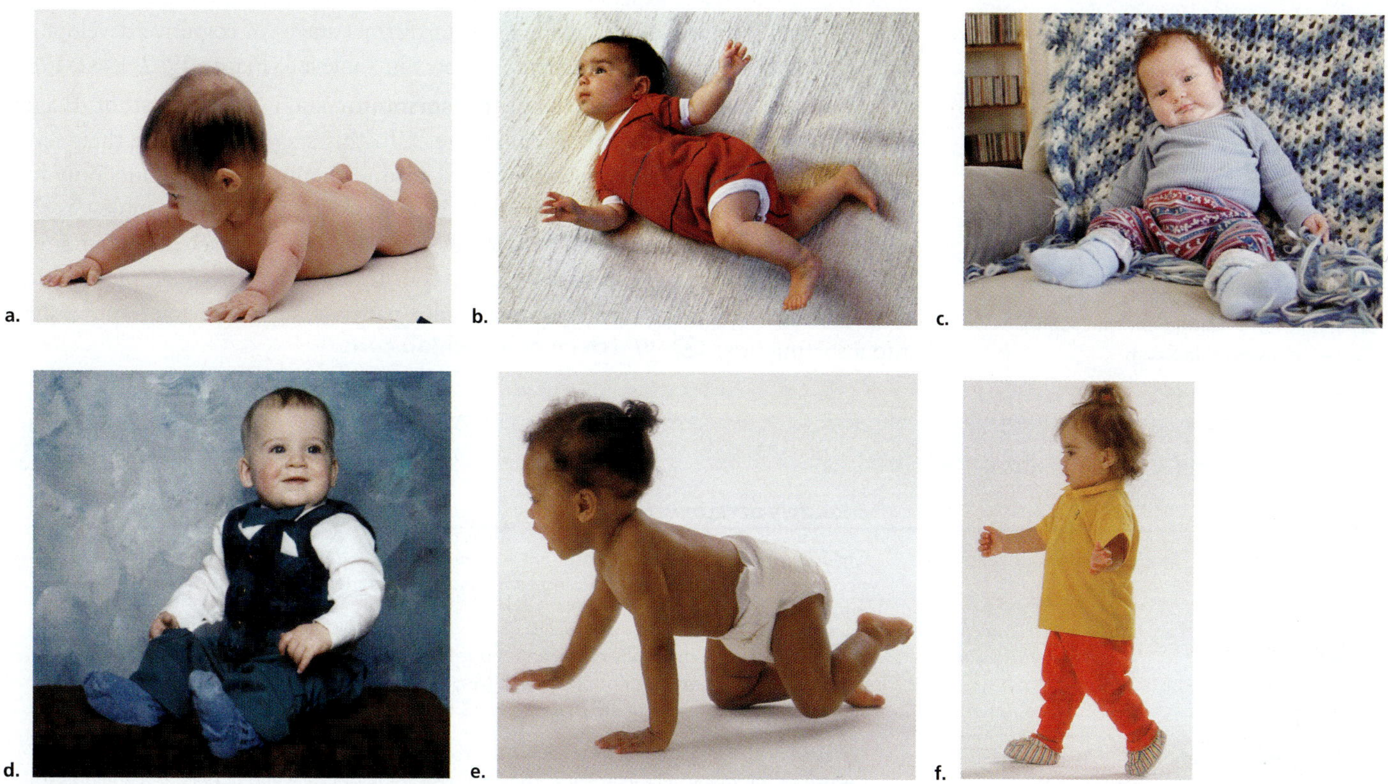

Figure 8.6 Six Motor Milestones

Shown here are (a) raising head and chest—2 to 4 months, (b) rolling over—2 to 5 months, (c) sitting up with support—4 to 6 months, (d) sitting up without support—6 to 7 months, (e) crawling—7 to 8 months, and (f) walking—8 to 18 months. The motor milestones develop as the infant gains greater voluntary control over the muscles in its body, typically from the top of the body downward. This pattern is seen in the early control of the neck muscles and the much later development of control of the legs and feet.

cognitive development the development of thinking, problem solving, and memory.

scheme in this case, a mental concept formed through experiences with objects and events.

sensorimotor stage Piaget's first stage of cognitive development in which the infant uses its senses and motor abilities to interact with objects in the environment.

COGNITIVE DEVELOPMENT

By the time the average infant has reached the age of 1 year, it has tripled its birth weight and added about another foot to its height. The brain triples its weight in the first 2 years, reaching about 75 percent of its adult weight. By age 5, the brain is at 90 percent of its adult weight. This increase makes possible a tremendous amount of major advances in **cognitive development**, including the development of thinking, problem solving, and memory.

8.6 What are two ways of looking at cognitive development, and how does language develop?

PIAGET'S THEORY: FOUR STAGES OF COGNITIVE DEVELOPMENT One of the three ways of examining the development of cognition that we will discuss in this chapter is found in the work of Jean Piaget. Early researcher Jean Piaget developed his theory from detailed observations of infants and children, most especially his own three children. Piaget made significant contributions to the understanding of how children think about the world around them; his theory shifted the commonly held view that children's thinking was that of "little adults" toward recognition that it was actually quite different from adult thinking. Piaget believed that children form mental concepts or **schemes** as they experience new situations and events. For example, if Sandy points to a picture of an apple and tells her child, "that's an apple," the child forms a scheme for "apple" that looks something like that picture. Piaget also believed that children first try to understand new things in terms of schemes they already possess, a process called *assimilation*. The child might see an orange and say "apple" because both objects are round. When corrected, the child might alter the scheme for apple to include "round" and "red." The process of altering or adjusting old schemes to fit new information and experiences is *accommodation* (Piaget, 1952, 1962, 1983).

Piaget also proposed that there are four distinct stages of cognitive development that occur from infancy to adolescence, as shown in Table 8.3 (Piaget, 1952, 1962, 1983).

The Sensorimotor Stage The **sensorimotor stage** is the first of Piaget's stages. It concerns infants from birth to age 2. In this stage, infants use their senses and motor abilities to learn about the world around them. At first, infants only have the involuntary reflexes present at birth to interact with objects and people. As their sensory and motor development progresses, they begin to interact deliberately with objects by grasping, pushing, tasting, and so on. Infants move from simple repetitive actions, such as grabbing their toes, to complex patterns, such as trying to put a shape into a sorting box. **Watch** on **mypsychlab.com**

Watch classic footage on sensorimotor development with Jean Piaget on **mypsychlab.com**

Table 8.3

Piaget's Stages of Cognitive Development

STAGE		COGNITIVE DEVELOPMENT
Sensorimotor	Birth to 2 years old	Children explore the world using their senses and ability to move. They develop object permanence and the understanding that concepts and mental images represent objects, people, and events.
Preoperational	2 to 7 years old	Young children can mentally represent and refer to objects and events with words or pictures and they can pretend. However, they can't conserve, logically reason, or simultaneously consider many characteristics of an object.
Concrete Operations	7 to 12 years old	Children at this stage are able to conserve, reverse their thinking, and classify objects in terms of their many characteristics. They can also think logically and understand analogies but only about concrete events.
Formal Operations	12 years old to adulthood	People at this stage can use abstract reasoning about hypothetical events or situations, think about logical possibilities, use abstract analogies, and systematically examine and test hypotheses. Not everyone can eventually reason in all these ways.

By the end of the sensorimotor stage, infants have fully developed a sense of **object permanence**, the knowledge that an object exists even when it is not in sight. For example, the game of "peek-a-boo" is important in teaching infants that Mommy's smiling face is always going to be behind her hands. This is a critical step in developing language (and eventually abstract thought), as words themselves are symbols of things that may not be present. Symbolic thought, which is the ability to represent objects in one's thoughts with symbols such as words, becomes possible by the end of this stage, with children at 2 years old capable of thinking in simple symbols and planning out actions.

object permanence the knowledge that an object exists even when it is not in sight.

preoperational stage Piaget's second stage of cognitive development in which the preschool child learns to use language as a means of exploring the world.

Why is it so easy for children to believe in Santa Claus and the Tooth Fairy when they're little?

Why is it so easy for children to believe in Santa Claus and the Tooth Fairy when they're little?

The Preoperational Stage The **preoperational stage** (ages 2–7) is a time of developing language and concepts. Children, who can now move freely about in their world, no longer have to rely only on senses and motor skills but now can ask questions and explore their surroundings more fully. Pretending and make-believe play become possible because children at this stage can understand, through symbolic thinking, that a line of wooden blocks can "stand in" for a train. They are limited, however, in several ways. They are not yet capable of logical thought—they can use simple mental concepts but are not able to use those concepts in a more rational, logical sense. They believe that anything that moves is alive, a quality called *animism*. They tend to believe that what they see is literally true, so when children of this age see Santa Claus in a book, on television, or at the mall, Santa Claus becomes real to them. It doesn't occur to them to think about how Santa might get to every child's house in one night or why those toys he delivers are the same ones they saw in the store just last week. They may be able to count up to 10 or 20, but they won't realize that in the bottom example in Figure 8.7 both rows have the same number of coins, because they focus on the longer *appearance* of the top row of coins.

Type of conservation	Initial presentation	Transformation	Question	Preoperational child's answer
Liquids	Two equal glasses of liquid 	Pour one into a taller, narrower glass. 	Which glass contains more?	The taller one.
Number	Two equal lines of pennies 	Increase spacing of pennies in one line. 	Which line has more pennies?	The longer one. 

Figure 8.7 Conservation Experiment

A typical conservation task consists of pouring equal amounts of water into two glasses of the same size and shape. When the water from one of these glasses is poured into a taller, narrower glass, children who cannot yet conserve tend to focus (centrate) on the height of the water in the second glass, assuming that the second glass now has more water than the first one. In the second example, pennies are laid out in two equal lines. When the pennies in the top line are spaced out, the child who cannot yet conserve will centrate on the top line and assume that there are actually more pennies in that line.

egocentrism the inability to see the world through anyone else's eyes.

centration in Piaget's theory, the tendency of a young child to focus only on one feature of an object while ignoring other relevant features.

conservation in Piaget's theory, the ability to understand that simply changing the appearance of an object does not change the object's nature.

irreversibility in Piaget's theory, the inability of the young child to mentally reverse an action.

concrete operations stage Piaget's third stage of cognitive development in which the school-age child becomes capable of logical thought processes but is not yet capable of abstract thinking.

formal operations stage Piaget's last stage of cognitive development, in which the adolescent becomes capable of abstract thinking.

Another limitation is **egocentrism**, the inability to see the world through anyone else's eyes but one's own. For the preoperational child, everyone else must see what the child sees, and what is important to the child must be important to everyone else. For example, 2-year-old Hiba, after climbing out of her crib for the third time, was told by her mother, "I don't want to see you in that living room again tonight!" So Hiba's next appearance was made with her hands over her eyes—if she couldn't see her mother, her mother couldn't see *her*. Egocentrism is not the same as being egotistical or selfish—it would also be egocentric, but completely unselfish, if 4-year-old Jamal wants to give his grandmother an action figure for her birthday because that's what *he* would want.

Remember that children in this stage are also overwhelmed by appearances, as in the coin example. A child who complains that his piece of pie is smaller than his brother's may be quite happy once his original piece is cut into two pieces—now he thinks he has "more" than his brother. He has focused only on the number of pieces, not the actual amount of the pie. Focusing only on one feature of some object rather than taking all features into consideration is called **centration**. In the coin example in Figure 8.7, children of this stage will focus (or center) on the *length* of the top line of coins only and ignore the *number* of coins. Centration is one of the reasons that children in this stage often fail to understand that changing the way something looks does not change its substance. The ability to understand that altering the appearance of something does not change its amount (as in the coin example), its volume, or its mass is called **conservation**.

Preoperational children fail at conservation not only because they centrate (focusing on just one feature, such as the number of pieces of pie) but also because they are unable to "mentally reverse" actions. This feature of preoperational thinking is called **irreversibility**. For example, if a preoperational child sees liquid poured from a short, wide glass into a tall, thin glass, the child will assume that the second glass holds more liquid. This failure to "conserve" (save) the volume of liquid as it takes on a different shape in the tall, thin glass is not only caused by the child's centration on the height of the liquid in the second glass but also by the inability of the child to imagine pouring the liquid back into the first glass and having it be the same amount again. Similar "reasoning" causes children of this age to assume that a ball of clay, when rolled out into a "rope" of clay, is now greater in mass.

Concrete Operations In the **concrete operations stage** (ages 7–12), children finally become capable of conservation and reversible thinking. Centration no longer occurs as children become capable of considering all the relevant features of any given object. They begin to think more logically about beliefs such as Santa Claus and ask questions, eventually coming to their own more rational conclusions about the fantasies of early childhood. They are in school, learning all sorts of science and math, and are convinced that they know more than their parents at this point.

The major limitation of this stage is the inability to deal effectively with *abstract concepts*. Abstract concepts are those that do not have some physical, *concrete*, touchable reality. For example, "freedom" is an abstract concept. People can define it, they can get a good sense of what it means, but there is no "thing" that they can point to and say, "This is freedom." *Concrete concepts*, which are the kind of concepts understood by children of this age, are about objects, written rules, and real things. Children need to be able to see it, touch it, or at least "see" it in their heads to be able to understand it.

These concrete operational children, seen in a science class, have begun to think logically and are able to solve many kinds of problems that were not possible for them to solve while in the preoperational stage.

Formal Operations In the last of Piaget's stages, **formal operations** (age 12 to adulthood), abstract thinking becomes possible. Teenagers not only understand concepts that have no physical reality, but also they get deeply involved in hypothetical thinking, or thinking about possibilities and even impossibilities. "What if everyone just got along?" "If women were in charge of countries, would there be fewer wars?"

Piaget did not believe that everyone would necessarily reach formal operations, and studies show that only about half of all adults in the United States reach formal operations (Sutherland, 1992). Adults who do not achieve formal operations tend to use a more practical, down-to-earth kind of intelligence that suits their particular lifestyle. Successful college students, however, need formal-operational thinking to succeed in their college careers, as most college classes require critical thinking, problem-solving abilities, and abstract thinking based on formal-operational skills (Powers, 1984).

Piaget saw children as active explorers of their surroundings, engaged in the discovery of the properties of objects and organisms within those surroundings. Educators have put Piaget's ideas into practice by allowing children to learn at their own pace, by "hands-on" experience with objects, and by teaching concepts that are at the appropriate cognitive level for those children (Brooks & Brooks, 1993). But Piaget's theory has also been criticized on several points. Some researchers believe that the idea of distinct stages of cognitive development is not completely correct and that changes in thought are more continuous and gradual rather than abruptly jumping from one stage to another (Courage & Howe, 2002; Feldman, 2003; Schwitzgebel, 1999; Siegler, 1996). Others point out that preschoolers are not as egocentric as Piaget seemed to believe (Flavell, 1999) and that object permanence exists much earlier than Piaget thought (Aguiar & Baillargeon, 2003; Baillargeon, 1986).

Piaget seemed to focus on the child's cognitive development as if the other people in the child's world were not all that necessary to the acquisition of knowledge and the development of skills. It is true, after all, that children are able to grasp many ideas and concepts through their own thought processes and interactions with objects, discovering basic principles and characteristics of objects in individual play. In contrast, psychologist Lev Vygotsky emphasized that other people, acting as teachers and mentors, were a crucial part of the cognitive development of the child (Duncan, 1995).

This boy is helping his younger sister learn to read a book. Vygotsky's view of cognitive development states that the help of skilled others aids in making cognitive advances such as this one.

VYGOTSKY'S THEORY: THE IMPORTANCE OF BEING THERE Russian psychologist Lev Vygotsky developed a theory of how children think that did not match the prevailing political ideas in Russia. After his death from tuberculosis in 1934, his ideas were suppressed by the government but kept alive by his students and later republished. Vygotsky's pioneering work in developmental psychology has had a profound influence on school education in Russia, and interest in his theories continues to grow throughout the world (Bodrova & Leong, 1996). Vygotsky wrote about children's cognitive development but differed from Piaget in his emphasis on the role of others in cognitive development (Vygotsky, 1934/1962, 1978, 1987). Whereas Piaget stressed the importance of the child's interaction with objects as a primary factor in cognitive development, Vygotsky stressed the importance of social interactions with other people, typically more highly skilled children and adults. Vygotsky believed that children develop cognitively when someone else helps them by asking leading questions and providing examples of concepts in a process called **scaffolding**. In scaffolding, the more highly skilled person gives the learner more help at the beginning of the learning process and then begins to withdraw help as the learner's skills improve (Rogoff, 1994).

Vygotsky also proposed that each developing child has a **zone of proximal development (ZPD)**, which is the difference between what a child can do alone versus what a child can do with the help of a teacher. For example, if little Jenny can do math problems up to the fourth-grade level on her own but with the help of a teacher can successfully work problems at a sixth-grade level, her ZPD is 2 years. Suzi might be the same age as Jenny (and might even score the same on a traditional IQ test), but if Suzi can only work math problems at a fifth-grade level with the help of the teacher, Suzi's ZPD is not as great as Jenny's. This might be a better way of thinking about intelligence: It isn't what you know (as measured by traditional tests), it's what you *can do*.

scaffolding process in which a more skilled learner gives help to a less skilled learner, reducing the amount of help as the less skilled learner becomes more capable.

zone of proximal development (ZPD) Vygotsky's concept of the difference between what a child can do alone and what that child can do with the help of a teacher.

Other researchers have applied Vygotsky's social focus on learning to the development of a child's memory for personal (autobiographical) events, finding evidence that children learn the culturally determined structures and purposes of personal stories from the early conversations they have with their parents. This process begins with the parent telling the story to the very young child, followed by the child repeating elements of the story as the child's verbal abilities grow. The child reaches the final stage at around age 5 or 6 when the child creates the personal story entirely—an excellent example of scaffolding (Fivush et al., 1996; Fivush & Nelson, 2004; Nelson, 1993). Vygotsky's ideas have been put into practice in education through the use of cooperative learning, in which children work together in groups to achieve a common goal, and in reciprocal teaching, in which teachers lead students through the basic strategies of reading until the students themselves become capable of teaching the strategies to others.

This infant has already learned some of the basics of language, including the use of gestures to indicate meaning and enhance communication.

STAGES OF LANGUAGE DEVELOPMENT The development of language is a very important milestone in the cognitive development of a child because language allows children to think in words rather than just images, to ask questions, to communicate their needs and wants to others, and to form concepts (L. Bloom, 1974; P. Bloom, 2000). Early views of language development were based on Skinnerian principles of reinforcement. However, Noam Chomsky argued strongly against this. He proposed a LAD (language acquisition device), an innate "program" that contained a *schema* for human language. The children matched the language they heard against this schema and, thus, language developed in a well-researched sequence (Chomsky, 1957, 1964, 1981, 1986).

Newer theories of language development are focusing on environmental influences on language such as *child-directed speech* (the way adults and older children talk to infants and very young children, with higher pitched, repetitious, sing-song speech patterns). Infants and toddlers attend more closely to this kind of speech, which creates a learning opportunity in the dialogue between caregiver and infant (Dominey & Dodane, 2004; Fernald, 1984, 1992; Küntay & Slobin, 2002). Other researchers are looking at the infant's use of gestures and signs (Behne et al., 2005; Lizskowski et al., 2006; Moll & Tomasello, 2007; Tomasello et al., 2007).

Infants also seem to understand far more than they can produce, a phenomenon known as the *receptive-productive lag* (Stevenson et al., 1988). They may be able to only produce one or two words, but they understand much longer sentences from their parents and others.

There are several stages of language development that all children experience, no matter what culture they live in or what language they will learn to speak (Brown, 1973):

1. **Cooing:** At around 2 months of age, babies begin to make vowel-like sounds.
2. **Babbling:** At about 6 months, infants add consonant sounds to the vowels to make a babbling sound, which at times can almost sound like real speech. Deaf children actually decrease their babbling after 6 months while increasing their use of primitive hand signs and gestures (Petitto & Marentette, 1991; Petitto et al., 2001).
3. **One-word speech:** Somewhere just before or around age 1, most children begin to say actual words. These words are typically nouns and may seem to represent an entire phrase of meaning. They are called *holophrases* (whole phrases in one word) for that reason. For example, a child might say "Milk!" and mean "I want some milk!" or "I drank my milk!"
4. **Telegraphic speech:** At around a year and a half, toddlers begin to string words together to form short, simple sentences using nouns, verbs, and adjectives. "Baby eat," "Mommy go," and "Doggie go bye-bye" are examples of telegraphic speech. Only the words that carry the meaning of the sentence are used.

5. **Whole sentences:** As children move through the preschool years, they learn to use grammatical terms and increase the number of words in their sentences, until by age 6 or so they are nearly as fluent as an adult, although the number of words they know is still limited when compared to adult vocabulary.

Before leaving the topic of cognitive development in infancy, let's briefly discuss a topic that has been making the news lately: the causes underlying autism spectrum disorder. Autism spectrum disorder (ASD) is actually a whole range of disorders (with what may be an equally broad range of causes), which cause problems in thinking, feeling, language, and social skills in relating to others. First diagnosed in early childhood, these disorders range from a severe form called autistic disorder to a much milder form called Asperger's syndrome (Atladóttir et al., 2009; Johnson & Myers, 2007). Rumors and misinformation about the causes of autism have been circulting on the internet for mant years. The following section describes the truth behind one of the most dangerous pieces of misinformation on this topic. Listen on mypsychlab.com

Listen to the Psychology in the News podcast about autism research on **mypsychlab.com**

issues in psychology

The Big Lie: Dr. Andrew Wakefield and the Vaccine Scandal

In 1998, British Dr. Andrew Wakefield (a gastroenterologist and certainly not an autism expert, nor even a pediatrician) published the results of two studies that seemed to link the MMR (measles, mumps, and rubella) vaccine to autism and bowel disease in children (Wakefield et al., 1998). The studies were quickly denounced as inadequate and dangerous by autism specialists and others: There were only 12 children considered in the research, hardly a large enough participant group from which to draw valid conclusions; there were no control groups; and neither study was blind—single or double (Fitzpatrick, 2004; Judelsohn, 2007; Matthew & Dallery, 2007; Novella, 2007; Stratton et al., 2001a, 2001b). LINK to Chapter One: The Science of Psychology, pp. 30–31. Nevertheless, Wakefield's publication was followed by measles epidemics due to parents refusing the MMR inoculation for their children. The myth of a link persists, in spite of numerous studies that have consistently failed to show any link between the MMR vaccine and autism (Gilberg & Coleman, 2000; Johnson & Myers, 2007; Madsen et al., 2002; Mars et al., 1998; Taylor et al., 1999; Thompson et al., 2007).

An investigation has been conducted in the past few years that continues to confirm these results (Burns, 2010; Gilberg & Coleman, 2000; Madsen et al., 2002; Taylor et al., 1999; Thompson et al., 2007).

Questions have been raised concerning Wakefield's motivation to discredit the MMR vaccine. Upon investigation, it was discovered that 2 years before Wakefield published his studies, he had received money from lawyers wanting to file lawsuits against the makers of the vaccine on behalf of parents who believed their autistic children were damaged by the vaccination. One year before the publication, Wakefield had applied for a patent for his own measles vaccine, which would be a competitor for the MMR and other existing measles vaccines. In 2009, the final blow came to Wakefield's credibility when it was discovered that he had falsified his data. In 2004, the other authors listed on the study formally retracted the 1998 paper.

As a result of the British Medical Council's investigation into Wakefield's actions, Wakefield's medical license was revoked in May of 2010, after the council found him guilty of "serious professional misconduct."

Questions for Further Discussion

1. How accountable do you believe Dr. Wakefield to be for the trend of refusing immunizations for one's child?
2. How accountable are the parents who refuse to vaccinate their children based on this misinformation?

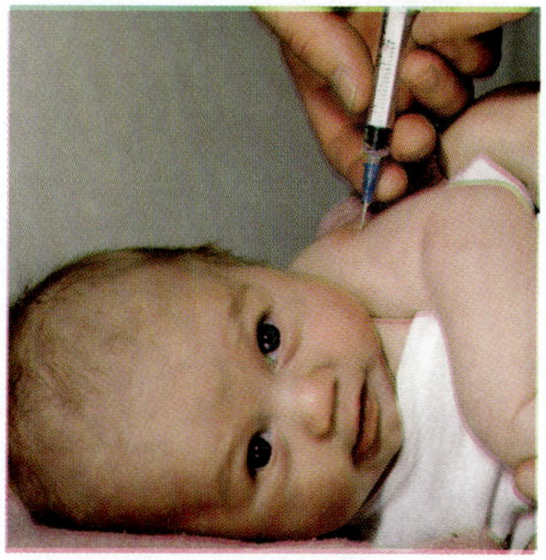

One of the most important things parents can do for the continued health and safety of their infant is to have the baby immunized, following an approved schedule for each type of vaccine. Immunizations today are safe and effective and prevent dangerous and often deadly childhood diseases, such as rubella.

8.5 8.6

CONCEPT MAP

- **physical development**
  - immediately after birth, body systems start to function (i.e., respiratory, circulatory, temperature regulation, digestive)
  - babies are born with (innate) reflex behaviors (see Fig. 8.4)
- **sensory development**
  - touch, taste, and smell are well developed
  - hearing is functional but not fully developed
  - vision is least developed (rods are functional, cones take about 6 months to fully develop)
- **motor development**
  - as with physical and sensory development, normal motor development is related to many factors, such as nutrition, care, and health
  - birth to 2 years = period of rapid development (see Fig. 8.6)

Infancy and Childhood Development

- **Piaget's theory**
  - suggests children form mental concepts or schemes as they experience new situations and events — understand new things in terms of schemes they already possess (assimilation) or through altering or adjusting old schemes to fit new information (accommodation)
  - proposes four distinct stages of cognitive development that span infancy to adolescence
    - **sensorimotor**
    - **preoperational**
    - **concrete operations**
    - **formal operations**
    - see Table 8.3
- **Vygotsky's theory**
  - stresses the importance of social interactions with others, typically more highly skilled children and adults
  - children's cognitive development occurs when someone helps them by asking leading questions and providing examples of concepts (scaffolding)
  - each child has a zone of proximal development—difference between what they can do alone vs. with aid of a teacher

Infancy and Childhood Development: Cognitive Development

- **stages of language development**
  - language allows children to think in words, ask questions, communicate needs and wants, and form concepts
  - various views of development
    - early views were based on principles of operant conditioning
    - Chomsky proposed innate language acquisition device (LAD) that contains schema for language
    - newer theories focus on environmental influences and possible lags in reception vs. production
  - universal progressive stages — cooing, babbling, one-word speech, telegraphic speech, whole sentences

PRACTICE quiz How much do you remember?

ANSWERS ON PAGE AK-2.

Pick the best answer.

1. Which sense is least functional at birth?
   a. touch
   b. taste
   c. smell
   d. vision
2. What is the first voluntary movement that allows an infant to get from one place to another?
   a. sitting without support
   b. rolling over
   c. raising the head when placed face down
   d. standing
3. In which of Piaget's stages would a child be who has just developed object permanence?
   a. sensorimotor
   b. preoperational
   c. concrete operations
   d. formal operations
4. Vygotsky defines __________ as the difference between what a child can do alone and what that child can do with help.
   a. scaffolding
   b. habituation
   c. zone of proximal development
   d. metamemory
5. "Daddy go bye-bye" is an example of __________.
   a. telegraphic speech.
   b. babbling.
   c. a holophrase.
   d. cooing.

PSYCHOSOCIAL DEVELOPMENT

8.7 How do infants and children develop personalities and form relationships with others, and what are Erikson's stages of psychosocial development for children?

The psychological and social development of infants and children involves the development of personality, relationships, and a sense of being male or female. Although these processes begin in infancy, they will continue, in many respects, well into adulthood.

Why are some children negative and whiny while others are sweet and good natured?

Why are some children negative and whiny while others are sweet and good natured?

TEMPERAMENT One of the first ways in which infants demonstrate that they have different personalities (i.e., the long-lasting characteristics that make each person different from others) is in their **temperament**, the behavioral and emotional characteristics that are fairly well established at birth. Researchers (Chess & Thomas, 1986; Thomas & Chess, 1977) have identified three basic temperament styles of infants:

1. **Easy:** "Easy" babies are regular in their schedules of waking, sleeping, and eating and are adaptable to change. Easy babies are happy babies and when distressed are easily soothed.
2. **Difficult:** "Difficult" babies are almost the opposite of easy ones. Difficult babies tend to be irregular in their schedules and are very unhappy about change of any kind. They are loud, active, and tend to be crabby rather than happy.
3. **Slow to warm up:** This kind of temperament is associated with infants who are less grumpy, quieter, and more regular than difficult children but who are slow to adapt to change. If change is introduced gradually, these babies will "warm up" to new people and new situations.

Of course, not all babies will fall neatly into one of these three patterns—some children may be a mix of two or even all three patterns of behavior, as Chess and Thomas (1986) discovered. Even so, longitudinal research strongly suggests that these temperament styles last well into adulthood (Kagan, 1998; Kagan et al., 2007; Korn, 1984; Scarpa et al., 1995), although they are somewhat influenced by the environment in which the infant is raised. For example, a "difficult" infant who is raised by parents who are themselves very loud and active may not be perceived as difficult by the parents, whereas a child who is slow to warm up might be perceived as difficult if the parents themselves like lots of change and noise. The first infant is in a situation in which the "goodness of fit" of the infant's temperament to the parents' temperament is very close, but the parents of the second infant are a "poor fit" in temperament for that less active child (Chess & Thomas, 1986). A poor fit can make it difficult to form an attachment, the important psychosocial–emotional bond we will discuss next.

ATTACHMENT The emotional bond that forms between an infant and a primary caregiver is called **attachment**. Attachment is an extremely important development in the social and emotional life of the infant, usually forming within the first 6 months of the infant's life and showing up in a number of ways during the second 6 months, such as wariness of strangers and fear of being separated from the caregiver. Although attachment to the mother is usually the primary attachment, infants can attach to fathers and to other caregivers as well.

Mary Ainsworth (Ainsworth, 1985; Ainsworth et al., 1978) devised a special experimental design to measure the attachment of an infant to the caregiver; she called it the "Strange Situation" (exposing an infant to a series of leave-takings and returns of the mother and a stranger). Through this measurement technique, Ainsworth and another colleague identified four attachment styles:

temperament the behavioral characteristics that are fairly well established at birth, such as "easy," "difficult," and "slow to warm up."

attachment the emotional bond between an infant and the primary caregiver.

This toddler shows reluctance to explore his environment, instead, clinging to his father's legs. Such clinging behavior, if common, can be a sign of an ambivalent attachment.

1. **Secure:** Infants labeled as secure were willing to get down from their mother's lap soon after entering the room with their mothers. They explored happily, looking back at their mothers and returning to them every now and then (sort of like "touching base"). When the stranger came in, these infants were wary but calm as long as their mother was nearby. When the mother left, the infants got upset. When the mother returned, the infants approached her, were easily soothed, and were glad to have her back.
2. **Avoidant:** In contrast, avoidant babies, although somewhat willing to explore, did not "touch base." They did not look at the stranger or the mother, and reacted very little to her absence or her return, seeming to have no interest or concern.
3. **Ambivalent:** The word *ambivalent* means to have mixed feelings about something. Ambivalent babies in Ainsworth's study were clinging and unwilling to explore, very upset by the stranger regardless of the mother's presence, protested mightily when the mother left, and were hard to soothe. When the mother returned, these babies would demand to be picked up, but at the same time push the mother away or kick her in a mixed reaction to her return.
4. **Disorganized–disoriented:** In subsequent studies, other researchers (Main & Hesse, 1990; Main & Solomon, 1990) found that some babies seemed unable to decide just how they should react to the mother's return. These disorganized–disoriented infants would approach her but with their eyes turned away from her, as if afraid to make eye contact. In general, these infants seemed fearful and showed a dazed and depressed look on their faces.

It should come as no surprise that the mothers of each of the four types of infants also behaved differently from one another. Mothers of secure infants were loving, warm, sensitive to their infant's needs, and responsive to the infant's attempts at communication. Mothers of avoidant babies were unresponsive, insensitive, and coldly rejecting. Mothers of ambivalent babies tried to be responsive but were inconsistent and insensitive to the baby's actions, often talking to the infant about something totally unrelated to what the infant was doing at the time. Mothers of disorganized–disoriented babies were found to be abusive or neglectful in interactions with the infants.

Attachment is not necessarily the result of the behavior of the mother alone, however. The temperament of the infant may play an important part in determining the reactions of the mothers (Goldsmith & Campos, 1982; Skolnick, 1986). For example, an infant with a difficult temperament is hard to soothe. A mother with this kind of infant might come to avoid unnecessary contact with the infant, as did the mothers of the avoidant babies in Ainsworth's studies.

Critics of Ainsworth's Strange-Situation research focus on the artificial nature of the design and wonder if infants and mothers would behave differently in the more familiar surroundings of home, even though Ainsworth's experimental observers also observed the infants and mothers in the home prior to the Strange Situation setting (Ainsworth, 1985). Other research has found results supporting Ainsworth's findings in home-based assessments of attachment (Blanchard & Main, 1979). Other studies have also found support for the concept of attachment styles and stability of attachment over the first 6 years of life (Lutkenhaus et al., 1985; Main & Cassidy, 1988; Owen et al., 1984; Wartner et al., 1994). Even adult relationships can be seen as influenced by the attachment style of the adult—those who are avoidant tend to have numerous shallow and brief relationships with different partners, whereas those who are ambivalent tend to have repeated break-ups and make-ups with the same person (Bartholomew, 1990; Hazan & Shaver, 1987).

As day care has become more widely acceptable and common, many parents have been concerned about the effect of day care on attachment. Psychologist Jay Belsky and colleagues (Belsky, 2005; Belsky & Johnson, 2005; Belsky et al., 2007) have studied the attachment of infants in day care and concluded that although higher quality of day care (small child-to-caregiver ratio, low turnover in caregivers, and caregivers educated in child-care techniques and theory) is important, especially for cognitive development, positive development including attachment was more clearly related to the quality of parenting that the infants and toddlers received at home.

Although there are some cultural differences in attachment—such as the finding that mothers in the United States tend to wait for a child to express a need before trying to fulfill that need, while Japanese mothers prefer to anticipate the child's needs (Rothbaum et al., 2000)—attachment does not seem to suffer in spite of the differences in sensitivity. Evidence that similar attachment styles are found in other cultures demonstrates the need to consider attachment as an important first step in forming relationships with others, one which may set the stage for all relationships that follow (Hu & Meng, 1996; Juffer & Rosenboom, 1997; Keromoian & Leiderman, 1986).

Before leaving the topic of attachment, let's take a look at one of the first studies that examined the key factors necessary for attachment.

classic studies in psychology

Harlow and Contact Comfort

As psychologists began to study the development of attachment, they at first assumed that attachment to the mother occurred because the mother was associated with satisfaction of primary drives such as hunger and thirst. The mother is always present when the food (a primary reinforcer) is presented, so the mother becomes a secondary reinforcer capable of producing pleasurable feelings. LINK to Chapter Five: Learning, p. 180.

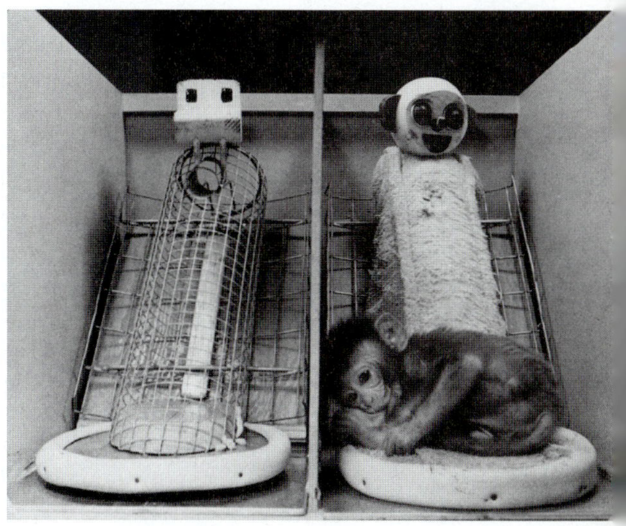

The wire surrogate "mother" provides the food for this infant rhesus monkey. But the infant spends all its time with the soft, cloth-covered surrogate. According to Harlow, this demonstrates the importance of contact comfort in attachment.

Psychologist Harry Harlow felt that attachment had to be influenced by more than just the provision of food. He conducted a number of studies of attachment using infant rhesus monkeys (Harlow, 1958). Noticing that the monkeys in his lab liked to cling to the soft cloth pad used to line their cages, Harlow designed a study to examine the importance of what he termed *contact comfort,* the seeming attachment of the monkeys to something soft to the touch.

He isolated eight baby rhesus monkeys shortly after their birth, placing each in a cage with two surrogate (substitute) "mothers." The surrogates were actually a block of wood covered in soft padding and terry cloth and a wire form, both heated from within. For half of the monkeys, the wire "mother" held the bottle from which they fed, while for the other half the soft "mother" held the bottle. Harlow then recorded the time each monkey spent with each "mother." If time spent with the surrogate is taken as an indicator of attachment, then learning theory would predict that the monkeys would spend more time with whichever surrogate was being used to feed them.

The results? Regardless of which surrogate was feeding them, all of the infant monkeys spent significantly more time with the soft, cloth-covered surrogate. In fact, all monkeys spent very little time with the wire surrogate, even if this was the one with the bottle. Harlow and his colleagues concluded that "contact comfort was an important basic affectional or love variable" (Harlow, 1958, p. 574).

Harlow's work represents one of the earliest investigations into the importance of touch in the attachment process and remains an important study in human development.

Questions for Further Discussion

1. Even though the cloth surrogate was warm and soft and seemed to provide contact comfort, do you think that the monkeys raised in this way would behave normally when placed into contact with other monkeys? How might they react?
2. What might be the implications of Harlow's work for human mothers who feed their infants with bottles rather than breast-feeding?

I've heard that you shouldn't pick a baby up every time it cries—that if you do, it might spoil the baby.

I've heard that you shouldn't pick a baby up every time it cries—that if you do, it might spoil the baby.

ERIKSON'S THEORY Unfortunately, a lot of people have not only heard this advice but also acted on it by frequently ignoring an infant's crying, which turns out to be a very bad thing for babies. When a baby under 6 months of age cries, it is an instinctive reaction meant to get the caregiver to tend to the baby's needs—hunger, thirst, pain, and even loneliness. Research has shown that babies whose cries are tended to consistently (that is, the infant is fed when hungry, changed when wet, and so on) in the early months are more securely attached at age 1 than those infants whose caregivers frequently allow the infants to cry when there is a need for attention—hunger, pain, or wetness, for example (Brazelton, 1992; Heinicke et al., 2000). Erikson, a psychodynamic theorist who emphasized the importance of social relationships in the development of personality, would certainly disagree with letting a baby "cry it out," although allowing an infant who has been fed, changed, burped, and checked to cry on occasion will not damage attachment.

Erikson, who trained as a Freudian psychoanalyst but became convinced that social interactions were more important in development than Freud's emphasis on sexual development, believed that development occurred in a series of eight stages, with the first four of these stages occurring in infancy and childhood (Erikson, 1950; Erikson & Erikson, 1997). (Freud's stages of psychosexual development are covered in detail in a later chapter.) LINK to Chapter Thirteen: Theories of Personality, pp. 495–500. Each of Erikson's stages is an emotional *crisis*, or a kind of turning point, in personality, and the crisis in each stage must be successfully met for normal, healthy psychological development.

Erikson focused on the relationship of the infant and the child to significant others in the immediate surroundings—parents and then later teachers and even peers. Table 8.4 summarizes the conflict in each of Erikson's eight stages and some of the implications for future development (Erikson, 1950; Erikson & Erikson, 1997). For now, look at the first four stages in particular.

When do little kids learn the difference between girls and boys?

GENDER-ROLE DEVELOPMENT

When do little kids learn the difference between girls and boys?

Most children begin to realize the difference between girls and boys at about age 2, and most can say which one they are at that age. But knowing one's *sex* (the physical characteristic of being male or female) is not the same thing as knowing the different behaviors expected of a male or a female (**gender**). The behavior that goes along with being male or female is heavily influenced by

gender the behavior associated with being male or female.

Table 8.4

Erikson's Psychosocial Stages of Development

STAGE	DEVELOPMENTAL CRISIS	SUCCESSFUL DEALING WITH CRISIS	UNSUCCESSFUL DEALING WITH CRISIS
1. Infant Birth to 1 year old	**Trust Versus Mistrust** Babies learn to trust or mistrust others based on whether or not their needs—such as food and comfort—are met.	If babies' needs are met, they learn to trust people and expect life to be pleasant.	If babies' needs are not met, they learn not to trust.
2. Toddler 1 to 3 years old	**Autonomy Versus Shame and Doubt** Toddlers realize that they can direct their own behavior.	If toddlers are successful in directing their own behavior, they learn to be independent.	If toddlers' attempts at being independent are blocked, they learn self-doubt and shame for being unsuccessful.
3. Preschool Age 3 to 5 years old	**Initiative Versus Guilt** Preschoolers are challenged to control their own behavior, such as controlling their exuberance when they are in a restaurant.	If preschoolers succeed in taking responsibility, they feel capable and develop initiative.	If preschoolers fail in taking responsibility, they feel irresponsible, anxious, and guilty.
4. Elementary School Age 5 to 12 years old	**Industry Versus Inferiority** School-aged children are faced with learning new social and academic skills. Social comparison is a primary source of information.	When children succeed at learning new skills, they develop a sense of industry, a feeling of competence and self-esteem arising from their work and effort.	If children fail to develop new abilities, they feel incompetent, inadequate, and inferior.
5. Adolescence 13 to early 20s	**Identity Versus Role Confusion** Adolescents are faced with deciding who or what they want to be in terms of occupation, beliefs, attitudes, and behavior patterns.	Adolescents who succeed in defining who they are and finding a role for themselves develop a strong sense of identity.	Adolescents who fail to define their identity become confused and withdraw or want to inconspicuously blend in with the crowd.
6. Early Adulthood 20s and 30s	**Intimacy Versus Isolation** The task facing those in early adulthood is to be able to share who they are with another person in a close, committed relationship.	People who succeed in this task will have satisfying intimate relationships.	Adults who fail at this task will be isolated from other people and may suffer from loneliness.
7. Middle Adulthood 40s and 50s	**Generativity Versus Stagnation** The challenge is to be creative, productive, and nurturant of the next generation.	Adults who succeed in this challenge will be creative, productive, and nurturant, thereby benefiting themselves, their family, community, country, and future generations.	Adults who fail will be passive, and self-centered, feel that they have done nothing for the next generation, and feel that the world is no better off for their being alive.
8. Late Adulthood 60s and beyond	**Ego Integrity Versus Despair** The issue is whether a person will reach wisdom, spiritual tranquility, a sense of wholeness, and acceptance of his or her life.	Elderly people who succeed in addressing this issue will enjoy life and not fear death.	Elderly people who fail will feel that their life is empty and will fear death.

Source: Erikson, 1950.

cultural expectations as well as biology, and is referred to as **gender identity**. One important way in which children learn about different gender roles is through play with their parents—fathers are more assertive during play, while mothers are more helpful and cooperative (Lindsey et al., 2010). Gender-role development is covered in more detail in Chapter Ten. LINK to Chapter Ten: Sexuality and Gender, pp. 385–386.

gender identity perception of one's gender and the behavior that is associated with that gender.

8.7 CONCEPT MAP

- **psychosocial development** — involves development of personality, relationships, and a sense of being male or female; process begins in infancy and continues into adulthood
  - **important early concepts**
    - infants demonstrate personality through their temperament (e.g., easy, difficult, slow to warm up), which can also affect, and is affected by, parenting and the environment
    - attachment (emotional bond between infant and a primary caregiver) is very important; different attachment styles have been identified by Ainsworth and others (e.g., secure, avoidant, ambivalent, disorganized–disoriented) that appear to be similar, but not identical, across different cultures
    - **Erikson's theory**
      - suggests development occurs in a series of eight stages (see Table 8.4)
      - at each stage an emotional crisis must be successfully met for normal development to occur
      - **gender-role development**
        - most children begin to realize difference between sexes at about age 2
        - knowing expectations for gender and development of gender identity takes much longer and is influenced by both biology and cultural expectations

Infancy and Childhood Development: Psychosocial Development

PRACTICE quiz How much do you remember? ANSWERS ON PAGE AK-2.

Pick the best answer.

1. According to Thomas and Chess, a child that is very irregular in sleeping and eating, resists change, and is negative and loud is labeled a(n) _________ child.
   a. easy **c.** slow-to-warm-up
   b. difficult **d.** negative
2. What kind of attachment, according to Ainsworth, is shown by a baby who explores the room, gets upset when the mother leaves but is easily soothed, and is happy to see the mother when she returns?
   a. secure **c.** ambivalent
   b. avoidant **d.** disorganized–disoriented
3. Mothers who were abusive and/or neglectful were associated with the _________ type of attachment.
   a. secure **c.** ambivalent
   b. avoidant **d.** disorganized–disoriented
4. In Erikson's _________ stage of psychosocial development, the child learns self-control and begins to feel more capable.
   a. trust versus mistrust
   b. autonomy versus shame and doubt
   c. initiative versus guilt
   d. industry versus inferiority

Adolescence

Adolescence is the period of life from about age 13 to the early 20s, during which a young person is no longer physically a child but is not yet an independent, self-supporting adult. Although in the past, adolescence was always defined as the "teens," from ages 13 to 19, adolescence isn't necessarily determined by chronological age. It also concerns how a person deals with life issues such as work, family, and relationships. So although there is a clear age of onset, the end of adolescence may come earlier or later for different individuals.

Isn't adolescence just the physical changes that happen to your body?

PHYSICAL DEVELOPMENT

Isn't adolescence just the physical changes that happen to your body?

PUBERTY

8.8 What are the physical, cognitive, and personality changes that occur in adolescence, including concepts of morality and Erikson's search for identity?

The clearest sign of the beginning of adolescence is the onset of **puberty**, the physical changes in both *primary sex characteristics* (growth of the actual sex organs such as the penis or the uterus) and *secondary sex characteristics* (changes in the body such

adolescence the period of life from about age 13 to the early 20s, during which a young person is no longer physically a child but is not yet an independent, self-supporting adult.

puberty the physical changes that occur in the body as sexual development reaches its peak.

as the development of breasts and body hair) that occur in the body as sexual development reaches its peak. LINK to Chapter Ten: Sexuality and Gender, p. 378. Puberty occurs as the result of a complex series of glandular activities, stimulated by the "master gland" or the pituitary gland, when the proper genetically determined age is reached. The thyroid gland increases the rate of growth, and the adrenal glands and sex glands stimulate the growth of characteristics such as body hair, muscle tissue in males, and the menstrual cycle in girls, for example (Grumbach & Kaplan, 1990; Grumbach & Styne, 1998). Puberty often begins about 2 years after the beginning of the *growth spurt*, the rapid period of growth that takes place at around age 10 for girls and around age 12 for boys.

In addition to an increase in height, physical characteristics related to being male or female undergo rapid and dramatic change. In fact, the rate of growth and development in puberty approaches that of development in the womb. LINK to Chapter Ten: Sexuality and Gender, pp. 378–379. After about 4 years, the changes of puberty are relatively complete.

COGNITIVE DEVELOPMENT

If I'm remembering correctly, teenagers should be in Piaget's formal operations stage. So why don't many teenagers think just like adults?

If I'm remembering correctly, teenagers should be in Piaget's formal operations stage. So why don't many teenagers think just like adults?

The cognitive development of adolescents is less visible than the physical development but still represents a major change in the way adolescents think about themselves, their peers and relationships, and the world around them.

PIAGET'S FORMAL OPERATIONS REVISITED Adolescents, especially those who receive a formal high school education, may move into Piaget's final stage of formal operations, in which abstract thinking becomes possible. This cognitive advance is feasible primarily due to the final development of the frontal lobes of the brain, the part of the brain that is responsible for organizing, understanding, and decision making (Giedd et al., 1999; Sowell et al., 1999). Teenagers begin to think about hypothetical situations, leading to a picture of what an "ideal" world would be like. Many become convinced that such a world is possible to achieve if only everyone else would just listen to the teenager. (It should be noted that although adolescents have reached the formal-operations stage, not all adolescents—or adults—use their formal-operational thought processes equally well. In a sense, they've graduated to "bigger and better" mental tools but don't necessarily know how to use those tools effectively. A more formal educational process or demanding life experiences help adolescents and adults become skilled "tool users.")

As discussed earlier, Piaget's concept of stages has been criticized as being too simplistic. The evidence now points to gradual, continuous cognitive development (Feldman, 2003; Siegler, 1996). Even so, Piaget's theory has had a tremendous impact in the education of children and in stimulating research about children's cognitive development (Satterly, 1987). Children in different cultures usually come to

personal fable type of thought common to adolescents in which young people believe themselves to be unique and protected from harm.

imaginary audience type of thought common to adolescents in which young people believe that other people are just as concerned about the adolescent's thoughts and characteristics as they themselves are.

preconventional morality first level of Kohlberg's stages of moral development in which the child's behavior is governed by the consequences of the behavior.

understand the world in the way that Piaget described, although the age at which this understanding comes varies from one child to another.

Although headed into an adult-style of thinking, adolescents are not yet completely free of egocentric thought. At this time in life, however, their egocentrism shows up in their preoccupation* with their own thoughts. They do a lot of introspection (turning inward) and may become convinced that their thoughts are as important to others as they are to themselves. Two ways in which this adolescent egocentrism emerges are the *personal fable* and the *imaginary audience* (Elkind, 1985; Lapsley et al., 1986; Vartanian, 2000).

In the **personal fable**, adolescents have spent so much time thinking about their own thoughts and feelings that they become convinced that they are special, one of a kind, and that no one else has ever had these thoughts and feelings before them. "You just don't understand me, I'm different from you" is a common feeling of teens. The personal fable is not without a dangerous side. Because they feel unique, teenagers may feel that they are somehow protected from the dangers of the world and so do not take the precautions that they should. This may result in an unwanted pregnancy, severe injury or death while racing in a car, drinking (or texting) and driving, and drug use, to name a few possibilities. "It can't happen to me, I'm special" is a risky but common thought.

The **imaginary audience** shows up as extreme self-consciousness in adolescents. They become convinced that *everyone is looking at them* and that they are always the center of everyone else's world, just as they are the center of their own. This explains the intense self-consciousness that many adolescents experience concerning what others think about how the adolescent looks or behaves.

MORAL DEVELOPMENT Another important aspect in the cognitive advances that occur in adolescence concerns the teenager's understanding of "right" and "wrong." Harvard University professor Lawrence Kohlberg was a developmental psychologist who, influenced by Piaget and others, outlined a theory of the development of moral thinking through looking at how people of various ages responded to stories about people caught up in moral dilemmas (see Figure 8.8 for a typical story). Kohlberg (1973) proposed three levels of moral development, or the knowledge of right and wrong behavior. These levels are summarized in Table 8.5, along with an example of each type of thinking. Although these stages are associated with certain age-groups, adolescents and adults can be found at all three levels. For example, a juvenile delinquent tends to be preconventional in moral thinking.

---

*preoccupation: extreme or excessive concern with something.

Example of a Moral Dilemma

A woman in Europe was dying from a rare disease. Her only hope was a drug that a local druggist had discovered. The druggist was charging ten times more than it cost him to make it. Heinz, the husband of the dying woman, had desperately tried to borrow money to buy the drug, but he could borrow only half of the amount he needed. He went to the druggist, told him that his wife was dying, and asked to let him pay the druggist later or to sell the drug at a lower cost. The druggist refused, saying that he had discovered the drug and he was going to make money from it. Later, Heinz broke into the druggist's store to steal the drug for his wife. Should Heinz have done that? Why?

Figure 8.8 Example of a Moral Dilemma

Source: Kohlberg, 1969, p. 379.

Table 8.5

Kohlberg's Three Levels of Morality

LEVEL OF MORALITY	HOW RULES ARE UNDERSTOOD	EXAMPLE
Preconventional morality (typically very young children)	The consequences determine morality; behavior that is rewarded is right; that which is punished is wrong.	A child who steals a toy from another child and does not get caught does not see that action as wrong.
Conventional* morality (older children, adolescents, and most adults)	Conformity to social norms is right; nonconformity is wrong.	A child criticizes his or her parent for speeding because speeding is against the stated laws.
Postconventional morality (about 20 percent of the adult population)	Moral principles determined by the person are used to determine right and wrong and may disagree with societal norms.	A reporter who wrote a controversial story goes to jail rather than reveal the source's identity.

*The term *conventional* refers to general standards or norms of behavior for a particular society, which will differ from one social group or culture to another.

Kohlberg's theory has been criticized as being male oriented, especially since he used only males in his studies (Gilligan, 1982). Carol Gilligan (1982) proposed that men and women have different perspectives on morality: Men tend to judge as moral the actions that lead to a fair or just end, whereas women tend to judge as moral the actions that are nonviolent and hurt the fewest people. Researchers, however, have not found consistent support for gender differences in moral thinking (Walker, 1991). Another criticism is that Kohlberg's assessment of moral development involves asking people what they think should be done in hypothetical moral dilemmas. What people say they will do and what people actually do when faced with a real dilemma are often two different things. **Read** on **mypsychlab.com**

conventional morality second level of Kohlberg's stages of moral development in which the child's behavior is governed by conforming to the society's norms of behavior.

postconventional morality third level of Kohlberg's stages of moral development in which the person's behavior is governed by moral principles that have been decided on by the individual and that may be in disagreement with accepted social norms.

identity versus role confusion stage of personality development in which the adolescent must find a consistent sense of self.

PSYCHOSOCIAL DEVELOPMENT

The development of personality and social relationships in adolescence primarily concerns the search for a consistent sense of self or personal identity.

ERIKSON'S IDENTITY VERSUS ROLE CONFUSION The psychosocial crisis that must be faced by the adolescent, according to Erikson, is that of **identity versus role confusion** (see Table 8.4 on p. 323). In this stage, the teenager must choose from among many options for values in life and beliefs concerning things such as political issues, career options, and marriage (Feldman, 2003). From those options, a consistent sense of self must be found. Erikson believed that teens who have successfully resolved the conflicts of the earlier four stages are much better "equipped" to resist peer pressure to engage in unhealthy or illegal activities and find their own identity during the adolescent years. Those teens who are not as successful come into the adolescent years with a lack of trust in others, feelings of guilt and shame, low self-esteem, and dependency on others. Peer pressure is quite effective on teenagers who desperately want to "fit in" and have an identity of a certain sort, and who feel that others will not want to be with them unless they conform to the expectations and demands of the peer group. They play the part of the model child for the parents, the good student for the teachers, and the "cool" juvenile delinquent to their friends and will be confused about which of the many roles they play really represent their own identity.

Read and learn more about Carol Gilligan's three stages of morality for women on **mypsychlab.com**

Actresses Lindsay Lohan, Amanda Seyfried, Lacey Chabert, and Rachel McAdams on the set of Mark S. Waters's comedy movie *Mean Girls*. This movie portrays the ins and outs of peer pressure and the desire to fit in that many adolescents face.

PARENT–TEEN CONFLICT Even for the majority of adolescents who end up successfully finding a consistent sense of self, there will be conflicts with parents. Many researchers believe that a certain amount of "rebellion" and conflict is a necessary step in breaking away from childhood dependence on the parents and becoming a self-sufficient* adult. Although many people think that these conflicts are intense and concern very serious behavior, the reality is that most parent–teen conflict is over trivial issues—hair, clothing, taste in music, and so on. On the really big moral issues, most parents and teens would be quite surprised to realize that they are in agreement. **Watch** on **mypsychlab.com**

Watch footage on adolescent behavior including egocentrism, teen drinking, and teen pregnancy on **mypsychlab.com**

*self-sufficient: able to function without outside aid; capable of providing for one's own needs.

8.8 CONCEPT MAP

Adolescence

(period of life from about age 13 to early 20s)

- **physical development**
  - increase in height and changes in both primary and secondary sex characteristics
  - occurs as the result of glandular and hormonal activities
  - tends to occur about 2 years after beginning of growth spurt
- **cognitive development**
  - final maturation of the frontal lobes allows cognitive advances (e.g., abstract thought/Piaget's formal operations)
  - despite advances, still have egocentric thought that emerges in a variety of ways
- **moral development**
  - understanding of what is "right" and "wrong"
  - early theory was proposed by Kohlberg; suggested three levels of moral development
    - **preconventional**
    - **conventional**
    - **postconventional**
    - see Table 8.5
  - some researchers (e.g., Gilligan) suggest that Kohlberg's ideas applied more to males; others suggest that assessment was based on hypothetical, rather than real-life, dilemmas
- **psychosocial development**
  - adolescence is largely marked by the search for a consistent sense of self or personal identity
  - Erikson: the psychosocial crisis that must be resolved is identity vs. role confusion
  - parent–teen conflict to be expected

PRACTICE quiz How much do you remember?

ANSWERS ON PAGE AK-2.

Pick the best answer.

1. Which of the following statements about adolescence is FALSE?
   a. It begins with the onset of puberty.
   b. It is a time during which the young person is no longer a child but is not yet an adult.
   c. It ends when puberty is complete.
   d. It is a time of preoccupation with one's own thoughts.
2. Which term refers to the feeling of being unique and protected?
   a. formal operations **c.** personal fable
   b. imaginary audience **d.** puberty
3. According to Kohlberg, most adolescents are at the _________ level of morality.
   a. preconventional **c.** postconventional
   b. conventional **d.** preliminary
4. According to Erikson, the task of the adolescent is to _________.
   a. find a consistent sense of self.
   b. develop a sense of initiative.
   c. find intimacy with another.
   d. develop a sense of industry.
5. Which of the following issues typically creates a lot of conflict between most teens and their parents?
   a. serious issues of drug and alcohol use
   b. trivial issues of hair, clothing, and music choices
   c. issues of postconventional morality
   d. issues of achieving an identity

Adulthood

PHYSICAL DEVELOPMENT: USE IT OR LOSE IT

When exactly does adulthood begin?

When exactly does adulthood begin?

Adulthood can be thought of as the period of life from the early 20s until old age and death. Exactly when adulthood begins is not always easy to determine. In some cultures, adulthood is reached soon after puberty (Bledsoe & Cohen, 1993; Ocholla-Ayayo et al., 1993). Some people feel that it begins after graduation from high school, whereas others would say adulthood doesn't begin until after graduation from college. Others define it as the point when a person becomes totally self-sufficient with a job and a home separate from his or her parents. In that case, some people are not adults until their late 30s.

8.9 What are the physical, cognitive, and personality changes that occur during adulthood and aging, including Erikson's last three psychosocial stages, and patterns of parenting?

Adulthood can also be divided into at least three periods: young adulthood, middle age, and late adulthood. Physical changes in young adulthood are relatively minimal. The good news is that the 20s are a time of peak physical health, sharp senses, fewer insecurities, and mature cognitive abilities. The bad news is that even in the early 20s, the signs of aging are already beginning. Oil glands in the neck and around the eyes begin to malfunction, contributing to wrinkles in those areas near the end of the 20s and beginning of the 30s. The 30s may not bring noticeable changes, but vision and hearing are beginning to decline and by around age 40, bifocal lenses may become necessary as the lens of the eye hardens, becoming unable to change its shape to shift focus. Hearing loss may begin in the 40s and 50s but often does not become noticeable until the 60s or 70s, when hearing aids may become necessary.

In the 40s, while most adults are able to experience some security and stability without the worries and concerns of adolescence and young adulthood, physical aging continues: Skin begins to show more wrinkles, hair turns gray (or falls out), vision and hearing decline further, and physical strength may begin to decline (Frontera et al., 1991). In the 50s, these changes continue. Throughout middle age, weight may increase as the rate at which the body functions slows down but eating increases and less time is spent exercising. Height begins to decrease, with about half an inch of height lost for every 10 years past age 40, although people with the bone-loss disease osteoporosis may lose up to 8 inches or more (Cummings & Melton, 2002). Although sexual functioning usually does not decline in middle age, opportunities for sexual activity may be fewer than in the days of young adulthood (Hodson & Skeen, 1994; Williams, 1995). Children, mortgages, and career worries can put a damper on middle-age romance.

MENOPAUSE In a woman's 40s, the levels of the female hormone estrogen decline as the body's reproductive system prepares to cease that function. Some women begin to experience "hot flashes," a sudden sensation of heat and sweating that may keep them awake at night. Interestingly, in some cultures, particularly those in which the diet contains high amounts of soy products, hot flashes are almost nonexistent (Cassidy et al., 1994; Lock, 1994). The changes that happen at this time are called the *climacteric*, and the period of 5 to 10 years over which these changes occur is called *perimenopause*. At an average age of 51, most women will cease ovulation altogether, ending their reproductive years. The cessation of ovulation and the menstrual cycle is called **menopause** (Mishell, 2001). Many women look forward to the freedom from monthly menstruation and fear of unplanned pregnancies (Adler et al., 2000; Hvas, 2001; Leon et al., 2007).

menopause the cessation of ovulation and menstrual cycles and the end of a woman's reproductive capability.

Do men go through anything like menopause?

Do men go through anything like menopause?

Men also go through a time of sexual changes, but it is much more gradual and less dramatic than menopause. In males, **andropause** (Carruthers, 2001) usually begins in the 40s with a decline in several hormones, primarily testosterone (the major male hormone). Physical symptoms are also less dramatic but no less troubling: fatigue, irritability, possible problems in sexual functioning, and reduced sperm count. Males, however, rarely lose all reproductive ability.

EFFECTS OF AGING ON HEALTH It is in middle age that many health problems first occur, although their true cause may have begun in the young adulthood years. Young adults may smoke, drink heavily, stay up late, and get dark tans, and the wear and tear that this lifestyle causes on their bodies will not become obvious until their 40s and 50s.

Some of the common health problems that may show up in middle age are high blood pressure, skin cancer, heart problems, arthritis, and obesity. High blood pressure can be caused by lifestyle factors such as obesity and stress but may also be related to hereditary factors (Rudd & Osterberg, 2002). Sleep problems, such as loud snoring and sleep apnea (in which breathing stops for 10 seconds or more), may also take their toll on physical health. There is some evidence that high blood pressure and apnea are linked, although the link very well may be the common factor of obesity (Nieto et al., 2000). Statistically, the most frequent causes of death in middle age are heart disease, cancer, and stroke—in that order (McGinnis & Foege, 1993).

COGNITIVE DEVELOPMENT

During this time, intellectual abilities do not decline overall, although speed of processing (or reaction time) does slow down. Compared to a younger adult, a middle-aged person may take a little longer to solve a problem. However, a middle-aged person also has more life experience and knowledge to bring to bear on a problem, which counters the lack of speed. In one study (Salthouse, 1984), for example, older typists were found to outperform younger typists, even though they typed more slowly than the younger subjects. The older typists, because of years of practice, had developed a skill of looking farther ahead in the document they were typing, so that they could type more continuously without looking back at the document. This allowed them to complete their typing more quickly than the younger typists.

CHANGES IN MEMORY Changes in memory ability are probably the most noticeable changes in middle-aged cognition. People find themselves having a hard time remembering a particular word or someone's name. This difficulty in retrieval is probably not evidence of a physical decline (or the beginning of Alzheimer's disease) but is more likely caused by the stresses a middle-aged person experiences and the sheer amount of information that a person of middle years must try to keep straight (Craik, 1994; Launer et al., 1995; Sands & Meredith, 1992). A recent study even suggests that thinking about the positive events of the past aids the formation of newer memories—the areas of the brain that are linked to processing emotional content seem to have a strong connection to the areas of the brain responsible for memory formation (Addis et al., 2010). Think positive!

HOW TO KEEP YOUR BRAIN YOUNG People who exercise their mental abilities have been found to be far less likely to develop memory problems or even more serious senile dementias, such as Alzheimer's, in old age (Ball et al., 2002; Colcombe et al., 2003; Fiatarone, 1996). "Use it or lose it" is the phrase to remember. Working challenging crossword puzzles, for example, can be a major factor in maintaining a healthy level of cognitive functioning. Reading, having an active social life, going to plays, taking classes, and staying physically active can all have a positive impact on the

andropause gradual changes in the sexual hormones and reproductive system of middle-aged males.

continued well-being of the brain (Bosworth & Schaie, 1997; Cabeza et al., 2002; Singh-Manoux et al., 2003).

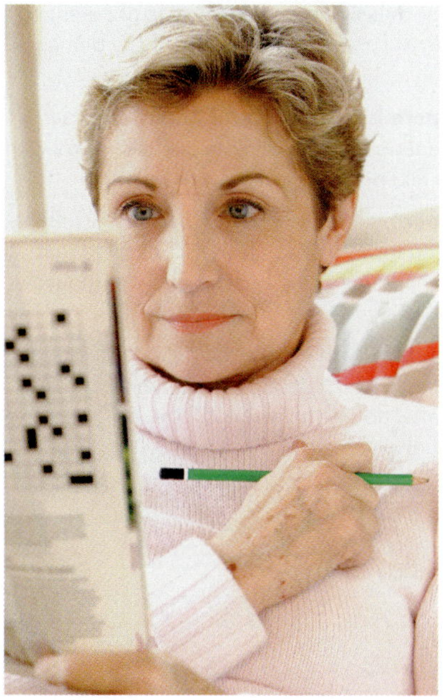

This middle-aged woman works on a crossword puzzle. Mental exercises such as this are one way to keep the brain healthy and fit. What might be some other ways to exercise one's brain?

PSYCHOSOCIAL DEVELOPMENT

In adulthood, concerns involve career, relationships, family, and approaching old age. The late teens and early 20s may be college years for many, although other young people go to work directly from high school. The task of choosing and entering a career is very serious and a task that many young adults have difficulty accomplishing. A college student may change majors more than once during the first few years of college, and even after obtaining a bachelor's degree many may either get a job in an unrelated field or go on to a different type of career choice in graduate school. Those who are working may also change careers several times (perhaps as many as five to seven times) and may experience periods of unemployment while between jobs.

ERIKSON'S INTIMACY VERSUS ISOLATION: FORMING RELATIONSHIPS Erikson saw the primary task in young adulthood to be that of finding a mate. True **intimacy** is an emotional and psychological closeness that is based on the ability to trust, share, and care (an ability developed during the earlier stages such as trust versus mistrust), while still maintaining one's sense of self. LINK to Chapter Twelve: Social Psychology, p. 476. Young adults who have difficulty trusting others and who are unsure of their own identities may find *isolation* instead of intimacy—loneliness, shallow relationships with others, and even a fear of real intimacy. For example, many marriages end in divorce within a few years, with one partner leaving the relationship—and even the responsibilities of parenting—to explore personal concerns and those unfinished issues of identity. Return to Table 8.4 on p. 323 for a summary of the adulthood stages in Erikson's theory.

ERIKSON'S GENERATIVITY VERSUS STAGNATION: PARENTING In middle adulthood, persons who have found intimacy can now turn their focus outward, toward others. Erikson saw this as parenting the next generation and helping them through their crises, a process he called **generativity**. Educators, supervisors, health-care professionals, doctors, and community volunteers might be examples of positions that allow a person to be generative. Other ways of being generative include engaging in careers or some major life work that can become one's legacy to the generations to come. Those who are unable to focus outward and are still dealing with issues of intimacy, or even identity, are said to be *stagnated*. People who frequently hand the care of their children over to grandparents or other relatives so that they can go out and "have fun" may be unable to focus on anyone else's needs but their own.

What kind of parent is the best parent—one who's really strict or one who's pretty easygoing?

What kind of parent is the best parent—one who's really strict or one who's pretty easygoing?

PARENTING STYLES Parenting children is a very important part of most people's middle adulthood. Diana Baumrind (1967) outlined three basic styles of parenting, each of which may be related to certain personality traits in the child raised by that style of parenting.

Authoritarian parenting tends to be overly concerned with rules. This type of parent is stern, rigid, demanding perfection, controlling, uncompromising,* and has a tendency to use physical punishment. Children raised in this way are often insecure, timid, withdrawn, and resentful. As teenagers, they will very often rebel against parental authority in very negative and self-destructive ways, such as delinquency (criminal acts committed by minor children), drug use, or premarital sex (Baumrind, 1991, 2005).

intimacy an emotional and psychological closeness that is based on the ability to trust, share, and care, while still maintaining a sense of self.

generativity providing guidance to one's children or the next generation, or contributing to the well-being of the next generation through career or volunteer work.

authoritarian parenting style of parenting in which parent is rigid and overly strict, showing little warmth to the child.

*uncompromising: not making or accepting any viewpoint other than one's own, allowing no other viewpoints.

permissive parenting style of parenting in which parent makes few, if any demands on a child's behavior.

permissive neglectful permissive parenting in which parents are uninvolved with child or child's behavior.

permissive indulgent permissive parenting in which parents are so involved that children are allowed to behave without set limits.

authoritative parenting style of parenting in which parents combine warmth and affection with firm limits on a child's behavior.

Permissive parenting occurs when parents put very few demands on their children for behavior. **Permissive neglectful** parents simply aren't involved with their children, ignoring them and allowing them to do whatever they want, until it interferes with what the parent wants. At that point, this relationship may become an abusive one. **Permissive indulgent** parents seem to be *too* involved with their children, allowing their "little angels" to behave in any way they wish, refusing to set limits on the child's behavior or to require any kind of obedience. Children from both kinds of permissive parenting tend to be selfish, immature, dependent, lacking in social skills, and unpopular with peers.

Authoritative parenting involves combining firm limits on behavior with love, warmth, affection, respect, and a willingness to listen to the child's point of view. Authoritative parents are more democratic, allowing the child to have some input into the formation of rules but still maintaining the role of final decision maker. Punishment tends to be nonphysical, such as restrictions, time-out, or loss of privileges. Authoritative parents set limits that are clear and understandable, and when a child crosses the limits, they allow an explanation and then agree upon the right way to handle the situation.

8.9 CONCEPT MAP

Adulthood

(period of life from early 20s until old age and death; age of onset can vary by culture)

- **physical development**
  - **young adulthood**
    - few changes; the 20s are typically associated with peak physical and cognitive health
  - **middle age**
    - hearing and vision begin to decline; weight increase is typical; height starts to decrease
    - women experience menopause; men experience less dramatic change called andropause
    - health problems related to genetics and lifestyle when younger start to appear
  - **late adulthood**
    - further decline in hearing; may need hearing aids
    - physical strength declines
    - people with osteoporosis may lose up to 8 inches in height
- **cognitive development**
  - cognitive skills often highest in 20s; processing and reaction time slow in middle age but are often compensated by greater life and situational knowledge
  - memory issues begin in middle age, likely due to stress and information overload
  - mental abilities aided by active cognitive engagement (challenging crossword puzzles, reading, etc.) and physical activity
- **psychosocial development**
  - typical life concerns involve career, relationships, family, and approaching old age
  - Erikson's stages (see Table 8.4)

PRACTICE quiz How much do you remember? ANSWERS ON PAGE AK-2.

Pick the best answer.

1. The period of 5 to 10 years during which a woman's reproductive system begins to decline is called _________.
   a. climacteric.
   b. perimenopause.
   c. menopause.
   d. all of the above.
2. Which of the following has NOT been shown to help maintain a healthy level of cognitive functioning?
   a. working crossword puzzles
   b. reading
   c. going to plays
   d. sedentary lifestyle
3. Today's worker may change careers as many as _________ times.
   a. one to two
   b. three to five
   c. five to seven
   d. eight to nine
4. According to Erikson, achieving true intimacy is difficult if one's _________ is not already established.
   a. identity
   b. independence
   c. career
   d. marriage
5. According to Baumrind, _________ parenting may lead to an abusive relationship.
   a. authoritarian
   b. authoritative
   c. permissive neglectful
   d. permissive indulgent

PRACTICE quiz How much do You remember? ANSWERS ON PAGE AK-2.

Pick the best answer.

1. In Erikson's last crisis, the life review is _________.
   a. a process of assigning blame.
   b. looking back on the life one has lived.
   c. an analysis of one's parents' lives.
   d. the writing of a biography.
2. A sense of completeness of one's ego, or identity, is called _________.
   a. life review.
   b. intelligence.
   c. integrity.
   d. generativity.
3. According to research, if an older person wants to adjust more positively to aging, he or she should _________.
   a. quietly withdraw from social life.
   b. limit his or her range of activities.
   c. disengage from life.
   d. remain active in some way.
4. In which theory of aging do telomeres become the major means of aging cells?
   a. wear-and-tear theory
   b. cellular-clock theory
   c. free-radical theory
   d. hormonal-imbalance theory
5. In the _________ stage of reaction to death and dying, a person may promise to do everything the doctor says if the doctor will say that the person can live a little longer.
   a. denial
   b. anger
   c. bargaining
   d. depression
   e. acceptance

Applying Psychology to Everyday Life: Cross-Cultural Views on Death

8.11 What are some cross-cultural differences in views of death and dying?

In the 1987 movie *The Princess Bride*, a character called Miracle Max (wonderfully played by comedian and actor Billy Crystal) says, "It just so happens that your friend here is only MOSTLY dead. There's a big difference between mostly dead and all dead. Mostly dead is slightly alive." As it turns out, that far-fetched idea of "mostly dead" is not unheard of in other cultures. While Westerners see a person as either dead or alive, in some cultures a person who, by Western standards is clearly alive, is mourned as already dead—as is the case in many Native American cultures. Let's take a look at three diverse cultures and their views on death and dying, remembering to contrast them with what you know of death and funeral rites common in your own culture.

- In a wealthy Hindu family in India, the dying person is surrounded by family members, even while in the hospital. In addition, many visitors will attend to the dying person, creating a nearly constant flow of visitors in and out of the room. Once the person has passed away, preparations for the funeral period—which can take nearly 2 weeks—are begun. The body is not sent to a funeral home, but rather is taken into the family home until the actual day of the funeral, where a cremation will take place. During the funeral preparation period, visitors and family stream in and out of the deceased's home and an abundance of food—all vegetarian at this time—are prepared and eaten. Until the day of the funeral, mattresses are placed on the floor, and all but the very old and infirm are expected to sleep there; the body of the deceased is also placed on the floor. The family members themselves will eventually wash the body in preparation for wrapping and the trip to the crematorium (Parkes et al., 1997). In Hinduism, it is believed that the dead person's soul will be reincarnated at either a higher level or a lower level of status, depending upon how the person lived his or her life.

The washed and wrapped body of a Hindu man is being carried to the crematorium by his family members.

- In the culture of the Northern Cheyenne Native American tribe, death is considered only the end of the physical body, while the self and one's Cheyenne nature will persist. The very old and the very young are said to be "close to the spirit," meaning that the infant has just come from the nonphysical world and the aged person is close to returning to it. The Cheyenne, like the Hindi, also believe in reincarnation, so many infants are seen to be the living embodiment of ancestors. Death itself is a long process, with various aspects of one's spirit leaving at different times. The first such "leaving" results in changes in the behavior and the mental activity of the dying person, but the person may still be able to walk and communicate. The second leads to loss of the senses, then consciousness, and finally, breathing. The very last essence to leave is the life principle, the first life given into an infant but the last to leave. This life principle stays in the skeleton until the bones begin to crumble into dust. Thus some Cheyenne believe that bones can become alive again (Strauss, 2004).

- In Navajo culture, a person who has died is believed to be in the underworld. Thus it is deemed possible for a dead person to visit the living; this is a feared situation, so the living try to avoid looking at the dead, and only a few people are permitted to touch or handle the body. A dying person is usually taken to a place removed from others, with only one or two very close relatives staying with the dying person—because to do so is to risk exposure to evil spirits. If a person dies in his or her own home, the home is destroyed—no one is allowed to live there afterward. At the time of death, two men prepare the body for burial, but prior to that ritual they must strip down to only their moccasins, and then cover themselves in ashes, which serves to protect them from the evil spirits. The body is then washed and dressed. Two additional men dig the grave; only these four men will attend the burial, which is held as quickly as possible—usually the next day. The men carry the body on their shoulders to the grave, warning others to stay away from the area. The deceased is then buried along with all his or her belongings, the dirt is returned to the grave, and all footprints are swept away. Even the tools used to dig the grave are destroyed (Downs, 1984).

Questions for Further Discussion

1. How has your own experience with death, if any, affected you and your outlook on life? What were the cultural trappings of the days leading up to the death and/or the funeral arrangements?
2. How do the customs of the wealthy Hindu family differ from those of the Cheyenne, and how are they alike? How do the two Native American cultures differ?

chapter summary

Listen on **mypsychlab.com** Listen to an audio file of your chapter **www.mypsychlab.com**

Issues in Studying Human Development

8.1 What are some of the special research methods used to study development?

- Three special methods used in developmental research are the longitudinal design, the cross-sectional design, and the cross-sequential design.

8.2 What is the relationship between heredity and environmental factors in determining development?

- Behavioral genetics is a field investigating the relative contributions to development of heredity (nature) and environment (nurture). Most developmental psychologists agree that development is a product of an interaction between nature and nurture.

The Basic Building Blocks of Development

8.3 How do chromosomes, genes, and DNA determine a person's characteristics or disorders, and what causes multiple births?

- Dominant genes control the expression of a trait, whereas recessive gene traits are only expressed when paired with another recessive gene for the same trait. Almost all traits are the result of combinations of genes working together in a process called polygenic inheritance.
- Chromosome disorders include Down syndrome, Klinefelter's syndrome, and Turner's syndrome, whereas genetic disorders include PKU, cystic fibrosis, sickle-cell anemia, and Tay-Sachs disease.

Prenatal Development

- The fertilized egg cell is called a zygote and divides into many cells, eventually forming the baby.
- Monozygotic twins are formed when the zygote splits into two separate masses of cells, each of which will develop into a baby identical to the other. When the two masses do not fully separate, conjoined twins occur.
- Dizygotic twins are formed when the mother's body releases multiple eggs and at least two are fertilized, or when another ovulation occurs even though the mother has already become pregnant.

PSYCHOLOGY IN THE NEWS: Abby and Brittany Hensel, Together for Life

- Conjoined twins Abby and Brittany Hensel are relatively healthy, well adjusted, and participate fully in many normal activities for young people of their age.

8.4 What happens during the germinal, embryonic, and fetal periods of pregnancy and what are some hazards in prenatal development?

- The germinal period is the first 2 weeks of pregnancy in which the dividing mass of cells (blastocyst) moves down the fallopian tube into the uterus.
- The embryonic period begins at 2 weeks after conception and ends at 8 weeks. The vital organs and structures of the baby form during this period, making it a critical one for teratogens to adversely affect the development of those developing organs and structures.
- The fetal period is from the beginning of the 9th week until the birth of the baby. During the fetal period, tremendous growth occurs, length and weight increase, and organs continue to become fully functional.

Infancy and Childhood Development

8.5 What kind of physical changes take place in infancy and childhood?

- Four critical areas of adjustment for the newborn are respiration, digestion, circulation, and temperature regulation.
- Infants are born with reflexes that help the infant survive until more complex learning is possible. These reflexes include sucking, rooting, Moro (startle), grasping, and stepping.
- The senses, except for vision, are fairly well developed at birth. Vision is blurry and lacking in full color perception until about 6 months of age. Gross- and fine motor skills develop at a fast pace during infancy and early childhood.

CLASSIC STUDIES IN PSYCHOLOGY: The Visual Cliff

- Gibson and Walk found that 81 percent of infants refused to crawl across an apparent "cliff," indicating that those infants were capable of seeing the world in three dimensions.

ISSUES IN PSYCHOLOGY: The Big Lie: Dr. Andrew Wakefield and the Vaccine Scandal

- Dr. Andrew Wakefield falsified data that led to parents refusing to have their children immunized against measles, mumps, and rubella, leading to epidemic outbreaks of these diseases.
- Wakefield was found guilty of gross misconduct and was stripped of his medical license, and his study was retracted.

8.6 What are two ways of looking at cognitive development, and how does language develop?

- Piaget's stages include the sensorimotor stage of sensory and physical interaction with the world, preoperational thought in which language becomes a tool of exploration, concrete operations in which logical thought becomes possible, and formal operations in which abstract concepts are understood and hypothetical thinking develops.
- Vygotsky believed that children learn best when being helped by a more highly skilled peer or adult in a process called scaffolding. The zone of proximal development is the difference between the mental age of tasks the child performs without help and those the child can perform with help.
- The stages of language development are cooing, babbling, one-word speech (holophrases), and telegraphic speech. Although some language is learned through imitation and reinforcement, infants may possess a language acquisition device that governs the learning of language during infancy and early childhood.

8.7 How do infants and children develop personalities and form relationships with others, and what are Erikson's stages of psychosocial development for children?

- The three basic infant temperaments are easy (regular, adaptable, and happy), difficult (irregular, nonadaptable, and irritable), and slow to warm up (need to adjust gradually to change).
- The four types of attachment are secure, avoidant (unattached), ambivalent (insecurely attached), and disorganized–disoriented (insecurely attached and sometimes abused or neglected).
- In trust versus mistrust, the infant must gain a sense of predictability and trust in caregivers or risk developing a mistrustful nature; in autonomy versus shame and doubt the toddler needs to become physically independent.
- In initiative versus guilt, the preschool child is developing emotional and psychological independence; in industry versus inferiority, school-age children are gaining competence and developing self-esteem.

CLASSIC STUDIES IN PSYCHOLOGY: Harlow and Contact Comfort

- Harlow's classic research with infant rhesus monkeys demonstrated the importance of contact comfort in the attachment process, contradicting the earlier view that attachment was merely a function of associating the mother with the delivery of food.

Adolescence

- Adolescence is the period of life from about age 13 to the early 20s during which physical development reaches completion.

8.8 What are the physical, cognitive, and personality changes that occur in adolescence, including concepts of morality and Erikson's search for identity?

- Puberty is a period of about 4 years during which the sexual organs and systems fully mature and during which secondary sex characteristics such as body hair, breasts, menstruation, deepening voices, and the growth spurt occur.
- Adolescents engage in two kinds of egocentric thinking called the imaginary audience and the personal fable.
- Kohlberg proposed three levels of moral development: preconventional morality, conventional morality, and postconventional morality. Gilligan suggested that Kohlberg's ideas applied more to males.

- In Erikson's identity versus role confusion crisis, the job of the adolescent is to achieve a consistent sense of self from among all the roles, values, and futures open to him or her.

Adulthood

8.9 What are the physical, cognitive, and personality changes that occur during adulthood and aging, including Erikson's last three psychosocial stages, and patterns of parenting?

- Adulthood begins in the early 20s and ends with death in old age. It can be divided into young adulthood, middle adulthood, and late adulthood.
- The 20s are the peak of physical health; in the 30s the signs of aging become more visible, and in the 40s visual problems may occur, weight may increase, strength may decrease, and height begins to decrease.
- Women experience a physical decline in the reproductive system called the climacteric, ending at about age 50 with menopause, when a woman's estrogen levels are at zero and her reproductive capabilities are at an end. Men go through andropause, a less dramatic change in testosterone and other male hormones, beginning in the 40s.
- Many health problems such as high blood pressure, skin cancers, and arthritis begin in middle age, with the most common causes of death in middle age being heart disease, cancer, and stroke.
- Reaction times slow down, but intelligence and memory remain relatively stable.
- Erikson's crisis of young adulthood is intimacy versus isolation, in which the young adult must establish an intimate relationship, usually with a mate.
- The crisis of middle adulthood is generativity versus stagnation, in which the task of the middle-aged adult is to help the next generation through its crises, either by parenting, mentoring, or a career that leaves some legacy to the next generation.
- Baumrind proposed three parenting styles: authoritarian (rigid and uncompromising), authoritative (consistent and strict but warm and flexible), and permissive (either indifferent and unconcerned with the daily activities of the child or indulgent and unwilling to set limits on the child).
- Erikson's final crisis is integrity versus despair, in which an older adult must come to terms with mortality.

8.10 How do psychologists explain why aging occurs, and what are the stages of death and dying?

- Research strongly indicates that remaining active and involved results in the most positive adjustment to aging.
- The cellular-clock theory is based on the idea that cells only have so many times that they can reproduce; once that limit is reached, damaged cells begin to accumulate.
- The wear-and-tear theory of physical aging states that as time goes by, repeated use and abuse of the body's tissues cause it to be unable to repair all the damage.
- The free-radical theory states that oxygen molecules with an unstable electron move around the cell, damaging cell structures as they go.
- The five stages of reaction to death and dying are denial, anger, bargaining, depression, and acceptance.

Applying Psychology to Everyday Life: Cross-Cultural Views on Death

8.11 What are some cross-cultural differences in views of death and dying?

- In wealthy Hindu families, a dying person is surrounded by family and friends and then honored with a funeral process of nearly 2 weeks.
- In Northern Cheyenne culture, death is seen as part of the process of the life cycle, and takes place in three stages.
- In Navajo culture, the dead are believed to move to the underworld, and contact with the body is strictly limited for fear of luring evil spirits to the world of the living.

test YOURSELF

ANSWERS ON PAGE AK-2.

Study and Review on **mypsychlab.com** Ready for your test? More quizzes and a customized study plan **www.mypsychlab.com**

Pick the best answer.

1. Differences between age-groups would cause the most serious problems for which developmental research method?
   a. longitudinal c. cross-sectional
   b. cross-cultural d. cross-sequential
2. If a person has one gene for cystic fibrosis but does not have the disease, cystic fibrosis must be a _________ disorder.
   a. dominant c. sex-linked
   b. recessive d. polygenic
3. In _________ syndrome, the 23rd pair of chromosomes is missing an X, resulting in short, infertile females.
   a. PKU c. Klinefelter's
   b. Down d. Turner's
4. Which of the following represents dizygotic twins?
   a. One egg is fertilized by two different sperm.
   b. One egg splits and is then fertilized by two different sperm.
   c. Two eggs get fertilized by two different sperm.
   d. Two eggs are fertilized by the same sperm.
5. The sponge-like organ that provides nourishment for the growing baby and filters away waste products is called the _________.
   a. fallopian tube. c. umbilical cord.
   b. uterus. d. placenta.
6. The critical period for pregnancy is the _________.
   a. germinal period. c. fetal period.
   b. embryonic period. d. last trimester.
7. Mary's baby was born with a smaller than normal head, some facial malformations, and is mentally retarded. Mary most likely _________ during her early pregnancy.
   a. ate fish with mercury in it c. drank alcohol
   b. drank too much caffeine d. smoked marijuana

8. In the __________ reflex, the baby moves its head toward any light touch to its face.
   a. sucking
   b. startle
   c. rooting
   d. grasping

9. Which of the newborn's senses is the most fully developed at birth?
   a. hearing
   b. vision
   c. smell
   d. touch

10. At what age can the typical infant sit without support?
   a. 3 months
   b. 6 months
   c. 8 months
   d. 12 months

11. By age 5, the brain is at __________ percent of its adult weight.
   a. 25
   b. 50
   c. 90
   d. 100

12. In which of Piaget's stages does the child become capable of understanding conservation?
   a. sensorimotor
   b. preoperational
   c. formal operations
   d. concrete operations

13. According to Vygotsky, giving a child help in the form of asking leading questions and providing examples is called __________.
   a. scaffolding.
   b. the zone of proximal development.
   c. private speech.
   d. habituation.

14. As children grow from the preschool years into middle childhood, the big changes in the capacity of short-term memory are most likely due to an increase in the use of __________.
   a. metamemory.
   b. control strategies.
   c. habituation.
   d. visual-recognition memory.

15. Little Kashif held his empty cup up to his mother and said, "Milk!" His use of this word is labeled ______.
   a. a holophrase.
   b. telegraphic speech.
   c. babbling.
   d. cooing.

16. As an infant, Liz never liked change, but if you introduce new things gradually, she will eventually accept them without too much fuss. Liz is most likely __________.
   a. easy.
   b. difficult.
   c. slow to warm up.
   d. securely attached.

17. In the Strange Situation, __________ babies were clinging, unwilling to explore, very upset when Mommy left the room, and demanded to be held but pushed her away at the same time when she returned.
   a. secure
   b. avoidant
   c. ambivalent
   d. disorganized–disoriented

18. In Erikson's crisis of __________, children are developing a sense of competence and self-esteem.
   a. trust versus mistrust
   b. autonomy versus shame and doubt
   c. initiative versus guilt
   d. industry versus inferiority

19. Samantha refuses to go to school because her chin has a "huge" pimple on it and she is afraid that everyone will laugh at her and point. Samantha is a victim of __________.
   a. the imaginary audience.
   b. the personal fable.
   c. abstract egocentrism.
   d. formal operations.

20. Erikson's fifth stage of psychosocial development is __________.
   a. identity versus role confusion.
   b. intimacy versus isolation.
   c. generativity versus stagnation.
   d. integrity versus despair.

21. Vision and hearing begin to decline in the __________.
   a. 20s.
   b. 30s.
   c. 40s.
   d. 50s.

22. A decline in testosterone in the 40s is called __________.
   a. perimenopause.
   b. menopause.
   c. climacteric.
   d. andropause.

23. The crisis of middle adulthood, according to Erikson, is __________.
   a. identity versus role confusion.
   b. generativity versus stagnation.
   c. intimacy versus isolation.
   d. integrity versus despair.

24. Rebellion in the teenage years is the most likely outcome of __________ parenting.
   a. authoritarian
   b. authoritative
   c. permissive neglectful
   d. permissive indulgent

25. Collagen, an elastic tissue that becomes less elastic as we get older, is a good example of the __________ theory of aging.
   a. wear-and-tear
   b. cellular-clock
   c. free-radical
   d. active

26. According to Kübler-Ross, when bargaining fails, __________ usually results.
   a. denial
   b. anger
   c. depression
   d. acceptance

27. Which culture discussed in the Applying Psychology section seems to have the greatest fear of the dead?
   a. Hindu
   b. Cheyenne
   c. Mexican
   d. Navajo

8 development across the life span

8.1 8.2 8.3 p. 303

Issues in Studying Human Development

(scientific study of changes that occur in people as they age)

- **research designs**
  - **longitudinal**
  - **cross-sectional**
  - **cross-sequential**
- **nature vs. nurture debate**
  - **nature/genetics**
  - **nurture/environment**
  - most developmental psychologists agree that the most likely explanation for most human development is based on the interaction between nature and nurture
- **basic building blocks of development**
  - **genetics** is the science of heredity
  - **DNA (deoxyribonucleic acid):** contains genetic codes and chromosomes
  - dominant and recessive genes
  - genetic and chromosome problems

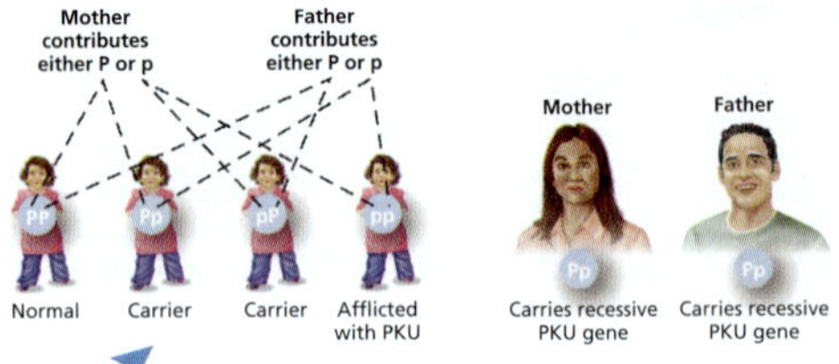

8.4 p. 307

Prenatal Development

- **zygote and twinning**
- **germinal period** (2-week period following fertilization)
  - zygote continues dividing and moving toward the uterus; cell differentiation is the process that results in specialized cells for all of the various parts of the body
- **embryonic period** (2 weeks after conception to 8 weeks)
  - once attached to the uterus, developing organism is called an embryo
  - embryo is vulnerable to hazards such as diseases and substances ingested by the mother as it receives nourishment through the placenta
- **fetal period** (from about 8 weeks to birth)
  - developing organism now called a fetus; time of tremendous growth and development
  - muscles begin to contract during the 3rd month, mother can start to feel "flutters" by 4th month, kicks felt by 5th month
  - full-term birth occurs around end of 38th week

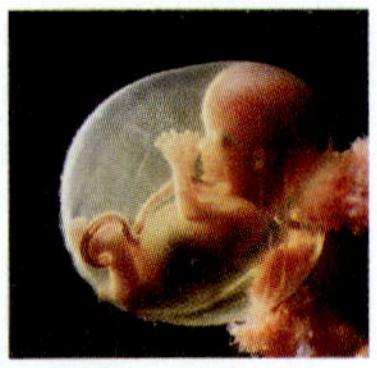

8.5 8.6 p. 318

Infancy and Childhood Development

- **physical development**
  - immediately after birth, body systems start to function (i.e., respiratory, circulatory, temperature regulation, digestive)
  - babies are born with (innate) reflex behaviors (see Fig. 8.4)
- **sensory development**
  - touch, taste, and smell are well developed
  - hearing is functional but not fully developed
  - vision is least developed
- **motor development**
  - normal motor development is related to many factors, such as nutrition, care, and health
  - birth to 2 years = period of rapid development (see Fig. 8.5)

Cognitive Development

- **Piaget's theory**
  - suggests children form mental concepts or schemes
  - proposes four distinct stages of cognitive development that span infancy to adolescence
- **Vygotsky's theory**
  - stresses the importance of social interactions with others
  - cognitive development occurs when others provide scaffolding and each child has a zone of proximal development
- **stages of language development**
  - language allows children to think in words, ask questions, communicate needs and wants, and form concepts
  - universal progressive stages but various views of development

8.7 p. 324

Infancy and Childhood Development: Psychosocial Development

- **psychosocial development** — involves development of personality, relationships, and a sense of being male or female; process begins in infancy and continues into adulthood
  - **Erikson's theory**
    - suggests development occurs in a series of eight stages (see Table 8.4)
    - at each stage an emotional crisis must be successfully met for normal development to occur
- **important early concepts**
  - infants demonstrate personality through their temperament (e.g., easy, difficult, slow to warm up), which can also affect, and is affected by, parenting and the environment
  - attachment (emotional bond between infant and a primary caregiver) is very important; different attachment styles have been identified by Ainsworth and others (e.g., secure, avoidant, ambivalent, disorganized–disoriented) that appear to be similar, but not identical, across different cultures
- **gender-role development**
  - most children begin to realize difference between sexes at about age 2
  - knowing expectations for gender and development of gender identity takes much longer and is influenced by both biology and cultural expectations

8.8 p. 328

Adolescence

(period of life from about age 13 to early 20s)

- **physical development**
  - increase in height and changes in both primary and secondary sex characteristics
  - occurs as the result of glandular and hormonal activities
  - tends to occur about 2 years after beginning of growth spurt

- **cognitive development**
  - final maturation of the frontal lobes allows cognitive advances (e.g., abstract thought/Piaget's formal operations)
  - despite advances, still have egocentric thought that emerges in a variety of ways
- **moral development**
  - understanding of what is "right" and "wrong"
  - early theory was proposed by Kohlberg; suggested three levels of moral development
  - some researchers (e.g., Gilligan) suggest that Kohlberg's ideas applied more to males; others suggest that assessment was based on hypothetical, rather than real-life, dilemmas
- **psychosocial development**
  - adolescence is largely marked by the search for a consistent sense of self or personal identity
  - Erikson: the psychosocial crisis that must be resolved is identity vs. role confusion
  - parent–teen conflict to be expected

8.9 p. 332

Adulthood

(period of life from early 20s until old age and death; age of onset can vary by culture)

- **physical development**
  - **young adulthood**
  - **middle age**
  - **late adulthood**
- **cognitive development**
  - cognitive skills often highest in 20s; processing and reaction time slow in middle age but are often compensated by greater life and situational knowledge
  - memory issues begin in middle age, likely due to stress and information overload
  - mental abilities aided by active cognitive engagement (challenging crossword puzzles, reading, etc.) and physical activity
- **psychosocial development**
  - typical life concerns involve career, relationships, family, and approaching old age
  - Erikson's stages (see Table 8.4)

8.10 p. 334

Adulthood: Aging

- **theories on aging** — vary focus from biological changes to influence on external stressors
  - **cellular-clock theory**
  - **wear-and-tear theory**
  - **free-radical theory**
- **activity theory** — positive psychological adjustment associated with continued activity and involvement
- **stages of death and dying** (based on work of Kübler-Ross)
  - **denial**
  - **anger**
  - **bargaining**
  - **depression**
  - **acceptance**

9 motivation and emotion

CHAPTER OUTLINE

MAKING THE GRADE

Jennifer had worked hard in high school, making straight A's her junior and senior years, and nothing less than a B throughout. She was involved in a variety of school activities but her classes and grades always came first. Good grades were her ticket for possibly getting a scholarship for college. This was a goal she really wanted but it would be impossible without a scholarship, her family simply couldn't afford it.

Jennifer's hard work paid off and she received an academic scholarship requiring her to maintain at least a 3.0 average on the university's 4-point grading scale. She needed B's or better. She was very thankful and did not think it would be too difficult.

Jennifer was excited about college and really enjoyed her courses and instructors. She also enjoyed the newfound freedoms of college life. With the seemingly more relaxed class schedule and abundance of social opportunities, she found several new extracurricular activities to pursue. She felt like she had plenty of time to do it all.

She got her first exam grade 4 weeks into the semester, a D. She was shocked; she had never received a D in high school. However, she admitted to herself she had not been prepared, relying on an intense cramming session the morning of the exam. She was disappointed but was sure it was only a fluke. Unfortunately, her behavior did not change and she finished her first semester with a B, three C's, and a D; a 2.0 GPA. The next semester was a bit better but her overall GPA was only a 2.2, and she lost her scholarship.

With the help of her academic advisor, Jennifer was ultimately able to identify specific time-management and studying strategies for improving her grades. More importantly, she renewed her personal focus and motivation. By learning to balance her academic and social lives, she was better able to prioritize the time her courses required. Her renewed focus enabled her to raise her GPA, later regain and maintain her scholarship, and ultimately graduate.

Why study
motivation and emotion?

The study of motivation not only helps us understand why we do the things we do but also why our behaviors can change when our focus shifts or gets redirected. Emotions are a part of everything we do, affecting our relationships with others and our own health, as well as influencing important decisions. In this chapter, we will explore the motives behind our actions and the origins and influences of emotions.

learning objectives

9.1 How do psychologists define motivation, and what are the key elements of the early instinct and drive-reduction approaches to motivation?

9.2 What are the characteristics of the three types of needs?

9.3 What are the key elements of the arousal and incentive approaches to motivation?

9.4 How do Maslow's hierarchy of needs and self-determination theories explain motivation?

9.5 What happens in the body to cause hunger, and how do social factors influence a person's experience of hunger?

9.6 What are some problems in eating behavior, and how are they affected by biology and culture?

9.7 What are the three elements of emotion?

9.8 How do the James-Lange and Cannon-Bard theories of emotion differ?

9.9 What are the key elements in cognitive arousal theory, the facial feedback hypothesis, and the cognitive-mediational theory of emotion?

Approaches to Understanding Motivation

9.1 How do psychologists define motivation, and what are the key elements of the early instinct and drive-reduction approaches to motivation?

Motivation is the process by which activities are started, directed, and continued so that physical or psychological needs or wants are met (Petri, 1996). The word itself comes from the Latin word *movere*, which means "to move." Motivation is what "moves" people to do the things they do. For example, when a person is relaxing in front of the television and begins to feel hungry, the physical need for food might cause the person to get up, go into the kitchen, and search for something to eat. If the hunger is great enough, the person might even cook something. The physical need of hunger caused the action (getting up), directed it (going to the kitchen), and sustained the search (finding or preparing something to eat). Hunger is only one example, of course. Loneliness may lead to calling a friend or going to a place where there are people. The desire to get ahead in life motivates many people to go to college. Just getting out of bed in the morning is motivated by the need to keep a roof over one's head and food on the table by going to work.

There are different types of motivation. Sometimes people are driven to do something because of an external reward of some sort (or the avoidance of an unpleasant consequence, as when someone goes to work at a job to make money and avoid losing possessions such as a house or a car) LINK to Chapter Five: Learning, pp. 181–182. When the motivation leads to an outcome that is outside of the self, it is called **extrinsic motivation**. In extrinsic motivation, a person performs an action because it leads to an outcome that is separate from the person (Ryan & Deci, 2000). Other examples would be giving a child money for every A grade received on a report card, offering a bonus to an employee for increased performance, or tipping a server in a restaurant for good service. The child, employee, and server are motivated to work for the external or extrinsic rewards. In contrast, **intrinsic motivation** is the type of motivation in which a person performs an action because the act itself is fun, rewarding, challenging, or satisfying in some internal manner. Both outcome and level of effort can vary depending on the type of motivation. Psychologist Teresa Amabile (Amabile et al., 1976) found that children's creativity was affected by the kind of motivation for which they worked: Extrinsic motivation decreased the degree of creativity shown in an experimental group's artwork when compared to the creativity levels of the children in an intrinsically motivated control group.

study tip

As you are reading this chapter, refer to I-4–I-9 in *Psychology in Action* for some ways to organize your study habits and improve your thinking and language skills.

"How much would you pay for all the secrets of the universe? Wait, don't answer yet. You also get this six-quart covered combination spaghetti pot and clam steamer. Now, how much would you pay?"

motivation the process by which activities are started, directed, and continued so that physical or psychological needs or wants are met.

extrinsic motivation type of motivation in which a person performs an action because it leads to an outcome that is separate from or external to the person.

intrinsic motivation type of motivation in which a person performs an action because the act itself is rewarding or satisfying in some internal manner.

INSTINCT APPROACHES

Early attempts to understand motivation focused on the biologically determined and innate patterns of behavior called **instincts** that exist in both people and animals. Just as animals are governed by their instincts to perform activities such as migrating, nest building, mating, and protecting their territory, early researchers proposed that human beings may also be governed by similar instincts (James, 1890; McDougall, 1908). According to **instinct approach** theorists, in humans the instinct to reproduce is responsible for sexual behavior, and the instinct for territorial protection may be related to aggressive behavior.

William McDougall (1908) actually proposed a total of 18 instincts for humans, including curiosity, flight (running away), pugnacity (aggressiveness), and acquisition (gathering possessions). As the years progressed, psychologists added more and more instincts to the list until there were thousands of proposed instincts. However, none of these early theorists did much more than give names to these instincts. Although there were plenty of descriptions, such as "submissive people possess the instinct of submission," there was no attempt to explain why these instincts exist in humans, if they exist at all (Petri, 1996).

Freud's psychoanalytic theory still includes the concept of instincts that reside in the id (the part of the personality containing all the basic human needs and drives). LINK to Chapter Thirteen: Theories of Personality, p. 496. Even so, instinct approaches have faded away because, although they could describe human behavior, they could not explain it. But these approaches did accomplish one important thing by forcing psychologists to realize that some human behavior is controlled by hereditary factors. This idea remains central in the study of human behavior today. For example, research on the genetics of both cognitive and behavioral traits suggests that hereditary factors can account for more than 50 percent of the variance in some aspects of human cognition, temperament, and personality; and much of this variance is due to the influence of multiple genes or hereditary factors, not just one (Kempf & Weinberger, 2009; Plomin et al., 1994; Plomin & Spinath, 2004).

DRIVE-REDUCTION APPROACHES

The next approach to understanding motivation focuses on the concepts of needs and drives. A **need** is a requirement of some material (such as food or water) that is essential for survival of the organism. When an organism has a need, it leads to a psychological tension as well as a physical arousal that motivates the organism to act in order to fulfill the need and reduce the tension. This tension is called a **drive** (Hull, 1943).

Drive-reduction theory proposes just this connection between internal physiological states and outward behavior. In this theory, there are two kinds of drives. **Primary drives** are those that involve survival needs of the body such as hunger and thirst, whereas **acquired (secondary) drives** are those that are learned through experience or conditioning, such as the need for money or social approval, or the need of recent former smokers to have something to put in their mouths. If this sounds familiar, it should. The concepts of primary and secondary reinforcers from Chapter Five are related to these drives. Primary reinforcers satisfy primary drives, and secondary reinforcers satisfy acquired, or secondary, drives. LINK to Chapter Five: Learning, pp. 181–182.

This theory also includes the concept of **homeostasis**, or the tendency of the body to maintain a steady state. One could think of homeostasis as the body's version of a thermostat—thermostats keep the temperature of a house at a constant level, and homeostasis does the same thing for the body's functions. When there is a primary drive need, the body is in a state of imbalance. This stimulates behavior that brings the body back into balance, or homeostasis. For example, if Jarrod's body needs food, he feels hunger and the

instincts the biologically determined and innate patterns of behavior that exist in both people and animals.

instinct approach the approach to motivation that assumes people are governed by instincts similar to those of animals.

need a requirement of some material (such as food or water) that is essential for survival of the organism.

drive a psychological tension and physical arousal arising when there is a need that motivates the organism to act in order to fulfill the need and reduce the tension.

drive-reduction theory approach to motivation that assumes behavior arises from physiological needs that cause internal drives to push the organism to satisfy the need and reduce tension and arousal.

primary drives those drives that involve needs of the body such as hunger and thirst.

acquired (secondary) drives those drives that are learned through experience or conditioning, such as the need for money or social approval.

homeostasis the tendency of the body to maintain a steady state.

(left) The human body needs water, especially when a person is working hard or under stress, as this man appears to be. Thirst is a survival need of the body, making it a primary drive, according to drive-reduction theory. What other kinds of needs might be primary drives?

(right) Some people are driven to do strenuous, challenging activities even when there is no physical need to do so. When a drive is acquired through learning, it is called an acquired or secondary drive. Fulfilling an acquired drive provides secondary reinforcement. What might this rock climber find reinforcing about scaling this steep cliff?

state of tension/arousal associated with that need. He will then seek to restore his homeostasis by eating something, which is the behavior stimulated to reduce the hunger drive (see Figure 9.1).

Although drive-reduction theory works well to explain the actions people take to reduce tension created by needs, it does not explain all human motivation. Why do people eat when they are not really hungry? People don't always seek to reduce their inner arousal either—sometimes they seek to increase it. Bungee-jumping, parachuting as a recreation, rock climbing, and watching horror movies are all activities that increase the inner state of tension and arousal, and many people love doing these activities. Why would people do such things if they don't reduce some need or restore homeostasis? The answer is complex: There are different types of needs, different effects of arousal, different incentives, and different levels of importance attached to many forms of behavior. The following theories explore some of these factors in motivation.

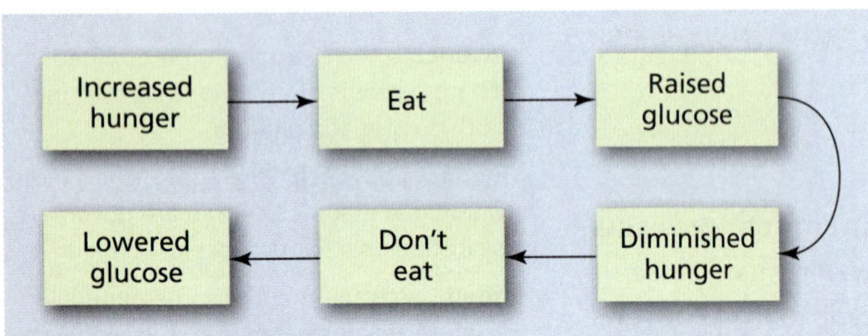

Figure 9.1 Homeostasis

In homeostasis, the body maintains balance in the body's physical states. For example, this diagram shows how increased hunger (a state of imbalance) prompts a person to eat. Eating increases the level of glucose (blood sugar), causing the feelings of hunger to reduce. After a period without eating, the glucose levels become low enough to stimulate the hunger drive once again, and the entire cycle is repeated.

DIFFERENT STROKES FOR DIFFERENT FOLKS: NEEDS Obviously, motivation is about needs. Drive-reduction theory talks about needs, and other theories of motivation include the concept of needs. In many of these theories, most needs are the result of some inner physical drive (such as hunger or thirst) that demands to be satisfied. Harvard University psychologist David C. McClelland (1961, 1987) proposed a theory of motivation that highlights the importance of three psychological needs not typically considered by the other theories: achievement, affiliation, and power.

9.2 What are the characteristics of the three types of needs?

Need for Achievement: How to Succeed by Excelling at Everything The **need for achievement** (abbreviated as **nAch** in McClelland's writings) involves a strong desire to succeed in attaining goals, not only realistic ones but also challenging ones. People who are high in nAch look for careers and hobbies that allow others to evaluate them because these high achievers also need to have feedback about their performance in addition to the achievement of reaching the goal. Although many of these people do become wealthy, famous, and publicly successful, others fulfill their need to achieve in ways that lead only to their own personal success, not material riches—they just want the challenge. Achievement motivation appears to be strongly

need for achievement (nAch) a need that involves a strong desire to succeed in attaining goals, not only realistic ones but also challenging ones.

related to success in school, occupational success, and the quality and amount of what a person produces (Collins et al., 2004; Gillespie et al., 2002; Spangler, 1992).

need for affiliation (nAff) the need for friendly social interactions and relationships with others.

need for power (nPow) the need to have control or influence over others.

Need for Affiliation: Popularity Rules Another psychological need is for friendly social interactions and relationships with others. Called the **need for affiliation (nAff)**, people high in this need seek to be liked by others and to be held in high regard by those around them. This makes high affiliation people good team players, whereas a person high in achievement just might run over a few team members on the way to the top. **Read** on **mypsychlab.com**

Read and learn more about the need for affiliation at **mypsychlab.com**

Need for Power: The One Who Dies With the Most Toys Wins The final psychological need proposed by McClelland is the **need for power (nPow)**. Power is not about reaching a goal but about having control over other people. People high in this need would want to have influence over others and make an impact on them. They want their ideas to be the ones that are used, regardless of whether or not their ideas will lead to success. Status and prestige are important, so these people wear expensive clothes, live in expensive houses, drive fancy cars, and dine in the best restaurants. Whereas someone who is a high achiever may not need a lot of money to validate the achievement, someone who is high in the need for power typically sees the money (and cars, houses, jewelry, and other "toys") as the achievement. The subtitle for this section is a saying from a popular bumper sticker but is really a comment on the more negative aspect of the need for power. For the person high in the need for power, it's all about who has the most expensive "toys" in the end.

How do people get to be high achievers?

Personality and nAch: Carol Dweck's Self-Theory of Motivation

How do people get to be high achievers?

According to motivation and personality psychologist Carol Dweck (1999), the need for achievement is closely linked to personality factors, including a person's view of how *self* can affect the understanding of how much a person's actions can influence his or her success. (Dweck defines *self* as the beliefs one holds about one's abilities and relationships to others.) This concept is related to the much older notion of *locus of control*, in which people who assume that they have control over what happens in their lives are considered to be *internal* in locus of control, and those who feel that their lives are controlled by powerful others, luck, or fate are considered to be *external* in locus of control (A. P. MacDonald, 1970; Rotter, 1966).

Donald Trump stands triumphant at the opening of his Trump International Hotel and Tower in New York. Many people who are as wealthy as "The Donald" continue to buy new houses, businesses, clothing, and cars (among other things) even though they do not need them. Such actions are examples of the need for power. How might this need for power be expressed in a person's relationships with others, such as a spouse, employee, or friend?

Dweck has amassed a large body of empirical research, particularly in the field of education, to support the idea that people's "theories" about their own selves can affect their level of achievement motivation and their willingness to keep trying to achieve success in the face of failure (Dweck, 1986; Dweck & Elliott, 1983; Dweck & Leggett, 1988; Elliott & Dweck, 1988). According to this research, people can form one of two belief systems about intelligence, which in turn affects their motivation to achieve. Those who believe intelligence is fixed and unchangeable often demonstrate an external locus of control when faced with difficulty, leading them to give up easily or avoid situations in which they might fail—often ensuring their own failure in the process. They are prone to developing learned helplessness, the tendency to stop trying to achieve a goal because past failure has led them to believe that they cannot succeed. LINK to Chapter Five: Learning, p. 199. Their goals involve trying to "look smart" and to outperform others ("See, at least I did better than she did"). For example, a student faced with a big exam may avoid coming to class that day, even though that might mean getting an even lower score on a makeup exam.

This does not mean that students with this view of intelligence are always unsuccessful. In fact, Dweck's research (1999) suggests that students who have had a long history of successes may be most at risk for developing a learned helplessness after a big

Many people are driven by a need to attain both realistic and challenging goals. This young girl seems eager to provide an answer to the teacher's question, and the teacher's positive feedback will help foster the girl's need for achievement.

failure, precisely because their previous successes have led them to believe in their own fixed intelligence. For example, a child who had never earned anything less than an A in school who then receives his first C might become depressed and refuse to do any more homework, ensuring future failure. Furthermore, students with this view of intelligence typically have an internal attribution for their intelligence (internal locus) and its fixed state; they simply don't see it as changeable by personal effort (Dweck & Molden, 2008).

The other type of person believes that intelligence is changeable and can be shaped by experiences and effort in small increases, or increments. These people also tend to show an internal locus of control, both in believing that their own actions and efforts will improve their intelligence, and in taking control or increasing their efforts when faced with challenges (Dweck & Molden, 2008). They work at developing new strategies and get involved in new tasks, with the goal of increasing their "smarts." They are motivated to master tasks and don't allow failure to destroy their confidence in themselves or prevent them from trying again and again, using new strategies each time.

Based on this and other research, Dweck recommends that parents and teachers encourage children to value the learning process more than "looking smart" by always having the right answer (and only responding when sure of that answer, for example). Errors should not be viewed as failures but as a way to improve future performance on the road to mastering whatever the goal in question is. Essentially, this means praising efforts and the methods that children use to make those efforts, not just successes or ability. Instead of saying, "You're right, how smart you are," the parent or teacher should say something such as, "You are really thinking hard," or "That was a very clever way to think about this problem." In the past, teachers and parents have been told that praise is good and criticism is bad—it might damage a child's self-esteem. Dweck believes that constructive criticism, when linked with praise of effort and the use of strategies, will be a better influence on the child's self-esteem than endless praise that can become meaningless when given indiscriminately.

9.1 9.2

CONCEPT MAP

- **types**
  - **intrinsic:** actions are rewarding or satisfying in and of themselves
  - **extrinsic:** actions are performed because they lead to some sort of external outcome

Motivation

(process by which activities are started, directed, and continued so that physical or psychological needs or wants are met)

- **instinct**
  - biologically determined/innate patterns of behavior
  - old approach: instincts are mainly descriptions, not explanations; idea that some behavior is hereditary remains an important focus
- **drive reduction**
  - **need:** requirement for something essential for survival; existence of need leads to psychological tension (drive) and physical arousal; satisfying need reduces drive/tension
  - **primary drives** involve survival needs (e.g., hunger, thirst) and maintaining homeostasis
  - **secondary (acquired) drives** are learned through experience or conditioning (e.g., money, social approval)
- **psychological needs**
  - psychological needs have been highlighted in some theories (e.g., McClelland)
    - need for **achievement**
    - need for **affiliation**
    - need for **power**
  - Dweck suggests that the need for achievement is linked to a person's view of self (fixed or changeable) and locus of control

Approaches to Understanding Motivation

PRACTICE quiz How much do you remember? ANSWERS ON PAGE AK-2.

Pick the best answer.

1. The process by which activities are started, directed, and sustained to meet a person's wants is called _________.
   a. drive. c. motivation.
   b. incentive. d. instinct.
2. Liz picked out "her" desk on the first day of class. But in the second class period, someone else is sitting in "her" chosen seat. Liz's territorial attitude about that desk and her negative feelings toward the "interloper" sitting there might best be explained by which of the following?
   a. extrinsic approach c. drive-reduction approach
   b. intrinsic approach d. instinct approach
3. People high in the need for _________ want to be liked by others and are good team players.
   a. achievement c. power
   b. affiliation d. emotion
4. Ronnie believes that people are just born smart or not smart, and he thinks of himself as "not smart." As a result, Ronnie doesn't really try all that hard to succeed in school. Dweck would say that Ronnie's achievement motivation is being affected by his _________.
   a. external locus of control. c. need for homeostasis.
   b. internal locus of control. d. centralized locus of control.

Brainstorming: How might the three types of needs discussed in this section relate to the goals of many politicians? Would some needs be more important than others?

AROUSAL APPROACHES

9.3 What are the key elements of the arousal and incentive approaches to motivation?

Another explanation for human motivation involves the recognition of yet another type of need, the need for stimulation. A **stimulus motive** is one that appears to be unlearned but causes an increase in stimulation. Examples would be curiosity, playing, and exploration.

In **arousal theory**, people are said to have an optimal (best or ideal) level of tension. Task performances, for example, may suffer if the level of arousal is too high (such as severe test anxiety) or even if the level of arousal is too low (such as boredom). For many kinds of tasks, a moderate level of arousal seems to be best. This relationship between task performance and arousal has been explained by the **Yerkes-Dodson law** (Teigen, 1994; Yerkes & Dodson, 1908), although Yerkes and Dodson formulated the law referring to stimulus intensity, not arousal level (Winton, 1987).

Of special interest to both sports psychologists and social psychologists, this arousal effect appears to be modified by the difficulty level of the task: Easy tasks demand a somewhat "high–moderate" level for optimal performance, whereas difficult tasks require a "low–moderate" level. Figure 9.2 shows this relationship in graphic form. A sports psychologist might work with an athlete to help them get "in the zone," where they are in that specific zone of arousal (not too low and not too high) and state of mental focus so as to maximize their athletic skills and performance. Social psychologists also examine the effect of the presence of other people on the facilitation or impairment of an individual's performance. LINK to Chapter Twelve: Social Psychology, p. 456. For example, imagine someone in a classroom speaking to a classmate seated nearby. The act of speaking directly to another person is a fairly easy task for many people and is accomplished without any difficulty or errors. However, ask that same individual to stand, turn, and address the entire classroom of students, and all of a sudden his or her arousal level spikes; many individuals in a similar situation may find themselves unable to put words together well enough to form coherent sentences, or to pronounce words correctly—in essence, they may become "tongue-tied," all because their arousal level has gotten too high.

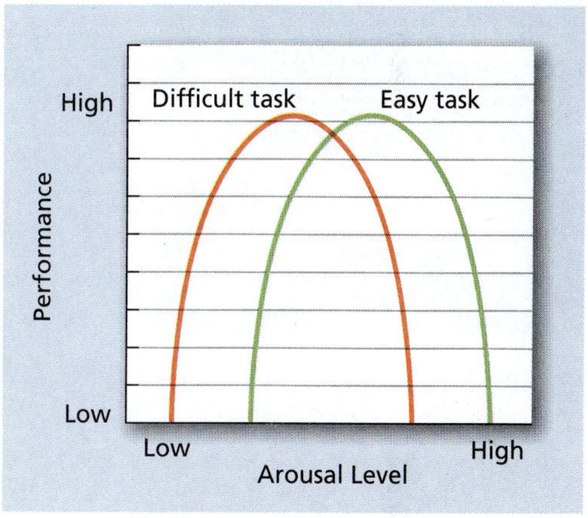

Figure 9.2 Arousal and Performance
The optimal level of arousal for task performance depends on the difficulty of the task. We generally perform easy tasks well if we are at a high–moderate level of arousal (green) and accomplish difficult tasks well if we are at a low–moderate level (red).

stimulus motive a motive that appears to be unlearned but causes an increase in stimulation, such as curiosity.

arousal theory theory of motivation in which people are said to have an optimal (best or ideal) level of tension that they seek to maintain by increasing or decreasing stimulation.

Yerkes-Dodson law law stating performance is related to arousal; moderate levels of arousal lead to better performance than do levels of arousal that are too low or too high. This effect varies with the difficulty of the task: Easy tasks require a high-moderate level whereas more-difficult tasks require a low-moderate level.

Maintaining an optimal level of arousal, then, may involve reducing tension or creating it (Hebb, 1955). For example, husbands or wives who are underaroused may pick a fight with their spouse. Students who experience test anxiety (a high level of arousal) may seek out ways to reduce that anxiety to improve their test performance. Students who are not anxious at all may not be motivated to study well, thus lowering their test performance. Many arousal theorists believe that the optimal level of arousal for most people under normal circumstances is somewhere in the middle, neither too high nor too low.

If people are supposed to be seeking a level of arousal somewhere around the middle, why do some people love to do things like bungee-jumping?

If people are supposed to be seeking a level of arousal somewhere around the middle, why do some people love to do things like bungee-jumping?

Even though the average person might require a moderate level of arousal to feel content, there are some people who need less arousal and some who need more. The person who needs more arousal is called a **sensation seeker** (Zuckerman, 1979, 1994). Sensation seekers seem to need more complex and varied sensory experiences than do other people. The need does not always have to involve danger. For example, students who travel to other countries to study tend to score higher on scales of sensation seeking than do students who stay at home (Schroth & McCormack, 2000). Sensation seeking may be related to temperament, as discussed in LINK Chapter Eight: Development Across the Life Span, pp. 319–320. Table 9.1 has some sample items from a typical sensation-seeking scale.

Does this look fun? If so, you may score relatively higher in sensation seeking.

In one study (Putnam & Stifter, 2002), researchers found evidence of "sensation-seeking" behavior in children as young as age 2. In this study, 90 children were studied at the ages of 6, 12, 24, and 25 months. In a test of the youngest participants, the babies were shown two sets of toys: a block, a plate, and a cup; or a flashing light, a toy beeper, and a wind-up dragon. The first set was considered a low-intensity stimulus whereas the second set was labeled a high-intensity stimulus. The infants who reached out for the toys more quickly, and reached for the high-intensity toys in particular, were labeled "approach motivated."

The same children at age 2 were given an opportunity to explore a black box with a hole in one side. The children who were labeled "low-approach motivated" at 6 and 12 months were unwilling to put their hands into the hole to see what might be in the box, whereas the "high-approach-motivated" children not only put their hands in but also in some cases tried to climb into the box.

This daring preschool boy has climbed high into this massive tree and looks as though he might try to climb higher still.

Is the tendency to be a sensation seeker something people have when they are born? Although it is tempting to think of 6-month-old children as having little in the way of experiences that could shape their personalities, the fact is that the first 6 months of life is full of experiences that might affect children's choices in the future. For example, a very young infant might, while being carried, stick a hand into some

Table 9.1

Sample Items From the Zuckerman-Kuhlman Personality Questionnaire

SCALE ITEM	SENSATION SEEKING
I sometimes do "crazy" things just for fun.	High
I prefer friends who are excitingly unpredictable.	High
I am an impulsive person.	High
Before I begin a complicated job, I make careful plans.	Low
I usually think about what I am going to do before doing it.	Low

Source: Adapted from Zuckerman, M. (2002).

sensation seeker someone who needs more arousal than the average person.

place that ends up causing pain. This experience might affect that infant's willingness in the future to put his or her hand in something else through the simple learning process of operant conditioning. LINK to Chapter Five: Learning, pp. 180–183. Determining the origins of sensation seeking will have to wait for further research.

INCENTIVE APPROACHES

Last Thanksgiving, I had eaten about all I could. Then my aunt brought out a piece of her wonderful pumpkin pie and I couldn't resist—I ate it, even though I was not at all hungry. What makes us do things even when we don't have the drive or need to do them?

Last Thanksgiving, I had eaten about all I could. Then my aunt brought out a piece of her wonderful pumpkin pie and I couldn't resist—I ate it, even though I was not at all hungry. What makes us do things even when we don't have the drive or need to do them?

It's true that sometimes there is no physical need present, yet people still eat, drink, or react as if they did have a need. Even though that piece of pie was not necessary to reduce a hunger drive, it was very rewarding, wasn't it? And on past occasions, that pie was also delicious and rewarding, so there is anticipation of that reward now. The pie, in all its glorious promise of flavor and sweetness, becomes, in itself, an incentive to eat. **Incentives** are things that attract or lure people into action. In fact, the dictionary (Merriam-Webster, 2003) lists *incentive* as meaning the same thing as *motive*.

In **incentive approaches**, behavior is explained in terms of the external stimulus and its rewarding properties. These rewarding properties exist independently of any need or level of arousal and can cause people to act only upon the incentive. Thus, incentive theory is actually based, at least in part, on the principles of learning that were discussed in Chapter Five. LINK to Chapter Five: Learning, pp. 181–183.

One of the earliest incentive approaches clearly demonstrates the relationship to learning, particularly the early cognitive learning theories found in the work of Edward Tolman (1932). **Expectancy-value theories** are a class of incentive theories based on the work of Tolman and others (Lewin, 1936; Rotter, 1954). In general, these theories assume that the actions of humans cannot be predicted or fully understood without understanding the beliefs, values, and the importance that people attach to those beliefs and values at any given moment in time. Tolman's work with animals (the latent learning studies with rats discussed in Chapter Five, pp. 197–198) demonstrated that organisms are capable of remembering what had happened in the past, anticipating future events, and adjusting their own actions according to those cognitive *expectancies* (a set of beliefs about what will happen in the future based on past experiences). Kurt Lewin (1936) applied these concepts to the estimated likelihood of future success or failure in his field theory of decision making. Julian Rotter's (1954) social learning theory included expectancy as one of the three factors that predict people's behavior—if Diego's past experiences with writing papers, for example, have led to an expectancy of failing to get a high grade, he is unlikely to take on the task of an extra term paper to earn bonus points.

By itself, the incentive approach does not explain the motivation behind all behavior. Many theorists today see motivation as a result of both the "push" of internal needs or drives and the "pull" of a rewarding external stimulus. For example, sometimes a person may actually be hungry (the push) but choose to satisfy that drive by selecting a candy bar instead of a celery stick. The candy bar has more appeal to most people, and it, therefore, has more pull than the celery. (Frankly, to most people, just about anything has more pull than celery.)

incentives things that attract or lure people into action.

incentive approaches theories of motivation in which behavior is explained as a response to the external stimulus and its rewarding properties.

expectancy-value theories incentive theories that assume the actions of humans cannot be predicted or fully understood without understanding the beliefs, values, and the importance that a person attaches to those beliefs and values at any given moment in time.

HUMANISTIC APPROACHES

9.4 How do Maslow's hierarchy of needs and self-determination theories explain motivation?

Some final approaches to the study of motivation are humanistic in nature. The first is based on the work of Abraham Maslow (1943, 1987). Maslow was one of the early

self-actualization according to Maslow, the point that is seldom reached at which people have sufficiently satisfied the lower needs and achieved their full human potential.

peak experiences according to Maslow, times in a person's life during which self-actualization is temporarily achieved.

humanistic psychologists who rejected the dominant theories of psychoanalysis and behaviorism in favor of a more positive view of human behavior. LINK to Chapter One: The Science of Psychology, p. 14. Maslow proposed that there are several levels of needs that a person must strive to meet before achieving the highest level of personality fulfillment. According to Maslow, **self-actualization** is the point that is seldom reached—at which people have satisfied the lower needs and achieved their full human potential.

These needs include both fundamental deficiency needs, such as the need for food or water, and growth needs, such as the desire for having friends or feeling good about oneself. For a person to achieve self-actualization, which is the highest level of growth needs, the primary, fundamental needs must first be fulfilled. Figure 9.3 shows the typical way to represent Maslow's series of needs as a pyramid with the most basic needs for survival at the bottom and the highest needs at the top. This type of ranking is called a hierarchy.* **Explore** on **mypsychlab.com**

Explore Maslow's Hierarchy of Needs on **mypsychlab.com**

The lowest level of the pyramid consists of physiological needs such as food, water, and rest. Once those needs are met, safety becomes important and involves feeling secure. Belongingness and love are the needs for friends and companions as well as to be accepted by others, and self-esteem is the need to feel that one has accomplished something good or earned the esteem of others. Just above the esteem needs on the hierarchy come the cognitive needs, or the need to know and understand the world (Maslow, 1971; Maslow & Lowery, 1998). This need is represented in people who learn for the sake of gathering knowledge, and all people who pursue their natural curiosity. Above the cognitive needs are the aesthetic needs, which include the need for order and beauty and are typical of artistic people. (It should be noted that all people also seem to like to express themselves artistically—even if it's only graffiti on a wall.) Once all these needs are met, it is possible to be concerned about self-actualization needs, or needs that help a person reach his or her full potential and capabilities as a human being. A final need, transcendence, involves helping others to achieve their full potential. People move up the pyramid as they go through life, gaining wisdom and the knowledge of how to handle many different situations. But a shift in life's circumstances can result in a shift down to a lower need. Moving up and down and then back up can occur frequently—even from one hour to the next. Times in a person's life in which self-actualization is achieved, at least temporarily, are called **peak experiences**. For Maslow, the process of growth and self-actualization is the striving to make peak experiences happen again and again.

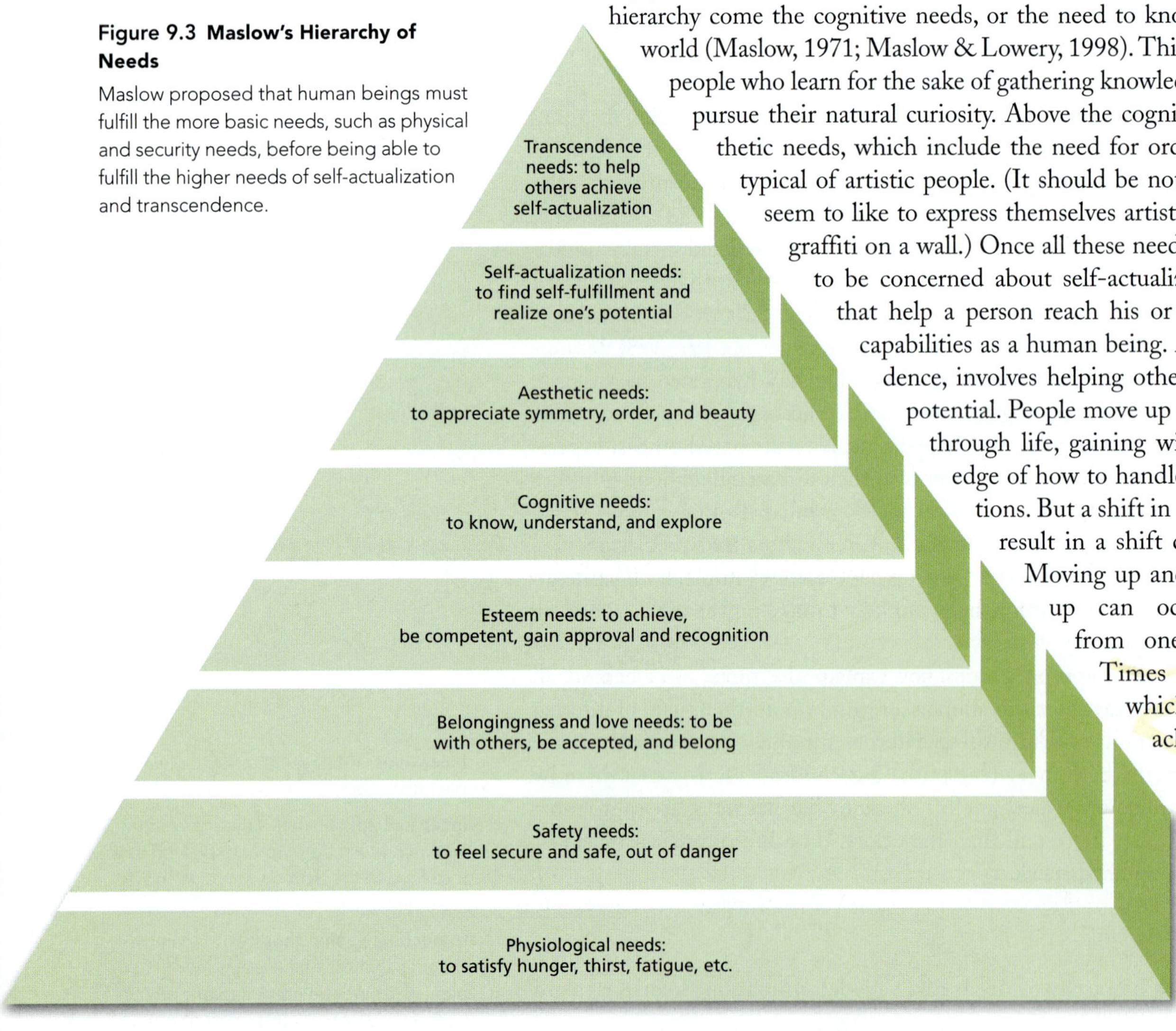

Figure 9.3 Maslow's Hierarchy of Needs
Maslow proposed that human beings must fulfill the more basic needs, such as physical and security needs, before being able to fulfill the higher needs of self-actualization and transcendence.

*hierarchy: a graded or ranked series.

Does this theory apply universally?

Does this theory apply universally?

Maslow's theory has had a powerful influence on the field of management (Heil et al., 1998) and has spawned new ideas and concepts of what might be an appropriate revised hierarchy. LINK to Appendix B: Applied Psychology. In spite of this influence, Maslow's theory is not without its critics. There are several problems that others have highlighted, and the most serious is that there is little scientific support (Drenth et al., 1984). Like Sigmund Freud, Maslow developed his theory based on his personal observations of people rather than any empirically gathered observations or research. Although many people report that while they were starving, they could think of nothing but food, there is anecdotal evidence in the lives of many people, some of them quite well known, that the lower needs do not have to be satisfied before moving on to a higher need (Drenth et al., 1984). For example, artists and scientists throughout history have been known to deny their own physical needs while producing great works (a self-actualization need).

Maslow's work was also based on his studies of Americans. Cross-cultural research suggests that the order of needs on the hierarchy does not always hold true for other cultures, particularly those cultures with a stronger tendency than the culture of the United States to avoid uncertainty, such as Greece and Japan. In those countries security needs are much stronger than self-actualization needs in determining motivation (Hofstede, 1980; Hofstede et al., 2002). This means that people in those cultures value job security more than they do job satisfaction (holding an interesting or challenging job). In countries such as Sweden and Norway, which stress the quality of life as being of greater importance than what a person produces, social needs may be more important than self-actualization needs (Hofstede et al., 2002). LINK to Chapter Thirteen: Theories of Personality, pp. 515–516.

In the movie *Castaway*, Tom Hanks's character is stranded on a deserted island. His first concern is to find something to eat and fresh water to drink—without those two things, he cannot survive. Even while he is building a crude shelter, he is still thinking about how to obtain food. Once he has those needs met, however, he gets lonely. He finds a volleyball, paints a handprint and then a crude face on it, and names it "Wilson." He talks to the volleyball as if it were a person, at first as a kind of way to talk out the things he needs to do and later as a way of staying relatively sane. The need for companionship is that strong.

Other theorists have developed and refined Maslow's hierarchy. Clayton Alderfer developed one of the more popular versions of this refinement. In his theory, the hierarchy has only three levels: *existence needs*, which include the physiological needs and basic safety needs that provide for the person's continued existence; *relatedness needs*, which include some safety issues as well as belongingness and self-esteem needs and are related to social relationships; and *growth needs*, which include some self-esteem issues and the self-actualization needs that help people develop their full potential as human beings (Alderfer, 1972). Alderfer believed that more than one need could be active at a time and that progression up and down the hierarchy is common as one type of need assumes greater importance at a particular time in a person's life than other needs.

Douglas Kenrick and colleagues have also recently suggested a modification to Maslow's original hierarchy that encompasses aspects of evolutionary biology, anthropology, and psychology. Their modification incorporates dynamics between internal motives and environmental threats and opportunities (Kenrick et al., 2010). However, their revision has not been without critique and has spawned further contemplation. Some elements of Kenrick's theory have been challenged, including a questioning of its focus on evolutionary aspects instead of human cultural influences (Kesebir et al., 2010), and its removal of self-actualization from both the pinnacle of the pyramid and from the hierarchy altogether as a stand-alone motive (Peterson & Park, 2010). Just as there are many aspects to motivation, any revision or discussion of an appropriate hierarchy of needs will need to take into account a wide variety of opinions and viewpoints.

SELF-DETERMINATION THEORY (SDT)

Another theory of motivation that is similar to Maslow's hierarchy of needs is the **self-determination theory (SDT)** of Ryan and Deci (2000). In this theory, there are three inborn and universal needs that help people gain a complete sense of self and whole, healthy relationships with others. The three needs are *autonomy*, or the need to be in

self-determination theory (SDT) theory of human motivation in which the social context of an action has an effect on the type of motivation existing for the action.

control of one's own behavior and goals (i.e., self-determination); *competence*, or the need to be able to master the challenging tasks of one's life; and *relatedness*, or the need to feel a sense of belonging, intimacy, and security in relationships with others. These needs are common in several theories of personality; the relatedness need is, of course, similar to Maslow's belongingness and love needs, and both autonomy and competence are important aspects of Erikson's theory of psychosocial personality development (Erikson, 1950, 1980). LINK to Chapter Eight: Development Across the Life Span, pp. 322–323.

"That is the correct answer, Bill, but I'm afraid you don't win anything for it."

Ryan, Deci, and their colleagues (Deci et al., 1994; Ryan & Deci, 2000) believe that satisfying these needs can best be accomplished if the person has a supportive environment in which to develop goals and relationships with others. Such satisfaction will not only foster healthy psychological growth but also increase the individual's intrinsic motivation (actions are performed because they are internally rewarding or satisfying). Evidence suggests that intrinsic motivation is increased or enhanced when a person not only feels competence (through experiencing positive feedback from others and succeeding at what are perceived to be challenging tasks) but also a sense of autonomy or the knowledge that his or her actions are self-determined rather than controlled by others (deCharms, 1968; Deci & Ryan, 1985).

Previous research has found a negative impact on intrinsic motivation when an external reward is given for the performance (Deci et al., 1999), but a more recent paper discusses the results of other studies that find negative effects only for tasks that are not interesting in and of themselves (Cameron et al., 2001). When the task itself is interesting to the person (as might be an assignment that an instructor or manager has explained in terms of its importance and future value), external rewards may increase intrinsic motivation, at least in the short term. Although this recent finding is intriguing, further research is needed to determine if the long-term effects of extrinsic rewards on intrinsic motivation are consistently negative, as the bulk of the research has shown up to now.

But don't we sometimes do things for both kinds of motives?

But don't we sometimes do things for both kinds of motives?

There are usually elements of both intrinsic and extrinsic motives in many of the things people do. Most teachers, for example, work for money to pay bills (the extrinsic motive) but may also feel that they are helping young children to become better adults in the future, which makes the teachers feel good about themselves (the intrinsic motive).

9.3 **9.4** CONCEPT MAP

- **arousal** need for stimulation
  - **arousal theory** suggests people have an optimal level of tension that they work to maintain
  - a moderate level is most commonly sought, but that level can range from low to high (sensation seeking)
- **incentive** things that attract or lure people into action, most often due to rewarding properties
  - based in part on principles of learning
  - early work by Tolman, Lewin, and Rotter focused on expectancy-values or how our beliefs, values, and importance we attach to these affect our actions
- **humanistic** based primarily on Maslow's hierarchy of needs; primary, basic needs must be met before higher levels can be met (see Fig. 9.3)
  - **Alderfer's modification:** only three levels: existence, relatedness, growth
  - **self-determination theory:** similar to Maslow's hierarchy, three universal needs are autonomy, competence, and relatedness

Approaches to Understanding Motivation (continued)

PRACTICE quiz How much do you remember? ANSWERS ON PAGE AK-2.

Pick the best answer.

1. In the _________ approach, people are said to have an optimal level of tension.
   a. drive-reduction
   b. arousal
   c. incentive
   d. humanistic
2. Which of the following approaches to motivation has ties to the basic principles of learning and the concept of reinforcement?
   a. arousal
   b. humanistic
   c. incentive
   d. self-determination
3. The most basic needs in Maslow's hierarchy are _________ needs.
   a. esteem
   b. love
   c. safety
   d. physiological
4. Jamal gets a new toy for every good grade on his report card in first grade. Toys are providing Jamal with _________.
   a. intrinsic motivation.
   b. extrinsic motivation.
   c. need motivation.
   d. intrinsic rewards.

Brainstorming: What motivates you while you are in this psychology course? In what ways are you intrinsically motivated? Extrinsically motivated?

What, Hungry Again? Why People Eat

Satisfying hunger is one of our most primary needs. The eating habits of people today have become a major concern and a frequent topic of news programs, talk shows, and scientific research. Countless pills, supplements, and treatments are available to "help" people eat less and others to eat more. Eating is not only a basic survival behavior that reduces a primary drive; it is also a form of entertainment for many and the attractive presentations and social environment of many eating experiences are a powerful incentive.

PHYSIOLOGICAL COMPONENTS OF HUNGER

Why do we eat? What causes us to feel hungry in the first place?

Why do we eat? What causes us to feel hungry in the first place?

There are actually several factors involved in the hunger drive. Cannon (Cannon & Washburn, 1912) believed that stomach contractions, or "hunger pangs," caused hunger and that the presence of food in the stomach would stop the contractions and appease the hunger drive. Oddly enough, having an empty stomach is not the deciding factor in many cases. Although the stomach does have sensory receptors that respond to the pressure of the stretching stomach muscles as food is piled in and that send signals to the brain indicating that the stomach is full (Geliebter, 1988), people who have had their stomachs removed still get hungry (Janowitz, 1967).

9.5 What happens in the body to cause hunger, and how do social factors influence a person's experience of hunger?

One factor in hunger seems to be the insulin response that occurs after we begin to eat. **Insulin** and **glucagon** are hormones that are secreted by the pancreas to control the levels of fats, proteins, and carbohydrates in the whole body, including glucose (blood sugar). Insulin reduces the level of glucose in the bloodstream, for example, whereas glucagon increases the level. Insulin, normally released in greater amounts after eating has begun, causes a feeling of more hunger because of the drop in blood sugar levels. Carbohydrates, especially those that are simple or highly refined (such as table sugar, fruit drinks, white flour, and white bread or pasta), cause the insulin level to spike even more than other foods do because there is such a large amount of glucose released by these foods at one time. High blood sugar leads to more insulin released, which leads to a low blood sugar level, increased appetite, and the tendency to overeat. That is the basic principle behind many of the newest diets that promote low-carbohydrate intake. The proponents of these new diets argue that if people control the carbohydrates, they can control the insulin reaction and prevent hunger cravings later on.

insulin a hormone secreted by the pancreas to control the levels of fats, proteins, and carbohydrates in the body by reducing the level of glucose in the bloodstream.

glucagon hormone that is secreted by the pancreas to control the levels of fats, proteins, and carbohydrates in the body by increasing the level of glucose in the bloodstream.

Figure 9.4 Obese Laboratory Rat

This rat has reached a high level of obesity because its ventromedial hypothalamus has been deliberately damaged in the laboratory. The result is a rat that no longer receives signals of being satiated, and so the rat continues to eat and eat and eat.

THE ROLE OF THE HYPOTHALAMUS The stomach and the pancreas are only two of the factors in hunger. In Chapter Two the role of the hypothalamus in controlling many kinds of motivational stimuli, including hunger, was seen as a result of its influence on the pituitary. But the hypothalamus itself has two separate areas, controlled by the levels of glucose and insulin in the body, which appear to control eating behavior.

The *ventromedial hypothalamus (VMH)* may be involved in stopping the eating response when glucose levels go up (Neary et al., 2004). In one study, rats whose VMH areas (located toward the bottom and center of the hypothalamus) were damaged would no longer stop eating—they ate and ate until they were quite overweight (Hetherington & Ranson, 1940). (See Figure 9.4 for a picture of a rat with this kind of damage.) However, they did not eat everything in sight. They actually got rather picky, only overeating on food that appealed to them (Ferguson & Keesey, 1975; Parkinson & Weingarten, 1990). In fact, if all the food available to them was unappealing, they did not become obese and in some cases even lost weight.

Another part of the hypothalamus, located on the side and called the *lateral hypothalamus (LH),* seems to influence the onset of eating when insulin levels go up (Neary et al., 2004). Damage to this area caused rats to stop eating to the point of starvation. They would eat only if force-fed and still lost weight under those conditions (Anand & Brobeck, 1951; Hoebel & Teitelbaum, 1966).

WEIGHT SET POINT AND BASAL METABOLIC RATE Obviously, the role of the hypothalamus in eating behavior is complex. Some researchers (Leibel et al., 1995; Nisbett, 1972) believe that the hypothalamus affects the particular level of weight that the body tries to maintain, called the **weight set point**. Injury to the hypothalamus does raise or lower the weight set point rather dramatically, causing either drastic weight loss or weight gain.

Metabolism, the speed at which the body burns available energy, and exercise also play a part in the weight set point. Some people are no doubt genetically wired to have faster metabolisms, and those people can eat large amounts of food without gaining weight. Others have slower metabolisms and may eat a normal or even less than normal amount of food and still gain weight or have difficulty losing it (Bouchard et al., 1990). (Some people swear they can gain weight just by *looking* at a piece of cake!) Regular, moderate exercise can help offset the slowing of metabolism and the increase in the weight set point that comes with it (Tremblay et al., 1999).

The rate at which the body burns energy when a person is resting is called the **basal metabolic rate (BMR)** and is directly tied to the set point. If a person's BMR decreases (as it does in adulthood and with decreased activity levels), that person's weight set point increases if the same number of calories is consumed. Table 9.2 shows the changes in BMR of a typical woman and man as age increases from 10 years to 80 years. Notice that the BMR decreases more dramatically as the age of the person increases. Adolescents typically have a very high BMR and activity level and, therefore, a lower weight set point, meaning they can eat far more than an adult of the same size and not gain weight. But when that adolescent becomes an adult, the BMR begins to decline. Adults should reduce the number of calories they consume and exercise most every day, but the tendency is to eat more and move less as income levels and job demands increase. Even if the eating habits of the teenage years are simply maintained, excessive weight gain is not far behind. (In some people, the excessive weight gain may be mostly "behind.")

weight set point the particular level of weight that the body tries to maintain.

basal metabolic rate (BMR) the rate at which the body burns energy when the organism is resting.

Table 9.2

Average Basal Metabolic Rates for a Female and Male

AGE RANGE	AGES 10–18	AGES 19–30	AGES 31–60	AGES 61–80
Female ($5\frac{1}{2}$ ft.)	1,770*	1,720	1,623	1,506
Male (6 ft.)	2,140	2,071	1,934	1,770

*Numbers in the table represent the number of calories a person needs to consume each day to maintain body weight (without exercise).

If you would like to calculate your own BMR, there are numerous Internet sites that allow a person to enter data such as height, age, weight, and activity level. The BMR is then automatically calculated according to a standard formula. Simply type "basal metabolic rate calculator" into your Web search engine to find these sites.

(top) Cultural factors play an important part in why people eat. Women in Japan have been found to be motivated to eat by hunger and social demands, illustrated by the interaction during a meal at this family gathering.

(bottom) Women in the United States may eat because they are depressed or for other emotional reasons, rather than just to appease hunger or as part of a social situation. Obviously, this woman does not need the social trappings of a bowl, dining table, and the company of others to motivate her eating habits—unless you count the cat.

SOCIAL COMPONENTS OF HUNGER

People often eat when they are not really hungry. There are all sorts of social cues that tell people to eat, such as the convention of eating breakfast, lunch, and dinner at certain times. A large part of that "convention" is actually the result of classical conditioning. LINK to Chapter Five: Learning, pp. 171–172. The body becomes conditioned to respond with the hunger reflex at certain times of the day; through association with the act of eating, those times of the day have become conditioned stimuli for hunger. Sometimes a person who has just eaten a late breakfast will still "feel" hungry at noon, simply because the clock says it's time to eat. People also respond to the appeal of food. How many times has someone finished a huge meal only to be tempted by that luscious-looking cheesecake on the dessert cart?

Food can also be used in times of stress as a comforting routine, an immediate escape from whatever is unpleasant (Dallman et al., 2003). Rodin (1981, 1985) found that the insulin levels that create hunger may actually increase *before* food is eaten (similar to the way Pavlov's dogs began salivating before they received their food). Like getting hungry at a certain time of day, this physiological phenomenon may also be due to classical conditioning: In the past, eating foods with certain visual and sensory characteristics led to an insulin spike, and this pairing occurred so frequently that now just looking at or smelling the food produces the spike before the food is consumed (Stockhorst, 1999). This may explain why some people (who are called "externals" because of their tendency to focus on the external features of food rather than internal hunger) are far more responsive to these external signals—they produce far more insulin in response to the *anticipation* of eating than do nonexternals, or people who are less affected by external cues (Rodin, 1985).

Cultural factors and gender also play a part in determining hunger and eating habits. In one study, a questionnaire about eating habits was given to both men and women from the United States and Japan. Although no significant differences in what initiates eating existed for men in either culture, women in the United States were found to be much more likely to start eating for emotional reasons, such as depression. Japanese women were more likely to eat because of hunger signals or social demands (Hawks et al., 2003). In this same study, both men and women from the United States were more likely to eat while watching television or movies than were Japanese men and women. Both culture and gender must be taken into account when studying why and under what circumstances people eat.

leptin a hormone that, when released into the bloodstream, signals the hypothalamus that the body has had enough food and reduces the appetite while increasing the feeling of being full.

MALADAPTIVE EATING PROBLEMS

9.6 What are some problems in eating behavior, and how are they affected by biology and culture?

It would be nice if people all over the world ate just the amount of food that they needed and were able to maintain a healthy, normal weight. Unfortunately, that is not the case for many people. Some people weigh far more than they should, whereas others weigh far less. Why do some people get so fat? Is it just overeating?

This family is becoming more typical in the United States as obesity rates continue to rise. How much of the excess weight on each of these family members is caused by poor choices in diet and lack of exercise, and how much might be caused by inherited biological factors?

OBESITY There are several factors that create *obesity*, a condition in which the body weight of a person is 20 percent or more over the ideal body weight for that person's height. Actual definitions of obesity vary. Some definitions consider 20 to 30 percent to be overweight and limit obesity to 30 percent. Others state that men are obese at 20 percent over the ideal weight and women at 30 percent. However it is defined, a significant factor in obesity is heredity. There appear to be several sets of genes, some on different chromosomes, which influence a person's likelihood of becoming obese (Barsh et al., 2000). If there is a history of obesity in a particular family, each family member has a risk of becoming obese that is double or triple the risk of people who do not have a family history of obesity (Bouchard, 1997).

Certainly, another obesity factor is overeating. Around the world, as developing countries build stronger economies and their food supplies become stable, the rates of obesity increase dramatically and quickly (Barsh et al., 2000). Foods become more varied and enticing* as well, and an increase in variety is associated with an increase in eating beyond the physiological need to eat (Raynor & Epstein, 2001). In industrialized societies when workers spend more hours in the workplace, there is less time available for preparing meals at home and more incentive to dine out (Chou et al., 2004). When the "dining out" choices include fast food and soft drinks, as is so often the case, obesity rates increase. In sum, as cultures become more industrialized and follow Western-culture lifestyles, negative aspects of those lifestyles, such as obesity, also increase. Over the last 20 years, rates of obesity in developing countries have tripled. Specifically, this is a trend in countries that have adopted the Western lifestyle of lower exercise rates and overeating—especially those foods that are cheap but high in fat and calories. In China, as well as many countries in the Middle East, Southeast Asia, and the Pacific Islands, 10 to 25 percent of children have been found to be overweight and another 2 to 10 percent are obese (Hossain et al., 2007).

As mentioned earlier, metabolism slows down as people age. Aside from not changing the eating habits of their youth and lowering their intake, as they earn more income people also often increase the amount of food they consume, thereby assuring a weight gain that may lead to obesity. The United States has the highest rate of obesity in the world: a third of its population is now obese (Flegal et al., 2010; Friedman, 2000, 2003; Marik, 2000; Mokdad et al., 2001).

In recent years, a hormone called **leptin** has been identified as one of the factors that controls appetite, which may also play an important role in obesity. When released into the bloodstream, leptin signals the hypothalamus that the body has had enough food, reducing appetite and increasing the feeling of being full, or satiated (Friedman & Halaas, 1998). In the body, problems with leptin production or detection can lead to overeating. **Read** on **mypsychlab.com**

Read and learn more about leptin and obesity on **mypsychlab.com**

*enticing: attractive; desirable.

Two other disorders of eating that cause weight fluctuations in the opposite direction of obesity are anorexia nervosa and bulimia nervosa. Both are classified as clinical (mental) disorders in the *Diagnostic and Statistical Manual of Mental Disorders, Fourth Edition, Text Revision* or *DSM-IV-TR* (American Psychiatric Association, 2000), which is a listing of disorders and their symptoms used by psychological professionals to make a diagnosis. Both disorders are discussed in a later chapter. LINK to Chapter Fourteen: Psychological Disorders, pp. 550–553.

Listen on **mypsychlab.com**

Listen to a Psychology in the News podcast on the biology of obesity on **mypsychlab.com**

psychology in the news

Cartoon Characters Influence Children's Food and Taste Preferences

Since the 1970s, rates of obesity have doubled for American preschoolers and more than tripled for children ages 6 to 11; these alarming statistics, not surprisingly, are of concern to parents and health-care professionals alike. Each year, food and beverage companies spend more than $1.6 billion targeting young consumers through television, the Internet, video games, and movie- or television-character licensing agreements (Roberto et al., 2010).

Many parents are all too familiar with the allure of cartoon and movie characters on a variety of food items. Whether it is the call of the character on the cereal box or the special toy in their child's meal, many American children are seemingly motivated primarily by the cartoon or movie character on the product packaging or the enticing toy or gadget associated with the character. Getting the special prize or toy is one thing, but can the use of licensed characters also affect food preferences? According to researchers at Yale University and a study of forty 4- to 6-year-old children, the answer is "yes!"

The researchers paired stickers of Dora the Explorer®, Scooby Doo®, and Shrek® with three different snacks: graham crackers, gummy fruit snacks, and baby carrots. Overall children preferred the taste of food items that were presented with cartoon characters as compared to plain packaging; they especially preferred the taste of gummy snacks and graham crackers paired with the characters. Although character stickers were not enough to influence taste preferences, children were more likely to choose baby carrots with character stickers as compared to those in plain packaging.

It is possible that cartoon and movie characters on fast food packaging can not only influence what children choose to eat, but affect their taste preferences as well.

Despite the relatively small sample size and a few other limitations noted by the researchers, the outcomes of this study provide preliminary support that the use of licensed characters can influence not only children's eating habits but their taste preferences as well. The researchers noted that recognition of the potential negative influences toward poorer nutritional choices should be acknowledged and has implications for the continued use of such characters in the marketing of lower nutritional food items (Roberto et al., 2010).

Questions for Further Discussion

1. Besides the influence of cartoon and movie characters, how might observational learning impact what a child chooses to eat?
2. This study focused on the eating habits of young children. What about teenagers and adults? Can you think of a food product or products that these age groups might be influenced to try or like as the result of influential figures (e.g., professional athletes?)

9.5 9.6

CONCEPT MAP

- **hunger**
  - impacted by insulin response; insulin (normally released more after onset of eating) reduces level of glucose in bloodstream (resulting in lower blood sugar and increased hunger); glucagon increases level of glucose
  - ventromedial area of the hypothalamus may be involved in stopping eating when glucose level goes up; lateral hypothalamus appears to influence onset of eating when insulin level goes up
  - person's weight set point and basal metabolic rate are tied to hypothalamus, and the hormone leptin appears to affect appetite
  - hunger and eating behaviors are influenced by social cues and convention (e.g., eating at certain times), culture, and gender

Why People Eat

- **maladaptive eating**
  - **obesity:** body weight 20% or more over ideal (based on height); significantly impacted by genetics, overeating, exercise, and changes in metabolism
  - **anorexia nervosa**
  - **bulimia nervosa**

LINK to Chapter Fourteen, Psychological Disorders

PRACTICE quiz How much do you remember? ANSWERS ON PAGE AK-2.

Pick the best answer.

1. Which of the following is not one of the physiological factors in hunger?
   a. stomach
   b. pancreas
   c. hypothalamus
   d. corpus callosum
2. If calorie intake stays the same, as the basal metabolic rate decreases, the weight set point __________.
   a. decreases.
   b. increases.
   c. stays the same.
   d. varies up and down.
3. People who are __________ respond to the anticipation of eating with higher insulin levels.
   a. internals
   b. externals
   c. intrinsic
   d. extrinsic
4. According to researchers at Yale, children are more likely to eat cereals with __________.
   a. more fiber.
   b. less sugar.
   c. cartoon characters on the box.
   d. a prize inside the box.

The first section of this chapter has looked at the motives that drive human behavior. But people do more than just behave—they experience feelings during every human action. The second section of the chapter explores the world of human emotions and how those emotions are connected to both thinking and actions.

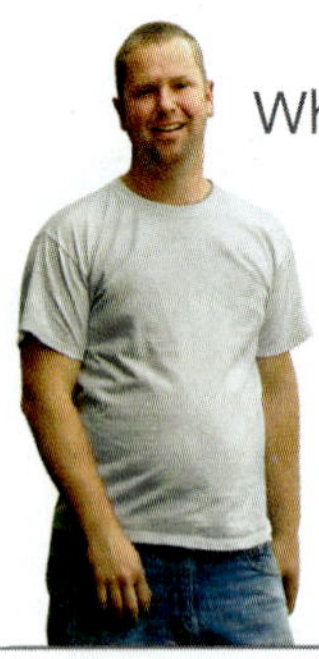

What part does the way we feel about things play in all of our daily activities—what exactly causes feelings?

Emotion

What part does the way we feel about things play in all of our daily activities—what exactly causes feelings?

Human beings are full of feelings, or emotions, and although emotions may be internal processes, there are outward physical signs of what people are feeling.

THE THREE ELEMENTS OF EMOTION

9.7 What are the three elements of emotion?

The Latin root word *mot*, meaning "to move," is the source of both of the words we use in this chapter over and over again—*motive* and *emotion*. **Emotion** can be defined as the "feeling" aspect of consciousness, characterized by three elements: a certain physical arousal, a certain behavior that reveals the feeling to the outside world, and an inner awareness of the feeling.

emotion the "feeling" aspect of consciousness, characterized by a certain physical arousal, a certain behavior that reveals the emotion to the outside world, and an inner awareness of feelings.

THE PHYSIOLOGY OF EMOTION Physically, when a person experiences an emotion, an arousal is created by the sympathetic nervous system. LINK to Chapter Two: The Biological Perspective, pp. 60–61. The heart rate increases, breathing becomes more rapid, the pupils dilate, and the mouth may become dry. Think about the last time you were angry and then about the last time you were frightened. Weren't the physical symptoms pretty similar? Although facial expressions do differ among various emotional responses (Ekman, 1980; Ekman et al., 1969; Ekman & Friesen, 1978), emotions are difficult to distinguish from one another on the basis of physiological reactions alone. However, in the laboratory using devices to measure the heart rate, blood pressure, and skin temperature, researchers have found that different emotions may be associated with different physiological reactions: Sadness, anger, and fear are associated with greater increases in heart rate than is disgust; higher increases in skin conductance occur during disgust as compared to happiness; and anger is more often associated with vascular measures, such as higher diastolic blood pressure, as compared to fear (Larsen et al., 2008; Levenson, 1992; Levenson et al., 1992).

Which parts of the brain are involved in various aspects of emotion? As discussed in Chapter Two, the *amygdala*, a small area located within the limbic system on each side of the brain, is associated with fear in both humans and animals (Davis & Whalen, 2001; Fanselow & Gale, 2003) and is also involved in the facial expressions of human emotions (Morris et al., 1998).

When portions of the amygdala are damaged in rats, the animals cannot be classically conditioned to fear new objects—they apparently cannot remember to be afraid (R. J. Davidson et al., 2000; Fanselow & Gale, 2003). In humans, damage to the amygdala has been associated with similar effects (LaBar et al., 1995) and with impairment of the ability to determine emotions from looking at the facial expressions of others (Adolphs & Tranel, 2003).

A lot of what we know about the amygdala's role in emotion comes from the work of Dr. Joseph LeDoux and his many colleagues and students. (NOTE for the curious, Dr. LeDoux's Ph.D. advisor was Dr. Michael Gazzaniga, whose work was discussed in Chapter Two) The amygdala is a complex structure with many different nuclei and subdivisions, whose roles have been investigated primarily through studies of fear conditioning (LeDoux & Phelps, 2008). Fear conditioning has been very helpful in relating behaviors to brain function because it results in stereotypical autonomic and behavioral responses. It is basically a classical conditioning procedure where an auditory stimulus (conditioned stimulus) is paired with foot shock (unconditioned stimulus) to elicit autonomic and behavioral conditioned responses (LeDoux, 1996; LeDoux & Phelps, 2008).

LeDoux's work has provided many insights into the brain's processing of emotional information and the role of the amygdala. Emotional stimuli travel to the amygdala by both a fast, crude "low road" (subcortical) and a slower but more involved cortical "high road" (LeDoux, 1996, 2007; LeDoux & Phelps, 2008). The direct route allows for quick responses to stimuli that are possibly dangerous, sometimes before we actually know what the stimuli are, but with the awareness provided by the indirect cortical route (specifically, processing by the prefrontal cortex), we can override the direct route and take control of our emotional responses (LeDoux, 1996; LeDoux & Phelps, 2008; Öhman, 2008).

LeDoux's work also provides a mechanism for understanding disorders of emotion, LINK to Chapter Fourteen: Psychological Disorders, pp. 541–546. It is possible that the direct route may be the primary processing pathway for individuals with emotional disorders and the indirect, cortical pathway is not able to override the processing initiated by the direct route. This would result in difficulty or inability to control our emotions, or the inability to extinguishing fears we've already acquired (LeDoux, 1996; LeDoux & Phelps, 2008).

Besides the amygdala, other subcortical and cortical areas of the brain are involved in the processing of emotional information. Research suggests that emotions may work differently depending on which side of the brain is involved. One area of investigation has been the frontal lobes. Researchers have found that positive emotions are associated with the left frontal lobe of the brain whereas negative feelings such as sadness, anxiety, and depression seem to be a function of the right frontal lobe (R. J. Davidson, 2003; Geschwind & Iacoboni, 2007; Heilman, 2002). In studies where the electrical activity of the brain has been tracked using an electroencephalograph, LINK to Chapter Two: The Biological Perspective, pp. 67–68, left frontal lobe activation has been associated with pleasant emotions while right frontal lobe activity has been associated with negative emotional states (R. J. Davidson, 2003). Furthermore, increased left frontal lobe activity has been found in individuals trained in meditation, and for the participants in this study, greater left frontal lobe activity was accompanied by a reduction in their anxiety as well as a boost in their immune system (R. J. Davidson et al., 2003).

The ability to interpret the facial expressions of others as a particular emotion also seems to be a function of one side of the brain more than the other. Researchers have found that when people are asked to identify the emotion on another person's face, the right hemisphere is more active than the left, particularly in women (Voyer & Rodgers, 2002). This difference begins weakly in childhood but increases in adulthood, with children being less able to identify negative emotions as well as they can positive emotions when compared to adults (Barth & Boles, 1999; Lane et al., 1995). This finding is consistent with early research that assigns the recognition of faces to the right hemisphere (Berent, 1977; Ellis, 1983).

Other types of emotional processing involve a variety of other brain areas. Have you ever been told to control your emotions? Or maybe you've heard the lyrics from the old Bobby McFerrin song, "Don't Worry, Be Happy." Different brain areas take primary roles based on the different ways you try to control your emotions, but there is a degree of overlap across several of the strategies. For example, some common strategies for regulating one's emotions include distraction, reappraisal, and controlling the influence of emotions on decision making. All three of these strategies take advantage of the lateral prefrontal cortex and anterior cingulate cortex and, as you might expect from the discussion before, the amygdala also comes into play (J. S. Beer, 2009).

However, distraction appears to be supported by activity in the anterior cingulate cortex, and reappraisal is supported by activity in the lateral orbitofrontal cortex; and both are accompanied by lower activity in the amygdala (J. S. Beer, 2009). Furthermore, distraction and reappraisal may engage more brain areas in general as compared to spontaneous control of emotions in decision making. Generally, brain areas associated with emotional control are the same brain areas responsible for control of non-emotional information (Beer, 2009). Read on **mypsychlab.com**

Read and learn more about hemisphere difference in the physiology of emotions on **mypsychlab.com**

THE BEHAVIOR OF EMOTION: EMOTIONAL EXPRESSION How do people behave when in the grip of an emotion? There are facial expressions, body movements, and actions that indicate to others how a person feels. Frowns, smiles, and sad expressions combine with hand gestures, the turning of one's body, and spoken words to produce an understanding of emotion. People fight, run, kiss, and yell, along with countless other actions stemming from the emotions they feel.

Facial expressions can vary across different cultures, although some aspects of facial expression seem to be universal. (See Figure 9.5 for some examples of universal facial expressions.) Charles Darwin (1898) was one of the first to theorize that emotions were a product of evolution and, therefore, universal—all human beings, no matter what their culture, would show the same facial expression because the

Figure 9.5 Facial Expressions of Emotion

Facial expressions appear to be universal. For example, these faces are consistently interpreted as showing (a) anger, (b) fear, (c) disgust, (d) happiness, (e) surprise, and (f) sadness by people of various cultures from all over the world. Although the situations that cause these emotions may differ from culture to culture, the expression of particular emotions remains strikingly the same.

facial muscles evolved to communicate specific information to onlookers. For example, an angry face would signal to onlookers that they should act submissively or expect a fight. Although Darwin's ideas were not in line with the behaviorist movement of the early and middle twentieth century, which promoted environment rather than heredity as the cause of behavior, other researchers have since found evidence that there is a universal nature to at least seven basic emotions, giving more support to the evolutionary perspective within psychology (Ekman, 1973; Ekman & Friesen, 1969, 1971). LINK to Chapter One: The Science of Psychology, pp. 16–17. Even children who are blind from birth can produce the appropriate facial expressions for any given situation without ever having witnessed those expressions on others, which strongly supports the idea that emotional expressions have their basis in biology rather than in learning (Charlesworth & Kreutzer, 1973; Fulcher, 1942). **Simulate** on **mypsychlab.com**

Simulate recognizing facial expressions of emotions on **mypsychlab.com**

In their research, Ekman and Friesen found that people of many different cultures (including Japanese, European, American, and the Fore tribe of New Guinea) can consistently recognize at least seven facial expressions: anger, fear, disgust, happiness, surprise, sadness, and contempt (Ekman & Friesen, 1969, 1971). Although the emotions and the related facial expressions appear to be universal, exactly when, where, and how an emotion is expressed may be determined by the culture. **Display rules** that can vary from culture to culture (Ekman, 1973; Ekman & Friesen, 1969) are learned ways of controlling displays of emotion in social settings. For example, Japanese people have strict social rules about showing emotion in public situations—they simply do not show emotion, remaining cool, calm, and collected, at least on the *outside*. But if in a more private situation, as a parent scolding a child within the

display rules learned ways of controlling displays of emotion in social settings.

home, the adult's facial expression would easily be recognized as "angry" by people of any culture. The emotion is universal and the way it is expressed on the face is universal, but whether it is expressed or displayed depends on the learned cultural rules for displaying emotion.

Display rules are different between cultures that are *individualistic* (placing the importance of the individual above the social group) and those that are *collectivistic* (placing the importance of the social group above that of the individual). Whereas the culture of the United States is individualistic, for example, the culture of Japan is collectivistic. At least part of the difference between the two types of display rules may be due to these cultural differences (Edelmann & Iwawaki, 1987; Hofstede, 1980; Hofstede et al., 2002). LINK to Chapter Thirteen: Theories of Personality, pp. 515–516.

Display rules are also different for males and females. Researchers looking at the display rules of boys and girls found that boys are reluctant to talk about feelings in a social setting, whereas girls are expected and encouraged to do so (Polce-Lynch et al., 1998). With adults, researchers looking at the expression of anger in the workplace found that women are generally less willing than men to express negative emotions, although factors such as status complicate the findings somewhat (Domagalski & Steelman, 2007).

SUBJECTIVE EXPERIENCE: LABELING EMOTION The third element of emotion is interpreting the subjective feeling by giving it a label: anger, fear, disgust, happiness, sadness, shame, interest, and so on. Another way of labeling this element is to call it the "cognitive element," because the labeling process is a matter of retrieving memories of previous similar experiences, perceiving the context of the emotion, and coming up with a solution—a label.

The label a person applies to a subjective feeling is at least in part a learned response influenced by their language and culture. Such labels may differ in people of different cultural backgrounds. For example, researchers in one study (J. L. Tsai et al., 2004) found that Chinese Americans who were still firmly rooted in their original Chinese culture were far more likely to use labels to describe their emotions that referred to bodily sensations (such as "dizzy") or social relationships (such as "friendship") than were more "Americanized" Chinese Americans and European Americans, who tended to use more directly emotional words (such as "liking" or "love").

In another study, even the subjective feeling of happiness showed cultural differences (Kitayama & Markus, 1994). In this study, Japanese students and students from the United States were found to associate a general positive emotional state with entirely different circumstances. In the case of the Japanese students, the positive state was more associated with friendly or socially engaged feelings. The students from the United States associated their positive emotional state more with feelings that were socially disengaged, such as pride. This finding is a further reflection of the differences between collectivistic and individualistic cultures. A major goal for psychologists engaged in cross-cultural research in emotions is to attempt to understand the meaning of other people's mental and emotional states without interpreting them incorrectly, or misleadingly, in the language or mindset of the researchers (Shweder et al., 2008).

So which of the three elements is the most important?

THEORIES OF EMOTION

So which of the three elements is the most important?

In the early days of psychology, it was assumed that feeling a particular emotion led first to a physical reaction and then to a behavioral one. According to this viewpoint—we'll call it the common sense theory of emotion—seeing a snarling dog in one's path causes the feeling of fear, which stimulates the body to arousal, followed by the behavioral act of running; that is, people are aroused because they are afraid. (See Figure 9.6.)

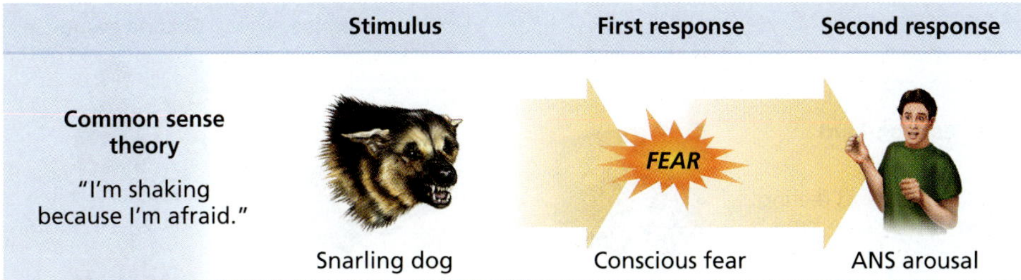

Figure 9.6 Common Sense Theory of Emotion

In the common sense theory of emotion, a stimulus (snarling dog) leads to an emotion of fear, which then leads to bodily arousal (in this case, indicated by shaking) through the autonomic nervous system (ANS).

9.8 How do the James-Lange and Cannon-Bard theories of emotion differ?

JAMES-LANGE THEORY OF EMOTION William James (1884, 1890, 1894), who was also the founder of the functionalist perspective in the early history of psychology, LINK to Chapter One: The Science of Psychology, pp. 7–8, disagreed with the common sense viewpoint. He believed that the order of the components of emotions was quite different. At nearly the same time, a physiologist and psychologist in Denmark, Carl Lange (1885), came up with an explanation of emotion so similar to that of James that the two names are used together to refer to the theory—the **James-Lange theory of emotion**. (See Figure 9.7.)

Figure 9.7 James-Lange Theory of Emotion

In the James-Lange theory of emotion, a stimulus leads to bodily arousal first, which is then interpreted as an emotion.

In this theory, a stimulus of some sort (for example, the large snarling dog) produces a physiological reaction. This reaction, which is the arousal of the "fight-or-flight" sympathetic nervous system (wanting to run), produces bodily sensations such as increased heart rate, dry mouth, and rapid breathing. James and Lange believed that the physical arousal led to the labeling of the emotion (fear). Simply put, "I am afraid because I am aroused," "I am embarrassed because my face is red," "I am nervous because my stomach is fluttering," and "I am in love because my heart rate increases when I look at her (or him)."

What about people who have spinal cord injuries that prevent the sympathetic nervous system from functioning? Although James-Lange would predict that these people should show decreased emotion because the arousal that causes emotion is no longer there, this does not in fact happen. Several studies of people with spinal cord injuries report that these people are capable of experiencing the same emotions after their injury as before, sometimes even more intensely (Bermond et al., 1991; Chwalisz et al., 1988).

CANNON-BARD THEORY OF EMOTION Physiologists Walter Cannon (1927) and Philip Bard (1934) theorized that the emotion and the physiological arousal occur more or less at the same time. Cannon, an expert in sympathetic arousal mechanisms, did not feel that the physical changes caused by various emotions were distinct enough to allow them to be perceived as different emotions. Bard expanded on this idea by stating that the sensory information that comes into the brain is sent simultaneously (by the thalamus) to both the cortex and the organs of the sympathetic nervous system. The fear and the bodily reactions are, therefore, experienced at the same time—not one after the other. "I'm afraid and running and aroused!" (See Figure 9.8.)

This theory, known as the **Cannon-Bard theory of emotion**, also had its critics. Lashley (1938) stated that the thalamus would have to be pretty sophisticated to make sense of all the possible human emotions and relay them to the proper areas of the cortex and

James-Lange theory of emotion theory in which a physiological reaction leads to the labeling of an emotion.

Cannon-Bard theory of emotion theory in which the physiological reaction and the emotion are assumed to occur at the same time.

Figure 9.8 Cannon-Bard Theory of Emotion

In the Cannon-Bard theory of emotion, a stimulus leads to activity in the brain, which then sends signals to arouse the body and interpret the emotion at the same time.

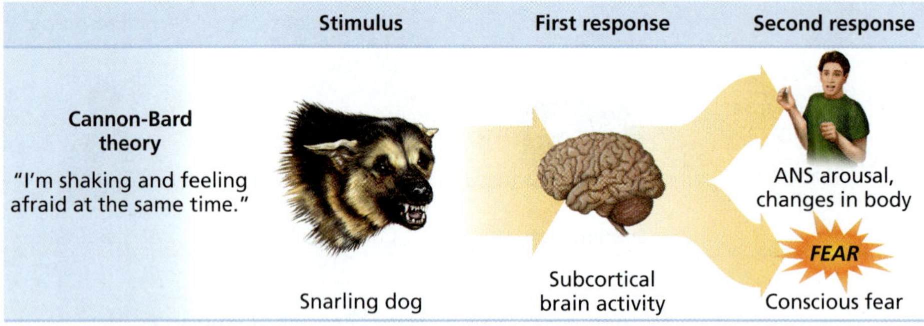

body. It would seem that other areas of the brain must be involved in processing emotional reactions. The studies of people with spinal cord injuries, which seem to suggest that emotions can be experienced without feedback from the sympathetic organs to the cortex and were cited as a criticism of the James-Lange theory, seem at first to support the Cannon-Bard version of emotions: People do not need feedback from those organs to experience emotion. However, there is an alternate pathway that does provide feedback from these organs to the cortex; this is the *vagus nerve*, one of the cranial nerves (LeDoux, 1994). The existence of this feedback pathway makes the case for Cannon-Bard a little less convincing.

9.9 What are the key elements in cognitive arousal theory, the facial feedback hypothesis, and the cognitive-mediational theory of emotion?

SCHACHTER-SINGER AND COGNITIVE AROUSAL THEORY OF EMOTION The early theories talked about the emotion and the physical reaction, but what about the mental interpretation of those components? In their **cognitive arousal theory**, Schachter and Singer (1962) proposed that two things have to happen before emotion occurs: the physical arousal and a labeling of the arousal based on cues from the surrounding environment. These two things happen at the same time, resulting in the labeling of the emotion. (See Figure 9.9.)

Figure 9.9 Schachter-Singer Cognitive Arousal Theory of Emotion

Schachter and Singer's cognitive arousal theory is similar to the James-Lange theory but adds the element of cognitive labeling of the arousal. In this theory, a stimulus leads to both bodily arousal and the labeling of that arousal (based on the surrounding context), which leads to the experience and labeling of the emotional reaction.

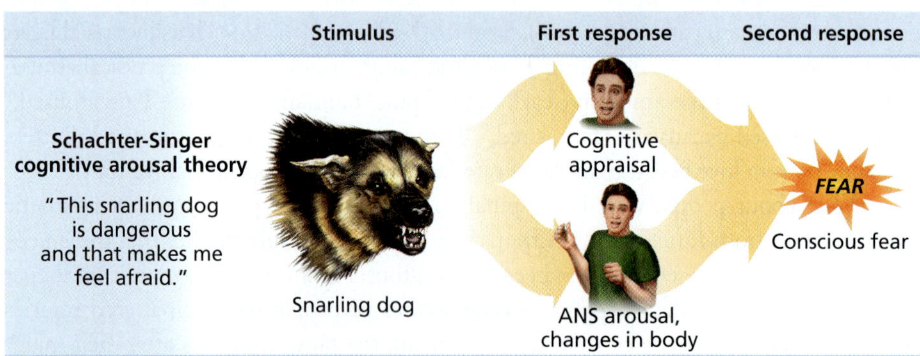

For example, if a person comes across a snarling dog while taking a walk, the physical arousal (heart racing, eyes opening wide) is accompanied by the thought (cognition) that this must be fear. Then and only then will the person experience the fear emotion. In other words, "I am aroused in the presence of a scary dog; therefore, I must be afraid." Evidence for this theory was found in what is now a classic experiment, described in the accompanying Classic Studies in Psychology. **Explore** on **mypsychlab.com**

Explore the different theories of emotion on **mypsychlab.com**

cognitive arousal theory theory of emotion in which both the physical arousal and the labeling of that arousal based on cues from the environment must occur before the emotion is experienced.

THE FACIAL FEEDBACK HYPOTHESIS: SMILE, YOU'LL FEEL BETTER In his (1898) book *The Expression of the Emotions in Man and Animals*, Charles Darwin stated that facial expressions evolved as a way of communicating intentions, such as threat or fear, and that these expressions are universal within a species rather than specific to a culture. He also believed (as in the James-Lange theory) that when such emotions are expressed freely on the face, the emotion itself intensifies—meaning that the more one smiles, the happier one feels.

classic studies in psychology

The Angry/Happy Man

In 1962, Stanley Schachter and Jerome Singer designed an experiment to test their theory that emotions are determined by an interaction between the physiological state of arousal and the label, or cognitive interpretation, that a person places on the arousal. Male student volunteers were told that they were going to answer a questionnaire about their reactions to a new vitamin called Suproxin. In reality, they were all injected with a drug called epinephrine, which causes physical arousal in the form of increased heart rate, rapid breathing, and a reddened face—all responses that happen during a strong emotional reaction.

Each student then participated in one of two conditions. In one condition, a confederate* posing as one of the participants started complaining about the experimenter, tearing up his questionnaire and storming out. In the other condition, there was one man who acted more like he was very happy, almost giddy and playing with some of the objects in the room. The "angry" man and the "happy" man in both conditions deliberately behaved in the two different ways as part of the experiment.

After both conditions had played out, participants in each of the two conditions were asked to describe their own emotions. The participants who had been exposed to the "angry" man interpreted their arousal symptoms as anger, whereas those exposed to the "happy" man interpreted their arousal as happiness. In all cases, the actual cause of arousal was the epinephrine and the physical symptoms of arousal were identical. The only difference between the two groups of participants was their exposure to the two different contexts. Schachter and Singer's theory would have predicted exactly these results: Physiological arousal has to be interpreted cognitively before it is experienced as a specific emotion.

Although this classic experiment stimulated a lot of research, much of that research has failed to find much support for the cognitive arousal theory of emotion (Reisenzein, 1983, 1994). But this theory did serve to draw attention to the important role that cognition plays in determining emotions. The role of cognition in emotion has been revisited in some more modern theories of emotion, as you will see in the remainder of the chapter.

Questions for Further Discussion

1. How might observing the emotions of others under more normal circumstances (i.e., not in a drugged state) affect a person's own emotional state?
2. According to Schachter and Singer's theory, for your first date with a person, should you choose a happy movie or a sad one?
3. In this experiment, what was the independent variable manipulated by the experimenters? What was the dependent variable?
4. This experiment used deception, as the participants were not told the true nature of the injection they received. What kind of ethical problems might have arisen from this deception? What problems would the experimenters have had in getting this study approved by an ethics committee today?

*confederate: someone who is cooperating with another person on some task.

Modern psychologists have proposed a theory of emotion that is consistent with much of Darwin's original thinking. Called the **facial feedback hypothesis**, this explanation assumes that facial expressions provide feedback to the brain concerning the emotion being expressed, which in turn not only intensifies the emotion but also actually *causes* the emotion (Buck, 1980; Ekman, 1980; Ekman & Friesen, 1978; Keillor et al., 2002). (See Figure 9.10.)

facial feedback hypothesis theory of emotion that assumes that facial expressions provide feedback to the brain concerning the emotion being expressed, which in turn causes and intensifies the emotion.

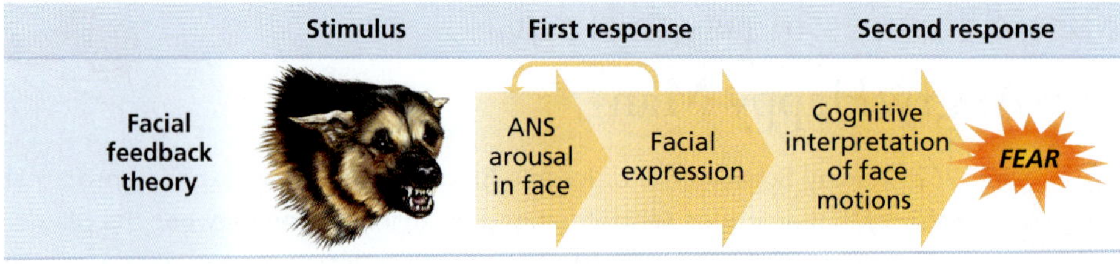

Figure 9.10 Facial Feedback Theory of Emotion

In the facial feedback theory of emotion, a stimulus such as this snarling dog causes arousal and a facial expression. The facial expression then provides feedback to the brain about the emotion. The brain then interprets the emotion and may also intensify it.

Does that mean that I don't smile because I'm happy—I'm happy because I smile?

Does that mean that I don't smile because I'm happy—I'm happy because I smile?

As the old song goes, "put on a happy face" and yes, you'll feel happier, according to the facial feedback hypothesis. One fairly recent study does cast some doubt on the validity of this hypothesis, however. If the facial feedback hypothesis is correct, then people who have facial paralysis on both sides of the face should be unable to experience emotions in a normal way. But a case study conducted on just such a person revealed that although she was unable to express emotions on her paralyzed face, she could respond emotionally to slides meant to stimulate emotional reactions, just as anyone else would (Keillor et al., 2002). Clearly, the question of how much the actual facial expression determines the emotional experience has yet to be fully answered.

The facial feedback hypothesis assumes that changing your own facial expression can change the way you feel. Smiling makes people feel happy, and frowning makes people feel sad. This effect seems to have an impact on the people around us as well. If this is true, this smiling woman may make the airline steward handing her the food feel good, too. Is it hard for you to stay in a bad mood when the people around you are smiling and laughing?

LAZARUS AND THE COGNITIVE-MEDIATIONAL THEORY As mentioned in the Classic Studies in Psychology section, Schachter and Singer's (1962) study stressed the importance of cognition, or thinking, in the determination of emotions. One of the more modern versions of cognitive emotion theories is Lazarus's **cognitive-mediational theory** of emotion (1991). In this theory, the most important aspect of any emotional experience is how the person interprets, or appraises, the stimulus that causes the emotional reaction. To *mediate* means to "come between" and in this theory, the cognitive appraisal mediates by coming between the stimulus and the emotional response to that stimulus.

For example, remember the person who encountered a snarling dog while walking through the neighborhood? According to Lazarus, the appraisal of the situation would come *before* both the physical arousal and the experience of emotion. If the dog is behind a sturdy fence, the appraisal would be something like "no threat." The most likely emotion would be annoyance, and the physical arousal would be minimal. But if the dog is not confined, the appraisal would more likely be "danger—threatening animal!" which would be followed by an increase in arousal and the emotional experience of fear. In other words, it's the *interpretation* of the arousal that results in the emotion of fear, not the labeling as in the Schachter-Singer model, and the interpretation comes first. (See Figure 9.11.)

Not everyone agrees with this theory, of course. Some researchers believe that emotional reactions to situations are so fast that they are almost instantaneous, which would leave little time for a cognitive appraisal to occur first (Zajonc, 1998). Others (Kilhstrom et al., 2000) have found that the human brain can respond to a physical threat before conscious thought enters the picture. The simple spinal cord reflex of pain withdrawal discussed in Chapter Two is an example of this—the reflex occurs so quickly that the brain itself is not involved, and the experience of pain is consciously felt *after* the injured body part is jerked away from the painful stimulus. LINK to Chapter Two: The Biological Perspective, pp. 56–57.

cognitive-mediational theory theory of emotion in which a stimulus must be interpreted (appraised) by a person in order to result in a physical response and an emotional reaction.

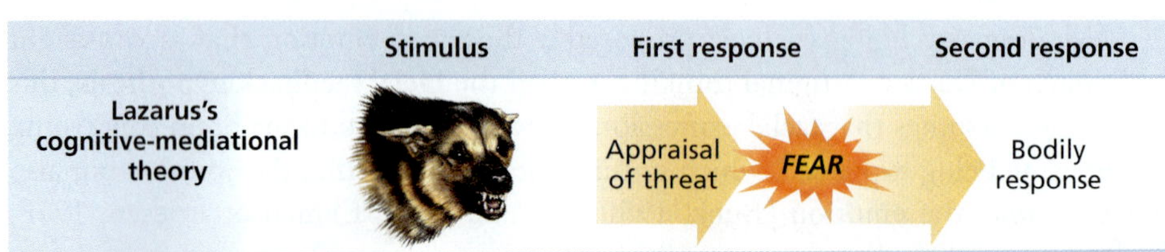

Figure 9.11 Lazarus's Cognitive-Mediational Theory

In Lazarus's cognitive-mediational theory of emotion, a stimulus causes an immediate appraisal (e.g., "The dog is snarling and not behind a fence, so this is dangerous"). The cognitive appraisal results in an emotional response, which is then followed by the appropriate bodily response.

Which theory is right?

Which theory is right?

Human emotions are so incredibly complex that it might not be out of place to say that all of the theories are correct to at least some degree. In certain situations, the cognitive appraisal might have time to mediate the emotion that is experienced (such as falling in love), whereas in other situations, the need to act first, and to think and feel later is more important. (See Figure 9.12.)

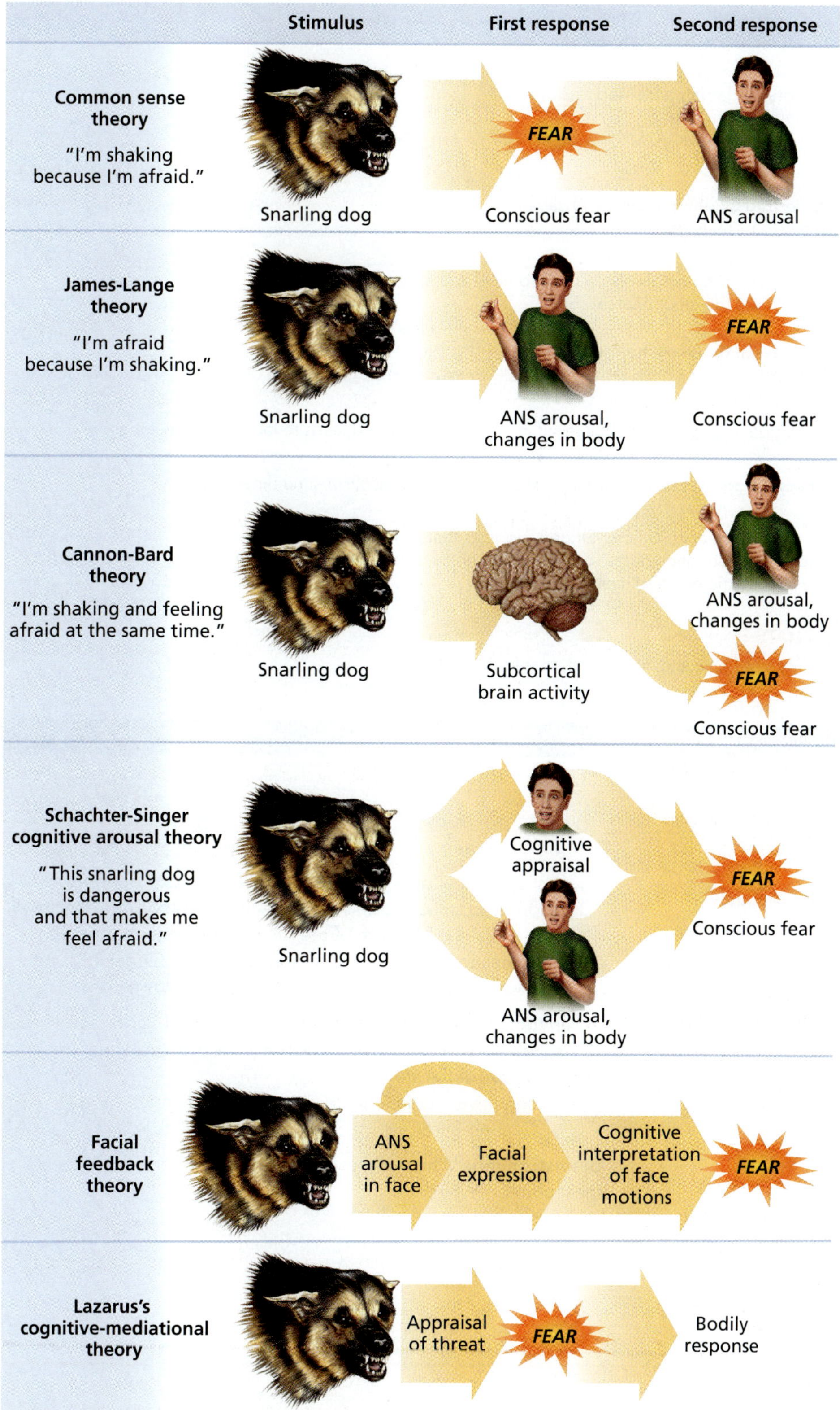

Figure 9.12 Comparison of Theories of Emotion

These figures represent the six different theories of emotion as discussed in the text.

9.7 9.8 9.9

CONCEPT MAP

- physiological arousal is created by the sympathetic nervous system and is associated with brain activity in specific areas (e.g., the amygdala) and right or left hemisphere activity
- emotional expressions can vary across cultures but some expressions seem to be universal; display rules also vary across cultures and according to gender
- subjective labeling of emotion is largely a learned response, influenced by both language and culture

Emotion

(is "feeling" aspect of consciousness, characterized by physiological arousal, specific expressive behavior, and inner awareness of feelings)

- Lazarus's **cognitive-mediational theory** places the emphasis on the cognitive appraisal and interpretation of the stimulus that causes the emotional reaction
- based on ideas from Darwin, the **facial feedback hypothesis** suggests that facial expressions (and other behaviors) provide feedback to the brain that can intensify or cause a specific emotion
- **James-Lange theory** suggests that specific stimuli result in physical arousal and leads to labeling of the emotion
- **Cannon-Bard theory** suggests that emotion and physiological arousal occur simultaneously
- **cognitive arousal theory** (Schacter-Singer) suggests that physiological arousal and the actual interpretation of that arousal based on cues from the environment must occur before the emotion itself is experienced

Various Theories of Emotion

have been suggested, each with a slightly different focus and interpretation (see Fig. 9.12)

PRACTICE quiz How much do you remember?

ANSWERS ON PAGE AK-2.

Pick the best answer.

1. Which of the following is NOT one of the three elements of emotion?
   a. subjective experience
   b. behavior
   c. attention
   d. physical reaction

2. Much of what we know about the amygdala's role in emotion comes from studies of autonomic and behavioral responses revealed through: __________.
   a. operant conditioning
   b. fear conditioning
   c. observational learning
   d. dream interpretation

3. The theory of emotion that states that the thalamus sends sensory information to the cortex and the sympathetic organs at the same time is the __________ theory.
   a. James-Lange
   b. Cannon-Bard
   c. Schachter-Singer
   d. facial feedback

4. In Schachter and Singer's classic study, participants who were exposed to the "angry" man interpreted their physiological arousal as __________, whereas those who were exposed to the "happy" man interpreted their arousal as __________.
   a. angry; happy.
   b. happy; angry.
   c. happy; happy.
   d. angry; angry.

5. Leslie smiles a lot in the classroom, which in turn prompts his students to smile, making them feel happier too. This effect is best explained by which of the following theories of emotion?
   a. James-Lange
   b. cognitive-mediational
   c. Schachter-Singer
   d. facial feedback

6. In the __________ theory of emotion, the most important aspect of an emotional experience is the interpretation, or appraisal, of the stimulus.
   a. cognitive-mediational
   b. Cannon-Bard
   c. James-Lange
   d. facial feedback

Brainstorming: Which of these theories of emotion do you feel is most correct? Why?

Applying Psychology to Everyday Life: When Motivation Is Not Enough

Now that we have discussed a variety of ways in which behavior gets initiated or maintained, what can you do to make sure you complete the tasks you need to finish or address the commitments you've made? Many college students find it difficult to keep track of all of their class assignments and projects, and to remember all of the things they are supposed to do—and when to do them. Keeping on task can be especially challenging when you might not be exactly thrilled about doing some of them in the first place. As such, if motivation is not enough to help you get things accomplished, what else can you do to ensure that you do what needs to be done?

There have been a variety of time- and task-management systems developed over the years, each with a slightly different focus on various aspects of motivation. One system suggests you should first identify key principles or important areas in your life (such as family, education, career, etc.); the next step is to sort your to-do list using those key categories, ranking your tasks by priority or in the order you need to do them. Finally, keep track of each item by plotting it on your calendar. This works for some people, for others it may sound like more steps than you want to do, or feel you need to do.

The book *Getting Things Done: The Art of Stress-Free Productivity* by David Allen and his "Getting Things Done" (or "GTD") methodology can provide a useful structure for a wide range of people who need help, well, in getting things done (Allen, 2001, 2008). Think back to Jennifer, the college student who ran into difficulties after starting college. With a system like GTD, she may have improved her chances of being more successful her first year.

How do you keep track of all of your class assignments, appointments, and deadlines?

The GTD method consists of five stages of processing your "stuff" into actual outcomes, identifying "next actions" you can actually take to gain and maintain control of your tasks and commitments. The five stages of the GTD method are:

1. Capture anything and everything that has your attention, getting it out of your head and physically collected in one place. This place can be a folder, notebook, computer program, spreadsheet, a set of index cards, or the like.
2. Process and define what you can take action on and identify the next steps. For example, instead of "do my research paper," identify actionable next steps such as "pinpoint topic, collect articles, schedule meeting to discuss ideas with classmates," for example.
3. Organize information and reminders into categories or contexts, based on how and when you need them. For example, if you need to send an email or text message to your group partners, you probably need to have your phone or computer to do so; "phone" or "computer" might be a context that you use.
4. Complete weekly reviews of your projects, next actions, and new items. To get things done, you need to review what you need to do.
5. Do your next actions, in the appropriate context or time frame for doing so.

Adapted from David Allen's (2001) *Getting Things Done: The Art of Stress-Free Productivity* (2001) and (2008) *Making It All Work.*

In this discussion we've only highlighted aspects of one specific approach for organizing and keeping on top of all those things you need to get done. There are a variety of time- and task-management systems and tools available, many more than we can cover in this textbook. Finding an approach or strategy that works best for you will likely pay off, not only now while you are in school but also in areas of your personal and future professional lives as well. Take some time now and investigate available strategies that will help you get organized and stay on track to meet your obligations in a timely manner. If you do, the next time you find that motivation and emotion are not enough to prompt you to get what you need done taken care of, you'll be glad you did.

chapter summary

Listen on mypsychlab.com Listen to an audio file of your chapter www.mypsychlab.com

Approaches to Understanding Motivation

9.1 How do psychologists define motivation, and what are the key elements of the early instinct and drive-reduction approaches to motivation?

- Motivation is the process by which activities are started, directed, and sustained so that physical and psychological needs are fulfilled.
- Instinct approaches proposed that some human actions may be motivated by instincts, which are innate patterns of behavior found in both people and animals.
- Drive-reduction approaches state that when an organism has a need (such as hunger), the need leads to psychological tension that motivates the organism to act, fulfilling the need and reducing the tension.
- Primary drives involve needs of the body whereas acquired (secondary) drives are those learned through experience. Homeostasis is the tendency of the body to maintain a steady state.

9.2 What are the characteristics of the three types of needs?

- The need for achievement is a strong desire to succeed in achieving one's goals, both realistic and challenging.
- The self-theory of emotion links the need for achievement to the concept of locus of control. A belief in control over one's life leads to more attempts to achieve, even in the face of failure. Those who believe that they have little control over what happens to them are more likely to develop learned helplessness.
- The need for affiliation is the desire to have friendly social interactions and relationships with others as well as the desire to be held in high regard by others.
- The need for power concerns having control over others, influencing them, and having an impact on them. Status and prestige are important to people high in this need.

9.3 What are the key elements of the arousal and incentive approaches to motivation?

- In arousal theory, a person has an optimal level of arousal to maintain. People who need more arousal than others are called sensation seekers.
- In the incentive approach, an external stimulus may be so rewarding that it motivates a person to act toward that stimulus even in the absence of a drive.

9.4 How do Maslow's hierarchy of needs and self-determination theories explain motivation?

- Maslow proposed a hierarchy of needs, beginning with basic physiological needs and ending with transcendence needs. The more basic needs must be met before the higher needs can be fulfilled.
- Self-determination theory (SDT) is a model of motivation in which three basic needs are seen as necessary to an individual's successful development: autonomy, competence, and relatedness.
- Intrinsic motivation occurs when people act because the act itself is satisfying or rewarding, whereas extrinsic motivation occurs when people receive an external reward (such as money) for the act.

What, Hungry Again? Why People Eat

9.5 What happens in the body to cause hunger, and how do social factors influence a person's experience of hunger?

- The physiological components of hunger include signals from the stomach and the hypothalamus, and the increased secretion of insulin.
- When the basal metabolic rate slows down, the weight set point increases and makes weight gain more likely.
- The social components of hunger include social cues for when meals are to be eaten, cultural customs and food preferences, and the use of food as a comfort device or as an escape from unpleasantness.
- Some people may be externals who respond to the anticipation of eating by producing an insulin response, increasing the risk of obesity.

9.6 What are some problems in eating behavior, and how are they affected by biology and culture?

- Maladaptive eating may lead to obesity.
- A third of the population of the U.S. is obese.

PSYCHOLOGY IN THE NEWS: Cartoon Characters Influence Children's Food and Taste Preferences

- Scientists studying children's eating habits have determined that the cartoons on boxes of cereal may be a powerful influence on which cereals children choose to eat.

Emotion

9.7 What are the three elements of emotion?

- Emotion is the "feeling" aspect of consciousness and includes physical, behavioral, and subjective (cognitive) elements.

9.8 How do the James-Lange and Cannon-Bard theories of emotion differ?

- The James-Lange theory states that a stimulus creates a physiological response that then leads to the labeling of the emotion.
- The Cannon-Bard theory asserts that the physiological reaction and the emotion are simultaneous, as the thalamus sends sensory information to both the cortex of the brain and the organs of the sympathetic nervous system.

9.9 What are the key elements in cognitive arousal theory, the facial feedback hypothesis, and the cognitive-mediational theory of emotion?

- In Schachter and Singer's cognitive arousal theory, both the physiological arousal and the actual interpretation of that arousal must occur before the emotion itself is experienced. This interpretation is based on cues from the environment.

CLASSIC STUDIES IN PSYCHOLOGY: The Angry/Happy Man

- In the facial feedback hypothesis, facial expressions provide feedback to the brain about the emotion being expressed on the face, intensifying the emotion.
- In the cognitive-mediational theory of emotion, the cognitive component of emotion (the interpretation) precedes both the physiological reaction and the emotion itself.
- Those participants who were exposed to the "angry" man interpreted their physical arousal as anger, whereas those who were exposed to the "happy" man interpreted their physical arousal as happiness.

Applying Psychology to Everyday Life: When Motivation Is Not Enough

- Motivation and emotion are sometimes not enough to prompt human behavior
- Time- or task-management systems can help you keep track of commitments and accomplish specific tasks and general goals.

test YOURSELF

ANSWERS ON PAGE AK-2.

Pick the best answer.

1. The approach to motivation that forced psychologists to consider the hereditary factors in motivation was the _________ approach.
   a. arousal c. instinct
   b. drive-reduction d. incentive
2. The need for money is an example of a(n) _________ drive.
   a. primary c. innate
   b. acquired d. instinctive
3. Jocelyn needs to be the one whose ideas are always used and craves prestige among others. She drives an expensive car and wears nothing but the most expensive clothes. Jocelyn is high in the need for _________.
   a. achievement. c. power.
   b. affiliation. d. attention.
4. People who are always looking for a challenge may be high in the need for _________.
   a. achievement. c. power.
   b. affiliation. d. attention.
5. Evidence from a study with 2-year-olds who were given an opportunity to explore a black box with a hole in it suggests that sensation seeking may be _________.
   a. learned. c. acquired over time.
   b. abnormal. d. innate.
6. Gene is trying to choose a snack. There is a bowl of fruit on the table, but there's also a candy bar that he bought yesterday. The fact that Gene feels drawn to choose the candy bar instead of the fruit is an example of the power of _________.
   a. needs. c. incentives.
   b. drives. d. arousal.
7. According to Maslow, a person who wants to become self-actualized must first satisfy _________.
   a. higher needs before other more primary needs.
   b. primary needs such as food and safety.
   c. needs for creativity, justice, and the appreciation of beauty.
   d. needs for achievement, affiliation, and power.
8. Shontia works at a day-care center. The pay is low and the hours are long, but she loves being around children and has no desire to look for a higher paying job. Shontia's motivation appears to be _________.
   a. intrinsic. c. selfish.
   b. extrinsic. d. external.
9. When we eat, the pancreas releases _________, which lowers blood sugar and can increase the feeling of hunger.
   a. glucose c. thyroxin
   b. insulin d. adrenaline
10. The structure in the brain that, when damaged, causes rats to stop eating is called the _________.
    a. ventromedial pituitary. c. ventromedial hypothalamus.
    b. lateral hippocampus. d. lateral hypothalamus.
11. The rate at which your body burns energy when at rest is called the _________.
    a. basal metabolic rate. c. basal set point.
    b. weight set point. d. weight metabolic rate.
12. According to Rodin, externals are people who may produce insulin in response to anticipating food as a result of _________.
    a. genetic tendencies. c. classical conditioning.
    b. biological sensitivity. d. operant conditioning.
13. If there is a history of obesity in a family, each family member has _________ of becoming obese compared to people without such a family history.
    a. the same risk c. five times the risk
    b. double or triple the risk d. less risk
14. Leptin is a _________ involved in appetite control.
    a. hormone c. organ
    b. fatty tissue d. neurotransmitter
15. Your heart is racing, your breathing is rapid, and your mouth is dry. What emotion are you experiencing?
    a. anger
    b. fear
    c. happiness
    d. It is not always possible to distinguish one emotion from another by physiological reactions only.
16. Dora is experiencing positive emotions while Milly is experiencing negative emotions. If researchers are examining EEG recordings of their brains, where are they most likely to see increases in activity?
    a. in Dora's left frontal lobe c. in their thalamic regions
    b. in Milly's right frontal lobe d. both a and b are correct.
17. The _________ is a brain structure that allows us to quickly and unconsciously respond to potentially dangerous stimuli before we are completely conscious of the threat.
    a. thalamus c. prefrontal cortex
    b. hippocampus d. amygdala
18. In Schachter and Singer's classic study, participants were physically aroused by _________.
    a. exposure to a "happy" man.
    b. exposure to an "angry" man.
    c. receiving epinephrine.
    d. watching an exciting film.
19. The theory of emotion that owes a lot to Darwin's work is the _________ theory.
    a. James-Lange c. Schachter-Singer
    b. Cannon-Bard d. facial feedback
20. Through pairing cartoon or movie characters with different food items, researchers have found characters can influence children's _________.
    a. television viewing habits. c. clothing choices.
    b. taste preferences. d. tantrum behavior.

9 motivation and emotion

9.1 9.2 p. 348

Motivation

(process by which activities are started, directed, and continued so that physical or psychological needs or wants are met)

- **types**
  - **intrinsic:** actions are rewarding or satisfying in and of themselves
  - **extrinsic:** actions are performed because they lead to some sort of external outcome

Approaches to Understanding Motivation

- **drive reduction**
  - **need**
  - **primary drives**
  - **secondary (acquired) drives**

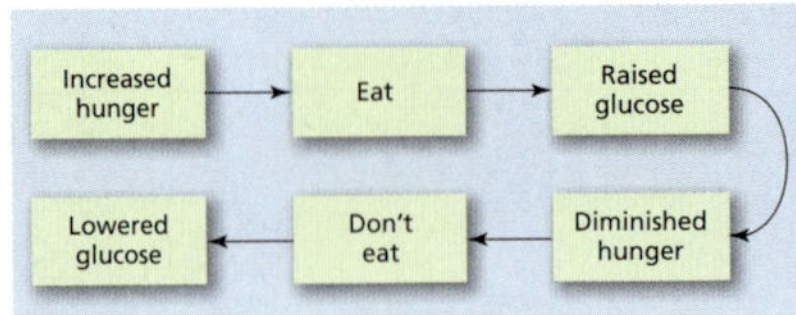

- **instinct**
  - biologically determined/innate patterns of behavior
  - old approach: instincts are mainly descriptions, not explanations; idea that some behavior is hereditary remains an important focus

- **psychological needs**
  - psychological needs have been highlighted in some theories (e.g., McClelland)
  - Dweck suggests that the need for achievement is linked to a person's view of self (fixed or changeable) and locus of control

9.3 9.4 p. 354

Approaches to Understanding Motivation (continued)

- **arousal** need for stimulation
  - **arousal theory** suggests people have an optimal level of tension that they work to maintain
  - a moderate level is most commonly sought, but that level can range from low to high (sensation seeking) →

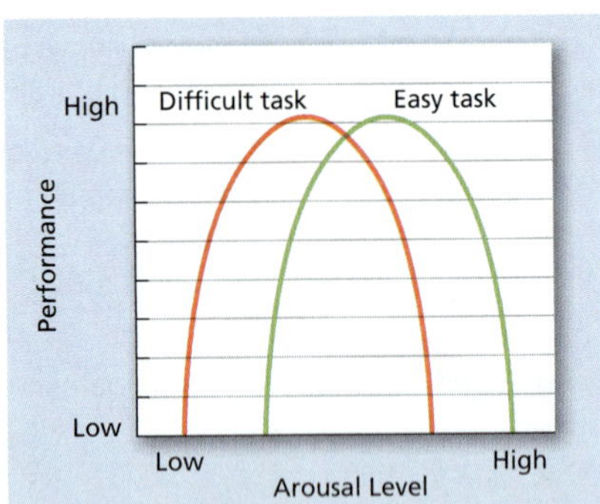

- **incentive** things that attract or lure people into action, most often due to rewarding properties
  - based in part on principles of learning
  - early work by Tolman, Lewin, and Rotter focused on expectancy-values or how our beliefs, values, and importance we attach to these affect our actions

- **humanistic** based primarily on Maslow's hierarchy of needs; primary, basic needs must be met before higher levels can be met →
  - **Alderfer's modification**
  - **self-determination theory**

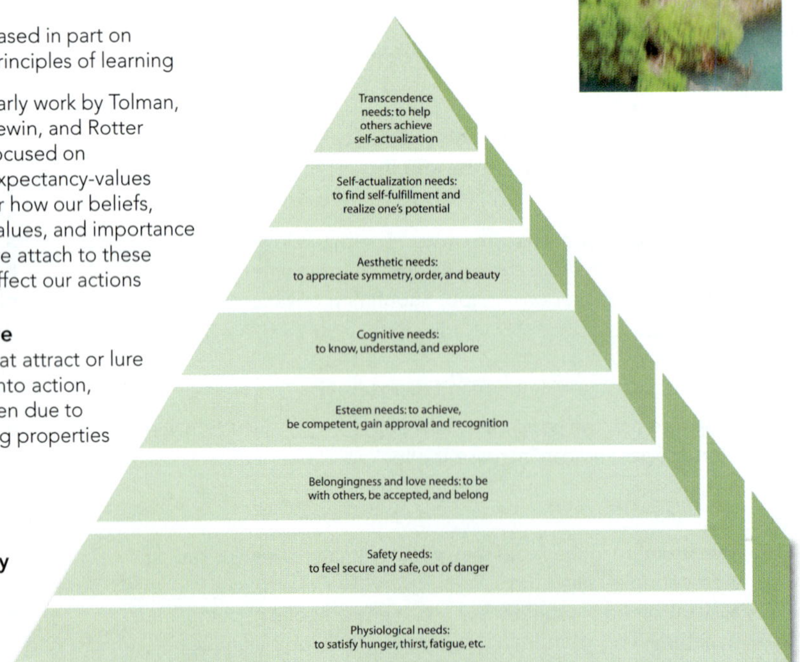

9.5 9.6 p. 360

Why People Eat

- **hunger**
  - impacted by insulin response; insulin (normally released more after onset of eating) reduces level of glucose in bloodstream (resulting in lower blood sugar and increased hunger); glucagon increases level of glucose
  - ventromedial area of the hypothalamus may be involved in stopping eating when glucose level goes up; lateral hypothalamus appears to influence onset of eating when insulin level goes up
  - person's weight set point and basal metabolic rate are tied to hypothalamus, and the hormone leptin appears to affect appetite
  - hunger and eating behaviors are influenced by social cues and convention (e.g., eating at certain times), culture, and gender
- **maladaptive eating**
  - **obesity:** body weight 20% or more over ideal (based on height); significantly impacted by genetics, overeating, exercise, and changes in metabolism
  - **anorexia nervosa**
  - **bulimia nervosa**

LINK to *Chapter Fourteen, Psychological Disorders*

9.7 9.8 9.9 p. 370

Emotion

(is "feeling" aspect of consciousness, characterized by physiological arousal, specific expressive behavior, and inner awareness of feelings)

- physiological arousal is created by the sympathetic nervous system and is associated with brain activity in specific areas (e.g., the amygdala) and right or left hemisphere activity

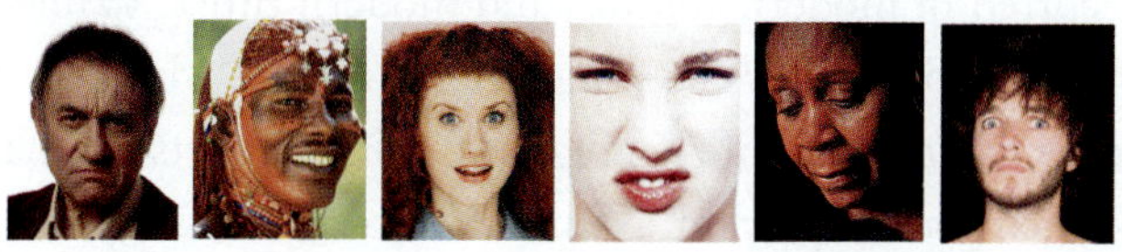

- emotional expressions can vary across cultures but some expressions seem to be universal; display rules also vary across cultures and according to gender
- subjective labeling of emotion is largely a learned response, influenced by both language and culture

Various Theories of Emotion

have been suggested, each with a slightly different focus and interpretation

- Lazarus's **cognitive-mediational theory**
- **facial feedback hypothesis** (based on ideas from Darwin)
- **James-Lange theory**
- **Cannon-Bard theory**
- **cognitive arousal theory** (Schacter-Singer)

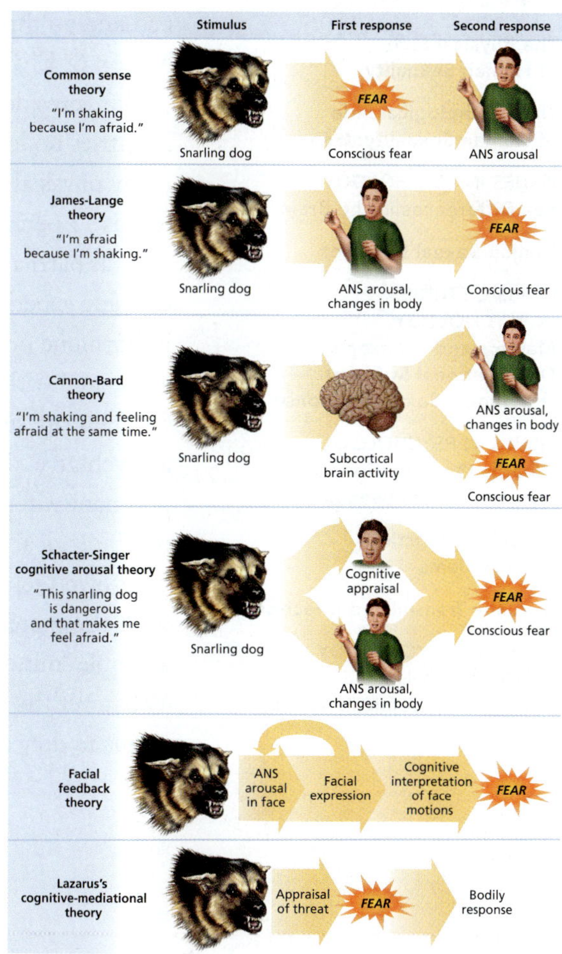

10 sexuality and gender

CHAPTER OUTLINE

UH-OH, MOM'S PREGNANT BUT SO IS DAD?

There is a gender-defying syndrome in which a man whose wife or mate is pregnant may experience a kind of "sympathy pregnancy." The syndrome is called *couvade,* from a French word meaning "to hatch or brood." Anthropologists have found this syndrome in many different cultures, often as a part of parenthood rituals. In Papua, New Guinea, for example, a father will build a hut away from the rest of the village, and when his wife is ready to give birth, he will stay in his bed and go through sympathy pains until his child is born (Budur et al., 2005; Mason & Elwood, 1995).

But couvade has occurred in modern cultures and modern times. While many countries no longer practice the ritual of couvade, there are men who experience many physical symptoms when their wife is pregnant. Some reports estimate as few as 11 percent or as many as 80 percent. Men in Western cultures, as their roles as participating fathers have changed, have actually shown an increase in couvade experiences. One study found that there are real and significant changes in hormone production in these men, including female hormones normally associated with the production of breast milk (Storey et al., 2000).

There are several possible explanations for couvade. Some believe it to be a psychiatric disorder—perhaps out of jealousy of the attention given to the pregnant wife. Some point to studies like Storey et al. (2000) as evidence for real biological changes. Still others see it as a way for men to work through their own feelings and reactions to pregnancy, which would certainly fit with the increasing incidence of couvade in Western society. It may be a simple "mind over body" reaction to the stresses of impending fatherhood. Whatever the cause or causes, couvade remains a fascinating condition which seems to defy ordinary gender roles.

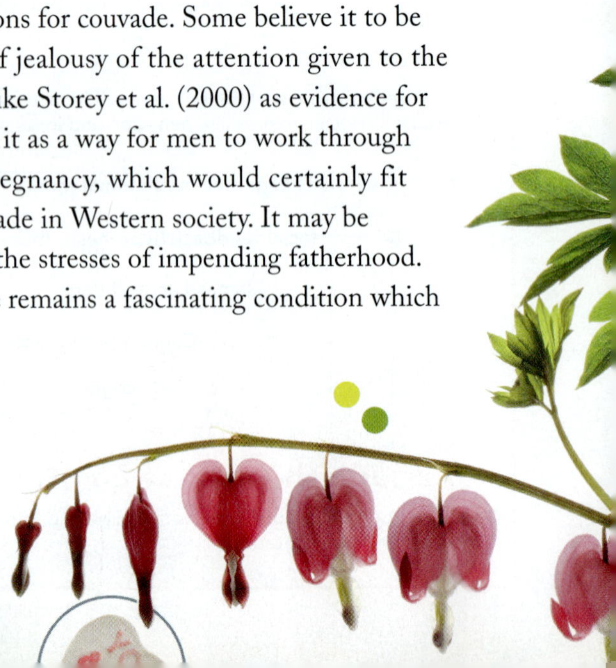

Why study
sexuality and gender?

Human sexual behavior is responsible for the reproduction of the human race, but it is also one of the most important motivators of human behavior. Gender, the psychological identification of a person as masculine or feminine, affects not only how people think of themselves but also their relationships with others as friends, lovers, and coworkers, and how those others think of them as well.

learning objectives

10.1 What are the physical differences between females and males?

10.2 What is gender, and how can biology and learning influence gender-role development?

10.3 How do gender roles develop, and how can they be influenced by stereotypes or an emphasis on androgyny?

10.4 How do men and women differ in thinking, social behavior, and personality?

10.5 What happens in the bodies of women and men during sexual intercourse?

10.6 What did the early and most recent surveys of human sexual behavior reveal?

10.7 How do different sexual orientations develop?

10.8 How do physical and psychological sexual problems differ?

10.9 What are sexually transmitted infections, and what can be done to prevent the spread of these disorders?

study tip

As you are reading this chapter, take a look back at pages I-5–I-6 in *Psychology in Action* for some ways to get more out of this chapter as you read through it.

The Physical Side of Human Sexuality

Before discussing gender and gender identity, it may help to understand the physical structures of the human sexual system and the function of those structures. These structures differ for females and males and develop at different times in an individual's life. As you read this next section, keep in mind that physical sex characteristics are not the same as the experience of *gender*, the psychological aspects of identifying oneself as male or female.

10.1 What are the physical differences between females and males?

THE PRIMARY SEX CHARACTERISTICS

The sexual organs include structures that are present at birth and those that develop during *puberty*, the period of physiological change that takes place in the sexual organs and reproductive system during late middle childhood and adolescence. LINK to Chapter Eight: Development Across the Life Span, pp. 324–325.

FEMALE PRIMARY SEX CHARACTERISTICS **Primary sex characteristics** are those physical characteristics that are present in the infant at birth. In the female, these characteristics include the **vagina** (the tube leading from the outside of the body to the opening of the womb), **uterus** (the womb), and **ovaries** (the female sex glands). (See Figure 10.1) Primary sex characteristics are directly involved in human reproduction.

MALE PRIMARY SEX CHARACTERISTICS In males, the primary sex characteristics include the **penis** (the organ through which males urinate and which delivers the male sex cells or sperm), the **testes** or **testicles** (the male sex glands), the **scrotum** (an external pouch that holds the testes), and the **prostate gland** (a gland that secretes most of the fluid that carries the sperm). (See Figure 10.1.)

THE SECONDARY SEX CHARACTERISTICS

Secondary sex characteristics develop during puberty and are only indirectly involved in human reproduction. These characteristics serve to distinguish the male from the female and may act as attractants to members of the opposite sex, ensuring that sexual activity and reproduction will occur. They are also, in many cases, a physical necessity for reproduction.

FEMALE SECONDARY SEX CHARACTERISTICS In females, secondary sex characteristics include a growth spurt that begins at about ages 10 to 12 and finished about 1 year following the first **menstrual cycle**, in which the blood and tissue lining of the uterus exit the body through the vagina if there is no pregnancy to support. This first cycle is known as *menarche* and occurs at an average age of about 12 in more-developed countries

primary sex characteristics sexual organs present at birth and directly involved in human reproduction.

vagina the tube that leads from the outside of a female's body to the opening of the womb.

uterus the womb in which the baby grows during pregnancy.

ovaries the female sexual glands.

penis the organ through which males urinate and which delivers the male sex cells or sperm.

testes (testicles) the male sex glands.

scrotum external sac that holds the testes.

prostate gland gland that secretes most of the fluid holding the male sex cells or sperm.

secondary sex characteristics sexual organs and traits that develop at puberty and are indirectly involved in human reproduction.

menstrual cycle monthly shedding of the blood and tissue that line the uterus in preparation for pregnancy when conception does not occur.

mammary glands glands within the breast tissue that produce milk when a woman gives birth to an infant.

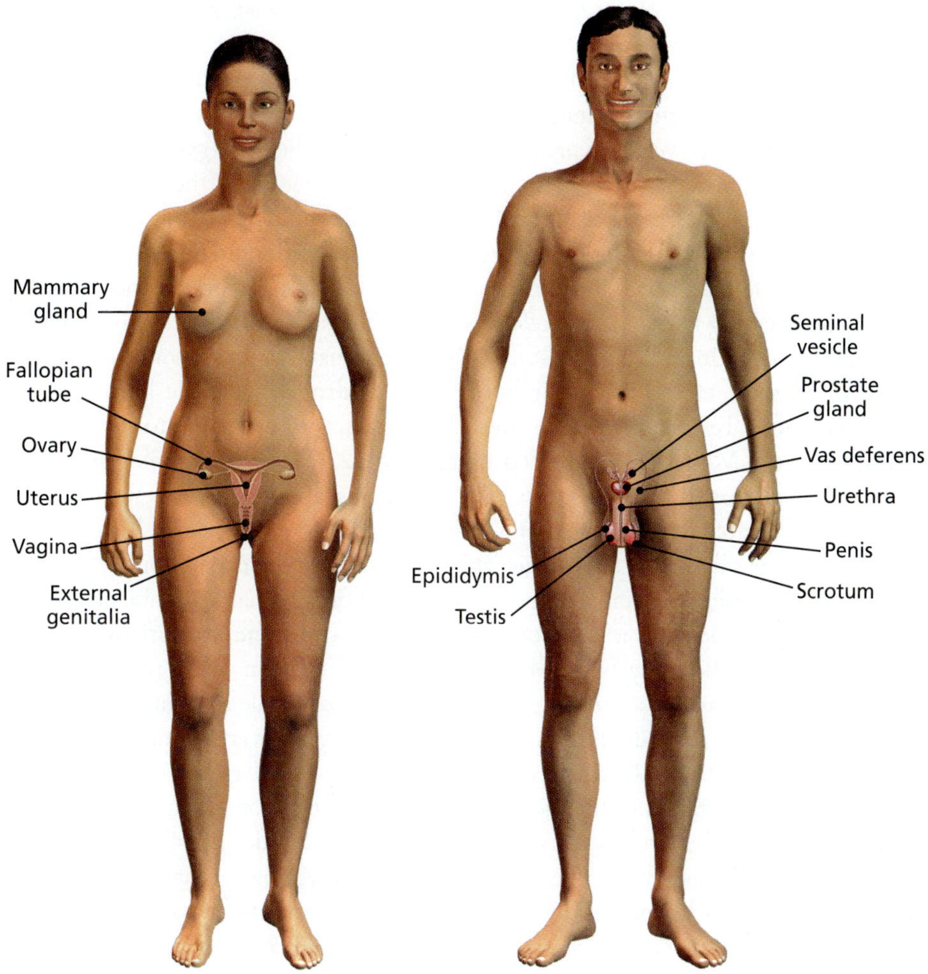

Figure 10.1 Male and Female Sexual Organs

These figures show the sexual organs of men and women. With the exception of breast-tissue development in the female, which occurs during puberty, all of these structures develop during the prenatal period.

such as the United States. In countries with poorer health care and nutrition, the average age of menarche may be later. Other changes include enlarged breasts about 2 years after the growth spurt, wider hips to allow the passage of the fetus through the pelvic bones, pubic hair, and fat deposits on the buttocks and thighs. Some secondary sex characteristics also involve the growth and development of the primary sexual organs. In females, this occurs when the **mammary glands** in the breasts become capable of producing milk for an infant and when the menstrual cycle begins (Kreipe, 1992; Lee, 1995). **Explore** on **mypsychlab.com**

Explore female reproductive organs on **mypsychlab.com**

MALE SECONDARY SEX CHARACTERISTICS The secondary sex characteristics of males include a deepening voice; emergence of facial, chest, and pubic hair; and the development of coarser skin texture. These changes are also accompanied by a large increase in height that continues beyond the growth spurt of the female. The male growth spurt occurs about 2 years later than the female growth spurt, but males continue to gain height until the late teens. Although the larynx (voice box) increases in size in both sexes, it increases so much in males that part of the tissue forming it becomes visible under the skin of the neck in a structure known as the Adam's apple. Primary sex characteristics also undergo changes during puberty, including the onset of the production of sperm (*spermarche,* occurring at a little over 14 years of age) and the growth of the penis and testes, which will eventually allow the male to function sexually and to reproduce (Kreipe, 1992; Lee, 1995).

Puberty changes come about 2 years earlier for girls than for boys, including the growth spurt. This dancing couple are both 13 years old, but the physical difference in height is quite obvious.

How does the person's body know which sexual characteristics to develop? Aren't some babies born with sex organs belonging to both sexes?

How does the person's body know which sexual characteristics to develop? Aren't some babies born with sex organs belonging to both sexes?

The primary sex characteristics develop as the embryo is growing in the womb as a result of the chromosomes contained within the embryonic cells as well as hormonal influences. At about 5 weeks of pregnancy, two organs called the *gonads* form in the embryo. Two sets of ducts (tubes) also develop next to the gonads, the Wolffian ducts (which can become the male sex organs) and the Müllerian ducts (which can become the female sex organs). At this point, the gonads are undifferentiated—neither fully male nor fully female—and the embryo could potentially become either male or female. The deciding factor is controlled by the chromosomes: If the chromosomes of the 23rd pair contain a Y chromosome, a gene on that Y chromosome causes the gonads to release *testosterone*, a male hormone or **androgen**. (Female hormones are called **estrogens**.) Testosterone causes the Wolffian ducts to develop into the male sex organs, while the Müllerian ducts deteriorate. If the 23rd pair of chromosomes contains two female or X chromosomes, the Y gene is absent so no testosterone is released, and the gonads will develop into the estrogen-secreting ovaries. The Müllerian ducts become the female sex organs while the Wolffian ducts deteriorate.

On rare occasions, an infant is born with sexual organs that are ambiguous—not clearly male or female. This is the more common form of **hermaphroditism**, the condition of possessing both male and female sex organs. (The term comes from the name of a Greek god, Hermaphroditus, who was said to have both male and female characteristics.) It is very rare to find a person who truly has both ovary and testicle material in their body. More commonly, the development of the external genitals is affected by either chromosome defects or the presence of the wrong hormones at a critical time in the development of the fetus in the womb (Hutcheson & Snyder, 2004). In this case, a female clitoris might look more like a penis, or a penis might be so small as to resemble a clitoris. People with hermaphroditism now prefer the term **intersexed** or **intersexual**, meaning "between the sexes." Approximately 1 out of 1,500 children are born with this condition (Dreger, 1998, 1999). **Read** on **mypsychlab.com**

Read and learn more about one such case with the story of David Reimer's life on **mypsychlab.com**

The Psychological Side of Human Sexuality: Gender

10.2 What is gender, and how can biology and learning influence gender role-development?

Whereas sex can be defined as the physical characteristics of being male or female, **gender** is defined as the psychological aspects of being masculine or feminine. The expectations of one's culture, the development of one's personality, and one's sense of identity are all affected by the concept of gender.

GENDER ROLES AND GENDER TYPING

Gender roles are the culture's expectations for behavior of a person who is perceived as male or female, including attitudes, actions, and personality traits associated with a particular gender within that culture (Tobach, 2001; Unger, 1979). **Gender typing** is the process by which people learn their culture's preferences and expectations for proper "masculine" and "feminine" behavior. The process of developing a person's **gender identity** (a sense of being male or female) is influenced by both biological and environmental factors (in the form of parenting and other child-rearing behaviors), although which type of factor has greater influence is still controversial.

Most researchers today would agree that biology has an important role in gender identity, at least in certain aspects of gender identity and behavior (Diamond &

androgens male hormones.

estrogens female hormones.

hermaphroditism the condition of possessing both male and female sexual organs.

intersexed, intersexual modern term for a hermaphrodite, a person who possesses ambiguous sexual organs, making it difficult to determine actual sex from a visual inspection at birth.

gender the psychological aspects of being male or female.

gender roles the culture's expectations for masculine or feminine behavior, including attitudes, actions, and personality traits associated with being male or female in that culture.

gender typing the process of acquiring gender-role characteristics.

gender identity the individual's sense of being male or female.

Sigmundson, 1997; Money, 1994; Reiner, 1999, 2000). In one study, 25 genetically male children who were born with ambiguous genitalia were surgically altered and raised as girls. Now, as older children and teenagers, they prefer male play activities such as sports. Fourteen of these children have openly declared themselves to be boys (Reiner, 2000).

This is We-Wa, a Zuni berdache (the Zuni version of winkte). This photograph was taken near the end of the 19th century.

Gender identity, like physical sex, is also not always as straightforward as males who are masculine and females who are feminine. People's sense of gender identity does not always match their external appearance or even the sex chromosomes that determine whether they are male or female (Califia, 1997; Crawford & Unger, 2004; White, 2000). Such people are typically termed *transgendered.* Biology and environment both have an influence on the concept of a person's gender identity. In a syndrome called *gender identity disorder (GID),* a person feels that he or she is occupying the body of the wrong sex; a man may feel that he was meant to be a woman or a woman may feel that she was meant to be a man (American Psychiatric Association, 2000). Some people with this disorder feel so strongly that they are the wrong sex that they have surgery to become the sex they feel they were always meant to be. These people are generally termed *transsexuals* because in addition to dressing as the gender they believe themselves to be, many receive hormone injections to change physical attributes to those of that gender, or may actually undergo sexual reassignment surgery.

Many Native American tribes have long recognized the role of the male *winkte* (a contraction of the Lakota word *winyanktehca,* meaning "to be as a woman or two-souls person") in their societies. These tribes traditionally were not only tolerant of such different individuals but also had important places for them in the social structure as caretakers of children, as cooks, and as menders and creators of clothing. The winkte also performed certain rituals for bestowing luck upon a hunt (Medicine, 2002). Although some winkte (now often referred to as people with two spirits) may have been homosexuals, many were not and would now be recognized as having an alternate gender identity or gender identity disorder. Unfortunately, as tribes have modernized and become more integrated into the larger European-dominated culture of the United States, the tolerant attitudes of other Native Americans toward the winkte have begun to be replaced with homophobic attitudes and aggressive behavior toward those who are different in this way (Medicine, 2002).

Although the causes of gender identity disorder are not fully understood, there is some evidence for both prenatal influences and early childhood experiences as causes (Stein, 1984; Ward, 1992; Zhou et al., 1995).

BIOLOGICAL INFLUENCES What are the biological influences on gender? Aside from the obvious external sexual characteristics of the genitals, there are also hormonal differences between men and women. Some researchers believe that exposure to these hormones during fetal development not only causes the formation of the sexual organs but also predisposes the infant to behavior that is typically associated with one gender or the other. There have been several studies of infant girls who were exposed to androgens before birth (for example, some drugs to prevent miscarriages are male hormones). In these studies, the girls were found to be tomboys during early childhood—preferring to play with typically "boy" toys, wrestling and playing rough, and playing with boys rather than with other girls (Berenbaum & Snyder, 1995; Money & Mathews, 1982; Money & Norman, 1987). However, when these girls grew up, they became more typically "female" in their desire for marriage and motherhood, which many of these same researchers took as evidence that upbringing won out over the hormonal influences.

Was their early tomboy nature due to the influence of the male hormones?

Was their early tomboy nature due to the influence of the male hormones?

This is difficult to prove, as the parents of these girls were told about their infants' exposure to male hormones during the pregnancy and may have formed assumptions about the effects of such masculinizing hormones on their children. It is entirely possible that these girls were simply allowed, or even encouraged, to be more "masculine" as small children because the parents were expecting them to be masculine. As these same girls grew older, they were exposed to the gender-role expectations of teachers, friends, and the media, which may have influenced them to become more like the feminine gender stereotype in contrast to their earlier "masculine" style of behavior.

Another study examined the way in which men and women respond to visual sexual stimuli and found that although men and women may report being equally aroused by erotic pictures, what happens in their brains is quite different (Hamann et al., 2004). Using a brain-scanning technique called *functional magnetic resonance imaging (fMRI)*, the researchers found that the amygdala and hypothalamus areas of the limbic system (areas involved in emotional and sexual responses) were more strongly active in men than in women who viewed the pictures. LINK to Chapter Two: The Biological Perspective, pp. 71–72. The researchers concluded that the male brain's enhanced reaction might be a product of natural selection, as early human males who could quickly recognize a sexually receptive female would have had a greater opportunity to mate and pass on their genes to their offspring.

"We don't believe in pressuring the children. When the time is right, they'll choose the appropriate gender."

ENVIRONMENTAL INFLUENCES Even if the girls who were exposed to androgens prenatally were initially influenced by these hormones, it seems fairly clear that their later "reversion" to more feminine ways was at least somewhat influenced by the pressures of society. In most cultures, there are certain roles that males and females are expected to play (gender roles, in other words), and the pressure that can be brought to bear on a person who does not conform to these expectations can be tremendous. In most Western cultures, the pressure to be masculine is even greater for males than the pressure to be feminine is for girls. The term *tomboy* is not generally viewed as an insult, but there are no terms for a boy who acts in a feminine manner that are not insulting—*sissy*, for example, is not a nice term at all. And although studies of parents' influence on their children's gender typing show that both parents have an impact, they also show that the fathers are almost always more concerned about their sons showing male gender behavior than they are about their daughters showing female gender behavior (Lytton & Romney, 1991).

Although Asian cultures are often more traditional in the roles that men and women play within society, even in these cultures gender roles are becoming more flexible, as this male preschool teacher in a Chinese classroom demonstrates. Why might gender roles in these traditional countries be changing?

CULTURE AND GENDER A person's culture is also an environmental influence. Although initial cross-cultural studies suggested that cultural differences had little effect on gender roles (Best & Williams, 2001), more recent research suggests that in the past few decades a change has occurred in cultures that are of different "personalities." Cultures that are more individualistic and have fairly high standards of living are becoming more nontraditional, especially for women in those cultures; research has shown that more-traditional views seem to be held by collectivistic cultures that have less wealth, although even in these cultures, women were more likely to be less traditional than men (Forbes et al., 2009; Gibbons et al., 1991; Shafiro et al., 2003). Other studies have found that the most nontraditional ideas about gender roles and gender behavior are found in countries such as the Netherlands, Germany, Italy, and England, whereas the most traditional ideas predominate in African and Asian countries such as Nigeria, Pakistan, and Japan (Best & Williams, 2001). The United States, often seen as very nontraditional by researchers, actually was somewhere in the middle in these studies, perhaps due to the large variation in subcultures that exists within this multicultural country. Environment, even in the form of culture, seems to play at least a partial and perhaps dominant role in gender behavior.

Biology, environment, and culture may all have an influence on differences in gender behavior. What about differences that originate within the brain itself? Are male and female brains really all that different? The following special section has a few possible answers. Watch on **mypsychlab.com**

Watch a video about gender versus sex on **mypsychlab.com**

issues in psychology

Sex Differences in the Brain

Several studies over the years have found differences in male and female brain activity: When doing language tasks, women use an area of the brain's right hemisphere that is not as active in men, leading some to speculate that this is why women seem to recover faster than men from left-hemisphere strokes that affect language (Jaeger et al., 1998; Skrandies et al., 1999). Women seem to be better at identifying emotions, especially fear and disgust, than are men, regardless of whether the emotional content is auditory, visual, or some combination (Collignon et al., 2010). Whereas men use the right side of the brain for emotional expression and the left side for visual–spatial perception, women seem to use both sides (Argyle, 1986; Cela-Conde et al., 2009; Fischer, 1993; Jaeger et al., 1998; Kimura, 2002; Pittam et al., 1995; Skrandies et al., 1999). Physical differences in male and female brains exist from birth with the male hypothalamus being somewhat larger than that of females in both rats and humans (Kimura, 2002). Women appear to have a far greater number of common receptors for the neurotransmitter serotonin, which is involved in mood and anxiety—both disorders from which women tend to suffer more than men (Jovanovic et al., 2008). Another physical difference involves the proportion of gray matter and white matter in the nervous system. Gray matter is composed of neurons, glial cells, dendrites, and both myelinated and nonmyelinated axons, and makes up the bulk of the brain and the interior of the spinal cord. The function of gray matter is to process incoming sensory information and form a response to that information. White matter is composed of myelinated axons and carries information to and from the neurons of the gray matter (Purves et al., 2008). It might help to think of gray matter as the "hardware" of a multicomputer system, and white matter as the "software network" connecting all the computers. Using various neuroimaging techniques, others have found that the actual volume of the male brain is greater than that of the female brain. However, even when volume is taken into account, women have more gray matter, while men have more white matter (Cosgrove et al., 2007).

Even in these biological differences, the influence of the environment in the form of parenting and cultural expectations cannot be ruled out as potential causes. For example, in Western cultures, girls are encouraged to express and use their emotions while boys are encouraged to hide emotions and be calm, which might contribute to the different emphasis placed on each hemisphere for the two sexes (Argyle, 1986; Fischer, 1993; Pittam et al., 1995). Psychologist Eleanor Maccoby (1998) believes that the biological differences between males and females help to create distinct contexts in which boys and girls are raised. The aggressive nature of boys, for example, causes them to engage in more rough-and-tumble play and competitive games than those in which girls would typically take part.

If there were sex differences in the brain prior to birth, they would be expected to be biologically based. A study that examined genetic expression in the cortex of the brain strongly suggests that there are prenatal sex differences, with many genes on the Y chromosome (which creates males) being expressed in parts of the brain before birth (Reinius & Jazin, 2009). One thing is clear: The issue of differences between men and women is one that will be discussed, debated, and researched for some time to come.

Questions for Further Discussion

1. How important do you think it is to determine whether or not differences between men and women are based in biology or based in learning?
2. How has your own behavior fit in with common ideas about masculine or feminine behavior? Can you think of experiences you have had growing up that would have influenced that behavior?
3. Can you think of possible differences in behavior that might be related to the different proportion of gray matter versus white matter as found in the Cosgrove et al. 2007 study?

CONCEPT MAP

10.1 10.2

- physical sex characteristics are not the same as gender, the psychological aspects of identifying as a male or female
- embryonic undifferentiated gonads develop into male or female sex organs as the result of chromosomes and hormones — chromosomal or hormonal defects can result in ambiguous sex organs/hermaphroditism/intersexed individuals
- **primary sexual characteristics:** present at birth, directly involved in reproduction
  - **female:** vagina, uterus, and ovaries
  - **male:** penis, testicles, scrotum, and prostate gland
- **secondary sexual characteristics:** develop during puberty (indirectly involved in reproduction)
  - **female:** breast enlargement, widening of hips, pubic hair, fat deposits on buttocks and thighs
  - **male:** deepening of voice, facial and chest hair, pubic hair, coarser skin texture, increase in height

The Physical Side of Human Sexuality

- **key concepts**
  - **gender roles:** cultural behavioral expectations for males or females
  - **gender typing:** process by which people learn gender roles
  - **gender identity:** sense of being male or female (influenced by both biology and environment)

The Psychological Side of Human Sexuality: Gender

- **gender** is defined as the psychological aspects of being masculine or feminine and is influenced by culture, individual personality, and self-identity
  - **biological influences:** sexual characteristics of the genitals, hormonal differences, and possible differences in brain structure and processing
  - **environmental influences:** parental influences and cultural expectations to adhere to gender roles
  - **culture:** individualistic/nontraditional versus collectivistic/traditional role adoption

PRACTICE quiz How much do you remember?

ANSWERS ON PAGE AK-2.

Pick the best answer.

1. Which of the following is not a primary sex characteristic?
   a. uterus
   b. penis
   c. enlarging breasts
   d. ovaries
2. Which of the following is FALSE concerning secondary sex characteristics?
   a. They are directly concerned with reproduction.
   b. They serve to attract members of the opposite sex.
   c. They typically develop during puberty.
   d. They include the appearance of pubic hair.
3. People who are intersexual __________.
   a. commonly have both ovaries and testes.
   b. are extremely rare—1 in a million births.

c. have a mixture of male and female sexual characteristics.
d. are people who suffer from gender identity disorder but are physically normal.

4. The development of a person's sense of being male or female is called _________.
   a. gender role.
   b. gender identity.
   c. gender typing.
   d. gender stereotyping.

5. Which of the following is not a biological influence on gender?
   a. hormones secreted during fetal development
   b. the influence of hormones taken by the pregnant mother
   c. exposure to playmates of a particular gender
   d. sex chromosomes

6. In _________ cultures, gender roles are seen as more traditional, whereas in _________ cultures they may be more nontraditional, especially for women.
   a. individualistic; collectivistic
   b. collectivistic; individualistic
   c. European; Asian
   d. affluent; poor

THEORIES OF GENDER-ROLE DEVELOPMENT

10.3 How do gender roles develop, and how can they be influenced by stereotypes or an emphasis on androgyny?

How do children acquire the knowledge of their society or culture's gender-role expectations? How does that knowledge lead to the development of a gender identity? Although early psychodynamic theorists such as Freud (LINK to Chapter Thirteen: Theories of Personality, p. 495) believed that children would learn their gender identities as a natural consequence of resolving the sexual conflicts of early childhood, many modern theorists focus on learning and cognitive processes for the development of gender identity and behavior.

As children develop the concept of gender, they begin to imitate the behavior of those they see as similar to themselves. This young girl is learning that women wear cosmetics while she plays at helping her mother put on her makeup. As she grows, she will incorporate more of her mother's behavior and ideas about what it is to be female into her own personality.

SOCIAL LEARNING THEORY Social learning theory, which emphasizes learning through observation and imitation of models, attributes* gender-role development to those processes. Children observe their same-sex parents behaving in certain ways and imitate that behavior. When the children imitate the appropriate gender behavior, they are reinforced with positive attention. Inappropriate gender behavior is either ignored or actively discouraged (Fagot & Hagan, 1991; Mischel, 1966).

Of course, parents are not the only gender-role models available to children. In addition to older brothers and sisters, family friends, teachers, and peers, children are exposed to male and female behavior on television and in other media. In fact, television, movies, and children's books are often filled with very traditional male and female roles. In these books, doctors are males and nurses are female far more often than the other way around, for example. Although some children's books and television programs make a genuine effort to present males and females in nontypical occupations, there are far more that maintain traditional roles for men and women.

GENDER SCHEMA THEORY A theory of gender-role development that combines social learning theory with cognitive development is called **gender schema theory** (Bem, 1987, 1993). In this theory based on the Piagetian concept of schemes (see Chapter Eight), children develop a schema, or mental pattern, for being male or female in much the same way that they develop schemas for other concepts such as "dog," "bird," and "big." As their brains mature, they become capable of distinguishing among various concepts. For example, a "dog" might at first be anything with four legs and a tail, but as a child encounters dogs and other kinds of animals and is given instruction, "dog" becomes more specific and the schema for "dog" becomes well defined.

gender schema theory theory of gender identity acquisition in which a child develops a mental pattern, or schema, for being male or female and then organizes observed and learned behavior around that schema.

*attributes: explains as a cause.

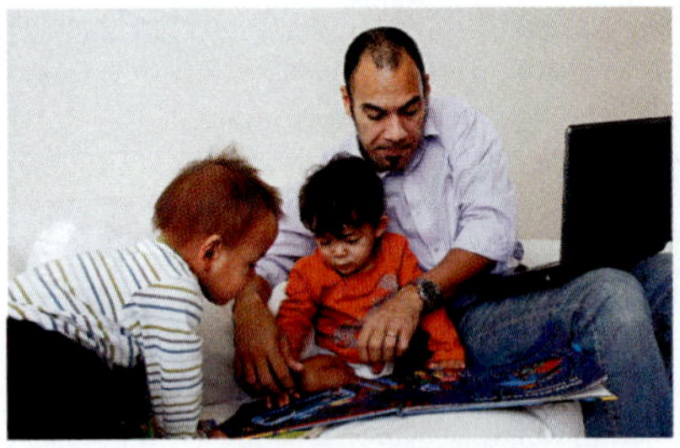

What are some of the ways in which this father may influence his sons' gender identities as they grow up?

In a similar manner, children develop a concept for "boy" and "girl." Once that schema is in place, children can identify themselves as "boy" or "girl" and will notice other members of that schema. They notice the behavior of other "boys" or "girls" and imitate that behavior. They play with their parents and pick up on differences in the behavior of fathers and mothers (Lindsey et al., 2010). Rather than being simple imitation and reinforcement, as in social learning theory, children acquire their gender-role behavior by organizing that behavior around the schema of "boy" or "girl." Evidence for this theory includes the finding that infants can discriminate between male and female faces and voices before age 1 (Martin, 2000), a sign that infants are already organizing the world into those two concepts.

GENDER STEREOTYPING

A **stereotype** is a concept that can be held about a person or group of people that is based on very superficial characteristics. A **gender stereotype** is a concept about males or females that assigns various characteristics to them on the basis of nothing more than being male or female. **Explore** on **mypsychlab.com**

Explore gender stereotypes on **mypsychlab.com**

MALE AND FEMALE GENDER STEREOTYPES The male gender stereotype generally includes the following characteristics: aggressive, logical, decisive, unemotional, insensitive, nonnurturing, impatient, and mechanically talented. The female stereotype typically includes these characteristics: illogical, changeable, emotional, sensitive, naturally nurturing, patient, and all-thumbs when it comes to understanding machines. Notice that each of these stereotypes has both positive and negative characteristics.

Some researchers believe that accepting stereotyping of any kind, even positive stereotyping, can lead to **sexism**, or prejudice about males and females. In fact, some researchers (Glick & Fiske, 2001) claim that acceptance of positive stereotypes can lead to **benevolent sexism**, prejudice that is more socially acceptable but still leads to men and women being treated unequally. Not all men are mechanically talented, nor are all women naturally nurturing, for example. A positive stereotype for men is that they are strong and protective of women, implying that women are weak and need protection, just as the positive female stereotype of natural nurturance of children implies that males cannot be nurturing. Such stereotypes, although somewhat "flattering" for the sex about whom they are held, can be harmful to the other sex.

ANDROGYNY Psychologist Sandra Bem (1975, 1981) has developed the concept of **androgyny** to describe a characteristic of people whose personalities reflect the characteristics of both males and females, regardless of gender. This allows them to be more flexible in everyday behavior and career choices. People who fall into the gender-role stereotypes, according to Bem, often find themselves limited in their choices for problem solving because of the stereotype's constraints on "proper" male or female behavior. An androgynous person, on the other hand, can make a decision based on the situation rather than on being masculine or feminine.

For example, let's say that a man, through an unhappy circumstance, is left to raise his three small children. If he is a male who has "bought into" the male stereotype, he has no confidence in his ability to bring up these children by himself. He may rush into another relationship with a woman just to provide his children with a "mother." Similarly, a "traditional" female who is left without a husband might have difficulty in dealing with raising sons and with a task as simple as mowing the lawn. Researchers have found that when traditional males, traditional females, and androgynous people are compared in terms of the degree of depression they experience when their lives are filled with many negative events, the androgynous people report less than half the depression exhibited by traditional men and only a third of the depression felt by traditional women (Roos & Cohen, 1987). Figure 10.2 shows the results of this study.

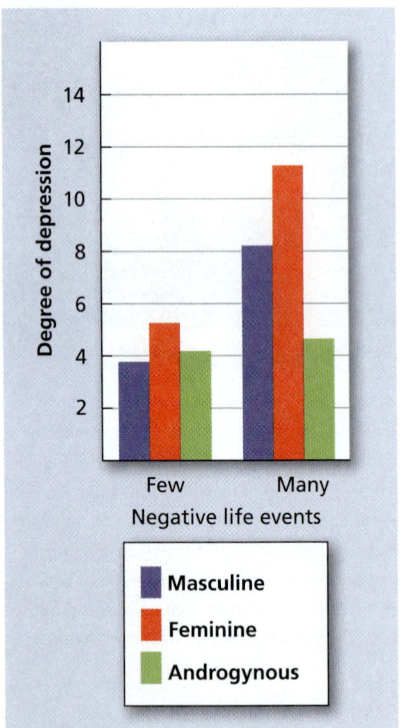

Figure 10.2 Depression as Influenced by Negative Life Events

The bar graph shows that men who are masculine and women who are feminine in their gender roles experience a significant increase in depression when they are exposed to an increased number of life events. The same is not true for people with an androgynous gender role. How might being androgynous allow a person to be more adaptable?

GENDER DIFFERENCES

10.4 How do men and women differ in thinking, social behavior, and personality?

Although there are clear biological differences in males and females, even to the point of affecting the size of certain structures in the brain (Allen & Gorski, 1991; Allen et al., 1989; Zhou et al., 1995), what sort of differences exist in the behavior of males and females? Are those differences due to biology, socialization, or a combination of the two influences?

COGNITIVE DIFFERENCES Researchers have long held that females score higher on tests of verbal abilities than do males, but that males score higher on tests of mathematical skills and spatial skills (Diamond, 1991; Voyer et al., 1995). Another study, using MRI technology, found that men listen with the left hemisphere only, whereas women listen with both hemispheres, suggesting that women pay attention to the tone and emotion of statements as well as the content (Lurito et al., 2000). Early explanations of these differences in cognitive functioning involved physical differences in the way each sex used the two hemispheres of the brain as well as hormonal differences (Witelson, 1991). Other research, however, strongly suggests that psychological and social issues may be more responsible for these differences, as these differences have become less and less obvious (Hyde & Plant, 1995; Kimura, 1999; Voyer et al., 1995; Watt, 2000). In particular, the supposed differences in math abilities between boys and girls have now been shown to be more the effect of girl's lack of confidence rather than any biological difference in the working of the brain (Else-Quest et al., 2010). That the disparities seem to be disappearing as society has begun to view the two genders as more equal in ability is taken as a sign that more equal treatment in society has reduced the gender difference.

More evidence that the gender differences between males and females in certain cognitive areas are disappearing comes from a study that showed that girls actually begin their school experience with math and science skills that are equal to those of the boys of their age group, but that by the time they finished high school, the girls had become less skilled in those two areas than boys (American Association of University Women, 1992; Sadker & Sadker, 1994). Six years later, a follow-up study showed that these differences had all but disappeared as the girls improved their skills (American Association of University Women, 1998).

SOCIAL AND PERSONALITY DIFFERENCES The differences normally cited between men and women in the ways they interact with others and in their personality traits are often the result of stereotyped thinking about the sexes. It is difficult to demonstrate differences that are not caused by the way boys and girls are socialized as they grow up. Boys are taught to hold in their emotions, not to cry, to be "strong" and "manly." Girls are encouraged to form emotional attachments, be emotional, and be open about their feelings with others.

In communication, research suggests that when men talk to each other, they tend to talk about current events, sports, and other events. This has been called a "report" style of communication and seems to involve switching topics frequently with attempts to dominate the conversation by certain members of the group. In contrast, women tend to use a "relate" style of communication with each other, revealing a lot about their private lives and showing concern and sympathy. They tend to interrupt each other less and let everyone participate in the conversation (Argamon et al., 2003; Coates, 1986; Pilkington, 1998; Swann, 1998).

stereotype a concept held about a person or group of people that is based on superficial, irrelevant characteristics.

gender stereotype a concept held about a person or group of people that is based on being male or female.

sexism prejudice about males and/or females leading to unequal treatment.

benevolent sexism acceptance of positive stereotypes of males and females that leads to unequal treatment.

androgyny characteristic of possessing the most positive personality characteristics of males and females regardless of actual sex.

"It's a guy thing."

It was long believed that the difference between girls and boys in math skills was a function of biology, but research now shows that psychological and social issues are the more likely causes.

10.3 10.4

CONCEPT MAP

The Psychological Side of Human Sexuality: Gender

- **theories of gender-role development**
  - **social learning theory:** gender roles learned through observation and imitation of models
  - **gender schema theory** (Bem): Piaget-like schemas and concepts for male and female develop and influence gender roles
  - **gender stereotyping:** positive or negative characteristics assigned on basis of being male or female; can lead to sexism (prejudice)
  - **androgyny** (based on Bem's work): positive aspects of both males and females, regardless of gender
- **gender differences**
  - **cognitive differences** (e.g., listening skills) may be present but are possibly due to psychological and social issues rather than biology
  - **social and personality differences** are often the result of stereotyped thinking about the sexes

PRACTICE quiz How much do you remember? ANSWERS ON PAGE AK-2.

Pick the best answer.

1. Studies have shown that __________ are more concerned about appropriate gender behavior in their children, particularly their __________ children.
   a. fathers; male
   b. fathers; female
   c. mothers; male
   d. mothers; female
2. Alex sees his father hammering some nails into a loose board on their house. Later, Alex takes his toy hammer and pretends to hammer in some imaginary nails. Of which theory of gender development would this be a good example?
   a. gender schema theory
   b. gender-role theory
   c. psychoanalytic theory
   d. social learning theory
3. In an older movie, a male character is suddenly left with a small baby for whom he must now care. Desperate for help, he calls his fiancée, thinking that she will know what to do because she's a woman, and women are natural mothers. The character's thinking in this instance is an example of __________.
   a. androgyny.
   b. schema error.
   c. benevolent sexism.
   d. negative stereotyping.
4. Susanna is a mother to her two children, but she also has a career as a professor at a university. She is nurturant and sensitive to her children's needs, able to express her emotions outwardly, independent and assertive, and thinks problems through calmly and logically. Susanna is a good example of a person who is __________.
   a. masculine.
   b. feminine.
   c. transsexual.
   d. androgynous.
5. Research has shown that men tend to talk to each other about __________.
   a. private concerns.
   b. their feelings.
   c. relationships.
   d. current events.

I've heard that men and women experience sex differently—is that true? What is different?

I've heard that men and women experience sex differently—is that true? What is different?

Human Sexual Behavior

10.5 What happens in the bodies of women and men during sexual intercourse?

In 1957, gynecologist Dr. William Masters and psychologist Dr. Virginia Johnson began what would become a controversial* study of the human sexual response in 700 men and women volunteers (Masters & Johnson, 1966). At that time in history, human sexuality was still a relatively forbidden topic to all but young adults, who were exploring the concepts of "free love" and engaging in premarital sex far more openly than in the past. Masters and Johnson devised equipment that would measure the

*controversial: leading to arguments or opposing viewpoints.

physical responses that occur during sexual activity. They used this equipment to measure physiological activity in both men and women volunteers who either were engaging in actual intercourse or masturbation. Although many conservative and religious people were outraged by this research, it remains as one of the most important studies of the human sexual response.

SEXUAL RESPONSE

Masters and Johnson (1966) identified four stages of a sexual-response cycle in their groundbreaking research. Although these stages are similar in both men and women, there are some differences. Also, the transition between the stages is not necessarily as well defined as the descriptions of the stages might seem to describe, and the length of time spent in any one phase can vary from experience to experience and person to person. Watch on **mypsychlab.com**

Watch video footage on sexual arousal in women on **mypsychlab.com**

PHASE 1: EXCITEMENT This first phase is the beginning of sexual arousal and can last anywhere from 1 minute to several hours. Pulse rate increases, blood pressure rises, breathing quickens, and the skin may show a rosy flush, especially on the chest or breast areas. In women, the clitoris swells, the lips of the vagina open, and the inside of the vagina moistens in preparation for intercourse. In men, the penis becomes erect, the testes pull up, and the skin of the scrotum tightens. Nipples will harden and become more erect in both sexes, but especially in the female.

PHASE 2: PLATEAU In the second phase of the sexual response, the physical changes that began in the first phase are continued. In women, the outer part of the vagina swells with increased amounts of blood to that area, while the clitoris retracts under the clitoral hood but remains highly sensitive. The outer lips of the vagina become redder in color. In men, the penis becomes more erect and may release a few drops of fluid. At this point, it is unlikely that the male will lose his erection. This phase may last only a few seconds to several minutes.

PHASE 3: ORGASM The third phase is the shortest of the three stages and involves a series of rhythmic muscular contractions known as the **orgasm**. In women, this involves the muscles of the vaginal walls and can happen multiple times, lasting slightly longer than the orgasm experience of the male. In men, the orgasmic contractions of the muscles in and around the penis trigger the release of **semen**, the fluid that contains the male sex cells, or sperm. Men typically have only one intense orgasm.

PHASE 4: RESOLUTION The final phase of the sexual response is **resolution**, the return of the body to its normal state before arousal began. The blood that congested the blood vessels in the various areas of the genitals recedes; the heart rate, blood pressure, and breathing all reduce to normal levels during this phase. In women, the clitoris retracts, the color of the vaginal lips returns to normal, and the lips close once more. In men, the erection is lost, the testes descend, and the scrotal sac thins again. Also, men have a **refractory period** during which they cannot achieve another erection, lasting anywhere from several minutes to several hours for different individuals. The older the man gets, the longer the refractory period tends to extend. Women do not have a refractory period and in fact may achieve another series of orgasms if stimulation continues.

Read the Classic Studies in Psychology section that follows for a more detailed look at the historic Masters and Johnson study and to learn how this landmark research was accomplished. (See also Figures 10.3 and 10.4.)

orgasm a series of rhythmic contractions of the muscles of the vaginal walls or the penis, also the third and shortest phase of sexual response.

semen fluid released from the penis at orgasm that contains the sperm.

resolution the final phase of the sexual response in which the body is returned to a normal state.

refractory period time period in males just after orgasm in which the male cannot become aroused or achieve erection.

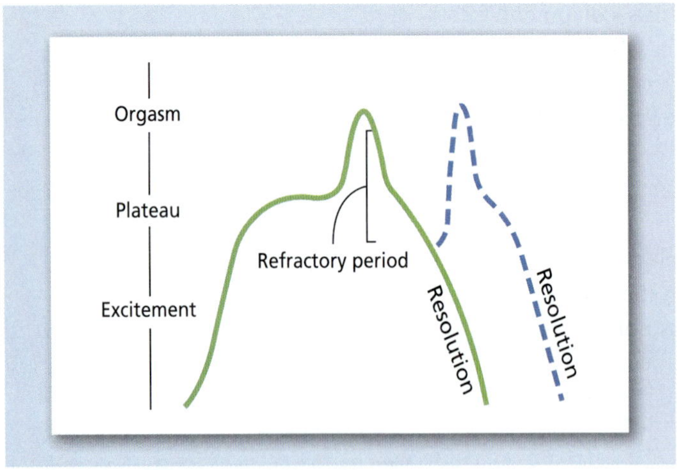

Figure 10.3 The Male Sexual-Response Cycle

A male experiences sexual arousal (excitement), a plateau lasting a few seconds to a few minutes, orgasm, and then experiences a refractory period during which another erection is not yet possible. This refractory period can last for several minutes to several hours and tends to increase in length with age. Resolution, in which the body returns to its prearousal state, is last.

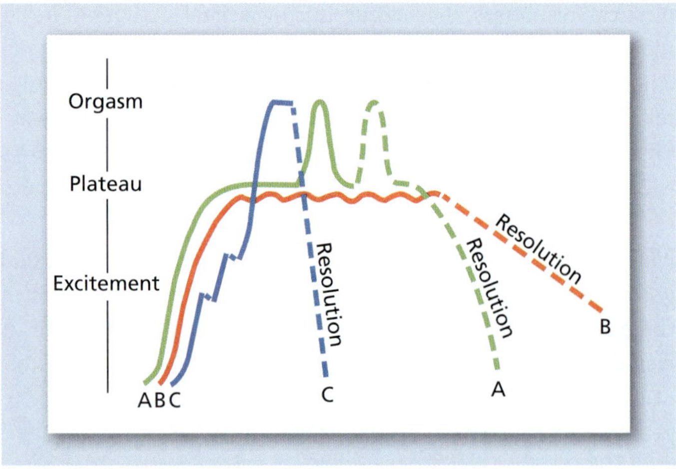

Figure 10.4 The Female Sexual-Response Cycle

Women can experience several different patterns of sexual response. In Pattern A, a woman experiences excitement, a plateau, and orgasm in a manner similar to a man. Unlike a man, the woman does not have a refractory period and can experience several orgasms before entering resolution. In Pattern B, there is a longer plateau period but no orgasm, and in Pattern C, the woman goes from excitement to orgasm to a quick resolution without experiencing a plateau period.

classic studies in psychology

Masters and Johnson's Observational Study of the Human Sexual Response

William Masters and Virginia Johnson pioneered the first direct observational study of human sexual behavior. Their study stirred up tremendous controversy in an era that feared that the study of human sexuality would undermine the structure of the family and society. Masters obtained permission from his department chair at the Washington University School of Medicine in St. Louis, Missouri, in 1954. He then assembled an advisory board composed of the police commissioner, a newspaper publisher, and several prominent religious leaders, in addition to the university's chancellor. Together, they accomplished a feat that seems incredible in today's media-driven world: They convinced the press to keep completely quiet about this research into human sexuality for the next 12 years (Kolodny, 2001).

Such research had to be conducted discreetly, as even Masters's choice of subjects was controversial. His initial studies in 1955 and 1956 were done entirely with prostitutes. He conducted interviews with them and observed them at work. Although this research was never published, he used the opportunity to think about what kind of instrumentation he would need to properly measure the sexual responses in a more controlled setting. Together with psychologist Virginia Johnson, Masters devised equipment that would allow them to measure sexual responses in humans in a laboratory setting. These machines were similar to a polygraph machine (a lie detector) but much more complex in their design and the particular physiological responses (for example, heart rate, body temperature) they measured. Masters and Johnson also used photography and direct observation in the laboratory settings, using prostitutes and other volunteers as subjects.

Dr. William Masters and Dr. Virginia Johnson examined human sexuality by measuring physiological responses in a laboratory. Their subjects were volunteers, many of whom were prostitutes, a fact that caused an uproar when their research became public.

The publication of *Human Sexual Response* in 1966 was the end result of the 12 years of research. Masters and Johnson became instant celebrities and the book itself became a best seller. This was the beginning of a partnership that lasted over 30 years. That partnership not only changed many people's attitudes about what was sexually normal but also challenged many sexual myths and created the field of sex therapy. Although direct observational studies can have the disadvantage of affecting the participant's behavior, the work of Masters and Johnson has remained some of the most important work in the field of human sexuality and is still used in sex therapy and sex education, and by infertility and conception experts (Kolodny, 2001; Masters, Johnson, & Kolodny, 1995).

Questions for Further Discussion

1. Would researchers today be able to convince the press (newspapers, magazines, and television) to keep research into human sexuality secret, as Masters did?
2. What problems with their research might have come from the fact that many of their participants were prostitutes?
3. In what ways might this kind of research be easier to conduct today?
4. In what ways might this kind of research be more difficult to conduct today?

10.5 CONCEPT MAP

- Masters and Johnson discovered the four stages of the human sexual-response cycle through direct observation and measurement; study was highly controversial

Human Sexual Behavior

- **sexual-response stages** are similar in both females and males but not identical (see Figs. 10.3 and 10.4)
  - **phase 1: excitement** — beginning of sexual arousal/preparation for intercourse (↑ pulse/blood pressure/breathing rate)
    - females: clitoris swells, vaginal lips open, vagina moistens
    - males: penis becomes erect, testes pull up, scrotum tightens
    - nipples harden/become erect in both sexes
  - **phase 2: plateau**
    - females: outer vagina swells and outer lips flush due to ↑ blood flow, clitoris retracts under clitoral hood
    - males: penis becomes more erect, may release a few drops of seminal fluid
  - **phase 3: orgasm**
    - shortest stage, consists of series of rhythmic muscular contractions
    - females can experience multiple orgasms; males typically only have one orgasm that results in release of seminal fluid/sperm
  - **phase 4: resolution** — return of the body to prearousal state; males have a refractory period during which another erection is not possible

PRACTICE quiz How much do you remember? ANSWERS ON PAGE AK-2.

Pick the best answer.

1. Which of the following was NOT one of the reasons that Masters and Johnson's research was considered controversial?
   a. They used prostitutes as participants.
   b. They were doing a study about sexual behavior.
   c. No one had ever studied sexual behavior before this.
   d. They were observing and taking pictures of people engaging in sexual activity.
2. In which of the phases of sexual response does the genital area undergo a series of muscular contractions?
   a. excitement
   b. plateau
   c. orgasm
   d. resolution
3. Which phase of the sexual response is typically the shortest, lasting a few seconds to several minutes?
   a. excitement
   b. plateau
   c. orgasm
   d. resolution
4. In which phase does the refractory period occur for men?
   a. excitement
   b. plateau
   c. orgasm
   d. resolution

DIFFERENT TYPES OF SEXUAL BEHAVIOR

10.6 What did the early and most recent surveys of human sexual behavior reveal?

While Masters and Johnson focused their research on the physiological responses that occur during the sexual act, other researchers had already been studying the different forms of sexual behavior. The study of sexual behavior is not the study of the sex act, but rather when, with whom, and under what circumstances sexual acts take place. Although there were other attempts to study human sexual behavior before the mid-twentieth-century studies of Alfred Kinsey (Kinsey et al., 1948; Kinsey et al., 1953), his original work remains an important source of information concerning the different ways in which people engage in the sex act. A movie based on Kinsey's life and work was released in the United States in 2004. Even more than half a century later, Kinsey's work is still so controversial that many movie theaters in the United States refused to show the film.

What were the findings of the report?

THE KINSEY STUDY In 1948, zoologist Alfred Kinsey published a controversial report on the results of a massive survey of sexual behavior collected from 1938 forward (Kinsey et al., 1948). His findings concerning the frequency of behavior such as masturbation, anal sex, and premarital sex rocked many people, who were apparently not ready to believe that so many people had tried alternative sexual behaviors. Kinsey believed that sexual orientation was not an either/or situation in which one is either completely heterosexual or completely homosexual but instead that sexual orientation is on a continuum,* with some people falling at either extreme and some falling closer to the middle. The idea that there were many people who fit into that middle range of sexual orientation was shocking and, for many at that time, unbelievable. (See Table 10.1.)

Kinsey used highly trained interviewers who conducted face-to-face interviews with the participants, who were all male in the original study. A later survey was published in 1953 that dealt exclusively with females (Kinsey et al., 1953). The participants were volunteers supposedly from both rural and urban areas and from different socioeconomic, religious, and educational backgrounds. In reality, a large portion of the participants were well-educated, urban, young Protestants. Table 10.2 lists some of the more interesting findings of the Kinsey study.

Although Kinsey's data are still quoted in many discussions of sexual behavior, his original surveys were far from perfect. As stated earlier, the participants were almost exclusively white, middle class, and college educated. Older people, those who lived in rural regions, and less educated people were not well represented. Some critics claimed that Kinsey gave far more attention to sexual behavior that was considered

Table 10.1

Kinsey and Colleagues' (1948) Rating Scale for Sexual Orientation

0	1	2	3	4	5	6
Exclusively heterosexual	Predominantly heterosexual; only incidentally homosexual	Predominantly heterosexual; more than incidentally homosexual	Equally heterosexual and homosexual	Predominantly homosexual; more than incidentally heterosexual	Predominantly homosexual; only incidentally heterosexual	Exclusively homosexual

Source: Reprinted with permission of the Kinsey Institute for Research in Sex, Gender, and Reproduction, Inc.

*continuum: a sequence of values, elements, or behavior that varies by small degrees.

Table 10.2

Key Findings From Kinsey's Sexual Behavior Surveys

Males reporting anal sex with spouse: 11 percent.
Nearly 46 percent of males had bisexual experiences.
Between 6 and 14 percent of females had bisexual experiences.
Whereas nearly 21 percent of the males had experienced intercourse at age 16, only 6 percent of females had done so.
Males reporting premarital sex: 67 to 98 percent (varied by economic level).
Females reporting premarital sex: 50 percent.
Nearly 50 percent of all married males had some extramarital experiences, whereas 26 percent of married females had extramarital experiences.
About 10 percent of males were predominantly homosexual.
Between 2 and 6 percent of females were predominantly homosexual.
Males who reported masturbating: 92 percent.
Females who reported masturbating: 62 percent.
Gebhard & Johnson (1979/1998).

unusual or abnormal than he did to "normal" sexual behavior (Geddes, 1954). Also, Kinsey's surveys were no less susceptible to the exaggerations, falsifications, and errors of any method using self-report techniques. Finally, a face-to-face interview might cause some people being interviewed to be inhibited about admitting to certain kinds of sexual behavior, or others might exaggerate wildly, increasing the likelihood of inaccurate data.

Alfred Kinsey conducted many of his interviews face to face, as seen here. How might having to answer questions about one's sexual behavior be affected by Kinsey's presence?

THE JANUS REPORT In 1993, Dr. Samuel S. Janus and Dr. Cynthia L. Janus published the results of the first large-scale study of human sexual behavior since those of Kinsey and colleagues (1948) and Masters and Johnson (1966). This national survey, begun in 1983, sampled 3,000 people from all 48 mainland states. Survey respondents ranged in age from 18 to over 65 years old from all levels of marital status, educational backgrounds, and geographical regions in the United States.

One finding of this massive survey was that nearly 80 percent of men and 70 percent of women had masturbated (although about a fourth to a third stated that this occurred rarely). Other responses indicated that 19 percent of men and nearly 8 percent of women had been involved in full sexual intercourse by age 14. Premarital sex was more commonly reported in men than in women (67 percent for males, 46 percent for females), and men were nearly twice as likely as women to report having had at least one extramarital affair. More than a fifth of the male respondents and only slightly fewer female respondents reported having at least one homosexual experience, but only 9 percent of males and 5 percent of females identified themselves as predominantly homosexual.

A more recent survey highlights the fact that age is not necessarily a barrier to being sexually active. The survey of over 3,000 people aged 57 to 85 found that many people are sexually active well into their 80s (Lindau et al., 2007). The most common barriers to sexual activity were health problems or lack of a partner rather than a lack of desire.

Of course, surveys have their problems as stated earlier. One possible problem might occur when asking the question, "at what age did you first have sex?" A recent study (Sanders et al., 2010) reports that not everyone means the same thing by the

sexual orientation a person's sexual attraction and affection for members of either the opposite or the same sex.

heterosexual person attracted to the opposite sex.

homosexual person attracted to the same sex.

bisexual person attracted to both men and women.

words, "have sex" or "had sex." In a sample of people 18 to 96 years old, 30 percent did not consider oral sex to be sex. Many older men—nearly a fourth of those surveyed—did not consider penile–vaginal intercourse to be sex! Some thought it wasn't sex if there was no orgasm. There was simply little agreement among survey participants as to what "having sex" really means, and researchers examining sexual behavior through the survey method should be very aware of this possible confounding.

SEXUAL ORIENTATION

The term **sexual orientation** refers to a person's sexual attraction and affection for members of either the opposite or the same sex. One of the more important questions that researchers are trying to answer is whether sexual orientation is the product of learning and experience or if it is biological in origin.

10.7 How do different sexual orientations develop?

HETEROSEXUAL The most common sexual orientation is **heterosexual**, in which people are sexually attracted to members of the opposite physical sex, as in a man being attracted to a woman or vice versa. (The Greek word *hetero* means "other," so *heterosexual* means "other sexual" or attraction for the other sex.) Heterosexuality is a socially acceptable form of sexual behavior in all cultures.

HOMOSEXUAL It is difficult to get an accurate percentage for **homosexual** orientation or sexual attraction to members of one's own sex. (The Greek word *homo* means "same.") The problem concerns the discrimination, prejudice, and mistreatment that homosexual people face in most cultures, making it more likely that a homosexual person will lie about his or her sexual orientation to avoid such negative treatment. A national survey estimates that about 2.3 percent of men and 1.3 percent of women aged 15 to 44 years consider themselves to be homosexuals, meaning that their sexual orientations are exclusively or predominantly homosexual (Mosher et al., 2005).

If people have had a homosexual experience as well as heterosexual ones, does that make them bisexuals?

If people have had a homosexual experience as well as heterosexual ones, does that make them bisexuals?

BISEXUAL A person who is **bisexual** may be either male or female and is attracted to both sexes. In the same national survey, only 1.8 percent of the men and 2.8 percent of the women considered themselves to be bisexual (Mosher et al., 2005). (It should be noted that many people experiment with alternative sexual behavior before deciding upon their true sexual identity; one bisexual experience does not make a person bisexual any more than one homosexual experience makes a person homosexual.)

Bisexual people do not necessarily have relationships with both men and women during the same period of time and may vary in the degree of attraction to one sex or the other over time. Many bisexuals may not act on their desires but instead have a long-term monogamous relationship with only one partner.

The survey also found that a nearly equal percentage of men and women—just fewer than 4 percent—considered themselves to be "something else." Obviously, sexual orientation is not as clearly defined as many people have assumed.

Homosexuality is a sexual orientation that has faced discrimination and prejudice in many cultures. Shelly Bailes and Ellen Pontac, partners for 34 years, highlight the fact that their "coupleness" and a sense of commitment are not limited to heterosexual pairs alone.

DEVELOPMENT OF SEXUAL ORIENTATION Although heterosexuality may be socially acceptable across cultures, there are various cultures in which homosexuality and bisexuality are not considered acceptable and in which people of those orientations have faced prejudice, discrimination, harassment, and much worse. Although attitudes in some of these cultures are beginning to change to more positive ones (Loftus, 2001; Tucker & Potocky-Tripodi, 2006), full acceptance of alternatives to heterosexuality is still a long way off.

Young people who are coming to terms with their identities and sexual orientation seem to have great difficulty when faced with being homosexual, bisexual, or transgender. These adolescents are at higher risk than their heterosexual peers for substance abuse, sexually risky behavior, eating disorders, suicidal thinking, and victimization by others (Coker et al., 2009; Zhao et al., 2010). When identification of one's sense of self as homosexual is paired with being another type of social minority (such as Asian American or Pacific Islanders living in the United States), the stresses and pressures are compounded (Hahm & Adkins, 2009). In the cultures from which these young people's families originate, traditional values make homosexuality a dishonor and shame to the family.

Is sexual orientation a product of the environment, biology, or both?

Is sexual orientation a product of the environment, biology, or both?

This is a very controversial issue for both heterosexuals and homosexuals (Diamond, 1995). If homosexuality is a product of upbringing and environmental experiences, it can be assumed to be a behavior that can be changed, placing a burden of choice to be "normal" or "abnormal" squarely on the shoulders of homosexual people. If it is biological, either through genetic influences or hormonal influences during pregnancy, then it can be seen as a behavior that is no more a choice than whether the infant is born a male or a female. The implications of homosexuality as biological lead to some volatile* issues: If it is not a choice or a learned behavior pattern, then society will no longer be able to expect or demand that homosexuals change their sexual behavior or orientation. Homosexuality becomes an issue of diversity rather than socially unacceptable behavior. See Table 10.3 for a look at when gay or bisexual college students said they first knew that they were different from their peers in their sexual orientation.

In the past several decades, a large body of research in the areas of biological differences in the brains of heterosexual and homosexual males, genetic influences on sexual orientation, and even prenatal influences on sexual orientation has been amassed by various scientists. One of the earliest studies, for example, found that severe stress experienced by pregnant women during the second trimester of pregnancy (the time during which the sexual differences in genitalia are formed) results in a significantly higher chance of any male children becoming homosexual in orientation (Ellis et al., 1988). Another study found that homosexual men and heterosexual women respond similarly (and quite differently than heterosexual men) to a testosterone-based pheromone (glandular chemical) that is secreted in perspiration (Savic et al., 2005). **Watch** on **mypsychlab.com**

Watch a video about sexual orientation on **mypsychlab.com**

Table 10.3

When Gay or Bisexual College Students Say They Became Aware of Their Sexual Orientation

AGE	FEMALE	MALE
Grade school	11%	17%
Junior high	6%	20%
High school	46%	50%
College	37%	13%

Source: Elliott & Brantley (1997).

*volatile: explosive.

Birth order has also been the subject of research in this area, with studies suggesting that the more older brothers a man has, the more likely the younger man is to be homosexual in orientation (Blanchard, 2001; McConaghy et al., 2006). The hypothesis is that with each male birth, the mother of these males develops a kind of "antibody" effect against the Y chromosome and these antibodies pass through the placenta and affect the sexual orientation of the later born males.

Finally, a recent study used neuroimaging techniques on heterosexual men and women and homosexual men and women, finding that the heterosexual men and homosexual women seemed neurologically similar when compared to homosexual men and heterosexual women, who were in turn neurologically similar to each other (Savic & Lindström, 2008).

The evidence for genetic influences on sexual orientation is increasingly convincing. In studies of male and female homosexuals who have identical twins, fraternal twins, or adopted siblings, researchers found that 52 percent of the identical twin siblings were also gay, compared to 22 percent of the fraternal twins and only 11 percent of the adopted brothers and sisters (Bailey & Pillard, 1991). In a similar study with lesbian women only, 48 percent of identical twins were also gay compared to 16 percent of the fraternal twins and 6 percent of the adopted siblings (Bailey et al., 1993). Other research along similar lines has supported these findings (Bailey et al., 2000; Dawood et al., 2000). However, these findings should be interpreted cautiously. Twin studies are difficult to conduct without the influence of environment on behavior. Even twins who are raised apart tend to be reared in similar environments, so that the influence of learning and experience on sexual orientation cannot be entirely ruled out.

Some research suggests that homosexuality may be transmitted by genes carried on the X chromosome, which is passed from mother to son but not from father to son. In 33 out of 40 homosexual brothers, Hamer and colleagues (Hamer et al., 1993) found an area on the X chromosome (in a location called Xq28) that contains several hundred genes that the homosexual brothers had in common in every case, even though other genes on that chromosome were different. This was taken as evidence that the brothers had both inherited a set of genes, donated on the mother's X chromosome, that might be responsible for their sexual orientation. These findings have been supported in other research as well (Hu et al., 1994; Turner, 1995).

One of the most common behavioral findings about male homosexuals is that they are consistently feminine as children, according to developmental psychologist J. Michael Bailey (Bailey & Zucker, 1995). Bailey has determined that about three fourths of feminine boys (defined as boys who are uninterested in sports or rough play, desire to be girls, or have a reputation as a "sissy") are homosexual as adults, a far greater rate than in the general population of males. Bailey and colleague Ken Zucker interpret these findings as further support for the biological foundations of sexual orientation. Of course, those differences in childhood behavior could also have been the result of attention and other forms of reinforcement from the social environment. It is simply a very difficult task to separate the environmental influences on any aspect of behavior from the biological ones. One thing is certain: The issue of what causes sexual orientation will continue to generate research and controversy for a long time to come.

Some scientists have wondered why homosexuality still exists, because from an evolutionary point of view—if it is genetic—the genes for homosexuality should have been removed from the gene pool long ago. The following special section takes a look at this issue.

issues in psychology

What Is the Evolutionary Purpose of Homosexuality?

Homosexuals do not often reproduce, so why hasn't the trait gone away? One recent theory has to do with something called the "kin selection hypothesis." Even though a homosexual member of a family may not reproduce himself or herself, by nurturing other family members such as nieces and nephews, they would be helping to continue many of their own genes through those kin (Iemmola & Camperio Ciani, 2008; Rahman & Hull, 2005). In Samoa, researchers Paul Vasey and Doug VanderLaan (Vasey & VanderLaan, 2010) studied the *fa'afafine*, men who prefer men as sexual partners and are accepted within that culture as neither man nor woman, much as the winkte in Lakota culture. The researchers wanted to see if the kin selection hypothesis was a valid hypothesis in this society, so they gave fa'afafine, women, and heterosexual men in this culture a survey to measure their willingness to help nieces and nephews in various ways, as well as their willingness to do these same things for unrelated children. The survey results strongly support the kin selection hypothesis, with the fa'afafine far more likely than the women or heterosexual men to help their own kin rather than children in general.

Questions for Further Discussion

1. Samoan culture is not like Western culture. Would the kin selection hypothesis work in the United States to explain homosexuality's continued existence?
2. How do Western homosexual men and women transmit or protect their own genetic material?

10.6 10.7 CONCEPT MAP

Human Sexual Behavior

differences in sexual behavior
- Kinsey pioneered the study of different types of sexual behavior through face-to-face surveys; study was highly controversial; sampling/representativeness questioned
  - suggested sexual orientation occurred on a continuum, not an either/or basis (see Table 10.1)
- the Janus Report (first large-scale survey since Kinsey) examined both normal and deviant sexual behavior

sexual orientation person's sexual attraction and affection for members of the opposite or same sex
- key concepts
  - **heterosexuality:** attraction to members of the opposite sex; most common and socially acceptable
  - **homosexuality:** attraction to members of one's own sex
  - **bisexuality:** attraction to members of both sexes
- sexual orientation is likely the product of both biology (i.e., brain structure, genetics) and environment; presence of biological foundations has implications for societal definitions of diversity versus deviance

PRACTICE quiz How much do you remember? ANSWERS ON PAGE AK-2.

Pick the best answer.

1. The first scientifically based survey of human sexual behavior was designed and carried out by ________.
   a. personality psychologists.
   b. a physiological psychologist.
   c. a zoologist.
   d. a psychiatrist.
2. In Kinsey's original data, more ________ than ________ reported having bisexual experiences.
   a. homosexuals; heterosexuals
   b. heterosexuals; homosexuals
   c. women; men
   d. men; women

(continued)

3. Which group was NOT one of the groups poorly represented in the Kinsey study?
   a. older people
   b. white, middle class
   c. people with little education
   d. people living in rural areas
4. Compared to the Kinsey data, the data from the Janus report revealed the age of the first sexual experience for about 20 percent of the men and 8 percent of the women to be ________.
   a. 14.
   b. 16.
   c. 17.
   d. 12.
5. The Savic et al. 2005 study found that homosexual men responded to a pheromone in the same way as
   a. heterosexual men
   b. transsexual men
   c. heterosexual women
   d. homosexual women

Sexual Dysfunctions and Problems

10.8 How do physical and psychological sexual problems differ?

What about when people have problems with sex, like impotence?

What about when people have problems with sex, like impotence?

A **sexual dysfunction** is a problem with sexual functioning, or with the actual physical workings of the sex act. Paraphilias are a category of sexual problems that are more behavioral than physical; they will be touched on a bit later. Sexual dysfunctions and problems can be caused by purely *organic factors* (i.e., illness or side effects from drugs), *sociocultural factors* (such as negative attitudes toward sexual behavior), or *psychological factors* stemming from either personality problems, traumatic events, or relationship problems. More commonly, such problems can stem from a combination of these influences.

Organic factors include physical problems such as illnesses, side effects from medication, the effects of surgeries, physical disabilities, and even the use of illegal and legal drugs, such as cocaine, alcohol, and nicotine. Chronic illnesses such as diabetes, cancer, or strokes also belong in this category of factors.

Former Surgeon General Joycelyn Elders advocated teaching young people masturbation as a safe alternative to sexual intercourse. One year later (1994) then President Clinton fired her as a result of this and other controversies.

Sociocultural influences on sexual attitudes and behavior also exist and may be a source of psychological stress leading to sexual dysfunction. In the United States and some other Western cultures, people may have experienced instruction from their parents (both direct and indirect teaching) that actually influenced them to form negative attitudes toward sex and sexual activities, such as masturbation. Some religious upbringing may also foster a sense of guilt about sex or an interest in sex. In one study, a relationship between conservative, religious traditionalism and sexual attitudes was found for married members of Jewish, Protestant, and Catholic faiths (Purcell, 1985). The research showed that the more conservative and traditional the married couples were, the less interest and pleasure they took in sexual activity and the more they experienced guilt, shame, and sexual inhibitions. In non-Western cultures, such as that of India, sex may be seen as not only a duty of married couples but also a joy to be celebrated within the context of producing children (Gupta, 1994). In particular, women in India may have an entirely different attitude toward sex because a woman's status in Indian culture depends greatly on her ability to bear children.

Psychological stressors also include individual psychological problems, such as low self-esteem, anxiety over performance of the sex act, depression, self-consciousness about one's body image, anxiety disorders, or a history of previous sexual abuse or assault. For example, women who were sexually molested in childhood are 2 to 4 times more likely to suffer from pain in the pelvic area on a chronic basis (Reiter & Milburn, 1994).

Another source of psychological stress leading to sexual dysfunctions is the relationship between the two sexual partners. The sexual dysfunction may be only an outward symptom of an underlying problem with the relationship. Examples of such problems might be unresolved arguments, resentment of the partner who feels he or she has less power and influence over the relationship, lack of trust, infidelities, lack of physical attractiveness to the partner, or even lack of sexual skills on the part of one or both partners (Alperstein, 2001).

sexual dysfunction a problem in sexual functioning.

ORGANIC OR STRESS-INDUCED DYSFUNCTIONS

Organic or **stress-induced dysfunctions** are types of sexual problems caused by physical disorders, such as nerve damage, or by psychological stress, such as worry and anxiety. (Because body and mind influence each other's functioning, it is difficult to separate these dysfunctions into purely organic and purely stress-induced disorders.) Sexual dysfunctions involve problems in three possible areas of sexual activity: sexual interest, arousal, and response.

How common are problems like these—aren't they pretty rare?

A nationwide survey found that about 43 percent of women and 31 percent of men report having some sort of sexual dysfunction at the time of this survey (Laumann et al., 1999). In the stress-filled world that many people live in today, it isn't all that surprising to find such a high degree of dysfunction. In fact, the figures may actually be higher than those reported in the survey. As stated in Chapter One, one of the hazards of doing survey research is that people don't always tell the truth. If a person is going to lie about sexual problems, the most likely lie (or distorted truth) would probably be to deny or minimize such problems.

Table 10.4 lists some of the more common physical sexual dysfunctions that may be caused by organic factors or psychological stressors such as those discussed at the beginning of this section.

For all of the sexual dysfunctions, treatment can include medication, psychotherapy, hormone therapy, stress reduction, and behavioral training. For example, Masters and Johnson (1970) recommended a technique called *sensate focus* for treatment of premature ejaculation, in which each member of a couple engages in a series of exercises meant to focus attention on his or her own sensual experiences during various stages of sexual arousal and activity. Male erectile disorder is now commonly treated with drug therapy.

THE PARAPHILIAS

The other major category of sexual problems is behavioral rather than organic in nature. **Paraphilia** (also called *atypical sexual behavior*) is a disorder in which the person either prefers, or must, achieve sexual arousal and fulfillment through sexual behavior that is unusual or not socially acceptable.

organic or **stress-induced dysfunction** sexual problem caused by physical disorder or psychological stress.

paraphilia a sexual disorder in which the person's preferred method of sexual arousal and fulfillment is through sexual behavior that is unusual or socially unacceptable.

How common are problems like these—aren't they pretty rare?

Erectile dysfunction is a major concern to many men who are unable to engage in sexual intercourse with their partners. Medications help some men function once again. Does this ad seem to promise more than just the revival of sexual functioning?

Table 10.4

Organic or Stress-Induced Dysfunctions

Sexual Desire Disorders	Hypoactive sexual desire disorder: Ongoing, abnormally low desire for sexual activity.
	Sexual aversion disorder: Fear and disgust of sexual contact.
Sexual Arousal Disorders	Female sexual arousal disorder: Desire for sexual activity is present, but physical discomfort and a lack of pleasure are experienced during sexual activity.
	Male erectile disorder: A male cannot maintain an erection long enough to complete the sexual act.
Orgasmic Disorders	Male orgasmic disorder: A male cannot achieve orgasm through vaginal stimulation, even though fully aroused.
	Female orgasmic disorder: A female cannot achieve an orgasm even though fully aroused.
	Premature ejaculation: Some men experience orgasm shortly after penetration, which can cause feelings of sexual inadequacy because the partner does not have time to achieve orgasm.
Sexual Pain Disorders	Vaginismus: Persistent contractions of the vaginal muscles, causing sexual intercourse to be painful or impossible.
	Dyspareunia: Pain in the genitals that can occur before, during, or after intercourse; can be experienced by either sex.

sexually transmitted infection (STI) an infection spread primarily through sexual contract.

AIDS or **acquired immune deficiency syndrome** sexually transmitted viral disorder that causes deterioration of the immune system and eventually results in death due to complicating infections that the body can no longer fight.

Sexually Transmitted Infections

10.9 **What are sexually transmitted infections, and what can be done to prevent the spread of these disorders?**

One of the consequences of unprotected sexual contact is the risk of contracting a **sexually transmitted infection (STI)**, an infection spread primarily through sexual contract. Some STIs affect the sex organs themselves, whereas others have broader and more life-threatening effects. The bacterial infections are quite treatable with antibiotics, but those caused by viruses are more difficult to treat and are often incurable. Even curable bacterial infections can cause serious problems if left untreated, and some bacterial infections are difficult to detect because the symptoms in at least one sex are not all that noticeable. For example, *chlamydia*, listed in Table 10.5, is the most common STI and is easily treated but may go undetected in women because there are few symptoms or no symptoms noticed. If left untreated, chlamydia can cause *pelvic inflammatory disorder (PID)*, a condition that can damage the lining of the uterus and the fallopian tubes as well as the ovaries and other nearby structures. Ten percent of women in the United States will develop PID during their childbearing years (Miller & Graves, 2000). Table 10.5 lists some of the more common sexually transmitted infections and their causes.

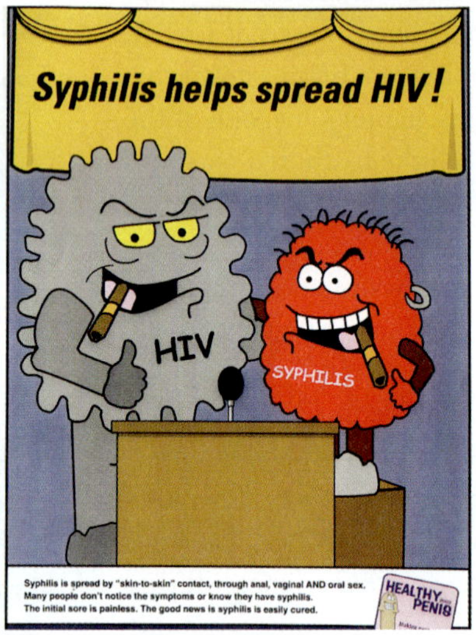

These posters warning against sexually transmitted infections hang in a youth center in San Francisco, California. Adolescents often fail to take precautions against such infections and are becoming sexually active at younger ages, making them a high-risk group for STIs.

AIDS

Without a doubt, the one sexually transmitted infection that nearly everyone knows something about is **AIDS**, or **acquired immune deficiency syndrome**. AIDS is caused by a viral infection, specifically the *human immunodeficiency virus*, or *HIV*. A person who has HIV does not necessarily have AIDS but is at risk for developing

Table 10.5
Common Sexually Transmitted Infections

STI	CAUSE	SYMPTOMS
Chlamydia	Bacterial infection that grows within the body's cells	Swollen testicles, discharge, burning during urination; women may experience no symptoms
Syphilis	Bacterial infection	Sores that appear on or in the genital area and can spread to other body parts and the brain
Gonorrhea	Bacterial infection that grows rapidly in warm, moist areas of the body (mouth, anus, throat, genitalia)	In men, a foul-smelling, cloudy discharge from the penis, burning upon urination; in women, inflamed cervix, light vaginal discharge
Genital Herpes	Herpes simplex virus	Sores on the genital area; itching, burning, throbbing, "pins-and-needles" sensations where sores are about to appear
Genital Warts	Human papillomavirus (HPV)	Warty growths on the genitalia
AIDS	Human immunodeficiency virus (HIV)	Severe malfunction and eventual breakdown of the immune system

AIDS in the future. HIV wears down the body's immune system, making the body vulnerable to "opportunistic" infections—infections caused by bacteria or viruses that, while harmless in a healthy immune system, will take hold when the immune system is weakened. When a person with HIV develops one of these types of infections or when their immune system's T-cell count goes below a certain level, the person is said to have AIDS (Folkman & Chesney, 1995).

I've heard a lot of stories about how people can get AIDS. What's the real story?

I've heard a lot of stories about how people can get AIDS. What's the real story?

HIV can be transmitted to a person from anyone who has the infection, even if that person doesn't look sick. He or she might not have tested positive for HIV yet but is still able to transmit the virus in one of three ways:

- Having unprotected vaginal, oral, or anal sexual contact.
- Sharing a needle (used to take drugs).
- Giving birth to a baby while infected. The virus can be transmitted to the baby in this way, as can breast-feeding the baby while infected (Kourtis et al., 2001).

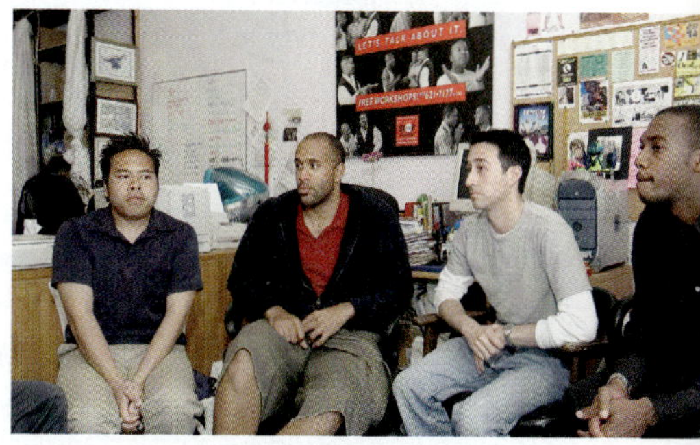

These young men are attending a counseling session at a community-based AIDS clinic. They do not necessarily have AIDS; the purpose of this particular group is to help educate these men and others like them in ways to prevent HIV infections. With no cure as yet, prevention is the best defense against AIDS. Remember, AIDS can affect women and men of all sexual orientations.

Blood, vaginal fluid, semen, and breast milk are the main ways in which HIV is passed from the infected person to an uninfected person. Contrary to a lot of myths about HIV, there is no scientific proof or documented cases of HIV being passed through tears or ordinary saliva. Kissing an infected person will not result in transmission, although it is possible to transmit the virus through oral sex or, rarely, through deep kissing when there are open sores or bleeding gums in the mouth of either party. More troubling is the finding that HIV can be transmitted to children who are fed by mothers who have "prechewed" food (a practice that occurs in several countries and cultures, including that of the United States). Although HIV cannot normally be transmitted through saliva, the women studied in this report all had sores or inflammations in their mouths, or the infants had cuts associated with teething in their mouths (Guar, 2008).

By the end of the year 2007, the number of estimated cases of AIDS in the United States had reached nearly half a million people, with the highest estimates by state existing in California, Florida, New York, and Texas (Centers for Disease Control and Prevention [CDC], 2009). Over a quarter of a million people in the United States are living with HIV but not AIDS. However, this number is probably a vast underestimate, as many HIV infections remain undiagnosed or unreported. The CDC estimates that about 1.1 million adults and adolescents in total are currently living with HIV in the United States (Centers for Disease Control, 2008).

In other cultures, AIDS is also taking a devastating toll. The most heavily hit areas in the world right now are the countries of sub-Saharan Africa, where an estimated 22.4 million people were living with HIV at the end of 2007—nearly two thirds of the total HIV infections in the world (Joint United Nations Programme on HIV/AIDS [UNAIDS, 2009b]). In 2008, 1.4 million people died from AIDS in these countries, and more than 14 million children were orphaned by AIDS (UNAIDS, 2007, 2009b). The Applying Psychology in Everyday Life section at the end of this chapter examines the course of AIDS in Russia—a region that is quickly becoming another AIDS "hot spot."

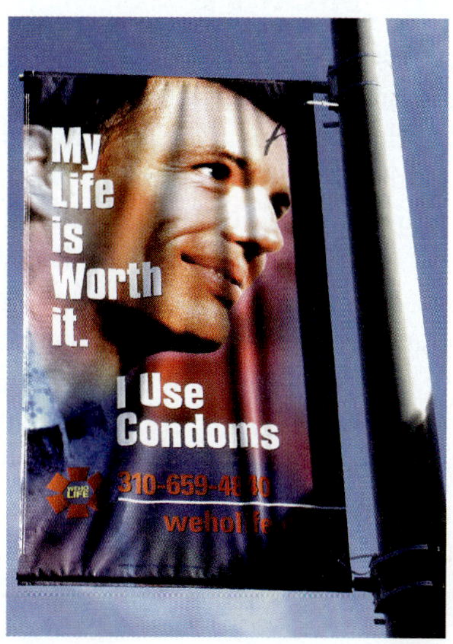

Not too many years ago, no one would have dared to advertise condoms in such a public manner. The only consequences of unsafe sex were unwanted pregnancies and serious, but not necessarily life-threatening, sexually transmitted infections. With the onslaught of the AIDS virus, safe sex has taken on a whole new meaning.

10.8 10.9

CONCEPT MAP

Sexual Dysfunctions, Problems, and Infections

- **sexual dysfunctions and problems**
  - sexual dysfunctions are problems with sexual functioning or physical aspects of the sex act (see Table 10.4)
  - paraphilias are disorders characterized by unusual or socially unacceptable sexual behaviors
- **sexually transmitted infections (STIs)**
  - infections spread through unprotected sexual contact (see Table 10.5)
    - affect sex organs or have broader, life-threatening effects
    - bacterial infections may be treatable with antibiotics if caught early; viruses are difficult to treat and may be incurable
  - acquired immune deficiency syndrome (AIDS)
    - caused by a viral infection, the human immunodeficiency virus (HIV)
    - first symptoms are often mistaken for the flu
    - onset often associated with opportunistic infections
    - has no known cure, can affect females and males of all sexual orientations, and continues to impact cultures world-wide

PRACTICE quiz How much do you remember? ANSWERS ON PAGE AK-2.

Pick the best answer.

1. Which of the following is not a sexual dysfunction stemming from an organic physical disorder?
   a. sexual desire disorder
   b. frotteurism
   c. male erectile disorder
   d. sexual aversion disorder
2. In __________, the person may have the desire for sexual activity but be unable to physically participate.
   a. sexual desire disorder
   b. sexual pain disorder
   c. sexual arousal disorder
   d. orgasmic disorder
3. If left untreated, __________ can cause pelvic inflammatory disorder in women.
   a. chlamydia
   b. syphilis
   c. genital warts
   d. AIDS
4. There is no scientific, documented proof of HIV being passed to another through __________.
   a. childbirth.
   b. blood transfusions.
   c. sharing a needle.
   d. tears or saliva.

Applying Psychology to Everyday Life: The AIDS Epidemic in Russia

While sub-Saharan Africa is still the focal point of AIDS and HIV infections for now, Russia and several surrounding countries in Eastern Europe and Central Asia are quickly becoming the center for a new and rapidly expanding epidemic of AIDS. Within the last decade, the prevalence of HIV in Russia and these other areas has nearly doubled (UNAIDS, 2009a).

What accounts for this horrific rise in AIDS cases? Drug users who often share needles are one cause. With the heavy opium-producing Afghanistan nearby, drug use is an ever-increasing problem in Russian and the surrounding region, with reports of over half a million registered drug users and nearly 30,000 drug-related deaths each year (Hamers & Downs, 2003; RIA Novosti, 2010). Then there are the sex workers: prostitutes who are not only at risk because of the nature of their work but also because of their lack of education about the transmission of HIV and their own drug use (UNAIDS, 2008b). Of course, the partners of these drug users and sex workers are also at risk. Nearly two thirds of the infections in women are caused by heterosexual contact with husbands or male lovers (Federal Service for Surveillance of Consumer Rights Protection and Human Well-Being of the Russian Federation and UNAIDS, 2008).

Another group at risk are prisoners (Dolan et al., 2007). The majority of the inmates were infected before entering the prison. Of note—one of the smallest groups responsible for the increase in AIDS and HIV infections are homosexuals (UNAIDS, 2008a). Homosexuality in Russia and the surrounding areas was once punishable by death, so it is not so surprising that there are either fewer homosexuals in those countries or, at the very least, few who are willing to reveal themselves as homosexuals.

Some researchers believe that between 2009 and 2015, Russia will experience its greatest number of AIDS-related deaths (Feshbach, 2008). Clearly, education about HIV and AIDS as well as a concerted effort to reduce the drug-using population, or, at the very least, giving them the tools necessary to reduce the risk of infection, must be a priority in the future—if there is to be one.

Questions for Further Discussion

1. Are there other countries around the world that you think might be the next site of an HIV/AIDS epidemic?
2. How would you go about trying to educate people who do not understand how HIV is spread?

chapter summary

Listen on **mypsychlab.com** Listen to an audio file of your chapter **www.mypsychlab.com**

The Physical Side of Human Sexuality

10.1 What are the physical differences between females and males?

- The female sexual organs present at birth are the primary sex characteristics of vagina, uterus, and ovaries.
- The female sexual organs that develop during puberty are secondary sex characteristics consisting of the growth spurt, onset of the menstrual cycle, breast development, widening hips, pubic hair, fat deposits, and further growth and development of the uterus, vagina, and ovaries.
- The primary male sex characteristics are the penis, scrotum, testicles, and prostate gland.
- The secondary male sex characteristics are an enlarged larynx (Adam's apple), deepening voice, facial and chest hair, pubic hair, coarser skin texture, and a large increase in height.

The Psychological Side of Human Sexuality: Gender

10.2 What is gender, and how can biology and learning influence gender-role development?

- Gender is the psychological aspects of being male or female.
- Gender roles are the culture's expectations for male and female behavior and personality.
- Gender typing is the process by which people in a culture learn the appropriate gender-role behavior.
- Gender identity is a person's sense of being male or female.
- Gender identities are formed by biological influences, in the form of hormones and chromosomes, as well as environmental influences, in the form of parenting, surroundings, and culture, on the formation of gender identity.

ISSUES IN PSYCHOLOGY: Sex Differences in the Brain

- Research has found differences between the function and structures of the male and female brain.
- Some sex differences in the brain appear to be prenatally influenced by the male and female chromosomes.

10.3 How do gender roles develop, and how can they be influenced by stereotypes or an emphasis on androgyny?

- Social learning theorists believe that gender identity is formed through reinforcement of appropriate gender behavior as well as imitation of gender models.
- Gender schema theorists believe that gender identity is a mental schema that develops gradually, influenced by the growth of the brain and organization of observed male or female behavior around the schema.
- Gender stereotyping occurs when people assign characteristics to a person based on the person's male or female status rather than actual characteristics.
- Androgyny describes people who do not limit themselves to the male or female stereotyped characteristics, instead possessing characteristics associated with both traditional masculine and feminine roles.

10.4 How do men and women differ in thinking, social behavior, and personality?

- Cognitive differences between men and women include a male advantage in mathematical and spatial skills and a female superiority in verbal skills. These differences are now less than they were previously.
- Males and females are socially taught to interact differently and express emotions differently. Men tend to talk with each other in a "report" style, whereas women tend to talk to each other in a "relate" style.

Human Sexual Behavior

10.5 What happens in the bodies of women and men during sexual intercourse?

- Masters and Johnson found four phases of human sexual response: arousal, plateau, orgasm, and resolution.

CLASSIC STUDIES IN PSYCHOLOGY: Masters and Johnson's Observational Study of the Human Sexual Response

- Masters and Johnson used volunteers, some of whom were prostitutes, and both observed and measured their physiological responses during all phases of sexual intercourse.

10.6 What did the early and most recent surveys of human sexual behavior reveal?

- Alfred Kinsey conducted a series of sexual-behavior surveys in the late 1940s and early 1950s, revealing some highly controversial findings about the kinds of sexual behavior common among people in the United States, including homosexuality, premarital sex, and extramarital sex.
- In the mid-1990s, Janus and Janus published the results of a large-scale survey of sexual behavior in the United States. Their survey results did not differ widely from those of Kinsey but they looked at many more types of sexual behavior and factors related to sexual behavior than did Kinsey's surveys.

10.7 How do different sexual orientations develop?

- Research suggests that there are biological differences between heterosexuals and homosexuals, and that there may be genetic influences as well.

ISSUES IN PSYCHOLOGY: What Is the Evolutionary Purpose of Homosexuality?

- Studies suggest that homosexuality may continue in the genetic pool because homosexuals protect their near kin, a theory called the kin selection hypothesis.

Sexual Dysfunctions and Problems

10.8 How do physical and psychological sexual problems differ?

- Sexual dysfunctions are problems with sexual functioning. They may be caused by physical problems, stress, or psychological problems.
- Organic or stress-induced dysfunctions are caused by a physical problem or by stress and can affect sexual interest, arousal, and response.
- These disorders include hypoactive sexual desire, sexual aversion, female sexual arousal disorder, male erectile disorder, male orgasmic disorder, female orgasmic disorder, premature ejaculation, vaginismus, and dyspareunia.
- The paraphilias are thought to be psychological in origin and involve sexual behavior that is unusual or not socially acceptable as a preferred way of achieving sexual pleasure.

Sexually Transmitted Infections

10.9 What are sexually transmitted infections, and what can be done to prevent the spread of these disorders?

- Sexually transmitted infections can affect the sexual organs and the ability to reproduce and may result in pain, disfigurement, and even death.
- Some common bacterial sexually transmitted infections are chlamydia, syphilis, and gonorrhea. These infections are treatable with antibiotics.
- Viral sexually transmitted infections include genital herpes (caused by the herpes simplex virus that also causes cold sores) and genital warts (caused by the human papillomavirus). Neither can be cured and both can lead to complications such as increased risk of cancer.
- Acquired immune deficiency syndrome (AIDS) is caused by a viral infection called human immunodeficency virus (HIV) that is transmitted through an exchange of blood, vaginal fluid, semen, or breast milk. Having unprotected sex with an infected person, sharing a needle with an infected person, or giving birth to or breast-feeding a baby while infected are the methods of transmission.
- AIDS wears down the immune system, opening the body up to infections that, over time, will result in death.

Applying Psychology to Everyday Life: The AIDS Epidemic in Russia

- Because of drug users, sex workers, and prisoners, HIV and AIDS have reached epidemic proportions in Russia and the surrounding countries.

test YOURSELF

ANSWERS ON PAGE AK-2.

Pick the best answer.

1. Which statement about primary sex characteristics is TRUE?
   a. They are directly involved in human reproduction.
   b. They develop during puberty.
   c. They are the same for males and females.
   d. They include the formation of breasts and growth of the beard.
2. The culture's expectations for male and female behaviors are called __________.
   a. gender roles.
   b. gender typing.
   c. gender identity.
   d. gender constancy.

3. What happened to the girls who were exposed to masculinizing hormones prenatally?
   a. They were unaffected by the hormones.
   b. They became lesbians.
   c. They became tomboys as adolescents and young adults.
   d. They became more traditionally feminine as they grew older.
4. In gender schema theory, gender identity _________.
   a. first forms as a mental concept of "boy" or "girl."
   b. is acquired through simple imitation of models.
   c. occurs through observational learning.
   d. is acquired through positive reinforcement of appropriate gender behavior.
5. Which characteristic is NOT one of the male stereotyped characteristics?
   a. aggressive
   b. unemotional
   c. changeable
   d. impatient
6. A person is said to be _________ if that person possesses both masculine and feminine personality traits that are typically positive.
   a. a hermaphrodite
   b. androgynous
   c. intersexed
   d. bisexual
7. Research suggests that differences between males and females in mathematics and verbal skills may be caused by psychological and social issues rather than biology because _________.
   a. these differences have increased in recent years.
   b. these differences have decreased in recent years.
   c. these differences have remained constant.
   d. females now score higher than males in mathematics.
8. An intersexed person is _________.
   a. a person who has sex with both men and women.
   b. another name for a homosexual.
   c. a person born with ambiguous sexual organs.
   d. another name for a heterosexual.
9. Orgasm occurs in _________.
   a. Phase 1.
   b. Phase 2.
   c. Phase 3.
   d. Phase 4.
10. The refractory period is a time during which _________.
    a. a woman cannot have another orgasm.
    b. a man cannot have another erection.
    c. a man can be erect but not have an orgasm.
    d. a woman cannot be aroused.
11. Which of the following studies of sexual behavior was not a survey?
    a. the Kinsey report
    b. the Janus report
    c. Masters and Johnson's study
    d. All of the above were surveys.
12. The most recent surveys indicate that about _________ percent of men and _________ percent of women are predominantly homosexual.
    a. 22; 17
    b. 15; 10
    c. 5; 9
    d. 9; 5
13. Bisexual people _________.
    a. have multiple relationships with men and women at the same time.
    b. are equally attracted to both sexes.
    c. can be either male or female.
    d. rarely have long-term, monogamous relationships.
14. Which of the following is not one of the three areas affected by sexual dysfunctions?
    a. sexual reproduction
    b. sexual arousal
    c. sexual interest
    d. sexual response
15. _________ is more a problem of timing than anything else.
    a. Male orgasmic disorder
    b. Female orgasmic disorder
    c. Dyspareunia
    d. Premature ejaculation
16. A woman who experiences intense contractions of the vaginal muscles, making intercourse painful, is suffering from _________.
    a. vaginismus.
    b. dyspareunia.
    c. sexual interest disorder.
    d. sexual aversion.
17. Which of the following sexually transmitted infections is not caused by a bacterial infection?
    a. genital herpes
    b. chlamydia
    c. syphilis
    d. gonorrhea
18. Charles has noticed a foul-smelling, cloudy discharge from his penis and burning when he urinates. Charles probably has _________.
    a. genital herpes.
    b. chlamydia.
    c. syphilis.
    d. gonorrhea.
19. A person is not said to have AIDS until _________.
    a. infected with HIV.
    b. the T-cell count goes below a certain level.
    c. Kaposi's sarcoma develops.
    d. the HIV bacteria count reaches a certain level.
20. Which of the following is not one of the recommendations for preventing the spread of sexually transmitted infections?
    a. Assume that your partner will take care of prevention.
    b. Have only one sexual partner; be sure that partner has currently has been tested as negative.
    c. Use condoms.
    d. Abstain from having sexual relations.

10 sexuality and gender

10.1 10.2

p. 384

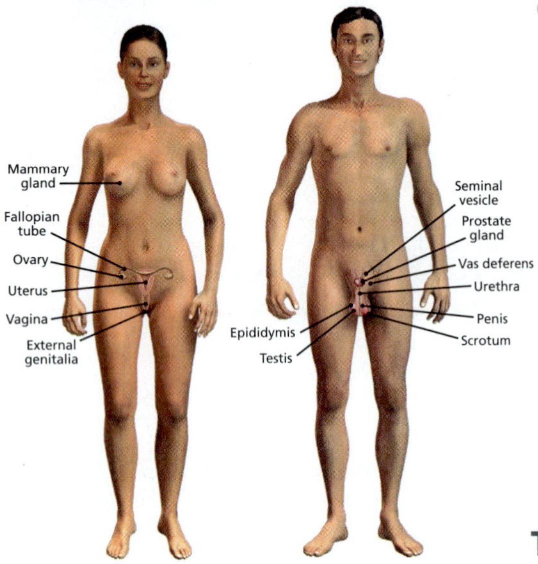

The Physical Side of Human Sexuality

- physical sex characteristics are not the same as gender, the psychological aspects of identifying as a male or female
- embryonic undifferentiated gonads develop into male or female sex organs as the result of chromosomes and hormones
  - chromosomal or hormonal defects can result in ambiguous sex organs/hermaphroditism/intersexed individuals
- **primary sexual characteristics:** present at birth, directly involved in reproduction
  - **female**
  - **male**
- **secondary sexual characteristics:** develop during puberty (indirectly involved in reproduction)
  - **female**
  - **male**

The Psychological Side of Human Sexuality: Gender

- **key concepts**
  - **gender roles:** cultural behavioral expectations for males or females
  - **gender typing:** process by which people learn gender roles
  - **gender identity:** sense of being male or female (influenced by both biology and environment)
- **gender** is defined as the psychological aspects of being masculine or feminine and is influenced by culture, individual personality, and self-identity
  - **biological influences**
  - **environmental influences**
  - **culture**

"We don't believe in pressuring the children. When the time is right, they'll choose the appropriate gender."

10.3 10.4

p. 388

The Psychological Side of Human Sexuality: Gender

- **theories of gender-role development**
  - **social learning theory**
  - **gender schema theory**
  - **gender stereotyping**
  - **androgyny**

- **gender differences**
  - **cognitive differences** (e.g., listening skills) may be present but are possibly due to psychological and social issues rather than biology
  - **social and personality differences** are often the result of stereotyped thinking about the sexes

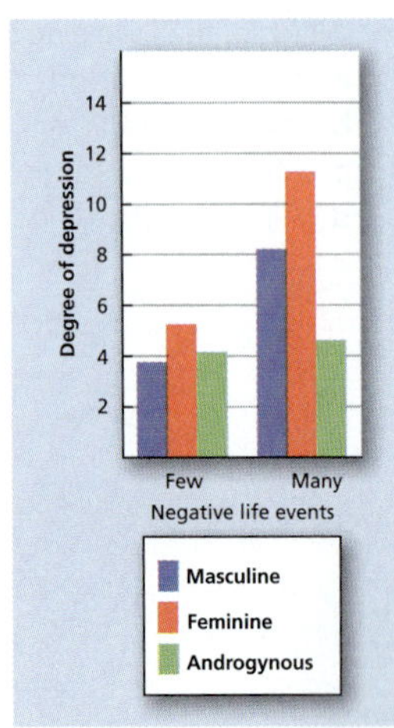

10.5 p. 391

Human Sexual Behavior

- Masters and Johnson discovered the four stages of the human sexual-response cycle through direct observation and measurement; study was highly controversial
- **sexual-response stages** are similar in both females and males but not identical
  - **phase 1: excitement**
  - **phase 2: plateau**
  - **phase 3: orgasm**
  - **phase 4: resolution**

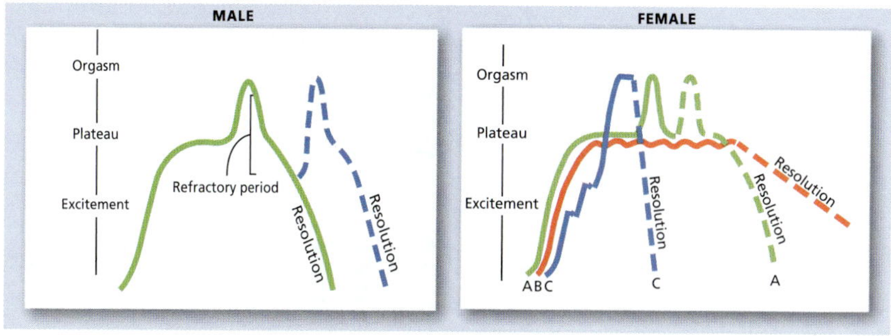

10.6 **10.7** p. 397

Human Sexual Behavior

- **differences in sexual behavior**
  - Kinsey pioneered the study of different types of sexual behavior through face-to-face surveys; study was highly controversial; sampling/representativeness questioned
  - the Janus Report (first large-scale survey since Kinsey) examined both normal and deviant sexual behavior
- **sexual orientation** person's sexual attraction and affection for members of the opposite or same sex
  - key concepts
    - **heterosexuality**
    - **homosexuality**
    - **bisexuality**
  - sexual orientation is likely the product of both biology (i.e., brain structure, genetics) and environment; presence of biological foundations has implications for societal definitions of diversity versus deviance

Table 10.3
When Gay or Bisexual College Students Say They Became Aware of Their Sexual Orientation

AGE	FEMALE	MALE
Grade school	11%	17%
Junior high	6%	20%
High school	46%	50%
College	37%	13%

Source: Elliott & Brantley (1997).

10.8 **10.9** p. 402

Sexual Dysfunctions, Problems, and Infections

- **sexual dysfunctions and problems**
  - sexual dysfunctions are problems with sexual functioning or physical aspects of the sex act (see Table 10.4)
  - paraphilias are disorders characterized by unusual or socially unacceptable sexual behaviors
- **sexually transmitted infections (STIs)**
  - infections spread through unprotected sexual contact (see Table 10.5)
  - acquired immune deficiency syndrome (AIDS)

11 stress and health

CHAPTER OUTLINE

- Stress and Stressors
- Physiological Factors: Stress and Health
- ISSUES IN PSYCHOLOGY: Health Psychology and Stress
- Coping With Stress
- APPLYING PSYCHOLOGY TO EVERYDAY LIFE: Exercising for Mental Health

LAUGHTER: THE BEST MEDICINE?

Secretary to psychologist: "Doctor, there is a patient here who thinks he is invisible."
Psychologist: "Tell him I can't see him right now."

I often dream about being carried away by a giant squirrel. Does that make me a nut?
Everyone has a photographic memory. Some just don't have film.

What's the difference between a behaviorist and a magician?
A behaviorist pulls habits out of rats!

They may not be the funniest jokes you've ever heard, but many of you probably chuckled a bit while reading them. Why begin a chapter on stress and health with a series of jokes? For many years now, psychologists and other researchers have known that humor is a great stress reliever (Berk et al., 1989, 2009; Dixon, 1980; Lefcourt et al., 1995; Wooten, 1980). In the last decade, researchers in **psychoneuroimmunology** (the study of the effects of psychological factors such as stress, emotions, thinking, and behavior on the body's disease-fighting system) have found two possible reasons for the stress-reducing benefits of laughter. In one study (Berk et al., 2008), researchers Dr. Lee Berk and Dr. Stanley Tan found that laughing significantly *increase level of* health-protecting hormones (beta-endorphins, a group of chemicals that help ease depression, and human growth hormone, which helps with immunity to diseases), but also just *looking forward* to a positive and humorous laughing experience can significantly *decrease* levels of potentially damaging hormones: cortisol, a major stress hormone, epinephrine (adrenaline), and dopac, a brain chemical that helps produce epinephrine. In another study, these researchers and their colleagues found that laughter has another health benefit: repetitive, joyous laughter causes the body to respond as if receiving moderate exercise, which enhances mood and immune system activity, lowers both bad cholesterol and blood pressure, raises good cholesterol, and decreases stress hormones (Berk et al., 2009). The moral of the story: Laugh it up!

psychoneuroimmunology the study of the effects of psychological factors such as stress, emotions, thoughts, and behavior on the immune system.

Why study health and stress?

How are they related? Stress is not a rare experience but something that all people experience in varying degrees every day. This chapter will explore the sources of stress in daily life, the factors that can make the experience of stress easier or more difficult, and how stress influences our physical and mental health. We'll finish by discussing various ways to cope with the stresses of everyday life as well as with the extraordinary experiences that arise in life that have the potential to induce stress.

learning objectives

11.1 How do psychologists define stress?

11.2 What kinds of external events can cause stress?

11.3 What are some psychological factors in stress?

11.4 How does stress affect the physical functioning of the body and its immune system?

11.5 How do cognitive factors and personality differences affect the experience of stress?

11.6 What social factors influence stress reactions?

11.7 What are some ways in which people cope with stress reactions?

11.8 How is coping with stress affected by culture and religion?

11.9 What are the psychological benefits of exercise?

study tip

As you are reading this chapter, take a look back at pages I-8–I-12 in *Psychology in Action* for some ways to reduce the stress and anxiety of studying and finishing assignments.

Stress and Stressors

Life is really about change. Every day, each person faces some kind of challenge, big or small. Just deciding what to wear to work or school can be a challenge for some people, whereas others find the drive to the workplace or school the most challenging part of the day. There are decisions to be made and changes that will require that you adapt already-made plans. Sometimes there are actual threats to well-being—an accident, a fight with the boss, a failed exam, or the loss of a job, to name a few. All of these challenges, threats, and changes require people to respond in some way.

DEFINITION OF STRESS

11.1 How do psychologists define stress?

Stress is the term used to describe the physical, emotional, cognitive, and behavioral responses to events that are appraised* as threatening or challenging.

Stress can show itself in many ways. Physical problems can include unusual fatigue, sleeping problems, frequent colds, and even chest pains and nausea. People under stress may behave differently, too: pacing, eating too much, crying a lot, smoking and drinking more than usual, or physically striking out at others by hitting or throwing things. Emotionally, people under stress experience anxiety, depression, fear, and irritability, as well as anger and frustration. Mental symptoms of stress include problems in concentration, memory, and decision making, and people under stress often lose their sense of humor.

I feel like that most of the time!

I feel like that most of the time!

Most people experience some degree of stress on a daily basis, and college students are even more likely to face situations and events that require them to make changes and adapt their behavior: Assigned readings, papers, studying for tests, juggling jobs, car problems, relationships, and dealing with deadlines are all examples of things that can cause a person to experience stress. Some people feel the effects of stress more than others because what is appraised as a threat by one person might be appraised as an opportunity by another. (For example, think of how you and your friends might respond differently to the opportunity to write a 10-page paper for extra credit in the last 3 weeks of the semester.) Stress-causing events are called **stressors**; they can come from within a person or from an external source and range from relatively mild to severe.

stress the term used to describe the physical, emotional, cognitive, and behavioral responses to events that are appraised as threatening or challenging.

stressors events that cause a stress reaction.

*appraised: in this sense, evaluated or judged in terms of importance or significance.

WHAT ARE STRESSORS?

Taking a test is just one of many possible stressors in a college student's life. What aspects of college life have you found to be stressful? Do other students experience the same degree of stress in response to the same stressors?

Events that can become stressors range from being stuck behind a person in the 10-items-or-less lane of the grocery store who has twice that amount, to dealing with the rubble left after a tornado or a hurricane destroys one's home. Stressors can range from the deadly serious (hurricanes, fires, crashes, combat) to the merely irritating and annoying (delays, rude people, losing one's car keys). Stressors can even be imaginary, as when a couple puts off doing their income tax return, imagining that they will have to pay a huge tax bill, or when a parent imagines the worst happening to a teenage child who isn't yet home from an evening out.

Actually, there are two kinds of stressors: those that cause **distress**, which occurs when people experience unpleasant stressors, and those that cause eustress, which results from positive events that still make demands on a person to adapt or change. Marriage, a job promotion, and having a baby may all be positive events for most people, but they all require a great deal of change in people's habits, duties, and often lifestyle, thereby creating stress. Hans Selye (1936) originally coined the term *eustress* to describe the stress experienced when positive events require the body to adapt.

In an update of Selye's original definition, researchers now define **eustress** as the optimal amount of stress that people need to promote health and well-being. The arousal theory, discussed in Chapter Nine, is based on the idea that a certain level of stress, or arousal, is actually necessary for people to feel content and function well (Zuckerman, 1994). LINK to Chapter Nine: Motivation and Emotion, p. 350. That arousal can be viewed in terms of eustress. Many students are aware that experiencing a little anxiety or stress is helpful to them because it motivates them to study, for example. Without the arousal created by the impending exam, many students might not study very much or at all. What about the student who is so stressed out that everything he's studied just flies right out of his head? Obviously, a high level of anxiety concerning an impending exam that actually interferes with the ability to study or to retrieve the information at exam time is distress. The difference is not only in the degree of anxiety but also in how the person interprets the exam situation. A number of events, great and small, good and bad, can cause us to feel "stressed out." The next section looks at how life's big deals and little hassles contribute to our overall stress experience. Simulate on mypsychlab.com

Simulate stress and stressors on mypsychlab.com

ENVIRONMENTAL STRESSORS: LIFE'S UPS AND DOWNS

11.2 What kinds of external events can cause stress?

CATASTROPHES Losing one's home in a tornado is an example of a stressor called a **catastrophe**, an unpredictable event that happens on a large scale and creates tremendous amounts of stress and feelings of threat. Wars, hurricanes, floods, fires, airplane crashes, and other disasters are catastrophes. The terrorist-driven destruction of the World Trade Center in New York City on September 11, 2001, is a prime example of a catastrophe. In one study, nearly 8 percent of the people living in the area near the attacks developed a severe stress disorder, and nearly 10 percent reported symptoms of depression even as late as 2 months after the attack (Galea et al., 2002). A study done 4 years later found a nearly 14 percent increase in stress disorders as well as continued persistence of previously diagnosed stress disorders (Pollack et al., 2006). LINK to Chapter Fourteen: Psychological Disorders, p. 544. Another example of a catastrophe was the devastation caused by Hurricane Katrina on August 29, 2005. A Category 3 hurricane, Katrina laid waste to the north-central coastal area of

distress the effect of unpleasant and undesirable stressors.

eustress the effect of positive events, or the optimal amount of stress that people need to promote health and well-being.

catastrophe an unpredictable, large-scale event that creates a tremendous need to adapt and adjust as well as overwhelming feelings of threat.

the Gulf of Mexico. In New Orleans, the damage from Katrina was increased by the failure of the levees to hold back flood waters. Eighty percent of the city and many neighboring areas were flooded for weeks (Swenson & Marshall, 2005). Rates of mental illness, including stress disorders, nearly doubled from pre-hurricane values (Kessler et al., 2006).

MAJOR LIFE CHANGES Thankfully, most people do not have to face the extreme stress of a catastrophe. But stress is present even in relatively ordinary life experiences and does not have to come from only negative events, such as job loss. Sometimes there are big events, such as marriage or going to college, that also require a person to make adjustments and changes—and adjustments and changes are really the core of stress, according to early researchers in the field (Holmes & Rahe, 1967).

The Social Readjustment Rating Scale (SRRS) Thomas Holmes and Richard Rahe (1967) believed that any life event that required people to change, adapt, or adjust their lifestyles would result in stress. Like Selye, they assumed that both negative events (such as getting fired) and positive events (such as getting a promotion) demand that a person adjust in some way, and so both kinds of events are associated with stress. Holmes and Rahe devised a scale to measure the amount of stress in a person's life by having that person add up the total "life change units" associated with each major event in their **Social Readjustment Rating Scale (SRRS)** (see Table 11.1). The researchers sampled 394 people, giving them a list of events, such as divorce, pregnancy, or taking a vacation. The people in the sample were told that, on a scale of 0 (no changes required of the person experiencing the event) to 100 (extreme changes required), marriage represented 50 "life change units." This gave those being sampled a "yardstick" of sorts, by which they could assign a number to each event, and these numbers became the life change units associated with each event on the SRRS.

When an individual adds up the points for each event that has happened to him or her within the past 12 months (and counting points for repeat events as well), the resulting score can provide a good estimate of the degree of stress being experienced by that person. The researchers found that certain ranges of scores on the SRRS could be associated with increased risk of illness or accidents. (Note: Table 11.1 is not a complete listing of the original 43 events and associated life change units and should not be used to calculate a stress "score"! If you would like to calculate your SRRS score, try this free Web site: **http://www.stresstips.com/lifeevents.htm**.)

Scores of 150 or below were not associated with any significant problems, but scores between 150 and 199 indicated a "mild life crisis" and were associated with a 33 percent increase in the risk of that person experiencing an illness or accident in the near future (when compared to persons not experiencing any crisis). Scores between 200 and 299 indicated a "moderate life crisis" and were associated with a 50 percent increase in risk, whereas scores over 300 indicated a "major life crisis" and represented an 80 percent increase in risk (Holmes & Masuda, 1973). Simply put, if a person's score is 300 or above, that person has a very high chance of becoming ill or having an accident in the near future. Illness includes not only physical conditions such as high blood pressure, ulcers, or migraine headaches but mental illness as well. In one study, researchers found that stressful life events of the kind listed in the SRRS were excellent predictors of the onset of episodes of major depression (Kendler & Prescott, 1999).

The SRRS was later revised (Miller & Rahe, 1997) to reflect changes in the ratings of the events in the 30 intervening years. Miller and Rahe found that overall stress associated with many of the items on the original list had increased by about 45 percent from the original 1967 ratings, citing changes in such issues as gender roles, economics, and social norms as possible reasons.

Social Readjustment Rating Scale (SRRS) assessment that measures the amount of stress in a person's life over a 1-year period resulting from major life events.

Table 11.1

Sample Items From the Social Readjustment Rating Scale (SRRS)

MAJOR LIFE EVENT	LIFE CHANGE UNITS
Death of spouse	100
Divorce	75
Marital separation	65
Jail term	63
Death of a close family member	63
Personal injury or illness	53
Marriage	50
Dismissal from work	47
Marital reconciliation	45
Pregnancy	40
Death of close friend	37
Change to different line of work	36
Change in number of arguments with spouse	36
Major mortgage	31
Foreclosure of mortgage or loan	30
Begin or end school	26
Change in living conditions	25
Change in work hours or conditions	20
Change in residence/schools/recreation	19
Change in social activities	18
Small mortgage or loan	17
Vacation	13
Christmas	12
Minor violations of the law	11

Source: Adapted and abridged from Holmes & Rahe (1967).

How can stress cause a person to have an accident? Many studies conducted on the relationship between stress and accidents in the workplace have shown that people under a lot of stress tend to be more distracted and less cautious and, therefore, place themselves at a greater risk for having an accident (Hansen, 1988; Sherry et al., 2003).

The SRRS as it was originally designed seems more appropriate for adults who are already established in their careers. There are versions of the SRRS that use as life events some of those things more likely to be experienced by college students. One of these more recent versions is the **College Undergraduate Stress Scale (CUSS)** that is represented in its entirety in Table 11.2 (Renner & Mackin, 1998). This scale looks quite different from Holmes and Rahe's original scale because the stressful events listed and rated include those that would be more common or more likely to happen to a college student. (Try it—add up the life change units from the events that you personally

College Undergraduate Stress Scale (CUSS) assessment that measures the amount of stress in a college student's life over a 1-year period resulting from major life events.

Table 11.2

College Undergraduate Stress Scale (CUSS)

EVENT	RATING
Being raped	100
Finding out that you are HIV-positive	100
Death of a close friend	97
Contracting a sexually transmitted infection (other than AIDS)	94
Concerns about being pregnant	91
Finals week	90
Oversleeping for an exam	89
Flunking a class	89
Having a boyfriend or girlfriend cheat on you	85
Financial difficulties	84
Writing a major term paper	83
Being caught cheating on a test	83
Two exams in one day	80
Getting married	76
Difficulties with parents	73
Talking in front of a class	72
Difficulties with a roommate	66
Job changes (applying, new job, work hassles)	65
A class you hate	62
Confrontations with professors	60
Maintaining a steady dating relationship	55
Commuting to campus or work, or both	54
Peer pressures	53
Being away from home for the first time	53
Getting straight A's	51
Fraternity or sorority rush	47
Falling asleep in class	40

Source: Adapted from Renner, M. J., & Mackin, R. S. (1998). A life stress instrument for classroom use. *Teaching of Psychology, 25*, 47

have experienced within the last year and then determine your level of risk according to Holmes and Rahe's original scoring system described earlier.)

I notice that Table 11.2 has "falling asleep in class" as its last item. How can falling asleep in class be stressful? It's what happens when the professor catches you that's stressful, isn't it?

I notice that Table 11.2 has "falling asleep in class" as its last item. How can falling asleep in class be stressful? It's what happens when the professor catches you that's stressful, isn't it?

Ah, but if you fall asleep in class, even if the professor doesn't catch on, you'll miss the lecture notes. You might then have to get the notes from a friend, find enough money to pay for the copy machine, try to read your friend's handwriting, and so on—all stressful situations. Actually, all the events listed on both the SRRS and the CUSS are stressful not just because some of them are emotionally intense but also because there are so many little details, changes, adjustments, adaptations, frustrations, and delays that are caused by the events themselves. The death of a spouse, for example, rates 100 life change units because it requires the greatest amount of adjustment in a person's life. A lot of those adjustments are going to be the little details: planning the funeral, deciding what to do with the spouse's clothes and belongings, getting the notice in the obituaries, answering all of the condolence cards with a thank-you card, dealing with insurance and changing names on policies, and on and on and on. In other words, major life events create a whole host of hassles. Simulate on mypsychlab.com

Simulate how stressed you are on mypsychlab.com

HASSLES Although it's easy to think about big disasters and major changes in life as sources of stress, the bulk of the stress we experience daily actually comes from little frustrations, delays, irritations, minor disagreements, and similar small aggravations. These daily annoyances are called **hassles** (Lazarus, 1993; Lazarus & Folkman, 1984). Experiencing major changes in one's life is like throwing a rock into a pond: There will be a big splash, but the rock itself is gone. What is left behind are all the ripples in the water that came from the impact of the rock. Those "ripples" are the hassles that arise from the big event.

Children in the preschool-age range find teasing by their peers to be the biggest daily hassle they experience. This boy is obviously upset by the teasing of the other children, who are making fun of his glasses. What other hassles might a child in this age range experience?

Lazarus and Folkman (1984) developed a *hassles scale* that has items such as "misplacing or losing things" and "troublesome neighbors." A person taking the test for hassles would rate each item in the scale in terms of how much of a hassle that particular item was for the person. The ratings range between 0 (no hassle or didn't occur) to 3 (extremely severe hassle). Whereas the major life events of Holmes and Rahe's scale (1967) may have a long-term effect on a person's chronic physical and mental health, the day-to-day minor annoyances, delays, and irritations that affect immediate health and well-being are far better predictors of short-term illnesses such as headaches, colds, backaches, and similar symptoms (Burks & Martin, 1985; DeLongis et al., 1988; Dunn et al., 2006). In one study, researchers found that among 261 participants who experienced headaches, scores on a scale measuring the number and severity of daily hassles were significantly better predictors of headaches than were scores on a life-events scale (Fernandez & Sheffield, 1996). The researchers also found that it was not so much the number of daily hassles that predicted headaches but rather the perceived severity of the hassles.

A recent study has indicated that hassles may also come from quite different sources depending on a person's developmental stage (Ellis et al., 2001). In this study, researchers surveyed 270 randomly selected people from ages 3 to 75. The participants were asked to check off a list of daily hassles and pleasures associated with having "bad days" and "good days," respectively, as well as ranking the hassles in terms of frequency and severity of impact. For children ages 3 to 5, getting teased was the biggest daily hassle. For children in the 6 to 10 age group, the biggest hassle was getting bad grades. Children 11 to 15 years old reported feeling pressured to use drugs, whereas older adolescents (ages 16 to 22) cited trouble at school or work. Adults found fighting among family members the greatest source of stress, whereas the elderly people in the study cited a lack of money.

In that same study, the researchers were somewhat surprised to find that elderly people were much more strongly affected by such hassles as going shopping, doctor's appointments, and bad weather than the children and younger adults were. It may be that while a young person may view going shopping as an opportunity to socialize, older adults find it threatening: Physically, they are less able to get to a place to shop and may have to rely on others to drive them and help them get around and, thus, may take much more time for shopping and doing errands than a younger person would. Mentally, shopping could be seen as threatening because of a lack of financial resources to pay for needed items. Even the need to make decisions might be seen as unpleasant to an older person.

hassles the daily annoyances of everyday life.

11.1 11.2

CONCEPT MAP

Stress and Stressors

- stress is the physical, emotional, cognitive, and behavioral response to events that are appraised as threatening or challenging; first studied systematically by Hans Selye
  - can include physical fatigue, recurring illness, over/under eating, smoking/drinking more than usual, mood swings, irritability, depression, anger, memory and concentration problems
- stress-causing events are called stressors; can come from external or internal sources; range from mild to severe
  - negative events cause distress; positive events cause eustress, the optimal level of stress required to facilitate healthy adaptation and well-being
  - external stress-causing events may include catastrophes, major life changes, and daily hassles (differ according to developmental stage)
  - can be assessed systematically (e.g., Social Readjustment Rating Scale, College Undergraduate Stress Scale)

PRACTICE quiz How much do you remember? ANSWERS ON PAGE AK-2.

Pick the best answer.

1. The optimal amount of stress that people need to promote their health and sense of well-being is called _________.
   a. intensity.
   b. distress.
   c. eustress.
   d. acute stress.
2. Which of the following is associated with the greatest degree of potential stress, according to Holmes and Rahe's original scale?
   a. minor violations of the law.
   b. marital reconciliation.
   c. death of a close friend.
   d. major mortgage.
3. Research has shown that _________ have a long-term effect on physical and mental health, but _________ have a greater impact on short-term health.
   a. hassles; major life events
   b. major life events; hassles
   c. major life events; catastrophes
   d. hassles; catastrophes
4. The College Undergraduate Stress Scale rates being raped as equally stressful when compared with which of the following?
   a. death of a close family member
   b. concerns about being pregnant
   c. being accused of rape
   d. finding out that one is HIV positive

Brainstorming: When during the school year are you most likely to come down with a cold or experience other symptoms such as headaches? What hassles and stressors are also present at those times? What steps could you take to minimize the effects of these stressors?

PSYCHOLOGICAL STRESSORS: WHAT, ME WORRY?

Although several specific stressors (such as marriage, car problems, etc.) have already been mentioned, the psychological reasons why people find these events stressful fall into several categories.

11.3 What are some psychological factors in stress?

PRESSURE When there are urgent demands or expectations for a person's behavior coming from an outside source, that person is experiencing **pressure**. Pressure occurs when people feel that they must work harder, faster, or do more, as when meeting a deadline or studying for final exams.

Time pressure is one of the most common forms of pressure. Although some people claim to "work well under pressure," the truth is that pressure can have a negative impact on a person's ability to be creative. Psychologist Teresa Amabile has gathered research within actual work settings strongly indicating that when time pressure is applied to workers who are trying to come up with creative, innovative ideas, creativity levels decrease dramatically—even though the workers may think they have been quite productive because of the effort they have made (Amabile et al., 2002).

pressure the psychological experience produced by urgent demands or expectations for a person's behavior that come from an outside source.

UNCONTROLLABILITY Another factor that increases a person's experience of stress is the degree of control that the person has over a particular event or situation. The less control a person has, the greater the degree of stress. Researchers in both clinical interviews and experimental studies have found that lack of control in a situation actually increases stress disorder symptoms (Breier et al., 1987).

In studies carried out in a nursing home with the elderly residents as the participants, researchers Rodin and Langer (Langer & Rodin, 1976; Rodin & Langer, 1977) found that those residents who were given more control over their lives (e.g., being able to choose activities and their timing) were more vigorous, active, and sociable than those in the control group. Employees at mental health clinics who have more input into and control over policy changes experience less stress than those who believe themselves to have little control (Johnson et al., 2006). A more recent study found that retirees experience more happiness and less stress when retirement is by their choice and not forced upon them, regardless of whether the retirement was rapid or gradual (Calvo et al., 2009).

Residents in retirement homes and nursing homes benefit both physically and psychologically when they can choose for themselves the activities in which they wish to participate, such as this exercise class. What are some other means of control residents might experience?

The stress-increasing effects of lack of control explain the relationship between unpredictability and stress as well. When potentially stressful situations are unpredictable, as in police work, the degree of stress experienced is increased. An unpredictable situation is one that is not controllable, which may at least partially explain the increase in stress. In one study, rats were either given an electric shock after a warning tone or given a shock with no warning. The rats receiving the unpredictable shocks developed severe stomach ulcers (Weiss, 1972).

FRUSTRATION **Frustration** occurs when people are blocked or prevented from achieving a desired goal or fulfilling a perceived need. As a stressor, frustration can be *external*, such as when a car breaks down, a desired job offer doesn't come through after all, or experiencing a theft of one's belongings. Losses, rejections, failures, and delays are all sources of external frustration.

Obviously, some frustrations are minor and others are more serious. The seriousness of a frustration is affected by how important the goal or need actually is. A person who is delayed in traffic while driving to the mall to do some shopping just for fun will be less frustrated than a person who is trying to get to the mall before it closes to get that last-minute forgotten and important anniversary gift.

Internal frustrations, also known as *personal frustrations*, occur when the goal or need cannot be attained because of internal or personal characteristics. For example, someone who wants to be an astronaut might find that severe motion sickness prevents him or her from such a goal. If a man wants to be a professional basketball player but is only 5 feet tall and weighs only 85 pounds, he may find that he cannot achieve that goal because of his physical characteristics. A person wanting to be an engineer but who has no math skills would find it difficult to attain that goal.

When frustrated, people may use several typical responses. The first is *persistence*, or the continuation of efforts to get around whatever is causing the frustration. Persistence may involve making more intense efforts or changing the style of response. For example, anyone who has ever put coins into a drink machine only to find that the drink does not come out has probably (1) pushed the button again, more forcefully, and (2) pushed several other buttons in an effort to get some kind of response from the machine. If neither of these strategies works, many people may hit or kick the machine itself in an act of aggression.

frustration the psychological experience produced by the blocking of a desired goal or fulfillment of a perceived need.

aggression actions meant to harm or destroy.

Aggression, or actions meant to harm or destroy, is unfortunately another typical reaction to frustration. Early psychologists in the field of behaviorism proposed a connection between frustration and aggression, calling it the *frustration–aggression hypothesis* (Dollard et al., 1939; Miller et al., 1941). LINK to Chapter Twelve: Social Psychology, p. 478. Although they believed that some form of frustration nearly always precedes aggression, that does not mean that frustration *always* leads to aggression. In fact, aggression is a frequent and persistent response to frustration, but it is seldom the first response. In a reformulation of the frustration–aggression hypothesis, Berkowitz (1993) stated that frustration creates an internal "readiness to aggress" but that aggression will not follow unless certain external cues are also present. For example, if the human source of a person's frustration is far larger and stronger in appearance than the frustrated person, aggression is an unlikely outcome!

Okay, so if the person who ticked you off is bigger than you—if aggression isn't possible—what can you do?

Okay, so if the person who ticked you off is bigger than you—if aggression isn't possible—what can you do?

One could try to reason with the person who is the source of frustration. Reasoning with someone is a form of persistence. Trying to "get around" the problem is another way in which people can deal with frustration. Another possibility is to take out one's frustrations on less threatening, more available targets, in a process called **displaced aggression**. Anyone who has ever been frustrated by things that occurred at work or school and then later yelled at another person (such as a spouse, parent, child, etc.) has experienced displaced aggression. The person one really wants to strike out at is one's boss, the teacher, or whoever or whatever caused the frustration in the first place. That could be dangerous, so the aggression is reserved for another less threatening or weaker target. For example, unemployment and financial difficulties are extremely frustrating, as they block a person's ability to maintain a certain standard of living and acquire desired possessions. In one study, male unemployment and single parenthood were the two factors most highly correlated to rates of child abuse (Gillham et al., 1998). Unemployment is also one of the factors correlated most highly with the murder of abused women, creating four times the risk of murder for women in abusive relationships (Campbell & Wolf, 2003). Both studies are examples of displaced aggression toward the weaker targets of children and women. Such targets often become *scapegoats*, or habitual targets of displaced aggression. Scapegoats are often pets, children, spouses, and even minority groups (who are seen as having less power). LINK to Chapter Twelve: Social Psychology, pp. 470–471.

These parents are fighting in front of their obviously distressed daughter. In some instances, a child who experiences this kind of frustration might act out aggressively toward a sibling or a pet in a form of displaced aggression.

Another possible reaction to frustration is **escape** or **withdrawal**. Escape or withdrawal can take the form of leaving, dropping out of school, quitting a job, or ending a relationship. Some people manage a psychological escape or withdrawal into apathy (ceasing to care about or act upon the situation), fantasy (which is only a temporary escape), or the use of drugs. Obviously the latter reaction can lead to even more problems. Others resort to what they see as the final escape: suicide. **Listen** on **mypsychlab.com**

Listen to a Psychology in the News podcast about suicide on **mypsychlab.com**

CONFLICT

Approach–Approach Conflict. In an **approach–approach conflict**, a person experiences desire for two goals, each of which is attractive. Typically, this type of conflict, often called a "win-win situation," is relatively easy to resolve and does not involve a great deal of stress. Because both goals are desirable, the only stress involved is having to choose between them, acquiring one and losing the other. An example of this might be the need to choose between the chocolate cake or key lime pie for dessert or from among several good choices for a date to the prom. "Six on one hand, half a dozen on the other" is a phrase that sums up this conflict nicely.

displaced aggression taking out one's frustrations on some less threatening or more available target.

escape or **withdrawal** leaving the presence of a stressor, either literally or by a psychological withdrawal into fantasy, drug abuse, or apathy.

approach–approach conflict conflict occurring when a person must choose between two desirable goals.

Avoidance–Avoidance Conflict. **Avoidance–avoidance conflicts** are much more stressful. In this conflict, the choice is between two or more goals or events that are unpleasant. This type of conflict is so common that there are numerous phrases to symbolize it, for example, "caught between a rock and a hard place," "between the devil and the deep blue sea," "out of the frying pan into the fire," and "lose-lose situation." People who are fearful of dental procedures might face the conflict of suffering the pain of a toothache or going to the dentist. Because neither alternative is pleasant, many people avoid making a choice by delaying decisions (Tversky & Shafir, 1992). For example, given the choice of risky back surgery or living with the pain, some people would wait, hoping that the pain would go away on its own and relieve them of the need to make a choice.

This couple has just purchased their first house, a rite of passage for many young couples. The decision to become a home owner, with the "pulls" of privacy and earning equity and the "pushes" of mortgage payments and upkeep, is often an approach–avoidance conflict.

Approach–Avoidance Conflict. **Approach–avoidance conflicts** are a bit different in that they only involve one goal or event. That goal or event may have both positive and negative aspects that make the goal appealing and yet unappealing at the same time. For example, marriage is a big decision to make for anyone and usually has both its attractive features, such as togetherness, sharing good times, and companionship, and also its negative aspects, such as disagreements, money issues, and mortgages. This is perhaps the most stressful of all of the types of conflict, causing many people to vacillate* or be unable to decide for or against the goal or event. The author of this text experienced a very stressful approach–avoidance conflict when deciding to write the book: On the one hand, there would be money, prestige, and the challenge of doing something new. On the other hand, a tremendous amount of effort and time would be required to write the text, which would take time and energy away from other areas of life. Another example is the offer of a promotion that would require a person to move to a city he or she doesn't like—more money and higher status but all the hassles of moving and living in a less than perfect place.

What if I have to choose between two things, and each of them has good points and bad points?

What if I have to choose between two things, and each of them has good points and bad points?

Multiple Approach–Avoidance Conflicts. When the choice is between two goals that have both positive and negative elements to each goal, it is called a **double approach–avoidance conflict**. For example, what if a person had the choice of buying a house out in the country or in the city? The house in the country has its attractions: privacy, fresh air, and quiet. But there would be a long commute to one's job in the city. A house in the city would make getting to work a lot easier, but then there are the negative aspects of pollution, noise, and crowded city streets. Each choice has both good and bad points. This type of conflict also tends to lead to vacillation. Other examples of this type of conflict might be trying to decide which of two people one wants to date or which of two majors one should choose.

It is fairly common to face **multiple approach–avoidance conflicts** in daily life. In a multiple approach–avoidance conflict, one would have more than two goals or options to consider, making the decision even more difficult and stressful. For many college students, deciding on a specific school or a career major is actually this type of conflict.

avoidance–avoidance conflict conflict occurring when a person must choose between two undesirable goals.

approach–avoidance conflict conflict occurring when a person must choose or not choose a goal that has both positive and negative aspects.

double approach–avoidance conflict conflict in which the person must decide between two goals, with each goal possessing both positive and negative aspects.

multiple approach–avoidance conflict conflict in which the person must decide between more than two goals, with each goal possessing both positive and negative aspects.

*vacillate: to go back and forth between one decision and another.

11.3

CONCEPT MAP

pressure
urgent demands or expectations and uncontrollability

frustration
due to external (losses, rejections, failures, delays) or internal (personal characteristics) factors; can result in several typical responses

- **persistence**
- **aggression**
- **escape/withdrawal** (**suicide** is a drastic form of escape)

conflict

- **approach–approach conflict** does not involve a great deal of stress; person experiences attraction to two or more desires or goals
- **avoidance–avoidance conflict** is more stressful; choice between two or more undesirable situations
- **approach–avoidance conflict** can be most stressful; single goal or event has both positive and negative aspects
- **multiple approach–avoidance conflicts** are fairly common in daily life (e.g., **double approach–avoidance**) due to life decisions affecting two or more goals

Stress and Stressors (continued)
(psychological stressors are often related to external events)

PRACTICE **quiz** How much do you remember?

ANSWERS ON PAGE AK-2.

Pick the best answer.

1. When people have to work harder, do more work, or work faster, they are experiencing _________.
   a. frustration.
   b. uncontrollability.
   c. pressure.
   d. conflict.
2. The stress-increasing effects of uncontrollability are related to the effects of _________ on stress.
   a. frustration
   b. unpredictability
   c. pressure
   d. conflict
3. Eduardo is on his way to an important job interview when his car breaks down on the highway. Eduardo is likely to experience what kind of frustration?
   a. external
   b. internal
   c. personal
   d. uncontrollable
4. The first response that people typically make to frustration is _________.
   a. persistence.
   b. increasing efforts.
   c. varying efforts.
   d. aggression.
5. Jasmine has just been offered an opportunity to teach at a small college in a rural area of Kansas. On the one hand, she really needs a job and the money it would bring would allow her to pay off some debts. But the college is in a very small town far away from any major cities and has very little to offer in the way of amusements. She would also be far away from her family and friends. Jasmine is facing what type of conflict in deciding whether or not to accept the job?
   a. approach–approach
   b. avoidance–avoidance
   c. approach–avoidance
   d. double approach–avoidance

Physiological Factors: Stress and Health

11.4 How does stress affect the physical functioning of the body and its immune system?

Chapter Two discussed in detail the function of the *autonomic nervous system* (ANS), the part of the human nervous system that is responsible for all automatic, involuntary, and life-sustaining activities. The ANS consists of two divisions, the *parasympathetic* and the *sympathetic*. It is the sympathetic nervous system (the "fight-or-flight" system) that reacts when the human body is subjected to stress: Heart rate increases, digestion slows or shuts down, and energy is sent to the muscles to help deal with whatever action the stressful situation requires. The parasympathetic system returns the body to normal, day-to-day functioning after the stress is ended. If the stress is great enough and lasts long enough, the parasympathetic system may shut the body down, causing a collapse into what some people might call "nervous exhaustion." Both systems figure prominently in a classic theory of the body's physiological reactions to stress, the general adaptation syndrome.

general adaptation syndrome (GAS) the three stages of the body's physiological reaction to stress, including alarm, resistance, and exhaustion.

THE GENERAL ADAPTATION SYNDROME

Psychologist Hans Selye was the founder of the field of research concerning stress and its effects on the human body. He studied the sequence of physiological reactions that the body goes through when adapting to a stressor. This sequence (see Figure 11.1) is called the **general adaptation syndrome (GAS)** and consists of three stages (Selye, 1956): Explore on **mypsychlab.com**

Explore Selye's General Adaptation Syndrome on **mypsychlab.com**

- **Alarm:** When the body first reacts to a stressor, the sympathetic nervous system is activated. The adrenal glands release hormones that increase heart rate, blood pressure, and the supply of blood sugar, resulting in a burst of energy. Reactions such as fever, nausea, and headache are common.

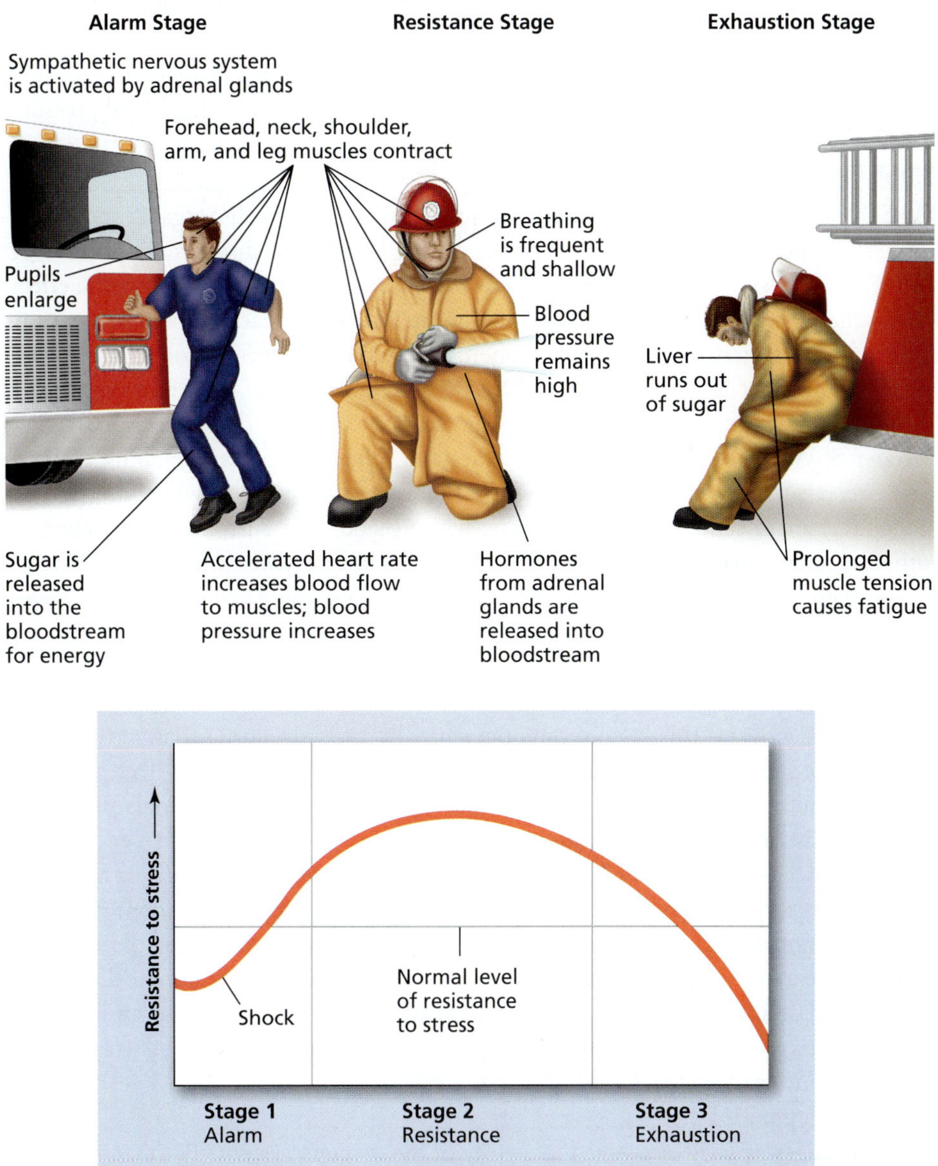

Figure 11.1 General Adaptation Syndrome
The diagram at the top shows some of the physical reactions to stress in each of the three stages of the general adaptation syndrome. The graph at the bottom shows the relationship of each of the three stages to the individual's ability to resist a stressor. In the alarm stage, resistance drops at first as the sympathetic system quickly activates. But resistance then rapidly increases as the body mobilizes its defense systems. In the resistance stage, the body is working at a much increased level of resistance, using resources until the stress ends or the resources run out. In the exhaustion stage, the body is no longer able to resist as resources have been depleted, and at this point disease and even death are possible.

immune system the system of cells, organs, and chemicals of the body that responds to attacks from diseases, infections, and injuries.

- **Resistance:** As the stress continues, the body settles into sympathetic division activity, continuing to release the stress hormones that help the body fight off, or resist, the stressor. The early symptoms of alarm lessen and the person or animal may actually feel better. This stage will continue until the stressor ends or the organism has used up all of its resources. Researchers have found that one of the hormones released under stress, noradrenaline (norepinephrine), actually seems to affect the brain's processing of pain, so that when under stress a person may experience a kind of analgesia (insensitivity to pain) if, for example, the person hits an arm or a shin (Delaney et al., 2007).
- **Exhaustion:** When the body's resources are gone, exhaustion occurs. Exhaustion can lead to the formation of stress-related diseases (i.e., high blood pressure or a weakened immune system) or the death of the organism if outside help is unavailable (Stein-Behrens et al., 1994). When the stressor ends, the parasympathetic division activates and the body attempts to replenish its resources.

Alarm and resistance are stages that people experience many times throughout life, allowing people to adapt to life's demands (Selye, 1976). It is the prolonged secretion of the stress hormones during the exhaustion stage that can lead to the most harmful effects of stress. It was this aspect of Selye's work that convinced other researchers of the connection between stress and certain *diseases of adaptation* as Selye termed them. The most common of these diseases are ulcers and high blood pressure.

IMMUNE SYSTEM AND STRESS

As Selye first discovered, the **immune system** (the system of cells, organs, and chemicals in the body that responds to attacks on the body from diseases and injuries) is affected by stress. The field of *psychoneuroimmunology* concerns the study of the effects of psychological factors such as stress, emotions, thinking, learning, and behavior on the immune system (Ader; 2003; Cohen & Herbert, 1996; Kiecolt-Glaser, 2009; Kiecolt-Glaser et al., 1995, 1996, 2002). Researchers in this field have found that stress triggers the same response in the immune system that infection triggers (Maier & Watkins, 1998). Certain enzymes and other chemicals (including antibodies) are created by immune cells when the immune cells, or white blood cells, encounter an infection in the body. The white blood cells surround the bacteria or other infectious material and release the chemicals and enzymes into the bloodstream. From there, these chemicals activate receptor sites on the *vagus nerve*, the longest nerve that connects the body to the brain. It is the activation of these receptor sites that signals the brain that the body is sick, causing the brain to respond by further activation of the immune system.

Stress activates this same system but starts in the brain rather than in the bloodstream. The same chemical changes that occur in the brain when it has been alerted by the vagus nerve to infection in the body occurred in laboratory animals when they were kept isolated from other animals or given electric shocks (Maier & Watkins, 1998). This has the effect of "priming" the immune system, allowing it to more successfully resist the effects of the stress, as in Selye's resistance stage of the GAS.

Hormones also play a part in helping the immune system fight the effects of stress. Researchers (Morgan et al., 2009) have found that a hormone called dehydroepiandrosterone (DHEA), known to provide antistress benefits in animals, also aids humans in stress toleration—perhaps by regulating the effects of stress on the hippocampus (part of the limbic system). LINK to Chapter Two: The Biological Perspective, pp. 71–72.

So stress actually increases the activity of the immune system? But then how does stress end up causing those diseases, like high blood pressure?

So stress actually increases the activity of the immune system? But then how does stress end up causing those diseases, like high blood pressure?

The positive effects of stress on the immune system only seem to work when the stress is not a continual, chronic condition. As stress continues, the body's resources begin to fail in the exhaustion phase of the general adaptation to stress (Kiecolt-Glaser et al., 1987, 1995, 1996; Prigerson et al., 1997). In one study, college students who were undergoing a stressful series of exams were compared to a group of similar students relaxing during a time of no classes and no exams (Deinzer et al., 2000). The exam group tested significantly lower for immune system chemicals that help fight off disease than did the relaxing control group, even as long as 14 days after the exams were over. The suppression of immune system functioning by stress apparently can continue even after the stress itself is over.

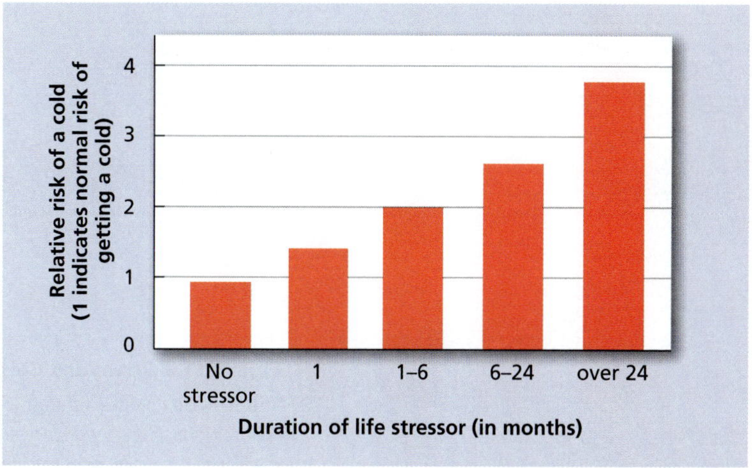

Figure 11.2 Stress Duration and Illness
In this graph, the risk of getting a cold virus increases greatly as the months of exposure to a stressor increase. Although a stress reaction can be useful in its early phase, prolonged stress has a negative impact on the immune system, leaving the body vulnerable to illnesses such as a cold.
Source: Cohen et al. (1998).

One reason that the early stress reaction is helpful but prolonged stress is not might be that the stress reaction, in evolutionary terms, is really only "designed" for a short-term response, such as running from a predator (Sapolsky, 2004). That level of intense bodily and hormonal activity isn't really meant to go on and on, as it does for human beings in the modern, stress-filled life we now know. Humans experience the stress reaction over prolonged periods of times and in situations that are not necessarily life threatening, leading to a breakdown in the immune system. (See Figure 11.2.)

HEART DISEASE Of course, anything that can weaken the immune system can have a negative effect on other bodily systems. Stress has been shown to put people at a higher risk for heart attacks and strokes at least in part because the liver, which is not activated while the sympathetic nervous system is aroused, does not have a chance to clear the fat and cholesterol from the bloodstream, leading to clogged arteries and eventually the possibility of heart attacks. In one study, middle-aged men were questioned about stress, diet, and lifestyle factors and were examined for biological risk factors for heart disease: obesity, high blood sugar, high triglycerides (a type of fatty acid found in the blood), and low levels of HDL or "good" cholesterol. (See Figure 11.3.) Stress and the production of stress hormones were found to be strongly linked to all four biological risk factors: The more stress the men were exposed to in their work environment and home life, the more likely they were to exhibit these risk factors (Brunner et al., 2002).

Other studies have produced similar findings. One study looked at the heart health of people who suffered acute stress reactions after the 9/11 terrorist attacks and found a 53 percent increase in heart ailments over the 3 years following the attacks (Holman et al., 2008), whereas another large-scale study found that work stress is highly associated with an increased risk of coronary heart disease due to negative effects of stress on the autonomic nervous system and glandular activity (Chandola et al., 2008). Prolonged stress is simply not good for the heart.

Stress can also lead to certain unhealthy behaviors, such as drinking alcohol; smoking; eating all the wrong, high-fat, high-calorie "comfort" foods; and avoiding exercise—all factors associated with poor health (Jackson et al., 2009).

DIABETES Review the last paragraph, and it becomes obvious that weight problems may also become associated with stress. One chronic illness sometimes associated with excessive weight gain is *diabetes*, specifically **Type 2 diabetes** (Type 1 diabetes is associated with failure of the pancreas to secrete enough insulin, necessitating medication, and is usually diagnosed before the age of 40). Type 2 diabetes is associated with excessive weight gain and occurs when pancreas insulin levels become less efficient as the body size increases. Type 2 diabetes can respond favorably to proper diet, exercise, and weight loss, but may

Type 2 diabetes disease involving failure of the pancreas to secrete enough insulin, necessitating medication, usually diagnosed before the age of 40 and can be associated with obesity.

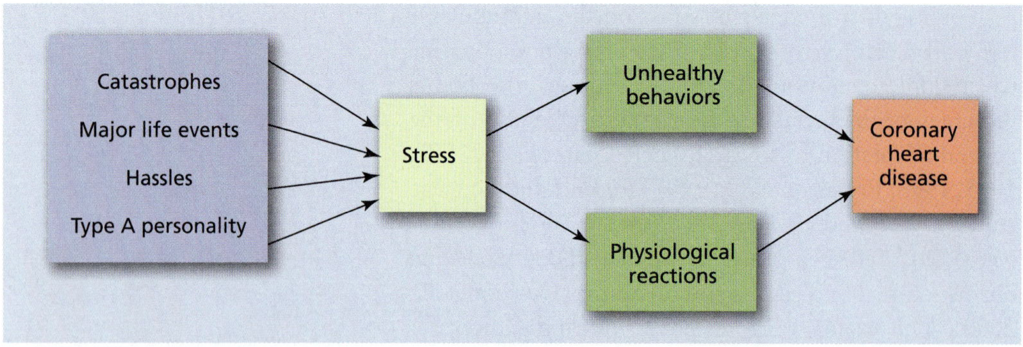

Figure 11.3 Stress and Coronary Heart Disease

The blue box on the left represents various sources of stress (Type A personality refers to someone who is ambitious, always working, and usually hostile). In addition to the physical reactions that accompany the stress reaction, an individual under stress may be more likely to engage in unhealthy behavior such as overeating, drinking alcohol or taking other kinds of drugs, avoiding exercise, and acting out in anger or frustration. This kind of behavior also contributes to an increased risk of coronary heart disease.

also require medication. Typically, it is associated with older adults, but with the rise in obesity among children, more cases of Type 2 diabetes in children are now occurring.

While controllable, diabetes is a serious disorder that has now been associated with an increased risk of Alzheimer's disease, although memory loss appears to be slower for diabetic Alzheimer patients than for nondiabetic Alzheimer's patients (Sanz et al., 2010). Several ongoing longitudinal studies strongly suggest that Type 2 diabetes not only is associated with mental decline in middle-aged individuals (Nooyens et al., 2010) but there is also indication that stress can compound the risk of that mental decline (Reynolds et al., 2010).

CANCER Cancer is not one disease but rather a collection of diseases that can affect any part of the body. Unlike normal cells, which divide and reproduce according to genetic instructions and stop dividing according to those same instructions, cancer cells divide without stopping. The resulting tumors affect the normal functioning of the organs and systems they invade, causing them to fail, eventually killing the organism. Cancer is found not only in humans and other animals, but also in plants.

Although stress itself cannot give a person cancer, stress can have a suppressing effect on the immune system, making the unchecked growth of cancer more likely. In particular, an immune-system cell called a **natural killer (NK) cell** has as its main functions the suppression of viruses and the destruction of tumor cells (Herberman & Ortaldo, 1981). Stress has been shown to depress the release of natural killer cells, making it more difficult for the body's systems to fight cancerous growths (Zorilla et al., 2001). The hormone adrenaline is released under stress and has been found to interfere with a protein that normally would suppress the growth of cancer cells (Sastry et al., 2007). In other research, stress has been linked to the accumulation of genetic errors that can lead to the formation of cancer cells and tumors: Stress causes the release of hormones such as adrenaline and noradrenaline that, over time, can cause mistakes (such as damage to the telomeres, structures at the ends of chromosomes that control the number of times a cell can reproduce) in the instructions given by the genes to the cells of the body. As these mistakes "pile up" over the years, cells can begin to grow out of control, causing the growth of tumors and possibly cancer (Kiecolt-Glaser et al., 2002).

natural killer (KT) cell immune-system cell responsible for suppressing viruses and destroying tumor cells.

OTHER HEALTH ISSUES Heart disease and cancer are not the only diseases affected by stress. Studies have shown that children in families experiencing ongoing stress are more likely to develop fevers with illness than are other children (Wyman et al., 2007). (Oddly enough, this same study showed that in children, stress actually seems to improve the function of their natural killer cells, just the opposite effect that is seen in adults.) A review of research and scientific literature (Cohen et al., 2007) found stress to be a contributing factor in a variety of human diseases and disorders, including heart disease, depression, and HIV/AIDS.

The physical effects of stress on the body and the immune system are only part of the picture of the influence of stress in daily life. The next section looks at how cognitive factors, such as how an individual interprets a stressful event, and psychological factors, such as personality type can affect the impact of stress. First, let's take a brief look at a field of psychology that has arisen in response to our increased understanding of health and its relationship to psychological and behavioral factors.

issues in psychology

Health Psychology and Stress

In the last 3 decades, people have become more aware of health issues and their relationship to what we do, what we eat, who we see, and how we think. A relatively new branch of psychology has begun to explore these relationships. **Health psychology** focuses on how our physical activities, psychological traits, and social relationships affect our overall health and rate of illnesses. Psychologists who specialize in this field are typically clinical or counseling psychologists and may work with medical doctors in a hospital or clinic setting, although there are health psychologists who are primarily engaged in teaching and research. Some health psychologists focus on health and wellness issues in the workplace or public health issues such as disease prevention through immunizations or nutrition education. Others are more concerned with health-care programs that service all levels of the socioeconomic layers of society (Marks et al., 2005).

Health psychologists seek to understand how behavior (such as use of drugs, optimism, personality, or the type of food one eats) can affect a person's ability to fight off illnesses—or increase the likelihood of getting sick. They want to know how to prevent illness, and how factors like poverty, wealth, religion, social support, personality, and even one's ethnicity can affect health. In this age of a new focus on health care, health psychology is destined to become a more important force in future research.

Questions for Further Discussion

1. How have some of the factors studied by health psychologists affected you in recent months?
2. What health issues might arise in the college or university setting that could have a positive or negative impact on your psychological and physical well-being?

THE INFLUENCE OF COGNITION AND PERSONALITY ON STRESS

11.5 How do cognitive factors and personality differences affect the experience of stress?

COGNITIVE FACTORS IN STRESS: LAZARUS'S COGNITIVE APPRAISAL APPROACH Cognitive psychologist Richard Lazarus developed a cognitive view of stress called the *cognitive–mediational theory* of emotions, in which the way people think about and appraise a stressor is a major factor in how stressful that particular stressor becomes (Lazarus, 1991, 1999; Lazarus & Folkman, 1984). LINK to Chapter Nine: Motivation and Emotion, p. 368. According to Lazarus, there is a two-step process in assessing the degree of threat or harm of a stressor and how one should react to that stressor. (See Figure 11.4.)

health psychology area of psychology focusing on how physical activities, psychological traits, and social relationships affect overall health and rate of illnesses.

Figure 11.4 Responses to a Stressor

Lazarus's Cognitive Appraisal Approach. According to this approach, there are two steps in cognitively determining the degree of stress created by a potential stressor. Primary appraisal involves determining if the potential stressor is a threat. If it is perceived as a threat, secondary appraisal occurs in addition to the bodily and emotional reactions. Secondary appraisal involves determining the resources one has to deal with the stress, such as time, money, physical ability, and so on. Inadequate resources lead to increased feelings of stress and the possibility of developing new resources to deal with the stress.

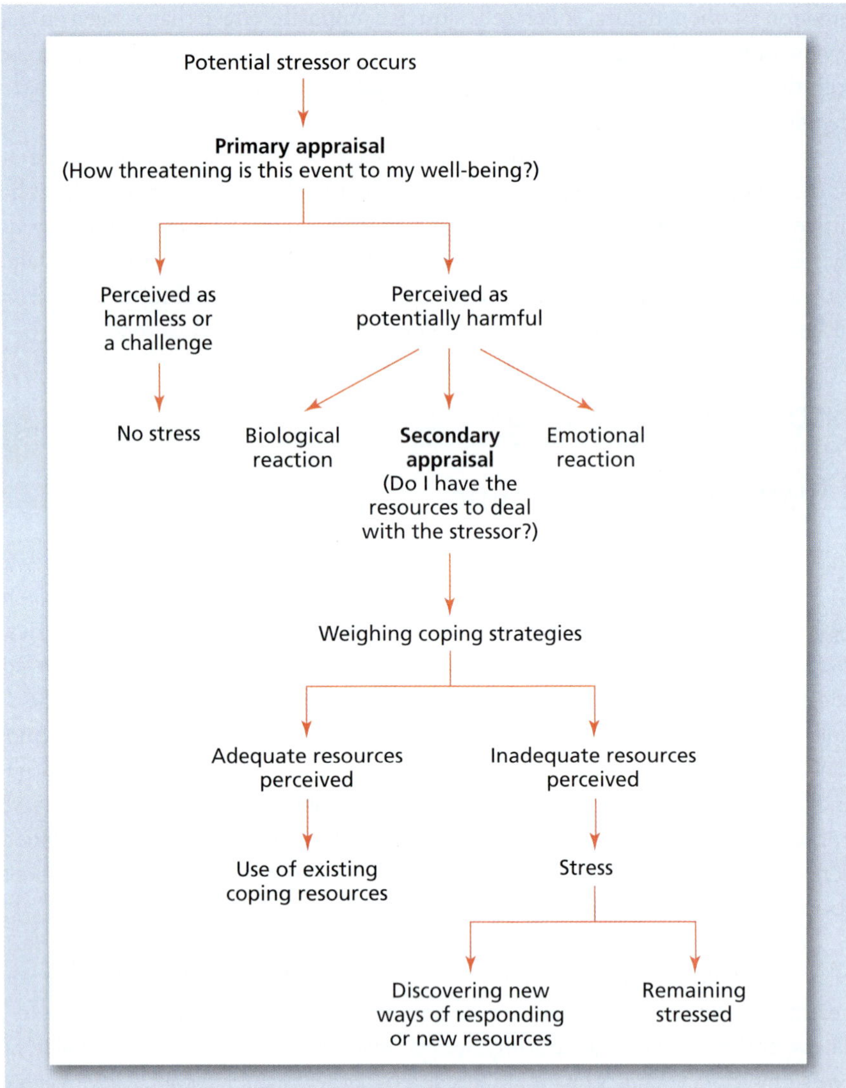

PRIMARY APPRAISAL The first step in appraising a stressor is called **primary appraisal**, which involves estimating the severity of the stressor and classifying it as a threat (something that could be harmful in the future), a challenge (something to be met and defeated), or a harm or loss that has already occurred. If the stressor is appraised as a threat, negative emotions may arise that inhibit the person's ability to cope with the threat. For example, a student who has not read the text or taken good notes will certainly appraise an upcoming exam as threatening. If the stressor is seen as a challenge, however, it is possible to plan to meet that challenge, which is a more positive and less stressful approach. For example, the student who has studied, read, and feels prepared is much more likely to appraise the upcoming exam as an opportunity to do well.

Perceiving a stressor as a challenge instead of a threat makes coping with the stressor (or the harm it may already have caused) more likely to be successful. Whereas perceiving the stressor as an embarrassment, or imagining future failure or rejection, is more likely to lead to increased stress reactions, negative emotions, and an inability to cope well (Folkman, 1997; Lazarus, 1993). Think positive!

primary appraisal the first step in assessing stress, which involves estimating the severity of a stressor and classifying it as either a threat or a challenge.

secondary appraisal the second step in assessing a threat, which involves estimating the resources available to the person for coping with the stressor.

SECONDARY APPRAISAL In **secondary appraisal**, people who have identified a threat or harmful effect must estimate the resources that they have available for coping with the stressor. Resources might include social support, money, time, energy, ability, or any number of potential resources, depending on the threat. If resources are perceived as adequate or abundant, the degree of stress will be considerably less than if resources are missing or lacking. Using the example of the student and the upcoming exam, a student who feels that she has the time to study and the ability to understand the material in that time will feel much less distress than the student who has little time to study and doesn't feel that she understood all the content of the lectures covered on the exam.

As another example, let's say that a person has just lost a job due to downsizing. That's a fairly big stressor in most situations, but the degree of stress experienced of that person and their coping abilities will depend on the individual's primary appraisal and secondary appraisal. In most cases, primary appraisal might go something like this: "I've lost my job! I need a job, so this is bad, very bad!" ("This is a threat!") The secondary appraisal might result in the following: "I don't have much money in savings, and the job market for my skills is pretty bad right now. I don't have anyone I can borrow money from or live with while I'm looking for more work. I'm going to lose everything!" ("I don't have the resources to deal with this!") Contrast that person's situation with this person's situation: "I've been let go, but that's not so bad. I wanted to look for a new job anyhow." ("This is a challenge.") The secondary appraisal might be: "I have some money in savings, and I can live with my brother for a while if nothing turns up quickly—I should be fine." ("I have the resources to deal with this.") Which person is going to experience more stress and have more health problems as a consequence?

PERSONALITY FACTORS IN STRESS

Of course, how one cognitively assesses a stressor has a lot to do with one's personality. People with certain kinds of personality traits—such as aggressiveness or a naturally high level of anxiety, for example—seem to create more stress for themselves than may exist in the actual stressor. Even as long ago as the early 1930s, psychologists have had evidence that personality characteristics are a major factor in predicting health. A longitudinal study begun in 1932 (Lehr & Thomae, 1987) found that personality was almost as important to longevity* as were genetic, physical, or lifestyle factors. Other researchers have found that people who live to be very old—into their 90s and even over 100 years—tend to be relaxed, easygoing, cheerful, and active. People who have the opposite personality traits, such as aggressiveness, stubbornness, inflexibility, and tenseness, typically do not live as long as the *average* life expectancy (Levy et al., 2002).

Those positive and negative personality traits are some of the factors associated with two personality types that have been related to how people deal with stress and the influence of certain personality characteristics on coronary heart disease.

"He always times 60 Minutes.*"*

*longevity: how long people live

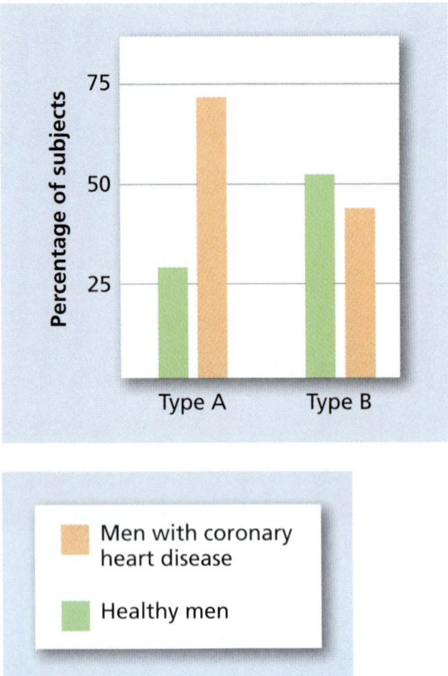

Figure 11.5 Personality and Coronary Heart Disease

The two bars on the left represent men with Type A personalities. Notice that within the Type A men, there are more than twice as many who suffer from coronary heart disease as those who are healthy. The two bars on the right represent men with Type B personalities. Far more Type B personalities are healthy than are Type A personalities, and there are far fewer Type B personalities with coronary heart disease when compared to Type A personalities.
Source: Miller et al. (1991, 1996).

TYPE A AND TYPE B In 1974, medical doctors Meyer Freidman and Ray Rosenman published a book titled *Type A Behavior and Your Heart*. The book was the result of studies spanning 3 decades of research into the influence of certain personality characteristics and coronary heart disease (Friedman & Kasanin, 1943; Friedman & Rosenman, 1959; Rosenman et al., 1975). Since then, numerous researchers have explored the link between what Friedman called Type A and Type B personalities.

Type A people are workaholics—they are very competitive, ambitious, hate to waste time, and are easily annoyed. They feel a constant sense of pressure and have a strong tendency to try to do several things at once. Often successful but frequently unsatisfied, they always seem to want to go faster and do more, and they get easily upset over small things. A typical Type A finds it difficult to relax and do nothing—Type A people take work with them on vacation, a laptop to the beach, and do business over the phone in the car.

In 1961, the *Western Collaborative Group Study* (Rosenman et al., 1975) assessed 3,500 men and followed them for 8 years. For example, participants were asked to agree or disagree with statements such as "I can relax without guilt," in which strong agreement indicates a Type B personality. The results were that Type A men were three times more likely to develop heart disease than were Type B men. **Type B** people are not that competitive or driven, tend to be easygoing and slow to anger, and seem relaxed and at peace. Type B people are more likely to take a book to the beach to cover up their face than to actually read the book. (See Figure 11.5.)

The *Framingham Heart Study* found that the risk of coronary heart disease for women who work and are also Type A is four times that of Type B working women (Eaker & Castelli, 1988). Other research has narrowed the key factors in Type A personality and heart disease to one characteristic: hostility* (Frederickson et al., 1999; Matthews et al., 2004; Williams, 1999; Williams et al., 1980). Williams and his colleagues used the *Minnesota Multiphasic Personality Inventory*, a personality test that looks for certain characteristics that include the level of hostility. LINK to Chapter Thirteen: Theories of Personality, p. 521. In this study, 424 patients who had undergone exploratory surgery for coronary heart disease were examined, and the presence of heart disease was related both to being Type A and to being hostile, with hostility being the more significant factor in the hardening of the arteries to the heart (Williams, 2001; Williams et al., 1980).

Numerous studies support the link between hostility and increased risk of coronary heart disease. A study of hostility levels and risk factors for heart disease in over 4,000 young adults found that increases in hostility over a 5-year follow-up study were associated with a rise in high blood pressure, one of the major risk factors of heart disease (Markovitz et al., 1997). Another study of anger in young men and their risk for premature heart disease found that over a period of slightly more than 3 decades, the young men who had exhibited high levels of hostility in their youth were far more likely to develop premature cardiovascular disease, particularly heart attacks, than were those men who had lower levels of anger and hostility (Chang et al., 2002). Similar studies found that hostility in college-aged male and females was significantly related to increased risk of heart disease, particularly if levels of hostility rose in middle age (Brondolo et al., 2003; Siegler et al., 2003).

Even children may not escape the hostility–heart disease link. A recent study has found that children and adolescents who scored high on assessments of hostility were more likely to show physical changes such as obesity, resistance to insulin, high blood pressure, and elevated levels of triglycerides 3 years after the initial measurements of hostility had been made (Raikkonen et al., 2003).

Type A personality person who is ambitious, time conscious, extremely hardworking, and tends to have high levels of hostility and anger as well as being easily annoyed.

Type B personality person who is relaxed and laid-back, less driven and competitive than Type A, and slow to anger.

Type C personality pleasant but repressed person, who tends to internalize his or her anger and anxiety and who finds expressing emotions difficult.

*hostility: feelings of conflict, anger, and ill will that are long lasting.

What about people who don't blow their top but try to keep everything "in" instead? Wouldn't that be bad for a person's health?

What about people who don't blow their top but try to keep everything "in" instead? Wouldn't that be bad for a person's health?

TYPE C A third personality type was identified by researchers Temoshok and Dreher (1992) as being associated with a higher incidence of cancer. **Type C** people tend to be very pleasant and try to keep the peace but find it difficult to express emotions, especially negative ones. They tend to internalize their anger and often experience a sense of despair over the loss of a loved one or a loss of hope. They are often lonely. These personality characteristics are strongly associated with cancer, and people who have cancer and this personality type often have thicker cancerous tumors as well (Eysenck, 1994; Temoshok & Dreher, 1992). Just as the stress of hostility puts the cardiovascular systems of Type A people at greater risk, the internalized negative emotions of the Type C personality may increase the levels of harmful stress hormones, weaken the immune system, and slow recovery.

A word of caution here: "personality-type" theories have come under criticism in recent years. Many consider them to be too simplistic—many people would not fall easily into one type or another. Nevertheless, many of the personality traits associated with these types do seem to be associated with stress and longevity. Many of the characteristics of the Type A personality, for example, fit the description of a major personality trait called *neuroticism,* the tendency to worry, be moody, and emotionally intense. LINK to Chapter Thirteen: Theories of Personality, p. 512. One recent longitudinal study's findings indicate that these characteristics are associated with an increased risk of an earlier death because people with these traits engage in poor health habits—poor diet, excessive drinking, smoking, and lack of exercise, to name a few (Mroczek et al., 2009). **Read** on **mypsychlab.com**

Read and learn more about Type C on **mypsychlab.com**

THE HARDY PERSONALITY Not all Type A people are prone to heart disease. Some people actually seem to thrive on stress instead of letting stress wear them down. These people have what is called the **hardy personality**, a term first coined by psychologist Suzanne Kobasa (1979). Hardy people (call them "Type H") differ from ordinary, hostile Type A people and others who suffer more ill effects due to stress in three ways:

hardy personality a person who seems to thrive on stress but lacks the anger and hostility of the Type A personality.

- Hardy people have a deep sense of *commitment* to their values, beliefs, sense of identity, work, and family life.
- Hardy people also feel that they are in *control* of their lives and what happens to them.
- Hardy people tend to interpret events in primary appraisal differently than people who are not hardy. When things go wrong, they do not see a frightening problem to be avoided but instead a *challenge* to be met and answered.

Why would those three characteristics (often known as the three "C's" of hardiness) lessen the negative impact of stress? Commitment makes a person more willing to make sacrifices and to deal with hardships than if commitment were lacking. Think about it: Have you ever had a job that you hated? Every little frustration and every snag was very stressful, right? Now think about doing something you love to do. The frustrations and snags that inevitably come with any endeavor just don't seem quite as bad when you are doing something you really want to do, do they?

As for control, uncontrollability is one of the major factors cited as increasing stress, as was discussed earlier in this chapter. Seeing events as challenges rather than problems also changes the level of stress experienced, a difference similar to that felt when riding a roller coaster: If riding the coaster is your own idea, it's fun; if someone makes you ride it, it's not fun.

Type Z behavior

The tendency for hardiness may even have genetic roots. Researchers have recently found that there seems to be a biochemical link between feeling miserable and an increased risk of death, and that there may be a genetic variation in some

Regular exercise—whether alone or in the company of family and friends—increases the functioning of the immune system and helps give people a sense of control over their health. Having a sense of control decreases feelings of stress, which also helps the immune system to function well.

individuals that actually severs that link, making that individual more biologically resilient or hardy (Cole et al., 2010).

The four personality types discussed so far could be summed up this way: If life gives you lemons,

- Type A people get enraged and throw the lemons back, having a minor heart attack while doing so.
- Type B people gather all the lemons and make lemonade.
- Type C people don't say anything but fume inside where no one can see.
- Type H people gather the lemons, make lemonade, sell it, turn it into a franchise business, and make millions. (Remember, laughing is good for you!)

EXPLANATORY STYLE: OPTIMISTS AND PESSIMISTS In addition to personality type, there are other personal factors that have an influence on people's reactions to stressors. One of these factors is the attitude that people have toward the things that happen to them in life.

Optimists are people who always tend to look for positive outcomes. **Pessimists** seem to expect the worst to happen. For an optimist, a glass is half full, whereas for a pessimist, the glass is half empty. Researchers have found that optimism is associated with longer life and increased immune-system functioning. Mayo Clinic researchers conducted a longitudinal study of optimists and pessimists (as assessed by a scale) over a period of 30 years (Maruta et al., 2002). The results for pessimists were not good: They had a much higher death rate than did the optimists, and those who were still living in 1994 had more problems with physical and emotional health, more pain, less ability to take part in social activities, and less energy than optimists. The optimists had a 50 percent lower risk of premature death and were more calm, peaceful, and happy than the pessimists (Maruta et al., 2002). Other studies link being optimistic to higher levels of helper T cells (immune system cells that direct and increase the functioning of the immune system) and higher levels of natural killer cells, the body's antivirus, anticancer cells (Segerstrom et al., 1998; Segerstrom & Sephton, 2010).

Martin Seligman is a social learning psychologist who developed the concept of *learned helplessness,* LINK to Chapter Five: Learning, pp. 199–201, and began the positive psychology movement. Seligman (2002) has outlined four ways in which optimism may affect how long a person lives:

1. Optimists are less likely to develop learned helplessness, the tendency to stop trying to achieve a goal that has been blocked in the past.
2. Optimists are more likely than pessimists to take care of their health by preventive measures (such as going to the doctor regularly, eating right, and exercising) because they believe that their actions make a difference in what happens to them. (Remember, this is a characteristic of hardy people as well.)
3. Optimists are far less likely than pessimists to become depressed, and depression is associated with mortality because of the effect of depression on the immune system.
4. Optimists have more effectively functioning immune systems than pessimists do, perhaps because they experience less psychological stress.

Whoa—optimistic students get better grades? How do I become an optimist?

Seligman (1998) has also found that optimists are more successful in their life endeavors than pessimists were. Optimistic politicians win more elections, optimistic students get better grades, and optimistic athletes win more contests.

Whoa—optimistic students get better grades? How do I become an optimist?

Sign me up! Optimism is mostly a matter of controlling mood or emotional reactions to situations. Psychiatrist Susan Vaughan (2000) has some good advice for optimistic people who want to keep a positive outlook:

optimists people who expect positive outcomes.

pessimists people who expect negative outcomes.

- **Alternative thinking:** Optimists tend to take bad things that happen less personally, coming up with alternative explanations for why the bad thing happened. For example, optimists tend to attribute poor exam grades to the difficulty of that particular material or to not having enough time to study. They appraise it as a challenge and assume that they will perform more successfully in the future.
- **Downward social comparison:** Many people make themselves feel better by comparing their performance to that of less competent others, making them feel better and protecting self-esteem. Optimists use *downward social comparison* frequently.
- **Relaxation:** Optimists use relaxation as a way to improve mood, such as exercising, meditating, or reading a good book.

HOW TO BECOME AN OPTIMISTIC THINKER The way to become an optimist is to monitor one's own thinking. Recognition of negative thoughts is the first step, followed by disputing those same negative thoughts (Seligman, 2002). The problem is that most people don't really think about their thoughts or characterize them as negative or pessimistic, which means that the damaging effects of such thinking are left uncontrolled. Here's a plan to follow to become an optimistic thinker:

1. When a bad mood strikes, stop and think about what just went through your head.
2. When you've recognized the negative statements, treat them as if they came from someone else—someone who is trying to make your life miserable. Think about the damage the statement is doing to you.
3. Argue with those thoughts. Challenge each negative statement and replace it with a more positive statement.
   Example:

1. "I'll never get this term paper finished, it's too hard and there's so much going on that it's impossible!" What words in this statement makes it pessimistic? "Never" is a long time. Why is it too hard? Is it really impossible, or just difficult? Is it just one part of the paper that seems so hard, or is it the whole thing?
2. That statement isn't going to help me at all, it just makes me feel worse and that makes me unmotivated to work on the paper.
3. I can finish the term paper. I'm just going to have to devote more time to working on it. I can make a timetable for finishing the different parts of the paper and stop spending so much time watching television and escaping into other activities that can wait until the paper is finished. I've been in situations like this before and managed, so I can manage now, too.

Notice that the third way of thinking is much more positive and hopeful. It includes ways to get around what seemed too hard or impossible in the negative statement. Essentially, the last step in becoming a more optimistic thinker is to learn to argue with yourself and correct distorted or faulty thinking.

How can I recognize distorted thinking when it's my own thoughts in the first place?

How can I recognize distorted thinking when it's my own thoughts in the first place?

Recognizing faulty thinking can be difficult at first. The following questions may help people to hone in on negative thinking:

1. In thinking about the thoughts you have had in the last few hours, how many of them were negative thoughts? How could you change those thoughts to be more positive?
2. When thinking about people you know who make a lot of negative self-statements or who are always minimizing their efforts or putting themselves down, how does their behavior make you feel? How do you think their behavior makes them feel?

11.4 11.5

CONCEPT MAP

Physiological Factors

- the **autonomic nervous system (ANS)** figures prominently in the body's physiological reactions to stress
- Hans Selye identified the **general adaption syndrome (GAS)**, the sequence of physiological reactions the body goes through when adapting to a stressor
  - **alarm:** sympathetic nervous system is first activated
  - **resistance:** continued activation of sympathetic activity until organism's resources are depleted
  - **exhaustion:** prolonged stress response coupled with depleted resources can lead to stress-related diseases or death of the organism; if stressor is stopped, parasympathetic division is activated and body attempts to replenish resources
- the field of **psychoneuroimmunology** focuses on the effects of stress on the immune system
  - stress-related responses similar to those triggered by infection—increase in white blood cell count, enzymes, and antibodies
  - body is engineered for short-term, acute stress; prolonged stress/depletion of resources results in reduced functioning of immune system

Cognitive and Personality Factors

- **Lazarus's cognitive–mediational theory of emotions** suggests an individual's appraisal of a stressor is a major factor in determining how stressful that stressor becomes
  - **primary appraisal** involves estimating severity of the stressor and classifying it as a threat, challenge, or loss already occurred
  - **secondary appraisal** involves estimation of resources available to cope with stressor
  - result of appraisal determines level of stress and emotional reaction
- **personality differences** affect how one assesses a stressor, the coping strategies used, and possible health outcomes
  - **Type A:** workaholic, competitive, ambitious, hate to waste time, easily annoyed; more likely to have health issues (e.g., heart disease), especially the more hostile an individual is
  - **Type B:** more easygoing, slower to anger, not as competitive or driven; less likely to have health issues
  - **Type C:** tend to be pleasant and at peace but find it difficult to express emotions, especially negative ones; associated with cancer
  - **"Type H":** hardy personality, appear to be like Type A but less prone to heart disease; appear to thrive on stress due to three factors: sense of commitment, control, and seeing stressors as a challenge
- **explanatory style** optimists tend to look for positive outcomes, whereas pessimists seem to expect the worst
  - Seligman (originally studied concept of learned helplessness) began the positive psychology movement; has suggested that optimism leads to longer life and greater success in life endeavors
  - optimism is associated with controlling mood or emotional reactions; can be a learned skill through alternative thinking, downward social comparison, relaxation, and correcting faulty thinking

PRACTICE quiz How much do you remember?

ANSWERS ON PAGE AK-2.

Pick the best answer.

1. In the _________ stage of the GAS, the person may actually start to feel better.
   a. alarm
   b. resistance
   c. exhaustion
   d. termination
2. The activation of the immune-system response by stress differs from the activation of that system by illness in that _________.
   a. illness activates areas in the brain first.
   b. stress increases the release of natural killer cells.
   c. stress activates a different immune response than does illness.
   d. stress activates areas in the brain first.
3. According to Lazarus, secondary appraisal involves _________.
   a. estimating the severity of the stressor.
   b. classifying the stressor as a threat or challenge.
   c. deciding whether the stressor is a problem.
   d. estimating the resources a person has available for coping.
4. Adam is very ambitious and driven to succeed. He is easily angered, always wants to be working, and finds it hard to relax. According to research, Adam _________.
   a. is at a high risk for coronary heart disease.
   b. is a hardy personality.
   c. is a Type B personality.
   d. is a Type C personality.
5. Which of the following is NOT one of the three "C's" of the hardy personality?
   a. commitment
   b. callousness
   c. control
   d. challenge
6. Optimism has been associated with all of the following except _________.
   a. taking care of one's health.
   b. increased rates of learned helplessness.
   c. lower rates of depression.
   d. healthy immune systems.

Poverty can lead to many conditions that increase the degree of stress experienced by both adults and children. These children, for example, may face an increased risk of malnutrition, illness, and exposure to violence because of the conditions under which they must live.

SOCIAL FACTORS IN STRESS: PEOPLE WHO NEED PEOPLE

11.6 What social factors influence stress reactions?

As stated earlier, much of the stress in everyday life comes from having to deal with other people and with the rules of social interaction. Overcrowding, for example, is a common source of stress and may be one reason for the increasing rise of *road rage*, or the tendency for drivers to become excessively enraged by ordinary traffic frustrations, sometimes resulting in serious injuries, assaults, and even death (AAA Foundation for Traffic Safety, 1997). Two of the more prominent social factors in creating stressful living conditions are both economically based: poverty and job stress.

POVERTY Living in poverty is stressful for many reasons. Lack of sufficient money to provide the basic necessities of life can lead to many stressors for both adults and children: overcrowding, lack of medical care, increased rates of disabilities due to poor prenatal care, noisy environments, increased rates of illness (such as asthma in childhood) and violence, and substance abuse (Aligne et al., 2000; Bracey, 1997; Leroy & Symes, 2001; Park et al., 2002; Renchler, 1993; Rouse, 1998; Schmitz et al., 2001).

JOB STRESS Even if a person has a job and is making an adequate salary, there are stresses associated with the workplace that add to daily stressors. Some of the typical sources of stress in the workplace include the workload, a lack of variety or meaningfulness in work, lack of control over decisions, long hours, poor physical work conditions, and lack of job security (Murphy, 1995). **Watch** on **mypsychlab.com**

Watch a video on rude atmospheres in the workplace on **mypsychlab.com**

Stress at work can result in the same symptoms as stress from any other source: headaches, high blood pressure, indigestion, and other physical symptoms; anxiety, irritability, anger, depression, and other psychological symptoms; and behavioral symptoms such as overeating, drug use, poor job performance, or changes in family relationships (Anschuetz, 1999).

There are times when I feel like I've just had it with school and all the work the teachers pile on—is that something like workplace stress?

There are times when I feel like I've just had it with school and all the work the teachers pile on—is that something like workplace stress?

One of the more serious effects of workplace stress is a condition called burnout. **Burnout** can be defined as negative changes in thoughts, emotions, and behavior as a result of prolonged stress or frustration (Miller & Smith, 1993). Symptoms of burnout are extreme dissatisfaction, pessimism, lowered job satisfaction, and a desire to quit. Although burnout is most commonly associated with job stress, college students can also suffer from burnout when the stresses of college life—term papers, exams, assignments and the like—become overwhelming. The emotional exhaustion associated

burnout negative changes in thoughts, emotions, and behavior as a result of prolonged stress or frustration.

This Buddhist group is celebrating Songkran, the New Year, by performing their cultural ritual of pouring water over their elder's palms. Although they are wearing clothing typical of people living in Los Angeles, California, where the ceremony is taking place, they still maintain some of their former cultural traditions. This is a good example of integration.

with burnout can be lessened when a person at risk of burnout is a member, within the work environment, of a social group that provides support and also the motivation to continue to perform despite being exhausted (Halbesleben & Bowler, 2007).

HOW CULTURE AFFECTS STRESS When a person from one culture must live in another culture, that person may experience a great deal of stress. *Acculturation* means the process of adapting to a new or different culture, often the dominant culture (Sodowsky et al., 1991). The stress resulting from the need to change and adapt to the dominant or majority culture is called **acculturative stress** (Berry & Kim, 1998; Berry & Sam, 1997).

The way in which a minority person chooses to enter into the majority culture can also have an impact on the degree of stress that person will experience (Berry & Kim, 1988). One method is called *integration*, in which the individual tries to maintain a sense of the original cultural identity while also trying to form a positive relationship with members of the majority culture. For example, an integrated person will maintain a lot of original cultural traditions within the home and with immediate family members but will dress like the majority culture and adopt some of those characteristics as well. For people who choose integration, acculturative stress is usually low (Ward & Rana-Deuba, 1999).

In *assimilation*, the minority person gives up the old cultural identity and completely adopts the majority culture's ways. In the early days of the United States, many immigrants were assimilated into the mainstream American culture, even changing their names to sound more "American." Assimilation leads to moderate levels of stress, most likely due to the loss of cultural patterns and rejection by other members of the minority culture who have not chosen assimilation (LaFromboise et al., 1993; Lay & Nguyen, 1998).

Separation is a pattern in which the minority person rejects the majority culture's ways and tries to maintain the original cultural identity. Members of the minority culture refuse to learn the language of the dominant culture, and they live where others from their culture live, socializing only with others from their original culture. An example of this might be seen in many "Chinatown" areas across the United States, in which there are some residents who do not speak any English and who rarely go outside their neighborhood. Separation results in a fairly high degree of stress, and that stress will be even higher if the separation is forced (by discrimination from the majority group) rather than voluntary (self-imposed withdrawal from the majority culture).

The greatest acculturative stress will most likely be experienced by people who have chosen to be *marginalized*, neither maintaining contact with their original culture nor joining the majority culture. They essentially live on the "margins" of both cultures without feeling or becoming part of either culture. Many Native Americans may feel marginalized, neither belonging to their original tribe of origin nor to the majority culture. Marginalized individuals do not have the security of the familiar culture of origin or the acceptance of the majority culture and may suffer a loss of identity and feel alienated from others (Roysircar-Sodowsky & Maestas, 2000). Obviously, marginalized people have little in the way of a social-support system to help them deal with both everyday stresses and major life changes.

I hear the term "social-support system" all the time now. Exactly what is it?

I hear the term "social-support system" all the time now. Exactly what is it?

THE POSITIVE BENEFITS OF SOCIAL SUPPORT A **social-support system** is the network of friends, family members, neighbors, coworkers, and others who can offer help to a person in need. That help can take the form of advice, physical or monetary

acculturative stress stress resulting from the need to change and adapt a person's ways to the majority culture.

social-support system the network of family, friends, neighbors, coworkers, and others who can offer support, comfort, or aid to a person in need.

support, information, emotional support, love and affection, or companionship. Research has consistently shown that having a good social-support system is of critical importance in a person's ability to cope with stressors: People with good social-support systems are less likely to die from illnesses or injuries than those without such support (Kulik & Mahler, 1989, 1993). Marriage, itself a form of social support, is a good predictor of healthy aging and longevity (Gardner & Oswald, 2004; Vaillant, 2002). Social support has been found to have a positive effect on the immune system (Holt-Lunstad et al., 2003); for example, it has been shown to improve the mental health and physical functioning of people who have *lupus*, a chronic inflammatory disease that can affect nearly any part of the body (Sutcliffe et al., 1999; M. M. Ward et al., 1999) as well as those with cancer and HIV (Carver & Antoni, 2004; Gonzalez et al., 2004).

Social support can make a stressor seem less threatening because people with such support know that there is help available. Having people to talk to about one's problems reduces the physical symptoms of stress—talking about frightening or frustrating events with others can help people think more realistically about the threat, for example, and talking with people who have had similar experiences can help put the event into perspective. LINK to Chapter Fifteen: Psychological Therapies, pp. 587–589. The negative emotions of loneliness and depression, which are less likely to occur with someone who has social support, can adversely affect one's ability to cope (Beehr et al., 2000; Weisse, 1992). Positive emotions, on the other hand, have a decidedly beneficial effect on health, helping people recover from stressful experiences more quickly and effectively (Tugade & Fredrickson, 2004). Positive emotions are more likely to occur in the presence of friends and family.

How people think about a stressor is also a powerful influence on their ability to cope, as the next section will discuss.

Coping with illness is always made easier when one has social support. Here, a man recovering in the hospital is visited by a volunteer and her dog. Animals are also a good source of social support, and people who have animals have been shown to recover from illnesses and stressors more quickly (Allen et al., 2002).

11.6 CONCEPT MAP

Social Factors in Stress

- a great deal of stress can come from dealing with other people and social interactions
- poverty and job stress are prominent, economically based social factors that lead to stressful living conditions
  - poverty results in lack of basic life necessities
  - job stress may be related to workload, lack of control or job security, work schedule, and low job satisfaction
- culturally, stress is affected by status of acculturation (adapting to a new, different, or often dominant culture) and the method chosen to adapt
  - **integration:** original identity maintained but forms positive relationships with members of dominant culture (lowest stress)
  - **assimilation:** individual gives up old culture and completely adopts ways of majority (moderate stress)
  - **separation:** majority culture is rejected and original cultural identity is maintained (high stress)
  - **marginalization:** does not maintain contact with original culture or join majority culture (greatest stress)
- in general, having a positive social support system that provides various forms of help (e.g., monetary, physical, emotional support) is a good predictor for healthy aging and longevity

(continued)

PRACTICE quiz How much do you remember? ANSWERS ON PAGE AK-2.

Pick the best answer.

1. Which of the following is NOT a typical source of stress in the workplace?
   - **a.** heavy workload
   - **b.** lack of variety
   - **c.** lack of shift work
   - **d.** lack of job security
2. Which of the following is NOT a symptom of burnout?
   - **a.** pessimism
   - **b.** dissatisfaction
   - **c.** optimism
   - **d.** desire to quit
3. Larysa moved from Ukraine to the United States. She learned to speak and write English, changed her last name so that it would sound more "American," and no longer maintains any of her old culture's styles of dress or customs. Larysa has used which method of entering the majority culture?
   - **a.** integration
   - **b.** assimilation
   - **c.** separation
   - **d.** marginalization
4. Social support ________.
   - **a.** has a positive benefit on health.
   - **b.** can improve the physical functioning of cancer patients.
   - **c.** can improve the physical functioning of people with HIV.
   - **d.** includes all of the above.

Brainstorming: In general, studies show that people who have social support are better able to deal with the effects of stress, but this does not mean that all social relationships have a positive effect on one's ability to cope. How can the people in your life interfere with your ability to handle stress, and what are some positive ways in which you can reduce that interference?

I have exams and my job and my relationship to worry about, so I feel pretty stressed out—how do people deal with all the stress they face every day?

Coping With Stress

I have exams and my job and my relationship to worry about, so I feel pretty stressed out—how do people deal with all the stress they face every day?

So far, this chapter has talked about what stress is and the factors that can magnify the effects of stress, as well as the effects of stress on a person's physical health. Part of dealing with stress is in knowing those kinds of things so that changes can be made in the factors that are controllable. **Coping strategies** are actions that people can take to master, tolerate, reduce, or minimize the effects of stressors, and they can include both behavioral strategies and psychological strategies.

An audience watches what is obviously a funny movie, one of the more popular choices for film-goers. A large part of the success of such comedies can be attributed to the human need to laugh—laughter helps us cope with many of life's stresses.

11.7 What are some ways in which people cope with stress reactions?

PROBLEM-FOCUSED COPING

One type of coping strategy is to work on eliminating or changing the stressor itself. When people try to eliminate the source of a stress or reduce its impact through their own actions, it is called **problem-focused coping** (Folkman & Lazarus, 1980; Lazarus, 1993). For example, a student might have a problem understanding a particular professor. The professor is knowledgeable but has trouble explaining the concepts of the course in a way that this student can understand. Problem-focused coping might include talking to the professor after class, asking fellow students to clarify the concepts, getting a tutor, or forming a study group with other students who are also having difficulty to pool the group's resources.

EMOTION-FOCUSED COPING

Problem-focused coping can work quite well but is not the only method people can use. Most people use both problem-focused coping and **emotion-focused coping** to successfully deal with controllable stressful events (Eschenbeck et al., 2008; Folkman & Lazarus, 1980; Lazarus, 1993; Stowell et al., 2001). Emotion-focused coping is a strategy that involves changing the way a person feels or emotionally reacts to a stressor. This reduces the emotional impact of the stressor and makes it possible to deal with the problem more effectively. For example, the student who is faced with a professor who isn't easy to understand might share his concerns with a friend, talking it through until calm enough to tackle the problem in a more direct manner. Emotion-focused coping also works for stressors that are uncontrollable and for which problem-focused coping is not possible. Someone using emotion-focused coping may decide to view the stressor as a challenge rather than a threat, decide that the problem is a minor one, write down concerns in a journal, or even ignore the problem altogether.

Ignore it? But won't that just make matters worse?

True, ignoring a problem is not a good strategy when there is something a person can actively do about solving the problem. But when it is not possible to change or eliminate the stressor, or when worrying about the stressor can be a problem itself, ignoring the problem is not a bad idea. Researchers working with people who had suffered heart attacks found that those people who worried about a future attack were more likely to suffer from symptoms of severe stress, such as nightmares and poor sleep (both factors that increase the risk of a future heart attack), than were the people who tried to ignore their worries (Ginzburg et al., 2003). LINK to Chapter Fourteen: Psychological Disorders, pp. 541–542.

Using humor can also be a form of emotion-focused coping, as the opening story to this chapter suggests. A study on the effects of laughter found that laughter actually boosted the action of the immune system by increasing the work of natural killer cells (cells that attack viruses in the body). In this study, participants were shown a humor video for 1 hour. Blood samples were taken 10 minutes before the viewing, 30 minutes into the viewing, 30 minutes after viewing, and 12 hours after viewing the humor video. There were significant increases in natural killer cell activity and nearly half a dozen other immune system cells and systems, with some effects lasting the full 12 hours after the video ended (Berk et al., 2001).

MEDITATION AS A COPING MECHANISM

Meditation is a mental series of exercises meant to refocus attention and achieve a trancelike state of consciousness. LINK to Chapter Four: Consciousness, p. 131. Meditation can produce a state of relaxation that can aid in coping with the physiological reactions to a stressful situation. When properly meditating, brain waves change to include more theta and alpha waves (indicating deep relaxation), but little to no delta waves, which would indicate deep sleep (Lagopoulos et al., 2009).

CONCENTRATIVE MEDITATION Have you ever found yourself staring out into space, or at some little spot on the wall or table, only to realize that your mind has been a complete blank for the last several minutes?

The state just described is really nothing more than **concentrative meditation**, the form of meditation best known to the general public. In concentrative meditation, the goal is to focus the mind on some repetitive or unchanging stimulus (such as a spot or the sound of one's own heart beating) so that the mind can forget daily hassles and problems and the body can relax. In fact, Herbert Benson (Benson, 1975; Benson et al., 1974a, 1974b) found that meditation produces a state of relaxation in which blood pressure is lowered, alpha waves (brain waves associated with relaxation) are increased, and the amounts of melatonin secreted at night (the hormone that helps induce sleep) are increased.

Some people say that if you meditate for only 20 minutes a day, you don't have to sleep at night. That would be nice—think how much more could be accomplished with those extra hours. Unfortunately, although certain meditation groups do make some rather wild claims for meditation, research has shown none of them to be true (Murphy & Donavan, 1997). What research does show is that concentrative meditation is a good way to relax and lower blood pressure in adolescents and

coping strategies actions that people can take to master, tolerate, reduce, or minimize the effects of stressors.

problem-focused coping coping strategies that try to eliminate the source of a stress or reduce its impact through direct actions.

emotion-focused coping coping strategies that change the impact of a stressor by changing the emotional reaction to the stressor.

meditation mental series of exercises meant to refocus attention and achieve a trancelike state of consciousness.

concentrative meditation form of meditation in which a person focuses the mind on some repetitive or unchanging stimulus so that the mind can be cleared of disturbing thoughts and the body can experience relaxation.

Ignore it? But won't that just make matters worse?

This man is practicing Zen yoga meditation. Meditation increases relaxation and helps to lower blood pressure and muscle tension.

These Peruvian villagers in a cemetery are honoring their loved ones who have passed away. The Day of the Dead is not only a celebration of the lives of those who have passed on but also a celebration for the living, who use this holiday to gain a sense of control over one of life's most uncontrollable events—death itself. What rituals or ceremonies do people of other cultures use to cope with death?

receptive meditation form of meditation in which a person attempts to become aware of everything in immediate conscious experience, or an expansion of consciousness.

adults, men and women, and both Whites and African Americans (Barnes et al., 1997; Rainforth et al., 2007; Schneider et al., 1995; Wenneberg et al., 1997). It isn't the only way, as reading a good book or taking a warm bath also produces relaxation. Even simply resting for the same amount of time as one might meditate can be just as relaxing. The advantage of meditation is that people can do it almost anywhere, even in the classroom just before a big test. (It would be a little difficult to take a warm bath then.)

Other research has suggested that concentrative meditation can reduce the levels of chronic pain (Brown & Jones, 2010; Kabat-Zinn et al., 1986), reduce the symptoms of anxiety, depression, and hostility (Kabat-Zinn et al., 1985), reduce the risk of heart disease (Schneider et al., 2010), and reduce stress levels in cancer patients (Speca et al., 2000). Reducing stress levels in cancer patients through meditation will increase the likelihood of recovery and reduce the incidence of recurrence.

RECEPTIVE MEDITATION The other kind of meditation is less well known and not as easily achieved. It is called **receptive meditation** and involves trying to expand consciousness outward. The best description of what this is like is to think about a time when you were overawed by nature. Perhaps you were standing at the ocean's edge on a starry night and became suddenly aware of how vast the universe really is. Or perhaps you were walking in the woods and listening to all the little sounds of the birds and animals surrounding you. Your attention was focused outward rather than inward, and this is similar to the state that this type of meditation tries to achieve.

THE EFFECTS OF MEDITATION Regardless of which form of meditation people choose to try, the effects are similar (Murphy & Donavan, 1997). Meditation for only 20 minutes can produce lowered blood pressure in people with hypertension (high blood pressure). It can calm anxiety, help people get to sleep, and help people deal with stress. **Explore** on **mypsychlab.com**

Explore coping strategies on **mypsychlab.com**

11.8 How is coping with stress affected by culture and religion?

HOW CULTURE AFFECTS COPING

Imagine this scene: You are driving out in the country when you come upon an elderly man working on a large wooden box, polishing it with great care. You stop to talk to the man and find out that the box is his own coffin, and he spends his days getting it ready, tending to it with great care. He isn't frightened of dying and doesn't feel strange about polishing his own coffin. How would you react?

If you were from the same rural area of Vietnam as the elderly man, you would probably think nothing strange is going on. For elderly people in the Vietnamese culture, thoughts of death and the things that go along with dying, such as a coffin, are not as stressful as they are to people from Western cultures. In fact, *stress* isn't all that common a term in Vietnamese society compared to Western societies (Phan & Silove, 1999).

In the case of people living in Vietnam and even Vietnamese immigrants in other countries, mental illness is explained by an imbalance between the male and female elements of a person, or by a loss of soul, evil spirits, or a weakening of the nerves. Coping with stress in Vietnamese culture may include rituals, consulting a fortune-teller, or eating certain foods (Phan & Silove, 1999). In many Asian cultures, meditation is a common stress-relief tool, including the art of tai chi, a form of meditational exercise (Yip, 2002).

Obviously, culture is an important factor in the kinds of coping strategies an individual may adopt and even in determining the degree of stress that is experienced. Mental-health professionals should make an effort to include an assessment of a person's cultural background as well as immediate circumstances when dealing with adjustment problems due to stress.

HOW RELIGION AFFECTS COPING

A belief in a higher power can also be a source of great comfort in times of stress. There are several ways that religious beliefs can affect the degree of stress people experience and the ability to cope with that stress (Hill & Butter, 1995; Pargament, 1997).

First, most people who hold strong religious beliefs belong to a religious organization and attend regular religious functions, such as services at a synagogue, mosque, temple, or church. This membership can be a vital part of a person's social-support system. People do not feel alone in their struggle, both literally because of the people who surround them in their religious community and spiritually because of the intangible presence of their deity (Koenig et al., 1999).

Another way that religion helps people cope involves the rituals and rites that help people feel better about personal weaknesses, failures, or feelings of inadequacy (Koenig et al., 2001). These include rituals such as confession of sins or prayer services during times of stress. Religion can also increase the likelihood that a person will volunteer to help others, feel stronger and better in many ways. Finally, religious beliefs can give meaning to things that otherwise seem to have no meaning or purpose, such as viewing death as a pathway to a paradise, or the destruction of one's home in a natural disaster as a reminder to place less attachment on material things.

Many religions also encourage healthy behavior and eating habits—eating wisely; limiting or foregoing the use of alcohol, tobacco, and other drugs; and sanctioning monogamous relationships. Some research even suggests that people with religious commitments live longer than those who have no such beliefs, although this is correlational research and should not be interpreted as concluding that religious belief causes longer life expectancies (Hummer et al., 1999; Koenig et al., 1999; Strawbridge et al., 1997; Thoresen & Harris, 2002). Simulate on mypsychlab.com

Simulate factors in stress reduction on mypsychlab.com

11.7 11.8

CONCEPT MAP

coping strategies
are behavioral and psychological actions taken to master, tolerate, reduce, or minimize the effect of stressors

problem-focused coping
involves working to change or eliminate the stressor itself

emotion-focused coping
involves changing the way a person feels or emotionally reacts to a stressor

various methods and behaviors exist to help individuals in dealing with stress

- meditation, in its various forms, helps to promote relaxatior calm anxiety, improve sleep, and lower blood pressure
- an individual's culture and/or religious beliefs can affect the appraisal of events as more or less stressful, the coping strategies adopted, and support systems that can offer assistance

Coping With Stress

PRACTICE quiz How much do you remember? ANSWERS ON PAGE AK-2.

Pick the best answer.

1. When a person tries to cope by eliminating or changing the stressor directly, it is known as __________.
   a. a defense mechanism.
   b. problem-focused coping.
   c. self-focused coping.
   d. emotion-focused coping.
2. Kareem is relaxing in a chair with his eyes closed. As he sits quietly, he is focusing on the sound of his own breathing and clearing his mind of other thoughts. Kareem is practicing __________.
   a. sensory deprivation.
   b. concentrative meditation.
   c. receptive meditation.
   d. implosive meditation.
3. Which of the following is NOT one of the ways that religion helps people reduce or cope with stress?
   a. Religion can provide a strong social-support system.
   b. Religion includes rituals that can help people feel better about their failings.
   c. Most religions promote healthy lifestyles.
   d. Religion isolates people from those who are different.

Brainstorming: Try to identify two or three behaviors in the past few weeks that may have been related to an unconscious defense mechanism. In hindsight, did the behavior(s) make the problem better or worse, and why?

Exercising regularly benefits not only physical health but mental health as well—both powerful motivators to get moving!

Applying Psychology to Everyday Life: Exercising for Mental Health

11.9 What are the psychological benefits of exercise?

You've heard it many times in your life: Exercise is good for you.

Exercise makes the heart healthier, raises the body's metabolic rate to help maintain a healthy weight, raises "good" cholesterol and lowers "bad" cholesterol, strengthens bones, improves sleep quality, reduces tiredness, increases natural killer cell activity to help ward off viruses and cancer, and is a great way to reduce the effects of stress (Courneya et al., 2009; Fiatarone et al., 1993; Manson et al., 2002; Peters et al., 2009). Aerobic exercise has also been found to reduce feelings of tiredness and increase energy in young adults who, because of a sedentary lifestyle, have been diagnosed with persistent fatigue (Puetz et al., 2008).

Now researchers are finding that exercise is good for your mental health as well as your physical health. Exercise has been found to help reduce symptoms in those menopausal women who experience anxiety or depression during the physical and chemical changes of menopause (Nelson et al., 2008). A survey of research on exercise and mental health has shown that exercise can also reduce the more severe symptoms of anxiety and depression disorders, with the author of the survey suggesting that exercise should be more widely prescribed by mental-health professionals (Ströhle, 2008). Individuals who exercise report not only lower levels of anxiety and depression, but also experience lower levels of stress and anger. One recent study found that regular exercise reduced the anxiety levels of patients suffering from a variety of chronic medical conditions by 20 percent, and this benefit was obtained with exercise programs of 30 minutes or less over a period of 3 to 12 weeks—anything longer and patients were less likely to continue (Herring et al., 2010).

An exercise program may be difficult to fit into one's busy schedule at first, but the benefits to physical and mental health are powerful persuaders to do so. And remember—joyous laughter counts as exercise, too.

chapter summary

Listen on **mypsychlab.com** Listen to an audio file of your chapter **www.mypsychlab.com**

Stress and Stressors

11.1 How do psychologists define stress?

- Stress is the physical, emotional, and behavioral responses that occur when events are identified as threatening or challenging.
- Stress that has a negative impact is called "distress." Eustress is the optimal amount of stress that people need to function well.

11.2 What kinds of external events can cause stress?

- Catastrophes are events such as floods or crashes that can result in high levels of stress.
- Major life changes create stress by requiring adjustments. Major life changes have an impact on chronic health problems and risk of accidents.
- Hassles are the daily frustrations and irritations that have an impact on day-to-day health.

11.3 What are some psychological factors in stress?

- Four sources of stress are pressure, uncontrollability, frustration, and conflict.
- Frustration, which can be internal or external, may result in persistence, aggression, displaced aggression, or withdrawal.

Physiological Factors: Stress and Health

- The autonomic nervous system consists of the sympathetic system, which responds to stressful events, and the parasympathetic system, which restores the body to normal functioning after the stress has ceased.

11.4 How does stress affect the physical functioning of the body and its immune system?

- The general adaptation syndrome is the body's reaction to stress and includes three stages of reaction: alarm, resistance, and exhaustion.
- Stress causes the immune system to react as though an illness or invading organism has been detected, increasing the functioning of the immune system.
- As the stress continues or increases, the immune system can begin to fail.

ISSUES IN PSYCHOLOGY: Health Psychology and Stress

- The relatively new field of health psychology focuses on the effects of physical activities, psychological traits, and social relationships on overall health and rate of illnesses.

11.5 How do cognitive factors and personality differences affect the experience of stress?

- The cognitive appraisal approach states that how people think about a stressor determines, at least in part, how stressful that stressor will become.
- The first step in appraising a stressor is called primary appraisal, in which the person determines whether an event is threatening, challenging, or of no consequence. Threatening events are more stressful than those seen as challenging.
- The second step is secondary appraisal, in which the person assesses the resources available to deal with the stressor, such as time, money, and social support.
- Type A personalities are ambitious, time conscious, hostile, and angry workaholics who are at increased risk of coronary heart disease, primarily due to their anger and hostility.
- Type B personalities are relaxed and easygoing and have one-third the risk of coronary heart disease as do Type A personalities, if male, and one-fourth the risk if female and working outside the home.
- Type C personalities are pleasant but repressed, internalizing their negative emotions.
- Hardy people are hard workers who lack the anger and hostility of the Type A personality, instead seeming to thrive on stress.
- Optimists look for positive outcomes and experience far less stress than pessimists, who take a more negative view.

11.6 What social factors influence stress reactions?

- Several social factors can be a source of stress or increase the effects of stress: poverty, stresses on the job or in the workplace, and entering a majority culture that is different from one's culture of origin.
- Burnout is a condition that occurs when job stress is so great that the person develops negative thoughts, emotions, and behavior as well as an extreme dissatisfaction with the job and a desire to quit.

- The four methods of acculturation are integration, assimilation, separation, and marginalization.
- Social-support systems are important in helping people cope with stress.

Coping With Stress

11.7 What are some ways in which people cope with stress reactions?

- Problem-focused coping is used when the problem can be eliminated or changed so that it is no longer stressful or so that the impact of the stressor is reduced.
- Emotion-focused coping is often used with problem-focused coping and involves changing one's emotional reactions to a stressor.
- Psychological defense mechanisms are unconscious distortions of perceived reality and can be a form of emotion-focused coping.
- Meditation can produce a state of relaxation and reduce the physical reactions common to stressful situations.
- Concentrative meditation involves focusing inward on some repetitive stimulus, such as one's breathing. Receptive meditation involves focusing outward to expand conscious awareness.

11.8 How is coping with stress affected by culture and religion?

- Different cultures perceive stressors differently, and coping strategies will also vary from culture to culture.
- People with religious beliefs also have been found to cope better with stressful events.

Applying Psychology to Everyday Life: Exercising for Mental Health

11.9 What are the psychological benefits of exercise?

- Exercise not only produces physical benefits such as reduction of heart disease, cancer, and weight, but also reduces anxiety and depression.

test YOURSELF

ANSWERS ON PAGE AK-2.

Study and Review on **mypsychlab.com** Ready for your test? More quizzes and a customized study plan **www.mypsychlab.com**

Pick the best answer.

1. Which of the following is a cognitive symptom of stress?
   a. frequent colds
   b. anxiety
   c. overeating
   d. memory problems
2. How do today's researchers differ from Selye in their view of eustress?
   a. They feel that eustress is more harmful than distress.
   b. They have not found evidence for eustress.
   c. They believe that a certain level of eustress is necessary to promote health.
   d. They believe that distress can be helpful instead of harmful.
3. Unpredictable, large-scale events that create a great deal of stress and feelings of threat are called _________.
   a. major life events.
   b. catastrophes.
   c. hassles.
   d. major hassles.
4. A score of 250 on the SRRS would indicate a ________, according to Holmes and Rahe.
   a. moderate life crisis.
   b. mild life crisis.
   c. major life crisis.
   d. noncrisis.
5. Lisa's score on the SRRS was 380. According to Holmes and Rahe, Lisa is probably suffering from a _________.
   a. mild life crisis.
   b. moderate life crisis.
   c. major life crisis.
   d. mild stress disorder.
6. Researchers found that the _________ of daily hassles was a far better predictor of headaches than were scores on a life-events scale.
   a. number
   b. type
   c. positive quality
   d. perceived severity
7. For which of the following groups of people would going shopping or experiencing bad weather be more stressful than for the other groups, according to Ellis et al. (2001)?
   a. children
   b. adolescents
   c. young adults
   d. elderly people
8. Which of the following is NOT a source of stress as discussed in the text?
   a. pressure
   b. uncontrollability
   c. predictability
   d. frustration
9. Who reformulated the frustration–aggression hypothesis?
   a. Dollard
   b. Berkowitz
   c. Miller
   d. Lazarus
10. Rachel's employer gives her a bad review, making Rachel feel lousy. When she arrives at home, she yells at her husband and children. Rachel is displaying _________.
    a. escape.
    b. withdrawal.
    c. displacement.
    d. projection.
11. Trying to decide between two of your favorite desserts is an example of a(n) _________ conflict.
    a. approach–approach
    b. avoidance–avoidance
    c. approach–avoidance
    d. multiple approach–avoidance
12. Phrases such as "caught between a rock and a hard place" and "out of the frying pan, into the fire" refer to _________ conflicts.
    a. approach–approach
    b. avoidance–avoidance
    c. approach–avoidance
    d. multiple approach–avoidance
13. When a person has to make a choice among several goals and each goal has both its good points and its bad points, the person is experiencing a(n) _________ conflict.
    a. approach–approach
    b. avoidance–avoidance
    c. approach–avoidance
    d. multiple approach–avoidance
14. In which of Selye's stages is death a possible outcome?
    a. alarm
    b. resistance
    c. reaction
    d. exhaustion

15. Appraising a stressor as a challenge results in _________ than if the stressor is appraised as a threat.
   a. more stress
   b. less stress
   c. less successful coping
   d. more negative emotions

16. Joe rarely takes any work home, preferring to leave his work worries at the office. He is not ambitious and likes to have a lot of leisure time when it is possible. He is also easygoing and doesn't lose his temper often, preferring to avoid conflict. Which of the following statements about Joe is most likely TRUE?
   a. Joe is a Type A personality.
   b. Joe is a Type B personality.
   c. Joe is a Type C personality.
   d. Joe's risk of coronary heart disease is high.

17. Tad seems to thrive on stress and feels very much in control of his life. He would probably be labeled a _________ personality.
   a. Type A
   b. Type B
   c. Type C
   d. hardy

18. Which of the following is NOT one of the three methods suggested by Vaughan to promote a positive, optimistic mood?
   a. alternative thinking
   b. relaxation
   c. using a scapegoat
   d. downward social comparison

19. Acculturative stress is lowest for people who choose _________ as their method of entering the majority culture.
   a. integration
   b. assimilation
   c. separation
   d. marginalization

20. Shawna is having trouble in algebra. She goes to the school's academic help center for tutoring and spends extra time working algebra problems at home. Shawna's method of coping is _________.
   a. problem focused.
   b. emotion focused.
   c. defensive focused.
   d. internal.

21. Meditation has been shown to accomplish all of the following except _________.
   a. relaxation.
   b. a reduction in blood pressure.
   c. reducing the need for sleep.
   d. reducing symptoms of anxiety.

22. Who among the following probably has the least ability to cope effectively with stress?
   a. Marian, a very religious person
   b. Mei Ling, who comes from a culture that emphasizes the family
   c. Jackie, who has few friends and whose family lives far away from her
   d. Lenora, who meditates every day

11 stress and health

11.1 11.2 p. 416

Stress and Stressors

- stress is the physical, emotional, cognitive, and behavioral response to events that are appraised as threatening or challenging; first studied systematically by Hans Selye
  - can include physical fatigue, recurring illness, over/under eating, smoking/drinking more than usual, mood swings, irritability, depression, anger, memory and concentration problems

- stress-causing events are called stressors; can come from external or internal sources; range from mild to severe
  - negative events cause distress; positive events cause eustress, the optimal level of stress required to facilitate healthy adaptation and well-being
  - external stress-causing events may include catastrophes, major life changes, and daily hassles (differ according to developmental stage)
  - can be assessed systematically (e.g., Social Readjustment Rating Scale, College Undergraduate Stress Scale)

Table 11.2
College Undergraduate Stress Scale (CUSS)

EVENT	RATING
Being raped	100
Finding out that you are HIV-positive	100
Death of a close friend	97
Contracting a sexually transmitted infection (other than AIDS)	94
Concerns about being pregnant	91
Finals week	90
Oversleeping for an exam	89
Flunking a class	89
Having a boyfriend or girlfriend cheat on you	85

11.3 p. 420

Stress and Stressors (continued)

(psychological stressors are often related to external events)

- **pressure**
  urgent demands or expectations and uncontrollability
- **frustration**
  due to external (losses, rejections, failures, delays) or internal (personal characteristics) factors; can result in several typical responses
  - **persistence**
  - **aggression**
  - **escape/withdrawal**
    (**suicide** is a drastic form of escape)
- **conflict**
  - **approach–approach conflict**
  - **avoidance–avoidance conflict**
  - **approach–avoidance conflict**
  - **multiple approach–avoidance conflicts**

11.4 p. 432

Physiological Factors

- the **autonomic nervous system (ANS)** figures prominently in the body's physiological reactions to stress
  - Hans Selye identified the **general adaptation syndrome (GAS)**, the sequence of physiological reactions the body goes through when adapting to a stressor
    - **alarm**
    - **resistance**
    - **exhaustion**

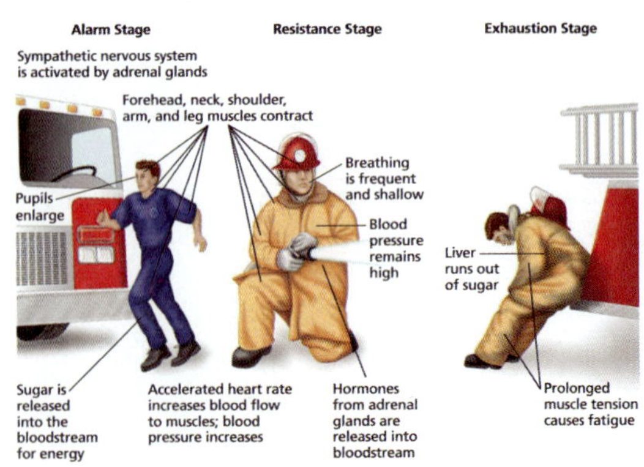

- the field of **psychoneuroimmunology** focuses on the effects of stress on the immune system
  - stress-related responses similar to those triggered by infection—increase in white blood cell count, enzymes, and antibodies
  - body is engineered for short-term, acute stress; prolonged stress/depletion of resources results in reduced functioning of immune system

Cognitive and Personality Factors

11.5 p. 432

- **Lazarus's cognitive–mediational theory of emotions** suggests an individual's appraisal of a stressor is a major factor in determining how stressful that stressor becomes
  - **primary appraisal**
  - **secondary appraisal**
- **personality differences** affect how one assesses a stressor, the coping strategies used, and possible health outcomes
  - **Type A**
  - **Type B**
  - **Type C**
  - **"Type H"**

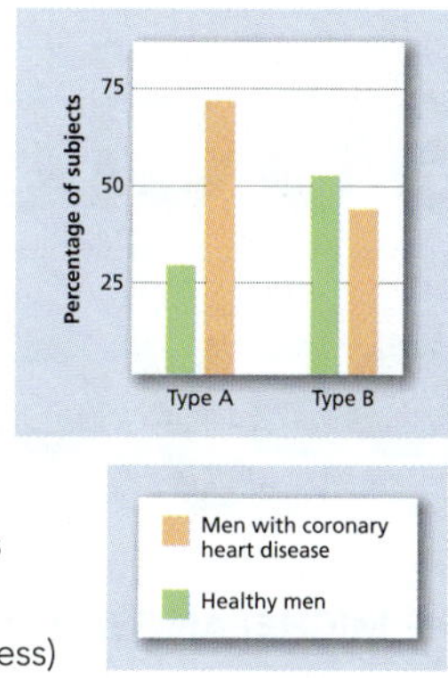

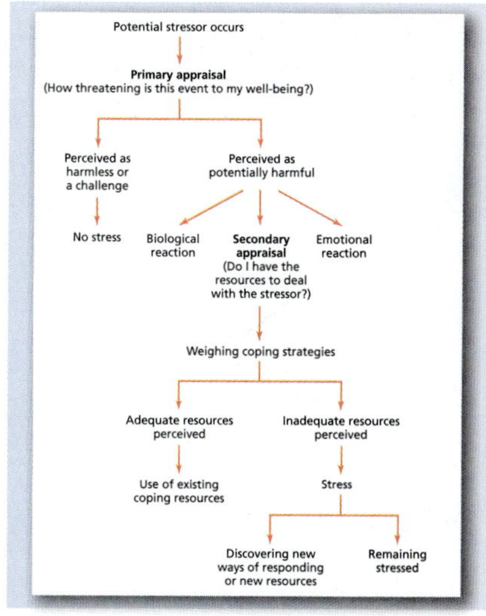

- **explanatory style** optimists tend to look for positive outcomes, whereas pessimists seem to expect the worst
  - Seligman (originally studied concept of learned helplessness) began the positive psychology movement; has suggested that optimism leads to longer life and greater success in life endeavors
  - optimism is associated with controlling mood or emotional reactions; can be a learned skill through alternative thinking, downward social comparison, relaxation, and correcting faulty thinking

Social Factors in Stress

11.6 p. 435

- a great deal of stress can come from dealing with other people and social interactions
  - poverty and job stress are prominent, economically based social factors that lead to stressful living conditions
    - poverty results in lack of basic life necessities
    - job stress may be related to workload, lack of control or job security, work schedule, and low job satisfaction
  - culturally, stress is affected by status of acculturation (adapting to a new, different, or often dominant culture) and the method chosen to adapt
    - **integration**
    - **assimilation**
    - **separation**
    - **marginalization**

- in general, having a positive social support system that provides various forms of help (e.g., monetary, physical, emotional support) is a good predictor for healthy aging and longevity

Coping With Stress

11.7 **11.8** p. 440

- **coping strategies** are behavioral and psychological actions taken to master, tolerate, reduce, or minimize the effect of stressors
  - **problem-focused coping** involves working to change or eliminate the stressor itself
  - **emotion-focused coping** involves changing the way a person feels or emotionally reacts to a stressor

- various methods and behaviors exist to help individuals in dealing with stress
  - meditation, in its various forms, helps to promote relaxation, calm anxiety, improve sleep, and lower blood pressure
  - an individual's culture and/or religious beliefs can affect the appraisal of events as more or less stressful, the coping strategies adopted, and support systems that can offer assistance

12 social psychology

CHAPTER OUTLINE

- Social Influence: Conformity, Compliance, Obedience and Group Behavior
- Social Cognition: Attitudes, Impression Formation, and Attribution
- Social Interaction: Prejudice and Aggression
- CLASSIC STUDIES IN PSYCHOLOGY: Brown Eyes, Blue Eyes
- Liking and Loving: Interpersonal Attraction
- PSYCHOLOGY IN THE NEWS: Facing Facebook—The Social Nature of Online Networking
- Aggression and Prosocial Behavior
- APPLYING PSYCHOLOGY TO EVERYDAY LIFE: Anatomy of a Cult

THE MICHELANGELO PHENOMENON: SCULPTING YOUR PARTNER

The concept of *self* is one that many psychologists have studied over the years. In this text, Carol Dweck's concept of self is discussed in Chapter Nine, and Carl Roger's concept of the real and ideal self is discussed in Chapter Thirteen. In both cases, however, the concept of self is an *intra*personal one—the beliefs that an individual holds about his or her own abilities and characteristics, including the *ideal self*, the abilities and characteristics that individual aspires to have. LINK to Chapter Thirteen: Theories of Personality, p. 508. But researchers are now looking at the *inter*personal self, the way in which an individual's close partners can help or hinder that person in the pursuit of the self's goals (Rusbult et al., 2009a, 2009b, 2009c).

In the *Michelangelo phenomenon* (famed sculptor Michelangelo Buonarroti felt that a sculptor merely releases the ideal figure from a block of stone), an individual's close friends, relatives, romantic partners, or colleagues help that individual "release" the ideal self that lies within by adapting to that person's basic traits and skills, providing opportunities for enhancement, and influencing the person's further personality development of those ideal aspects (Rusbult et al., 2009a). For example, if Latashia would like to become less shy and more outgoing, her boyfriend Antoine might encourage that aspect of her ideal self to develop by providing her with opportunities to tell their friends a funny story she had told to him. Antoine is in a sense "directing" Latashia's development. Over time, Latashia's behavior in these specific situations will become stable components of her sense of self. This effect of the significant other or others on a person's self-concept is particularly effective when it involves affirmation—the positive support of a person's goals for the ideal self (Drigotas et al., 1999; Kumashiro et al., 2009). (Of course, if Antoine's "directing" takes the form of negative criticism or belittling, Latashia's sense of self will no doubt suffer.)

In a very real sense, then, we look into the "mirror" of our partners' eyes and see ourselves as they see us. This is simply one example of the influence that others can have upon the individual, one area of study in the broad field of social psychology.

Why study social psychology?

If people lived in total isolation from other people, there would be no reason to study the effect that other people have on the behavior of individuals and groups. But human beings are social creatures—we live with others, work with others, and play with others. The people who surround us all of our lives have an impact on our beliefs and values, decisions and assumptions, and the way we think about ourselves and about other people in general. Why are some people prejudiced toward certain other people? Why do we obey some people but not others? What causes us to like, to love, or to hate others? The answers to all these questions and many more can be found in the study of social psychology.

learning objectives

12.1 What factors influence people to conform to the actions of others?

12.2 How is compliance defined, and what are four common ways to gain the compliance of another?

12.3 What factors make obedience more likely?

12.4 What are the three components of an attitude, how are attitudes formed, and how can attitudes be changed?

12.5 How do people react when attitudes and behavior are not the same?

12.6 What are social categorization and implicit personality theories?

12.7 How do people try to explain the actions of others?

12.8 How are prejudice and discrimination different?

12.9 Why are people prejudiced, and how can prejudice be stopped?

12.10 What factors govern attraction and love, and what are some different kinds of love?

12.11 How is aggressive behavior determined by biology and learning?

12.12 What is altruism, and how is deciding to help someone related to the presence of others?

12.13 Why do people join cults?

study tip

As you are reading this chapter, take a look back at page I-6 in *Psychology in Action* for some study strategies involving social relationships.

Chapter One defined psychology as the scientific study of behavior and mental processes, including how people think and feel. The field of social psychology also looks at behavior and mental processes but includes as well the social world in which we exist, as we are surrounded by others to whom we are connected and by whom we are influenced in so many ways. It is not the same field as *sociology*, which is the study and classification of human societies. Sociology studies the big picture: how entire groups of people live, work, and play. Although social psychology does look at group behavior, it is more concerned with the individual person within the group and the influence of the group on the person.

Social psychology is the scientific study of how a person's behavior, thoughts, and feelings are influenced by the real, imagined, or implied presence of others. Although there are several sections in this chapter, there are really only three main areas under discussion: *social influence*, the ways in which a person's behavior can be affected by other people; *social cognition*, the ways in which people think about other people; and *social interaction*, the positive and negative aspects of people relating to others.

Social Influence: Conformity, Compliance, Obedience, and Group Behavior

Each of us lives in a world filled with other people. An infant is born into a world with adults who have an impact on the infant's actions, personality, and growth. Adults must interact with others on a daily basis. Such interactions provide ample opportunity for the presence of other people to directly or indirectly influence the behavior, feelings, and thoughts of each individual in a process called **social influence**. There are many forms of social influence. People can influence others to follow along with their own actions or thoughts, to agree to do things even when the person might prefer to do otherwise, and to be obedient to authorities. The mere presence of others can even influence the way people perform tasks successfully or unsuccessfully.

social psychology the scientific study of how a person's thoughts, feelings, and behavior are influenced by the real, imagined, or implied presence of others.

social influence the process through which the real or implied presence of others can directly or indirectly influence the thoughts, feelings, and behavior of an individual.

CONFORMITY

12.1 What factors influence people to conform to the actions of others?

Have you ever noticed someone looking up at something? Did the urge to look up to see what that person was looking at become so strong that you actually found yourself looking up? This common practical joke always works, even when people suspect that it's a joke. It clearly demonstrates the power of **conformity**: changing one's own behavior to more closely match the actions of others.

"Sure, I follow the herd—not out of brainless obedience, mind you, but out of a deep and abiding respect for the concept of community."

In 1936, social psychologist Muzafer Sherif conducted a study in which participants were shown into a darkened room and exposed to a single point of light. Under those conditions, a point of light will seem to move because of tiny, involuntary movements of the eye. LINK to Chapter Three: Sensation and Perception, p. 119. The participants were not told of this effect and reported the light moved anywhere from a few inches to several feet. When a confederate (a person chosen by the experimenter to deliberately manipulate the situation) also gave estimates, the original participants began to make estimates of motion that were more and more similar to those of the confederate (Sherif, 1936). This early experiment on conformity has been criticized because the judgments being made were ambiguous* (i.e., the light wasn't really moving so any estimate within reason would sound good). Would participants be so easily swayed if the judgments were more specifically measurable and certain?

ASCH'S CLASSIC STUDY ON CONFORMITY Solomon Asch (1951) conducted the first of his classic studies on conformity by having seven participants gather in a room. They were told that they were participating in an experiment on visual judgment. They were then shown a white card with only one line on it followed by another white card with three lines of varying lengths. The task was to determine which line on the second card was most similar to the line on the first card (see Figure 12.1).

In reality, only the next-to-the-last person in the group was a real participant. The others were all confederates (people following special directions from the experimenter) who were instructed to pick the same *incorrect* line from the comparison lines. Would the real participant, having heard the others pick what seemed to be the

conformity changing one's own behavior to match that of other people.

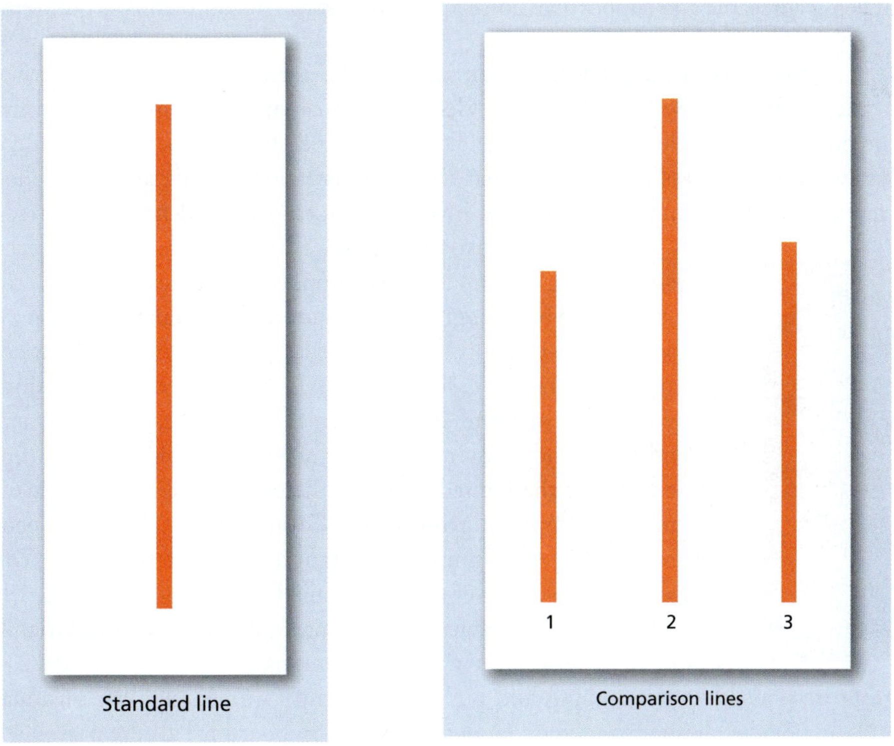

Figure 12.1 Stimuli Used in Asch's Study

Participants in Asch's famous study on conformity were first shown the standard line. They were then shown the three comparison lines and asked to determine to which of the three was the standard line most similar. Which line would you pick? What if you were one of several people, and everyone who answered ahead of you chose line 3? How would that affect your answer?

Source: Adapted from Asch (1956).

*ambiguous: having no clear interpretation or able to be interpreted in many ways rather than just one way.

groupthink kind of thinking that occurs when people place more importance on maintaining group cohesiveness than on assessing the facts of the problem with which the group is concerned.

wrong answer, change to conform to the group's opinion? Surprisingly, the participants conformed to the group answer a little over one third of the time. Asch also found that the number of confederates mattered: Conformity increased with each new confederate until there were four confederates; more than that did not increase the participants' tendency to conform (Asch, 1951). In a later experiment, Asch (1956) found that conformity greatly decreased if there was just one confederate who gave the correct answer—apparently, if participants knew that there was at least one other person whose answer agreed with their own, the evidence of their own eyes won out over the pressure to conform to the group. **Watch** on **mypsychlab.com**

Watch a video conformity on **mypsychlab.com**

Subsequent research in the United States has found less conformity among participants, perhaps suggesting that the Asch conformity effect was due to the more conforming nature of people in the era and culture of the United States in the 1950s (Lalancette & Standing, 1990; Nicholson et al., 1985; Perrin & Spencer, 1980, 1981). In other cultures, however, studies have found conformity effects similar to those in Asch's study (Neto, 1995). Still others have found even greater effects of conformity in collectivist cultures, such as Hong Kong, Japan, and Zimbabwe (Bond & Smith, 1996; Kim & Markus, 1999). This cultural difference may exist only when face-to-face contact is a part of the task, however. A recent study found that when the Asch judgment task is presented in an online format (participants were in communication but not able to see each other), the cultural difference disappears (Cinnirella & Green, 2007).

What about gender—are men or women more conforming?

What about gender—are men or women more conforming?

Research shows that gender differences are practically nonexistent unless the situation involves behavior that is not private. If it is possible to give responses in private, conformity is no greater for women than for men, but if a public response is required, women do tend to show more conformity than men (Eagly, 1987; Eagly et al., 2000; Eagly & Carly, 2007). This effect may be due to the socialization that women receive in being agreeable and supportive; however, the difference in conformity is quite small.

THE HAZARDS OF GROUPTHINK Shortly after the terrorist attack on the World Trade Center in New York, President George W. Bush and his administration made the decision to invade Iraq, find Saddam Hussein, and stop him before he could use his "weapons of mass destruction" that the administration and its advisors believed were hidden in Iraq. This decision to invade a country that had not committed an open act of war against the United States was made and executed *without* building any broad-based support from allies. Although there were advisors who thought the action to be a mistake, no one person was willing to stand up to the rest of the group and challenge the group's decision and assumptions. Many now see this decision (a costly decision in terms of lost lives and casualties, huge monetary expenditures, and—according to many—the tarnishing of the diplomatic status of the United States in the eyes of the rest of the world) as a prime example of **groupthink**. Groupthink occurs when people within a group feel it is more important to maintain the group's cohesiveness than to consider the facts realistically (Hogg & Hains, 1998; Janis, 1972, 1982; Kamau & Harorimana, 2008; Schafer & Crichlow, 1996). Other examples include the sinking of the *Titanic* in 1912 (the group responsible for designing and building the ship assumed she was unsinkable and did not even bother to include enough lifeboats on board for all the passengers), the *Challenger* disaster of 1986 in which a part on the shuttle was known by a few to be unacceptable (but no one spoke up to delay the launch), and the disastrous Bay of Pigs invasion of Cuba during the Kennedy administration.

On April 20, 2010, an explosion on the Deepwater Horizon oil drilling rig in the Gulf of Mexico. Oil flowed into the Gulf for three months, but the environmental impact will no doubt be felt for years. How might groupthink apply in this situation?

Table 12.1

Characteristics of Groupthink

CHARACTERISTIC	DESCRIPTION
Invulnerability	Members feel they cannot fail.
Rationalization	Members explain away warning signs and help each other rationalize their decision.
Lack of introspection	Members do not examine the ethical implications of their decision because they believe that they cannot make immoral choices.
Stereotyping	Members stereotype their enemies as weak, stupid, or unreasonable.
Pressure	Members pressure each other not to question the prevailing opinion.
Lack of disagreement	Members do not express opinions that differ from the group consensus.
Self-deception	Members share in the illusion that they all agree with the decision.
Insularity	Members prevent the group from hearing disruptive but potentially useful information from people who are outside the group.

Source: Janis (1972, 1982).

Why does groupthink happen? Social psychologist Irving Janis (1972, 1982), who originally gave this phenomenon its name, lists several "symptoms" of groupthink. For example, group members may come to feel that the group can do no wrong, is morally correct, and will always succeed, creating the illusion of invulnerability.* Group members also tend to hold stereotyped views of those who disagree with the group's opinions, causing members to think that those who oppose the group have no worthwhile opinions. They exert pressure on individual members to conform to group opinion, prevent those who might disagree from speaking up, and even censor themselves so that the group's mind-set will not be disturbed in a "don't rock the boat" mentality. Self-appointed "mind guards" work to protect the leader of the group from contrary viewpoints. (See Table 12.1.)

Several things can be done to minimize the possibility of groupthink (Hart, 1998; McCauley, 1998; Moorhead et al., 1998). For example, leaders should remain impartial and the entire group should seek the opinions of people outside the group. Any voting should be done on secret ballots rather than by a show of hands, and it should be made clear that group members will be held responsible for decisions made by the group.

COMPLIANCE

12.2 How is compliance defined, and what are four common ways to gain the compliance of another?

I have a friend who watches all those infomercials on the shopping channels and buys stuff that isn't worth the money or that doesn't work like it's supposed to work. Why do people fall for pitches like that?

I have a friend who watches all those infomercials on the shopping channels and buys stuff that isn't worth the money or that doesn't work like it's supposed to work. Why do people fall for pitches like that?

Marketing products is really very much a psychological process. In fact, the whole area of **consumer psychology** is devoted to figuring out how to get people to buy things that someone is selling. LINK to Appendix B: Applied Psychology, p. B-12. But infomercials are not the only means by which people try to get others to do what

consumer psychology branch of psychology that studies the habits of consumers in the marketplace.

*invulnerability: quality of being unable to be attacked or harmed.

they want them to do. **Compliance** occurs when people change their behavior as a result of another person or group asking or directing them to change. The person or group asking for the change in behavior typically doesn't have any real authority or power to command a change; when that authority does exist and behavior is changed as a result, it is called *obedience*, which is the topic of the next major section of this chapter.

A number of techniques that people use to get the compliance of others clearly show the relationship of compliance to the world of marketing, as they refer to techniques that door-to-door salespersons would commonly use.

FOOT-IN-THE-DOOR TECHNIQUE Let's say that a neighbor asks you to keep an eye on his house while he is on vacation. You agree, thinking that it's a rather small request. Later that day, or perhaps even in the same conversation, the neighbor asks if you would kindly water his plants while he's gone. This is a little bit more involved and requires more of your time and energy—will you do it? If you are like most people, you probably will comply with this second, larger request.

When compliance with a smaller request is followed by a larger request, people are quite likely to comply because they have already agreed to the smaller one and they want to behave consistently with their previous response (Cialdini et al., 1995; Dillard, 1990, 1991; Freedman & Fraser, 1966; Meineri & Guéguen, 2008). This is called the **foot-in-the-door technique** because the first small request acts as an opener. (Door-to-door salespeople once literally stuck a foot in the door to prevent the occupant from shutting it so they could continue their sales pitch, hence, the name.)

DOOR-IN-THE-FACE TECHNIQUE Closely related to the foot-in-the-door technique is its opposite: the **door-in-the-face technique** (Cialdini et al., 1975). In this method, the larger request comes first, which is usually refused. This is followed by a second smaller and more reasonable request that often gets compliance. An example of this would be if the neighbor first asked you to take care of his dog and cat in your home. After you refused to do so, the neighbor might ask if you would at least water his plants, which you would probably do.

This technique relies on the **norm of reciprocity**, which basically assumes that if someone does something for a person, the person should do something in return (Burger et al., 2009; Fehr et al., 2000; Gouldner, 1960). This is also the principle used by those organizations that give out free, unasked-for samples, such as the free address stickers that come with many requests for charitable donations.

LOWBALL TECHNIQUE Another compliance technique, also common in the world of sales, is called the **lowball technique** (Bator & Cialdini, 2006; Burger & Petty, 1981; Weyant, 1996). In this technique, once a commitment is made, the cost of that commitment is increased. (In the sense used here, *cost* does not necessarily mean money; *cost* can also mean time, effort, or other kinds of sacrifices.) For example, let's say that a professor agrees to write a textbook for a publishing company. Once committed to that process, the professor discovers that the task involves not only writing but also traveling to meet with editors, working nights and weekends to meet deadlines, and making the commitment to take time off from her teaching job to finish the text on time for publication. (This example is purely hypothetical, of course.)

A more common example will occur to anyone who has ever bought a car. The commitment to buy the car at one low price is quickly followed by the addition of other costs: extended warranties, additional options, taxes and fees, and so on, causing the buyer to spend more money than originally intended.

compliance changing one's behavior as a result of other people directing or asking for the change.

foot-in-the-door technique asking for a small commitment and, after gaining compliance, asking for a bigger commitment.

door-in-the-face technique asking for a large commitment and being refused and then asking for a smaller commitment.

norm of reciprocity assumption that if someone does something for a person, that person should do something for the other in return.

lowball technique getting a commitment from a person and then raising the cost of that commitment.

THAT'S-NOT-ALL TECHNIQUE Finally, there is the now familiar technique of the infomercial salesperson: the **that's-not-all technique**. In this compliance tactic, the person doing the persuading makes an offer, but before the target of the offer can make a decision, the persuader throws in something extra to make the deal look even better (Burger, 1986). See if this sounds familiar:

> *"But wait—that's not all! If you act now, we'll send you this 15-piece set of genuine faux carving knives as a bonus!"*

By offering something that the consumer did not ask for in the first place, the persuader has once again activated the norm of reciprocity. Now the consumer feels as though the persuader has "given" something and the consumer should respond by giving in to the persuader's request to buy the product.

Cultural differences exist in people's susceptibility to these techniques. For the foot-in-the door technique in particular, research has shown that people in individualist cultures (such as the United States) are more likely to comply with the second request than are people in collectivist cultures (such as Japan). The research suggests that people in collectivist cultures are not as concerned with being consistent with previous behavior because they are less focused on their inner motivation than are people in individualist cultures, who are more concerned with their inner motives and consistency (Cialdini et al., 1999; Petrova et al., 2003). LINK to Chapter Thirteen: Theories of Personality, pp. 515–516.

OBEDIENCE

12.3 What factors make obedience more likely?

There is a difference between the concepts of compliance, which is agreeing to change one's behavior because someone else asks for the change, and **obedience**, which is changing one's behavior at the direct order of an authority figure. A salesperson who wants a person to buy a car has no real power to force that person to buy, but an authority figure is a person with social power—such as a police officer, a teacher, or a work supervisor—who has the right to demand certain behavior from the people under the authority figure's command or supervision.

How far will people go in obeying the commands of an authority figure? What factors make obedience more or less likely? These are some of the questions that researchers have been investigating for many years. The answers to these questions became very important not only to researchers but also to people everywhere after the atrocities committed by the soldiers in Nazi Germany—soldiers who were "just following orders."

MILGRAM'S SHOCKING RESEARCH In what is now a classic study, social psychologist Stanley Milgram set out to find answers to these questions. He was aware of Asch's studies of conformity and wondered how much impact social influence could have on a behavior that was more meaningful than judging the length of lines on cards. He designed what has become one of the most famous (even notorious*) experiments in the history of psychology.

Through ads placed in the local newspaper, Milgram recruited people who were told that they would be participating in an experiment to test the effects of punishment on learning behavior (Milgram, 1964a, 1974). Although there were several different forms of this experiment with different participants, the basic premise was the same: The participants believed that they had randomly been assigned to either the

*notorious: widely and unfavorably known.

that's-not-all technique a sales technique in which the persuader makes an offer and then adds something extra to make the offer look better before the target person can make a decision.

obedience changing one's behavior at the command of an authority figure.

Figure 12.2 Control Panel in Milgram's Experiment

In Stanley Milgram's classic study on obedience, the participants were presented with a control panel like this one. Each participant ("teacher") was instructed to give electric shocks to another person (the "learner," who only pretended to be shocked). At what point do you think you would have refused to continue the experiment?

"teacher" role or the "learner" role, when in fact the learner was an actor already aware of the situation. The teacher was given a sample 45-volt shock from the chair in which the learner was strapped during the experiment. The task for the learner was a simple memory test for paired words.

The teacher was seated in front of a machine through which the shocks would be administered and the level of the shocks changed. (See Figure 12.2.) For each mistake made by the learner, the teacher was instructed to increase the level of shock by 15 volts. The learner (who was not actually shocked) followed a carefully arranged script, showing discomfort, asking for the experiment to end, screaming, and even falling silent as if unconscious—or dead. (See Table 12.2 for samples of the scripted responses of the learner.) As the teachers became reluctant to continue administering the shocks, the experimenter in his authoritative white lab coat said, for example, "The experiment requires you to continue" or "You must continue," and reminded the teacher that the experimenter would take full responsibility for the safety of the learner.

Table 12.2

Sample Script Items From Milgram's Classic Experiment

VOLTAGE OF "SHOCK"	LEARNER'S SCRIPT
150	"Ugh!! Experimenter! That's all. Get me out of here. I told you I had heart trouble. My heart's starting to bother me now. Get me out of here, please. My heart's starting to bother me. I refuse to go on. Let me out."
210	"Ugh!! Experimenter! Get me out of here. I've had enough. I *won't* be in this experiment any more."
300	(*Agonized scream*) "I absolutely refuse to answer any more. Get me out of here. You can't hold me here. Get me out. Get me out of here."
330	(*Intense and prolonged agonized scream*) "Let me out of here. Let me out of here. My heart's bothering me. Let me out, I tell you. (*Hysterically*) Let me out of here. Let me out of here. You have no right to hold me here. Let me out! Let me out! Let me out of here! Let me out! Let me out!"

Source: Milgram (1964a, 1974).

12.1 12.2 12.3

CONCEPT MAP

Social Influence

(the ways in which a person's behavior can be affected by other people)

- **conformity** changing one's own behavior to more closely match the actions of others
  - several classic studies (i.e., Sherif, Asch) suggest that individuals will change their behaviors to conform to those of a group
  - may be influenced by private vs. face-to-face contact, gender, or culture
  - **groupthink:** occurs when people within a group feel it is more important to maintain group cohesiveness rather than critically evaluate facts when making decisions often with dire consequences
- **compliance** person changing their behavior due to another person or group asking or directing them to change, often in the absence of any real authority or power
  - **foot-in-the-door technique**
  - **door-in-the-face technique**
  - **lowball technique**
  - **that's-not-all technique**
- **group polarization** risky shift phenomenon
  - presence of others increases extreme positions
- **obedience** changing one's behavior at the direct order of an authority figure
  - a classic study by Milgram (i.e., teacher/learner electrical shock study) indicated that 65% of "teachers" went all the way through shock levels, despite protest from "learners"
- **task performance** can be affected by social influence
  - **social facilitation** = positive influence
  - **social impairment** = negative influence
    - presence of others increases arousal
  - **social loafing** occurs when people do not work hard when others are also working; easy to "hide" in a group

PRACTICE quiz How much do you remember?

ANSWERS ON PAGE AK-2.

Pick the best answer.

1. A person's conformity in a situation like the Asch line study is most likely to be strongest when __________.
   a. the person is in the room with only one other person.
   b. at least one other person agrees with the person.
   c. that person is from Hong Kong.
   d. that person is from the United States.
2. In groupthink, members of the group __________.
   a. have an illusion of invulnerability.
   b. avoid stereotyping those who hold an opposing viewpoint.
   c. like to "rock the boat" every now and then.
   d. sometimes question the moral "rightness" of the group.
3. When members of a cult are trying to enlist a new recruit, they start by asking the recruit to make a small commitment, such as attending a short meeting or helping out at a social function. Then the commitments get more involved, such as staying for a longer period of time and eventually for major donations of money and moving in with the cult members. This is most like which of the following techniques?
   a. foot-in-the-door technique
   b. door-in-the-face technique
   c. lowball technique
   d. that's-not-all technique
4. Which of the following has been shown to be true concerning the "teachers" in Milgram's experiment?
   a. Most of the "teachers" were sorry to have been a part of the experiment.
   b. They were found to be psychologically weak-minded people.
   c. A follow-up psychiatric exam found no signs of psychological problems after 1 year.
   d. They were not ordinary people.
5. Alex, who is in the honors program, failed to do his share of the work on the group project with his four classmates. Alex was most likely engaging in __________.
   a. social facilitation.
   b. social impairment.
   c. social loafing.
   d. group polarization.

Brainstorming: Can you think of a time when you obeyed someone in uniform? What went through your mind when you decided to obey? Was there a time when you changed your mind about something because everyone else disagreed with you? How might Asch's conformity effect come into play when a jury is trying to get a unanimous vote of guilty or not guilty?

Social Cognition: Attitudes, Impression Formation, and Attribution

Social cognition focuses on the ways in which people think about other people and how those cognitions influence behavior toward those other people. In this section, we'll concentrate on how we perceive others and form our first impressions of them, as well as how we explain the behavior of others and ourselves.

ATTITUDES

One area of social cognition concerns the formation and influence of attitudes on the behavior and perceptions of others. An **attitude** can be defined as a tendency to respond positively or negatively toward a certain idea, person, object, or situation (Triandis, 1971). This tendency, developed through peoples' experiences as they live and work with others, can affect the way they behave toward those ideas, people, objects, and situations and can include opinions, beliefs, and biases. In fact, attitudes influence the way people view these things *before* they've actually been exposed to them (Petty et al., 2003).

What do you mean—how can an attitude have an effect on something that hasn't happened yet?

What do you mean—how can an attitude have an effect on something that hasn't happened yet?

Attitudes are not something people have when they are born. They are learned through experiences and contact with others and even through direct instruction from parents, teachers, and other important people in a person's life. Because attitudes involve a positive or negative evaluation of things, it's possible to go into a new situation, meet a new person, or be exposed to a new idea with one's "mind already made up" to like or dislike, agree or disagree, and so on (Eagly & Chaiken, 1993; Petty et al., 2003). For example, children are known for making up their minds about certain foods before ever tasting them, simply because the foods are "green." Those children may have tried a green food in the past and disliked it and now are predisposed* to dislike any green food whether they've tasted it or not.

THE ABC MODEL OF ATTITUDES

12.4 What are the three components of an attitude, how are attitudes formed, and how can attitudes be changed?

Attitudes are actually made up of three different parts, or components, as shown in Figure 12.3. These components should not come as a surprise to anyone who has been reading the other chapters in this text because, throughout the text, references have been made to personality and traits being composed of the ways people think, feel, and act. By using certain terms to describe these three things, psychologists have come up with a handy way to describe the three components of attitudes (Eagly & Chaiken, 1993, 1998).

AFFECTIVE COMPONENT The *affective component* of an attitude is the way a person feels toward the object, person, or situation. *Affect* is used in psychology to mean "emotions" or "feelings," so the affective component is the emotional component. For example, some people might feel that country music is fun and uplifting.

BEHAVIOR COMPONENT The *behavior component* of an attitude is the action that a person takes in regard to the person, object, or situation. For example, a person who feels that country music is fun is likely to turn to a country music station on the car radio, buy country music CDs, or go to a country music concert.

attitude a tendency to respond positively or negatively toward a certain person, object, idea, or situation.

*predisposed: referring to a tendency to respond in a particular way based on previous experience.

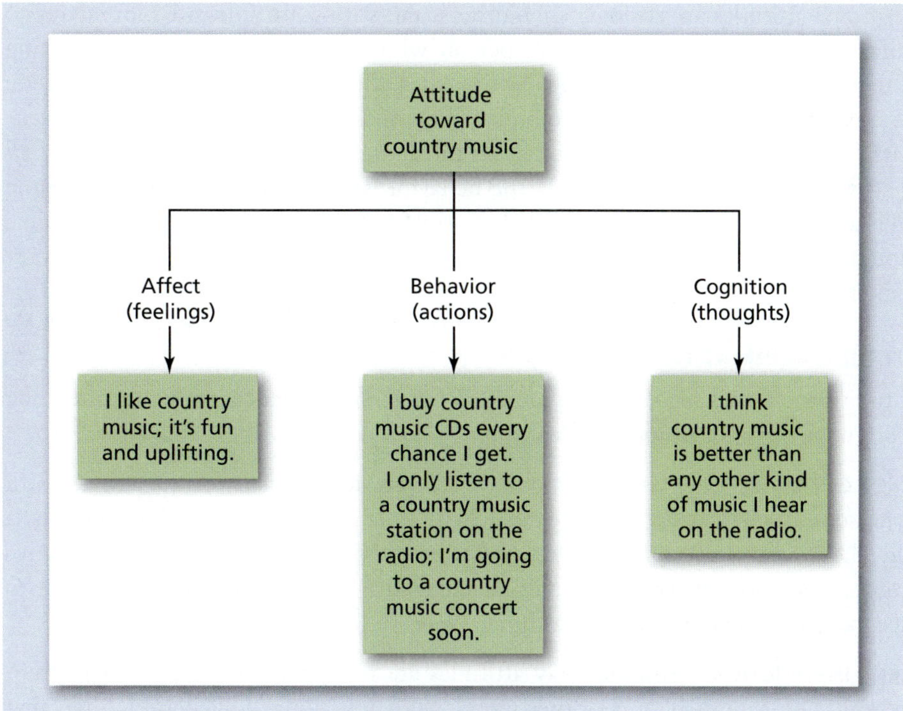

Figure 12.3 Three Components of an Attitude

Attitudes consist of the way a person feels and thinks about something, as well as the way the person chooses to behave. If you like country music, you are also likely to think that country music is good music. You are also more likely to listen to this style of music, buy this type of music, and even go to a performance. Each of the three components influences the other two.

COGNITIVE COMPONENT Finally, the *cognitive component* of an attitude is the way a person thinks about himself, an object, or a situation. These thoughts, or cognitions, include beliefs and ideas about the focus of the attitude. For example, the country music lover might believe that country music is superior to other forms of music.

So if you know what someone thinks or feels about something, you can predict what that person will do, right?

So if you know what someone thinks or feels about something, you can predict what that person will do, right?

Oddly enough, attitudes turn out to be pretty poor predictors of actual behavior in a number of controlled research studies. The results of several decades of research indicate that what people say and what people do are often two very different things (van de Garde-Perik et al., 2008; Wicker, 1971). Studies conducted in the decades that followed found that attitudes predict behavior only under certain conditions. For example, in one study researchers found that a randomly chosen sample of people indicated on a survey that they believed in protecting the environment and would be willing to pay more for fruits and vegetables raised under environmentally friendly conditions. When the people of that same sample were studied for their actual buying habits, the only sample members who bought the ecofriendly fruit did so only in grocery stores in areas of higher income levels. These consumers actually had the financial means to "put their money where their mouth was" (A. Clarke et al., 1999). Those members of the sample who did not live in a higher income area gave what they probably saw as a socially desirable answer on the survey but in practice, their lower income influenced their actual behavior—they did NOT buy the more expensive ecofriendly fruit.

While many people may believe in helping the environment by using organically grown products, one study found that only those with the money to buy these more expensive products did so.

Another factor in matching attitudes and behavior concerns how specific the attitude itself is. People may hold a general attitude about something without reflecting that attitude in their actual behavior. For example, doctors generally hold the attitude that people should do everything they can to protect their health and promote wellness, yet many doctors still smoke tobacco, fail to exercise, and often get too little sleep. But a very specific attitude, such as "exercise is important to my immediate health," will more likely be associated with the behavior of exercising (Ajzen, 2001; Ajzen & Fishbein, 2000).

Some attitudes are stronger than others, and strong attitudes are more likely to predict behavior than weak ones. A person who quit smoking because of failing health might have a stronger attitude toward secondhand smoking than someone who quit smoking on a dare, for example. The importance, or salience*, of a particular attitude in a given situation also has an impact on behavior—the more important the attitude appears, the more likely the behavior will match the attitude. Someone who is antismoking might be more likely to confront a smoker breaking the rules in a hospital, for example, than they would a smoker outside the building (Eagly & Chaiken, 1998).

ATTITUDE FORMATION

Attitude formation is the result of a number of different influences with only one thing in common: They are all forms of learning.

DIRECT CONTACT One way in which attitudes are formed is by direct contact with the person, idea, situation, or object that is the focus of the attitude. For example, a child who tries brussels sprouts for the first time and dislikes them will form a negative attitude about brussels sprouts. Later that negative attitude may be generalized to other foods that are green or have a similar taste.

DIRECT INSTRUCTION Another way attitudes are formed is through direct instruction, either by parents or some other individual. Parents may tell their children that smoking cigarettes is dangerous and unhealthy, for example. Some children will form a negative attitude about smoking as a result.

INTERACTION WITH OTHERS Sometimes attitudes are formed because the person is around other people with that attitude. If a person's friends, for example, all hold the attitude that smoking is cool, that person is more likely to think that smoking is cool as well (Brenner, 2007; Eddy et al., 2000; Hill, 1990). The attitudes and behavior of teachers, parents, and siblings matter as well. Researchers found that a nonsmoking mother, teacher, or brother had a strong influence on both girls and boys, making both genders less likely to smoke. Unfortunately, the influence of all three social groups on boys seemed to fade over a 7-year follow-up study (Shean et al., 1994).

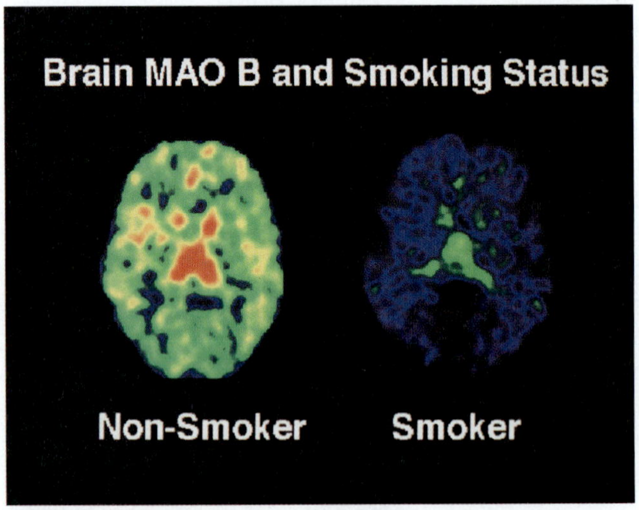

Direct instruction, such as this brain scan showing the severe difference between the brain activity of a smoker and a non-smoker, is only one way attitudes can be formed.

VICARIOUS CONDITIONING (OBSERVATIONAL LEARNING) Many attitudes are learned through the observation of other people's actions and reactions to various objects, people, or situations. Just as a child whose mother shows a fear of dogs may develop a similar fear, a child whose mother or father shows a positive attitude toward classical music may grow into an adult with a similarly positive attitude. The emotional components of an attitude can be learned by observing the emotional reactions of others, and the behavioral components can be observed and imitated.

Attitudes are not only influenced by other people in a person's immediate world but also by the larger world of the educational system (many attitudes may be learned in school or through reading books) and the mass media of magazines, television, and the movies—a fact of which advertisers and marketing experts are well aware (Gresham & Shimp, 1985; MacKenzie et al., 1986).

*salience: importance or having the quality of being obvious or easily seen.

ATTITUDE CHANGE: THE ART OF PERSUASION

Sometimes people learn attitudes that aren't necessarily good ones, right? So can attitudes change?

Sometimes people learn attitudes that aren't necessarily good ones, right? So can attitudes change?

Because attitudes are learned, they are also subject to change with new learning. The world is full of people, companies, and other organizations that want to change peoples' attitudes. It's all about the art of **persuasion**, the process by which one person tries to change the belief, opinion, position, or course of action of another person through argument, pleading, or explanation.

Persuasion is not a simple matter. There are several factors that become important in predicting how successful any persuasive effort at attitude change might be. These factors include the following:

- **Source:** The *communicator* is the person delivering the message. There is a strong tendency to give more weight to people who are perceived as experts, as well as those who seem trustworthy, attractive, and similar to the person receiving the message (Eagly & Chaiken, 1975; O'Keefe, 2009; Petty & Cacioppo, 1986, 1996; Priester & Petty, 1995).
- **Message:** The actual message should be clear and well organized (Booth-Butterfield, 1996). It is usually more effective to present both sides of an argument to an audience that has not yet committed to one side or the other (Crowley & Hoyer, 1994; O'Keefe, 2009; Petty & Cacioppo, 1996; Petty et al., 2003). Messages that are directed at producing fear are more effective if they produce only a moderate amount of fear and also provide information about how to avoid the fear-provoking consequences (Kleinot & Rogers, 1982; Meyrick, 2001; Petty, 1995; Rogers & Mewborn, 1976).
- **Target Audience:** The characteristics of the people who are the intended target of the message of persuasion are also important in determining the effectiveness of the message. The age of the audience members can be a factor, for example. Researchers have found that people who are in the young adult stage of the late teens to the mid-20s are more susceptible to persuasion than are older people (O'Keefe, 2009; Visser & Krosnick, 1998).

How the jurors in this courtroom interpret and process the information they are given will determine the outcome of the trial. Those who listen carefully to what is said by persons involved in the trial are using central-route processing. There may be some jurors, however, who are more affected by the appearance, dress, attractiveness, or tone of voice of the lawyers, defendant, and witnesses. When people are persuaded by factors other than the message itself, it is called peripheral-route processing.

How easily influenced a person is will also be related to the way people tend to process information. In the **elaboration likelihood model** of persuasion (Petty & Cacioppo, 1986), it is assumed that people either elaborate (add details and information) based on what they hear (the facts of the message) or they do not elaborate at all, preferring to pay attention to the surface characteristics of the message (length, who delivers it, how attractive the message deliverer is, etc.). Two types of processing are hypothesized in this model: **central-route processing**, in which people attend to the content of the message; and **peripheral-route processing**, a style of information processing that relies on peripheral cues (cues outside of the message content itself), such as the expertise of the message source, the length of the message, and other factors that have nothing to do with the message content. This style of processing causes people not to pay attention to the message itself but instead to base their decisions on those peripheral factors (Petty & Cacioppo, 1986; Stiff & Mongeau, 2002). For example, the author once participated on a jury panel in which one woman voted "guilty" because the defendant had "shifty eyes" and not because of any of the evidence presented.

persuasion the process by which one person tries to change the belief, opinion, position, or course of action of another person through argument, pleading, or explanation.

elaboration likelihood model model of persuasion stating that people will either elaborate on the persuasive message or fail to elaborate on it and that the future actions of those who do elaborate are more predictable than those who do not.

central-route processing type of information processing that involves attending to the content of the message itself.

peripheral-route processing type of information processing that involves attending to factors not involved in the message, such as the appearance of the source of the message, the length of the message, and other noncontent factors.

COGNITIVE DISSONANCE: WHEN ATTITUDES AND BEHAVIOR CLASH

12.5 How do people react when attitudes and behavior are not the same?

As stated earlier, sometimes what people say and what they do are very different. I once pointed this out to a friend of mine who was behaving this way, and he got really upset over it. Why did he get so upset?

As stated earlier, sometimes what people say and what they do are very different. I once pointed this out to a friend of mine who was behaving this way, and he got really upset over it. Why did he get so upset?

When people find themselves doing things or saying things that don't match their idea of themselves as smart, nice, or moral, for example, they experience an emotional discomfort (and physiological arousal) known as **cognitive dissonance** (Aronson, 1997; Festinger, 1957; Kelly et al., 1997). When people are confronted with the knowledge that something they have done or said was dumb, immoral, or illogical, they suffer an inconsistency in cognitions. For example, they may have a cognition that says "I'm pretty smart" but also the cognition "That was a dumb thing to do," which causes a dissonance. (*Dissonance* is a term referring to an inconsistency or lack of agreement.)

When people experience cognitive dissonance, the resulting tension and arousal are unpleasant, and their motivation is to change something so that the unpleasant feelings and tension are reduced or eliminated. There are three basic things that people can do to reduce cognitive dissonance:

1. Change their conflicting behavior to make it match their attitude.
2. Change their current conflicting cognition to justify their behavior.
3. Form new cognitions to justify their behavior.

Take the example of Larry, who is a college graduate and a cigarette smoker. On one hand, Larry is educated enough to know that cigarette smoking is extremely harmful, causing lung problems, cancer, and eventually death. On the other hand, Larry enjoys smoking, feeling that it calms him and helps him deal with stress—not to mention the fact that he's thoroughly addicted and finds it difficult to quit. His attitude (smoking is bad for you) doesn't match his behavior. Larry is experiencing cognitive dissonance and knows he needs to do something to resolve his dilemma.*

If Larry chooses the first way of dealing with cognitive dissonance, he'll quit smoking, no matter how difficult it is (Option 1). As long as he is working at changing the conflicting behavior, his dissonance will be reduced. But what if he can't quit? He might decide that smoking isn't as bad as everyone says it is, which changes his original conflicting attitude (Option 2). He might also form a new attitude by deciding that if he smokes "light" cigarettes, he's reducing his risk enough to justify continuing smoking (Option 3). **Explore** on **mypsychlab.com**

Explore cognitive dissonance and attitude change on **mypsychlab.com**

In a classic experiment conducted at Stanford University by psychologist Leo Festinger and colleague James Carlsmith (1959), each male student volunteer was given an hour-long, very boring task of sorting wooden spools and turning wooden pegs. After the hour, the experimenters asked the participant to tell the female volunteer in the waiting room that the task was enjoyable. While half of the participants were paid only $1 to try to convince the waiting woman, the other participants were paid $20. (In the late 1950s, $20 was a considerable sum of money—the average income was $5,000, the average car cost $3,000, and gas was only 25 cents a gallon.)

At the time of this study, many researchers would have predicted that the more the participants were paid to lie, the more they would come to like the task, because they were getting more reinforcement ($20) for doing so. But what actually happened was that those participants who were paid only $1 for lying actually convinced them-

cognitive dissonance sense of discomfort or distress that occurs when a person's behavior does not correspond to that person's attitudes.

*dilemma: a problem involving a difficult choice.

selves that the task was interesting and fun. The reason is cognitive dissonance: Participants who were paid only $1 experienced discomfort at thinking that they would lie to someone for only a dollar. Therefore, they must not be lying—the task really was pretty interesting, after all, and fun, too! Those who were paid more experienced no dissonance, because they knew exactly why they were lying—for lots of money—and the money was a sufficient amount to explain their behavior to their satisfaction. Although most people don't want to be thought of as liars, back then, getting paid enough money to fill the gas tank of one's car three or four times over was incentive enough to tell what probably seemed to be a harmless fib. Those who were paid only $1 had to change their attitude toward the task so that they would not really be lying and could maintain their self-image of honesty. (See Figure 12.4.)

Inducement	Attitude
$1	+1.35
$20	– 0.5
Control	– .45

*Based on a –5 to +5 scale, where –5 means "extremely boring" and +5 means "extremely interesting"

Figure 12.4 Cognitive Dissonance: Attitude Toward a Task

After completing a boring task, some participants were paid $1 and some $20 to convince others waiting to do the same task that the task was interesting and fun. Surprisingly, the participants who were paid only $1 seemed to change their own attitude toward the task, rating it as interesting, whereas those who were paid $20 rated the task no differently than a control group did.
Source: Adapted from Festinger and Carlsmith (1959).

Cognitive dissonance theory has been challenged over the last 50 years by other possible explanations. Bem's self-perception theory says that instead of experiencing negative tension, people look at their own actions and then infer their attitudes from those actions (Bem, 1972). New research on dissonance still occurs, much of it focusing on finding the areas of the brain that seem to be involved when people are experiencing dissonance. These studies have found that the left frontal cortex (where language and much of our decision making occurs) is particularly active when people have made a decision that reduces dissonance and then acted upon that decision (Harmon-Jones, 2000, 2004, 2006; Harmon-Jones et al., 2008). Since reducing cognitive dissonance is mainly a function of people "talking" themselves into or out of a particular course of action, this neurological finding is not surprising. But researchers at Yale University have found surprising evidence for cognitive dissonance in both 4-year-old humans and capuchin monkeys—two groups that are not normally associated with having the developed higher level mental abilities thought to be in use during the resolution of dissonance (Egan et al., 2007; Egan et al., 2010). Are monkeys and preschool humans more complex thinkers than we had assumed? Or are the cognitive processes used to resolve dissonance a lot simpler than previously indicated? Obviously, there are still questions to be answered with new research in cognitive dissonance.

12.4 12.5

CONCEPT MAP

Social Cognition

- focuses on the ways in which people think about other people and how those cognitions affect behavior
- **attitudes**
  tendency to respond positively or negatively toward a certain idea, person, object, or situation; learned through experience
  - comprise affective, behavioral, and cognitive components
  - are not great predictors of behavior although tend to have more influence as they become more specific and salient
  - attitude formation can be the result of several processes
    - **direct contact**
    - **direct instruction**
    - **interaction with others**
    - **vicarious learning**
  - can change through persuasion and are contingent upon both the message and the target audience; elaboration likelihood model suggests that the route/level of information processing (central vs. peripheral) influences ease of persuasion
- **cognitive dissonance**
  emotional discomfort as the result of engaging in behavior that is inconsistent with personal cognitions
  - can be reduced by (1) changing behavior, (2) changing cognition, or (3) forming new cognitions to justify behavior

(continued)

PRACTICE quiz How much do you remember? ANSWERS ON PAGE AK-2.

Pick the best answer.

1. Which of the following represents the cognitive component of an attitude?
   a. "I just love Italian food!"
   b. "Tonight, we're going to that new Italian restaurant."
   c. "Italian food is the best of the European cuisines."
   d. "I'm going to make lasagna tonight."
2. Lilly's mother always listens to the classic rock station on her car radio, so Lilly has grown up hearing that music and noticing how much her mother enjoys it. Now Lilly says that classic rock is her favorite music, too. Lilly's attitude toward classic rock was most likely acquired through _________.
   a. direct contact.
   b. direct instruction.
   c. interaction with others.
   d. vicarious conditioning.
3. Physical attractiveness is most involved in which of the following aspects of persuasion?
   a. the source
   b. the message
   c. the audience
   d. the media
4. Which of the following is not one of the elements of effective persuasion?
   a. the source or communicator
   b. characteristics of the message
   c. presence of supporters
   d. characteristics of the audience
5. "I didn't like the sermon at all today. It was too long, and that preacher wasn't dressed up enough" would be an example of which type of processing?
   a. central-route processing
   b. peripheral-route processing
   c. cognitive-route processing
   d. visual-route processing
6. In the famous Festinger experiment, participants were paid either $1 or $20 to lie to a woman in the waiting room about how interesting the task really was. The participants who convinced themselves that the task really was fun were the ones who were _________.
   a. paid immediately.
   b. paid after one day.
   c. paid only $1.
   d. paid $20.

IMPRESSION FORMATION

When one person meets another for the first time, it is the first opportunity either person will have to make initial evaluations and judgments about the other. That first opportunity is a very important one in **impression formation**, the forming of the first knowledge a person has about another person. Impression formation includes assigning the other person to a number of categories and drawing conclusions about what that person is likely to do—it's really all about prediction. In a sense, when first meeting another person, the observer goes through a process of concept formation similar to that discussed in Chapter Seven. Impression formation is another kind of social cognition.

There is a *primacy effect* in impression formation: The first time people meet someone, they form an impression of that person that persists even though they may later have other contradictory information about that person (DeCoster & Claypool, 2004; Luchins, 1957). So the old saying is pretty much on target: First impressions do count.

Impression formation is one of a number of phenomena that are all part of **social cognition**, the mental processes that people use to make sense out of the social world around them. **Simulate** on **mypsychlab.com**

Simulate impression formation and attribution on **mypsychlab.com**

impression formation the forming of the first knowledge that a person has concerning another person.

social cognition the mental processes that people use to make sense of the social world around them.

social categorization the assignment of a person one has just met to a category based on characteristics the new person has in common with other people with whom one has had experience in the past.

12.6 What are social categorization and implicit personality theories?

SOCIAL CATEGORIZATION

One of the processes that occur when people meet someone new is the assignment of that person to some kind of category or group. This assignment is usually based on characteristics the new person has in common with other people or groups with whom the perceiver has had prior experience. This **social categorization** is mostly automatic and occurs without conscious awareness of the process (Macrae & Bodenhausen, 2000). Although this is a natural process (human beings are just born categorizers, LINK to Chapter Seven: Cognition, pp. 255-258), sometimes it can cause problems. When the characteristics used to categorize the person are superficial* ones that have become improperly

*superficial: on the surface.

At this job fair in Shanghai, China, thousands of applicants wait hopefully in line for an opportunity to get a job interview. Making a good first impression is important in any job interview situation, but when the competition numbers in the thousands, the people who will most likely get interviews are those who are neatly dressed and well-groomed.

attached to certain ideas, such as "red hair equals a bad temper," social categorization can result in a **stereotype**, a set of characteristics that people believe is shared by all members of a particular social category (Fiske, 1998). Stereotypes (although not always negative) are very limiting, causing people to misjudge what others are like and often to treat them differently as a result. Add the process of stereotyping to the primacy effect and it becomes easy to see how important first impressions really are. That first impression not only has more importance than any other information gathered about a person later on but may include a stereotype that is resistant to change as well (Hilton & von Hipple, 1996; Hugenberg & Bodenhausen, 2003).

It sounds as though we'd be better off if people didn't use social categorization.

It sounds as though we'd be better off if people didn't use social categorization.

Social categorization does have an important place in the perception of others. It allows people to access a great deal of information that can be useful about others, as well as helping people to remember and organize information about the characteristics of others (Macrae & Bodenhausen, 2000). The way to avoid falling into the trap of negatively stereotyping someone is to be aware of existing stereotypes and apply a little critical thinking: "Okay, so he's a guy with a lot of piercings. That doesn't mean that he's overly aggressive—it just means he has a lot of piercings."

IMPLICIT PERSONALITY THEORIES

The categories into which people place others are based on something called an **implicit personality theory**. Implicit personality theories are sets of assumptions that people have about how different types of people, personality traits, and actions are all related and form in childhood (Dweck et al., 1995; Erdley & Dweck, 1993). For example, many people have an implicit personality theory that includes the idea that happy people are also friendly people and people who are quiet are shy. Although these assumptions or beliefs are not necessarily true, they do serve the function of helping to organize *schemas*, or mental patterns that represent (in this case) what a person believes about certain "types" of people. (The concept of schema here is similar to the complex schemes proposed by Piaget. LINK to Chapter Eight: Development Across the Life Span, p. 312.) Of course, the schemas formed in this way can easily become

stereotype a set of characteristics that people believe is shared by all members of a particular social category.

implicit personality theory sets of assumptions about how different types of people, personality traits, and actions are related to each other.

stereotypes when people have limited experience with others who are different from them, especially in superficial ways such as skin color or other physical characteristics (Levy et al., 1998).

Some evidence to suggests that implicit personality theories may differ from culture to culture as well as from individual to individual. For example, one study found that Americans and Hong Kong Chinese people have different implicit personality theories about how much the personality of an individual is able to change. Whereas Americans assume that personality is relatively fixed and unchanging, Chinese people native to Hong Kong assume that personalities are far more changeable (Chiu et al., 1997).

ATTRIBUTION

12.7 How do people try to explain the actions of others?

Another aspect of social cognition is the need people seem to have to explain the behavior of other people. Have you ever watched someone who was doing something you didn't understand? Chances are you were going through a number of possible explanations in your head: "Maybe he's sick, or maybe he sees something I can't see," and so on. It seems to be human nature to want to know why people do the things they do so that we know how to behave toward them and whom we might want to use as role models. If no obvious answer is available, people tend to come up with their own reasons. People also need an explanation for their own behavior. This need is so great that if an explanation isn't obvious, it causes the distress known as cognitive dissonance. The process of explaining both one's own behavior and the behavior of other people is called **attribution**. Explore on **mypsychlab.com**

Explore internal and external attribution on **mypsychlab.com**

CAUSES OF BEHAVIOR **Attribution theory** was originally developed by social psychologist Fritz Heider (1958) as a way of not only explaining why things happen but also why people choose the particular explanations of behavior that they do. There are basically two kinds of explanations—those that involve an external cause and those that assume that causes are internal.

When the cause of behavior is assumed to be from external sources, such as the weather, traffic, educational opportunities, and so on, it is said to be a **situational cause**. The observed behavior is assumed to be caused by whatever situation exists for the person at that time. For example, if John is late, his lateness might be explained by heavy traffic or car problems.

On the other hand, if the cause of behavior is assumed to come from within the individual, it is called a **dispositional cause**. In this case, it is the person's internal personality characteristics that are seen as the cause of the observed behavior. Someone attributing John's behavior to a dispositional cause, for example, might assume that John was late because his personality includes being careless of his and other people's time.

There's an emotional component to these kinds of attributions as well. When people are happy in a marriage, for example, researchers have found that when a spouse's behavior has a positive effect, the tendency is to attribute it to an internal cause ("he did it because he wanted me to feel good"). When the effect is negative, the behavior is attributed to an external cause ("she must have had a difficult day"). But if the marriage is an unhappy one, the opposite attributions occur: "He is only being nice because he wants something from me" or "She's being mean because it's her nature to be crabby" (Fincham et al., 2000; Karney & Bradbury, 2000).

attribution the process of explaining one's own behavior and the behavior of others.

attribution theory the theory of how people make attributions.

situational cause cause of behavior attributed to external factors, such as delays, the action of others, or some other aspect of the situation.

dispositional cause cause of behavior attributed to internal factors such as personality or character.

FUNDAMENTAL ATTRIBUTION ERROR

But what else determines which type of cause a person will use? For example, what determines how people explain the behavior of someone they don't already know or like?

But what else determines which type of cause a person will use? For example, what determines how people explain the behavior of someone they don't already know or like?

The best known attributional bias is the **fundamental attribution error**, which is the tendency for people to overestimate the influence of another person's internal characteristics on behavior and underestimate the influence of the situation (whereas in explaining our own behavior, the tendency to use situational attributions instead of personal is called the *actor-observer bias*). In other words, people tend to explain the actions of others based on what "kind" of person they are rather than looking for outside causes, such as social influences or situations (Blanchard-Fields et al., 2007; Harman, 1999; Jones & Harris, 1967; Leclerc & Hess, 2007; Weiner, 1985). (For example, people hearing about Milgram's "shock" study tend to assume that something is wrong with the "teachers" in the study rather than explaining their behavior within the circumstances of the situation.)

But why do we do that? Why not assume an external cause for everyone?

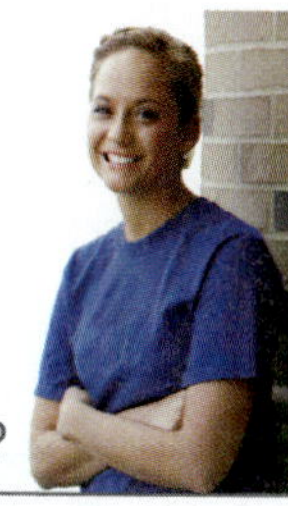

But why do we do that? Why not assume an external cause for everyone?

When people observe themselves, they are very aware of the situational influences on their own behavior. For example, Tardy John was actually the one driving to work, and he knows that heavy traffic and a small accident made him late to work—he was *there*, after all. But someone else looking at John's behavior doesn't have the opportunity to see all of the possible situational influences and has only John himself in focus and, thus, assumes that John's tardiness is caused by some internal personality flaw.

Other research has shown that when students are given an opportunity to make attributions about cheating, they make the fundamental attribution error and actor-observer bias: If others are cheating, it's because they are not honest people, but if the students themselves are cheating it is be because of the situation (Bogle, 2000).

Can the tendency to make these errors be reduced? There are several strategies for making errors in attribution less likely. One is to notice how many other people are doing the same thing. As a college professor, the author often has students who come in late. When it is only one student and it happens frequently, the assumption is that the student is not very careful about time (dispositional cause). But when a large number of students come straggling in late, the assumption becomes "there must be a wreck on the bridge," which is a situational attribution. In other words, if a lot of people are doing it, it is probably caused by an outside factor.

Another trick is to think about what you would do in the same situation. If you think that you might behave in the same way, the cause of behavior is probably situational. People should also make the effort of looking for causes that might not be obvious. If John were to look particularly "stressed out," for example, the assumption might be that something stressed him out, and that "something" might have been heavy traffic.

Although the fundamental attribution error has been found in American culture (Jones & Harris, 1967), would the same error occur in a culture very different from that of America's, such as Japan's? This is the question asked by researchers Masuda and Kitayama (2004), who had both American and Japanese participants ask a target person to read a prewritten attitudinal statement. The participants were then asked to give their opinion on the target's real attitude. American participants made the classic error, assuming that the target's attitude matched the reading. The Japanese participants, however, assumed that the person's attitude might be different from the statement—the person might have been under social obligation to write the piece. Japanese society is a collectivistic culture, and a Japanese person might expect to write a paper to please a teacher or employer even though the paper's contents do not necessarily express the writer's attitudes. A summary of the research in

fundamental attribution error the tendency to overestimate the influence of internal factors in determining behavior while underestimating situational factors.

cross-cultural differences in attribution provides further support for the idea that the fundamental attribution error is not a universal one (Peng et al., 2000). The work of Miller (1984) and many other researchers (Blanchard-Fields et al., 2007; Cha & Nam, 1985; Choi & Nisbett, 1998; Choi et al., 1999; Lee et al., 1996; Morris & Peng, 1994; Morris et al., 1995; Norenzayan et al., 1999) strongly suggests that in more interdependent, collectivist cultures found in China, Hong Kong, Japan, and Korea people tend to assume that external situational factors are more responsible for the behavior of other people than are internal dispositional factors—a finding that is exactly the reverse of the fundamental attribution error so common in the United States and other individualist Western cultures.

Even age is a factor in how likely someone is to fall prey to the fundamental attribution error. Several studies (Blanchard-Fields & Horhota, 2005; Follett & Hess, 2002; Leclerc & Hess, 2007) have found that older adults show a stronger bias toward attributing the actions of another to internal causes than do younger people.

12.6 12.7

CONCEPT MAP

Social Cognition: (continued) Impression Formation and Attribution

- **impression formation** forming of first knowledge about another person; influenced by primacy effect
- **social categorization** automatic and unconscious assignment of a new acquaintance to some category or group
  - **stereotypes:** set of characteristics believed to be shared by all members of a particular category; can be useful (by limiting information processing)
  - categories assigned are based on implicit personality theory, the set of assumptions formed in childhood about different types of people
- attribution is process by which we explain both our own behavior and the behavior of others; based on attribution theory (Heider)
  - **situational:** cause of behavior is assumed to come from external sources
  - **dispositional:** cause of behavior is assumed to come from within the individual
  - **fundamental attribution error** is the tendency to overestimate the influence of another person's internal characteristics on behavior and underestimate the external/situational factors; influenced by age and culture

PRACTICE quiz How much do you remember? ANSWERS ON PAGE AK-2.

Pick the best answer.

1. Which of the following statements about stereotypes is FALSE?
   a. Stereotypes are forms of social categories.
   b. Stereotypes are sets of characteristics that people believe are true for all members of a particular social category.
   c. Stereotypes are governed by the recency effect.
   d. Stereotypes are very limiting and can cause discrimination.
2. Mental patterns that represent what a person believes about certain types of people are called __________.
   a. schemas.
   b. stereotypes.
   c. attributions.
   d. attitudes.
3. Elizabeth's room is almost always a mess. Her parents attribute this to Elizabeth's laziness. This is an example of a __________ cause.
   a. situational
   b. dispositional
   c. dispensational
   d. superficial
4. John was late to class, and his friend Eddie assumes that John simply doesn't care about being on time. But when Eddie is late the next day, he blames it on heavy traffic. Eddie has made the __________.
   a. egocentric error.
   b. fundamental attribution error.
   c. assumption error.
   d. false consensus error.
5. In Asian cultures, people tend to explain the behavior of others as a result of __________.
   a. bad genes.
   b. internal dispositions.
   c. situational factors.
   d. personality traits.

Social Interaction: Prejudice and Aggression

Social influence and social cognition are two of three main areas included in the field of social psychology. The third major area has to do with social interactions with others, or the relationships between people, both casual and intimate. Social interactions include prejudice and discrimination, liking and loving, and aggression and prosocial behavior.

PREJUDICE AND DISCRIMINATION

12.8 How are prejudice and discrimination different?

In talking about attitudes, the idea that some attitudes—stereotypes—can be formed by using only superficial information about a person or group of people was discussed. When a person holds an unsupported and often negative stereotyped attitude about the members of a particular social group, it is called **prejudice**. When prejudicial attitudes cause members of a particular social group to be treated differently than others in situations that call for equal treatment, it is called **discrimination**. Prejudice is the attitude and discrimination is the behavior that can result from that attitude. Although laws can be made to minimize discriminatory behavior, it is not possible to have laws against holding certain attitudes. In other words, discrimination can be controlled and in some cases eliminated, but the prejudicial attitude that is responsible for the discrimination cannot be so easily controlled or eliminated.

On September 6, 1957, this high school in Little Rock, Arkansas, became integrated, allowing African American students to attend school with White students. The practice of segregating Black and White school children was discrimination, and the desegregation laws were aimed at stopping that discrimination. But the attitudes of prejudice persisted even after the legal discrimination was stopped and to some degree still exist today. The courts can make laws against discrimination, but changing prejudicial attitudes is much more difficult.

TYPES OF PREJUDICE AND DISCRIMINATION

There are many kinds of prejudice. There are also many kinds of discrimination that occur as a result of prejudice. There's ageism, or prejudicial attitudes toward the elderly or teenagers (among others); sexism; racism, or prejudice toward those from different ethnic groups; prejudice toward those from different religions, those from different economic levels, those who are overweight, those who are too thin, and so on. Prejudice can also vary in terms of what type of people or groups make the most likely targets. In any society, there will always be **in-groups** and **out-groups**, or "us" versus "them." The in-group is all the people with whom a particular person identifies and the out-groups are everyone else (Brewer, 2001; Hewstone et al., 2002; Tajfel & Turner, 1986). The formation of in-groups and out-groups begins in childhood (Ruble et al., 2004) and continues as children become adults.

"First, can we agree that it's a big backyard?"

Once an in-group is established, prejudice toward and discriminatory treatment of the out-group or groups soon follow (Brewer, 2001). Members of the out-groups are usually going to become stereotyped according to some superficial characteristic, such as skin color or hair color, and getting rid of a stereotype once formed is difficult at best (Cameron et al., 2001; Hamilton & Gifford, 1976).

The **realistic conflict theory** of prejudice states that increasing prejudice and discrimination are closely tied to an increasing degree of conflict between the in-group and the out-group when those groups are seeking a common resource, such as land or available jobs (Horowitz, 1985; Taylor & Moghaddam, 1994). Because the examples of this from history and modern times are so numerous, it is possible to list only a few: the conflict between the early Crusaders and the Muslims, between the Jewish people and the Germans, the hatred between the Irish Catholics and the Irish Protestants, and the conflict between the native population of you-name-the-country and the colonists who want that land. The section that follows is a classic study that illustrates how easily in-groups and out-groups can be formed and how quickly prejudice and discrimination follow.

prejudice negative attitude held by a person about the members of a particular social group.

discrimination treating people differently because of prejudice toward the social group to which they belong.

in-groups social groups with whom a person identifies; "us."

out-groups social groups with whom a person does not identify; "them."

realistic conflict theory theory stating that prejudice and discrimination will be increased between groups that are in conflict over a limited resource.

classic studies in psychology

Brown Eyes, Blue Eyes

In a small town in Iowa in 1968, a few days after the assassination of Dr. Martin Luther King, Jr., a second-grade teacher named Jane Elliot tried to teach her students a lesson in prejudice and discrimination. She divided her students into two groups, those with blue eyes and those with brown eyes.

On the first day of the lesson, the blue-eyed children were given special privileges, such as extra time at recess and getting to leave first for lunch. She also told the blue-eyed children that they were superior to the brown-eyed children, telling the brown-eyed children not to bother taking seconds at lunch because it would be wasted. She kept the blue-eyed children and the brown-eyed children apart (Peters, 1971).

Although Elliot tried to be critical of the brown-eyed out-group, she soon found that the blue-eyed children were also criticizing, belittling, and were quite vicious in their attacks on the brown-eyed children. By the end of the day, the blue-eyed children felt and acted superior, and the brown-eyed children were miserable. Even the lowered test scores of the brown-eyed children reflected their misery. Two days later, the brown-eyed children became the favored group and the effects from the first two days appeared again but in reverse this time: The blue-eyed children began to feel inferior and their test scores dropped.

The fact that test scores reflected the treatment received by the out-group is a stunning one, raising questions about the effects of prejudice and discrimination on the education of children who are members of stereotyped out-groups. That the children were so willing to discriminate against their own classmates, some of whom were their close friends before the experiment, is also telling. In his book about this classroom experiment, *A Class Divided*, Peters (1971) reported that the students who were part of the original experiment, when reunited 15 years later to talk about the experience, said that they believed that this early experience with prejudice and discrimination helped them to become less prejudiced as young adults.

These Korean demonstrators were protesting the riots that followed the 1992 not guilty verdict of the four police officers who were videotaped beating Rodney King. The riots lasted 6 days, killing 42 people and damaging 700 buildings in mainly Korean and other Asian American neighborhoods. As the most recent immigrants to the area, the Asian American population of Los Angeles, California, became the scapegoats for aggression.

Questions for Further Discussion

1. Is there anything about this experiment that you find disturbing?
2. How do you think adults might react in a similar experiment?
3. Are there any ethical concerns with what Elliot did in her classroom?
4. What kinds of changes might have occurred in the personalities and performances of the children if the experiment had continued for more than 2 days with each group?

SCAPEGOATING Conflicts between groups are usually greater when there are other pressures or stresses going on, such as war, economic difficulties, or other misfortunes. When such pressures exist, the need to find a *scapegoat* becomes stronger. A scapegoat is a person or a group, typically a member or members of an out-group, who serves as the target for the frustrations and negative emotions of members of the in-group. (The term comes from the ancient Jewish tradition of sending a goat out into the wilderness with the symbolic sins of all the people on its head.)

Scapegoats are going to be the group of people with the least power, and the newest immigrants to any area are typically those who have the least power at that time. That is why many social psychologists believe that the rioting that took place in Los Angeles, California, in the spring of 1992 occurred in the areas it did. This was the time of the infamous Rodney King beating. Rodney King was an African American man who was dragged out of his car onto the street and severely beaten by four police officers. The beating was caught on tape by a bystander. At the trial, the officers were found not guilty of assault with a deadly weapon. This decision was followed by a series of violent riots (Knight, 1996).

The puzzling thing about these riots is that the greatest amount of rioting and violence did not take place in the neighborhoods of the mostly White police officers or in the African American neighborhoods. The rioting was greatest in the neighborhoods of the Asian Americans and Asians who were the most recent immigrants to the area. When a group has only recently moved into an area, as the Asians had, that group has the least social power and influence in that new area. So the rioters took out their frustrations *not* on the people seen as directly responsible for those frustrations but on the group of people with the least power to resist.

HOW PEOPLE LEARN PREJUDICE

12.9 Why are people prejudiced, and how can prejudice be stopped?

As was clearly demonstrated in the brown eyes–blue eyes experiment discussed in the Classic Studies in Psychology section, even children are, under the right circumstances, prone to developing prejudiced attitudes. Is all prejudice simply a matter of learning, or are there other factors at work? Several theories have been proposed to explain the origins and the persistence of prejudice. In **social cognitive theory** (using cognitive processes in relation to understanding the social world), prejudice is seen as an attitude that is formed as other attitudes are formed, through direct instruction, modeling, and other social influences on learning.

SOCIAL IDENTITY THEORY In **social identity theory**, three processes are responsible for the formation of a person's identity within a particular social group and the attitudes, concepts, and behavior that go along with identification with that group (Tajfel & Turner, 1986). The first process is *social categorization*, as discussed earlier in this chapter. Just as people assign categories to others (such as Black, White, student, teacher, and so on) to help organize information about those others, people also assign themselves to social categories to help determine how they should behave. The second element of social identity theory is *identification*, or the formation of one's **social identity**. A social identity is the part of the self-concept that includes the view of oneself as a member of a particular social group within the social category—typically, the in-group. The third aspect of social identity theory is **social comparison**, Festinger's (1954) concept in which people compare themselves favorably to others to improve their own self-esteem: "Well, at least I'm better off than that person." Members of the out-group make handy comparisons. (Remember, social comparison is one of the factors in group polarization, discussed earlier.)

With respect to prejudice, social identity theory helps to explain why people feel the need to categorize or stereotype others, producing the in-group sense of "us versus them" that people adopt toward out-groups. Prejudice may result, at least in part, from the need to increase one's own self-esteem by looking down on others.

STEREOTYPE VULNERABILITY As discussed previously, stereotypes are the widespread beliefs a person has about members of another group. Not only do stereotypes affect the way people perceive other people, but also stereotypes can affect the way people see themselves and their performance (Snyder et al., 1977). **Stereotype vulnerability** refers to the effect that a person's knowledge of another's stereotyped opinions can have on that person's behavior (Osborne, 2007; Steele, 1992, 1997). Research has shown that when people are aware of stereotypes that are normally applied to their own group by others, they may feel anxious about behaving in ways that might support that stereotype. This fear results in anxiety and self-consciousness that have negative effects on their performance in a kind of **self-fulfilling prophecy**, or the effect that expectations can have on outcomes.

Stereotype vulnerability is highly related to *stereotype threat*, in which members of a stereotyped group are made anxious and wary of any situation in which their behavior might confirm a stereotype (Hyde & Kling, 2001; Steele, 1999). In one study, researchers administered a difficult verbal test to both Caucasian and African American

Social comparison involves comparing yourself to others so that your self esteem is protected. What do you think each of these young girls might be thinking?

social cognitive theory referring to the use of cognitive processes in relation to understanding the social world.

social identity theory theory in which the formation of a person's identity within a particular social group is explained by social categorization, social identity, and social comparison.

social identity the part of the self-concept including one's view of self as a member of a particular social category.

social comparison the comparison of oneself to others in ways that raise one's self-esteem.

stereotype vulnerability the effect that people's awareness of the stereotypes associated with their social group has on their behavior.

self-fulfilling prophecy the tendency of one's expectations to affect one's behavior in such a way as to make the expectations more likely to occur.

participants (Steele & Aronson, 1995). Half of the African American participants were asked to record their race on a demographic* question before the test, making them very aware of their minority status. Those participants showed a significant decrease in scores on the test when compared to the other participants, both African American and Caucasian, who did not answer such a demographic question. They had more incorrect answers, had slower response times, answered fewer questions, and demonstrated more anxiety when compared to the other participants (Steele & Aronson, 1995).

Similar effects of stereotype threat on performance have been found in women (Gonzales et al., 2002; Steele, 1997; Steele et al., 2002), and for athletes in academic settings (Yopyk & Prentice, 2005). A recent study did find that some people can overcome feelings of stereotype threat by identifying themselves with a different social identity, such as a woman who identifies herself with "college students" when taking a math exam rather than with "females," since the latter group is often stereotyped as being math deficient (Rydell & Boucher, 2010). This effect only held for those women with fairly high self-esteem, however. **Watch** on **mypsychlab.com**

Watch a video about prejudice on **mypsychlab.com**

OVERCOMING PREJUDICE

The best weapon against prejudice is education: learning about people who are different from you in many ways. The best way to learn about others is to have direct contact with them and to have the opportunity to see them as people rather than "as outsiders or strangers." *Intergroup contact* is very common in college settings, for example, where students and faculty from many different backgrounds live, work, and study together. Because they go through many of the same experiences (midterms, finals, and so on), people from these diverse** backgrounds find common ground to start building friendships and knowledge of each other's cultural, ethnic, or religious differences.

Intergroup contact is one of the best ways to combat prejudice. When people have an opportunity to work together, as the students in this diverse classroom do, they get to know each other on common ground. Can you think of the first time you had direct contact with someone who was different from you? How did that contact change your viewpoint?

EQUAL STATUS CONTACT Contact between social groups can backfire under certain circumstances, however, as seen in a famous study (Sherif et al., 1961) called the "Robber's Cave." In this experiment conducted at a summer camp called Robber's Cave, 22 White, well-adjusted 11- and 12-year-old boys were divided into two groups. The groups each lived in separate housing and were kept apart from each other for daily activities. During the second week, after in-group relationships had formed, the researchers scheduled highly competitive events pitting one group against the other. Intergroup conflict quickly occurred, with name-calling, fights, and hostility emerging between the two groups.

The third week involved making the two groups come together for pleasant, noncompetitive activities, in the hopes that cooperation would be the result. Instead, the groups used the activities of the third week as opportunities for more hostility. It was only after several weeks of being forced to work together to resolve a series of crises (created deliberately by the experimenters) that the boys lost the hostility and formed friendships between the groups. When dealing with the crises, the boys were forced into a situation of **equal status contact**, in which they were all in the same situation with neither group holding power over the other. Equal status contact has been shown to reduce prejudice and discrimination. It appears that personal involvement with people from another group must be cooperative and occur when all groups are equal in terms of power or status to have a positive effect on reducing prejudice (Pettigrew & Tropp, 2000; Robinson & Preston, 1976).

equal status contact contact between groups in which the groups have equal status with neither group having power over the other.

THE "JIGSAW CLASSROOM" One way to ensure that contact between people from different backgrounds will occur in a cooperative fashion is to make success at a task dependent on the cooperation of each person in a group of people of mixed abilities or statuses. If each member of the group has information that is needed to solve the

*demographic: having to do with the statistical characteristics of a population.

**diverse: different, varied.

problem at hand, a situation is created in which people must depend on one another to meet their shared goals (Aronson et al., 1978). Ordinarily, school classrooms are not organized along these lines but are instead more competitive and, therefore, more likely to create conflict between people of different abilities and backgrounds.

In a **"jigsaw classroom,"** students have to work together to reach a specific goal. Each student is given a "piece of the puzzle," or information that is necessary for solving the problem and reaching the goal (Aronson et al., 1978; Clarke, 1994). Students then share their information with other members of the group. Interaction between diverse students is increased, making it more likely that those students will come to see each other as partners and form friendly relationships rather than labeling others as members of an out-group and treating them differently. This technique works at the college level as well as in the lower school grades (Johnson et al., 1991; Lord, 2001).

"jigsaw classroom" educational technique in which each individual is given only part of the information needed to solve a problem, causing the separate individuals to be forced to work together to find the solution.

12.8 12.9

CONCEPT MAP

Social Interaction: Prejudice and Discrimination

- **prejudice** unsupported and negative stereotypes (e.g., ageism, sexism, racism, etc.) about members of a particular social group
  - **social cognitive theory** suggests that prejudice is an attitude formed as others are formed
  - **social identity theory** suggests three processes are responsible for the formation of a person's identity within a social group—categorization, identification, and comparison
  - **stereotype vulnerability** (knowledge of someone else's stereotyped opinions) can result in self-fulfilling prophecy and is related to stereotype threat when situational anxiety occurs if a person's behavior might confirm a stereotype
  - **prejudice** can be overcome through education, equal status intergroup contact, and working together to achieve a specific goal (e.g., the "jigsaw classroom")
- **discrimination** occurs when prejudicial attitudes cause members of a social group to be treated differently than others in situations calling for equal treament
- can vary based on existence of in-groups and out-groups
  - **scapegoating** (target for frustrations and negative emotions) typically occurs for members of an out-group
- **realistic conflict theory** suggests that when resources are limited, prejudice and discrimination are closely tied to an increasing degree of conflict between groups that seek common resources

PRACTICE quiz How much do you remember?

ANSWERS ON PAGE AK-2.

Pick the best answer.

1. The behavioral component of prejudice is _________.
   a. discrimination.
   b. stereotyping.
   c. implicit personality theorizing.
   d. holding a negative attitude toward a person.
2. The most likely predictor of the development of prejudice and discrimination between two groups is the degree of _________ between the groups.
   a. differences
   b. conflict
   c. distance
   d. emotionality
3. In teacher Jane Elliot's classic study, the most startling finding was that the _________.
   a. blue-eyed children were kinder to their brown-eyed peers.
   b. brown-eyed children were less prejudiced.
   c. test scores of each group decreased when it was the out-group.
   d. children were unwilling to discriminate with respect to the others.
4. Which of the following is not an element of social identity theory?
   a. reference group
   b. social identity
   c. social comparison
   d. superordinate goals
5. Which situation would be least likely to result in a decrease of prejudice?
   a. asking people to work on separate projects but in the same room
   b. asking people to work on a common task
   c. giving each person a piece of information to share with the others to solve a problem
   d. people of various backgrounds helping rescue others from a flood

Brainstorming: What was the first time you became aware that you had a prejudiced attitude toward something or someone? How did you confront that knowledge?

interpersonal attraction liking or having the desire for a relationship with another person.

proximity physical or geographical nearness.

reciprocity of liking tendency of people to like other people who like them in return.

Liking and Loving: Interpersonal Attraction

Prejudice pretty much explains why people don't like each other. What does psychology say about why people like someone else? There are some "rules" for those whom people like and find attractive. Liking or having the desire for a relationship with someone else is called **interpersonal attraction**, and there's a great deal of research on the subject. (Who wouldn't want to know the rules?)

THE RULES OF ATTRACTION

12.10 What factors govern attraction and love, and what are some different kinds of love?

Several factors are involved in the attraction of one person to another, including both superficial physical characteristics, such as physical beauty and proximity, as well as elements of personality. **Watch** on **mypsychlab.com**

Watch a video about attraction on **mypsychlab.com**

PHYSICAL ATTRACTIVENESS When people think about what attracts them to others, one of the topics that usually arises is the physical attractiveness of the other person. Some research suggests that physical beauty is one of the main factors that influence individuals' choices for selecting people they want to know better, although other factors may become more important in the later stages of relationships (Eagly et al., 1991; Feingold, 1992; White, 1980).

PROXIMITY—CLOSE TO YOU The closer together people are physically, such as working in the same office building or living in the same dorm, the more likely they are to form a relationship. **Proximity** refers to being physically near someone else. People choose friends and lovers from the pool of people available to them, and availability depends heavily on proximity.

One theory about why proximity is so important involves the idea of repeated exposure to new stimuli. The more people experience something, whether it is a song, a picture, or a person, the more they tend to like it. The phrase "it grew on me" refers to this reaction. When people are in physical proximity to each other, repeated exposure may increase their attraction to each other.

BIRDS OF A FEATHER—SIMILARITY Proximity does not guarantee attraction, just as physical attractiveness does not guarantee a long-term relationship. People tend to like being around others who are *similar* to them in some way. The more people find they have in common with others—such as attitudes, beliefs, and interests—the more they tend to be attracted to those others (Hartfield & Rapson, 1992; Moreland & Zajonc, 1982; Neimeyer & Mitchell, 1998). Similarity as a factor in relationships makes sense when seen in terms of validation of a person's beliefs and attitudes. When other people hold the same attitudes and beliefs and do the same kinds of actions, it makes a person's own concepts seem more correct or valid.

WHEN OPPOSITES ATTRACT

Isn't there a saying about "opposites attract"? Aren't people sometimes attracted to people who are different instead of similar?

Isn't there a saying about "opposites attract"? Aren't people sometimes attracted to people who are different instead of similar?

There is often a grain of truth in many old sayings, and "opposites attract" is no exception. Some people find that forming a relationship with another person who has *complementary* qualities (characteristics in the one person that fill a need in the other) can be very rewarding (Carson, 1969; Schmitt, 2002). Research does not support this view of attraction, however. It is similarity, not complementarity, that draws people together and helps them stay together (Berscheid & Reis, 1998; McPherson et al., 2001).

RECIPROCITY OF LIKING Finally, people have a very strong tendency to like people who like them, a simple but powerful concept referred to as **reciprocity of liking**. In one experiment, researchers paired college students with other students (Curtis &

Miller, 1986). Neither student in any of the pairs knew the other member. One member of each pair was randomly chosen to receive some information from the experimenters about how the *other* student in the pair felt about the first member. In some cases, target students were led to believe that the other students liked them and, in other cases, that the targets disliked them.

When the pairs of students were allowed to meet and talk with each other again, they were friendlier, disclosed more information about themselves, agreed with the other person more, and behaved in a warmer manner *if they had been told* that the other student liked them. The other students came to like these students better as well, so liking produced more liking.

The only time that liking someone does not seem to make that person like the other in return is if a person suffers from feelings of low self-worth. In that case, finding out that someone likes you when you don't even like yourself makes you question his or her motives. This mistrust can cause you to act unfriendly to that person, which makes the person more likely to become unfriendly to you in a kind of self-fulfilling prophecy (Murray et al., 1998).

psychology in the news

Facing Facebook—The Social Nature of Online Networking

There are some interesting research findings concerning the online networking phenomenon. For example, people using particular sites seem to have certain things in common. The findings of one study suggest that which social network sites a college student selects is related to racial identity, ethnic identity, and the education level of the student's parents (Hargittai, 2007). White students prefer Facebook, and Hispanic students prefer MySpace; and while Asian and Asian American students use Facebook more than MySpace, they use less popular sites like Xanga and Friendster more than any other ethnic group does. The more education the parents have, the more likely the student is to use Facebook and Xanga, and the less likely to use MySpace.

In another study, researchers found that young people who already experience positive social relationships use the online sites to enhance those same relationships, contrary to the stereotyped view that it would be the socially inept who would gravitate toward the anonymous nature of online networking (Mikami et al., 2010). In fact, those who are less well-adjusted either did not use social networking sites or used them in more negative ways: excessive bad language, hostile remarks, aggressive gestures, or posting of unflattering or suggestive photographs.

Finally, a recent study's findings suggest that users of social networking sites spend a lot more time on "social searching," which is defined as searching a site for specific information about a certain person, group, or event, than they do on "social browsing," defined as surveying the site without any specific target in mind (Wise et al., 2010). Users were also found to be more emotionally and positively engaged when searching rather than browsing. Again, this runs counter to the complaints of some who feel that such sites encourage time-wasting browsing. Instead, people are actively searching for information they desire.

Questions for Further Discussion

1. Why might certain networking sites be more attractive to one ethnicity over another?
2. How do you find yourself using networking sites, and how does that relate to the findings of these studies?

LOVE IS A TRIANGLE—ROBERT STERNBERG'S TRIANGULAR THEORY OF LOVE

Dictionary definitions of love refer to a strong affection for another person due to kinship, personal ties, sexual attraction, admiration, or common interests.

But those aren't all the same kind of relationships. I love my family and I love my friends, but in different ways.

But those aren't all the same kind of relationships. I love my family and I love my friends, but in different ways.

Psychologists generally agree that there are different kinds of love. One psychologist, Robert Sternberg, outlined a theory of what he determined were the three main components of love and the different types of love that combinations of these three components can produce (Sternberg, 1986, 1988b, 1997).

THE THREE COMPONENTS OF LOVE According to Sternberg, love consists of three basic components: intimacy, passion, and commitment.

Intimacy, in Sternberg's view, refers to the feelings of closeness that one has for another person or the sense of having close emotional ties to another. Intimacy in this sense is not physical but psychological. Friends have an intimate relationship because they disclose things to each other that most people might not know, they feel strong emotional ties to each other, and they enjoy the presence of the other person.

Passion is the physical aspect of love. Passion refers to the emotional and sexual arousal a person feels toward the other person. Passion is not simply sex; holding hands, loving looks, and hugs can all be forms of passion.

Commitment involves the decisions one makes about a relationship. A short-term decision might be, "I think I'm in love." An example of a more long-term decision is, "I want to be with this person for the rest of my life." **Watch** on **mypsychlab.com**

Watch a video on Sternberg's triangular theory of love on **mypsychlab.com**

THE LOVE TRIANGLES A love relationship between two people can involve one, two, or all three of these components in various combinations. The combinations can produce seven different forms of love, as can be seen in Figure 12.5.

Two of the more familiar and more heavily researched forms of love from Sternberg's theory are romantic love and companionate love. When intimacy and passion are combined, the result is the more familiar **romantic love**, which is sometimes called passionate love by other researchers (Bartels & Zeki, 2000; Diamond, 2003; Hartfield, 1987). Romantic love is often the basis for a more lasting relationship. In many

romantic love type of love consisting of intimacy and passion.

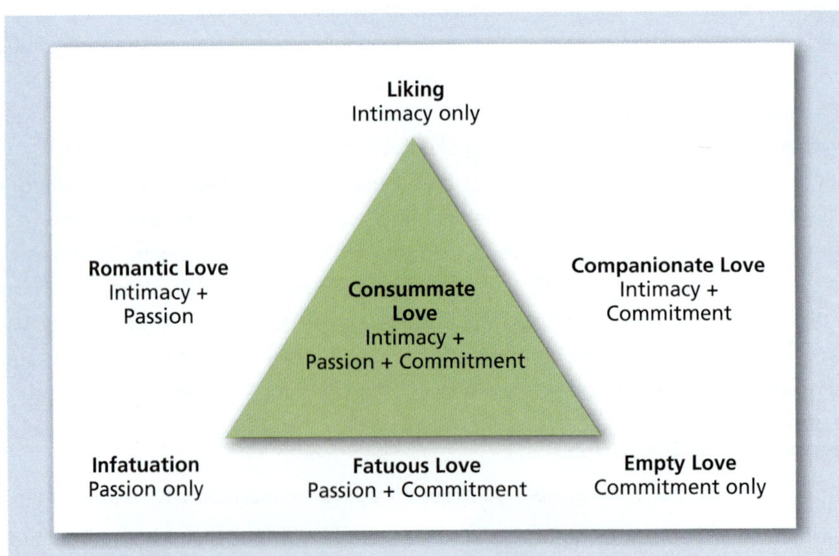

Figure 12.5 Sternberg's Triangular Theory of Love

This diagram represents the seven different kinds of love that can result from combining the three components of love: intimacy, passion, and commitment. Notice that some of these types of love sound less desirable or positive than others. What is the one key element missing from the less positive types of love?

Source: Adapted from Sternberg (1986).

Western cultures, the ideal relationship begins with liking, then becomes romantic love as passion is added to the mix, and finally becomes a more enduring form of love as a commitment is made.

When intimacy and commitment are the main components of a relationship, it is called **companionate love**. In companionate love, people who like each other, feel emotionally close to each other, and understand one another's motives have made a commitment to live together, usually in a marriage relationship. Companionate love is often the binding tie that holds a marriage together through the years of parenting, paying bills, and lessening physical passion (Gottman & Krokoff, 1989; Steinberg & Silverberg, 1987). In many non-Western cultures, companionate love is seen as more sensible. Choices for a mate on the basis of compatibility are often made by parents or matchmakers rather than the couple themselves (Duben & Behar, 1991; Hortaçsu, 1999; Jones, 1997; Thornton & Hui-Sheng, 1994). **Read** on **mypsychlab.com**

Finally, when all three components of love are present, the couple has achieved *consummate love*, the ideal form of love that many people see as the ultimate goal. This is also the kind of love that may evolve into companionate love when the passion lessens during the middle years of a relationship's commitment.

Read and learn more about the labeling theory of passionate love on **mypsychlab.com**

companionate love type of love consisting of intimacy and commitment.

12.10 CONCEPT MAP

Social Interaction: (continued) Interpersonal Attraction

- liking or having the desire for a relationship with someone else; can be influenced by a variety of factors
  - physical attractiveness
  - proximity
  - similarity
  - complementary qualities
  - reciprocity of liking
- **love** strong affection for another person due to kinship, personal ties, sexual attraction, admiration, or common interests
  - **Sternberg's triangular theory** suggests different components and types of love
    - three components
      - intimacy
      - passion
      - commitment
    - three types
      - **romantic** (intimacy and passion)
      - **companionate** (intimacy and commitment)
      - **consummate** (intimacy, passion, and commitment)

PRACTICE **quiz** How much do you remember? ANSWERS ON PAGE AK-2.

Pick the best answer.

1. Which of the following is not one of the reasons given by the text for interpersonal attraction?
   a. physical attractiveness
   b. similarity
   c. personality
   d. proximity
2. The more you see someone, the more likely you are to _________ that person.
   a. dislike
   b. like
   c. grow tired of
   d. be annoyed by
3. A person who is very low in self-worth is less likely to be affected by the _________.
   a. halo effect.
   b. mere exposure effect.
   c. need complementarity effect.
   d. reciprocity of liking effect.
4. According to Sternberg, the emotional and physical arousal a person feels for another is the _________ component of love.
   a. intimacy
   b. passion
   c. commitment
   d. psychological

aggression behavior intended to hurt or destroy another person.

Aggression and Prosocial Behavior

Unfortunately, violence toward others is another form of social interaction. When one person hurts or tries to destroy another person deliberately, either with words or with physical behavior, psychologists call it **aggression**. One common cause of aggressive behavior is frustration, which occurs when a person is prevented from reaching some desired goal. The concept of aggression as a reaction to frustration is known as the frustration–aggression hypothesis (Berkowitz, 1993; Miller et al., 1941). Many sources of frustration can lead to aggressive behavior. Pain, for example, produces negative sensations that are often intense and uncontrollable, leading to frustration and often aggressive acts against the nearest available target (Berkowitz, 1993). Loud noises, excessive heat, the irritation of someone else's cigarette smoke, and even awful smells can lead people to act out in an aggressive manner (Anderson, 1987; Rotton & Frey, 1985; Rotton et al., 1979; Zillmann et al., 1981).

Frustration is not the only source of aggressive behavior. Many early researchers, including Sigmund Freud (1930), believed that aggression was a basic human instinct. In Freud's view, aggression was part of the death instinct that drove human beings to destroy both others and themselves, and he believed that if aggression were not released it would cause illness. But if aggression is an instinct present in all humans, it should occur in far more similar patterns across cultures than it does. Instinctual behavior, as often seen in animals, is not modifiable by environmental influences. Modern approaches try to explain aggression as a biological phenomenon or a learned behavior.

AGGRESSION AND BIOLOGY

12.11 How is aggressive behavior determined by biology and learning?

There is some evidence that human aggression has, at least partially, a genetic basis. Studies of twins reared together and reared apart have shown that if one identical twin has a violent temper, the identical sibling will most likely also have a violent temper. This agreement between twins' personalities happens more often with identical twins than with fraternal twins (Miles & Carey, 1997; Rowe et al., 1999). It may be that some gene or complex of genes makes certain people more susceptible to aggressive responses under the right environmental conditions.

As discussed in Chapter Two, certain areas of the brain seem to control aggressive responses. The amygdala and other structures of the limbic system have been shown to trigger aggressive responses when stimulated in both animals and humans (Adams, 1968; Albert & Richmond, 1977; LaBar et al., 1995; Scott et al., 1997). Charles Whitman, the Texas Tower sniper, who in 1966 killed his mother, his wife, and then shot and killed 12 more people before finally being killed by law enforcement officers, left a note asking for an examination of his brain. An autopsy did reveal a tumor that was pressing into his amygdala (Lavergne, 1997).

There are also chemical influences on aggression. Testosterone, a male sex hormone, has been linked to higher levels of aggression in humans (Archer, 1991). This may help to explain why violent criminals tend to be young, male, and muscular. They typically have high levels of testosterone and low levels of serotonin, another important chemical found in the brain (Alexander et al., 1986; Brown & Linnoila, 1990; Coccaro & Kavoussi, 1996; Dabbs et al., 2001; Robins, 1996).

Don't some people get pretty violent after drinking too much? Does alcohol do something to those brain chemicals?

● *Don't some people get pretty violent after drinking too much? Does alcohol do something to those brain chemicals?*

Alcohol does have an impact on aggressive behavior. Psychologically, alcohol acts to release inhibitions, making people less likely to control their behavior even if they are not yet intoxicated. Biologically, alcohol affects the functioning of many neurotransmitters and in particular is associated with a decrease in serotonin (Virkkunen & Linnoila, 1996). LINK to Chapter Two: The Biological Perspective, p. 53. In one study, volunteers were asked to administer electric shocks to an unseen "opponent" in a study reminiscent of Milgram's shock experiment. The actual responses to the shock were simulated by a computer, although the volunteers believed that the responses were coming from a real person. The volunteers were told it was a test of reaction time and learning (Bushman, 1997). Volunteers participated both before consuming alcohol and after consuming alcohol. Participants were much more aggressive in administering stronger shocks after drinking.

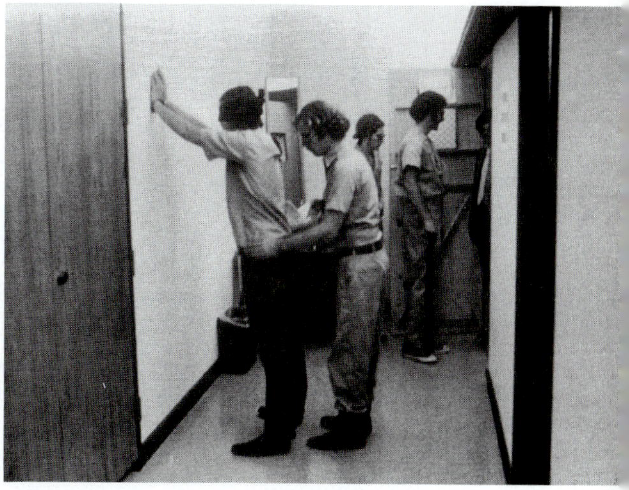

This photograph shows a "guard" searching a "prisoner" in Zimbardo's famous Stanford prison experiment. The students in the experiment became so deeply involved in their assigned roles that Zimbardo had to cancel the experiment after only 5 days—less than half the time originally scheduled for the study.

THE POWER OF SOCIAL ROLES

Although frustration, genetics, body chemicals, and even the effects of drugs can be blamed for aggressive behavior to some degree, much of human aggression is also influenced by learning. The social learning theory explanation for aggression states that aggressive behavior is learned (in a process called observational learning) by watching aggressive models get reinforced for their aggressive behavior (Bandura, 1980; Bandura et al., 1961). LINK to Chapter Five: Learning, pp. 201–203. Aggressive models can be parents, siblings, friends, or people on television or in computerized games.

Some evidence suggests that even taking on a particular *social role*, such as that of a soldier, can lead to an increase in aggressive behavior. A **social role** is the pattern of behavior that is expected of a person who is in a particular social position. For example, "doctor" is a social role that implies wearing a white coat, asking certain types of questions, and writing prescriptions, among other things. A deeply disturbing experiment was conducted by famed social psychologist Philip Zimbardo at Stanford University in 1971. The experiment was recorded on film from the beginning to its rather abrupt end. About 70 young men, most of whom were college students, volunteered to participate for 2 weeks. They were told that they would be randomly assigned the social role of either a guard or a prisoner in the experiment. The "guards" were given uniforms and instructions not to use violence but to maintain control of the "prison." The "prisoners" were booked at a real jail, blindfolded, and transported to the campus "prison," actually the basement of one of the campus buildings. On Day 2, the prisoners staged a revolt (not planned as part of the experiment), which was quickly crushed by the guards. The guards then became increasingly more aggressive, using humiliation to control and punish the prisoners. For example, prisoners were forced to clean out toilet bowls with their bare hands. The staff observing the experiment had to release five of the prisoners who became so upset that they were physically ill. The entire experiment was canceled on the fifth day, after one of the prisoners reported to Zimbardo that what the experimenters were doing to the young men was terrible (Zimbardo, 1971).

The conclusions of Zimbardo and his colleagues highlighted the influence that a social role, such as that of "guard," can have on perfectly ordinary people. Although history is full of examples of people behaving horribly to others while filling a particular role; one need not travel very far into the past to find an example. **Watch** on **mypsychlab.com**

Watch classic footage of Zimbardo's Stanford prison experiment on **mypsychlab.com**

During the war in Iraq in 2003, an army reserve general was suspended from duty while an investigation into reported prisoner abuses was conducted. Between October and December 2003, investigators found numerous cases of cruel, humiliating, and other startling abuses of the Iraqi prisoners by the army military police stationed at the prison of Abu Ghraib (Hersh, 2004). Among the cruelties reported were pouring cold water on naked detainees, beating them with a broom handle or chair, threatening them with rape, and one case of actually carrying out the threat. How could any normal person have done such things? The "guards" in the Stanford prison study were normal people, but the

social role the pattern of behavior that is expected of a person who is in a particular social position.

A U.S. soldier mistreats an Iraqi prisoner at the Abu Ghraib prison in Iraq. Investigators into alleged abuses at this prison found numerous sadistic and brutal acts committed by U.S. military personnel upon the prisoners.

Read and learn more about child abuse on **mypsychlab.com**

effect of putting on the uniform and taking on the social role of guard changed their behavior radically. Is it possible that a similar factor was at work at Abu Ghraib? The behavior of the guards at Abu Ghraib was not part of a formal, controlled study, so further research will be needed to determine to what degree the social roles at work in situations like this influence the kind of behavior seen in this real-life example.

No one can deny that abused children are exposed to powerful models of aggression. Unfortunately, the parents who abuse them are reinforced for their aggressive behavior when they get what they want from the child. No one can deny that there are people who were abused as children who then go on to become abusers. Contrary to popular belief, most children who suffer abuse do *not* grow up to become abusers themselves—in fact, only one third of abused children do so (Glasser et al., 2001; Kaufman & Zigler, 1993; Oliver, 1993). Instead of becoming the abuser, some abused children receive help in the form of counseling and/or removal from the abusive situation, overcoming the damage from their childhood, whereas others withdraw, isolating themselves rather than becoming abusive (Dodge et al., 1990). **Read** on **mypsychlab.com**

VIOLENCE IN THE MEDIA AND AGGRESSION

I've heard that violent television programs can cause children to become more aggressive. How true is that?

I've heard that violent television programs can cause children to become more aggressive. How true is that?

Bandura's early study on the effects of an aggressive model viewed over a movie screen on small children was one of the first attempts to investigate the effect of violence in the media on children's aggressive behavior (Bandura et al., 1963). LINK to Chapter Five: Learning, pp. 201–203. Since then, researchers have examined the impact of television and other media violence on the aggressive behavior of children of various ages. The conclusions have all been similar: Children who are exposed to high levels of violent media are more aggressive than children who are not (Baron & Reiss, 1985; Bushman & Huesmann, 2000; Centerwall, 1989; Geen & Thomas, 1986; Huesmann & Miller, 1994; Huesmann et al., 1997; Huesmann et al., 2003; Villani, 2001). These studies have found that there are several contributing factors involving the normal aggressive tendencies of the child, with more aggressive children preferring to watch more aggressive media as well as the age at which exposure begins: The younger the child, the greater the impact. Parenting issues also have an influence, as the aggressive impact of television is lessened in homes where hostile behavior is not tolerated and punishment is not physical.

Violent video games have also come under fire as causing violent acting-out in children, especially young adolescents. The tragic shootings at schools all over the United States have, at least in part, been blamed on violent video games that the students seemed to be imitating. This was especially a concern in the Littleton, Colorado, shootings because the adolescent boys involved in those incidents had not only played a violent video game in which two shooters killed people who could not fight back but also had made a video of themselves in trench coats, shooting school athletes. This occurred less than a year before these same boys killed 13 of their fellow students at Columbine High School and wounded 23 others (Anderson & Dill, 2000). In one study, second-grade boys were allowed to play either an aggressive or a nonaggressive video game. After playing the game, the boys who had played the aggressive video game demonstrated more verbal and physical aggression both to objects around them and to their playmates while playing in a free period than did the boys who had played the nonagressive video game (Irwin & Gross, 1995). **Listen** on **mypsychlab.com**

Listen to the Psychology in the News podcast about violent video games and their effect on the brain on **mypsychlab.com**

In a massive meta-analysis of research into the connection between violent media and aggressive behavior in children, social psychologist Craig Anderson and colleagues found clear and consistent evidence that even short-term exposure to violent media significantly increases the likelihood that children will engage in both physical and verbal aggression as well as aggressive thoughts and emotions (Anderson et al., 2003). Clearly, violent video games do correlate with increased aggression levels of the children who play them, both young children and adolescents (Anderson, 2003; Anderson & Bushman, 2001; Anderson et al., 2008; Bartlett et al., 2008; Ferguson et al., 2008). (Remember, correlation does NOT prove causation—the studies mentioned here have not proven that playing violent video games *causes* increased aggression! LINK to Chapter One: The Science of Psychology, pp. 26–27).

PROSOCIAL BEHAVIOR

Another and far more pleasant form of human social interaction is **prosocial behavior**, or socially desirable behavior that benefits others rather than brings them harm.

12.12 What is altruism, and how is deciding to help someone related to the presence of others?

ALTRUISM One form of prosocial behavior that almost always makes people feel good about other people is **altruism**, or helping someone in trouble with no expectation of reward and often without fear for one's own safety. Although no one is surprised by the behavior of a mother who enters a burning house to save her child, some people are often surprised when total strangers step in to help, risking their own lives for people they do not know.

Sociobiologists, scientists who study the evolutionary and genetic bases of social organizations in both animals and humans, see altruistic behavior as a way of preserving one's genetic material, even at the cost of one's own life. This is why the males of certain species of spiders, for example, seem to willingly become "dinner" for the female mates they have just fertilized, ensuring the continuation of their genes through the offspring she will produce (Koh, 1996). It also explains the mother or father who risks life and limb to save a child. But why do people risk their own lives to help total strangers? More importantly, why do people sometimes refuse to help when their own lives are not at risk?

WHY PEOPLE WON'T HELP On March 13, 1964, at about 3:15 in the morning, a man who didn't even know Catherine "Kitty" Genovese caught her in the parking lot of her apartment complex, stabbed her, left, and then came back nearly half an hour later to rape and stab her to death in the entryway of the complex. A police investigation determined that at least 38 people heard or watched some part of the fatal attack from their apartment windows. Not one of these people—Kitty's neighbors—called the police until after the attack was over (Delfiner, 2001; Gado, 2004; Rosenthal, 1964).

People were outraged by the apparent indifference and lack of sympathy for the poor woman's plight. Why did those people simply stand by and watch or listen? Social psychologists would explain that the lack of response to Kitty Genovese's screams for help was not due to indifference or a lack of sympathy but instead to the presence of other people.

Forty-three years later on June 23, 2007, 27-year-old LaShanda Calloway was stabbed to death during an argument in a convenience store. It took two minutes for someone to call 9-1-1. Surveillance video captured the attack, including the five shoppers who stepped over her bleeding form and continued shopping. One customer did stop—to take a picture of Ms. Calloway as she lay dying on the floor (Hegeman, 2007). When other people are present at the scene or are assumed to be present, individuals are affected by two basic principles of social psychology: the bystander effect and diffusion of responsibility.

prosocial behavior socially desirable behavior that benefits others.

altruism prosocial behavior that is done with no expectation of reward and may involve the risk of harm to oneself.

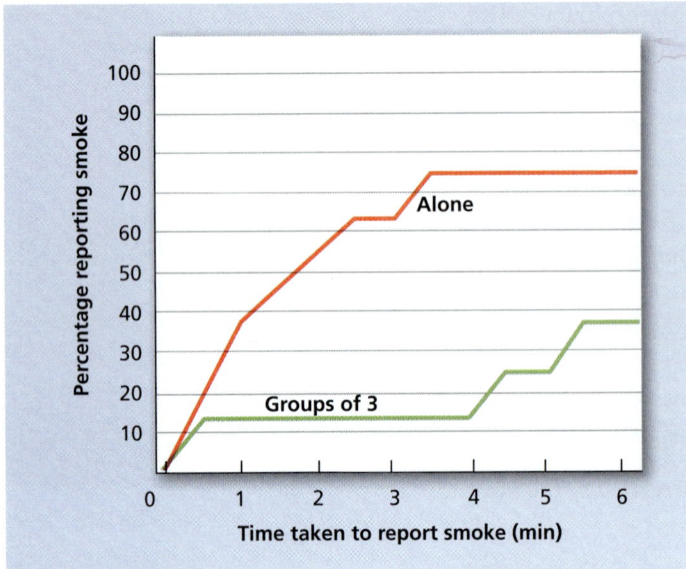

Figure 12.6 Elements Involved in Bystander Response

In a classic experiment, participants were filling out surveys as the room began to fill with smoke. As you can see in the accompanying graph, the time taken to report smoke and the percentage of people reporting smoke both depended on how many people were in the room at the time the smoke was observed. If a person was alone, he or she was far more likely to report the smoke and report it more quickly than when there were three people.
Source: Latané & Darley (1969).

The **bystander effect** refers to the finding that the likelihood of a bystander (someone observing an event and close enough to offer help) to help someone in trouble decreases as the number of bystanders increases. If only one person is standing by, that person is far more likely to help than if there is another person, and the addition of each new bystander decreases the possibility of helping behavior even more (Darley & Latané, 1968; Eagly & Crowley, 1986; Latané & Darley, 1969). In the case of Kitty Genovese, there were 38 "bystanders" at the windows of the apartment buildings, and none of them helped. There is some evidence that only six or seven people actually *saw* parts of the attack, while others heard what some interpreted as a lover's quarrel. No one apparently witnessed the entire event from start to finish, and the greater part of the assault actually took place out of the hearing of any witnesses (Rasenberger, 2006). Still, not one person called the police.

Social psychologists Bibb Latané and John Darley conducted several classic experiments about the bystander effect. In one study, participants were filling out questionnaires in a room that began to fill with smoke. Some participants were alone in the room, whereas in another condition there were three participants in the room. In a third condition one participant was in the room with two confederates of the experimenter, who were instructed to notice the smoke but ignore it afterwards. In the "participant alone" condition, three-fourths of the participants left the room to report the smoke. In the "three participants" condition, only a little over one-third of the participants reported the smoke, whereas only one-tenth of the participants who were in the room with confederates did so (Figure 12.6).

But why does the number of bystanders matter?

But why does the number of bystanders matter?

Diffusion of responsibility is the phenomenon in which a person fails to take responsibility for either action or inaction because of the presence of other people who are seen to share the responsibility (Leary & Forsyth, 1987). Diffusion of responsibility is a form of attribution in which people explain why they acted (or failed to act) as they did because of others. "I was just following orders," "Other people were doing it," and "There were a lot of people there, and I thought one of them would do something" are all examples of statements made in such situations. Kitty Genovese and LaShanda Calloway received no help because there were too many potential "helpers," and not one of the people listening to cries for help took the responsibility to intervene—they thought surely someone else was doing something about it.

FIVE DECISION POINTS IN HELPING BEHAVIOR What kind of decision-making process do people go through before deciding to help? What are the requirements for deciding when help is needed? Darley and Latané (1968) identified several cognitive decision points that a bystander must face before helping someone in trouble. These decision points are outlined in Table 12.3 and are still considered valid over forty years later.

Aside from the factors listed in the table, there are other influences on the decision to help. For example, the more ambiguity* in a situation, the less likely it will be defined as an emergency. (Remember, many of those who heard the attack on Kitty Genovese were not sure if it was a lover's quarrel or not.) If there are other people nearby, especially if the situation is ambiguous, bystanders may rely on the actions of

bystander effect referring to the effect that the presence of other people has on the decision to help or not help, with help becoming less likely as the number of bystanders increases.

diffusion of responsibility occurring when a person fails to take responsibility for actions or for inaction because of the presence of other people who are seen to share the responsibility.

*ambiguity: having the quality of being difficult to identify specific elements of the situation.

Table 12.3

Help or Don't Help: Five Decision Points

DECISION POINT	DESCRIPTION	FACTORS INFLUENCING DECISION
Noticing	Realizing that there is a situation that might be an emergency.	Hearing a loud crash or a cry for help.
Defining an Emergency	Interpreting the cues as signaling an emergency.	Loud crash is associated with a car accident, people are obviously hurt.
Taking Responsibility	Personally assuming the responsibility to act.	A single bystander is much more likely to act than when others are present (Latané & Darley, 1969).
Planning a Course of Action	Deciding how to help and what skills might be needed.	People who feel they have the necessary skills to help are more likely to help.
Taking Action	Actually helping.	Costs of helping (e.g., danger to self) must not outweigh the rewards of helping.

the others to help determine if the situation is an emergency or not. Since all the bystanders may be doing this, it is very likely that the situation will be seen as a non-emergency because no one is moving to help.

Another factor is the mood of the bystanders. People in a good mood are generally more likely to help than people in a bad mood, but oddly enough, they are not as likely to help if helping would destroy the good mood. Gender of the victim is also a factor, with women more likely to receive help than men if the bystander is male, but not if the bystander is female. Physically attractive people are more likely to be helped. Victims who look like "they deserve what is happening" are also less likely to be helped. For example, a man lying on the side of the street who is dressed in shabby clothing and appears to be drunk will be passed by, but if he is dressed in a business suit, people are more likely to stop and help. Racial and ethnicity differences between victim and bystander also decrease the probability of helping (Richards & Lowe, 2003; Tukuitonga & Bindman, 2002).

12.11 12.12 **CONCEPT MAP**

Social Interaction: (continued) Aggression and Prosocial Behavior

- **aggression** occurs when one person verbally or physically hurts or tries to destroy another person; often the result of frustration
  - aggression may be partly attributed to genetics and can be triggered by variations in brain functic (i.e., amygdala activation) and internal or external chemical influences (e.g., testosterone, alcohol)
  - much of aggression is influenced by learning but not totally deterministic
    - partially explained by social learning theory—social roles (expected behavior in particular social situation) determine much of behavior (e.g., Zimbardo's Stanford Prison study)
    - childhood exposure to abuse does not necessarily mean that one will grow up to be an abuser
    - short-term exposure to violent media (video games, television, movies) has been correlated with increases in both physical and verbal aggression and aggressive thoughts and emotions
- prosocial, or socially desirable, behavior benefits others
  - **altruism:** helping someone with no expectation of reward and often at personal risk
  - can be influenced by helper's mood and victim's gender, attractiveness, or "just rewards"; racial and ethnic differences can decrease probability of helping
  - refusal to help another can be negatively affected by the presence of others (bystander effect/diffusion of responsibility) rather than indifference or a lack of sympathy; also influenced by individual's appraisal of situation (see Table 12.3)

(continued)

PRACTICE quiz How much do you remember? ANSWERS ON PAGE AK-2.

Pick the best answer.

1. According to the text, which of the following has not been studied as a cause of aggressive behavior?
   a. frustration
   b. pain
   c. alcohol
   d. marijuana
2. The area of the brain that is most involved in aggression is the _________.
   a. amygdala.
   b. pineal gland.
   c. cerebellum.
   d. cortex.
3. Which of the following statements is TRUE?
   a. Abused children always grow up to become abusers.
   b. Abused children rarely grow up to become abusers.
   c. Abused children grow up to become abusers about one third of the time.
   d. Children who were not abused do not grow up to become abusers.
4. According to the bystander effect, Leshan is more likely to get help if there is (are) _________.
   a. no other people standing nearby.
   b. only one other person standing nearby.
   c. several people standing nearby.
   d. a crowd of people standing nearby.
5. In the Latané and Darley experiment, subjects were most likely to help when _________.
   a. they were alone in the room.
   b. they were with a friend.
   c. there were three other people in the room.
   d. there was one stranger in the room.
6. Once a situation has been defined as an emergency, the next step in the decision-making process is _________.
   a. noticing.
   b. taking action.
   c. taking responsibility.
   d. planning a course of action.

Applying Psychology to Everyday Life: Anatomy of a Cult

12.13 Why do people join cults?

In 1978, the Reverend Jim Jones, leader of the People's Temple in Jonestown, Guyana, ordered his followers to drink poisoned drinks or shoot each other. Of the cult members, 640 adults died and 274 children were either killed by their own hands or those of their parents.

The term **cult** literally refers to any group of people with a particular religious or philosophical set of beliefs and identity. In the strictest sense of the word, the Roman Catholic Church and Protestantism are cults within the larger religion of Christianity. But most people associate the term *cult* with a negative connotation*: A group of people whose religious or philosophical beliefs and behavior are so different from that of mainstream organizations that they are viewed with suspicion and seen as existing on the fringes of socially acceptable behavior. Although many cults exist without much notice from more mainstream groups, at times members of cults have horrified the public with their actions.

One of the best remembered and often cited examples of a cult gone horribly wrong was that of the People's Temple in Jonestown, Guyana, headed by Jim Jones. Originally a Christian offshoot, the People's Temple became a cult under Jones's dictatorial leadership. In 1978, Jones felt threatened by a group of several reporters and a Congressman who had visited the Guyana compound to take home any members who wanted to leave. He sent some of his guards to try to stop them from leaving, and the result was that they shot and killed five people, including the Congressman. Jones then told the entire cult of over 900 people that conspirators would soon arrive to attack and torture them, including their children. Jones instructed them to commit suicide by either drinking cyanide-laced drinks or shooting each other. A total of 914 people died, including 274 children (Chidester, 2003).

Nineteen years later, the followers of the Heaven's Gate cult, who believed that aliens in a spaceship were coming in the tail of the Hale-Bopp comet in 1997,

cult any group of people with a particular religious or philosophical set of beliefs and identity.

*connotation: the meaning of a word or concept that is more suggestive than directly stated.

committed suicide under the leadership of Marshall Applewhite. They believed that their souls would be taken up by the comet aliens.

Why would any person get so caught up in cult beliefs that suicide, and in some cases, murder becomes a desired behavior? What kind of person joins a cult in the first place? Although there is no particular personality profile associated with cult membership, cult members do appear to have been in some psychological distress at the time of recruitment by the cult. People who are under a lot of stress, dissatisfied with their lives, unassertive, gullible, dependent, feel a desire to belong to a group, and who are unrealistically idealistic ("we can solve all the world's problems if everyone will just love each other") are the most likely targets of cult recruitment (Langone, 1996). Young people rebelling against parental authority or trying to become independent of families are prime targets.

Cult leaders also have certain techniques of persuasion that are common to most cult organizations. The first step is usually something called "love-bombing" by current cult members, who shower the recruits with affection and attention and claim to understand just how the potential cult members feel. Then efforts are made to isolate the recruits from family and friends who might talk them out of joining. This is accomplished in part by keeping the recruits so busy with rigid rituals, ways of dress, meditations, and other activities that they do not allow the recruits time to think about what is happening. All of these activities also serve to wear down the resistance of the recruits. Cults also teach their members how to stop questioning thoughts or criticisms, which are typically seen as sins or extremely undesirable behavior. Access to people and information outside the cult is either kept to a well-guarded minimum or totally shut off (Singer & Lalich, 1995; Zimbardo & Hartley, 1985).

Commitments to the cult are small at first, such as attending a music concert or some other cult function. Eventually, a major step is requested by the cult, such as quitting one's job, turning over money or property to the cult, or similar commitments. Leaving a cult is quite difficult, as members of the cult in good standing will often track down a "deserter."

Parents, friends, and other family members have been known to hire special "deprogrammers" to help their loved one recover from cult membership, willingly or unwillingly. Sometimes people actually have to "kidnap" their loved one out of the cult environment. Nevertheless, as difficult as it is to leave, 90 percent or more of cult members do eventually get out (Barker, 1983, 2007; Galanter, 1983).

Cults have existed all through recorded history and will probably continue to exist in the future. Most cults do not pose a physical threat to their members or others, but the examples of the followers of Jim Jones, Marshall Applewhite, and David Koresh (the Waco, Texas, disaster in 1993) clearly demonstrate that cults, like any group of people, can become deadly.

Questions for Further Discussion

1. In what ways are the methods used by cults on new recruits similar to the methods used by the military when training new soldiers?
2. Is it ethical for the family members of an adult to "kidnap" and deprogram a cult member?
3. Which methods of compliance do cults seem to use to recruit new members?
4. Do you think that Osama bin Laden and his followers constitute a cult? Why or why not?

chapter summary

Listen on mypsychlab.com Listen to an audio file of your chapter www.mypsychlab.com

- Social psychology is the scientific study of how a person's thoughts, feelings, and behavior are influenced by the real, imagined, or implied presence of other people.

Social Influence: Conformity, Compliance, Obedience, and Group Behavior

12.1 What factors influence people to conform to the actions of others?

- Asch used a set of comparison lines and a standard line to experiment with conformity, finding that subjects conformed to group opinion about one third of the time, increased as the number of confederates rose to four, and decreased if just one confederate gave the correct answer.
- Cross-cultural research has found that collectivistic cultures show more conformity than individualistic cultures. Gender differences do not exist in conformity unless the response is not private, in which case women are more conforming than men.
- Groupthink occurs when a decision-making group feels that it is more important to maintain group unanimity and cohesiveness than to consider the facts realistically.
- Minimizing groupthink involves impartial leadership, seeking outside opinions, stating problems in an objective manner, breaking large groups into subgroups, encouraging questions and alternate solutions, using secret ballots, and holding group members responsible for the decisions made by the group.

12.2 How is compliance defined, and what are four common ways to gain the compliance of another?

- Compliance occurs when a person changes behavior as a result of another person asking or directing that person to change.
- Four common ways of getting compliance from others are the foot-in-the-door technique, the door-in-the-face technique, the lowball technique, and the that's-not-all technique.

12.3 What factors make obedience more likely?

- Milgram did experiments in which he found that 65 percent of people obeyed the authority figure of a psychology professor even if it meant hurting, injuring, or possibly killing another person with an electric shock.
- When the performance of an individual on a relatively easy task is improved by the presence of others, it is called social facilitation. When the performance of an individual on a relatively difficult task is negatively affected by the presence of others, it is called social impairment.
- When a person who is lazy is able to work in a group of people, that person often performs less well than if the person were working alone, in a phenomenon called social loafing.

Social Cognition: Attitudes, Impression Formation, and Attribution

12.4 What are the three components of an attitude, how are attitudes formed, and how can attitudes be changed?

- Attitudes are tendencies to respond positively or negatively toward ideas, persons, objects, or situations.
- The three components of an attitude are the affective (emotional) component, the behavioral component, and the cognitive component.
- Attitudes are often poor predictors of behavior unless the attitude is very specific or very strong.
- Direct contact with the person, situation, object, or idea can help form attitudes.
- Attitudes can be formed through direct instruction from parents or others.
- Interacting with other people who hold a certain attitude can help an individual form that attitude.
- Attitudes can also be formed through watching the actions and reactions of others to ideas, people, objects, and situations.
- Persuasion is the process by which one person tries to change the belief, opinion, position, or course of action of another person through argument, pleading, or explanation.
- The key elements in persuasion are the source of the message, the message itself, and the target audience.
- In the elaboration likelihood model, central-route processing involves attending to the content of the message itself, whereas peripheral-route processing involves attending to factors not involved in the message, such as the appearance of the source of the message, the length of the message, and other noncontent factors.

12.5 How do people react when attitudes and behavior are not the same?

- Cognitive dissonance is discomfort or distress that occurs when a person's actions do not match the person's attitudes.
- Cognitive dissonance is lessened by changing the conflicting behavior, changing the conflicting attitude, or forming a new attitude to justify the behavior.
- Impression formation is the forming of the first knowledge a person has about another person.
- The primacy effect in impression formation means that the very first impression one has about a person tends to persist even in the face of evidence to the contrary.
- Impression formation is part of social cognition, or the mental processes that people use to make sense out of the world around them.

12.6 What are social categorization and implicit personality theories?

- Social categorization is a process of social cognition in which a person, upon meeting someone new, assigns that person to a category or group on the basis of characteristics the person has in common with other people or groups with whom the perceiver has prior experience.
- One form of a social category is the stereotype, in which the characteristics used to assign a person to a category are superficial and believed to be true of all members of the category.
- An implicit personality theory is a form of social cognition in which a person has sets of assumptions about different types of people, personality traits, and actions that are assumed to be related to each other.
- Schemas are mental patterns that represent what a person believes about certain types of people. Schemas can become stereotypes.

12.7 How do people try to explain the actions of others?

- Attribution is the process of explaining the behavior of others as well as one's own behavior.
- A situational cause is an explanation of behavior based on factors in the surrounding environment or situation.
- A dispositional cause is an explanation of behavior based on the internal personality characteristics of the person being observed.
- The fundamental attribution error is the tendency to overestimate the influence of internal factors on behavior while underestimating the influence of the situation.

Social Interaction: Prejudice and Aggression

12.8 How are prejudice and discrimination different?

- Prejudice is a negative attitude that a person holds about the members of a particular social group. Discrimination occurs when members of a social group are treated differently because of prejudice toward that group.
- There are many forms of prejudice, including ageism, sexism, racism, and prejudice toward those who are too fat or too thin.
- In-groups are the people with whom a person identifies, whereas out-groups are everyone else at whom prejudice tends to be directed.
- Conflict between groups increases prejudice and discrimination according to realistic conflict theory.
- Scapegoating refers to the tendency to direct prejudice and discrimination at out-group members who have little social power or influence. New immigrants are often the scapegoats for the frustration and anger of the in-group.

CLASSIC STUDIES IN PSYCHOLOGY: Brown Eyes, Blue Eyes

- A schoolteacher divided her class into brown-eyed children and blue-eyed children to teach them a lesson about prejudice. The children quickly began to discriminate toward whichever group was the out-group during a certain time period.

12.9 Why are people prejudiced, and how can prejudice be stopped?

- Social cognitive theory views prejudice as an attitude acquired through direct instruction, modeling, and other social influences.
- Social identity theory sees a person's formation of a social sense of self within a particular group as being due to three things: social categorization (which may involve the use of reference groups), social identity (the person's sense of belonging to a particular social group), and social comparison (in which people compare themselves to others to improve their own self-esteem).
- Stereotype vulnerability refers to the effect that a person's knowledge of the stereotypes that exist against his or her social group can have on that person's behavior.
- People who are aware of stereotypes may unintentionally come to behave in a way that makes the stereotype real in a self-fulfilling prophecy.
- Intergroup contact is more effective in reducing prejudice if the groups have equal status.
- Prejudice and discrimination can also be reduced when a superordinate goal that is large enough to override all other goals needs to be achieved by all groups.
- Prejudice and discrimination are reduced when people must work together to solve a problem because each person has an important key to solving the problem, creating a mutual interdependence. This technique used in education is called the "jigsaw classroom."
- Interpersonal attraction refers to liking or having the desire for a relationship with another person.

Liking and Loving: Interpersonal Attraction

12.10 What factors govern attraction and love, and what are some different kinds of love?

- People tend to form relationships with people who are in physical proximity to them.
- People are attracted to others who are similar to them in some way.
- People may also be attracted to people who are different from themselves, with the differences acting as a complementary support for areas in which each may be lacking.
- People tend to like other people who like them in return, a phenomenon called the reciprocity of liking.
- Love is a strong affection for another person due to kinship, personal ties, sexual attraction, admiration, or common interests.
- Sternberg states that the three components of love are intimacy, passion, and commitment.
- Romantic love is intimacy with passion, companionate love is intimacy with commitment, and consummate love contains all three components.

PSYCHOLOGY IN THE NEWS: Facing Facebook—The Social Nature of Online Networking

- Social networking at online sites is associated with race, ethnicity, and education level of one's parents, with some sites being more likely to be used by certain groups.
- Other research has found that people use these sites in positive or negative way according to the nature of their face-to-face interactions with others.
- People also tend to search through these sites for specific purposes rather than just aimless browsing.

Aggression and Prosocial Behavior

12.11 How is aggressive behavior determined by biology and learning?

- Aggression is behavior intended to hurt or destroy another person in a way that may be physical or verbal. Frustration is a major source of aggression.
- Biological influences on aggression may include genetics, the amygdala and limbic system, and testosterone and serotonin levels.
- Social roles are powerful influences on the expression of aggression. Social learning theory states that aggression can be learned through direct reinforcement and through the imitation of successful aggression by a model.
- Studies have concluded that violent television, movies, and video games stimulate aggressive behavior, both by increasing aggressive tendencies and providing models of aggressive behavior.
- Prosocial behavior is behavior that is socially desirable and benefits others.

12.12 What is altruism, and how is deciding to help someone related to the presence of others?

- Altruism is prosocial behavior in which a person helps someone else without expectation of reward or recognition, often without fear for his or her own safety.
- The bystander effect means that people are more likely to get help from others if there are one or only a few people nearby rather than a larger number. The more people nearby, the less likely it is that help will be offered.

- When others are present at a situation in which help could be offered, there is a diffusion of responsibility among all the bystanders, reducing the likelihood that any one person or persons will feel responsibility for helping.
- Researchers Latané and Darley found that people who were alone were more likely to help in an emergency than people who were with others.
- The five steps in making a decision to help are noticing, defining an emergency, taking responsibility, planning a course of action, and taking action.

Applying Psychology to Everyday Life: Anatomy of a Cult

12.13 Why do people join cults?

- People who join cults tend to be under stress, unhappy, unassertive, gullible, dependent, idealistic, and they want to belong. Young people are also likelier to join cults than are older people.
- Cults use love-bombing, isolation, rituals, and activities to keep the new recruits from questioning and critical thinking. Cults also use the foot-in-the-door technique.

test YOURSELF

ANSWERS ON PAGE AK-2.

Study and Review on **mypsychlab.com** Ready for your test? More quizzes and a customized study plan **www.mypsychlab.com**

Pick the best answer.

1. Studies have found the degree of conformity to be greater in __________ cultures.
a. collectivistic **c.** Western
b. individualistic **d.** European

2. To prevent groupthink, members of a group should do all but which of the following?
a. Have the leader of the group remain impartial.
b. Seek outside opinions.
c. Discourage questions and alternate solutions.
d. Use secret ballots.

3. Maria's fellow professor asked her to teach an honors class in the spring. Maria agreed only to find out after agreeing that teaching such a course also meant that she would have to attend meetings of the honors professors, go to honors-oriented conventions, and take on special advising duties. Maria had fallen victim to the __________ technique.
a. foot-in-the-door **c.** lowball
b. door-in-the-face **d.** that's-not-all

4. Some researchers believe that Milgram's results were a form of the __________ technique of persuasion.
a. foot-in-the-door **c.** lowball
b. door-in-the-face **d.** that's-not-all

5. Sandy loves to play pool and has become quite good at the game. Lately, she has noticed that she seems to play better when there are people watching her than when she is playing alone. This difference in Sandy's playing is most likely the result of __________.
a. social facilitation. **c.** social loafing.
b. social impairment. **d.** social laziness.

6. Jerry goes to a lot of dog races because he enjoys them and loves to see the dogs run. For Jerry, going to the dog races a lot represents the __________ component of an attitude.
a. psychological **c.** cognitive
b. behavioral **d.** affective

7. The public service messages that encourage parents to sit down with their children and talk frankly about drugs are promoting which method of attitude formation?
a. direct contact **c.** vicarious conditioning
b. direct instruction **d.** observational learning

8. Researchers have found that a __________ degree of fear in a message makes it more effective, particularly when it is combined with __________.
a. maximum; information about how to prevent the fearful consequences
b. minimum; threats
c. moderate; threats
d. moderate; information about how to prevent the fearful consequences

9. Sandy was a juror in the trial for a man accused of stealing guns from a sporting goods store. The defendant was not very well-spoken and came from a very poor background, but Sandy listened carefully to the evidence presented and made her decision based on that. Sandy was using __________ processing.
a. central-route **c.** cognitive-route
b. peripheral-route **d.** visual-route

10. Which of the following is not one of the three things people do to reduce cognitive dissonance?
a. change their behavior **c.** form a new attitude
b. change their attitude **d.** ignore the conflict

11. Gerard goes to his job interview dressed in patched blue jeans, a torn t-shirt, and sandals. His hair is uncombed and he hasn't shaved in a few days. Obviously, Gerard knows nothing about __________.
a. cognitive dissonance. **c.** impression formation.
b. attitude formation. **d.** groupthink.

12. Sets of assumptions that people have about how different types of people, personality traits, and actions are all related to each other are called __________.
a. social categorization. **c.** urban legends.
b. implicit personality theories. **d.** stereotypes.

13. If behavior is assumed to be caused by internal personality characteristics, this is known as __________.
a. a situational cause.
b. a dispositional cause.
c. a fundamental attribution error.
d. actor-observer bias.

14. The people with whom a person identifies most strongly are called the _________.
a. referent group. **c.** out-group.
b. in-group. **d.** "them" group.

15. Prejudice and discrimination are least likely to develop in which of the following situations?
a. two different groups of immigrants competing for jobs
b. two different religious groups, in which each believes that its religion is the right one
c. two different groups, with one group being blamed for the economic difficulties of the other
d. two different groups dealing with the aftermath of a hurricane

16. The _________ explanation of prejudice assumes that the same processes that help form other attitudes form prejudiced attitudes.
a. scapegoat **c.** social cognitive
b. authoritarian **d.** psychodynamic

17. Patrick is very proud of his Irish heritage and thinks of himself as an Irish American. Patrick has a strong _________.
a. social identity. **c.** social category.
b. reference group. **d.** stereotype vulnerability.

18. The self-fulfilling prophecy is a negative outcome of _________.
a. social identity. **c.** scapegoating.
b. reference grouping. **d.** stereotype vulnerability.

19. The "Robber's Cave" experiment showed the value of _________ in combating prejudice.
a. "jigsaw classrooms" **c.** subordinate goals
b. equal status contact **d.** stereotyping vulnerability

20. Sarah found her soul mate, Jon, when she moved to a small town in Florida. According to research in interpersonal attraction, the most likely explanation for them to "find" each other is _________.
a. karma. **c.** fate.
b. personal attractiveness. **d.** proximity.

21. According to Sternberg, married (committed) people who also have intimacy and passion are in the form of love called _________ love.
a. companionate **c.** affectionate
b. romantic **d.** consummate

22. The concept of aggression as a basic human instinct driving people to destructive acts was part of early _________ theory.
a. humanistic **c.** psychoanalytical
b. behavioral **d.** cognitive

23. The neurotransmitter that seems most involved in aggression is _________.
a. testosterone. **c.** dopamine.
b. serotonin. **d.** norepinephrine.

24. Violent video games have been blamed for all but which of the following?
a. increased levels of aggression in children
b. increased levels of aggression in adolescents
c. increased levels of altruism in children
d. increased incidents of school shootings

25. To which two processes do most social psychologists attribute the failure of Kitty Genovese's neighbors to help her?
a. bystander effect and altruism
b. aggression and diffusion of responsibility
c. altruism and diffusion of responsibility
d. bystander effect and diffusion of responsibility

26. Cries for help, shouting, and loud noises all help with which step in the decision process for helping?
a. noticing **c.** taking responsibility
b. defining an emergency **d.** taking action

27. Cults use all of the following except _________ to gain new members.
a. love-bombing
b. isolation
c. "foot-in-the-door" technique
d. talking with parents of the recruit

12 social psychology

12.1 12.2 12.3

p. 457

Social Influence

(the ways in which a person's behavior can be affected by other people)

- **conformity** changing one's own behavior to more closely match the actions of others
  - several classic studies (i.e., Sherif, Asch) suggest that individuals will change their behaviors to conform to those of a group
  - may be influenced by private vs. face-to-face contact, gender, or culture
  - **groupthink**
- **compliance** person changing their behavior due to another person or group asking or directing them to change, often in the absence of any real authority or power
  - **foot-in-the-door technique**
  - **door-in-the-face technique**
  - **lowball technique**
  - **that's-not-all technique**
- **obedience** changing one's behavior at thedirect order of an authority figure
  - a classic study by Milgram (i.e., teacher/learner electrical shock study) indicated that 65% of "teachers" went all the way through shock levels, despite protest from "learners"

- **task performance** can be affected by social influence
  - **social facilitation** = positive influence
  - **social impairment** = negative influence
  - **social loafing** occurs when people do not work hard when others are also working; easy to "hide" in a group
- **group polarization** risky shift phenomenon
  - presence of others increases extreme positions

12.4 12.5

p. 464

Social Cognition

- focuses on the ways in which people think about other people and how those cognitions affect behavior
- **attitudes** tendency to respond positively or negatively toward a certain idea, person, object, or situation; learned through experience
  - comprise affective, behavioral, and cognitive components
  - are not great predictors of behavior although tend to have more influence as they become more specific and salient
  - attitude formation can be the result of several processes
  - can change through persuasion and are contingent upon both the message and the target audience; elaboration likelihood model suggests that the route/level of information processing (central vs. peripheral) influences ease of persuasion

- **cognitive dissonance** emotional discomfort as the result of engaging in behavior that is inconsistent with personal cognitions
  - can be reduced by (1) changing behavior, (2) changing cognition, or (3) forming new cognitions to justify behavior

12.6 12.7

p. 468

Social Cognition: (continued) Impression Formation and Attribution

- **impression formation** forming of first knowledge about another person; influenced by primacy effect
- **social categorization** automatic and unconscious assignment of a new acquaintance to some category or group
  - **stereotypes**
  - categories assigned are based on implicit personality theory, the set of assumptions formed in childhood about different types of people
- **attribution** is process by which we explain both our own behavior and the behavior of others; based on attribution theory (Heider)
  - **situational**
  - **dispositional**
  - **fundamental attribution error**

12.8 12.9 p. 473

Social Interaction Prejudice and Discrimination

prejudice
unsupported and negative stereotypes (e.g., ageism, sexism, racism, etc.) about members of a particular social group

- **social cognitive theory**
- **social identity theory**
- **stereotype vulnerability**
- **prejudice**

discrimination
occurs when prejudicial attitudes cause members of a social group to be treated differently than others in situations calling for equal treament

can vary based on existence of in-groups and out-groups
- **scapegoating** (target for frustrations and negative emotions) typically occurs for members of an out-group

realistic conflict theory
suggests that when resources are limited, prejudice and discrimination are closely tied to an increasing degree of conflict between groups that seek common resources

12.10 p. 477

Social Interaction: (continued) Interpersonal Attraction

liking or having the desire for a relationship with someone else; can be influenced by a variety of factors
- **physical attractiveness**
- **proximity**
- **similarity**
- **complementary qualities**
- **reciprocity of liking**

love
strong affection for another person due to kinship, personal ties, sexual attraction, admiration, or common interests

Sternberg's triangular theory suggests different components and types of love

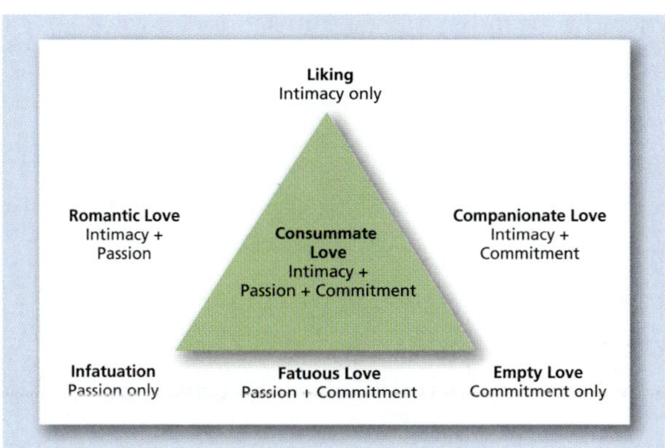

12.11 12.12 p. 483

Social Interaction: (continued) Aggression and Prosocial Behavior

aggression
occurs when one person verbally or physically hurts or tries to destroy another person; often the result of frustration
- aggression may be partly attributed to genetics and can be triggered by variations in brain function (i.e., amygdala activation) and internal or external chemical influences (e.g., testosterone, alcohol)
- much of aggression is influenced by learning but not totally deterministic

prosocial, or socially desirable, behavior benefits others
- **altruism:** helping someone with no expectation of reward and often at personal risk
- can be influenced by helper's mood and victim's gender, attractiveness, or "just rewards"; racial and ethnic differences can decrease probability of helping
- refusal to help another can be negatively affected by the presence of others (bystander effect/diffusion of responsibility) rather than indifference or a lack of sympathy; also influenced by individual's appraisal of situation (see Table 12.3)

13 theories of personality

CHAPTER OUTLINE

NOT-SO-IDENTICAL TWINS

Many people have heard the story of the "Jim" twins, James Arthur Springer and James Edward Lewis, identical twins separated at the age of 1 month. At age 39 Springer and Lewis were the first set of twins studied by University of Minnesota psychologist Thomas Bouchard, who examined the differences and similarities between identical and fraternal twins raised apart from each other (Bouchard et al., 1990).

The two "Jims" shared interests in mechanical drawing and carpentry, a love of math and a dread of spelling in high school, and smoked and drank the same amount. It is understandable that many researchers attribute these similarities to the shared genetic material of the "Jim" twins. But Springer and Lewis were both raised in Ohio by parents from relatively similar socioeconomic backgrounds—how much of their similarity to each other might be due to those conditions? And how would genetics explain that they both divorced women named Linda before marrying women named Betty? Are there genes for "divorce Linda, marry Betty?" Obviously not.

Then there's the case of identical twins Oskar and Jack. Like the "Jim" twins, they also exhibited a number of similarities in personality and behavior. No one would accuse Oskar and Jack of being raised in similar environments, however. Born in Trinidad at the time Hitler was rising to power, Jack Yufe was raised by their Jewish father in Trinidad as a Jew, while their mother took Oskar Stohr to occupied Czechoslovakia, where he attended a Nazi-run school and was at one time a Hitler youth. In terms of environment, Oskar and Jack were not-so-identical twins.

If the researchers in the twin study had dug a little deeper, they would also have found countless differences between the twins in the study. To automatically assume that similarities between identical twins are all caused by genetic influences and that differences are caused by environmental influences is bad science. The fact is that any two randomly selected people will find that they have countless things in common, none of which is likely to be caused by hereditary factors.

Why study personality?

Personality is the sum total of who you are—your attitudes and reactions, both physical and emotional. It's what makes each person different from every other person in the world. How can any study of human behavior not include the study of who we are and how we got to be that way?

learning objectives

13.1 What is personality, and how do the various perspectives in psychology view personality?

13.2 How did Freud's historical view of the mind and personality form a basis for psychodynamic theory?

13.3 How did Jung, Adler, Horney, and Erikson modify Freud's theory?

13.4 How does modern psychoanalytic theory differ from that of Freud?

13.5 How do behaviorists and social cognitive theorists explain personality?

13.6 How do humanists such as Carl Rogers explain personality?

13.7 What are the history and current views of the trait perspective?

13.8 What part do biology, heredity, and culture play in personality?

13.9 What are the advantages and disadvantages of the following measures of personality: interviews, projective tests, behavioral assessment, personality inventories, and online personality tests?

study tip

As you are reading this chapter, remember to use the SQ3R method discussed on pages I-7–I-8 in *Psychology in Action*. Breaking your reading into small sections will help you get more out of every chapter.

Theories of Personality

13.1 What is personality, and how do the various perspectives in psychology view personality?

Personality is the unique way in which each individual thinks, acts, and feels throughout life. Personality should not be confused with **character**, which refers to value judgments made about a person's morals or ethical behavior; nor should it be confused with **temperament**, the enduring characteristics with which each person is born, such as irritability or adaptability. Temperament is based in one's biology, either through genetic influences, prenatal influences, or a combination of those influences, and forms the basis upon which one's larger personality is built. Both character and temperament are vital parts of personality, however. Every adult personality is a combination of temperaments and personal history of family, culture, and the time during which they grew up (Kagan, 2010).

Personality is an area of the still relatively young field of psychology in which there are several ways in which the characteristic behavior of human beings can be explained. However, the investigation of personality goes back quite some time. For example, the physiological roots of personality were postulated as early as the fourth century B.C.E. by Empedocles and later by Hippocrates, with Hippocrates' work later influencing Galen in the second century C.E. (Dumont, 2010). Hippocrates and Galen believed that temperament or personality was related to the relative balance of the four physical humors of the body: blood, black bile, yellow bile, and phlegm.

One reason no single explanation of personality exists is because personality is still difficult to measure precisely and scientifically, and different perspectives of personality have arisen. There are four traditional perspectives in personality theory:

- The *psychodynamic perspective* had its beginnings in the work of Sigmund Freud and still exists today. It focuses on the role of the unconscious mind in the development of personality. This perspective is also heavily focused on biological causes of personality differences.
- The *behaviorist perspective* is based on the theories of learning as discussed in Chapter Five. This approach focuses on the effect of the environment on behavior.
- The *humanistic perspective* first arose as a reaction against the psychoanalytic and behaviorist perspectives and focuses on the role of each person's conscious life experiences and choices in personality development.

personality the unique and relatively stable ways in which people think, feel, and behave.

character value judgments of a person's moral and ethical behavior.

temperament the enduring characteristics with which each person is born.

The *trait perspective* differs from the other three in its basic goals: The psychoanalytic, behaviorist, and humanistic perspectives all seek to explain the process that causes personality to form into its unique characteristics, whereas trait theorists are more concerned with the end result—the characteristics themselves. Although some trait theorists assume that traits are biologically determined, others make no such assumption.

The Man and the Couch: Sigmund Freud and the Psychodynamic Perspective

FREUD'S CULTURAL BACKGROUND

It's hard to understand how Freud developed his ideas about personality unless we have some knowledge of the world in which he and his patients lived. Born in the Austro-Hungarian Empire in 1856, Freud's family moved to Vienna when he was only 4 years old. He lived there until 1938, when Germany occupied Austria, and Freud, of Jewish background, moved to England to escape the Nazis. During this time period, Europe was in what is commonly known as the Victorian Age, named for Queen Victoria of Great Britain. The Victorian Age was a time of sexual repression. People growing up in this period were told by their church that sex should take place only in the context of marriage and then only to make babies. To enjoy sexual intercourse was considered a sin.

Sigmund Freud (1856–1939) was the founder of the psychodynamic movement in psychology. Many of his patients sat or reclined on the couch above while he sat in a chair, listening to them and developing his psychoanalytic theory of personality.

Men were understood to be unable to control their "animal" desires at times, and a good Victorian husband would father several children with his wife and then turn to a mistress for sexual comfort, leaving his virtuous* wife untouched. Women, especially those of the upper classes, were not supposed to have sexual urges. It is no wonder that many of Freud's patients were wealthy women with problems stemming from unfulfilled sexual desires or sexual repression. Freud's "obsession" with sexual explanations for abnormal behavior seems more understandable in light of his cultural background and that of his patients.

Freud came to believe that there were layers of consciousness in the mind. His belief in the influence of the unconscious mind on conscious behavior, published in *The Psychopathology of Everyday Life* (Freud, 1901), shocked the Victorian world.

13.2 How did Freud's historical view of the mind and personality form a basis for psychodynamic theory?

THE UNCONSCIOUS MIND

Freud believed that the mind was divided into three parts: the preconscious, conscious, and unconscious minds (Freud, 1904). (See Figure 13.1.) While no one really disagreed with the idea of a conscious mind in which one's current awareness exists, or even of a preconscious mind containing memories, information, and events of which one can easily become aware, the **unconscious mind** (also called "the unconscious") was the real departure for the professionals of Freud's day. Freud theorized that there is a part of the mind that remains hidden at all times, surfacing only in symbolic form in dreams and in some of the behavior people engage in without knowing why they have done so. Even when a person makes a determined effort to bring a memory out of the unconscious mind, it will not appear directly, according to Freud. Freud believed that the unconscious mind was the most important determining factor in human behavior and personality.

unconscious mind level of the mind in which thoughts, feelings, memories, and other information are kept that are not easily or voluntarily brought into consciousness.

*virtuous: morally excellent.

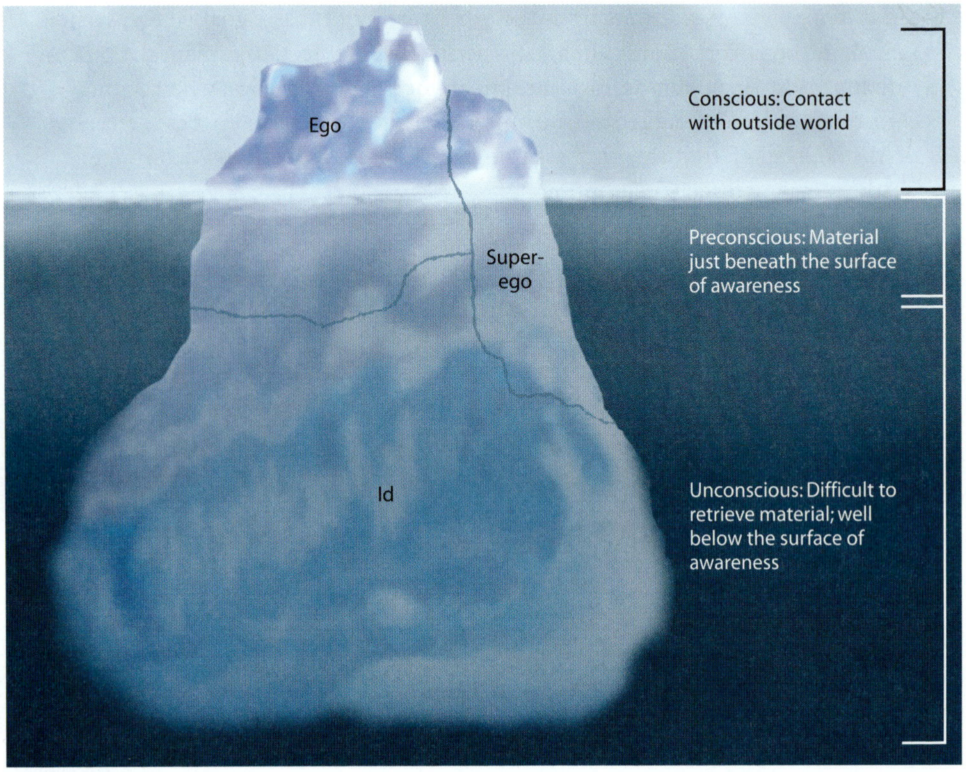

Figure 13.1 Freud's Conception of the Personality

This iceberg represents the three levels of the mind. The part of the iceberg visible above the surface is the conscious mind. Just below the surface is the preconscious mind, everything that is not yet part of the conscious mind. Hidden deep below the surface is the unconscious mind, feelings, memories, thoughts, and urges that cannot be easily brought into consciousness. While two of the three parts of the personality (ego and superego) exist at all three levels of awareness, the id is completely in the unconscious mind.

FREUD'S DIVISIONS OF THE PERSONALITY

Freud believed, based on observations of his patients, that personality itself could be divided into three parts, each existing at one or more levels of conscious awareness (see Figure 13.1). The way these three parts of the personality develop and interact with one another became the heart of his theory (Freud, 1923, 1933, 1940).

ID: IF IT FEELS GOOD, DO IT The first and most primitive part of the personality, present in the infant, is the **id**. *Id* is a Latin word that means "it." The id is a completely unconscious, pleasure-seeking, amoral part of the personality that exists at birth, containing all of the basic biological drives: hunger, thirst, self-preservation, and sex, for example.

Wait a minute—Freud thought babies have sex drives?

Wait a minute—Freud thought babies have sex drives?

Yes, Freud thought babies have sex drives, which shocked and outraged his colleagues and fellow Victorians. By "sex drive" he really meant "pleasure drive," the need to seek out pleasurable sensations. People do seem to be pleasure-seeking creatures, and even infants seek pleasure from sucking and chewing on anything they can get into their mouths. In fact, thinking about what infants are like when they are just born provides a good picture of the id. Infants are demanding, irrational, illogical, and impulsive. They want their needs satisfied immediately, and they don't care about anyone else's needs or desires. (A word of caution: The fact that infant behavior seems to fit Freud's concept of the id is not proof that the id exists. It simply means that Freud came up with the concept of the id to fit what he already knew about infants.)

Freud called this need for satisfaction the **pleasure principle**, which can be defined as the desire for immediate gratification of needs with no regard for the consequences. The pleasure principle can be summed up simply as "if it feels good, do it."

✓**id** part of the personality present at birth and completely unconscious.

✓**pleasure principle** principle by which the id functions; the immediate satisfaction of needs without regard for the consequences.

EGO: THE EXECUTIVE DIRECTOR People normally try to satisfy an infant's needs as quickly as possible. Infants are fed when hungry, changed when wet, and tended to whenever they cry. But as infants begin to grow, adults start denying them their every wish. There will be things they cannot touch or hold, and they must learn to wait for certain things, such as food. Freud would say that reality has reared its ugly head, and the id simply cannot deal with the reality of having to wait or not getting what it wants. Worse still would be the possibility of punishment as a result of the id's unrestrained actions.

According to Freud, to deal with reality, a second part of the personality develops called the **ego**. The ego, from the Latin word for "I," is mostly conscious and is far more rational, logical, and cunning than the id. The ego works on the **reality principle**, which is the need to satisfy the demands of the id only in ways that will not lead to negative consequences. This means that sometimes the ego decides to deny the id its desires because the consequences would be painful or too unpleasant.

For example, while an infant might reach out and take an object despite a parent's protests, a toddler with the developing ego will avoid taking the object when the parent says, "No!" to avoid punishment—but may go back for the object when the parent is not looking. A simpler way of stating the reality principle, then, is "if it feels good, do it, but only if you can get away with it."

SUPEREGO: THE MORAL WATCHDOG

If everyone acted on the pleasure principle, the world would be pretty scary. How does knowing right from wrong come into Freud's theory?

If everyone acted on the pleasure principle, the world would be pretty scary. How does knowing right from wrong come into Freud's theory?

Freud called the third and final part of the personality, the moral center of personality, the **superego**. The superego (also Latin, meaning "over the self") develops as a preschool-aged child learns the rules, customs, and expectations of society. The super ego contains the **conscience**, the part of the personality that makes people feel guilt, or *moral anxiety*, when they do the wrong thing. It is not until the conscience develops that children have a sense of right and wrong. (Note that the term *conscience* is a different word from *conscious*. They may look and sound similar, but they represent totally different concepts.) **Explore** on **mypsychlab.com**

Explore the id, ego, and superego on **mypsychlab.com**

THE ANGEL, THE DEVIL, AND ME: HOW THE THREE PARTS OF THE PERSONALITY WORK TOGETHER Anyone who has ever watched cartoons while growing up has probably seen these three parts of the personality shown in animated form—the id is usually a little devil, the superego an angel, and the ego is the person or animal caught in the middle, trying to decide what action to take. Images such as these appear often in animated films, with one of the more recent examples in *The Emperor's New Groove* when a character argues with his angel and devil over disposing of the emperor.

So, the id makes demands, the superego puts restrictions on how those demands can be met, and the ego has to come up with a plan that will quiet the id but satisfy the superego. Sometimes the id or the superego does not get its way, resulting in a great deal of anxiety for the ego itself. This constant state of conflict is Freud's view of how personality works; it is only when the anxiety created by this conflict gets out of hand that disordered behavior arises.

The **psychological defense mechanisms** are ways of dealing with stress through unconsciously distorting one's perception of reality. These defense mechanisms were mainly outlined and studied by Freud's daughter, Anna Freud, who was a psychoanalyst (Benjafield, 1996; A. Freud, 1946). In order for the three parts of the personality to function, the constant conflict among them must be managed, and Freud assumed that the defense mechanisms were one of the most important tools for dealing with the anxiety caused by this conflict. A list of the defense mechanisms, their definitions, and examples of each appears in Table 13.1.

ego part of the personality that develops out of a need to deal with reality, mostly conscious, rational, and logical.

reality principle principle by which the ego functions; the satisfaction of the demands of the id only when negative consequences will not result.

superego part of the personality that acts as a moral center.

conscience part of the superego that produces guilt, depending on how acceptable behavior is.

psychological defense mechanisms unconscious distortions of a person's perception of reality that reduce stress and anxiety.

denial psychological defense mechanism in which the person refuses to acknowledge or recognize a threatening situation.

repression psychological defense mechanism in which the person refuses to consciously remember a threatening or unacceptable event, instead pushing those events into the unconscious mind.

rationalization psychological defense mechanism in which a person invents acceptable excuses for unacceptable behavior.

projection psychological defense mechanism in which unacceptable or threatening impulses or feelings are seen as originating with someone else, usually the target of the impulses or feelings.

reaction formation psychological defense mechanism in which a person forms an opposite emotional or behavioral reaction to the way he or she really feels to keep those true feelings hidden from self and others.

displacement redirecting feelings from a threatening target to a less threatening one.

regression psychological defense mechanism in which a person falls back on childlike patterns of responding in reaction to stressful situations.

identification defense mechanism in which a person tries to become like someone else to deal with anxiety.

compensation (substitution) defense mechanism in which a person makes up for inferiorities in one area by becoming superior in another area.

sublimation channeling socially unacceptable impulses and urges into socially acceptable behavior.

fixation disorder in which the person does not fully resolve the conflict in a particular psychosexual stage, resulting in personality traits and behavior associated with that earlier stage.

psychosexual stages five stages of personality development proposed by Freud and tied to the sexual development of the child.

oral stage first stage occurring in the first year to year and a half of life in which the mouth is the erogenous zone and weaning is the primary conflict.

Table 13.1
The Psychological Defense Mechanisms

DEFENSE MECHANISM AND DEFINITION	EXAMPLE
Denial: refusal to recognize or acknowledge a threatening situation.	Ben is an alcoholic who denies being an alcoholic.
Repression: "pushing" threatening or conflicting events or situations out of conscious memory.	Elise, who was sexually abused as a child, cannot remember the abuse at all.
Rationalization: making up acceptable excuses for unacceptable behavior.	"If I don't have breakfast, I can have that piece of cake later on without hurting my diet."
Projection: placing one's own unacceptable thoughts onto others, as if the thoughts belonged to them and not to oneself.	Keisha is attracted to her sister's husband but denies this and believes the husband is attracted to her.
Reaction formation: forming an emotional reaction or attitude that is the opposite of one's threatening or unacceptable actual thoughts.	Matt is unconsciously attracted to Ben but outwardly voices an extreme hatred of homosexuals.
Displacement: expressing feelings that would be threatening if directed at the real target onto a less threatening substitute target.	Sandra gets reprimanded by her boss and goes home to angrily pick a fight with her husband.
Regression: falling back on childlike patterns as a way of coping with stressful situations.	Four-year-old Jeff starts wetting his bed after his parents bring home a new baby.
Identification: trying to become like someone else to deal with one's anxiety.	Marie really admires Suzy, the most popular girl in school, and tries to copy her behavior and dress.
Compensation (substitution): trying to make up for areas in which a lack is perceived by becoming superior in some other area.	Reggie is not good at athletics, so he puts all of his energies into becoming an academic scholar.
Sublimation: turning socially unacceptable urges into socially acceptable behavior.	Alain, who is very aggressive, becomes a professional hockey player.

STAGES OF PERSONALITY DEVELOPMENT

So the id exists at birth, but the other two parts of the personality develop later—how much later? When is personality finished?

So the id exists at birth, but the other two parts of the personality develop later—how much later? When is personality finished?

For Freud, the three parts of the personality develop in a series of stages. Because he focused heavily on the sex drive, he believed that the stages were determined by the developing sexuality of the child. At each stage, a different *erogenous zone*, or area of the body that produces pleasurable feelings, becomes important and can become the source of conflicts. Conflicts that are not fully resolved can result in **fixation**, or getting "stuck" to some degree in a stage of development. The child may grow into an adult but will still carry emotional and psychological "baggage" from that earlier fixated stage.

Because the personality, or *psyche*, develops as a result of sexual development, Freud called these the **psychosexual stages** of personality development.

ORAL STAGE: WEANING AND ORAL FIXATION The first stage is called the **oral stage** because the erogenous zone is the mouth. This stage occurs from the birth of the infant to about 1 or $1\frac{1}{2}$ years and is dominated by the id. The conflict that can arise here, according to Freud, will be over weaning (taking the mother's breast away from the child, who will now drink from a cup). Weaning that occurs too soon or too late can result in too little or too much satisfaction of the child's oral needs, resulting in the activities and personality traits associated with an orally fixated adult personality: overeating, drinking too much, chain smoking, talking too much, nail biting, gum chewing, and a tendency to be either too dependent and optimistic (when the oral needs are overindulged) or too aggressive and pessimistic (when the oral needs are denied)

ANAL STAGE: TOILET TRAINING AND ANAL FIXATION As the child becomes a toddler (1 or $1\frac{1}{2}$ years to 3 years), Freud believed that the erogenous zone moves from the mouth to the anus, because he also believed that children got a great deal of pleasure from both withholding and releasing their feces at will. This stage is, therefore, called the **anal stage**.

Obviously, Freud thought that the main area of conflict here is toilet training, the demand that the child use the toilet at a particular time and in a particular way. This invasion of reality is part of the process that stimulates the development of the ego during this stage. Fixation in the anal stage, from toilet training that is too harsh, can take one of two forms. The child who rebels openly against the demands of the parents and other adults will refuse to go in the toilet, instead defecating where and when he or she feels like doing it. According to Freud, this translates in the adult as a person who sees messiness as a statement of personal control and who is somewhat destructive and hostile. These *anal expulsive personalities* (so called because as children they expelled their feces purposefully) are what most people would call "slobs." Some children, however, are terrified of making a mess and rebel passively—refusing to go at all or retaining the feces. No mess, no punishment. As adults, they are stingy, stubborn, and excessively neat. This type is called the *anal retentive personality*.

PHALLIC STAGE As the child grows older (3 to 6 years), the erogenous zone shifts to the genitals. Children have discovered the differences between the sexes by now, and most have also engaged in perfectly normal self-stimulation of the genitals, or masturbation. One can only imagine the horror of the Victorian parent who discovered a child engaged in masturbation. People of that era believed that masturbation led to all manner of evils, including mental illness.

This awakening of sexual curiosity and interest in the genitals is the beginning of what Freud termed the **phallic stage**. (The word *phallic* comes from the Greek word *phallos* and means "penis.") Freud believed that when boys realized that the little girl down the street had no penis they developed a fear of losing the penis called *castration anxiety,* while girls developed *penis envy* because they were missing a penis. If this seems an odd focus on male anatomy, remember the era—the Western world at that time was very male oriented and male dominated. Fortunately, nearly all psychoanalysts have long since abandoned the concept of penis envy (Horney, 1939, 1973; Slipp, 1993). The conflict in the phallic stage centers on the awakening sexual feelings of the child. Freud essentially believed that boys develop both sexual attraction to their mothers and jealousy of their fathers during this stage, a phenomenon called the **Oedipus complex**. (Oedipus was a king in a Greek tragedy who unknowingly killed his father and married his mother.)

The sexual attraction is not that of an adult male for a female but more of a sexual curiosity that becomes mixed up with the boy's feelings of love and affection for his mother. Of course, his jealousy of his father leads to feelings of anxiety and fears that his father, a powerful authority figure, might get angry and do something terrible—remember that castration anxiety? To deal with this anxiety, two things must occur by the time the phallic stage ends. The boy will *repress* his sexual feelings for his mother

anal stage second stage occurring from about 1 or $1\frac{1}{2}$ years of age, in which the anus is the erogenous zone and toilet training is the source of conflict.

phallic stage third stage occurring from about 3 to 6 years of age, in which the child discovers sexual feelings.

Oedipus complex/Electra complex situation occurring in the phallic stage in which a child develops a sexual attraction to the opposite-sex parent and jealousy of the same-sex parent. Males develop an Oedipus complex whereas females develop an Electra complex.

According to Freud, children in the phallic stage develop a natural curiosity about sexual differences. These girls and boys are at just the right age to have noticed that they have physical differences.

and *identify* with his father. (*Identification* is one of the defense mechanisms used to combat anxiety.) The boy tries to be just like his father in every way, taking on the father's behavior, mannerisms, values, and moral beliefs as his own, so that Daddy won't be able to get angry with the boy. Girls go through a similar process called the **Electra complex** with their father as the target of their affections and their mother as the rival. The result of identification is the development of the superego, the internalized moral values of the same-sex parent.

What happens when things go wrong? If a child does not have a same-sex parent with whom to identify, or if the opposite-sex parent encourages the sexual attraction, fixation can occur. Fixation in the phallic stage usually involves immature sexual attitudes as an adult. People who are fixated in this stage, according to Freud, will often exhibit promiscuous* sexual behavior and be very vain. The vanity is seen as a cover-up for feelings of low self-worth arising from the failure to resolve the complex, and the lack of moral sexual behavior stems from the failure of identification and the inadequate formation of the superego. Additionally, men with this fixation may be "mama's boys" who never quite grow up, and women with this fixation may look for much older father figures to marry.

Now the child is about 6 years old and, if passage through the first three stages was successfully accomplished, has all three parts of the personality in place. What next? The personality may be in place, but the place it is in is only 6 years old. Freud named two more periods, one a kind of "holding pattern" and the other the final coming to terms with one's own sexuality.

LATENCY STAGE: BOYS HAVE COOTIES AND GIRLS ARE YUCKY Remember that by the end of the phallic stage, children have pushed their sexual feelings for the opposite sex into the unconscious in another defensive reaction, repression. From age 6 to the onset of puberty, children will remain in this stage of hidden, or *latent*, sexual feelings, so this stage is called **latency**. In this stage, children grow and develop intellectually, physically, and socially but not sexually. This is the age at which boys play with other boys, girls play only with girls, and each thinks the opposite sex is pretty awful.

GENITAL STAGE When puberty does begin, the sexual feelings that were once repressed can no longer be ignored. Bodies are changing and sexual urges are once more allowed into consciousness, but these urges will no longer have the parents as their targets. When children are 3, their parents are their whole world. When they are 13, their parents have to walk 20 paces behind them in the mall so none of the 13-year-olds' friends will see them. Instead, the focus of sexual curiosity and attraction will become other adolescents or music stars, movie stars, and other objects of adoration. Since Freud tied personality development into sexual development, the genital stage represented the final process in Freud's personality theory, as well as the entry into adult social and sexual behavior. Table 13.2 summarizes the stages of the psychosexual theory of personality development.

THE NEO-FREUDIANS

13.3 How did Jung, Adler, Horney, and Erikson modify Freud's theory?

At first Freud's ideas were met with resistance and ridicule by the growing community of doctors and psychologists. Eventually, a number of early psychoanalysts, objecting to Freud's emphasis on biology and particularly on sexuality, broke away from a strict interpretation of psychoanalytic theory, instead altering the focus of **psychoanalysis**

latency fourth stage occurring during the school years, in which the sexual feelings of the child are repressed while the child develops in other ways.

psychoanalysis Freud's term for both the theory of personality and the therapy based on it.

*promiscuous: having sexual relations with more than one partner.

Table 13.2

Freud's Psychosexual Stages

STAGE	AGE	FOCUS OF PLEASURE	FOCUS OF CONFLICTS	DIFFICULTIES AT THIS STAGE AFFECT LATER
Oral	Birth to 1 or $1\frac{1}{2}$ years old	Oral activities (such as sucking, feeding, and making noises with the mouth)	Weaning	• Ability to form interpersonal attachments • Basic feelings about the world • Tendency to use oral forms of aggression, such as sarcasm • Optimism or pessimism • Tendency to take charge or be passive
Anal	1 or $1\frac{1}{2}$ to 3 years old	Bowel and bladder control	Toilet training	• Sense of competence and control • Stubbornness or willingness to go along with others • Neatness or messiness • Punctuality or tardiness
Phallic	3 to 6 years old	Genitals	Sexual awareness	• Development of conscience through identification with same-sex parent • Pride or humility
Latency	6 years old to puberty	Social skills (such as the ability to make friends) and intellectual skills; dormant period in terms of psychosexual development	School, play, same-sex friendships	• Ability to get along with others
Genital	Puberty to death	Sexual behavior	Sexual relationship with partner	• Immature love or indiscriminate hate • Uncontrollable working or inability to work

Note: Freud thought that the way a person finds pleasure or is prevented from satisfying urges for pleasure at each stage affects personality. Thus, like Erikson's stage model described in Chapter Eight, Freud's model argues that the way a person deals with particular psychological challenges or potential areas of conflict has long-term effects on personality.

(the term Freud applied to both his explanation of the workings of the unconscious mind and the development of personality and the therapy he based on that theory) to the impact of the social environment. At the same time they retained many of Freud's original concepts such as the id, ego, superego, and the defense mechanisms. These early psychoanalysts became the **neo-Freudians**, or "new" Freudian psychoanalysts. This section briefly covers some of the more famous neo-Freudians.

JUNG Carl Gustav Jung ("YOONG") disagreed with Freud about the nature of the unconscious mind. Jung believed that the unconscious held much more than personal fears, urges, and memories. He believed that there was not only a **personal unconscious**, as described by Freud, but a **collective unconscious** as well (Jung, 1933).

According to Jung, the collective unconscious contains a kind of "species" or "racial" memory, memories of ancient fears and themes that seem to occur in many folktales and cultures. These collective, universal human memories were called **archetypes** by Jung. There are many archetypes, but two of the more well known are the *anima/animus* (the feminine side of a man/the masculine side of a woman) and the *shadow* (the dark side of personality, called the "devil" in Western cultures). The side of one's personality that is shown to the world is termed the *persona.*

ADLER Alfred Adler was also in disagreement with Freud over the importance of sexuality in personality development. Adler (1954) developed the theory that as young, helpless children, people all develop feelings of inferiority when comparing themselves to the more powerful, superior adults in their world. The driving force behind all human endeavors, emotions, and thoughts for Adler was not the seeking of pleasure but the seeking of superiority. The defense mechanism of *compensation*, in which people try to overcome feelings of inferiority in one area of life by striving to be superior in another area, figured prominently in Adler's theory (see Table 13.1).

neo-Freudians followers of Freud who developed their own competing psychodynamic theories.

personal unconscious Jung's name for the unconscious mind as described by Freud.

collective unconscious Jung's name for the memories shared by all members of the human species.

archetypes Jung's collective, universal human memories.

Adler (1954) also developed a theory that the birth order of a child affected personality. Firstborn children with younger siblings feel inferior once those younger siblings get all the attention and often overcompensate by becoming overachievers. Middle children have it slightly easier, getting to feel superior over the dethroned older child while dominating younger siblings. They tend to be very competitive. Younger children are supposedly pampered and protected but feel inferior because they are not allowed the freedom and responsibility of the older children. Although some researchers have found evidence to support Adler's birth order theory (Stein, 2001; Sulloway, 1996), and some have even linked birth order to career choices (Leong et al., 2001; Watkins & Savickas, 1990), other researchers point to sloppy methodology and the bias of researchers toward the birth-order idea (Beer & Horn, 2001; Freese et al., 1999; Ioannidis, 1998).

According to Horney, of the three ways children deal with anxiety, which way do you think this child might be using?

HORNEY Karen Horney (horn-EYE) did not study directly with Freud but studied his work and taught psychoanalysis at the Psychoanalytic Institutes of Berlin and New York (1967, 1973). She left the institute because of disagreements with Freud over the differences between males and females and the concept of penis envy, with which she strongly disagreed. She countered with her own concept of "womb envy," stating that men felt the need to compensate for their lack of childbearing ability by striving for success in other areas (Burger, 1997).

Rather than focusing on sexuality, Horney focused on the child's sense of **basic anxiety**, the anxiety created in a child born into a world that is so much bigger and more powerful than the child. While people whose parents gave them love, affection, and security would overcome this anxiety, others with less secure upbringings would develop **neurotic personalities** and maladaptive ways of dealing with relationships. Some children, according to Horney, try to deal with their anxiety by moving toward people, becoming dependent and clingy. Others move against people, becoming aggressive, demanding, and cruel. A third way of coping would be to move away from people by withdrawing from personal relationships.

ERIKSON Erik Erikson (1950, 1959, 1982) was an art teacher who became a psychoanalyst by studying with Anna Freud. He also broke away from Freud's emphasis on sex, preferring instead to emphasize the social relationships that are important at every stage of life. Erikson's eight psychosocial stages are discussed in detail in Chapter Eight. LINK to Chapter Eight: Development Across the Life Span, pp. 322–323.

It sounds as if all of these theorists became famous by ditching some of Freud's original ideas. Is Freud even worth studying anymore?

It sounds as if all of these theorists became famous by ditching some of Freud's original ideas. Is Freud even worth studying anymore?

CURRENT THOUGHTS ON FREUD AND THE PSYCHODYNAMIC PERSPECTIVE

13.4 How does modern psychoanalytic theory differ from that of Freud?

Although Freud's psychoanalytic theory seems less relevant in today's sexually saturated world, many of his concepts have remained useful and still form a basis for many modern personality theories. The idea of the defense mechanisms has had some research support and has remained useful in clinical psychology as a way of describing people's defensive behavior and irrational thinking. The concept of an unconscious mind also has some research support.

As strange as the idea of an unconscious mind that guides behavior must have seemed to Freud's contemporaries, modern researchers have had to admit that there are influences on human behavior that exist outside of normal conscious awareness. Although much of this research has taken place in the area of hypnosis and

basic anxiety anxiety created when a child is born into the bigger and more powerful world of older children and adults.

neurotic personalities personalities typified by maladaptive ways of dealing with relationships in Horney's theory.

subliminal perception (Borgeat & Goulet, 1983; Bryant & McConkey, 1989; Kihlstrom, 1987, 1999, 2001), other researchers have looked at the concept of implicit memory and implicit learning (Frensch & Runger, 2003). LINK to Chapter Six: Memory, p. 225.

CRITICISMS OF THE PSYCHODYNAMIC PERSPECTIVE This might be a good time to point out a very important fact about Freud's theory: He did no experiments to arrive at his conclusions about personality. His theory is based on his own observations (case studies) of numerous patients. Basing his suppositions on his patients' detailed memories of their childhoods and life experiences, he interpreted their behavior and reminiscences to develop his theory of psychoanalysis. He felt free to interpret what his patients told him of their childhoods as fantasy or fact, depending on how well those memories fit in with his developing theory. For example, many of Freud's patients told him that they were sexually abused by fathers, brothers, and other close family members. Freud was apparently unable to accept these memories as real and decided that they were fantasies, making them the basis of the Oedipal conflict. He actually revised his original perceptions of his patients' memories of abuse as real in the face of both public and professional criticism from his German colleagues (Masson, 1984).

Freud based much of his diagnoses of patients' problems on the interpretations of dreams (LINK to Chapter Four: Consciousness, pp. 143–144) and the results of the patient's free association (talking about anything without fear of negative feedback). These "sources" of information are often criticized as being too ambiguous and without scientific support for the validity of his interpretations. The very ambiguity of these sources of information allowed Freud to fit the patient's words and recollections to his own preferred interpretation, as well as increasing the possibility that his own suggestions and interpretations, if conveyed to the patient, might alter the actual memories of the patient, who would no doubt be in a very suggestible state of mind during therapy (Grünbaum, 1984).

Another criticism of Freud's theory concerns the people upon whose dreams, recollections, and comments the theory of psychoanalysis was based. Freud's clients were almost all wealthy Austrian women living in the Victorian era of sexual repression. Critics state that basing his theory on observations made with such a demographically limited group of clients promoted his emphasis on sexuality as the root of all problems in personality, as women of that social class and era were often sexually frustrated. Freud rarely had clients who did not fit this description, and so his theory is biased in terms of sexual frustrations (Robinson, 1993).

Although most professionals today view Freud's theory with a great deal of skepticism, his influence on the modern world cannot be ignored. Freudian concepts have had an impact on literature, movies, and even children's cartoons. People who have never taken a course in psychology are familiar with some of Freud's most basic concepts, such as the defense mechanisms. He was also one of the first theorists to emphasize the importance of childhood experiences on personality development—in spite of the fact he did not work extensively with children (he did have at least one case study of a five-year-old boy, "Little Hans," in which Freud gained much of his information from the boy's father, who was providing the actual treatment).

It has only been in the last several decades that people have had the necessary tools to examine the concepts of the unconscious mind. One can only wonder how Freud might have changed his theory in light of what is known about the workings of the human brain and the changes in society that exist today.

13.1 13.2 13.3 13.4

CONCEPT MAP

Theories of Personality

- **personality**
  unique way in which each individual thinks, acts, and feels throughout life
- **perspectives/theories**
  different ways of viewing and explaining personality
  - **psychodynamic:** based on work of Freud; primary focus is on role of unconscious mind
  - **behavioral and social cognitive views:** focus on the effect of the environment on behavior; based on theories of learning
  - **humanistic:** focuses on conscious life experiences and choices
  - **trait:** focuses on characteristics themselves, not roots of personality

Psychodynamic Perspective

- **basic aspects**
  - mind made up of different levels of awareness—conscious, preconscious, and unconscious
  - personality stems from interplay and conflict between demands made by the id, restrictions set forth by the superego, and direction by the ego
  - disordered behavior is product of constant conflict and anxiety; ego uses unconscious defense mechanisms as ways to manage anxiety/conflict between three parts of personality (see Table 13.1)
- **psychosexual stages of personality development**
  - id exists at birth; ego and superego develop in childhood
  - different erogenous zones are sources of conflict as individual ages; unresolved conflicts result in individuals getting stuck or fixated at that stage
    - **oral**
    - **anal**
    - **phallic**
    - **latency**
    - **genital**

    see Table 13.2
- a group of Freud's students and followers of the psychoanalytic perspective, called the neo-Freudians, modified his theory and altered the focus of psychoanalysis
  - **Jung:** believed in both a personal unconscious and a collective unconscious that holds universal human memories called archetypes
  - **Adler:** focused on feelings of inferiority and seeking feelings of superiority as opposed to importance of sexuality; birth order also important
  - **Horney:** disagreed with concept of penis envy, developed womb envy; rather than sexuality, focused on basic anxiety
  - **Erikson:** emphasized social relationships at every stage of life (see Table 8.4)
- modern psychodynamic theory maintains focus on unconscious mind, concept of defense mechanisms is still useful
- despite several criticisms, Freud's theory still important—first to suggest that personality develops through stages, that we are not always consciously aware of reasons for behavior, and that early life experiences influence who we are later in life

PRACTICE quiz How much do you remember?

ANSWERS ON PAGE AK-2.

Pick the best answer.

1. When we refer to someone's __________, we are specifically referring to the unique and consistent way they think, feel, and behave.
   a. temperament
   b. character
   c. personality
   d. mood
2. Although Chien's parents have told him that he attended his grandmother's funeral when he was 9 years old, he has no memory of the funeral. According to Freud, Chien's memory of the funeral may be in the __________ mind.
   a. preconscious
   b. conscious
   c. conscience
   d. unconscious
3. According to Freud, which part of the personality makes the person feel guilt when doing the wrong thing?
   a. ego
   b. superego
   c. conscious
   d. conscience
4. In Freud's view of the personality, the part that is present at birth and focused on pleasure is the __________.
   a. conscience.
   b. id.
   c. ego.
   d. superego.

5. Kelly is convinced that a supervisor in her office is very attracted to her, even though he has shown no outward signs of interest in her. She watches the supervisor frequently and makes excuses to be near him or to talk to him. She interprets everything he says as a veiled reference to his desire for her. If Kelly's supervisor actually has no romantic interest in her, we might conclude that Kelly is __________.
   - **a.** rationalizing.
   - **b.** repressing.
   - **c.** projecting.
   - **d.** regressing.
6. In which psychosexual stage might fixation result in a person who is excessively neat and fussy?
   - **a.** oral
   - **b.** anal
   - **c.** phallic
   - **d.** genital
7. In which psychosexual stage does the defense mechanism of identification figure prominently?
   - **a.** oral
   - **b.** anal
   - **c.** phallic
   - **d.** latency
8. According to Jung, the part of the mind containing universal human memories is called the __________ unconscious.
   - **a.** personal
   - **b.** cognitive
   - **c.** collective
   - **d.** animistic

Brainstorming: What aspects of psychodynamic theory do you think still have relevance in today's world? Was there one neo-Freudian whose theory appealed to you, and if so, why?

The Behaviorist and Social Cognitive View of Personality

At the time that Freud's theory was shocking the Western world, another psychological perspective was also making its influence known. In Chapter Five the theories of classical and operant conditioning were discussed in some detail. *Behaviorists* (researchers who use the principles of conditioning to explain the actions and reactions of both animals and humans) and *social cognitive theorists* (researchers who emphasize the influence of social and cognitive factors on learning) have a very different view of personality. Read on **mypsychlab.com**

Read and learn more about behaviorists Dollard and Miller's four critical situations on **mypsychlab.com**

13.5 How do behaviorists and social cognitive theorists explain personality?

For the behaviorist, personality is nothing more than a set of learned responses or **habits** (DeGrandpre, 2000; Dollard & Miller, 1950). In the strictest traditional view of Watson and Skinner, everything a person or animal does is a response to some environmental stimulus that has been reinforced or strengthened by a reward in some way.

So how does a pattern of rewarding certain behavior end up becoming part of some kind of personality pattern?

So how does a pattern of rewarding certain behavior end up becoming part of some kind of personality pattern?

Think about how a traditional behaviorist might explain a shy personality. Beginning in childhood, a person might be exposed to a parent with a rather harsh discipline style (stimulus). Avoiding the attention of that parent would result in fewer punishments and scoldings, so that avoidance response is negatively reinforced—the "bad thing" or punishment is avoided by keeping out of sight and quiet. Later, that child might generalize that avoidance response to other authority figures and adults, such as teachers. In this way, a pattern (habit) of shyness would develop.

Of course, many learning theorists today do not use only classical and operant conditioning to explain the development of the behavior patterns referred to as personality. **Social cognitive learning theorists**, who emphasize the importance of both the influences of other people's behavior and of a person's own expectancies on learning, hold that observational learning, modeling, and other cognitive learning techniques can lead to the formation of patterns of personality. LINK to Chapter Five: Learning, p. 197.

One of the more well-researched learning theories that includes the concept of cognitive processes as influences on behavior is the social cognitive theory of Albert Bandura. In the **social cognitive view**, behavior is governed not just by the influence of external stimuli and response patterns but also by cognitive processes such as anticipating, judging, and memory as well as learning through the imitation of models. In fact, you might remember Bandura's work with observation learning and imitation of models from his Bobo doll study. LINK to Chapter Five: Learning, pp. 201–202.

habits in behaviorism, sets of well-learned responses that have become automatic.

social cognitive learning theorists theorists who emphasize the importance of both the influences of other people's behavior and of a person's own expectancies of learning.

social cognitive view learning theory that includes cognitive processes such as anticipating, judging, memory, and imitation of models.

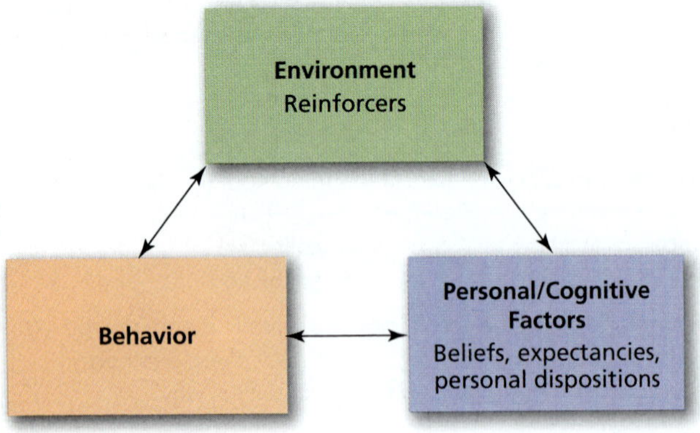

Figure 13.2 Reciprocal Determinism

In Bandura's model of reciprocal determinism, three factors influence behavior: the environment, which consists of the physical surroundings and the potential for reinforcement; the person (personal/cognitive characteristics that have been rewarded in the past); and the behavior itself, which may or may not be reinforced at this particular time and place.

BANDURA'S RECIPROCAL DETERMINISM AND SELF-EFFICACY

Bandura (1989) believes that three factors influence one another in determining the patterns of behavior that make up personality: the environment, the behavior itself, and personal or cognitive factors that the person brings into the situation from earlier experiences (see Figure 13.2). These three factors each affect the other two in a reciprocal, or give-and-take, relationship. Bandura calls this relationship **reciprocal determinism**.

Take a look at Figure 13.2, the environment includes the actual physical surroundings, the other people who may or may not be present, and the potential for reinforcement in those surroundings. The intensity and frequency of the behavior will not only be influenced by the environment but will also have an impact on that environment. The person brings into the situation previously reinforced responses (personality, in other words) and mental processes such as thinking and anticipating.

Here's how this might work: Richard walks into a classroom filled with other students, but no teacher is present at this time. (This is the *environment*.) Part of Richard's *personal* characteristics includes the desire to have attention from other people by talking loudly and telling jokes, which has been very rewarding to him in the past (past reinforcements are part of his cognitive processes, or expectancies of future rewards for his behavior). Also in the past, he has found that he gets more attention when an authority figure is not present. His *behavior* will most likely be to start talking and telling jokes, which will continue if he gets the reaction he expects from his fellow students. If the teacher walks in (the *environment* changes), his behavior will change. If the other students don't laugh, his behavior will change. In the future Richard might be less likely to behave in the same way because his expectations for reward (a cognitive element of his *personal* variables) are different.

One of the more important personal variables that Bandura talks about is **self-efficacy**, a person's expectancy of how effective his or her efforts to accomplish a goal will be in any particular circumstance (Bandura, 1998). (Self-efficacy is not the same concept as *self-esteem*, which is the positive values a person places on his or her sense of worth.)

People's sense of self-efficacy can be high or low, depending on what has happened in similar circumstances in the past (success or failure), what other people tell them about their competence, and their own assessment of their abilities. For example, if Fiona has an opportunity to write an extra-credit paper to improve her grade in psychology, she will be more likely to do so if her self-efficacy is high: She has gotten good grades on such papers in the past, her teachers have told her that she writes well, and she knows she can write a good paper. According to Bandura, people high in self-efficacy are more persistent and expect to succeed, whereas people low in self-efficacy expect to fail and tend to avoid challenges (Bandura, 1998).

ROTTER'S SOCIAL LEARNING THEORY: EXPECTANCIES

Julian Rotter (1966, 1978, 1981, 1990) devised a theory based on a basic principle of motivation derived from Thorndike's law of effect: People are motivated to seek reinforcement and avoid punishment. He viewed personality as a relatively stable set of *potential* responses to various situations. If in the past, a certain way of responding led to a reinforcing or pleasurable consequence, that way of responding would become a pattern of responding, or part of the "personality" as learning theorists see it.

reciprocal determinism Bandura's explanation of how the factors of environment, personal characteristics, and behavior can interact to determine future behavior.

self-efficacy individual's expectancy of how effective his or her efforts to accomplish a goal will be in any particular circumstance.

One very important pattern of responding in Rotter's view became his concept of **locus of control**, the tendency for people to assume that they either have control or do not have control over events and consequences in their lives. LINK to Chapter Nine: Motivation and Emotion, p. 347. People who assume that their own actions and decisions directly affect the consequences they experience are said to be *internal* in locus of control, whereas people who assume that their lives are more controlled by powerful others, luck, or fate are *external* in locus of control (MacDonald, 1970; Rotter, 1966). Rotter associated people high in internal locus of control with the personality characteristics of high achievement motivation (the will to succeed in any attempted task). Those who give up too quickly or who attribute events in their lives to external causes can fall into patterns of learned helplessness and depression (Abramson et al., 1978, 1989; Gong-Guy & Hammen, 1980).

locus of control the tendency for people to assume that they either have control or do not have control over events and consequences in their lives.

expectancy a person's subjective feeling that a particular behavior will lead to a reinforcing consequence.

humanistic perspective the "third force" in psychology that focuses on those aspects of personality that make people uniquely human, such as subjective feelings and freedom of choice.

Like Bandura, Rotter (1978, 1981) also believed that an interaction of factors would determine the behavioral patterns that become personality for an individual. For Rotter, there are two key factors influencing a person's decision to act in a certain way given a particular situation: expectancy and reinforcement value. **Expectancy** is fairly similar to Bandura's concept of self-efficacy in that it refers to the person's subjective feeling that a particular behavior will lead to a reinforcing consequence. A high expectancy for success is similar to a high sense of self-efficacy and is also based on past experiences with successes and failures.

According to Rotter, what would be the most likely form of locus of control experienced by this young woman?

CURRENT THOUGHTS ON THE BEHAVIORIST AND SOCIAL COGNITIVE VIEWS

Behaviorism as an explanation of the formation of personality has its limitations. The classic theory does not take mental processes into account when explaining behavior, nor does it give weight to social influences on learning. The social cognitive view of personality, unlike traditional behaviorism, does include social and mental processes and their influence on behavior. Unlike psychoanalysis, the concepts in this theory can and have been tested under scientific conditions (Backenstrass et al., 2008; Bandura, 1965; Catanzaro et al., 2000; DeGrandpre, 2000; Domjan et al., 2000; Skinner, 1989). Some of this most recent research has investigated how people's expectancies can influence their control of their own negative moods. Although some critics think that human personality and behavior are too complex to explain as the result of cognitions and external stimuli interacting, others point out that this viewpoint has enabled the development of therapies based on learning theory that have become effective in changing undesirable behavior. LINK to Chapter Fifteen: Psychological Therapies, pp. 581–585.

"It's always 'Sit,' 'Stay,' 'Heel'—never 'Think,' 'Innovate,' 'Be yourself.'"

The Third Force: Humanism and Personality

13.6 How do humanists such as Carl Rogers explain personality?

As first discussed in Chapter One, in the middle of the twentieth century the pessimism of Freudian psychodynamic theory with its emphasis on conflict and animalistic needs, together with the emphasis of behaviorism on external control of behavior, gave rise to a third force in psychology: the **humanistic perspective**. Humanists such as Carl Rogers and Abraham Maslow wanted psychology to focus on the things that make people uniquely human, such as subjective emotions and the freedom to choose one's own destiny. As Maslow's theory was discussed more fully in Chapter Nine, in this chapter the discussion of the humanistic view of personality will focus on the theory of Carl Rogers.

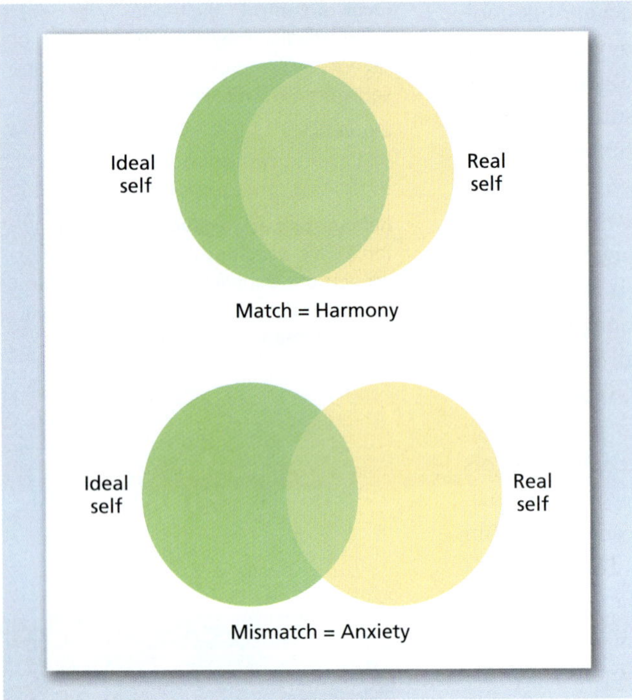

Figure 13.3 Real and Ideal Selves

According to Rogers, the self-concept includes the real self and the ideal self. The real self is a person's actual perception of traits and abilities, whereas the ideal self is the perception of what a person would like to be or thinks he or she should be. When the ideal self and the real self are very similar (matching), the person experiences harmony and contentment. When there is a mismatch between the two selves, the person experiences anxiety and may engage in neurotic behavior.

self-actualizing tendency the striving to fulfill one's innate capacities and capabilities.

self-concept the image of oneself that develops from interactions with important, significant people in one's life.

self an individual's awareness of his or her own personal characteristics and level of functioning.

real self one's perception of actual characteristics, traits, and abilities.

ideal self one's perception of whom one should be or would like to be.

positive regard warmth, affection, love, and respect that come from significant others in one's life.

unconditional positive regard positive regard that is given without conditions or strings attached.

conditional positive regard positive regard that is given only when the person is doing what the providers of positive regard wish.

CARL ROGERS AND SELF-CONCEPT

Both Maslow and Rogers (1961) believed that human beings are always striving to fulfill their innate capacities and capabilities and to become everything that their genetic potential will allow them to become. This striving for fulfillment is called the **self-actualizing tendency**. An important tool in human self-actualization is the development of an image of oneself, or the **self-concept**. The self-concept is based on what people are told by others and how the sense of **self** is reflected in the words and actions of important people in one's life, such as parents, siblings, coworkers, friends, and teachers.

REAL AND IDEAL SELF Two important components of the self-concept are the **real self** (one's actual perception of characteristics, traits, and abilities that form the basis of the striving for self-actualization) and the **ideal self** (the perception of what one should be or would like to be). The ideal self primarily comes from those important, significant others in a person's life, most often the parents. Rogers believed that when the real self and the ideal self are very close or similar to each other, people feel competent and capable, but when there is a mismatch between the real self and ideal self, anxiety and neurotic behavior can be the result. (See Figure 13.3.)

The two halves of the self are more likely to match if they aren't that far apart at the start. When a person has a realistic view of the real self, and the ideal self is something that is actually attainable, there usually isn't a problem of a mismatch. It is when a person's view of self is distorted or the ideal self is impossible to attain that problems arise. Once again, it is primarily how the important people (who can be either good or bad influences) in a person's life react to the person that determines the degree of agreement between real and ideal selves.

CONDITIONAL AND UNCONDITIONAL POSITIVE REGARD Rogers defined **positive regard** as warmth, affection, love, and respect that come from the significant others (parents, admired adults, friends, and teachers) in people's experience. Positive regard is vital to people's ability to cope with stress and to strive to achieve self-actualization. Rogers believed that **unconditional positive regard**, or love, affection, and respect with no strings attached, is necessary for people to be able to explore fully all that they can achieve and become. Unfortunately, some parents, spouses, and friends give **conditional positive regard**, which is love, affection, respect, and warmth that depend, or seem to depend, on doing what those people want.

Here is an example: As a freshman, Sasha was thinking about becoming a math teacher, a computer programmer, or an elementary school teacher. Karen, also a freshman, already knew that she was going to be a doctor. Whereas Sasha's parents had told her that what she wanted to become was up to her and that they would love her no matter what, Karen's parents had made it very clear to her as a small child that they expected her to become a doctor. She was under the very strong impression that if she tried to choose any other career, she would lose her parents' love and respect. Sasha's parents were giving her unconditional positive regard, but Karen's parents (whether they intended to do so or not) were giving her conditional positive regard. Karen was obviously not as free as Sasha to explore her potential and abilities.

For Rogers, a person who is in the process of self-actualizing, actively exploring potentials and abilities and experiencing a match between the real self and ideal self, is a **fully functioning person**. Fully functioning people are in touch with their own feelings and abilities and are able to trust their innermost urges and intuitions (Rogers, 1961). To become fully functioning, a person needs unconditional positive regard. In Rogers's view, Karen would not have been a fully functioning person.

What kind of people are considered to be fully functioning? Is it the same thing as being self-actualized?

What kind of people are considered to be fully functioning? Is it the same thing as being self-actualized?

Although the two concepts are highly related, there are some subtle differences. Self-actualization is a goal that people are always striving to reach, according to Maslow (1987). LINK to Chapter Nine: Motivation and Emotion, p. 352. In Rogers's view, only a person who is fully functioning is capable of reaching the goal of self-actualization. To be fully functioning is a necessary step in the process of self-actualization. Maslow (1987) listed several people who he considered to be self-actualized people: Albert Einstein, Mahatma Gandhi, and Eleanor Roosevelt, for example. These were people who Maslow found to have the self-actualized qualities of being creative, autonomous, and unprejudiced. In Rogers's view, these same people would be seen as having trusted their true feelings and innermost needs rather than just going along with the crowd.

These proud parents are giving their daughter unconditional positive regard.

fully functioning person a person who is in touch with and trusting of the deepest, innermost urges and feelings.

CURRENT THOUGHTS ON THE HUMANISTIC VIEW OF PERSONALITY

Humanistic views of personality paint a very rosy picture. Some critics believe that the picture is a little too rosy, ignoring the more negative aspects of human nature. For example, would humanistic theory easily explain the development of sociopathic personalities who have no conscience or moral nature? Or could a humanist explain the motivation behind terrorism?

Humanistic theory is also very difficult to test scientifically. Little research support exists for this viewpoint, which could be considered more a philosophical view of human behavior than it is a psychological explanation. Its greatest impact has been in the development of therapies designed to promote self-growth and help people better understand themselves and others. LINK to Chapter Fifteen: Psychological Therapies, pp. 578–580.

13.5 13.6 CONCEPT MAP

Behavioral, Social Cognitive, and Humanistic Perspectives

- **behavioral and social cognitive**
  - for behaviorists, personality is a set of learned responses and habits, gained through classical and operant conditioning
  - in social cognitive view, both learning (individual and through imitation of models) and cognitive processes (such as anticipation, judgment, and memory) are important
    - **Bandura:** concept of self-efficacy; believed three factors were important: the environment, the behavior itself, and personal or cognitive experiences from earlier experiences; each affect the other two in a reciprocal way—reciprocal determinism (see Figure 13.2)
    - **Rotter:** theory based on principles of motivation derived from Thorndike's law of effect; personality is set of potential responses to various situations, including one's locus of control (internal vs. external) and sense of expectancy
- **humanistic**
  referred to as the third force in psychology (after psychoanalysis and behaviorism); based largely on work of Rogers and Maslow
  - **Rogers:** believed that humans are always striving to fulfill their innate capacities and capabilities (self-actualizing tendency)
  - **self-concept** is based on an individual's view of his or her real self and ideal self; when close/similar, people feel capable and competent; when there is mismatch, anxiety and neurotic behavior can occur
  - **self-actualization** is facilitated through positive regard, especially unconditional positive regard
  - when there is congruence between real and ideal selves, one is considered to be fully functioning and capable of reaching the goal of self-actualization

(continued)

PRACTICE quiz How much do you remember? ANSWERS ON PAGE AK-2.

Pick the best answer.

1. According to behaviorists, personality is _________.
   - **a.** driven by unconscious forces.
   - **b.** a set of learned responses.
   - **c.** motivated by a striving for success.
   - **d.** a collection of specific traits.
2. Which of the following is not one of Bandura's three factors in reciprocal determinism?
   - **a.** environment
   - **b.** the person
   - **c.** traits
   - **d.** behavior
3. Sandy is playing a trivia game with her friends. When it is her turn, she gets the category of geography. She knows very little about geography and has never done well in this category in the past, so her sense of self-efficacy is likely to be _________.
   - **a.** low.
   - **b.** high.
   - **c.** just right.
   - **d.** unaffected by the game.
4. Eddie knows that he is pretty good at art, but his parents have never encouraged him to develop art as a career because they don't feel that artists have "real" jobs. As a result, Eddie feels that he should concentrate on a more practical career to please his parents. If Eddie is working to be who he should be, according to his parents, he is being influenced by his _________.
   - **a.** self-concept.
   - **b.** real self.
   - **c.** superego.
   - **d.** ideal self.
5. Rogers believed that in order for people to become fully functioning, they must receive _________ from the important people in their lives.
   - **a.** unconditional positive regard
   - **b.** conditional positive regard
   - **c.** positive reinforcement
   - **d.** positive modeling

"Can't you give him one of those personalities in a bottle I keep reading about?"

Trait Theories: Who Are You?

13.7 What are the history and current views of the trait perspective?

As discussed in the introduction to this chapter, **trait theories** are less concerned with the explanation for personality development and changing personality than they are with describing personality and predicting behavior based on that description. A **trait** is a consistent, enduring way of thinking, feeling, or behaving, and trait theories attempt to describe personality in terms of a person's traits.

ALLPORT

One of the earliest attempts to list and describe the traits that make up personality can be found in the work of Gordon Allport (Allport & Odbert, 1936). Allport and his colleague H. S. Odbert literally scanned the dictionary for words that could be traits, finding about 18,000, then paring that down to 200 traits after eliminating synonyms. Allport believed (with no scientific evidence, however) that these traits were literally wired into the nervous system to guide one's behavior across many different situations and that each person's "constellation" of traits was unique. (In spite of Allport's lack of evidence, behavioral geneticists have found support for the heritability of personality traits, and these findings are discussed in the next section of this chapter.) **Watch** on **mypsychlab.com**

Watch classic video footages on personality traits with Allport on **mypsychlab.com**

trait theories theories that endeavor to describe the characteristics that make up human personality in an effort to predict future behavior.

trait a consistent, enduring way of thinking, feeling, or behaving.

surface traits aspects of personality that can easily be seen by other people in the outward actions of a person.

CATTELL AND THE 16PF

Two hundred traits is still a very large number of descriptors. How might an employer be able to judge the personality of a potential employee by looking at a list of 200 traits? A more compact way of describing personality was needed. Raymond Cattell (1990) defined two types of traits as *surface traits* and *source traits*. **Surface traits** are like those found by Allport, representing the personality characteristics easily seen by other people. **Source traits** are those more basic traits that underlie the surface traits. For example, shyness, being quiet, and disliking crowds might all be surface traits related to the more basic source trait of **introversion**, a tendency to withdraw from excessive stimulation.

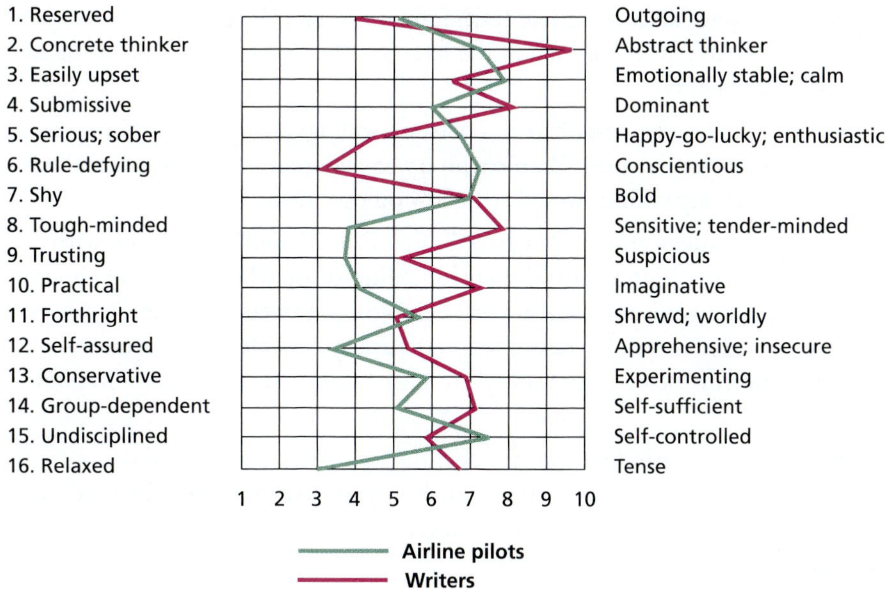

Figure 13.4 Cattell's Self-Report Inventory

This is an example of personality profiles based on Cattell's 16PF self-report inventory. The two groups represented are airline pilots and writers. Notice that airline pilots, when compared to writers, tend to be more conscientious, relaxed, self-assured, and far less sensitive. Writers, on the other hand, are more imaginative and better able to are think abstractly.

Source: Cattell (1973).

Using a statistical technique that looks for groupings and commonalities in numerical data called *factor analysis*, Cattell identified 16 source traits (Cattell, 1950, 1966), and although he later determined that there might be another seven source traits to make a total of 23 (Cattell & Kline, 1977), he developed his assessment questionnaire, *The Sixteen Personality Factor (16PF) Questionnaire* (Cattell, 1995) based on just 16 source traits (see Figure 13.4). These 16 source traits are seen as trait dimensions, or continuums, in which there are two opposite traits at each end with a range of possible degrees for each trait measurable along the dimension. For example, someone scoring near the "reserved" end of the "reserved/outgoing" dimension would be more introverted than someone scoring in the middle or at the opposite end.

THE BIG FIVE: OCEAN, OR THE FIVE-FACTOR MODEL OF PERSONALITY

Sixteen factors are still quite a lot to discuss when talking about someone's personality. Later researchers attempted to reduce the number of trait dimensions to a more manageable number, with several groups of researchers arriving at more or less the same five trait dimensions (Botwin & Buss, 1989; Jang et al., 1998; McCrae & Costa, 1996). These five dimensions have become known as the **five-factor model**, or the **Big Five** (see Table 13.3), and represent the core description of human personality—that is, the only dimensions necessary to understand what makes us tick.

✓**source traits** the more basic traits that underlie the surface traits, forming the core of personality.

✓**introversion** dimension of personality in which people tend to withdraw from excessive stimulation.

✓**five-factor model (Big Five)** model of personality traits that describes five basic trait dimensions.

Table 13.3

The Big Five

HIGH SCORER CHARACTERISTICS	FACTOR (OCEAN)	LOW SCORER CHARACTERISTICS
Creative, artistic, curious, imaginative, nonconforming	**Openness (O)**	Conventional, down-to-earth, uncreative
Organized, reliable, neat, ambitious	**Conscientiousness (C)**	Unreliable, lazy, careless, negligent, spontaneous
Talkative, optimistic, sociable, affectionate	**Extraversion (E)**	Reserved, comfortable being alone, stays in the background
Good-natured, trusting, helpful	**Agreeableness (A)**	Rude, uncooperative, irritable, aggressive, competitive
Worrying, insecure, anxious, temperamental	**Neuroticism (N)**	Calm, secure, relaxed, stable

Source: Adapted from McCrae & Costa (1990).

openness one of the five factors; willingness to try new things and be open to new experiences.

conscientiousness the care a person gives to organization and thoughtfulness of others; dependability.

extraversion dimension of personality referring to one's need to be with other people.

extraverts people who are outgoing and sociable.

introverts people who prefer solitude and dislike being the center of attention.

agreeableness the emotional style of a person that may range from easygoing, friendly, and likeable to grumpy, crabby, and unpleasant.

neuroticism degree of emotional instability or stability.

trait–situation interaction the assumption that the particular circumstances of any given situation will influence the way in which a trait is expressed.

Explore the five-factor model on **mypsychlab.com**

As shown in the table, these five trait dimensions can be remembered by using the acronym OCEAN, in which each of the letters is the first letter of one of the five dimensions of personality.

- **Openness** can best be described as a person's willingness to try new things and be open to new experiences. People who try to maintain the status quo and who don't like to change things would score low on openness.
- **Conscientiousness** refers to a person's organization and motivation, with people who score high in this dimension being those who are careful about being places on time and careful with belongings as well. Someone scoring low on this dimension, for example, might always be late to important social events or borrow belongings and fail to return them or return them in poor condition.
- **Extraversion** is a term first used by Carl Jung (1933), who believed that all people could be divided into two personality types: **extraverts** and **introverts**. Extraverts are outgoing and sociable, whereas introverts are more solitary and dislike being the center of attention.
- **Agreeableness** refers to the basic emotional style of a person, who may be easygoing, friendly, and pleasant (at the high end of the scale) or grumpy, crabby, and hard to get along with (at the low end).
- **Neuroticism** refers to emotional instability or stability. People who are excessive worriers, overanxious, and moody would score high on this dimension, whereas those who are more even-tempered and calm would score low.

Costa and McCrae proposed that these five traits are not interdependent. In other words, knowing someone's score on extraversion would not give any information about scores on the other four dimensions, allowing for a tremendous amount of variety in personality descriptions. **Explore** on **mypsychlab.com**

CURRENT THOUGHTS ON THE TRAIT PERSPECTIVE

Some theorists have cautioned that personality traits will not always be expressed in the same way across different situations. Walter Mischel, a social cognitive theorist, has emphasized that there is a **trait–situation interaction** in which the particular circumstances of any given situation are assumed to influence the way in which a trait is expressed (Mischel & Shoda, 1995). An outgoing extravert, for example, might laugh, talk to strangers, and tell jokes at a party. That same person, if at a funeral, would still talk and be open, but the jokes and laughter would be less likely to occur. However, the five-factor model provides a dimensional approach to classifying personality structure (as opposed to a categorical approach), which is consistent with proposed changes for the upcoming edition of the *Diagnostic and Statistical Manual of Mental Disorders* (*DSM-5*), and has implications for the diagnosis of personality disorders (Widiger & Trull, 2007)

As mentioned earlier, the five-factor model has been studied and tested by numerous researchers. Cross-cultural studies have found evidence of these five trait dimensions in 11 different cultures, including Japan, the Philippines, Germany, China, and Peru (Digman, 1990; John et al., 1988; McCrae et al., 2000; 2005; McCrae & Terracciano, 2007; Paunonen et al., 1996; Piedmont et al., 2002). This cultural commonality raises the question of the origins of the Big Five trait dimensions: Are child-rearing practices across all those cultures similar enough to result in these five aspects of personality, or could these five dimensions have a genetic component that transcends cultural differences? The next section will discuss the evidence for a genetic basis of the Big Five.

13.7 CONCEPT MAP

- a trait is a consistent, enduring way of thinking, feeling, or behaving; trait theories attempt to describe personality in terms of a person's traits
- **Allport:** believed there were 200 traits that were wired into the nervous system to guide a person's behavior
- **Cattell:** developed concept of surface traits and source traits; identified 16 source traits through factor analysis (later suggested 23); developed assessment questionnaire to identify original 16 trait dimensions (16PF)
- several groups' work resulted in the **five-factor model** (Big Five, OCEAN)—openness, conscientiousness, extraversion, agreeableness, neuroticism (see Table 13.3)
- Mischel and others have suggested that there is a trait–situation interaction; there is evidence of the Big Five trait dimensions across various cultures

Trait Theories

PRACTICE quiz How much do you remember? ANSWERS ON PAGE AK-2.

Pick the best answer.

1. Who believed that traits existed as part of the nervous system?
   a. Costa and McCrae
   b. Allport
   c. Cattell
   d. Rogers
2. According to Cattell, traits that are numerous and can easily be seen by other people are called _________ traits.
   a. central
   b. cardinal
   c. surface
   d. source
3. In the Big Five theory of personality, "C" stands for _________.
   a. conscientiousness.
   b. consciousness.
   c. contrariness.
   d. complexity.
4. Elsie's daughter gave her a microwave oven for her birthday. Elsie has never used a microwave and is scared to use this one. Instead, she lets it sit in her kitchen and refuses to let her daughter teach her how to use it. Elsie would probably score very low on _________.
   a. agreeableness.
   b. neuroticism.
   c. introversion.
   d. openness.

The Biology of Personality: Behavioral Genetics

What about genetics? How much of our personality is inherited?

The field of **behavioral genetics** is devoted to the study of just how much of an individual's personality is due to inherited traits. Animal breeders have known for a long time that selective breeding of certain animals with specific desirable traits can produce changes not only in size, fur color, and other physical characteristics but also in the temperament of the animals (Isabel, 2003; Trut, 1999). As stated earlier in this chapter, temperament consists of the characteristics with which each person is born and is, therefore, determined by biology to a great degree. If the temperaments of animals can be influenced by manipulating patterns of genetic inheritance, then it is only one small step to assume that at least those personality characteristics related to temperament in human beings may also be influenced by heredity.

Animal breeders have an advantage over those who are studying the influence of genes in human behavior. Those who breed animals can control the mating of certain animals and the conditions under which those animals are raised. Human research cannot ethically or practically develop that degree of control and so must fall back on the accidental "experiments" of nature and opportunity, studies of twins and adopted persons.

What about genetics? How much of our personality is inherited?

behavioral genetics field of study devoted to discovering the genetic bases for personality characteristics.

13.8 What part do biology, heredity, and culture play in personality?

James Arthur Springer and James Edward Lewis, otherwise known as the "Jim" twins. Although separated shortly after birth and reunited at age 39, they exhibited many similarities in personality and personal habits. Although genetics may explain some of these similarities, what other factors might also be at work?

TWIN STUDIES

The difference between monozygotic (identical) and dizygotic (fraternal) twins was discussed in Chapter Eight. LINK to Chapter Eight: Development Across the Life Span, p. 304. As discussed previously, identical twins share 100 percent of their genetic material, having come from one fertilized egg originally, whereas fraternal twins share only about 50 percent of their genetic material as any other pair of siblings would. By comparing identical twins to fraternal twins, especially when twins can be found who were not raised in the same environment (like Oskar and Jack or the "Jim" twins in the opening story), researchers can begin to find evidence of possible genetic influences on various traits, including personality. (See Figure 13.5.)

The results of the Minnesota twin study have revealed that identical twins are more similar than fraternal twins or unrelated people in intelligence, leadership abilities, the tendency to follow rules, and the tendency to uphold traditional cultural expectations (Bouchard, 1997; Finkel & McGue, 1997); nurturance,* empathy,** and assertiveness (Neale et al., 1986); and aggressiveness (Miles & Carey, 1997). This similarity holds even if the twins are raised in separate environments. Watch on **mypsychlab.com**

Watch a video about twin studies on **mypsychlab.com**

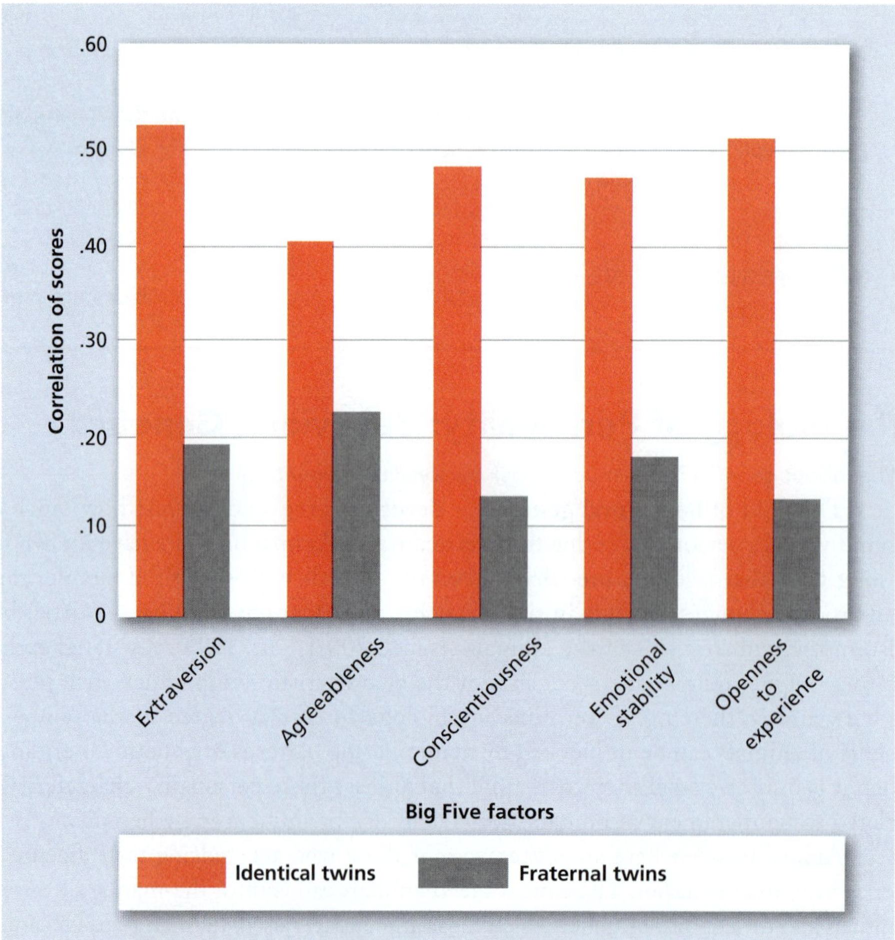

Figure 13.5 Personalities of Identical and Fraternal Twins

Identical and fraternal twins differ in the way they express the Big Five personality factors. The scores of identical twins have a correlation of about 50 percent, whereas those of fraternal twins have a correlation of only about 15 to 20 percent. These findings give support to the idea that some aspects of personality are genetically based.

Source: Loehlin (1992)

*nurturance: affectionate care and attention.

**empathy: the ability to understand the feelings of others.

ADOPTION STUDIES

Another tool of behavioral geneticists is to study adopted children and their adoptive and birth families. If studying genetically identical twins raised in different environments can help investigators understand the genetic influences on personality, then studying *unrelated* people who are raised in the *same* environment should help investigators discover the influence of environment. By comparing adopted children to their adoptive parents and siblings and, if possible, to their biological parents who have not raised them, researchers can uncover some of the shared and nonshared environmental and genetic influences on personality.

Adoption studies have confirmed what twin studies have shown: Genetic influences account for a great deal of personality development, regardless of shared or nonshared environments (Hershberger et al., 1995; Loehlin et al., 1985; Loehlin et al., 1998). Through this kind of study, for example, a genetic basis has been suggested for shyness (Plomin et al., 1988) and aggressiveness (Brennan et al., 1997).

CURRENT FINDINGS

Several studies have found that the five personality factors of the five-factor model have nearly a 50 percent rate of heritability* across several cultures (Bouchard, 1994; Herbst et al., 2000; Jang et al., 1996; Loehlin, 1992; Loehlin et al., 1998). Personality's relationship to psychopathology is also being investigated via genetic techniques (Plomin & Spinath, 2004). Together with the results of the Minnesota twin study and other research (Lubinski, 2000; Lykken & Tellegen, 1996; Plomin, 1994), the studies of genetics and personality seem to indicate that variations in personality traits are about 25 to 50 percent inherited (Jang et al., 1998). This also means that environmental influences apparently account for about half of the variation in personality traits as well.

Although the five factors have been found across several cultures, this does not mean that different cultures do not have an impact on personality. For more on this topic, see the Classic Studies in Psychology section that follows.

*heritability: the degree to which the changes in some trait within a population can be considered to be due to genetic influences.

classic studies in psychology

Geert Hofstede's Four Dimensions of Cultural Personality

In the early 1980s, organizational management specialist Geert Hofstede conducted a massive study into the work-related values of employees of IBM, a multinational corporation (Hofstede, 1980; Hofstede et al., 2002). The study surveyed workers in 64 countries across the world. Hofstede analyzed the data collected from this survey and found four basic dimensions of personality along which cultures differed.

1. **Individualism/collectivism:** *Individualistic cultures* tend to have loose ties between individuals, with people tending to look after themselves and their immediate families only. Members of such cultures have friends based on shared activities and interests and may belong to many different loosely organized social groups. Autonomy,* change, youth, security of the individual, and equality are all highly

*autonomy: the quality of being self-directed or self-controlled.

valued. In contrast, in a *collectivistic culture,* people are from birth deeply tied into very strong in-groups, typically extended families that include grandparents, aunts and uncles, and cousins. Loyalty to the family is highly stressed, and the care of the family is placed before the care of the individual. Group membership is limited to only a few permanent groups that have tremendous influence over the individual. The values of this kind of culture are duty, order, tradition, respect for the elderly, group security, and respect for the group status and hierarchy.* Whereas the United States and Great Britain are examples of individualistic cultures, Japan, China, Korea, Mexico, and Central America are much more collectivistic.

2. **Power distance:** This dimension refers to the degree to which the less powerful members of a culture accept and even expect that the power within the culture is held in the hands of a select few rather than being more evenly distributed. Countries such as the Philippines, Mexico, many Arab countries, and India were found to be high in such expectations, whereas countries such as Austria, Sweden, Australia, Great Britain, and the United States were low in power distance.
3. **Masculinity/femininity:** Referring to how a culture distributes the roles played by men and women within a culture, this dimension varies more for the men within a culture than for the women. "Masculine" cultures are assertive and competitive, although more so for men than for women, and "feminine" cultures are more modest and caring. Both men and women in "feminine" countries have similar, caring values, but in "masculine" countries, the women are not quite as assertive and competitive as the men, leading to a greater difference between the sexes in masculine countries. Japan, Austria, Venezuela, Italy, Switzerland, Mexico, Ireland, Jamaica, the United States, Great Britain, and Germany were found to be masculine countries, whereas Sweden, Norway, the Netherlands, Denmark, Costa Rica, Yugoslavia, Finland, Chile, Portugal, Thailand, and Guatemala were ranked as more feminine.
4. **Uncertainty avoidance:** Some cultures are more tolerant of uncertainty, ambiguity,** and unstructured situations. Cultures that do not tolerate such uncertainty and lack of structure tend to have strict rules and laws with lots of security and safety measures and tend toward a philosophical/religious belief of One Truth (and "we have it!"). Cultures that are more accepting of uncertainty are more tolerant of different opinions and have fewer rules. They tend to allow many different religious beliefs to exist side by side and are less anxious and emotional than people in uncertainty-avoiding countries. Uncertainty–avoiding countries include Greece, Portugal, Guatemala, Uruguay, Belgium, El Salvador, Japan, Yugoslavia, and Peru, whereas those that are more tolerant of uncertainty include Singapore, Jamaica, Denmark, Sweden, Hong Kong, Ireland, Great Britain, Malaysia, India, Philippines, the United States, Canada, and Indonesia.

Note that the Big Five personality dimensions of Costa and McCrae (2000) are not necessarily in competition with Hofstede's dimensions. Hofstede's dimensions are *cultural* personality traits, whereas those of the Big Five refer to individuals.

Questions for Further Discussion

1. Was your own culture listed for any of these dimensions? If so, do you agree with the personality dimension assigned to your culture?
2. If your culture was not listed for a personality dimension, where do you think your culture would fall on that dimension?

*hierarchy: in this sense, a body of persons in authority over others.

**ambiguity: the quality of being uncertain and indistinct.

Assessment of Personality

13.9 What are the advantages and disadvantages of the following measures of personality: interviews, projective tests, behavioral assessment, personality inventories, and online personality tests?

With all the different theories of personality, how do people find out what kind of personality they have?

The methods for measuring or assessing personality vary according to the theory of personality used to develop those methods, as one might expect. However, most psychological professionals doing a personality assessment on a client do not necessarily tie themselves down to one theoretical viewpoint only, preferring to take a more *eclectic* view of personality. The eclectic view is a way of choosing the parts of different theories that seem to best fit a particular situation, rather than using only one theory to explain a phenomenon. In fact, looking at behavior from all four perspectives can often bring insights into a person's behavior that would not easily come from taking only one perspective. Many professionals will not only use several different perspectives but also several of the assessment techniques that follow. Even so, certain methods are more commonly used by certain kinds of theorists, as can be seen in Table 13.4.

Personality assessments may also differ in the purposes for which they are conducted. For example, sometimes a researcher may administer a personality test of some sort to participants in a research study so that the participants may be classified according to certain personality traits. There are tests available to people who simply want to learn more about their own personalities. Finally, clinical and counseling psychologists, psychiatrists, and other psychological professionals use these personality assessment tools in the diagnosis of disorders of personality. LINK to Chapter Fourteen: Psychological Disorders, pp. 560–562. **Listen** on **mypsychlab.com**

With all the different theories of personality, how do people find out what kind of personality they have?

Listen to the Psychology in the News podcast about online personality testing on **mypsychlab.com**

Table 13.4
Who Uses What Method?

TYPE OF ASSESSMENT	MOST LIKELY USED BY . . .
Interviews	Psychoanalysts, humanistic therapists
Projective Tests Rorschach Thematic Apperception Test	Psychoanalysts
Behavioral Assessments Direct observation Rating scales Frequency counts	Behavioral and social cognitive therapists
Personality Inventories Sixteen Personality Factor Questionnaire (16PF) Neuroticism/Extraversion/Openness Personality Inventory (NEO-PI) Myers-Briggs Type Indicator (MBTI) Eysenck Personality Questionnaire (EPQ) Keirsey Temperament Sorter II California Psychological Inventory (CPI) Minnesota Multiphasic Personality Inventory, Version II (MMPI-2)	Trait theorists

So an interview is a kind of self-report process?

INTERVIEWS

Some therapists ask questions and note down the answers in a survey process called an **interview**. LINK to Chapter One: The Science of Psychology, p. 4. This type of interview, unlike a job interview, is likely to be *unstructured* and flow naturally from the beginning dialog between the client and the psychologist.

PROBLEMS WITH INTERVIEWS

So an interview is a kind of self-report process?

Yes, when psychologists interview clients, clients must report on their innermost feelings, urges, and concerns—all things that only they can directly know. The same problems that exist with self-report data (such as surveys) exist with interviews. Clients can lie, distort the truth, misremember, or give what they think is a socially acceptable answer instead of true information. Interviewers themselves can be biased, interpreting what the client says in light of their own belief systems or prejudices. Freud certainly did this when he refused to believe that his patients had actually been sexually molested as children, preferring to interpret that information as a fantasy instead of reality (Russell, 1986).

Another problem with interviews is something called the **halo effect**, which is a tendency to form a favorable or unfavorable impression of someone at the first meeting, so that all of a person's comments and behavior after that first impression will be interpreted to agree with the impression—positively or negatively. The halo effect can happen in any social situation, including interviews between a psychological professional and a client. First impressions really do count, and people who make a good first impression because of clothing, personal appearance, or some other irrelevant* characteristic will seem to have a "halo" hanging over their heads—they can do no wrong after that (Lance et al., 1994; Thorndike, 1920). (Sometimes the negative impression is called the "horn effect.")

PROJECTIVE TESTS

Psychoanalysts have a goal in dealing with their clients that other personality theorists do not share: The psychoanalyst wishes to uncover the unconscious conflicts, desires, and urges that affect the client's conscious behavior. No other theorist assigns such importance to the unconscious mind, so psychoanalysts use assessment methods that are meant to "get at" those unconscious, hidden emotions and events.

Think about the definition of the defense mechanism of **projection**: placing, or "projecting," one's own unacceptable thoughts onto others, as if the thoughts actually belonged to those others. What if a person could project unacceptable, unconscious thoughts onto some harmless, ambiguous stimulus, like a picture? For example, have you ever tried to see "shapes" in the clouds? You might see a house where another person might see the same cloud as a horse. The cloud isn't really either of those things but can be *interpreted* as one or the other, depending on the person doing the interpretation. That makes a cloud an ambiguous stimulus—one that is capable of being interpreted in more than one way.

In just this way, psychoanalysts (and a few other psychologists) show their clients ambiguous visual stimuli and ask the clients to tell them what they see. The hope is that the client will project those unconscious concerns and fears onto the visual stimulus, revealing them to the analyst. Tests using this method are called **projective tests**. Although such tests can be used to explore a client's personality, they are more commonly used as a diagnostic tool to uncover problems in personality.

*irrelevant: not applying to the case or example at hand.

interview method of personality assessment in which the professional asks questions of the client and allows the client to answer, either in a structured or unstructured fashion.

halo effect tendency of an interviewer to allow positive characteristics of a client to influence the assessments of the client's behavior and statements.

projection defense mechanism involving placing, or "projecting," one's own unacceptable thoughts onto others, as if the thoughts actually belonged to those others and not to oneself.

projective tests personality assessments that present ambiguous visual stimuli to the client and ask the client to respond with whatever comes to mind.

Rorschach inkblot test projective test that uses 10 inkblots as the ambiguous stimuli.

Thematic Apperception Test (TAT) projective test that uses 20 pictures of people in ambiguous situations as the visual stimuli.

subjective referring to concepts and impressions that are only valid within a particular person's perception and may be influenced by biases, prejudice, and personal experiences.

THE RORSCHACH INKBLOTS One of the more well-known projective tests is the **Rorschach inkblot test**, developed in 1921 by Swiss psychiatrist Hermann Rorschach (ROR-shok). There are 10 inkblots, 5 in black ink on a white background and 5 in colored inks on a white background. (See Figure 13.6 for an image similar to a Rorschach-type inkblot.)

People being tested are asked to look at each inkblot and simply say whatever it might look like to them. Using predetermined categories and responses commonly given by people to each picture (Exner, 1980), psychologists score responses on key factors, such as reference to color, shape, figures seen in the blot, and response to the whole or to details.

Rorschach tested thousands of inkblots until he narrowed them down to the 10 in use today. They are still frequently used to describe personality, diagnose mental disorders, and predict behavior (Watkins et al., 1995; Weiner, 1997).

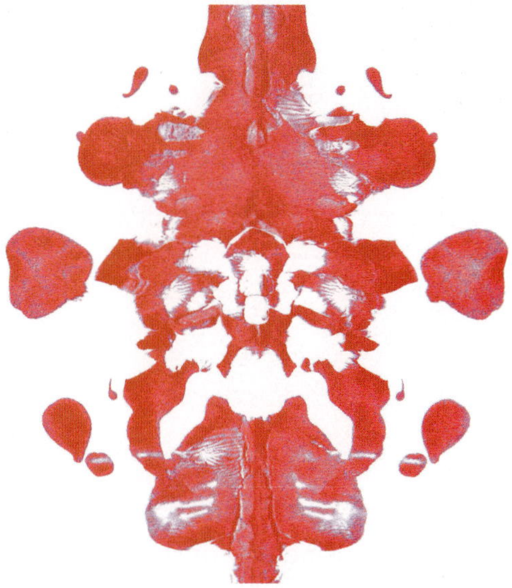

Figure 13.6 Rorschach Inkblot Example

A facsimile of a Rorschach inkblot. A person being tested is asked to tell the interviewer what he or she sees in an inkblot similar to the one shown. Answers are neither right nor wrong but may reveal unconscious concerns. What do you see in this inkblot?

THE TAT First developed in 1935 by psychologist Henry Murray and his colleagues (Morgan & Murray, 1935), the **Thematic Apperception Test (TAT)** consists of 20 pictures, all black and white, that are shown to a client. The client is asked to tell a story about the person or people in the picture, who are all deliberately drawn in ambiguous situations (see Figure 13.7). Again, the story developed by the client is interpreted by the psychoanalyst, who looks for revealing statements and projection of the client's own problems onto the people in the pictures.

These are only two of the more well-known projective tests. Other types of projective tests include the Sentence Completion test, Draw-A-Person, and House-Tree-Person. In the Sentence Completion test, the client is given a series of sentence beginnings, such as "I wish my mother . . ." or "Almost every day I feel . . ." and asked to finish the sentence, whereas in the Draw-A-Person and House-Tree-Person, the client is asked to draw the named items.

But how can anyone know if the interpretation is correct? Isn't there a lot of room for error?

But how can anyone know if the interpretation is correct? Isn't there a lot of room for error?

PROBLEMS WITH PROJECTIVE TESTS Projective tests are by their nature very **subjective** (valid only within the person's own perception), and interpreting the answers of clients is almost an art. It is certainly not a science and is not known for

Figure 13.7 Thematic Apperception Test Example

A sample from the Thematic Apperception Test (TAT). When you look at this picture, what story does it suggest to you? Who are the people? What is their relationship?

its accuracy. Problems lie in the areas of reliability and validity. In Chapter Seven, *reliability* was defined as the tendency of a test to give the same score every time it is administered to the same person or group of people, and *validity* was defined as the ability of the test to measure what it is intended to measure. Projective tests, with no standard grading scales, have both low reliability and low validity (Gittelman-Klein, 1978; Lilienfield, 1999; Wood et al., 1996). A person's answers to the Rorschach, for example, might be quite different from one day to the next, depending on the person's mood and what scary movie might have been on television the previous night.

Projective tests may sound somewhat outdated in today's world of MRIs and PET scans, but many practicing clinical psychologists and psychiatrists still use this type of testing (Butcher & Rouse, 1996; Camara et al., 2000). Some psychologists believe that the latest versions of these tests and others like them still have practical use and some validity (Ganellen, 1996; Weiner, 1997), especially when a client's answers on these tests are used as a starting point for digging deeper into the client's recollections, concerns, and anxieties. However, more-reliable and objective methods for assessing personality are available, as the next section discusses.

Somehow, I can't see a behaviorist using any of these tests, they're too "mental"—do behaviorists even measure personality?

Somehow, I can't see a behaviorist using any of these tests, they're too "mental"—do behaviorists even measure personality?

BEHAVIORAL ASSESSMENTS

Behaviorists do not typically want to "look into the mind." Because behaviorists assume that personality is merely habitually learned responses to stimuli in the environment, the preferred method for a behaviorist would be to watch that behavior unfold in the real world.

In **direct observation**, the psychologist observes the client engaging in ordinary, everyday behavior, preferably in the natural setting of home, school, or workplace, for example. A therapist who goes to the classroom and observes that tantrum behavior only happens when a child is asked to do something involving fine motor abilities (like drawing or writing) might be able to conclude that the child has difficulty with those skills and throws a tantrum to avoid the task.

Other methods often used by behavioral therapists and other assessors are rating scales and frequency counts. In a **rating scale**, a numerical rating is assigned, either by the assessor or the client, for specific behaviors (Nadeau et al., 2001). In a **frequency count**, the assessor literally counts the frequency of certain behaviors within a specified time limit. Educators make use of both rating scales and frequency counts to diagnose behavioral problems such as attention-deficit/hyperactivity disorder (ADHD) and aspects of personality such as social-skill level through the various grade levels.

PROBLEMS WITH BEHAVIORAL ASSESSMENTS Problems with these assessments can include the observer effect (when a person's behavior is affected by being watched) and observer bias, which can be controlled by having multiple observers and correlating their observations with each other. LINK to Chapter One: The Science of Psychology, pp. 22–23. As with any kind of observational method, there is no control over the external environment. A person observing a client for a particular behavior may not see that behavior occur within the observation time—much as some car problems never seem to show up when the mechanic is examining the car.

direct observation assessment in which the professional observes the client engaged in ordinary, day-to-day behavior in either a clinical or natural setting.

rating scale assessment in which a numerical value is assigned to specific behavior that is listed in the scale.

frequency count assessment in which the frequency of a particular behavior is counted.

personality inventory paper and pencil or computerized test that consists of statements that require a specific, standardized response from the person taking the test.

PERSONALITY INVENTORIES

Trait theorists are typically more interested in personality descriptions. They tend to use an assessment known as a **personality inventory**, a questionnaire that has a standard list of questions and only requires certain specific answers, such as "yes," "no," and "can't decide." The standard nature of the questions (everyone gets the same list) and the lack of open-ended answers make these assessments far more objective and reliable than projective tests (Garb et al., 1998), although they are still a form of self-report. One such personality inventory is Cattell's 16PF, described earlier in this chapter. Costa and McCrae (2000) have recently revised their original *Neuroticism/Extraversion/Openness Personality Inventory (NEO-PI)*, which is based on the five-factor model of personality traits (discussed on pages 511–512).

Another inventory in common use is the *Myers-Briggs Type Indicator (MBTI)*. This inventory is based on the ideas of Carl Jung and looks at four personality dimensions. The *sensing/intuition* (S/I) dimension includes people who prefer to rely on what they can see, hear, and so on through their own physical senses (sensing) and, on its opposite end, those who look for patterns and trust their hunches (intuition). Sensing people are very detail oriented, preferring to work only with the known facts, whereas intuitive people are more willing to use metaphors, analogies, and look for possibilities. The *thinking/feeling* (T/F) dimension runs from those who prefer to use logic, analysis, and experiences that can be verified as facts (thinkers) to those who tend to make decisions based on their personal values and emotional reactions (feeling). *Introversion/extraversion* (I/E) is the same classic dimension that began with Jung and is represented in nearly every personality theory, including the Big Five. *Perceiving/judging* (P/J) describes those who are willing to adapt and modify decisions, be spontaneous, and who are naturally curious and tend to put off making a final decision so that all possibilities are covered (perceiving) as well as those who are the opposite: the action-oriented, decisive, get-the-task-done-and-don't-look-back type (judging). These four dimensions can differ for each individual, resulting in 16 (4 × 4) possible personality types: ISTJ, ISTP, ISFP, ISFJ, and so on (Briggs & Myers, 1998).

The Myers-Briggs is often used to assess personality to help people know the kinds of careers for which they may best be suited. For example, a person who scored high on the extravert, sensing, thinking, and judging dimensions would be an ESTJ. A typical description of this personality type would be a person who needs to analyze information and bring order to the outer world. Such people are organizers, energetic in completing tasks, and practical. They also take their responsibilities seriously and expect others to do so as well. School administrators, for example, are often ESTJs.

Other common personality tests include the Eysenck Personality Questionnaire (Eysenck & Eysenck, 1993), the Keirsey Temperament Sorter II (Keirsey, 1998), the California Psychological Inventory (Gough, 1995), and the Sixteen Personality Factor Questionnaire (Cattell, 1994).

THE MMPI-2 By far the most common personality inventory is the *Minnesota Multiphasic Personality Inventory, Version II*, or *MMPI-2*, which specifically tests for abnormal behavior patterns in personality (Butcher & Rouse, 1996; Butcher et al., 2000, 2001). This questionnaire consists of 567 statements such as "I am often very tense" or "I believe I am being plotted against." The person taking the test must answer "true," "false," or "cannot say." The MMPI has 10 clinical scales and 8 validity scales in addition to numerous subscales. Each scale tests for a particular kind of behavior. The behavior patterns include relatively mild personality problems such as excessive worrying and shyness as well as more-serious disorders such as schizophrenia and depression. LINK to Chapter Fourteen: Psychological Disorders, pp. 546, 556.

How can you tell if a person is telling the truth on a personality inventory?

How can you tell if a person is telling the truth on a personality inventory?

Validity scales, which are built into any well-designed psychological inventory, are intended to indicate whether or not a person taking the inventory is responding honestly. Responses to certain items on the test will indicate if people are trying to make themselves look better or worse than they are, for example, and certain items are repeated throughout the test in a slightly different form, so that anyone trying to "fake" the test will have difficultly responding to those items consistently (Butcher et al., 2001). For example, if one of the statements is "I am always happy" and a person responds "true" to that statement, the suspicion would be that this person is trying to look better than he or she really is. If several of the validity scale questions are answered in this way, the conclusion is that the person is not being honest. **Read** on **mypsychlab.com**

Read and learn more about the clinical scales of the MMPI-2 on **mypsychlab.com**

PROBLEMS WITH PERSONALITY INVENTORIES The advantage of personality inventories over projective tests and interviews is that inventories are standardized (i.e., everyone gets exactly the same questions and the answers are scored in exactly the same way). In fact, responses to inventories are often scored on a computer. Observer bias and bias of interpretation are simply not possible because this kind of assessment is objective rather than subjective. The validity and reliability of personality inventories are generally recognized as being greatly superior to those of projective tests (Anastasi & Urbina, 1997).

There are some problems, however. The validity scales, for example, are a good check against cheating, but they are not perfect. Some people are still able to fake their answers and respond in what they feel are the socially appropriate ways (Anastasi & Urbina, 1997; Hicklin & Widiger, 2000). Despite the best intentions of the test creators, individual responses to specific questions may also vary as they may be interpreted in different ways by different individuals, and are very likely to be subject to cultural influences (Kagan, 2010). Other problems have to do with human nature itself: Some people may develop a habit of picking a particular answer rather than carefully considering the statement, whereas others may simply grow tired of responding to all those statements and start picking answers at random.

13.8 13.9

CONCEPT MAP

biology of personality

- behavioral genetics studies how much of an individual's personality is due to inherited traits
- identical twins are more similar than fraternal twins or unrelated people in many facets of personality
- adoption studies of twins have confirmed that genetic influences account for a great deal of personality development, regardless of shared or nonshared environments
- personality factors of the five-factor model have nearly a 50% rate of heritability across cultures; variations in personality are about 25–50% inherited

Personality: Biological Roots and Assessment

personality assessment can be assessed through various methods, based on perspective endorsed

- **interview:** largely self-report through unstructured or semistructured interview; problems—people can lie or interviewer can be biased (halo effect)
- **projective tests:** ambiguous visual stimuli are used and clients are asked to describe what they see, unconscious concerns or fears are "projected" onto stimulus (e.g., Rorschach Inkblot Test and TAT); problems—nature of tests result in possible subjectivity in interpretation; reliability is suspect
- **behavioral assessments:** direct observation is used to quantify behavior through rating scales and frequency counts; problems—observer bias and lack of environmental control
- **personality inventories:** standard list of questions, often with "yes/true" or "no/false" answers, typically more objective and reliable, many have validity and reliability scales built in; problems—still able to provide false answers and, although difficult, can "fake bad" or "fake good"
  - NEO-PI
  - MBTI
  - MMPI-2

see Table 13.4

PRACTICE quiz How much do you remember? ANSWERS ON PAGE AK-2.

Pick the best answer.

1. Which of the following is not one of the traits found to have a genetic component in studies of identical twins?
   a. intelligence
   b. leadership abilities
   c. antagonism
   d. aggressiveness
2. The five-factor model trait dimensions have been shown to have _________.
   a. no relevance in other cultures.
   b. only a 20 percent rate of heritability.
   c. relevance only for Western cultures.
   d. about a 50 percent rate of heritability across cultures.
3. Which of the following countries would be most likely to have an individualistic trait, according to Hofstede?
   a. Japan
   b. Vietnam
   c. England
   d. Brazil
4. Which of the following methods would NEVER be used by a behaviorist?
   a. interview
   b. projective test
   c. direct observation
   d. personality inventory
5. Which method of personality assessment offers the most objective measurement?
   a. interview
   b. projective test
   c. direct observation
   d. personality inventory
6. Observer bias would be a problem for any of the following methods except _________.
   a. interview.
   b. projective test.
   c. direct observation.
   d. personality inventory.

Brainstorming: Should employers require prospective employees to take a personality test? Why or why not? Would such a requirement make more sense in certain professions, and what professions might those be?

Applying Psychology to Everyday Life: The Biological Basis of the Big Five

In 1796, Dr. Franz Joseph Gall, a German physician, developed a theory of personality traits based on the shape of a person's skull. This theory became very popular in the nineteenth century and was known as *phrenology.* Gall believed that certain areas of the brain were responsible for certain aspects of personality, and that the skull itself would bulge out according to which of these traits were dominant (Finger, 1994; Simpson, 2005). As psychology became a scientific area of its own, nonscience-based ideas such as phrenology were soon relegated to the realm of pseudoscience.

How odd, then, that a recent study by Dr. Colin DeYoung and colleagues (DeYoung et al., 2010) seems to suggest that there are indeed certain areas of the brain associated with certain personality traits. Specifically, DeYoung and colleagues believe they have evidence for the biological seat of four of the Big Five: extraversion, neuroticism, agreeableness, and conscientiousness.

In their study, 116 volunteers answered a questionnaire about their Big Five personality traits. The participants were then subjected to a structural magnetic resonance imaging technique for identifying the volume of specific areas of the brain. One participant was found to be near the group average for personality traits, and that individual's brain image was used as a reference image to which the other participants' scans were compared.

The trait of *extraversion* was associated with a higher volume in the medial orbitofrontal cortex (underside of frontal lobe, directly above the eyes). This area of the brain is associated with recognizing the value of rewarding information. *Neuroticism* was associated with lower brain volume in several areas responding to threat, punishment, and negative emotions. Reduced volumes were found in the dorsomedial prefrontal cortex (toward the top and middle of the prefrontal cortex) and in the left posterior hippocampus. Neuroticism was also associated with higher brain volume in the middle cingulate cortex (cortical component of limbic system), associated with error detection and response to pain. Areas of the brain associated with the intentions of actions and mental states of others were correlated to *agreeableness,* with the area of the posterior cingulate cortex showing a greater volume in individuals high in that trait and a lesser volume in the left superior temporal sulcus.

Conscientiousness seemed associated with the left lateral prefrontal cortex, an area located on the side of the frontal lobes involved in planning, working memory, and voluntary control of behavior. (The researchers did look at areas that might be associated with the fifth of the Big Five traits, *openness,* but failed to find any significant differences.)

This study, and the others like it that are sure to follow, is part of the growing area of personality neuroscience and an important step in linking personality to the physical structure and functioning of the brain. No skull bulges needed! **Simulate** on **mypsychlab.com**

Simulate the biological basis of the "Big Five" personality factors on **mypsychlab.com**

Questions for Further Discussion

1. We use personality assessments to make predictions about employment, marriage, and stability among others. What might it mean for the future if a brain scan becomes part of personality assessment?
2. If personality traits are so closely linked with brain structure, what does that say about the plasticity of personality? Are people able to change their traits? Their behavior?

chapter summary

Listen on **mypsychlab.com** Listen to an audio file of your chapter **www.mypsychlab.com**

Theories of Personality

13.1 What is personality, and how do the various perspectives in psychology view personality?

- Personality is the unique way individuals think, feel, and act. It is different from character and temperament but includes those aspects.
- The four traditional perspectives in the study of personality are the psychodynamic, behavioristic (including social cognitive theory), humanistic, and trait perspectives.

The Man and the Couch: Sigmund Freud and the Psychodynamic Perspective

13.2 How did Freud's historical view of the mind and personality form a basis for psychodynamic theory?

- The three divisions of the mind are the conscious, preconscious, and unconscious. The unconscious can be revealed in dreams.
- The three parts of the personality are the id, ego, and superego.
- The id works on the pleasure principle and the ego works on the reality principle.
- The superego is the moral center of personality, containing the conscience, and is the source of moral anxiety.
- The conflicts between the demands of the id and the rules and restrictions of the superego lead to anxiety for the ego, which uses defense mechanisms to deal with that anxiety.
- The personality develops in a series of psychosexual stages: oral (id dominates), anal (ego develops), phallic (superego develops), latency (period of sexual repression), and genital (sexual feelings reawaken with appropriate targets).
- The Oedipus and Electra complexes (sexual "crushes" on the opposite-sex parent) create anxiety in the phallic stage, which is resolved through identification with the same-sex parent.
- Fixation occurs when conflicts are not fully resolved during a stage, resulting in adult personality characteristics reflecting childhood inadequacies.

13.3 How did Jung, Adler, Horney, and Erikson modify Freud's theory?

- The neo-Freudians changed the focus of psychoanalysis to fit their own interpretation of the personality, leading to the more modern version known as the psychodynamic perspective.
- Jung developed a theory of a collective unconscious.
- Adler proposed feelings of inferiority as the driving force behind personality and developed birth order theory.
- Horney developed a theory based on basic anxiety and rejected the concept of penis envy.
- Erikson developed a theory based on social rather than sexual relationships, covering the entire life span.

13.4 How does modern psychoanalytic theory differ from that of Freud?

- Current research has found support for the defense mechanisms and the concept of an unconscious mind that can influence conscious behavior, but other concepts cannot be scientifically researched.

The Behaviorist and Social Cognitive View of Personality

13.5 How do behaviorists and social cognitive theorists explain personality?

- Behaviorists define personality as a set of learned responses or habits.
- The social cognitive view of personality includes the concept of reciprocal determinism, in which the environment, characteristics of the person, and the behavior itself all interact.

- Self-efficacy is a characteristic in which a person perceives a behavior as more or less effective based on previous experiences, the opinions of others, and perceived personal competencies.
- Locus of control is a determinant of personality in which one either assumes that one's actions directly affect events and reinforcement one experiences or that such events and reinforcements are the result of luck, fate, or powerful others.
- Personality, in the form of potential behavior patterns, is also determined by an interaction between one's expectancies for success and the perceived value of the potential reinforcement.
- Behaviorist personality theory has scientific support but is criticized as being too simplistic.

The Third Force: Humanism and Personality

13.6 How do humanists such as Carl Rogers explain personality?

- Humanism developed as a reaction against the negativity of psychoanalysis and the deterministic nature of behaviorism.
- Carl Rogers proposed that self-actualization depends on proper development of the self-concept.
- The self-concept includes the real self and the ideal self. When these two components do not match or agree, anxiety and disordered behavior result.
- Unconditional positive regard from important others in a person's life helps the formation of the self-concept and the congruity of the real and ideal selves, leading to a fully functioning person.
- Humanistic theory is not scientifically researched but has been effective in therapy situations.

Trait Theories: Who Are You?

13.7 What are the history and current views of the trait perspective?

- Trait theorists describe personality traits in order to predict behavior.
- Allport first developed a list of about 200 traits and believed that these traits were part of the nervous system.
- Cattell reduced the number of traits to between 16 and 23 with a computer method called factor analysis.
- Several researchers have arrived at five trait dimensions that have research support across cultures, called the Big Five or five-factor model. The five factors are openness, conscientiousness, extraversion, agreeableness, and neuroticism.
- Cross-cultural research has found support for the five-factor model of personality traits in a number of different cultures.
- Future research will explore the degree to which child-rearing practices and heredity may influence the five personality factors.
- Behavior genetics is a field of study of the relationship between heredity and personality.

The Biology of Personality: Behavioral Genetics

13.8 What part do biology, heredity, and culture play in personality?

- Studies of twins and adopted children have found support for a genetic influence on many personality traits, including intelligence, leadership abilities, traditionalism, nurturance, empathy, assertiveness, neuroticism, and extraversion.

CLASSIC STUDIES IN PSYCHOLOGY: Geert Hofstede's Four Dimensions of Cultural Personality

- Hofstede's cross-cultural management study revealed four basic dimensions of personality along which cultures may vary: individualism/collectivism, power distance, masculinity/femininity, and uncertainty avoidance.

Assessment of Personality

13.9 What are the advantages and disadvantages of the following measures of personality: interviews, projective tests, behavioral assessment, personality inventories, and online personality tests?

- Interviews are used primarily by psychoanalysts and humanists and can include structured or unstructured interviews.
- Disadvantages of interviews can include the halo effect and bias of the interpretation on the part of the interviewer.
- Projective tests are based on the defense mechanism of projection and are used by psychoanalysts. Projective tests include the Rorschach inkblot test and the Thematic Apperception Test.
- Projective tests can be useful in finding starting points to open a dialogue between therapist and client but have been criticized for being low in reliability and validity.
- Behavioral assessments are primarily used by behaviorists and include direct observation of behavior, rating scales of specific behavior, and frequency counts of behavior.
- Behavioral assessments have the disadvantage of the observer effect, which causes an observed person's behavior to change, and observer bias on the part of the person doing the assessment.
- Personality inventories are typically developed by trait theorists and provide a detailed description of certain personality traits. They are objective tests rather than subjective.
- The NEO-PI is based on the five-factor model, whereas the Myers-Briggs Type Indicator is based on Jung's theory of personality types.
- The MMPI-2 is designed to detect abnormal personality.
- Personality inventories include validity scales to prevent cheating, but such measures are not perfect and cheating is sometimes possible.

Applying Psychology to Everyday Life: The Biological Basis of the Big Five

- Personality neuroscience is a growing area of research and brain structure differences associated with some aspects of the Big Five dimensions of personality have been identified using structural MRI.

test YOURSELF

ANSWERS ON PAGE AK-2.

Pick the best answer.

1. Which of the following is the definition of personality?
   - a. the characteristics with which each person is born
   - b. the moral and ethical behavior of a person
   - c. the unique way an individual thinks, feels, and acts
   - d. changes in behavior according to experiences
2. Freud's emphasis on sex and sexual development was mostly due to _________.
   - a. his own problems with sexuality.
   - b. the culture within which he and his patients existed at the time.
   - c. an increase in sexual deviancy across Europe in the nineteenth century.
   - d. the influence of his colleagues.
3. Which of Freud's parts of the personality is the most like short-term memory?
   - a. conscious
   - b. preconscious
   - c. unconscious
   - d. subconscious
4. Stephen wants a new cell phone he saw in the local electronics store, but he doesn't have enough money to pay for it. Which structure of Stephen's personality would urge him to take the phone while no one in the store was looking?
   - a. id
   - b. ego
   - c. superego
   - d. libido
5. Which structure of the personality, according to Freud, works on the reality principle?
   - a. id
   - b. ego
   - c. superego
   - d. libido
6. The _________ develops in the _________ stage as a result of identification.
   - a. ego; oral
   - b. id; oral
   - c. superego; phallic
   - d. superego; latency
7. Tina's boss gives her a bad review, making Tina feel lousy. When she arrives at home, she yells at her husband and children. Tina is likely displaying _________.
   - a. escape.
   - b. withdrawal.
   - c. displacement.
   - d. projection.
8. Jerome, an 8-year-old boy, constantly teases one of the girls in his third-grade classroom. He calls her names and chases her on the playground, telling other boys that she has "cooties." If Jerome's real feelings are more like attraction to this girl, we can say that Jerome is exhibiting _________.
   - a. displacement.
   - b. projection.
   - c. reaction formation.
   - d. sublimation.
9. Three-year-old Brandon has watched his father, a chef, when he prepares meals for the family. This year, Brandon has asked for a play kitchen for his birthday. Freud would say that Brandon is beginning the process of _________ as a way of resolving his Oedipal conflict.
   - a. compensation
   - b. identification
   - c. sublimation
   - d. denial
10. According to Adler, middle children tend to be _________.
    - a. overachieving.
    - b. competitive.
    - c. resentful of the freedom of the older child.
    - d. filled with feelings of inferiority.
11. Research has begun to show some support for which of Freud's concepts?
    - a. the existence of an id, ego, and superego
    - b. the order of the psychosexual stages
    - c. the concept of an unconscious mind
    - d. the existence of the Oedipus complex
12. To explain a person's personality, behaviorists would look to _________.
    - a. early childhood emotional traumas.
    - b. the kind of love, warmth, and affection given to the person by his or her parents.
    - c. the early experiences of rewards and punishments for certain behavior.
    - d. the constellation of personality traits possessed by the person.
13. For Bandura, one of the most important person variables in determining personality is _________.
    - a. self-efficacy.
    - b. expectancy.
    - c. reinforcement value.
    - d. self-motivation.
14. Unlike the psychodynamic view, the social cognitive view of personality _________.
    - a. tries to explain how people become the people they are.
    - b. stresses the importance of early childhood in personality development.
    - c. is fully able to explain all the complexities of human behavior.
    - d. has been scientifically tested.
15. The striving for fulfillment of one's potential is called _________.
    - a. self-concept.
    - b. self-efficacy.
    - c. self-actualization.
    - d. locus of control.
16. According to Rogers, anxiety and neurotic behavior result from _________.
    - a. unconscious conflicts and desires.
    - b. a mismatch between the real self and ideal self.
    - c. receiving too much unconditional positive regard from significant others.
    - d. learned habits of behavior.
17. Which of the following viewpoints has different goals from the other three?
    - a. psychoanalytic
    - b. behaviorism
    - c. humanism
    - d. trait theory
18. How many source traits did Cattell use in developing his personality inventory?
    - a. 5
    - b. 10
    - c. 16
    - d. 23

19. The five-factor model of personality traits includes all but which of the following?
a. openness
b. self-sufficiency
c. extraversion
d. neuroticism

20. Dr. Jackson is constantly late for her classes and often shows up late for her office hours, leaving students waiting in the hallway outside her door for nearly an hour at times. Using the five-factor model, which dimension would show a very low score for Dr. Jackson?
a. self-sufficiency
b. openness
c. agreeableness
d. conscientiousness

21. The study of the inherited portions of personality is called __________.
a. twin studies.
b. adoptive studies.
c. behavioral genetics.
d. adoptive genetics.

22. According to Hofstede, cultures that have many strict rules and laws with lots of security and safety measures and that tend to hold only one philosophical or religious belief are high in __________.
a. individualism.
b. power distance.
c. masculinity.
d. uncertainty avoidance.

23. If a patient is having trouble talking about what is bothering them, a psychoanalyst might turn to a(n) __________ to probe the patient's unconscious conflicts.
a. objective test
b. projective test
c. personality inventory
d. observational study

24. The Rorschach test requires test-takers to __________.
a. tell stories about a picture with people in it.
b. answer hundreds of questions about their feelings and thoughts.
c. perform tasks while an observer watches through a one-way mirror.
d. look at ambiguous visual stimuli and tell what they think it is.

25. Which type of assessment would have the least problem with reliability?
a. subjective test
b. projective test
c. personality inventory
d. observational study

26. Which of the following is not a type of behavioral assessment?
a. direct observation
b. Thematic Apperception Test
c. rating scale
d. frequency count

27. Which of the following is based on the five-factor model?
a. NEO-PI
b. MBTI
c. MMPI-2
d. 16PF

28. Personality neuroscience is an emerging field, offering evidence of a possible relationship between various aspects of personality with __________.
a. brain structure and function
b. the structure and function of individual neurons
c. skull shape and size
d. neuroticism

13 theories of personality

13.1 13.2 13.3 13.4 p. 504

personality
unique way in which each individual thinks, acts, and feels throughout life

Theories of Personality

perspectives/theories
different ways of viewing and explaining personality
- **psychodynamic**
- **behavioral and social cognitive views**
- **humanistic**
- **trait**

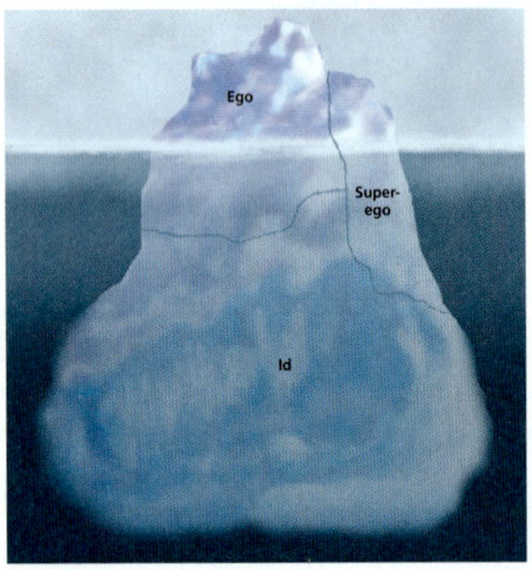

Psychodynamic Perspective

basic aspects
- mind made up of different levels of awareness—conscious, preconscious, and unconscious
- personality stems from interplay and conflict between demands made by the id, restrictions set forth by the superego, and direction by the ego
- disordered behavior is product of constant conflict and anxiety; ego uses unconscious defense mechanisms as ways to manage anxiety/conflict between three parts of personality (see Table 13.1)

psychosexual stages of personality development
- id exists at birth; ego and superego develop in childhood
- different erogenous zones are sources of conflict as individual ages; unresolved conflicts result in individuals getting stuck or fixated at that stage

Table 13.2
Freud's Psychosexual Stages

STAGE	AGE	FOCUS OF PLEASURE	FOCUS OF CONFLICTS	DIFFICULTIES AT THIS STAGE AFFECT LATER
Oral	Birth to 1 or $1\frac{1}{2}$ years old	Oral activities (such as sucking, feeding, and making noises with the mouth)	Weaning	• Ability to form interpersonal attachments • Basic feelings about the world • Tendency to use oral forms of aggression, such as sarcasm • Optimism or pessimism • Tendency to take charge or be passive
Anal	1 or $1\frac{1}{2}$ to 3 years old	Bowel and bladder control	Toilet training	• Sense of competence and control • Stubbornness or willingness to go along with others • Neatness or messiness • Punctuality or tardiness
Phallic	3 to 6 years old	Genitals	Sexual awareness	• Development of conscience through identification with same-sex parent • Pride or humility
Latency	6 years old to puberty	Social skills (such as the ability to make friends) and intellectual skills; dormant period in terms of psychosexual development	School, play, same-sex friendships	• Ability to get along with others
Genital	Puberty to death	Sexual behavior	Sexual relationship with partner	• Immature love or indiscriminate hate • Uncontrollable working or inability to work

Note: Freud thought that the way a person finds pleasure or is prevented from satisfying urges for pleasure at each stage affects personality. Thus, like Erikson's stage model described in Chapter Eight, Freud's model argues that the way a person deals with particular psychological challenges or potential areas of conflict has long-term effects on personality.

a group of Freud's students and followers of the psychoanalytic perspective, called the neo-Freudians, modified his theory and altered the focus of psychoanalysis
- **Jung**
- **Adler**
- **Horney**
- **Erikson**

modern psychodynamic theory maintains focus on unconscious mind, concept of defense mechanisms is still useful

despite several criticisms, Freud's theory still important—first to suggest personality develops through stages, that we are not always consciously aware of reasons for behavior, and early life experiences influence who we are later in life

13.5 13.6 p. 509

Behavioral, Social Cognitive, and Humanistic Perspectives

behavioral and social cognitive
- for behaviorists, personality is a set of learned responses and habits, gained through classical and operant conditioning
- in social cognitive view, both learning (individual and through imitation of models) and cognitive processes (such as anticipation, judgment, and memory) are important
  - **Bandura**
  - **Rotter**

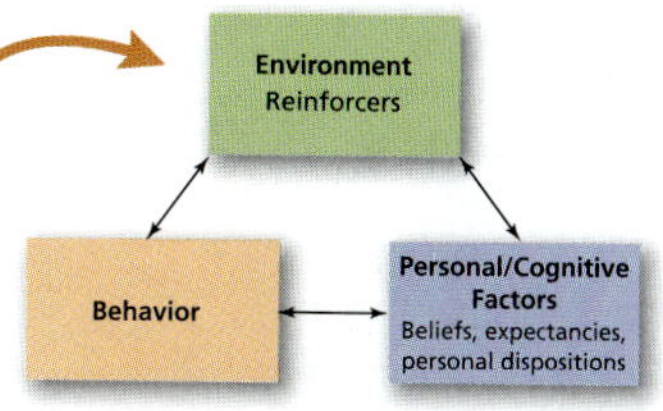

humanistic
referred to as the third force in psychology (after psychoanalysis and behaviorism); based largely on work of Rogers and Maslow
- **Rogers**
- **self-concept**
- **self-actualization**
- when there is congruence between real and ideal selves, one is considered to be fully functioning and capable of reaching the goal of self-actualization

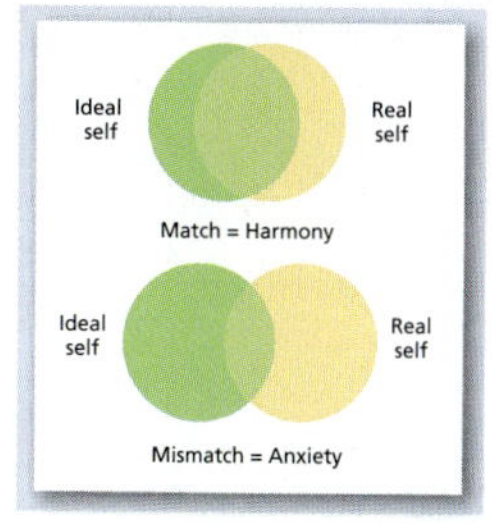

13.7 p. 513

Trait Theories

- a trait is a consistent, enduring way of thinking, feeling, or behaving; trait theories attempt to describe personality in terms of a person's traits
- **Allport:** believed there were 200 traits that were wired into the nervous system to guide a person's behavior
- **Cattell:** developed concept of surface traits and source traits; identified 16 source traits through factor analysis (later suggested 23); developed assessment questionnaire to identify original 16 trait dimensions (16PF)
- several groups' work resulted in the **five-factor model** (Big Five, OCEAN)—openness, conscientiousness, extraversion, agreeableness, neuroticism
- Mischel and others have suggested that there is a trait–situation interaction; there is evidence of the Big Five trait dimensions across various cultures

Table 13.3
The Big Five

HIGH SCORER CHARACTERISTICS	FACTOR (OCEAN)	LOW SCORER CHARACTERISTICS
Creative, artistic, curious, imaginative, nonconforming	Openness (O)	Conventional, down-to-earth, uncreative
Organized, reliable, neat, ambitious	Conscientiousness (C)	Unreliable, lazy, careless, negligent, spontaneous
Talkative, optimistic, sociable, affectionate	Extraversion (E)	Reserved, comfortable being alone, stays in the background
Good-natured, trusting, helpful	Agreeableness (A)	Rude, uncooperative, irritable, aggressive, competitive
Worrying, insecure, anxious, temperamental	Neuroticism (N)	Calm, secure, relaxed, stable

Source: Adapted from McCrae & Costa (1990).

13.8 13.9 p. 522

Personality: Biological Roots and Assessment

biology of personality
- behavioral genetics studies how much of an individual's personality is due to inherited traits
- identical twins are more similar than fraternal twins or unrelated people in many facets of personality
- adoption studies of twins have confirmed that genetic influences account for a great deal of personality development, regardless of shared or nonshared environments
- personality factors of the five-factor model have nearly a 50% rate of heritability across cultures; variations in personality are about 25–50% inherited

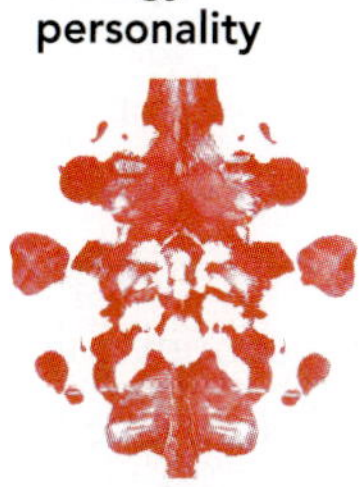

personality assessment
personality can be assessed through various methods, based on perspective endorsed

14 psychological disorders

CHAPTER OUTLINE

THE PSYCHOLOGICAL IMPACT OF DISASTERS

When disaster strikes, it leaves in its wake both physical and psychological damage. Hurricane Katrina, a Category 3 hurricane that ripped across the Gulf Coast of the United States in August of 2005, is still causing serious emotional disturbances for many people, especially children and adolescents who experienced the devastation (McLaughlin et al., 2009; McLaughlin et al., in press).

Now a new disaster has unfolded in the Gulf of Mexico, far more slowly but in many ways, no less devastating. On April 20, 2010, a deep-water oil rig in the Gulf exploded and began to release anywhere from 35,000 to 60,000 barrels of crude oil each day—and possibly more—the equivalent, some say, of more than fifteen *Exxon Valdez* spills, the Alaskan disaster of 1989, which is still causing psychological problems of its own today (Macdonald et al., 2010; National Wildlife Federation, 2010).

Dr. Steven Picou, a sociology professor at the University of South Alabama, has been studying the psychological impact of the *Valdez* oil spill for 21 years. He and other researchers found that the unfolding effects of that disaster included escalation of depression, posttraumatic stress disorder, anxiety disorders and other mental-health problems long after the original spill. An oil-spill related suicide occurred 4 full years *after* the *Valdez* spill. A charter boat captain in Alabama became severely depressed over the loss of his livelihood and committed suicide just a little over *2 months* after the BP spill (Kam, 2010).

The BP spill is expected to set off a chain reaction of tragedies and mental disorders relating to the stresses of failing fishing industries, decreased tourism, and health issues caused by the oil that is lingering in the Gulf (and beyond) as well as washing up on shore; it is a chain reaction that may be felt for decades. Within 4 months of the spill, an increase in number of reported deaths has been seen in the population of chronically homeless people of the Gulf Coast area. Many of the deaths are believed to have been caused by stress-induced heart attacks, as well as the result of suicide (Kam, 2010). To date, there have been hundreds of claims filed against BP for the stress, anxiety, and psychophysiological disorders brought on by the psychological ramifications of the oil spill. The litigation over these claims is a major stressor in and of itself, and there may be decades of unfolding psychological harm ahead.

Why study abnormal behavior?

Because it is all around us, which raises many questions: How should one react? What should be done to help? What kind of person develops a mental illness? Could this happen to someone close to you? The key to answering these questions is to develop an understanding of just what is meant by abnormal behavior and the different ways in which behavior can depart from the "normal" path.

learning objectives

14.1 How has mental illness been explained in the past, how is abnormal behavior defined today, and what is the impact of cultural differences in defining abnormality?

14.2 How can psychological disorders be explained within the biological and psychological models?

14.3 What are the different types of psychological disorders and how common are they?

14.4 What are the different types of anxiety disorders, their symptoms, and causes?

14.5 What are the different types of mood disorders and their causes?

14.6 What are the two primary types of eating disorders, how do they differ, and who are they most likely to affect?

14.7 How do the various dissociative disorders differ, and how do they develop?

14.8 What are the main symptoms, types, and causes of schizophrenia?

14.9 How do the various personality disorders differ, and what is thought to be the cause of personality disorders?

14.10 What are some of the future directions in psychopathology?

study tip

As you are reading this chapter, take a look back at pages I-11–I-12 in *Psychology in Action* for some ways to reduce the stress and anxiety of studying and finishing assignments.

What Is Abnormality?

I've heard people call the different things other people do "crazy" or "weird." How do psychologists decide when people are really mentally ill and not just a little odd?

I've heard people call the different things other people do "crazy" or "weird." How do psychologists decide when people are really mentally ill and not just a little odd?

Exactly what is meant by the term *abnormal behavior*? Abnormal compared to what? Who gets to decide what is normal and what is not? Has the term always meant what it means now? These are just a few questions that come to mind when thinking about the study of abnormal behavior, or **psychopathology**.

A VERY BRIEF HISTORY OF PSYCHOLOGICAL DISORDERS

14.1 How has mental illness been explained in the past, how is abnormal behavior defined today, and what is the impact of cultural differences in defining abnormality?

Dating from as early as 3000 B.C.E., archaeologists have found human skulls with small holes cut into them, and close examination indicates that the holes were made while the person was still alive. Many of the holes show evidence of healing, meaning that the person survived the process. The process of cutting holes into the skull of a living person is called "trepanning" (also spelled *trephining*). Although trepanning is still done today to relieve pressure of fluids on the brain, in ancient times the reason may have had more to do with releasing the "demons" possessing the poor victim (Gross, 1999). Ancient peoples might well have assumed that some among them who were behaving oddly were possessed by evil spirits.

Hippocrates (460–377 B.C.E.), a Greek physician during the time in which the rest of the world and even many Greeks believed in the demonic possession explanation of mental illness, challenged that belief with his assertion that illnesses of both the body and the mind were the result of imbalances in the body's vital fluids, or *humors*. Although Hippocrates was not correct in his assumptions about the humors of the body (phlegm, black bile, blood, and yellow bile), his was the first recorded attempt to explain abnormal behavior as due to some biological process.

Moving forward in time, people of the Middle Ages believed in spirit possession (a belief influenced by the teachings of the Roman Catholic Church and the remnants of other religious/cultural systems) as one cause of abnormal behavior. The treatment of choice for such maladies was a religious one: *exorcism*, or the formal casting out of the demon through a religious ritual (Lewis, 1995). During the Renaissance, belief in demonic possession (in which the possessed person was seen as a victim) gave way to a belief in witchcraft, and mentally ill persons were most likely called witches and put to

psychopathology the study of abnormal behavior.

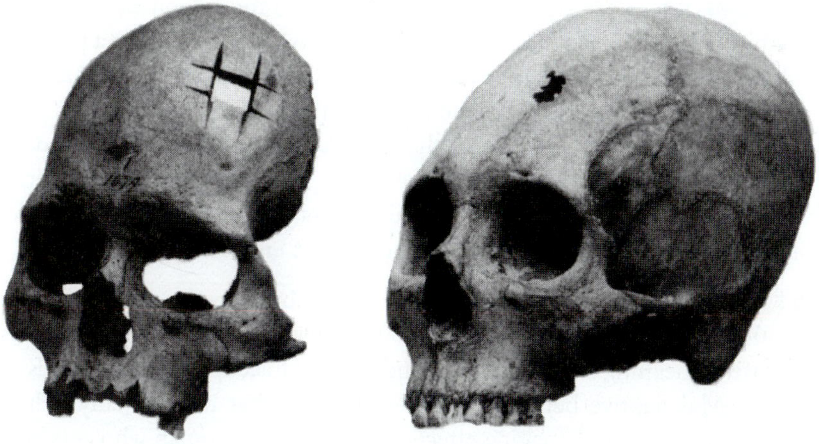

These human skulls clearly show the signs of trepanning, a process in which ancient priests or medicine men cut holes into the skulls of a living person, perhaps to release the "demons" that were making the person's behavior odd or disturbed. Some who were treated in this way must have survived, as the holes show some evidence of healing.
American Museum of Natural History.

death. Although there is wide disagreement about exactly how many people were hanged, burned, stoned, or drowned as witches, some estimates place the number at around 100,000 (Barstow, 1995).

WHAT IS ABNORMAL?

Defining abnormal behavior or abnormality is not as simple as it might seem at first. The easy way out is to say that abnormal behavior is behavior that is not normal, but what does that mean? It's complicated, as you'll see by considering different criteria for determining abnormality.

By what criterion (or criteria) of abnormality might this person be considered abnormal? Would your perception of him change if the context were a Fourth of July celebration?

STATISTICAL DEFINITION One way to define *normal* and *abnormal* is to use a statistical definition. Frequently occurring behavior would be considered normal, and behavior that is rare would be abnormal. That kind of definition works fine with a behavior such as talking to others, as the two rarer possibilities would be not talking to anyone at all and talking too much to too many people—both of which would be considered abnormal. But what about a behavior such as happiness? Should a person who is very happy be labeled abnormal? Statistical definitions of abnormality wouldn't work for intelligence either, as only intellectual disability or mental retardation (the lower end of a distribution of intelligence in a population) would be considered undesirable and abnormal (Troisi & McGuire, 2002). People possessing a higher degree of intelligence than is "normal" are actually highly respected.

SOCIAL NORM DEVIANCE Another way of defining abnormality is to see it as something that goes against the norms or standards of the society in which the individual lives. For example, refusing to wear clothing in a society that does not permit nudity would be seen as abnormal. But deviance (variation) from social norms is not always labeled as negative, abnormal behavior. For instance, a person who decides to become a monk and live in a monastery in the United States would be exhibiting unusual behavior, and certainly not what the society considers a standard behavior, but it wouldn't be a sign of abnormality.

The **situational context** (the social or environmental setting of a person's behavior) can also make a difference in how behavior is labeled. For example, if a man comes to a therapist complaining of people listening in on his phone conversations and spying on all his activities, the therapist's first thought might be that the man is suffering from feelings of persecution. But if the man then explains that he is in a witness protection program, the complaints take on an entirely different and quite understandable tone.

situational context the social or environmental setting of a person's behavior.

subjective discomfort emotional distress or emotional pain.

maladaptive anything that does not allow a person to function within or adapt to the stresses and everyday demands of life.

sociocultural perspective perspective in which abnormal behavior (as well as normal behavior) is seen as the product of the learning and shaping of behavior within the context of the family, the social group to which one belongs, and the culture within which the family and social group exist.

cultural relativity the need to consider the unique characteristics of the culture in which behavior takes place.

culture-bound syndromes disorders found only in particular cultures.

SUBJECTIVE DISCOMFORT One sign of abnormality is when the person experiences a great deal of **subjective discomfort**, or emotional distress while engaging in a particular behavior. A woman who suffers from a fear of going outside her house, for example, would experience a great deal of anxiety when trying to leave home and distress over being unable to leave. However, all behavior that might be considered abnormal does not necessarily create subjective discomfort in the person committing the act—a serial killer, for example, does not experience emotional distress after taking someone's life, and some forms of disordered behavior involve showing no emotions at all.

INABILITY TO FUNCTION NORMALLY Behavior that does not allow a person to fit into society or function normally can also be labeled abnormal. This kind of behavior is termed **maladaptive**, meaning that the person finds it hard to adapt to the demands of day-to-day living. Maladaptive behavior includes behavior that may initially help a person cope but has harmful or damaging effects. For example, a woman who cuts herself to relieve anxiety does experience initial relief but is harmed by the action. Maladaptive behavior is a key element in the definition of abnormality.

A migrant farming background has been found to be related to increased symptoms of anxiety and depression among college students of Mexican heritage when compared to those without a migrant background.

THE SOCIOCULTURAL PERSPECTIVE What's normal in one culture may be abnormal in another culture. In the **sociocultural perspective** of abnormality, abnormal behavior (as well as normal behavior) is seen as the product of behavioral shaping within the context of family influences, the social group to which one belongs, and the culture within which the family and social group exist. In particular, cultural differences in abnormal behavior must be addressed when psychological professionals are attempting to assess and treat members of a culture different from that of the professional. **Cultural relativity** is a term that refers to the need to consider the unique characteristics of the culture in which the person with a disorder was nurtured to be able to correctly diagnose and treat the disorder (Castillo, 1997). For example, in most traditional Asian cultures, mental illness is often seen as a shameful thing that brings disgrace to one's family. It may be seen as something inherited and, therefore, something that would hurt the marriage chances of other family members, or it may be seen as stemming from something the family's ancestors did wrong in the past (Ritts, 1999; Ying, 1990). This leads many Asian people suffering from disorders that would be labeled as depression or even schizophrenia to report bodily symptoms rather than emotional or mental ones because bodily ailments are more socially acceptable (Fedoroff & McFarlane, 1998; Lee, 1995; Ritts, 1999). Furthermore, there are disorders unique to specific cultures called **culture-bound syndromes**, that are only found in particular cultures. For example, anorexia nervosa and bulimia nervosa are most often found in Western societies. **Read** on **mypsychlab.com**

Read and learn more about culture-bound syndromes on **mypsychlab.com**

It is important to take into account other background and influential factors such as socioeconomic status and education level. Another area of awareness should be primary language and if applicable, degree of acculturation. Psychosocial functioning has been part of the diagnostic process for some time now, but traditionally, greater attention has been paid to specifically identifying symptoms of pathology rather than focusing on the environmental factors that influence an individual's overall level of functioning (Ro & Clark, 2009). For example, in one recent study, college students of Mexican heritage with migrant farming backgrounds reported more symptoms of anxiety and depression as compared to nonmigrant college students of Mexican heritage (Mejía & McCarthy, 2010). The nature of migrant farming poses different stressors than those faced by nonmigrant families.

So how do psychologists decide what is abnormal?

A WORKING DEFINITION OF ABNORMALITY

So how do psychologists decide what is abnormal?

To get a clear picture of abnormality, it is often necessary to take all of the factors discussed in the preceding section into account. Psychologists and other psychological professionals must consider several different criteria when determining whether or not a behavior is abnormal (at least two of these criteria must be met to form a diagnosis of abnormality):

1. Is the behavior unusual, such as experiencing severe panic when faced with a stranger or being severely depressed in the absence of any stressful life situations?
2. Does the behavior go against social norms? (And keep in mind that social norms change over time—e.g., homosexuality was once considered a psychological disorder rather than a variation in sexual orientation.)
3. Does the behavior cause the person significant subjective discomfort?
4. Is the behavior maladaptive or result in an inability to function?
5. Does the behavior cause the person to be dangerous to self or others, as in the case of someone who tries to commit suicide or who attacks other people without reason?

Abnormal behavior that includes at least two of these five criteria is perhaps best classified by the term **psychological disorder**, which is defined as any pattern of behavior that causes people significant distress, causes them to harm themselves or others, or harms their ability to function in daily life.

Before moving on, it is important to clarify how the term *abnormality* is different from the term *insanity*. Simulate on mypsychlab.com

psychological disorder any pattern of behavior that causes people significant distress, causes them to harm others, or harms their ability to function in daily life.

Simulate the definition of psychological disorders on **mypsychlab.com**

issues in psychology

Abnormality Versus Insanity

Although only psychological professionals can diagnose disorders and determine the best course of treatment for someone who suffers from mental illness, lawyers and judges are charged with determining how the law should address crimes committed under the influence of mental illness. Psychologists and psychiatrists determine whether or not certain behavior is abnormal, but they do not decide whether a certain person is insane. In the United States, *insanity* is not a psychological term; it is a legal term used to argue that a mentally ill person who has committed a crime should not be held responsible for his or her actions because that person was unable to understand the difference between right and wrong at the time of the offense. This argument is called the *insanity defense*.

Many people are diagnosed with psychological disorders either before or after committing crimes. If an individual with schizophrenia burns down a house because he believes God has told him to do it, he has certainly committed a crime—but is he truly guilty? Supporters of the insanity defense might argue that he is not.

It is important to keep in mind that not everyone who has been diagnosed with a psychological disorder is a good candidate to use the insanity defense to plead innocent to a criminal charge. Very few people use the insanity defense in court, and, of those people, only a small percentage are found innocent by reason of insanity.

This photograph shows Keith, Deanna, Joshua, and Luck Laney of New Chapel Hill, Texas, in seemingly happier times. On May 12, 2003, Deanna Laney killed her two young sons by crushing their heads with rocks, believing that God had ordered her to kill her children. On the day of the killings, Deanna suffered a number of visual and auditory hallucinations. She was found innocent by reason of insanity in 2004 and has been committed to a maximum security state hospital, where she is undergoing treatment for paranoid schizophrenia.

Questions for Further Discussion

1. Should the insanity defense be permitted? Why or why not?
2. In what situations should a person exonerated of a crime due to the insanity defense still be required to face some sort of penalty, such as community service or financial restitution?

What causes psychological disorders?

Models of Abnormality

What causes psychological disorders?

In Chapter Thirteen several different theories of personality were discussed. These theories of personality can be used to describe and explain the formation of not only ordinary behavior and personality but disordered behavior and abnormal personality as well. How one explains disordered behavior, then, depends on which theoretical model is used to explain personality in general.

14.2 How can psychological disorders be explained within the biological and psychological models?

THE BIOLOGICAL MODEL: MEDICAL CAUSES FOR PSYCHOLOGICAL DISORDERS

One model that was not discussed in Chapter Thirteen is the **biological model**, which proposes that psychological disorders have a biological or medical cause (Gamwell & Tomes, 1995). This model explains disorders such as anxiety, depression, and schizophrenia as caused by chemical imbalances, genetic problems, brain damage and dysfunction, or some combination of those causes. For example, as you may recall from the discussion of trait theory and the five-factor theory of personality traits, LINK to Chapter Thirteen: Theories of Personality, pp. 511–512, a growing body of evidence suggests that basic personality traits are as much influenced by genetic inheritance as they are by experience and upbringing, even across cultures (Bouchard, 1994; Herbst et al., 2000; Jang et al., 1996; Loehlin, 1992; Loehlin et al., 1998). One of the Big Five factors was neuroticism, for example, and it is easy to see how someone who scores high in neuroticism would be at greater risk for anxiety-based disorders.

The biological or medical model has had a great deal of influence, especially in the language used to describe disorders: *mental illness*, *symptoms of disorder*, and terms such as *diagnosis*, *mental patient*, *mental hospital*, *therapy*, and *remission* all come from medical terminology. The use of such terms, although still widespread, may tend to bias the assumptions of professionals who are not psychiatrists or medical doctors toward a biological cause for disordered behavior or the idea that disorders might be diseases that can be "cured." Many disorders can effectively be controlled but may not be fully resolved. LINK to Chapter Fifteen: Psychological Therapies, p. 601.

THE PSYCHOLOGICAL MODELS

Although biological explanations of psychological disorders are influential, they are not the only ways or even the first ways in which disorders are explained. Several psychological models explain disordered behavior as the result of various forms of emotional, behavioral, or thought-related malfunctioning.

PSYCHODYNAMIC VIEW: HIDING PROBLEMS The psychodynamic model, based on the work of Freud and his followers, LINK to Chapter Thirteen: Theories of Personality, pp. 495-503, explains disordered behavior as the result of repressing one's threatening thoughts, memories, and concerns in the unconscious mind (Carducci, 1998). These repressed thoughts and urges try to resurface, and disordered behavior develops as a way of keeping the thoughts repressed. According to this view, a woman who has unacceptable thoughts of sleeping with her brother-in-law might feel "dirty" and be compelled to wash her hands every time those thoughts threaten to become conscious, ridding herself symbolically of the "dirty" thoughts.

BEHAVIORISM: LEARNING PROBLEMS Behaviorists, who define personality as a set of learned responses, have no trouble explaining disordered behavior as being learned just like normal behavior (Skinner, 1971; Watson, 1913). For example, when Emma was a

biological model model of explaining behavior as caused by biological changes in the chemical, structural, or genetic systems of the body.

small child, a spider dropped onto her leg, causing her to scream and react with fear. Her mother made a big fuss over her, giving her lots of attention. Each time Emma saw a spider after this, she screamed again, drawing attention to herself. Behaviorists would say that Emma's fear of the spider was classically conditioned, and her screaming reaction was positively reinforced by all the attention.

COGNITIVE PERSPECTIVE: THINKING PROBLEMS **Cognitive psychologists** study the way people think, remember, and mentally organize information; they see abnormal behavior as resulting from illogical thinking patterns (Mora, 1985). A cognitive psychologist might explain Emma's fear of spiders as distorted thinking: "All spiders are vicious and will bite me, and I will die!" Emma's particular thinking patterns put her at a higher risk of depression and anxiety than those of a person who thinks more logically.

BIOPSYCHOSOCIAL PERSPECTIVE: ALL OF THE ABOVE

In recent years, the biological, psychological, and sociocultural influences on abnormality are no longer seen as independent causes of abnormal behavior. Instead, these influences interact with one another to cause the various forms of disorders. For example, a person may have a genetically inherited tendency for a type of disorder, such as anxiety, but may not develop a full-blown disorder unless the family and social environments produce the right stressors at the right time in development. How accepting of such disorders the particular culture is will also play a part in determining the exact degree and form that anxiety disorder might take. This is known as the **biopsychosocial model** of disorder, which has become a very influential way to view the connection between mind and body.

Diagnostic and Statistical Manual of Mental Disorders, Fourth Edition, Text Revision (DSM-IV-TR)

14.3 **What are the different types of psychological disorders and how common are they?**

In 1952, the first edition of the *Diagnostic and Statistical Manual of Mental Disorders (DSM)* was published to help psychological professionals diagnose psychological disorders. The current version of the *DSM* is called the *Diagnostic and Statistical Manual of Mental Disorders, Fourth Edition, Text Revision (DSM-IV-TR)* (American Psychiatric Association, 2000). (The Text Revision version did not change any categories from the older *DSM-IV* but added new text material to the existing categories.)

CATEGORIES IN THE *DSM-IV-TR*

The *DSM-IV-TR* describes about 250 different psychological disorders. Each disorder is described in terms of its symptoms, the typical path the disorder takes as it progresses, and a checklist of specific criteria that must be met in order for the diagnosis of that disorder to be made. The manual also divides these disorders and relevant facts about the person being diagnosed along five different categories, or axes. A psychologist or psychiatrist assesses the person on each of these five axes.

Axis I, Clinical Disorders, contains the disorders that bring most people to the attention of a psychological professional. With the exception of personality disorders, all of the psychological disorders are listed on this axis. Axis II lists personality disorders along with mental retardation (most often now called *intellectual disability*). Personality disorders are a part of the individual's personality and are relatively stable and enduring, affecting relationships, careers, and behavior. The stability and enduring nature of personality disorders seem more similar to a condition

cognitive psychologists psychologists who study the way people think, remember, and mentally organize information.

biopsychosocial model perspective in which abnormal behavior is seen as the result of the combined and interacting forces of biological, psychological, social, and cultural influences.

Table 14.1

Axis I Disorders of the *DSM-IV-TR*

DISORDER	EXAMPLES
Disorders usually first diagnosed in infancy, childhood, or adolescence	Learning disabilities, ADHD, bed-wetting, speech disorders, conduct disorder, oppositional defiant disorder
Delirium, dementia, amnesia, and other cognitive disorders	Alzheimer's, Parkinson's, amnesia due to physical causes
Psychological disorders due to a general medical condition	Personality change because of a brain tumor
Substance-related disorders	Alcoholism, drug addictions
Schizophrenia and other psychotic disorders	Schizophrenia, delusional disorders, paranoid psychosis
Mood disorders	Depression, mania, bipolar disorders
Anxiety disorders	Panic disorder, phobias, stress disorders
Somatoform disorders	Hypochondriasis, conversion disorder
Factitious disorders	Pathological lying, Munchausen syndrome
Dissociative disorders	Dissociative identity disorder (formerly multiple personality), amnesia not due to physical causes
Sexual and gender identity disorders	Sexual desire disorders, paraphilias (sexual arousal to objects or unusual situations)
Eating disorders	Anorexia, bulimia
Sleep disorders	Insomnia, sleep terror disorder, sleepwalking, narcolepsy
Impulse-control disorders not classified elsewhere	Kleptomania, pathological gambling, pyromania
Adjustment disorders	Mixed anxiety, conduct disturbances

Adapted from the American Psychiatric Association, *DSM-IV-TR* (2000).

Explore the axes of the *DSM-IV-TR* on **mypsychlab.com**

such as mental retardation, which is a developmental disorder affecting many areas of the individual's life. **Explore** on **mypsychlab.com**

Axis III includes physical disorders that affect a person's psychological well-being, such as juvenile diabetes, chromosome disorders such as Klinefelter's syndrome, and high blood pressure. Axis IV contains information about problems in the person's life that might affect adjustment, such as the death of a loved one, the loss of a job, or poverty. Finally, Axis V, Global Assessment of Functioning, is an overall judgment made by the psychological professional of the person's mental health and adjustment, literally a rating on a scale of 0 to 100. For example, scores of 91–100 would be interpreted as superior functioning, 71–80 as temporary problems due to stress, and 41–50 would indicate serious symptoms or impairment in functioning.

For a listing and brief description of the disorders found on Axis I, see Table 14.1.

That table has a pretty long list of disorders, but most people don't get these problems, right?

HOW COMMON ARE PSYCHOLOGICAL DISORDERS?

That table has a pretty long list of disorders, but most people don't get these problems, right?

Actually, psychological disorders are more common than most people might think. In any given year, about 26.2 percent of American adults over age 18 suffer from a mental disorder; that comes to about 57.7 million people in the United States. Statistically, mental disorders are the leading cause of disability in the United States and Canada (National Institute of Mental Health, 2010). In fact, it is quite common for people to suffer from more than one mental disorder at a time, such as a person with depression who also has a substance-abuse disorder, or a person with an anxiety disorder who also suffers from sleep disorders. Approximately 45 percent of individuals with a mental disorder meet criteria for 2 or more disorders (National Institute of Mental Health, 2010). Table 14.2 has percentages of selected psychological disorders in the United States. (Note that this table does not include all of the disorders that occur in the 57.7 million adults in the United States mentioned earlier in this paragraph.)

Statistically speaking, about 1 out of every 5 of the people in this crowd probably suffers from some form of psychological disorder.

THE PROS AND CONS OF LABELS

With its lists of disorders and their corresponding symptoms, the *DSM-IV-TR* helps psychological professionals diagnose patients and provide those patients with labels that explain their conditions. In the world of psychological diagnosis and treatment, labels like *depression, anxiety*, and *schizophrenia* can be very helpful: They make up a common language in the mental-health community, allowing psychological professionals to communicate with each other clearly and efficiently. Labels establish distinct diagnostic categories that all professionals recognize and understand, and they help patients receive effective treatment.

However, labels can also be dangerous—or, at the very least, overly prejudicial. In 1972, researcher David Rosenhan asked healthy participants to enter psychiatric hospitals and complain that they were hearing voices. All of the participants, whom Rosenhan called "pseudopatients," were admitted into the hospitals and diagnosed with either schizophrenia or manic depression. Once the pseudopatients were admitted, they stopped pretending to be ill and acted as they normally would, but the hospital staff's

Table 14.2

Yearly Occurrence of Psychological Disorders in the United States

CATEGORY OF DISORDER	SPECIFIC DISORDER	PERCENTAGE OF U.S. POPULATION AND NUMBER AFFECTED*
Depressive disorders	All types	9.5% or 20.9 million
	Major depressive disorder	6.7% or 14.8 million
	Dysthymic disorder	1.5% or 3.3 million
	Bipolar disorder	2.6% or 5.7 million
Schizophrenia	All types	1.1% or 2.4 million
Anxiety disorders	All types	18.1% or 40 million
	Panic disorder	2.7% or 6 million
	Obsessive-compulsive disorder	1% or 2.2 million
	Posttraumatic stress disorder	3.5% or 7.7 million
	Generalized anxiety disorder	3.1% or 6.8 million
	Social phobia	6.8% or 15 million
	Agoraphobia	0.8% or 1.8 million
	Specific phobia	8.7% or 19.2 million

*Percentage of adults over age 18 affected annually and approximate number within the population based on 2004 United States Census data.

Adapted from National Institute of Mental Health (2010).

interpretation of the pseudopatients' normal behavior was skewed by the label of mental illness. For example, hospital workers described one pseudopatient's relatively normal relationships with family and friends as evidence of a psychological disorder, and another pseudopatient's note-taking habits were considered to be a pathological behavior. The pseudopatients had been diagnosed and labeled, and those labels stuck, even when actual symptoms of mental illness disappeared. Rosenhan concluded that psychological labels are long lasting and powerful, affecting not only how other people see mental patients but how patients see themselves (Rosenhan, 1973).

Labels can be time-saving and even life-saving tools, but they can also bias us, affect our judgment, and give us preconceived notions that may very well turn out to be false. Just to be clear, the diagnostic labels listed in the *DSM-IV-TR* are intended to help both psychologists and patients, and they *do* help. As you read on, remember the power that labels have to shape our perceptions of reality.

Before describing the various categories and types of disorders, here is a word of caution: It's very easy to see oneself in these disorders. Medical students often become convinced that they have every one of the symptoms for some rare, exotic disease they have been studying. Psychology students studying abnormal behavior can also become convinced that they have some mental disorder, a problem that can be called "psychology student's syndrome." The problem is that so many psychological disorders are really ordinary variations in human behavior taken to an extreme. For example, some people are natural-born worriers. They look for things that can go wrong around every corner. That doesn't make them disordered—it makes them pessimistic worriers. Remember, it doesn't become a disorder until the worrying causes them significant distress, causes them to harm themselves or others, or harms their ability to function in everyday life. So if you start "seeing" yourself or even your friends and family in any of the following discussions, don't panic—all of you are *probably* okay.

14.1 14.2 14.3

CONCEPT MAP

Psychological Disorders

- **what is abnormality?**
  - **psychopathology** is the study of abnormal behavior; mental illness has been defined in various ways throughout history (e.g., possession, evil spirits, bodily imbalances)
  - current definitions of abnormality are based on several factors
    - **statistical definition**
    - **social norm deviance**
    - **subjective discomfort**
    - **inability to function normally**
  - disorders vary according to culture; cultural sensitivity and relativity are necessary in diagnosing and treating psychological disorders
  - overall, psychological disorders are any pattern of behavior that causes significant distress, causes them to harm themselves or others, or harms their ability to function in daily life
- **models of abnormality**
  explanations for disordered behavior depend on theoretical model used to explain personality in general
  - **biological model:** proposes that psychological disorders have a biological or medical cause
  - **psychological models:** propose that disordered behavior is the result of various forms of emotional, behavioral, or thought-related malfunctioning
    - **psychodynamic**
    - **behavioral**
    - **cognitive**
  - **biopsychosocial perspective:** incorporates biological, psychological, and sociocultural factors
- ***Diagnostic and Statistical Manual of Mental Disorders, Fourth Edition, Text Revision (DSM–IV–TR)***
  - *DSM* first published in 1952, current version *(DSM–IV–TR)* published in 2000
  - currently describes approximately 250 different psychological disorders and includes diagnostic criteria along five different categories, or axes (see Table 14.1)
  - in general, approximately 26% of adults over age 18 in the United States suffer from a mental disorder (see Table 14.2)

PRACTICE quiz How much do you remember? ANSWERS ON PAGE AK-2.

Pick the best answer.

1. Who would be most likely to assume that psychological disorders are caused by an imbalance in the fluids of the body?
   a. an ancient Egyptian physician
   b. a modern psychiatrist
   c. an ancient Greek physician
   d. a physician of the Middle Ages
2. Lisa has started having feelings of fearfulness about going to school. She has begun to suffer from headaches and stomachaches and has missed several days of school already. Lisa's condition is abnormal from the _________ definition.
   a. statistical
   b. situational context
   c. social deviance
   d. subjective discomfort
3. In the United States, insanity is not a _________ term; it is a _________ term.
   a. behavioral; psychoanalytic
   b. legal; medical
   c. legal; psychological
   d. psychological; legal
4. Elliot is attracted to his beautiful cousin, Ginny, but knows that she is too closely related to him. He believes he has successfully overcome this forbidden attraction but still finds that every time Ginny is near him he is overwhelmed with feelings of anxiety and feels the need to wash his hands. Which model of abnormality would most likely explain Elliot's behavior?
   a. psychodynamic
   b. cognitive
   c. behavioral
   d. biological
5. Which model of abnormality explains abnormal behavior as caused by illogical thinking?
   a. psychodynamic
   b. cognitive
   c. behavioral
   d. biopsychosocial

Brainstorming: What might be the advantages of explaining disorders within the biopsychosocial model rather than using a biological or psychological model only?

Anxiety Disorders: What, Me Worry?

14.4 What are the different types of anxiety disorders, their symptoms, and causes?

The category of **anxiety disorders** includes all disorders in which the most dominant symptom is excessive or unrealistic anxiety. Anxiety can take very specific forms, such as a fear of a specific object, or it can be a very general emotion, such as that experienced by someone who is worried and doesn't know why.

But doesn't everybody have anxiety sometimes? What makes it a disorder?

But doesn't everybody have anxiety sometimes? What makes it a disorder?

Everyone does have anxiety, and some people have a great deal of anxiety at times. When talking about anxiety disorders, the anxiety is either excessive—greater than it should be given the circumstances—or unrealistic. If final exams are coming up and a student hasn't studied enough, that student's anxiety is understandable and realistic. But a student who has studied, has done well on all the exams, and is very prepared and still worries *excessively* about passing is showing an unrealistic amount of anxiety. For more about test anxiety, see the Applying Psychology to Everyday Life section in this chapter. People who are in danger of losing their job might experience quite a bit of anxiety, but its source is obvious and understandable. But someone whose life is going well, and for whom nothing bad is looming in the future, and who still feels extremely anxious may be experiencing an anxiety disorder. **Free-floating anxiety** is the term given to anxiety that seems to be unrelated to any realistic, known factor, and it is often a symptom of an anxiety disorder (Freud & Gay, 1977).

anxiety disorders disorders in which the main symptom is excessive or unrealistic anxiety and fearfulness.

free-floating anxiety anxiety that is unrelated to any realistic, known source.

phobia an irrational, persistent fear of an object, situation, or social activity.

PHOBIC DISORDERS: WHEN FEARS GET OUT OF HAND

One of the more specific anxiety disorders is a **phobia**, an irrational, persistent fear of something. The "something" might be an object or a situation or may involve social interactions. For example, many people would feel fear if they suddenly came upon a live snake as they were walking and would take steps to avoid the snake. Although those same people would not necessarily avoid a *picture* of a snake in a book, a person with a phobia of snakes would. Avoiding a live snake is rational; avoiding a picture of a snake is not. **Read** on **mypsychlab.com**

Read and learn more about phobias on **mypsychlab.com**

Many people get nervous when they have to speak in front of an audience. Fear of public speaking is a common social phobia. Can you remember a time when you experienced a fear like this?

SOCIAL PHOBIAS (SOCIAL ANXIETY DISORDER) **Social phobias** (also called *social anxiety disorders*) involve a fear of interacting with others or being in a social situation and are some of the most common phobias people experience (World Health Organization International Consortium in Psychiatric Epidemiology, 2000). People with a social phobia are afraid of being evaluated in some negative way by others, so they tend to avoid situations that could lead to something embarrassing or humiliating. They are very self-conscious as a result. Common types of social phobia are stage fright, fear of public speaking, and fear of urinating in a public restroom. Not surprisingly, people with social phobias often have a history of being shy as children (Sternberger et al., 1995).

SPECIFIC PHOBIAS A **specific phobia** is an irrational fear of some object or specific situation, such as a fear of dogs, or a fear of being in small, enclosed spaces (**claustrophobia**). Other specific phobias include a fear of injections (*trypanophobia*), fear of dental work (*odontophobia*), fear of blood (*hematophobia*), and fear of heights (**acrophobia**). For a listing of common phobias, see Table 14.3.

AGORAPHOBIA A third type of phobia is **agoraphobia**, a Greek name that literally means "fear of the marketplace." Although that makes it sound like a social phobia, agoraphobia is a little more complicated. It is actually the fear of being in a place or situation (social or not) from which escape is difficult or impossible if something should go wrong (American Psychiatric Association, 2000). So individuals with agoraphobia are often afraid of not only crowds but also of crossing bridges, traveling in a car or plane, eating in restaurants, and sometimes even of leaving the house. To be in any of these situations or to even think about being in such situations can lead to extreme feelings of anxiety and even panic attacks (see the following section about panic attacks).

If a person has agoraphobia, it might be difficult to even go to work or to the store, right?

If a person has agoraphobia, it might be difficult to even go to work or to the store, right?

Exactly. People with specific phobias can usually avoid the object or situation without too much difficulty and people with social phobias may simply avoid jobs and situations that involve meeting people face to face. But people with agoraphobia cannot avoid their phobia's source because it is simply being outside in the real world. A severe case of agoraphobia can make a person's home a prison, leaving the person trapped inside unable to go to work, shop, or engage in any kind of activity that requires going out of the home.

Agoraphobia includes a fear of crossing bridges, although this bridge is enough to test anyone's courage.

social phobia fear of interacting with others or being in social situations that might lead to a negative evaluation.

specific phobia fear of objects or specific situations or events.

claustrophobia fear of being in a small, enclosed space.

Table 14.3

Common Phobias and Their Scientific Names

FEAR OF	SCIENTIFIC NAME
Washing and bathing	Ablutophobia
Spiders	Arachnophobia
Lightning	Ceraunophobia
Dirt, germs	Mysophobia
Snakes	Ophidiophobia
Darkness	Nyctophobia
Fire	Pyrophobia
Foreigners, strangers	Xenophobia
Animals	Zoophobia

Source: Adapted from Culbertson (2003).

PANIC DISORDER

Fourteen-year-old Dariya was sitting in science class watching a film. All of a sudden, she started feeling really strange. Her ears seemed to be stuffed with cotton and her vision was very dim. She was cold, had broken out in a sweat, and felt extremely afraid for no good reason. Her heart was racing and she immediately became convinced that she was dying. A friend sitting behind her saw how pale she had become and tried to ask her what was wrong, but Dariya couldn't speak. She was in a state of panic and couldn't move.

Dariya's symptoms are the classic symptoms of a **panic attack**, a sudden onset of extreme panic with various physical symptoms: racing heart, rapid breathing, a sensation of being "out of one's body," dulled hearing and vision, sweating, and dry mouth (Kumar & Oakley-Browne, 2002). Many people who have a panic attack think that they are having a heart attack and can experience pain as well as panic, but the symptoms are caused by the panic, not by any actual physical disorder. Psychologically, the person having a panic attack is in a state of terror, thinking that this is it, death is happening, and many people may feel a need to escape. The attack happens without warning and quite suddenly. Although some panic attacks can last as long as half an hour, some last only a few minutes, with most attacks peaking within 10 to 15 minutes.

Having a panic attack is not that unusual, especially for adolescent girls and young adult women (Eaton et al., 1994; Hayward et al., 1989, 2000). Researchers have also found evidence that cigarette smoking greatly increases the risk of panic attacks in adolescents and young adults (Johnson, 2000; Zvolensky et al., 2003). Regardless of the age of onset, it is only when panic attacks become so frequent that they affect a person's ability to function in day-to-day life that they become a **panic disorder**. When a fear of having panic attacks in a public place prevents the person from going out into unfamiliar or exposed places, it is called **panic disorder with agoraphobia**.

Many people try to figure out what triggers a panic attack and then do their best to avoid the situation if possible. If driving a car sets off an attack, they don't drive. If being in a crowd sets off an attack, they don't go where crowds are. It is easy to see how having panic disorder can often lead to agoraphobia. Psychologists and psychiatrists will classify a person as having either a panic disorder with agoraphobia or a panic disorder without agoraphobia.

OBSESSIVE-COMPULSIVE DISORDER

Sometimes people get a thought running through their head that just won't go away, like when a song gets stuck in one's mind. If that particular thought causes a lot of anxiety, it can become the basis for an **obsessive-compulsive disorder** or OCD. OCD is a disorder in which intruding* thoughts that occur again and again (obsessions, such as a fear that germs are on one's hands) are followed by some repetitive, ritualistic behavior or mental acts (compulsions, such as repeated hand washing, counting, etc.). The compulsions are meant to lower the anxiety caused by the thought (Soomro, 2001).

I knew someone who had just had a baby, and she spent the first few nights home with the baby checking it to see if it was breathing—is that an obsessive-compulsive disorder?

No, almost all new parents check their infant's breathing frequently at first. Remember psychology student's syndrome? Everyone experiences a little obsessive thinking from time to time or has some small ritual that just makes them feel better. The difference is whether or not a person *likes* to do the ritual (but doesn't *have* to do it) or feels *compelled* to do the ritual and feels extreme anxiety if unable to complete it.

*intruding: forcing one's way in; referring to something undesirable that enters awareness.

acrophobia fear of heights.

agoraphobia fear of being in a place or situation from which escape is difficult or impossible.

panic attack sudden onset of intense panic in which multiple physical symptoms of stress occur, often with feelings that one is dying.

panic disorder disorder in which panic attacks occur frequently enough to cause the person difficulty in adjusting to daily life.

panic disorder with agoraphobia fear of leaving one's familiar surroundings because one might have a panic attack in public.

obsessive-compulsive disorder disorder in which intruding, recurring thoughts or obsessions create anxiety that is relieved by performing a repetitive, ritualistic behavior or mental act (compulsion).

"RONALD IS EXTREMELY COMPULSIVE."

www.cartoonstock.com

I knew someone who had just had a baby, and she spent the first few nights home with the baby checking it to see if it was breathing—is that an obsessive-compulsive disorder?

acute stress disorder (ASD) a disorder resulting from exposure to a major stressor, with symptoms of anxiety, dissociation, recurring nightmares, sleep disturbances, problems in concentration, and moments in which people seem to "relive" the event in dreams and flashbacks for as long as 1 month following the event.

posttraumatic stress disorder (PTSD) a disorder resulting from exposure to a major stressor, with symptoms of anxiety, dissociation, nightmares, poor sleep, reliving the event, and concentration problems, lasting for more than 1 month.

generalized anxiety disorder disorder in which a person has feelings of dread and impending doom along with physical symptoms of stress, which lasts 6 months or more.

The distress caused by a failure or inability to successfully complete the compulsive behavior or mental act is a defining feature of OCD.

ACUTE STRESS DISORDER (ASD) AND POSTTRAUMATIC STRESS DISORDER (PTSD)

Both general and specific stressors were discussed in Chapter Eleven, Stress and Health. Two anxiety disorders—*Acute Stress Disorder* and *Posttraumatic Stress Disorder*—are related to exposure to significant and traumatic stressors. The severe stress and anxiety experienced by people after 9/11, Hurricane Katrina, and the April 2010 oil spill in the Gulf of Mexico can lead to **acute stress disorder (ASD)**. The symptoms of ASD occur within 4 weeks of the traumatic event and include anxiety, dissociative symptoms (such as emotional numbness/lack of responsiveness, not being aware of surroundings, dissociative amnesia), recurring nightmares, sleep disturbances, problems in concentration, and moments in which people seem to "relive" the event in dreams and flashbacks for as long as 1 month following the event. One recently published study gathered survey information from Katrina evacuees at a major emergency shelter and found that 62 percent of those sampled met the criteria for having acute stress disorder (Mills et al., 2007).

After the BP oil spill in April of 2010, anywhere from 35 to 45 percent of people living around or near the Gulf of Mexico reported suffering symptoms of stress (Abramson et al., 2010).

When the symptoms associated with ASD last for more than 1 month, the disorder is then called **posttraumatic stress disorder (PTSD)**. In the same study (Mills et al., 2007), researchers concluded that it was likely that anywhere from 38 to 49 percent of all the evacuees sampled were at risk of developing PTSD that would still be present 2 years after the disaster. Furthermore, whereas the onset of ASD occurs within 4 weeks of the traumatic event, the symptoms of PTSD may not occur until 6 months or later after the event (American Psychiatric Association, 2000). Treatment of these stress disorders may involve psychotherapy and the use of drugs to control anxiety. LINK to Chapter Fifteen: Psychological Therapies, pp. 596–597.

Researchers have found that women have almost twice the risk of developing PTSD than do men and that the likelihood increases if the traumatic experience took place before the woman was 15 years old (Breslau et al., 1997, 1999). Children may also suffer different effects from stress than do adults. Severe PTSD has been linked to a decrease in the size of the hippocampus in children with the disorder (Carrion et al., 2007). The hippocampus is important in the formation of new long-term declarative memories (LINK to Chapter Six: Memory, pp. 225–226) and this may have a detrimental effect on learning and the effectiveness of treatments for these children. One recent study of older veterans over a 7-year period (Yaffe et al., 2010) found that those with PTSD were more likely to develop dementia (10.6 percent risk) when compared to those without PTSD (only 6.6 percent risk). Some life experiences lend themselves to people experiencing traumatic events. For example, the rate of PTSD (self-reported) among combat-exposed military personnel has tripled since 2001 (Smith et al., 2008).

What about people who are just worriers? Can that become a disorder?

GENERALIZED ANXIETY DISORDER

What about people who are just worriers? Can that become a disorder?

Remember free-floating anxiety? That's the kind of anxiety that has no real external source and may be experienced by people with **generalized anxiety disorder**, in which excessive anxiety and worries (apprehensive expectations) occur more days than not for at least 6 months. People with this disorder may also experience anxiety about a number of events or activities (such as work or school performance). These feelings of anxiety persist 6 months or more and have no real source that can be pinpointed, nor can the person control the feelings even if an effort is made to do so.

People with this disorder are just plain worriers (Ruscio et al., 2001). They worry *excessively* about money, their children, their lives, their friends, the dog, as well as things no one else would see as a reason to worry. They feel tense, edgy, get tired easily, and may have trouble concentrating. They have muscle aches, they experience sleeping problems, and are often irritable—all signs of stress. General anxiety disorder is often found occurring with other anxiety disorders and depression.

magnification the tendency to interpret situations as far more dangerous, harmful, or important than they actually are.

all-or-nothing thinking the tendency to believe that one's performance must be perfect or the result will be a total failure.

overgeneralization the tendency to interpret a single negative event as a never-ending pattern of defeat and failure.

minimization the tendency to give little or no importance to one's successes or positive events and traits.

CAUSES OF ANXIETY DISORDERS

Different perspectives on how personality develops offer different explanations for anxiety disorders. For example, the *psychodynamic model* sees anxiety as a kind of danger signal that repressed urges or conflicts are threatening to surface (Freud & Gay, 1977). A phobia is seen as a kind of displacement, in which the phobic object is actually only a symbol of whatever the person has buried deep in his or her unconscious mind—the true source of the fear. A fear of knives might mean a fear of one's own aggressive tendencies, or a fear of heights may hide a suicidal desire to jump.

Behaviorists believe that anxious behavioral reactions are learned. They see phobias, for example, as nothing more than classically conditioned fear responses, as was the case with "Little Albert" (Rachman, 1990; Watson & Rayner, 1920). LINK to Chapter Five: Learning, p. 177. *Cognitive psychologists* see anxiety disorders as the result of illogical, irrational thought processes. One way in which people with anxiety disorders show irrational thinking (Beck, 1976, 1984) is through **magnification**, or the tendency to "make mountains out of molehills" by interpreting situations as being far more harmful, dangerous, or embarrassing than they actually are. In panic disorder, for example, a person might interpret a racing heartbeat as a sign of a heart attack instead of just a momentary arousal.

Another distorted thought process is **all-or-nothing thinking**, in which a person believes that his or her performance must be perfect or the result will be a total failure. **Overgeneralization** (a single negative event interpreted as a never-ending pattern of defeat), jumping to conclusions without facts to support that conclusion, and **minimization** (giving little or no emphasis to one's successes or positive events and traits) are other examples of irrational thinking.

Growing evidence exists that *biological* factors contribute to anxiety disorders. Generalized anxiety disorder, for example, has been linked to an imbalance in several neurotransmitters in the nervous system, including lower levels of both serotonin and GABA (Brawman-Mintzer & Lydiard, 1997; Rynn et al., 2000). Lower levels of these neurotransmitters may reduce the ability to calm reactions to stress. Research has linked panic disorder to a possible defect in the way serotonin binds to its receptors in the nervous system (Neumeister et al., 2004). Recent studies with mice have indicated that an area of the hippocampus known as the ventral hippocampus (vHPC) may help control anxiety by "talking" to the medial prefrontal cortex, the area of the brain important in processing emotional awareness (Adhikari et al., 2010). LINK to Chapter Two: The Biological Perspective, p. 76.

Some evidence suggests that these chemical imbalances may have a genetic component, meaning that anxiety disorders such as obsessive-compulsive disorder, phobias, and panic disorder can be passed from parent to child through more than just observational learning (Karayiorgou et al., 1997; Lesch et al., 1996; Logue et al., 2003). Twin studies have provided more evidence for a genetic basis for anxiety disorders, particularly panic disorder and the phobias, with

Anxiety disorders affect children as well as adults.

affect in psychology, a term indicating "emotion" or "mood."

mood disorders disorders in which mood is severely disturbed.

major depression severe depression that comes on suddenly and seems to have no external cause, or is too severe for current circumstances.

some studies finding that the heritability of panic disorder is about 44 percent, agoraphobia about 39 percent, and anxiety disorder about 30 percent (Hettema et al., 2001; Tsuang et al., 2004; Villafuerte & Burmeister, 2003). Neuroimaging studies using the scanning techniques of PET and fMRI, LINK to Chapter Two: The Biological Perspective, pp. 68–69, have revealed that the amygdala, an area of the limbic system, is more active in phobic people responding to pictures of spiders than in nonphobic people (LeDoux, 2003; Rauch et al., 2003).

Anxiety disorders are found around the world, although the particular form the disorder takes might be different in various cultures. For example, in some Latin American cultures anxiety can take the form of *ataque de nervios*, or "attack of nerves," in which the person may have fits of crying, shout uncontrollably, experience sensations of heat, and become very aggressive, either verbally or physically. These attacks usually come after some stressful event such as the death of a loved one (American Psychiatric Association, 2000). Several syndromes that are essentially types of phobias are specific to certain cultures. For example, *koro* (found primarily in China and a few other South Asian and East Asian countries) involves a fear that one's genitals are shrinking (Pfeiffer, 1982), and TKS (found primarily in Japan) involves excessive fear and anxiety, but in this case it is the fear that one will do something in public that is socially inappropriate or embarrassing, such as blushing, staring, or having an offensive body odor (Kirmayer, 1991). Panic disorder is found almost universally at about the same rate all over the world (Weissman et al., 1997). **Watch** on **mypsychlab.com**

Watch a video about anxiety disorders on **mypsychlab.com**

Mood Disorders: The Effect of Affect

14.5 What are the different types of mood disorders and their causes?

In psychological terms, the word **affect** is used to mean "emotion" or "mood." **Mood disorders** are a disturbance in emotion and are also referred to as affective disorders. Although the range of human emotions runs from deep, intense sadness and despair to extreme happiness and elation, under normal circumstances people stay in between those extremes—neither too sad nor too happy, but content (see Figure 14.1). It is when stress or some other factor pushes a person to one extreme or the other that mood disorders can result. Mood disorders can be relatively mild or moderate (straying only a short distance from the "average") or they can be extreme (existing at either end of the full range). Mild to moderate depression is called *dysthymia*, while moderate mood swings (from sad to elated) are called *cyclothymia* (D. Klein et al., 2000). Both forms are chronic* and usually last 2 years or more.

MAJOR DEPRESSION

When a deeply depressed mood comes on fairly suddenly and either seems to be too severe for the circumstances or exists without any external cause for sadness, it is called **major depression**. Major depression would fall at the far extreme of sadness on Figure 14.1. People suffering from major depression are depressed for most of every day, take little or no pleasure in any activities, feel tired, have trouble sleeping or sleep too much, experience changes in appetite and significant weight changes, experience excessive guilt or feelings of worthlessness, have trouble concentrating, and may have thoughts of death or suicide, including suicide attempts. Death by suicide is a real risk

*chronic: long-lasting or occurring frequently over a long period of time.

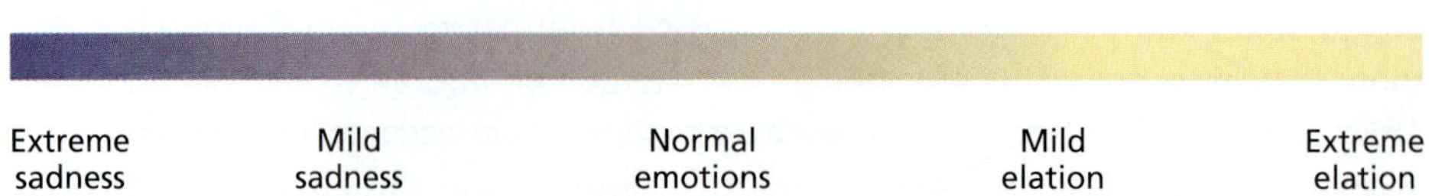

Figure 14.1 The Range of Emotions

Most people experience a range of emotions over the course of a day or several days, such as mild sadness, calm contentment, or mild elation and happiness. A person with a mood disorder experiences emotions that are extreme and, therefore, abnormal.

faced by people suffering from major depression. Some people with this disorder also suffer from delusional thinking and may experience hallucinations. Most of these symptoms occur on a daily basis, lasting for the better part of the day (American Psychiatric Association, 2000).

Major depression is the most common of the diagnosed mood disorders (see Figure 14.2) and is about twice as common in women as it is in men (American Psychiatric Association, 2000). This is true even across various cultures (Blazer et al., 1994; Weissman et al., 1993). Many possible explanations have been proposed for this gender difference, including the different hormonal structure of the female system (menstruation, hormonal changes during and after pregnancy, menopause, etc.) and different social roles played by women in the culture (Blehar & Oren, 1997). Research has found little support for hormonal influences in general, instead finding that the role of hormones and other biological factors in depression is unclear. Instead, studies have found that the degree of differences between male and female rates of depression is decreasing and is nonexistent in college students and single adults, leading some to conclude that social factors such as marital status, career type, and number of children may have more importance in creating the gender difference than biological differences (McGrath et al., 1992; Nolen-Hoeksema, 1990; Weissman & Klerman, 1977).

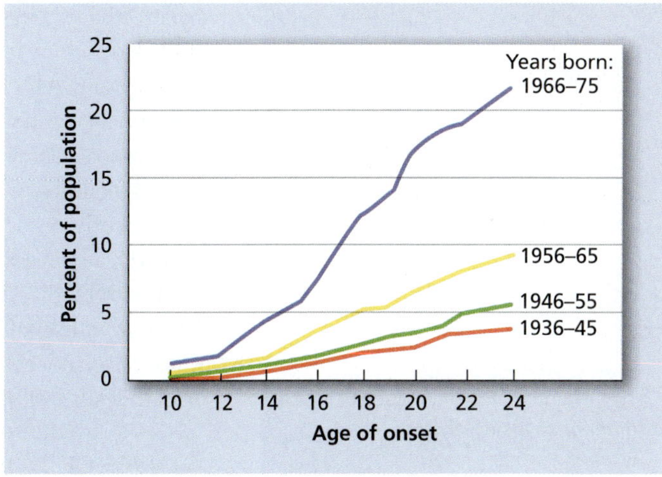

Figure 14.2 Prevalence of Major Depressive Disorder

As the most common mood disorder, major depressive disorder has seen an increase in diagnosis with each decade. From 1936 to 1945, the prevalence of major depression in the population was about 3 percent, with the onset of symptoms occurring at around ages 18 to 20. By 1966 to 1975, the prevalence had jumped to about 23 percent of the population, and the age of onset had dropped to the early teens.

BIPOLAR DISORDERS

Major depression is sometimes referred to as a *unipolar disorder* because the emotional problem exists at only one end, or "pole," of the emotional range. When a person suffers from severe mood swings that go all the way from severe depression to **manic** episodes (excessive excitement, energy, and elation), that person is said to suffer from a **bipolar disorder**, meaning that emotions cycle between the two poles of possible emotions (American Psychiatric Association, 2000). Unlike mild or moderate mood disorders, there is usually no external cause for the extreme ups and downs of the bipolar person. The depressive phases of a bipolar person are indistinguishable from major depression but give way to manic episodes that may last from a few weeks to a few months. In these manic episodes, the person is extremely happy or euphoric* without any real cause to be so happy. Restlessness, irritability, an inability to sit still or remain inactive, and seemingly unlimited energy are also common. The person may seem silly to others and can become aggressive when not allowed to carry out the grand (and sometimes delusional) plans that are often the hallmark of the manic phase. Speech may be rapid and jump from one topic to another. Oddly, people in the manic state are often very creative until their lack of organization renders their attempts at being creative useless (Blumer, 2002; McDermott, 2001; Rothenberg, 2001).

That sounds almost like a description of an overactive child—can't sit still, can't concentrate—are the two disorders related?

That sounds almost like a description of an overactive child—can't sit still, can't concentrate—are the two disorders related?

The answer to that question is actually part of an ongoing controversy. There does seem to be a connection between attention-deficit/hyperactivity disorder (ADHD) and the onset of bipolar disorder in adolescence (Carlson et al., 1998), but only a small percentage of children with ADHD go on to develop bipolar disorder. The symptoms of bipolar disorder include irrational thinking and other manic symptoms that are not present in ADHD (Geller ct al., 1998). Confusion between the two disorders arises because

manic having the quality of excessive excitement, energy, and elation or irritability.

bipolar disorder severe mood swings between major depressive episodes and manic episodes.

*euphoric: having a feeling of vigor, well-being, or high spirits.

hyperactivity (excessive movement and an inability to concentrate) is a symptom of both disorders. In one recent study, researchers compared children diagnosed with both bipolar disorder and ADHD to children diagnosed with ADHD only on measures of academic performance and a series of neurological tests (Henin et al., 2007). They found that the two groups responded in very similar ways, showing the same deficits in information processing abilities, with only one exception: The children with both disorders performed more poorly on one measure of processing speed when compared to children with only ADHD. The researchers concluded that the neurological deficits often observed in children with bipolar disorder are more likely to be due to the ADHD rather than the bipolar disorder itself. Children with bipolar disorder also seem to suffer from far more severe emotional and behavioral problems than those with ADHD (Ferguson-Noyes, 2005; McDougall, 2009). Watch on **mypsychlab.com**

Watch a video on bipolar disorder on **mypsychlab.com**

CAUSES OF MOOD DISORDERS

Explanations of depression and other mood disorders today come from the perspectives of behavioral, social cognitive, and biological theories as well as genetics.

Behavioral theorists link depression to learned helplessness (Seligman, 1975, 1989), whereas social cognitive theorists point to distortions of thinking such as blowing negative events out of proportion and minimizing positive, good events (Beck, 1976, 1984). In the social cognitive view, depressed people continually have negative, self-defeating thoughts about themselves, which depress them further in a downward spiral of despair. Learned helplessness (discussed in Chapter Five) has been linked to an increase in such self-defeating thinking and depression in studies with people who have experienced uncontrollable, painful events (Abramson et al., 1978, 1980). This link does not necessarily mean that negative thoughts *cause* depression; it may be that depression increases the likelihood of negative thoughts (Gotlib et al., 2001). One study found that when comparing adolescents who were depressed to those who were not, the depressed group faced risk factors specifically associated with the social cognitive environment, such as being female or a member of an ethnic minority, living in poverty, regular use of drugs (including tobacco and alcohol), and engaging in delinquent behavior (Costello et al., 2008). In contrast, those in the nondepressed group of adolescents were more likely to come from two-parent households; had higher self-esteem; and felt connected to parents, peers, and school. Clearly, learned helplessness in the face of discrimination, prejudice, and poverty may be associated with depression in these adolescents. A recent study has also found that when therapists focus on helping clients to change their way of thinking, depression improves significantly when compared to therapy that focuses only on changing behavior; these results lend support to the cognitive explanation of distorted thinking as the source of depression (Strunk et al., 2010).

Depression may be caused by conflicts with others, learned reactions, illogical thought patterns, or chemical imbalances—or some combination of all of these factors.

Biological explanations of mood disorders focus on the effects of brain chemicals such as serotonin, norepinephrine, and dopamine; drugs used to treat depression and mania typically affect the levels of these three neurotransmitters, either alone or in combination (Cohen, 1997; Cummings & Coffey, 1994; Ruhe et al., 2007).

Some people find that they only get depressed at certain times of the year. In particular, depression seems to set in during the winter months and goes away with the coming of spring and summer. **Seasonal affective disorder (SAD)** is a mood disorder that is caused by the body's reaction to low levels of light present in the winter months (Partonen & Lonnqvist, 1998). Read on **mypsychlab.com**

Read and learn more about seasonal affective disorder on **mypsychlab.com**

seasonal affective disorder (SAD) a mood disorder caused by the body's reaction to low levels of sunlight in the winter months.

Genes also play a part in mood disorders. The fact that the more severe mood disorders are not a reaction to some outside source of stress or anxiety but rather seem to come from within the person's own body, together with the tendency of mood disorders to appear in genetically related individuals at a higher rate, suggests rather strongly that inheritance may play a significant part in these disorders (Barondes, 1998; Farmer,

1996). Evidence exists for specific genes associated with major depression on chromosome 11 and with bipolar disorder on chromosome 18 (Levinson, 2006; McMahon et al., 2001; Stine et al., 1995). More than 65 percent of people with bipolar disorder have at least one close relative with either bipolar disorder or major depression (Craddock et al., 2005; National Institute of Mental Health Genetics Workgroup, 1998; Sullivan et al., 2000). Twin studies have shown that if one identical twin has either major depression or bipolar disorder, the chances that the other twin will also develop a mood disorder are about 40 to 70 percent (Muller-Oerlinghausen et al., 2002).

14.4 14.5

CONCEPT MAP

Anxiety and Mood Disorders

- **anxiety disorders** most dominant symptom is excessive or unrealistic anxiety
  - anxiety can be free-floating (nonspecific, anxious in general) or more specific, as in the case of phobias
    - **social phobias**
    - specific phobias (e.g., **claustrophobia, acrophobia)**
    - **agoraphobia**
  - **panic disorder** consists of an individual having frequent panic attacks that interfere with normal daily functioning; **panic disorder with agoraphobia** occurs when a fear of having panic attacks in public prevents an individual from going out
  - **obsessive-compulsive disorder (OCD)** consists of recurring anxiety-provoking thoughts or obsessions that are only relieved through ritualistic or repetitive behaviors or mental events
  - **generalized anxiety disorder** involves excessive worry about lots of things and occurs more days than not
  - causes
    - **behavioral:** anxious behavioral reactions are learned
    - **cognitive:** anxiety is result of illogical, irrational thought processes
      - **magnification**
      - **all-or-none thinking**
      - **overgeneralization**
      - **minimization**
    - **biological:** anxiety is due to imbalance in several neurotransmitters (e.g., serotonin, GABA) and/or difference in brain activation; panic disorder is also hereditary
    - **cultural:** anxiety disorders found around the world but particular forms vary across cultures
- **mood disorders** involve a disturbance in mood or emotion; can be mild or severe
  - **major depression:** deeply depressed mood; most commonly diagnosed mood disorder, twice as common in women
  - **bipolar disorders** involve extreme mood swings, ranging from severe depression to manic episodes
  - causes
    - **psychodynamic:** depression is repressed anger originally aimed at parents or other authority figures
    - **behavioral:** depression is linked to learned helplessness
    - **social cognitive:** distorted thinking and negative, self-defeating thoughts
    - **biological:** variation in neurotransmitter levels (e.g., serotonin, norepinephrine, dopamine) or specific brain activity; genes and heritability also play a part

PRACTICE quiz How much do you remember?

ANSWERS ON PAGE AK-2.

Pick the best answer.

1. An irrational fear of blood would be a _________.
   a. social phobia.
   b. specific phobia.
   c. type of agoraphobia.
   d. type of acrophobia.
2. Jennifer worries that someone might come into her house at night while she is sleeping and helpless. She checks the locks on the doors and windows several times before she can relax enough to go to bed. Her constant checking of the locks is most similar to _________.
   a. a compulsion.
   b. an obsession.
   c. a panic disorder.
   d. a phobia.
3. Anxiety, recurring nightmares, sleep disturbances, and concentration problems that occur for more than 1 month after a major stressor are symptoms of _________.
   a. acute stress disorder.
   b. posttraumatic stress disorder.
   c. pretraumatic stress disorder.
   d. general stress disorder.

(continued)

4. Bud's relatives are concerned that he worries too much. He worries about little things going wrong, he worries about big things going wrong, and sometimes it seems as though he's worrying because there's nothing to worry about. He worries so much that he has a hard time getting things done. Bud most likely has __________.
   - **a.** panic disorder.
   - **b.** obsessive-compulsive disorder.
   - **c.** generalized anxiety disorder.
   - **d.** posttraumatic stress disorder.

5. Sandy has the tendency to make everything seem so much worse than it usually is. Beck would say that Sandy has a tendency to __________.
   - **a.** overgeneralize.
   - **b.** minimize.
   - **c.** do all-or-nothing thinking.
   - **d.** magnify.

6. Jorge lost his father 3 years ago. Since then, he has experienced occasional bouts of sadness and depression. Although he usually feels quite happy, sometimes the sadness returns. Jorge's relatively mild mood swings most likely indicate __________.
   - **a.** dysthymia.
   - **b.** cyclothymia.
   - **c.** major depression.
   - **d.** bipolar disorder.

7. Macha woke up one morning in a very sad mood and couldn't think of any reason why she should feel that way. The feeling got worse as the day went on, and although in the days and weeks to follow she occasionally felt normal, she had more sad days than normal. Her feelings were so intense that she couldn't sleep, ate too much, and couldn't take joy in anything. Macha is most likely suffering from __________.
   - **a.** dysthymia.
   - **b.** cyclothymia.
   - **c.** major depression.
   - **d.** bipolar disorder.

8. Vicki was always coming up with grand plans for making money, none of which lasted very long before she abandoned them. The latest scheme is to buy a huge tract of land and build an expensive "dude" ranch where people can come to learn how to train their horses, eat at a four-star restaurant, and stay in luxury accommodations—all this in spite of the fact that Vicki and her husband don't have the money to buy the land, knowledge of how to run a hotel, or have a four-star chef handy. Vicki may have __________.
   - **a.** dysthymia.
   - **b.** cyclothymia.
   - **c.** major depression.
   - **d.** bipolar disorder.

Brainstorming: Individuals with symptoms of anxiety may also have symptoms of depression. How might this affect the day-to-day life of a college student?

This young model is not merely thin; by medical standards she is probably at a weight that would allow her to be labeled as anorexic. The "thin is in" mentality that dominates the field of fashion design models is a major contributor to the Western cultural concept of very thin women as beautiful and desirable. The model pictured here is a far cry from the days of sex symbol Marilyn Monroe, who was rumored to be a size 12.

Eating Disorders

14.6 What are the two primary types of eating disorders, how do they differ, and who are they most likely to affect?

ANOREXIA NERVOSA

Anorexia nervosa, often called **anorexia**, is a condition in which a person (typically young and female) reduces eating to the point that a weight loss of 15 percent below expected body weight or more is the result (Rideout, 2005). At a weight loss of 40 percent below expected body weight, hospitalization is necessary. Hormone secretion becomes abnormal, especially in the thyroid and adrenal glands. The heart muscles become weak and heart rhythms may alter. Other physical effects of anorexia include diarrhea, loss of muscle tissue, loss of sleep, low blood pressure, and lack of menstruation in females.

Some individuals with anorexia will eat in front of others (whereas individuals with bulimia tend to binge eat as secretly as possible) but then force themselves to throw up or take large doses of laxatives. They are often obsessed with exercising and with food—cooking elaborate meals for others while eating nothing themselves. They have extremely distorted body images, seeing fat where others see only skin and bones.

What causes anorexia is not yet fully understood. Some theories involve biological explanations. Others point to psychological factors such as sexual abuse, perfectionism with a desire to control as many aspects of one's life as possible, and family dysfunction (Abraham & Llewellyn-Jones, 2001; Mitchell, 1985).

What can be done to treat anorexia? If the anorexic weight loss is severe (40 percent or more below expected normal weight), dehydration, severe chemical imbalances, and possibly organ damage may result. Hospitalization should occur before this dangerous point is reached. In the hospital the anorexic's physical needs will be treated, even to the point of force-feeding in extreme cases. Psychological counseling will also be part of the hospital treatment, which may last from 2 to 4 months. Those individuals with anorexia who are not so severely malnourished as to be in immediate danger can be treated outside of the hospital setting, typically receiving supportive psychotherapy, behavioral therapy, and perhaps group therapy. Family therapy is nearly always appropriate when the family of the individual with anorexia is contributing in some way to the behavior. LINK to Chapter Fifteen: Psychological Therapies, p. 588. The prognosis for full recovery is not as hopeful as it should be; only 40 to 60 percent of all individuals with anorexia who receive treatment will make a recovery. For some individuals with anorexia who do gain weight, the damage already done to the heart and other body systems may still be so great that an early death is a possibility (Neumarker, 1997). **Watch** on **mypsychlab.com**

anorexia nervosa (anorexia) a condition in which a person reduces eating to the point that a weight loss of 15 percent below the ideal body weight or more occurs.

bulimia nervosa (bulimia) a condition in which a person develops a cycle of "binging," or overeating enormous amounts of food at one sitting, and then using unhealthy methods to avoid weight gain.

Watch a video on anorexia on **mypsychlab.com**

The following Web sites provide access to information, help, and professional referrals for people with anorexia and other eating disorders:

- http://www.nationaleatingdisorders.org/
  (information about eating disorders and professional referrals)
- http://www.womenshealth.gov/FAQ/anorexia-nervosa.cfm
  (information and links to other organizations)
- http://www.nami.org/Content/ContentGroups/Helpline1/Anorexia_Nervosa.htm

BULIMIA NERVOSA

Bulimia nervosa, often called **bulimia**, is a condition in which a person develops a cycle of "binging" or overeating enormous amounts of food at one sitting, and then using inappropriate methods for avoiding weight gain (American Psychiatric Association, 2000; Rideout, 2005). Most individuals with bulimia engage in "purging" behaviors, such as deliberately vomiting after the binge or misuse of laxatives, but some may not, using other inappropriate methods to avoid weight gain such as fasting the day or two after the binge or engaging in excessive exercise (American Psychiatric Association, 2000). There are some similarities to anorexia: The victims are usually female, are obsessed with their appearance, diet excessively, and believe themselves to be fat even when they are quite obviously not fat. But individuals with bulimia are typically a little older than individuals with anorexia at the onset of the disorder—early 20s rather than early puberty. Individuals with bulimia often maintain a normal weight, making the disorder difficult to detect. The most obvious difference between the two conditions is that the bulimic individual will eat, and eat to excess, binging on huge amounts of food—an average of 3,500 calories in a single binge and as much as 50,000 calories in one day (Humphries, 1987; Mitchell et al., 1981; Oster, 1987). A typical binge may include a gallon of ice cream, a package of cookies, and a gallon of milk—all consumed as quickly as possible.

But wait a minute—if individuals with bulimia are so concerned about gaining weight, why do they binge at all?

But wait a minute—if individuals with bulimia are so concerned about gaining weight, why do they binge at all?

The binge itself may be prompted by an anxious or depressed mood, social stressors, feelings about body weight or image, or intense hunger after attempts to diet. The binge continues due to a lack of, or impairment in, self-control once the binge begins. The individual is unable to control when to stop eating or how much to eat. Eating one cookie while trying to control weight can lead to a binge—after all, since the diet is completely blown, why not go all out? This kind of thought process is another example of the cognitive distortion of all-or-nothing thinking.

One might think that bulimia is not as damaging to the health as anorexia. After all, the bulimic is in no danger of starving to death. But bulimia comes with many serious health consequences: severe tooth decay and erosion of the lining of the esophagus from the acidity of the vomiting, enlarged salivary glands, potassium, calcium, and sodium imbalances that can be very dangerous, damage to the intestinal tract from overuse of laxatives, heart problems, fatigue, and seizures (Berg, 1999).

As with anorexia, there have been many proposed causes for bulimia. Several research studies indicate a genetic component for both bulimia and anorexia (Fumeron et al., 2001; Strober et al., 2000; Vink et al., 2001). Psychological issues of control have also been cited, but biological evidence suggests that brain chemistry, and in particular low levels of the neurotransmitter *serotonin*, is involved in both bulimia and anorexia (Fumeron et al., 2001; Jimerson et al., 1997; Kaye, 2005). Other studies point to the role of leptin, a hormone that has also been implicated in obesity (Ferron et al., 1997; Monteleone, 2002). Individuals with anorexia may have too much leptin whereas individuals with bulimia may have too little (Frederich et al., 2002).

Treatment of bulimia can involve many of the same measures taken to treat anorexia: hospitalization, drug therapy to affect serotonin levels, and psychotherapy. The prognosis for the individual with bulimia's recovery is somewhat more hopeful than that of anorexia. Cognitive therapy, which involves helping clients understand how illogical and irrational their thought patterns have become, has been successful in treating bulimia (DeAngelis, 2002). A cognitive therapist is very direct, forcing clients to see how their beliefs do not stand up when considered in "the light of day" and helping them form new, more constructive ways of thinking about themselves and their behavior. LINK to Chapter Fifteen: Psychological Therapies, p. 585. Table 14.4 lists just a few of the more visible signs and symptoms of eating disorders.

CULTURE AND EATING DISORDERS Although many researchers have believed eating disorders, especially anorexia, are culture-bound syndromes that only show up in cultures obsessed with being thin (as many Western cultures are), eating disorders are also

Table 14.4

Possible Signs of Eating Disorders
Dramatic weight loss in a relatively short period of time
Obsession with calories and fat content of food
Hiding food in strange places
Hair loss, pale appearance to the skin
Bruised or callused knuckles, bloodshot eyes with light bruising under the eyes
Frequent trips to the bathroom following meals
Obsession with continuous exercise
Wearing baggy clothes to hide body shape or weight loss
Reading books about weight loss and eating disorders
Complaints of often feeling cold

found in non-Western cultures (Miller & Pumariega, 1999). What differs between Western and non-Western cultures is the rate at which such disorders appear. For example, Chinese and Chinese American women are far less likely to suffer from eating disorders than are non-Hispanic White women (Pan, 2000). Why wouldn't Chinese American women be more likely to have eating disorders after being exposed to the Western cultural obsession with thinness? Pan (2000) assumes that whatever Chinese cultural factors "protect" Chinese women from developing eating disorders may also still have a powerful influence on Chinese American women.

One problem with studying anorexia and bulimia in other cultures is that the behavior of starving oneself may be seen in other cultures as having an entirely different purpose than in Western cultures. One key component of anorexia, for example, is a fear of being fat, a fear that is missing in many other cultures. Yet women in those cultures have starved themselves for other socially recognized reasons: religious fasting or unusual ideas about nutrition (Castillo, 1997).

Anorexia and bulimia have also been thought to occur only rarely in African American women, but that characterization seems to be changing. Researchers are seeing an increase in anorexia and bulimia among young African American women of all socioeconomic levels (Crago et al., 1996; Mintz & Betz, 1998; Pumariega & Gustavson, 1994). If clinicians and doctors are not aware that these disorders can affect more than the typical White, young, middle-class to upper-middle-class woman, important signs and symptoms of eating disorders in non-White or non-Western people may allow these disorders to go untreated until it is too late.

Dissociative Disorders: Altered Identities

14.7 How do the various dissociative disorders differ, and how do they develop?

Dissociative disorders involve a break, or dissociation, in consciousness, memory, or a person's sense of identity. This "split" is easier to understand when thinking about how people sometimes drive somewhere and then wonder how they got there—they don't remember the trip itself at all. This sort of "automatic pilot" driving happens when the route is familiar and frequently traveled. One part of the conscious mind was thinking about work, school, or whatever was uppermost in the mind while lower centers of consciousness were driving the car, stopping at signs and lights, and turning when needed. This split in conscious attention is very similar to what happens in dissociative disorders. The difference is that in these disorders the dissociation is much more pronounced and involuntary. Read on mypsychlab.com

Read and learn more about dissociative amnesia on mypsychlab.com

DISSOCIATIVE AMNESIA: WHO AM I?

In **dissociative amnesia**, the individual cannot remember personal information such as one's own name or specific personal events—the kind of information contained in episodic long-term memory. LINK to Chapter Six: Memory, pp. 225–226. Dissociative amnesia may sound like retrograde amnesia, but it differs in its cause. In retrograde amnesia, the memory loss is typically caused by a physical injury, such as a blow to the head. In dissociative amnesia, the cause is psychological rather than physical. The "blow" is a mental one, not a physical one. The reported memory loss is usually associated with a stressful or emotionally traumatic experience, such as rape or childhood abuse (Chu et al., 1999; Kirby et al., 1993), and cannot be easily explained by simple forgetfulness. It can be a loss of memory for only one small segment of time, or it can involve a total loss of one's past personal memories. For example, a soldier might be

dissociative disorders disorders in which there is a break in conscious awareness, memory, the sense of identity, or some combination.

dissociative amnesia loss of memory for personal information, either partial or complete.

Edward Lighthart, or, as he prefers, Jon Doe, pauses during an interview Monday, Sept. 14, 2009, in a public relations office in Seattle, Washington. Doe says memories have been slowly trickling back in the nearly seven weeks since he walked out of a Seattle park with no idea of who he was and how he got there. This is clearly a case of dissociative fugue.

able to remember being in combat but cannot remember witnessing a friend get killed, or a person might forget his or her entire life. These memories usually resurface, sometimes quickly, and sometimes after a long delay. In one case, a veteran of the Second World War had amnesia for the time during which he was captured, tortured, and escaped from the Far East. He did not recall these memories, or the fact that he had been an intelligence agent at the time, until 37 years later (Cassiday & Lyons, 1992).

DISSOCIATIVE FUGUE: WHO AM I AND HOW DID I GET HERE?

The Latin word *fugere* means "flight" and is the word from which the term *fugue* is taken. A **dissociative fugue** occurs when a person suddenly travels away from home (the flight) and afterwards cannot remember the trip or even personal information such as identity. The individual may become confused about identity, sometimes even taking on a whole new identity in the new place (Nijenhuis, 2000). Such flights usually take place after an emotional trauma and are more common in times of disasters or war.

As an example, look at the story of John Doe, so named by the physician who first saw him in the emergency room. John had no belongings, didn't know his name, and had no memories about his life before waking up on a park bench that morning, 8 hours before. He seemed physically healthy, in his 40s, and was dressed neatly and casually. He was clear, coherent, and seemed mentally stable, except for his loss of memory. Following a lead provided by the tag in his jacket, John was identified as a lawyer from a town 500 miles away who had been reported missing by his wife 2 days earlier. He had been criminally charged with embezzling from his clients and had been under such pressure that he had told his wife, "I don't know if I can take much more of this without losing my mind." Instead of losing his mind, John lost himself (Morrison, 1995).

DISSOCIATIVE IDENTITY DISORDER: HOW MANY AM I?

Perhaps the most controversial dissociative disorder is **dissociative identity disorder** (DID), formerly known as multiple personality disorder. In this disorder, a person seems to experience at least two or more distinct personalities existing in one body. There may be a "core" personality, who usually knows nothing about the other personalities and is the one who experiences "blackouts" or losses of memory and time. Fugues are common in dissociative identity disorder, with the core personality experiencing unsettling moments of "awakening" in an unfamiliar place or with people who call the person by another name (Kluft, 1984).

With the publication of several famous books such as *The Three Faces of Eve* (Thigpen & Cleckley, 1992) and *Sybil* (Schreiber, 1973) and movies made from those books, dissociative identity disorder became well known to the public. Throughout the 1980s, psychological professionals began to diagnose this condition at an alarming rate—"multiple personality," as it was then known, had become the "fad" disorder of the late twentieth century, according to some researchers (Aldridge-Morris, 1989; Boor, 1982; Cormier & Thelen, 1998; Showalter, 1997).

In the last decade, the diagnosis of dissociative identity disorder has come under scrutiny with many (but not all) professionals now doubting the validity of previous diagnoses. Even the famous case of "Sybil" has been criticized as a case of the therapist actually "creating" the multiple personalities in her client through suggestion and even

dissociative fugue traveling away from familiar surroundings with amnesia about the trip and possible amnesia for personal information.

dissociative identity disorder disorder occurring when a person seems to have two or more distinct personalities within one body.

direct instruction. Some psychological professionals believe that dissociative identity disorder is actually a misdiagnosis of borderline personality disorder or some other form of anxiety disorder (Lauer et al., 1993). Watch on mypsychlab.com

Watch Watch classic footage on *The Three Faces of Eve* on **mypsychlab.com**

CAUSES OF DISSOCIATIVE DISORDERS

Psychodynamic theory sees the repression of threatening or unacceptable thoughts and behavior as a defense mechanism at the heart of all disorders, and the dissociative disorders in particular seem to have a large element of repression—motivated forgetting—in them. In the psychodynamic view, loss of memory or disconnecting one's awareness from a stressful or traumatic event is adaptive in that it reduces the emotional pain (Dorahy, 2001).

Cognitive and behavioral explanations for dissociative disorders are connected: The person may feel guilt, shame, or anxiety when thinking about disturbing experiences or thoughts and start to avoid thinking about them. This "thought avoidance" is negatively reinforced by the reduction of the anxiety and unpleasant feelings and eventually will become a habit of "not thinking about" these things. This is similar to what many people do when faced with something unpleasant, such as an injection or a painful procedure such as having a root canal. They "think about something else." In doing that, they are deliberately not thinking about what is happening to them at the moment and the experience of pain is decreased. People with dissociative disorders may simply be better at doing this sort of "not thinking" than other people are.

Also, consider the positive reinforcement possibilities for a person with a dissociative disorder: attention from others and help from professionals. Shaping may also play a role in the development of some cases of dissociative identity disorder. The therapist may unintentionally pay more attention to a client who talks about "feeling like someone else," which may encourage the client to report more such feelings and even elaborate on them.

There are some possible biological sources for dissociations, as well. Researchers have found that people with **depersonalization disorder** (a mild dissociative disorder in which people feel detached and disconnected from themselves, their bodies, and their surroundings) have lower brain activity in the areas responsible for their sense of body awareness than do people without the disorder (Simeon et al., 2000). Others have found evidence that people with dissociative identity disorders show significant differences in PET scan activity taken when different "personalities" are present (Reinders et al., 2001; Tsai et al., 1999). A recent review also suggests that individuals with DID may be more elaborative when forming memories and are better at memory recall as a result (García-Campayo et al., 2009).

Another study proposes that the neurological differences might result from the childhood abuse so common to persons diagnosed with DID (Teicher et al., 2002). These studies, if successfully replicated in future research, may one day put an end to the controversy over the validity of dissociative identity disorder.

Dissociative disorders can also be found in other cultures. The trancelike state known as *amok* in which a person suddenly becomes highly agitated and violent (found in Southeast Asia and Pacific Island cultures) is usually associated with no memory for the period during which the "trance" lasts (Suryani & Jensen, 1993). But a study that reviewed historical literature throughout the centuries found no mention or tales of what would be labeled as dissociative amnesia in the stories or nonfiction writings of any culture prior to the 1800s (Pope et al., 2007). The authors concluded that dissociative amnesia may be more of a nineteenth-century culture-bound phenomenon than a neuropsychological one.

depersonalization disorder dissociative disorder in which individuals feel detached and disconnected from themselves, their bodies, and their surroundings.

14.6 14.7

CONCEPT MAP

Eating and Dissociative Disorders

- **eating disorders**
  - **anorexia nervosa** is disordered eating that causes weight loss 15% or more below body weight
  - **bulimia nervosa** involves cycles of binging and use of unhealthy methods to avoid weight gain; unlike anorexia, those with bulimia will tend to maintain a normal body weight
    - → typically female, obsessed with appearance, diet excessively, and have distorted body images; biological, psychological, and cultural factors are likely
  - social influences on "thinness" and fear of being fat impacts prevalence rates across various cultures
- **dissociative disorders** involve a dissociation in consciousness, memory, or sense of identity, often associated with extreme stress or trauma
  - **dissociative amnesia:** one cannot remember personal information
  - **dissociative fugue:** person takes sudden trip and cannot remember traveling or personal information
  - **dissociative identity disorder:** person seems to experience at least two or more distinct personalities; validity of actual disorder has been topic of debate
  - causes
    - **psychodynamic:** repressed thoughts and behavior is primary defense mechanism and reduces emotional pain
    - **cognitive and behavioral:** trauma-related thought avoidance is negatively reinforced by reduction in anxiety and emotional pain
    - **biological:** support for brain activity differences in body awareness has been found in individuals with **depersonalization disorder**

PRACTICE quiz How much do you remember? ANSWERS ON PAGE AK-2.

Pick the best answer.

1. One of the main differences between anorexia nervosa and bulimia nervosa is that the individual with anorexia nervosa ________.
   a. is obsessed about body weight.
   b. tends to be female.
   c. weighs 15 percent or more below expected body weight.
   d. can suffer from heart problems.
2. Bulimia nervosa, unlike anorexia nervosa, ________.
   a. produces an obsession with food.
   b. is hard to detect because the person's weight is often normal.
   c. is not physically harmful.
   d. involves starvation.
3. Carlo wakes up in a strange motel room. He doesn't know where he is or how he got there, and he's not sure what day it is. This is most likely an episode of dissociative ________.
   a. amnesia.
   b. fugue.
   c. identity disorder.
   d. multiple personality.
4. The fact that the dissociative disorders seem to have a large element of repression in them is related to the ________ explanation of disorders.
   a. behavioral
   b. cognitive
   c. biological
   d. psychodynamic

Brainstorming: How might the proliferation of various media and the Internet affect the development of eating disorders in cultures not previously impacted by them?

Schizophrenia: Altered Reality

Once known as *dementia praecox*, a Latin-based term meaning "out of one's mind before one's time," **schizophrenia** was renamed by Eugen Bleuler, a Swiss psychiatrist, to better illustrate the division (*schizo-*) within the brain (*phren*) among thoughts, feelings, and behavior that seems to take place in people with this disorder (Bleuler, 1911; Möller & Hell, 2002). Because the term literally means "split mind," it has often been confused with dissociative identity disorder, which was at one time called "split personality." A more modern definition of schizophrenia describes it as a long-lasting **psychotic** disorder (involving a severe break with reality), in which there is an inability to distinguish what is real from fantasy as well as disturbances in thinking, emotions, behavior, and perception.

schizophrenia severe disorder in which the person suffers from disordered thinking, bizarre behavior, hallucinations, and inability to distinguish between fantasy and reality.

psychotic term applied to a person who is no longer able to perceive what is real and what is fantasy.

14.8 What are the main symptoms, types, and causes of schizophrenia?

SYMPTOMS

Schizophrenia includes several different kinds of symptoms. Disorders in thinking are a common symptom and are called **delusions**. Although delusions are not prominent in all forms of schizophrenia, they are the symptom that most people associate with this disorder. Delusions are false beliefs about the world that the person holds and that tend to remain fixed and unshakable even in the face of evidence that disproves the delusions. Common schizophrenic delusions include *delusions of persecution*, in which people believe that others are trying to hurt them in some way; *delusions of reference*, in which people believe that other people, television characters, and even books are specifically talking to them; *delusions of influence*, in which people believe that they are being controlled by external forces, such as the devil, aliens, or cosmic forces; and *delusions of grandeur* (or *grandiose delusions*), in which people are convinced that they are powerful people who can save the world or have a special mission (American Psychiatric Association, 2000).

Dr. John Nash is a famous mathematician who won the Nobel Prize for mathematics in 1994. His fame, however, is more due to the fact that Nash once suffered from a form of schizophrenia in which he experienced delusions of persecution. He at one time believed that aliens were trying to contact him through the newspaper (delusions of reference). His life story and remarkable recovery from schizophrenia are portrayed in the 2001 movie *A Beautiful Mind*, which starred Russell Crowe as Nash.

Delusional thinking alone is not enough to merit a diagnosis of schizophrenia, as there is a separate category of psychotic disorders called **delusional disorders**, in which the primary symptom is some form of delusion. In schizophrenia, other symptoms must be present (American Psychiatric Association, 2000; Black & Andreason, 1999). Speech disturbances are common: People with schizophrenia will make up words, repeat words or sentences persistently, string words together on the basis of sounds (called *clanging*, such as "come into house, louse, mouse, mouse and cheese, please, sneeze"), and experience sudden interruptions in speech or thought. Thoughts are significantly disturbed as well, with individuals with schizophrenia having a hard time linking their thoughts together in a logical fashion.

People with schizophrenia may also have **hallucinations**, in which they hear voices or see things or people that are not really there. Hearing voices is actually more common and one of the key symptoms in making a diagnosis of schizophrenia (Kuhn & Nasar, 2001; Nasar, 1998). Hallucinations involving touch, smell, and taste are less common but also possible. Emotional disturbances are also a key feature of schizophrenia. **Flat affect** is a condition in which the person shows little or no emotion. Emotions can also be excessive and/or inappropriate—a person might laugh when it would be more appropriate to cry or show sorrow, for example.

The person's behavior may also become disorganized and extremely odd. For example, some forms of schizophrenia are accompanied by periods of complete immobility, whereas others may involve weird facial grimaces and odd gesturing. According to the American Psychiatric Association (2000), at least two or more of the following symptoms must be present frequently for at least 1 month to diagnose schizophrenia: delusions, hallucinations, disturbed speech, disturbed emotions, and disturbed behavior.

Attention is also a problem for many people with schizophrenia. They seem to have trouble "screening out" information and stimulation that they don't really need, causing them to be unable to focus on information that is relevant (Asarnow et al., 1991; Luck & Gold, 2008).

CATEGORIES OF SCHIZOPHRENIA

Although all people with schizophrenia share the symptoms already discussed to a certain degree, the way in which these symptoms show up in behavior can be used to distinguish among several different types of schizophrenia. There are five subtypes of

delusions false beliefs held by a person who refuses to accept evidence of their falseness.

delusional disorder a psychotic disorder in which the primary symptom is one or more delusions.

hallucinations false sensory perceptions, such as hearing voices that do not really exist.

flat affect a lack of emotional responsiveness.

Nathaniel Ayers, a homeless musician, is pictured in 2003 in front of The Midnight Mission shelter in Los Angeles, California. Mr. Ayers's life is the subject of the 2009 movie *The Soloist* starring Jamie Foxx. Mr. Ayers was a Julliard-trained musician who became mentally ill.

schizophrenia and two categories of symptoms (American Psychiatric Association, 2000). Three of the subtypes will be highlighted along with the two symptom categories that are seen across the different subtypes.

DISORGANIZED People suffering from **disorganized** schizophrenia are very confused in speech, have vivid and frequent hallucinations, and tend to have very inappropriate affect (emotion) or flat affect. They are very socially impaired, unable to engage in the normal social rituals of daily life. Giggling, silliness, nonsensical speech, and neglect of cleanliness are common. They may not bathe or change clothing and may have problems with urinating or defecating in public, either because of incontinence or a deliberate wish to shock those watching.

CATATONIC **Catatonic** schizophrenia is less common and involves very disturbed motor behavior. The person doesn't respond to the outside world and either doesn't move at all, maintaining often odd-looking postures for hours on end (a condition known as *catatonia*) or moves about wildly in great agitation. It's as if there are only two "speeds" for the catatonic, totally off or totally on.

PARANOID People diagnosed with **paranoid** schizophrenia suffer from hallucinations and delusions. Auditory hallucinations are common, and the delusions are typically persecution, grandeur, or extreme jealousy of another or several other persons. Although their thinking is not as scattered as that of someone with disorganized schizophrenia, their delusions tend to be bizarre but very systematic.

Another way of categorizing schizophrenia is to look at the kind of symptoms that predominate. **Positive symptoms** appear to reflect an excess or distortion of normal functions, such as hallucinations and delusions. **Negative symptoms** appear to reflect a decrease of normal functions, such as poor attention or lack of affect (American Psychiatric Association, 2000).

Positive symptoms are associated with overactivity in the subcortical dopamine areas of the brain. Dopamine-reducing drugs used to treat schizophrenia are usually effective on these symptoms and the outlook for recovery is generally good (Davis et al., 1991; Penn, 1998).

Negative symptoms include the inability to filter out stimuli to focus attention, flat affect, problems with producing speech, apathy, and withdrawal from others. Negative symptoms, unlike positive symptoms, are associated with *lower* than normal activity in the cortical dopamine systems of the brain and problems in the functioning of the frontal lobe. Studies have found that those with schizophrenia and primarily negative symptoms have decreased blood flow to the frontal lobe areas (Davis et al., 1991; Perlstein et al., 2001) and enlarged ventricles (the fluid-filled spaces within the brain) when compared to people without schizophrenia (Serban et al., 1990). Unfortunately, this also means that the outlook for recovery from schizophrenia with predominantly negative symptoms is not good, as these symptoms do not respond well to medications that are effective with schizophrenia with predominantly positive symptoms. Read on **mypsychlab.com**

CAUSES OF SCHIZOPHRENIA

When trying to explain the cause or causes of schizophrenia, the biopsychological model prevails. Biological explanations of schizophrenia have generated a significant amount of research pointing to genetic origins, inflammation in the brain, chemical influences (dopamine, GABA, glutamate, and other neurotransmitters), and brain structural defects (frontal lobe defects, deterioration of neurons, and reduction in white matter integrity) as the causes of schizophrenia (Gottesman & Shields, 1982; Harrison, 1999; Kety et al., 1994; Nestor et al., 2008; Söderlund et al., 2009). Dopamine was first suspected when amphetamine users began to show schizophrenia-like psychotic symptoms. One of the side effects of amphetamine usage is to increase

Read and learn more about undifferentiated and residual categories of schizophrenia on **mypsychlab.com**

disorganized type of schizophrenia in which behavior is bizarre and childish, and thinking, speech, and motor actions are very disordered.

catatonic type of schizophrenia in which the person experiences periods of statue-like immobility mixed with occasional bursts of energetic, frantic movement, and talking.

paranoid type of schizophrenia in which the person suffers from delusions of persecution, grandeur, and jealousy, together with hallucinations.

positive symptoms symptoms of schizophrenia that are excesses of behavior or occur in addition to normal behavior; hallucinations, delusions, and distorted thinking.

negative symptoms symptoms of schizophrenia that are less than normal behavior or an absence of normal behavior; poor attention, flat affect, and poor speech production.

the release of dopamine in the brain. Drugs used to treat schizophrenia decrease the activity of dopamine in areas of the brain responsible for some of the positive symptoms such as overactivity. However, the prefrontal cortex (an area of the brain involved in planning and organization of information) of people with schizophrenia has been shown to produce lower levels of dopamine than normal (Harrison, 1999), resulting in attention deficits (Luck & Gold, 2008) and poor organization of thought, negative symptoms of the disorder.

Further support for a biological explanation of schizophrenia comes from studies of the incidence of the disorder across different cultures. If schizophrenia were caused mainly by environmental factors, the expectation would be that rates of schizophrenia would vary widely from culture to culture. In fact, about 7 to 8 individuals out of 1,000 will develop schizophrenia in their lifetime, regardless of the culture (Saha et al., 2005; Torrey, 1987).

Family, twin, and adoption studies have provided strong evidence that genes are a major means of transmitting schizophrenia. The highest risk for developing schizophrenia if one has a blood relative with the disorder is faced by monozygotic (identical) twins, who share 100 percent of their genetic material, with a risk factor of about 50 percent (Cardno & Gottesman, 2000; Gottesman & Shields, 1976, 1982; Gottesman et al., 1987). Dizygotic twins, who share about 50 percent of their genetic material, have about a 17 percent risk, the same as a child with one parent with schizophrenia. As genetic relatedness decreases, so does the risk (see Figure 14.3). Twin studies are not perfect tools, however; identical twins share the same womb but are not necessarily exposed to the same exact prenatal environment, causing some to urge caution in interpreting the 50 percent figure; and even twins reared apart are often raised in similar childhood environments (Davis et. al., 1995).

Adoption studies also support the genetic basis of schizophrenia (Sullivan, 2005; Tienari et al., 2004). In one study, the biological and adoptive relatives of adoptees with schizophrenia were compared to a control group of adoptees without schizophrenia but from similar backgrounds and conditions (Kety et al., 1994). The adoptees with schizophrenia had relatives with schizophrenia but *only among their biological relatives.* When the prevalence of schizophrenia was compared between the biological relatives of the adoptees with schizophrenia and the biological relatives of the control group, the rate of the disorder in the relatives of the group with schizophrenia was 10 times higher than in the control group (Kety et al., 1994). **Simulate** on **mypsychlab.com**

Simulate the diagnosis of schizophrenia on **mypsychlab.com**

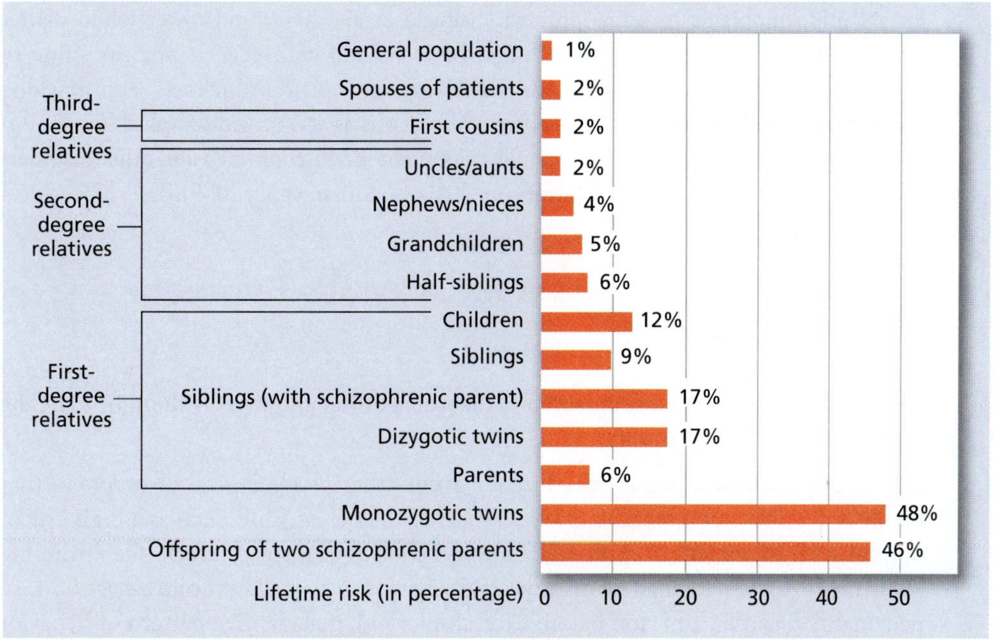

Figure 14.3 Genetics and Schizophrenia

This graph shows a definite pattern: The greater the degree of genetic relatedness, the higher the risk of schizophrenia in individuals related to each other. The only individual to carry a risk even close to that of identical twins (who share 100 percent of their genes) is a person who is the child of two parents with schizophrenia.

Source: Gottesman (1991).

There's something I don't understand. If one identical twin has the gene and the disorder, shouldn't the other one always have it, too? Why is the rate only 50 percent?

There's something I don't understand. If one identical twin has the gene and the disorder, shouldn't the other one always have it, too? Why is the rate only 50 percent?

If schizophrenia were entirely controlled by genes, identical twins would indeed both have the disorder at a risk of 100 percent, not merely 50 percent. Obviously, there is some influence of environment on the development of schizophrenia. One model that has been proposed is the **stress-vulnerability model**, which assumes that persons with the genetic "markers" for schizophrenia have a physical vulnerability to the disorder but will not develop schizophrenia unless they are exposed to environmental or emotional stress at critical times in development, such as puberty (Harrison, 1999; Weinberger, 1987). That would explain why only one twin out of a pair might develop the disorder when both carry the genetic markers for schizophrenia—the life stresses for the affected twin were different from those of the one who remained healthy. The immune system is activated during stress, and one recent study has found that in recent-onset schizophrenia (the early stages of the disorder) the brain's immune system secretes high levels of an inflammation fighting substance, indicating a possible infection (Söderlund et al., 2009). This leads to the possibility that schizophrenia might one day be treatable with anti-inflammatory medications.

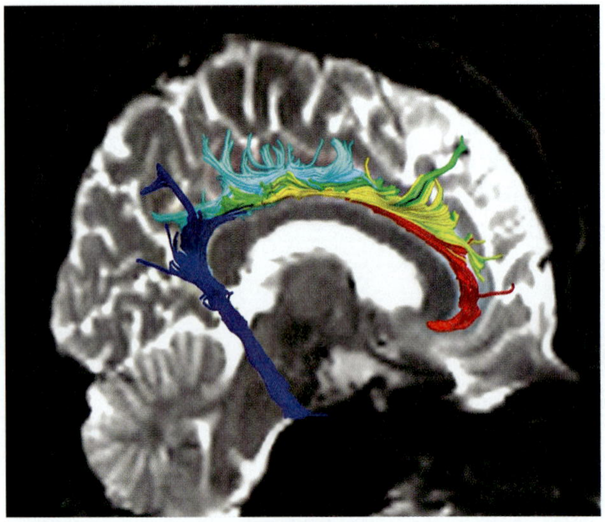

Nestor et al. (2008) used diffusion tensor imaging to investigate schizophrenia. Two of the brain areas examined were the cingulum bundle (CB) and the uncinate fasciculus (UF), two fiber pathways. The cingulum bundle is depicted in the image above. For individuals with schizophrenia, both the CB and UF fiber pathways were found to have neurons with significantly less myelin, making them less efficient in information transfer, and resulting in decreased memory and decision-making ability. Image courtesy of Dr. Paul Nestor.

The development of brain-scanning techniques such as magnetic resonance imaging (MRI) and functional MRI (fMRI) has made studies of the structure as well as the functioning of the brains of those with schizophrenia possible. In one study, researchers using *diffusion tensor imaging* (DTI), LINK to Chapter Two: The Biological Perspective, p. 67, in addition to other neurological testing found that, when compared to healthy control participants, participants with schizophrenia showed structural differences in two particular areas of the brain (Nestor et al., 2008). Specifically, areas known as the cingulum bundle (CB, consisting of fibers underlying the cingulate gyrus linking parts of the limbic system) and the uncinate fasciculus (UF, neural fibers linking the frontal lobe to the temporal lobe) were found to have significantly less myelin coating on the axons of the neurons within the bundle. This makes these areas of the brain less efficient in sending neural messages to other cells, resulting in decreased memory and decision-making ability. The CB has been implicated in other studies of schizophrenia using DTI and suggest that the less myelin and lower neural efficiency is partly responsible for attention problems in schizophrenia (Kubicki et al., 2009) and lower white matter integrity in areas of the frontal lobe might be associated with genetic predisposition to schizophrenia (Camchong et al., 2009). Measuring cortical thickness and tracking changes in the volume of gray matter and white matter is also providing valuable information about the abnormal patterns of brain development in schizophrenia and other disorders (Gogtay et al., 2008; Gogtay & Thompson, 2010; Goldman et al., 2009).

Personality Disorders: I'm Okay, It's Everyone Else Who's Weird

14.9 How do the various personality disorders differ, and what is thought to be the cause of personality disorders?

Personality disorders are a little different from other psychological disorders in that the disorder does not affect merely one aspect of the person's life, such as a higher than normal level of anxiety or a set of distorted beliefs, but instead affects the entire life adjustment of the person. The disorder is the personality itself, not one aspect of it. In personality disorder, a person has an excessively rigid, maladaptive pattern of behavior

stress-vulnerability model explanation of disorder that assumes a biological sensitivity, or vulnerability, to a certain disorder will result in the development of that disorder under the right conditions of environmental or emotional stress.

personality disorders disorders in which a person adopts a persistent, rigid, and maladaptive pattern of behavior that interferes with normal social interactions.

and ways of relating to others (American Psychiatric Association, 2000). This rigidity and inability to adapt to social demands and life changes make it very difficult for the individual with a personality disorder to fit in with others or have relatively normal social relationships. There are three basic categories of personality disorders listed in the *DSM-IV-TR* (American Psychiatric Association, 2000): those in which the people are seen as odd or eccentric by others, those in which the behavior of the person is very dramatic or erratic, and those in which the main emotion is anxiety or fearfulness. There are 10 recognized types of personality disorders (see Table 14.5).

antisocial personality disorder disorder in which a person has no morals or conscience and often behaves in an impulsive manner without regard for the consequences of that behavior.

ANTISOCIAL PERSONALITY DISORDER

One of the most well researched of the personality disorders is **antisocial personality disorder**. People with antisocial personality disorder are literally "against society." The antisocial person, sometimes called a *sociopath*, habitually breaks the law, disobeys rules, tells lies, and uses other people without worrying about their rights or feelings. The person with antisocial personality seems to have no real conscience to create guilt feelings when the person does something morally wrong. As a consequence, people with this disorder typically feel no remorse or guilt at lying, cheating, stealing, or even more serious crimes such as murder.

The first thing that usually comes to most people's minds when they hear the term *sociopath* is the *serial killer*, a person who kills others for the excitement and thrill of killing without feeling any guilt. However, most antisocial personalities are not killers. Typically they borrow money or belongings and don't bother to repay the debt or return the items,

Table 14.5

The Personality Disorders

PERSONALITY DISORDER	DESCRIPTION
Odd or Eccentric Types	
Paranoid	Extreme suspicion of others; mistrustful, often jealous
Schizoid	Loners who are cool, distant, and unwilling and unable to form close relationships with others
Schizotypal	Difficulty in forming social relationships, odd and eccentric behavior, tendency to hold magical beliefs, slightly increased risk of developing schizophrenia later on
Dramatic or Erratic Types	
Antisocial	Lacking in conscience or morals; users and con artists who experience no regret or strong emotions
Borderline	Moody, unstable, lacking in a clear sense of identity, clinging to others
Histrionic	Tendency to overreact and use excessive emotions to draw attention from and manipulate others; love to be the center of attention
Narcissistic	Extremely vain and self-involved
Anxious or Fearful Types	
Avoidant	Fearful of social relationships, tend to avoid social contacts unless absolutely necessary
Dependent	Needy, want others to make decisions for them
Obsessive-Compulsive	Controlling, focused on neatness and order to an extreme degree

Adapted from the American Psychiatric Association, *DSM-IV-TR* (2000).

they are impulsive, they don't keep their commitments either socially or in their jobs, and they tend to be very selfish, self-centered, manipulative, and unable to feel deep emotions.

There is a definite gender difference in antisocial personality disorder with nearly three times to six times as many males diagnosed with this disorder as females (American Psychiatric Association, 2000; Paris, 2004).

BORDERLINE PERSONALITY DISORDER

People with **borderline personality disorder** have relationships with other people that are intense and relatively unstable. They are often moody, manipulative, and untrusting of others. Periods of depression are not unusual, and some may engage in excessive spending, drug abuse, or suicidal behavior (suicide attempts may be part of the manipulation the borderline personality uses against others in a relationship). Emotions are often inappropriate and excessive, leading to confusion with *histrionic personality disorder.* What makes the individual with borderline personality different is the confusion over identity issues, in which the person may be unable to focus on consistent life goals, career choices, friendships, and even sexual behavior (American Psychiatric Association, 2000).

The frequency of this disorder in women is nearly two to three times greater than in men (American Psychiatric Association, 2000; Swartz et al., 1990). Numerous causes such as genetic or hormonal influences, childhood experiences with incest or other abuse, and a poor mother–infant relationship during the years in which the identity is forming have all been suggested as a cause of the disorder (Torgersen, 2000; Widiger & Weissman, 1991; Zanarini, 2000).

CAUSES OF PERSONALITY DISORDERS

Cognitive-behavioral theorists talk about how specific behavior can be learned over time through the processes of reinforcement, shaping, and modeling. More cognitive explanations involve the belief systems formed by the personality disordered persons, such as the paranoia, extreme self-importance, and fear of being unable to cope by oneself of the paranoid, narcissistic, and dependent personalities, for example.

There is some evidence of genetic factors in personality disorders (Reichborn-Kjennerud, 2008). Close biological relatives of people with disorders such as antisocial, schizotypal, and borderline are more likely to have these disorders than those who are not related (American Psychiatric Association, 2000; Battaglia et al., 1995; Faraone et al., 1999; Nigg & Goldsmith, 1994). Adoption studies of children whose biological parents had antisocial personality disorder show an increased risk for that disorder in those children, even though raised in a different environment by different people (American Psychiatric Association, 2000). A longitudinal study has linked the temperaments of children at age 3 to antisocial tendencies in adulthood, finding that those children with lower fearfulness and inhibitions were more likely to show antisocial personality characteristics in a follow-up study at age 28 (Glenn et al., 2007).

Other causes of personality disorders have been suggested. Antisocial personalities are emotionally unresponsive to stressful or threatening situations when compared to others, which may be one reason that they are not afraid of getting caught (Arnett et al., 1997; Blair et al., 1995; Lykken, 1995). This unresponsiveness seems to be linked to lower than normal levels of stress hormones in antisocial persons (Fairchild et al., 2008; Lykken, 1995). **Read** on **mypsychlab.com**

Disturbances in family relationships and communication have also been linked to personality disorders and, in particular, to antisocial personality disorder (Benjamin, 1996; Livesley, 1995). Childhood abuse, neglect, overly strict parenting, overprotective parenting, and parental rejection have all been put forth as possible causes, making the picture of the development of personality disorders a complicated one. It is safe to say that many of the same factors (genetics, social relationships, and parenting) that help to create ordinary personalities also create disordered personalities.

Read and learn more about psychological disorders in the *DSM* on **mypsychlab.com**

borderline personality disorder maladaptive personality pattern in which the person is moody, unstable, lacks a clear sense of identity, and often clings to others.

14.8 14.9

CONCEPT MAP

- **schizophrenia** psychotic disorder involving a break with reality and disturbances in thinking, emotions, behavior, and perceptions
  - primary symptoms are often classified as positive (in excess or in addition to normal functions) or negative (absence or decrease in normal functions)
    - **delusions:** false beliefs about the world (e.g., delusions of persecution, delusions of grandeur, delusions of reference)
    - **disturbed or disorganized thoughts:** often lacking structure or relevance, most often displayed through disorganized speech
    - **hallucinations:** can occur in any sensory modality but auditory hallucinations are most common
    - **changes in mood:** including flat affect (displaying little or no emotion)
    - **disorganized or odd behavior:** ranging from periods of immobility to odd gesturing or facial grimaces
  - categories
    - **disorganized**
    - **catatonic**
    - **paranoid**
  - causes
    - positive symptoms appear to be associated with overactivity of dopamine areas of brain; negative with lower dopamine activity; related to dopamine hypothesis
    - genetics and brain structural defects have been implicated
    - biological roots supported by universal lifetime prevalence across cultures of approximately 7–8 people out of 1,000; genetics supported by twin and adoption studies
    - **stress-vulnerability model:** suggests people with genetic markers for schizophrenia will not develop the disorder unless they are exposed to environmental or emotional stress at critical times in development

Schizophrenia and Personality Disorders

- **personality disorders** involve excessively rigid and maladaptive patterns of behavior and ways of relating to others (see Table 14.5)
  - **antisocial personality disorder:** sociopath; minimal to no regard for value of others' rights or feelings; more common in men
  - **borderline personality disorder:** relationships with others that are intense and unstable; often moody, manipulative, and untrusting of others; more common in women
  - causes
    - **psychodynamic:** inadequate resolution of Oedipus complex
    - **cognitive-behavioral:** specific behaviors learned over time, associated with maladaptive belief systems
    - genetic factors play a role, with many showing increased rates of heritability
    - variances in stress tolerance and disturbances in family relationships and communication have also been linked to personality disorders

PRACTICE quiz How much do you remember?

ANSWERS ON PAGE AK-2.

Pick the best answer.

1. Charles believed that a famous song by a popular musical group carried a special, secret message meant only for him. This would be an example of a delusion of __________.
   a. persecution.
   b. reference.
   c. influence.
   d. grandeur.
2. In an old movie, a madman made weird faces and sounds, jumped about wildly in his cell, and laughed and giggled constantly. This bizarre behavior is typical of __________ schizophrenia.
   a. disorganized
   b. catatonic
   c. paranoid
   d. depressed
3. In which type of schizophrenia is an individual most likely to have delusions of grandeur?
   a. disorganized
   b. catatonic
   c. paranoid
   d. depressed
4. Which of the following statements about antisocial personality disorder is TRUE?
   a. Most people with this disorder are vicious killers.
   b. Most people with this disorder are men.
   c. People with this disorder suffer terrible guilt but commit crimes anyway.
   d. People with this disorder feel emotions very deeply and intensely.

Brainstorming: Do you think it is possible for someone with a personality disorder to change his or her maladaptive behavior with the help of psychotherapy? Are there any personality disorders that might be more changeable than others?

FUTURE DIRECTIONS IN PSYCHOPATHOLOGY

14.10 What are some of the future directions in psychopathology?

The *DSM-5* is currently in development and will likely include a variety of updates associated with current research and changes in perspectives over the years. The name itself "DSM-5," using Arabic instead of Roman numerals, is in line with how future updates will be created such as *DSM-5.1*, *DSM-5.2*, and so forth (American Psychiatric Association, 2010). As with other areas of science, what people once believed to be true—or to be most important—can change after collecting enough correct data. Greater awareness can also come as the result of shifts in perspective. For example, it was once believed that very young children were incapable of experiencing the primary symptoms of depression. However, data is accumulating that suggests the opposite, and research is ongoing related to the early detection and recognition of depression in young children, coupled with early intervention (Luby, 2010).

Some changes in the study of the various disorders are in the language, or nomenclature, related to symptoms and conceptualizations, such as recasting "mental retardation" as "intellectual disability." Other modifications reflect systematic changes in the conceptualization of disorders. The personality disorders are one area under review and will likely move to a dimensional spectrum approach (American Psychiatric Association, 2009). Spectrum, or dimensional approaches are likely to characterize many different areas in the *DSM-5* as some symptoms have a broad range of manifestation and many disorders don't lend themselves to neatly fitting in their prescribed categories. For example, differentiation between depression being a chronic disorder versus it being an episodic disorder has been raised (D. N. Klein, 2010).

Finally, there has been a push for greater sociocultural relevance and incorporation of a soicocultural framework into the diagnostic and treatment process; it is a factor for all individuals, not just racial and ethnic minorities (Alarcón et al., 2009). Specifically for the *DSM-5*, recognition of factors that cut across all diagnoses, such as gender and cultural issues, will be a primary goal along with closer alliance with other diagnostic systems such as the World Health System's International Classification of Diseases (Kupfer & Reger, 2009).

Applying Psychology to Everyday Life: Taking the Worry Out of Exams

Imagine this scenario: You sit down to take your midterm exam, feeling that you are prepared and ready. Once you get the test in front of you, well, maybe you start to feel just a bit more nervous, your hands get sweaty, your stomach may ache; and when you look at the first question—your mind becomes a complete blank!

These are a few of the common symptoms of *test anxiety*, the personal experience of possible negative consequences or poor outcomes on an exam or evaluation, accompanied by a cluster of cognitive, affective, and behavioral symptoms (Zeidner & Matthews, 2005). *Cognitive* symptoms may consist of worrying excessively about an exam, expecting to do poorly no matter how hard you study, or even finding it hard to start studying in the first place. Then, while taking the test, you might find you do not understand certain directions or questions, "go blank" when looking at the items, or feel like you cannot concentrate on the exam in front of you because your mind keeps wandering. *Affective* or emotional symptoms may include body tension and heightened physiological arousal including sweaty palms, upset stomach, difficulty breathing, and the like, prior to and/or during the exam. *Behavioral* aspects may include procrastination, deficient study skills, or avoiding studying altogether.

While not yet recognized as a clinical disorder in the *DSM-IV-TR*, test anxiety has caused countless students considerable stress and agony over the years. Remember "psychology student's syndrome"? You may not really have any of the psychological disorders we've discussed in this chapter, but chances are good that you *have* experienced test anxiety a time or two. One way to make the development of a true anxiety disorder less likely is to deal realistically with milder forms of anxiety *before* they escalate, and the main intent of this section is to help you achieve that.

So, what can you do if you experience test anxiety and want to get your worrying under control? First, determine why you want to do well on the test in the first place. Do you really want to demonstrate your understanding of the material or are you hoping just to pass? Try to find an internal motivation to do well on the exam rather than simply relying on extrinsic reasons. Even if you are taking a test in a subject you don't necessarily enjoy, try to identify something **you** want to accomplish, and get your focus off the goal of simply earning a passing grade.

Second, develop some type of strategy for controlling both your cognitive state and behavior, before and during the exam. Review the study tips we presented in the Psychology in Action section of this book. As mentioned there, if you are well prepared, you are less likely to worry. Avoid cramming and take advantage of the additive effects of distributed practice. Refer back to that information and review suggestions that will help you manage your tasks and your time. Schedule regular study sessions and avoid or limit distractions (email, phone, text messages, television, noisy roommates, and the like may seem to provide welcome escapes from studying, but they will only keep you from your intended goal). You've read the chapter on Learning (or at least you should have!) and now know that spacing out your study and using meaningful, elaborative rehearsal over multiple study periods is going to yield much better results than an all-out cramming marathon the night before an exam. LINK to Psychology in Action: Secrets for Surviving College and Improving Your Grades, pp. I-10–I-12.

The way you approach an exam can have a significant impact on the testing experience and how you manage yourself during that exam (Davis et al., 2008). Instead of focusing on how nervous you are and how sure you are that you aren't going to be able to remember anything, turn that thinking around and recognize how much energy you have going in to the exam (Dundas et al., 2009). Positive self-talk can be very valuable in this kind of situation (and is a good example of cognitive therapy at work). A recent study demonstrated that competence-priming (imagining a person who is successful at a related task), lowered the relationship between test anxiety and test performance (Lang & Lang, 2010). Lastly, instead of focusing on the whole exam, take control and address one question at a time, first answering the questions you know—that will build your confidence and help you progress through the test. Also control your body, try to stay relaxed and breathe normally. If you get distracted, consciously redirect yourself back to the next question. Before you know it, you will have completed the entire exam—whew!

chapter summary

((•• Listen on mypsychlab.com Listen to an audio file of your chapter **www.mypsychlab.com**

What Is Abnormality?

- Psychopathology is the study of abnormal behavior.

14.1 How has mental illness been explained in the past, how is abnormal behavior defined today, and what is the impact of cultural differences in defining abnormality?

- In ancient times holes were cut in an ill person's head to let out evil spirits in a process called trepanning. Hippocrates believed that mental illness came from an imbalance in the body's four humors, whereas in the Middle Ages the mentally ill were labeled as witches.
- Abnormal behavior can be defined as behavior that is statistically rare, is deviant from social norms, causes subjective discomfort, does not allow day-to-day functioning, or causes a person to be dangerous to self or others.
- Cultural relativity refers to the need to consider the norms and customs of another culture when diagnosing a person from that culture with a disorder.
- In the United States, *insanity* is a legal term, not a psychological term.

ISSUES IN PSYCHOLOGY: Abnormality Versus Insanity

Models of Abnormality

14.2 How can psychological disorders be explained within the biological and psychological models?

- In biological models of abnormality, the assumption is that mental illnesses are caused by chemical or structural malfunctions in the nervous system.
- Psychodynamic theorists assume that abnormal behavior stems from repressed conflicts and urges that are fighting to become conscious.
- Behaviorists see abnormal behavior as learned.
- Cognitive theorists see abnormal behavior as coming from irrational beliefs and illogical patterns of thought.

Diagnostic and Statistical Manual of Mental Disorders, Fourth Edition, Text Revision (*DSM-IV-TR*)

14.3 What are the different types of psychological disorders and how common are they?

- *Diagnostic and Statistical Manual of Mental Disorders, Fourth Edition, Text Revision (DSM-IV-TR)* is a manual of psychological disorders and their symptoms.
- There are five axes in the *DSM-IV-TR*, which include clinical disorders, personality disorders and mental retardation, general medical conditions, psychosocial and environmental problems, and a global assessment of functioning.
- Over one fifth of all adults over age 18 suffer from a mental disorder in any given year. Major depression is one of the most common psychological disorders worldwide.

Anxiety Disorders: What, Me Worry?

14.4 What are the different types of anxiety disorders, their symptoms, and causes?

- Anxiety disorders are all disorders in which the most dominant symptom is excessive and unrealistic anxiety.
- Phobias are irrational, persistent fears. The three types of phobias are social phobias, specific phobias, and agoraphobia.
- Obsessive-compulsive disorder consists of an obsessive, recurring thought that creates anxiety and a compulsive, ritualistic, and repetitive behavior that reduces that anxiety.
- Panic disorder is the sudden and recurrent onset of intense panic for no reason, with all the physical symptoms that can occur in sympathetic nervous system arousal, and is sometimes accompanied by agoraphobia.
- Generalized anxiety disorder is a condition of intense and unrealistic anxiety that lasts 6 months or more.
- Psychodynamic explanations point to repressed urges and desires that are trying to come into consciousness, creating anxiety that is controlled by the abnormal behavior.
- Behaviorists state that disordered behavior is learned through both operant conditioning and classical conditioning techniques.
- Cognitive psychologists believe that excessive anxiety comes from illogical, irrational thought processes.
- Biological explanations of anxiety disorders include chemical imbalances in the nervous system, in particular serotonin and GABA systems.
- Genetic transmission may be responsible for anxiety disorders among related persons.

Mood Disorders: The Effect of Affect

14.5 What are the different types of mood disorders and their causes?

- Mood disorders, also called affective disorders, are severe disturbances in emotion.
- Dysthymia is a moderate depression that is typically a reaction to some external stressor, whereas cyclothymia consists of moderate mood swings usually tied to an external stressor.
- Major depression has a sudden onset and is extreme sadness and despair, typically with no obvious external cause. It is the most common of the mood disorders and is twice as common in women as in men.
- Bipolar disorders are severe mood swings from major depressive episodes to manic episodes of extreme elation and energy with no obvious external cause.
- Psychodynamic theories see depression as anger at authority figures from childhood turned inward on the self.

- Learning theories link depression to learned helplessness.
- Cognitive theories see depression as the result of distorted, illogical thinking.
- Biological explanations of mood disorders look at the function of serotonin, norepinephrine, and dopamine systems in the brain.
- Mood disorders are more likely to appear in genetically related people with higher rates of risk for closer genetic relatives.

Eating Disorders

14.6 What are the two primary types of eating disorders, how do they differ, and who are they most likely to affect?

- Maladaptive eating problems include anorexia and bulimia.
- Genetics, low levels of serotonin, and insensitivity to leptin (a hormone that influences appetite) may play a part in anorexia and bulimia.

Dissociative Disorders: Altered Identities

14.7 How do the various dissociative disorders differ, and how do they develop?

- Dissociative disorders involve a break in consciousness, memory, or both. These disorders include dissociative amnesia, dissociative fugue, and dissociative identity disorder.
- Psychodynamic explanations point to repression of memories, seeing dissociation as a defense mechanism against anxiety.
- Cognitive and behavioral explanations see dissociative disorders as a kind of avoidance learning.
- Biological explanations point to lower than normal activity levels in the areas responsible for body awareness in people with dissociative disorders.

Schizophrenia: Altered Reality

- Schizophrenia is a split between thoughts, emotions, and behavior. It is a long-lasting psychotic disorder in which reality and fantasy become confused.

14.8 What are the main symptoms, types, and causes of schizophrenia?

- Symptoms of schizophrenia include delusions (false beliefs about the world), hallucinations, emotional disturbances, attentional difficulties, disturbed speech, and disordered thinking.
- The three types of schizophrenic behavior are disorganized, catatonic, and paranoid.
- Positive symptoms are excesses of behavior associated with increased dopamine activity, whereas negative symptoms are deficits in behavior associated with decreased dopamine activity.
- Psychodynamic theories see schizophrenia as resulting from a severe breakdown of the ego, which has become overwhelmed by the demands of the id and results in childish, infantile behavior.
- Behaviorists focus on how reinforcement, observational learning, and shaping affect the development of the behavioral symptoms of schizophrenia.
- Cognitive theorists see schizophrenia as severely irrational thinking.
- Biological explanations focus on dopamine, structural defects in the brain, and genetic influences in schizophrenia. Rates of risk of developing schizophrenia increase drastically as genetic relatedness increases with the highest risk faced by an identical twin whose twin sibling has schizophrenia.

Personality Disorders: I'm Okay, It's Everyone Else Who's Weird

14.9 How do the various personality disorders differ, and what is thought to be the cause of personality disorders?

- Personality disorders are extremely rigid, maladaptive patterns of behavior that prevent a person from normal social interactions and relationships.
- In antisocial personality disorder a person has no conscience and uses people for personal gain. A rare form is the serial killer.
- In borderline personality disorder a person is clingy, moody, unstable in relationships, and suffers from problems with identity.
- Cognitive-learning theorists see personality disorders as a set of learned behavior that has become maladaptive—bad habits learned early on in life. Belief systems of the personality disordered person are seen as illogical.
- Biological relatives of people with personality disorders are more likely to develop similar disorders, supporting a genetic basis for such disorders.
- Biological explanations look at the lower than normal stress hormones in antisocial personality disordered persons as responsible for their low responsiveness to threatening stimuli.
- Other possible causes of personality disorders may include disturbances in family communications and relationships, childhood abuse, neglect, overly strict parenting, overprotective parenting, and parental rejection.

14.10 What are some of the future directions in psychopathology?

- The *DSM* is constantly being revised to include the findings of current research.
- Some changes involve the terminology used to describe disorders and their symptoms.
- There is a push for greater social relevance and attention to cultural differences.

Applying Psychology to Everyday Life: Taking the Worry Out of Exams

- Test anxiety is a common and very distressing experience for many students.
- There are several things that can be done to reduce test anxiety, including preparation and relaxation exercises.

test YOURSELF

ANSWERS ON PAGE AK-2.

Study and Review on **mypsychlab.com** Ready for your test? More quizzes and a customized study plan **www.mypsychlab.com**

Pick the best answer.

1. Survivors of natural disasters like Hurricane Katrina in 2005 and the 2010 BP oil spill in the Gulf of Mexico may experience higher incidences of _________:
- **a.** depression
- **b.** posttraumatic stress disorder
- **c.** anxiety disorders
- **d.** all of the above

2. What was the most likely reason that ancient peoples performed trepanning on others?
- **a.** to relieve fluid pressure on the brain
- **b.** to look into the brain to see what was wrong
- **c.** to release evil spirits that were in the person's head
- **d.** to restore balance to the body's humors

3. Michael decided to give up his job teaching at a small community college in Florida and become a monk. He moved to a nearby town with a monastery, took his vows, and is now living quite happily as a member of that religious order. By what definition might Michael's behavior be considered abnormal?
- **a.** statistical
- **b.** subjective discomfort
- **c.** maladaptive
- **d.** harmful to self

4. Which model of abnormality talks about rewards, shaping, and imitation as ways of developing abnormal behavior?
- **a.** psychodynamic
- **b.** behavioral
- **c.** cognitive
- **d.** biological

5. Which axis of the *DSM-IV-TR* would a therapist use to classify the loss of a person's job?
- **a.** I
- **b.** II
- **c.** III
- **d.** IV

6. When anxiety is unrelated to any known, realistic factor, it is called _________.
- **a.** free-floating anxiety.
- **b.** panic.
- **c.** a phobia.
- **d.** acute.

7. Alisa hates to go over bridges. This is a mild form of _________.
- **a.** social phobia.
- **b.** specific phobia.
- **c.** agoraphobia.
- **d.** claustrophobia.

8. Professor Albus always checked the door to his office before leaving for class, lunch, or home. He would pull it closed and then rattle the doorknob three times to make sure that it was locked. He does this because he keeps thinking that he hasn't really locked it well. His thoughts about this are a form of _________.
- **a.** obsession.
- **b.** compulsion.
- **c.** anxiety attack.
- **d.** door phobia.

9. When a person experiences sudden attacks of intense fear, racing heart, dizziness, and other physical signs of stress, and refuses to go away from home for fear one of these attacks will happen again, it is most properly called _________.
- **a.** an anxiety attack.
- **b.** a panic attack.
- **c.** panic disorder.
- **d.** panic disorder with agoraphobia.

10. Lori went to great lengths to plan a surprise party for her mother's 70th birthday. "Oh, if she finds out about this, the whole thing will be ruined, it'll be a disaster!" Her sister tried to tell her that even if the party ended up not being a surprise, their mother would be happy and have fun, but Lori was convinced that it would be horrible. According to a cognitive theorist, Lori is engaging in _________.
- **a.** minimization.
- **b.** all-or-nothing thinking.
- **c.** overgeneralization.
- **d.** magnification.

11. Which term does not belong?
- **a.** bipolar
- **b.** hypochondria
- **c.** dysthymia
- **d.** major depression

12. Which mood disorder consists of mostly manic episodes with only a few episodes of depression?
- **a.** bipolar
- **b.** unipolar
- **c.** dysthymia
- **d.** major depression

13. Which mood disorder consists of a consistent, extremely sad mood?
- **a.** bipolar
- **b.** cyclothymia
- **c.** mania
- **d.** major depression

14. Unlike individuals with anorexia, individuals with bulimia _________.
- **a.** often purge themselves to stay thin.
- **b.** are obsessed with being too thin.
- **c.** can do damage to their health.
- **d.** may appear to be normal in weight.

15. The role of _________, a neurotransmitter, may provide clues to both bulimia and anorexia.
- **a.** serotonin
- **b.** insulin
- **c.** dopamine
- **d.** norepinephrine

16. Dissociative amnesia is different from retrograde amnesia because _________.
- **a.** only memories of the past are lost in retrograde amnesia.
- **b.** the ability to form new memories is lost in retrograde amnesia.
- **c.** dissociative amnesia is caused by a physical blow to the head.
- **d.** dissociative amnesia is caused by psychological trauma.

17. The fact that people with dissociative identity disorder have different PET scan activity when in their different "personalities" is evidence for the _________ explanation of dissociative disorders.
- **a.** biological
- **b.** psychodynamic
- **c.** behavioral
- **d.** cognitive

18. A character in an old movie was a street person who wore aluminum foil on his head to protect his brain from the thought-controlling rays of the government. This is an example of a _________ delusion.
- **a.** persecution
- **b.** reference
- **c.** influence
- **d.** grandeur

19. Which of the following is not a typical symptom of schizophrenia?
 a. overly rational thinking
 b. inappropriate emotions
 c. delusions
 d. hallucinations

20. In which category of schizophrenia would a person be who remains motionless for long periods of time?
 a. catatonic
 b. disorganized
 c. paranoid
 d. undifferentiated

21. David Koresh, leader of the ill-fated Branch Davidians in Waco, Texas, believed that he was "God's Anointed One," who would bring about the end of the world. This is a __________ delusion.
 a. jealous
 b. grandiose
 c. persecutory
 d. somatic

22. Relatives of people who have schizotypal personality disorder have an increased risk of developing __________ when compared to unrelated persons.
 a. major depression
 b. affective psychosis
 c. antisocial personality disorder
 d. schizophrenia

23. Erik gets really anxious before and during exams. What are two strategies he might focus on?
 a. not sleeping the night before an exam and skipping breakfast
 b. improving his studying/preparation beforehand and learning relaxation techniques
 c. really focusing on how anxious he is and breathing rapidly
 d. waiting until his anxiety is at its worst and then just ignoring it

CONCEPT SUMMARY

14 psychological disorders

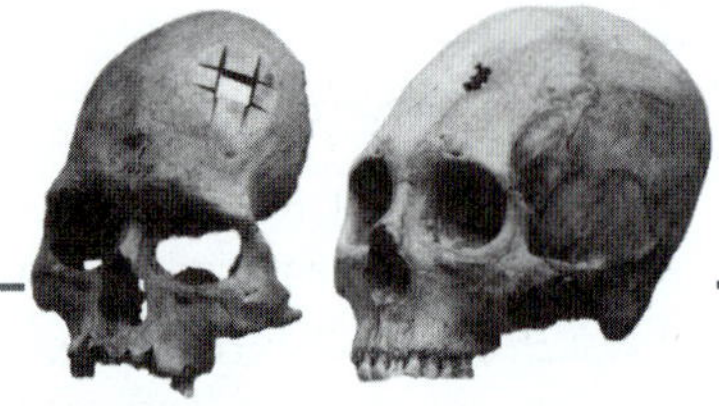

14.1 14.2 14.3 p. 540

Psychological Disorders

- **what is abnormality?**
  - **psychopathology** is the study of abnormal behavior; mental illness has been defined in various ways throughout history (e.g., possession, evil spirits, bodily imbalances)
  - current definitions of abnormality are based on several factors
  - disorders vary according to culture; cultural sensitivity and relativity are necessary in diagnosing and treating psychological disorders
  - overall, psychological disorders are any pattern of behavior that causes significant distress, causes individuals to harm themselves or others, or harms their ability to function in daily life
- **models of abnormality**
  explanations for disordered behavior depend on theoretical model used to explain personality in general
  - **biological model**
  - **psychological models**
  - **biopsychosocial perspective**
- ***Diagnostic and Statistical Manual of Mental Disorders, Fourth Edition, Text Revision (DSM–IV–TR)***
  - *DSM* first published in 1952, current version *(DSM–IV–TR)* published in 2000
  - currently describes approximately 250 different psychological disorders and includes diagnostic criteria along five different categories, or axes (see Table 14.1)
  - in general, approximately 26% of adults over age 18 in the United States suffer from a mental disorder (see Table 14.2)

Table 14.1
Axis I Disorders of the *DSM-IV-TR*

DISORDER	EXAMPLES
Disorders usually first diagnosed in infancy, childhood, or adolescence	Learning disabilities, ADHD, bed-wetting, speech disorders, conduct disorder, oppositional defiant disorder
Delirium, dementia, amnesia, and other cognitive disorders	Alzheimer's, Parkinson's, amnesia due to physical causes
Psychological disorders due to a general medical condition	Personality change because of a brain tumor
Substance-related disorders	Alcoholism, drug addictions
Schizophrenia and other psychotic disorders	Schizophrenia, delusional disorders, paranoid psychosis
Mood disorders	Depression, mania, bipolar disorders
Anxiety disorders	Panic disorder, phobias, stress disorders
Somatoform disorders	Hypochondriasis, conversion disorder

14.4 14.5 p. 549

Anxiety and Mood Disorders

- **anxiety disorders**
  most dominant symptom is excessive or unrealistic anxiety
  - anxiety can be free-floating (nonspecific, anxious in general) or more specific, as in the case of phobias
  - **panic disorder** consists of an individual having frequent panic attacks that interfere with normal daily functioning; **panic disorder with agoraphobia** occurs when a fear of having panic attacks in public prevents an individual from going out
  - **obsessive-compulsive disorder (OCD)** consists of recurring anxiety-provoking thoughts or obsessions that are only relieved through ritualistic or repetitive behaviors or mental events
  - **generalized anxiety disorder** involves excessive worry about lots of things and occurs more days than not
  - causes
    - **behavioral**
    - **cognitive**
    - **biological**
    - **cultural**

- **mood disorders**
  involve a disturbance in mood or emotion; can be mild or severe
  - **major depression:** deeply depressed mood; most commonly diagnosed mood disorder, twice as common in women
  - **bipolar disorders** involve extreme mood swings, ranging from severe depression to manic episodes
  - causes
    - **psychodynamic**
    - **behavioral**
    - **social cognitive**
    - **biological**

14.6 14.7 p. 556

Eating and Dissociative Disorders

- **eating disorders**
  - **anorexia nervosa** is disordered eating that causes weight loss 15% or more below body weight
  - **bulimia nervosa** involves cycles of binging and use of unhealthy methods to avoid weight gain; unlike anorexia, those with bulimia will tend to maintain a normal body weight

- **dissociative disorders** involve a dissociation in consciousness, memory, or sense of identity, often associated with extreme stress or trauma
  - **dissociative amnesia:** one cannot remember personal information
  - **dissociative fugue:** person takes sudden trip and cannot remember traveling or personal information
  - **dissociative identity disorder:** person seems to experience at least two or more distinct personalities; validity of actual disorder has been topic of debate
  - causes
    - **psychodynamic**
    - **cognitive and behavioral**
    - **biological**

14.8 14.9 p. 563

Schizophrenia and Personality Disorders

- **schizophrenia** psychotic disorder involving a break with reality and disturbances in thinking, emotions, behavior, and perceptions
  - primary symptoms are often classified as positive (in excess or in addition to normal functions) or negative (absence or decrease in normal functions)
    - **delusions**
    - **disturbed or disorganized thoughts**
    - **hallucinations**
    - **changes in mood**
    - **disorganized or odd behavior**
  - categories
    - **disorganized**
    - **catatonic**
    - **paranoid**
  - causes
    - positive symptoms appear to be associated with overactivity of dopamine areas of brain; negative with lower dopamine activity; related to dopamine hypothesis
    - genetics and brain structural defects have been implicated
    - biological roots supported by universal lifetime prevalence across cultures of approximately 7–8 people out of 1,000; genetics supported by twin and adoption studies
    - **stress-vulnerability model:** suggests people with genetic markers for schizophrenia will not develop the disorder unless they are exposed to environmental or emotional stress at critical times in development

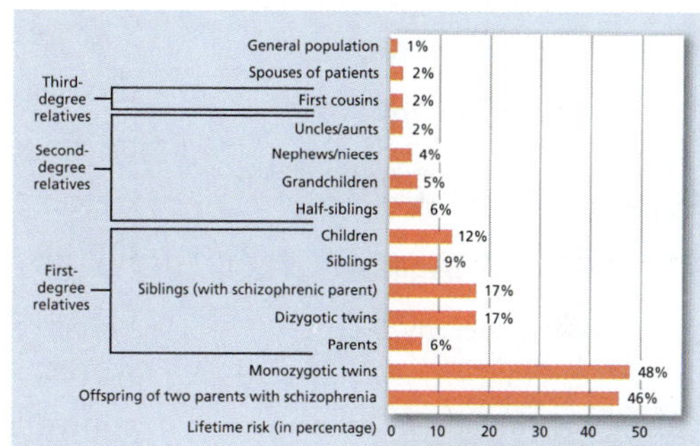

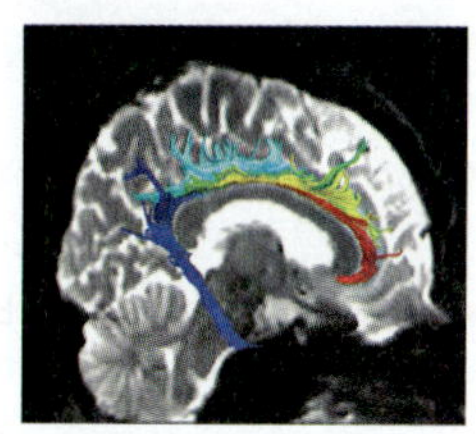

- **personality disorders** involve excessively rigid and maladaptive patterns of behavior and ways of relating to others (see Table 14.5)
  - **antisocial personality disorder**
  - **borderline personality disorder**
  - causes
    - **psychodynamic**
    - **cognitive-behavioral**
    - genetic factors play a role, with many showing increased rates of heritability
    - variances in stress tolerance and disturbances in family relationships and communication have also been linked to personality disorders

Odd or Eccentric Types
Paranoid
Schizoid
Schizotypal

Dramatic or Erratic Types
Antisocial
Borderline
Histrionic
Narcissistic

Anxious or Fearful Types
Avoidant
Dependent
Obsessive-Compulsive

15 psychological therapies

CHAPTER OUTLINE

- Two Kinds of Therapy
- The Early Days: Ice-Water Baths and Electric Shocks
- Psychotherapy Begins
- Humanistic Therapy: To Err Is Human
- Behavior Therapies: Learning One's Way to Better Behavior
- Cognitive Therapies: Thinking Is Believing
- Group Therapies: Not Just for the Shy
- PSYCHOLOGY IN THE NEWS: Mental Health on Campus
- Does Psychotherapy Really Work?
- Biomedical Therapies
- APPLYING PSYCHOLOGY TO EVERYDAY LIFE: Virtual Realities

Have you noticed how often television programs, especially medical dramas, take their plots almost directly from newspaper headlines or real situations? A number of years ago, there was an excellent but short-lived medical show called *Chicago Hope.* On one episode, the neurosurgeon worked with a psychiatrist to help a young boy who suffered from obsessive-compulsive disorder (OCD), which caused him to count constantly and left him unable to live a normal life. The neurosurgeon severed some of the neural fibers in an area of the brain called the *cingulate gyrus,* believed to be responsible for the obsessive behavior. In the television program, of course, the surgery is successful.

In real life, this surgery is seen as a treatment of last resort for not only certain OCDs, but also chronic pain. It is called *bilateral anterior cingulotomy* and is discussed near the end of this chapter (Christmas et al., 2004). When this surgery works, its success is attributed to the involvement of this area of the brain in controlling tasks that demand attention (Crottaz-Herbette & Menon, 2006; Davis et al., 2000).

Unfortunately, further research has shown that this procedure does not have as positive a result as the magical world of television might lead you to believe. In a long-term follow up of 44 patients, each the recipient of a cingulotomy for OCD, only 32 percent of the 44 patients actually responded to the surgery with significant improvement; another 14 percent showed modest signs of improvement, and there were side effects of the surgery: memory problems, apathy, urinary problems, and seizures (Dougherty et al., 2002). The researchers concluded that cingulotomy was perhaps not the best treatment for OCD.

This anecdote illustrates the difficulty of finding the right therapy or combination of therapies to treat disorders. Different disorders require different kinds of therapies, and not all disorders can be completely eliminated. Therapies can take many forms, depending on the particular psychological explanation and approach to the disorder—which will then determine the basis of the therapy. In this chapter, we'll explore many of these forms of therapy and their relative success for various disorders.

Why study therapies for psychological disorders?

There are almost as many therapy methods as there are disorders. Correctly matching the type of therapy to the disorder can mean the difference between a cure or a crisis. It is important to know the choices available for treatment and how they relate to the different kinds of disorders so that an informed decision can be made and the best possible outcome can be achieved for mental health and wellness.

learning objectives

15.1 What are the two modern ways in which psychological disorders can be treated, and how have they been treated in the past?

15.2 What were the basic elements of Freud's psychoanalysis, and how does psychoanalysis differ today?

15.3 What are the basic elements of the humanistic therapies known as person-centered therapy and Gestalt therapy?

15.4 How do behavior therapists use classical and operant conditioning to treat disordered behavior?

15.5 How successful are behavior therapies?

15.6 What are the goals and basic elements of cognitive therapies such as cognitive–behavioral therapy and rational–emotive behavior therapy?

15.7 What are the various types of group therapies and the advantages and disadvantages of group therapy?

15.8 How effective is psychotherapy, and how is the effectiveness of psychotherapy influenced by cultural, ethnic, and gender differences?

15.9 What are the various types of drugs used to treat psychological disorders?

15.10 How are electroconvulsive therapy and psychosurgery used to treat psychological disorders today?

15.11 How might computers be used in psychotherapy?

study tip

As you are reading this chapter, take a look back at page I-5–I-8 in *Psychology in Action* for some ways to get more out of this chapter as you read through it.

Two Kinds of Therapy

When talking about treating psychological disorders, there are two main types of **therapy** (treatment methods aimed at making people feel better and function more effectively). In one type of therapy based in psychological techniques, people tell the therapist about their problems, and the therapist listens and tries to help them understand those problems or assists them in changing the behaviors related to the problem. The other type of therapy uses medical interventions to bring the symptoms under control. Although we can separate treatments into these two larger categories, many effective treatments combine facets of both. Just as there as is no one single "cause" of a disorder (Maxmen et al., 2009), different psychological treatments are often used in tandem or combined with biomedical interventions.

15.1 What are the two modern ways in which psychological disorders can be treated, and how have they been treated in the past?

The kind of therapy that involves application of psychological principles is called **psychotherapy**, whereas the kind of therapy that uses medical methods is called **biomedical therapy**.

PSYCHOTHERAPY

The goal of most psychotherapy is to help both mentally healthy and psychologically disordered persons understand themselves better (Goin, 2005; Wolberg, 1977). Because understanding of one's motives and actions is called *insight*, therapies aimed mainly at this goal are called **insight therapies**. A therapy that is directed more at changing behavior than providing insights into the reasons for that behavior is called **action therapy**. Many psychological professionals use a combination of insight and action therapeutic methods.

BIOMEDICAL THERAPY

The other main type of therapy uses some biological treatment in the form of a medical procedure to bring about changes in the person's disordered behavior. Biomedical therapies include the use of drugs, surgical methods, and electric shock treatments. It is important to understand that biomedical therapy often

therapy treatment methods aimed at making people feel better and function more effectively.

psychotherapy therapy for mental disorders in which a person with a problem talks with a psychological professional.

biomedical therapy therapy for mental disorders in which a person with a problem is treated with biological or medical methods to relieve symptoms.

insight therapies therapies in which the main goal is helping people to gain insight with respect to their behavior, thoughts, and feelings.

action therapy therapy in which the main goal is to change disordered or inappropriate behavior directly.

eliminates or alleviates the symptoms of a disorder while psychotherapy addresses issues associated with the disorder, and when used together, these two types of therapy facilitate each other (Maxmen et al., 2009). For example, when medications are needed, individuals taking the proper medications are going to benefit more from psychotherapy as their symptoms will be better controlled. Furthermore, psychotherapy, not medication, is going to help them better understand what the symptoms of their disorder are and facilitate adjustment, other coping strategies, and proactive ways of addressing the disorder or its related outcomes (Maxmen et al., 2009).

The Early Days: Ice-Water Baths and Electric Shocks

As discussed in Chapter Fourteen, although psychological or social causes might have been identified for some disorders, until the late 1700s, people suffering severe mental illnesses were sometimes thought to be possessed by demons or evil spirits, and the "treatments" to rid the person of these spirits were severe and deadly. Even within the last 200 years, a period of supposedly more "enlightened" awareness, the mentally ill did not always receive humane* treatment. **Watch** on **mypsychlab.com**

Watch a video on the history of mental institutions in the United States on **mypsychlab.com**

EARLY TREATMENT OF THE MENTALLY ILL

I've seen movies about mental hospitals, and they didn't look like great places to be in even now—how bad was it back then? What did people do with relatives who were ill that way?

I've seen movies about mental hospitals, and they didn't look like great places to be in even now—how bad was it back then? What did people do with relatives who were ill that way?

The first truly organized effort to do something with mentally ill persons began in England in the middle of the sixteenth century. Bethlehem Hospital in London (later known as "Bedlam") was converted into an asylum (a word meaning "place of safety") for the mentally ill. In reality, the first asylums were little more than prisons where the mentally ill were chained to their beds. "Treatments" consisted of bloodletting (which more often than not led to death or the need for lifelong care for the patient), beatings, ice baths in which the person was submerged until passing out or suffering a seizure, and induced vomiting in a kind of spiritual cleansing (Hunt, 1993). This cleansing or purging was meant to rid the body of physical impurities so that the person's mind and soul could function more perfectly.

In this famous painting by French artist Robert Fleury, French psychiatrist Dr. Philippe Pinel orders the chains removed from patients at a Paris asylum for insane women. Pinel was one of the first psychiatrists to recommend humane treatment of the mentally ill.

PINEL'S REFORMS

It was not until 1793 that efforts were made to treat the mentally ill with kindness and guidance—known as "moral treatment"—rather than beating them or subjecting them to the harsh physical purging that had been commonplace. It was at this time that Philippe Pinel personally unchained the inmates at La Bicêtre Asylum in Paris, France, beginning the movement of humane treatment of the mentally ill (Brigham, 1844; Curtis, 1993).

*humane: marked by compassion, sympathy, or consideration for humans (and animals).

So what exactly happens in psychoanalysis? I've heard lots of stories about it, but what's it really like?

Psychotherapy Begins

So what exactly happens in psychoanalysis? I've heard lots of stories about it, but what's it really like?

In a sense, Freud took the old method of physical cleansing to a different level. Instead of a physical purge, cleansing for Freud meant removing all the "impurities" of the unconscious mind that he believed were responsible for his patients' psychological and nervous disorders. (Freud was a medical doctor and referred to the people who came to him for help as "patients.") The impurities of the unconscious mind were considered to be disturbing thoughts, socially unacceptable desires, and immoral urges that originated in the id, the part of the personality that is itself unconscious and driven by basic needs for survival and pleasure. LINK to Chapter Thirteen: Theories of Personality, p. 495.

"Why do you think you cross the road?"

PSYCHOANALYSIS

Freud believed that his patients used these unconscious thoughts to prevent anxiety, and as such, the thoughts would not be easily brought into conscious awareness. Freud designed a therapy technique to help his patients feel more relaxed, open, and able to explore their innermost feelings without fear of embarrassment or rejection. This method was called **psychoanalysis**, and it is an insight therapy that emphasizes revealing the unconscious conflicts, urges, and desires that are assumed to cause disordered emotions and behavior (Freud, 1904; Mitchell & Black, 1996). This is the original reason for the couch in Freud's version of psychoanalysis; people lying on the couch were more relaxed and would, Freud thought, feel more dependent and childlike, making it easier for them to "get at" those early childhood memories. An additional plus was that he could sit behind the patients at the head of the couch and take notes. Without the patients being able to see his reactions to what they said, they remained unaffected by his reactions.

15.2 **What were the basic elements of Freud's psychoanalysis, and how does psychoanalysis differ today?**

Freud also made use of two techniques to try to reveal the repressed information in his patients' unconscious minds. These techniques were the interpretation of dreams and allowing patients to talk freely about anything that came to mind.

DREAM INTERPRETATION

Dream interpretation, or the analysis of the elements within a patient's reported dream, formed a large part of Freud's psychoanalytic method. LINK to Chapter Four: Consciousness, pp. 143–144. Freud believed that repressed material often surfaced in dreams, although in symbolic form. The **manifest content** of the dream was the actual dream and its events, but the **latent content** was the hidden, symbolic meaning of those events that would, if correctly interpreted, reveal the unconscious conflicts that were creating the nervous disorder (Freud, 1900).

FREE ASSOCIATION

The other technique for revealing the unconscious mind was a method originally devised by Freud's coworker, Josef Breuer (Breuer & Freud, 1895). Breuer encouraged his patients to freely say whatever came into their minds without fear of being negatively evaluated or

psychoanalysis an insight therapy based on the theory of Freud, emphasizing the revealing of unconscious conflicts.

manifest content the actual content of one's dream.

latent content the symbolic or hidden meaning of dreams.

condemned. As the patients talked, they began to reveal things that were loosely associated with their flow of ideas, often revealing what Breuer felt were hidden, unconscious concerns. Freud adopted this method of **free association**, believing that repressed impulses and other material were trying to "break free" into consciousness and would eventually surface using this technique.

RESISTANCE AND TRANSFERENCE Other components of Freud's original psychoanalytic method were **resistance** (the point at which the patient becomes unwilling to talk about certain topics) and **transference** (when the therapist becomes a symbol of a parental authority figure from the past). Therapists can also experience *countertransference,* in which the therapist has a transference reaction to the patient. This reaction might not always be to the benefit of the patient. As in all of the therapeutic approaches, peer and professional supervision helps therapists recognize potential issues in providing effective therapy.

free association psychoanalytic technique in which a patient was encouraged to talk about anything that came to mind without fear of negative evaluations.

resistance occurring when a patient becomes reluctant to talk about a certain topic, by either changing the subject or becoming silent.

transference In psychoanalysis, the tendency for a patient or client to project positive or negative feelings for important people from the past onto the therapist.

directive therapy in which the therapist actively gives interpretations of a client's statements and may suggest certain behavior or actions.

psychodynamic therapy a newer and more general term for therapies based on psychoanalysis with an emphasis on transference, shorter treatment times, and a more direct therapeutic approach.

interpersonal therapy (IPT) form of therapy for depression which incorporates multiple approaches and focuses on interpersonal problems.

EVALUATION OF PSYCHOANALYSIS AND PSYCHODYNAMIC APPROACHES

Freud's original theory, on which he based his interpretations of his patients' revelations, has been criticized as having several flaws, which were discussed in Chapter Thirteen. These included the lack of scientific research to support his claims, his unwillingness to believe some of the things revealed by his patients when those revelations did not fit into his view of the world, and his almost obsessive need to assume that problems with sex and sexuality were at the heart of nearly every nervous disorder.

Although some psychoanalysts today still use Freud's original methods, which could take years to produce results, most modern psychoanalysts have greatly modified the way a psychoanalytic session is conducted. The couch is gone, and the *client* (a term used to support the active role of the person seeking help and to avoid implying "sickness," as might result when using the term *patient*) may sit face-to-face with the therapist. The client may also stand or walk about. Rather than remaining quiet until the client says something revealing, the modern psychoanalyst is far more **directive**, asking questions, suggesting helpful behavior, and giving opinions and interpretations earlier in the relationship, which helps speed up the therapeutic process. Today's psychoanalysts also focus less on the id as the motivator of behavior, instead looking more at the ego or sense of self as the motivating force behind all actions (Prochaska & Norcross, 2003). Some psychoanalysts also focus on the process of transference more than on other typical aspects of traditional psychoanalysis, leading to the more general method called **psychodynamic therapy**. Psychodynamic therapy is typically shorter in duration than traditional psychoanalysis.

Even so, all of the psychodynamic techniques require the client to be fairly intelligent and verbally able to express his or her ideas, feelings, and thoughts effectively. People who are extremely withdrawn or who suffer from the more severe psychotic disorders are not good candidates for this form of psychotherapy. People who have nonpsychotic adjustment disorders, such as anxiety, somatoform, or dissociative disorders, are more likely to benefit from psychodynamic therapy.

Psychotherapy often takes place one-on-one, with a client and therapist exploring various issues together to achieve deeper insights or to change undesirable behavior.

INTERPERSONAL PSYCHOTHERAPY

Interpersonal psychotherapy (IPT) is a psychotherapy, developed to address depression. It is an insight therapy focusing on relationships of the individual with others and the interplay between mood and the events of everyday life (Bleiberg & Markowitcz, 2008). It is based on the interpersonal theories of Adolph Meyer and Harry Stack Sullivan along with the attachment theory of John Bowlby, and focuses on interpersonal relationships and functioning (Bleiberg & Markowitcz, 2008). It is one of the

A Rogerian person-centered therapist listens with calm acceptance to anything the client says. A sense of empathy with the client's feelings is also important.

few theories derived from psychodynamic thinking that does have some research support for its effectiveness in treating depression, particularly when combined with medication (Mufson et al., 2004; Reynolds et al., 1999). Despite its origins, IPT is not considered to be a psychodynamic therapy as it combines aspects of humanistic and cognitive–behavioral therapies, making it truly **eclectic**.

Humanistic Therapy: To Err Is Human

Unlike psychodynamic therapists, humanistic theorists do not focus on unconscious, hidden conflicts. Instead, humanists focus on conscious, subjective experiences of emotion and people's sense of self, as well as the more immediate experiences in their daily lives rather than early childhood experiences of the distant past (Cain & Seeman, 2001; Rowan, 2001; Schneider et al., 2001). LINK to Chapter One: The Science of Psychology, p. 14. Humanistic therapy emphasizes the importance of the choices made by individuals and the potential to change one's behavior. The two most common therapy styles based on humanistic theory are Carl Rogers's person-centered therapy and Fritz Perls's Gestalt therapy; both are primarily insight therapies.

15.3 What are the basic elements of the humanistic therapies known as person-centered therapy and Gestalt therapy?

TELL ME MORE: ROGERS'S PERSON-CENTERED THERAPY

Chapter Thirteen discussed the basic elements of Rogers's theory of personality, which emphasizes the sense of self (Rogers, 1961). To sum it up quickly, Rogers proposed that everyone has a *real self* (how people see their actual traits and abilities) and an *ideal self* (how people think they should be). The closer the real and ideal selves match up, the happier and more well adjusted the person. To have these two self-concepts match, people need to receive *unconditional positive regard*, which is love, warmth, respect, and affection without any conditions attached. If people think that there are conditions put on the love and affection they receive, their ideal selves will be determined by those conditions and become more difficult to achieve, resulting in a mismatch of selves and unhappiness.

So the key to getting over unhappiness would be to get the real and ideal selves closer together? How does a therapist do that?

So the key to getting over unhappiness would be to get the real and ideal selves closer together? How does a therapist do that?

Rogers believed that the goal of the therapist should be to provide the unconditional positive regard that has been absent from the troubled person's life and to help the person recognize the discrepancies between the real and ideal selves. He also believed that the person would actually have to do most of the work, talking out problems and concerns in an atmosphere of warmth and acceptance from the therapist, so he originally called the people in this therapy relationship "clients" instead of "patients," to put the therapeutic* relationship on a more equal footing. As a result, Rogers's therapy is very **nondirective** because the person actually does all the real work, with the therapist merely acting as a sounding board. Later, the term *client* was changed to the even more neutral term *person*. His therapy is now called **person-centered therapy** because the person is truly the center of the process.

FOUR BASIC ELEMENTS Rogers saw four key elements as being necessary in any successful person–therapist relationship.

Reflection **Reflection** refers to the technique the therapist must use to allow clients to continue to talk and have insights without the interference of the therapist's interpretations and possible biases. The only way to ensure that a therapist will not control the stream of ideas coming from clients is for the therapist to simply restate what

eclectic approach to therapy that results from combining elements of several different approaches or techniques.

nondirective therapy style in which the therapist remains relatively neutral and does not interpret or take direct actions with regard to the client, instead remaining a calm, nonjudgmental listener while the client talks.

person-centered therapy a nondirective insight therapy based on the work of Carl Rogers in which the client does all the talking and the therapist listens.

reflection therapy technique in which the therapist restates what the client says rather than interpreting those statements.

*therapeutic: providing or assisting in a cure.

people have already said in slightly different words but with the same exact meaning. Reflection is literally a kind of mirroring of clients' statements. Here's an example from one of Rogers's own therapy sessions with a client (Meador & Rogers, 1984, p. 143):

CLIENT: I just ain't no good to nobody, never was, and never will be.

ROGERS: Feeling that now, hm? That you're just no good to yourself, no good to anybody. Never will be any good to anybody. Just that you're completely worthless, huh?—Those really are lousy feelings. Just feel that you're no good at all, hm?

CLIENT: Yeah.

Unconditional Positive Regard Another key element of person-centered therapy is the warm, accepting, completely uncritical atmosphere that the therapist must create for clients. Having respect for clients and their feelings, values, and goals, even if they are different from those of the therapist, is called **unconditional positive regard**.

Empathy The therapist also has to be able to acknowledge what clients are feeling and experiencing by using a kind of understanding called **empathy**. This involves listening carefully and closely to what clients are saying and trying to feel what they feel. Therapists must also avoid getting their own feelings mixed up with clients' feelings (e.g., countertransference).

Authenticity Finally, the therapist must show **authenticity** in a genuine, open, and honest response to the client. It is easier for some professionals to "hide" behind the role of the therapist, as was often the case in psychoanalysis. In person-centered therapy, the therapist has to be able to tolerate a client's differences without being judgmental.

MOTIVATIONAL INTERVIEWING A variation of client-centered therapy is *motivational interviewing*, or MI (Miller & Rollnick, 2002), which has been described by Hal Arkowitz and William R. Miller as "client-centered therapy with a twist" (p. 6). In contrast to client-centered, MI has specific goals, to reduce ambivalence about change and to increase intrinsic motivation to bring that change about (Arkowitcz & Miller, 2008). For a therapist, the four principles of MI are express empathy, develop discrepancy between the client's present behaviors and values, roll with resistance, and support the client's self-efficacy (Miller & Rollnick, 2002).

unconditional positive regard referring to the warmth, respect, and accepting atmosphere created by the therapist for the client in person-centered therapy.

empathy the ability of the therapist to understand the feelings of the client.

authenticity the genuine, open, and honest response of the therapist to the client.

Gestalt therapy form of directive insight therapy in which the therapist helps clients to accept all parts of their feelings and subjective experiences, using leading questions and planned experiences such as role-playing.

GESTALT THERAPY

Another therapy based on humanistic ideas is called **Gestalt therapy**. The founder of this therapeutic method is Fritz Perls, who believed that people's problems often stemmed from hiding important parts of their feelings from themselves. If some part of a person's personality, for example, is in conflict with what society says is acceptable, the person might hide that aspect behind a false "mask" of socially acceptable behavior. As happens in Rogers's theory when the real and ideal selves do not match, in Gestalt theory the person experiences unhappiness and maladjustment when the inner self does not match the mask (Perls, 1951, 1969).

That sounds pretty much like the same thing, only with slightly different words. How is Gestalt therapy different from person-centered therapy?

That sounds pretty much like the same thing, only with slightly different words. How is Gestalt therapy different from person-centered therapy?

The two therapy types are similar because they are both based in humanism. But whereas person-centered therapy is nondirective, allowing the client to talk out concerns and eventually come to insights with only minimal guidance from the therapist, Gestalt therapists are very directive, often confronting clients about the statements they have made. This means that a Gestalt therapist does more than simply reflect back clients' statements; instead, a Gestalt therapist actually leads clients through a number of planned experiences, with the goal of helping clients to become more aware of their own feelings and take responsibility for their own choices in life, both now and in the past. These experiences might

In Gestalt therapy, it is not unusual to find a client talking to an empty chair. The chair represents some person from the past with whom the client has unresolved issues, and this is the opportunity to deal with those issues.

Explore the different schools of therapy on **mypsychlab.com**

include a dialogue* that clients have with their own conflicting feelings in which clients actually argue both sides of those feelings. Clients may talk with an empty chair to reveal their true feelings toward the person represented by the chair or take on the role of a parent or other person with whom they have a conflict so that the clients can see things from the other person's point of view. The Gestalt therapist pays attention to body language as well as to the events going on in the client's life at the time of therapy. Unlike psychoanalysis, which focuses on the *hidden past*, Gestalt therapy focuses on the *denied past*. Gestalt therapists do not talk about the unconscious mind. They believe everything is conscious but that it is possible for some people to simply refuse to "own up" to having certain feelings or to deal with past issues. By looking at the body language, feelings both stated and unstated, and the events in the life of the client, the therapist gets a *gestalt*—a whole picture—of the client.

EVALUATION OF THE HUMANISTIC THERAPIES

Humanistic therapies have been used to treat psychological disorders, help people make career choices, deal with workplace problems, and in marriage counseling. Person-centered therapy in particular can be a very "hands-off" form of therapy because it is so nondirective: Most often, there's nothing that the therapist says that the client has not already said, so the therapist runs a lower risk of misinterpretation. However, omission or not reflecting some things back might be a source of error.

Unfortunately, humanistic therapies have several of the same drawbacks as Freudian psychoanalysis and other forms of modern psychodynamic therapy. There is little experimental research to support the basic ideas on which this type of therapy is founded, but humanists have always preferred to use case studies to build their theories. People must be intelligent, verbal, and able to express their thoughts, feelings, and experiences in a logical manner, which makes humanistic therapies a somewhat less practical choice for treating the more serious mental disorders such as schizophrenia. **Explore** on **mypsychlab.com**

*dialogue: a conversation or exchange of ideas between two or more persons.

15.1 15.2 15.3

CONCEPT MAP

Psychological Therapies

- **modern treatments**
  - **psychotherapy:** based on psychological techniques, individuals talk about their problems and the therapist assists them in understanding and changing behavior
    - **insight therapies**
    - **action therapies**
  - **biomedical therapy:** uses medical interventions to bring symptoms under control
- **early interventions**
  - historically, psychological or social causes identified for some disorders; for others, individuals with mental illness were believed to be possessed by demons or evil spirits
  - organized treatment began in England around the middle 1500s
  - Pinel started the "moral treatment" movement in France
- **Freud's psychoanalysis and related techniques**
  - Freud developed the technique of **psychoanalysis**, an insight therapy aimed at revealing unconscious conflicts, urges, and desires
  - **dream interpretation:** involved deciphering the hidden, latent content from the manifest content, the actual dream itself
  - **free association:** originally developed by Breuer, involved patients freely talking about whatever came to mind; believed to reveal hidden, unconscious concerns
  - **modern psychodynamic approach:** more directive than it was historically and typically focuses more on the ego or sense of self rather than the id, when looking at reasons behind behavior
  - **evaluation:** although techniques have been modified, still lacks scientific support for basic premises and requires client to be fairly intelligent and verbally expressive
- **interpersonal therapy (IPT)**
  - eclectic therapy with some theoretical roots in the psychodynamic approach but combines aspects from humanistic and cognitive–behavioral therapies

Psychological Therapies (continued)

- **humanistic therapy** — focuses on the conscious, subjective experience of emotion and people's sense of self; promotes insight and emphasizes the importance of individual choice and the potential to change one's behavior
  - **person-centered therapy**
    - developed by Carl Rogers; focuses on match between real self and ideal self; maladjustment is result of not matching; unconditional positive regard is important for congruence between real and ideal selves
    - therapist uses a nondirective approach and four basic elements to develop the person–therapist relationship
      - **reflection**
      - **unconditional positive regard**
      - **empathy**
      - **authenticity**
  - **Gestalt therapy**
    - developed by Fritz Perls; focuses on match between actual and ideal self; focuses on the gestalt, or "whole picture"
    - therapist uses a very directive approach to lead the client through a number of planned experiences (e.g., self-dialogue, "empty chair" technique), with the goal of increasing self-awareness
    - although aspects of the individual's past are examined, the focus is on denied past, not hidden past; everything is conscious but possibly not in the "here and now"
  - **evaluation:** little scientific support for basic premises and requires client to be fairly intelligent and verbally expressive
- **motivational interviewing** — "client-centered with a twist"; has specific goals to reduce ambivalence about change and increase intrinsic motivation

PRACTICE quiz How much do you remember?

ANSWERS ON PAGE AK-2.

Pick the best answer.

1. Psychotherapies that attempt to change disordered behavior directly are known as __________ therapies.
   a. insight **c.** biomedical
   b. action **d.** psychoanalytic
2. In the sixteenth century, purging or __________ was sometimes used as a means to rid the body of physical impurities so that the person's mind and soul could improve.
   a. ice bathing **c.** beating
   b. bloodletting **d.** spiritual cleansing
3. In __________, a psychoanalyst encouraged the patient to talk about whatever came to mind.
   a. free association **c.** resistance
   b. dream interpretation **d.** transference
4. Compared to traditional psychoanalysis, modern psychodynamic therapy is __________.
   a. more directive. **c.** more action oriented.
   b. less directive. **d.** more focused on the id.
5. Humanistic therapies are different from psychoanalysis because the humanistic therapies are __________.
   a. more directive.
   b. action oriented.
   c. focused only on conscious thoughts and behavior.
   d. insight therapies.
6. Which of the following is not one of the four basic elements of Rogers's person-centered therapy?
   a. conditional positive regard **c.** reflection
   b. empathy **d.** authenticity
7. Which of the following types of therapy makes the greatest use of body language?
   a. psychoanalysis **c.** Gestalt therapy
   b. person-centered therapy **d.** Rogerian therapy

Brainstorming: Which of the forms of psychotherapy discussed so far would probably work best for a very shy and withdrawn person? Why?

Behavior Therapies: Learning One's Way to Better Behavior

The last chapter talked about how behaviorists have a very different way of looking at abnormality—it's all learned. So do behaviorists do any kind of therapy?

The last chapter talked about how behaviorists have a very different way of looking at abnormality—it's all learned. So do behaviorists do any kind of therapy?

behavior therapies action therapies based on the principles of classical and operant conditioning and aimed at changing disordered behavior without concern for the original causes of such behavior.

That's right—the basic concept behind behaviorism is that all behavior, whether "normal" or "abnormal," is learned through the same processes of classical and operant conditioning. Unlike the psychodynamic and humanistic therapies, **behavior therapies** are action based rather than insight based. Their aim is to change behavior through the use of the same kinds of learning techniques that people (and

animals) use to learn any new responses. The abnormal or undesirable behavior is not seen as a symptom of anything else but rather is the problem itself. Learning created the problem, and new learning can correct it (Onken et al., 1997; Skinner, 1974; Sloan & Mizes, 1999).

15.4 How do behavior therapists use classical and operant conditioning to treat disordered behavior?

THERAPIES BASED ON CLASSICAL CONDITIONING

Classical conditioning is the learning of involuntary responses by pairing a stimulus that normally causes a particular response with a new, neutral stimulus. After enough pairings, the new stimulus will also cause the response to occur. LINK to Chapter Five: Learning, pp. 171–179. Through classical conditioning, old and undesirable reflex responses can be replaced by desirable ones. There are several techniques that have been developed using this type of learning to treat disorders such as phobias, obsessive-compulsive disorder, and similar anxiety disorders.

Using learning techniques to change undesirable behavior and increase desirable behavior has a long history (Hughes, 1993; Lovaas, 1987; Lovaas et al., 1966). Originally called **behavior modification**, the more recent adaptation of these techniques is **applied behavior analysis**. The newer term better highlights the need for a functional analysis of the behavior to be modified, which is then followed by the use of conditioning techniques to modify the behavior.

behavior modification or **applied behavior analysis** the use of learning techniques to modify or change undesirable behavior and increase desirable behavior.

systematic desensitization behavior technique used to treat phobias, in which a client is asked to make a list of ordered fears and taught to relax while concentrating on those fears.

aversion therapy form of behavioral therapy in which an undesirable behavior is paired with an aversive stimulus to reduce the frequency of the behavior.

SYSTEMATIC DESENSITIZATION **Systematic desensitization**, in which a therapist guides the client through a series of steps meant to reduce fear and anxiety, is normally used to treat phobic disorders and consists of a three-step process. First, the client must learn to relax through deep muscle relaxation training. Next, the client and the therapist construct a list, beginning with the object or situation that causes the least fear to the client, eventually working up to the object or situation that produces the greatest degree of fear. Finally, under the guidance of the therapist the client begins at the first item on the list that causes minimal fear and looks at it, thinks about it, or actually confronts it, all while remaining in a relaxed state. By pairing the old conditioned stimulus (the fear object) with a new relaxation response that is incompatible* with the emotions and physical arousal associated with fear, the person's fear is reduced and relieved. The person then proceeds to the next item on the list of fears (called a *hierarchy of fears*) until the phobia is gone. It is even possible to use a computer-generated virtual reality technique for desensitization (Rothbaum et al., 1995).

This device allows the delivery of high levels of nicotine to the smoker in a process known as rapid smoking. Rapid smoking is an aversive technique for helping people to quit smoking and is based on the classical conditioning principle of counterconditioning.

AVERSION THERAPY Another way to use classical conditioning is to reduce the frequency of undesirable behaviors, such as smoking or overeating, by teaching the client to pair an aversive (unpleasant) stimulus with the stimulus that results in the undesirable response in a process called **aversion therapy**. For example, someone who wants to stop smoking might go to a therapist who uses a *rapid-smoking* technique, in which the client is allowed to smoke but must take a puff on the cigarette every 5 or 6 seconds. As nicotine is a poison, such rapid smoking produces nausea and dizziness, both unpleasant effects.

*incompatible: referring to two or more things that cannot exist together or at the same time.

Could you use aversion therapy to help someone with a phobia?

Because phobias are already very unpleasant, aversive conditioning is not the most useful method of therapy. But although desensitization remains one of the more common therapies for phobias, it does not always bring quick results.

Could you use aversion therapy to help someone with a phobia?

EXPOSURE THERAPIES Behavioral techniques that introduce the client to situations, under carefully controlled conditions, which are related to their anxieties or fears are called **exposure therapies**. Exposure can be accomplished through a variety of routes and is intended to promote new learning. It can be *in vivo* ("in life"), where the client is exposed to the actual anxiety-related stimulus; *imaginal*, where the client visualizes or imagines the stimulus; and even *virtual*, where virtual reality (VR) technology is used (Najavits, 2007). (For more on virtual reality in psychology, see the Applying Psychology to Everyday Life section at the end of this chapter.)

For example, if Chang-sun has social phobia (fairly rare for Korean males at a lifetime prevalence of only about 0.1 percent) (Sadock et al., 2007), for in vivo exposure he might have to attend a social event; for imaginal exposure he might be asked to visualize himself attending a social event; and for virtual exposure, Chang-sun might experience a social event, such as attending a dinner party, through VR technology.

Exposure methods can introduce the feared stimulus gradually, or quite suddenly. A gradual, or *graded* exposure, involves the client and therapist developing a fear hierarchy as in systematic desensitization: Exposure begins at the least feared event and progresses through to the most feared, similar to desensitization. If the exposure is rapid and intense, it begins with the most feared event and is called **flooding** (Gelder, 1976; Olsen, 1975). Flooding is used under very controlled conditions and, like graded exposure, produces extinction of the conditioned fear response by preventing an escape or avoidance response (e.g., Chang-sun would not be allowed to leave the party). Exposure therapy is sometimes called "exposure and response prevention" for that reason.

Eye-movement desensitization reprocessing, or EMDR, is a type of exposure therapy used in the treatment of posttraumatic stress disorder (PTSD). It involves imaginal flooding, cognitive reprocessing and desensitization of the fearful event, and rapid eye movements or other bilateral stimulation (Shapiro, 2001). It is also used with phobias, and other anxiety-related disorders, although PTSD remains a primary disorder for which this therapy is most commonly used. Read on **mypsychlab.com**

Read and learn more about EMDR on **mypsychlab.com**

THERAPIES BASED ON OPERANT CONDITIONING

Operant conditioning techniques include reinforcement, extinction, shaping, and modeling to change the frequency of voluntary behavior. LINK to Chapter Five: Learning, pp. 192–195, 201–203. In the treatment of psychological disorders, the goal is to reduce the frequency of undesirable behavior and increase the frequency of desirable responses.

One of the advantages of using operant conditioning to treat a problem behavior is that results are usually quickly obtained rather than having to wait through years of more insight-oriented forms of therapy. When bringing the behavior under control (rather than finding out why it occurs in the first place) is the goal, operant and other behavioral techniques are very practical. There's an old joke about a man whose fear of things hiding under his bed is cured by a behavioral therapist in one night. The therapist simply cut the legs off the bed.

MODELING **Modeling**, or learning through the observation and imitation of a model, is discussed in Chapter Five. The use of modeling as a therapy is based on the work of Albert Bandura, which states that a person with specific fears or someone who

exposure therapies behavioral techniques that expose individuals to anxiety- or fear-related stimuli, under carefully controlled conditions, to promote new learning.

flooding technique for treating phobias and other stress disorders in which the person is rapidly and intensely exposed to the fear-provoking situation or object and prevented from making the usual avoidance or escape response.

modeling learning through the observation and imitation of others.

This boy is sitting in the "time-out" corner at his school. By removing the attention that he found rewarding, the teacher is attempting to extinguish the behavior that earned the boy a time-out. Do you see anything in this time-out corner that might make it less effective?

needs to develop social skills can learn to do so by watching someone else (the model) confront those fears or demonstrate the needed social skills (Bandura et al., 1969). In **participant modeling**, a model demonstrates the desired behavior in a step-by-step, gradual process. The client is encouraged by the therapist to imitate the model in the same gradual, step-by-step manner (Bandura, 1986; Bandura et al., 1974). The model can be a person actually present in the same room with the client or someone viewed on video. For example, a model might first approach a dog, then touch the dog, then pet the dog, and finally hug the dog. A child (or adult) who fears dogs would watch this process and then be encouraged to repeat the steps that the model demonstrated.

Behavioral therapists can give parents or others advice and demonstrations on how to carry out behavioral techniques. Once a person knows what to do, modeling is a fairly easy technique. Modeling has been effective in helping children with dental fears (Klorman et al., 1980; Ollendick & King, 1998), social withdrawal (O'Connor, 1972), obsessive-compulsive disorder (Roper et al., 1975), and phobias (Hintze, 2002).

USING REINFORCEMENT **Reinforcement** is the strengthening of a response by following it with some pleasurable consequence (positive reinforcement) or the removal of an unpleasant stimulus (negative reinforcement). Reinforcement of both types can form the basis for treatment of people with behavioral problems.

Token Economies In a **token economy**, objects that can be traded for food, candy, treats, or special privileges are called *tokens*. Clients earn tokens for behaving correctly or accomplishing behavioral goals and can later exchange those tokens for things that they want. They may also lose tokens for inappropriate behavior. This trading system is a token economy. LINK to Chapter Five: Learning, p. 195. Token economies have also been used successfully in modifying the behavior of relatively disturbed persons in mental institutions, such as people with schizophrenia or depressed persons (Dickerson et al., 1994; Glynn, 1990; McMonagle & Sultana, 2002).

Contingency Contracting Another method based on the use of reinforcement involves making a **contingency contract** with the client (Salend, 1987). This contract is a formal agreement between therapist and client (or teacher and student, or parent and child) in which both parties' responsibilities and goals are clearly stated. Such contracts are useful in treating specific problems such as drug addiction (Talbott & Crosby, 2001), educational problems (Evans & Meyer, 1985; Evans et al., 1989), and eating disorders (Brubaker & Leddy, 2003). Because the stated tasks, penalties, and reinforcements are clearly stated and consistent, both parties are always aware of the consequences of acting or failing to act within the specifications of the contract, making this form of behavioral treatment fairly effective. Consistency is one of the most effective tools in using both rewards and punishments to mold behavior. LINK to Chapter Five: Learning, p. 190–191.

USING EXTINCTION **Extinction** involves the removal of a reinforcer to reduce the frequency of a particular response. In modifying behavior, operant extinction often involves removing one's attention from the person when that person is engaging in an inappropriate or undesirable behavior. With children, this removal of attention may be a form of **time-out**, in which the child is removed from the situation that provides reinforcement (Kazdin, 1980). In adults, a simple refusal by the other persons in the room to acknowledge the behavior is often successful in reducing the frequency of that behavior.

participant modeling technique in which a model demonstrates the desired behavior in a step-by-step, gradual process while the client is encouraged to imitate the model.

reinforcement the strengthening of a response by following it with a pleasurable consequence or the removal of an unpleasant stimulus.

token economy the use of objects called tokens to reinforce behavior in which the tokens can be accumulated and exchanged for desired items or privileges.

contingency contract a formal, written agreement between the therapist and client (or teacher and student) in which goals for behavioral change, reinforcements, and penalties are clearly stated.

extinction the removal of a reinforcer to reduce the frequency of a behavior.

time-out an extinction process in which a person is removed from the situation that provides reinforcement for undesirable behavior, usually by being placed in a quiet corner or room away from possible attention and reinforcement opportunities.

EVALUATION OF BEHAVIOR THERAPIES

15.5 **How successful are behavior therapies?**

Behavior therapies may be more effective than other forms of therapy in treating specific behavioral problems, such as bed-wetting, overeating, drug addictions, and phobic reactions (Burgio, 1998; Wetherell, 2002). More-serious psychological disorders, such as severe depression or schizophrenia, do not respond as well overall to behavioral treatments, although improvement of specific symptoms can be achieved (Glynn, 1990; McMonagle & Sultana, 2002). Bringing symptoms under control is an important step in allowing a person to function normally in the social world, and behavior therapies are a relatively quick and efficient way to eliminate or greatly reduce such symptoms.

Cognitive Therapies: Thinking Is Believing

15.6 **What are the goals and basic elements of cognitive therapies such as cognitive–behavioral therapy and rational–emotive behavior therapy?**

Cognitive therapy (Beck, 1979; Freeman et al., 1989) was developed by Aaron T. Beck and is focused on helping people change their ways of thinking. Rather than focusing on the behavior itself, the cognitive therapist focuses on the distorted thinking and unrealistic beliefs that lead to maladaptive behavior (Hollon & Beck, 1994), especially those distortions relating to depression (Abela & D'Allesandro, 2002; McGinn, 2000). The goal is to help clients test, in a more objective, scientific way, the truth of their beliefs and assumptions, as well as their attributions concerning both their own behavior and the behavior of others in their lives. LINK to Chapter Twelve: Social Psychology, pp. 466–467. Then they can recognize thoughts that are distorted and negative and replace them with more-positive, helpful thoughts. Because the focus is on changing thoughts rather than gaining deep insights into their causes, this kind of therapy is primarily an action therapy.

BECK'S COGNITIVE THERAPY

What are these unrealistic beliefs?

What are these unrealistic beliefs?

Cognitive therapy focuses on the distortions of thinking. LINK to Chapter Thirteen: Theories of Personality, pp. 505-507. Here are some of the more common distortions in thought that can create negative feelings and unrealistic beliefs in people:

- **Arbitrary inference:** This refers to "jumping to conclusions" without any evidence. Arbitrary means to decide something based on nothing more than personal whims. Example: "Suzy canceled our lunch date—I'll bet she's seeing someone else!"
- **Selective thinking:** In selective thinking, the person focuses only on one aspect of a situation, leaving out other relevant facts that might make things seem less negative. Example: Peter's teacher praised his paper but made one comment about needing to check his punctuation. Peter assumes that his paper is lousy and that the teacher really didn't like it, ignoring the other praise and positive comments.
- **Overgeneralization**: Here a person draws a sweeping conclusion from one incident and then assumes that the conclusion applies to areas of life that have nothing to do with the original event. Example: "I insulted my algebra teacher. I'll flunk and I'll never be able to get a decent job—I'll end up on welfare."
- **Magnification and minimization:** Here a person blows bad things out of proportion while not emphasizing good things. Example: A student who has received good grades on every other exam believes that the C she got on the last quiz means she's not going to succeed in college.

cognitive therapy therapy in which the focus is on helping clients recognize distortions in their thinking and replace distorted, unrealistic beliefs with more realistic, helpful thoughts.

arbitrary inference distortion of thinking in which a person draws a conclusion that is not based on any evidence.

selective thinking distortion of thinking in which a person focuses on only one aspect of a situation while ignoring all other relevant aspects.

overgeneralization distortion of thinking in which a person draws sweeping conclusions based on only one incident or event and applies those conclusions to events that are unrelated to the original.

magnification and minimization distortions of thinking in which a person blows a negative event out of proportion to its importance (magnification) while ignoring relevant positive events (minimization).

personalization distortion of thinking in which a person takes responsibility or blame for events that are unconnected to the person.

cognitive–behavioral therapy (CBT) action therapy in which the goal is to help clients overcome problems by learning to think more rationally and logically.

rational–emotive behavior therapy (REBT) cognitive–behavioral therapy in which clients are directly challenged in their irrational beliefs and helped to restructure their thinking into more rational belief statements.

Don't those questions sound like critical thinking, which was discussed in Chapter One?

- **Personalization:** In personalization, an individual takes responsibility or blame for events that are not really connected to the individual. Example: When Sandy's husband comes home in a bad mood because of something that happened at work, she immediately assumes that he is angry with her.

A cognitive therapist tries to get clients to look at their beliefs and test them to see how accurate they really are. The first step is to identify an illogical or unrealistic belief, which the therapist and client do in their initial talks. Then the client is guided by the therapist through a process of asking questions about that belief, such as "When did this belief of mine begin?" or "What is the evidence for this belief?"

Don't those questions sound like critical thinking, which was discussed in Chapter One?

Cognitive therapy really is critical thinking applied to one's own thoughts and beliefs. Just as cognitive psychology grew out of behaviorism, LINK to Chapter One: The Science of Psychology, pp. 10–11, 14–15, therapies using cognitive methods have behavioral elements within them as well, leading to the term **cognitive–behavioral therapy (CBT)**.

Cognitive–behavioral therapy, or CBT, focuses on the present rather than the past (like behaviorism) but also assumes that people interact with the world with more than simple, automatic reactions to external stimuli. People observe the world and the people in the world around them, make assumptions and inferences* based on those observations or cognitions, and then decide how to respond (Rachman & Hodgson, 1980). As a form of cognitive therapy, CBT also assumes that disorders come from illogical, irrational cognitions and that changing the thinking patterns to more rational, logical ones will relieve the symptoms of the disorder, making it an action therapy. Cognitive–behavioral therapists may also use any of the tools that behavioral therapists use to help clients alter their actions. The three basic goals of any cognitive–behavioral therapy follow.

1. Relieve the symptoms and help clients resolve the problems.
2. Help clients develop strategies that can be used to cope with future problems.
3. Help clients change the way they think from irrational, self-defeating thoughts to more rational, self-helping, positive thoughts.

ELLIS AND RATIONAL–EMOTIVE BEHAVIOR THERAPY (REBT)

Albert Ellis proposed a version of CBT called **rational–emotive behavioral therapy (REBT)**, in which clients are taught a way to challenge their own irrational beliefs with more-rational, helpful statements (Ellis, 1997, 1998). Here are some examples of irrational beliefs:

- Everyone should love and approve of me (if they don't, I am awful and unlovable).
- When things do not go the way I wanted and planned, it is terrible and I am, of course, going to get very disturbed. I can't stand it!

But I've felt that way at times. Why are these statements so irrational?

But I've felt that way at times. Why are these statements so irrational?

Notice that these statements have one thing in common: It's either all or nothing. Can a person really expect the love and affection of every single person? Is it realistic to expect things to work as planned every time? Rational–emotive behavioral therapy is about challenging these types of "my way or nothing" statements, helping people to realize that life can be good without being "perfect." In REBT, therapists take a very directive role, challenging the client when the client makes statements like those listed earlier, assigning homework, using behavioral techniques to modify behavior, and arguing with clients about the rationality of their statements.

*inferences: conclusions drawn from observations and facts.

Table 15.1

Characteristics of Psychotherapies

TYPE OF THERAPY	GOAL	KEY PEOPLE
Psychodynamic therapy	Insight	Freud
Person-centered therapy	Insight	Rogers
Gestalt therapy	Insight	Perls
Behavior therapy	Action	Watson, Jones, Skinner, Bandura
Cognitive therapy	Action	Beck
CBT	Action	Various professionals
REBT	Action	Ellis

EVALUATION OF COGNITIVE AND COGNITIVE–BEHAVIORAL THERAPIES

Cognitive and cognitive–behavioral therapies are less expensive than the typical insight therapy because they are comparatively short-term therapies. As in behavior therapy, clients do not have to dig too deep for the hidden sources of their problems. Instead, cognitive-based therapies get right to the problems themselves, helping clients deal with their symptoms more directly. In fact, one of the criticisms of these therapies as well as behavior therapies is that they treat the symptom, not the cause. However, it should be noted that in the cognitive viewpoint, the maladaptive thoughts are seen as the cause of the problems, not merely the symptoms. There is also an element of potential bias because of the therapist's opinions as to which thoughts are rational and which are not (Westen, 2005).

Nevertheless, cognitive and cognitive–behavioral therapies have considerable success in treating many types of disorders, including depression, stress disorders, eating disorders, anxiety disorders, personality disorders, and even—in addition to other forms of therapy—some types of schizophrenia (Barlow et al., 2007; Beck, 2007; Clark et al., 1989, 2009; DeRubeis et al., 1999; Holcomb, 1986; Jay & Elliot, 1990; Kendall, 1983; Kendall et al., 2008; McGinn, 2000; Meichenbaum, 1996; Mueser et al., 2008; Resick et al., 2008; Turk et al., 2008; Young et al., 2008). As an offshoot of behaviorism, the learning principles that are the basis of cognitive–behavioral therapies are considered empirically sound (Barlow et al., 2007; Masters et al., 1987). For a summary of the various types of psychotherapies discussed up to this point, see Table 15.1.

In group therapy, several people who share similar problems gather with a therapist to discuss their feelings and concerns. The presence of others who are going through the same kind of emotional difficulties can be comforting as well as provide the opportunity for insights into one's own problems by hearing about the problems of others.

Group Therapies: Not Just for the Shy

An alternative to individual therapy, in which the client and the therapist have a private, one-on-one session, is to gather a group of clients with similar problems together and have the group discuss problems under the guidance of a single therapist (Yalom, 1995).

15.7 What are the various types of group therapies and the advantages and disadvantages of group therapy?

TYPES OF GROUP THERAPIES

Group therapy can be accomplished in several ways. The therapist may use either an insight or cognitive–behavioral style, although person-centered, Gestalt, and behavior therapies seem to work better in group settings than psychodynamic and cognitive–behavioral therapies (Andrews, 1989).

In addition to the variations in the style of therapy, the group structure can also vary. There may be small groups formed of related persons or other groups of unrelated persons that meet without the benefit of a therapist. Their goal is to share their problems and provide social and emotional support for each other.

FAMILY COUNSELING One form of group therapy is **family counseling** or **family therapy**, in which all of the members of a family who are experiencing some type of problem—marital problems, problems in child discipline, or sibling rivalry, for example—are seen by the therapist as a group. The therapist may also meet with one or more family members individually at times, but the real work in opening the lines of communication among family members is accomplished in the group setting (Frankel & Piercy, 1990; Pinsoff & Wynne, 1995). The family members may include grandparents, aunts and uncles, and in-laws as well as the core family. This is because family therapy focuses on the family as a whole unit or system of interacting "parts." No one person is seen as "the problem" because all members of the family system are part of the problem: They are experiencing it, rewarding it, or by their actions or inactions causing it to occur in the first place.

The goal in family therapy, then, is to discover the unhealthy ways in which family members interact and communicate with one another and change those ways to healthier, more productive means of interaction. Family therapists work not only with families but also with couples who are in a committed relationship with the goal of improving communication, helping the couple to learn better ways of solving their problems and disagreements, and increasing feelings of intimacy and emotional closeness (Christensen et al., 1995; Heavey et al., 1993).

In self-help groups, the person or persons leading a group are not specialists or therapists but just members of the group. They often have the same problem as all of the other people in the room, which is the strength of this type of program—people may be more likely to trust and open up to someone who has struggled as they have.

SELF-HELP GROUPS Therapists are often in short supply, and they also charge a fee for leading group-therapy sessions. In addition, many people may feel that a therapist who has never had, for example, a drug problem would be unable to truly understand their situation; and they may also feel that someone who has experienced addiction and beaten it is more capable of providing real help. This, rather than just concerns about the cost of therapy, is the main reason some people choose to meet with others who have problems similar to their own, with no therapist in charge. Called **self-help groups** or **support groups**, these groups are usually formed around a particular problem. Some examples of self-help groups are Alcoholics Anonymous, Overeaters Anonymous, and Narcotics Anonymous, all of which have groups meeting all over the country at almost any time of the day or night. There are countless smaller support groups for nearly every condition imaginable, including anxiety, phobias, having a parent with dementia, having difficult children, depression, and dealing with stress—to name just a few. The advantages of self-help groups are that they are free and provide the social and emotional support that any group session can provide (Bussa & Kaufman, 2000). Self-help groups do not have leaders but instead have people who volunteer monthly or weekly to lead individual meetings. So the person who is in charge of organizing the meetings is also a member of the group with the same problem as all the other members.

family counseling (family therapy) a form of group therapy in which family members meet together with a counselor or therapist to resolve problems that affect the entire family.

self-help groups (support groups) a group composed of people who have similar problems and who meet together without a therapist or counselor for the purpose of discussion, problem solving, and social and emotional support.

ADVANTAGES OF GROUP THERAPY

There are several advantages to group therapy:

- Lower cost. Because the therapist can see several clients at one time, this type of therapy is usually less expensive than individual therapy.
- Exposure to the ways in which other people view and handle the same kinds of problems.
- The opportunity for both the therapist and the person to see how that person interacts with others.

- Social and emotional support from people who have problems that are similar or nearly identical to one's own. This advantage is an important one; studies have shown that breast cancer patients who were part of a group-therapy process had much higher survival and recovery rates than those who received only individual therapy or no psychotherapy (Fawzy et al., 1993; Spiegel et al., 1989). Another study found that adolescent girls in Africa, suffering from depression due to the stresses of the war in Uganda, experienced significant reductions in depression when treated with group therapy (Bolton et al., 2007).
- An extremely shy person may initially have great difficulty speaking up in a group setting but cognitive–behavioral group therapy can be effective for social phobia (Heimberg & Becker, 2002; Turk et al., 2008).

DISADVANTAGES OF GROUP THERAPY

Group therapy is not appropriate for all situations, and there can be disadvantages:

- The therapist is no longer the only person to whom secrets and fears are revealed, which may make some people reluctant to speak freely.
- The client must share the therapist's time during the session.
- People with severe psychiatric disorders involving paranoia, such as schizophrenia, may not be able to tolerate group-therapy settings.

A survey and comparison of the effectiveness of both individual and group therapy found that group therapy is only effective if it is long term and that it is more effective when used to promote skilled social interactions rather than as an attempt to decrease the more bizarre symptoms of delusions and hallucinations (Evans et al., 2000).

EVALUATION OF GROUP THERAPY Group therapy can provide help to people who might be unable to afford individual psychotherapy. It can also provide social and emotional support to people who may improve significantly from simply knowing that they are not the only people to suffer from whatever their particular problem may be. People who are not comfortable in social situations or who have trouble speaking in front of others may not find group therapy as helpful as those who are more verbal and social by nature. It is also important to note that group therapy can be used in combination with individual and biomedical therapies. **Read** on **mypsychlab.com**

Read and learn more about different kinds of self-help groups on **mypsychlab.com**

15.4 15.5 15.6 15.7

CONCEPT MAP

- **behavior therapies** action-based therapies operating on the premise that all behaviors, both normal and abnormal, are learned; applied behavior analysis involves functional analysis and learning techniques to increase desirable behaviors and decrease undesirable behaviors
  - techniques based on classical conditioning—pairing of stimuli
    - **systematic desensitization**
    - **aversion therapy**
    - **exposure therapies:** expose individual to anxiety-provoking stimulus in real or imagined form, in a gradual or sudden (**flooding**) manner
  - techniques based on operant conditioning—reinforcement, extinction, shaping, and modeling
    - **participant modeling**
    - **token economies (reinforcement)**
    - **contingency contracting (reinforcement)**
    - **time-out (extinction)**
  - **evaluation:** more effective than others for specific behavioral problems (e.g., bed-wetting, overeating, drug addictions, phobic reactions)

Action Therapies

(continued)

Action Therapies (continued)

cognitive therapies action-based therapies that focus on helping people change their ways of thinking; emphasis on identifying distorted and unrealistic beliefs that lead to maladaptive behavior and problem emotions and then replacing them with more-positive, helpful thoughts

- **Beck's cognitive therapy** identifies several common distortions
  - **arbitrary inference (jumping to conclusions)**
  - **selective thinking**
  - **overgeneralization**
  - **magnification and minimization**
  - **personalization**
- **cognitive–behavioral therapy (CBT)** uses cognitive methods that have behavioral elements within them as well
- **rational–emotive behavior therapy (REBT)** was developed by Albert Ellis; teaches clients to challenge their own irrational beliefs with more-rational, helpful statements
- **evaluation:** typically shorter and less expensive than insight therapies; treating the symptom, not the cause, is both a feature and a criticism; especially effective for many disorders, including depression, anxiety disorders, and personality disorders

Group Therapies

- alternative to individual therapy; group of clients meet together to discuss similar problems with a single therapist or pair of therapists
  - may use a variety of styles, but person-centered, Gestalt, and behavioral seem to work best; may also take several different forms
    - **family therapy**
    - **problem-based groups**
- **self-help groups** may also be effective; do not have a therapist directly involved
- **evaluation:** advantages include lower cost, exposure to ways other people view and handle same type of problems, social and emotional support; disadvantages include greater exposure, less one-on-one contact with therapist, and some problems hard to treat in group setting

PRACTICE quiz How much do you remember?

ANSWERS ON PAGE AK-2.

Pick the best answer.

1. Jeremy is trying to stop biting his fingernails. He wears a rubber band around each of his wrists and, whenever he finds himself biting his nails, he snaps the band. Jeremy is using a form of __________ to modify his nail-biting behavior.
   a. systematic desensitization
   b. aversion therapy
   c. flooding
   d. extinction
2. The reality television shows that deliberately force people to face their "worst fears" are most similar to which therapy technique?
   a. systematic desensitization
   b. aversion therapy
   c. flooding
   d. extinction
3. At Skinner Elementary School, teachers pass out "skinner bucks" to students who turn in papers on time, obey the teacher, and finish their homework. The paper "bucks" can be used at the end of the week to trade for special treats or game-playing time on the classroom computer. This system most resembles a __________.
   a. participant modeling technique.
   b. contingency contract.
   c. group extinction procedure.
   d. token economy.
4. Which of the following would be an unlikely strategy for a rational–emotive behavior therapist to use in treating a client?
   a. arguing with the client's statements
   b. repeating what the client has just said without interpreting it
   c. giving the client homework
   d. pointing out irrational beliefs to the client
5. Maya is upset because her supervisor teased her about turning in her report several hours late. Although her supervisor was quite pleased with the report itself and told Maya that her work was excellent, Maya remains unhappy. Beck would say that Maya is guilty of __________.
   a. arbitrary inference.
   b. selective thinking.
   c. personalization.
   d. defective thinking.
6. Which person might benefit the least from a group-therapy environment?
   a. Azul, who has a phobia of cats
   b. Richard, who has a drinking problem
   c. Jasmine, who is experiencing auditory hallucinations
   d. Elena, who suffers from depression
7. Six members of Ron's statistics class would meet every Saturday to go over their notes and try to figure out what the teacher had told them during his rambling lectures. If part of every Saturday's session is spent sharing feelings about the teacher and venting their anger and resentment, Ron's study group could be said to serve as __________.
   a. a support group.
   b. family therapy.
   c. an awareness training group.
   d. a guided-discovery group.

psychology in the news

Mental Health on Campus

The college experience is supposed to be one of intellectual and social development but it is also a time of strife and stress for many. From exams to living conditions (commuting, new roommates, living in a dorm), relationship issues (immediate family, significant others), and adjustment in general, college life can be quite stressful. The shootings and other campus crises over the past few years are just one indicator of the level of psychological dysfunction that can occur in extreme circumstances.

These circumstances can make preexisting conditions worse or prompt the development of new psychological disorders. According to the American College Counseling Association's 2009 National Survey of Counseling Center Directors, of the 2.6 million students represented in the survey, approximately 270,000 sought counseling (Gallagher, 2009). Of those students receiving services in college counseling centers, 16 percent are referred for psychiatric evaluation and 25 percent are on psychiatric medication. The majority of counseling center directors believe there is an increase in the number of students coming to campus already on psychiatric medication, and there is a trend toward a greater number of students on campus recognized with severe psychological problems. Increases are being noted in medication management, crisis intervention, learning disabilities, self-injury (e.g., self-cutting), illicit drug use, alcohol abuse, eating disorders, and sexual assault concerns or problems related to earlier sexual abuse (Gallagher, 2009).

As revealed by the 2009–2010 Community College Counselors Survey, these increases are especially troublesome given the added stress of the ongoing economic situation in the United States. Consequences of economic stressors include increases in enrollment, more signs of anxiety and depression in both students and college employees, and an increased need for mental-health services (American College Counseling Association's Community College Task Force, 2010). The top four presenting problems were stress, depression, anxiety disorders, and academic problems.

So what can you do with this information? First, if you are not familiar with your college's counseling resources, learn more about what is offered. Even if you do not have a serious psychological disorder, counselors can assist you in identifying and developing effective coping strategies. Second, take care of yourself, get enough sleep, eat healthy foods (not just instant noodles or macaroni and cheese), exercise, and take time for yourself to relax. Finally, know that you are not alone if you do experience difficulties and that a variety of resources are likely available to help you along the path to your college degree.

Questions for Further Discussion

1. Do you know any of your fellow students who have used your college's counseling center? If so, what was their experience like?
2. What do you believe to be the greatest stressor in college life today?

Does Psychotherapy Really Work?

There sure are a lot of psychotherapies, but do any of them really work?

There sure are a lot of psychotherapies, but do any of them really work?

In the 1950s, Hans Eysenck did one of the earliest studies of the effectiveness of therapy. His conclusion—that the people receiving psychotherapy did not recover at any higher rate than those who had no psychotherapy and that the passage of time alone could account for all recovery.

STUDIES OF EFFECTIVENESS

15.8 How effective is psychotherapy, and how is the effectiveness of psychotherapy influenced by cultural, ethnic, and gender differences?

Eysenck's classic survey created a major controversy within the world of clinical and counseling psychology. Other researchers began their own studies to find evidence that would contradict Eysenck's findings. One such effort reviewed studies that the researchers considered to be well controlled and concluded that the psychotherapies did not differ from one another in effectiveness (Luborsky et al., 1975). Of course, that can mean either that the psychotherapies were all equally effective or that they were all equally ineffective. (Note—many psychological professionals take an eclectic approach, using more than one psychotherapy technique.)

There are numerous problems with studying the effectiveness of psychotherapy. Controlled studies can be done using an experimental group of people who receive a particular psychotherapy and a control group of people who are put on a waiting list, but this is less than ideal. The control group is not getting the attention from the therapist, for one thing, and so there would be no placebo-effect expectations about getting better because of therapy (Shapiro & Shapiro, 1997). Also, not all therapies take the same amount of time to be effective. For example, psychoanalysis, even in its short form, takes longer than a behavioral therapy. In a short-term study, behavioral therapy would obviously look more effective. Action therapies such as behavior therapy measure the success of the therapy differently than do insight therapies; in a behavioral therapy the reduction of the undesired behavior is easy to objectively measure, but gaining insights and feelings of control, self-worth, self-esteem, and so on are not as easily evaluated (Shadish et al., 2002).

Studies that do not use empirical* procedures but instead try to determine if the clients who have been helped by the therapy in general are plagued by problems such as experimenter bias (the therapist expects the therapy to work and is also the one assessing the progress of the client), the inaccuracies of self-report information, and the same placebo-effect expectations cited by Shapiro and Shapiro (Seligman, 1995; Wampold, 1997).

Nevertheless, more-recent surveys have shown that people who have received psychotherapy believe that they have been helped more often than not (*Consumer Reports*, 1995; Kotkin et al., 1996). The *Consumer Reports* research was a survey of the magazine's readers in which those who had been or were currently clients in psychotherapy rated the effectiveness of the therapy they received. Here are the findings from a summary of this and several other similar surveys (Lambert & Ogles, 2004; Seligman, 1995; Thase, 1999):

- An estimated 75–90 percent of people feel that psychotherapy has helped them.
- The longer a person stays in therapy, the greater the improvement.

Other studies have found that some psychotherapies are more effective for certain types of disorders (Clarkin et al., 2007; Hollon et al., 2002) but that no one psychotherapy is the most effective or works for every type of problem.

THE SEVEN DWARFS AFTER THERAPY

*empirical: capable of being verified or disproved by observation or experiment.

CHARACTERISTICS OF EFFECTIVE THERAPY

So how does a person with a problem know what kind of therapist to go to? How do you pick a good one?

So how does a person with a problem know what kind of therapist to go to? How do you pick a good one?

As discussed before, many psychological professionals today take an eclectic view of psychotherapy, using a combination of methods or switching methods to fit the particular client's needs or specific problems.

The *common factors approach* in psychotherapy is a modern approach to eclecticism and focuses on those factors common to successful outcomes from different forms of therapy (Norcross, 2005). These factors are seen as the source of the success rather than specific differences among therapies. The most important common factor of a successful psychotherapy may be the relationship between the client and the therapist, known as the **therapeutic alliance**. This relationship should be caring, warm, and accepting, and be characterized by empathy, mutual respect, and understanding. Therapy should also offer clients a *protected setting* in which to release emotions and reveal private thoughts and concerns and should help clients understand why they feel they way they do and provide them with ways to feel better. Other common factors in therapy effectiveness are *opportunity for catharsis* (relieving pent-up emotions), *learning and practice of new behaviors*, and *positive experiences* for the client (Norcross, 2005).

"I like to think that each generation will need a little less therapy than the generation before."

An ongoing area of research in psychology is related to identifying those treatments and other aspects of treatment that work best for specific disorders. Especially in today's modern age of managed health care and tight budgets, clients benefit through evidence-based practice, or empirically validated treatment. Evidence-based practice includes systematic reviews of relevant and valid information that ranges from assessment to intervention (American Psychological Association, 2005; Hunsley & Mash, 2008; Nathan & Gorman, 2007). Some examples of evidence-based, or empirically validated, treatments are exposure therapies, cognitive–behavioral, and cognitive processing for PTSD (Ehlers et al., 2010; Najavits, 2007; Resick et al., 2008), cognitive–behavioral treatment for panic disorder with agoraphobia (Barlow et al., 2007; Craske & Barlow, 2008), cognitive–behavioral group therapy for social anxiety disorder (Turk et al., 2008), cognitive therapy for depression (Young et al., 2008), antipsychotic drugs for schizophrenia (Sharif et al., 2007), and interpersonal psychotherapy for depression (Bleiberg & Markowitcz, 2008).

CULTURAL, ETHNIC, AND GENDER CONCERNS IN PSYCHOTHERAPY

Consider the following situation (adapted from Wedding, 2004).

> *K. is a 24-year-old Korean American. She lived with her parents, who were both born and reared in Korea before moving to the United States as adults. She came to a therapist because she was depressed and unhappy with her lack of independence. Her father was angry about her plans to marry a non-Korean. Her therapist immediately began assertiveness training and role-playing to prepare K. to deal with her father. The therapist was disappointed when K. failed to keep her second appointment.*

This example of an actual case demonstrates a problem that exists in the therapist–client relationship for many clients when the ethnicity or culture of the client is different from that of the therapist. This cultural difference makes it difficult for therapists to understand the exact nature of their clients' problems and for clients to benefit from therapies that do not match their needs (Matsumoto, 1994; Moffic; 2003; Wedding, 2004). The values of different cultures and ethnic groups are not universally the same. How, for example, could a female therapist who is White, from a upper-middle-class

therapeutic alliance the relationship between therapist and client that develops as a warm, caring, accepting relationship characterized by empathy, mutual respect, and understanding.

family, and well educated understand the problems of a Hispanic adolescent boy from a poor family living in substandard housing if she did not acknowledge the differences between them? In this case, gender, ethnicity, and economic background of client and therapist are all vastly different.

In the case of K., for example, the therapist mistakenly assumed that the key to improving K.'s situation was to make her more assertive and independent from her family, particularly her father. This Western idea runs counter to Korean cultural values. Korean culture stresses interdependence, not independence. The family comes first, obedience to one's elders is highly valued, and "doing one's own thing" is not acceptable. K.'s real problem may have been her feelings of guilt about her situation and her father's anger. She may have wanted help in dealing with her family situation and her feelings about that situation, not help in becoming more independent.

For therapy to be effective, the client must continue in treatment until a successful outcome is reached. K. never came back after the first session. One of the problems that can occur when the culture or ethnic backgrounds of the client and therapist are mismatched, as in K.'s case, is that the therapist may project his or her values onto the client, failing to achieve true empathy with the client's feelings or even to realize what the client's true feelings are, thus causing the client to drop out of therapy. Studies of such situations have found that members of minority racial or ethnic groups drop out of therapy at a significantly higher rate than the majority group clients (Brown et al., 2003; Cooper et al., 2003; Flaherty & Adams, 1998; Sue, 1977, 1992; Sue et al., 1994; Vail, 1976; Vernon & Roberts, 1982).

Traditional forms of psychotherapy, developed mainly in Western, individualistic cultures may need to be modified to fit the more collectivistic, interdependent cultures. For example, Japanese psychologist Dr. Shigeru Iwakabe has pointed out that the typical "talking cure" practiced by many psychotherapists—including psychodynamic and humanistic therapists—may have to be altered to a nontalking cure and the use of nonverbal tasks (like drawing) due to the reluctance of many traditional Japanese people to talk openly about private concerns (Iwakabe, 2008).

Are differences in gender that important? For example, do women prefer female therapists, but men would rather talk to another man?

Are differences in gender that important? For example, do women prefer female therapists, but men would rather talk to another man?

Research on gender and therapist–client relationships varies. When talking about White, middle-class clients, it seems that both men and women prefer a female therapist (Jones et al., 1987). But African American clients were more likely to drop out of therapy if the therapist was the *same* sex as the client (Vail, 1976); male Asian clients seemed to prefer a male therapist; and female Asian clients stayed in therapy equally long with either male or female therapists (Flaherty & Adams, 1998; Flaskerud, 1991). (Although several of the references cited are older ones, they represent the most recent studies for these specific findings.)

Four barriers to effective psychotherapy exist when the culture or ethnic backgrounds of client and therapist are different (Sue & Sue, 2008):

1. **Culture-bound values.** Including individual centered versus other (or others) centered, verbal/emotional/behavioral expressiveness, communication patterns from client to counselor, nuclear family, and so forth (Sue & Sue, 2008). Differing cultural values can cause therapists to fail at forming an empathetic relationship (Sattler, 1977; Wedding, 2004).
2. **Class-bound values.** Adherence to time schedules, ambiguous approach to problems, looking for long-range goals (Sue & Sue, 2008). Clients from impoverished backgrounds may have values and experiences that the therapist cannot understand (Wedding, 2004).

3. **Language.** Use of Standard English, emphasis on verbal communication (Sue & Sue, 2008). Speaking different languages becomes a problem in understanding what both client and therapist are saying and in psychological testing (Betancourt & Jacobs, 2000; Lewis, 1996).
4. **Nonverbal communication.** Body language, or nonverbal communication, can also differ between cultures and ethnicities. The physical distance between the client and therapist, the use of gestures, and eye contact, for example, can cause misunderstandings during the session and in interpretation of the client's moods and intentions (Galanti, 1997; Like et al., 1996). People in some cultures are content with long periods of silence whereas others are not, direct eye contact is desirable in some cultures and offensive in others, and even facial expressions of emotion vary from very expressive (as with Hispanic people) to nonexpressive (as with many Asian people).

The American Psychiatric Association (2000a) has included a guide for therapists concerning cultural issues and culture-bound syndromes such as *koro*. LINK to Chapter Fourteen: Psychological Disorders, p. 534. All therapists need to make an effort to become aware of cultural differences, culture-bound syndromes, and possible gender issues. Sociopolitical issues should also be examined (Sue & Sue, 2008).

CYBERTHERAPY: THERAPY IN THE COMPUTER AGE

Although psychotherapy is usually accomplished by the client or clients speaking face-to-face with the therapist, a new type of therapy is now available to people in need who own a computer. **Cybertherapy** refers to psychotherapy that is offered on the Internet, and the people who practice it are called *cybertherapists*. Although this method of delivery may have the advantages of lower or no cost, availability of therapy opportunities for those unable to get to a therapist easily (such as people living in a remote or rural area), access to support groups online, and relative anonymity, there are dangers. There is no guarantee that the cybertherapist has any credentials or training in psychotherapy. Although some therapists use voice or video conferencing, some only use text-based chat. When there is no face-to-face or voice-to-voice contact, the therapist has no access to body language or vocal tones in trying to assess a client's emotional and psychological state. For further information on this subject, an excellent list of the various forms that cybertherapy can take and the strengths and weaknesses of each has been developed by Dr. Azy Barak, a psychologist at the University of Haifa in Israel and an expert in Internet psychotherapy (Barak, 1999; Barak & Hen, 2008; Barak & Suler, 2008). (For more on the application of computers in psychology, see the Applying Psychology to Everyday Life section.)

A group of researchers in Germany found that people who were treated as inpatients and then allowed to "meet" with a group therapist in an Internet chat room showed a significantly lower risk of negative changes in their mental status than a control group (Golkaramnay et al., 2007). The dropout rate from the Internet group was very low, and most patients "attended" the chat room sessions, which suggests that the ease of using a computer to connect to a group-therapy session may be a viable option for some people needing continued therapy opportunities.

Biomedical Therapies

Just as a therapist trained in psychoanalysis is more likely to use that technique, a therapist whose perspective on personality and behavior is biological will most likely turn to medical techniques to manage disordered behavior. Even psychotherapists who are not primarily biological in orientation may combine psychotherapy with medical treatments that are supervised by a medical doctor working with the

cybertherapy psychotherapy that is offered on the Internet. Also called online, Internet, or Web therapy or counseling.

biomedical therapies therapies that directly affect the biological functioning of the body and brain.

psychopharmacology the use of drugs to control or relieve the symptoms of psychological disorders.

antipsychotic drugs drugs used to treat psychotic symptoms such as delusions, hallucinations, and other bizarre behavior.

Simulate different biomedical therapies on **mypsychlab.com**

psychologist. As medical doctors, psychiatrists are almost inevitably biological in perspective and, thus, use **biomedical therapies** (directly affecting the biological functioning of the body and brain) in addition to any psychotherapy technique they may favor. The biomedical therapies fall into three categories: drug therapy, shock therapy, and surgical treatments.

PSYCHOPHARMACOLOGY

15.9 What are the various types of drugs used to treat psychological disorders?

The use of drugs to control or relieve the symptoms of a psychological disorder is called **psychopharmacology**. Although these drugs are sometimes used alone, they are more often combined with some form of psychotherapy and are more effective as a result (Kearney & Silverman, 1998; Keller et al., 2000). There are four basic categories of drugs used to treat psychotic disorders, anxiety disorders, the manic phase of mood disorders, and depression. Simulate on **mypsychlab.com**

ANTIPSYCHOTIC DRUGS Drugs used to treat psychotic symptoms, such as hallucinations, delusions, and bizarre behavior, are called **antipsychotic drugs**. The three categories of antipsychotic drugs are *typical neuroleptics, atypical neuroleptics*, and *partial dopamine agonists*. The first of the typical neuroleptics to be developed was *chlorpromazine* (Jones & Pilowsky, 2002). The term *neuroleptic* comes from the French word *neuroleptique*, which means "to have an effect on neurons." Table 15.2 lists several of these antipsychotic drugs and their side effects.

These drugs work by blocking certain dopamine receptors in the brain, thereby reducing the effect of dopamine in synaptic transmission (Csernansky et al., 2002). However, because they block more pathways in the dopamine system than are involved in psychosis, with prolonged use they tend to cause problems such as *tardive dyskinesia*, a syndrome causing the person to make repetitive, involuntary jerks and movements of the face, lips, legs, and body (Jones & Pilowsky, 2002).

Table 15.2

Types of Drugs Used in Psychopharmacology

CLASSIFICATION	TREATMENT AREAS	SIDE EFFECTS	EXAMPLES
Antipsychotic: Typical Neuroleptic	Positive (excessive) symptoms such as delusions or hallucinations	Motor problems, tardive dyskinesia	chlorpromazine, droperidol, haloperidol
Antipsychotic: Atypical Neuroleptic	Positive and some negative symptoms of psychoses	Fewer than typical neuroleptics; clozapine may cause serious blood disorder	risperidone, clozapine, aripiprazole
Antianxiety: Minor Tranquilizers	Symptoms of anxiety and phobic reactions	Slight sedative effect; potential for physical dependence	alprazolam, lorazepam, diazepam
Antimanic	Manic behavior	Potential for toxic buildup	lithium, anticonvulsant drugs
Antidepressants: MAOIs	Depression	Weight gain, constipation, dry mouth, dizziness, headache, drowsiness, insomnia, some sexual arousal disorders	iproniazid, isocarboxazid, phenelzine sulfite, tranylcypromine sulfate
Antidepressants: Tricyclics	Depression	Skin rashes, blurred vision, lowered blood pressure, weight loss	imipramine, desipramine, amitriptyline, doxepin
Antidepressants: SSRIs	Depression	Nausea, nervousness, insomnia, diarrhea, rash, agitation, some sexual arousal problems	fluoxetine, sertraline, paroxetine

The atypical neuroleptics also suppress dopamine but to a much greater degree in the one dopamine pathway that seems to cause psychotic problems. These drugs also block or partially block certain serotonin receptors, resulting in fewer negative side effects and occasionally some improvement in the more negative symptoms of schizophrenia such as withdrawal, apathy, and reduced communication (Jones & Pilowsky, 2002).

Clozapine, an atypical neuroleptic, can cause a potentially fatal reduction in the white blood cells of the body's immune system in a very small percentage of people. For this reason, the blood of patients on clozapine is closely monitored (Jones & Pilowsky, 2002).

How long do people generally have to take these antipsychotic medications?

How long do people generally have to take these antipsychotic medications?

In some cases, a person might have a psychotic episode that lasts only a few months or a few years and may need drug treatment only for that time. But in most cases, especially in schizophrenia that starts in adolescence or young adulthood, the medication must be taken for the rest of the person's life.

Long-term use of neuroleptics, particularly the older typical drugs, has been associated with a decrease in cognitive functioning (Terry et al., 2002, 2003). A newer class of atypical neuroleptics called partial dopamine agonists affects the release of dopamine rather than blocking its receptors in the brain (Tamminga, 2002). (An *agonist* is any chemical substance that can stimulate a reaction within the synapse.) LINK to Chapter Two: The Biological Perspective, p. 52. By 2005 the only one of these drugs that had been approved by the Food and Drug Administration for use in the treatment of schizophrenia was aripiprazole (Abilify). The hope is that these newer drugs will not only produce fewer negative side effects but also have less impact on the thought processes of those persons taking these drugs. In one recent study, the atypical neuroleptics were also found to lower the risk of violent behavior in patients with schizophrenia who are receiving their medication through community-based treatment centers (Swanson et al., 2004).

ANTIANXIETY DRUGS There are currently two kinds of drugs used to treat anxiety disorders from mild anxiety to the more serious anxiety of social phobias, simple phobias, and panic disorder. The traditional **antianxiety drugs** are the minor tranquilizers or *benzodiazepines* such as Xanax, Ativan, and Valium. All of these drugs have a sedative effect and in the right dose can relieve symptoms of anxiety within half an hour of taking the drug (Uretsky, 2002). Although many side effects are possible, the main concern in using these drugs is their potential for addiction as well as abuse in the form of taking larger doses to "escape" (National Institute on Drug Abuse [NIDA], 2002).

In the last several years the use of the benzodiazepines to treat anxiety has declined, and physicians and therapists have begun to prescribe **antidepressant drugs** to treat anxiety disorders such as panic disorder, obsessive-compulsive disorder, and posttraumatic stress disorder. Although the antidepressants take from 3 to 5 weeks to show any effect, they are not as subject to abuse as the minor tranquilizers and have fewer of the same side effects.

ANTIMANIC DRUGS For many years, the treatment of choice for bipolar disorder and episodes of mania has been *lithium*, a metallic chemical element that in its salt form (lithium carbonate) evens out both the highs and the lows of bipolar disorder. It is generally recommended that treatment with lithium continue at maintenance levels in people with recurring bipolar disorder. Lithium affects the way sodium ions in neuron and muscle cells are transported, although it is not clear exactly how this affects mood. Side effects typically disappear quickly, although the use of lithium has been associated with weight gain. Diet needs to be controlled when taking lithium because lowered levels of sodium in the diet can cause lithium to build up to toxic levels, as can any substance that removes water from the body such as the caffeine in sodas, tea, and coffee.

antianxiety drugs drugs used to treat and calm anxiety reactions, typically minor tranquilizers.

antidepressant drugs drugs used to treat depression and anxiety.

Anticonvulsant drugs, normally used to treat seizure disorders, have also been used to treat mania. Examples are carbamazepine, valproic acid (Depakote), and lamotrigine. These drugs can be as effective in controlling mood swings as lithium and can also be used in combination with lithium treatments (Bowden et al., 2000; Thase & Sachs, 2000). When bouts of mania include psychotic symptoms (as in affective psychosis), patients are often treated with antipsychotic drugs in addition to a combination of anticonvulsants or antidepressants (Tohen et al., 2003).

ANTIDEPRESSANT DRUGS As is so often the case in scientific discoveries, the first types of drugs used in the treatment of depression were originally developed to treat other disorders. Iproniazid, for example, was used to treat tuberculosis symptoms in the early 1950s and was found to have a positive effect on mood, becoming the first modern *antidepressant* (Trujillo & Chinn, 1996). This drug became the first of the *monamine oxidase inhibitors (MAOIs)*, a class of antidepressants that blocks the activity of an enzyme called monamine oxidase. Monamine oxidase is the brain's "cleanup worker" because its primary function is to break down the neurotransmitters norepinephrine, serotonin, and dopamine—the three neurotransmitters most involved in control of mood. Under normal circumstances, the excess neurotransmitters are broken down *after* they have done their "job" in mood control. In depression, these neurotransmitters need more time to do their job, and the MAOIs allow them that time by inhibiting the enzyme's action.

Some common MAOIs in use today are isocarboxazid (Marplan), phenelzine sufate (Nardil), and tranylcypromine sulfate (Parnate). These drugs can produce some unwanted side effects, although in most cases the side effects decrease or disappear with continued treatment: weight gain, constipation, dry mouth, dizziness, headache, drowsiness or insomnia, and sexual arousal disorders are possible. People taking MAOIs should also be careful about eating certain smoked, fermented, or pickled foods, drinking certain beverages, or taking some other medications due to a risk of severe high blood pressure in combination with these substances (Geddes & Butler, 2002).

The second category of antidepressant drug to be developed is called the *tricyclic antidepressants*. These drugs were discovered in the course of developing treatments for schizophrenia (Trujillo & Chinn, 1996). Tricyclics, so called because of their molecular structure consisting of three rings (cycles), increase the activity of serotonin and norepinephrine in the nervous system by inhibiting their reuptake into the synaptic vesicles of the neurons. LINK to Chapter Two: The Biological Perspective, pp. 53–55. Some common tricyclics are imipramine (Tofranil), desipramine (Norpramin, Pertofrane), amitriptyline (Elavil), and doxepin (Sinequan, Adapin). Side effects of these drugs, which may also decrease over the course of treatment, are very similar to those of the MAOIs but can also include skin rashes, blurred vision, lowered blood pressure, and weight loss (American Psychiatric Association, 2000b; Geddes & Butler, 2002).

The effect of the MAOIs and the tricyclics on the action of the three critical neurotransmitters led researchers to try to develop drugs that would more specifically target the critical neural activity involved in depression with fewer negative side effects. This led to the development of the *selective serotonin reuptake inhibitors (SSRIs)*, drugs that inhibit the reuptake process of only serotonin. This causes fewer side effects while still providing effective antidepressant action, making these drugs relatively safe when compared to the older antidepressants. But like the other two classes of antidepressants, the SSRIs may take from 2 to 6 weeks to produce effects. Some of the better-known SSRIs are fluoxetine (Prozac), sertraline (Zoloft), and paroxetine (Paxil). Listen on **mypsychlab.com**

Listen to the Psychology in the News podcast on treating children and adolescents with antidepressant drugs on **mypsychlab.com**

15.10 How are electroconvulsive therapy and psychosurgery used to treat psychological disorders today?

ELECTROCONVULSIVE THERAPY

Many people are—well—*shocked* to discover that **electroconvulsive therapy (ECT)** is still in use to treat cases of severe depression. ECT involves the delivery of an electric shock to either one side or both sides of a person's head, resulting in a seizure or convulsion of the body and the release of a flood of neurotransmitters in the brain (American Psychiatric Association [APA] Committee on Electroconvulsive Therapy, 2001). The result is an almost immediate improvement in mood, and ECT is used not only in severe cases of depression that have not responded to drug treatments, the side effects of medication, or psychotherapy but also in the treatment of several other severe disorders that are not responding to those alternate treatments, such as schizophrenia and severe mania (APA Committee on Electroconvulsive Therapy, 2001).

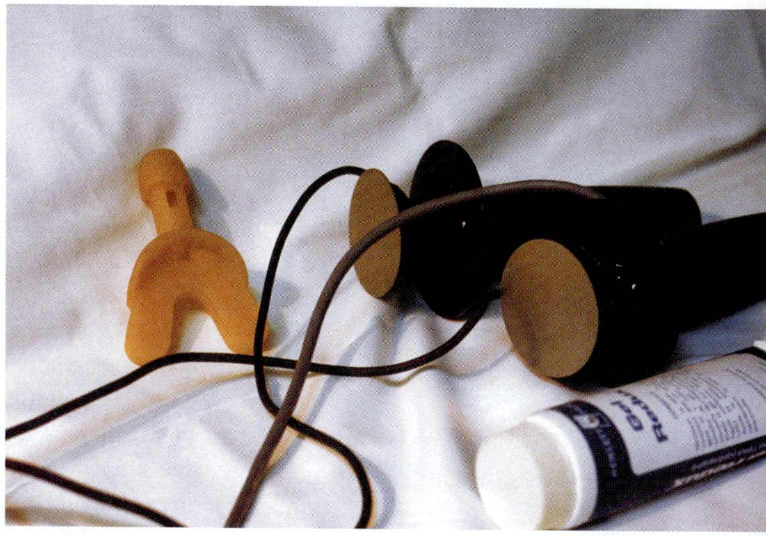

Electroconvulsive therapy consists of applying an electric shock to one or both sides of the head. The result is rapid improvement in mood. It has been shown to be most effective in treating severe depression that has not responded to medication or where medication side effects cannot be tolerated.

In the 1930s, doctors actually were researching the possible uses of inducing seizures in treating schizophrenia, although the seizures were induced through means of a drug (camphor) in those early experiments. It was Italian researchers Cerletti and Bini who first used electricity to induce a seizure in a man with schizophrenia, who fully recovered after only 11 such treatments (Endler, 1988; Fink, 1984; Shorter, 1997). Soon doctors were using ECT on every kind of severe mental disorder. In those early days, no anesthesia was used because the shock was severe enough to result in a loss of consciousness (most of the time). Broken bones, bitten tongues, and fractured teeth were not untypical "side effects."

Today's ECT is far more controlled and humane. It is only used to treat severe disorders and written and informed consent is required in most states. ECT has been found to be most useful for severe depression that has not responded to medications or psychotherapy and in cases where suicide is a real possibility or has already been attempted. ECT works more quickly than antidepressant medications, so it can play an important role in helping to prevent suicide attempts (APA Committee on Electroconvulsive Therapy, 2001). However, ECT should not be considered a "cure." It is a way to get a person suffering from severe depression into a state of mind that is more receptive to other forms of therapy or psychotherapy.

What are some of the side effects? Wasn't there something from an earlier chapter about this therapy affecting memory?

What are some of the side effects? Wasn't there something from an earlier chapter about this therapy affecting memory?

ECT does have several negative side effects, some of which last longer than others. Memory is definitely affected, as ECT disrupts the consolidation process and prevents the formation of long-term memories. LINK to Chapter Six: Memory, pp. 243–244. This causes both retrograde amnesia, the loss of memories for events that happen close to the time of the treatment, and anterograde amnesia, the rapid forgetting of new material (APA Committee on Electroconvulsive Therapy, 2001; Lisanby et al., 2000; Weiner, 2000). The retrograde effects can extend to several months before and a few weeks after treatment and the older memories may return with time, whereas the anterograde amnesia is more temporary, clearing up in a few weeks after treatment. Only a very few patients suffer more severe and long-lasting cognitive difficulties, and it is not easy to determine whether these difficulties originate with the treatment or the disorder the person exhibits (Smith, 2001).

electroconvulsive therapy (ECT) form of biomedical therapy to treat severe depression in which electrodes are placed on either one or both sides of a person's head and an electric current is passed through the electrodes that is strong enough to cause a seizure or convulsion.

psychosurgery surgery performed on brain tissue to relieve or control severe psychological disorders.

prefrontal lobotomy psychosurgery in which the connections of the prefrontal lobes of the brain to the rear portions are severed.

bilateral anterior cingulotomy psychosurgical technique in which an electrode wire is inserted into the anterior cingulate gyrus with the guidance of a magnetic resonance imaging machine for the purpose of destroying that area of brain tissue with an electric current.

When ECT is used today an effort is made to reduce as many side effects as possible. The modern patient is given muscle relaxants to reduce the effects of the convulsion as well as a very short-term anesthetic.

PSYCHOSURGERY

Just as surgery involves cutting into the body, **psychosurgery** involves cutting into the brain to remove or destroy brain tissue for the purpose of relieving symptoms of mental disorders. One of the earliest and best-known psychosurgical techniques is the **prefrontal lobotomy**, in which the connections of the prefrontal lobes of the brain to the rest of the brain are severed. The lobotomy was developed in 1935 by Portuguese neurologist Dr. Antonio Egas Moniz, who was awarded the Nobel Prize in medicine for his contribution to psychosurgery (Cosgrove & Rauch, 1995; Freeman & Watts, 1937). Walter Freeman and James W. Watts modified Moniz's technique and developed a procedure called the *transorbital lobotomy*, during which an instrument resembling an ice pick, called a leucotome, was inserted through the back of the eye socket and into the brain to sever the brain fibers. It was this technique that became widely used, and unfortunately sometimes overused, in the pursuit of relief for so many people suffering from mental illness.

But I thought lobotomies left most people worse off than before—didn't it take away their emotions or something?

But I thought lobotomies left most people worse off than before—didn't it take away their emotions or something?

Although it is true that some of the early lobotomy patients did seem less agitated, anxious, and delusional, it is also true that some early patients did not survive the surgery (about 6 percent died, in fact) and others were left with negative changes in personality: apathy, lack of emotional response, intellectual dullness, and childishness, to name a few. Fortunately, the development of antipsychotic drugs, beginning with chlorpromazine, together with the results of long-term studies that highlighted serious side effects of lobotomies, led to the discontinuation of lobotomies as a psychosurgical technique (Cosgrove & Rauch, 1995; Swayze, 1995). Some famous recipients of the last decades of lobotomies (and the disorders for which the procedure was performed) were Rosemary Kennedy, sister of John F. Kennedy (mild intellectual disability), and Rose Williams, sister of playwright Tennessee Williams (schizophrenia).

Are there any psychosurgical techniques in use today since the lobotomy is no longer used?

Are there any psychosurgical techniques in use today since the lobotomy is no longer used?

The lobotomy is gone, but there is a different, and more modern technique that was mentioned in the chapter opener called **bilateral anterior cingulotomy**, in which magnetic resonance imaging, LINK to Chapter Two: The Biological Perspective, p. 67, is used to guide an electrode to a specific area of the brain called the cingulate gyrus. This area connects the frontal lobes to the limbic system, which controls emotional reactions. By running a current through the electrode, a very small and specific area of brain cells can be destroyed. This process is called *deep lesioning*. LINK to Chapter Two: The Biological Perspective, p. 65. Cingulotomies have been shown to be effective in about one third to one half of cases of major depression, bipolar disorder, and certain forms of obsessive-compulsive disorder that have not responded to any other therapy techniques (Dougherty et al., 2002; Kuhn et al., 2010; Spangler et al., 1996). Because this is deliberate brain damage and quite permanent, all other possible treatments must be exhausted before a bilateral cingulotomy will be performed and, unlike the early days of lobotomies, it can be performed only with the patient's full and informed consent (Rodgers, 1992; Spangler et al., 1996). In fact, because of the ethical, social, and legal implications of psychosurgery in general, today only a very small number of such surgeries are carried out in a few medical centers across the world (Cosgrove & Rauch, 1995). Read on mypsychlab.com

The woman on the left is Rosemary Kennedy, sister of President John F. Kennedy. The man on the right is her father, U.S. Ambassador to Great Britain Joseph Kennedy. About 6 years after this photograph was taken, Rosemary, who had mild intellectual disability and whose behavior had become difficult to control, was subjected to a prefrontal lobotomy. The results were disastrous, and she remained institutionalized until her death on January 7, 2005.

Read and learn more about the history of lobotomy on **mypsychlab.com**

EMERGING TECHNIQUES Some new noninvasive techniques for effecting changes in the brain were discussed in LINK Chapter Two including *repetitive transcranial magnetic stimulation* (rTMS), where magnetic pulses are applied to the cortex and *transcranial direct current stimulation* (tDCS), which uses scalp electrodes to pass very low amplitude direct currents to the brain. These new and exciting strategies are being evaluated as possible treatment options for a variety of psychological disorders including PTSD and depression (Boggio et al., 2009; Nitsche et al., 2009). Another technique highlighted in LINK Chapter Two was *deep brain stimulation* and it is being evaluated as a treatment modality for both depression and OCD (Harvard Mental Health Letter, 2010; Huff et al., 2010).

Many psychological professionals today believe that combining psychotherapy with medical therapies—particularly drug therapy—is a more effective approach to treating many disorders. A person dealing with depression may be given an antidepressant drug to alleviate symptoms but may also still need to talk about what it's like to deal with depression and with needing the medication. Cognitive–behavioral therapy in combination with drug therapy has been shown to be particularly effective in treating depression (Dew et al., 2007; Frank et al., 2007; Rohde et al., 2008). Another study has found that women with recurrent depression benefit from a combination of treatment with antidepressants and monthly maintenance psychotherapy (Frank et al., 2007).

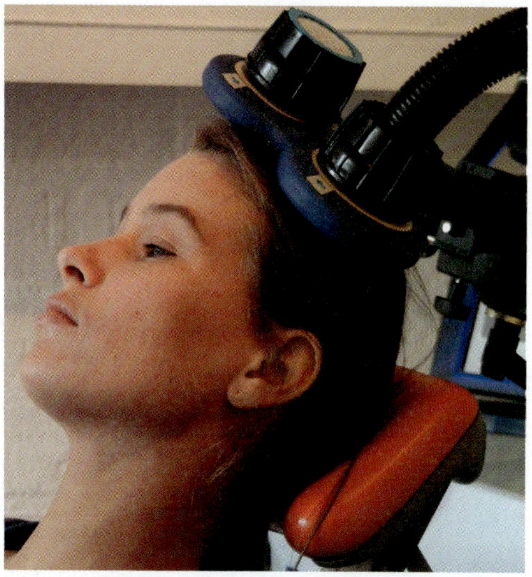

Repetitive transcranial magnetic stimulation (rTMS) uses a pulsating magnetic field to activate specific parts of the brain's surface. As seen above, by placing an electromagnet on the scalp, rTMS can be used to stimulate small areas of the cortex and is being evaluated as a way to control some psychological symptoms, such as those related to depression and PTSD. Photo courtesy of Martijn Arns, http://www.brainclinics.com

CONCEPT MAP

15.8 15.9 15.10

- effectiveness is not easy to study due to different theories, techniques, time frames for success, etc.; tendency of some therapists to be eclectic (using variety of techniques) is also a challenge
  - common factors approach: focuses on those factors common to successful outcomes from different forms of therapy
  - clients benefit through evidence-based practice, or empirically validated treatment—identification of treatments and other aspects of treatment that work best for specific disorders
- where effective, greater success is often tied to the relationship between the therapist and client (therapeutic alliance), a sense of safety, and longer time in therapy
- cultural, ethnic, and gender concerns should also be examined; these factors can affect not only the therapeutic alliance but also identification of actual problem(s) and treatment options

Does Psychotherapy Work?

- **psychopharmacology** the use of drugs to control or relieve the symptoms of a psychological disorder; may be used alone or in combination with other therapies (see Table 15.2)
  - **antipsychotic drugs:** treat psychotic symptoms such as hallucinations, delusions, and bizarre behavior; include the typical neuroleptics, atypical neuroleptics, and partial dopamine agonists; work by blocking certain dopamine receptors in the brain; long-term use has variety of risks, both behavioral and cognitive
  - **antianxiety drugs:** address anxiety disorders; include the minor tranquilizers (benzodiazepines) that have a sedative effect—also have potential for addiction and abuse; antidepressant drugs also used to treat anxiety disorders
  - **antimanic drugs:** address the manic episodes associated with bipolar disorder; most common is lithium; may also include anticonvulsants and antidepressants
  - **antidepressant drugs:** are used to treat symptoms of depression and include monoamine oxidase inhibitors (MAOIs), tricyclic antidepressants, and selective serotonin reuptake inhibitors (SSRIs)

Biomedical Therapies

(continued)

Biomedical Therapies (continued)

- **electroconvulsive therapy**
  - still used to treat severe depression and a few other disorders that have not responded to other forms of treatment
  - involves the application of an electric shock and resulting seizure that appears to normalize the balance of neurotransmitters within the brain
  - traditional side effects (extreme memory loss, broken bones) have been minimized by lower levels of current and the use of both muscle relaxers and anesthesia
- **psychosurgery**
  - used as a last resort, involves cutting into the brain to remove or destroy brain tissues associated with symptoms of a mental disorder
  - prefrontal lobotomies were widely used in the mid-1900s up until the development of antipsychotic drugs
  - at present, bilateral anterior cingulotomy (involves selective areas of cingulate gyrus) is used, primarily for obsessive-compulsive disorder; has also been used with depression and bipolar disorder
- **emerging technologies**
  - repetitive transcranial magnetic stimulation (rTMS)
  - transcranial direct current stimulation (tDCS)
    - → being evaluated as treatment options for PTSD and depression, and other disorders
  - deep brain stimulation for depression and OCD

PRACTICE quiz How much do you remember?

ANSWERS ON PAGE AK-2.

Pick the best answer.

1. Which of the following statements about the effectiveness of psychotherapy is FALSE?
   a. In surveys, 75 to 90 percent of people reported that therapy has helped them.
   b. The longer a person stays in therapy, the less effective it is.
   c. Psychotherapy without drugs seems to work as well as psychotherapy with drugs.
   d. No one psychotherapy is effective for all disorders.
2. For psychotherapy to be effective, __________.
   a. the therapist must provide a protected setting for clients to reveal their feelings.
   b. the therapist should maintain emotional distance from the client.
   c. clients and therapists should avoid warmth in their relationship.
   d. therapists should choose one style of therapy for all of their clients.
3. Of the following, all are potential barriers to effective therapy listed by Sue and Sue (2008) when culture or ethnic backgrounds of therapist and client are different except __________.
   a. language. **c.** social class.
   b. cultural values. **d.** age.
4. The newest drugs being developed to treat psychotic symptoms are the __________.
   a. typical neuroleptics. **c.** anticonvulsants.
   b. atypical neuroleptics. **d.** partial dopamine agonists.
5. For which disorders have antidepressants NOT been used?
   a. panic disorder
   b. dissociative amnesia
   c. obsessive-compulsive disorder
   d. posttraumatic stress disorder
6. Electroconvulsive shock therapy is useful in preventing suicide attempts because it __________.
   a. is more effective than drug therapies.
   b. has few negative side effects.
   c. works more quickly than antidepressants.
   d. makes people happy.
7. The risk of permanent brain damage is greatest with __________.
   a. cybertherapy. **c.** psychosurgery.
   b. ECT. **d.** bilateral ECT.

Brainstorming: What are some of the possible drawbacks of using medication to treat disordered behavior, beyond any side effects of the medications themselves?

Applying Psychology to Everyday Life: Virtual Realities

15.11 How might computers be used in psychotherapy?

Virtual reality is a software generated three-dimensional simulated environment. Imagine yourself playing a video game, but instead of viewing your character on the screen in front of you, you are immersed in the visual and auditory world

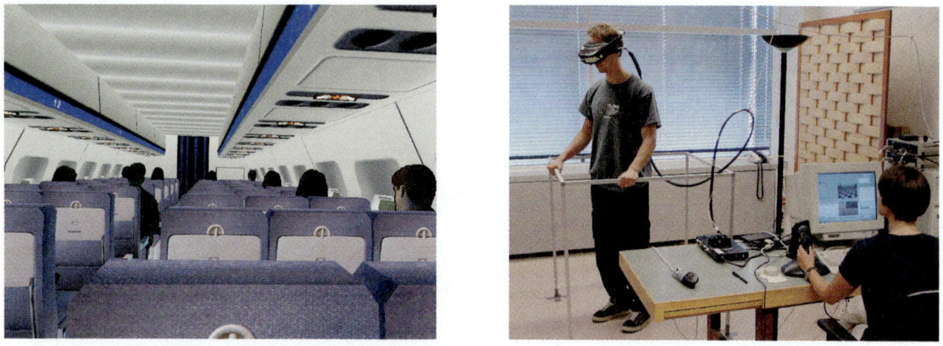

Some behavioral therapists now use virtual reality to expose patients to phobic objects and situations—like the cabin of an airplane. As part of systematic desensitization, this patient receives exposure to anxiety-provoking visual displays through a virtual reality headset.
Credit: Charles Undermost, Delft University of Technology.

created by the game designers, seeing and hearing through the eyes and ears of your character. While playing a video game in this manner might be a lot of fun, there are some very practical uses of virtual reality (VR) for treating psychological disorders.

One of the main uses of VR as a therapy incorporates exposure therapy of some form. Exposure therapy involves preventing a person with a phobia, for example, from avoiding the presentation of the phobic object—preventing the typical avoidance response and eventually resulting in extinction of the conditioned fear. Using VR ensures that the person being treated cannot avoid exposure as the sight and sound of the animal, open spaces, or whatever the phobia involves is always right in front of him or her. A study that is being conducted at the University of Manchester, England, and led by Professor Nick Tarrier is focused on helping people with phobias about driving cars by having them wear sophisticated goggles that allow them to experience a virtual driving environment (University of Manchester, 2009). Special sensors on chest and fingers measure anxiety levels. The real advantage of VR psychotherapy here is that there is no physical risk to the phobic driver, therapist, or other drivers on a real road.

Posttraumatic stress disorder (PTSD) is another mental-health issue benefiting from the use of VR psychotherapy. Cases of this disorder are rising (and with the BP oil spill disaster discussed in Chapter Fourteen and other such stressors, psychologists expect the number of PTSD cases to continue to rise), and traditional treatments are not always effective. Virtual reality psychotherapy allows the safe use of exposure therapy, already thought to be a highly promising treatment for PTSD (Mary Ann Liebert, Inc./Genetic Engineering News, 2010). Another advantage is the more-vivid and realistic imagery possible with VR, especially for patients who are asked to "imagine" the scenarios that disturb them who may not be highly skilled in visualization. Think also of the portability of VR: there are currently handheld VR devices that eventually could be used to deliver therapy for PTSD, for example, to survivors of earthquakes, tsunamis, hurricanes, and other massive disasters around the world.

Questions for Further Discussion

1. What other disorders can you think of that might benefit from virtual reality psychotherapy?
2. Can you think of any disadvantages to this method of therapy?

chapter summary

((•• Listen on mypsychlab.com Listen to an audio file of your chapter www.mypsychlab.com

Two Kinds of Therapy

15.1 What are the two modern ways in which psychological disorders can be treated, and how have they been treated in the past?

- Psychotherapy involves a person talking to a psychological professional about the person's problems.
- Psychotherapy for the purpose of gaining understanding into one's motives and actions is called insight therapy, whereas psychotherapy aimed at changing disordered behavior directly is called action therapy.
- Biomedical therapy uses a medical procedure to bring about changes in behavior.

The Early Days: Ice-Water Baths and Electric Shocks

- Mentally ill people began to be confined to institutions called asylums in the mid-1500s. Treatments were harsh and often damaging.
- Philippe Pinel became famous for demanding that the mentally ill be treated with kindness, personally unlocking the chains of inmates at Bicêtre Asylum in Paris, France.

Psychotherapy Begins

- Sigmund Freud developed a treatment called psychoanalysis that focused on releasing a person's hidden, repressed urges and concerns from the unconscious mind.

15.2 What were the basic elements of Freud's psychoanalysis, and how does psychoanalysis differ today?

- Psychoanalysis uses interpretation of dreams, free association, positive and negative transference, and resistance to help patients reveal their unconscious concerns.
- Freud's original therapy technique is criticized for its lack of scientific research and his own personal biases that caused him to misinterpret much of what his patients revealed.
- Modern psychodynamic therapists have modified the technique so that it takes less time and is much more direct, and they do not focus on the id and sexuality as Freud did.

Humanistic Therapy: To Err Is Human

15.3 What are the basic elements of the humanistic therapies known as person-centered therapy and Gestalt therapy?

- Humanistic therapies focus on the conscious mind and subjective experiences to help clients gain insights.
- Person-centered therapy is very nondirective, allowing the client to talk through problems and concerns while the therapist provides a supportive background.
- The four basic elements of person-centered therapy are reflection of the client's statements by the therapist, unconditional positive regard given to the client by the therapist, the empathy of the therapist for the client, and the authenticity of the therapists in the client's perception.
- Gestalt therapy is more directive, helping clients to become aware of their feelings and to take responsibility for their choices in life.
- Gestalt therapists try to help clients deal with things in their past that they have denied and will use body language and other nonverbal cues to understand what clients are really saying.
- Humanistic therapies are also not based in experimental research and work best with intelligent, highly verbal persons.

Behavior Therapies: Learning One's Way to Better Behavior

- Behavior therapies are action therapies that do not look at thought processes but instead focus on changing the abnormal or disordered behavior itself through classical or operant conditioning.

15.4 How do behavior therapists use classical and operant conditioning to treat disordered behavior?

- Classical conditioning techniques for changing behavior include systematic desensitization, aversion therapy, and flooding.
- Therapies based on operant conditioning include modeling, reinforcement and the use of token economies, and extinction.

15.5 How successful are behavior therapies?

- Behavior therapies can be effective in treating specific problems, such as bed-wetting, drug addictions, and phobias, and can help improve some of the more troubling behavioral symptoms associated with more severe disorders.

Cognitive Therapies: Thinking Is Believing

15.6 What are the goals and basic elements of cognitive therapies such as cognitive–behavioral therapy and rational–emotive behavior therapy?

- Cognitive therapy is oriented toward teaching clients how their thinking may be distorted and helping clients to see how inaccurate some of their beliefs may be.
- Some of the cognitive distortions in thinking include arbitrary inference, selective thinking, overgeneralization, magnification and minimization, and personalization.
- Cognitive–behavioral therapies are action therapies that work at changing a person's illogical or distorted thinking.
- The three goals of cognitive–behavioral therapies are to relieve the symptoms and solve the problems, to develop strategies for solving future problems, and to help change irrational, distorted thinking.
- Rational–emotive behavior therapy is a directive therapy in which the therapist challenges clients' irrational beliefs, often arguing with clients and even assigning them homework.

- Although CBT has seemed successful in treating depression, stress disorders, and anxiety, it is criticized for focusing on the symptoms and not the causes of disordered behavior.

Group Therapies: Not Just for the Shy

15.7 What are the various types of group therapies and the advantages and disadvantages of group therapy?

- Group therapy has the advantages of low cost, exposure to other people with similar problems, social interaction with others, and social and emotional support from people with similar disorders or problems. It has also been demonstrated to be very effective for people with social anxiety.
- Disadvantages of group therapy can include the need to share the therapist's time with others in the group, the lack of a private setting in which to reveal concerns, and the inability of people with severe disorders to tolerate being in a group.
- Group therapy can be accomplished using many styles of psychotherapy and may involve treating people who are all part of the same family, as in family counseling.
- Group therapy can also be accomplished without the aid of a trained therapist in the form of self-help or support groups composed of other people who have the same or similar problems.
- Group therapy is most useful to persons who cannot afford individual therapy and who may obtain a great deal of social and emotional support from other group members.

PSYCHOLOGY IN THE NEWS: Mental Health on Campus

- Campus life is often very stressful, and many students arrive on campus already in therapy for a diagnosed disorder.
- Students should make use of the available resources on college campuses, such as counseling centers.

Does Psychotherapy Really Work?

- Eysenck's early survey of client improvement seemed to suggest that clients would improve as time passed, with or without therapy.

15.8 How effective is psychotherapy, and how is the effectiveness of psychotherapy influenced by cultural, ethnic, and gender differences?

- Surveys of people who have received therapy suggest that psychotherapy is more effective than no treatment at all.
- Surveys reveal that from 75 to 90 percent of people who receive therapy improve, the longer a person stays in therapy the better the improvement, and psychotherapy works as well alone as with drugs.
- Some types of psychotherapy are more effective for certain types of problems, and no one psychotherapy method is effective for all problems.
- Effective therapy should be matched to the particular client and the particular problem, there should exist a therapeutic alliance between therapist and client, and a protected setting in which clients can release emotions and reveal private thoughts is essential.
- When the culture, ethnic group, or gender of the therapist and the client differs, misunderstandings and misinterpretations can occur due to differences in cultural/ethnic values, socioeconomic differences, gender roles, and beliefs.
- The four barriers to effective psychotherapy that exist when the backgrounds of client and therapist differ are language, cultural values, social class, and nonverbal communication.
- Cybertherapy is therapy that is offered on the Internet. Cybertherapists may or may not be trained in psychotherapy, but cybertherapy offers the advantages of anonymity and therapy for people who cannot otherwise get to a therapist.

Biomedical Therapies

- Biomedical therapies include the use of drugs, induced convulsions, and surgery to relieve or control the symptoms of mental disorders.

15.9 What are the various types of drugs used to treat psychological disorders?

- Antipsychotic drugs are used to control delusions, hallucinations, and bizarre behavior and include the typical neuroleptics, atypical neuroleptics, and partial dopamine agonists.
- Antianxiety drugs are used to treat anxiety disorders and include the benzodiazepines and certain antidepressant drugs.
- Antimanic drugs are used to treat bipolar disorder and include lithium and certain anticonvulsant drugs.
- Antidepressant drugs are used in the treatment of depression and include monamine oxidase inhibitors (MOAIs), tricyclic antidepressants, and selective serotonin reuptake inhibitors (SSRIs).

15.10 How are electroconvulsive therapy and psychosurgery used to treat psychological disorders today?

- Electroconvulsive therapy, or ECT, is used to treat severe depression, bipolar disorder, and schizophrenia and involves the use of a muscle relaxant, a short-term anesthetic, and induction of a seizure under contolled conditions.
- One of the earliest psychosurgeries was the prefrontal lobotomy, in which the front part of the frontal lobe was cut away from the back part of the brain, producing effects ranging from a disappearance of symptoms to a lack of emotional response and dulling of mental functions.
- Modern psychosurgery includes the bilateral cingulotomy, used to treat major depression, bipolar disorders, and certain forms of obsessive-compulsive disorder that have not responded to other forms of treatment.
- Emerging technologies for treatment of psychological disorders include repetitive transcranial magnetic stimulation (rTMS), transcranial direct current stimulation (tDCS), and deep brain stimulation

Applying Psychology to Everyday Life: Virtual Realities

15.11 How might computers be used in psychotherapy?

- Virtual reality therapy is a computer-based simulation of environments that can be used to treat disorders such as phobias and PTSD with less risk than that of actual exposure to anxiety-provoking stimuli.
- VRT is particularly useful as a delivery system for exposure therapy.

test YOURSELF

ANSWERS ON PAGE AK-2.

Pick the best answer.

1. Larisa is going to a therapist to gain a better understanding of what makes her do the things she does. This type of therapy is known as _________ therapy.
   a. insight c. behavioral
   b. action d. biomedical
2. It was _________ who is most credited with the "moral treatment" movement for using kindness and guidance with the mentally ill.
   a. Sigmund Freud c. Jean Martin Charcot
   b. Josef Breuer d. Philippe Pinel
3. The actual content of a dream is the _________ content, according to Freud.
   a. repressed c. manifest
   b. latent d. sexual
4. A psychoanalyst may rely on the technique of _________, which allows the patient to talk about anything that comes to mind.
   a. positive transference c. free association
   b. negative transference d. dream analysis
5. In _________, a person-centered therapist must show an honest and open response to the client and not hide behind the professional role of therapist.
   a. reflection
   b. unconditional positive regard
   c. empathy
   d. authenticity
6. Gestalt therapy differs from person-centered therapy because _________.
   a. it is based in humanistic theory.
   b. it focuses on the unconscious mind.
   c. it is directive rather than nondirective.
   d. it is an insight therapy.
7. What kind of person would probably get the least benefit from a humanistic therapy?
   a. one who is bright but confused about self-image
   b. one who is very talkative and open in discussing feelings
   c. one who enjoys exploring the inner workings of the mind
   d. one who has a hard time putting things into words in a logical manner
8. Megan was afraid of dogs. She wanted to get over this fear, so she began by thinking about seeing a dog but staying calm. Then she walked past her neighbor's dog in its fenced yard until she no longer felt afraid. Next, she visited a pet store and petted a dog while the salesclerk held it. Finally, she bought herself a puppy and was no longer afraid. Megan's method is most like _________.
   a. systematic desensitization. c. flooding.
   b. aversion therapy. d. extinction.
9. When the exposure to a feared object is rapid and intense rather than slow and gradual, it is called _________.
   a. systematic desensitization. c. flooding.
   b. aversion therapy. d. extinction.
10. Carra sat down with her daughter, Morgan, and together they wrote out a list of things that Morgan was expected to do each day and the rewards she would get if she accomplished them, as well as the penalties she would face if she did not do them. This is most like which technique?
   a. token economy c. extinction
   b. time-out d. contingency contracting
11. Which therapy style can be compared to a drill sergeant–private style of therapeutic relationship?
   a. person-centered c. rational–emotive behavioral
   b. Gestalt d. cognitive
12. Which of the following is not one of the three goals of cognitive–behavioral therapy?
   a. helping the client gain insight
   b. relieving the symptoms and resolving the problems
   c. helping the client develop strategies for future problem solving
   d. helping the client to think in a more rational, self-helping way
13. Stephan sees a text message from a phone number he does not recognize on his girlfriend's phone. He immediately assumes his girlfriend is seeing someone else and the phone number belongs to that person. Beck would say that Stephan has engaged in what type of distorted thinking?
   a. arbitrary inference c. overgeneralization
   b. selective thinking d. personalization
14. Which of the following is a disadvantage of group therapy?
   a. Clients share the therapist's time.
   b. Clients see how other people have handled the problem.
   c. Clients get social support from others.
   d. Clients interact with others socially.
15. When Carson began acting out, her parents took her to a therapist who suggested that her parents may have caused the problem by using the wrong kind of discipline. The kind of therapy that might best help Carson would probably be _________.
   a. a support group of other disturbed children.
   b. an insight therapy.
   c. a cognitive therapy.
   d. family therapy.
16. Which of the following is not one of the problems in studying the effectiveness of psychotherapy?
   a. All therapies take the same amount of time to be effective.
   b. Control groups have no expectations about getting better.
   c. Some therapies measure success differently and are not easily evaluated.
   d. There may be experimenter bias.
17. Cindy is a White, upper-middle-class graduate student in clinical psychology doing her first internship in juvenile court. Her first client is an angry 15-year-old African American boy. Which of the following might be barriers to effective therapy in this situation?
   a. social class c. cultural values
   b. nonverbal communication d. All of these might be barriers.

18. When a person on an antipsychotic drug develops repetitive, involuntary jerks and movements of the face, lips, legs, and body, this is called __________.
   a. the "Thorazine" shuffle.
   b. neuroleptic syndrome.
   c. tardive dyskinesia.
   d. psychotic syndrome.

19. The use of antianxiety drugs to treat anxiety disorders is gradually being phased out in favor of treatment with __________ drugs.
   a. antidepressant
   b. antimanic
   c. antipsychotic
   d. sedative

20. Which neurotransmitter is not one of the three that seems to be involved in depression and the drugs that treat depression?
   a. norepinephrine
   b. serotonin
   c. dopamine
   d. epinephrine

21. Before the use of electricity, seizures were induced in psychotic patients by means of __________.
   a. ice cold water.
   b. bloodletting.
   c. camphor.
   d. opium.

22. In bilateral anterior cingulotomy __________.
   a. the front of the brain is cut away from the back.
   b. a thin wire electrode is used to destroy a small area of brain tissue.
   c. an electric shock is used to stimulate certain areas of the brain.
   d. a drug is injected into the brain to destroy a small area of brain tissue.

23. Virtual reality (VR) techniques have been useful in the treatment of which of the following disorders?
   a. phobias
   b. mania
   c. posttraumatic stress disorder
   d. both a and c

15 psychological therapies

15.1 15.2 15.3 p. 580

Psychological Therapies

- **modern treatments**
  - psychotherapy
  - biomedical therapy
- **early interventions**
  - historically, psychological or social causes identified for some disorders; for others, individuals with mental illness were believed to be possessed by demons or evil spirits
  - organized treatment began in England around the middle 1500s
  - Pinel started the "moral treatment" movement in France

- **Freud's psychoanalysis and related techniques**
  - Freud developed the technique of **psychoanalysis**, an insight therapy aimed at revealing unconscious conflicts, urges, and desires
  - **dream interpretation**
  - **free association**
  - **modern psychodynamic approach**

"Why do you think you cross the road?"

- **interpersonal therapy (IPT)**
  - eclectic therapy with some theoretical roots in the psychodynamic approach but combines aspects from humanistic and cognitive–behavioral therapies

- **humanistic therapy**
  - focuses on the conscious, subjective experience of emotion and people's sense of self; promotes insight and emphasizes the importance of individual choice and the potential to change one's behavior
  - **person-centered therapy**
    - developed by Carl Rogers; focuses on match between real self and ideal self; maladjustment is result of not matching; unconditional positive regard is important for congruence between real and ideal selves
    - therapist uses a nondirective approach and four basic elements to develop the person–therapist relationship

  - **Gestalt therapy**
    - developed by Fritz Perls; focuses on match between actual and ideal self; focuses on the gestalt, or "whole picture"
    - therapist uses a very directive approach to lead the client through a number of planned experiences (e.g., self-dialogue, "empty chair" technique), with the goal of increasing self-awareness
    - although aspects of the individual's past are examined, the focus is on denied past, not hidden past; everything is conscious but possibly not in the "here and now"

  - **motivational interviewing**
    - "client-centered with a twist"; has specific goals to reduce ambivalence about change and increase intrinsic motivation

evaluation: little scientific support for basic premises and requires client to be fairly intelligent and verbally expressive

15.4 15.5 p. 589

Action Therapies

- **behavior therapies**
  action-based therapies operating on the premise that all behaviors, both normal and abnormal, are learned; applied behavior analysis involves functional analysis and learning techniques to increase desirable behaviors and decrease undesirable behaviors
  - techniques based on classical conditioning—pairing of stimuli
  - techniques based on operant conditioning—reinforcement, extinction, shaping, and modeling
  - **evaluation:** more effective than others for specific behavioral problems (e.g., bed-wetting, overeating, drug addictions, phobic reactions)

15.6 15.7 p. 590

Action Therapies

cognitive therapies action-based therapies that focus on helping people change their ways of thinking; emphasis on identifying distorted and unrealistic beliefs that lead to maladaptive behavior and problem emotions and then replacing them with more-positive, helpful thoughts

- **Beck's cognitive therapy**
- **cognitive–behavioral therapy (CBT)**
- **rational–emotive behavior therapy (REBT)**
- **evaluation:** typically shorter and less expensive than insight therapies; treating the symptom, not the cause, is both a feature and a criticism; especially effective for many disorders, including depression, anxiety disorders, and personality disorders

Table 15.1
Characteristics of Psychotherapies

TYPE OF THERAPY	GOAL	KEY PEOPLE
Psychodynamic therapy	Insight	Freud
Person-centered therapy	Insight	Rogers
Gestalt therapy	Insight	Perls
Behavior therapy	Action	Watson, Jones, Skinner, Bandura
Cognitive therapy	Action	Beck
CBT	Action	Various professionals
REBT	Action	Ellis

Group Therapies

- alternative to individual therapy; group of clients meet together to discuss similar problems with a single therapist or pair of therapists
- may use a variety of styles, but person-centered, Gestalt, and behavioral seem to work best; may also take several different forms
- **self-help groups** may also be effective; do not have a therapist directly involved

- **evaluation:** advantages include lower cost, exposure to ways other people view and handle same type of problems, social and emotional support; disadvantages include greater exposure, less one-on-one contact with therapist, and some problems hard to treat in a group setting

15.8 15.9 15.10 p. 601

Does Psychotherapy Work?

- effectiveness is not easy to study due to different theories, techniques, time frames for success, etc.; tendency of some therapists to be eclectic (using variety of techniques) is also a challenge
  - where effective, greater success is often tied to the relationship between the therapist and client (therapeutic alliance), a sense of safety, and longer time in therapy
- cultural, ethnic, and gender concerns should also be examined; these factors can affect not only the therapeutic alliance but also identification of actual problem(s) and treatment options

Biomedical Therapies

psychopharmacology the use of drugs to control or relieve the symptoms of a psychological disorder; may be used alone or in combination with other therapies (see Table 15.2)

electroconvulsive therapy

- still used to treat severe depression and a few other disorders that have not responded to other forms of treatment
- involves the application of an electric shock and resulting seizure that appears to normalize the balance of neurotransmitters within the brain
- traditional side effects (extreme memory loss, broken bones) have been minimized by lower levels of current and the use of both muscle relaxers and anesthesia

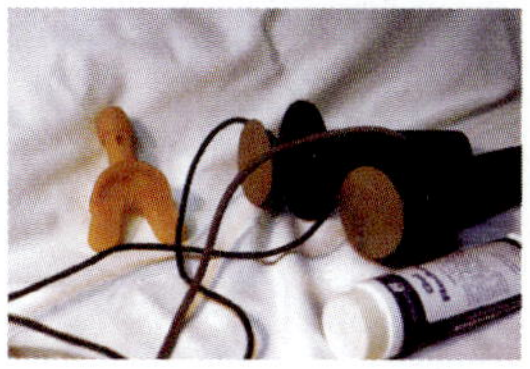

psychosurgery

- used as a last resort, involves cutting into the brain to remove or destroy brain tissues associated with symptoms of a mental disorder
- prefrontal lobotomies were widely used in the mid-1900s up until the development of antipsychotic drugs
- at present, bilateral anterior cingulotomy (involves selective areas of cingulate gyrus) is used, primarily for obsessive-compulsive disorder; has also been used with depression and bipolar disorder

emerging technologies

- repetitive transcranial magnetic stimulation (rTMS)
- transcranial direct current stimulation (tDCS)
  - being evaluated as treatment options for PTSD and depression, and other disorders
- deep brain stimulation for depression and OCD

appendix A
statistics in psychology

A.1 Why do psychologists use statistics?

Why study statistics?

Psychology is a science, and scientists must have ways of describing, summarizing, and analyzing the numerical data gathered through systematic observation and experimentation. Statistics allow researchers to do all of these things in a meaningful, logical fashion.

Many students in psychology wonder why the field uses seemingly such complicated mathematics. The answer is easy. Psychologists base their field on research findings. Data are collected and they have to be analyzed. *Statistics* is the field that gives us the tools to do that.

Psychologists have to be able to do two things with the data they collect. The first is to summarize the information from a study or experiment. This is the role of **descriptive statistics**. The second is to make judgments and decisions about the data. We are interested if groups differ from each other. We are also interested in how one group of variables is related to another. This second emphasis is known as **inferential statistics**.

Statistical analysis is a way of trying to account for the error that exists in almost any body of data. A **statistic** is typically a number that represents some measure of central tendency or variability. These are described later. Statistics are calculated from a **sample**. The same number calculated from a population is called a **parameter**. If you asked what the average height of teenage males was, and you calculated the average from just your high school, that average would be a statistic. If you tested every teenage male on earth, the average would be a parameter. As you can see parameters are very rarely calculated. Thus, **statistics** is the branch of mathematics that is concerned with the collection and interpretation of data from samples (Agresti & Finlay, 1997; Aron et al., 2005). Psychology is only one of many fields that use the following types of statistics.

Descriptive Statistics

Descriptive statistics are a way of organizing numbers and summarizing them so that they can be understood. There are two main types of descriptive statistics:

- **Measures of Central Tendency.** Measures of central tendency are used to summarize the data and give you one score that seems typical of your sample.
- **Measures of Variability.** Measures of variability are used to indicate how spread out the data are. Are they tightly packed or are they widely dispersed?

The actual descriptive statistics are best understood after we explain the concept of a frequency distribution.

A.1 Why do psychologists use statistics?

DESCRIPTIVE STATISTICS

A.2 What types of tables and graphs represent patterns in data?

A.3 What types of statistics examine central tendencies in data?

A.4 What types of statistics examine variations in data?

INFERENTIAL STATISTICS

A.5 How can statistics be used to determine if differences in sets of data are large enough to be due to something other than chance variation?

A.6 How are statistics used to predict one score from another?

A.7 Why are skills in statistics important to psychology majors?

descriptive statistics a way of organizing numbers and summarizing them so that patterns can be determined.

inferential statistics statistical analysis of two or more sets of numerical data to reduce the possibility of error in measurement and to determine if the differences between the data sets are greater than chance variation would predict.

statistic a measure of central tendency or variability computed from a sample.

sample group of subjects selected from a larger population of subjects, usually selected randomly.

parameter a number representing some measure of central tendency or variability within a population.

statistics branch of mathematics concerned with the collection and interpretation of numerical data.

frequency distribution a table or graph that shows how often different numbers or scores appear in a particular set of scores.

histogram a bar graph showing a frequency distribution.

polygon line graph showing a frequency distribution.

normal curve a special frequency polygon in which the scores are symmetrically distributed around the mean, and the mean, median, and mode are all located on the same point on the curve with scores decreasing as the curve extends from the mean.

bell curve alternate name for the normal curve, which is said to be shaped like a bell.

A.2 What types of tables and graphs represent patterns in data?

One way psychologists get started in a research project is to look at their data, but just looking at a list of numbers wouldn't do much good. So we make a graph or chart. Then we can look for patterns.

FREQUENCY DISTRIBUTIONS

A **frequency distribution** is a table or graph that shows how often different numbers, or scores, appear in a particular set of scores. For example, let's say that you have a sample of 30 people, the size of some psychology classes. You ask them how many glasses of water they drink each day. You could represent the answers as shown in Table A.1. Just by looking at this table, it is clear that typical people drink between 4 to 8 glasses of water a day.

Tables can be useful, especially when dealing with small sets of data. Sometimes a more visual presentation gives a better "picture" of the patterns in a data set, and that is when researchers use graphs to plot the data from a frequency distribution. One common graph is a **histogram**, or a bar graph. Figure A.1 shows how the same data from Table A.1 would look in a bar graph.

Another type of graph used in frequency distributions is the **polygon**, a line graph. Figure A.2 shows the same data in a polygon graph.

Table A.1

A Frequency Distribution

NUMBER OF GLASSES PER DAY	NUMBER OF PEOPLE OUT OF 30 (FREQUENCY)
1	0
2	1
3	2
4	4
5	5
6	6
7	5
8	4
9	2
10	1

THE NORMAL CURVE

Frequency polygons allow researchers to see the shape of a set of data easily. For example, the number of people drinking glasses of water in Figure A.2 is easily seen to be centered about 6 glasses (central tendency) but drops off below 4 glasses and above 8 glasses a day (variability). Our frequency polygon has a high point and the frequency decreases on both sides.

A common frequency distribution of this type is called the **normal curve**. It has a very specific shape and is sometimes called the **bell curve**. Look at Figure A.3. This curve is almost a perfect normal curve, and many things in life are not that perfect. The normal curve is used as a model for many things that are measured, such as intelligence,

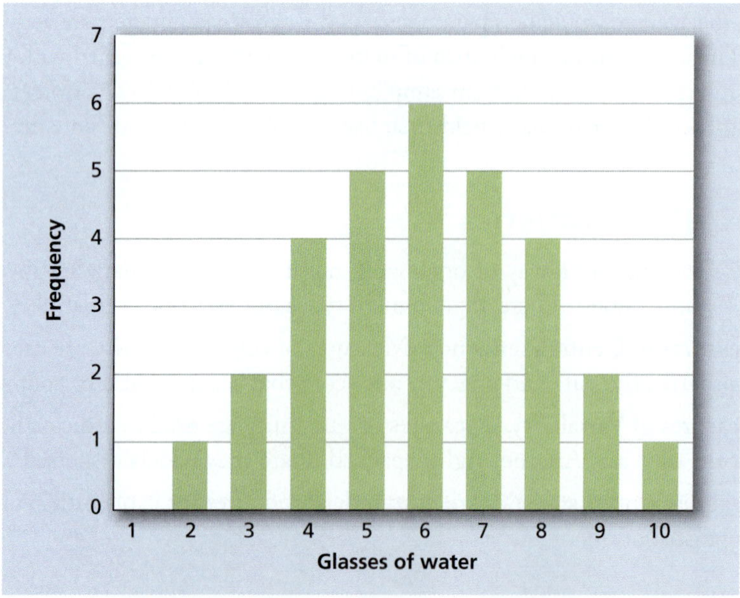

Figure A.1 A Histogram

Histograms, or bar graphs, provide a visual way to look at data from frequency distributions. In this graph, for example, the height of the bars indicates that most people drink between 4 to 8 glasses of water (represented by the five highest bars in the middle of the graph).

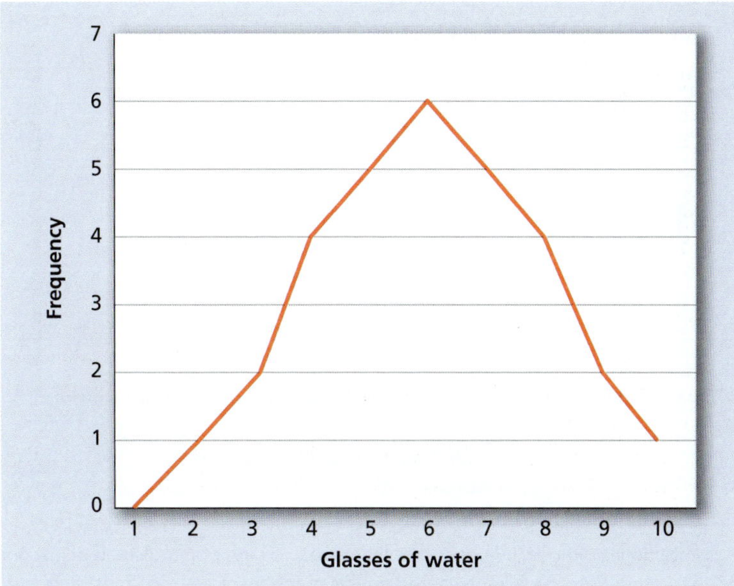

Figure A.2 A Polygon

A polygon is a line graph that can represent the data in a frequency distribution in much the same way as a bar graph but allows the shape of the data set to be easily viewed.

height, or weight, but even those measures only come close to a perfect distribution (provided large numbers of people are measured). One of the reasons that the normal curve is so useful is that it has very specific relationships to measures of central tendency and a measurement of variability, known as the standard deviation.

OTHER DISTRIBUTION TYPES Distributions aren't always normal in shape. Some distributions are described as *skewed*. This occurs when the distribution is not even on both sides of a central score with the highest frequency (like in our example). Instead, the scores are concentrated toward one side of the distribution. For example, what if a study of people's water-drinking habits in a different class revealed that most people drank around 7 to 8 glasses of water daily, with no one drinking more than 8? The frequency polygon shown in Figure A.4 reflects this very different distribution.

In this case, scores are piled up in the high end with most people drinking 7 or 8 glasses of water a day. The graphs in Figure A.5 show a **skewed distribution**. Skewed distributions are called positively or negatively skewed, depending on where the scores are concentrated. A concentration in the high end would be called **negatively skewed**. A

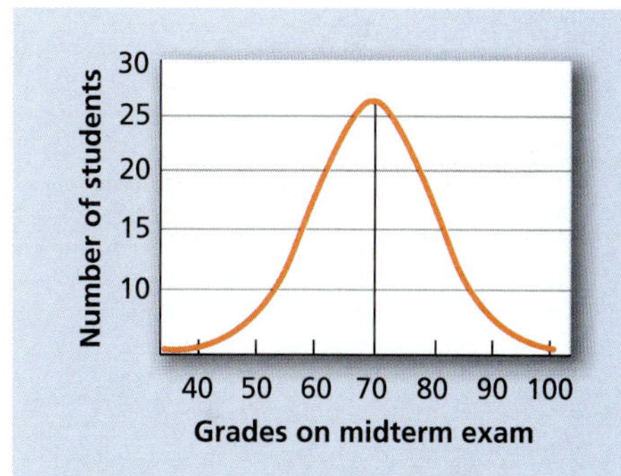

Figure A.3 The Normal Curve

The normal curve, also known as the bell curve because of its unique shape, is often the way in which certain characteristics such as intelligence or weight are represented in the population. The highest point on the curve typically represents the average score in any distribution.

skewed distribution frequency distribution in which most of the scores fall to one side or the other of the distribution.

negatively skewed a distribution of scores in which scores are concentrated in the high end of the distribution.

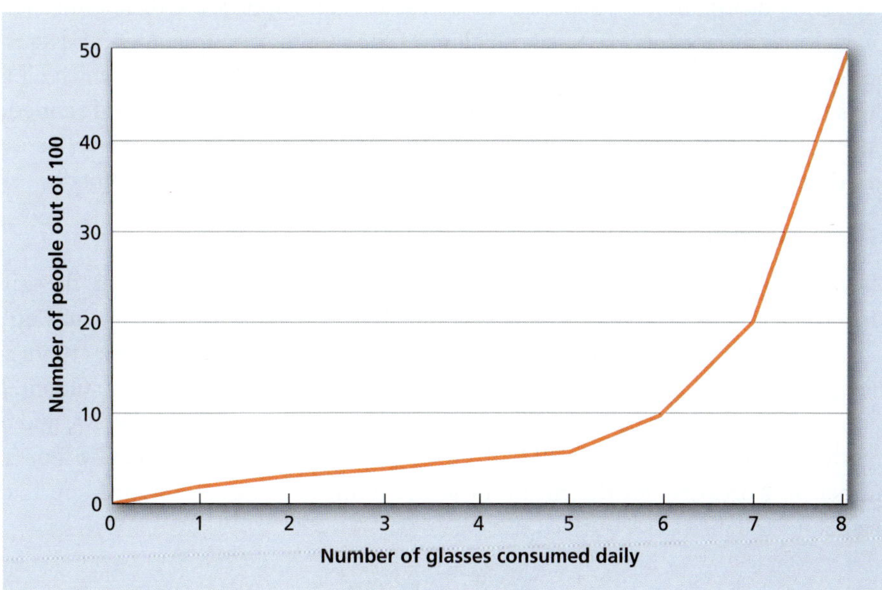

Figure A.4 A Frequency Polygon

Skewed distributions are those in which the most frequent scores occur at one end or the other of the distribution, as represented by this frequency polygon in which most people are seen to drink at least 7 to 8 glasses of water each day.

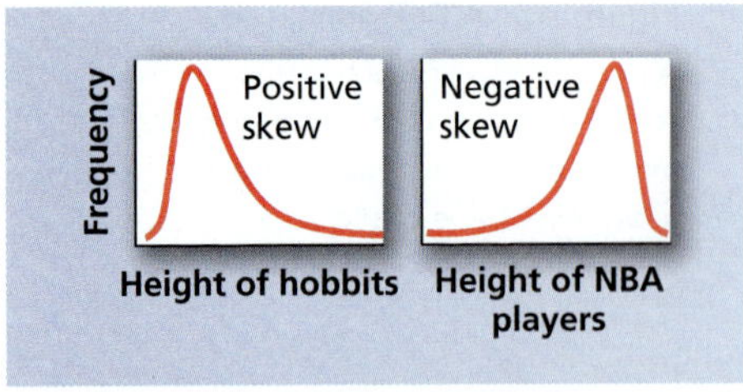

Figure A.5 Skewed Distribution

These frequency polygons show how distributions can be skewed in two different directions. The graph on the left represents the frequency of heights among hobbits (the little people from the fantasy *The Lord of the Rings*) and is positively skewed because the long "tail" goes to the right, or positive direction. The graph on the right shows the frequency of heights among NBA basketball players and is negatively skewed—the tail points to the left.

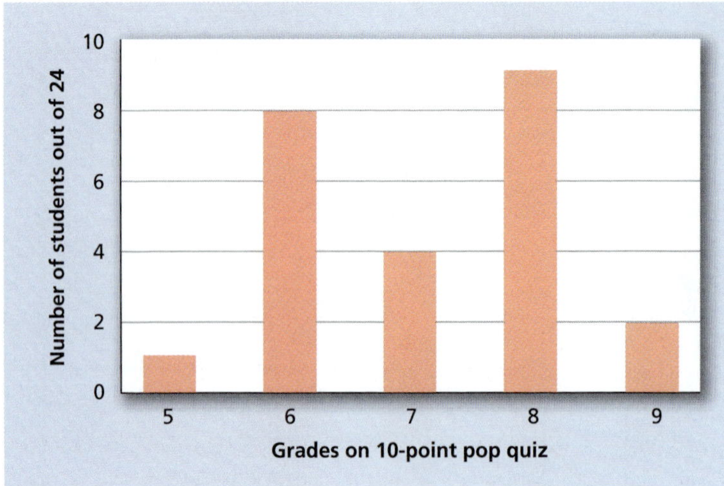

Figure A.6 A Bimodal Distribution

When a distribution is bimodal, it means that there are two high points instead of just one. For example, in the pop-quiz scores represented on this graph there are two "most frequent" scores—6 and 8. This most likely represents two groups of students, with one group being less successful than the other.

concentration in the low end would be called **positively skewed**. The direction of the extended tail determines whether it is positively (tail to right) or negatively (tail to left) skewed. Here's an example. What do you think about the distribution of heights of hobbits (the little guys from *The Lord of the Rings*) and NBA basketball players (who are usually tall)? Might not these frequency distributions of height in Figure A.5 be appropriate?

Some frequency polygons show two high points rather than just one (see Figure A.6) and are called **bimodal distributions**. In this example, we have a distribution of scores from a 10-point pop quiz and we see that one group of students seemed to do well and one group didn't. Bimodal distributions usually indicate that you have two separate groups being graphed in one polygon. What would the distribution of height for men and women look like?

MEASURES OF CENTRAL TENDENCY

A frequency distribution is a good way to look at a set of numbers, but there's still a lot to look at—isn't there some way to sum it all up? One way to sum up numerical data is to find out what a "typical" score might be, or some central number around which all the others seem to fall. This kind of summation is called a **measure of central tendency**, or the number that best represents the central part of a frequency distribution. There are three different measures of central tendency: the mean, the median, and the mode.

A.3 What types of statistics examine central tendencies in data?

MEAN The most commonly used measure of central tendency is the **mean**, the arithmetic average of a distribution of numbers. That simply indicates that you add up all the numbers in a particular set and then divide them by how many numbers there are. This is usually the way teachers get the grade point average for a particular student, for example. If Rochelle's grades on the tests she has taken so far are 86, 92, 87, and 90, then the teacher would add $86 + 92 + 87 + 90 = 335$, and then divide 355 by four (the number of scores) to get the mean, or grade point average, of 88.75. Here is the formula for the mean:

$$\text{Mean} = \Sigma X/N$$

positively skewed a distribution of scores in which scores are concentrated in the low end of the distribution.

bimodal distributions frequency distribution in which there are two high points rather than one.

measure of central tendency numbers that best represent the most typical score of a frequency distribution.

mean the arithmetic average of a distribution of numbers.

What does this mean?

- Σ is a symbol called sigma. It is a Greek letter and it is also called the summation sign.
- X represents a score. Rochelle's grades are represented by X.
- ΣX means add up or sum all the X scores or $\Sigma X = 86 + 92 + 87 + 90 = 355$.
- N means the number of scores. In this case, there are four grades.

We then divide the sum of the scores (ΣX) by N to get the mean or

$$\text{Mean} = \Sigma X/\text{N} = \frac{355}{4} = 88.75$$

The mean is a good way to find a central tendency if the set of scores clusters around the mean with no extremely different scores that are either far higher or far lower than the mean.

MEDIAN

I remember that sometimes my teacher would "curve" the grades for a test, and it was always bad when just one person did really well and everyone else did lousy—is that what you mean about extremely different scores?

I remember that sometimes my teacher would "curve" the grades for a test, and it was always bad when just one person did really well and everyone else did lousy—is that what you mean about extremely different scores?

Yes, the mean doesn't work as well when there are extreme scores, as you would have if only two students out of an entire class had a perfect score of 100 and everyone else scored in the 70s or lower. If you want a truer measure of central tendency in such a case, you need one that isn't affected by extreme scores. The **median** is just such a measure. A median is the score that falls in the middle of an *ordered* distribution of scores. Half of the scores will fall above the median, and half of the scores will fall below it. If the distribution contains an odd number of scores, it's just the middle number, but if the number of scores is even, it's the average of the two middle scores. The median is also the 50th percentile. Look at Table A.2 for an example of the median.

The mean IQ of this group would be 114.6, but the median would be 101 (the average between Evan with 102 and Fethia with 100, the average of the two middle numbers). This may not look like much of a difference, but it's really a change of about 13.6 IQ points—a big difference. Also, think about measures of income in a particular area. If most people earn around $35,000 per year in a particular area, but there are just a few extremely wealthy people in the same area who earn $1,000,000 a year, a mean of all the annual incomes would no doubt make the area look like it was doing much better than it really is economically. The median would be a more accurate measure of the central tendency of such data.

MODE The **mode** is another measure of central tendency in which the most frequent score is taken as the central measure. In the numbers given in the below example, the mode would be 100 because that number appears more times in the distribution than any other. Three people have that score. This is the simplest measure of central ten-

median the middle score in an ordered distribution of scores, or the mean of the two middle numbers; the 50th percentile.

mode the most frequent score in a distribution of scores.

Table A.2

Intelligence Test Scores For 10 People

NAME	ALLISON	BEN	CAROL	DENISE	EVAN	FETHIA	GEORGE	HAL	INGA	JAY
IQ	160	150	139	102	102	100	100	100	98	95

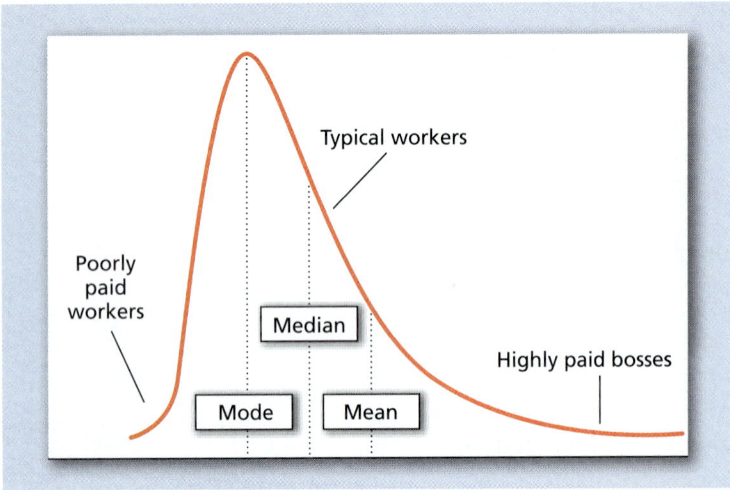

Figure A.7 Positively Skewed Distribution

In a skewed distribution, the high scores on one end will cause the mean to be pulled toward the tail of the distribution, making it a poor measure of central tendency for this kind of distribution. For example, in this graph many workers make very little money (represented by the mode) while only a few workers make a lot of money (the tail). The mean in this case would be much higher than the mode because of those few high scores distorting the average. In this case, the median is a much better measure of central tendency because it tends to be unaffected by extremely high or extremely low scores such as those in this distribution.

dency and is also more useful than the mean in some cases, especially when there are two sets of frequently appearing scores. For example, suppose a teacher notices that on the last exam the scores fall into two groups, with about 15 students making a 95 and another 14 students making a 67. The mean *and* the median would probably give a number somewhere between those two scores—such as 80. That number tells the teacher a lot less about the distribution of scores than the mode would because, in this case, the distribution is **bimodal**—there are two very different yet very frequent scores (See Figure A.6 for another example.)

MEASURES OF CENTRAL TENDENCY AND THE SHAPE OF THE DISTRIBUTION When the distribution is normal or close to it, the mean, median, and mode are the same or very similar. There is no problem. When the distribution is not normal, then the situation requires a little more explanation.

SKEWED DISTRIBUTIONS If the distribution is skewed, then the mean is pulled in the direction of the tail of the distribution. The mode is still the highest point and the median is between the two. Let's look at an example. In Figure A.7 we have a distribution of salaries at a company. A few people make a low wage, most make a midlevel wage, and the bosses make a lot of money. This gives us a positively skewed distribution with the measures of central tendency placed as in the figure. As mentioned earlier, with such a distribution, the median would be the best measure of central tendency to report. If the distribution were negatively skewed (tail to the left), the order of the measures of central tendency would be reversed.

BIMODAL DISTRIBUTIONS If you have a bimodal distribution, then none of the measures of central tendency will do you much good. You need to discover why you have seemingly two groups in your one distribution.

MEASURES OF VARIABILITY

A.4 What types of statistics examine variations in data?

Descriptive statistics can also determine how much the scores in a distribution differ, or vary, from the central tendency of the data. These **measures of variability** are used to discover how "spread out" the scores are from each other. The more the scores cluster around the central scores, the smaller the measure of variability will be, and the more widely the scores differ from the central scores, the larger this measurement will be.

There are two ways that variability is measured. The simpler method is by calculating the **range** of the set of scores, or the difference between the highest score and the lowest score in the set of scores. The range is somewhat limited as a measure of variability when there are extreme scores in the distribution. For example, if you look at Table A.2, the range of those IQ scores would be 160–95, or 65. But if you just look at the numbers, you can see that there really isn't that much variation except for the three highest scores of 139, 150, and 160.

The other measure of variability that is commonly used is the one that is related to the normal curve, the **standard deviation**. This measurement is simply the square root of the average squared difference, or deviation, of the scores from the mean of the distribution. The mathematical formula for finding the standard deviation looks

bimodal condition in which a distribution has two modes.

measures of variability measurement of the degree of differences within a distribution or how the scores are spread out.

range the difference between the highest and lowest scores in a distribution.

standard deviation the square root of the average squared deviations from the mean of scores in a distribution; a measure of variability.

complicated, but it is really nothing more than taking each individual score, subtracting the mean from it, squaring that number (because some numbers will be negative and squaring them gets rid of the negative value), and adding up all of those squares. Then this total is divided by the number of scores and the square root of that number is the standard deviation. In the IQ example, it would go like this:

$$\text{Standard Deviation Formula} \quad SD = \sqrt{[\Sigma(X - M)^2/N]}$$

The mean (M) of the 10 IQ scores is 114.6. To calculate the standard deviation we

1. Subtract each score from the mean to get a deviation score $\rightarrow (X - M)$
2. We square each deviation score $\rightarrow (X - M)^2$
3. We add them up. Remember that's what the sigma (Σ) indicates $\rightarrow \Sigma(X - M)^2$
4. We divide the sum of the squared deviation by N (the number of scores) $\rightarrow \Sigma(X - M)^2/N$
5. We take the square root $(\sqrt{\ })$ of the sum for our final step. $\sqrt{[\Sigma(X - M)^2/N]}$

The process is laid out in Table A.3.

The standard deviation is equal to 23.5. What that tells you is that this particular group of data deviates, or varies, from the central tendencies quite a bit—there are some very different scores in the data set, or in this particular instance, three noticeably different scores.

Table A.3

Finding the Standard Deviation

SCORE	DEVIATION FROM THE MEAN ($X \pm M$)	SQUARED DEVIATION
160.00	45.40	2,061.16
	(ex. 160 − 114.60 = 45.40)	(45.40^2 = 2,061.16)
150.00	35.4	1,253.16
139.00	24.4	595.36
102.00	−12.60	158.76
102.00	−12.60	158.76
100.00	−14.60	213.16
100.00	−14.60	213.16
100.00	−14.60	213.16
98.00	−16.60	275.56
95.00	−19.60	384.16
Sum of Scores (ΣX) = 1,146.00 Mean = (ΣX)/N = 1,146/10 = 114.60	($\Sigma X - M$) = 0.00	($\Sigma X - M)^2$ = 5,526.40 Standard Deviation = $\sqrt{[\Sigma(X - M)^2/N]}$ = $\sqrt{5{,}526.40/10}$ = 23.5

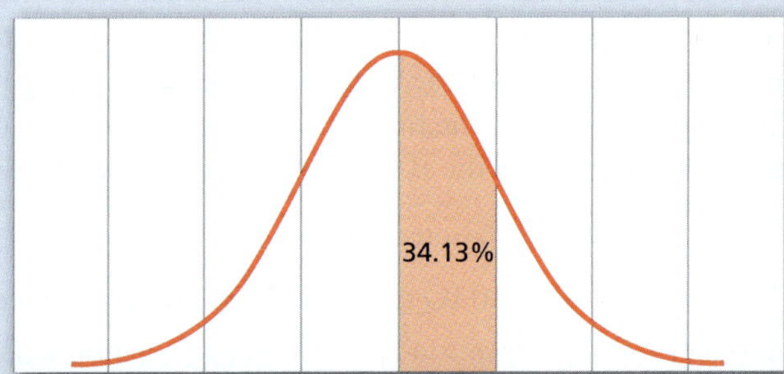

Standard Deviations	-4	-3	-2	-1	0	1	2	3	4
Wechsler IQ	40	55	70	85	100	115	130	145	160
Stanford-Binet IQ	36	52	68	84	100	116	132	148	164
Cumulative %	0.003	0.135	2.275	15.856	50.00	84.134	97.725	99.865	99.997

Figure A.8 IQ Normal Curve
Scores on intelligence tests are typically represented by the normal curve. The dotted vertical lines each represent one standard deviation from the mean, which is always set at 100. For example, an IQ of 116 on the Stanford-Binet Fourth Edition (Stanford-Binet 4) represents one standard deviation above the mean, and the area under the curve indicates that 34.13 percent of the population falls between 100 and 116 on that test. The Stanford-Binet Fifth Edition was published in 2003 and it now has a mean of 100 and a standard deviation of 15 for composite scores.

This procedure may look very complicated. Let us assure you that computers and inexpensive calculators can figure out the standard deviation simply by entering the numbers and pressing a button. No one does a standard deviation by hand anymore.

How does the standard deviation relate to the normal curve? Let's look at the classic distribution of IQ scores. It has a mean of 100 and a standard deviation of 15 as set up by the test designers. It is a bell curve. With a true normal curve, researchers know exactly what percent of the population lies under the curve between each standard deviation from the mean. For example, notice that in the percentages in Figure A.8, one standard deviation above the mean has 34.13 percent of the population represented by the graph under that section. These are the scores between the IQs of 100 and 115. One standard deviation below the mean (–1) has exactly the same percent, 34.13, under that section—the scores between 85 to 100. This means that 68.26 percent of the population falls within one standard deviation from the mean, or one average "spread" from the center of the distribution. For example, "giftedness" is normally defined as having an IQ score that is two standard deviations *above* the mean. On the Wechsler Intelligence Scales, this means having an IQ of 130 or greater because the Wechsler's standard deviation is 15. But if the test a person took to determine giftedness was the Stanford-Binet Fourth Edition (the previous version of the test), the IQ score must have been 132 or greater because the standard deviation of that test was 16, not 15. The current version, the Stanford-Binet Fifth Edition, was published in 2003 and it now has a mean of 100 and a standard deviation of 15 for composite scores.

Although the "tails" of this normal curve seem to touch the bottom of the graph, in theory they go on indefinitely, never touching the base of the graph. In reality, though, any statistical measurement that forms a normal curve will have 99.72 percent of the population it measures falling within three standard deviations either above or below the mean. Because this relationship between the standard deviation and the normal curve does not change, it is always possible to compare different test scores or sets of data that come close to a normal curve distribution. This is done by computing a ***z* score,** which indicates how many standard deviations you are away from the mean. It is calculated by subtracting the mean from your score and dividing by the standard deviation. For example, if you had an IQ of 115, your z score would be 1.0. If you had an IQ of 70, your z score would –2.0. So on any exam, if you had a positive z score you did relatively well. A negative z score means you didn't do as well. The formula for a z score is:

$$Z = (X - M)/SD$$

***z* score** a statistical measure that indicates how far away from the mean a particular score is in terms of the number of standard deviations that exist between the mean and that score.

Inferential Statistics

A.5 How can statistics be used to determine if differences in sets of data are large enough to be due to something other than chance variation?

Descriptive methods of statistics are not useful when it comes to comparing sets of numbers or scores to see if there are differences between them that are great enough to be caused by something other than chance variation. Inferential statistics consist of statistical techniques that allow researchers to determine the difference between results of a study that are meaningful and those that are merely due to chance variations. Inferential statistics also allow researchers to draw conclusions, or make *inferences*, about the results of research and about whether those results are only true for the specific group of animals or people involved in the study or whether the results can be applied to, or *generalized* to, the larger population from which the study participants were selected.

For example, in the Cheryan (Cheryan et al., 2009) study described in Chapter One, there were a lot of variables that simply could not be controlled completely, even with random assignment of participants to the two conditions. LINK to Chapter One: The Science of Psychology, pp. 5–6. For example, there was no guarantee that random assignment would account for the interfering effects of female participants who might have really liked the science fiction toys, posters, and pizza they saw in one of the test conditions. Maybe any difference found between the males and females was due to pure luck or chance and not to the variables under study.

In any analysis that compares two or more sets of data, there's always the possibility of error in the data that comes from either within the group (all participants in one group, for example, will not be exactly like each other) or differences between groups (the experimental group and the control group are formed with different people, so there are differences between the two groups that have nothing to do with the manipulations of the experimenter). When researchers want to know if the differences they find in the data that come from studies like the Cheryan experiment are large enough to be caused by the experimental manipulation and *not* just by the chance differences that exist within and between groups, they have to use a kind of statistical technique that can take those chance variations into account. These kinds of statistical analysis use inferential statistics.

Inferential statistical analysis also allows researchers to determine how much confidence they should have in the results of a particular experiment. As you might remember, results from other kinds of studies that look for relationships—observations, surveys, and case studies—are often analyzed with descriptive statistics, especially correlations. But experiments look for *causes* of relationships, and researchers want to have some evidence that the results of their experiments really mean what they think they mean.

There are many different kinds of inferential statistical methods. The method that is used depends on the design of the experiment, such as the number of independent and dependent variables or the number of experimental groups. All inferential statistics have one thing in common—they look for differences in group measurements that are **statistically significant**. Statistical significance is a way to test differences to see how likely those differences are to be real and not just caused by the random variations in behavior that exist in everything animals and people do.

For example, in a classic study investigating the effects of intrinsic versus extrinsic motivation on children's creativity, Dr. Teresa Amabile's 1982 study showed that the collages of the children who were promised prizes (an extrinsic reward) were judged to be less creative than those of the children who created collages just for fun.

statistically significant referring to differences in data sets that are larger than chance variation would predict.

t-test type of inferential statistical analysis typically used when two means are compared to see if they are significantly different.

significant difference a difference between groups of numerical data that is considered large enough to be due to factors other than chance variation.

correlation coefficient a number that represents the strength and direction of a relationship existing between two variables.

But was that difference between the creativity scores of the two groups a real difference, or was it merely due to chance variations in the children's artistic creations? Dr. Amabile used an inferential test on her results that told her that the difference was too big to be just chance variations, which means her results were *significant*—they were most likely to be real differences. How likely? Tests of significance give researchers the probability that the results of their experiment were caused by chance and not by their experimental manipulation. For example, in one test called a ***t*-test**, the scores of the children's artwork would have been placed into a formula that would result in a single number (t) that evaluates the probability that the difference between the two group means is due to pure chance or luck. That number would be compared to a value that exists in a table of possible t values, which tells researchers the probability of the result is due to chance or luck. If the number obtained by the calculation is bigger than the value in the table, there will be a probability associated with that number in the table. The probability, symbolized by the letter p, will tell researchers the probability of the difference was due to chance. In Dr. Amabile's case, the probability was $p < .05$ which means the probability that the results were due to chance alone was less than 5 out of 100. Another way of stating the same result is that Dr. Amabile could be 95 percent certain that her results were real and not due to chance. Dr. Amabile would, thus, report that the study found a **significant difference**, which means a difference thought not to be due to chance.

There are several statistic techniques to test if groups are different from each other. Here are some common ones you might encounter if you read journal articles.

- *t*-test—determines if two means are different from each other
- *F*-test or analysis of variance—determines if three or more means are different from each other. Can also evaluate more than one independent variable at a time.
- chi-square—compares frequencies of proportions between groups to see if they are different. For example, the proportion of women hired at a company is too low and might indicate discrimination. *Chi* is pronounced like the beginning of the word *kite*. Don't say "chee." It will be ugly.

If you do take a statistics course, you will find out that most analyses are done by computers and you don't have to manually go through the long formulas.

A.6 How are statistics used to predict one score from another?

We've already talked about the correlation coefficient. Let's see how psychologists can predict one variable from another by using it. LINK to Chapter One: The Science of Psychology, pp. 26–28.

THE CORRELATION COEFFICIENT

A *correlation* is a measure of the relationship between two or more variables. For example, if you wanted to know if scores on the SAT are related to grade point average, you could get SAT scores and GPAs from a group of people and enter those numbers into a mathematical formula, which will produce a number called the **correlation coefficient**. The correlation coefficient represents the direction of the relationship and its strength. Chapter One (pages 26–27) discusses correlation in more detail and also emphasizes that correlation does not allow the assumption that one variable causes the other.

Is the formula for the correlation coefficient really complicated?

Is the formula for the correlation coefficient really complicated?

Actually, the definitional formula for finding a correlation coefficient is not very complicated. Here it is:

$$r = \frac{\Sigma Z_x Z_y}{n}$$

The r is the *correlation coefficient*, the number representing the strength and direction of the relationship between the two variables. Z_x and Z_y are the z scores for each score. If you remember, the z score tells you how many standard deviations a score is away from the mean. You would calculate the Z_x and Z_y for each subject, multiply, and add them up. Then divide by the number of subjects. There is a very complicated-looking formula based on the raw scores.

$$r = \frac{\Sigma XY - \dfrac{\Sigma X \Sigma Y}{N}}{\sqrt{\left(\Sigma X^2 - \dfrac{(\Sigma X)^2}{N}\right)\left(\Sigma Y^2 - \dfrac{(\Sigma Y)^2}{N}\right)}}$$

Don't worry. You can do all this work on inexpensive calculators or on computers using common statistical programs or spreadsheets. Let's take the following example of two sets of scores, one on a test of drawing ability with scores from 1 (poor) to 5 (excellent) and the other on a test of writing ability using the same scale.

	Drawing (*X*)	**Writing (*Y*)**
Student 1	3	5
Student 2	1	2
Student 3	2	3
Student 4	4	4
Student 5	1	3
Student 6	4	6
Student 7	2	3
Student 8	3	4
Student 9	5	5
Student 10	1	2

If we plugged our data set into our calculator or spreadsheet, we would find that r (the correlation coefficient) equals 0.86. That would indicate a fairly strong correlation. If you continue studies in statistics, you will find out how to see if the correlation coefficient we calculated is statistically significant or, if you recall, not due to just dumb luck when we picked our subjects. In our case, the r is very significant and would happen by chance only 1 in 100 times!

Remember that the correlation coefficient has values that range between +1.0 and −1.0. The closer the r is to these values, the stronger the relationship. A positive r means a positive relationship, whereas a negative r means a negative relationship.

Our example had us trying to see if two scores were related. It is also possible to see if three or more scores are related with various techniques. The most common one is called multiple regression.

A.7 Why are skills in statistics important to psychology majors?

We have taken a look at describing data—seeing if groups differ from each other and seeing if two variables are related to each other. Those are the basic ideas of psychological statistics. The more advanced techniques are just bigger and better versions of these ideas. Many psych students sometimes panic at the thought of taking statistics. However, it is crucial to the field and not really that hard if you put your mind to it and don't freeze yourself up. Here's a practical hint. Students with good research and statistical skills are much more employable and make more money than those who don't try to master research skills. It's nice to care about people but you need all the skills you can get in today's world. Statistics and research design is one really profitable set of skills.

chapter summary

Listen on **mypsychlab.com** Listen to an audio file of your chapter **www.mypsychlab.com**

A.1 Why do psychologists use statistics?

- Statistics is a branch of mathematics that involves the collection, description, and interpretation of numerical data.

Descriptive Statistics

- Descriptive statistics are ways of organizing numbers and summarizing them so that they can be understood.
- Inferential statistics are ways of determining if groups are different and if two or more variables are related.

A.2 What types of tables and graphs represent patterns in data?

- Frequency distributions are tables or graphs that show the patterns in a set of scores and can be a table, a bar graph or histogram, or a line graph or polygon.

A.3 What types of statistics examine central tendencies in data?

- Measures of central tendency are ways of finding numbers that best represent the center of a distribution of numbers and include the mean, median, and mode.
- The normal curve is a special frequency polygon that is symmetrical and has the mean, median, and mode as the highest point on the curve.

A.4 What types of statistics examine variations in data?

- Measures of variability provide information about the differences within a set of numbers and include the range and the standard deviation.

Inferential Statistics

A.5 How can statistics be used to determine if differences in sets of data are large enough to be due to something other than chance variation?

- Inferential statistics involves statistical analysis of two or more sets of numerical data to reduce the possibility of error in measurement and determine statistical significance of the results of research.

A.6 How are statistics used to predict one score from another?

- The correlation coefficient is a number that represents the strength and direction of a relationship existing between two variables.

A.7 Why are skills in statistics important to psychology majors?

- Students who understand the process of research and the statistical methods used in research are more desirable to many university and business institutions than those who lack such skills.

test YOURSELF

ANSWERS ON PAGE AK-2.

Study and Review on **mypsychlab.com** Ready for your test? More quizzes and a customized study plan **www.mypsychlab.com**

Pick the best answer.

1. The correlation coefficient provides all of the following types of information EXCEPT ________.
   a. whether or not there is a relationship between the variables.
   b. the strength of the relationship between the variables.
   c. the cause of the relationship between the variables.
   d. the direction of the relationship between the variables.
2. Another name for a bar graph is a ________.
   a. polygon.
   b. histogram.
   c. normal curve.
   d. line graph.
3. A table that shows how often different scores appear in a set of scores is called a frequency ________.
   a. polygon.
   b. histogram.
   c. normal curve.
   d. distribution.
4. In the set of numbers 2, 2, 2, 3, 5, 5, 6, 8, 15, the median would be ________.
   a. 5.75.
   b. 5.33.
   c. 5.
   d. 2.
5. In the same set of numbers in Question 4, the mode would be ________.
   a. 5.75.
   b. 5.33.
   c. 5.
   d. 2.
6. In a skewed distribution, the scores ________.
   a. have two high points instead of one.
   b. fall to one side of the distribution.
   c. are evenly distributed around the mean.
   d. fall on both sides of the mean.

7. The normal curve is a special kind of ________.
   a. frequency distribution.
   b. scattergram.
   c. measure of central tendency.
   d. pie chart.
8. The normal curve has a special relationship with the ________.
   a. range.
   b. median.
   c. standard deviation.
   d. mode.
9. In the normal curve, ________.
   a. the mean, median, and mode are all on the highest point of the curve.
   b. the mean is on the highest point while the median and mode are on either side of the mean.
   c. the median is on the highest point while the mean and mode are on either side of the median.
   d. the standard deviation is located at the highest point of the curve.
10. What approximate percent of the population is said to fall between one standard deviation above and one standard deviation below the mean on a normal curve?
    a. 50 percent
    b. 34 percent
    c. 100 percent
    d. 68 percent
11. Errors in data ________.
    a. come only from within a group.
    b. come only from between different groups.
    c. come from both between and within groups.
    d. can be completely eliminated by random assignment.
12. When the goal is to compare sets of numbers or scores to see if the differences between them are greater than chance variations, researchers use ________.
    a. descriptive statistics.
    b. inferential statistics.
    c. analytical statistics.
    d. their intuition.
13. Inferential statistics are used when researchers want to know about ________.
    a. the range of the highest to lowest scores.
    b. causes of differences in data.
    c. central tendencies in data.
    d. variability in data.
14. Dr. Asimov finds that the results of his *t*-test are significant at $p < .01$. That means that he can be ________.
    a. totally certain that the results are not due to chance.
    b. totally certain that the results are due to chance.
    c. 1 percent certain that the results are not due to chance.
    d. 1 percent certain that the results are due to chance.

appendix B
applied psychology and psychology careers

Why study applied psychology?

Many different kinds of psychologists study or work in many different fields. Whereas early psychologists were still discovering the processes that govern the human mind, today's psychologists are more often applying information and principles gained from research to people in the real world. Why study careers in psychology? With so many different areas of focus, a career in psychology can be varied and exciting. There is much more to psychology than helping people who have mental health problems.

Professor John Gambon of Ozarks Technical Community College in Springfield, Missouri, is an industrial/organizational psychologist who has been studying violence in the workplace and gathering data for presentation to his classes. Recently, Gambon has found himself moving into another area of applied psychology: forensic psychology. He has had the opportunity to be an expert witness for the defense in two different trials, testifying about the accuracy and problems with eyewitness testimony as outlined by psychologist Elizabeth Loftus. LINK to Chapter Six: Memory, pp. 232–233. In one trial, the defendant was accused of an armed robbery that had taken place at night. In the other trial, the defendant was accused of a double homicide. The kinds of things Gambon spoke about on the witness stand included the length of time between the incidents and the questioning of the eyewitnesses, the concept of "weapons focus" and its tendency to wipe out memories of the face of the perpetrator, the lighting at the scene of the crime, and so on. He also showed an instructional video he had made in which people rush into Gambon's classroom and hit him with water balloons, yelling, "That was for last fried eggs!" Later, when answering a survey about the incident, the students witnessing this incident in the video all reported in writing that the statement yelled at the end was "That was for last Friday!" Clearly, this is one example of the flaws inherent in eyewitness testimony. Forensic psychology is just one of many areas in which psychological principles can be applied to issues and concerns of everyday life. This appendix will look at several areas of applied psychology, as well as the types of careers that are open to someone who studies psychology today. We will also return to the issue of workplace violence later in this appendix.

WHAT IS APPLIED PSYCHOLOGY?

B.1 What is the definition of applied psychology?

PSYCHOLOGY AS A CAREER

B.2 What are the different types of psychological professionals?

B.3 What kinds of careers are available to someone with a master's degree in psychology?

B.4 What kinds of careers are available to someone with a bachelor's degree in psychology?

B.5 What are the areas of specialization in psychology?

PSYCHOLOGY BEYOND THE CLASSROOM

B.6 How does psychology interact with other career fields?

PSYCHOLOGY AND WORK

B.7 What are industrial/organizational psychology and human factors psychology?

APPLYING PSYCHOLOGY TO EVERYDAY LIFE: Techniques Used by Sports Psychologists

B.8 What are some techniques used in sports psychology?

What Is Applied Psychology?

B.1 What is the definition of applied psychology?

The term **applied psychology** refers to using findings from psychological research to solve real-world problems. The psychological professional, who might be a psychiatrist, psychologist, or even a psychiatric social worker (as described later in this appendix), may do testing or use some other type of assessment and then describe a plan of action intended to solve whatever problem is of concern. As is evident in the opening comments about John Gambon, you can see that his training in psychology and his specialized knowledge enabled him to testify in court as an expert witness. This is a practical application of psychological tools to a real problem—the professional literally "applies" psychology.

It seems to me that psychology could be useful in a lot of different areas, not just education. In fact, wasn't that what all those "Applying Psychology" sections at the end of each chapter were about?

It seems to me that psychology could be useful in a lot of different areas, not just education. In fact, wasn't that what all those "Applying Psychology" sections at the end of each chapter were about?

Every chapter in this text (and even this appendix) does end with some application of psychology to the real world. The field of applied psychology isn't just one field but rather a lot of different areas that all share the common goal of using psychology in a practical way. A large number of areas can be considered applied psychology, including one of the broadest areas of psychology: clinical and counseling psychology. For example, health psychologists examine the effects of stress on physical as well as mental health; educational and school psychologists look for ways to improve student learning and apply the findings to the classroom; sports psychologists help athletes prepare themselves mentally for competition; human-factors psychologists deal with the way people and machines interact; forensic psychologists deal with psychological issues within the legal system; and industrial/organizational (I/O) psychologists deal with the work environment. In addition, environmental psychologists examine the interaction of people with their surroundings at work, in social settings, and in schools, homes, and other buildings. Those surroundings include not just the physical structures but also the particular population of people who live, work, and play in those surroundings. Other psychologists look at the factors that influence people to buy certain products, analyze the best ways to market a product, and examine the buying habits of the typical consumer.

This appendix includes information on the different roles of psychological professionals and the type of education required for many professions, along with a brief overview of many of the specialized areas in psychology. The remainder of this appendix briefly explores how psychology can be used in practical ways in several different areas of life: the environment, law, education, the military, sports, and the world of work.

Psychology as a Career

When most people think of psychology as a potential career, they assume certain things about the profession: For example, to help people with their problems one has to be a psychologist, all psychologists are doctors, and all psychologists counsel mentally ill people. None of these assumptions is completely true.

applied psychology the use of psychological concepts in solving real-world problems.

TYPES OF PSYCHOLOGICAL PROFESSIONALS

B.2 What are the different types of psychological professionals?

There are several types of professionals who work in psychology. These professionals have different training with different focuses and may have different goals.

PSYCHIATRISTS A **psychiatrist** has a medical doctorate (M.D.) degree and is a medical doctor who has specialized in the diagnosis and treatment of psychological disorders. Like any other medical doctor who may specialize in emergency medicine, treating the diseases of the elderly, treating infants and children, or any other special area of medicine, psychiatrists are able to write prescriptions and perform medical procedures on their patients. They simply have special training in the diagnosis and treatment of disorders that are considered to be mental disorders, such as schizophrenia, depression, or extreme anxiety. Because they are medical doctors, they tend to have a biopsychological perspective on the causes and treatments for such disorders.

PSYCHIATRIC SOCIAL WORKERS A **psychiatric social worker** is trained in the area of social work and usually possesses a master of social work (M.S.W.) degree and may be licensed in the state they work as a licensed clinical social worker (L.C.S.W.). These professionals focus more on the social conditions that can have an impact on mental disorders, such as poverty, overcrowding, stress, and drug abuse. They may administer psychotherapy (talking with clients about their problems) and often work in a clinical setting where other types of psychological professionals are available.

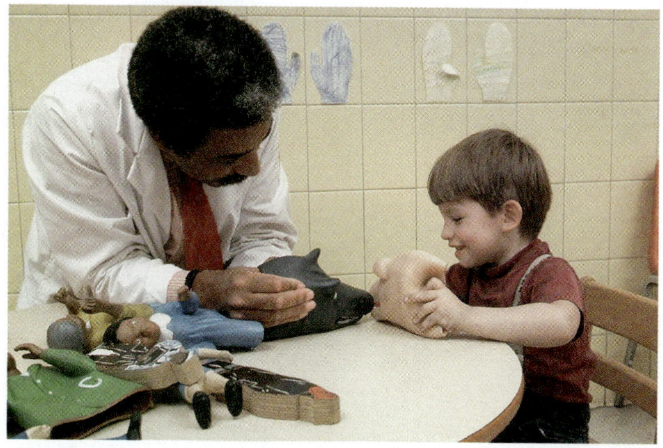

Psychologists specialize in many different areas and work in many different settings. This child psychologist is evaluating the young boy by using puppets and dolls to encourage the boy to talk about his feelings.

PSYCHOLOGISTS A **psychologist** doesn't have medical training but instead undergoes intense academic training, learning about many different areas of psychology before choosing an area in which to specialize. Psychologists may have either a doctor of philosophy (Ph.D.) or doctor of psychology (Psy.D.) degree. (People who hold a master of science or M.S. degree are not usually called psychologists except in a few states. They can be called therapists or counselors, or they may be teachers or researchers.)

What's the difference between a Ph.D. and a Psy.D.?

What's the difference between a Ph.D. and a Psy.D.?

The Ph.D. is a type of degree that usually indicates the highest degree of learning available in almost any subject area—psychology, the study of languages, education, philosophy, the sciences, and many others. It is typically very research oriented, and earning the degree usually requires a previous master's degree in addition to course work for the doctorate itself, as well as a dissertation—a scholarly work of research in the area of focus that is as long as a book and may even be published as a book.

The Psy.D. is a type of degree developed in the late 1970s that is focused less on research and more on the practical application of psychological principles (Peterson, 1976, 1982). In addition to academic course work such as that required for the Ph.D., this degree may require a major paper instead of a dissertation, with the difference being that the paper is not a report of research designed and conducted by the student but is rather a large-scale term paper. Each year of a Psy.D. program will also require the student to participate in a *practicum,* an actual experience with observing and eventually conducting therapy and treatments under supervision.

Unlike psychiatrists, psychologists typically cannot prescribe medicines or perform medical procedures. Some states are seeking legislative changes to allow psychologists to prescribe psychotropic medications if they receive special education in the use of prescription drugs. Such privileges were first pursued by the U.S. military. The reasoning

psychiatrist a medical doctor who specializes in the diagnosis and treatment of psychological disorders.

psychiatric social worker a social worker with some training in therapy methods who focuses on the environmental conditions that can have an impact on mental disorders, such as poverty, overcrowding, stress, and drug abuse.

psychologist a professional with an academic degree and specialized training in one or more areas of psychology.

behind this move, for which the American Psychological Association has been lobbying since 1984, involves both cost and the delay in receiving mental health services. If a person sees a psychologist and then has to go to a psychiatrist for medical prescriptions, the cost can be prohibitive. There are also fewer psychiatrists in some states than in others, causing long waits for mental health services from those doctors—delays that can sometimes lead to an increase in suicide rates for patients who are not getting the help they need. As of August 2010, only two states (New Mexico and Louisiana) have successfully afforded prescription privileges to psychologists.

Some psychologists provide counseling or therapy and use a variety of techniques and approaches. LINK to Chapter Fifteen: Psychological Therapies, pp. 574–589. However, many psychologists do no counseling at all. There are psychologists who only engage in assessment, those who teach at colleges or universities, those who do only research in those same institutions or for industries, and those who do a combination of teaching and research (and some that do a combination of teaching, research, and counseling or clinical practice.) Other psychologists are involved in designing equipment and workplaces, developing educational methods, or working as consultants to businesses and the court system.

Although becoming a psychologist requires a doctorate degree of some kind, many career fields can benefit from a 4-year college degree in psychology as the basis of that career or going on to obtain a master's degree in psychology.

CAREERS WITH A MASTER'S DEGREE IN PSYCHOLOGY

B.3 What kinds of careers are available to someone with a master's degree in psychology?

While individuals earning a master's degree in psychology are not typically able to engage in the level of independent research or practice of psychology as someone with a doctoral degree, they can still work in a variety of areas, both within and beyond the field of psychology. They may work directly under the supervision of a doctoral psychologist if engaged in clinical, counseling, school psychology, or engaged in assessment. Others work outside of the field in jobs requiring research or analysis skills and work in health, industry, or government areas.

For those interested in counseling or providing therapy, many states allow individuals with master's degrees and prerequisite training and supervision experiences to become licensed to provide unsupervised counseling and therapy. Titles may vary by state but some of the areas and titles associated with licensed master's level work include licensed marriage and family therapist (LMFT), licensed professional counselor (LPC), licensed mental health counselor (LMHC), or licensed clinical social worker (LCSW). These individuals may work in a larger organization or work independently in private practice. Beyond these areas, some individuals with a master's degree in psychology become certified or licensed to serve as school counselors at various levels and may work in an elementary school, middle school, or high school.

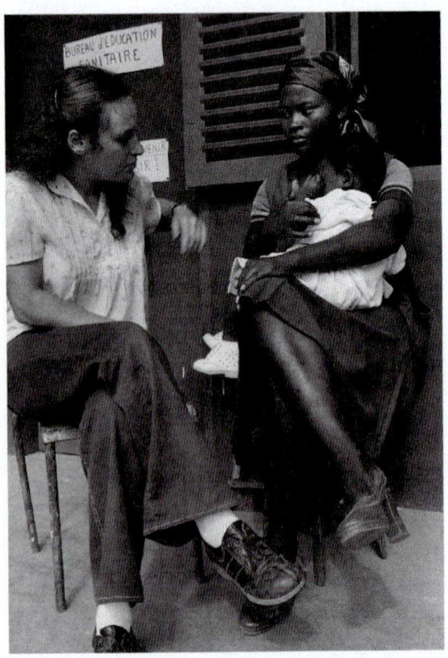

Constance Newman (left) is a Peace Corps volunteer. Using skills she developed while obtaining a bachelor's degree in psychology, Constance is trying to help this Mbankono woman understand the importance of having her child immunized against diseases such as measles.

CAREERS WITH A BACHELOR'S DEGREE IN PSYCHOLOGY

B.4 What kinds of careers are available to someone with a bachelor's degree in psychology?

Although people earning only the baccalaureate (bachelor's) degree in psychology cannot be called psychologists or provide therapy in a private practice, there are many career fields open to such a person. More than 1 million bachelor's degrees in psychology have been awarded since 1970, and since 2000 the number has increased each year (Landrum, 2009; Snyder & Dillow, 2010). A bachelor's degree in psychology can be

Many people with a bachelor's degree in psychology work in health-related fields, such as this woman who is lecturing about depression at a medical clinic.

highly flexible and adaptable to many different kinds of careers (Landrum, 2009; Landrum & Davis, 2007; Schwartz, 2000). While surveys, both by the American Psychological Association and others, reveal many may work in health-related or social fields, individuals with a bachelor's degree in psychology may be employed in research development or research management, administration, business, education and teaching, professional services, sales, or management (Grocer & Kohout, 1997; Landrum, 2009),

Other possible careers include marketing researcher, social worker, and communications specialist (Landrum & Davis, 2007; Schwartz, 2000). With its emphasis on critical thinking and empirical observation, psychology trains people for a variety of potential workplace environments and requirements. Psychology is an excellent major even if you intend to do graduate work in some other career: Business, law, child care, teaching, and management are only a few of the areas that relate to psychology.

AREAS OF SPECIALIZATION

You said that some psychologists teach or do research. What kind of research do they do?

You said that some psychologists teach or do research. What kind of research do they do?

There are many different areas in which psychologists may focus their energies. They conduct experiments, surveys, observations, and so on to gather more information for their particular field of interest, to find support for current theories, or to develop new ones. Let's look at some of the areas in which psychologists may specialize.

B.5 What are the areas of specialization in psychology?

CLINICAL PSYCHOLOGY Even though not all psychologists do counseling or therapy, many psychologists do. **Clinical psychology** is the most similar of the areas to psychiatry in that professionals with this focus traditionally work with individuals with more-serious forms of mental illness. It is also the area of specialization with the largest number of psychologists. Clinical psychologists, like psychiatrists, diagnose and treat psychological disorders in people. However, the clinical psychologist cannot prescribe drugs or medical therapies (with the exceptions discussed earlier, of course) but instead relies on listening or observing the client's problems, possibly administering psychological tests, and then providing explanations for the client's behavior and feelings or directing them in specific actions to make positive changes in his or her life.

clinical psychology area of psychology in which the psychologists diagnose and treat people with psychological disorders that may range from mild to severe.

COUNSELING PSYCHOLOGY **Counseling psychology** is similar to clinical psychology in that this type of psychologist diagnoses and treats problems. The difference is that a counseling psychologist usually works with relatively healthy people who have less severe forms of mental illness or problems, such as adjustment to college, marriage, family life, work problems, and so on. As of 2008, nearly 73 percent of surveyed psychologists currently providing health services identified themselves as clinical psychologists or counseling psychologists (Michalski et al., 2010). LINK to Chapter One: The Science of Psychology, p. 17.

DEVELOPMENTAL PSYCHOLOGY **Developmental psychology** is an area that focuses on the study of change, or development. Developmental psychologists are interested in changes in the way people think, in how people relate to others, and in the ways people feel over the entire span of life. These psychologists work in academic settings such as colleges and universities and may do research in various areas of development. They do not provide therapy. LINK to Chapter Eight: Development Across the Life Span, pp. 298–299.

EXPERIMENTAL PSYCHOLOGY **Experimental psychology** encompasses several different areas such as learning, memory, thinking, perception, motivation, and language. The focus of these psychologists, however, is on doing research and conducting studies and experiments with both people and animals in these various areas. They tend to work in academic settings, especially in large universities. LINK to Chapter One: The Science of Psychology, p. 17.

SOCIAL PSYCHOLOGY **Social psychology** is an area that focuses on how human behavior is affected by the presence of other people. For example, social psychologists explore areas such as prejudice, attitude change, aggressive behavior, and interpersonal attraction. Although most social psychologists work in academic settings teaching and doing research, some work in federal agencies and big business doing practical (applied) research. In fact, many social psychologists are experimental psychologists who perform their experiments in real-world settings rather than the laboratory to preserve the natural reactions of people. When people are in an artificial setting, they often behave in self-conscious ways, which is not the behavior the researcher wishes to study. LINK to Chapter Twelve: Social Psychology, p. 448.

PERSONALITY PSYCHOLOGY **Personality psychology** focuses on the differences in personality among people. These psychologists may look at the influence of heredity on personality. They study the ways in which people are both alike and different. They look at the development of personality and do personality assessment. They may be involved in forming new theories of how personality works or develops. Personality psychologists work in academic settings, doing research and teaching. LINK to Chapter Thirteen: Theories of Personality, p. 494.

PHYSIOLOGICAL PSYCHOLOGY **Physiological psychology** is an area that focuses on the study of the biological bases of behavior. Many professionals now refer to this area as *behavioral neuroscience* or *biopsychology*. Physiological psychologists study the brain, nervous system, and the influence of the body's chemicals, such as hormones and the chemicals in the brain, on human behavior. They study the effects of drug use and possible genetic influences on some kinds of abnormal and normal human behavior, such as schizophrenia or aspects of intelligence. Most physiological psychologists, like experimental psychologists, work in an academic setting. LINK to Chapter Two: The Biological Perspective, p. 46.

NEUROPSYCHOLOGY **Neuropsychology** is an area within the field of psychology in which professionals explore the relationships between the brain systems and behavior. Neuropsychologists may be engaged in research or more focused on the assessment, diagnosis, treatment, and/or rehabilitation of individuals with various neurological,

counseling psychology area of psychology in which the psychologists help people with problems of adjustment.

developmental psychology area of psychology in which the psychologists study the changes in the way people think, relate to others, and feel as they age.

experimental psychology area of psychology in which the psychologists primarily do research and experiments in the areas of learning, memory, thinking, perception, motivation, and language.

social psychology area of psychology in which the psychologists focus on how human behavior is affected by the presence of other people.

personality psychology area of psychology in which the psychologists study the differences in personality among people.

physiological psychology area of psychology in which the psychologists study the biological bases of behavior.

neuropsychology area of psychology in which psychologists specialize in the research or clinical implications of brain-behavior relationships.

medical, neurodevelopmental or psychiatric conditions (National Academy of Neuropsychology, 2001). LINK to Chapter Seven: Cognition, pp. 273–274.

COMPARATIVE PSYCHOLOGY **Comparative psychology** is an area that focuses exclusively on animals and animal behavior. By comparing and contrasting animal behavior with what is already known about human behavior, comparative psychologists can contribute to the understanding of human behavior by studying animals. Research in animal behavior also helps people to learn how to treat animals more humanely and to coexist with the animals in a common environment. Comparative psychologists might work in animal laboratories in a university or may do observation and studies of animals in the animals' natural habitats.

Psychologists in these areas may do research that is directed at discovering basic principles of human behavior (basic research) or they may engage in research designed to find solutions to practical problems of the here and now (applied research). There are many other areas in which psychologists may specialize that focus almost exclusively on applied research. These areas are those most often associated with applied psychology.

Psychology Beyond the Classroom

B.6 How does psychology interact with other career fields?

PSYCHOLOGY AND HEALTH

Health psychology focuses on the relationship of human behavior patterns and stress reactions to physical health with the goal of improving and helping to maintain good health while preventing and treating illness. For example, a health psychologist might design a program to help people lose weight or stop smoking. Stress management techniques are also a major focus of this area. Health psychologists may work in hospitals, clinics, medical schools, health agencies, academic settings, or private practice.

In a recent study (Kerwin et al., 2010), researchers found an association between obesity in older women and a decline in memory functioning in those women. This finding was particularly true for women carrying the excess weight around their hips (pear shapes) and less so for women carrying the excess weight around their waists (apple shapes). The study controlled for other health variables, such as diabetes, heart disease, and stroke. This is a good example of the kind of research that health psychologists conduct. Other areas studied by health psychologists include the influence of optimistic attitudes on the progress of disease, the link between mental distress and health, and the promotion of wellness and hope in an effort to prevent illness. LINK to Chapter Eleven: Stress and Health, p. 425.

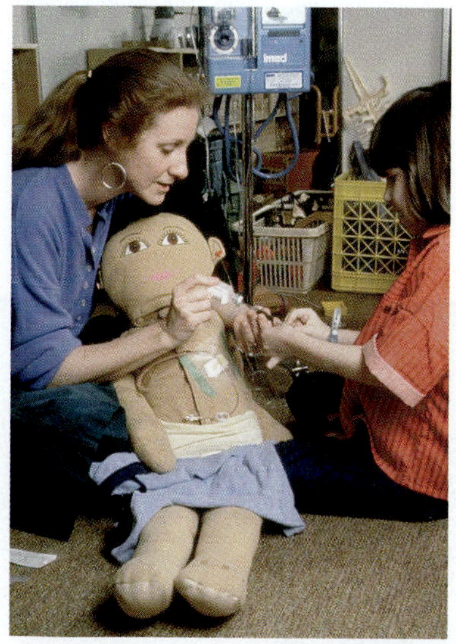

This woman is a health psychologist. She is helping this girl to control her fear of receiving an injection by letting her act out giving an injection to a special doll.

PSYCHOLOGY AND EDUCATION

Educational psychology is concerned with the study of human learning. As educational psychologists come to understand some of the basic aspects of learning, they develop methods and materials for aiding the process of learning. For example, educational psychologists helped to design the phonics method of teaching children to read. This type of psychologist may have a doctorate of education (Ed.D.) rather than a Ph.D. and typically works in academic settings.

What types of research might an educational psychologist conduct? The May 2010 issue of *Journal of Educational Psychology* included articles on the role that speech-rhythm sensitivity plays on children's reading ability, strategy-based intervention for adolescents with reading difficulties, the impact of conceptual and procedural knowledge when learning fractions, and investigation of Bandura's ideas of self-efficacy and reciprocal determinism, LINK to Chapter Thirteen: Theories of Personality, pp. 505–506,

comparative psychology area of psychology in which the psychologists study animals and their behavior for the purpose of comparing and contrasting it to human behavior.

health psychology area of psychology in which the psychologists focus on the relationship of human behavior patterns and stress reaction to physical health.

educational psychology area of psychology in which the psychologists are concerned with the study of human learning and development of new learning techniques.

School psychologists often administer tests to assess a child's intelligence or psychological well-being. The young boy's description of the drawing he is holding will help this psychologist determine the boy's emotional state.

and performance in mathematics in students from 33 different countries—just to name a few.

School psychology is related to, but not at all the same as, educational psychology. Whereas educational psychologists may do research and develop new learning techniques, school psychologists may take the results of that research or those methods and apply them in the actual school system. School psychologists work directly with children in the school setting. They do testing and other forms of assessment to place children in special programs or to diagnose educational problems such as dyslexia or attention-deficit/hyperactivity disorder. They may act as consultants to teachers, parents, and educational administrators. Counseling students is actually a relatively small part of the job of a school psychologist, although counseling takes a much bigger role when tragedies strike a school. When traumatic events such as the unexpected and tragic death of a classmate or even larger-scale tragedies such as the numerous school shootings of the past decade take place, school psychologists are often called on to offer help and counseling to students.

PSYCHOLOGY AND SPORTS

Sports psychology is a relatively new and fast-growing field in which the main focus is on helping athletes and others involved in sports activities prepare mentally, rather than just physically, for participation in sports. The idea behind this field is that a superior physical performance is not enough to guarantee success; rather, the mind must be prepared for the activity by setting clear, short-term goals, holding positive thoughts, using visualization of the goal, stopping negative thoughts, and other techniques based primarily in the cognitive perspective. For example, a sports psychologist might have a golfer, who has been having trouble with the accuracy of his drives, perform visualization exercises, mentally seeing himself hit the ball down the fairway again and again. Sports psychologists work in athletic organizations and may have a private practice or do consulting work. (For more on the techniques used in sports psychology, see the Applying Psychology to Everyday Life section at the end of this appendix.)

A Fort Lewis Army psychologist demonstrates a headset from the "Virtual Reality Iraq" therapy program on April 18, 2007, in Spanaway, Washington. The virtual-reality program, which simulates the sights, sounds and smells of combat, will be used in working with soldiers suffering from post-traumatic stress disorder.

PSYCHOLOGY AND THE MILITARY

Within the military, psychologists work in a variety of areas ranging from assessment, teaching, management, research, and the provision of mental health services. The variety of psychologists in this field may include clinical, counseling, experimental, I/O, or human factors, among others, and may reflect any specialty area in the field of psychology. In short, they apply psychological skills to human issues in military environments, working with both military personnel and their families (American Psychological Association, Division 19, 2010). One poignant example, the rise of suicides in the armed forces associated with the conflicts in Iraq and Afghanistan have placed demands on both the military and military families at a level not seen before (Berman et al., 2010). For more on the work of psychologists (specifically neuropsychologists) in the military, see the Psychology in the News section of Chapter Seven, pp. 273–274.

PSYCHOLOGY AND THE LAW

Psychologists have often been involved in the world of legal matters in various ways. Social psychologists often do research in the areas of criminal behavior and may

school psychology area of psychology in which the psychologists work directly in the schools, doing assessments, educational placement, and diagnosing educational problems.

sports psychology area of psychology in which the psychologists help athletes and others to prepare themselves mentally for participation in sports activities.

consult with attorneys or other agents of the court system on such topics as witness credibility, jury selection, and the kind of influences that exist for decision-making processes. Developmental psychologists may become involved in determining the accuracy of and influences on the testimony of children and adolescents, as well as the needs of children caught up in a custody battle between divorced or divorcing parents. Cognitive psychologists may become expert witnesses on the accuracy of memory and eyewitness testimony or ways to determine the truth or falsehood of statements made by witnesses or defendants. Clinical psychologists may deliver their services directly to incarcerated prisoners or may conduct assessments of intelligence and/or mental status to determine whether or not a person charged with a crime should stand trial.

All of the forms of psychological involvement in legal matters mentioned here can be considered as part of the growing field of **forensic psychology**. Forensic psychology is the practice of psychology related to the legal system and it involves examining criminal evidence and aiding law enforcement investigations into criminal activities. Some forensic psychologists provide information and advice to officials in the legal system, such as lawyers or judges; some act as expert witnesses (like Professor John Gambon in the opening story); some actually diagnose and treat criminals within the prison system; and others may administer psychological tests to criminal defendants. Forensic psychologists may aid either the prosecution or the defense in a trial by helping determine which potential jurors would be the best or worst choices. This type of professional may do consulting work in addition to maintaining a regular private practice in clinical or counseling psychology, or may work entirely within the justice system as a police psychologist, a profiler of serial criminals for federal agencies, or a full-time jury expert, for example.

forensic psychology area of psychology concerned with people in the legal system, including profiling of criminals, jury selection, and expert witnessing.

environmental psychology area of psychology in which the focus is on how people interact with and are affected by their physical environments.

PSYCHOLOGY AND THE ENVIRONMENT

Another broad area in which psychological principles can be applied to solve practical problems is the area of managing the environment. **Environmental psychology** is an area that focuses on the relationship between human behavior and the environment in which the behavior takes place, such as an office, store, school, dormitory, or hospital. Because the concern of researchers in this field deals directly with behavior in a particular setting, research is always conducted in that setting rather than in a laboratory. Environmental psychologists may work with other professionals such as urban or city planners, economists, engineers, and architects, helping those professionals to plan the most efficient buildings, parks, housing developments, or plants.

PRACTICE quiz How much do you remember?

ANSWERS ON PAGE AK-2.

Pick the best answer.

1. Which of the following professionals in psychology focuses more on the social conditions that affect mental disorders?
   a. psychiatrist
   b. therapist
   c. psychiatric social worker
   d. psychologist
2. Which of the following specialties in psychology is most similar to the medical field of psychiatry?
   a. clinical
   b. counseling
   c. personality
   d. experimental
3. Max is interested in becoming a psychologist. He is most interested in how people become attracted to other people. He would most likely specialize in _________ psychology.
   a. comparative
   b. developmental
   c. sports
   d. social
4. The study of the effects of psychological stress on the growth rate of cancer cells would most likely be the work of _________ psychologists.
   a. environmental
   b. forensic
   c. health
   d. military
5. Which type of psychologist would be more likely to administer an IQ test to a child to determine the child's eligibility for a gifted program?
   a. educational
   b. school
   c. developmental
   d. personality

Psychology and Work

B.7 What are industrial/organizational psychology and human factors psychology?

Work is a tremendous part of many people's lives. People often spend more time at work than they do with their families or in social activities. One of the largest branches of applied psychology focuses on how psychology can help people in management, productivity, morale, and many other areas of the world of work.

Industrial/organizational (I/O) psychology is concerned with the relationships between people and their work environments. I/O psychologists may help in personnel selection, administer job performance assessments, design work schedules that help workers adjust to new time periods of work hours with less difficulty, or design new work areas to increase morale and productivity. Psychologists in this field may study the behavior of entire organizations. They are often hired by corporations and businesses to deal with the hiring and assessment of employees. They may research and develop ways for workers to be more efficient and productive. They may work in business, government agencies, and academic settings.

Human factors psychologists design machines that are more practical and comfortable for people to use. For example, this keyboard is designed to reduce the risk of pain in the wrists and increase accuracy in typing.

A specific kind of I/O specialist, called a *human factors engineer*, focuses on designing machines, furniture, and other devices that people have to use so that those devices are the most practical, comfortable, and logical for human use. **Human factors psychology** consists of these researchers and designers who study the way humans and machines interact with each other. They may work directly in the companies involved in the design of appliances, airplane controls, and the operation of computers or other mechanical devices.

Psychologists working in I/O settings apply psychological principles and theories to the workplace. For example, Maslow's humanistic theory and hierarchy of needs has had a powerful influence on the field of management (Heil et al., 1998). Douglas McGregor, in his explanations of two different styles of management (McGregor, 1960), relates the older and less productive "Theory X" (workers are unmotivated and need to be managed and directed) to Maslow's lower needs and the newer, more productive style of management called "Theory Y" (workers want to work and want that work to be meaningful) to the higher needs.

Industrial/organizational psychology got its start near the beginning of the twentieth century with the work of Walter D. Scott, a former student of famed physiologist and founder of the first psychological laboratory, Wilhelm Wundt. Scott applied psychological principles to hiring, management, and advertising techniques (Schultz & Schultz, 2004). He also wrote one of the first books about the application of psychology to industry and advertising, called *The Theory and Practice of Advertising* (Scott, 1908). Another early figure in the newly developing field of industrial/organizational psychology was Hugo Munsterberg, a psychologist also trained by Wundt, who conducted research on such varied topics as the power of prayer and eyewitness testimony (Hothersall, 1995). Munsterberg wrote a book about eyewitness testimony called *On the Witness Stand* (1907) and later wrote *Psychology and Industrial Efficiency* (1913).

The I/O field became important during World War I when the army needed a way to test the intelligence of potential recruits. Psychologist Robert Yerkes, who would later become known for his groundbreaking research in comparative psychology while working with the great apes, developed the Army Alpha and Army Beta tests. The Army Alpha test was used with applicants who were able to read, whereas the Army Beta test was administered to applicants who were illiterate (McGuire, 1994; Yerkes, 1921).

industrial/organizational (I/O) psychology area of psychology concerned with the relationships between people and their work environment.

human factors psychology area of industrial/organizational psychology concerned with the study of the way humans and machines interact with each other.

In the mid-1920s a series of studies conducted by Elton Mayo for the Western Electric Company (Franke & Kaul, 1978; Parsons, 1992; Roethlisberger & Dickson, 1939) broadened the field. These were the first studies to view the workplace as a social system rather than as just a production line. Instead of treating workers as simply other pieces of equipment, these studies suggested that allowing workers some input into the decision-making process not only improved worker morale* but also reduced workers' resistance to changes in the workplace. These studies led the way for others to examine how management of employees and production could be improved. Management theories and strategies may also be applied to other kinds of settings such as schools, colleges, and universities. The following section takes a closer look at the development of these theories.

*morale: a sense of common purpose, enthusiasm, confidence, and loyalty.

These women were participants in one of the early industrial/organizational psychology experiments conducted by Elton Mayo for the Western Electric Company.

issues in psychology

Workplace Violence

Acts of violence in the workplace have increased dramatically in the past few decades—nearly tripling in the 1980s alone (Baron, 1993). Psychologists are devoting time and energy to studying the reasons for this violence and are looking for ways to recognize and prevent future incidents. Some highlights from research in workplace violence show that people in some types of jobs face a higher probability of becoming a victim of a crime because of the characteristics of the job. For example, three of the most likely occupations are police officers, corrections officers, and taxi drivers (Centers for Disease Control and Prevention, 2009). For taxi drivers (along with convenience-store clerks), it is the availability of cash and the solitary nature of the job that entices many criminals to attempt robbery. In the case of police and correctional officers, violence is part of the very nature of their job. Consider the following statistics:

- Between 1992 and 2006, there were 11,613 workplace homicide victims reported.
- Of those homicides, 11.6 police officers out of every 100,000 were killed on the job compared to 4.0 out of every 100,000—the national average for all occupations.
- From 2004 to 2008 there was an average of 564 work-related homicides each year—10 percent of all fatal work injuries.
- Four out of every 5 homicide victims in 2008 were male.
- Men were more likely to be killed by an assailant, while women were more likely to be killed by a relative or personal acquaintance.
- In 2008, there were 30 multiple-fatality workplace homicide incidents, with an average of 2 people dying in each incident. Most were shot, and in 12 percent of the shootings the assailants were coworkers or former coworkers (Bureau of Labor Statistics, 2010).

Industrial/organizational psychologists have developed a term for the employee who becomes highly violent and commits violent crimes resulting in serious injury or death to other employees: the *berserker*. What are the characteristics of persons who "go berserk" in the workplace? Typically, they have at least a high school diploma or some college. Their self-esteem, or sense of worth as a person, is intimately tied to their job. They tend to like watching violent television or movies. There is a small correlation between berserkers and those with delusional disorders: People who become violent in the workplace are also somewhat likely to suffer from a delusional disorder, such as paranoia. LINK to Chapter Fourteen: Psychological Disorders, pp. 557–558.

The aftermath of workplace violence: a somber crowd gathers at a candlelight vigil Sunday Aug. 8, 2010 in honor of the victims of a workplace shooting at a Connecticut beer distribution company, which took place on August 8, 2010. Only one week prior to this vigil, Omar Thornton killed eight co-workers and wounded two others before killing himself at the Hartford Distributors building.

Prevention of violence in the workplace can include some simple, commonsense steps as well as more-complicated training and preparation (Arbury, 2005; Harvey & Keashly, 2003; Security Director's Report, 2008; Vandenbos & Bulatao, 1996):

- entrances and exits that are well lighted
- presence of video cameras or security guards, especially at night
- criminal background checks performed on all potential new employees
- training managers and supervisors to identify signs of potential workplace violence, including such things as employees (1) who have a tendency to use verbal threats or who use low-grade acts of violence, such as pushing or shoving; (2) who are fascinated with and have access to firearms; or (3) who appear desensitized to television and movie violence and show a preference for watching such media.

OTHER AREAS IN INDUSTRIAL/ORGANIZATIONAL PSYCHOLOGY

There are many other areas of research and study in the field of industrial/organization psychology. Table B.1 briefly lists some of the areas of specialization.

Table B.1
Areas in I/O Psychology

AREAS IN INDUSTRY	AREAS IN ORGANIZATIONS
Job analysis	Social behavior of work teams
Job evaluation and compensation	Job satisfaction
Characteristics critical to effective management	Personality characteristics critical to job performance
Personnel recruiting, selection, and placement	Relationships between management and workers
Occupational training	Leadership characteristics and training
Examination of working conditions	Consumer psychology
Interviewing and testing	Motivational concerns
Performance appraisal and feedback	Conflict management

PRACTICE quiz How much do you remember? ANSWERS ON PAGE AK-2.

Pick the best answer.

1. Bernard works in a factory and is responsible for making sure that the office equipment made in the factory is practical and easy to use. He sometimes suggests changes in the design of certain equipment to accomplish this goal. Bernard is most likely what type of psychologist?
   a. forensic
   b. human factors
   c. industrial/organizational
   d. management/design
2. One of the early figures in I/O psychology who examined the behavior of eyewitnesses in the courtroom was _________.
   a. Wilhelm Wundt.
   b. Walter D. Scott.
   c. Hugo Munsterberg.
   d. Robert Yerkes.
3. Violence in the workplace can come from which of the following sources?
   a. a fellow employee
   b. a disgruntled lover or spouse
   c. an outside person, such as a robber
   d. all of the above

Applying Psychology to Everyday Life: Techniques Used by Sports Psychologists

B.8 What are some techniques used in sports psychology?

Many athletes become frustrated when their performance seems to be less than it could be or when they reach some "roadblock" on their way to achieving new goals. The techniques that follow are designed to help athletes get around the roadblocks and get the most out of their performance. The same techniques are also helpful in the careers of acting, musical performance, professional speaking, teaching, or any career in which there is an element of performance in front of others.

1. *Visualization.* In this technique, athletes try to "see" their performance in their minds as if watching from the sidelines before actually doing it.
2. *Imagery/mental rehearsal.* Similar to visualization, imagery can be used to mentally rehearse the desired performance. Instead of visualizing oneself as if from the sidelines, however, imagery/mental rehearsal involves actually "seeing" and "feeling" the performance in one's mind from one's own viewpoint. This helps prepare the muscles that will be used for action.
3. *Distraction desensitization.* Athletes can be trained to ignore distractions, such as the shouts of spectators.
4. *Thought stopping.* People often have negative thoughts about things that might happen: "I'm going to miss it, I just know it!" is a good example of a negative, self-defeating thought. Sports psychologists train athletes to stop such thoughts in the making, replacing them with more positive thoughts: "I can do this. I've done it before and it was easy."
5. *Confidence training.* Another thing that sports psychologists do is try to build confidence and self-esteem in the athletes who come to them for help. Lack of confidence in one's own abilities is a major roadblock.
6. *Focus training.* Athletes can also be trained to focus attention, often through the use of hypnosis, concentrative meditation, or similar psychological techniques.
7. *Relaxation training.* Athletes can be trained to use special breathing methods, tension and relaxation of muscles, and other tricks for relaxation to reduce anxiety and tension before a performance.
8. *Autogenic training.* Autogenic essentially means "from within the self." In the sense used here, autogenic training involves helping athletes learn about their physiological responses to stress. Once learned, athletes can gain control over these responses, such as learning to slow one's heart rate or to lower anxiety.
9. *Fostering realistic goals and expectations.* Sports psychologists try to teach athletes that although setting goals is important, setting unrealistic goals can lead to burnout, frustration, and feelings of failure. Sports psychologists try to help athletes modify their expectations and goals to be more realistic.
10. *Fostering team unity.* Sports psychologists may also work with entire teams of athletes, helping them to become a unit that works as one single "organism" while still providing support for each individual athlete.

Relaxation training is becoming a very important part of any athlete's training. Here the Wisconsin Badgers college football team participates in a relaxation exercise before the big game. What other career areas might be improved by relaxation training?

chapter summary

Listen on **mypsychlab.com** Listen to an audio file of your chapter **www.mypsychlab.com**

What Is Applied Psychology?

B.1 What is the definition of applied psychology?

- Applied psychology refers to using psychological principles and research to solve problems in the real world.

Psychology as a Career

B.2 What are the different types of psychological professionals?

- Different types of psychological professionals vary by level of education and training. Examples include psychiatrists, psychiatric social workers, and psychologists.
- Psychologists hold either a Ph.D. or Psy.D. degree.

B.3 What kinds of careers are available to someone with a master's degree in psychology?

- Individuals with a master's degree may work under the supervision of a doctoral-level psychology professional, practice independently if licensed, or in private or educational settings.

B.4 What kinds of careers are available to someone with a bachelor's degree in psychology?

- Education, statistical consulting, administration and other business occupations, as well as health services are examples of careers that a person with a bachelor's degree in psychology might enter.

B.5 What are the areas of specialization in psychology?

- Areas of specialization include clinical and counseling psychology, developmental, experimental, social, personality, physiological, neuropsychology, and comparative psychology.

Psychology Beyond the Classroom

B.6 How does psychology interact with other career fields?

- Health psychology is an area in which the goal is to discover relationships between human behavior, including stress factors, and physical health with the intention of preventing and treating ill health.
- Educational psychologists study the processes of human learning to develop new techniques and methods, whereas school psychologists apply those methods in the school, administer assessments, recommend placement, and provide counseling and diagnosis of educational problems.
- Sports psychologists help athletes prepare themselves mentally for participation in sports.
- Psychologists working in the military represent most all subfields of psychology and work with both military personnel and their families in military environments.
- Psychologists may act as expert witnesses for legal matters, help in jury selection, provide clinical services to defendants or prisoners, or produce personality profiles of various types of criminals in the field of forensic psychology.
- Environmental psychology looks at the relationship between human behavior and the physical environment in which that behavior takes place.

Psychology and Work

B.7 What are industrial/organizational psychology and human factors psychology?

- Industrial/organizational psychology is concerned with how people function in and are affected by their work environments.
- Human factors is a type of I/O psychology in which the focus is on the way humans and machines interact with each other, designing or helping to design the machines used by people in various science and industrial settings.

Applying Psychology to Everyday Life: Techniques Used by Sports Psychologists

B.8 What are some techniques used in sports psychology?

- Sports psychologists use many techniques to help athletes better their performances, including visualization, imagery, thought stopping, confidence training, relaxation training, and fostering team unity.

test YOURSELF

ANSWERS ON PAGE AK-2.

Study and Review on **mypsychlab.com** Ready for your test? More quizzes and a customized study plan **www.mypsychlab.com**

Pick the best answer.

1. Carrie would like to work as a psychological professional, but she is not interested in scientific research or in becoming a medical doctor. She would like to be able to call herself a psychologist and provide therapy for her clients. What type of degree would be best for Carrie to pursue?
   a. a master's degree in psychology
   b. a Ph.D.
   c. a Psy.D.
   d. a master's degree in social work
2. What type of professional would help people with adjustments to stress, work problems, or marital difficulties?
   a. clinical psychologist
   b. personality psychologist
   c. developmental psychologist
   d. counseling psychologist
3. Dr. Trentenelli is studying the changes that occur in people's memories as they age from youth to late adulthood. Dr. Trentenelli's area of specialization is most likely in _________ psychology.
   a. social c. comparative
   b. personality d. developmental
4. _________ psychologists do research and conduct experiments with people and animals in the areas of learning, memory, thought processes, perception, and language.
   a. Experimental c. Developmental
   b. Comparative d. Social
5. The view that panic attacks occur because of a malfunction in a small area of the brain normally responsible for alerting the person to real danger is most compatible with which area of specialization in psychology?
   a. developmental c. physiological
   b. health d. human factors
6. What type of psychologist would be most likely to put together a personality profile of a criminal for the FBI?
   a. industrial/organizational c. forensic
   b. clinical d. environmental
7. City planners who want the new public library to be accessible to all and logically organized into different areas, each with a different function, might consult what type of psychologist?
   a. developmental c. social
   b. physiological d. environmental
8. Which type of psychologist is most concerned with increasing productivity of workers by increasing morale and manipulating work shifts?
   a. industrial/organizational c. forensic
   b. clinical d. environmental
9. Suzanne is about to compete on the balance beam and begins to have second thoughts about her ability. She realizes that such negative thoughts will not help and tells herself that this is something she has done perfectly in practice and that she can do it perfectly now. Suzanne's ability to replace her negative thinking with more helpful, positive thinking is a form of _________.
   a. visualization. c. distraction desensitization.
   b. thought stopping. d. autogenic training.
10. The psychologist tells Michaela that she needs to "be the ball," or try to see herself actually hitting the ball over the net. The psychologist is using _________.
    a. distraction desensitization. c. imagery/mental rehearsal.
    b. thought stopping. d. focus training.

answer key

PSYCHOLOGY IN ACTION

Practice Quiz page I-9
1. c 2. c 3. a

Practice Quiz page I-14
1. d 2. c

Test Yourself page I-17
1. c 2. a 3. c 4. a 5. b

CHAPTER 1

Practice Quiz page 13
1. c 2. d 3. b 4. b 5. d 6. a 7. b

Practice Quiz pages 19–20
1. b 2. d 3. d 4. c 5. c 6. c

Practice Quiz page 25
1. b 2. c 3. a 4. c 5. d

Practice Quiz page 36
1. a 2. b 3. b 4. d 5. c 6. c 7. b 8. d

Test Yourself pages 40–42
1. a 2. b 3. c 4. b 5. d 6. d 7. a 8. a 9. d 10. a 11. c 12. d 13. d 14. a 15. b 16. d 17. a 18. d 19. c 20. b 21. a 22. b 23. a 24. d 25. d 26. b 27. c 28. c 29. b 30. c 31. c

CHAPTER 2

Practice Quiz page 56
1. b 2. d 3. a 4. d 5. c 6. c

Practice Quiz page 65
1. a 2. c 3. d 4. b 5. a 6. b 7. a 8. a

Practice Quiz page 74
1. d 2. b 3. a 4. c 5. a

Practice Quiz page 80
1. b 2. a 3. a 4. c 5. c

Test Yourself pages 84–85
1. a 2. b 3. d 4. b 5. c 6. d 7. c 8. a 9. a 10. b 11. a 12. d 13. d 14. c 15. a 16. c 17. d 18. b 19. c 20. d 21. a 22. c 23. b 24. b

CHAPTER 3

Practice Quiz page 93
1. b 2. d 3. a 4. d

Practice Quiz page 100
1. b 2. c 3. d 4. b 5. a

Practice Quiz page 105
1. a 2. c 3. a 4. d

Practice Quiz page 112
1. c 2. a 3. b 4. b 5. a 6. c

Practice Quiz page 121
1. b 2. c 3. a 4. c 5. a 6. b

Test Yourself pages 124–125
1. b 2. c 3. a 4. d 5. c 6. a 7. b 8. b 9. b 10. c 11. d 12. c 13. b 14. a 15. a 16. d 17. c 18. a 19. a 20. c 21. b 22. d 23. a 24. c

CHAPTER 4

Practice Quiz page 136
1. b 2. c 3. a 4. c 5. b

Practice Quiz page 143
1. c 2. c 3. d 4. a 5. d 6. b

Practice Quiz page 146
1. b 2. c 3. d 4. a 5. b

Practice Quiz page 149
1. a 2. c 3. c 4. b

Practice Quiz page 161
1. c 2. b 3. a 4. a 5. c 6. b 7. b 8. b 9. a 10. a 11. d 12. a

Test Yourself pages 164–165
1. b 2. c 3. a 4. c 5. a 6. d 7. b 8. d 9. b 10. d 11. a 12. c 13. d 14. a 15. c 16. a 17. d 18. d 19. a 20. b 21. c 22. c 23. a 24. b 25. b

CHAPTER 5

Practice Quiz page 176
1. a 2. b 3. b 4. d 5. a 6. b

Practice Quiz pages 179-180
1. b 2. c 3. c 4. a 5. d

Practice Quiz page 183
1. d 2. a 3. c 4. d

Practice Quiz pages 196–197
1. a 2. c 3. d 4. c 5. d 6. a 7. c 8. a

Practice Quiz page 204
1. c 2. b 3. d 4. b 5. a 6. b

Test Yourself pages 208–209
1. c 2. b 3. a 4. d 5. c 6. b 7. a 8. b 9. a 10. c 11. d 12. d 13. c 14. a 15. a 16. c 17. b 18. c 19. d 20. a 21. b 22. a 23. c 24. d 25. c

CHAPTER 6

Practice Quiz page 217
1. c 2. a 3. a 4. b

Practice Quiz page 228
1. d 2. b 3. d 4. a 5. b 6. c

Practice Quiz pages 234–235
1. a 2. b 3. d 4. d 5. c

Practice Quiz page 238
1. b 2. d 3. b 4. a

Practice Quiz page 245
1. a 2. c 3. b 4. c 5. d 6. d 7. a 8. a

Test Yourself pages 248–249
1. c 2. b 3. b 4. c 5. b 6. a 7. a 8. c 9. d 10. d 11. c 12. c 13. c 14. d 15. d 16. a 17. d 18. b 19. c 20. c 21. a 22. a 23. d 24. c

CHAPTER 7

Practice Quiz page 261
1. b 2. c 3. a 4. b 5. d

Practice Quiz page 265
1. a 2. b 3. c 4. b

Practice Quiz page 275
1. c 2. b 3. a 4. d 5. b 6. b 7. a

Practice Quiz page 284
1. b 2. d 3. c 4. b 5. d

Practice Quiz page 289
1. c 2. a 3. b 4. d 5. c

Test Yourself page 293
1. c 2. b 3. d 4. a 5. b 6. a 7. c 8. c 9. b 10. c 11. a 12. d 13. b 14. d 15. a 16. c 17. b 18. c 19. b 20. a 21. d 22. d

CHAPTER 8

Practice Quiz page 303
1. b 2. c 3. b 4. d 5. a

Practice Quiz page 308
1. c 2. d 3. b 4. b 5. d

Practice Quiz page 318
1. d 2. b 3. a 4. c 5. a

Practice Quiz page 324
1. b 2. a 3. d 4. c

Practice Quiz page 328
1. c 2. c 3. b 4. a 5. b

Practice Quiz page 332
1. b 2. d 3. c 4. a 5. c

Practice Quiz page 335
1. b 2. c 3. d 4. b 5. c

Test Yourself pages 338–339
1. c 2. b 3. d 4. c 5. d 6. b 7. c 8. c 9. d 10. b 11. c 12. d 13. a 14. b 15. a 16. c 17. c 18. d 19. a 20. a 21. b 22. d 23. b 24. a 25. a 26. c 27. d

CHAPTER 9

Practice Quiz page 349
1. c 2. d 3. b 4. a

Practice Quiz page 355
1. b 2. c 3. d 4. b

Practice Quiz page 360
1. d 2. b 3. b 4. c

Practice Quiz page 370
1. c 2. b 3. a 4. d 5. a

Test Yourself page 373
1. c 2. b 3. c 4. a 5. c 6. c 7. b 8. a 9. b 10. d 11. a 12. c 13. b 14. a 15. d 16. d 17. d 18. c 19. d 20. b

CHAPTER 10

Practice Quiz pages 384–385
1. c 2. a 3. c 4. b 5. c 6. b

Practice Quiz page 388
1. a 2. d 3. c 4. d 5. d

Practice Quiz page 391
1. c 2. c 3. c 4. d

Practice Quiz pages 397–398
1. c 2. d 3. b 4. a 5. c

Practice Quiz page 402
1. b 2. c 3. a 4. d

Test Yourself page 404–405
1. a 2. a 3. d 4. a 5. c 6. b 7. b 8. c 9. c 10. b 11. c 12. d 13. c 14. a 15. d 16. a 17. a 18. d 19. b 20. a

CHAPTER 11

Practice Quiz page 416
1. c 2. b 3. b 4. d

Practice Quiz page 420
1. c 2. b 3. a 4. a 5. c

Practice Quiz page 432
1. b 2. d 3. d 4. a 5. b 6. b

Practice Quiz page 436
1. c 2. c 3. b 4. d

Practice Quiz page 440
1. b 2. b 3. d

Test Yourself pages 442–443
1. d 2. c 3. b 4. a 5. c 6. d 7. d 8. c 9. b 10. c 11. a 12. b 13. d 14. d 15. b 16. b 17. d 18. c 19. a 20. a 21. c 22. c

CHAPTER 12

Practice Quiz page 457
1. c 2. a 3. a 4. c 5. c

Practice Quiz page 464
1. c 2. d 3. a 4. c 5. b 6. c

Practice Quiz page 468
1. c 2. a 3. b 4. b 5. c

Practice Quiz page 473
1. a 2. b 3. c 4. d 5. a

Practice Quiz page 477
1. c 2. b 3. d 4. b

Practice Quiz page 484
1. d 2. a 3. c 4. b 5. a 6. c

Test Yourself pages 488–489
1. a 2. c 3. c 4. a 5. a 6. b 7. b 8. d 9. a 10. d 11. c 12. b 13. b 14. b 15. d 16. c 17. a 18. d 19. b 20. d 21. d 22. c 23. b 24. c 25. d 26. b 27. d

CHAPTER 13

Practice Quiz pages 504–505
1. c 2. d 3. d 4. b 5. c 6. b 7. c 8. c

Practice Quiz page 510
1. b 2. c 3. a 4. d 5. a

Practice Quiz page 513
1. b 2. c 3. a 4. d

Practice Quiz page 523
1. c 2. d 3. c 4. b 5. d 6. d

Test Yourself pages 526–527
1. c 2. b 3. a 4. a 5. b 6. c 7. c 8. b 9. b 10. b 11. c 12. c 13. a 14. d 15. c 16. b 17. d 18. c 19. b 20. d 21. c 22. d 23. b 24. d 25. c 26. b 27. a 28. a

CHAPTER 14

Practice Quiz page 541
1. c 2. d 3. d 4. a 5. b

Practice Quiz pages 549–550
1. b 2. a 3. b 4. c 5. d 6. b 7. c 8. d

Practice Quiz page 556
1. c 2. b 3. b 4. d

Practice Quiz page 563
1. b 2. a 3. c 4. b

Test Yourself pages 568–569
1. d 2. c 3. a 4. b 5. d 6. a 7. c 8. b 9. d 10. b 11. b 12. a 13. d 14. d 15. a 16. d 17. a 18. c 19. a 20. a 21. b 22. d 23. b

CHAPTER 15

Practice Quiz page 581
1. b 2. d 3. a 4. a 5. a

Practice Quiz page 590
1. b 2. c 3. d 4. b 5. b 6. c 7. a

Practice Quiz page 602
1. b 2. a 3. d 4. d 5. b 6. c 7. c

Test Yourself pages 606–607
1. a 2. d 3. c 4. c 5. d 6. c 7. d 8. a 9. c 10. d 11. c 12. a 13. c 14. a 15. d 16. a 17. d 18. c 19. a 20. d 21. c 22. b 23. d

APPENDIX A

Test Yourself pages A-12–A-13
1. c 2. b 3. d 4. c 5. d 6. b 7. a 8. c 9. a 10. d 11. c 12. b 13. b 14. d.

APPENDIX B

Practice Quiz page B-9
1. c 2. a 3. d 4. c 5. b

Practice Quiz page B-12
1. b 2. c 3. d

Test Yourself page B-14
1. c 2. d 3. d 4. a 5. c 6. c 7. d 8. a 9. b 10. c

glossary

absolute threshold the lowest level of stimulation that a person can consciously detect 50 percent of the time the stimulation is present. 91

accommodation as a monocular cue, the brain's use of information about the changing thickness of the lens of the eye in response to looking at objects that are close or far away. 116

acculturative stress stress resulting from the need to change and adapt a person's ways to the majority culture. 434

acquired (secondary) drives those drives that are learned through experience or conditioning, such as the need for money or social approval. 345

acrophobia fear of heights. 543

action potential the release of the neural impulse consisting of a reversal of the electrical charge within the axon. 49

action therapy therapy in which the main goal is to change disordered or inappropriate behavior directly. 574

activation-information-mode model (AIM) revised version of the activation-synthesis explanation of dreams in which information that is accessed during waking hours can have an influence on the synthesis of dreams. 145

activation-synthesis hypothesis premise that states that dreams are created by the higher centers of the cortex to explain the activation by the brain stem of cortical cells during REM sleep periods. 145

activity theory theory of adjustment to aging that assumes older people are happier if they remain active in some way, such as volunteering or developing a hobby. 333

acute stress disorder (ASD) a disorder resulting from exposure to a major stressor, with symptoms of anxiety, dissociation, recurring nightmares, sleep disturbances, problems in concentration, and moments in which people seem to "relive" the event in dreams and flashbacks for as long as 1 month following the event. 544

adaptive theory theory of sleep proposing that animals and humans evolved sleep patterns to avoid predators by sleeping when predators are most active. 134

adolescence the period of life from about age 13 to the early 20s, during which a young person is no longer physically a child but is not yet an independent, self-supporting adult. 324

adrenal glands endocrine glands located on top of each kidney that secrete over 30 different hormones to deal with stress, regulate salt intake, and provide a secondary source of sex hormones affecting the sexual changes that occur during adolescence. 64

aerial (atmospheric) perspective the haziness that surrounds objects that are farther away from the viewer, causing the distance to be perceived as greater. 116

affect in psychology, a term indicating "emotion" or "mood." 546

afferent (sensory) neuron a neuron that carries information from the senses to the central nervous system. 57

afterimages images that occur when a visual sensation persists for a brief time even after the original stimulus is removed. 98

aggression actions meant to harm or destroy. 417

aggression behavior intended to hurt or destroy another person. 478

agonists chemical substances that mimic or enhance the effects of a neurotransmitter on the receptor sites of the next cell, increasing or decreasing the activity of that cell. 52

agoraphobia fear of being in a place or situation from which escape is difficult or impossible. 543

agreeableness the emotional style of a person that may range from easygoing, friendly, and likeable to grumpy, crabby, and unpleasant. 512

AIDS or **acquired immune deficiency syndrome** sexually transmitted viral disorder that causes deterioration of the immune system and eventually results in death due to complicating infections that the body can no longer fight. 400

alcohol the chemical resulting from fermentation or distillation of various kinds of vegetable matter. 155

algorithms very specific, step-by-step procedures for solving certain types of problems. 258

all-or-none referring to the fact that a neuron either fires completely or does not fire at all. 51

all-or-nothing thinking the tendency to believe that one's performance must be perfect or the result will be a total failure. 545

alpha waves brain waves that indicate a state of relaxation or light sleep. 136

altered state of consciousness state in which there is a shift in the quality or pattern of mental activity as compared to waking consciousness. 131

altruism prosocial behavior that is done with no expectation of reward and may involve the risk of harm to oneself. 481

amphetamines stimulants that are synthesized (made) in laboratories rather than being found in nature. 151

amygdala brain structure located near the hippocampus, responsible for fear responses and memory of fear. 72

anal stage second stage occurring from about 1 or 1½ years of age, in which the anus is the erogenous zone and toilet training is the source of conflict. 499

analytical intelligence the ability to break problems down into component parts, or analysis, for problem solving. 267

androgens male hormones. 380

androgyny characteristic of possessing the most positive personality characteristics of males and females regardless of actual sex. 387

andropause gradual changes in the sexual hormones and reproductive system of middle-aged males. 330

anorexia nervosa a condition in which a person reduces eating to the point that a weight loss of 15 percent below the ideal body weight or more occurs. 551

antagonists chemical substances that block or reduce a cell's response to the action of other chemicals or neurotransmitters. 52

anterograde amnesia loss of memory from the point of injury or trauma forward, or the inability to form new long-term memories. 224

antianxiety drugs drugs used to treat and calm anxiety reactions, typically minor tranquilizers. 597

antidepressant drugs drugs used to treat depression and anxiety. 597

antipsychotic drugs drugs used to treat psychotic symptoms such as delusions, hallucinations, and other bizarre behavior. 596

antisocial personality disorder disorder in which a person has no morals or conscience and often behaves in an impulsive manner without regard for the consequences of that behavior. 561

anxiety disorders disorders in which the main symptom is excessive or unrealistic anxiety and fearfulness. 541

applied behavior analysis (ABA) modern term for a form of functional analysis and behavior modification that uses a variety of behavioral techniques to mold a desired behavior or response. 195

approach–approach conflict conflict occurring when a person must choose between two desirable goals. 418

approach–avoidance conflict conflict occurring when a person must choose or not choose a goal that has both positive and negative aspects. 419

arbitrary inference distortion of thinking in which a person draws a conclusion that is not based on any evidence. 585

archetypes Jung's collective, universal human memories. 501

arousal theory theory of motivation in which people are said to have an optimal (best or ideal) level of tension that they seek to maintain by increasing or decreasing stimulation. 349

association areas areas within each lobe of the cortex responsible for the coordination and interpretation of information, as well as higher mental processing. 76

attachment the emotional bond between an infant and the primary caregiver. 319

attitude a tendency to respond positively or negatively toward a certain person, object, idea, or situation. 458

attribution the process of explaining one's own behavior and the behavior of others. 466

attribution theory the theory of how people make attributions. 466

auditory canal short tunnel that runs from the pinna to the eardrum. 102

auditory nerve bundle of axons from the hair cells in the inner ear. 102

authenticity the genuine, open, and honest response of the therapist to the client. 579

authoritarian parenting style of parenting in which parent is rigid and overly strict, showing little warmth to the child. 331

authoritative parenting style of parenting in which parents combine warmth and affection with firm limits on a child's behavior. 332

autobiographical memory the memory for events and facts related to one's personal life story. 244

automatic encoding tendency of certain kinds of information to enter long-term memory with little or no effortful encoding. 233

autonomic nervous system (ANS) division of the PNS consisting of nerves that control all of the involuntary muscles, organs, and glands. 59

availability heuristic estimating the frequency or likelihood of an event based on how easy it is to recall relevant information from memory or how easy it is for us to think of related examples. 259

aversion therapy form of behavioral therapy in which an undesirable behavior is paired with an aversive stimulus to reduce the frequency of the behavior. 582

avoidance–avoidance conflict conflict occurring when a person must choose between two undesirable goals. 419

axon tubelike structure that carries the neural message to other cells. 47

axon terminals branches at the end of the axon. 51

barbiturates depressant drugs that have a sedative effect. 154

basal metabolic rate (BMR) the rate at which the body burns energy when the organism is resting. 356

basic anxiety anxiety created when a child is born into the bigger and more powerful world of older children and adults. 502

basic level type an example of a type of concept around which other similar concepts are organized, such as "dog," "cat," or "pear." 256

behavior modification the use of operant conditioning techniques to bring about desired changes in behavior. 194

behavior modification or **applied behavior analysis** the use of learning techniques to modify or change undesirable behavior and increase desirable behavior. 582

behavior therapies action therapies based on the principles of classical and operant conditioning and aimed at changing disordered behavior without concern for the original causes of such behavior. 581

behavioral genetics field of study devoted to discovering the genetic bases for personality characteristics. 513

behaviorism the science of behavior that focuses on observable behavior only. 11

benevolent sexism acceptance of positive stereotypes of males and females that leads to unequal treatment. 387

benzodiazepines drugs that lower anxiety and reduce stress. 155

beta waves smaller and faster brain waves, typically indicating mental activity. 136

bilateral anterior cingulotomy psychosurgical technique in which an electrode wire is inserted into the anterior cingulate gyrus with the guidance of a magnetic resonance imaging machine for the purpose of destroying that area of brain tissue with an electric current. 600

binocular cues cues for perceiving depth based on both eyes. 115

binocular disparity the difference in images between the two eyes, which is greater for objects that are close and smaller for distant objects. 117

biofeedback using feedback about biological conditions to bring involuntary responses, such as blood pressure and relaxation, under voluntary control. 195

biological model model of explaining behavior as caused by biological changes in the chemical, structural, or genetic systems of the body. 536

biological preparedness referring to the tendency of animals to learn certain associations, such as taste and nausea, with only one or few pairings due to the survival value of the learning. 178

biological psychology or **behavioral neuroscience** branch of neuroscience that focuses on the biological bases of psychological processes, behavior, and learning. 47

biomedical therapies therapies that directly affect the biological functioning of the body and brain. 596

biomedical therapy therapy for mental disorders in which a person with a problem is treated with biological or medical methods to relieve symptoms. 574

biopsychological perspective perspective that attributes human and animal behavior to biological events occurring in the body, such as genetic influences, hormones, and the activity of the nervous system. 15

biopsychosocial model perspective in which abnormal behavior is seen as the result of the combined and interacting forces of biological, psychological, social, and cultural influences. 537

bipolar disorder severe mood swings between major depressive episodes and manic episodes. 547

bisexual person attracted to both men and women. 394

blind spot area in the retina where the axons of the three layers of retinal cells exit the eye to form the optic nerve, insensitive to light. 96

borderline personality disorder maladaptive personality pattern in which the person is moody, unstable, lacks a clear sense of identity, and often clings to others. 562

bottom-up processing the analysis of the smaller features to build up to a complete perception. 121

brightness constancy the tendency to perceive the apparent brightness of an object as the same even when the light conditions change. 112

Broca's aphasia condition resulting from damage to Broca's area, causing the affected person to be unable to speak fluently, to mispronounce words, and to speak haltingly. 77

bulimia nervosa a condition in which a person develops a cycle of "binging," or overeating enormous amounts of food at one sitting, and then using unhealthy methods to avoid weight gain. 551

burnout negative changes in thoughts, emotions, and behavior as a result of prolonged stress or frustration. 433

bystander effect referring to the effect that the presence of other people has on the decision to help or not help, with help becoming less likely as the number of bystanders increases. 482

caffeine a mild stimulant found in coffee, tea, and several other plant-based substances. 153

Cannon-Bard theory of emotion theory in which the physiological reaction and the emotion are assumed to occur at the same time. 365

case study study of one individual in great detail. 23

catastrophe an unpredictable, large-scale event that creates a tremendous need to adapt and adjust as well as overwhelming feelings of threat. 411

catatonic type of schizophrenia in which the person experiences periods of statue-like immobility mixed with occasional bursts of energetic, frantic movement, and talking. 558

central nervous system (CNS) part of the nervous system consisting of the brain and spinal cord. 57

central-route processing type of information processing that involves attending to the content of the message itself. 461

centration in Piaget's theory, the tendency of a young child to focus only on one feature of an object while ignoring other relevant features. 314

cerebellum part of the lower brain located behind the pons that controls and coordinates involuntary, rapid, fine motor movement. 70

cerebral hemispheres the two sections of the cortex on the left and right sides of the brain. 74

cerebrum the upper part of the brain consisting of the two hemispheres and the structures that connect them. 78

character value judgments of a person's moral and ethical behavior. 494

chromosome tightly wound strand of genetic material or DNA. 300

circadian rhythm a cycle of bodily rhythm that occurs over a 24-hour period. 132

classical conditioning learning to make an involuntary (reflex) response to a stimulus other than the original, natural stimulus that normally produces the reflex. 171

claustrophobia fear of being in a small, enclosed space. 542

closure the tendency to complete figures that are incomplete. 113

cocaine a natural drug derived from the leaves of the coca plant. 152

cochlea snail-shaped structure of the inner ear that is filled with fluid. 102

cognitive dissonance sense of discomfort or distress that occurs when a person's behavior does not correspond to that person's attitudes. 462

cognitive arousal theory theory of emotion in which both the physical arousal and the labeling of that arousal based on cues from the environment must occur before the emotion is experienced. 366

cognitive–behavioral therapy (CBT) action therapy in which the goal is to help clients overcome problems by learning to think more rationally and logically. 586

cognitive-mediational theory theory of emotion in which a stimulus must be interpreted (appraised) by a person in order to result in a physical response and an emotional reaction. 368

cognitive development the development of thinking, problem solving, and memory. 312

cognitive neuroscience study of the physical changes in the brain and nervous system during thinking. 15

cognitive perspective modern perspective that focuses on memory, intelligence, perception, problem solving, and learning. 14

cognitive perspective modern theory in which classical conditioning is seen to occur because the conditioned stimulus provides information or an expectancy about the coming of the unconditioned stimulus. 179

cognitive psychologists psychologists who study the way people think, remember, and mentally organize information. 537

cognitive therapy therapy in which the focus is on helping clients recognize distortions in their thinking and replace distorted, unrealistic beliefs with more realistic, helpful thoughts. 585

cognitive universalism theory that concepts are universal and influence the development of language. 287

collective unconscious Jung's name for the memories shared by all members of the human species. 501

College Undergraduate Stress Scale (CUSS) assessment that measures the amount of stress in a college student's life over a 1-year period resulting from major life events. 413

companionate love type of love consisting of intimacy and commitment. 477

compensation (substitution) defense mechanism in which a person makes up for inferiorities in one area by becoming superior in another area. 498

compliance changing one's behavior as a result of other people directing or asking for the change. 452

computed tomography (CT) brain-imaging method using computer-controlled X-rays of the brain. 67

concentrative meditation form of meditation in which a person focuses the mind on some repetitive or unchanging stimulus so that the mind can be cleared of disturbing thoughts and the body can experience relaxation. 437

concepts ideas that represent a class or category of objects, events, or activities. 255

concrete operations stage Piaget's third stage of cognitive development in which the school-age child becomes capable of logical thought processes but is not yet capable of abstract thinking. 314

conditional positive regard positive regard that is given only when the person is doing what the providers of positive regard wish. 508

conditioned emotional response (CER) emotional response that has become classically conditioned to occur to learned stimuli, such as a fear of dogs or the emotional reaction that occurs when seeing an attractive person. 177

conditioned response (CR) learned reflex response to a conditioned stimulus. 172

conditioned stimulus (CS) stimulus that becomes able to produce a learned reflex response by being paired with the original unconditioned stimulus. 172

conditioned taste aversion development of a nausea or aversive response to a particular taste because that taste was followed by a nausea reaction, occurring after only one association. 177

cones visual sensory receptors found at the back of the retina, responsible for color vision and sharpness of vision. 95

confirmation bias the tendency to search for evidence that fits one's beliefs while ignoring any evidence that does not fit those beliefs. 262

conformity changing one's own behavior to match that of other people. 449

conscience part of the superego that produces guilt, depending on how acceptable behavior is. 497

conscientiousness the care a person gives to organization and thoughtfulness of others; dependability. 512

consciousness a person's awareness of everything that is going on around him or her at any given moment, which is used to organize behavior. 130

conservation in Piaget's theory, the ability to understand that simply changing the appearance of an object does not change the object's nature. 314

consolidation the changes that take place in the structure and functioning of neurons when a memory is formed. 242

constructive processing referring to the retrieval of memories in which those memories are altered, revised, or influenced by newer information. 235

consumer psychology branch of psychology that studies the habits of consumers in the marketplace. 451

contiguity the tendency to perceive two things that happen close together in time as being related. 113

contingency contract a formal, written agreement between the therapist and client (or teacher and student) in which goals for behavioral change, reinforcements, and penalties are clearly stated. 584

continuity the tendency to perceive things as simply as possible with a continuous pattern rather than with a complex, broken-up pattern. 113

continuous reinforcement the reinforcement of each and every correct response. 184

control group subjects in an experiment who are not subjected to the independent variable and who may receive a placebo treatment. 29

conventional morality second level of Kohlberg's stages of moral development in which the child's behavior is governed by conforming to the society's norms of behavior. 326

convergence the rotation of the two eyes in their sockets to focus on a single object, resulting in greater convergence for closer objects and lesser convergence if objects are distant. 116

convergent thinking type of thinking in which a problem is seen as having only one answer, and all lines of thinking will eventually lead to that single answer, using previous knowledge and logic. 263

coping strategies actions that people can take to master, tolerate, reduce, or minimize the effects of stressors. 437

corpus callosum thick band of neurons that connects the right and left cerebral hemispheres. 74

correlation a measure of the relationship between two variables. 26

correlation coefficient a number derived from the formula for measuring a correlation and indicating the strength and direction of a correlation. 26

cortex outermost covering of the brain consisting of densely packed neurons, responsible for higher thought processes and interpretation of sensory input. 73

creative intelligence the ability to deal with new and different concepts and to come up with new ways of solving problems. 267

creativity the process of solving problems by combining ideas or behavior in new ways. 263

critical periods times during which certain environmental influences can have an impact on the development of the infant. 306

critical thinking making reasoned judgments about claims. 36

cross-sectional design research design in which several different participant age-groups are studied at one particular point in time. 298

cross-sequential design research design in which participants are first studied by means of a cross-sectional design but are also followed and assessed longitudinally. 298

cult any group of people with a particular religious or philosophical set of beliefs and identity. 484

cultural relativity the need to consider the unique characteristics of the culture in which behavior takes place. 534

culture-bound syndromes disorders found only in particular cultures. 534

curve of forgetting a graph showing a distinct pattern in which forgetting is very fast within the first hour after learning a list and then tapers off gradually. 239

cybertherapy psychotherapy that is offered on the Internet. Also called online, Internet, or Web therapy or counseling. 595

dark adaptation the recovery of the eye's sensitivity to visual stimuli in darkness after exposure to bright lights. 96

decay loss of memory due to the passage of time, during which the memory trace is not used. 240

declarative memory type of long-term memory containing information that is conscious and known. 225

deep lesioning insertion of a thin, insulated wire into the brain through which an electrical current is sent that destroys the brain cells at the tip of the wire. 65

delta waves long, slow waves that indicate the deepest stage of sleep. 137

delusional disorder a psychotic disorder in which the primary symptom is one or more delusions. 557

delusions false beliefs held by a person who refuses to accept evidence of their falseness. 557

dendrites branchlike structures that receive messages from other neurons. 47

denial psychological defense mechanism in which the person refuses to acknowledge or recognize a threatening situation. 498

dependent variable variable in an experiment that represents the measurable response or behavior of the subjects in the experiment. 29

depersonalization disorder dissociative disorder in which individuals feel detached and disconnected from themselves, their bodies, and their surroundings. 555

depressants drugs that decrease the functioning of the nervous system. 151

depth perception the ability to perceive the world in three dimensions. 114

deviation IQ scores a type of intelligence measure that assumes that IQ is normally distributed around a mean of 100 with a standard deviation of about 15. 271

diffusion process of molecules moving from areas of high concentration to areas of low concentration. 49

diffusion of responsibility occurring when a person fails to take responsibility for actions or for inaction because of the presence of other people who are seen to share the responsibility. 482

direct observation assessment in which the professional observes the client engaged in ordinary, day-to-day behavior in either a clinical or natural setting. 520

directive therapy in which the therapist actively gives interpretations of a client's statements and may suggest certain behavior or actions. 577

discrimination treating people differently because of prejudice toward the social group to which they belong. 174

discriminative stimulus any stimulus, such as a stop sign or a doorknob, that provides the organism with a cue for making a certain response in order to obtain reinforcement. 192

disorganized type of schizophrenia in which behavior is bizarre and childish, and thinking, speech, and motor actions are very disordered. 558

displaced aggression taking out one's frustrations on some less threatening or more available target. 418

displacement redirecting feelings from a threatening target to a less threatening one. 498

display rules learned ways of controlling displays of emotion in social settings. 363

dispositional cause cause of behavior attributed to internal factors such as personality or character. 466

dissociative amnesia loss of memory for personal information, either partial or complete. 553

dissociative disorders disorders in which there is a break in conscious awareness, memory, the sense of identity, or some combination. 553

dissociative fugue traveling away from familiar surroundings with amnesia for the trip and possible amnesia for personal information. 554

dissociative identity disorder disorder occurring when a person seems to have two or more distinct personalities within one body. 554

distress the effect of unpleasant and undesirable stressors. 411

distributed practice spacing the study of material to be remembered by including breaks between study periods. 239

disuse another name for decay, assuming that memories that are not used will eventually decay and disappear. 240

divergent thinking type of thinking in which a person starts from one point and comes up with many different ideas or possibilities based on that point. 263

dizygotic twins often called fraternal twins, occurring when two individual eggs get fertilized by separate sperm, resulting in two zygotes in the uterus at the same time. 304

DNA (deoxyribonucleic acid) special molecule that contains the genetic material of the organism. 300

dominant referring to a gene that actively controls the expression of a trait. 301

door-in-the-face technique asking for a large commitment and being refused and then asking for a smaller commitment. 452

double approach–avoidance conflict conflict in which the person must decide between two goals, with each goal possessing both positive and negative aspects. 419

double-blind study study in which neither the experimenter nor the subjects know if the subjects are in the experimental or control group. 31

drive a psychological tension and physical arousal arising when there is a need that motivates the organism to act in order to fulfill the need and reduce the tension. 345

drive-reduction theory approach to motivation that assumes behavior arises from physiological needs that cause internal drives to push the organism to satisfy the need and reduce tension and arousal. 345

echoic memory the brief memory of something a person has just heard. 219

eclectic approach to therapy that results from combining elements of several different approaches or techniques. 578

efferent (motor) neuron a neuron that carries messages from the central nervous system to the muscles of the body. 57

ego part of the personality that develops out of a need to deal with reality, mostly conscious, rational, and logical. 497

ego integrity sense of wholeness that comes from having lived a full life possessing the ability to let go of regrets; the final completion of the ego. 333

egocentrism the inability to see the world through anyone else's eyes. 314

eidetic imagery the ability to access a visual memory for 30 seconds or more. 218

elaboration likelihood model model of persuasion stating that people will either elaborate on the persuasive message or fail to elaborate on it and that the future actions of those who do elaborate are more predictable than those who do not. 461

elaborative rehearsal a method of transferring information from STM into LTM by making that information meaningful in some way. 223

electroconvulsive therapy (ECT) form of biomedical therapy to treat severe depression in which electrodes are placed on either one or both sides of a person's head and an electric current is passed through the electrodes that is strong enough to cause a seizure or convulsion. 599

electroencephalogram (EEG) a recording of the electrical activity of large groups of cortical neurons just below the skull, most often using scalp electrodes. 67

electroencephalograph machine designed to record the electroencephalogram (EEG). 67

embryo name for the developing organism from 2 weeks to 8 weeks after fertilization. 305

embryonic period the period from 2 to 8 weeks after fertilization, during which the major organs and structures of the organism develop. 305

emotion the "feeling" aspect of consciousness, characterized by a certain physical arousal, a certain behavior that reveals the emotion to the outside world, and an inner awareness of feelings. 360

emotion-focused coping coping strategies that change the impact of a stressor by changing the emotional reaction to the stressor. 437

emotional intelligence the awareness of and ability to manage one's own emotions as well as the ability to be self-motivated, able to feel what others feel, and socially skilled. 280

empathy the ability of the therapist to understand the feelings of the client. 579

encoding the set of mental operations that people perform on sensory information to convert that information into a form that is usable in the brain's storage systems. 214

encoding failure failure to process information into memory. 240

encoding specificity the tendency for memory of information to be improved if related information (such as surroundings or physiological state) that is available when the memory is first formed is also available when the memory is being retrieved. 229

endocrine glands glands that secrete chemicals called hormones directly into the bloodstream. 62

enzymatic degradation process by which structure of neurotransmitter is altered so it can no longer act on a receptor. 54

episodic memory type of declarative memory containing personal information not readily available to others, such as daily activities and events. 225

equal status contact contact between groups in which the groups have equal status with neither group having power over the other. 472

escape or **withdrawal** leaving the presence of a stressor, either literally or by a psychological withdrawal into fantasy, drug abuse, or apathy. 418

estrogens female hormones. 380

eustress the effect of positive events, or the optimal amount of stress that people need to promote health and well-being. 411

evolutionary perspective perspective that focuses on the biological bases of universal mental characteristics that all humans share. 16

excitatory synapse synapse at which a neurotransmitter causes the receiving cell to fire. 52

expectancy a person's subjective feeling that a particular behavior will lead to a reinforcing consequence. 507

expectancy-value theories incentive theories that assume the actions of humans cannot be predicted or fully understood without understanding the beliefs, values, and the importance that a person attaches to those beliefs and values at any given moment in time. 351

experiment a deliberate manipulation of a variable to see if corresponding changes in behavior result, allowing the determination of cause-and-effect relationships. 28

experimental group subjects in an experiment who are subjected to the independent variable. 29

experimenter effect tendency of the experimenter's expectations for a study to unintentionally influence the results of the study. 30

explicit memory memory that is consciously known, such as declarative memory. 226

exposure therapies behavioral techniques that expose individuals to anxiety- or fear-related stimuli, under carefully controlled conditions, to promote new learning. 583

extinction the disappearance or weakening of a learned response following the removal or absence of the unconditioned stimulus (in classical conditioning) or the removal of a reinforcer (in operant conditioning). 174

extinction the removal of a reinforcer to reduce the frequency of a behavior. 584

extraversion dimension of personality referring to one's need to be with other people. 512

extraverts people who are outgoing and sociable. 512

extrinsic motivation type of motivation in which a person performs an action because it leads to an outcome that is separate from or external to the person. 344

facial feedback hypothesis theory of emotion that assumes that facial expressions provide feedback to the brain concerning the emotion being expressed, which in turn causes and intensifies the emotion. 367

false positive error of recognition in which people think that they recognize some stimulus that is not actually in memory. 232

family counseling (family therapy) a form of group therapy in which family members meet together with a counselor or therapist to resolve problems that affect the entire family. 588

fertilization the union of the ovum and sperm. 304

fetal period the time from about 8 weeks after conception until the birth of the baby. 307

fetus name for the developing organism from 8 weeks after fertilization to the birth of the baby. 307

figure–ground the tendency to perceive objects, or figures, as existing on a background. 113

five-factor model (Big Five) model of personality traits that describes five basic trait dimensions. 511

fixation disorder in which the person does not fully resolve the conflict in a particular psychosexual stage, resulting in personality traits and behavior associated with that earlier stage. 498

fixed interval schedule of reinforcement schedule of reinforcement in which the interval of time that must pass before reinforcement becomes possible is always the same. 184

fixed ratio schedule of reinforcement schedule of reinforcement in which the number of responses required for reinforcement is always the same. 186

flashbulb memories type of automatic encoding that occurs because an unexpected event has strong emotional associations for the person remembering it. 233

flat affect a lack of emotional responsiveness. 557

flooding technique for treating phobias and other stress disorders in which the person is rapidly and intensely exposed to the fear-provoking situation or object and prevented from making the usual avoidance or escape response. 583

foot-in-the-door technique asking for a small commitment and, after gaining compliance, asking for a bigger commitment. 452

formal concepts concepts that are defined by specific rules or features. 256

formal operations stage Piaget's last stage of cognitive development, in which the adolescent becomes capable of abstract thinking. 314

free association psychoanalytic technique in which a patient was encouraged to talk about anything that came to mind without fear of negative evaluations. 577

free-floating anxiety anxiety that is unrelated to any realistic, known source. 541

frequency count assessment in which the frequency of a particular behavior is counted. 520

frequency theory theory of pitch that states that pitch is related to the speed of vibrations in the basilar membrane. 103

frontal lobes areas of the cortex located in the front and top of the brain, responsible for higher mental processes and decision making as well as the production of fluent speech. 76

frustration the psychological experience produced by the blocking of a desired goal or fulfillment of a perceived need. 417

fully functioning person a person who is in touch with and trusting of the deepest, innermost urges and feelings. 509

functional fixedness a block to problem solving that comes from thinking about objects in terms of only their typical functions. 262

functional magnetic resonance imaging (fMRI) MRI-based brain-imaging method that allows for functional examination of brain areas through changes in brain oxygenation. 69

functionalism early perspective in psychology associated with William James, in which the focus of study is how the mind allows people to adapt, live, work, and play. 8

fundamental attribution error the tendency to overestimate the influence of internal factors in determining behavior while underestimating situational factors. 467

g factor the ability to reason and solve problems, or general intelligence. 266

gender the behavior associated with being male or female. 322

gender the psychological aspects of being male or female. 380

gender identity perception of one's gender and the behavior that is associated with that gender. 323

gender identity the individual's sense of being male or female. 380

gender roles the culture's expectations for masculine or feminine behavior, including attitudes, actions, and personality traits associated with being male or female in that culture. 380

gender schema theory theory of gender identity acquisition in which a child develops a mental pattern, or schema, for being male or female and then organizes observed and learned behavior around that schema. 385

gender stereotype a concept held about a person or group of people that is based on being male or female. 387

gender typing the process of acquiring gender-role characteristics. 380

gene section of DNA having the same arrangement of chemical elements. 300

general adaptation syndrome (GAS) the three stages of the body's physiological reaction to stress, including alarm, resistance, and exhaustion. 421

generalized anxiety disorder disorder in which a person has feelings of dread and impending doom along with physical symptoms of stress, which lasts 6 months or more. 544

generativity providing guidance to one's children or the next generation, or contributing to the well-being of the next generation through career or volunteer work. 331

genetics the science of inherited traits. 300

germinal period first 2 weeks after fertilization, during which the zygote moves down to the uterus and begins to implant in the lining. 305

Gestalt psychology early perspective in psychology focusing on perception and sensation, particularly the perception of patterns and whole figures. 10

Gestalt therapy form of directive insight therapy in which the therapist helps clients to accept all parts of their feelings and subjective experiences, using leading questions and planned experiences such as role-playing. 579

gifted the 2 percent of the population falling on the upper end of the normal curve and typically possessing an IQ of 130 or above. 277

glial cells cells that provide support for the neurons to grow on and around, deliver nutrients to neurons, produce myelin to coat axons, clean up waste products and dead neurons, influence information processing, and, during prenatal development, influence the generation of new neurons. 48

glucagon hormone that is secreted by the pancreas to control the levels of fats, proteins, and carbohydrates in the body by increasing the level of glucose in the bloodstream. 355

gonads sex glands; secrete hormones that regulate sexual development and behavior as well as reproduction. 64

grammar the system of rules governing the structure and use of a language. 285

group polarization the tendency for members involved in a group discussion to take somewhat more extreme positions and suggest riskier actions when compared to individuals who have not participated in a group discussion. 456

groupthink kind of thinking that occurs when people place more importance on maintaining group cohesiveness than on assessing the facts of the problem with which the group is concerned. 450

gustation the sensation of a taste. 105

habits in behaviorism, sets of well-learned responses that have become automatic. 505

habituation tendency of the brain to stop attending to constant, unchanging information. 92

hallucinations false sensory perceptions, such as hearing voices that do not really exist. 557

hallucinogenics drugs including hallucinogens and marijuana that produce hallucinations or increased feelings of relaxation and intoxication. 151

hallucinogens drugs that cause false sensory messages, altering the perception of reality. 158

halo effect tendency of an interviewer to allow positive characteristics of a client to influence the assessments of the client's behavior and statements. 518

hardy personality a person who seems to thrive on stress but lacks the anger and hostility of the Type A personality. 429

hassles the daily annoyances of everyday life. 415

health psychology area of psychology focusing on how physical activities, psychological traits, and social relationships affect overall health and rate of illnesses. 425

hermaphroditism the condition of possessing both male and female sexual organs. 380

heroin narcotic drug derived from opium that is extremely addictive. 157

hertz (Hz) cycles or waves per second, a measurement of frequency. 101

heterosexual person attracted to the opposite sex. 394

heuristic an educated guess based on prior experiences that helps narrow down the possible solutions for a problem. Also known as a "rule of thumb." 259

higher-order conditioning occurs when a strong conditioned stimulus is paired with a neutral stimulus, causing the neutral stimulus to become a second conditioned stimulus. 175

hindsight bias the tendency to falsely believe, through revision of older memories to include newer information, that one could have correctly predicted the outcome of an event. 236

hippocampus curved structure located within each temporal lobe, responsible for the formation of long-term memories and the storage of memory for location of objects. 72

homeostasis the tendency of the body to maintain a steady state. 345

homosexual person attracted to the same sex. 394

hormones chemicals released into the bloodstream by endocrine glands. 62

human development the scientific study of the changes that occur in people as they age from conception until death. 298

humanistic perspective the "third force" in psychology that focuses on those aspects of personality that make people uniquely human, such as subjective feelings and freedom of choice. 507

hypnosis state of consciousness in which the person is especially susceptible to suggestion. 147

hypothalamus small structure in the brain located below the thalamus and directly above the pituitary gland, responsible for motivational behavior such as sleep, hunger, thirst, and sex. 72

hypothesis tentative explanation of a phenomenon based on observations. 20

iconic memory visual sensory memory, lasting only a fraction of a second. 218

id part of the personality present at birth and completely unconscious. 496

ideal self one's perception of whom one should be or would like to be. 508

identification defense mechanism in which a person tries to become like someone else to deal with anxiety. 498

identity versus role confusion stage of personality development in which the adolescent must find a consistent sense of self. 323

imaginary audience type of thought common to adolescents in which young people believe that other people are just as concerned about the adolescent's thoughts and characteristics as they themselves are. 326

immune system the system of cells, organs, and chemicals of the body that responds to attacks from diseases, infections, and injuries. 422

implicit memory memory that is not easily brought into conscious awareness, such as procedural memory. 225

implicit personality theory sets of assumptions about how different types of people, personality traits, and actions are related to each other. 225

impression formation the forming of the first knowledge that a person has concerning another person. 464

in-groups social groups with whom a person identifies; "us." 469

incentive approaches theories of motivation in which behavior is explained as a response to the external stimulus and its rewarding properties. 351

incentives things that attract or lure people into action. 351

independent variable variable in an experiment that is manipulated by the experimenter. 29

infantile amnesia the inability to retrieve memories from much before age 3. 244

information-processing model model of memory that assumes the processing of information for memory storage is similar to the way a computer processes memory in a series of three stages. 215

inhibitory synapse synapse at which a neurotransmitter causes the receiving cell to stop firing. 52

insight the sudden perception of relationships among various parts of a problem, allowing the solution to the problem to come quickly. 199

insight therapies therapies in which the main goal is helping people to gain insight with respect to their behavior, thoughts, and feelings. 574

insomnia the inability to get to sleep, stay asleep, or get a good quality of sleep. 141

instinct approach the approach to motivation that assumes people are governed by instincts similar to those of animals. 345

instinctive drift tendency for an animal's behavior to revert to genetically controlled patterns. 194

instincts the biologically determined and innate patterns of behavior that exist in both people and animals. 345

insulin a hormone secreted by the pancreas to control the levels of fats, proteins, and carbohydrates in the body by reducing the level of glucose in the bloodstream. 355

intellectual disability condition in which a person's behavioral and cognitive skills exist at an earlier developmental stage than the skills of others who are the same chronological age; may also be referred to as developmentally delayed. This condition was formerly known as mental retardation. 276

intelligence the ability to learn from one's experiences, acquire knowledge, and use resources effectively in adapting to new situations or solving problems. 265

intelligence quotient (IQ) a number representing a measure of intelligence, resulting from the division of one's mental age by one's chronological age and then multiplying that quotient by 100. 268

interneuron a neuron found in the center of the spinal cord that receives information from the afferent neurons and sends commands to the muscles through the efferent neurons. Interneurons also make up the bulk of the neurons in the brain. 57

interpersonal attraction liking or having the desire for a relationship with another person. 474

interpersonal therapy (IPT) form of therapy for depression which incorporates multiple approaches and focuses on interpersonal problems. 577

intersexed, intersexual modern term for a hermaphrodite, a person who possesses ambiguous sexual organs, making it difficult to determine actual sex from a visual inspection at birth. 380

interview method of personality assessment in which the professional asks questions of the client and allows the client to answer, either in a structured or unstructured fashion. 518

intimacy an emotional and psychological closeness that is based on the ability to trust, share, and care, while still maintaining a sense of self. 331

intrinsic motivation type of motivation in which a person performs an action because the act itself is rewarding or satisfying in some internal manner. 344

introversion dimension of personality in which people tend to withdraw from excessive stimulation. 511

introverts people who prefer solitude and dislike being the center of attention. 512

irreversibility in Piaget's theory, the inability of the young child to mentally reverse an action. 314

James-Lange theory of emotion theory in which a physiological reaction leads to the labeling of an emotion. 365

"jigsaw classroom" educational technique in which each individual is given only part of the information needed to solve a problem, causing the separate individuals to be forced to work together to find the solution. 473

just noticeable difference (jnd or the **difference threshold)** the smallest difference between two stimuli that is detectable 50 percent of the time. 90

kinesthetic sense sense of the location of body parts in relation to the ground and each other. 108

language a system for combining symbols (such as words) so that an unlimited number of meaningful statements can be made for the purpose of communicating with others. 285

latency fourth stage occurring during the school years, in which the sexual feelings of the child are repressed while the child develops in other ways. 500

latent content the symbolic or hidden meaning of dreams. 576

latent learning learning that remains hidden until its application becomes useful. 198

law of effect law stating that if an action is followed by a pleasurable consequence, it will tend to be repeated, and if followed by an unpleasant consequence, it will tend not to be repeated. 181

learned helplessness the tendency to fail to act to escape from a situation because of a history of repeated failures in the past. 199

learning/performance distinction referring to the observation that learning can take place without actual performance of the learned behavior. 202

leptin a hormone that, when released into the bloodstream, signals the hypothalamus that the body has had enough food and reduces the appetite while increasing the feeling of being full. 358

levels-of-processing model model of memory that assumes information that is more "deeply processed," or processed according to its meaning rather than just the sound or physical characteristics of the word or words, will be remembered more efficiently and for a longer period of time. 215

light adaptation the recovery of the eye's sensitivity to visual stimuli in light after exposure to darkness. 97

limbic system a group of several brain structures located under the cortex and involved in learning, emotion, memory, and motivation. 71

linear perspective the tendency for parallel lines to appear to converge on each other. 115

linguistic relativity hypothesis the theory that thought processes and concepts are controlled by language. 287

locus of control the tendency for people to assume that they either have control or do not have control over events and consequences in their lives. 507

longitudinal design research design in which one participant or group of participants is studied over a long period of time. 298

long-term memory (LTM) the system of memory into which all the information is placed to be kept more or less permanently. 222

lowball technique getting a commitment from a person and then raising the cost of that commitment. 452

LSD (lysergic acid diethylamide) powerful synthetic hallucinogen. 158

magnetic resonance imaging (MRI) brain-imaging method using radio waves and magnetic fields of the body to produce detailed images of the brain. 67

magnification the tendency to interpret situations as far more dangerous, harmful, or important than they actually are. 545

magnification and minimization distortions of thinking in which a person blows a negative event out of proportion to its importance (magnification) while ignoring relevant positive events (minimization). 585

maintenance rehearsal practice of saying some information to be remembered over and over in one's head in order to maintain it in short-term memory. 222

major depression severe depression that comes on suddenly and seems to have no external cause, or is too severe for current circumstances. 546

maladaptive anything that does not allow a person to function within or adapt to the stresses and everyday demands of life. 534

mammary glands glands within the breast tissue that produce milk when a woman gives birth to an infant. 378

manic having the quality of excessive excitement, energy, and elation or irritability. 547

manifest content the actual content of one's dream. 576

marijuana mild hallucinogen (also known as "pot" or "weed") derived from the leaves and flowers of a particular type of hemp plant. 159

MDMA (Ecstasy or **X)** designer drug that can have both stimulant and hallucinatory effects. 159

means–end analysis heuristic in which the difference between the starting situation and the goal is determined and then steps are taken to reduce that difference. 260

meditation mental series of exercises meant to refocus attention and achieve a trancelike state of consciousness. 437

medulla the first large swelling at the top of the spinal cord, forming the lowest part of the brain, which is responsible for life-sustaining functions such as breathing, swallowing, and heart rate. 69

memory an active system that receives information from the senses, puts that information into a usable form, and organizes it as it stores it away, and then retrieves the information from storage. 214

memory trace physical change in the brain that occurs when a memory is formed. 240

menopause the cessation of ovulation and menstrual cycles and the end of a woman's reproductive capability. 329

menstrual cycle monthly shedding of the blood and tissue that line the uterus in preparation for pregnancy when conception does not occur. 378

mental images mental representations that stand for objects or events and have a picturelike quality. 254

mental set the tendency for people to persist in using problem-solving patterns that have worked for them in the past. 262

mescaline natural hallucinogen derived from the peyote cactus buttons. 159

microsleeps brief sidesteps into sleep lasting only a few seconds. 133

minimization the tendency to give little or no importance to one's successes or positive events and traits. 545

mirror neurons neurons that fire when an animal or person performs an action and also when an animal or person observes that same action being performed by another. 76

misinformation effect the tendency of misleading information presented after an event to alter the memories of the event itself. 236

modeling learning through the observation and imitation of others. 583

monocular cues (pictorial depth cues) cues for perceiving depth based on one eye only. 115

monozygotic twins identical twins formed when one zygote splits into two separate masses of cells, each of which develops into a separate embryo. 304

mood disorders disorders in which mood is severely disturbed. 546

morphemes the smallest units of meaning within a language. 285

morphine narcotic drug derived from opium, used to treat severe pain. 157

motion parallax the perception of motion of objects in which close objects appear to move more quickly than objects that are farther away. 116

motivation the process by which activities are started, directed, and continued so that physical or psychological needs or wants are met. 344

motor cortex section of the frontal lobe located at the back, responsible for sending motor commands to the muscles of the somatic nervous system. 76

motor pathway nerves coming from the CNS to the voluntary muscles, consisting of efferent neurons. 59

multiple approach–avoidance conflict conflict in which the person must decide between more than two goals, with each goal possessing both positive and negative aspects. 419

myelin fatty substances produced by certain glial cells that coat the axons of neurons to insulate, protect, and speed up the neural impulse. 48

Müller-Lyer illusion illusion of line length that is distorted by inward-turning or outward-turning corners on the ends of the lines, causing lines of equal length to appear to be different. 118

narcolepsy sleep disorder in which a person falls immediately into REM sleep during the day without warning. 142

narcotics a class of opium-related drugs that suppress the sensation of pain by binding to and stimulating the nervous system's natural receptor sites for endorphins. 151

natural concepts concepts people form as a result of their experiences in the real world. 256

natural killer (KT) cell immune system cell responsible for suppressing viruses and destroying tumor cells. 424

nature the influence of our inherited characteristics on our personality, physical growth, intellectual growth, and social interactions. 299

need a requirement of some material (such as food or water) that is essential for survival of the organism. 345

need for achievement (nAch) a need that involves a strong desire to succeed in attaining goals, not only realistic ones but also challenging ones. 346

need for affiliation (nAff) the need for friendly social interactions and relationships with others. 347

need for power (nPow) the need to have control or influence over others. 347

negative reinforcement the reinforcement of a response by the removal, escape from, or avoidance of an unpleasant stimulus. 183

negative symptoms symptoms of schizophrenia that are less than normal behavior or an absence of normal behavior; poor attention, flat affect, and poor speech production. 558

neo-Freudians followers of Freud who developed their own competing psychodynamic theories. 501

nerves bundles of axons coated in myelin that travel together through the body. 48

nervous system an extensive network of specialized cells that carries information to and from all parts of the body. 46

neurofeedback form of biofeedback using brain-scanning devices to provide feedback about brain activity in an effort to modify behavior. 196

neuron the basic cell that makes up the nervous system and that receives and sends messages within that system. 47

neuroplasticity the ability within the brain to constantly change both the structure and function of many cells in response to experience or trauma. 58

neuroscience a branch of the life sciences that deals with the structure and function of neurons, nerves, and nervous tissue. 15

neurotic personalities personalities typified by maladaptive ways of dealing with relationships in Horney's theory. 502

neuroticism degree of emotional instability or stability. 512

neurotransmitter chemical found in the synaptic vesicles that, when released, has an effect on the next cell. 52

neutral stimulus (NS) stimulus that has no effect on the desired response. 171

nicotine the active ingredient in tobacco. 153

night terrors relatively rare disorder in which the person experiences extreme fear and screams or runs around during deep sleep without waking fully. 140

nightmares bad dreams occurring during REM sleep. 139

non-REM (NREM) sleep any of the stages of sleep that do not include REM. 134

nondirective therapy style in which the therapist remains relatively neutral and does not interpret or take direct actions with regard to the client, instead remaining a calm, nonjudgmental listener while the client talks. 578

norm of reciprocity assumption that if someone does something for a person, that person should do something for the other in return. 452

nurture the influence of the environment on personality, physical growth, intellectual growth, and social interactions. 299

obedience changing one's behavior at the command of an authority figure. 453

object permanence the knowledge that an object exists even when it is not in sight. 313

objective introspection the process of examining and measuring one's own thoughts and mental activities. 6

observational learning learning new behavior by watching a model perform that behavior. 201

observer bias tendency of observers to see what they expect to see. 23

observer effect tendency of people or animals to behave differently from normal when they know they are being observed. 22

obsessive-compulsive disorder disorder in which intruding, recurring thoughts or obsessions create anxiety that is relieved by performing a repetitive, ritualistic behavior or mental act (compulsion). 543

occipital lobe section of the brain located at the rear and bottom of each cerebral hemisphere containing the visual centers of the brain. 74

Oedipus complex/Electra complex situation occurring in the phallic stage in which a child develops a sexual attraction to the opposite-sex parent and jealousy of the same-sex parent. Males develop an Oedipus complex whereas females develop an Electra complex. 499

olfaction (olfactory sense) the sensation of smell. 107

olfactory bulbs two bulb-like projections just under the front of the brain that receive information from the receptors in the nose. 72

olfactory bulbs areas of the brain located just above the sinus cavity and just below the frontal lobes that receive information from the olfactory receptor cells. 108

openness one of the five factors; willingness to try new things and be open to new experiences. 512

operant any behavior that is voluntary. 181

operant conditioning the learning of voluntary behavior through the effects of pleasant and unpleasant consequences to responses. 180

operational definition definition of a variable of interest that allows it to be directly measured. 28

opium substance derived from the opium poppy from which all narcotic drugs are derived. 157

opponent-process theory theory of color vision that proposes visual neurons (or groups of neurons) are stimulated by light of one color and inhibited by light of another color. 98

optimists people who expect positive outcomes. 430

oral stage first stage occurring in the first year to year and a half of life in which the mouth is the erogenous zone and weaning is the primary conflict. 498

organic or **stress-induced dysfunction** sexual problem caused by physical disorder or psychological stress. 399

orgasm a series of rhythmic contractions of the muscles of the vaginal walls or the penis, also the third and shortest phase of sexual response. 389

out-groups social groups with whom a person does not identify; "them." 469

ovaries the female gonads. 64

ovaries the female sexual glands. 378

overgeneralization the tendency to interpret a single negative event as a never-ending pattern of defeat and failure. 545

overgeneralization distortion of thinking in which a person draws sweeping conclusions based on only one incident or event and applies those conclusions to events that are unrelated to the original. 585

overlap (interposition) the assumption that an object that appears to be blocking part of another object is in front of the second object and closer to the viewer. 116

ovum the female sex cell, or egg. 304

pancreas endocrine gland; controls the levels of sugar in the blood. 63

panic attack sudden onset of intense panic in which multiple physical symptoms of stress occur, often with feelings that one is dying. 543

panic disorder disorder in which panic attacks occur frequently enough to cause the person difficulty in adjusting to daily life. 543

panic disorder with agoraphobia fear of leaving one's familiar surroundings because one might have a panic attack in public. 543

parallel distributed processing (PDP) model a model of memory in which memory processes are proposed to take place at the same time over a large network of neural connections. 215

paranoid type of schizophrenia in which the person suffers from delusions of persecution, grandeur, and jealousy, together with hallucinations. 558

paraphilia a sexual disorder in which the person's preferred method of sexual arousal and fulfillment is through sexual behavior that is unusual or socially unacceptable. 399

parasympathetic division part of the ANS that restores the body to normal functioning after arousal and is responsible for the day-to-day functioning of the organs and glands. 60

parietal lobes sections of the brain located at the top and back of each cerebral hemisphere containing the centers for touch, taste, and temperature sensations. 75

partial reinforcement effect the tendency for a response that is reinforced after some, but not all, correct responses to be very resistant to extinction. 184

participant modeling technique in which a model demonstrates the desired behavior in a step-by-step, gradual process while the client is encouraged to imitate the model. 584

participant observation a naturalistic observation in which the observer becomes a participant in the group being observed. 23

PCP synthesized drug now used as an animal tranquilizer that can cause stimulant, depressant, narcotic, or hallucinogenic effects. 158

peak experiences according to Maslow, times in a person's life during which self-actualization is temporarily achieved. 352

penis the organ through which males urinate and which delivers the male sex cells or sperm. 378

perception the method by which the sensations experienced at any given moment are interpreted and organized in some meaningful fashion. 112

perceptual set (perceptual expectancy) the tendency to perceive things a certain way because previous experiences or expectations influence those perceptions. 120

peripheral nervous system (PNS) all nerves and neurons that are not contained in the brain and spinal cord but that run through the body itself. 59

peripheral-route processing type of information processing that involves attending to factors not involved in the message, such as the appearance of the source of the message, the length of the message, and other noncontent factors. 461

permissive indulgent permissive parenting in which parents are so involved that children are allowed to behave without set limits. 332

permissive neglectful permissive parenting in which parents are uninvolved with child or child's behavior. 332

permissive parenting style of parenting in which parent makes few, if any demands on a child's behavior. 332

person-centered therapy a nondirective insight therapy based on the work of Carl Rogers in which the client does all the talking and the therapist listens. 578

personal fable type of thought common to adolescents in which young people believe themselves to be unique and protected from harm. 326

personal unconscious Jung's name for the unconscious mind as described by Freud. 501

personality the unique and relatively stable ways in which people think, feel, and behave. 428

personality disorders disorders in which a person adopts a persistent, rigid, and maladaptive pattern of behavior that interferes with normal social interactions. 560

personality inventory paper and pencil or computerized test that consists of statements that require a specific, standardized response from the person taking the test. 520

personalization distortion of thinking in which a person takes responsibility or blame for events that are unconnected to the person. 586

persuasion the process by which one person tries to change the belief, opinion, position, or course of action of another person through argument, pleading, or explanation. 461

pessimists people who expect negative outcomes. 430

phallic stage third stage occurring from about 3 to 6 years of age, in which the child discovers sexual feelings. 499

phobia an irrational, persistent fear of an object, situation, or social activity. 541

phonemes the basic units of sound in language. 285

physical dependence condition occurring when a person's body becomes unable to function normally without a particular drug. 150

pineal gland endocrine gland located near the base of the cerebrum; secretes melatonin. 63

pinna the visible part of the ear. 102

pitch psychological experience of sound that corresponds to the frequency of the sound waves; higher frequencies are perceived as higher pitches. 103

pituitary gland gland located in the brain that secretes human growth hormone and influences all other hormone-secreting glands (also known as the master gland). 63

place theory theory of pitch that states that different pitches are experienced by the stimulation of hair cells in different locations on the organ of Corti. 103

placebo effect the phenomenon in which the expectations of the participants in a study can influence their behavior. 30

pleasure principle principle by which the id functions; the immediate satisfaction of needs without regard for the consequences. 496

pons the larger swelling above the medulla that connects the top of the brain to the bottom and that plays a part in sleep, dreaming, left–right body coordination, and arousal. 70

population the entire group of people or animals in which the researcher is interested. 24

positive regard warmth, affection, love, and respect that come from significant others in one's life. 508

positive reinforcement the reinforcement of a response by the addition or experiencing of a pleasurable stimulus. 182

positive symptoms symptoms of schizophrenia that are excesses of behavior or occur in addition to normal behavior; hallucinations, delusions, and distorted thinking. 558

positron emission tomography (PET) brain-imaging method in which a radioactive sugar is injected into the subject and a computer compiles a color-coded image of the activity of the brain. 68

postconventional morality third level of Kohlberg's stages of moral development in which the person's behavior is governed by moral principles that have been decided on by the individual and that may be in disagreement with accepted social norms. 327

posttraumatic stress disorder (PTSD) a disorder resulting from exposure to a major stressor, with symptoms of anxiety, dissociation, nightmares, poor sleep, reliving the event, and concentration problems, lasting for more than 1 month. 544

practical intelligence the ability to use information to get along in life and become successful. 267

pragmatics aspects of language involving the practical ways of communicating with others, or the social "niceties" of language. 286

preconventional morality first level of Kohlberg's stages of moral development in which the child's behavior is governed by the consequences of the behavior. 326

prefrontal lobotomy psychosurgery in which the connections of the prefrontal lobes of the brain to the rear portions are severed. 600

prejudice negative attitude held by a person about the members of a particular social group. 469

preoperational stage Piaget's second stage of cognitive development in which the preschool child learns to use language as a means of exploring the world. 313

pressure the psychological experience produced by urgent demands or expectations for a person's behavior that come from an outside source. 416

primacy effect tendency to remember information at the beginning of a body of information better than the information that follows. 231

primary appraisal the first step in assessing stress, which involves estimating the severity of a stressor and classifying it as either a threat or a challenge. 426

primary drives those drives that involve needs of the body such as hunger and thirst. 345

primary reinforcer any reinforcer that is naturally reinforcing by meeting a basic biological need, such as hunger, thirst, or touch. 182

primary sex characteristics sexual organs present at birth and directly involved in human reproduction. 378

proactive interference memory problem that occurs when older information prevents or interferes with the learning or retrieval of newer information. 241

problem solving process of cognition that occurs when a goal must be reached by thinking and behaving in certain ways. 258

problem-focused coping coping strategies that try to eliminate the source of a stress or reduce its impact through direct actions. 437

procedural (nondeclarative) memory type of long-term memory including memory for skills, procedures, habits, and conditioned responses. These memories are not conscious but are implied to exist because they affect conscious behavior. 224

projection psychological defense mechanism in which unacceptable or threatening impulses or feelings are seen as originating with someone else, usually the target of the impulses or feelings. 498

projection defense mechanism involving placing, or "projecting," one's own unacceptable thoughts onto others, as if the thoughts actually belonged to those others and not to oneself. 518

projective tests personality assessments that present ambiguous visual stimuli to the client and ask the client to respond with whatever comes to mind. 518

prosocial behavior socially desirable behavior that benefits others. 481

prostate gland gland that secretes most of the fluid holding the male sex cells or sperm. 378

prototype an example of a concept that closely matches the defining characteristics of a concept. 257

proximity the tendency to perceive objects that are close to each other as part of the same grouping. 113

proximity physical or geographical nearness. 474

psilocybin natural hallucinogen found in certain mushrooms. 159

psychiatric social worker a social worker with some training in therapy methods who focuses on the environmental conditions that can have an impact on mental disorders, such as poverty, overcrowding, stress, and drug abuse. 18

psychiatrist a medical doctor who has specialized in the diagnosis and treatment of psychological disorders. 18

psychoactive drugs drugs that alter thinking, perception, and memory. 150

psychoanalysis the theory and therapy based on the work of Sigmund Freud. 11

psychoanalysis Freud's term for both the theory of personality and the therapy based on it. 500

psychoanalysis an insight therapy based on the theory of Freud, emphasizing the revealing of unconscious conflicts. 576

psychodynamic perspective modern version of psychoanalysis that is more focused on the development of a sense of self and the discovery of motivations behind a person's behavior other than sexual motivations. 13

psychodynamic therapy a newer and more general term for therapies based on psychoanalysis with an emphasis on transference, shorter treatment times, and a more direct therapeutic approach. 577

psychological defense mechanisms unconscious distortions of a person's perception of reality that reduce stress and anxiety. 497

psychological dependence the feeling that a drug is needed to continue a feeling of emotional or psychological well-being. 151

psychological disorder any pattern of behavior that causes people significant distress, causes them to harm others, or harms their ability to function in daily life. 535

psychologist a professional with an academic degree and specialized training in one or more areas of psychology. 17

psychology the scientific study of behavior and mental processes. 4

psychoneuroimmunology the study of the effects of psychological factors such as stress, emotions, thoughts, and behavior on the immune system. 408

psychopathology the study of abnormal behavior. 532

psychopharmacology the use of drugs to control or relieve the symptoms of psychological disorders. 596

psychosexual stages five stages of personality development proposed by Freud and tied to the sexual development of the child. 498

psychosurgery surgery performed on brain tissue to relieve or control severe psychological disorders. 600

psychotherapy therapy for mental disorders in which a person with a problem talks with a psychological professional. 574

psychotic term applied to a person who is no longer able to perceive what is real and what is fantasy. 556

puberty the physical changes that occur in the body as sexual development reaches its peak. 324

punishment any event or object that, when following a response, makes that response less likely to happen again. 188

punishment by application the punishment of a response by the addition or experiencing of an unpleasant stimulus. 188

punishment by removal the punishment of a response by the removal of a pleasurable stimulus. 188

random assignment process of assigning subjects to the experimental or control groups randomly, so that each subject has an equal chance of being in either group. 29

rapid eye movement (REM) sleep stage of sleep in which the eyes move rapidly under the eyelids and the person is typically experiencing a dream. 134

rating scale assessment in which a numerical value is assigned to specific behavior that is listed in the scale. 520

rational–emotive behavior therapy (REBT) cognitive–behavioral therapy in which clients are directly challenged in their irrational beliefs and helped to restructure their thinking into more rational belief statements. 586

rationalization psychological defense mechanism in which a person invents acceptable excuses for unacceptable behavior. 498

reaction formation psychological defense mechanism in which a person forms an opposite emotional or behavioral reaction to the way he or she really feels to keep those true feelings hidden from self and others. 498

real self one's perception of actual characteristics, traits, and abilities. 508

realistic conflict theory theory stating that prejudice and discrimination will be increased between groups that are in conflict over a limited resource. 469

reality principle principle by which the ego functions; the satisfaction of the demands of the id only when negative consequences will not result. 497

recall type of memory retrieval in which the information to be retrieved must be "pulled" from memory with very few external cues. 230

recency effect tendency to remember information at the end of a body of information better than the information at the beginning of it. 231

receptive meditation form of meditation in which a person attempts to become aware of everything in immediate conscious experience, or an expansion of consciousness. 438

receptor sites 3-dimensional proteins on the surface of the dendrites or certain cells of the muscles and glands, which are shaped to fit only certain neurotransmitters. 52

recessive referring to a gene that only influences the expression of a trait when paired with an identical gene. 301

reciprocal determinism Bandura's explanation of how the factors of environment, personal characteristics, and behavior can interact to determine future behavior. 506

reciprocity of liking tendency of people to like other people who like them in return. 474

recognition the ability to match a piece of information or a stimulus to a stored image or fact. 230

reflection therapy technique in which the therapist restates what the client says rather than interpreting those statements. 578

reflex an involuntary response, one that is not under personal control or choice. 171

reflex arc the connection of the afferent neurons to the interneurons to the efferent neurons, resulting in a reflex action. 57

refractory period time period in males just after orgasm in which the male cannot become aroused or achieve erection. 389

regression psychological defense mechanism in which a person falls back on childlike patterns of responding in reaction to stressful situations. 498

reinforcement any event or stimulus, that when following a response, increases the probability that the response will occur again. 181

reinforcement the strengthening of a response by following it with a pleasurable consequence or the removal of an unpleasant stimulus. 584

reinforcers any events or objects that, when following a response, increase the likelihood of that response occurring again. 182

relative size perception that occurs when objects that a person expects to be of a certain size appear to be small and are, therefore, assumed to be much farther away. 115

reliability the tendency of a test to produce the same scores again and again each time it is given to the same people. 270

REM behavior disorder a rare disorder in which the mechanism that blocks the movement of the voluntary muscles fails, allowing the person to thrash around and even get up and act out nightmares. 139

REM paralysis the inability of the voluntary muscles to move during REM sleep. 138

REM rebound increased amounts of REM sleep after being deprived of REM sleep on earlier nights. 138

replicate in research, repeating a study or experiment to see if the same results will be obtained in an effort to demonstrate reliability of results. 22

representative heuristic assumption that any object (or person) sharing characteristics with the members of a particular category is also a member of that category. 259

representative sample randomly selected sample of subjects from a larger population of subjects. 24

repression psychological defense mechanism in which the person refuses to consciously remember a threatening or unacceptable event, instead pushing those events into the unconscious mind. 498

resistance occurring when a patient becomes reluctant to talk about a certain topic, by either changing the subject or becoming silent. 577

resolution the final phase of the sexual response in which the body is returned to a normal state. 389

resting potential the state of the neuron when not firing a neural impulse. 49

restorative theory theory of sleep proposing that sleep is necessary to the physical health of the body and serves to replenish chemicals and repair cellular damage. 134

reticular formation (RF) an area of neurons running through the middle of the medulla and the pons and slightly beyond that is responsible for general attention, alertness, and arousal. 70

retrieval getting information that is in storage into a form that can be used. 215

retrieval cue a stimulus for remembering. 229

retroactive interference memory problem that occurs when newer information prevents or interferes with the retrieval of older information. 241

retrograde amnesia loss of memory from the point of some injury or trauma backwards, or loss of memory for the past. 243

reuptake process by which neurotransmitters are taken back into the synaptic vesicles. 54

reversible figures visual illusions in which the figure and ground can be reversed. 113

rods visual sensory receptors found at the back of the retina, responsible for noncolor sensitivity to low levels of light. 95

romantic love type of love consisting of intimacy and passion. 476

Rorschach inkblot test projective test that uses 10 inkblots as the ambiguous stimuli. 518

s factor the ability to excel in certain areas, or specific intelligence. 266

scaffolding process in which a more skilled learner gives help to a less skilled learner, reducing the amount of help as the less skilled learner becomes more capable. 315

scheme in this case, a mental concept formed through experiences with objects and events. 312

schizophrenia severe disorder in which the person suffers from disordered thinking, bizarre behavior, hallucinations, and inability to distinguish between fantasy and reality. 556

scientific method system of gathering data so that bias and error in measurement are reduced. 20

scrotum external sac that holds the testes. 378

seasonal affective disorder (SAD) a mood disorder caused by the body's reaction to low levels of sunlight in the winter months. 548

secondary appraisal the second step in assessing a threat, which involves estimating the resources available to the person for coping with the stressor. 426

secondary reinforcer any reinforcer that becomes reinforcing after being paired with a primary reinforcer, such as praise, tokens, or gold stars. 182

secondary sex characteristics sexual organs and traits that develop at puberty and are indirectly involved in human reproduction. 378

selective attention the ability to focus on only one stimulus from among all sensory input. 219

selective thinking distortion of thinking in which a person focuses on only one aspect of a situation while ignoring all other relevant aspects. 585

self an individual's awareness of his or her own personal characteristics and level of functioning. 508

self-actualization according to Maslow, the point that is seldom reached at which people have sufficiently satisfied the lower needs and achieved their full human potential. 352

self-actualizing tendency the striving to fulfill one's innate capacities and capabilities. 508

self-concept the image of oneself that develops from interactions with important, significant people in one's life. 508

self-determination theory (SDT) theory of human motivation in which the social context of an action has an effect on the type of motivation existing for the action. 353

self-efficacy individual's expectancy of how effective his or her efforts to accomplish a goal will be in any particular circumstance. 506

self-fulfilling prophecy the tendency of one's expectations to affect one's behavior in such a way as to make the expectations more likely to occur. 471

self-help groups (support groups) a group composed of people who have similar problems and who meet together without a therapist or counselor for the purpose of discussion, problem solving, and social and emotional support. 588

semantic memory type of declarative memory containing general knowledge, such as knowledge of language and information learned in formal education. 225

semantic network model model of memory organization that assumes information is stored in the brain in a connected fashion, with concepts that are related stored physically closer to each other than concepts that are not highly related. 227

semantics the rules for determining the meaning of words and sentences. 285

semen fluid released from the penis at orgasm that contains the sperm. 389

sensation the process that occurs when special receptors in the sense organs are activated, allowing various forms of outside stimuli to become neural signals in the brain. 90

sensation seeker someone who needs more arousal than the average person. 350

sensorimotor stage Piaget's first stage of cognitive development in which the infant uses its senses and motor abilities to interact with objects in the environment. 312

sensory adaptation tendency of sensory receptor cells to become less responsive to a stimulus that is unchanging. 92

sensory conflict theory an explanation of motion sickness in which the information from the eyes conflicts with the information from the vestibular senses, resulting in dizziness, nausea, and other physical discomfort. 111

sensory memory the very first stage of memory, the point at which information enters the nervous system through the sensory systems. 217

sensory pathway nerves coming from the sensory organs to the CNS consisting of afferent neurons. 59

serial position effect tendency of information at the beginning and end of a body of information to be remembered more accurately than information in the middle of the body of information. 230

sexism prejudice about males and/or females leading to unequal treatment. 387

sexual dysfunction a problem in sexual functioning. 380

sexual orientation a person's sexual attraction and affection for members of either the opposite or the same sex. 394

sexually transmitted infection (STI) an infection spread primarily through sexual contract. 400

shape constancy the tendency to interpret the shape of an object as being constant, even when its shape changes on the retina. 112

shaping the reinforcement of simple steps in behavior that lead to a desired, more complex behavior. 192

short-term memory (STM) the memory system in which information is held for brief periods of time while being used. 219

similarity the tendency to perceive things that look similar to each other as being part of the same group. 113

single photon emission computed tomography (SPECT) neuroimaging method that is similar to PET but uses a different radioactive tracer and can be used to examine brain blood flow. 68

single-blind study study in which the subjects do not know if they are in the experimental or the control group. 31

situational cause cause of behavior attributed to external factors, such as delays, the action of others, or some other aspect of the situation. 466

situational context the social or environmental setting of a person's behavior. 533

size constancy the tendency to interpret an object as always being the same actual size, regardless of its distance. 112

skin senses the sensations of touch, pressure, temperature, and pain. 108

sleep apnea disorder in which the person stops breathing for nearly half a minute or more. 142

sleep deprivation any significant loss of sleep, resulting in problems in concentration and irritability. 133

sleepwalking (somnambulism) occurring during deep sleep, an episode of moving around or walking around in one's sleep. 140

social categorization the assignment of a person one has just met to a category based on characteristics the new person has in common with other people with whom one has had experience in the past. 464

social cognition the mental processes that people use to make sense of the social world around them. 464

social cognitive learning theorists theorists who emphasize the importance of both the influences of other people's behavior and of a person's own expectancies of learning. 505

social cognitive theory referring to the use of cognitive processes in relation to understanding the social world. 471

social cognitive view learning theory that includes cognitive processes such as anticipating, judging, memory, and imitation of models. 505

social comparison the comparison of oneself to others in ways that raise one's self-esteem. 471

social facilitation the tendency for the presence of other people to have a positive impact on the performance of an easy task. 456

social identity the part of the self-concept including one's view of self as a member of a particular social category. 471

social identity theory theory in which the formation of a person's identity within a particular social group is explained by social categorization, social identity, and social comparison. 471

social impairment the tendency for the presence of other people to have a negative impact on the performance of a difficult task. 456

social influence the process through which the real or implied presence of others can directly or indirectly influence the thoughts, feelings, and behavior of an individual. 448

social loafing the tendency for people to put less effort into a simple task when working with others on that task. 456

social phobia fear of interacting with others or being in social situations that might lead to a negative evaluation. 542

social psychology the scientific study of how a person's thoughts, feelings, and behavior are influenced by the real, imagined, or implied presence of others. 448

Social Readjustment Rating Scale (SRRS) assessment that measures the amount of stress in a person's life over a 1-year period resulting from major life events. 412

social role the pattern of behavior that is expected of a person who is in a particular social position. 479

social-cognitive theory of hypnosis theory that assumes that people who are hypnotized are not in an altered state but are merely playing the role expected of them in the situation. 149

social-support system the network of family, friends, neighbors, coworkers, and others who can offer support, comfort, or aid to a person in need. 434

sociocultural perspective perspective that focuses on the relationship between social behavior and culture. 15

sociocultural perspective perspective in which abnormal behavior (as well as normal behavior) is seen as the product of the learning and shaping of behavior within the context of the family, the social group to which one belongs, and the culture within which the family and social group exist. 534

soma the cell body of the neuron responsible for maintaining the life of the cell. 47

somatic nervous system division of the PNS consisting of nerves that carry information from the senses to the CNS and from the CNS to the voluntary muscles of the body. 59

somatosensory cortex area of neurons running down the front of the parietal lobes responsible for processing information from the skin and internal body receptors for touch, temperature, body position, and possibly taste. 75

somesthetic senses the body senses consisting of the skin senses, the kinesthetic sense, and the vestibular senses. 108

source traits the more basic traits that underlie the surface traits, forming the core of personality. 511

spatial neglect condition produced by damage to the association areas of the right hemisphere resulting in an inability to recognize objects or body parts in the left visual field. 77

specific phobia fear of objects or specific situations or events. 542

spinal cord a long bundle of neurons that carries messages between the body and the brain and is responsible for very fast, lifesaving reflexes. 57

spontaneous recovery the reappearance of a learned response after extinction has occurred. 174

stem cells special cells found in all the tissues of the body that are capable of becoming other cell types when those cells need to be replaced due to damage or wear and tear. 59

stereotype a concept held about a person or group of people that is based on superficial, irrelevant characteristics. 387

stereotype a set of characteristics that people believe is shared by all members of a particular social category. 465

stereotype vulnerability the effect that people's awareness of the stereotypes associated with their social group has on their behavior. 471

stimulants drugs that increase the functioning of the nervous system. 151

stimulatory hallucinogenics drugs that produce a mixture of psychomotor stimulant and hallucinogenic effects. 159

stimulus discrimination the tendency to stop making a generalized response to a stimulus that is similar to the original conditioned stimulus because the similar stimulus is never paired with the unconditioned stimulus. 174

stimulus generalization the tendency to respond to a stimulus that is only similar to the original conditioned stimulus with the conditioned response. 173

stimulus motive a motive that appears to be unlearned but causes an increase in stimulation, such as curiosity. 349

stimulus substitution original theory in which Pavlov stated that classical conditioning occurred because the conditioned stimulus became a substitute for the unconditioned stimulus by being paired closely together. 178

storage holding onto information for some period of time. 214

stress the term used to describe the physical, emotional, cognitive, and behavioral responses to events that are appraised as threatening or challenging. 410

stressors events that cause a stress reaction. 410

stress-vulnerability model explanation of disorder that assumes a biological sensitivity, or vulnerability, to a certain disorder will result in the development of that disorder under the right conditions of environmental or emotional stress. 560

structuralism early perspective in psychology associated with Wilhelm Wundt and Edward Titchener, in which the focus of study is the structure or basic elements of the mind. 7

subjective referring to concepts and impressions that are only valid within a particular person's perception and may be influenced by biases, prejudice, and personal experiences. 518

subjective discomfort emotional distress or emotional pain. 534

sublimation channeling socially unacceptable impulses and urges into socially acceptable behavior. 498

subordinate concept the most specific category of a concept, such as one's pet dog or a pear in one's hand; subordinate refers to lowest in status or standing. 256

successive approximations small steps in behavior, one after the other, that lead to a particular goal behavior. 192

superego part of the personality that acts as a moral center. 497

superordinate concept the most general form of a type of concept, such as "animal" or "fruit"; superordinate refers to highest in status or standing. 256

surface traits aspects of personality that can easily be seen by other people in the outward actions of a person. 510

sympathetic division (fight-or-flight system) part of the ANS that is responsible for reacting to stressful events and bodily arousal. 60

synapse (synaptic gap) microscopic fluid-filled space between the synaptic knob of one cell and the dendrites or surface of the next cell. 52

synaptic knob rounded areas on the end of the axon terminals. 51

synaptic vesicles saclike structures found inside the synaptic knob containing chemicals. 51

synesthesia disorder in which the signals from the various sensory organs are processed in the wrong cortical areas, resulting in the sense information being interpreted as more than one sensation. 88

syntax the system of rules for combining words and phrases to form grammatically correct sentences. 285

systematic desensitization behavior technique used to treat phobias, in which a client is asked to make a list of ordered fears and taught to relax while concentrating on those fears. 582

temperament the behavioral characteristics that are fairly well established at birth, such as "easy," "difficult," and "slow to warm up." 319

temperament the enduring characteristics with which each person is born. 494

temporal lobes areas of the cortex located just behind the temples containing the neurons responsible for the sense of hearing and meaningful speech. 75

teratogen any factor that can cause a birth defect. 306

testes (testicles) the male sex glands. 378

testes the male gonads. 64

texture gradient the tendency for textured surfaces to appear to become smaller and finer as distance from the viewer increases. 116

thalamus part of the limbic system located in the center of the brain, this structure relays sensory information from the lower part of the brain to the proper areas of the cortex and processes some sensory information before sending it to its proper area. 71

that's-not-all technique a sales technique in which the persuader makes an offer and then adds something extra to make the offer look better before the target person can make a decision. 453

Thematic Apperception Test (TAT) projective test that uses 20 pictures of people in ambiguous situations as the visual stimuli. 518

therapeutic alliance the relationship between therapist and client that develops as a warm, caring, accepting relationship characterized by empathy, mutual respect, and understanding. 593

therapy treatment methods aimed at making people feel better and function more effectively. 574

theta waves brain waves indicating the early stages of sleep. 136

thinking (cognition) mental activity that goes on in the brain when a person is organizing and attempting to understand information and communicating information to others. 254

thyroid gland endocrine gland found in the neck; regulates metabolism. 63

time-out an extinction process in which a person is removed from the situation that provides reinforcement for undesirable behavior, usually by being placed in a quiet corner or room away from possible attention and reinforcement opportunities. 584

token economy type of behavior modification in which desired behavior is rewarded with tokens. 195

token economy the use of objects called tokens to reinforce behavior in which the tokens can be accumulated and exchanged for desired items or privileges. 584

top-down processing the use of preexisting knowledge to organize individual features into a unified whole. 120

trait a consistent, enduring way of thinking, feeling, or behaving. 510

trait theories theories that endeavor to describe the characteristics that make up human personality in an effort to predict future behavior. 510

trait–situation interaction the assumption that the particular circumstances of any given situation will influence the way in which a trait is expressed. 512

transduction the process of converting outside stimuli, such as light, into neural activity. 90

transference In psychoanalysis, the tendency for a patient or client to project positive or negative feelings for important people from the past onto the therapist. 577

trial and error (mechanical solution) problem-solving method in which one possible solution after another is tried until a successful one is found. 258

triarchic theory of intelligence Sternberg's theory that there are three kinds of intelligence: analytical, creative, and practical. 267

trichromatic theory theory of color vision that proposes three types of cones: red, blue, and green. 97

Type 2 diabetes disease involving failure of the pancreas to secrete enough insulin, necessitating medication, usually diagnosed before the age of 40 and can be associated with obesity. 423

Type A personality person who is ambitious, time conscious, extremely hardworking, and tends to have high levels of hostility and anger as well as being easily annoyed. 428

Type B personality person who is relaxed and laid-back, less driven and competitive than Type A, and slow to anger. 428

Type C personality pleasant but repressed person, who tends to internalize his or her anger and anxiety and who finds expressing emotions difficult. 428

unconditional positive regard positive regard that is given without conditions or strings attached. 508

unconditional positive regard referring to the warmth, respect, and accepting atmosphere created by the therapist for the client in person-centered therapy. 579

unconditioned response (UCR) an involuntary (reflex) response to a naturally occurring or unconditioned stimulus. 171

unconditioned stimulus (UCS) a naturally occurring stimulus that leads to an involuntary (reflex) response. 171

unconscious mind level of the mind in which thoughts, feelings, memories, and other information are kept that are not easily or voluntarily brought into consciousness. 495

uterus the womb in which the baby grows during pregnancy. 378

vagina the tube that leads from the outside of a female's body to the opening of the womb. 378

validity the degree to which a test actually measures what it's supposed to measure. 270

variable interval schedule of reinforcement schedule of reinforcement in which the interval of time that must pass before reinforcement becomes possible is different for each trial or event. 185

variable ratio schedule of reinforcement schedule of reinforcement in which the number of responses required for reinforcement is different for each trial or event. 186

vestibular senses the sensations of movement, balance, and body position. 108

vicarious conditioning classical conditioning of a reflex response or emotion by watching the reaction of another person. 177

visual accommodation the change in the thickness of the lens as the eye focuses on objects that are far away or close. 95

volley principle theory of pitch that states that frequencies from about 400 Hz to 4000 Hz cause the hair cells (auditory neurons) to fire in a volley pattern, or take turns in firing. 103

waking consciousness state in which thoughts, feelings, and sensations are clear, organized, and the person feels alert. 131

weight set point the particular level of weight that the body tries to maintain. 356

Wernicke's aphasia condition resulting from damage to Wernicke's area, causing the affected person to be unable to understand or produce meaningful language. 77

withdrawal physical symptoms that can include nausea, pain, tremors, crankiness, and high blood pressure, resulting from a lack of an addictive drug in the body systems. 150

working memory an active system that processes the information in short-term memory. 220

Yerkes-Dodson law law stating performance is related to arousal; moderate levels of arousal lead to better performance than do levels of arousal that are too low or too high. This effect varies with the difficulty of the task: Easy tasks require a high-moderate level whereas more-difficult tasks require a low-moderate level. 349

zone of proximal development (ZPD) Vygotsky's concept of the difference between what a child can do alone and what that child can do with the help of a teacher. 315

zygote cell resulting from the uniting of the ovum and sperm. 304

references

AAA Foundation for Traffic Safety. (1997). *Aggressive driving: Three studies.* Washington, DC: Louis Mizell.

Abadinsky, H. (1989). *Drug abuse: An introduction.* Chicago: Nelson-Hall Series in Law, Crime, and Justice.

Abbott, L., Nadler, J., & Rude, R. K. (1994). Magnesium deficiency in alcoholism: Possible contribution to osteoporosis and cardiovascular disease in alcoholics. *Alcoholism, Clinical & Experimental Research, 18*(5), 1076–1082.

Abe, K., Amatomi, M., & Oda, N. (1984). Sleepwalking and recurrent sleep talking in children of childhood sleepwalkers. *American Journal of Psychiatry, 141*, 800–801.

Abel, G. G., & Osborn, C. A. (1992). The paraphilias: The extent and nature of sexually deviant and criminal behavior. In J. M. W. Bradford (Ed.), *Psychiatric Clinics of North America, 15*(3) (pp. 675–687). Philadelphia: W. B. Saunders Company.

Abela, J. R. Z., & D'Allesandro, D. U. (2002). Beck's cognitive theory of depression: The diathesis-stress and causal mediation components. *British Journal of Clinical Psychology, 41*, 111–128.

Åberg, M. A., Pedersen, N. L., Torén, K., Svartengren, M., Bäckstrand, B., Johnsson, T., Cooper-Kuhn, C. M., Åberg, N. D., Nilsson, M., & Kuhn, H. G. (2009). Cardiovascular fitness is associated with cognition in young adulthood. *Proceedings of the National Academy of Sciences, 106*(49), 20906–20911.

Abraham, S., & Llewellyn-Jones, D. (2001). *Eating disorders, the facts* (5th ed). London: Oxford University Press.

Abraham, W. C., & Williams, J. M. (2003). Properties and mechanisms of LTP maintenance. *The Neuroscientist, 9*(6), 463–474.

Abramson, L. Y., Garber, J., & Seligman, M. E. P. (1980). Learned helplessness in humans: An attributional analysis. In J. Garber & M. E. P. Seligman (Eds.), *Human Helplessness* (pp. 3–34). New York: Academic Press.

Abramson, L. Y., Seligman, M. E. P., & Teasdale, J. D. (1978). Learned helplessness in humans: Critique and reformulation. *Journal of Abnormal Psychology, 87*, 49–74.

Acheson, D. J., MacDonald, M. C., & Postle, B. R. (2010). The interaction of concreteness and phonological similarity in verbal working memory. *Journal of Experimental Psychology: Learning, Memory and Cognition, 36*(1), 17–36.

Adam, K. (1980). Sleep as a restorative process and a theory to explain why. *Progressive Brain Research, 53*, 289–305.

Adams, D. B. (1968). The activity of single cells in the midbrain and hypothalamus of the cat during affective defense behavior. *Archives Italiennes de Biologie, 106*, 243–269.

Adams, R. J. (1987). An evaluation of colour preferences in early infancy. *Infant Behaviour and Development, 10*, 143–150.

Addis, D. R., Leclerc, C. M., Muscatell, K., & Kensinger, E. A. (2010). There are age-related changes in neural connectivity during the encoding of positive, but not negative, information. *Cortex, 46*: 9.

Ader R. (2003). Conditioned immunomodulation: Research needs and directions. *Brain, Behavior, and Immunity, 17*(1), 51–57.

Adhikari, A., Topiwala, M. A., & Gordon, J. A. (2010). Synchronized activity between the ventral hippocampus and the medial prefrontal cortex during anxiety. *Neuron, 65*(2), 257–269.

Adler, A. (1954). *Understanding human nature.* New York: Greenburg Publisher.

Adler, S. R., Fosket, J. R., Kagawa-Singer, M., McGraw, S. A., Wong-Kim, E., Gold, E., & Sternfeld, B. (2000) Conceptualizing menopause and midlife: Chinese American and Chinese women in the U.S. *Maturitas 35*(1), 11–23.

Adolphs, R., Gosselin, F., Buchanan, T. W., Tranel, D., Schyns, P., & Damasio, A. R. (2005). A mechanism for impaired fear recognition after amygdala damage. *Nature, 433*, 68–72.

Adolphs, R., & Tranel, D. (2003). Amygdala damage impairs emotion recognition from scenes only when they contain facial expressions. *Neuropsychologia, 41*, 1281–1289.

Aghajanian, G. K., & Marek, G. J. (1999). Serotonin and hallucinogens. *Neuropsychopharmacology, 21*, 16S–23S.

Agnati, L. F., Bjelke, B., & Fuxe, K. (1992). Volume transmission in the brain. *American Scientist, 80*, 362–373.

Agresti, A., & Finlay, B. (1997). *Statistical Methods for the Social Sciences*, New Jersey, Prentice Hall.

Aguiar, A., & Baillargeon, R. (2003). Perseverative responding in a violation-of-expectation task in 6.5-month-old infants. *Cognition, 88*(3), 277–316.

Ahlskog, J. E. (2003). Slowing Parkinson's disease progression: Recent dopamine agonist trials. *Neurology, 60*(3), 381–389.

Ahn, W. (1998). Why are different features central for natural kinds and artifacts? The role of causal status in determining feature centrality. *Cognition, 69*, 135–178.

Aiello, J. R., & Douthitt, E. A. (2001). Social facilitation from Triplett to electronic performance monitoring. *Group Dynamics: Theory, Research, and Practice, 5*(3), 163–180.

Ainsworth, M. D. S. (1985). Attachments across the life span. *Bulletin of the New York Academy of Medicine, 61*, 792–812.

Ainsworth, M. D. S., Blehar, M. C., Waters, E., & Wall, S. (1978). *Patterns of attachment: A study of the strange situation.* Hillsdale, NJ: Erlbaum.

Aitchison, J. (1992). Good birds, better birds, and amazing birds: The development of prototypes. In P. J. Arnaud & H. Béjoint (Eds.), *Vocabulary and applied linguistics* (pp. 71–84). London: Macmillan.

Ajzen, I. (2001). Nature and operation of attitudes. *Annual Review of Psychology, 52*, 27–58.

Ajzen, I., & Fishbein, M. (2000). Attitudes and the attitude–behavior relation: Reasoned and automatic processes. In W. Stroebe & M. Hewstone (Eds.), *European review of social psychology* (pp. 1–33). New York: John Wiley & Sons.

Akil, M., Kolachana, B. S., et al. (2003). Catechol-o-methyltransferase genotype and dopamine regulation in the human brain. *Journal of Neuroscience, 23*(6), 2008–2013.

Alarcón, R. D., Becker, A. E., Lewis-Fernández, R., Like, R. C., Desai, P., Foulks, E., Gonzales, J., Hansen, H., Kopelowicz, A., Lu, F. G., Oquendo, M. A., & Primm, A. (2009). Issues for *DSM-V*: The role of culture in psychiatric diagnosis. *The Journal of Nervous and Mental Disease, 197*(8), 559–660.

Albert, D. J., & Richmond, S. E. (1977). Reactivity and aggression in the rat: Induction by alpha–adrenergic blocking agents injected ventral to anterior septum but not into lateral septum. *Journal of Comparative and Physiological Psychology, 91*, 886–896 [DBA] *Physiology and Behavior, 20*, 755–761.

Alderfer, C. P. (1972). *Existence, relatedness and growth: Human needs in organisational settings.* New York: Free Press.

Aldridge-Morris, R. (1989). *Multiple personality: An exercise in deception.* Hillsdale, NJ: Erlbaum.

Alexander, G., DeLong, M. R., & Strick, P. L. (1986). Parallel organization of functionally segregated circuits linking basal ganglia and cortex. *Annual Review of Neuroscience, 9*, 357–381.

Aligne, C. A., Auinger, P., Byrd, R. S., & Weitzman, M. (2000). Risk factors for pediatric asthma contributions of poverty, race, and urban residence. *American Journal of Respiratory Critical Care Medicine, 162*(3), 873–877.

Alkon, D. (1989). Memory storage and neural systems. *Scientific American, 261*(1), 42–50.

Allen, D. (2001). *Getting things done: the art of stress-free productivity.* New York: Viking Adult.

Allen, D. (2008). *Making it all work.* New York: Viking Adult.

Allen, F. (1994). *Secret formula.* New York: HarperCollins.

Allen, G., & Parisi, P. (1990). Trends in monozygotic and dizygotic twinning rates by maternal age and parity. Further analysis of Italian data, 1949–1985, and rediscussion of U.S. data, 1964–1985. *Acta Genetic Medicine & Gemellology, 39*, 317–328.

Allen, G. E. (2006). *Intelligence tests and immigration to the United States, 1900–1940.* Hoboken, NJ: John Wiley and Sons.

Allen, K., Blascovich, J., & W. Mendes. (2002). Cardiovascular reactivity and the presence of pets, friends, and spouses: The truth about cats and dogs. *Psychosomatic Medicine, 64*, 727–739.

Allen, L. S., & Gorski, R. A. (1991). Sexual dimorphism of the anterior commissure and massa intermedia of the human brain. *Journal of Comparative Neurology, 312*, 97–104.

Allen, L. S., Hines, M., Shryne, J. E., & Gorski, R. A. (1989). Two sexually dimorphic cell groups in the human brain. *Journal of Neuroscience, 9*(9), 496–506.

Alloway, T. P., Rajendran, G., & Archibald, L. (2009). Working memory in children with developmental disorders. *Journal of Learning Disabilities, 42*(4), 372–382.

Alloy, L. B., & Clements, C. M. (1998). Hopelessness theory of depression: Tests of the symptom component. *Cognitive Therapy and Research, 22*, 303–335.

Allport, G. W., & Odbert, H. S. (1936). Trait names: A psycho-lexical study. *Psychological Monographs, 47*(211).

Alm, H., & Nilsson, L. (1995). The effects of a mobile telephone conversation on driver behaviour in a car following situation. *Accident Analysis and Prevention, 27*(5), 707–715.

Alperstein, L. (2001, May). *For two: Some basic perspectives and skills for couples therapy.* Paper presented at the XXXIII Annual Conference of the American Association of Sex Educators, Counselors, and Therapists, San Francisco.

Alzheimer's Association. (2010). Alzheimer's disease facts and figures. *Alzheimer's & Dementia, 6*, 4–54.

Amabile, T., Hadley, C. N., & Kramer, S. J. (2002). Creativity under the gun. *Harvard Business Review, 80*(8), 52–60.

Amabile, T. M. (1982). The social psychology of creativity: A consensual assessment technique. *Journal of Personality and Social Psychology, 43*, 997–1013.

Amabile, T. M., DeJong, W., & Lepper, M. R. (1976). Effects of externally imposed deadlines on subsequent intrinsic motivation. *Journal of Personality and Social Psychology, 34*, 92–98.

Amat, J., Baratta, M. V., Paul, E., Bland, S. T., Watkins, L. R., & Maier, S. F. (2005). Medial prefrontal cortex determines how stressor controllability affects behavior and dorsal raphe nucleus. *Nature Neuroscience, 8*(3), 365–371.

American Academy of Pediatrics. (1995). Health supervision for children with Turner syndrome. *Pediatrics, 96*(6), 1166–1173.

American Association of University Women. (1992). *How schools shortchange girls.* Washington, DC: AAUW Educational Foundation, The Wellesley College Center for Research on Women.

American Association of University Women. (1998). *Separated by sex: A critical look at single-sex education for girls.* Washington, DC: AAUW Educational Foundation, The Wellesley College Center for Research on Women.

American Association on Intellectual and Developmental Disabilities [AAIDD]. (2009). FAQ on intellectual disability. Retrieved June 8, 2010, from www.aamr.org/content_104.cfm

American Association on Intellectual and Developmental Disabilities [AAIDD]. (2007). Definition of mental retardation. Retrieved December 6, 2007, from www.aamr.org/Policies/faq_mental_retardation.shtml.

American College Counseling Association's (ACCA) Community College Task Force (2010). *2009–2010 Community college counselors survey.* Retrieved August 12, 2010, from www.collegecounseling.org/pdf/2009-2010_Community_College_Counselors_Survey_Results.pdf

American Psychiatric Association. (2000). *DSM-IV-TR: Diagnostic and statistical manual of mental disorders* (4th ed., Text Revision). Washington, DC: American Psychicatric Association.

American Psychiatric Association. (2000a). Appendix I: Outline for cultural formulation and glossary of culture-bound syndromes. In *DSM-IV-TR: Diagnostic and statistical manual of mental disorders* (4th ed., Text Revision). Washington, DC: American Psychicatric Association.

American Psychiatric Association. (2000b). Practice guidelines for the treatment of patients with major depressive disorder (revision). *American Journal of Psychiatry, 157*(Suppl. 4), 1–45.

American Psychiatric Association. (2009, April). Report of the *DSM-V* Neurodevelopmental disorders work group [Electronic version] from www.psych.org/MainMenu/Research/DSMIV/DSMV/DSMRevisionActivities/DSM-V-Work-Group-Reports/Neurodevelopmental-Disorders-Work-Group-Report.aspx

American Psychiatric Association (2009). Report of the *DSM-5* Personality and Personality Disorders Work Group Retrieved from http://www.dsm5.org/ProgressReports/Pages/0904ReportoftheDSM-VPersonalityandPersonalityDisordersWorkGroup.aspx

American Psychiatric Association (2010). APA modifies *DSM* naming convention to reflect publication changes. Retrieved September 23, 2010, from http://www.dsm5.org/Newsroom/Documents/DSM-Name-Change.pdf

American Psychiatric Association Committee on Electroconvulsive Therapy. (2001). *The practice of electroconvulsive therapy: Recommendations for treatment, training, and privileging*, (2nd ed.). Washington, DC: American Psychiatric Association.

American Psychological Association. (2002). Ethical principles of psychologists and code of conduct. *American Psychologist, 57*, 1060–1073.

American Psychological Association (2005). Policy statement on evidence-based practice in psychology. Retrieved September 22, 2010, from http://www.apa.org/practice/guidelines/evidence-based.pdf

American Psychological Association Division 19 (2010). Society for Military Psychology. Retrieved from http://www.apadivision19.org/about.htm

Anand, B. K., & Brobeck, J. R. (1951.) Hypothalamic control of food intake in rats and cats. *Yale Journal of Biological Medicine, 24*, 123–146.

Anastasi, A., & Urbina, S. (1997). *Psychological testing* (7th ed.). Upper Saddle River, NJ: Prentice-Hall.

Anderson, C., Sakamoto, A., Gentile, D., Ihori, N., Shibuya, A., Yukawa, S., Naito, M., & Kobayashi, K. (2008). Longitudinal effects of violent video games on aggression in Japan and the United States, *Pediatrics, 122*(5), e1067–e1072.

Anderson, C. A. (1987). Temperature and aggression: Effects on quarterly, yearly, and city rates of violent and nonviolent crime. *Journal of Personality and Social Psychology, 52*(6), 1161–1173.

Anderson, C. A. (2003). Video games and aggressive behavior. In D. Ravitch & J. P. Viteritti (Eds.), *Kid stuff: Marketing sex and violence to America's children* (p. 157). Baltimore/London: The Johns Hopkins University Press.

Anderson, C. A., & Bushman, B. J. (2001). Effects of violent video games on aggressive behavior, aggressive cognition, aggressive affect, physiological arousal, and prosocial behavior: A meta-analytic review of the scientific literature. *Psych Science, 12*(5), 353–359.

Anderson, C. A., & Dill, K. E. (2000). Video games and aggressive thoughts, feelings, and behavior in the laboratory and in life. *Journal of Personality and Social Psychology, 78*(4), 772–790.

Anderson, C. A., Berkowitz, L., Donnerstein, E., Huesmann, L. R., Johnson, J. D., Linz, D., Malamuth, N. M., & Wartella, E. (2003). The influence of media violence on youth. *Psychological Science in the Public Interest, 4*(3), 81–110.

Anderson, L. W., Krathwohl, D. R., Airasian, P. W., Cruikshank, K. A., Mayer, R. E., Pintrich, P. R., Raths, J., & Wittrock, M. C. (Eds.). (2001). *A taxonomy for learning, teaching, and assessing—A revision of Bloom's Taxonomy of Educational Objectives.* New York: Addison Wesley Longman.

Anderson, M. C., & Neely, J. H. (1995). Interference and inhibition in memory retrieval. In E. L. Bjork & R. A. Bjork (Eds.). *Handbook of perception and cognition, Vol. 10. Memory.* San Diego, CA: Academic Press.

Andrews, J. D. W. (1989). Integrating visions of reality: Interpersonal diagnosis and the existential vision. *American Psychologist, 44*, 803–817.

Anschuetz, B. L. (1999). The high cost of caring: Coping with workplace stress. *The Journal, the Newsletter of the Ontario Association of Children's Aid Societies, 43*(3), 1–63.

Antuono, P. G., Jones, J. L., Wang, Y., & Li, S. (2001). Decreased glutamate [plus] glutamine in Alzheimer's disease detected in vivo with (1)H-MRS at 0.5 T. *Neurology, 56*(6), 737–742.

Arbury, S. (2005). Workplace Violence: Training Young Workers in Preventative Strategies. *NFIB Business Toolbox, March 4.*

Archer, J. (1991). The influence of testosterone on human aggression. *British Journal of Psychology, 82*, 1–28.

Argamon, S., Koppel, M., Fine, J., & Shimoni, A. (2003, August). Gender, genre, and writing style in formal written texts. *Text, 23*(3).

Argyle, M. (1986). Rules for social relationships in four cultures. *Australian Journal of Psychology, 38*, 309–318.

Arkowitcz, H., & Miller, W. R. (2008). Learning, applying, and extending motivational interviewing. In H. Arkowitcz, H. A. Westra, W. R. Miller, & S. Rollnick (Eds.). *Motivational interviewing in the treatment of psychological disorders* (pp. 1–25). New York: Guilford Press.

Armstrong, R. (1997). When drugs are used for rape. *Journal of Emergency Nursing, 23*(4), 378–381.

Arnett, P. A., Smith, S. S., & Newman, J. P. (1997). Approach and avoidance motivation in psychopathic criminal offenders during passive avoidance. *Journal of Personality and Social Psychology, 72*(6), 1413–1428.

Aron, A., Aron, E., & Coups, E. (2005). *Statistics for the behavioral and social sciences: Brief course.* (4th edition). Upper Saddle River, NJ: Prentice-Hall.

Aronson, E. (1997). Back to the future. Retrospective review of Leon Festinger's—A theory of cognitive dissonance. *American Journal of Psychology, 110*, 127–137.

Aronson, E., Blaney, N., Stephan, C., Sikes, J., & Snapp, M. (1978). *The jigsaw classroom*. Beverly Hills, CA: Sage.

Asarnow, R. F., Granholm, E., & Sherman, T. (1991). Span of apprehension in schizophrenia. In H. A. Nasrallah (Ed.), *Handbook of Schizophrenia, Vol. 5*. In S. R. Steinhauer, J. H. Gruzelie, & J. Zubin (Eds.), *Neuropsychology, psychophysiology and information processing* (pp. 335–370). Amsterdam: Elsevier.

Asch, S. E. (1951). Effects of group pressure upon the modification and distortion of judgement. In H. Guetzkow (Ed.), *Groups, leadership and men*. Pittsburgh: Carnegie Press.

Asch, S. E. (1956). Studies of independence and conformity: A minority of one against a unanimous majority. *Psychological Monographs, 70* (Whole no. 416).

Aserinsky, E., & Kleitman, N. (1953). Regularly occurring periods of eye motility, and concomitant phenomena, during sleep. *Science, 118*, 273–274.

Ash, M. G. (1998). *Gestalt psychology in German culture, 1890–1967: Holism and the quest for objectivity*. Cambridge: Cambridge University Press.

Assaf, Y., & Pasternak, O. (2008). Diffusion tensor imaging (DTI)-based white matter mapping in brain research: A review. *Journal of Molecular Neuroscience, 34*(1), 51–61.

Atkinson, R. C., & Shiffrin, R. M. (1968). Human memory: A proposed system and its control processes. In K. W. Spence & J. T. Spence (Eds.). *The psychology of learning and motivation* (Vol. 2, pp. 89–105). New York: Academic Press.

Atladóttir, H. O., Pedersen, M. G., Thorsen, C., Mortensen, P. B., Deleuran, B., Eaton, W. W., & Parner, E. T. (2009). Association of family history of autoimmune diseases and autism spectrum disorders. *Pediatrics, 124*(2), 687–694.

Babiloni, C., Vecchio, F., Buffo, P., Buttiglione, M., Cibelli, G., & Rossini, P. M. (2010). Cortical responses to consciousness of schematic emotional facial expressions: A high-resolution EEG study. *Human Brain Mapping, 8*, 8.

Backenstraß, M., Pfeiffer, N., Schwarz, T., Catanzaro, S. J., & Mearns, J. (2008). Reliability and validity of the German version of the Generalized Expectancies for Negative Mood Regulation (NMR) Scale. *Diagnostica, 54,* 43–51.

Backer, B., Hannon, R., & Russell, N. (1994). *Death and dying: Understanding and care* (2nd ed.). Albany, NY: Delmar.

Baddeley, A. (1988). Cognitive psychology and human memory. *Trends in Neurosciences, 11*, 176–181.

Baddeley, A. D. (1986). *Working memory.* London/New York: Oxford University Press.

Baddeley, A. D. (1996). Exploring the central executive. *Quarterly Journal of Experimental Psychology, 49A*, 5–28.

Baddeley, A. D. (2003). Working memory: Looking back and looking visual forward. *Nature Reviews Neuroscience, 4*(10), 829–839.

Baddeley, A. D., & Hitch, G. (1974). Working memory. In G. A. Bower (Ed.), *The psychology of learning and motivation, 8* (pp. 47–89). New York: Academic Press.

Baddeley, A. D., & Larson, J. D. (2007). The phonological loop unmasked? A comment on the evidence for a "perceptual-gestural" alternative. *Quarterly Journal of Experimental Psychology, 60*(4), 497–504.

Baehr, E. K., Revelle, W., & Eastman, C. I. (2000). Individual difference in the phase amplitude of the human circadian temperature rhythm: With an emphasis on morningness-eveningness. *Journal of Sleep Research, 9*, 117–127.

Baer, D. M., Wolf, M. M., & Risley, T. R. (1968). Some current dimensions of applied behavior analysis. *Journal of Applied Behavior Analysis, 1*, 91–97.

Bahrick, H. (1984). Fifty years of second language attrition: Implications for programmatic research. *Modern Language Journal, 68*, 105–118.

Bahrick, H. P., Hall, L. K., & Berger, S. A. (1996, September). Accuracy and distortion in memory for high school grades. *Psychological Science, 7*, 265–271.

Bailey, J., Dunne, M. P., & Martin, N. G. (2000). Genetic and environmental influences on sexual orientation and its correlates in an Australian twin sample. *Journal of Personality and Social Psychology Volume, 78*(3), 524–536.

Bailey, J. M., & Pillard, R. C. (1991). A genetic study of male sexual orientation. *Archives of General Psychiatry, 48*, 1089–1096.

Bailey, J. M., Pillard, R. C., Neale, M. C., & Agyei, Y. (1993). Heritable factors influence sexual orientation in women. *Archives of General Psychiatry, 50*, 217–223.

Bailey, J. M., & Zucker, K. J. (1995). Childhood sex-typed behavior and sexual orientation: A conceptual analysis and quantitative review. *Developmental Psychology, 31*, 43–55.

Baillargeon, R. (1986). Representing the existence and the location of hidden objects: Object permanence in 6- and 8-month-old infants. *Cognition,* 23, 21-41.

Baker, L. D., Frank, L. L., Foster-Schubert, K., Green, P. S., Wilkinson, C. W., McTiernan, A., et al. (2010). Effects of aerobic exercise on mild cognitive impairment: A controlled trial. *Archives of Neurology, 67*(1), 71–79.

Ball, K., Berch, D. B., Helmers, K. F., Jobe, J. B., Leveck, M. D., Marsiske, M., Morris, J. N., Rebok, G. W., Smith, D. M., Tennstedt, S. L., Unverzagt, F. W., & Willis, S. L. (2002). Advanced Cognitive Training for Independent and Vital Elderly Study Group. Effects of cognitive training interventions with older adults: A randomized controlled trial. *Journal of the American Medical Association, 288*, 2271–2281.

Baltes, P. B., Reese, H. W., & Nesselroade, J. R. (1988). *Introduction to research methods, life-span developmental psychology.* Hillsdale, NJ: Lawrence Erlbaum

Bandura, A. (1965). Influence of models' reinforcement contingencies on the acquisition of imitative responses. *Journal of Social Psychology, 1*, 589–595.

Bandura, A. (1980). The social learning theory of aggression. In R. A. Falk & S. S. Kim (Eds.), *The war system: An interdisciplinary approach* (p. 146). Boulder, CO: Westview Press.

Bandura, A. (1986). *Social foundations of thought and action: A social cognitive theory*. Englewood Cliffs, NJ: Prentice Hall.

Bandura, A. (1989). Human agency in social cognitive theory. *American Psychologist, 44*, 1175–1184.

Bandura, A. (1998). Exploration of fortuitous determinants of life paths. *Psychological Inquiry, 9*, 95–99.

Bandura, A., Blanchard, E. B., & Ritter, B. (1969). Relative efficacy of desensitization and modeling approaches for inducing behavioral, affective, and attitudinal changes. *Journal of Personality and Social Psychology, 13*, 173–199.

Bandura, A., Jeffrey, R. W., & Wright, C. L. (1974). Efficacy of participant modeling as a function of response induction aids. *Journal of Abnormal Psychology, 83*, 56–64.

Bandura, A., & Rosenthal, T. L. (1966). Vicarious classical conditioning as a functioning of arousal level. *Journal of Personality and Social Psychology, 3*, 54–62.

Bandura, A., Ross, D., & Ross, S. A. (1961). Transmission of aggression through imitation of aggressive models. *Journal of Abnormal and Social Psychology, 63*, 575–582.

Bandura, A., Ross, D., & Ross, S. A. (1963). Imitation of film-mediated aggressive models. *Journal of Abnormal and Social Psychology, 66*, 3–11.

Barak, A. (1999). Psychological applications on the Internet: A discipline on the threshold of a new millennium. *Applied and Preventive Psychology, 8*, 231–246.

Barak, A., & Hen, L. (2008). Exposure in cyberspace as means of enhancing psychological assessment. In A. Barak (Ed.), *Psychological aspects of cyberspace: Theory, research, applications* (pp. 129–162). Cambridge, UK: Cambridge University Press.

Barak, A., & Suler, J. (2008). Reflections on the psychology and social science of cyberspace. In A. Barak (Ed.), *Psychological aspects of cyberspace: Theory, research, applications* (pp. 1–12). Cambridge, UK: Cambridge University Press.

Bard, P. (1934). On emotional expression after decortication with some remark on certain theoretical views. *Psychological Review, 41*, 309–329, 424–449.

Bargh, J. A., Chen, M., & Burrows, C. (1996). Automaticity of social behavior: Direct effects of trait construct and stereotype activation on action. *Journal of Personality & Social Psychology, 71*(2), 230–244.

Barker, E. (1983). The ones who got away: People who attend Unification Church workshops and do not become Moonies. In E. Barker (Ed.), *Of gods and men: New religious movements in the West.* Macon, GA: Mercer University Press.

Barkley, R. A., Murphy, K. R., & Fischer, M. (2008). *ADHD in adults: What the science says.* New York: Guilford Press.

Barlow, D. H., Allen, L. B., & Basden, S. L. (2007). Psychological treatments for panic disorders, phobias, and generalized anxiety disorder. In P. E. Nathan & J. M. Gorman (Eds.), *A guide to treatments that work* (3rd ed., pp. 351–394). New York: Oxford University Press.

Barnes, A. M., & Carey, J. C. (2002, January). Common problems of babies with trisomy 18 or 13. Rochester, NY, *Support Organization for Trisomy 18, 13, and Related Disorders,* January 11, New York: Soft Publications.

Barnes, V., Schneider, R., Alexander, C., & Staggers, F. (1997). Stress, stress reduction, and hypertension in African Americans: An updated review. *Journal of the National Medical Association, 89*(7), 464–476.

Barnyard, P., & Grayson, A. (1996). *Introducing psychological research.* London: MacMillan Press.

Baron, J. N., & Reiss, P. C. (1985). Same time, next year: Aggregate analyses of the mass media and violent behavior. *American Sociological Review, 50,* 347–363.

Baron, S. A. (1993). *Violence in the workplace.* Ventura, CA: Pathfinder Publishing of California.

Barondes, S. H. (1998). *Mood genes: Hunting for origins of mania and depression.* New York: W. H. Freeman.

Barone, J. J., & Roberts, H. R. (1996). Caffeine consumption. *Food Chemistry and Toxicology, 34,* 119–129.

Barsalou, L. W. (1992). *Cognitive psychology: An overview for cognitive scientists.* Hillsdale, NJ: Lawrence Erlbaum.

Barsch, J. (1996). *Barsch learning style inventory (rev. ed.).* Novato, CA: Academic Therapy Publications.

Barsh, G. S., Farooqi, I. S., & O'Rahilly, S. (2000). Genetics of body-weight regulation. *Nature, 404,* 644–651.

Barstow, A. L. (1995). *Witchcraze: A new history of the European witch hunts.* London: Pandora.

Bartels, A., & Zeki, S. (2000). The neural basis of romantic love. *NeuroReport, 11,* 3829–3834.

Barth, J. M., & Boles, D. B. (1999, September,). *Positive relations between emotion recognition skills and right hemisphere processing.* Paper presented at the 11th Annual Convention of the American Psychological Society, Denver, CO.

Bartholomew, K. (1990). Avoidance of intimacy: An attachment perspective. *Journal of Social and Personal Relationships, 7,* 147–178.

Bartlett, C., Harris, R., & Bruey, C. (2008). The effect of the amount of blood in a violent video game on aggression, hostility, and arousal. *Journal of Experimental Social Psychology, 44*(3), 539–546.

Bartlett, F. C. (1932). *Remembering: A study in experimental ad social psychology.* Cambridge, U.K.: Cambridge University Press.

Bartlett, N. R. (1965). Dark and light adaptation. In C. H. Graham (Ed.), *Vision and visual perception.* New York: John Wiley & Sons

Barton, M. E., & Komatsu, L. K. (1989). Defining features of natural kinds and artifacts. *Journal of Psycholinguistic Research, 18,* 433–447.

Bartoshuk, L. M. (1993). The biological basis for food perception and acceptance. *Food Quality and Preference, 4*(1/2), 21–32.

Bartoshuk, L. M., Duffy, V. B., Hayes, J. E., Moskowitz, H. R., & Snyder, D. J. (2006). Psychophysics of sweet and fat perception in obesity: Problems, solutions and new perspectives. *Philosophical transactions of the Royal Society of London. Series B, Biological sciences, 361*(1471), 1137–1148.

Bartoshuk, L. M., Fast, K., & Snyder, D. J. (2005). Differences in our sensory worlds. *Current Directions in Psychological Science, 14*(3), 122–125.

Basadur, M., Pringle, P., & Kirkland, D. (2002). Crossing cultures: Training effects on the divergent thinking attitudes of Spanish-speaking South American managers. *Creativity Research Journal, 14*(3, 4), 395–408.

Bastien, C. H., Morin, C. M., Ouellet, M., Blais, F. C., Bouchard, S. (2004). Cognitive-behavioral therapy for insomnia: Comparison of individual therapy, group therapy, and telephone consultations. *Journal of Consulting and Clinical Psychology, 72*(4), 653–659.

Battaglia, M., Bernardeschi, L., Franchini, L., Bellodi, L., & Smeraldi, E. (1995). A family study of schizotypal disorder. *Schizophrenia Bulletin, 2*(1)1, 133–146.

Baumrind, D. (1964). Some thoughts on ethics of research: After reading Milgram's "Behavioral Study of Obedience." *American Psychologist, 19,* 421–423.

Baumrind, D. (1967). Child care practices anteceding three patterns of preschool behavior. *Genetic Psychology Monograph, 75,* 43–88.

Baumrind, D. (1991). The influence of parenting style on adolescent competence and substance abuse. *Journal of Early Adolescence, 11*(1), 56–95.

Baumrind, D. (1997). Necessary distinctions. *Psychological Inquiry, 8,* 176–182.

Baumrind, D. (2005). Patterns of parental authority and adolescent autonomy. In J. Smetana (Ed.), *New directions for child development: Changes in parental authority during adolescence* (pp. 61–69). San Francisco: Jossey-Bass.

Bayliss, D. M., Baddeley, J. C., & Gunn, D. M. (2005). The relationship between short-term memory and working memory: Complex span made simple? *Memory, 13*(3–4), 414–421.

Beardsley, T. (1995, January). For whom the bell curve really tolls. *Scientific American,* 14–17.

Bechtel, W. & Abrahamsen, A. (2002). *Connectionism and the mind: Parallel processing, dynamics, and evolution in networks* (2nd ed.). Oxford, UK: Basil Blackwell.

Beck, A. T. (1976). *Cognitive therapy and the emotional disorders.* New York: International Universities Press.

Beck, A. T. (1979). *Cognitive therapy and the emotional disorders.* New York: Penguin Books.

Beck, A. T. (1984). Cognitive approaches to stress. In C. Lehrer & R. L. Woolfolk (Eds.), *Clinical guide to stress management.* New York: Guilford Press.

Beck, J. S. (2007). Cognitive therapy for personality disorders. Retrieved November 17, 2010, from http://www.academyofct.org/Library/InfoManage/Guide.asp?FolderID=196.

Beckman, M. & Pierrehumbert, J. (1986). Intonational structure in English and Japanese. *Phonology Year Book III,* 15–70.

Beehr, T. A., Jex, S. M., Stacy, B. A., & Murray, M. A. (2000). Work stressors and coworker support as predictors of individual strain and job performance. *Journal of Organizational Behavior, 21*(4), 391–405.

Beer, J. M., & Horn, J. M. (2001). The influence of rearing order on personality development within two adoption cohorts. *Journal of Personality, 68,* 789–819.

Beer, J. S. (2009). The neural basis of emotion regulation: Making emotion work for you and not against you. In M. S. Gazzaniga (Ed.), *The Cognitive Neurosciences* (pp. 961–972). Cambridge, MA: The MIT Press.

Behne, T., Carpenter, M., & Tomasello, M. (2005). One-year-olds comprehend the communicative intentions behind gestures in a hiding game. *Developmental Science, 8,* 492–499.

Békésy, G. V. (1960). *Experiments in Hearing* (E. G. Wever, Trans.). New York: McGraw-Hill Book Company.

Belsky, J. (2005). Differential susceptibility to rearing influence: An evolutionary hypothesis and some evidence. In B. Ellis & D. Bjorklund (Eds.), *Origins of the social mind: Evolutionary psychology and child development* (pp. 139–163). New York: Guilford.

Belsky, J., & Johnson, C. D. (2005). Developmental outcome of children in day care. In J. Murph, S. D. Palmer, & D. Glassy (Eds.), *Health in child care: A manual for health professionals* (4th ed., pp. 81–95). Elks Grove Village, IL: American Academy of Pediatrics.

Belsky, J., Vandell, D., Burchinal, M., Clarke-Stewart, K. A., McCartney, K., Owen, M., & NICHD Early Child Care Research Network. (2007). Are there long-term effects of early child care? *Child Development, 78,* 681–701.

Bem, D. J. (1972). Self-perception theory. In L. Berkowitz (Ed.), *Advances in experimental social psychology* (Vol. 6, pp. 1–62). New York: Academic Press.

Bem, S. L. (1975). Sex role adaptability: The consequence of psychological androgyny. *Journal of Personality and Social Psychology, 31,* 634–643.

Bem, S. L. (1981). Gender schema theory: A cognitive account of sex typing. *Psychological Review, 88*, 354–364.

Bem, S. L. (1987). Gender schema theory and the romantic tradition. In P. Shaver & C. Hendrick (Eds.), *Review of personality and social psychology* (Vol. 7, pp. 251-271). Newbury Park, CA: Sage.

Bem, S. L. (1993). Is there a place in psychology for a feminist analysis of the social context? *Feminism & Psychology, 3*, 247–251.

Benjafield, J. J. G. (1996). *A history of psychology*. Boston: Allyn and Bacon.

Benjamin, S. L. (1996). An interpersonal theory of personality disorders. In J. F. Clarkin & M. F. Lenzenweger (Eds.), *Major theories of personality disorder*. New York: Guilford Press.

Benowitz, N. L. (1988). Pharmacologic aspects of cigarette smoking and nicotine addiction. *New England Journal of Medicine, 319*, 1318–1330.

Benowitz, N. L. (1996). Pharmacology of nicotine: Addiction and therapeutics. *Annual Review of Pharmacology and Toxicology, 36*, 597–613.

Ben-Shakhar, G., Bar-Hillel, M., Bliu, Y., Ben-Abba, E., & Flug, A. (1986). Can graphology predict occupational success? Two empirical studies and some methodological ruminations. *Journal of Applied Psychology, 71*, 645–653.

Benson, H. (1975). *The relaxation response*. New York: Morrow.

Benson, H., Beary, J., & Carol, M. (1974a). The relaxation response. *Psychiatry, 37*, 37–46.

Benson, H., Rosner, B. A., Marzetta, B. R., & Klemchuk, H. M. (1974b). Decreased blood pressure in pharmacologically treated hypertensive patients who regularly elicited the relaxation response. *Lancet, 1*(7852), 289–291.

Benton, D., & Parker P. (1998). Breakfast, blood glucose and cognition. American Journal of Clinical Nutrition, 67(Suppl:772S).

Berenbaum, S. A., & Snyder, E. (1995). Early hormonal influences on childhood sex-typed activity and playmate preferences: Implications for the development of sexual orientation. *Developmental Psychology, 31*, 31–42.

Berent, S. (1977). Functional asymmetry of the human brain in the recognition of faces. *Neuropsychologia, 15*, 829–831.

Berg, F. (1999). Health risks associated with weight loss and obesity treatment programs. *Journal of Social Issues, 55*(2), 277–297.

Berk, L., Prowse, M., Petrofsky, J. S., Batt, J., Laymon, M., Bains, G., Daher, N., Tan, S., & Berk, D. (2009, May). *Laughercise: Health benefits similar of exercise lowers cholesterol and systolic blood pressure*. Presented at the Association for Psychological Science 21st Annual Convention, San Francisco, California.

Berk L., Tan, S. A., & Berk, D. (2008, April). *Cortisol and catecholamine stress hormone decrease is associated with the behavior of perceptual anticipation of mirthful laughter.* Presented at the 121st Annual Meeting of the American Physiological Society, San Diego, California.

Berk, L. E. (1992). Children's private speech: An overview of theory and the status of research. In R. M. Diaz & L. E. Berk (Eds.), *Private speech: From social interaction to self-regulation* (pp. 17–53). Hillsdale, NJ: Erlbaum.

Berk, L. E., & Spuhl, S. T. (1995). Maternal interaction, private speech, and task performance in preschool children. *Early Childhood Research Quarterly, 10*, 145–169.

Berk, L. S., Felten, D. L., Tan, S. A., Bittman, B. B., & Westengard, J. (2001). Modulation of neuroimmune parameters during the eustress of humor-associated mirthful laughter. *Alternative Therapy Health Medicines, 7*(2), 62–72, 74–76.

Berk, L. S., Tan, S. A., Fry, W. F., Napier, B., J., Lee, J. W., Hubbard, R. W., Lewis, J. E., & Eby, W. C. (1989). Neuroendrocrine and stress hormone changes during mirthful laughter. *American Journal of the Medical Sciences. 298*(6), 390–396.

Berkowitz, L. (1993). *Aggression: Its causes, consequences and control.* New York: McGraw-Hill.

Berman, A., Bradley, J. C., Carroll, B., Certain, R. D., Gabrelcik, J. C., Green, R., et al. (2010). *The challenge and the promise: Strengthening the force, preventing suicide and saving lives. Final report of the Department of Defense task force on the prevention of suicide by members of the armed forces.* Washington, DC.

Bermond, B., Nieuwenhuyse, B., Fasotti, L., & Schuerman, J. (1991). Spinal cord lesions, peripheral feedback, and intensities of emotional feelings. *Cognition and Emotion, 5*, 201–220.

Bernat, E., Shevrin, H., & Snodgrass, M. (2001). Subliminal visual oddball stimuli evoke a P300 component. *Clinical Neurophysiology, 112*, 159–171.

Berry, J. W., & Kim, U. (1998). Acculturation and mental health. In P. R. Dasen, J. W. Berry, & N. Sartorius (Eds.), *Health and cross-cultural psychology: Toward applications* (pp. 207–236). Newbury Park, CA: Sage.

Berry, J. W., & Sam, D. L. (1997). Acculturation and adaptation. In J. W. Berry, M. H. Segall, & C. Kagitcibasi (Eds.), *Handbook of cross-cultural psychology, Vol. 3: Social behaviour and applications* (2nd ed., pp. 291–326). Boston: Allyn & Bacon.

Berscheid, E., & Reis, H. T. (1998). Attraction and close relationships. In D. T. Gilbert & S. T. Fiske et al. (Eds.), *The handbook of social psychology, Vol. 2* (4th ed., pp. 193–281), New York: McGraw-Hill.

Berteretche, M. V., Dalix, A. M., Cesar d'Ornano, A. M., Bellisle, F., Khayat, D., & Faurion, A. (2004). Decreased taste sensitivity in cancer patients under chemotherapy. *Supportive Care in Cancer, 12*(8), 571–576.

Bertram, L., & Tanzi, R. E. (2005). The genetic epidemiology of neurodegenerative disease. *The Journal of Clinical Investigation, 115*(6), 1449–1457.

Best, D. L., & Williams, J. E. (2001). Gender and culture. In D. Matsumoto (Ed.), *The handbook of culture and psychology* (pp. 195–212). New York: Oxford University Press.

Betancourt, J. R., & Jacobs, E. A. (2000). Language barriers to informed consent and confidentiality: The impact on women's health. *Journal of American Medical Women's Association, 55*, 294–295.

Beyer, B. K. (1995). *Critical thinking.* Bloomington, IN: Phi Delta Kappa Educational Foundation.

Beyreuther, K., Biesalski, H. K., Fernstrom, J. D., Grimm, P., Hammes, W. P., Heinemann, U., Kempski, O., Stehle, P., Steinhart, H., & Walker, R. (2007). Consensus meeting: Monosodium glutamate, an update. *European Journal of Clinical Nutrition, 61*, 304–313.

Bidinosti, M., Ran, I., Sanchez-Carbente, M. R., Martineau, Y., Gingras, A. C., Gkogkas, C., Raught, B., Bramham, C. R., Sossin, W. S., Costa-Mattioli, M., DesGroseillers, L., Lacaille, J. C., & Sonenberg, N. (2010). Postnatal deamidation of 4E-BP2 in brain enhances its association with raptor and alters kinetics of excitatory synaptic transmission. *Molecular Cell: 37*(6), 797–808.

Bigler, E. D., Johnson, S. C., Anderson, C. V., Blatter, D. D., Gale, S. D., Russo, A. A., Ryser, D. K., Macnamara, S. E., Bailey, B. R., & Hopkins, R. O. (1996). Traumatic brain injury and memory: The role of hippocampal atrophy. *Neuropsychology, 10*, 333–342.

Binet, A., & Simon, T. (1916). *The development of intelligence in children.* Baltimore: Williams & Wilkins.

Bivens, J. A., & Berk, L. E. (1990). A longitudinal study of the development of elementary school children's private speech. *Merill-Palmer Quarterly, 36*, 443–463.

Bjork, R. A., & Bjork, E. L. (1992). A new theory of disuse and an old theory of stimulus fluctuation. In A. Healy, S. Kosslyn, & R. Shiffrin (Eds.), *From learning processes to cognitive processes: Essays in honor of William K. Estes* (Vol. 2, pp. 35–67). Hillsdale, NJ: Erlbaum.

Bjork, R. A., & Whitten, W. B. (1974). Recency-sensitive retrieval processes in long-term free recall. *Cognitive Psychology, 6*, 173–189.

Black, D. W., & Andreasen, N. C. (1999). Schizophrenia, schizophreniform disorder, and delusional (paranoid) disorders. In R. E. Hales et al. (Eds.), *Textbook of psychiatry* (3rd ed., pp. 425–477). Washington, DC: American Psychiatric Press.

Blackmon, L. R., Batton, D. G., Bell, E. F., Engle, W. A., Kanto, W. P., Martin, G. I., Rosenfeld, W. N., Stark, A. R., & Lemons, J. A. (Committee on Fetus and Newborn). (2003). *Apnea, sudden infant death syndrome, and home monitoring. Pediatrics, 111*(4), 914–917.

Blair, R. J. R., Sellars, C., Strickland, I., Clark, F., Williams, A. O., Smith, M., & Jones, L. (1995). Emotion attributions in the psychopath. *Personality and Individual Differences, 19*(4), 431–437.

Blanchard, M., & Main, M. (1979). Avoidance of the attachment figure and social-emotional adjustment in day-care infants. *Developmental Psychology, 15*, 445–446.

Blanchard, R. (2001). Fraternal birth order and the maternal immune hypothesis of male homosexuality. *Hormones and Behavior, 40*(2), 105–114.

Blanchard-Fields, F., Chen, Y., Horhota, M., & Wang, M. (2007). Cultural differences in the relationship between aging and the correspondence bias. *Journals of Gerontology Series B: Psychological Sciences and Social Sciences, 62*(6), 362–365.

Blanchard-Fields, F., & Horhota, M. (2005). Age differences in the correspondence bias: When a plausible explanation matters. *Journals of Gerontology Series B: Psychological Sciences and Social Sciences, 60*(5), 259–267.

Blass, T. (1991). Understanding behavior in the Milgram obedience experiment: The role of personality, situations, and their interactions. *Journal of Personality and Social Psychology, 60*, 398–413.

Blass, T. (1999). The Milgram paradigm after 35 years: Some things we now know about obedience to authority. *Journal of Applied Social Psychology, 25*, 955–978.

Blazer, D. G., Kessler, R. C., McGonagle, K. A., & Swartz, M. S. (1994). The prevalence and distribution of major depression in a national community sample: The National Comorbidity Survey. *American Journal of Psychiatry, 151*, 979–986.

Bledsoe, C. H., & Cohen, B. (1993). *Social dynamics of adolescent fertility in sub-Saharan Africa.* Washington DC: National Academy Press.

Blehar, M. C., & Oren, D. A. (1997). Gender differences in depression. *Medscape General Medicine, 1*(2). Retrieved June 27, 2004, from http://www.medscape.com/viewarticle/719236

Bleiberg, K. L., & Markowitcz, J. C. (2008). Interpersonal psychotherapy for depression. In D. H. Barlow (Ed.), *Clinical handbook of psychological disorders* (pp. 306–327). New York: Guilford Press.

Bleuler, E. (1911, reissued 1950). *Dementia praecox or the group of schizophrenias.* New York: International Universities Press.

Blits, B., & Bunge, M. B. (2006). Direct gene therapy for repair of the spinal cord. *Journal of Neurotrauma, 23*(3–4), 508–520.

Block, N. (2005). Two neural correlates of consciousness. *Trends in Cognitive Sciences*, 9, 41–89.

Bloom, B. S. (Ed.). (1956) Taxonomy of educational objectives, the classification of educational goals—Handbook I: Cognitive domain. New York: McKay.

Bloom, L. (1974). Talking, understanding and thinking. In R. Schiefelbusch & L. L. Lloyd (Eds.), *Language perspectives: Acquisition, retardation and intervention.* New York: Macmillan.

Bloom, P. (2000). *How children learn the meaning of words.* Cambridge, MA: MIT Press.

Blumenfeld, H. (2002). *Neuroanatomy through clinical cases.* Sunderland, MA: Sinauer.

Blumer, D. (2002). The illness of Vincent van Gogh. *American Journal of Psychiatry, 159*(4), 519–526.

Bock, R. (1993, August). *Understanding Klinefelter syndrome: A guide for XXY males and their families.* NIH Publication No. 93-3202. National Institutes of Health, Office of Research Reporting. Washington, DC: Retrieved August 10, 2010, from http://www.nichd.nih.gov/publications/pubs/klinefelter.cfm

Bodrova, E., & Leong, D. J. (1996). *Tools of the mind: The Vygotskian approach to early childhood education.* Englewood Cliffs, NJ: Prentice Hall.

Boggio, P. S., Campanha, C., Valasek, C. A., Fecteau, S., Pascual-Leone, A., & Fregni, F. (2010). Modulation of decision-making in a gambling task in older adults with transcranial direct current stimulation. *The European Journal of Neuroscience, 31*(3), 593–597.

Boggio, P. S., Fregni, F., Valasek, C., Ellwood, S., Chi, R., Gallate, J., et al. (2009). Temporal lobe cortical electrical stimulation during the encoding and retrieval phase reduces false memories. *PLoS One, 4*(3), e4959.

Boggio, P. S., Rocha, M., Oliveira, M. O., Fecteau, S., Cohen, R. B., Campanha, C., Ferreira-Santos, E., Meleiro, A., Corchs, F., Zaghi, S., Pascual-Leone, A., & Fregni, F. (2009). Noninvasive brain stimulation with high-frequency and low-intensity repetitive transcranial magnetic stimulation treatment for post-traumatic stress disorder. *The Journal of Clinical Psychiatry, 29*, 29.

Bogle, K. D. (2000). Effect of perspective, type of student, and gender on the attribution of cheating. *Proceedings of the Oklahoma Academy of Science, 80*, 91–97.

Bolton, P., Bass, J., Betancourt, T., Speelman, L., Onyango, G., Clougherty, K. F., et. al. (2007). Interventions for depression symptoms among adolescent survivors of war and displacement in northern Uganda. *Journal of Medical Association, 298,* 519–527.

Bond, R. A., & Smith, P. B. (1996). Culture and conformity: A meta-analysis of studies using Asch's (1952, 1956) line judgment task. *Psychological Bulletin, 119*, 111–137.

Bondarenko, L. A. (2004). Role of methionine in nocturnal melatonin peak in the pineal gland. *Bulletin of Experimental Biological Medicine, 137*(5), 431–432.

Bonnelykke, B. (1990). Maternal age and parity as predictors of human twinning. *Acta Genetic Medicine & Gemellology, 39*, 329–334.

Boor, M. (1982). The multiple personality epidemic: Additional cases and inferences regarding diagnosis, etiology, dynamics, and treatment. *Journal of Nervous and Mental Disease, 170*, 302–304.

Booth-Butterfield, S. (1996). Message characteristics. *Steve's primer of practical persuasion and influence.* Retrieved August 2, 2004, from http://www.austincc.edu/colangelo/1311/persuasivecharacteristics.htm

Borgeat, F., & Goulet, J. (1983, June). Psychophysiological changes following auditory subliminal suggestions for activation and deactivation. *Perceptual & Motor Skills, 56*(3), 759–766.

Borges, M. A., Stepnowsky, M. A., & Holt, L. H. (1977). Recall and recognition of words and pictures by adults and children. *Bulletin of the Psychonomic Society, 9*, 113–114.

Boroditsky, L. (2001). Does language shape thought? Mandarin and English speakers' conceptions of time. *Cognitive Psychology, 43*(1), 1–22.

Boroditsky, L. (2009). How does our language shape the way we think? In M. Brockman (Ed.), What's next? Dispatches on the future of science (pp. 116–129). New York: Vintage.

Bosworth, H. B., & Schaie, K. W. (1997). The relationship of social environment, social networks, and health outcomes in the Seattle Longitudinal Study: Two analytical approaches. *Journals of Gerontology Series B: Psychological Sciences and Social Sciences, 52*(5), 197–205.

Botwin, M. D., & Buss, D. M. (1989). The structure of act data: Is the Five-Factor Model of personality recaptured? *Journal of Personality and Social Psychology, 56*, 988–1001.

Bouchard, C., Tremblay, A., Nadeau, A., Dussault, J., Despres, J. P., Theriault, G., Lupien, P. J., Serresse, O., Boulay, M. R., & Fournier, G. (1990). Long-term exercise training with constant energy intake. 1: Effect on body composition and selected metabolic variables. *International Journal on Obesity, 14*(1), 57–73.

Bouchard, T. (1994). Genes, environment, and personality. *Science, 264*, 1700–1701.

Bouchard, T. J., Jr. (1997). Whenever the twain shall meet. *The Science, 37*(5), 52–57.

Bouchard, T. J., & Segal, N. L. (1985). Environment and IQ. In B. B. Wolman (Ed.), *Handbook of intelligence: Theories, measurements, and applications* (pp. 391–464). New York: John Wiley.

Bowden, C. L., Calabrese, J. R., McElroy, S. L., Gyulai, L., Wassef, A., Petty, F., Pope, H. G., Jr., Chou, J. C., Keck, P. E., Jr., Rhodes, L. J., Swann, A. C., Hirschfeld, R. M., & Wozniak, P. J. (2000). For the Divalproex Maintenance Study Group. A randomized, placebo-controlled 12-month trial of divalproex and lithium in treatment of outpatients with bipolar I disorder. *Archives of General Psychiatry, 57*(5), 481–489.

Bowers, K. S., & Woody, E. Z. (1996). Hypnotic amnesia and the paradox of intentional forgetting. *Journal of Abnormal Psychology, 105*, 381–390.

Bowman, E. S. (1996). Delayed memories of child abuse: Part II: An overview of research findings relevant to understanding their reliability and suggestibility. *Dissociation: Progress in the Dissociative Disorders, 9*, 232–243.

Boyd, C. H., & Peeler, C. M. (May, 2004). *Highlighting vs note taking: A comparison of students' performance on tests.* Poster presented at 16th Annual Convention of the American Psychological Society, Chicago, Illinois, USA.

Boyd, L. A., & Winstein, C. J. (2004). Cerebellar stroke impairs temporal but not spatial accuracy during implicit motor learning. *Neurorehabilitation and Neural Repair, 18*(3), 134–143.

Boyson-Bardies, B., deHalle, P., Sagart, L., & Durand, C. (1989). A cross-linguistic investigation of vowel formats in babbling. *Journal of Child Language, 16*, 1–17.

Bracey, G. (1997). A few facts about poverty. *Phi Delta Kappan, 79*, 163–164.

Braio, A., Beasley, T. M., Dunn, R., Quinn, P., & Buchanan, K. (1997). Incremental implementation of learning style strategies among urban low achievers. *The Journal of Educational Research, 91,* 15–25.

Braun, S. R. (1996). *Buzz: the science and lore of alcohol and caffeine,* pp. 137-169. New York: Oxford University Press.

Brawman-Mintzer, O., & Lydiard, R. B. (1997). Biological basis of generalized anxiety disorder. *Journal of Clinical Psychiatry, 58*(3), 16–25.

Brazelton, T. B. (1992). *Touchpoints: Your child's emotional and behavioral development.* Reading, MA: Addison-Wesley.

Brecher, M., Wang, B. W., Wong, H., & Morgan, J. P. (1988). Phencyclidine and violence: Clinical and legal issues. *Journal of Clinical Psychopharmacology, 8*, 397–401.

Breier, A., Albus, M., Pickar, D., Zahn, T. P., Wolkowitz, O. M., & Paul, S. M. (1987). Controllable and uncontrollable stress in humans: Alterations in mood, neuroendocrine and psychophysiological function. *American Journal of Psychiatry, 144*, 1419–1425.

Breland, K., & Breland, M. (1961). The misbehavior of organisms. *American Psychologist. 16*, 681–684.

Bremmer, J. D. (2005). *Brain imaging handbook.* New York: W. W. Norton.

Brennan, J. F. (2002). *History and systems of psychology* (6th ed.). Upper Saddle River, NJ: Prentice Hall.

Brennan, P. A., Raine, A., Schulsinger, F., Kirkegaard-Sorensen, L., Knop, J., Hutchings, B., Rosenberg, R., & Mednick, S. A. (1997). Psychophysiological protective factors for male subjects at high risk for criminal behavior. *American Journal of Psychiatry, 154*, 853–855.

Brenner, J. (2007, August).Parental impact on attitude formation—A siblings study on worries about immigration. *Ruhr Economic Paper No. 22*. Available at Social Science Research Network (SSR) at http://ssrn.com/abstract=1012110

Breslau, N., Chilcoat, H. D., Kessler, R. C., Peterson, E. L., & Lucia, V. C. (1999). Vulnerability to assaultive violence: Further specification of the sex difference in posttraumatic stress disorder. *Psychological Medicine, 29*, 813–821.

Breslau, N., Davis, G. C., Andreski, P., & Peterson, E. L. (1997). Sex differences in posttraumatic stress disorder. *Archives of General Psychiatry, 54*(11), 1044–1048.

Breuer, J., & Freud, S. (1895). *Studies on hysteria (cathartic method). Special Edition, 2*, 1–309.

Brewer, M. B. (2001). Ingroup identification and intergroup conflict: When does in-group love become outgroup hate? In R. D. Ashmore, L. Jussim, & D. Wilder (Eds.), *Social identity, intergroup conflict, and conflict reduction*. New York: Oxford University Press.

Brick, J. (2003). The characteristics of alcohol: Chemistry, use and abuse. In J. Brick (Ed.), *Handbook of the medical consequences of alcohol and drug abuse* (pp. 1–11). New York: Haworth Medical Press.

Briem, V., & Hedman, L. R. (1995). Behavioural effects of mobile telephone use during simulated driving. *Ergonomics, 38*, 2536–2562.

Briggs, K. C., & Myers, I. B. (1998). *The Myers-Briggs Type Indicator-Form M.* Palo Alto, CA: Consulting Psychologists Press.

Brigham, A. (1844). Asylums exclusively for the incurably insane. Classic article in *The American Journal of Psychiatry, 151*, 50–70.

Broadbent, D. (1958). *Perception and communication.* Elmsford, NY: Pergamon.

Brondolo, E., Rieppi, R., Erickson, S. A., Bagiella, E., Shapiro, P. A., McKinley, P., & Sloan, R. P. (2003). Hostility, interpersonal interactions, and ambulatory blood pressure. *Psychosomatic Medicine, 65*, 1003–1011.

Bronkhorst, A. W. (2000). The cocktail party phenomenon: A review on speech intelligibility in multiple-talker conditions. *Acta Acustica united with Acustica 86*, 117–128. PDF available from http://eaa-fenestra.org/products/acta-acustica/most-cited/acta_86_2000_Bronkhorst.pdf

Brooks, J. G., & Brooks, M. G. (1993). *In search of understanding: The case for constructivist classrooms.* Alexandria, VA: The Association for Supervision and Curriculum Development.

Brown, C., Taylor, J., Green, A., Lee, B. E., Thomas, S. B., & Ford, A. (2003). *Managing depression in African Americans: Consumer and provider perspectives.* (Final Report to Funders). Pittsburgh: Mental Health Association of Allegheny County.

Brown, C. A., & Jones, A. K. P. (in press). Meditation experience predicts less negative appraisal of pain: Electrophysiological evidence for the involvement of anticipatory neural responses. *Pain*. doi: 10.1016/j.pain.2010.04.017

Brown, G., Lawrence, T. B., & Robinson, S. L. (2005). Territoriality in management organizations. *Academy of Management Review, 30*(3), 577–594.

Brown, G. L., & Linnoila, M. I. (1990). CSF serotonin metabolite (5–HIAA) studies in depression, impulsivity, and violence. *Journal of Clinical Psychiatry, 51*(4), 31–43.

Brown, J. (1958). Some tests of the decay theory of immediate memory. *Quarterly Journal of Experimental Psychology, 10*, 12–21.

Brown, P. K., & Wald, G. (1964). Visual pigments in single rods and cones of the human retina. *Science, 144*, 45.

Brown, R. (1973). *A first language: The early stages.* Cambridge, MA: Harvard University Press.

Brown, R., & McNeill, D. (1966). The "tip of the tongue" phenomenon. *Journal of Verbal Learning & Verbal Behavior, 5*(4), 325–337.

Brown, W. M., Finn, C. J., Cooke, B. M., & Breedlove, S. M. (2002). Differences in finger length ratios between self-identified "butch" and "femme" lesbians. *Archives of Sexual Behavior, 31*(1), 123–127.

Browne, D. (2004). Do dolphins know their own minds? *Biology & Philosophy, 19*, 633–653.

Browne, M. N., & Keeley, S. M. (2009). *Asking the right questions: A guide to critical thinking* (9th ed., pp. 37–129). Upper Saddle River, NJ: Pearson Prentice-Hall.

Broyles, S. (2006). Subliminal advertising and the perpetual popularity of playing to people's paranoia. *Journal of Consumer Affairs, 40*(2), 392–406.

Brubaker, D. A., & Leddy, J. J. (2003). Behavioral contracting in the treatment of eating disorders. *The Physician and Sportsmedicine, 31*(9).

Brunner, E. J., Hemingway, H., Walker, B., Page, M., Clarke, P., Juneja, M., Shipley, M. J., Kumari, M., Andrew, R., Seckl, J. R., Papadopoulos, A., Checkley, S., Rumley, A., Lowe, G. D., Stansfeld, S. A., & Marmot, M. G. (2002). Adrenocortical, autonomic and inflammatory causes of the metabolic syndrome: Nested case-control study. *Circulation, 106*, 2659–2665.

Bryan, E. B., & Hallett, F. (2001). *Guidelines for professionals. Twins and triplets: The first five years and beyond.* London: Multiple Births Foundation.

Bryan, J., & Freed, F. (1982). Corporal punishment: Normative data and sociological and psychological correlates in a community college population. *Journal of Youth and Adolescence, 11*(2), 77–87.

Bryant, R. A., & McConkey, K. M. (1989). Hypnotic blindness: A behavioral and experimental analysis. *Journal of Abnormal Psychology, 98*, 71–77.

Brzustowicz, L. M., Simone, J., Mohseni, P., Hayter, J. E., Hodgkinson, K. A., Chow, E. W., & Bassett, A. S. (2004). Linkage disequilibrium mapping of schizophrenia susceptibility to the CAPON region of chromosome 1q22. *American Journal of Human Genetics, 74*(5), 1057–1063.

Buccino, G., Binkofski, F., Fink, G. R., Fadiga, L., Fogassi, L., Gallese, V., et al. (2001). Action observation activates premotor and parietal areas in a somatotopic manner: An fMRI study. *European Journal of Neuroscience, 13*(2), 400–404.

Buccino, G., Binkofski, F., & Riggio, L. (2004). The mirror neuron system and action recognition. *Brain and Language, 89*(2), 370–376.

Bucher, B. D., & Lovaas, O. I. (1967). Use of aversive stimulation in behavior modification. In M. R. Jones (Ed.), *Miami Symposium on the Prediction of Behavior 1967: Aversive Stimulation*, 77–145. Coral Gables: University of Miami Press.

Buck, R. (1980). Nonverbal behavior and the theory of emotion: The facial feedback hypothesis. *Journal of Personality and Social Psychology, 38*, 811–824.

Budur, K., Mathews, M., & Mathews, M. (2005). Couvade syndrome equivalent? *Psychosomatics, 46*(1), 71–72.

Bullock, T. H., Bennett, M. V., Johnston, D., Josephson, R., Marder, E., & Fields, R. D. (2005). Neuroscience. The neuron doctrine, redux. *Science, 310*(5749), 791–793.

Bunge, M. (1984). What is pseudoscience? *The Skeptical Inquirer, 9*(1), 36–46.

Bunge, M. B., & Pearse, D. D. (2003). Transplantation strategies to promote repair of the injured spinal cord. *Journal of Rehabilitative Research & Development, 40*(4), 55–62.

Bureau of Labor Statistics. (2010). *Census of fatal occupational injuries.* Retrieved August 9, 2010, from http://www.bls.gov/iif/oshcfoi1.htm

Burger, J. J. M. (1997). The psychoanalytic approach: Neo-Freudian theory, application, and assessment. *Personality* (4th ed.). Pacific Grove, CA: Brooks/Cole.

Burger, J. M. (1986). Increasing compliance by improving the deal: The that's not all technique. *Journal of Personality and Social Psychology, 51*, 277–283.

Burger, J. M., & Petty, R. E. (1981). The low-ball compliance technique: Task or person commitment? *Journal of Personality and Social Psychology, 40*, 492–500.

Burgio, K. L. (1998). Behavioral vs. drug treatment for urge urinary incontinence in older women: A randomized controlled trial. *Journal of the American Medical Association, 280*, 1995–2000.

Burke, D. M., MacKay, D. G., Worthley, J. S., & Wade, E. (1991). On the tip of the tongue: What causes word finding failures in young and older adults. *Journal of Memory and Language, 30*, 542–579.

Burks, N., & Martin, B. (1985). Everyday problems and life change events: Ongoing versus acute sources of stress. *Journal of Human Stress, 11*, 27–35.

Burns, J. F. (May 24, 2010). British medical council bars doctor who linked vaccine with autism. *New York Times.*

Bush, G., Frazier, J. A., Rauch, S. L., Seidman, L. J., Whalen, P. J., Jenike, M. A., et al. (1999). Anterior cingulate cortex dysfunction in attention-deficit/hyperactivity disorder revealed by fMRI and the Counting Stroop. *Biological Psychiatry, 45*(12), 1542–1552.

Bush, G., Spencer, T. J., Holmes, J., Shin, L. M., Valera, E. M., Seidman, L. J., et al. (2008). Functional magnetic resonance imaging of methylphenidate and placebo in attention-deficit/hyperactivity disorder during the Multi-Source Interference Task. *Archives of General Psychiatry, 65*(1), 102–114.

Bushman, B. J. (1997). Effects of alcohol on human aggression: Validity of proposed explanations. In M. Galanter (Ed.), Recent developments in alcoholism. Vol. 1: Alcohol and violence—Epidemiology, neurobiology, psychology, family issues (pp. 227–243). New York: Plenum Press.

Bushman, B. J., & Huesmann, L. R. (2001). Effects of televised violence on aggression. In D. G. Singer & J. L. Singer (Eds.), *Handbook of children and the media* (Ch. 11, pp. 223–254). Thousand Oaks, CA: Sage.

Buss, D. M., Larsen, R. J., Westen, D., & Semmelroth, J. (1992). Sex differences in jealousy: Evolution, physiology, and psychology. *Psychological Science, 3*, 251–255.

Bussa, B., & Kaufman, C. (2000). What can self-help do? *The Journal of the California Alliance of the Mentally Ill, 2*(2), 34–45.

Butcher, J. N., & Rouse, S. V. (1996). Personality: Individual differences and clinical assessment. *Annual Review of Psychology, 47*, 87–111.

Butcher, J. N., Graham, J. R., Ben-Poarth, Y. S., Tellegen, A., Dahlstrom, W. G., & Kaemmer, B. (2001). *Minnesota Multiphasic Personality Inventory-2. Manual for administration, scoring, and interpretation* (Rev. ed.). Minneapolis, MN: University of Minnesota Press.

Butcher, J. N., Rouse, S. V., & Perry, J. N. (2000). Empirical description of psychopathology in therapy clients: Correlates of MMPI-2 scales. In J. N. Butcher (Ed.), *Basic sources on the MMPI-2* (pp. 487–500). Minneapolis, MN: University of Minnesota Press.

Cabeza, R., Anderson, N. D., Locantore, J. K. & McIntosh, A. R. (2002). Aging gracefully: Compensatory brain activity in high-performing older adults. *NeuroImage, 17*(3), 1394–1402.

Cabeza, R., & Nyberg, L. (2000). Imaging cognition II: An empirical review of 275 PET and fMRI studies. *Journal of Cognitive Neuroscience, 12*(1), 1–47.

Cain, D., & Seeman, J. (Eds.). (2001). *Humanistic psychotherapies: Handbook of research and practice*. Washington, DC: APA Publications.

Califia, P. (1997). *Sex changes: The politics of transgenderism*. San Francisco: Cleis Press.

Calvo, E. Haverstick, K. & Sass, S. A. (2009). Gradual retirement, sense of control, and retirees' happiness. *Research on Aging, 31*, 112–135.

Camara, W. J., Nathan, J. S., & Puente, A. E. (2000). Psychological test usage: Implications in professional psychology. *Professional Psychology: Research and Practice, 31*(2), 141–154.

Camchong, J., Lim, K. O., Sponheim, S. R., & Macdonald, A. W. (2009). Frontal white matter integrity as an endophenotype for schizophrenia: Diffusion tensor imaging in monozygotic twins and patients' nonpsychotic relatives. *Frontiers in Human Neuroscience, 3*, 35.

Cameron, J., Banko, K. M., & Pierce, W. D. (2001). Pervasive negative effects of rewards on intrinsic motivation: The myth continues. *The Behavior Analyst, 24*, 1–44.

Cameron, J. A., Alvarez, J. M., Ruble, D. N., & Fuligni, A. J. (2001). Children's lay theories about ingroups and outgroups: Reconceptualizing research on prejudice. *Personality and Social Psychology Review, 5*, 118–128.

Cami, J., Farre, M., Mas, M., Roset, P. N., Poudevida, S., Mas, A., San, L., & de la Torre, R. (2000). Human pharmacology of 3,4-methylenedioxymethamphetamine ("ecstasy"): Psychomotor performance and subjective effects. *Journal of Clinical Psychopharmacology, 20*, 455–466.

Campbell, J. C., & Wolf, A. D. (2003). Risk factors for femicide in abusive relationships: Results from a multisite case control study. *American Journal of Public Health, 93*(7).

Cannon, W. B. (1927). The James-Lange theory of emotion: A critical examination and an alternative theory. *American Journal of Psychology, 39*, 10–124.

Cannon, W. B., & Washburn, A. L. (1912). An explanation of hunger. *American Journal of Physiology, 29*, 444–454.

Carducci, B. (1998). *The psychology of personality*. Pacific Grove, CA: Brooks/Cole Publishing Co.

Carey, B. (2009, December 21). Building a search engine of the brain, slice by slice. *New York Times*. Retrieved June 10, 2010, from http://www.nytimes.com/2009/12/22/health/22brain.html?ref=henry_gustav_molaison

Carlson, G. A., Jensen, P. S., & Nottelmann, E. D. (Eds.). (1998). Current issues in childhood bipolarity [Special issue]. *Journal of Affective Disorders, 51*.

Carnot, M. J., Dunn, B., Cañas, A. J., Graham, P. & Muldoon, J. (2001). Concept Maps vs. Web Pages for Information Searching and Browsing. Manuscript in preparation. Institute for Human and Machine Cognition.

Carpenter, P. A., Just, M. A., & Shell, P. (1990). What one intelligence test measures: A theoretical account of the processing in the Raven Progressive Matrices test. *Psychological Review, 97*(3), 404–431.

Carr, E. G., & Lovaas, O. I. (1983). Contingent electric shock as a treatment for severe behavior problems. In S. Axelrod & J. Apsche (Eds.), *The effects of punishment on human behavior* (pp. 221–245). New York: Academic Press.

Carrion, V. G., Weems, C. F., & Reiss, A. L. (2007). Stress predicts brain changes in children: A pilot longitudinal study on youth stress, posttraumatic stress disorder, and the hippocampus. *Pediatrics, 119*(3), 509–516.

Carruthers, M. (2001). A multifactorial approach to understanding andropause. *Journal of Sexual and Reproductive Medicine, 1*, 69–74.

Carskadon, M. A., & Dement, W. C. (2005). Normal human sleep overview. In M. H. Kryger, T. Roth, & W. C. Dement (Eds.), *Principles and practice of sleep medicine* (4th ed., pp. 13–23). Philadelphia: Elsevier/Saunders.

Carson, R. C. (1969). *Interaction concepts of personality*. Chicago: Aldine.

Carter, C., Bishop, J., & Kravits, S. L. (2006). Keys to success: Building successful intelligence for college, career, and life (5th ed.). Englewood Cliffs, NJ: Prentice Hall.

Carter, C., Bishop, J., Kravits, S. L., & D'Agostino, J. V. (Ed. consultant). (2002). *Keys to college studying: Becoming a lifelong learner*. Upper Saddle River, NJ: Prentice Hall.

Carver, C. S., & Antoni, M. H. (2004). Finding benefit in breast cancer during the year after diagnosis predicts better adjustment 5 to 8 years after diagnosis. *Health Psychology, 26*, 595–598.

Carver, L. J., & Bauer, P. J. (2001). The dawning of a past: The emergence of long-term explicit memory in infancy. *Journal of Experimental Psychology: General, 130*, 726–745.

Cassiday, K. L., & Lyons, J. A. (1992). Recall of traumatic memories following cerebral vascular accident. *Journal of Traumatic Stress, 5*, 627–631.

Cassidy, A., Bingham, S., & Setchell, K. D. R. (1994). Biological effects of a diet of soy protein rich in isoflavones on the menstrual cycle of premenopausal women. *American Journal of Clinical Nutrition, 60*, 333–340.

Castillo, R. J. (1997). Eating disorders. In R. J. Castillo (Ed.), *Culture and mental illness: A client-centered approach* (p. 152). Pacific Grove, CA: Brooks/Cole.

Catanzaro, S. J., Wasch, H. H., Kirsch, I., & Mearns, J. (2000). Coping-related expectancies and dispositions as prospective predictors of coping responses and symptoms: Distinguishing mood regulation expectancies, dispositional coping, and optimism. *Journal of Personality, 68*, 757–788.

Cattell, R. B. (1950). *Personality: A systematic, theoretical, and factual study*. New York: McGraw-Hill.

Cattell, R. B. (Ed.). (1966). *Handbook of multivariate experimental psychology*. Chicago: Rand McNally.

Cattell, R. B. (1973). *Personality and mood by questionnaire*. San Francisco: Jossey-Bass.

Cattell, R. B. (1990). Advances in Cattellian personality theory. In L. A. Pervin (Ed.), *Handbook of personality: Theory and research* (pp. 101–110). New York: Guilford.

Cattell, R. B. (1994). *Sixteen Personality Factor Questionnaire* (5th ed.). Champaign, IL: Institute for Personality and Ability Testing, Inc.

Cattell, R. B. (1995). Personality structure and the new fifth edition of the 16PF. *Educational & Psychological Measurement, 55*(6), 926–937.

Cattell, R. B., & Kline, P. (1977). *The scientific analysis of personality and motivation*. New York: Academic Press.

Cave, K. R., & Kim, M. (1999). Top-down and bottom-up attentional control: On the nature of interference from a salient distractor. *Perception & Psychophysics, 61*, 1009–1023.

Cela-Conde, C. J., Ayala, F. J., Munar, E., Maestú, F., Nadal, M., Capó, M. A., del Río, D., López-Ibor, J. J., Ortiz, T., Mirasso, C., & Marty, G. (2009). Sex-related similarities and differences in the neural correlates of beauty. *Proceedings of the National Academy of Sciences, USA, 106*(10), 3847–3852.

Centers for Disease Control and Prevention (CDC). (1992). *Smoking and health in the Americas: The Surgeon General's report*. National Center for Chronic Disease Prevention and Health Promotion. Atlanta, Georgia.

Centers for Disease Control and Prevention (CDC). (2008). National Health and Nutrition Survey. Retrieved February 8, 2008, from http://www.cdc.gov/nchs/data/nhanes/survey_content_99_10.pdf

Centers for Disease Control and Prevention (CDC). (2008). Annual smoking-attributable mortality, years of potential life lost, and economic costs—United States, 2000–2004. *Morbidity and Mortality Weekly Report, 57*(45), 1226–1228.

Centers for Disease Control and Prevention. (2008, October 3). Morbidity and Mortality Weekly Report. HIV Prevalence Estimates—United States, 2006 Centers for Disease Control and Prevention. Atlanta, GA: U.S. Centers for Disease Control and Prevention.

Centers for Disease Control and Prevention. (2009a). HIV/AIDS Surveillance Report 2007 (Vol. 19). National Center for Chronic Disease Prevention and Health Promotion. Atlanta, Georgia.

Centers for Disease Control and Prevention. (2009b). Health effects of cigarette smoking. Retrieved January 13, 2010, from http://www.cdc.gov/tobacco/data_statistics/fact_sheets/health_effects/effects_cig_smoking/index.htm

Centers for Disease Control and Prevention. (2009c). Down syndrome. Retrieved June 19, 2010, from www.cdc.gov/ncbddd/birthdefects/DownSyndrome.htm

Centers for Disease Control and Prevention. (2009d). Occupational violence. Retrieved August 9, 2010, from http://www.cdc.gov/niosh/topics/violence

Centerwall, B. S. (1989). Exposure to television as a risk factor for violence. *American Journal of Epidemiology, 129*, 643–652.

Cepeda, N. J., Pashler, H., Vul, E., Wixted, J. T., & Rohrer, D. (2006). Distributed practice in verbal recall tasks: A review and quantitative synthesis. *Psychological Bulletin, 132,* 354–380.

Cermak, L., & Craik, F. (1979). *Levels of processing in human memory*. Hillsdale, NJ: Erlbaum.

Cha, J. H., & Nam, K. D. (1985). A test of Kelley's cube theory of attribution: A cross-cultural replication of McArthur's study. *Korean Social Science Journal, 12*, 151–180.

Chaddock, L., Hillman, C. H., Buck, S. M., & Cohen, N. J. (2010). Aerobic fitness and executive control of relational memory in preadolescent children. *Medicine and Science in Sports and Exercise.* doi: 10.1249/MSS.0b013e3181e9af48

Chandola, T., Britton, A., Brunner, E., Hemingway, H., Malik, M., Kumari, M., Badrick, E., Kivimaki, M., & Marmot, M. (2008). Work stress and coronary heart disease: What are the mechanisms? *European Heart Journal.,* doi:10.1093/eurheartj/ehm584

Chang, P. P., Ford, D. E., Meoni, L. A., Wang, N., & Klag, M. J. (2002). Anger in young men and subsequent premature cardiovascular disease: The precursors study. *Archives of Internal Medicine, 162*, 901–906.

Chapelon-Clavel, F., Paoletti, C., & Benhamou, S. (1997). Smoking cessation rates 4 years after treatment by nicotine gum and acupuncture. *Preventive Medicine, 26*, 25–28.

Charlesworth, W. R., & Kreutzer, M. A. (1973). Facial expression of infants and children. In P. Ekman (Ed.), *Darwin and facial expression: A century of research in review.* New York: Academic.

Chee, M. W. L., & Choo, W. C. (2004, April 24–May 1). Functional imaging of working memory following 24 hours of total sleep deprivation. *Program and abstracts of the 56th Annual Meeting of the American Academy of Neurology.* San Francisco.

Chen, J. Y. (2007). Do Chinese and English speakers think about time differently? Failure of replicating Boroditsky (2001). *Cognition, 104*(2), 427–436.

Chen, L. Y., Rex, C. S., Sanaiha, Y., Lynch, G., & Gall, C. M. (2010). Learning induces neurotrophin signaling at hippocampal synapses. *Proceedings of the National Academy of Sciences, USA 107*(15), 7030–7035.

Chen, R., & Ende, N. (2000). The potential for the use of mononuclear cells from human umbilical cord blood in the treatment of amyotrophic lateral sclerosis in SOD1 mice. *Journal of Medicine, 31*, 21–31.

Cheng, H., Cao, Y., & Olson, L. (1996). Spinal cord repair in adult paraplegic rats: Partial restoration of hind limb function. *Science, 273*, 510–513.

Cherry, E. C. (1953). Some experiments on the recognition of speech, with one and with two ears. *Journal of the Acoustical Society of America, 25*(5), 975–979.

Cheryan, S., Plaut, V., Davis, P., & Steele, C. (2009). Ambient belonging: How stereotypical cues impact gender participation in computer science. *Journal of Personality and Social Psychology, 97*(6), 1045–1060.

Chess, S., & Thomas, A. (1986). *Temperament in clinical practice.* New York: Guilford Press.

Chesterton, L. S., Barlas, P., Foster, N. E., Baxter, G. D., & Wright, C. C. (2003). Gender differences in pressure pain threshold in healthy humans. *Pain, 101*, 259–266.

Cheyne, J. A. (2003). Sleep paralysis and the structure of waking-nightmare hallucinations. *Dreaming, 13*(3), 163–179.

Chidester, D. (2003). *Salvation and suicide: Jim Jones, the Peoples Temple, and Jonestown* (Rev. ed., pp. 1–51). Bloomington, IN: Indiana University Press.

Chinn, A.B. & Trujillo, K.A. (1996). Drugs and the brain: A World Wide Web tutorial in neuropsychopharmacology. *Society for Neuroscience Abstracts, 22,* 246.

Chiu, C., Hong, Y., & Dweck, C. S. (1997). Lay dispositionism and implicit theories of personality. *Journal of Personality and Social Psychology, 73*, 19–30.

Choi, I., & Nisbett, R. E. (1998). Situational salience and cultural differences in the correspondence bias and in the actor–observer bias. *Personality and Social Psychology Bulletin, 24*, 949–960.

Choi, I., Nisbett, R. E., & Norenzayan, A. (1999). Causal attribution across cultures: Variation and universality. *Psychological Bulletin, 125*, 47–63.

Chomsky, N. (1957). *Syntactic structures*. The Hague: Mouton.

Chomsky, N. (1964). *Current issues in linguistic theory*. The Hague: Mouton.

Chomsky, N. (1981). Principles and parameters in syntactic theory. In N. Hornstein & D. Lightfoot (Eds.), *Explanation in linguistics: The logical problem of language acquisition.* London: Longman.

Chomsky, N. (1986). *Knowledge of language: Its nature, origin and use.* New York: Praeger.

Chomsky, N. (2006). *Language and mind* (3rd ed.). New York: Cambridge University Press.

Chomsky, N., Belletti, A., & Rizzi, L. (2002). *On nature and language.* New York: Cambridge University Press.

Chou, S. Y., Grossman, M., & Saffer, H. (2004). An economic analysis of adult obesity: Results from the behavioral risk factor surveillance system. *Journal of Health Economics, 23*, 565–587.

Christensen, A., Jacobson, N. S., & Babcock, J. C. (1995). Integrative behavioral couple therapy. In N. S. Jacobson & A. S. Gurman (Eds.), *Clinical handbook of couple therapy* (pp. 31–64). New York: Norton.

Christmas, D., Morrison, C., Eljamel, M. S., & Matthews, K. (2004). Neurosurgery for mental disorders. Advances in Psychiatric Treatment, 10, 189-199.

Chu, J. A., Frey, L. M., Ganzel, B. L., & Matthews, J. A. (1999). Memories of childhood abuse: Dissociation, amnesia, and corroboration. *American Journal of Psychiatry, 156*, 749–755.

Chwalisz, K., Diener, E., & Gallagher, D. (1988). Autonomic arousal feedback and emotional experience: Evidence from the spinal cord injured. *Journal of Personality and Social Psychology, 54*, 820–828.

Cialdini, R., Vincent, J., Lewis, S., Catalan, J., Wheeler, D., & Darby, B. (1975). Reciprocal concessions procedure for inducing compliance: The door–in–the–face technique. *Journal of Personality and Social Psychology, 31*, 206–215.

Cialdini, R., Wosinska, W., Barrett, D., Butner, J., & Gornik–Durose, M. (1999). Compliance with a request in two cultures: The differential influence of social proof and commitment/consistency on collectivists and individualists. *Personality and Social Psychology Bulletin, 25*, 1242–1253.

Cialdini, R. B., Trost, M. R., & Newsom, J. T. (1995). Preference for consistency: The development of a valid measure and the discovery of surprising behavioral implications. *Journal of Personality and Social Psychology, 69*, 318–328.

Ciardiello, A. (1998). Did you ask a good question today? Alternative cognitive and metacognitive strategies. *Journal of Adolescent & Adult Literacy, 42*, 210–219.

Cincirpini, P. M., Lapitsky, L., Seay, S., Wallfisch, A., & Kitchens, K. V. V. H. (1995). The effects of smoking schedules on cessation outcome: Can we improve on common methods of gradual and abrupt nicotine withdrawal? *Journal of Consulting and Clinical Psychology, 63*(3), 388–399.

Cinnirella, M., & Green, B. (2007). Does "cyber-conformity" vary cross-culturally? Exploring the effect of culture and communication medium on social conformity. *Computers in Human Behavior, 23*(4), 2011–2025.

Clancy, S. A., McNally, R. J., Schacter, D. L., Lenzenweger, M. F., & Pitman, R. K. (2002). Memory distortion in people reporting abduction by aliens. *Journal of Abnormal Psychology, 111*(3), 455–461.

Clark, A. (1991). *Microcognition: Philosophy, cognitive science, and parallel distributed processing.* Cambridge, MA: MIT Press, reprint edition (1989).

Clark, D. A., Beck, A. T., & Brown, G. (1989). Cognitive mediation in general psychiatric outpatients: A test of the content-specificity hypothesis. *Journal of Personality and Social Psychology, 56*, 958–964.

Clark, D. A., Hollifield, M., Leahy, R. L., & Beck, J. S. (2009). Theory of cognitive therapy. In G. Gabbard, J. S. Beck, & J. Wright (Eds.), Textbook of psychotherapeutic treatments in psychiatry, pp. 165–200. Washington, DC: American Psychiatric Press.

Clarke, A., Harvey, M. L., & Kane, D. J. (1999). *Attitudes and behavior: Are produce consumers influenced by eco-labels?* Paper presented at a National Conference on Eco-labels, "Making Change in the Marketplace," October 22–23, 1998. Retrieved August 1, 2004, from http://www.ssi.nrcs.usda.gov/ssienvpsy/nrcs/ecolabel.pdf

Clarke, A. R., Barry, R. J., McCarthy, R., Selikowitz, M., Johnstone, S. J., Hsu, C. I., et al. (2007). Coherence in children with Attention-Deficit/Hyperactivity Disorder and excess beta activity in their EEG. *Clinical Neurophysiology, 118*(7), 1472–1479.

Clarke, J. (1994). Pieces of the puzzle: The jigsaw method. In S. Sharan (Ed.), *Handbook of cooperative learning methods* (pp. 34–50). Westport, CT: Greenwood Press.

Clarkin, J. F., Levy, K. N., Lenzenweger, M. F., & Kernberg, O. F. (2007). Evaluating three treatments for borderline personality disorder: A multiwave study. *American Journal of Psychiatry, 164*(6), 922–928.

Coates, J. (1986). *Women, men, and language*. New York: Longman.

Coccaro, E. F., & Kavoussi, R. J. (1996). Neurotransmitter correlates of impulsive aggression. In D. M. Stoff & R. B. Cairns (Eds.), *Aggression and violence* (pp. 67–86). Mahwah, NJ: Lawrence Erlbaum.

Coffield, F., Moseley, D., Hall, E., Ecclestone, K. (2004). Learning styles and pedagogy in post-16 learning. A systematic and critical review. London: Learning and Skills Research Centre.

Cohen, L. J. (1997). Rational drug use in the treatment of depression. *Pharmacotherapy, 17*, 45–61.

Cohen, N. J., Eichenbaum, R., Decedo, J. C., & Corkin, S. (1985). Preserved learning capacity in amnesia: Evidence for multiple memory systems. In L. S. Squire & N. Butters (Eds.), *Neuropsychology of memory*. New York: Gilford Press.

Cohen, S., Frank, E., Doyle, B. J., Skoner, D. P., Rabin, B. S., & Gwaltney, J. M. (1998). Types of stressors that increase susceptibility to the common cold. *Health Psychology, 17,* 214–223.

Cohen, S., & Herbert, T. B. (1996). Health psychology: Psychological factors and physical disease from the perspective of human psychoneuroimmunology. *Annual Review of Psychology, 47*, 113–142.

Cohen, S., Janicki-Deverts, D., & Miller, G. E. (2007). Psychological stress and disease. *Journal of the American Medical Association, 298*(14), 1685–1687.

Coker, T., Austin, S., & Schuster, M. (2009). The health and health care of lesbian, gay, and bisexual adolescents. *Annual Review of Public Health, 31*, 457–477.

Colcombe, S. J., Erickson, K. I., Raz, N., Webb, A. G., Cohen, N. J., McAuley, E., & Kramer, A. F. (2003). Aerobic fitness reduces brain tissue loss in aging humans. *Journal of Gerontology Series A: Biological Sciences and Medical Sciences, 58*, 176–180.

Cole, S. W., Arevalo, J. M. G., Takahashi, R., Sloan, E. K., Lutgendorf, S. K., Sood, A. K., Sheridan, J. F., & Seeman, T. E. (2010). *Computational identification of gene-social environment interaction oat the human IL6 locus. Proceedings of the National Academy of Sciences of the United States of America.* Retrieved September 27, 2010, from http://www.pnas.org/content/107/12/5681.full.

Colligan, J. (1983). Musical creativity and social rules in four cultures. *Creative Child and Adult Quarterly, 8,* 39–44.

Collignon, O., Girard, S., Gosselin, F., Saint-Amour, D., Lepore, F., & Lassonde, M. (2010). Women process multisensory emotion expressions more efficiently than men. *Neuropsychologia, 48*, 220–225.

Collins, A. M., & Loftus, E. F. (1975). A spreading activation theory of semantic processing. *Psychological Review, 82*, 407–428.

Collins, A. M., & Quillian, M. R. (1969). Retrieval time from semantic memory. *Journal of Verbal Learning and Verbal Behaviour, 8*, 240–247.

Collins, C. J., Hanges, P. J., & Locke, E. A. (2004). The relationship of achievement motivation to entrepreneurial behavior: A meta-analysis. *Human Performance, 17*(1), 95–117.

Colom, R., Shih, P. C., Flores-Mendoza, C., & Quiroga, M. A. (2006). The real relationship between short-term memory and working memory. *Memory, 14*(7), 804–813.

Committee on Animal Research and Ethics. (2004). *Research with animals in psychology*. Retrieved October 12, 2004, from www.apa.org/science/animal2.html

Cone-Wesson, B. (2005). Prenatal alcohol and cocaine exposure: Influences on cognition, speech, language, and hearing. *Journal of Communication Disorders, 38*(4), 279–302.

Conrad, R., & Hull, A. J. (1964). Information, acoustic confusion, and memory span. *British Journal of Psychology, 55*, 429–432.

Consumer Reports. (1995, November). Mental health: Does psychotherapy help? 734–739.

Conway, M. A., Cohen, G., & Stanhope, N. (1992). Very long-term memory for knowledge acquired at school and university. *Applied Cognitive Psychology, 6*, 467–482.

Coolidge, F. L. (2006). *Dream interpretation as a psychotherapeutic technique*. London: Radcliffe.

Cooper, L. A., Gonzales, J. J., Gallo, J. J., Rost, K. M., Meredith, L. S., Rubenstein, L. V., Wang, N. Y., & Ford, D. E. (2003). The acceptability of treatment for depression among African-American, Hispanic, and White primary care patients. *Medical Care, 41*(4), 479–489.

Corbetta, M., Kincade, M. J., Lewis, C., Snyder, A. Z., & Sapir, A. (2005). Neural basis and recovery of spatial attention deficits in spatial neglect. *Nature Neuroscience, 8*, 1603–1610.

Cormier, J. F., & Thelen, M. H. (1998). Professional skepticism of multiple personality disorder. *Professional Psychology: Research and Practice, 29*, 163–167.

Cosgrove, G. R., & Rauch, S. L. (1995). Psychosurgery. *Neurosurgery Clinics of North America, 6*, 167–176.

Cosgrove, K. P., Mazure, C. M., & Staley, J. K. (2007). Evolving knowledge of sex differences in brain structure, function, and chemistry. *Biological Psychiatry, 62*(8), 847–855.

Costa, P. T., Jr., & McCrae, R. R. (2000). The Revised NEO Personality Inventory (NEO PI-R). In J. Cheek & E. M. Donahue (Eds.), *Handbook of personality inventories.* New York: Plenum.

Costello, D. M., Swendsen, J., Rose, J. S., & Dierker, L. C. (2008). Risk and protective factors associated with trajectories of depressed mood from adolescence to early adulthood. *Journal of Consulting and Clinical Psychology, 76*(2), 173–183.

Courage, M. L., & Howe, M. L. (2002). From infant to child: The dynamics of cognitive change in the second year of life. *Psychological Bulletin, 128*, 250–277.

Courneya, K. S., Sellar, C. M., Stevinson, C., McNeely, M. L., Peddle, C. J., Friedenreich, C. M., Tankey, K., Basi, S., Chua, N., Mazurek, A., & Reiman, T. (2009). Randomized controlled trial of the effects of aerobic exercise on physical functioning and quality of life in lymphoma patients. *Journal of Clinical Oncology, 27*(27), 4605–4612.

Cowan, N. (1988). Evolving conceptions of memory storage, selective attention, and their mutual constraints within the human information processing system. *Psychological Bulletin, 104*, 163–191.

Cowan, N. (2001). The magical number 4 in short-term memory: A reconsideration of mental storage capacity. *Behavioral and Brain Sciences*, 24, 97–185.

Cowan, N., Elliott, E. M., Saults, J. S., Morey, C. C., Mattox, S., Hismjatullina, A., & Conway, A. R. A. (2005). On the capacity of attention: Its estimation and its role in working memory and cognitive aptitudes. *Cognitive Psychology*, 51(1), 42–100.

Craddock, N., O'Donovan, M. C., & Owen, M. J. (2005). The genetics of schizophrenia and bipolar disorder: Dissecting psychosis. *Journal of Medical Genetics, 42*, 288–299.

Crago, M. B., Shisslak, C. M., & Estes, L. S. (1996). Eating disturbances among American minority groups: A review. *International Journal of Eating Disorders, 19*, 239–248.

Craik, F. I. M. (1970). The fate of primary memory items in free recall. *Journal of Verbal Learning and Verbal Behavior, 9*, 143–148.

Craik, F. I. M. (1994). Memory changes in normal aging. *Current Directions in Psychological Science, 3*(5), 155–158.

Craik, F. I. M., & Lockhart, R. S. (1972). Levels of processing. A framework for memory research. *Journal of Verbal Learning and Verbal Behaviour, 11*, 671–684.

Craik, F. I. M., & Tulving, E. (1975). Depth of processing and the retention of words in episodic memory. *Journal of Experimental Psychology: General, 104*, 268–294.

Craske, M. G., & Barlow, D. H. (2008). Panic disorder and agoraphobia. In D. H. Barlow (Ed.), *Clinical handbook of psychological disorders* (pp. 1–64). New York: Guilford Press.

Crawford, M., & Unger, R. (2004). *Women and gender: A feminist psychology* (4th ed.). Boston: McGraw-Hill.

Crick, F., & Koch, C. (1990). Towards a neurobiological theory of consciousness. *Seminars in the Neurosciences, 2*, 263–275.

Crick, F. & Koch, C. (2003). A framework for consciousness. *Nature Neuroscience, 6*, 119–127.

Critchfield, T. S., Haley, R., Sabo, B., Colbert, J., & Macropoulis, G. (2003). A half century of scalloping in the work habits of the United States Congress. *Journal of Applied Behavior Analysis, 36*(4), 465–486.

Croft, A. P., & Przyborski, S. A. (2006). Formation of neurons by non-neural adult stem cells: Potential mechanism implicates an artifact of growth in culture. *Stem Cells, 24*(8), 1841–1851.

Crottaz-Herbette S., Menon V. (2006). Where and when the anterior cingulate cortex modulates attentional response: combined fMRI and ERP evidence. *Journal of Cognitive Neuroscience, 18*(5), 766-780.

Crowley, A. E., & Hoyer, W. D. (1994). An integrative framework for understanding two-sided persuasion. *Journal of Consumer Research, 20*, 561–574.

Csernansky, J. G., Mahmoud, R., & Brenner, R. (2002). A comparison of reperidone and haloperidol for the prevention of relapse in patients with schizophrenia. *New England Journal of Medicine, 346*, 16–22.

Csikszentmihalyi, M. (1996). *Creativity: Flow and the psychology of discovery and invention*. New York: Harper Perennial.

Csikszentmihalyi, M. (1997). *Finding flow: The psychology of engagement with everyday life*. New York: Basic Books.

Cua, A. B., Wilhelm, K. P., & Maibach, H. I. (1990). Elastic properties of human skin: Relation to age, sex and anatomical region. *Archives of Dermatology Research, 282*, 283–288.

Culbertson, F. (2003). *The phobia list*. Retrieved June 22, 2004, from www.phobialist.com

Cummings, J. L., & Coffey C. E. (1994). Neurobiological basis of behavior. In C. E. Coffey & J. L. Cummings (Eds.), *Textbook of geriatric neuropsychiatry* (pp. 72–96). Washington, DC: American Psychiatric Press.

Cummings, S. R., & Melton, L. J., III. (2002). Epidemiology and outcomes of osteoporotic fractures. *Lancet, 359*(9319), 1761–1767.

Curtis, R. C., & Miller, K. (1986). Believing another likes or dislikes you: Behaviors making the beliefs come true. *Journal of Personality and Social Psychology, 51*, 284–290.

Curtis, R. H. (1993). *Great lives: Medicine*. New York: Charles Scribner's Sons Books for Young Readers.

Cytowic, R. E. (1989). Synesthesia and mapping of subjective sensory dimensions. *Neurology, 39*, 849–850.

Czeisler, C. A. (1995). The effect of light on the human circadian pacemaker. In D. J. Chadwick & K. Ackrill (Eds.), *Circadian clocks and their adjustment* (pp. 254–302). West Sussex, England: John Wiley & Sons.

Czeisler, C. A., Moore-Ede, M. C., & Coleman, R. M. (1982). Rotating shift work schedules that disrupt sleep are improved by applying circadian principles. *Science, 217*, 460–463.

Czeisler, C. A., Weitzman, E. D., Moore-Ede, M. C., Zimmerman, J. C., & Knauer, R. S. (1980). Human sleep: Its duration and organization depend on its circadian phase. *Science, 210*, 1264–1267.

Dabbs, J. M., Jr., Bernieri, F. J., Strong, R. K., Campo, R., & Milun, R. (2001). Going on stage: Testosterone in greetings and meetings. *Journal of Research in Personality, 35*, 27–40.

Dalenberg, C. J. (1996). Accuracy, timing and circumstances of disclosure in therapy of recovered and continuous memories of abuse. *The Journal of Psychiatry and Law, 24*(2), 229–275.

Dallman, M., Pecoraro, N., Akana, S., la Fleur, S. E., Gomez, F., Houshyar, H., Bell, M. E., Bhatnagar, S., Laugero, K. D., & Manalo, S. (2003). Chronic stress and obesity: A new view of "comfort food." *Proceedings of the National Academy of Sciences, USA, 100*(20), 11696–11701.

Daly, M., Wilson, M., & Weghorst, S. J. (1982). Male sexual jealousy. *Ethology and Sociobiology, 3*, 11–27.

Damasio, H., Grabowski, T., Frank, R., Galaburda, A. M., & Damasion, A. R. (1994). The return of Phineas Gage: Clues about the brain from the skull of a famous patient. *Science, 264*, 1102–1105.

Dani, J., Burrill, C., & Demmig-Adams, B. (2005). The remarkable role of nutrition in learning and behavior. *Nutrition & Food Science, 35*(4), 258-263.

Darley, J. M., & Latané, B. (1968). Bystander intervention in emergencies: Diffusion of responsibility. *Journal of Personality and Social Psychology, 8*, 377–383.

Darvill, T., Lonky, E., Reihman, J., Stewart, P., & Pagano, J. (2000). Prenatal exposure to PCBs and infant performance on the Fagan test of infant intelligence. *Neurotoxicology, 21*(6), 1029–1038.

Darwin, C. (1859). *The origin of species by means of natural selection*. London: John Murray.

Darwin, C. (1898). *The expression of the emotions in man and animals*. New York: D. Appleton.

Daum, I., & Schugens, M. M. (1996). On the cerebellum and classical conditioning. *Current Directions in Psychological Science, 5*, 58–61.

Davidson, R., Kabat-Zinn, J., Schumacher, J., Rosenkranz, M., Muller, D., Santorelli, S., Urbanowski, F., Harrington, A., Bonus, K. & Sheridan, J. (2003). Alterations in brain and immune function produced by mindfulness meditation. *Psychosomatic Medicine, 65*, 564–570.

Davidson, R. J. (2003). Affective neuroscience and psychophysiology: Toward a synthesis. *Psychophysiology, 40*(5), 655–665.

Davidson, R. J., Putman, K. M., & Larson, C. L. (2000). Dysfunction in the neural circuitry of emotion regulation—A possible prelude to violence. *Science, 289*, 591–594.

Davies, I. R. L., Laws, G., Corbett, G. G., & Jerrett, D. J. (1998a). Cross-cultural differences in colour vision: Acquired "colour blindness" in Africa. *Personality and Individual Differences, 25*, 1153–1162.

Davies, I. R. L., Sowden, P., Jerrett, D. T., Jerrett, T., & Corbett, G. G. (1998b). A cross-cultural study of English and Setswana speakers on a colour triads task: A test of the Sapir-Whorf hypothesis. *British Journal of Psychology, 89*, 1–15.

Davis, H. A., DiStefano, C., & Schutz, P. A. (2008). Identifying patterns of appraising tests in first-year college students: Implications for anxiety and emotion regulation during test taking. *Journal of Educational Psychology, 100*(4), 942–960. doi: 10.1037/a0013096

Davis, J. O., Phelps, J. A., & Bracha, H. S. (1995). Prenatal development of monozygotic twins and concordance for schizophrenia. *Schizophrenia Bulletin, 21*, 357–366.

Davis, K. D., Hutchison, W. D., Lozano, A. M., Tasker, R. R., & Dostrovsky, J. O. (2000). Human anterior cingulate cortex neurons modulated by attention-demanding tasks. *Journal of Neurophysiology, 83*(6), 2575–2577.

Davis, K. F., Parker, K. P., & Montgomery, G. (2004). Sleep in infants and young children: Part 1: Normal sleep. *Journal of Pediatric Healthcare, 18*(2), 65–71.

Davis, K. L., Kahn, R. S., Ko, G., & Davidson, M. (1991). Dopamine in schizophrenia: A review and reconceptualization. *American Journal of Psychiatry, 148*, 1474–1486.

Davis, M., & Whalen, P. J. (2001). The amygdala: Vigilance and emotion. *Molecular Psychiatry, 6*, 13–34.

Dawood, K., Pillard, R. C., Horvath, C., Revelle, W., & Bailey, J. M. (2000). Familial aspects of male homosexuality. *Archives of Sexual Behavior, 29*(2).

De Valois, R. L., & De Valois, K. K. (1993). A multi-stage color model. *Vision Research, 33*(8), 1053–1065.

De Valois, R. L., & Jacobs, G. H. (1968). Primate color vision, *Science, 162*, 553–540.

Dean, G., & Kelly, I. W. (2000). Does astrology work? Astrology and skepticism 1975–2000. In P. Kurtz (Ed.), *Skepticism: A 25 Year Retrospective* (pp. 191–207). Amherst, NY: Prometheus Books.

Dean, G., Kelly, I. W., Sakolfske, D. H., & Furnham, A. (1992). Graphology and human judgment. In B. L. Beyerstein & D. F. Beyerstein (Eds.), *The write stuff: Evaluations of graphology—The study of handwriting analysis* (pp. 342–396). Amherst, NY: Prometheus Books.

DeAngelis, T. (2002). Promising treatments for anorexia and bulimia: Research boosts support for tough-to-treat eating disorders. *APA Monitor on Psychology, 33*(3), 38–43.

Dębiec, J., Díaz-Mataix, L., Bush, D. E. A., Doyère, V., & LeDoux, J. E. (2010). The amygdala encodes specific sensory features of an aversive reinforcer. *Nature Neuroscience, 13*, 536–537.

DeCasper, A. J., & Fifer, W. P. (1980). Of human bonding: Newborns prefer their mothers' voices. *Science, 208*, 1174–1176.

DeCasper, A. J., & Spence, M. J. (1986). Prenatal maternal speech influence on newborns' perception of sounds. *Infant Behaviour and Development, 9*, 133–150.

deCharms, R. (1968). *Personal causation.* New York: Academic Press.

Deci, E. L., & Ryan, R. M. (1985). *Intrinsic motivation and self-determination in human behavior.* New York: Plenum.

Deci, E. L., Eghrari, H., Patrick, B. C., & Leone, D. R. (1994). Facilitating internalization: The self-determination theory perspective. *Journal of Personality, 62*, 119–142.

Deci, E. L., Koestner, R., & Ryan, R. M. (1999). A meta-analytic review of experiments examining the effects of extrinsic rewards on intrinsic motivation. *Psychological Bulletin, 125*, 627–668.

DeCoster, J., & Claypool, H. M. (2004). A meta-analysis of priming effects on impression formation supporting a general model of informational biases. *Personality and Social Psychology Review, 8*(1), 2–27.

DeGrandpre, R. J. (2000). A science of meaning: Can behaviorism bring meaning to psychological science? *American Psychologist, 55*, 721–739.

Deinzer, R., Kleineidam, C. H., Winkler, R., Idel, H., & Bachg, D. (2000). Prolonged reduction of salivary immunoglobulin A (slgA) after a major academic exam. *International Journal of Psychophysiology, 37*, 219–232.

Delagrange, P., & Guardiola-Lemaitre, B. (1997). Melatonin, its receptors, and relationships with biological rhythm disorders. *Clinincal Neuropharmacology, 20*, 482–510.

Delaney, A. J., Crane, J. W., & Sah, P. (2007). Noradrenaline modulates transmission at a central synapse by a presynaptic mechanism. *Neuron, 56*(6), 880–892.

Delfiner, R. (2001, November 16). "Kitty Left at Death's Door." *New York Post.*

DeLongis, A., Lazarus, R. S., & Folkman, S. (1988). The impact of daily stress on health and mood: Psychological and social resources as mediators. *Journal of Personality and Social Psychology, 54*(3), 486–495.

Dement, W. C. (1960). The effect of dream deprivation. *Science, 131*, 1705–1707.

Dement, W. C. (1974). *Some must watch while some must sleep.* New York: W. H. Freeman & Co. Ltd.

Dement, W. C., Henry, P., Cohen, H., & Ferguson, J. (1969). Studies on the effect of REM deprivation in humans and animals. In K. H. Pribram (Ed.), *Mood, states, and mind.* Baltimore: Penguin.

Demers, R. A. (1988). Linguistics and animal communication. In F. J. Newmeyer (Ed.), *Language form and language function* (pp. 314–335). Cambridge, MA: MIT Press.

Dempster, F. N., & Farris, R. (1990). The spacing effect: Research and practice. *Journal of Research and Development in Education 23*(2), 97–101.

Dennett, D. C. (1991). *Consciousness explained.* New York: Little, Brown.

Denno, D. W. (2002). Crime and consciousness: Science and involuntary acts. *Minnesota Law Review, 87*, 269–399.

Deregowski, J. B. (1969). Perception of the two-pronged trident by two- and three-dimensional perceivers. *Journal of Experimental Psychology, 82*, 9–13.

DeRubeis, R. J., Gelfand, L. A., Tang, T. Z., & Simons, A. D. (1999). Medications versus cognitive behavior therapy for severely depressed outpatients: Mega-analysis of four randomized comparisons. *American Journal of Psychiatry, 156*(7), 1007–1013.

Dew, M. A., Whyte, E. M., Lenze, E. J., Houck, P. R., Mulsant, B. H., Pollock, B. G., Stack, J. A., Bensasi, S., & Reynolds, C. F. (2007). Recovery from major depression in older adults receiving augmentation of antidepressant pharmacotherapy. *American Journal of Psychiatry, 164*(6), 892–899.

DeYoung, C. G., Hirsh, J. B., Shane, M. S., Papademetris, X., Rajeevan, N., & Gray, J. R. (2010). Testing predictions from personality neuroscience: Brain structure and the Big Five. *Psychological Science, 21*(6), 820–828.

Diamond, L. M. (2003). What does sexual orientation orient? A biobehavioral model distinguishing romantic love and sexual desire. *Psychological Review, 110*, 173–192.

Diamond, M. (1995). Biological aspects of sexual orientation and identity. In L. Diamant & R. McAnulty (Eds.), *The psychology of sexual orientation, behavior, and identity: A handbook* (pp. 45–80). Westport, CT: Greenwood Press.

Diamond, M., & Sigmundson, H. K. (1997). Sex reassignment at birth. Long-term review and clinical implications. *Archives of Pediatric Adolescent Medicine, 151*(3), 298–304.

Diamond, M. C. (1991). Hormonal effects on the development of cerebral lateralization. *Psychoneuroendocrinology, 16*, 121–129.

Dickens, W. T., & Flynn, J. R. (2001 April). Heritability estimates vs. large environmental effects: The IQ paradox resolved. *Psychological Review, 108*(2), 346–369.

Dickerson, F., Ringel, N., Parente, F., & Boronow, J. (1994). Seclusion and restraint, assaultiveness, and patient performance in a token economy. *Hospital and Community Psychiatry, 45*, 168–170.

Digman, J. M. (1990). Personality structure: Emergence of the five-factor model. *Annual Review of Psychology, 41*, 417–440.

Dillard, J. (1990). Self-inference and the foot-in-the-door technique: Quantity of behavior and attitudinal mediation. *Human Communication Research, 16*, 422–447.

Dillard, J. (1991). The current status of research on sequential–request compliance techniques. *Personality and Social Psychology Bulletin, 17*, 282–288.

Dinges, D. F. (1995). An overview of sleepiness and accidents. *Journal of Sleep Research, 4*(2), 4–14.

Dixon, N. F. (1980). Humor: A cognitive alternative to stress? In I. Sarason and C. D. Spielberger (Eds.), *Stress and Anxiety* (Vol. 7, pp. 281–289). Washington, DC: Hemisphere.

Dodge, K. A., Bates, J. E., & Pettit, G. S. (1990). Mechanisms in the cycle of violence. *Science, 250*, 1678–1683.

Doidge, N. (2007). *The brain that changes itself.* New York: Viking.

Dolan, K., Kite, B., Black, E., Aceijas, C., & Stimson, G. V. (2007). HIV in prison in low-income and middle-income countries. *The Lancet: Infectious Diseases, 7*(1), 32-41.

Dolcos, F., LaBar, K. S., Cabeza, R. & Purves, D. (2005). Remembering one year later: Role of the amygdala and the medial temporal lobe memory system in retrieving emotional memories. *Proceedings of the National Academy of Sciences, USA.* doi: 10.1073/pnas.0409848102

Dollard, J., & Miller, N. F. (1950). *Personality and psychotherapy.* New York: McGraw-Hill.

Dollard, J., Doob, L. W., Miller, N. E., Mowrer, O. H., & Sears, R. R. (1939). *Frustration and aggression.* New Haven, CT: Yale University Press.

Domagalski, T. A., & Steelman, L. A. (2007). The impact of gender and organizational status on workplace anger expression. *Management Communication Quarterly, 20*(3), 297–315.

Domhoff, G. W. (1996). *Finding meaning in dreams: A quantitative approach.* New York: Plenum Publishing.

Domhoff, G. W. (2005). The content of dreams: Methodologic and theoretical implications. In M. Kryger, T. Roth, & W. Dement (Eds.), *Principles and practices of sleep medicine* (4th ed., pp. 522–534). Philadelphia: Saunders.

Dominey, P. F., & Dodane, C. (2004). Indeterminacy in language acquisition: The role of child-directed speech and joint attention. *Journal of Neurolinguistics, 17*(2–3), 121–145.

Domjan, M., Cusato, B., & Villarreal, R. (2000). Pavlovian feed-forward mechanisms in the control of social behavior. *Behavioral and Brain Sciences, 23*, 235–282.

Donovan, J. J., & Radosevich, D. R. (1999). A meta-analytic review of the distribution of practice effect: Now you see it, now you don't. *Journal of Applied Psychology, 84*, 795–805.

Dorahy, M. J. (2001). Dissociative identity disorder and memory dysfunction: The current state of experimental research and its future directions. *Clinical Psychology Review, 21*(5), 771–795.

Dougherty, D. D., Baer, L., Cosgrove, G. R., Cassem, E. H., Price, B. H., Nierenberg, A. A., Jenike, M. A., & Rauch, S. L. (2002). Prospective long-term follow-up of 44 patients who received cingulotomy for treatment-refractory obsessive-compulsive disorder. *The American Journal of Psychiatry, 159*(2), 269–275.

Dove, A. (1971). The "Chitling" Test. In L. R. Aiken Jr. (Ed.), *Psychological and educational testings.* Boston: Allyn and Bacon.

Downs, J. F.(1984). *The Navajo* (p. 108). Prospect Heights, IL: Waveland Press, International.

Dreger, A. D. (1998). "Ambiguous sex"—or ambivalent medicine? Ethical issues in the treatment of intersexuality. *Hastings Center Report, 28*(3), 24–35.

Dreger, A. D. (1999). *Intersex in the age of ethics.* Hagerstown, MD: University Publishing Groups.

Drenth, P. J., Thierry, H., Willems, P. J., & de Wolff, C. J. (1984). *Handbook of work and organizational psychology.* Chichester, England: John Wiley and Sons.

Drigotas, S. M., Rusbult, C. E., Wieselquist, J., & Whitton, S. (1999). Close partner as sculptor of the ideal self: Behavioral affirmation and the Michelangelo phenomenon. *Journal of Personality and Social Psychology, 77*, 293–323.

Druckman, D., & Bjork, R. A. (Eds.). (1994). *Learning, remembering, believing: Enhancing human performance.* (Study conducted by the National Research Council). Washington, DC: National Academy Press.

Drysdale, M. T., Ross, J. L., & Schulz, R. A. (2001). Cognitive learning styles and academic performance in 19 first-year university courses: Successful students versus students at risk. Journal of Education for Students Placed at Risk, 6, 271–289.

Duben, A., & Behar, C. (1991). *Istanbul households: Marriage, family and fertility 1880–1940.* Cambridge, NY: Cambridge University Press.

Dubowitz, H., & Bennett, S. (2007). Physical abuse and neglect of children. *Lancet, 369*(9576), 1891–1899.

Dudai, Y. (2004). The neurobiology of consolidations, or, how stable is the engram? *Annual Review of Psychology,* 55, 51–86.

Duker, P. C. & Seys, D. M. (1996). Long-term use of electrical aversion treatment with self-injurious behaviors. *Research in Developmental Disabilities, 17*, 293–301.

Dumont, F. (2010). *A history of personality psychology.* New York: Cambridge University Press.

Duncan, R. M. (1995). Piaget and Vygotsky revisited: Dialogue or assimilation? *Developmental Review, 15*, 458–472.

Dundas, I., Wormnes, B. R., & Hauge, H. (2009). Making exams a manageable task. *Nordic Psychology, 61*(1), 26–41.

Dunn, J. C., Whelton, W. J., & Sharpe, D. (2006). Maladaptive perfectionism, hassles, coping, and psychological distress in university professors. *Journal of Counseling Psychology, 53*(4), 511–523.

Dunn, R. S., Beaudry, J. S., & Klavas, A. (1989). Survey of research on learning styles. Educational Leadership, 46(6), 50–58.

Dunn, R. S., Denig, S. J., & Lovelace, M. K. (2001). Two sides of the same coin or different strokes for different folks? Teacher Librarian, 28(3), 9–16.

Durrant, M. (Ed.). (1993). *Aristotle's De anima in focus.* London: Routledge.

Durso, F., Rea, C., & Dayton, T. (1994). Graph-theoretic confirmation of restructuring during insight. *Psychological Science, 5*, 94–98.

Durston, S. (2003). A review of the biological bases of ADHD: What have we learned from imaging studies? *Mental Retardation and Developmental Disabilities Research Reviews, 9*, 184–195.

Dweck, C. (1986). Motivational processes affecting learning. *American Psychologist, 41*(10), 1040–1048.

Dweck, C., & Elliott, E. (1983). Achievement motivation. In P. Mussen (Ed.), *Handbook of child psychology: Vol. 4. Socialization, personality, and social development* (pp. 643–691). New York: Wiley.

Dweck, C. S. (1999). *Self-theories: Their role in motivation, personality and development.* Philadelphia: Psychology Press.

Dweck, C. S., Chiu, C., & Hong, Y. (1995). Implicit theories and their role in judgments and reactions: A world from two perspectives. *Psychological Inquiry, 6*, 267–285.

Dweck, C. S., & Leggett, E. L. (1988). A social-cognitive approach to motivation and personality. *Psychological Review, 95*, 256–273.

Dweck, C. S., & Molden, D. C. (2008). Self-theories: The construction of free will. In J. Baer, J. C. Kaufman, & R. F. Baumeister (Eds.), *Are we free? Psychology and free will* (pp. 44–64). New York: Oxford University Press.

Dykens, E. M., Hodapp, R. M., & Leckman, J. F. (1994). *Behavior and development in fragile X syndrome.* Thousand Oaks, CA: Sage.

Eagleman, D. M. (2001). Visual illusions and neurobiology. *Nature reviews: Neuroscience, 2*(12), 920–926.

Eagly, A., & Chaiken, S. (1975). An attribution analysis of the effect of communicator characteristics on opinion change: The case of communicator attractiveness. *Journal of Personality and Social Psychology, 37*, 136–144.

Eagly, A., & Crowley, M. (1986). Gender and helping behavior: A meta-analytic review of the social psychological literature. *Psychological Bulletin, 100*, 283–308.

Eagly, A. H. (1987). *Sex difference in social behavior: A social-role interpretation.* Hillsdale, NJ: Lawrence Erlbaum.

Eagly, A. H., & Chaiken, S. (1993). *The psychology of attitudes.* Fort Worth, TX: Harcourt Brace.

Eagly, A. H., & Chaiken, S. (1998). Attitude structure and function. In D. T. Gilbert, S. T. Fiske, & G. Lindzey (Eds.), *The handbook of social psychology* (4th ed., pp. 269–322). New York: McGraw-Hill.

Eagly, A. H., Ashmore, R. D., Makhijani, M. G., & Longo, L. C. (1991). What is beautiful is good, but . . . : A meta-analytic review of the physical attractiveness stereotype. *Psychological Bulletin, 110*, 109–128.

Eagly, A. H., Wood, W., & Diekman, A. B. (2000). Social role theory of sex differences and similarities: A current appraisal. In T. Eckes & H. M. Trautner (Eds.), *The developmental social psychology of gender* (pp. 123–174). Mahwah, NJ: Lawrence Erlbaum.

Eaker, E. D., & Castelli, W. P. (1988). Type A behavior and mortality from coronary disease in the Framingham Study. *New England Journal of Medicine, 319*, 1480–1481.

Eastern Virginia Medical School (2009, May 5). Texting while driving can be deadly, study shows. *ScienceDaily*. Retrieved May 5, 2010, from http://www.sciencedaily.com/releases/2009/05/090504094434.htm

Eaton, W. W., Kessler, R. C., Wittchen, H. U., & Magee, W. J. (1994). Panic and panic disorder in the United States. *American Journal of Psychiatry 151*(3), 413–420.

Ebbinghaus, H. (1885). *Memory: A contribution to experimental psychology.* New York: Dover Publications.

Ebbinghaus, H. (1913). *Memory: A contribution to experimental psychology.* New York: Teachers College Press. (Translated from the 1885 German original.)

Eddy, J., Fitzhugh, E., & Wang, M. (2000). Smoking acquisition: Peer influence and self-selection. *Psychological Reports, 86*, 1241–1246.

Edelmann, R. J., & Iwawaki, S. (1987). Self-reported expression of embarrassment in five European cultures. *Psychologia: An International Journal of Psychology, 30*, 205–216.

Edlund, J. E., Heider, J. D., Scherer, C. R., Farc, M.-M., & Sagarin, B. J. (2006). Sex differences in jealousy in response to actual infidelity. *Evolutionary Psychology, 4*, 462–470.

Edwards, R. (Producer), & Williams, E. (Writer/Director). (2010). *Unforgettable: The memorable adventures of "the Human Google"* [Documentary]. Available from Let'sgetouttahere Productions, U.S.

Egan, L. C., Bloom, P., & Santos, L. R. (2010). Choice-induced preferences in the absence of choice: Evidence from a blind two choice paradigm with young children and capuchin monkeys. *Journal of Experimental Social Psychology, 46*(1), 204–207.

Egan, L. C., Santos, L. R., & Bloom, P. (2007). The origins of cognitive dissonance. Evidence from children and monkeys. *Psychological Science, 18*(11), 978–983.

Ehlers, A., Bisson, J., Clark, D. M., Creamer, M., Pilling, S., Richards, D., Schnurr, P. P., Turner, S., & Yule, W. (2010). Do all psychological treatments really work the same in posttraumatic stress disorder? *Clinical Psychology Review, 30*(2), 269–276.

Eich, E., & Metcalfe, J. (1989). Mood dependent memory for internal vs. external events. *Journal of Experimental Psychology: Learning, Memory and Cognition, 15*, 443–455.

Eiden, R. D., McAuliffe, S., Kachadourian, L., Coles, C., Colder, C., & Schuetze, P. (2009). Effects of prenatal cocaine exposure on infant reactivity and regulation. *Neurotoxicology and Teratology, 31*, 60–68.

Ekman, P. (1973). Darwin and cross-cultural studies of facial expression. In P. Ekman (Ed.), *Darwin and facial expression: A century of research in review.* New York: Academic Press.

Ekman, P. (1980). Asymmetry in facial expression. *Science, 209*, 833–834.

Ekman, P., & Friesen, W. (1969). The repertoire of nonverbal behavior: Categories, origins, usage, and coding. *Semiotica, 1*, 49–98.

Ekman, P., & Friesen, W. (1971). Constants across cultures in the face and emotion. *Journal of Personality and Social Psychology, 17*(2), 124–129.

Ekman, P., & Friesen, W. V. (1978). *The facial action coding system.* Palo Alto, CA: Consulting Psychologists Press.

Ekman, P., Sorensen, E. R., & Friesen, W. V. (1969). Pan-cultural elements in facial displays of emotion. *Science, 164*, 86–88.

Elkind, D. (1985). Egocentrism redux. *Developmental Review, 5*, 218–226.

Ellenbogen, J. M., Payne, J. D., & Stickgold, R. (2006). The role of sleep in declarative memory consolidation: Passive, permissive, active or none? *Current Opinions in Neurobiology, 16*, 716–722.

Elliott, E., & Dweck, C. (1988). Goals: An approach to motivation and achievement. *Journal of Personality and Social Psychology, 54*, 5–12.

Elliott, L., & Brantley, C. (1997). *Sex on campus: The naked truth about the real sex lives of college students*. New York: Random House.

Ellis, A. (1997). *The practice of rational emotive behavior therapy*. New York: Springer.

Ellis, A. (1998). *The Albert Ellis reader: A guide to well-being using rational emotive behavior therapy*. Secaucus, NJ: Carol Publishing Group.

Ellis, H. D. (1983). The role of the right hemisphere in face perception. In A. W. Young (Ed.), *Functions of the right cerebral hemisphere* (pp. 33–64). London: Academic Press.

Ellis, L., Ames, M. A., Peckham, W., & Burke, D. (1988). Sexual orientation of human offspring may be altered by severe maternal stress during pregnancy. *The Journal of Sex Research, 25*, 152–157.

Ellis, L. K., Gay, P. E., & Paige, E. (2001). Daily pleasures and hassles across the lifespan. Poster presented at the September annual meeting of the American Psychological Association, San Francisco.

Else-Quest, N., Shibley Hyde, J., Linn, M. C. (2010). Cross-national patterns of gender differences in mathematics: A meta-analysis. *Psychological Bulletin, 136*(1), 103–127.

Endler, N. S. (1988). The origins of electroconvulsive therapy (ECT). *Convulsive Therapy, 4*, 5–23.

Engle, R. W., & Kane, M. J. (2004). Executive attention, working memory capacity, and a two-factor theory of cognitive control. *The Psychology of Learning and Motivation, 44*, 145–199.

Enns, J. T., & Coren, S. (1995). The box alignment illusion: An orientation illusion induced by pictorial depth. *Perception & Psychophysics, 57*, 1163–1174.

Ephraim, P. L., Wegener, S. T., MacKenzie, E. J., Dillingham, T. R., & Pezzin, L. E. (2005). Phantom pain, residual limb pain and back pain in persons with limb loss: Results of a national survey. *Archives of Physical Medicine and Rehabilitation, 86*, 1910–1919.

Epping-Jordan, M., Waltkins, S. S., Koob, G. F., & Markou, A. (1998). Dramatic decreases in brain reward function during nicotine withdrawal. *Nature, 393*, 76–79.

Erdley, C. A., & Dweck, C. S. (1993). Children's implicit personality theories as predictors of their social judgments. *Child Development, 64*, 863–878.

Erickson, K. I., Prakash, R. S., Voss, M. W., Chaddock, L., Hu, L., Morris, K. S., et al. (2009). Aerobic fitness is associated with hippocampal volume in elderly humans. *Hippocampus, 19*(10), 1030–1039.

Erikson, E. (1980). Elements of a psychoanalytic theory of psychosocial development. In S. Greenspan & G. Pollock (Eds.), *The Course of Life, Vol. 1* (pp. 11–61). Washington, DC: U.S. Dept. of Health and Human Services.

Erikson, E. H. (1950). *Childhood and society*. New York: Norton.

Erikson, E. H. (1959). Growth and crises of the healthy personality. *Psychological Issues, 1*, 50–100.

Erikson, E. H. (1982). *The life cycle completed*. New York: Norton.

Erikson, E. H., & Erikson, J. M. (1997). *The life cycle completed*. New York: Norton.

Eriksson, P., Ankarberg, E., Viberg, H., & Fredriksson, A. (2001). The developing cholinergic system as target for environmental toxicants, nicotine and polychlorinated biphenyls (PCBs): Implications for neurotoxicological processes in mice. *Neurotoxicity Research, 3*(1), 37–51.

Ertelt, D., Small, S., Solodkin A., McNamara A., Binkofski F., & Buccino, G. (in press). Action observation has a positive impact on rehabilitation of motor deficits after stroke. *Neuroimage.*

Escandon, A., Al-Hammadi, N., Galvin, J. E. (2010). Effect of cognitive fluctuation on neuropsychological performance in aging and dementia. *Neurology, 74*, 210–217.

Eschenbeck, H., Kohlmann, C.-W., & Lohaus, A. (2008). Gender differences in coping strategies in children and adolescents. *Journal of Individual Differences, 28*(1), 18–26.

Eskenazi, B., Bradman, A., & Castorina, R. (1999). Exposures of children to organophosphate pesticides and their potential adverse health effects. *Environmental Health Perspectives, 107*(Suppl. 3), 409–419.

Espiard, M. L., Lecardeur, L., Abadie, P., Halbecq, I., & Dollfus, S. (2005). HPPD after psilocybin consumption: A case study. *European Psychiatry, 20*(5–6), 458–460.

Evans, D., Hodgkinson, B., O'Donnell, A., Nicholson, J., & Walsh, K. (2000). The effectiveness of individual therapy and group therapy in the treatment of schizophrenia. In *Best Practice, 5*(3), 1–54.

Evans, I. M., & Meyer, L. H. (1985). *An educative approach to behavior problems: A practical decision model for interventions with severely handicapped learners*. Baltimore: Paul H. Brookes.

Evans, W. H., Evans, S. S., & Schmid, R. E. (1989). *Behavior and instructional management: An ecological approach*. Boston: Allyn and Bacon.

Everson, S. (1995). Psychology. In J. Barnes (Ed.), *The Cambridge companion to Aristotle* (pp. 168–194). Cambridge, England: Cambridge University Press.

Exner, J. E. (1980). But it's only an inkblot. *Journal of Personality Assessment, 44*, 562–577.

Eysenck, H. (1994a). *Test your IQ*. Toronto: Penguin Books.

Eysenck, H. J. (1957). The effects of psychotherapy: An evaluation. *Journal of Consulting Psychology, 16*, 319–324.

Eysenck, H. J. (1994b). Synergistic interaction between psychosocial and physical factors in the causation of lung cancer. In C. Lewis, C. O'Sullivan, & J. Barraclough (Eds.), *The psychoimmunology of human cancer* (pp. 163–178). London: Oxford University Press.

Eysenck, H. J., & Eysenck, S. B. G. (1993). *Eysenck Personality Questionnaire* [Revised]. London: Hodder & Stoughton Educational.

Fagot, B. I., & Hagan, R. (1991). Observations of parent reactions to sex-stereotyped behaviours: Age and sex effects. *Child Development, 62*, 617–628.

Fairchild, G., Van Goozen, S. H., Stollery, S. J., & Goodyer, I. M. (2008). Fear conditioning and affective modulation of the startle reflex in male adolescents with early-onset or adolescence-onset conduct disorder and healthy control subjects. *Biological Psychiatry 63*(3), 279–285.

Fanselow, M. S., & Gale, G. D. (2003). The amygdala, fear, and memory. *Annals of the New York Academy of Sciences, 985*, 125–134.

Fantz, R. L. (1961). The origin of form perception. *Scientific American, 204*, 66–72.

Fantz, R. L. (1964). Visual experience in infants: Decreased attention to familiar patterns relative to novel ones. *Science, 146*, 668–670.

Faraone, S. V., Tsuang, M. T., & Tsuang, D. W. (1999). *Genetics of mental disorders: A guide for students, clinicians, and researchers*. New York: Guilford Press.

Farmer, A. E. (1996). The genetics of depressive disorders. *International Review of Psychiatry, 8*(4).

Farthing, W. (1992). *The psychology of consciousness*. Upper Saddle River, NJ: Prentice-Hall.

Faucett, J., Gordon, N., & Levine, J. (1994). Differences in postoperative pain severity among four ethnic groups. *Journal of Pain Symptom Management, 9*, 383–389.

Fawzy, F. I., Fawzy, N. W., Hyun, C. S., Elashoff, R., Guthrie, D., Fahey, J. L., & Morton, D. L. (1993). Malignant melanoma effects of an early structured psychiatric intervention, coping, and affective state on recurrence and survival 6 years later. *Archives of General Psychiatry, 50*(9), 681–689.

Fazel-Rezai, R., & Peters, J. F. (2005). P300 wave feature extraction: Preliminary results, in *Proceedings of the 18th Annual Canadian Conference on Electrical and Computer Engineering (CCECE '05*, pp. 390–393). Saskatoon, Saskatchewan, Canada.

Fechner, G. T. (1860). *Elemente der Psykophysik*. Leipzig: Breitkopf und Härtel.

Federal Service for Surveillance of Consumer Rights Protection and Human Well-Being of the Russian Federation and UNAIDS. (2008)., *Country progress report of the Russian Federation on the implementation of the declaration of commitment on HIV/AIDS*. Adopted at the 26th United Nations General Assembly Special Session, June 2001. Moscow, Russia: UNAIDS.

Fedoroff, I. C., & McFarlane, T. (1998). Cultural aspects of eating disorders. In S. S. Kazarian & D. R. Evans (Eds.), *Cultural clinical psychology: Theory, research and practice* (pp. 152–176). New York: Oxford University Press.

Fehr, E., & Gächter, S. (Summer 2000). Fairness and retaliation: The economics of reciprocity. *Journal of Economic Perspectives 14*(3), 159–181.

Feingold, A. (1992). Good-looking people are not what we think. *Psychological Bulletin, 111*, 304–341.

Felder, R. M., & Spurlin, J. E. (2005). Applications, reliability and validity of the index of learning styles. *International Journal of Engineering Education, 21*(1), 103–112.

Feldman, D. H. (2003). Cognitive development in childhood. In R. M. Lerner, M. A. Easterbrooks et al. (Eds.), *Handbook of psychology: Developmental psychology: Vol. 6* (pp. 195–201). New York: Wiley.

Ferguson, C., Rueda, S., Cruz, A., Ferguson, D., & Fritz, S. (2008). Violent video games and aggression: Causal relationship or byproduct of family violence and intrinsic violence motivation? *Criminal Justice and Behavior, 35*(3), 311–332.

Ferguson, N. B., & Keesey, R. E. (1975). Effect of a quinine-adulterated diet upon body weight maintenance in male rats with ventromedial hypothalamic lesions. *Journal of Comparative Physiological Psychology, 89*(5), 478–488.

Ferguson-Noyes, N. (2005). Bipolar disorder in children. *Advanced Nurse Practitioner, 13*, 35.

Fernald, A. (1984). The perceptual and affective salience of mothers' speech to infants. In L. Feagans, C. Garvey, & R. Golinkoff (Eds.), *The origins and growth of communication*. Norwood, NJ: Ablex.

Fernald, A. (1992) Human maternal vocalizations to infants as biologically relevant signals: An evolutionary perspective. In J. H. Barkow, L. Cosmides, & J. Tooby (Eds.), *The adapted mind: Evolutionary psychology and the generation of culture*. New York: Oxford University Press.

Fernandez, E., & Sheffield, J. (1996). Relative contributions of life events versus daily hassles to the frequency and intensity of headaches. *Headache, 36*(10), 595–602.

Feroah, T. R., Sleeper, T., Brozoski, D., Forder, J., Rice, T. B., & Forster, H. V. (2004). *Circadian slow wave sleep and movement behavior are under genetic control in inbred strains of rat*. Paper presented at the American Physiological Society Annual Conference, April 17–21, 2004, Washington, DC.

Ferron, F., Considine, R. V., Peino, R., Lado, I. G., Dieguez, C., & Casanueva, F. F. (1997). Serum leptin concentrations in patients with anorexia nervosa, bulimia nervosa and non-specific eating disorders correlate with the body mass index but are independent of the respective disease. *Clinical Endocrinology (Oxford), 46*, 289–293.

Feshbach, M. (2008, August 13), What's in a number? A new projection by Pokrovskiy's Center for HIV prevention and treatment and some consequences for Russia, Johnson's Russia List. Retrieved June 17, 2010, from http://www.cdi.org/russia/johnson/2008-153-36.cfm.

Festinger, L. (1954). A theory of social comparison processes. *Human Relations, 7*, 117–140.

Festinger, L. (1957). *A theory of cognitive dissonance*. Stanford, CA: Stanford University Press.

Festinger, L., & Carlsmith, J. (1959). $1/$20 experiment: Cognitive consequences of forced compliance. *Journal of Abnormal and Social Psychology, 58*(2), 203–210.

Fiatarone, M. (1996). Physical activity and functional independence in aging. *Research Quarterly for Exercise & Sport, 67*, 70–75.

Fiatarone, M. A., O'Neill, E. F., Doyle, N., Clements, K. M., Roberts, S. B., Kehayias, J. J., Lipsitz, L. A., & Evans, W. J. (1993). The Boston FICSIT study: The effects of resistance training and nutritional supplementation on physical frailty in the oldest old. *Journal of American Geriatrics, 41*, 333–337.

Fincham, F. D., Harold, G. T., & Gano-Phillips, S. (2000). The longitudinal association between attributions and marital satisfaction: Direction of effects and role of efficacy expectations. *Journal of Family Psychology, 14*, 267–285.

Finger, S. (1994). *Origins of neuroscience: A history of explorations into brain function*. New York: Oxford University Press.

Fink, M. (1984). Meduna and the origins of convulsive therapy. *American Journal of Psychiatry, 141*, 1034–1041.

Finke, R. (1995). Creative realism. In S. Smith, T. Ward & R. Finke (Eds.), *The creative cognition approach* (pp. 301–326). Cambridge, MA.: Cambridge University Press.

Finkel, D., & McGue, M. (1997). Sex differences and nonadditivity in heritability of the Multidimensional Personality Questionnaire scales. *Journal of Personality and Social Psychology, 72*, 929–938.

Fiore, M. C., Jaén, C. R., Baker, T. B., Bailey, W. C., Benowitz, N. L., Curry, S. J., et al. (2008). Treating tobacco use and dependence: 2008 update. *U.S. Department of Health and Human Services. Public Health Service*. Retrieved January 6, 2009, from www.surgeongeneral.gov/tobacco/treating_tobacco_use08.pdf

Fischer, A. (1993). Sex differences in emotionality: Fact or stereotype? *Feminism & Psychology, 3*, 303–318.

Fischl, B., Liu, A., & Dale, A. M. (2001). Automated manifold surgery: Constructing geometrically accurate and topologically correct models of the human cerebral cortex. *IEEE Transactions on Medical Imaging, 20*, 70–80.

Fisher, M., Holland, C., Merzenich, M. M., & Vinogradov, S. (2009). Using neuroplasticity-based auditory training to improve verbal memory in schizophrenia. *The American Journal of Psychiatry, 166*(7), 805–811.

Fisher, R., Salanova, V., Witt, T., Worth, R., Henry, T., Gross, R., et al. (2010). Electrical stimulation of the anterior nucleus of thalamus for treatment of refractory epilepsy. *Epilepsia, 17*, 17.

Fiske, S. T. (1998). Stereotyping, prejudice, and discrimination. In D. T. Gilbert & S.T. Fiske (Eds.), *The handbook of social psychology* (4th ed., Vol. 2, pp. 357–411). New York: McGraw-Hill.

Fitzpatrick, M. (2004). MMR and autism (pp. 133–149). New York: Routledge.

Fivush, R., Haden, C., & Reese, E. (1996). Remembering, recounting, and reminiscing: The development of autobiographical memory in social context. In D. C. Rubin (Ed.), *Remembering our past: Studies in autobiographical memory* (pp. 341–359). New York: Cambridge University Press.

Fivush, R., & Nelson, K. (2004). Culture and language in the emergence of autobiographical memory. *Psychological Science, 15*(9), 573.

Flaherty, J. A., & Adams, S. A. (1998). Therapist–patient race and sex matching: Predictors of treatment duration. *Psychiatric Times, 15*(1).

Flaskerud, J. H. (1991). Effects of an Asian client–therapist language, ethnicity and gender match on utilization and outcome of therapy. *Community Mental Health Journal, 27*, 31–42.

Flavell, J. H. (1999). Cognitive development: Children's knowledge about the mind. *Annual Review of Psychology, 50*, 21–45.

Fleming, M. F., & Barry, K. L. (1992). Clinical overview of alcohol and drug disorders. In M. F. Fleming & K. L. Barry (Eds.), *Addictive disorders*. St. Louis: Mosby Year Book.

Flemons, W. W. (2002). Obstructive sleep apnea. *New England Journal of Medicine, 347*, 498–504.

Folkman, S. (1997). Positive psychological states and coping with severe stress. *Social Science & Medicine, 45*, 1207–1221.

Folkard, S., Arendt, J., & Clark, M. (1993). Can melatonin improve shift workers' tolerance of the night shift? Some preliminary findings. *Chronobiology International: The Journal of Biological and Medical Rhythm Research, 10*(5), 315–320.

Folkard, S., Lombardi, D. A., & Spencer, M. B. (2006). Estimating the circadian rhythm in the risk of occupational injuries and accidents. *Chronobiology International: The Journal of Biological and Medical Rhythm Research, 23*(6), 1181–1192.

Folkard, S., Lombardi, D. A., & Tucker, P. (2005). Shiftwork: Safety, sleepiness, and sleep. *Industrial Health, 43*(1), 20–23.

Folkard, S., & Tucker, P. (2003). Shift work, safety, and productivity. *Medicine, 53*, 95–101.

Folkman, S., & Chesney, M. A. (1995). Coping with HIV infection. In M. Stein & A. Baum (Eds.), *Perspectives in behavioral medicine* (pp. 115–133). Hillsdale, NJ: Lawrence Erlbaum.

Folkman, S., & Lazarus, R. S. (1980). An analysis of coping in a middle-aged community sample. *Journal of Health and Social Behavior, 21*(3), 219–239.

Follett, K. J., & Hess, T. M. (2002). Aging, cognitive complexity, and the fundamental attribution error. *Journals of Gerontology Series B: Psychological Sciences and Social Sciences, 57*, 312–323.

Forbes, G., Zhang, X., Doroszewicz, K., & Haas, K. (2009). Relationships between individualism-collectivism, gender, and direct or indirect aggression: a study in China, Poland, and the U.S. *Aggressive Behavior, 35*(1), 24–30.

Ford, N., & Chen, S. Y. (2001). Matching/mismatching revisited: An empirical study of learning and teaching styles. *British Journal of Educational Technology, 32*(1), 5–22.

Fornito, A., Yucel, M., & Pantelis, C. (2009). Reconciling neuroimaging and neuropathological findings in schizophrenia and bipolar disorder. *Current Opinion in Psychiatry, 22*(3), 312–319.

Foulkes, D. (1982). *Children's dreams*. New York: Wiley.

Foulkes, D., & Schmidt, M. (1983). Temporal sequence and unit comparison composition in dream reports from different stages of sleep. *Sleep, 6*, 265–280.

Frank, D. A., Augustyn, M., Knight, W. G., Pell, T., & Zuckerman, B. (2001). Growth, development, and behavior in early childhood following prenatal cocaine exposure. *Journal of the American Medical Association, 285*(12), 1613–1625.

Frank, E., Kupfer, D. J., Buysse, D. J., Swartz, H. A., Pilkonis, P. A., Houck, P. R., Rucci, P., Novick, D. M., Grochocinski, V. J., & Stapf, D. M. (2007). Randomized trial of weekly, twice-monthly, and monthly interpersonal psychotherapy as maintenance treatment for women with recurrent depression. *American Journal of Psychiatry, 164*(5), 761–767.

Franke, R. H., & Kaul, J. D. (1978). The Hawthorne experiments: First statistical interpretation. *American Sociological Review, 43,* 623–643.

Frankel, B. R., & Piercy, F. P. (1990). The relationship among selected supervisor, therapist, and client behaviors. *Journal of Marital and Family Therapy, 16,* 407–421.

Franklin, D. (1990). Hooked: Why isn't everyone an addict? *In Health, 4*(6), 38–52.

Fredrickson, B. L., Maynard, K. E., Helms, M. J., Haney, T. L., Seigler, I. C. & Barefoot, J. C. (2000). Hostility predicts magnitude and duration of blood pressure response to anger. *Journal of Behavioral Medicine, 23,* 229–243.

Freedman, J., & Fraser, S. (1966). Compliance without pressure: The foot-in-the-door technique. *Journal of Personality and Social Psychology, 4,* 195–202.

Freeman, A., Simon, K. M., Beutler, L. E., & Arkowitz, H. (Eds.). (1989). *Comprehensive handbook of cognitive therapy*. New York: Plenum Press.

Freeman, J. (2001). *Gifted children grown up*. London: David Fulton.

Freeman, W., & Watts, J. W. (1937). Prefrontal lobotomy in the treatment of mental disorders. *Southern Medical Journal, 30,* 23–31.

Freese, J., Powell, B., & Steelman, L. C. (1999). Rebel without a cause or effect: Birth order and social attitudes. *American Sociological Review, 64,* 207–231.

Frensch, P. A., & Runger, D. (2003). Implicit learning. *Current Directions in Psychological Science, 12,* 13–18.

Fresquet, N., Angst, M., & Sandner, G. (2004, August). Insular cortex lesions alter conditioned taste avoidance in rats differentially when using two methods of sucrose delivery. *Behavioral Brain Research, 153*(2), 357–365.

Freud, A. (1946). *The ego and the mechanisms of defense. American Edition,* New York: I.U.P.

Freud, S. (1900). The interpretation of dreams. *S.E., 4–5.* (cf. J. Crick, Trans., 1999). London: Oxford University Press.

Freud, S. (1901). The psychopathology of everyday life. *S.E., 6,* 1–290.

Freud, S. (1904a). *Psychopathology of everyday life.* New York: Macmillan; London: Fisher Unwin.

Freud, S. (1904b). Freud's psycho-analytic procedure. *S.E., 7,* 249–254.

Freud, S. (1915/1974). *Repression, The standard edition of the complete psychological works of Sigmund Freud: Vol. 14.* J. Strachey (Ed.). London: Hogart Press and the Institute of Psychoanalysis.

Freud, S. (1923). The ego and the id. *S.E., 19,* 12–66.

Freud, S. (1930). *Civilization and its discontents.* New York: Jonathon Cape and Co.

Freud, S. (1931) Female sexuality. *Pelican Freud Library, 7,* 367.

Freud, S. (1933). *New introductory lectures on psycho-analysis.* London: Hogarth.

Freud, S. (1940). Splitting of the ego in the process of defence. *International Journal of Psychoanalysis, 22,* 65 [1938], S.E., 23, 275–278.

Freud, S., & Gay, P. (1977). *Inhibitions, symptoms and anxiety. Standard edition of the complete works of Sigmund Freud.* New York: W. W. Norton.

Freud, S., Strachey, J., & Riviere, J. (1990). *The ego and the id (The standard edition of the complete psychological works of Sigmund Freud).* New York: W. W. Norton and Company.

Friedman, J. M. (2000). Obesity in the new millennium. *Nature, 404,* 632–634.

Friedman, J. M. (2003). A war on obesity, not the obese. *Science, 299*(5608), 856–858.

Friedman, J. M., & Halaas, J. L. (1998). Leptin and the regulation of body weight in mammals. *Nature, 395,* 763.

Friedman, M., & Kasanin, J. D. (1943). Hypertension in only one of identical twins. *Archives of Internal Medicine, 72,* 767–774.

Friedman, M., & Rosenman, R. H. (1959). Association of specific behavior pattern with blood and cardiovascular findings. *Journal of the American Medical Association, 169,* 1286–1296.

Friedman, M., & Rosenman, R. (1974). *Type A behavior and your heart.* New York: Knopf.

Frontera, W. R., Hughes, V. A., Lutz, K. J., & Evans, W. J. (1991). A cross-sectional study of muscle strength and mass in 45- to 78-year-old men and women. *Journal of Applied Physiology, 71,* 644–650.

Fulcher, J. S. (1942). "Voluntary" facial expression in blind and seeing children. *Archives of Psychology, 38,* 1–49.

Fumeron, F., Betoulle, D., Aubert, R., Herbeth, B., Siest, G., & Rigaud, D. (2001). Association of a functional 5–HT transporter gene polymorphism with anorexia nervosa and food intake. *Molecular Psychiatry, 6,* 9–10.

Furumoto, L. (1979). Mary Whiton Calkins (1863–1930): Fourteenth president of the American Psychological Association. *Journal of the History of Behavioral Sciences, 15,* 346–356.

Furumoto, L. (1991). Portraits of pioneers in psychology. In G. A. Kimble, M. Wertheimer, & C. White (Eds.), *From "Paired associates" to a psychology of self: The intellectual odyssey of Mary Whiton Calkins* (pp. 57–72). Washington, DC: American Psychological Association.

Fuster, J. M. (2008). *The prefrontal cortex* (4th ed.). London: Academic Press.

Gable, R. S. (2004). Acute toxic effects of club drugs. *Journal of Psychoactive Drugs. 36*(1), 303–313.

Gado, M. (2004). A cry in the night: The Kitty Genovese murder. *Court TV's Crime Library: Criminal Minds and Methods.* Retrieved August 2, 2004, from www.crimelibrary.com/serial_killers/predators/kitty_genovese/1.html?sect=2.

Galanter, M. (1983). Unification Church ("Moonie") dropouts: Psychological readjustment after leaving a charismatic religious group. *American Journal of Psychiatry, 140*(8), 984–989.

Galanti, G. A. (1997). *Caring for patients from different cultures* (2nd ed.). Philadelphia: University of Pennsylvania Press.

Galea, S., Resnick, H., Kilpatrick, D., Bucuvalas, M., Gold, J., & Vlahov, D. (2002, March 28). Psychological sequelae of the September 11 terrorist attacks in New York City. *New England Journal of Medicine, 346*(13), 982–987.

Gallagher, R. P. (2009). National Survey of Counseling Center Directors, 2009. *The American College Counseling Association (ACCA).* Retrieved from http://www.iacsinc.org/2009%20National%20Survey.pdf

Gamwell, L., & Tomes, N. (1995). *Madness in America: Cultural and medical perspectives of mental illness before 1914.* Ithaca, NY: Cornell University Press.

Ganchrow, J. R., Steiner, J. E., & Munif, D. (1983). Neonatal facial expressions in response to different qualities and intensities of gustatory stimuli. *Infant Behavior Development, 6,* 473–478.

Ganellen, R. J. (1996). *Integrating the Rorschach and the MMPI-2 in personality assessment.* Mahwah, NJ: Erlbaum.

Ganis, G., Thompson, W. L., & Kosslyn, S. M. (2004). Brain areas underlying visual mental imagery and visual perception: An fMRI study. *Cognitive Brain Research, 20*(2), 226–241.

Garb, H. N., Florio, C. M., & Grove, W. M. (1998). The validity of the Rorschach and the Minnesota Multiphasic Personality Inventory: Results from meta-analyses. *Psychological Science, 9,* 402–404.

Garcia, J., & Koelling, R. A. (1966). Relation of cue to consequence in avoidance learning. *Psychonomic Science, 4,* 123.

Garcia, J., Brett, L. P., & Rusiniak, K. W. (1989). Limits of Darwinian conditioning. In S. B. Klein & R. R. Mowrer (Eds.), *Contemporary learning theories: Instrumental conditioning theory and the impact of biological constraints on learning* (pp. 237–275). Hillsdale, NJ: Erlbaum.

García-Campayo, J., Fayed, N., Serrano-Blanco, A., & Roca, M. (2009). Brain dysfunction behind functional symptoms: Neuroimaging and somatoform, conversive, and dissociative disorders. *Current Opinion in Psychiatry, 22*(2), 224–231.

Gardner, H. (1993a). *Creating minds: An anatomy of creativity seen through the lives of Freud, Einstein, Picasso, Stravinsky, Eliot, Graham, and Ghandi.* New York: Basic Books.

Gardner, H. (1993b). *Multiple intelligences: The theory in practice.* New York: Basic Books.

Gardner, H. (1998). Are there additional intelligences? The case for naturalist, spiritual, and existential intelligences. In J. Kane (Ed.), *Education, information, and transformation* (pp. 111–131). Upper Saddle River, NJ: Merrill-Prentice Hall.

Gardner, H. (1999a). *Intelligence reframed: Multiple intelligences for the 21st century.* New York: Basic Books.

Gardner, H. (1999b, February). Who owns intelligence? *Atlantic Monthly,* 67–76.

Gardner, H., & Moran, S. (2006). The science in multiple intelligences: A response to Lynn Waterhouse. *Educational Psychologist, 41,* 227–232.

Gardner, H., Kornhaber, M. L., & Wake, W. K. (1996). *Intelligence: Multiple perspectives.* Orlando, FL: Harcourt Brace & Co.

Gardner, J., & Oswald, A. J. (2004). How is mortality affected by money, marriage, and stress? *Journal of Health Economics, 23*(6), 1181–1207.

Gardner, R. J. M., & Sutherland, G. R. (1996). Chromosome abnormalities and genetic counseling. *Oxford Monographics on Medical Genetics No. 29.* New York: Oxford University Press.

Garland, E. J., & Smith, D. H. (1991). Simultaneous prepubertal onset of panic disorder, night terrors, and somnambulism. *Journal of American Academic Child and Adolescent Psychiatry, 30*(4), 553–555.

Gazzaniga, M. S. (2006). *The ethical brain: The science of our moral dilemmas.* New York: HarperCollins.

Gazzaniga, M. S. (2009). *Human: The science behind what makes us unique.* New York: Harper Perennial.

Geake, J. (2008). Neuromythologies in education. *Educational Research, 50,* 123–133.

Geary, D. C. (2000). Evolution and proximate expression of human paternal investment. *Psychological Bulletin, 126,* 55–77.

Geary, D. C. (in press). Sex differences. In V. S. Ramachandran (Editor-in-chief), *Encyclopedia of human behavior* (2nd ed.). San Diego, CA: Elsevier.

Gebhard, P. H., & Johnson, A. B. (1979/1998). *The Kinsey data: Marginal tabulations of 1938–1963 interviews conducted by the Institute for Sex Research.* Philadelphia: W. B. Saunders.

Geddes, D. P. (Ed.) (1954). *An analysis of the Kinsey reports.* New York: New American Library.

Geddes, J., & Butler, R. (2002). Depressive disorders. *Clinical Evidence, 7,* 867–882.

Geen, R. G., & Thomas, S. L. (1986). The immediate effects of media violence on behavior. *Journal of Social Issues, 42,* 7–27.

Geier, J., Bernáth, L., Hudák, M., & Sára, L. (2008). Straightness as the main factor of the Hermann grid illusion. *Perception, 37*(5), 651–665.

Gelder, M. (1976). Flooding. In T. Thompson & W. Dockens (Eds.), *Applications of behavior modification* (pp. 250–298). New York: Academic Press.

Geliebter, A. (1988). Gastric distension and gastric capacity in relation to food intake in humans. *Physiological Behavior, 44,* 665–668.

Geller, B., Williams, M., Zimerman, B., Frazier, J., Beringer, L., & Warner, K. L. (1998). Prepubertal and early adolescent bipolarity differentiate from ADHD by manic symptoms, grandiose delusions, ultra-rapid or ultradian cycling. *Journal of Affective Disorders, 51*(2), 81–91.

Gelman, S. A. (1988). The development of induction within natural kind and artifact categories. *Cognitive Psychology, 20,* 65–95.

Gelman, S. A., & Markman, E. M. (1986). Categories and induction in young children. *Cognition, 23,* 183–209.

Gershoff, E. T. (2000). The short- and long-term effects of corporal punishment on children: A meta-analytical review. In D. Elliman & M. A. Lynch, *The physical punishment of children* (pp. 196–198).

Gershoff, E. T. (2002). Corporal punishment by parents: Effects on children and links to physical abuse. *Child Law Practice, 21* (10), 154-157.

Geschwind, D. H., & Iacoboni, M. (2007). Structural and functional asymmetries of the frontal lobes. In B. L. Miller & J. K. Cummings (Eds.), *The human frontal lobes* (2nd ed., pp. 68–91). New York: Guilford Press.

Gessel, L. M., Fields, S. K., Collins, C. L., Dick, R. W., & Comstock, R. D. (2007). Concussions among United States high school and collegiate athletes. *Journal of Athletic Training, 42*(4), 495–503.

Gibbons, J. L., Stiles, D. A., & Shkodriani, G. M. (1991). Adolescents' attitudes toward family and gender roles: An international comparison. *Sex Roles, 25,* 625–643.

Gibson, E. J., & Walk, R. D. (1960). The "visual cliff." *Scientific American, 202,* 67–71.

Giedd, J. N., Blumenthal, J., Jeffries, N. O., Castellanos, F. X., Liui, H., Zijdenbos, A., Paus, T., Evans, A. C., & Rapoport, J. L. (1999). Brain development during childhood and adolescence: A longitudinal MRI study. *Nature Neuroscience, 2*(10), 861–863.

Gilberg, C., & Coleman, M. (2000). *The biology of the autistic syndromes* (3rd ed.). London: Mac Keith Press.

Gilbert, S. J. (1981). Another look at the Milgram obedience studies: The role of the graduated series of shocks. *Personality and Social Psychology Bulletin, 7*(4), 690–695.

Gill, S. T. (1991). Carrying the war into the never-never land of psi. *Skeptical Inquirer, 15*(1), 269–273.

Gillespie, M. A., Kim, B. H., Manheim, L. J., Yoo, T., Oswald, F. L., & Schmitt, N. (June, 2002). The development and validation of biographical data and situational judgment tests in the prediction of college student success. Presented in A. M. Ryan (Chair), *Beyond g: Expanding thinking on predictors of college success.* Symposium conducted at the 14th Annual Convention of the American Psychological Society, New Orleans, LA.

Gillham, B., Tanner, G., Cheyne, B., Freeman, I., Rooney, M., & Lambie, A. (1998). Unemployment rates, single parent density, and indices of child poverty: Their relationship to different categories of child abuse and neglect. *Child Abuse and Neglect, 22*(2), 79–90.

Gilligan, C. (1982). *In a different voice: Psychological theory and women's development.* Cambridge, MA: Harvard University Press.

Gillund, G., & Shiffrin, R. M. (1984). A retrieval model for both recognition and recall. *Psychological Review, 91,* 1–67.

Gilmour, J., & Skuse, D. (1999). A case-comparison study of the characteristics of children with a short stature syndrome induced by stress (hyperphagic short stature) and a consecutive series of unaffected "stressed" children. *Journal of Child Psychology and Psychiatry and Allied Disciplines, 40*(6), 969–978.

Ginzburg, K., Solomon, Z., Koifman, B., Keren, G., Roth, A., Kriwisky, M., Kutz, I., David, D., & Bleich, A. (2003). Trajectories of post-traumatic stress disorder following myocardial infarction: A prospective study. *Journal of Clinical Psychiatry, 64*(10), 1217–1223.

Gittelman-Klein, R. (1978). Validity in projective tests for psychodiagnosis in children. In R. L. Spitzer & D. F. Klein (Eds.), *Critical issues in psychiatric diagnosis* (pp. 141–166). New York: Raven Press.

Glenn, A. L., Raine, A., Mednick, S. A., & Venables, P. (2007). Early temperamental and psychophysiological precursors of adult psychopathic personality. *Journal of Abnormal Psychology, 116*(3), 508–518.

Glenn, D. (2009). Matching teaching style to learning style may not help students. *The Chronicle of Higher Education, December 15th, 2009.* Retrieved January, 6, 2010, from http://chronicle.com/article/Matching-Teaching-Style-to/49497/

Glick, P., & Fiske, S. (2001). An ambivalent alliance: Hostile and benevolent sexism as complementary justifications for gender inequality. *American Psychologist, 56,* 109–118.

Glucksman, M.L. (2006). Psychoanalytic and psychodynamic education in the 21st century. *Journal of American Academy of Psychoanalysis, 34,* 215–22.

Glynn, S. M. (1990). Token economy approaches for psychiatric patients: Progress and pitfalls over 25 years. *Behavior Modification, 14,* 383–407.

Godden, D. R., & Baddeley, A. D. (1975). Context-dependent memory in two natural environments: On land and underwater. *British Journal of Psychology, 66,* 325–331.

Goel, V., & Grafman, J. (1995). Are the frontal lobes implicated in "planning" functions? Interpreting data from the Tower of Hanoi. *Neuropsychologia, 33*(5), 623–642.

Gogtay, N., & Thompson, P. M. (2010). Mapping gray matter development: Implications for typical development and vulnerability to psychopathology. *Brain and Cognition, 72*(1), 6–15.

Gogtay, N., Lu, A., Leow, A. D., Klunder, A. D., Lee, A. D., Chavez, A., Greenstein, D., Giedd, J. N., Toga, A. W., Rapoport, J. L., & Thompson, P. M. (2008). Three-dimensional brain growth abnormalities in childhood-onset schizophrenia visualized by using tensor-based morphometry. *Proceedings of the National Academy of Sciences, USA, 105*(41), 15979–15984.

Goin, M. K. (2005). Practical psychotherapy: A current perspective on the psychotherapies. *Psychiatric Services, 56*(3), 255–257.

Goldman, A. L., Pezawas, L., Mattay, V. S., Fischl, B., Verchinski, B. A., Chen, Q., Weinberger, D. R., & Meyer-Lindenberg, A. (2009). Widespread reductions of cortical thickness in schizophrenia and spectrum disorders and evidence of heritability. *Archives of General Psychiatry, 66*(5), 467–477.

Goldman-Rakic, P. S. (1998). The prefrontal landscape: Implications of functional architecture for understanding human mentation and the central executive. In A. C. Roberts, T. W. Robbins, & L. Weiskrantz (Eds.), *The prefrontal cortex: Executive and cognitive functions* (pp. 87–102). Oxford, UK: Oxford University Press.

Goleman, D. (1982). Staying up: The rebellion against sleep's gentle tyranny. *Psychology Today, 3,* 24–35.

Goleman, D. (1995). *Emotional intelligence: Why it can matter more than IQ.* New York: Bantam Books.

Golkaramnay, V., Bauer, S., Haug, S., Wolf, M., & Kordy, H. (2007). The exploration of the effectiveness of group therapy through an Internet chat as aftercare: A controlled naturalistic study. *Pychotherapy and Psychosomatics, 76*, 219–225.

Gong-Guy, E., & Hammen, C. (1980). Causal perceptions of stressful events in depressed and nondepressed outpatients. *Journal of Abnormal Psychology, 89*, 662–669.

Gonsalves, B., Reber, P. J., Gitelman, D. R., Parrish, T. B., Mesulam, M. M., & Paller, K. A. (2004). Neural evidence that vivid imagining can lead to false remembering. *Psychological Science, 15*, 655–660.

Gonzales, P. M., Blanton, H., & Williams, K. J. (2002). The effects of stereotype threat and double–minority status on the test performance of Latino women. *Personality and Social Psychology Bulletin, 28*(5), 659–670.

Gonzalez, J. S., Penedo, F. J., Antoni, M. H., Durán, R. E., Fernandez, M. I., McPherson-Baker, S., Ironson, G., Klimas, N. G., Fletcher, M. A., & Schneiderman, N. (2004). Social support, positive states of mind, and HIV treatment adherence in men and women living with HIV/AIDS. *Health Psychology, 23*(4), 413–418.

Goodglass, H., Kaplan, E., & Barresi, B. (2001). *The assessment of aphasia and related disorders* (3rd ed.). Baltimore: Lippincott, Williams & Wilkins.

Goodman, E. S. (1980). Margaret Floy Washburn (1871–1939) first woman Ph.D. in psychology. *Psychology of Women Quarterly, 5*, 69–80.

Gosselin, R. E., Smith, R. P., Hodge, H. C., & Braddock, J. E. (1984). *Clinical toxicology of commercial products* (5th ed.). Sydney, Australia: Williams & Wilkins.

Gotlib, I. H., Sivers, H., Canli, T., Kasch, K. L., & Gabrieli, J. D. E. (November, 2001). Neural activation in depression in response to emotional stimuli. In I. H. Gotlib (Chair), *New directions in the neurobiology of affective disorders.* Symposium conducted at the annual meeting of the Society for Research in Psychopathology, Madison, WI.

Gottesman, I. I. (1991). *Schizophrenia genesis: The origins of madness.* New York: Freeman.

Gottesman, I. I., McGuffin P. & Farmer, A. E. (1987). Clinical genetics as clues to the "Real" genetics of schizophrenia (A decade of modest gains while playing for time). *Schizophrenia Bulletin, 13*, 23-47.

Gottesman, I. I., & Shields, J. (1976). A critical review of recent adoption, twin and family studies of schizophrenia: Behavioural genetics perspectives. *Schizophrenia Bulletin, 2*, 360–401.

Gottesman, I., & Shields, J. (1982). *Schizophrenia: The epigenetic puzzle.* New York: Cambridge University Press.

Gottman, J. M., & Krokoff, L. J. (1989). Marital interaction and satisfaction: A longitudinal view. *Journal of Consulting and Clinical Psychology, 57*, 47–52.

Gough, H. G. (1995). *California Psychological Inventory* (3rd ed.). Palo Alto, CA: Consulting Psychologist-Press.

Gould, J. L., & Gould, C. G. (1994). *The animal mind.* New York: Scientific American Library.

Gould, S. J. (1981). *The mismeasure of man.* New York: Norton.

Gould, S. J. (1996). *The mismeasure of man.* New York: W. W. Norton.

Gouldner, A. W. (1960). The norm of reciprocity: A preliminary statement. *American Sociological Review, 25*, 161–178.

Grandjean, P., Weihe, P., White, R. F., Debes, F., Araki, S., Yokoyama, K., Murata, K., Sorensen, N., Dahl, R., & Jorgensen, P. J. (1997). Cognitive deficit in 7-year-old children with prenatal exposure to methylmercury. *Neurotoxicology and Teratology, 19*(6), 417–428.

Greeley, A. (1987). Mysticism goes mainstream. *American Health, 1*, 47–49.

Gregory, R. L. (1990). *Eye and brain, the psychology of seeing.* Princeton, NJ: Princeton University Press.

Gresham, L. G., & Shimp, T. A. (1985). Attitude toward the advertisement and brand attitudes: A classical conditioning prospective. *Journal of Advertising, 14*(1), 10–17, 49.

Gribbons, B., & Herman, J. (1997) True and quasi-experimental designs. Washington, DC: ERIC Clearinghouse on Assessment and Evaluation.

Griffiths, R. R., Richards, W. A., McCann, U., & Jesse, R. (2006). Psilocybin can occasion mystical-type experiences having substantial and sustained personal meaning and spiritual significance. *Psychopharmacology*, 187(3), 1432–2072.

Grocer, S., & Kohout, J. (1997). The 1995 APA survey of 1992 baccalaureate recipients. Washington, DC: American Psychological Association.

Gross, C. G. (1999). A hole in the head. *The Neuroscientist, 5*, 263–269.

Grünbaum, A. (1984). *The foundations of psychoanalysis: A philosophical critique.* Berkeley, CA: University of California Press.

Grumbach, M. M., & Kaplan, S. L. (1990). The neuroendocrinology of human puberty: An ontogenetic perspective. In M. M. Grumbach, P. C. Sizonenko, & M. L. Aubert (Eds.), *Control of the onset of puberty* (pp. 1–6). Baltimore: Williams & Wilkins.

Grumbach, M. M., & Styne, D. M. (1998). Puberty: Ontogeny, neuroendocrinology, physiology, and disorders. In J. D. Wilson, D. W. Foster, H. M. Kronenberg, & P. R. Larsen (Eds.), *Williams textbook of endocrinology* (9th ed. pp. 1509–1625). Philadelphia: W. B. Saunders.

Guar, A., Dominguez, K., Kalish, M., Rivera-Hernandez, D., Donohoe, M., & Mitchell, C. (2008, February). *Practice of offering a child pre-masticated food: An unrecognized possible risk factor for HIV transmission.* Paper presented at the 15th Conference on Retroviruses and Opportunistic Infections, Boston, MA.

Guilford, J. P. (1967). *The nature of human intelligence.* New York: McGraw-Hill.

Gupta, M. (1994). Sexuality in the Indian sub-continent. *Sex and Marital Therapy, 9*, 57–69.

Guskiewicz, K. M., Marshall, S. W., Bailes, J., McCrea, M., Cantu, R. C., Randolph, C., & Jordan, B. D. (2005). Association between recurrent concussion and late-life cognitive impairment in retired professional football players. *Neurosurgery, 57*(4), 719–726.

Guskiewicz, K. M., Marshall, S. W., Bailes, J., McCrea, M., Harding, H. P., Jr., Matthews, A., Mihalik, J. R., & Cantu, R. C. (2007). Recurrent concussion and risk of depression in retired professional football players. *Medicine and Science in Sports and Exercise, 39*(6), 903–909.

Gustavson, C. R., Kelly, D. J., Seeney, M., & Garcia, J. (1976). Prey lithium aversions I: Coyotes and wolves. *Behavioral Biology, 17*, 61–72.

Guthrie, R. V. (2004). *Even the rat was white: A historical view of psychology.* Boston: Allyn & Bacon.

Haber, R. N. (1979). Twenty years of haunting eidetic imagery: Where's the ghost? *The Behavioral and Brain Sciences, 2*, 583–619.

Hahm, H. C., & Adkins, C. (2009). A model of Asian and Pacific Islander sexual minority acculturation. *Journal of LGBT Youth, 6*, 155–173.

Halbesleben, J. R. B., & Bowler, W. M. (2007). Emotional exhaustion and job performance: The mediating role of motivation. *Journal of Applied Psychology, 91*, 93–106.

Hall, C. (1966). Studies of dreams collected in the laboratory and at home. *Institute of Dream Research Monograph Series* (No. 1). Santa Cruz, CA: Privately printed.

Hall, W., & Degenhardt, L. (2009). Adverse health effects of non-medical cannabis use. *Lancet*, 374, 1383–1391.

Hamann, S., Herman, R. A., Nolan, C. L., & Wallen, K. (2004). Men and women differ in amygdale response to visual sexual stimuli. *Nature Neuroscience, 7*(4), 411–419.

Hamer, D. H., Hu, S., Magnuson, V. L., Hu, N., & Pattatucci, A. M. L. (1993). A linkage between DNA markers on the X chromosome and male sexual orientation. *Science, 261*, 321–327.

Hamers, F. F., and Downs, A. M. (2003, March). HIV in central and eastern Europe. *Lancet, 362*, 9362.

Hamilton, D. L., & Gifford, R. K. (1976). Illusory correlation in interpersonal perception: A cognitive basis of stereotypic judgments. *Journal of Experimental Social Psychology, 12*, 392–407.

Hampton, J. A. (1998). Similarity-based categorization and fuzziness of natural categories. *Cognition, 65*, 137–165.

Handel, S. (1989). *Listening: An introduction to the perception of auditory events.* Cambridge, MA: MIT Press.

Hansen, C. P. (1988). Personality characteristics of the accident involved employee. *Journal of Business and Psychology, 2*(4), 346–365.

Hargittai, E. (2007). Whose space? Differences among users and non-users of social network sites. *Journal of Computer-Mediated Communication, 13*(1), article 14. Retrieved from http://jcmc.indiana.edu/vol13/issue1/hargittai.html

Harlow, H. F. (1958). The nature of love. *American Psychologist, 13*, 573–685.

Harman, G. (1999). Moral philosophy meets social psychology: Virtue ethics and the fundamental attribution error. *Proceedings of the Aristotelian Society, 1998–99, 99*, 315–331.

Harmon-Jones, E. (2000). Cognitive dissonance and experienced negative affect: Evidence that dissonance increases experienced negative affect even in the absence of aversive consequences. *Personality and Social Psychology Bulletin, 26,* 1490–1501.

Harmon-Jones, E. (2004). Insights on asymmetrical frontal brain activity gleaned from research on anger and cognitive dissonance. *Biological Psychology, 67,* 51–76.

Harmon-Jones, E. (2006). Integrating cognitive dissonance theory with neurocognitive models of control. *Psychophysiology, 43,* S16.

Harmon-Jones, E., Harmon-Jones, C., Fearn, M., Sigelman, J. D., & Johnson, P. (2008). Action orientation, relative left frontal cortical activation, and spreading of alternatives: A test of the action-based model of dissonance. *Journal of Personality and Social Psychology, 94*(1), 1–15.

Harrison, P. J. (1999). The neuropathology of schizophrenia: A critical review of the data and their interpretation. *Brain, 122,* 593–624.

Hart, P. (1998). Preventing groupthink revisited: Evaluating and reforming groups in government. *Organizational Behavior & Human Decision Processes, 73*(2–3), 306–326.

Hartfield, E. (1987). Passionate and companionate love. In R. J. Sternberg & M. L. Barnes (Eds.), *The psychology of love* (pp. 191–217). New Haven, CT: Yale University Press.

Hartfield, E., & Rapson, R. L. (1992). Similarity and attraction in intimate relationships. *Communication Monographs, 59,* 209–212.

Harvard Mental Health Letter (2010). Experts urge caution in using deep brain stimulation. *Harvard Mental Health Letter, 26*(8), 6–7.

Harvey, S. & Keashly, L. (2003). Predicting the risk for aggression in the workplace: Risk factors, self-esteem and time at work. *Social Behaviour & Personality: An International Journal, 31*(8), 807–814.

Hauck, S. J., & Bartke, A. (2001). Free radical defenses in the liver and kidney of human growth hormone transgenic mice. *Journal of Gerontology and Biological Science, 56,* 153–162.

Havighurst R. J., Neugarten B. L., & Tobin S. N. S. (1968). Disengagement and patterns of aging. In B. L. Neugarten (Ed.), *Middle age and aging: A reader in social psychology* (pp. 161–172). Chicago: University of Chicago Press.

Hawks, S. R., Madanat, H. N., Merrill, R. M., Goudy, M. B., & Miyagawa, T. (2003). A cross-cultural analysis of "motivation for eating" as a potential factor in the emergence of global obesity: Japan and the United States. *Health Promotion International, 18*(2), 153–162.

Hayflick, L. (1977). The cellular basis for biological aging. In C. E. Finch & L. Hayflick (Eds.), *Handbook of biology of aging* (p. 159). New York: Van Nostrand Reinhold.

Hayward, C., Killen, J. D., Kraemer, H. C., & Taylor, C. B. (2000). Predictors of panic attacks in adolescents. *Journal of the American Academy of Child and Adolescent Psychiatry, 39*(2), 207–214.

Hayward, C., Killen, J., & Taylor, C. B. (1989). Panic attacks in young adolescents. *American Journal of Psychiatry, 146*(8), 1061–1062.

Hazan, C., & Shaver, P. (1987). Romantic love conceptualized as an attachment process. *Journal of Personality and Social Psychology, 52,* 511–524.

Heavey, C. L., Layne, C., & Christensen, A. (1993). Gender and conflict structure in marital interaction: A replication and extension. *Journal of Consulting and Clinical Psychology, 61,* 16–27.

Hebb, D. O. (1955). Drives and the CNS (Conceptual Nervous System). *Psychological Review, 62,* 243–254.

Heider, F. (1958). *The psychology of interpersonal relations.* New York: John Wiley & Sons.

Heil, G., Maslow, A., & Stephens, D. (1998). *Maslow on management.* New York: John Wiley and Sons.

Heilman, K., Watson, R., & Valenstein, E. (1993). Neglect and related disorders. In K. Heilman and E. Valenstein (Eds.), *Clinical neuropsychology.* New York: Oxford University Press.

Heilman, K. M. (2002). *Matter of mind: A neurologist's view of brain-behavior relationships.* New York: Oxford University Press.

Heimberg, R. G., & Becker, R. E. (2002). *Cognitive-behavioral group therapy for social phobia: Basic mechanisms and clinical strategies.* New York: Guilford Press.

Heinicke, C. M., Goorsky, M., Moscov, S., Dudley, K., Gordon, J., Schneider, C., & Guthrie, D. (2000). Relationship-based intervention with at-risk mothers: Factors affecting variations in outcome. *Infant Mental Health Journal, 21,* 133–155.

Heinrich, B. (2000). Testing insight in ravens. In C. Heyes & L. Huber (Eds.), *The evolution of cognition.* Cambridge, MA: MIT Press.

Helms, J. E. (1992). Why is there no study of cultural equivalence in standardized cognitive ability testing? *American Psychologist, 47*(9), 1083–1101.

Henin, A., Mick, E., Biederman, J., Fried, R., Wozniak, J., Faraone, S. V., Harrington, K., Davis, S., & Doyle, A. E. (2007). Can bipolar disorder-specific neuropsychological impairments in children be identified? *Journal of Consulting and Clinical Psychology, 75*(2), 210–220.

Henning, H. (1916). Die qualitätenreihe des geschmacks. *Zsch. f. Psychol., 74,* 203–219.

Henningfield, J. E. (1995). Nicotine medications for smoking cessation. *New England Journal of Medicine, 333*(18), 1196–1203.

Henningfield., J. E., Clayton, R., & Pollin, W. (1990). Involvement of tobacco in alcoholism and illicit drug use. *British Journal of Addition, 85,* 279–292.

Henningfield, J. E., Cohen, C., Slade, J. D. (1991). Is nicotine more addictive than cocaine? *British Journal of Addiction, 86,* 565–569.

Henry, J. (2007, July 30). Professor pans "learning style" teaching method. [London] *Telegraph.* Retrieved March 24, 2010, from http://www.telegraph.co.uk/news/uknews/1558822/Professor-pans-learning-style-teaching-method.html

Herberman, R. B., & Ortaldo, J. R. (1981). Natural killer cells: Their role in defenses against disease. *Science, 214,* 24–30.

Herbst, J. H., Zonderman, A. B., McCrae, R. R., & Costa, P. T., Jr. (2000). Do the dimensions of the Temperament and Character Inventory map a simple genetic architecture? Evidence from molecular genetics and factor analysis. *American Journal of Psychiatry, 157,* 1285–1290.

Herman, L. M., Pack, A. A., & Morrell-Samuels, P. (1993). Representational and conceptual skills of dolphins. In H. L. Roitblatt, L. M. Herman, & P. E. Nachtigall (Eds.), *Language and communication: Comparative perspectives.* Hillsdale, NJ: Erlbaum.

Hermann, A., Maisel, M., Wegner, F., Liebau, S., Kim, D.-W., Gerlach, M., Schwarz, J., Kim, K.-S., & Storch, A. (2006). Multipotent neural stem cells from the adult tegmentum with dopaminergic potential develop essential properties of functional neurons. *Stem Cells, 24*(4), 949–964.

Hernandez, D., & Fisher, E. M. (1996). Down syndrome genetics: Unravelling a multifactorial disorder. *Human Molecular Genetics, 5,* 1411–1416.

Herring, M. P., O'Connor, P. J., & Dishman, R. K. (2010). The effect of exercise training on anxiety symptoms among patients: A systematic review. *Archives of Internal Medicine, 170*(4), 321–331.

Herrnstein, R. J., & Murray, C. (1994). *The bell curve: The reshaping of American life by differences in intelligence.* New York: Free Press.

Hersh, S. M. (2004, May 10). Annals of national security: Torture at Abu Ghraib. *The New Yorker.*

Hershberger, S. L., Plomin, R., & Pedersen, N. L. (1995, October). Traits and metatraits: Their reliability, stability, and shared genetic influence. *Journal of Personality and Social Psychology, 69*(4), 673–685.

Herxheimer, A., & Petrie, K. J. (2001). Melatonin for preventing and treating jet lag. *Cocharane Database of Systematic Reviews* (1), CD 001520.

Heslegrave, R. J., & Rhodes. W. (1997). Impact of varying shift schedules on the performance and sleep in air traffic controllers. *Sleep Research, 26,* 198.

Hetherington, A. W., & Ranson, S. W. (1940). Hypothalamic legions and adiposity in rats. *Anatomical Records, 78,* 149–172.

Hettema, J. M., Neale, M. C., & Kendler, K. S. (2001). A review and meta-analysis of the genetic epidemiology of anxiety disorders. *American Journal of Psychiatry, 158,* 1568–1578.

Hewstone, M., Rubin, M., & Willis, H. (2002). Intergroup bias. *Annual Review of Psychology, 53,* 575–604.

Heyes, C. M. (1998). Theory of mind in nonhuman primates. *Behavior and Brain Science, 21,* 101–148.

Hicklin, J., & Widiger, T. A. (2000). Convergent validity of alternative MMPI-2 personality disorder scales. *Journal of Personality Assessment, 75*(3), 502–518.

Hilgard E. R. (1965). Hypnotic susceptibility. New York: Harcourt, Brace & World.

Hilgard, E. R. (1991). A neodissociation interpretation of hypnosis. In S. J. Lynn & J. W. Rhue (Eds.), *Theories of hypnosis* (pp. 83–104). New York: Guilford Press.

Hilgard, E. R., & Hilgard, J. R. (1994). *Hypnosis in the relief of pain* (Rev. ed.). New York: Brunner/Mazel.

Hill, D. (1990). Causes of smoking in children. In B. Durston & K. Jamrozik, *Smoking and health 1990—The global war. Proceedings of the 7th World Conference on Smoking and Health*, 1–5 April. Perth: Health Department of Western Australia, 205–209.

Hill, J. A. (1998). Miscarriage risk factors and causes: What we know now. *OBG Management, 10*, 58–68.

Hill, P. C., & Butter E. M. (1995). The role of religion in promoting physical health. *Journal of Psychology and Christianity, 14*(2), 141–155.

Hillman, C. H., Pontifex, M. B., Raine, L. B., Castelli, D. M., Hall, E. E., & Kramer, A. F. (2009). The effect of acute treadmill walking on cognitive control and academic achievement in preadolescent children. *Neuroscience, 159*(3), 1044–1054.

Hilton, J. L., & von Hipple, W. (1996). Stereotypes. *Annual Review of Psychology, 47*, 237–271.

Hilts, P. J. (August 2, 1998). Is nicotine addictive? It depends on whose criteria you use. *New York Times*, p. C3.

Hines, T. (2003). *Pseudoscience and the paranormal: A critical examination of the evidence.* Amherst, NY: Prometheus.

Hintze, J. M. (2002). Interventions for fears and anxiety problems. In M. R. Shinn, H. R. Walker, & G. Stoner (Eds.), *Interventions for academic and behavior problems II: Preventive and remedial approaches* (pp. 939–954). Bethesda, MD: National Association of School Psychologists.

Hobson, J. (1988). *The dreaming brain*. New York: Basic Books.

Hobson, J., Pace-Schott, E., & Stickgold, R. (2000). Dreaming and the brain: Towards a cognitive neuroscience of conscious states. *Behavioral and Brain Sciences, 23*(6), 793–1121.

Hobson, J. A., & McCarley, R. (1977). The brain as a dream state generator: An activation-synthesis hypothesis of the dream process. *American Journal of Psychiatry, 134*, 1335–1348.

Hochman, J. (1994). Buried memories challenge the law. *National Law Journal, 1*, 17–18.

Hodges, J. R. (1994). Retrograde amnesia. In A. Baddeley, B. A. Wilson, & F. Watts (Eds.), *Handbook of memory disorders* (pp. 81–107). New York: Wiley.

Hodgson, B. (2001). *In the arms of Morpheus: The tragic history of laudanum, morphine, and patent medicines.* New York: Firefly Books.

Hodson, D. S., & Skeen, P. (1994). Sexuality and aging: The hammerlock of myths. *The Journal of Applied Gerontology, 13*, 219–235.

Hoebel, B. G., & Teitelbaum, P. (1966). Weight regulation in normal and hypothalamic hyperphagic rats. *Journal of Comparative Physiological Psychology, 61*, 189–193.

Hoffer, T. B., Hess, M.,Welch, V., Jr., & Williams, K. (2007). *Doctorate Recipients from United States Universities: Summary Report 2006*. Chicago: National Opinion Research Center.

Hoffmann, A. (1998). *Paradigms of artificial intelligence: A Methodological and computational analysis.* London: Springer-Verlag.

Hoffrage, U., Hertwig, R., & Gigerenzer, G. (2000). Hindsight bias: A by-product of knowledge updating? *Journal of Experimental Psychology: Learning, Memory, and Cognition, 26*, 566–581.

Hofstede, G. H. (1980). *Culture's consequences, international differences in work-related values.* Beverly Hills, CA: Sage .

Hofstede, G. J., Pedersen, P. B., & Hofstede, G. H. (2002). *Exploring culture: Exercises, stories, and synthetic cultures.* Yarmouth, ME: Intercultural Press.

Hoge, C. W., McGurk, D., Thomas, J. L., Cox, A. L., Engel, C. C., & Castro, C. A. (2008). Mild traumatic brain injury in U.S. soldiers returning from Iraq. *The New England Journal of Medicine, 358*(5), 453–463.

Hogg, M. A., & Hains, S. C. (1998). Friendship and group identification: A new look at the role of cohesiveness in groupthink. *European Journal of Social Psychology, 28*(1), 323–341.

Holahan, C. K., & Sears, R. R. (1996). *The gifted group at later maturity*. Stanford, CA: Stanford University Press.

Holcomb, W. R. (1986). Stress inoculation therapy with anxiety and stress disorders of acute psychiatric patients. *Journal of Clinical Psychology, 42*, 864–872.

Holden, C., & Vogel, G. (2002). Plasticity: Time for a reappraisal? *Science, 296*, 2126–2129.

Hollon, S., These, M., & Markowitz, J. (2002). Treatment and prevention of depression. *Psychological Science in the Public Interest, 3*, 39–77.

Hollon, S. D., & Beck, A. T. (1994). Cognitive and cognitive-behavioral therapies. In A. E. Bergin & and S. L. Garfield (Eds.), *Handbook of psychotherapy and behavior change* (4th ed., p. 428). Chichester, UK: John Wiley & Sons.

Holman, E. A., Silver, R. C., Poulin, M., Andersen, J., Gil-Rivas, V., & McIntosh, D. N. (2008). Terrorism, acute stress, and cardiovascular health: A 3-year national study following the September 11th attacks. *Archives of General Psychiatry, 65*, 73–80.

Holmes, C. B., Wurtz, P. J., Waln, R. F., Dungan, D. S., & Joseph, C. A. (1984). Relationship between the Luscher Color Test and the MMPI. *Journal of Clinical Psychology, 40*, 126–128.

Holmes, T. H., & Masuda, M. (1973). Psychosomatic syndrome: When mothers-in-law or other disasters visit, a person can develop a bad, bad cold. *Psychology Today, 5*(11), 71–72, 106.

Holmes, T. H., & Rahe, R. H. (1967). The Social Readjustment Rating Scale. *Journal of Psychosomatic Research II*, 213–218.

Holroyd, J. (1996). Hypnosis treatment of clinical pain: Understanding why hypnosis is useful. *International Journal of Clinical and Experimental Hypnosis, 44*, 33–51.

Holt-Lunstad, J., Uchino, B. N., Smith, T. W., Cerny, C. B., & Nealey-Moore, J. B. (2003). Social relationships and ambulatory blood pressure: Structural and qualitative predictors of cardiovascular function during everyday social interactions. *Health Psychology, 22*, 388–397.

Hood, D. C. (1998). Lower-level visual processing and models of light adaptation. *Annual Review of Psychology, 49*, 503–535.

Hootman, J. M., Dick, R., & Agel, J. (2007). Epidemiology of collegiate injuries for 15 sports: Summary and recommendations for injury prevention initiatives. *Journal of Athletic Training, 42*(2), 311–319.

Hopfinger, J. B., Buonocore, M. H., & Mangun, G. R. (2000). The neural mechanisms of top-down attentional control. *Nature Neuroscience, 3*, 284–291.

Horne, J. A., & Staff, C. H. (1983). Exercise and sleep: Body heating effects. *Sleep, 6*, 36–46.

Horney, K. (1939). *New ways in psychoanalysis*, New York: W. W. Norton.

Horney, K. (1967/1973). *Feminine psychology.* New York: W. W. Norton.

Horowitz, D. L. (1985). *Ethnic groups in conflict*. Berkeley: University of California Press.

Hortaçsu, N. (1999). The first year of family and couple initiated marriages of a Turkish sample: A longitudinal investigation. *International Journal of Psychology, 34*(1), 29–41.

Hossain, P., Kawar, B., & El Nahas, M. (2007). Obesity and diabetes in the developing world—A growing challenge. *New England Journal of Medicine, 356*(9), 973.

Hothersall, D. (1995). *History of psychology* (pp. 162–165). New York: McGraw-Hill, Inc.

Hovland, C. I. (1937). The generalization of conditioned responses. I. The sensory generalization of conditioned responses with varying frequencies of tone. *Journal of General Psychology, 17*,125–48.

Hu, P., & Meng, Z. (August, 1996). *An examination of infant–mother attachment in China.* Poster session presented at the meeting of the International Society for the Study of Behavioral Development, Quebec City, Quebec, Canada.

Hu, S., & Stern, R. M. (1999). Retention of adaptation to motion sickness eliciting stimulation. *Aviation, Space, and Environmental Medicine, 70*, 766–768.

Hu, S., Pattatucci, A. M. L., Patterson, C., Li, L., Fulker, D. W., Cherny, S. S., Kruglyak, L., & Hamer, D. H. (1994). Linkage between sexual orientation and chromosome Xq28 in males but not in females. *Nature Genetics, 11*, 248–256.

Hubel, D. H., & Wiesel, T. N. (1959). Receptive fields of single neurons in the cat's striate cortex. *The Journal of Physiology, 148*, 574–591.

Huesmann, L. R., & Eron, L. (1986). *Television and the aggressive child: A cross-national comparison.* Hillsdale, NJ: Erlbaum.

Huesmann, L. R., & Miller, L. S. (1994). Long-term effects of repeated exposure to media violence in childhood. In L. R. Huesmann (Ed.), *Aggressive behavior: Current perspectives* (pp. 153–183). New York: Plenum Press.

Huesmann, L. R., Moise, J. F., & Podolski, C. L. (1997). The effects of media violence on the development of antisocial behavior. In D. M. Stoff, J. Breiling, & J. D. Maser (Eds.), *Handbook of antisocial behavior* (pp. 181–193). New York: John Wiley.

Huesmann, L. R., Moise-Titus, J., Podolski, C. L., & Eron, L. D. (2003). Longitudinal relations between children's exposure to TV violence and their aggressive and violent behavior in young adulthood: 1977–1992. *Developmental Psychology, 39*(2), 201–221.

Huff, W., Lenartz, D., Schormann, M., Lee, S. H., Kuhn, J., Koulousakis, A., Mai, J., Daumann, J., Maarouf, M., Klosterkotter, J., & Sturm, V. (2010). Unilateral deep brain stimulation of the nucleus accumbens in patients with treatment-resistant obsessive-compulsive disorder: Outcomes after one year. *Clinical Neurology and Neurosurgery, 112*(2), 137–143.

Hugenberg, K., & Bodenhausen, G. V. (2003). Facing prejudice: Implicit prejudice and the perception of facial threat. *Psychological Science, 14*, 640–643.

Hughes, J. (1993). Behavior therapy. In T. R. Kratochwill & R. J. Morris (Eds.), *Handbook of psychotherapy with children and adolescents* (pp. 185–220). Boston: Allyn and Bacon.

Hughes, S. M., Harrison, M. A., & Gallup, G. G., Jr. (2007). Sex differences in romantic kissing among college students: An evolutionary perspective. *Evolutionary Psychology 5*(3), 612–631.

Hull, C. L. (1943). *Principles of behavior*. New York: Appleton-Century.

Hummer, R. A., Rogers, R. G., Nam, C. B., & Ellison, C. G. (1999). Religious involvement and U.S. adult mortality. *Demography, 36*(2), 273–285.

Humphries, L. L. (1987). Bulimia: Diagnosis and treatment. *Comprehensive Therapy, 13*, 12–15.

Hunsley, J., & Mash, E. J. (2008). Developing criteria for evidence-based assessment: An introduction to assessments that work. In J. Hunsley & E. J. Mash (Eds.), *A guide to assessments that work* (3rd ed.). New York: Guilford Press.

Hunt, E. (2001). Multiple views of multiple intelligence. [Review of Intelligence reframed: Multiple intelligence in the 21st century.] *Contemporary Psychology, 46*, 5–7.

Hunt, M. (1993). *The story of psychology*. New York: Doubleday.

Hurley, D. (1989). The search for cocaine's methadone. *Psychology Today, 23*(7/8), 54.

Hurley, S., & Nudds, M. (Eds.). (2006). *Rational animals?* Oxford, UK: Oxford University Press.

Hurvich, L. M., & Jameson, D. (1957). An opponent-process theory of color vision. *Psychological Review, 64*, 384–404.

Hutcheson, J., & Snyder, H. M. (2004). Ambiguous genitalia and intersexuality. *eMedicine Journal, 5*(5). Retrieved November 17, 2004, from http://author.emedicine.com/PED/topic1492.htm

Hvas, L. (2001). Positive aspects of menopause: A qualitative study. *Maturitas 39*(1), 11–17.

Hyde, J. S., & Kling, K. C. (2001). Women, motivation, and achievement. *Psychology of Women Quarterly, 25*, 264–378.

Hyde, J. S., & Plant, E. A. (1995). Magnitude of psychological gender differences. *American Psychologist, 50*, 159–161.

Hygge, S. A., & Öhman, A. (1976). The relation of vicarious to direct instigation and conditioning of electrodermal responses. *Scandanavian Journal of Psychology, 17*(1), 217–222.

Hyman, I. E., Gilstrap, L. L., Decker, K., & Wilkinson, C. (1998). Manipulating remember and know judgements of autobiographical memories. *Applied Cognitive Psychology, 12*, 371–386

Hyman, I. E., Jr. (1993). Imagery, reconstructive memory, and discovery. In B. Roskos-Ewoldsen, M. J. Intons-Peterson, & R. E. Anderson (Eds.), *Imagery, creativity, and discovery: A cognitive perspective* (pp. 99–121). The Netherlands: Elsevier Science.

Hyman, I. E., Jr., & Loftus, E. F. (1998). Errors in autobiographical memories. *Clinical Psychology Review, 18*, 933–947.

Hyman, I. E., Jr., & Loftus, E. F. (2002). False childhood memories and eyewitness memory errors. In M. L. Eisen, J. A. Quas, & G. S. Goodman (Eds.), *Memory and suggestibility in the forensic interview* (pp. 63–84). Mahwah, NJ: Erlbaum.

Iacoboni, M., Woods, R. P., Brass, M., Bekkering, H., Mazziotta, J. C., & Rizzolatti, G. (1999). Cortical mechanisms of human imitation. *Science, 286*, 2526–2528.

Iber, C., Ancoli-Israel, S., Chesson Jr., A. L., & Quan, S. F. (2007). The AASM Manual for the scoring of sleep and associated events: Rules, terminology and technical specifications. Westchester, IL: American Academy of Sleep Medicine

Iemmola, F., & Camperio Ciani, A. (2008). New evidence of genetic factors influencing sexual orientation in men: Female fecundity increase in the maternal line. *Archives of Sexual Behavior, 38*(3), 393–399.

Imaizumi, Y. (1998). A comparative study of twinning and triplet rates in 17 countries, 1972–1996. *Acta Genetic Medicine & Gemellology, 47*, 101–114.

Insel, T. R., & Wang, P. S. (2010). Rethinking mental illness. *The Journal of the American Medical Association, 303*(19). 1970–1971.

Ioannidis, J. P. A. (1998, January 28). Effect of the statistical significance of results on the time to completion and publication of randomized efficacy trials. *Journal of the American Medical Association, 279*, 281–286.

Irwin, A. R., & Gross, A. M. (1995). Cognitive tempo, violent video games, and aggressive behavior in young boys. *Journal of Family Violence, 10*(3), 337–350.

Irwin, M., Cole, J., & Nicassio, P. (2006). Comparative meta-analysis of behavioral intervention for insomnia and their efficacy in middle aged adults and in older adults 55+ years of age. *Health Psychology, 25*, 3–14.

Isabel, J. (2003). *Genetics: An introduction for dog breeders.* Loveland, CO: Alpine.

Isenberg, D. J. 1986. Group Polarization: A Critical Review and Meta-Analysis. *Journal of Personality and Social Psychology, 50*(6), 1141–1151.

Iwakabe, S. (2008). Psychotherapy integration in Japan. *Journal of Psychotherapy Integration, 18*(1), 103–125.

Iwamoto, E. T., & Martin, W. (1988). A critique of drug self-administration as a method for predicting abuse potential of drugs. *National Institute on Drug Abuse Research Monograph, 1046*, 81457–81465.

Izard, C. (1988). Emotion-cognition relationships and human development. In C. Izard, J. Kagan, & R. Zajonc (Eds.), *Emotions, cognition, and behavior*. New York: Cambridge University Press.

Jackson, J. S., Knight, K. M., & Rafferty, J. A. (2009). Race and unhealthy behaviors: Chronic stress, the HPA axis, and physical and mental health disparities over the life course. *American Journal of Public Health, 100*(5), 933.

Jackson, R. (2001). *Plato: A beginner's guide*. London: Hoder & Stroughton.

Jackson, T., Iezzi, T., Gunderson, J., Fritch, A., & Nagasaka, T. (2002). Gender differences in pain perception: The mediating role of self-efficacy beliefs. *Sex Roles, 47*, 561–568.

Jacobson, S. G., Cideciyan A. V., Regunath, G., et al. (1995). Night blindness in Sorsby's fundus dystrophy reversed by vitamin A. *Nature Genetics, 11,* 27–32.

Jaeger, J. J., Lockwood, A. H., Van Valin, R. D., Kemmerer, D. L., Murphy, B. W., & Wack, D. S. (1998). Sex differences in brain regions activated by grammatical and reading tasks. *Neuroreport, 9*, 2803–2807.

Jaeggi, S. M., Buschkuehl, M., Jonides, J., & Perrig, W. J. (2008). Improving fluid intelligence with training on working memory. *Proceedings of the National Academy of Sciences, USA, 105*(19), 6829–6833.

James, W. (1884). What is an emotion? *Mind, 9*, 188–205.

James, W. (1890). *Principles of psychology*. New York: Henry Holt.

James, W. (1890, 2002). *The principles of psychology (Vols. 1 and 2)*. Cambridge, MA: Harvard University Press.

James, W. (1894). The physical basis of emotion. *Psychological Review, 1*, 516–529.

Jameson, M., Diehl, R., & Danso, H. (2007). Stereotype threat impacts college athletes' academic performance. *Current Research in Social Psychology, 12*(5), 68–79

Jang, K. L., Livesley, W. J., & Vernon, P. A. (1996). Heritability of the Big Five personality dimensions and their facets: A twin study. *Journal of Personality, 64*, 577–591.

Jang, K. L., McCrae, R. R., Angleitner, A., Riemann, R., & Livesley, W. J. (1998). Heritability of facet-level traits in a cross-cultural twin sample: Support for a hierarchical model of personality. *Journal of Personality and Social Psychology, 74*, 1556–1565.

Janis, I. (1972). *Victims of groupthink*. Boston: Houghton-Mifflin.

Janis, I. (1982). *Groupthink* (2nd ed.). Boston: Houghton-Mifflin.

Janos, P. M. (1987). A fifty-year follow-up of Terman's youngest college students and IQ-matched agemates. *Gifted Child Quarterly, 31*, 55–58.

Janowitz, H. D. (1967). Role of gastrointestinal tract in the regulation of food intake. In C. F. Code (Ed.), *Handbook of physiology: Alimentary canal 1*. Washington, DC: American Physiological Society.

January, D., & Kako, E. (2007). Re-evaluating evidence for linguistic relativity: Reply to Boroditsky (2001). *Cognition, 104*(2), 417–426.

Janus, S. S., & Janus, C. L. (1993). *The Janus report on sexual behavior.* New York: John Wiley & Sons.

Jay, S. M., & Elliot, C. H. (1990). A stress inoculation program for parents whose children are undergoing medical procedures. *Journal of Consulting and Clinical Psychology, 58*, 799–804.

Jehn, K., Northcraft, G., & Neale, M. (1999). Why differences make a difference: A field study of diversity, conflict, and performance in workgroups. *Administrative Science Quarterly, 44*, 741–763.

Jensen, A. R. (1969). How much can we boost IQ and scholastic achievement? *Harvard Educational Review, 39*, 1–123.

Jimerson, D. C., Wolfe, B. E., Metzger, E. D., Finkelstein, D. M., Cooper, T. B., & Levine, J. M. (1997). Decreased serotonin function in bulimia nervosa. *Archives of General Psychiatry, 54*, 529–534.

Joanna Briggs Institute. (2001). Smoking cessation interventions and strategies. *Best Practice, 5*(3), 1329–1874. New York: Wiley-Blackwell.

John, O. P., Angleitner, A., & Ostendorf, F. (1988). The lexical approach to personality: A historical review of trait taxonomic research. *European Journal of Personality, 2*, 171–203.

Johnson, C. P., Myers, S. M. (Council on Children with Disabilities). (2007). Identification and evaluation of children with autism spectrum disorders. *Pediatrics, 120*(5), 1183–1215.

Johnson, D., Johnson, R., & Smith, K. (1991). *Active learning: Cooperation in the college classroom*. Edna, MN: Interaction Book Company.

Johnson, G. (1995, June 6). Chimp talk debate: Is it really language? *New York Times*.

Johnson, J., Cohen, P., Pine, D. S., Klein, D. F., Kasen, S., & Brook, J. S. (2000). Association between cigarette smoking and anxiety disorders during adolescence and early adulthood. *Journal of the American Medical Association, 284*(18), 2348–2351.

Johnson, M. E., Brems, C., Mills, M. E., Neal, D. B., & Houlihan, J. L. (2006). Moderating effects of control on the relationship between stress and change. *Administration and Policy in Mental Health and Mental Health Services Research, 33*(4), 499–503.

Johnson, W., Bouchard, T. J., Jr., McGue, M., Segal, N. L., Tellegen, A., Keyes, M., & Gottesman, I. I. (2007). Genetic and environmental influences on the Verbal-Perceptual-Image Rotation (VPR) model of the structure of mental abilities in the Minnesota Study of Twins Reared Apart. *Intelligence, 35*(6), 542–562.

Johnston, L. D., O'Malley, P. M., Bachman, J. G., Schulenberg, J. E. (2007). *Monitoring the Future national survey results on drug use, 1975–2006: Vol. 1. Secondary school students 2006*. Bethesda, MD: National Institute on Drug Abuse; September 2007.

Joiner, W. J., Crocker, A., White, B. H,. & Sehgal, A. (2006). Sleep in *Drosophila* is regulated by adult mushroom bodies. *Nature, 441*, 757–760.

Jones, E., Fear, N. T., & Wessely, S. (2007). Shell shock and mild traumatic brain injury: A historical review. *The American Journal of Psychiatry, 164*(11), 1641–1645.

Jones, E. E., & Harris, V. A. (1967). The attribution of attitudes. *Journal of Experimental Social Psychology, 3*, 1–24.

Jones, E. J., Krupnick, J. L., & Kerig, P. K. (1987). Some gender effects in a brief psychotherapy. *Psychotherapy, 24*, 336–352.

Jones, G. W. (1997). Modernization and divorce: Contrasting trends in Islamic Southeast Asia and the West. *Population and Development Review, 23*(1), 95–113.

Jones, H. M., & Pilowsky, L. S. (2002). Dopamine and antipsychotic drug action revisited. *British Journal of Psychiatry, 181*, 271–275.

Jones, M. C. (1924). A laboratory study of fear: The case of Peter. *Pedagogical Seminary, 31*, 308–315.

Jones, M. K., & Menzies, R. G. (1995). The etiology of fear of spiders. *Anxiety, Stress and Coping, 8*, 227–234.

Jovanovic, H., Lundberg, J., Karlsson, P., Cerin, A., Saijo, T., Varrone, A., Halldin, C., & Nordstrom, A.-L. (2008). Sex differences in the serotonin 1A receptor and serotonin transporter binding in the human brain measured by PET. *NeuroImage, 39*(3), 1408–1419.

Judelsohn, R. G. (2007). Vaccine Safety: Vaccines are one of public health's great accomplishments. *Skeptical Inquirer*, 31.6 (November/December), Retrieved June 13, 2010, from http://www.csicop.org/si/show/vaccine_safety_vaccines_are_one_of_public_healthrsquos_great_accomplishment/

Juffer, F., & Rosenboom, L. G. (1997). Infant–mother attachment of internationally adopted children in the Netherlands. *International Journal of Behavioral Development, 20*(1), 93–107.

Julien, R. M., Advokat, C. D., & Comaty, J. E. (2008). *A primer of drug action: A comprehensive guide to the actions, uses, and side effects of psychoactive drugs* (11th ed.). New York: Worth.

Jung, C. (1933). *Modern man in search of a soul.* New York: Harcourt Brace.

Kabat-Zinn, J., Lipworth, L., & Burney, R. (1985). The clinical use of mindfulness meditation for the self-regulation of chronic pain. *Journal of Behavioral Medicine, 8*, 163–190.

Kabat-Zinn, J., Lipworth, L., Burney, R., & Sellers, W. (1986). Four year follow-up of a meditation-based program for the self regulation of chronic pain: Treatment outcomes and compliance. *Clinical Journal of Pain, 2*, 159–173.

Kable, J. A., Coles, C. D., Lynch, M. E., & Platzman, K. (2008). Physiological responses to social and cognitive challenges in 8-year olds with a history of prenatal cocaine exposure. *Developmental Psychobiology, 50*(3), 251–265.

Kagan, J. (1998). *Galen's prophecy: Temperament in human nature*. (pp. 237–260, 270–274). New York: Basic Books.

Kagan, J. (2010). *The temperamental thread*. New York: Dana Press.

Kagan, J., Snidman, N., Kahn, V., & Towsley, S. (2007). The preservation of two infant temperaments into adolescence. *SRCD Monographs, 72*(2), 76-80.

Kahan, M., & Sutton, N. (1998). Overview: Methadone treatment for the opioid-dependent patient. In B. Brands & J. Brands (Eds.), *Methadone maintenance: A physician's guide to treatment* (pp. 1–15). Toronto, ON: Addiction Research Foundation.

Kahneman, D., & Tversky, A. (1973). On the psychology of prediction. *Psychological Review, 80*, 237–251.

Kahneman, D., Slovic, P., & Tversky, A. (1982). *Judgment under uncertainty: Heuristics and biases.* New York: Cambridge University Press.

Kail, R. & Hall, L. K. (2001). Distinguishing short-term memory from working memory. *Memory & Cognition, 29*(1), 1–9.

Kakko, J., Svanborg, K. D., Kreek, M. J., & Heilig, M. (2003). 1-year retention and social function after buprenorphine-associated relapse prevention treatment for heroin dependence in Sweden: A randomised, placebo-controlled trial. *Lancet, 361*, 662–668.

Kales, A., Soldatos, C., Bixler, E., Ladda, R. L., Charney, D. S., Weber, G., & Schweitzer, P. K. (1980). Hereditary factors in sleepwalking and night terrors. *British Journal of Psychiatry, 137*, 111–118.

Kam, D. (2010, June 29). Valdez expert: Psychological impact of Gulf oil spill won't fully emerge for years. *The Palm Beach Post.* Retrieved July 9, 2010, from http://www.palmbeachpost.com/news/valdez-expert-psychological-impact-of-gulf-oil-spill-776588.html

Kamau, C., & Harorimana, D. (2008) Does knowledge sharing and withholding of information in organizational committees affect quality of group decision making? *Proceedings of the 9th European Conference on Knowledge Management* (pp. 341–348). Reading, PA: Academic.

Kamin, L. J. (1995, February). Behind the curve. *Scientific American*, 99–103.

Kandel, E. R., & Schwartz, J. H. (1982). Molecular biology of learning: Modulation of transmitter release. *Science, 218*, 433–443.

Kanne, S. M., Balota, D. A., Storandt, M., McKeel, D. W., Jr., & Morris, J. C. (1998). Relating anatomy to function in Alzheimer's disease: Neuropsychological profiles predict regional neuropathology 5 years later. *Neurology, 50*(4), 979–985.

Karau, S. J., & Williams, K. D. (1993). Social loafing: A meta-analytic review and theoretical integration. *Journal of Personality and Social Psychology, 65*, 681–706.

Karau, S. J., & Williams, K. D. (1997). The effects of group cohesiveness on social loafing and social compensation. *Group Dynamics: Theory, Research and Practice, 1*, 156–168.

Karayiorgou, M., Altemus, M., Galke, B., Goldman, D., Murphy, D., Ott, J., & Gogos, J. (1997). Genotype determining low catechol-O-methyltransferase activity as a risk factor for obsessive-compulsive disorder. *Proceedings of the National Academy of Sciences, USA, 94*, 4572–4575.

Karney, B. R., & Bradbury, T. N. (2000). Attributions in marriage: State or trait? A growth curve analysis. *Journal of Personality and Social Psychology, 78*, 295–309.

Kastenbaum, R., & Costa, P. T., Jr. (1977). Psychological perspective on death. *Annual Review of Psychology, 28*, 225–249.

Katz, V. L. (2007). Spontaneous and recurrent abortion: Etiology, diagnosis, treatment. In V. L. Katz, G. M. Lentz, R. A. Lobo, & D. M. Gershenson (Eds.), *Comprehensive Gynecology* (5th ed). Philadelphia: Mosby Elsevier

Kaufman, J., & Zigler, E. (1993). The intergenerational transmission of abuse is overstated. In R. J. Gelles & D. R. Loseke (Eds.), *Current controversies on family violence*. Newbury Park, CA: Sage.

Kaveny, M. C. (2001). The case of conjoined twins: Embodiment, individuality, and dependence. *Theological Studies, 62.*

Kaye, W. H., Frank, G. K., Bailer, U. F., Henry, S. E., Meltzer, C. C., Price, J. C., Mathis, C. A., & Wagner, A. (2005). Serotonin alterations in anorexia and bulimia nervosa: New insights from imaging studies. *Physiology & Behavior, 85*, 73–81.

Kazdin, A. E. (1980). Acceptability of time out from reinforcement procedures for disruptive behavior. *Behavior Therapy, 11*(3), 329–344.

Kearney, C. A., & Silverman, W. K. (1998). A critical review of pharmacotherapy for youth with anxiety disorders: Things are not as they seem. *Journal of Anxiety Disorders, 12*, 83–102.

Keillor, J., Barrett, A., Crucian, G., Kortenkamp, S., & Heilman, K. (2002). Emotional experience and perception in the absence of facial feedback. *Journal of the International Neuropsychological Society, 8*(1), 130–135.

Keirsey, D.(1998). *Please understand me ii: Temperament character intelligence.* Del Mar, CA: Prometheus Nemesis Book Company.

Keller, M. B., McCullough, J. P., Klein, D. N., Arnow, B., Dunner, D., Gelenberg, A., Markowitz, J. C., Nemeroff, C. B., Russell, J. M., Thase, M. E., Trivedi, M. H., & Zajecka, J. (2000). A comparison of nefazodone, the cognitive behavioral-analysis system of psychotherapy, and their combination for the treatment of chronic depression. *New England Journal of Medicine, 342*(20), 1462–1470.

Kelly, I. (1980). The scientific case against astrology. *Mercury, 10*(13), 135.

Kelly, J. A., McAuliffe, T. L., Sikkema, K. J., Murphy, D. A., Somlai, A. M., Mulry, G., Miller, J. G., Stevenson, L. Y., & Fernandez, M. I. (1997). Reduction in risk behavior among adults with severe mental illness who learned to advocate for HIV prevention. *Psychiatric Services, 48*(10), 1283–1288.

Kempf, L., & Weinberger, D. R. (2009). Molecular genetics and bioinformatics: An outline for neuropsychological genetics. In T. E. Goldberg & D. R. Weinberger (Eds.), *The genetics of cognitive neuroscience* (pp. 3–26). Cambridge, MA: MIT Press.

Kendall, P. (1983). Stressful medical procedures: Cognitive-behavioral strategies for stress management and prevention. In D. Meichenbaum & M. Jaremko (Eds.), *Stress reduction and prevention.* (pp. 159–190). New York: Plenum Press.

Kendall, P. C., Hudson, J. L., Gosch, E., Flannery-Schroeder, E., & Suveg, C. (2008). Cognitive-behavioral therapy for anxiety disordered youth: A randomized clinical trial evaluating child and family modalities. *Journal of Consulting and Clinical Psychology, 76*(2), 282–297.

Kendler, K. S. (1985). Diagnostic approaches to schizotypal personality disorders: A historical perspective. *Schizophrenia Bulletin, 11*, 538–553.

Kendler, K. S., & Prescott, C. A. (1999). A population-based twin study of lifetime major depression in men and women. *Archives of General Psychiatry, 56*(1), 39–44.

Kenny, A. (1968). Mind and body, In *Descartes: A study of his philosophy* (p. 279). New York: Random House.

Kenny, A. (1994). Descartes to Kant. In A. Kenny (Ed.), *The Oxford history of western philosophy* (pp. 107–192). Oxford, England: Oxford University Press.

Kenrick, D. T., Griskevicius, V., Neuberg, S. L., & Schaller, M. (2010). Renovating the pyramid of needs: Contemporary extensions built upon ancient foundations. *Perspectives on Psychological Science, 5*(3), 292–314.

Kensinger, E. A., Shearer, D. K., Locascio, J. J., Growdon, J. H., & Corkin, S. (2003). Working memory in mild Alzheimer's disease and early Parkinson's disease. *Neuropsychology, 17*(2), 230–239.

Keromoian, R., & Leiderman, P. H. (1986). Infant attachment to mother and child caretaker in an East African community. *International Journal of Behavioral Development, 9*, 455–469.

Kerwin, D. R., Zhang, Y., Kotchen, J. M., Espeland, M. A., Van Horn, L., McTigue, K. M., Robinson, J. G., Powell, L., Kooperberg, C., Coker, L. H., & Hoffmann, R. (2010). The cross-sectional relationship between body mass index, waist–hip ratio, and cognitive performance in postmenopausal women enrolled in the women's health initiative. *Journal of the American Geriatric Society, 58*, 1427–1432. [Article first published online July 14, 2010]. doi: 10.1111/j.1532-5415.2010.02969.x

Kesebir, S., Graham, J., & Oishi, S. (2010). A theory of human needs should be human-centered, not animal-centered. *Perspectives on Psychological Science, 5*(3), 315–319.

Kety, S. S., Wender, P. H., Jacobsen, B., Ingaham, L. J., Jansson, L., Faber, B., & Kinney, D. K. (1994). Mental illness in the biological and adoptive relatives of schizophrenic adoptees. *Archives of General Psychiatry, 51*, 442–455.

Kiecolt-Glaser, J. K. (2009). Psychoneuroimmunology: Psychology's gateway to the biomedical future. *Perspectives on Psychological Science, 4*(4), 367.

Kiecolt-Glaser, J. K., Fisher, L. D., Ogrocki, P., Stout, J. C., Speicher, C. E., & Glaser, R. (1987). Marital quality, marital disruption, and immune function. *Psychosomatic Medicine, 49*, 13–34.

Kiecolt-Glaser, J. K., Glaser, R., Gravenstein, S., Malarkey, W. B., & Sheridan, J. (1996). Chronic stress alters the immune response to influenza virus vaccine in older adults. *Proceedings of the National Academy of Sciences, USA, 93*(7), 3043–3047.

Kiecolt-Glaser, J. K., Marucha, P. T., Malarkey, W. B., & Marcado, A. M. (1995). Slowing of wound healing by psychological stress. *Lancet, 346*, 1194–1196.

Kiecolt-Glaser, J. K., McGuire, L., Robles, T., & Glaser, R. (2002). Psychoneuroimmunology: Psychological influences on immune function and health. *Journal of Consulting and Clinical Psychology, 70*, 537–547.

Kihlstrom, J., Mulvaney, S., Tobias, B., & Tobis, I. (2000). The emotional unconscious. In E. Eich, J. Kihlstrom, G. Bower, J. Forgas, & P. Niedenthal (Eds.), *Cognition and emotion* (pp. 30–86). New York: Oxford University Press.

Kihlstrom, J. F. (1985). Hypnosis. *Annual Review of Psychology, 36*, 385–418.

Kihlstrom, J. F. (1987). The cognitive unconscious. *Science, 237*, 1445–1452.

Kihlstrom, J. F. (1999). Conscious and unconscious cognition. In R. J. Sternberg (Ed.), *The nature of cognition* (pp. 173–203). Cambridge, MA: MIT Press.

Kihlstrom, J. F. (2001). Hypnosis and the psychological unconscious. In Howard S. Friedman (Ed.), *Assessment and therapy: Specialty articles from the encyclopedia of mental health* (pp. 215–226). San Diego, CA: Academic Press.

Kihlstrom, J. F. (2002). Memory, autobiography, history. *Proteus: A Journal of Ideas, 19*(2), 1–6.

Kim, H., & Markus, H. R. (1999). Deviance or uniqueness, harmony or conformity? A cultural analysis. *Journal of Personality and Social Psychology, 77*, 785–800.

Kimura, D. (1999). *Sex and cognition.* Cambridge, MA: MIT Press.

Kimura, D. (2002, May 13). Sex differences in the brain. In *The hidden mind* [Special issue]. *Scientific American. 12*, 32–37.

Kinsey, A. C., Pomeroy, W. B., & Martin, C. E. (1948). *Sexual behavior in the human male.* Philadelphia: W. B. Saunders.

Kinsey, A. C., Pomeroy, W. B., Martin, C. E., & Gebhard, P. H. (1953). *Sexual behavior in the human female.* New York: W. B. Saunders.

Kirby, J. S., Chu, J. A., & Dill, D. L. (1993). Correlates of dissociative symptomatology in patients with physical and sexual abuse histories. *Comprehensive Psychiatry 34*, 250–263.

Kirmayer, L. J. (1991). The place of culture in psychiatric nosology: *Taijin kyofusho* and the *DSM-III-TR*. *Journal of Nervous and Mental Disease, 179*, 19–28.

Kirsch, I. (2000). The response set theory of hypnosis. *American Journal of Clinical Hypnosis, 42* (3/42), 4, 274–292.

Kirsch, I., & Lynn, S. J. (1995). The altered state of hypnosis: Changes in the theoretical landscape. *American Psychologist, 50*, 846–858.

Kitamura, T., Saitoh, Y., Takashima, N., Murayama, A., Niibori, Y., Ageta, H., Sekiguchi, M., Sugiyama, H., & Inokuchi, K. (2009). Adult neurogenesis modulates the hippocampus-dependent period of associative fear memory. *Cell*, 139(4), 814–827.

Kitayama, S., & Markus, H. R. (1994). Introduction to cultural psychology and emotion research. In S. Kitayama & H. R. Markus (Eds.), *Emotion and culture: Empirical studies of mutual influence* (pp. 1–22). Washington, DC: American Psychological Association.

Klaver, C. C., Wolfs, R. C., Vingerling, J. R., Hofman, A., & de Jong, P. T. (1998). Age-specific prevalence and causes of blindness and visual impairment in an older population: The Rotterdam Study. *Archives of Ophthalmology, 116*, 653–658.

Klein, D. N. (2010). Chronic depression: Diagnosis and classification. *Current Directions in Psychological Science, 19*(2), 96–100.

Klein, D., Schwartz, J., Rose, S., & Leader, J. (2000). Five-year course and outcome of dysthymic disorder: A prospective, naturalistic follow-up study. *American Journal of Psychiatry, 157*(6), 931–939.

Klein, S. B., & Mowrer, R. R. (1989). *Contemporary learning theories: Pavlovian conditioning and the status of traditional learning theory.* Hillsdale, NJ: Lawrence Erlbaum.

Kleinot, M. C., & Rogers, R. W. (1982). Identifying effective components of alcohol misuse prevention programs. *Journal of Studies on Alcohol, 43*, 802–811.

Kligman, A. M., & Balin, A. K. (1989). Aging of human skin. In A. K. Balin & A. M. Kligman (Eds.), *Aging and the skin* (pp. 1–42). New York: Raven Press.

Klorman, R., Hilpert, P. L., Michael, R., LaGana, C., & Sveen, O. B. (1980). Effects of coping and mastery modeling on experienced and inexperienced pedodontic patients' disruptiveness. *Behavior Therapy, 11*, 156–168.

Klüver, H., & Bucy, P. C. (1939). Preliminary analysis of functions of the temporal lobes in monkeys. *Archives of Neurological Psychiatry, 42*, 979–1000.

Kluft, R. P. (1984). Introduction to multiple personality disorder. *Psychiatric Annals, 14*, 19–24.

Knight, A. (1996). *The life of the law: The people and cases that have shaped our society, from King Alfred to Rodney King*. New York: Crown Publishing Group.

Knight, J. A. (1998). Free radicals: Their history and current status in aging and disease. *Annals of Clinical and Laboratory Science, 28*, 331–346.

Kobasa, S. (1979). Stressful life events, personality, and health: An inquiry into hardiness. *Journal of Personality and Social Psychology, 37*(1), 1–11.

Koch C. & Mormann F. (2010). The neurobiology of consciousness. In G. Mashour (Ed.), *Consciousness, awareness, and anesthesia* (pp. 24–46). New York: Cambridge University Press.

Koenig, H. G., Hays, J. C., Larson, D. B., George, L. K., Cohen, H. J., McCullough, M. E., Meador, K. G., & Blazer, D. G. (1999). Does religious attendance prolong survival? A six-year follow-up study of 3,968 older adults. *Journal of Gerontology, 54A*, M370–M377.

Koenig, H. G., McCullough, M. E., & Larson, D. B. (2001). *Handbook of religion and health*. Oxford, UK: Oxford University Press.

Koh, J. K. (1996). A guide to common Singapore spiders. *BP Guide to Nature* series. Singapore: Singapore Science Center.

Kohlberg, L. (1969). Stage and sequence: the cognitive-developmental approach to socialization. In D. A. Goslin (Ed.), *Handbook of socialization: Theory in research* (pp. 347–480). Boston: Houghton-Mifflin.

Kohlberg, L. (1973). Continuities in childhood and adult moral development revisited. In P. Baltes & K. W. Schaie (Eds.), *Life-span development psychology: Personality and socialization*. San Diego, CA: Academic Press.

Köhler, W. (1925, 1992). *Gestalt psychology: An introduction to new concepts in modern psychology (reissue)*. New York: Liveright.

Kolodny, R. C. (2001, August). In memory of William H. Masters. *Journal of Sex Research*.

Konowal, N. M., Van Dongen, H. P. A., Powell, J. W., Mallis, M. M., & Dinges, D. F. (1999). Determinants of microsleeps during experimental sleep deprivation. *Sleep, 22* (Suppl. 1), 328.

Korn, S. (1984). Continuities and discontinuities in difficult/easy temperament: Infancy to young adulthood. *Merrill Palmer Quarterly, 30*, 189–199.

Kosslyn, S. M. (1983). Mental imagery. In Z. Rubin (Ed.), *The psychology of being human*. New York: Harper & Row.

Kosslyn, S. M., Alpert, N. M., Thompson, W. L., Maljkovic, V., Weise, S. B., Chabris, C. F., Hamilton, S. E. and Buonano, F. S. (1993). Visual mental imagery activates topographically organized visual cortex: PET investigations. *Journal of Cognitive Neuroscience 5*, 263–287.

Kosslyn, S. M., Ball, T. M., & Reiser, B. J. (1978). Visual images preserve metric spatial information: Evidence from studies of image scanning. *Journal of Experimental Psychology: Human Perception and Performance, 4*, 47–60.

Kosslyn, S. M., Ganis, G., & Thompson, W. L. (2001). Neural foundations of imagery. *Nature Reviews Neuroscience 2*, 635–642.

Kosslyn, S. M., Pascual-Leone, A., Felician, O., Camposano, S., Keenan, J. P., Thompson, W. L., Ganis, G., Sukel, K. E., & Alpert, N. M. (1999). The role of area 17 in visual imagery: Convergent evidence from PET and rTMS. *Science 284*, 167–170.

Kosslyn, S. M., Thompson, W. L., Wraga, M. J., & Alpert, N. M. (2001). Imagining rotation by endogenous and exogenous forces: Distinct neural mechanisms for different strategies. *Neuroreport*, 12, 2519–2525.

Kotkin, M., Daviet, C., & Gurin, J. (1996). The *Consumer Reports* mental health survey. *American Psychologist, 51*(10), 1080–1082.

Kouri, E. M., Pope, H. G., & Lukas, S. E. (1999). Changes in aggressive behavior during withdrawal from long-term marijuana use. *Psychopharmacology, 143*, 302–308.

Kourtis, A. P., Bulterys, M., Nesheim, S. R., & Lee, F. K. (2001). Understanding the timing of HIV transmission from mother to infant. *Journal of the American Medical Association, 285*(6), 709–712.

Kratofil, P. H., Baberg, H. T., & Dimsdale, J. E. (1996). Self-mutilation and severe self-injurious behavior associated with amphetamine psychosis. *General Hospital Psychiatry, 18*, 117–120.

Kreipe, R. E. (1992). Normal somatic adolescent growth and development. In E. McAnarney, R. E. Kreipe, D. Orr, & G. Comerci (Eds.), *Textbook of adolescent medicine* (pp. 44–68). Philadelphia: W.B. Saunders & Co.

Kriegstein, A., & Alvarez-Buylla, A. (2009). The glial nature of embryonic and adult neural stem cells. *Annual Review of Neuroscience, 32*(1), 149–184.

Kristensen, P., & Bjerkedal, T. (2007). Explaining the relation between birth order and intelligence. *Science, 316*(5832), 1717.

Kryger, M., Lavie, P., & Rosen, R. (1999). Recognition and diagnosis of insomnia. *Sleep, 22*, S421–S426.

Kubicki, M., Niznikiewicz, M., Connor, E., Nestor, P., Bouix, S., Dreusicke, M., Kikinis, R., McCarley, R., & Shenton, M. (2009). Relationship between white matter integrity, attention, and memory in schizophrenia: A diffusion tensor imaging study. *Brain Imaging and Behavior, 3*(2), 191–201.

Kübler-Ross, E. (1997). *The wheel of life: A memoir of living and dying*. New York: Touchstone.

Küntay, A., & Slobin, D. I. (2002). Putting interaction back into child language: Examples from Turkish. *Psychology of Language and Communication,* 6, 5–14.

Kuhn, H. W., & Nasar, S. (Eds.). (2001). *The essential John Nash*. Princeton, NJ: Princeton University Press.

Kuhn, J., Gründler, T. O. J., Lenartz, D., Sturm, V., Klosterkötter, J., & Huff, W. (2010). Deep brain stimulation for psychiatric disorders. *Deutsches Ärzteblatt International, 107* (7), 105–113.

Kulik, J. A., & Mahler, H. I. M. (1989). Social support and recovery from surgery. *Health Psychology, 8*, 221–238.

Kulik, J. A., & Mahler, H. I. M. (1993). Emotional support as a moderator of adjustment and compliance after coronary bypass surgery: A longitudinal study. *Journal of Behavioral Medicine, 16*, 45–63.

Kumar, R. (1994). Postnatal mental illness: A transcultural perspective. *Social Psychiatry and Psychiatric Epidemiology, 29*(6), 250–264.

Kumar, S., & Oakley-Browne, M. (2002). Panic disorder. *Clinical Evidence, 7*, 906–912.

Kumashiro, M., Rusbult, C. E., Coolsen, M. K., Wolf, S. T., van den Bosch, M., & van der Lee, R. (2009). Partner affirmation, verification, and enhancement as determinants of attraction to potential dates: Experimental evidence of the unique effect of affirmation. Unpublished manuscript, Goldsmiths, University of London.

Kupfer, D. J., & Reger, D. A. (2009). Current activities: Report of the DSM-5 task force. Retrieved from http://www.dsm5.org/ProgressReports/Pages/CurrentActivitiesReportoftheDSM-VTaskForce%28March2009%29.aspx

Kupfer, D. J., & Reynolds, C. F., III. (1997). Management of insomnia. *New England Journal of Medicine, 336*(5), 341–346.

Kuriki, I., Ashida, H., Murakami, I., & Kitaoka, A. (2008). Functional brain imaging of the Rotating Snakes illusion by fMRI. *Journal of Vision, 8*(10), 16 11–10.

Kvavilashvili, L., Mirani, J., Schlagman, S., Foley, K., & Dornbrot, D. E. (2009). Consistency of flashbulb memories of September 11 over long delays: Implications for consolidation and wrong time slice hypotheses. *Journal of Memory and Language*, 61(4), 556–572.

LaBar, K. S., LeDoux, J. E., Spencer, D. D., & Phelps, E. A. (1995). Impaired fear conditioning following unilateral temporal lobectomy to humans. *Journal of Neuroscience, 15*, 6846–6855.

LaBerge, D. (1980). Unitization and automaticity in perception. In J. H. Flowers (Ed.), *Nebraska Symposium on Motivation* (pp. 53–71). Lincoln: University of Nebraska Press.

Lacayo, A. (1995). Neurologic and psychiatric complications of cocaine abuse. *Neuropsychiatry, Neuropsychology, and Behavioral Neurology, 8*(1), 53–60.

LaFromboise, T., Coleman, H. L. K., & Gerton J. (1993). Psychological impact of biculturalism: Evidence and theory. *Psychological Bulletin, 114*, 395–412.

Lagopoulos, J., Xu, J., Rasmussen, I., Vik, A., Malhi, G. S., Eliassen, C. F., Arntsen, I. E., Sæther, J. G., Hollup, S., Holen, A., Davanger, S., & Ellingsen, Ø. (2009). Increased theta and alpha EEG activity during nondirective meditation. *The Journal of Alternative and Complementary Medicine, 15*(11), 1187.

Lal, S. (2002). Giving children security: Mamie Phipps Clark and the radicalization of child psychology. *American Psychologist, 57*(1), 20–28.

Lalancette, M.-F., & Standing, L. G. (1990). Asch fails again. *Social Behavior and Personality, 18*(1), 7–12.

Lambert, M. J., & Ogles, B. M. (2003). The efficacy and effectiveness of psychotherapy. In M. J. Lambert (Ed.), *Handbook of psychotherapy and behavior change* (5th ed.) (pp. 139–193). New York: Wiley.

Lance, C. J., LaPointe, J. A., & Fisicaro, S. (1994). Tests of three causal models of halo rater error. *Organizational Behavior and Human Decision Performance, 57*, 83–96.

Laungani, P. (1997). Death in a Hindu family. In C. M. Parkes, P. Laungani, & B. Young (Eds.), *Death and bereavement across cultures* (pp. 52–72). London: Routledge.

Landrum, R. E. (2009). Finding jobs with a psychology bachelor's degree. Washington, DC: American Psychological Association.

Landrum, R. E., & Davis, S. F. (2007). *The psychology major: Career options and strategies for success,* 3rd ed. Upper Saddle River, NJ: Prentice Hall.

Lane, R. D., Kivley, L. S., DuBois, M. A. Shamasundara, P., & Schwartz, G. E. (1995). Levels of emotional awareness and the degree of right hemisphere dominance in the perception of facial emotion. *Neuropsychologia, 33*, 525–538.

Lang, J. W. B., & Lang, J. (2010). Priming competence diminishes the link between cognitive test anxiety and test performance. *Psychological Science, 21*(6), 811–819.

Lange, C. (1885. The emotions. Reprinted in C. G. Lange & W. James (Eds.), *The emotions*. New York: Harner.

Langer, E. J., & Rodin, J. (1976). The effects of enhanced personal responsibility for the aged: A field experiment in an institutional setting. *Journal of Personality and Social Psychology, 34*, 191–198.

Langone, M. C. (1996). Clinical update on cults. *Psychiatric Times, 13*(7), 1–3.

Lanphear, B. P., Dietrich, K., Auinger, P., & Cox, C. (2000). Cognitive deficits associated with blood lead concentrations <10 micrograms/dL in U.S. children and adolescents. *Public Health Reports, 115*(6), 521–529.

Lapsley, D. K., Milstead, M., Quintana, S. M., Flannery, D., & Buss, R. R. (1986). Adolescent egocentricism and formal operations: Tests of a theoretical assumption. *Developmental Psychology, 22*, 800–807.

Larsen, J. T., Berntson, G. G., Poehlmann, K. M., Ito, T. A., & Cacioppo, J. T. (2008). The psychophysiology of emotion. In M. Lewis, J. M. Haviland-Jones, & L. F. Barrett (Eds.), *Handbook of Emotions* (3rd ed., pp. 180–195). New York: Guilford Press.

Larzelere, R. (1986). Moderate spanking: Model or deterrent of children's aggression in the family? *Journal of Family Violence, 1*(1), 27–36.

Lashley, K. S. (1938). The thalamus and emotion. *The Psychological Review, 45*, 21–61.

Lasnik, H. (1990). Metrics and morphophonemics in early English verse. *University of Connecticut Working Papers in Linguistics: Vol. 3* (pp. 29–40). Storrs: University of Connecticut.

Latané, B., & Darley, J. M. (1969). Bystander "apathy." *American Scientist, 57*(2), 244–268.

Latané, B., Williams, K., & Harkins, S. (1979). Many hands make light the work: The causes and consequences of social loafing. *Journal of Personality & Social Psychology, 37*(6), 822–832.

Lauer, J., Black, D. W., & Keen, P. (1993). Multiple personality disorder and borderline personality disorder: Distinct entities or variations on a common theme? *Annals of Clinical Psychiatry, 5*, 129–134.

Laumann, E. O., Paik, A., & Rosen, R. C. (1999). Sexual dysfunction in the United States: Prevalence and predictors. *Journal of the American Medical Association, 281*(6), 537–544.

Launer, L., Masaki, K., Petrovitch, H., Foley, D., & Havlik, R. (1995). The association between midlife blood pressure levels and late-life cognitive function. *Journal of the American Medical Association, 272*(23), 1846–1851.

Lavergne, G. M. (1997). *A sniper in the tower: The true story of the Texas Tower massacre*. New York: Bantam.

Laws, G., Davies, I., & Andrews, C. (1995). Linguistic structure and nonlinguistic cognition: English and Russian blues compared. *Language and Cognitive Processes, 10*, 59–94.

Lay, C., & Nguyen, T. T. I. (1998). The role of acculturation-related and acculturation non-specific daily hassles: Vietnamese-Canadian students and psychological distress. *Canadian Journal of Behavioural Science, 30*(3), 172–181.

Lazarus, R. S. (1991). *Emotion and adaptation*. New York: Oxford University Press.

Lazarus, R. S. (1993). From psychological stress to the emotions: A history of changing outlooks. *Annual Review of Psychology, 44*, 1–22.

Lazarus, R. S. (1999). *Stress and emotion: A new synthesis*. New York: Springer.

Lazarus, R. S., & Folkman, S. (1984). *Stress, appraisal and coping*. New York: Springer.

Leary, M. R., & Forsyth, D. R. (1987). Attributions of responsibility for collective endeavors. *Review of Personality and Social Psychology, 8*, 167–188.

Leask, J., Haber, R. N., & Haber, R. B. (1969). Eidetic imagery in children: II. Longitudinal and experimental results. *Psychonomic Monograph Supplements, 3*, 25–48.

Leccese, A. P., Pennings, E. J. M., & De Wolff, F. A. (2000). *Combined use of alcohol and psychotropic drugs. A review of the literature.* Leiden, The Netherlands: Academisch Ziekenhuis Leiden (AZL).

Leclerc, C. M., & Hess, T. M. (2007). Age differences in the bases for social judgments: Tests of a social expertise perspective. *Experimental Aging Research, 33*(1), 95–120.

LeDoux, J. (1994). Emotion, memory and the brain. *Scientific American, 270*, 32–39.

LeDoux, J. (2003). The emotional brain, fear, and the amygdala. *Cellular and Molecular Neurobiology, 23*(4–5), 727–738.

LeDoux, J. E. (1996). *The emotional brain: The mysterious underpinnings of emotional life*. New York: Simon & Schuster.

LeDoux, J. E. (2007). The amygdala. *Current Biology, 17*(20), R868–R874.

LeDoux, J. E., & Phelps, E. A. (2008). Emotional networks in the brain. In M. Lewis, J. M. Haviland-Jones, & L. F. Barrett (Eds.), *Handbook of emotions* (3rd ed., pp. 159–179). New York: Guilford Press.

Lee, F., Hallahan, M., & Herzog, T. (1996). Explaining real life events: How culture and domain shape attributions. *Personality and Social Psychology Bulletin, 22*, 732–741.

Lee, M., & Shlain, B. (1986). *Acid dreams: The complete social history of LSD: The CIA, the sixties, and beyond*. New York: Grove Press.

Lee, P. A. (1995). Physiology of puberty. In K. L. Becker (Ed.), *Principles and practice of endocrinology and metabolism* (pp. 822–830). Philadelphia: J.B. Lippincott.

Lee, S. H., Kim, E. Y., Kim, S., & Bae, S. M. (2010). Event-related potential patterns and gender effects underlying facial affect processing in schizophrenia patients. *Neuroscience Research, 7*, 7.

Lefcourt, H. M., Davidson, K., Shepherd, R., & Phillips, M. (1995). Perspective-taking humor: Accounting for stress moderation. *Journal of Social and Clinical Psychology 14*(4), 373–391.

Lehnert, B. (2007). Joint wave-particle properties of the individual photon. *Progress in Physics, 4*(10), 104–108.

Lehr, U., & Thomae, H. (1987). Patterns of psychological aging. *Results from the Bonne Aging Longitudinal Study (BOLSA)*. Stuttgart, Germany: Enke.

Leibel, R. L., Rosenbaum, M., & Hirsch, J. (1995). Changes in energy expenditure resulting from altered body weight. *The New England Journal of Medicine, 332*, 621–628.

Leon, P., Chedraui, P., Hidalgo, L., & Ortiz, F. (2007). Perceptions and attitudes toward the menopause among middle-aged women from Guayaquil, Ecuador. *Maturitas, 57*(3), 233–238.

Leonard, L. (1997). *Children with specific language impairment.* Cambridge, MA: MIT Press.

Leong, F. T. L., Hartung, P. J., Goh, D., & Gaylor, M. (2001). Appraising birth order in career assessment: Linkages to Holland's and Super's models. *Journal of Career Assessment, 9*, 25–39.

Leroy, C., & Symes, B. (2001). Teachers' perspectives on the family backgrounds of children at risk. *McGill Journal of Education, 36*(1), 45–60.

Lesch, K. P., Bengel, D., Heils, A., Sabol, S. Z., Greenberg, B. D., Petri, S., Benjamin, J., Muller, C. R., Hamer, D. H., & Murphy, D. L. (1996). Association of anxiety-related traits with a polymorphism in the serotonin transporter gene regulatory region. *Science, 274*(5292), 1527–1531.

Leslie, M. (2000, July/August). The vexing legacy of Louis Terman. *Stanford Magazine.* Retrieved on August 12, 2010, from http://www.stanfordalumni.org/news/magazine/2000/julaug/articles/terman.html

Levenson, R. W. (1992). Autonomic nervous system differences among emotions. *Psychological Sciences, 3*, 23–27.

Levenson, R. W., Ekman, P., Heider, K., & Friesen, W. V. (1992). Emotion and autonomic nervous system activity in the Minangkabau of West Sumatra. *Journal of Personality and Social Psychology, 62*, 972–988.

Levinson, D. F. (2006). The genetics of depression: A review. *Biological Psychiatry, 60*(2), 84–92.

Levy, B. R., Slade, M. D., Kunkel, S. R., & Kasl, S. V. (2002). Longevity increased by positive self-perceptions of aging. *Journal of Personality and Social Psychology, 83*, 261–269.

Levy, S. R., Stroessner, S. J., & Dweck, C. S. (1998). Stereotype formation and endorsement: The role of implicit theories. *Journal of Personality and Social Psychology, 74*, 1421–1436.

Lewin, K. (1936). *Principles of topological psychology*. New York: McGraw-Hill.

Lewis, J. R. (1995) *Encyclopedia of afterlife beliefs and phenomenon*. Detroit, MI: Visible Ink Press.

Light, K. R, Kolata, S., Wass, C., Denman-Brice, A., Zagalsky, R., & Matzel, L. D. (2010). Working memory training promotes general cognitive abilities in genetically heterogeneous mice. *Current Biology, 20*(8), 777–782.

Like, R., Steiner, P., & Rubel, A. (1996). Recommended core curriculum guidelines on culturally sensitive and competent care. *Family Medicine, 27*, 291–297.

Lilienfeld, S. O. (1999). Projective measures of personality and psychopathology: How well do they work? *Skeptical Inquirer, 23*(5), 32–39.

Lilienfeld, S. O., Lynn, S. J., & Lohr, J. M. (2004). Science and pseudoscience in clinical psychology: Initial thoughts, reflections, and considerations. In S. O. Lilienfeld, S. J. Lynn, & J. M. Lohr (Eds.), *Science and pseudoscience in clinical psychology* (p. 2). New York: Guilford Press.

Lim, J., Choo, W. C., & Chee, M. W. L. (2007). Reproducibility of changes in behavior and fMRI activation associated with sleep deprivation in a working memory task. *Sleep, 30*, 61–70.

Lin, C. S., Lyons, J. L., and Berkowitz, F. (2007). Somatotopic identification of language-SMA in language processing via fMRI. *Journal of Scientific and Practical Computing 1*(2), 3–8.

Lin, P. J., & Schwanenflugel, P. J. (1995). Cultural familiarity and language factors in the structure of category knowledge. *Journal of Cross-Cultural Psychology, 26*, 153–168.

Lin, P. J., Schwanenflugel, P. J. & Wisenbaker, J. M. (1990). Category typicality, cultural familiarity, and the development of category knowledge. *Developmental Psychology, 26*, 805–813.

Lindau, S. T., Schumm, P., Laumann, E. O., Levinson, W., O'Muircheartaigh, C. A., & Waite, L. J. (2007). A study of sexuality and health among older adults in the United States. *New England Journal of Medicine, 357*(8), 762–764.

Lindsey, E. W., Cremeens, P. R., & Caldera, Y. M. (2010). Gender Differences in mother–toddler and father–toddler verbal initiations and responses during a caregiving and play context. *Sex Roles.* Retrieved June 21, 2010, from http://www.springerlink.com/content/q261154773764443/

Lindsey, E. W., Cremeens, P. R., & Caldera, Y. M. (2010). Gender differences in mother–toddler and father–toddler verbal initiations and responses during a caregiving and play context. *Sex Roles, 62*(11–12), 746–759.

Lisanby, S. H., Maddox, J. H., Prudic, J., Devanand, D. P., & Sackeim, H. A. (2000). The effects of electroconvulsive therapy on memory of autobiographical and public events. *Archives of General Psychiatry, 57*, 581–590.

Livesley, J. W. (Ed.). (1995). *The DSM-IV Personality disorders*. New York: Guilford Press.

Lizskowski, U., Carpenter, M., Striano, T., & Tomasello, M. (2006). 12- and 18-month-olds point to provide information for others. *Journal of Cognition and Development, 7*, 173–187.

Lock, M. (1994). Menopause in cultural context. *Experimental Gerontology, 29*(3–4), 307–317.

Loehlin, J. C. (1992). *Genes and environment in personality development*. Newbury Park, CA: Sage.

Loehlin, J. C., McCrae, R. R., Costa, P. T., Jr., & John, O. P. (1998). Heritabilities of common and measure-specific components of the Big Five personality factors. *Journal of Research in Personality, 32*, 431–453.

Loehlin, J. C., Willerman, L., & Horn, J. M. (1985). Personality resemblances in adoptive families when the children are late-adolescent or adult. *Journal of Personality and Social Psychology, 48*, 376–392.

Loftus, E. (1975). Leading questions and the eyewitness report. *Cognitive Psychology, 7*, 560–572.

Loftus, E. (1987, June 29). Trials of an expert witness. *Newsweek, 109:* 10–11.

Loftus, E. F., & Loftus, G. R. (1980). On the permanence of stored information in the human brain. *American Psychologist, 35*, 409–420.

Loftus, E. F., Miller, D. G., & Burns H. J. (1978). Semantic integration of verbal information into a visual memory. *Journal of Experimental Psychology: Human Learning, 4*, 19–31.

Loftus, J. (2001). America's liberalization in attitudes toward homosexuality, 1973 to 1998. *American Sociological Review, 66*(5), 762–782.

Logue, M. W., Vieland, V. J., Goedken, R. J., & Crowe, R. R. (2003). Bayesian analysis of a previously published genome screen for panic disorder reveals new and compelling evidence for linkage to chromosome 7. *American Journal of Medical Genetics, 121B*, 95–99.

Loo, S. K., Hale, T. S., Macion, J., Hanada, G., McGough, J. J., McCracken, J. T., et al. (2009). Cortical activity patterns in ADHD during arousal, activation and sustained attention. *Neuropsychologia, 47*(10), 2114–2119.

Lord, T. R. (2001). 101 reasons for using cooperative learning in biology teaching. *The American Biology Teacher, 63*(1), 30–38.

Lovaas, O. I. (1964). Cue properties of words: The control of operant responding by rate and content of verbal operants. *Child Development, 35*, 245–256.

Lovaas, O. I. (1987). Behavioral treatment and normal educational and intellectual functioning in young autistic children. *Journal of Consulting and Clinical Psychology, 55*, 3–9.

Lovaas, O. I., Berberich, J. P., Perloff, B. F., & Schaffer, B. (1966). Acquisition of imitative speech by schizophrenic children. *Science, 151*, 705–707.

Lu, S., & Ende, N. (1997). Potential for clinical use of viable pluripotent progenitor cells in blood bank stored human umbilical cord blood. *Life Sciences, 61*, 1113–1123.

Lubinski, D. (2000). Scientific and social significance of assessing individual differences: "Sinking shafts at a few critical points." *Annual Review of Psychology, 51*, 405–444.

Luborsky, L., Singer, B., & Luborsky, L. (1975). Comparative studies of psychotherapies: Is it true that "everyone has won and all must have prizes"? *Archives of General Psychiatry, 32*, 995–1008.

Luby, J. L. (2010). Preschool depression: The importance of identification of depression early in development. *Current Directions in Psychological Science, 19*(2), 91–95.

Luchins, A. S. (1957). Primacy-recency in impression formation. In C. Hovland (Ed.), *The order of presentation in persuasion* (pp. 33–40, 55–61). New Haven, CT: Yale University Press.

Luck, S. J., & Gold, J. M. (2008). The construct of attention in schizophrenia. *Biological Psychiatry, 64*(1), 34–39.

Lucy, J. A., & Shweder, R. A. (1979). Whorf and his critics: Linguistic and nonlinguistic influences on color memory. *American Anthropologist, 81*, 581–615.

Luria, A. R. (1968). *The mind of a mnemonist* (pp. 24, 25). New York: Basic Books.

Lurito, J. T., Dzemidzic, M., Mathews, V. P., Lowe, M. J., Kareken, D. A., Phillips, M. D., & Wang, Y. (2000). Comparison of hemispheric lateralization using four language tasks. *Neuroimage, 11*, S358.

Lutkenhaus, P., Grossmann, K. E., & Grossman, K. (1985). Infant–mother attachment at twelve months and style of interaction with a stranger at the age of three years. *Child Development, 56*, 1538–1542.

Lydiard, R. B. (2003). The role of GABA in anxiety disorders. *The Journal of Clinical Psychiatry, 64*(Suppl. 3), 21–27.

Lykken, D. T. (1995). *The antisocial personalities*. Hillsdale, NJ: Laurence Erlbaum.

Lykken, D. T., & Tellegen, A. (1996). Happiness is a stochastic phenomenon. *Psychological Science, 7*, 186–189.

Lynch, E. B., Coley, J. D., & Medin, D. L. (2000). Tall is typical: Central tendency, ideal dimensions, and graded category structure among tree experts and novices. *Memory & Cognition, 28*(1), 41–50.

Lytton, H., & Romney, D. M. (1991). Parents' sex-differentiated socialization of boys and girls: A meta-analysis. *Psychological Bulletin, 109*, 267–296.

Lyvers, M. (2003). The neurochemistry of psychedelic experiences. *Science & Consciousness Review, 1*, 1–5.

Lyznicki, J. M., Doege, T. C., Davis, R. M., & Williams, M. A. (Council on Scientific Affairs, American Medical Association). (1998). Sleepiness, driving, and motor-vehicle crashes. *Journal of the American Medical Association, 279*(23), 1908–1913.

Maccoby, E. E. (1998). *The two sexes: Growing up apart: Coming together.* Cambridge, MA: Belknap Press.

MacCoun, R. J.; Kerr, N. L. (1988). Asymmetric influence in mock jury deliberation: Jurors' bias for leniency. *Journal of Personality and Social Psychology*, 54, 21–33.

MacDonald, A. P. (1970). Internal-external locus of control and the practice of birth control. *Psychological Reports, 27*, 206.

MacDonald, D., Kabani, N., Avis, D., & Evens, A. C. (2000). Automated 3D extraction of inner and outer surfaces of cerebral cortex from MRI. *NeuroImage, 12*, 340–356.

Macdonald, I., Amos, J., Crone, T., Wereley, S. (2010, May 21). The measure of an oil disaster. [Electronic version]. *New York Times.* Retrieved June 9, 2010, from http://www.nytimes.com/2010/05/22/opinion/22macdonald.html

Mack, J. E. (1994). *Abduction.* New York: Scribner.

MacKenzie, S. B., Lutz, R. J., & Belch, G. E. (1986, May). The role of attitude toward the ad as a mediator of advertising effectiveness: A test of competing explanations. *Journal of Marketing Research, 23*, 130–143.

Macknik, S. L., King, M., Randi, J., Robbins, A., Teller, Thompson, J., & Martinez-Conde, S. (2008). Attention and awareness in stage magic: Turning tricks into research. *Nature Reviews: Neuroscience, 9*(11), 871–879.

Macknik, S. L., & Martinez-Conde, S. (2009). Real magic: Future studies of magic should be grounded in neuroscience. *Nature reviews: Neuroscience, 10*(3), 241–241.

Macquet, P., & Franck, G. (1996). Functional neuroanatomy of human rapid eye movement sleep and dreaming. *Nature, 383*, 163–166.

Macrae, C. N., & Bodenhausen, G. V. (2000). Social cognition: Thinking categorically about others. *Annual Review of Psychology, 51*, 93–120.

Madsen, K. M., Hviid, A., Vestergaard, M., Schendel, D., Wohlfahrt, J., Thorsen, P., Olsen, J., & Melbye, M. (2002). A population-based study of measles, mumps, rubella vaccine and autism. *New England Journal of Medicine, 347*, 1477–1482.

Maguire, E. A., Burgess, N., Donnett, J. G., O'Keefe, J., & Frith, C. D. (1998). Knowing where things are: Parahippocampal involvement in encoding object locations in virtual large-scale space. *Journal of Cognitive Neuroscience, 10*(1), 61–76.

Mahowald, M. W., & Schenck, C. H. (1996). NREM sleep parasomnias. *Neurologic Clinics, 14*, 675–696.

Mai, J. K., Triepel, J., & Metz, J. (1987). Neurotensin in the human brain. *Neuroscience, 22*, 499–524.

Maier, S. F., Amat, J., Baratta, M. V., Paul, E., & Watkins, L. R. (2006). Behavioral control, the medial prefrontal cortex, and resilience. *Dialogues in Clinical Neuroscience, 8*(4), 397–406.

Maier, S. F., & Watkins, L. R. (1998). Cytokines for psychologists: Implications of bidirectional immune-to-brain communication for understanding behavior, mood, and cognition. *Psychological Review, 105*, 83–107.

Maier, S. F., & Watkins, L. R. (2005). Stressor controllability and learned helplessness: The roles of the dorsal raphe nucleus, serotonin, and corticotropin-releasing factor. *Neuroscience & Biobehavioral Reviews, 29*(4–5), 829–841.

Main, M., & Cassidy, J. (1988). Categories of response to reunion with the parent at age 6: Predictable from infant attachment classifications and stable over a 1 month period. *Developmental Psychology, 24*, 415–426.

Main, M., & Hesse, E. (1990). Parents' unresolved traumatic experiences are related to infant disorganized attachment status; Is frightened and/or frightening parental behaviour the linking mechanism? In M. T. Greenberg, D. Cicchetti, & E. M. Cummings (Eds.), *Attachment in the preschool years: Theory, research and intervention* (pp. 161–182). Chicago: University of Chicago Press.

Main, M., & Solomon, J. (1990). Procedures for identifying infants as disorganized/disoriented during the Ainsworth Strange Situation. In M. T. Greenberg, D. Cicchetti, & E. M. Cummings (Eds.), *Attachment in the preschool years: Theory, research and intervention* (pp. 121–160). Chicago: University of Chicago Press.

Maletic, V., Robinson, M., Oakes, T., Iyengar, S., Ball, S. G., & Russell, J. (2007). Neurobiology of depression: An integrated view of key findings. *The International Journal of Clinical Practice, 61*(12), 2030–2040.

Mandler, G. (1967). Organization and memory. In K. W. Spence & J. T. Spence (Eds.), *The psychology of learning and motivation, Vol. 1* (pp. 327–372). New York: Academic Press.

Mandler, J. M. (2000). Perceptual and conceptual processes. *Journal of Cognition and Development, 1*, 3–36.

Mandler, J. M. (2003). Conceptual categorization. In D. H. Rakison & L. M. Oakes (Eds.), *Early category and concept development: Making sense of the blooming, buzzing confusion* (pp. 103–131). Oxford, England: Oxford University Press.

Manson, J., Greenland, P., LaCroix, A. Z., Stefanick, M. L., Mouton, C. P., Oberman, A., Perri, M. G., Sheps, D. S., Pettinger, M. B., & Siscovick, D. S. (2002). Walking compared with vigorous exercise for the prevention of cardiovascular events in women. *The New England Journal of Medicine, 347*(10), 716–725.

Manusov, V., & Patterson, M. L. (Eds.). (2006). *The Sage handbook of nonverbal communication* (p. 289). Thousand Oaks, CA: Sage.

Manzo, L., Locatelli, C., Candura, S. M., & Costa, L. G. (1994). Nutrition and alcohol neurotoxicity. *Neurotoxicology, 15*(3), 555–565.

Maquet, P., Schwartz, S., Passingham, R., & Frith, C. (2003). Sleep-related consolidation of a visuomotor skill: Brain mechanisms as assessed by functional magnetic resonance imaging. *The Journal of Neuroscience, 23*(4), 1432.

Marcus, G. F. (2001). *The algebraic mind: Integrating connectionism and cognitive science (learning, development, and conceptual change).* Cambridge, MA: MIT Press.

Maren, S., & Fanselow, M. S. (1996). The amygdala and fear conditioning: Has the nut been cracked? *Neuron, 16*, 237–240.

Margolin, S., & Kubic, L. S. (1944). An apparatus for the use of breath sounds as a hypnogogic stimulus. *American Journal of Psychiatry, 100*, 610.

Marik, P. E. (2000). Leptin, obesity, and obstructive sleep apnea. *Chest, 118*, 569–571.

Markovitz, J. H., Lewis, C. E., Sanders, P. W., Tucker, D., & Warnock, D. G. (1997). Relationship of diastolic blood pressure with cyclic GMP excretion among young adults (the CARDIA study): Influence of a family history of hypertension. *Journal of Hypertension, 15*(9), 955–962.

Marks, D. F., Murray, M., Evans, B., Willig, C., Sykes, C. M., & Woodall, C. (2005). *Health Psychology: Theory, research & practice* (pp. 3–25). London: Sage.

Marks, K. (2010). Round-the-world teenage sailor Jessica Watson gets hero's welcome in Australia. *The Christian Science Monitor*, May 16, 2010. Retrieved June 27, 2010, from http://www.csmonitor.com/World/Asia-Pacific/2010/0516/Round-the-world-teenage-sailor-Jessica-Watson-gets-hero-s-welcome-in-Australia

Mars, A. E., Mauk, J. E., & Dowrick, P. (1998). Symptoms of pervasive developmental disorders as observed in prediagnostic home videos of infants and toddlers. *Journal of Pediatrics, 132*, 500–504.

Martin, C. L. (2000). Cognitive theories of gender development. In T. Eckes & H. M. Trautner (Eds.), *The developmental social psychology of gender* (pp. 91–121). Mahwah, NJ: Lawrence Erlbaum.

Martin, J. A., & Buckwalter, J. J. (2001). Telomere erosion and senescence in human articular cartilage chondrocytes. *Journal of Gerontology and Biological Science, 56*(4), 172–179.

Martin, L. (2004). Can sleepwalking be a murder defense? Retrieved October 19, 2004, from http://www.lakesidepress.com/pulmonary/Sleep/sleep-murder.htm

Martinussen, R., Hayden J., Hogg-Johnson, S., & Tannock, R. (2005). A meta-analysis of working memory components in children with Attention-Deficit/Hyperactivity Disorder. *Journal of the American Academy of Child & Adolescent Psychiatry, 44*(4), 377–384.

Maruta, T., Colligan, R. C., Malinchoc, M., & Offord, K. P. (2002, August). Optimism-pessimism assessed in the 1960s and self-reported health status 30 years later. *Mayo Clinic Proceedings*. 77, 748–753.

Maslow, A. (1943). A theory of human motivation. *Psychological Review, 50*, 370–396.

Maslow, A. (1971). *The farther reaches of human nature.* New York: Viking Press.

Maslow, A. (1987). *Motivation and personality* (3rd ed.). New York: Harper & Row.

Maslow, A., & Lowery, R. (Ed.). (1998). *Toward a psychology of being* (3rd ed.). New York: Wiley & Sons.

Mason, C., & Elwood, R. (1995). Is there a physiological basis for the couvades and onset of paternal care? *International Journal of Nursing Studies, 32*(4), 137–148.

Massaro, D. W., & Cowan, N. (1993). Information processing models: Microscopes of the mind. *Annual Review of Psychology, 44*, 383–426.

Masson, J. M. (1984). *The assault on truth: Freud's suppression of the seduction theory.* New York: Farrar, Straus & Giroux.

Masters, J. C., Burish, T. G., Holton, S. D., & Rimm, D. C. (1987). *Behavior therapy: Techniques and empirical finding.* San Diego, CA: Harcourt Brace Jovanovich.

Masters, W., & Johnson, V. (1966). *Human sexual response.* Boston: Little, Brown.

Masters, W. H., & Johnson, V. E. (1970). *Human sexual inadequacy.* Boston: Little, Brown.

Masters, W., Johnson, V., & Kolodny, R. (1995). *Human sexuality* (5th ed.). New York: HarperCollins.

Masuda, T., & Kitayama, S. (2004). Perceiver-induced constraint and attitude attribution in Japan and the U.S.: A case for the cultural dependence of the correspondence bias. *Journal of Experimental Social Psychology, 40*, 409–416.

Matsumoto, D. (1994). *People: Psychology from a cultural perspective* (pp. 144–147). Pacific Grove, CA: Brooks-Cole.

Matthew, N. & Dallery, J. (2007). Mercury rising: Exploring the vaccine–autism myth. *Skeptic, 13*(3), Retrieved May 3, 2010, from http://www.skeptic.com/eskeptic/07-06-20/#feature

Matthews, K. A., Gump, B. B., Harris, K. F., Haney, T. L., & Barefoot, J. C. (2004). Hostile behaviors predict cardiovascular mortality among men enrolled in the Multiple Risk Factor Intervention trial. *Circulation, 109*, 66–70.

Maurer, D., & Young, R. (1983). Newborns' following of natural and distorted arrangements of facial features. *Infant Behaviour and Development, 6*, 127–131.

Mavromatis, A. (1987). *Hypnagogia: The unique state of consciousness between wakefulness and sleep*. London: Routledge & Kegan Paul.

Mavromatis, A., & Richardson, J. T. E. (1984). Hypnagogic imagery. *International Review of Mental Imagery, 1*, 159–189.

Maxmen, J. S., Ward, N. G., & Kilgus, M. D. (2009). *Essential psychopathology and its treatment*. New York: W. W. Norton.

Mayer, J. D. (1999). Emotional Intelligence: Popular or scientific psychology? *APA Monitor, 30*(8), 50.

Mayer, J. D., & Geher, G. (1996). Emotional intelligence and the identification of emotion. *Intelligence, 22*, 89–113.

Mayer, J. D., Salovey, P., & Caruso, D. R. (2000). Models of emotional intelligence. In R. J. Sternberg (Ed.), *Handbook of human intelligence* (2nd ed., pp. 396–420). New York: Cambridge University Press.

Maziade, M., Bissonnette, L., Rouillard, E., Martinez, M., Turgeon, M., Charron, L., Pouliot, V., Boutin, P., Cliché, D., Dion, C., Fournier, J. P., Garneau, Y., Lavallee, J. C., Montgrain, N., Nicole, L., Pires, A., Ponton, A. M., Potvin, A., Wallot, H., Roy, M. A., & Merette, C. (Le Groupe IREP). (1997). 6p24–22 region and major psychoses in the Eastern Quebec population. *American Journal of Medical Genetics, 74*, 311–318.

Mazzoni, G. A. L., Loftus, E. F., & Kirsch, I. (2001). Changing beliefs about implausible autobiographical events: A little plausibility goes a long way. *Journal of Experimental Psychology: Applied, 7*(1), 51–59.

McCann, S. J. H., & Stewin, L. L. (1988). Worry, anxiety, and preferred length of sleep. *Journal of Genetic Psychology, 149*, 413–418.

McCauley, C. (1998). Group dynamics in Janis's theory of groupthink: Backward and forward. *Organizational Behavior & Human Decision Processes, 73*(2–3), 142–162.

McClelland, D. C. (1961). *The achieving society*. Princeton, NJ: Van Nostrand.

McClelland, D. C. (1987). *Human motivation*. Cambridge, MA: Cambridge University Press.

McClelland, J. L., & Rumelhart, D. E. (1988). Explorations in parallel distributed processing. Cambridge, MA: MIT Press.

McConaghy, N., Hadzi-Pavlovic, D., Stevens, C., Manicavasagar, V., Buhrich, N., & Vollmer-Conna, U. (2006). Fraternal birth order and ratio of heterosexual/homosexual feelings in women and men. *Journal of Homosexuality, 51*(4), 161–174.

McCrae, R. R., & Costa, P. T. (1990). *Personality in adulthood*. New York: Guilford Press.

McCrae, R. R., & Costa, P. T., Jr. (1996). Toward a new generation of personality theories: Theoretical contexts for the five-factor model. In J. S. Wiggins (Ed.), *The five-factor model of personality: Theoretical perspectives* (pp. 51–87). New York: Guilford.

McCrae, R. R., Costa, P. T., Jr., Ostendorf, F., Angleitner, A., Hrebickova, M., Avia, M. D., Sanz, J., Sanchez-Bernardos, M. L., Kusdil, M. E., Woodfield, R., Saunders, P. R, & Smith, P. B. et al. (2000). Nature over nurture: Temperament, personality, and life span development. *Journal of Personality and Social Psychology, 78*, 173–186.

McCrae R. R., Terracciano A., & 78 Members of the Personality Profiles of Cultures Project (2005). Universal features of personality traits from the observer's perspective: Data from 50 cultures. *Journal of Personality and Social Psychology, 88,* 547–561.

McCrae, R. R., & Terracciano, A. (2007). The Five-Factor model and its correlates in individuals and cultures. In F. J. R. van de Vijver, D. A. van Hemert, & Y. Poortinga (Eds.), *Individuals and cultures in multi-level analysis* (pp. 247–281). Mahwah, NJ: Erlbaum.

McDaniel, M. A., Howard, D. C., & Einstein, G. O. (2009). The read-recite-review study strategy: Effective and portable. *Psychological Science, 20*(4), 516–522.

McDermott, J. F. (2001). Emily Dickinson revisited: A study of periodicity in her work. *American Journal of Psychiatry, 158*(5), 686–690.

McDonald, J., Becker, D., Sadowsky, C., Jane, J., Conturo, T., & Schultz, L. (2002). Late recovery following spinal cord injury. *Journal of Neurosurgery: Spine, 97*, 252–265.

McDougall, T. (2009). Nursing children and adolescents with bipolar disorder. *Journal of Child and Adolescent Psychiatric Nursing, 22*, 33–39.

McDougall, W. (1908). *An introduction to social psychology*. London: Methuen & Co.

McEwen, B. S. (2000). The neurobiology of stress: From serendipity to clinical relevance. *Brain Research, 886*, 172–189.

McGaugh, J. L. (2004). The amygdala modulates the consolidation of memories of emotionally arousing experiences, *Annual Review Neuroscience*, 27, 1–28.

McGinn, L. K. (2000). Cognitive behavioral therapy of depression: Theory, treatment, and empirical status. *American Journal of Psychotherapy, 54*, 254–260.

McGinnis, J. M., & Foege, W. H. (1993). Actual causes of death in the United States. *Journal of the American Medical Association, 270*(18), 2207–2212.

McGrath, E., Keita, G. P., Strickland, B. R., & Russo, N. F. (1992). *Women and depression: Risk factors and treatment issues.* Washington, DC: American Psychological Association.

McGregor, D. (1960). *The human side of enterprise*. New York: McGraw-Hill.

McGuire, F. (1994). Army alpha and beta tests of intelligence. In R. J. Sternberg (Ed.), *Encyclopedia of intelligence* (Vol. 1, pp. 125–129.) New York: Macmillan.

McKee, A. C., Cantu, R. C., Nowinski, C. J., Hedley-Whyte, E. T., Gavett, B. E., Budson, A. E., Santini, V. E., Lee, H. S., Kubilus, C. A., & Stern, R. A. (2009). Chronic traumatic encephalopathy in athletes: Progressive tauopathy after repetitive head injury. *Journal of Neuropathology and Experimental Neurology, 68*(7), 709–735.

McLaughlin, K. A., Fairbank, J. A., Gruber, M. J., Jones, R. T., Lakoma, M. D., Pfefferbaum, B., Sampson, N. A., & Kessler, R. C. (2009). Serious emotional disturbance among youths exposed to Hurricane Katrina 2 years postdisaster. *Journal of the American Academy of Child and Adolescent Psychiatry*, 48(11), 1069–1078.

McLaughlin, K. A., Fairbank, J. A., Gruber, M. J., Jones, R. T., Osofsky, J. D., Pfefferbaum, B., Sampson, N. A., Kessler, R. C. (2010). Trends in serious emotional disturbance among youths exposed to Hurricane Katrina. *Journal of the American Academy of Child Adolescent Psychiatry,* 49(10), 990–1000.

McLaughlin, S. K. & Margolskee, R. F. (1994). Vertebrate taste transduction. *American Scientist, 82*, 538–545.

McMahon, F. J., Simpson, S. G., McInnis, M. G., Badner, J. A., MacKinnon, D. F., & DePaulo, J. R. (2001). Linkage of bipolar disorder to chromosome 18q and the validity of bipolar II disorder. *Archives of General Psychiatry, 58*, 1025–1031.

McMonagle, T., & Sultana, A. (2002). Token economy for schizophrenia (Cochrane Review). In *The Cochrane Library, Issue 2*. Oxford: Update Software.

Meador, B. D., & Rogers, C. R. (1984). Person-centered therapy. In R. J. Corsini (Ed.), *Current psychotherapies* (3rd ed., pp. 142–195). Itasca, IL: Peacock.

Medicine, B. (2002). Directions in gender research in American Indian societies: Two spirits and other categories. In W. J. Lonner, D. L. Dinnel, S. A. Hayes, & D. N. Sattler (Eds.), *Online Readings in Psychology and Culture* (Unit 3, Chapter 2) (www.wwu.edu/~culture), Center for Cross-Cultural Research, Western Washington University, Bellingham, WA.

Mehrabian, A. (2000). Beyond IQ: Broad-based measurement of individual success potential or "emotional intelligence." *Genetic, Social, and General Psychology Monographs, 126*, 133–239.

Meichenbaum, D. (1996). Stress inoculation training for coping with stressors. *The Clinical Psychologist, 49*, 4–7.

Mejía, O. L., & McCarthy, C. J. (2010). Acculturative stress, depression, and anxiety in migrant farmwork college students of Mexican heritage. *International Journal of Stress Management, 17*(1), 1–20.

Melzack, R., & Wall, P. D. (1965). Pain mechanisms: A new theory. *Science, 150*, 971–979.

Melzack, R., & Wall, P. D. (1996). *The challenge of pain*. London: Penguin Books.

Menon, T., Morris, M., Chiu, C. Y., & Hong, Y. I. (1999). Culture and the construal of agency: Attribution to individual versus group dispositions. *Journal of Personality and Social Psychology, 76*, 701–727.

Merikle, M. P. (2000). Subliminal perception. In A. E. Kazdin (Ed.), *Encyclopedia of Psychology* (Vol. 7, pp. 497–499). New York: Oxford University Press.

Merriam-Webster. (2003). *Merriam-Webster's collegiate dictionary* (11th ed.). Springfield, MA: Merriam-Webster.

Mervis, C. B., & Rosch, E. (1981). Categorization of natural objects. *Annual Review of Psychology, 32*, 89–115.

Meyrick, J. (2001). Forget the blood and gore: An alternative message strategy to help adolescents avoid cigarette smoking. *Health Education, 101*(3), 99–107.

Michaels, J. W., Blommel, J. M., Brocato, R. M., Linkous, R. A., & Rowe, J. S. (1982). Social facilitation and inhibition in a natural setting. *Replications in Social Psychology, 2*, 21–24.

Michalski, D., Mulvey, T., & Kohoout, J. (2010). *2008 American Psychological Association survey of psychology health service providers*. Retrieved April 5, 2010, from http://www.apa.org/workforce/publications/08-hsp/report.pdf

Mikami, A. Y., Szwedo, D. E., Allen, J. P., Evans, M. A., & Hare, A. L. (2010). Adolescent peer relationships and behavior problems predict young adults' communication on social networking websites. *Developmental Psychology, 46*, 46–56.

Miles, D. R., & Carey, G. (1997). Genetic and environmental architecture of human aggression. *Journal of Personality and Social Psychology, 72*, 207–217.

Milgram, S. (1964a). Behavioral study of obedience. *Journal of Abnormal and Social Psychology, 67*, 371–378.

Milgram, S. (1964b). Issues in the study of obedience: A reply to Baumrind. *American Psychologist, 19*, 848–852.

Milgram, S. (1974). *Obedience to authority: An experimental view*. New York: Harper & Row.

Miller, G. (2009). Neuropathology. A late hit for pro football players. *Science, 325*(5941), 670–672.

Miller, G. A. (1956). The magical number seven, plus or minus two: Some limits on our capacity for processing information. *Psychological Review, 63*, 81–97.

Miller, J. G. (1984). Culture and the development of everyday social explanation. *Journal of Personality and Social Psychology, 46*, 961–978.

Miller, K., & Doman, J. M. R. (1996, April). Together forever. *Life Magazine*, 46–56.

Miller, K. E., & Graves, J. C. (2000). Update on the prevention and treatment of sexually transmitted diseases. *American Family Physician, 61*, 379–386.

Miller, L. H., & Smith, A. D. (1993). *The stress solution*. New York: Pocket Books.

Miller, M., & Rahe, R. H. (1997). Life changes scaling for the 1990s. *Journal of Psychosomatic Research, 43*(3), 279–292.

Miller, M. E., & Bowers, K. S. (1993). Hypnotic analgesia: Dissociated experience or dissociated control? *Journal of Abnormal Psychology, 102*, 29–38.

Miller, M. N., & Pumariega, A. (1999). Culture and eating disorders. *Psychiatric Times, 16*(2), 1–4.

Miller, N. E., Sears, R. R., Mowrer, O. H., Doob, L. W., & Dollard, J. (1941). The frustration-aggression hypothesis. *Psychological Review, 48*, 337–342.

Miller, T. Q., Smith, T. W., Turner, C. W., Guijarro, M. L., & Hallet, A. J. (1996). A meta-analytic review of research on hostility and physical health. *Psychological Bulletin, 119*, 322–348.

Miller, T. Q., Turner, C. W., Tindale, R. S., Posavac, E. J., & Dugoni, B. L. (1991). Reasons for the trend toward null findings in research on Type A behavior. *Psychological Bulletin, 110*, 469–485.

Miller, W. R., & Rollnick, S. (2002). *Motivational interviewing: Preparing people for change* (2nd ed.). New York: Guilford Press.

Mills, M. A., Edmondson, D., & Park, C. L. (2007). Trauma and stress response among Hurricane Katrina evacuees. *American Journal of Public Health, 97*(1), 116–123.

Milner, B., Corkin, S., & Teuber, H. L. (1968). Further analysis of the hippocampal syndrome: 14-year follow-up study of H. M. *Neuropsychologia, 6*, 215–234.

Milner, J. (1992, January). Risk for physical child abuse: Adult factors. *Violence Update*, pp. 9–11.

Mintz, L. B., & Betz, N. E. (1988). Prevalence and correlates of eating disordered behaviors among undergraduate women. *Journal of Counseling Psychology, 35*, 463–471.

Mischel, W. (1966). A social learning view of sex differences in behaviour. In E. E. Maccoby (Ed.), *The development of sex differences* (pp. 56–81). Stanford, CT: Stanford University Press.

Mischel, W., & Shoda, Y. (1995). A cognitive-affective system theory of personality: Reconceptualizing situations, dispositions, dynamics, and invariances in personality structure. *Psychological Review, 102*, 246–268.

Mishell, D. R. (2001). Menopause. In M. A. Stenchever et al. (Eds.), *Comprehensive gynecology* (4th ed., pp. 1217–1258). St. Louis, MO: Mosby.

Mitchell, J. E. (1985). *Anorexia nervosa & bulimia, diagnosis and treatment*. Minneapolis: University of Minnesota Press.

Mitchell, J. E., Pyle, R. L., Eckert, E. D. (1981). Frequency and duration of binge-eating episodes in patients with bulimia. *American Journal of Psychiatry, 138*, 835–836.

Mitchell, S. A., & Black, M. J. (1996). *Freud and beyond: A history of modern psychoanalytic thought* [Reprint ed.]. New York: HarperCollins.

Miyatake, A., Morimoto Y., Oishi, T., Hanasaki, N., Sugita, Y., Iijima, S., Teshima. Y., Hishikawa, Y., & Yamamura, Y. (1980). Circadian rhythm of serum testosterone and its relation to sleep: Comparison with the variation in serum luteinizing hormone, prolactin, and cortisol in normal men. *Journal of Clinical Endocrinology and Metabolism, 51*(6), 1365–1371.

Moffic, H. S. (2003). Seven ways to improve "cultural competence." *Current Psychiatry, 2*(5), 78.

Mogil, J. S. (1999). The genetic mediation of individual differences in sensitivity to pain and its inhibition. *Proceedings of the National Academy of Sciences, USA, 96*(14), 7744–7751.

Mokdad, A. H., Bowman, B. A., Ford, E. S., Dietz, W. H., Vinicor, F., Bales, V. S., & Marks, J. S. (2001). Prevalence of obesity, diabetes, and obesity related health risk factors. *Journal of the American Medical Association, 289*, 76–79.

Moldofsky, H. (1995). Sleep and the immune system. *International Journal of Immunopharmacology, 17*(8), 649–654.

Moll, H., & Tomasello, M. (2007). How 14- and 18-month-olds know what others have experienced. *Developmental Psychology, 43*, 309–317.

Möller, A., & Hell, D. (2002). Eugen Bleuler and forensic psychiatry. *International Journal of Law and Psychiatry*, 25, 351–360.

Money, J. (1994). *Sex errors of the body and related syndromes*. Baltimore: Paul H. Brookes.

Money, J., & Mathews, D. (1982). Prenatal exposure to virilizing progestins: An adult follow-up study of 12 women. *Archives of Sexual Behavior, 11*(1), 73–83.

Money, J., & Norman, B. F. (1987). Gender identity and gender transposition: Longitudinal outcome study of 24 male hermaphrodites assigned as boys. *Journal of Sex and Marriage Therapy, 13*, 75–79.

Monteleone, P., Martiadis, V., Colurcio, B., & Maj, M. (2002). Leptin secretion is related to chronicity and severity of the illness in bulimia nervosa. *Psychosomatic Medicine, 64*, 874–879.

Moody, R., & Perry, P. (1993). *Reunions: Visionary encounters with departed loved ones*. London: Little, Brown.

Moore, T. E. (1988). The case against subliminal manipulation. *Psychology and Marketing, 5*, 297–316.

Moore, T. H., Zammit, S., Lingford-Hughes, A., Barnes, T. R., Jones, P. B., Burke, M., & Lewis, G. (2007). Cannabis use and risk of psychotic or affective mental health outcomes: A systematic review. *Lancet, 370*, 293–294, 319–328.

Moore-Ede, M. C., Sulzman, F. M., & Fuller, C. A. (1982). *The clocks that time us*. Cambridge, MA: Harvard University Press.

Moorhead, G., Neck, C. P., & West, M. S. (1998). The tendency toward defective decision making within self-managing teams: The relevance of groupthink for the 21st century. *Organizational Behavior & Human Decision Processes, 73*(2–3), 327–351.

Mora, G. (1985). History of psychiatry. In H. I. Kaplan & B. J. Sadock (Eds.), *Comprehensive textbook of psychiatry* (pp. 2034–2054). Baltimore: Williams & Wilkins.

Moreland, R. L., & Zajonc, R. B. (1982). Exposure effects in person perceptions: Familiarity, similarity, and attraction. *Journal of Experimental Social Psychology, 18*(5), 395–415.

Morgan, C. A., Rasmusson, A., Pietrzak, R. H., Coric, V., Southwick, S. M. (2009). Relationships among plasma dehydroepiandrosterone and dehydroepiandrosterone sulfate, cortisol, symptoms of dissociation, and objective performance in humans exposed to underwater navigation stress. *Biological Psychiatry, 66*(4), 334–340.

Morgan, C. D., & Murray, H. A. (1935). A method for investigating fantasies: The Thematic Apperception Test. *Archives of Neurology and Psychiatry, 34*, 298–306.

Morin, C. M., Bootzin, R. R., Buysse, D. J., Edinger, J. D., Espie, C. A., & Lichstein, K. L. (2006). Psychological and behavioral treatment of insomnia: Update of the recent evidence (1998–2004). *Sleep, 29*(11), 1398–1414.

Morris, J. S., Friston, K. J., Buche, L. C., Frith, C. D., Young, A. W., Calder, A. J., & Dolan, R. J. (1998). A neuromodulatory role for the human amygdala in processing emotional facial expressions. *Brain, 121*, 47–57.

Morris, M., Nisbett, R. E., & Peng, K. (1995). Causal understanding across domains and cultures. In D. Sperber, D. Premack, & A. J. Premack (Eds.), *Causal cognition: A multidisciplinary debate* (pp. 577–612). Oxford, UK: Oxford University Press.

Morris, M. W., & Peng, K. (1994). Culture and cause: American and Chinese attributions social and physical events. *Journal of Personality and Social Psychology, 67*, 949–971.

Morris, S. (2009, November 20). Devoted husband who strangled wife in his sleep walks free from court. Retrieved April 9, 2010, from http://www.guardian.co.uk/uk/2009/nov/20/brian-thomas-dream-strangler-tragedy

Morrison, J. (1995). *The clinician's guide to diagnosis.* New York: Guilford Press.

Morrow, C. E., Culbertson, J. L., Accornero, V. H., Xue, L., Anthony, J. C., & Bandstra, E. S. (2006). Learning disabilities and intellectual functioning in school-aged children with prenatal cocaine exposure. *Developmental Neuropsychology, 30*(3), 905–931.

Moruzzi, G., & Magoun, H. W. (1949). Brainstem reticular formation and activation of the EEG. *Electroencephalographs in Clinical Neurophysiology, 1*, 455–473.

Moscovici, S., & Zavalloni, M. (1969). The group as a polarizer of attitudes. *Journal of Personality and Social Psychology 12*, 125–135.

Mosher, W. D., Chandra, A., & Jones, J. (2005). Sexual behavior and selected health measures: Men and women 15–44 years of age, United States, 2002. *Advance data from vital and health statistics; no 362*. Hyattsville, MD: National Center for Health Statistics.

Mowat, F. (1988). *Woman in the mists: The story of Dian Fossey and the mountain gorillas of Africa.* New York: Warner Books.

Mroczek, D. K., Spiro, A., & Turiano, N. A. (2009). Do health behaviors explain the effect of neuroticism on mortality? Longitudinal findings from the VA Normative Aging Study. *Journal of Research in Personality, 43*(4), 653.

Mueser, K. T., Rosenberg, St. D., Xie, H., Jankowski, M. K., Bolton, E. E., Lu, E., Hamblen, J. L., Rosenberg, H. J., McHugo, G. J., & Wolfe, R. (2008). A randomized controlled trial of cognitive-behavioral treatment for posttraumatic stress disorder in severe mental illness. *Journal of Consulting and Clinical Psychology, 76*(2), 259–271.

Mufson, L. H., Dorta, K. P., Olfson, M., Weissman, M. M., & Hoagwood, K. (2004). Effectiveness research: Transporting interpersonal psychotherapy for depressed adolescents (IPT-A) from the lab to school-based health clinics. *Clinical Child and Family Psychology Review, 7*(4), 251–261.

Muhlberger, A., Herrmann, M. J., Wiedemann, G. C., Ellgring. H., & Pauli, P. (2001). Repeated exposure of flight phobics to flights in virtual reality. *Behaviour Research and Therapy, 39*(9), 1033–1050.

Mukamel, R., Ekstrom, A. D., Kaplan, J., Iacoboni, M., & Fried, I. (2010). Single-neuron responses in humans during execution and observation of actions. *Current Biology, 20*, 750–756.

Muller-Oerlinghausen, B., Berghofer, A., & Bauer, M. (2002). Bipolar disorder. *Lancet, 359*, 241–247.

Munoz, Daniel (15 May 2010). Australian teenager finishes round-world solo sail. *Reuters.* Retrieved May 15, 2010, from http://www.reuters.com/article/idUSTRE64E0D920100515.

Münsterberg, H. (1908). *On the witness stand.* New York: Clark, Boardman.

Münsterberg, H. (1913). *Psychology and industrial efficiency.* Boston & New York: Houghton Mifflin

Murdock, B. B., Jr. (1962). The serial position effect in free recall. *Journal of Experimental Psychology, 64*, 482–488.

Murphy, C. C., Boyle, C., Schendel, D., Decouflé, P., & Yeargin-Allsopp, M. (1998). Epidemiology of mental retardation in children. *Mental Retardation and Developmental Disabilities Research Reviews, 4*, 6–13.

Murphy, L. R. (1995). Managing job stress: An employee assistance/human resource management partnership. *Personnel Review, 24*(1), 41–50.

Murphy, M., & Donavan, S. (1997). *The physical and psychological effects of meditation: A review of contemporary research with a comprehensive bibliography.* Petaluma, CA: Institute of Noetic Sciences.

Murray, S. L., Holmes, J. G., MacDonald, G., & Ellsworth, P. C. (1998). Through the looking glass darkly? When self-doubts turn into relationship insecurities. *Journal of Personality and Social Psychology, 75*, 1459–1480.

Muter, P. (1978). Recognition failure of recallable words in semantic memory. *Memory & Cognition, 6*(1), 9–12.

Nadeau, K. G., Quinn, P., & Littman, E. (2001). *AD/HD self-rating scale for girls.* Springfield, MD: Advantage Books.

Naitoh, P., Kelly, T. L., & Englund, C. E. (1989). *Health effects of sleep deprivation* (Naval Health Research Centre, Rep. No. 89-46), San Diego, CA: NHRC.

Najavits, L. M. (2007). Psychosocial treatments for postraumatic stress disorder. In P. E. Nathan & J. M. Gorman (Eds.), *A guide to treatments that work* (3rd ed., pp. 513–530). New York: Oxford University Press.

Naqvi, N., Tranel, D., & Bechara, A. (2006). Visceral and decision-making functions of the ventromedial prefontal cortex. In D. H. Zald & S. L. Rauch (Eds.), *The orbitofrontal cortex* (pp. 325–353). New York: Oxford University Press.

Nasar, S. (1998). *A beautiful mind: A biography of John Forbes Nash, Jr., winner of the Nobel Prize in economics 1994.* New York: Simon & Schuster.

Nathan, P. E., & Gorman, J. M. (2007). *Psychosocial treatments for postraumatic stress disorder* (3rd ed.). New York: Oxford University Press.

National Academy of Neuropsychology. (May, 2001). NAN definition of a clinical neuropsychologist [Electronic version]. Retrieved April 13, 2010, from http://www.nanonline.org/NAN/Files/PAIC/PDFs/NANPositionDefNeuro.pdf

National Center for Health Statistics (NCHS) (2007). Alcohol use. Retrieved July 25, 2007, from http://www.cdc.gov/nchs/fastats/alcohol.htm

National College Athletic Association (2002). 2002 NCAA graduation rates report. Retrieved September 21, 2007, from NCAA—The National Collegiate Athletic Association: The online resource for the National Collegiate Athletic Association Web site: http://web1.ncaa.org/web_files/grad_rates/2002/index.html

National Institute of Mental Health (NIMH) (2010). The numbers count: Mental disorders in America. Retrieved from http://www.nimh.nih.gov/health/publications/the-numbers-count-mental-disorders-in-america/index.shtml

National Institute of Mental Health (NIMH) Genetics Workgroup. (1998). *Genetics and mental disorders* (NIH Publication No. 98-4268). Rockville, MD: National Institute of Mental Health.

National Institute on Alcoholism and Alcohol Abuse (NIAAA) (2007). Data/Statistical Tables. Retrieved July 25, 2007, from http://www.niaaa.nih.gov/Resources/DatabaseResources/QuickFacts/default.htm

National Institute on Drug Abuse (NIDA). (2002). Research report series—Prescription drugs: Abuse and addiction. National Institutes of Health (NIH). Retrieved July 19, 2008, from www.drugabuse.gov/ResearchReports/Prescription/prescription5.html

National Institute on Drug Abuse. (2006, May). NIDA InfoFacts: MDMA (Ecstasy). Retrieved May 5, 2010, from http://www.nida.nih.gov/Infofacts/ecstasy.html

National Institutes of Health. (2007). *Stem cell basics.* Retrieved February 6, 2008, from http://stemcells.nih.gov/info/basics/

National Safety Council. (2010). National safety council estimates that at least 1.6 million crashes are caused each year by drivers using cell phones and texting. Retrieved March 3, 2010, from http://www.nsc.org/Pages/NSCestimates16millioncrashescausedbydriversusingcellphonesandtexting.aspx

National Sleep Foundation (2009). Can't sleep? What to know about insomnia. Retrieved May 5, 2010, from http://www.sleepfoundation.org/article/sleep-related-problems/insomnia-and-sleep

Neale, M. C., Rushton, J. P., & Fulker, D. W. (1986). The heritability of items from the Eysenck Personality Questionnaire. *Personality and Individual Differences, 7*, 771–779.

Neary, N. M., Goldstone, A. P., & Bloom, S. R. (2004). Appetite regulations: From the gut to the hypothalamus. *Clinical Endocrinology, 60*(2), 153–160.

Neimark, J. (1996). The diva of disclosure, memory researcher Elizabeth Loftus. *Psychology Today, 29*(1), 48–80.

Neimeyer, R. A., & Mitchell, K. A. (1998). Similarity and attraction: A longitudinal study. *Journal of Social and Personality Relationships, 5*, 131–148.

Neisser, U. (1982). Snapshots or benchmarks? In U. Neisser (Ed.), *Memory observed: Remembering in natural contexts* (pp. 43–48). San Francisco: W. H. Freeman.

Neisser, U., & Harsch, N. (1992). Phantom flashbulbs: False recollections of hearing the news about *Challenger.* In E. Winograd & U. Neisser (Eds.), *Affect and accuracy in recall: Studies of "flashbulb memories"* (pp. 9–31). New York: Cambridge University Press.

Neisser, U., Boodoo, G., Bouchard, T. J., Boykin, A. W., Brody, N., Ceci, S. J., Halpern, D. F., Loehlin, J. C., Perloff, R., Sternberg, R. J., & Urbina, S. (1996). Intelligence: Knowns and unknowns. *American Psychologist, 51*, 77–101.

Nelson, D. B., Sammel, M. D., Freeman, E. W., Lin, H., Gracia, C. R., & Schmitz, K. H. (2008). Effect of physical activity on menopausal symptoms among urban women. *Medicine & Science in Sports & Exercise, 40*(1), 50–58.

Nelson, K. (1993). The psychological and social origins of autobiographical memory. *Psychological Science, 4*, 7–14.

Nestor, P. G., Kubicki, M., Niznikiewicz, M., Gurrera, R. J., McCarley, R. W., & Shenton, M. E. (2008). Neuropsychological disturbance in schizophrenia: A diffusion tensor imaging study. *Neuropsychology, 22*(2), 246–254.

Neto, F. (1995). Conformity and independence revisited. *Social Behavior and Personality, 23*(3), 217–222.

Neumarker, K. (1997). Mortality and sudden death in anorexia nervosa. *International Journal of Eating Disorders, 21*, 205–212.

Neumeister, A., Bain, E., Nugent, A. C., Carson, R. E., Bonne, O., Luckenbaugh, D. A., Eckelman, W., Herscovitch, P., Charney, D. S., & Drevets, W. C. (2004). Reduced serotonin Type 1a receptor binding in panic disorder. *The Journal of Neuroscience, 24*(3), 589–591.

Neville, H. J., & Bavelier, D. (2000). Specificity and plasticity in neurocognitive development in humans. In M. S. Gazzaniga (Ed.), *The New Cognitive Neurosciences* (2nd ed., pp. 83–99). Cambridge, MA: MIT Press.

Nicholson, N., Cole, S., & Rocklin, T. (1985). Conformity in the Asch situation: A comparison between contemporary British and U.S. students. *British Journal of Social Psychology, 24*, 59–63.

Nickell, J. 1995. Crop circle mania wanes: An investigative update. *Skeptical Inquirer 19*(3), 41–43.

Nickerson, R. S., & Adams, J. J. (1979). Long-term memory for a common object. *Cognitive Psychology, 11*, 287–307.

Niedermeyer, E. (2005). Historical aspects. In E. Niedermeyer & F. Lopes da Silva (Eds.), *Electroencephalography: Basic principles, clinical applications, and related fields* (5th ed., pp. 1–15). Philadelphia: Lippincott, Williams & Wilkins.

Nieto, F., Young, T. B., Lind, B. K., Shahar, E., Samet, J. M., Redline, S., D'Agostino, R. B., Newman, A. B., Lebowitz, M. D., & Pickering, T. G. (2000). Association of sleep-disordered breathing, sleep apnea, and hypertension in a large, community-based study. *Journal of the American Medical Association, 283*(14), 1829–1836.

Nigg, J. T. (2010). Attention-Deficit/Hyperactivity Disorder: Endophenotypes, structure, and etiological pathways. *Current Directions in Psychological Science, 19*(1), 24–29.

Nigg, J. T., & Goldsmith, H. H. (1994). Genetics of personality disorders: Perspectives from personality and psychopathology research. *Psychological Bulletin, 115*, 346–380.

Nijenhuis, E. R. (2000). Somatoform dissociation: Major symptoms of dissociative disorders. *Journal of Trauma and Dissociation, 1*(4), 7–29.

Nikolajsen, L., & Jensen, T. S. (2001). Phantom limb pain. *British Journal of Anaesthesia, 87*, 107–116.

Nisbett, R. E. (1972). Hunger, obesity, and the ventromedial hypothalamus. *Psychological Review, 79*, 433–453.

Nitsche, M. A., Boggio, P. S., Fregni, F., & Pascual-Leone, A. (2009). Treatment of depression with transcranial direct current stimulation (tDCS): A review. *Experimental Neurology, 219*(1), 14–19.

Nolen-Hoeksema, S. (1990). *Sex differences in depression.* Palo Alto, CA: Stanford University Press.

Nooyens, A. C. J., Baan, C. A., Spijkerman, A. M. W., & Verschuren, W. M. M. (in press). *Type 2 diabetes mellitus and cognitive decline in middle-aged men and women—The Doetinchem Cohort Study.* American Diabetes Association: Diabetes Care.

Norcross, J. C. (2005). A primer on psychotherapy integration. In J. C. Norcross & M. R. Goldfried (Eds.), *Handbook of psychotherapy integration* (2nd ed., pp. 3–23). New York, Oxford University Press.

Norenzayan, A., Choi, I., & Nisbett, R. E. (1999). Eastern and Western perceptions of causality for social behavior: Lay theories about personalities and situations. In D. A. Prentice & D. T. Miller (Eds.), *Cultural divides* (pp. 239–272). New York: Russell Sage Foundation.

Norrbrink Budh, C., Lund, I., Hultling, C., Levi, R., Werhagen, L., Ertzgaard, P., & Lundeberg, T. (2003). Gender-related differences in pain in spinal cord injured individuals. *Spinal Cord, 41*, 122–128.

Nosich, G. M. (2008). Learning to think things through: A guide to critical thinking across the curriculum (3rd ed., pp. 2–16). Upper Saddle River, NJ: Prentice-Hall.

Novak, J. D. (1995). Concept maps to facilitate teaching and learning. *Prospects, 25*, 95–11.

Novella, S. (2007, November/December). The Anti-Vaccination Movement. *Skeptical Inquirer.* Retrieved May 21, 2010, from http://www.csicop.org/si/show/anti-vaccination_movement/www.guardian.co.uk/science/2007/feb/24/badscience.uknews

Nyberg, L., & Tulving, E. (1996). Classifying human long-term memory: Evidence from converging dissociations. *European Journal of Cognitive Psychology, 8*(2), 163–183.

Oberman, L. M. & Ramachandran, V. S. (2007). The simulating social mind: The role of simulation in the social and communicative deficits of autism spectrum disorders, *Psychological Bulletin, 133*, 310–327.

Ocholla-Ayayo, A. B. C., Wekesa, J. M., & Ottieno, J. A. M. (1993). *Adolescent pregnancy and its implications among ethnic groups in Kenya.* In International Population Conference, Montreal, Canada: International Union for the Scientific Study of Population, *1:* 381–395.

Ochsner, K., & Kosslyn, S. M. (1994). Mental imagery. In V. S. Ramaschandran (Ed.), *Encyclopedia of human behavior.* New York: Academic Press.

O'Connor, R. D. (1972). Relative efficacy of modeling, shaping, and the combined procedures for modification of social withdrawal. *Journal of Abnormal Psychology, 79*, 327–334.

Ohayon, M. M., Priest, R. G., Caulet, M., & Guilleminault, C. (1996). Hypnagogic and hypnopompic hallucinations: pathological phenomena? *British Journal of Psychiatry,169*, 459–67.

Öhman, A. (2008). Fear and anxiety. In M. Lewis, J. M. Haviland-Jones & L. F. Barrett (Eds.), *Handbook of emotion* (3rd ed., pp. 709–729). New York: Guiford Press.

O'Keefe, D. J. (2009). Theories of persuasion. In R. L. Nabi & M. B. Oliver (Eds.), *The Sage handbook of media processes and effects* (pp. 277–278). Los Angeles: Sage.

Okie, S. (2005). Traumatic brain injury in the war zone. *The New England Journal of Medicine, 352*(20), 2043–2047.

Oliver, J. E. (1993). Intergenerational transmission of child abuse: Rates, research, and clinical interpretations. *American Journal of Psychiatry, 150*, 1315–1324.

Ollendick, T. H., & King, N. J. (1998). Empirically supported treatments for children with phobic and anxiety disorders: Current status. *Journal of Clinical Child Psychology, 27*(2), 156–167.

Olsen, P. (1975). *Emotional flooding.* Baltimore: Penguin Books.

Olson, H. C., & Burgess, D. M. (1997). Early intervention for children prenatally exposed to alcohol and other drugs. In M. J. Guralnick (Ed.), *The effectiveness of early intervention* (pp. 109–146). Baltimore: Brookes.

Oman, C. M. (1990). Motion sickness: A synthesis and evaluation of the sensory conflict theory. *Canadian Journal of Physiological Pharmacology, 68*, 294–303.

Onken, L. S., Blaine, J. D., & Battjes, R. J. (1997). Behavioral therapy research: A conceptualization of a process. In S. W. Henggeler & A. B. Santos (Eds.), *Innovative approaches for difficult-to-treat populations* (pp. 477–485). Washington, DC: American Psychiatric Press.

Osborne, J. W. (2007). Linking stereotype threat and anxiety. *Educational Psychology, 27*, 135–154.

Oster, J.R. (1987). The binge-purge syndrome: A common albeit unappreciated cause of acid-base and fluid-electrolyte disturbances. *Southern Medical Journal, 80*, 58–67.

Oswald, I. (1959). Sudden bodily jerks on falling asleep. *Brain, 82*, 92–103.

Oswalt, R., Anderson, M., Hagstrom, K., & Berkowitz, B. (1993). Evaluation of the one-session eye-movement desensitization reprocessing procedure for eliminating traumatic memories. *Psychological Reports, 73*, 99–104.

Overeem, S., Mignot, E., Gert van Dijk, J., & Lammers, G. J. (2001). Narcolepsy: Clinical features, new pathophysiological insights, and future perspectives. *Journal of Clinical Neurophysiology, 18*(2), 78–105.

Overmier, J. B., & Seligman, M. E. P. (1967). Effects of inescapable shock on subsequent escape and avoidance behavior. *Journal of Comparative Physiology and Psychology, 63*, 23–33.

Owen, A. M., Hampshire, A., Grahn, J. A., Stenton, R., Dajani, S., Burns, A. S., Howard, R. J., & Ballard, C. G. (2010). Putting brain training to the test [Electronic version]. *Nature.* DOI 10.1038/nature09042

Owen, M. T., Easterbrooks, M. A., Chase-Lansdale, L., & Goldberg, W. A. (1984). The relation between maternal employment status and the stability of attachments to mother and to father. *Child Development, 55*, 1894–1901.

Paivio, A. (1971). *Imagery and verbal processes.* New York: Holt, Rinehart & Winston.

Paivio, A. (1986). *Mental representations: A dual coding approach.* New York: Oxford University Press.

Pajonk, F. G., Wobrock, T., Gruber, O., Scherk, H., Berner, D., Kaizl, I., Kierer, A., Muller, S., Oest, M., Meyer, T., Backens, M., Schneider-Axmann, T., Thornton, A. E., Honer, W. G., & Falkai, P. (2010). Hippocampal plasticity in response to exercise in schizophrenia. *Archives of General Psychiatry,* 67(2), 133–143.

Palmer, S. E. (1992). Common region: A new principle of perceptual grouping. *Cognitive Psychology, 24*(3), 436–447.

Palva, J. M., Monto, S., Kulashekhar, S., & Palva, S. (2010). Neuronal synchrony reveals working memory networks and predicts individual memory capacity. *Proceedings of the National Academy of Sciences, USA,* 107(16), 7580–7585.

Pan, A. S. (2000). Body image, eating attitudes, and eating behaviors among Chinese, Chinese-American and non-Hispanic White women. *Dissertation Abstracts International, Section B: The Sciences and Engineering, 61*(1-B), 544.

Pargament, K. I. (1997). *The psychology of religion and coping: Theory, research, and practice.* New York: Guilford Press.

Paris, J. (2004). Gender differences in personality traits and disorders. *Current Psychiatry Reports, 6*, 71–74.

Park, J., Turnbull, A. P., & Turnbull, H. R. (2002). Impacts of poverty on quality of life in families of children with disabilities. *Exceptional Children, 68*, 151–170.

Parker, E. S., Cahill, L., & McGaugh, J. L. (February 2006). A case of unusual autobiographical remembering. *Neurocase 12*(1), 35–49.

Parkinson, W. L., & Weingarten, H. P. (1990). Dissociative analysis of ventromedial hypothalamic obesity syndrome. *American Journal of Physiology: Regulatory, Integrative, and Comparative Physiology, 259*, R829–R835.

Parsons, H. M. (1992). Hawthorne: An early OBM experiment. *Journal of Organizational Behavior Management, 12*(1), 27–43.

Partonen, T., & Lonnqvist, J. (1998). Seasonal affective disorder. *Lancet, 352*(9137), 1369–1374.

Pashler, H., McDaniel, M., Rohrer, D., & Bjork, R. (2009). Learning styles: concepts and evidence. *Psychological Science in the Public Interest, 9*(3), 106–119.

Paul, B. M., ElvevÅg, B., Bokat, C. E., Weinberger, D. R., & Goldberg, T. E. (2005). Levels of processing effects on recognition memory in patients with schizophrenia. *Schizophrenia Research, 74*(1), 101–110.

Paunonen, S. V., Keinonen, M., Trzbinski, J., Forsterling, F., Grishenko-Roze, N., Kouznetsova, L., & Chan, D. W., et al. (1996). The structure of personality in six cultures. *Journal of Cross Cultural Psychology, 27*, 339–353.

Pavlov, I. (1926). *Conditioned reflexes.* London: Oxford University Press.

Pavlov, I. P. (1906). The scientific investigation of the psychical faculties or processes in the higher animals. *Science, 24*, 613–619.

Pavlov, I. P. (1927). *Conditioned Reflexes: An Investigation of the Physiological Activity of the Cerebral Cortex. Translated and Edited by G. V. Anrep.* London: Oxford University Press.

Peng, K., Ames, D. R., & Knowles, E. D. (2000). Culture and human inference: Perspectives from three traditions. In D. Matsumoto (Ed.) (2001). *The handbook of culture and psychology* (pp. 245–264). New York: Oxford University Press.

Penn, D. L. (1998). Assessment and treatment of social dysfunction in schizophrenia. *Clinicians Research Digest, Supplemental Bulletin, 18*, 1–2.

Peplau, L. A., & Taylor, S. E. (1997). *Sociocultural perspectives in social psychology: Current readings.* Upper Saddle River, NJ: Prentice-Hall.

Pepperberg, I. M. (1998). Talking with Alex: Logic and speech in parrots. *Scientific American Presents: Exploring Intelligence, 9*(4), 60–65.

Pepperberg, I. M. (2005). An avian perspective on language evolution: Implications of simultaneous development of vocal and physical object combinations by a grey parrot (*Psittacus erithacus*). In M. Tallerman (Ed.), *Language origins: Perspectives on evolution* (pp. 239–261). New York: Oxford University Press.

Pepperberg, I. M. (2006). Grey Parrot *(Psittacus erithacus)* numerical abilities: Addition and further experiments on a zero-like concept. *Journal of Comparative Psychology, 120*(1), 1–11.

Pepperberg, I. M. (2007). Grey parrots do not always "parrot": The roles of imitation and phonological awareness in the creation of new labels from existing vocalizations. *Language Sciences, 29*(1), 1–13.

Pereira, M. A., Kartashov, A. I., Van Horn, L., Slattery, M., Jacobs, D. R. Jr., & Ludwig, D. S. (2003, March). *Eating breakfast may reduce risk of obesity, diabetes, heart disease.* Paper presented at the American Heart Association's Annual Conference on Cardiovascular Disease Epidemiology and Prevention, Miami, FL.

Perls, F. (1951). *Gestalt therapy.* New York: Julian Press.

Perls, F. (1969). *Gestalt therapy verbatim.* Moab, UT: Real People Press.

Perlstein, W. M., Carter, C. S., Noll, D. C., & Cohen, J. D. (2001). Relation of prefrontal cortex dysfunction to working memory and symptoms in schizophrenia. *American Journal of Psychiatry, 156*, 1105–1113.

Perrin, S., & Spencer, C. (1980). The Asch effect—A child of its time. *Bulletin of the British Psychological Society, 33*, 405–406.

Perrin, S., Spencer, C. P. (1981). Independence or conformity in the Asch experiment as a reflection of cultural and situational factors. *British Journal of Social Psychology*, 20(3), 205–209.

Perrine, D. M. (1997). *The chemistry of mind-altering drugs.* Washington, DC: American Chemical Society.

Persaud, R. (2001). *Staying sane: How to make your mind work for you.* New York: Bantam.

Peters, T. M., Moore, S. C., Gierach, G. L., Wareham, N. J., Ekelund, U., Hollenbeck, A. R., Schatzkin, A., & Leitzmann, M. F. (2009). Intensity and timing of physical activity in relation to postmenopausal breast cancer risk: The prospective NIH=AARP Diet and Health Study. *BMC Cancer*, 9, 349.

Peters, W. A. (1971). *A class divided.* Garden City, NY: Doubleday.

Peterson, C., & Park, N. (2010). What happened to self-actualization? *Perspectives on Psychological Science, 5*(3), 320–322.

Peterson, D. R. (1976). Need for the Doctor of Psychology degree in professional psychology. *American Psychologist, 31,* 792–798.

Peterson, D. R. (1982). Origins and development of the Doctor of Psychology concept. In G. R. Caddy, D. C. Rimm, N. Watson, & J. H. Johnson (Eds.), *Educating professional psychologists* (pp. 19-38). New Brunswick, NJ: Transaction Books.

Peterson, L. R., & Peterson, M. J. (1959). Short-term retention of individual items. *Journal of Experimental Psychology, 58*, 193–198.

Petitto, L. A., & Marentette, P. F. (1991). Babbling in the manual mode: Evidence for the ontogeny of language. *Science, 251*, 1493–1496.

Petitto, L. A., Holowka, S., Sergio, L. E., & Ostry, D. (2001). Language rhythms in baby hand movements. *Nature, 413*, 35.

Petrakis, I. L, Gonzalez, G., Rosenheck, R., & Krystal, J. H. (2002). Comorbidity of alcoholism and psychiatric disorders. *Alcohol Research and Health, 26*(2), 81–89.

Petri, H. (1996). *Motivation: Theory, research and application* (4th ed.), Belmont, CA: Wadsworth.

Petrova, P. K., Cialdini, R. B., & Sills S., J. (2007). Compliance, consistency, and culture: Personal consistency and compliance across cultures. *Journal of Experimental Social Psychology 43*: 104–111.

Pettigrew, T. F., & Tropp, L. R. (2000). Does intergroup contact reduce prejudice? Recent meta-analytic findings. In S. Oskamp (Ed.), *Reducing prejudice and discrimination: Social psychological perspectives* (pp. 93–114). Mahwah, NJ: Erlbaum.

Petty, R., & Cacioppo, J. (1986). *Communication and persuasion: Central and peripheral routes to attitude change.* New York: Springer-Verlag.

Petty, R., & Cacioppo, J. (1996). *Attitudes and persuasion: Classic and contemporary approaches* (reprint). Boulder, CO: Westview Press.

Petty, R. E. (1995). Attitude change. In A. Tesser (Ed.), *Advances in social psychology* (pp. 194–255). New York: McGraw-Hill.

Petty, R. E., Wheeler, S. C., & Tormala, Z. L. (2003). Persuasion and attitude change. In T. Millon & M. J. Lerner (Eds.), *Handbook of psychology: Volume 5: Personality and social psychology* (pp. 353–382). Hoboken, NJ: John Wiley & Sons.

Pezdek, K., & Hodge, D. (1999). Planting false childhood memories in children: The role of event plausibility. *Child Development, 70*, 887–895.

Pezdek, K., Finger, K., & Hodge, D. (1997). Planting false childhood memories: The role of event plausibility. *Psychological Science, 8*, 437–441

Pfeiffer, W. M. (1982). Culture-bound syndromes. In I. Al-Issa (Ed.), *Culture and psychopathology* (pp. 201–218). Baltimore: University Park Press.

Pfurtscheller, G., Allison, B. Z., Bauernfeind, G., Brunner, C., Solis Escalante, T., Scherer, R., Zander, T. O., Mueller-Putz, G., Neuper, C., & Birbaumer, N. (2010). The hybrid BCI. *Frontiers in Neuroprosthetics, 4:* 30.

Phan, T., & Silove, D. (1999). An overview of indigenous descriptions of mental phenomena and the range of traditional healing practices amongst the Vietnamese. *Transcultural Psychiatry, 36*, 79–94.

Piaget, J. (1926). *The language and thought of the child.* New York: Harcourt Brace.

Piaget, J. (1952). *The origins of intelligence in children.* New York: W. W. Norton.

Piaget, J. (1962). *Play, dreams and imitation in childhood.* New York: W. W. Norton.

Piaget, J. (1983). Piaget's theory. In W. Kessen (Ed.), *Handbook of child psychology: Volume 1. Theoretical models of human development* (pp. 103–128). New York: Wiley.

Piedmont, R. L., Bain, E., McCrae, R. R., & Costa, P. T., Jr. (2002). The applicability of the Five-Factor Model in a sub-Saharan culture: The NEO-PI-R in Shona. In R. R. McCrae & J. Allik (Eds.), *The Five-Factor Model across cultures* (pp. 105–126). New York: Kluwer Academic/Plenum Publishers.

Pilkington, J. (1998). "Don't try and make out that I'm nice": The different strategies women and men use when gossiping. In J. Coates (Ed.), *Language and gender: A reader* (pp. 254–269). Oxford, UK: Blackwell.

Pinker, S. (1995). Language acquisition. In Gleitman et al. (Eds.), *An invitation to cognitive science* (2nd ed., pp. 135–182). Cambridge: MIT Press.

Pinker, S., & Bloom, P. (1990). Natural language and natural selection. *Behavioral and Brain Sciences, 13*(4), 707–784.

Pinsof, W. M., & Wynne, L. C. (1995). The efficacy of marital and family therapy: An empirical overview, conclusions, and recommendations. *Journal of Marital and Family Therapy, 21*, 585–613.

Pittam, J., Gallois, C., Iwawaki, S., & Kroonenberg, P. (1995). Australian and Japanese concepts of expressive behavior. *Journal of Cross-Cultural Psychology, 26*(5), 451–473.

Plaut, D. C., & McClelland, J. L. (2010). Locating object knowledge in the brain: A critique of Bowers' (2009) attempt to revive the grandmother cell hypothesis. *Psychological Review, 117*, 284–288.

Plomin, R. (1994). The nature of nurture: The environment beyond the family. In R. Plomin (Ed.), *Genetics and experience: The interplay between nature and nurture* (pp. 82–107). Thousand Oaks, CA: Sage.

Plomin, R., & DeFries, J. C. (1998, May). Genetics of cognitive abilities and disabilities. *Scientific American*, 62–69.

Plomin, R., & Spinath, F. M. (2004). Intelligence: Genetics, genes, and genomics. *Journal of Personality and Social Psychology, 86*(1), 112–129.

Plomin, R., Owen, M. J., & McGuffin, P. (1994). The genetic basis of complex human behaviors. *Science, 264*(5166), 1733–1739.

Plomin, R. N. L., Pederson, G. E., McClearn, J. R., Nesselroade, C. S., & Bergman, H. F. (1988). EAS temperaments during the last half year of the life span: Twins reared apart and twins raised together. *Psychology of Aging, 4*, 43–50.

Plug, C., & Ross, H. E. (1994). The natural moon illusion: A multi-factor angular account. *Perception, 23*, 321–333.

Plum, F., & Posner, J. B. (1985). *The diagnosis of stupor and coma.* Philadelphia: F. A. Davis.

Pogue-Geile, M. F., & Yokley, J. L. (2010). HYPERLINK "http://cdp.sagepub.com/content/19/4/214.abstract". Current Research on the Genetic Contributors to Schizophrenia. *Current Directions in Psychological Science, 19*, 214–219. doi: 10.1177/0963721410378490.

Polce-Lynch, M., Myers, B. J., Kilmartin, C. T., Forssmann-Falck, R., & Kliewer, W. (1998) Gender and age patterns in emotional expression, body image, and self-esteem: A qualitative analysis. *Sex Roles, 38*, 1025–1050.

Polewan, R. J., Vigorito, C. M., Nason, C. D., Block, R. A., & Moore, J. W. (2006). A cartesian reflex assessment of face processing. *Behavioral and Cognitive Neuroscience Reviews, 3*(5), 3–23.

Pollack, M. H., Simon, N. M., Fagiolini, A., Pitman, R., McNally, R. J., Nierenberg, A. A., Miyahara, S., Sachs, G. S., Perlman, C., Ghaemi, S. N., Thase, M. E., & Otto, M. W. (2006). Persistent posttraumatic stress disorder following September 11 in patients with bipolar disorder. *Journal of Clinical Psychiatry, 67*(3), 394–399.

Pollitt, E., Mathews, R. 1998. Breakfast and cognition: an integrative summary. *The American Journal of Clinical Nutrition*. V67: 804S -13S.

Pope, H. G., Poliakoff, M. B., Parker, M. P., Boynes, M., & Hudson, J. I. (2007). Is dissociative amnesia a culture-bound syndrome? Findings from a survey of historical literature. *Psychological Medicine, 37*(2), 225–233.

Pormerleau, C. S., & Pormerleau, O. F. (1994). Euphoriant effects of nicotine. *Tobacco Control, 3*, 374.

Posthuma, D., de Geus, E. J. C., & Deary, I. J. (2009). The genetics of intelligence. In T. E. Goldberg & D. R. Weinberger (Eds.), *The Genetics of Cognitive Neuroscience*. Cambridge, MA: MIT Press.

Postman, L. (1975). Tests of the generality of the principle of encoding specificity. *Memory & Cognition, 3*, 663–672.

Powers, M. H. (1984). A computer-assisted problem-solving method for beginning chemistry students. *The Journal of Computers in Mathematics and Science Teaching, 4*(1), 13–19.

Pratkanis, A. R. (1992). The cargo-cult science of subliminal persuasion. *Skeptical Inquirer, 16*, 260–272.

Pratkanis, A. R., & Greenwald, A. G. (1988). Recent perspectives on unconscious processing: Still no marketing applications. *Psychology and Marketing, 5*, 337–353.

Pratt, J. A. (1991). Psychotropic drug tolerance and dependence: Common underlying mechanisms? In E. Pratt (Ed.), *The biological bases of drug tolerance and dependence* (pp. 2–28). London: Academic Press/Harcourt Brace Jovanovich.

Premack, D. (2004). Is language the key to human intelligence? *Science, 303*(5656), 318–320.

Preston, J. D., O'Neal, J. H., & Talaga, M. C. (2008). *Handbook of clinical psychopharmacology for therapists* (5th ed.). Oakland, CA: New Harbinger.

Priester, J. M., & Petty, R. E. (1995). Source attributions and persuasion: Perceived honesty as a determinant of message scrutiny. *Personality and Social Psychology Bulletin, 21*, 637–654.

Prigerson, H. G., Bierhals, A. J., Kasi, S. V., Reynolds, C. F., Shear, M. K., Day, N., Beery, L. C., Newsome, J. T., & Jacobs, S. (1997). Traumatic grief as a risk factor for mental and physical morbidity. *American Journal of Psychiatry, 154I*, 616–623.

Prochaska, J. O., & Norcross, J. C. (2003). *Systems of psychotherapy* (5th ed.). Belmont, CA: Wadsworth.

Puetz, T. W., Flowers, S. S., & O'Connor, P. J. (2008). A randomized controlled trial of the effect of aerobic exercise training on feelings of energy and fatigue in sedentary young adults with persistent fatigue. *Psychotherapy and Psychosomatics, 77*(3), 167–174.

Pullum, G. K. (1991). *The great Eskimo vocabulary hoax: And other irreverent essays on the study of language.* Chicago: University of Chicago Press.

Pumariega, A. J., & Gustavson, C. R. (1994). Eating attitudes in African-American women: The essence. *Eating Disorders: Journal of Treatment and Prevention, 2*, 5–16.

Purcell, S. (1985, August). *Relation between religious orthodoxy and marital sexual functioning.* Paper presented at the meeting of the American Psychological Association, Los Angeles.

Purdy, D., Eitzen, D., & Hufnagel, R. (1982). Are athletes also students? The educational attainment of college athletes. *Social Problems, 29*, 439–448.

Purves, D., Augustine, G. J., Fitzpatrick, D., Hall, W. C., LaMantia, A.-S., McNamara, J. O., & White, L. E. (2008). *Neuroscience* (4th ed., pp. 15–16). Sunderland, ME: Sinauer.

Putnam, S. P., & Stifter, C. A. (2002). Development of approach and inhibition in the first year: Parallel findings for motor behavior, temperament ratings and directional cardiac response. *Developmental Science, 5*, 441–451.

Puts, D. A., Jordan, C. L., & Breedlove, S. M. (2006). O brother, where art thou? The fraternal birth-order effect on male sexual orientation. *Proceedings of the National Academy of Sciences, USA, 103*(28), 10531–10532.

Quintero, J. E., Kuhlman, S. J., & McMahon, D. G. (2003). The biological clock nucleus: A multiphasic oscillator network regulated by light. *Journal of Neuroscience, 23*, 8070–8076.

Raaijmakers, J. G. W., & Shiffrin, R. M. (1992). Models for recall and recognition. *Annual Review of Psychology, 43*, 205–234.

Rabins, P., Appleby, B. S., Brandt, J., DeLong, M. R., Dunn, L. B., Gabriels, L., et al. (2009). Scientific and ethical issues related to deep brain stimulation for disorders of mood, behavior, and thought. *Archives of General Psychiatry, 66*(9), 931–937.

Rachman, S. (1990). The determinants and treatments of simple phobias. *Advances in Behavioral Research and Therapy, 12*(1), 1–30.

Rachman, S. J., & Hodgson, R. J. (1980). *Obsessions and compulsions.* Englewood Cliffs, NJ: Prentice Hall.

Rahman, Q., & Hull, M. S. (2005). An empirical test of the kin selection hypothesis for male homosexuality. *Archives of Sexual Behavior, 34*, 461–467.

Raikkonen, K., Matthews, K. A., & Salomon, K. (2003). Hostility predicts metabolic syndrome risk factors in children and adolescents. *Health Psychology, 22*, 279–286.

Rainforth, M. V., Schneider, R. H., Nidich, S. I., Gaylord-King, C., Salerno, J. W., & Anderson, J. W. (2007). Stress reduction programs in patients with elevated blood pressure: A systematic review and meta-analysis. *Current Hypertension Reports, 9*, 520–528.

Ramachandran, V. S., & Blakeslee, S. (1998). *Phantoms in the brain*. New York: Quill William Morrow.

Ramachandran, V. S., & Hubbard, E. M. (2003). Hearing colors, tasting shapes. *Scientific American, 5*, 52–59.

Ranke, M. B., & Saenger, P. (2001, July 28). Turner's syndrome. *Lancet, 358*(9278), 309–314.

Rao, S. C., Rainer, G., & Miller, E. K. (1997) Integration of what and where in the primate prefrontal cortex. *Science, 276*, 821–824.

Rasenberger, J. (2006). Nightmare on Austin Street. *American Heritage Magazine, 57*(5), Retrieved July 8, 2010, from http://www.americanheritage.com/articles/magazine/ah/2006/5/2006_5_65.shtml

Ratey, J. J., & Hagerman, E. (2008). *Spark: The revolutionary new science of exercise and the brain*. New York: Little, Brown.

Rauch, S. L., Shin, L. M., & Wright, C. I. (2003). Neuroimaging studies of amygdala function in anxiety disorders. *Annals of the New York Academy of Sciences, 985*, 389–410.

Raynor, H. A., & Epstein, L. H. (2001). Dietary variety, energy regulation and obesity. *Psychological Bulletin, 127*(3), 325–341.

Reason, J. T., & Brand, J. J. (1975). *Motion sickness*. London: Academic Press.

Reder, L. M., Anderson, J. R., & Bjork, R. A. (1974). A semantic interpretation of encoding specificity. *Journal of Experimental Psychology, 102*, 648–656.

Reichborn-Kjennerud, T. (2008). Genetics of personality disorders. *Psychiatric Clinics of North America, 31*, 421.

Reinders, A., Quak, J., Nijenhuis, E. R., Korf, J., Paans, A. M., Willemsen, A. T., & den Boer, J. A. (2001, June). *Identity state-dependent processing of neutral and traumatic scripts in dissociative identity disorder as assessed by PET*. Oral presentation at the 7th Annual Meeting of the Organisation for Human Brain Mapping, Brighton, UK. *NeuroImage 13*(Suppl.), S1093.

Reiner, W. G. (1999). Assignment of sex in neonates with ambiguous genitalia. *Current Opinions in Pediatrics, 11*(4), 363–365.

Reiner, W. G. (September 29, 2000). *The genesis of gender identity in the male: Prenatal androgen effects on gender identity and gender role*. Oral presentation at New York University Child Study Center, Grand Rounds Summary.

Reinius, B. & Jazin, E. (2009). mRNA expression of Y-linked transcripts in 12 regions of the prenatal human male brain. *Molecular Psychiatry, 14*(11), 987.

Reisenzein, R. (1983). The Schachter theory of emotion: Two decades later. *Psychological Bulletin, 94*, 239–264.

Reisenzein, R. (1994). Pleasure-arousal theory and the intensity of emotions. *Journal of Personality and Social Psychology, 7*(6), 1313–1329.

Reiter, R., & Milburn, A. (1994). Exploring effective treatment for chronic pelvic pain. *Comtemporary Ob/Gyn, 3*, 84–103.

Renchler, R. (1993). Poverty and learning. *ERIC Digest No. 83*, Eugene, OR: ERIC Clearinghouse on Educational Management. (ERIC Document Reproduction Service No. ED 357 433).

Renner, M. J., & Mackin, R. S. (1998). A life stress instrument for classroom use. *Teaching of Psychology, 25*, 47.

Rescorla, R. (1988). Pavlovian conditioning—It's not what you think. *American Psychologist, 43*, 151–160.

Rescorla, R. A. (1968). Probability of shock in the presence and absence of CS in fear conditioning. *Journal of Comparative and Physiological Psychology, 66*, 1–5.

Resick, P. A., Monson, C. M., & Rizvi, S. (2008). Posttraumatic stress disorder. In D. H. Barlow (Ed.), *Clinical handbook of psychological disorders* (pp. 65–122). New York: Guilford Press.

Reynolds, C. F.; Frank, E.; Perel, J. M.; Imber, S. D.; Cornes, C.; Miller, M. D.; Mazumdar, S.; Houck, P. R.; Dew, M. A.; Stack, J. A.; Pollock, B. G.; & Kuper, D. J. (1999). Nortriptyline and interpersonal psychotherapy as maintenance therapies for recurrent depression: A randomized controlled trial in patients older than 59 years. *Journal of the American Medical Association 281* (1), 39–45.

Reynolds, J. A. (2002). *Succeeding in college: study skills and strategies, 2e*. Needham Heights: Allyn and Bacon.

Reynolds, R. M., Strachan, M Frier, B. M., Fowkes, F. G., Mitchell, R., Seckl, J. R., Deary, I. J., Walker, B. R., & Prices, J. F. (2010). Morning cortisol levels and cognitive abilities in people with Type 2 diabetes. *American Diabetes Association: Diabetes Care, 33*(4), 714–720.

Rezvani, A. H., & Levin, E. D. (2001). Cognitive effects of nicotine. *Biological Psychiatry, 49*, 258–267.

Rhine, J. B. (1935). *Extrasensory perception*. Boston: Bruce Humphries.

RIA Novosti. (2010, January 7). Some 80 people die from drug abuse in Russia every day—minister. Retrieved June 30, 2010, from http://en.rian.ru/russia/20100616/159443005.html

Richards, C. F., & Lowe, R. A. (2003). Researching racial and ethnic disparities in emergency medicine. *Academic Emergency Medicine, 10*(11), 1169–1175.

Richardson, J., & Morgan, R. (1997). *Reading to learn in the content areas*. Belmont, CA: Wadsworth.

Rideout, T. M. (2005). Eating disorders: Anorexia and bulimia. Eating Disorders Infocenter, Holistic online.com. Retrieved March 30, 2005, from www.holistic-online.com/Remedies/EatingD/EatD_anorexia-bulemia.htm

Rideout, V. J., Foehr, U. G., & Roberts, D. F. (2010). *Generation M2: Media in the lives of 8- to 18-year-olds*: Menlo Park, CA: Henry J. Kaiser Family Foundation.

Ridley, H. (2002). Crop Circle Confession. *Scientific American*. Retrieved February 17, 2010, from http://www.sciam.com/article.cfm?chanID=sa006&articleID=00038B16-ED5F-1D29-97CA809EC588EEDF

Ridley, M. (1999). *Genome: The autobiography of a species in 23 chapters*. London: Fourth Estate.

Rieber, R. W., & Robinson, D. K. (2001). *Wilhelm Wundt in history: The making of a scientific psychology*. New York: Kluwer Academic.

Rizzolatti, G., Fabbri-Destro, M., & Cattaneo, L. (2009). Mirror neurons and their clinical relevance. *Nature Clinical Practice Neurology, 5*(1), 24–34.

Ro, E., & Clark, L. A. (2009). Psychosocial functioning in the context of diagnosis: Assessment and theoretical issues. *Psychological Assessment, 21*(3), 313–324.

Roberto, C. A., Baik, J., Harris, J. L., & Brownell, K. D. (2010). Influence of licensed characters on children's taste and snack preferences. *Pediatrics*. Retrieved from http://pediatrics.aappublications.org/cgi/content/abstract/peds.2009-3433v1.doi:10.1542/peds.2009-3433

Robins, L. N. (1996). *Deviant children grown up*. Baltimore: Williams & Wilkins.

Robinson, F. P. (1946). *Effective study*. New York: Harper & Bros.

Robinson, J. W., & Preston, J. D. (1976). Equal status contact and modification of racial prejudice: A reexamination of the contact hypothesis. *Social Forces, 54*, 911–924.

Robinson, P. (1993). *Freud and his critics*. Berkeley: University of California Press.

Rodgers, J. E. (1992). *Psychosurgery: Damaging the brain to save the mind*. New York: HarperCollins.

Rodin, J. (1981). Current status of the internal-external hypothesis for obesity. *American Psychologist, 36*, 361–372.

Rodin, J. (1985). Insulin levels, hunger, and food intake: An example of feedback loops in body weight regulation. *Health Psychology, 4*, 1–24.

Rodin, J., & Langer, E. J. (1977). Long-term effects of a control-relevant intervention among the institutionalized aged. *Journal of Personality and Social Psychology, 35*, 275–282.

Roediger, H. L. (1990). Implicit memory: Retention without remembering. *American Psychologist, 45*, 1043–1056.

Roediger, H. L., III (2000). Why retrieval is the key process to understanding human memory. In E. Tulving (Ed.), *Memory, consciousness and the brain: The Tallinn Conference* (pp. 52–75). Philadelphia: Psychology Press.

Roediger, H. L., III, & Crowder, R. G. (1976). A serial position effect in recall of United States presidents. *Bulletin of the Psychonomic Society, 8*, 275–278.

Roediger, H. L., III, & Guynn, M. J. (1996). Retrieval processes. In E. L. Bjork & R. A. Bjork (Eds.), *Memory* (pp. 197–236). New York: Academic Press.

Roethlisberger, F. J. & Dickson, W. J. (1939) *Management and the Worker*. Cambridge, MA: Harvard University Press.

Roffman, R. A., Stephens, R. S., Simpson, E. E., & Whitaker, D. L. (1988). Treatment of marijuana dependence: Preliminary results. *Journal of Psychoactive Drugs, 20*(1), 129–137.

Roffwarg, H. P., Muzio, J. N., & Dement, W. C. (1966). Ontogenetic development of the human sleep-dream cycle. *Science, 152*(3722), 604–619.

Rogers, C. (1961). *On becoming a person: A therapist's view of psychotherapy.* Boston: Houghton/Mifflin.

Rogers, R. W., & Mewborn, C. R. (1976). Fear appeals and attitude change: Effects of a threat's noxiousness, probability of occurrence, and the efficacy of the coping responses. *Journal of Personality and Social Psychology, 34,* 54–61.

Rogoff, B. (1994). Developing understanding of the idea of communities of learners. *Mind, Culture, and Activity, 1*(4), 209–229.

Rohde, A., & Marneros, A. (1993). Postpartum psychoses: Onset and long-term course. *Psychopathology, 26,* 203–209.

Rohde, P., Silva, S. G., Tonev, S. T., Kennard, B. D., Vitiello, B., Kratochvil, C. J., Reinecke, M. A., Curry, J. F., Simons, A. D., March, J. S. (2008). Achievement and maintenance of sustained improvement during TADS continuation and maintenance therapy. *Archives of General Psychiatry, 65*(4), 447–455.

Roid, G. H. (2003). *Stanford-Binet intelligence scales* (5th ed.). Itasca, IL: Riverside.

Roos, P. E., & Cohen, L. H. (1987). Sex roles and social support as moderators of life stress adjustment. *Journal of Personality and Social Psychology, 3,* 576–585.

Rosch, E. (1973). On the internal structure of perceptual and semantic categories. In T. E. Moore (Ed.), *Cognitive development and the acquisition of language* (pp. 111–144). New York: Academic Press.

Rosch, E. (1977). Human categorization. In N. Warren (Ed.), *Advances in cross-cultural psychology, 1* (pp. 1–72). London: Academic Press.

Rosch, E., & Mervis, C. (1975). Family resemblances: Studies in the internal structures of categories. *Cognitive Psychology, 7,* 573–605.

Rosch, E., Mervis, C. B., Gray, W. D., Johnson, D. M., & Boyes-Braem, P. (1976). Basic objects in natural categories. *Cognitive Psychology, 8,* 382–439.

Rosch-Heider, E. (1972). Universals in color naming and memory. *Journal of Experimental Psychology, 93,* 10–20.

Rosch-Heider, E., & Olivier, D. C. (1972). The structure of the color space in naming and memory for two languages. *Cognitive Psychology, 3,* 337–354.

Rose, S., Kamin, L. J., & Lewontin, R. C. (1984). *Not in our genes: Biology, ideology and human nature.* Harmondsworth, UK: Penguin.

Rosenfeld, J. P., Labkovsky, E., Winograd, M., Lui, M. A., Vandenboom, C., & Chedid, E. (2008). The Complex Trial Protocol (CTP): A new, countermeasure-resistant, accurate, P300-based method for detection of concealed information. *Psychophysiology, 45*(6), 906–919.

Rosenhan, D. L. (1973), On being sane in insane places, *Science, 179,* 250–258.

Rosenman, R. H., Brand, R. I., Jenkins, C. D., Friedman, M., Straus, R., & Wurm, M. (1975). Coronary heart disease in the Western Collaborative Group Study, final follow-up experience of 2 years. *Journal of the American Medical Association, 233,* 812–817.

Rosenthal, A. M. (1964). *Thirty-eight witnesses: The Kitty Genovese case.* New York: McGraw-Hill.

Rosenthal, R., & Jacobson, L. (1968). *Pygmalion in the classroom.* New York: Holt, Rinehart & Winston.

Ross, H. E., & Ross, G. M. (1976). Did Ptolemy understand the moon illusion? *Perception, 5,* 377–385.

Rossini, P. M., Altamura, C., Ferreri, F., Melgari, J. M., Tecchio, F., Tombini, M., Pasqualetti, P., & Vernieri, F. (2007). Neuroimaging experimental studies on brain plasticity in recovery from stroke. *Eura Medicophys, 43*(2), 241–254.

Rothbaum, B. O., Hodges, L. F., Kooper, R., Opdyke, D., Williford, J. S., & North, M. (1995). Effectiveness of computer-generated (virtual reality) graded exposure in the treatment of acrophobia. *American Journal of Psychiatry, 152,* 626–628.

Rothbaum, R., Weisz, J., Pott, M., Miyake, K., & Morelli, G. (2000). Attachment and culture: Security in Japan and the U.S. *American Psychologist, 55,* 1093–1104.

Rothenberg, A. (2001). Bipolar illness, creativity, and treatment. *Psychiatric Quarterly, 72*(2), 131–147.

Rotter, J. B. (1954). *Social learning and clinical psychology.* New York: Prentice Hall.

Rotter, J. B. (1966). Generalized expectancies for internal versus external control of reinforcements. *Psychological Monographs, 80* [Whole no. 609].

Rotter, J. B. (1978). Generalized expectancies for problem solving and psychotherapy. *Cognitive Therapy and Research, 2,* 1–10.

Rotter, J. B. (1981). The psychological situation in social learning theory. In D. Magnusson (Ed.), *Toward a psychology of situations: An interactional perspective.* Hillsdale, NJ: Lawrence Erlbaum.

Rotter, J. B. (1990). Internal versus external control of reinforcement: A case history of a variable. *American Psychologist, 45,* 489–493.

Rotton, J., & Frey, J. (1985). Air pollution, weather, and violent crime: Concomitant time-series analysis of archival data. *Journal of Personality and Social Psychology, 49,* 1207–1220.

Rotton, J., Frey, J., Barry, T., Milligan, M., & Fitzpatrick, M. (1979). The air pollution experience and physical aggression. *Journal of Applied Social Psychology, 9,* 397–412.

Rouse, B. A. (1998). *Substance and mental health statistics source book.* Rockville, MD: Department of Health and Human Services, Substance Abuse and Mental Health Services Administration (SAMHSA).

Rouw, R., & Scholte, H. S. (2007, May 21). Increased structural connectivity in grapheme-color synesthesia. *Nature Neuroscience 10,* 792–797.

Rovet, J. (1993). The psychoeducational characteristics of children with Turner's syndrome. *Journal of Learning Disabilities, 26,* 333–341.

Rowan, J. (2001). *Ordinary ecstacsy.* Hove, UK: Brunner-Routledge.

Rowe, D. C., Almeida, D. A., & Jacobson, K. C. (1999). School context and genetic influences on aggression in adolescence. *Psychological Science, 10,* 277–280.

Roysircai-Sodowsky, G. R., & Maestas, M. V. (2000). Acculturation, ethnic identity, and acculturative stress: Evidence and measurement. In R. H. Dana (Ed.), *Handbook of cross-cultural and multicultural assessment* (pp. 131–172). Mahwah, NJ: Lawrence Erlbaum.

Ruble, D., Alvarez, J., Bachman, M., Cameron, J., Fuligni, A., Garcia Coll, C., & Rhee, E. (2004). The development of a sense of "we": The emergence and implications of children's collective identity. In M. Bennett & F. Sani (Eds.), *The development of the social self.* New York: Psychology Press.

Rudd, P., & Osterberg, L. G. (2002). Hypertension: Context, pathophysiology, and management. In E. J. Topol (Ed.), *Textbook of cardiovascular medicine* (pp. 91–122). Philadelphia: Lippincott Williams & Wilkins.

Ruff, R. M., Iverson, G. L., Barth, J. T., Bush, S. S., & Broshek, D. K. (2009). Recommendations for diagnosing a mild traumatic brain injury: A National Academy of Neuropsychology education paper. *Archives of Clinical Neuropsychology, 24*(1), 3–10.

Ruhe, H. G., Mason, N. S., & Schene, A. H. (2007). Mood is indirectly related to serotonin, norepinephrine and dopamine levels in humans: A meta-analysis of monoamine depletion studies. *Molecular Psychiatry, 12*(4), 331–359.

Rumelhart, D. E., Hinton, G. E., & McClelland, J. L. (1986). A general framework for parallel distributed processing. In D. E. Rumelhart, J. L. McClelland, & the PDP Research Group (Eds.), *Parallel distributed processing: Explorations in the microstructure of cognition: Vol. 1. Foundations* (pp. 45–76). Cambridge, MA: MIT Press.

Rundus, D. (1971). An analysis of rehearsal processes in free recall. *Journal of Experimental Psychology, 89,* 63–77.

Rusbult, C. E., Finkey, E. J., & Kumashiro, M. (2009a). The Michelangelo phenomenon. *Current Directions in Psychological Science, 18*(1), 305–309.

Rusbult, C. E., Kumashiro, M., Finkel, E., Kirchner, J., Coolsen, M., Stocker, S., & Clarke, J. (2009b). *A longitudinal study of the Michelangelo phenomenon in marital relationships.* Unpublished manuscript, Vrije Universiteit Amsterdam, The Netherlands.

Rusbult, C. E., Kumashiro, M., Kubacka, K. E., & Finkel, E. J. (2009c). "The part of me that you bring out": Ideal similarity and the Michelangelo phenomenon. *Journal of Personality and Social Psychology, 96,* 61–82.

Ruscio, A. M., Borkovec, T. D., & Ruscio, J. (2001). A taxometric investigation of the latent structure of worry. *Journal of Abnormal Psychology, 110,* 413–422.

Russell, D. E. (1986). *The secret trauma: Incest in the lives of girls and women.* New York: Basic Books.

Rutherford, A. (2000). Mary Cover Jones (1896–1987). *The Feminist Psychologist, 27*(3), 25.

Ryan, R. M., & Deci, E. L. (2000). Intrinsic and extrinsic motivations: Classic definitions and new directions. *Contemporary Educational Psychology, 25,* 54–67.

Rydell, R. J., & Boucher, K. L. (2010). Capitalizing on multiple social identities to prevent stereotype threat: The moderating role of self-esteem. *Personality and Social Psychology Bulletin, 36*(2), 239–250.

Sabatini, E., Della Penna, S., Franciotti, R., Ferretti, A., Zoccolotti, P., Rossini, P. M., Romani, G. L., & Gainotti, G. (2009). Brain structures activated by overt and covert emotional visual stimuli. *Brain Research Bulletin, 79*(5), 258–264.

Sacks, O. (1990). *The man who mistook his wife for a hat and other clinical tales.* New York: HarperPerennial.

Sadker, M., & Sadker, D. (1994). *Failing at fairness: How America's schools cheat girls.* New York: Scribner.

Sadock, B. J., Kaplan, H. I., & Sadock, V. A. (2007). *Kaplan & Sadock's synopsis of psychiatry: Behavioral sciences/clinical psychiatry* (10th ed.). Philadelphia: Lippincott Williams & Wilkins.

Sagan, C. (1977). *The dragons of Eden: Speculations on the evolution of human intelligence.* New York: Random House.

Saha, S., Chant, D., Welham, J., & McGrath, J. (2005). A systematic review of the prevalence of schizophrenia. *PLoS Medicine, 2*(5), e141.

Salend, S. J. (1987). Contingency management systems. *Academic Therapy, 22,* 245–253.

Salovey, P., & Mayer, J. D. (1990). Emotional intelligence. *Imagination, cognition, and personality, 9,* 185–211.

Salthouse, T. A. (1984). The skill of typing. *Scientific American, 250*(2), 128–135.

Sanders, L. D., Weber-Fox, C. M., & Neville, H. J. (2008). Varying degrees of plasticity in different subsystems within language. In J. R. Pomerantz & M. Crair (Eds.), *Topics in integrative neuroscience: From cells to cognition.* New York: Cambridge University Press.

Sanders, S., Hill, B., Yarber, W., Graham, C., Crosby, R., & Milhausen, R. (2010). Misclassification bias: Diversity in conceptualisations about having "had sex." *Sexual Health, 7*(1), 31–34.

Sands, L. P., & Meredith, W. (1992). Intellectual functioning in late midlife. *Journal of Gerontological and Psychological Science, 47,* 81–84.

Sanz, C., Andrieu, S., Sinclair, A., Hanaire, H., & Vellas, B. (2009). Diabetes is associated with a slower rate of cognitive decline in Alzheimer disease. *Neurology, 73,* 1359–1366.

Saper, C. B., Chou, T. C., & Scammell, T. E. (2001). The sleep switch: Hypothalamic control of sleep and wakefulness. *Trends in Neurosciences, 24,* 726–731.

Sapir, E. S. (1921). *Language: An introduction to the study of speech.* New York: Harcourt, Brace.

Sapolsky, R. M. (2004). *Why zebras don't get ulcers* (3rd ed., pp. 1, 144–145). New York: Owl Books.

Sarbin, T. R., & Coe, W. C. (1972). *Hypnosis: A social psychological analysis of influence communication.* New York: Holt, Rinehart, & Winston.

Sastry, K. S., Karpova, Y., Prokopovich, S., Smith, A. J., Essau, B., Gersappe, A., Carson, J. P., Weber, M. J., Register, T. C., Chen, Y. Q., Penn, R. B., & Kulik, G. (2007). Epinephrine protects cancer cells from apoptosis via activation of cAMP-dependent protein kinase and BAD phosphorylation. *Journal of Biological Chemistry, 282*(19), 14094–14100.

Satterly, D. (1987). Piaget and education. In R. L. Gregory (Ed.), *The Oxford companion to the mind* (pp. 110–143). Oxford: Oxford University Press.

Sattler, J. M. (1977). The effects of therapist–client racial similarity. In A. S. Gurman & A. M. Razin (Eds.), *Effective psychotherapy: A handbook of research* (pp. 252–290). Elmsford, NY: Pergamon.

Saunders, B., & Goddard, C. R. (1998). Why do we condone the "physical punishment" of children? *Children Australia, 23,* 23–28.

Savage-Rumbaugh, S., & Lewin, R. (1994). *Kanzi.* New York: Wiley.

Savage-Rumbaugh, S., Shanker, S., & Taylor, T. J. (1998). *Apes, language and the human mind.* Oxford, UK: Oxford University Press.

Savic, I. & Lindstrom, P. (2008). PET and MRI show differences in cerebral asymmetry and functional connectivity between homo- and heterosexual subjects. *Proceedings of the National Academy of Sciences, USA, 105*(27), 9403–9408.

Savic, I., Berglund, H., & Lindstrom, P. (2005). Brain response to putative pheromones in homosexual men. *Proceedings of the National Academy of Sciences, USA, 102*(20), 7356–7361.

Scarmeas, N., Luchsinger, J. A., Mayeux, R., & Stern, Y. (2007). Mediterranean diet and Alzheimer disease mortality. *Neurology, 69,* 1084–1093.

Scarpa, A., Raine, A., Venables, P. H., & Mednick, S. A. (1995). The stability of inhibited/uninhibited temperament from ages 3 to 11 years in Mauritian children. *Journal of Abnormal Child Psychology, 23,* 607–618.

Schachter, S., & Singer, J. E. (1962). Cognitive, social and physiological determinants of emotional states. *Psychological Review, 69,* 379–399.

Schafer, M., & Crichlow S. (1996). Antecedents of groupthink: A quantitative study. *Journal of Conflict Resolution, 40,* 415–435.

Schalock, R. L., Borthwick-Duffy, S. A., Buntinz, W. H. E., Coultier, D. L., & Craig, E. M. P. (2010). *Intellectual disability: Definition, classification, and systems of supports* (11th ed.): American Association on Intellectual and Developmental Disabilities.

Schapiro, A. C. & McClelland, J. L. (2009). A connectionist model of a continuous developmental transition in the balance scale task. Cognition, *110*(1), 395–411.

Schiller, P. H., & Carvey, C. E. (2005). The Hermann grid illusion revisited. Perception, 34(11), 1375–1397.

Schmitt, D. P. (2002). Personality, attachment and sexuality related to dating relationship outcomes: Contrasting three perspectives on personal attribute interaction. *British Journal of Social Psychology, 41*(4), 589–610.

Schmitz, C., Wagner, J., & Menke, E. (2001). The interconnection of childhood poverty and homelessness: Negative impact/points of access. *Families in Society, 82*(1), 69–77.

Schnabel, J. (1994). *Round in circles* (pp. 267–277). London: Hamish Hamilton.

Schneider, K. J., Bugental, J. F. T., & Fraser, J. F. (Eds.). (2001). *Handbook of humanistic psychology.* Thousand Oaks, CA: Sage.

Schneider, R. H., Staggers, F., Alexander, C. N., Sheppard, W., Rainforth, M., Kondwani, K., Smith, S., & King, C. G. (1995). A randomized controlled trial of stress reduction for hypertension in older African Americans. *Hypertension, 26*(5), 820–827.

Schneider, R., Nidich, S., Kotchen, J. M., Kotchen, T., Grim, C., Rainforth, M., King, C. G., & Salerno, J. (2009). Abstract 1177: Effects of stress reduction on clinical events in African Americans with coronary heart disease: A randomized controlled trial, *Circulation, 120,* S461.

Schneider, W., Dumais, S., & Shriffrin, R. (1984). *Automatic and control processing and attention.* London: Academic Press.

Schneidman, E. (1983). *Death of man.* New York: Jason Aronson.

Schneidman, E. (1994). *Death: Current perspectives.* New York: McGraw-Hill.

Schols, L., Haan, J., Riess, O., Amoiridis, G., & Przuntek, H. (1998). Sleep disturbance in spinocerebellar ataxias: Is the SCA3 mutation a cause of restless legs syndrome? *Neurology, 51,* 1603–1607

Schreiber, F. R. (1973, reissued 1995). *Sybil.* New York: Warner.

Schroeder, S. R. (2000). Mental retardation and developmental disabilities influenced by environmental neurotoxic insults. *Environmental Health Perspectives 108*(Suppl. 3), 395–399.

Schroth, M. L., & McCormack, W. A. (2000). Sensation seeking and need for achievement among study-abroad students. *The Journal of Social Psychology, 140,* 533–535.

Schultz, D. P., & Schultz, S. E. (2004). *A History of Modern Psychology,* pp. 239–242. Belmont, CA: Wadsworth.

Schwanenflugel, P., & Rey, M. (1986). Interlingual semantic facilitation: Evidence from common representational system in the bilingual lexicon. *Journal of Memory and Language, 25,* 605–618.

Schwartz, S. K. (2000). *Working your degree.* Retrieved March 6, 2010, from http:/ /cnnfn.cnn.com/2000/12/08/career/q_degreepsychology/

Schweickert, R. (1993). A multinomial processing tree model for degradation and redintegration in immediate recall. *Memory and Cognition, 21,* 168–175.

Schwitzgebel, E. (1999). Representation and desire: A philosophical error with consequences for theory-of-mind research. *Philosophical Psychology, 12,* 157–180.

Scott, W. D. (1908). *The theory and practice of advertising.* Boston, MA: Small, Maynard, & Company,

Scott, S. K., Young, A. W., Calder, A. J., Hellawell, D. J., Aggleton, J. P., & Johnson, M. (1997). Impaired auditory recognition of fear and anger following bilateral amygdala lesions. *Nature, 385*(6613), 254–257.

Security Director's Report (2008). Experts identify four trends in workplace violence. *Institute of Management and Administration, Inc., 8*(6), 1–15.

Segall, M. H., Campbell, D. T., & Herskovits, M. J. (1966). *The influence of culture on perception.* Indianapolis, IN: Bobbs-Merrill.

Segerstrom, S. C., Taylor, S. E., Kemeny, M. E., & Fahey, J. L. (1998). Optimism is associated with mood, coping, and immune change in response to stress. *Journal of Personality and Social Psychology, 74*(6), 1646–1655.

Segerstrom, S.C., & Sephton, S.E. (2010). Optimistic expectancies and cell-mediated immunity: The role of positive affect. *Psychological Science, 21*(3), 448–455.

Seligman, M. (1975). *Helplessness: Depression, development and death.* New York: W. H. Freeman.

Seligman, M. (1989). *Helplessness.* New York: W. H. Freeman.

Seligman, M. (1970). On the generality of the laws of learning. *Psychological Review, 77,* 406–418.

Seligman, M. (1995). The effectiveness of psychotherapy: The *Consumer Reports* study. *American Psychologist, 50*, 965–975.

Seligman, M. (1998). *Learned optimism: How to change your mind and your life* (2nd ed.). New York: Pocket Books.

Seligman, M., & Maier, S. F. (1967). Failure to escape traumatic shock. *Journal of Experimental Psychology, 74*, 1–9.

Seligman, M. (2002). *Authentic happiness*. New York: Free Press.

Selye, H. (1956). *The stress of life*. New York: McGraw-Hill.

Selye, H. (1976). *The stress of life* (Rev. ed.). New York: McGraw-Hill.

Selye, H. A. (1936). Syndrome produced by diverse nocuous agents. *Nature, 138*, 32.

Serban, G., George, A., Siegel, S., DeLeon, M., & Gaffney, M. (1990). Computed tomography scans and negative symptoms in schizophrenia: Chronic schizophrenics with negative symptoms and nonenlarged lateral ventricles. *Acta Psychiatrica Scandinavica, 81*(5), 441–447.

Shackelford, T. K., Buss, D. M., & Bennett, K. (2002). Forgiveness or breakup: Sex differences in responses to a partner's infidelity. *Cognition and Emotion, 16*(2), 299–307.

Shadish, R., Cook, T. D., & Campbell, D. T. (2002). *Experimental and quasi-experimental designs for generalized causal inferences*. New York: Houghton Mifflin.

Shafiro, M. V., Himelein, M. J., & Best, D. L. (2003). Ukrainian and U.S. American females: Differences in individualism/collectivism and gender attitudes. *Journal of Cross-Cultural Psychology, 34*(3), 297–303.

Shafto, P., & Coley, J. D. (2003). Development of categorization and reasoning in the natural world: Novices to experts, naïve similarity to ecological knowledge. *Journal of Experimental Psychology: Learning, Memory & Cognition, 29*, 641–649.

Shafton, A. (1995). *Dream reader: Contemporary approaches to the understanding of dreams (SUNY series in dream studies)* (pp. 40–46). New York: State University of New York Press.

Shah, P. M. (1991). Prevention of mental handicaps in children in primary health care. *Bulletin of the World Health Organization, 69*, 779–789.

Shapiro, A. K., & Shapiro, E. (1997). *The powerful placebo*. Baltimore: Johns Hopkins University Press.

Shapiro, F. (2001). *Eye movement desensitization and reprocessing: Basic principles, protocols, and procedures*. New York: Guilford Press.

Shapiro, K. L., Jacobs, W. J., & LoLordo, V. M. (1980). Stimulus relevance in Pavlovian conditioning in pigeons. *Animal Learning and Behavior, 8*, 586–594.

Sharif, Z., Bradford, D., Stroup, S., & Lieberman, J. (2007). Pharmacological treatment of schizophrenia. In P. E. Nathan & J. M. Gorman (Eds.), *A guide to treatments that work* (3rd ed., pp. 203–241). New York: Oxford University Press.

Sharot, T., Delgado, M. R. & Phelps, E. A. (2004). How emotion enhances the feeling of remembering, *Nature Neuroscience, 7*(12), 1376–1380.

Shean, R. E., de Klerk, N. H., Armstrong, B. K., & Walker, N. R. (1994). Seven-year follow-up of a smoking-prevention program for children. *Australian Journal of Public Health, 18*, 205–208.

Shekelle, P. G., Hardy, M. L., Morton, S. C., Maglione, M., Mojica, W. A., Suttorp, M. J., Rhodes, S. L., Jungvig, L., & Gagné, J. (2003). Efficacy and safety of ephedra and ephedrine for weight loss and athletic performance: A metaanalysis. *Journal of the American Medical Association, 289*(12), 1537–1545.

Sheldon, S. H. (2002). Sleep in infants and children. In T. L. Lee-Chiong, M. J. Sateia, & M. A. Carskadon (Eds.), *Sleep medicine* (pp. 99–103). Philadelphia: Hanley & Belfus.

Shepard, R. N., & Metzler, J. (1971). Mental rotation of three-dimensional objects. *Science, 171*, 701–703.

Shepard, T. H. (2001). *Catalog of teratogenic agents* (10th ed.). Baltimore: Johns Hopkins University Press.

Sherif, M. (1936). *The psychology of social norms*. New York: Harper & Row.

Sherif, M., Harvey, O. J., White, B. J., Hood, W. R., & Sherif, C. W. (1961). *Intergroup conflict and cooperation: The Robber's Cave experiment*. Norman: University of Oklahoma Book Exchange.

Sherry, P. (1991). Person environment fit and accident prediction. *Journal of Business and Psychology, 5*, 411–416.

Sherry, P., Gaa, A., Thurlow-Harrison, S., Graber, K., Clemmons, J., & Bobulinski, M. (2003). *Traffic accidents, job stress, and supervisor support in the trucking industry*. Paper presented at the International Institute for Intermodal Transportation, University of Denver, CO.

Shields, B. J., & Smith, G. A. (2009). Cheerleading-related injuries in the United States: A prospective surveillance study. *Journal of Athletic Training, 44*(6), 567–577.

Shore, L. A. (1990). Skepticism in light of scientific literacy. *Skeptical Inquirer, 15*(1), 3–4.

Shorey, G. (2001). Bystander non-intervention and the Somalia incident. *Canadian Military Journal*, 19–27.

Shorter E. (1997). *A history of psychiatry: From the era of the asylum to the age of Prozac*. New York: John Wiley & Sons.

Showalter, E. (1997). *Hystories: Hysterical epidemics and modern culture*. New York: Columbia University Press.

Shuglin, A. (1986). The background chemistry of MDMA. *Journal of Psychoactive Drugs, 18*(4), 291–304.

Shurkin, J. N. (1992). *Terman's kids; The groundbreaking study of how the gifted grow up*. Boston: Little, Brown.

Shweder, R. A., Haidt, J., Horton, R., & Joseph, C. (2008). The cultural psychology of the emotions. In M. Lewis, J. M. Haviland-Jones & L. F. Barrett (Eds.), *Handbook of emotions* (3rd ed., pp. 409–427). New York: Guilford Press.

Siegel, J. M. (2001). The REM sleep-memory consolidation hypothesis. *Science, 294*, 1058–1063.

Siegel, R. K., & West, L. J., Eds. (1975). *Hallucinations: Behavior, experience, and theory* (2nd ed.). New York: Wiley.

Siegel, S. (1969). Effects of CS habituation on eyelid conditioning. *Journal of Comparative and Physiological Psychology, 68*(2), 245–248.

Siegler, I. C., Costa, P. T., Brummett, B. H., Helms, M. J., Barefoot, J. C., Williams, R. B., Dahlstrom, G., Kaplan, B. H., Vitaliano, P. P., Nichaman, M. Z., Day, S., & Rimer, B. K. (2003). Patterns of change in hostility from college to midlife in the UNC alumni heart study predict high-risk status. *Psychosomatic Medicine, 65*, 738–745.

Siegler, R. S. (1996). *Emerging minds: The process of change in children's thinking*. New York: Oxford University Press.

Silva, C. E., & Kirsch, I. (1992). Interpretive sets, expectancy, fantasy proneness, and dissociation as predictors of hypnotic response. *Journal of Personality & Social Psychology, 63*, 847–856.

Simeon, D., Guralnik, O., Hazlett, E. A., Spiegel-Cohen, J., Hollander, E., & Buchsbaum, M. S. (2000). Feeling unreal: A PET study of depersonalization disorder. *American Journal of Psychiatry, 157*, 1782–1788.

Simon, D. A., & Bjork, R. A. (2001). Metacognition in motor learning. *Journal of Experimental Psychology: Learning, memory, and cognition, 27*(4), 907–912.

Simpson, D. (2005). Phrenology and the neurosciences: Contributions of F. J. Gall and J. G. Spurzheim. *ANZ Journal of Surgery, 75*(6), 475–482.

Singer, M. T., & Lalich, J. (1995). *Cults in our midst*. San Francisco: Jossey-Bass.

Singh-Manoux, A., Richards, M., & Marmot, M. (2003). Leisure activities and cognitive function in middle age: Evidence from the Whitehall II study. *Journal of Epidemiology and Community Health, 57*, 907–913.

Skinner, B. F. (1938). *The behavior of organisms: An experimental analysis*. New York: Appleton-Century-Crofts.

Skinner, B. F. (1956). A case history in scientific method. *American Psychologist, 11*, 221–233.

Skinner, B. F. (1961). *Cumulative record: Definitive edition*. New York: Appelton-Century-Crofts.

Skinner, B. F. (1971). *Beyond freedom and dignity*. New York: Alfred A. Knopf.

Skinner, B. F. (1974). *About behaviorism*. New York: Alfred A. Knopf.

Skinner, B. F. (1989) The origins of cognitive thought. *Recent Issues in the Analysis of Behavior*, Princeton, NC: Merrill Publishing Company.

Slater, A. (2000). Visual perception in the young infant: Early organisation and rapid learning. In D. Muir & A. Slater (Eds.), *Infant development: The essential readings*. Oxford, UK: Blackwell.

Slater M., Antley, A., Davison, A., Swapp, D., Guger, C., Barker, C., Pistrang, N., & Sanchez-Vives, M. V. (2006). A virtual reprise of the Stanley Milgram obedience experiments. *PLoS ONE 1*(1), e39. doi:10.1371/journal.pone.0000039

Slipp, S. (1993). *The Freudian mystique: Freud, women and feminism*. New York: New York University Press.

Sloan, D. M., & Mizes, J. S. (1999). Foundations of behavior therapy in the contemporary healthcare context. *Clinical Psychology Review, 19*, 255–274.

Smith, D. (2001). Shock and disbelief. *Atlantic Monthly, 2*, 79–90.

Smith, J. D., & Mitchell, A. (2001). "Me? I'm not a drooler. I'm the assistant": Is it time to abandon mental retardation as a classification? *Mental Retardation, 39*(2), 144–146.

Smith, T. C., Ryan, M. A. K., Wingard, D. L., Sallis, J. F., & Kritz-Silverstein, D. (2008). New onset and persistent symptoms of post-traumatic stress disorder self-reported after deployment and combat exposures: Prospective population based U.S. military cohort study. *British Medical Journal, 336*(7640), 366–371.

Smolen, P., Baxter, D. A., Byrne, J. H., (2006) A model of the roles of essential kinases in the induction and expression of late long-term potentiation. *Biophysical Journal, 90*, 2760–2775.

Snyder, D. J., & Bartoshuk, L. M. (2009). Epidemiological studies of taste function: Discussion and perspectives. *Annals of the New York Academy of Sciences*, 1170, 574–580.

Snyder, M., Tanke, E. D., & Berscheid, E. (1977). Social perception and interpersonal behavior: On the self-fulfilling nature of social stereotypes. *Journal of Personality and Social Psychology, 35*, 656–666.

Snyder, T. D., & Dillow, S. A. (2010). Digest of education statistics 2009 (NCES Publication No. NCES 2010-013). Washington, DC: National Center for Education Statistics, Institute of Education Sciences, U.S. Department of Education.

Snyder, S. H. (2002), Forty years of neurotransmitters. *Archives of General Psychiatry, 59,* 983-994.

Söderlund, J., Schröder, J., Nordin, C., Samuelsson, M., Walther-Jallow, L., Karlsson, H., Erhardt, S., & Engberg, G. (2009). Activation of brain interleukin-1β in schizophrenia. *Molecular Psychiatry, 14*(12), 1069.

Sodowsky, G. R., Lai, E. W., & Plake, B. S. (1991). Moderating effects of socio-cultural variables on acculturation attitudes of Hispanics and Asian Americans. *Journal and Counseling and Development, 70*, 194–204.

Soomro, G. M. (2001). Obsessive-compulsive disorder. *Clinical Evidence, 6*, 754–762.

Sowell, E. R., Thompson, P. M., Holmes, C. J., Jernigan, T. L., & Toga, A. W. (1999). In vivo evidence for post-adolescent brain maturation in frontal and striatal regions. *Nature Neuroscience, 2*(10), 859–861.

Spangler, W. D. (1992). Validity of questionnaire and TAT measures of need for achievement: Two meta-analyses. *Psychological Bulletin, 112*, 140–154.

Spangler, W. J., Cosgrove, G. R., Ballantine, H. T., Jr., Cassem, E. H., Rauch, S. L., Nierenberg, A., & Price, B. H. (1996). Magnetic resonance image-guided stereotactic cingulotomy for intractable psychiatric disease. *Neurosurgery, 38*, 1071–1076.

Sparing, R., Mottaghy, F., Ganis, G., Thompson, W. L., Toepper, R., Kosslyn, S. M., & Pascual-Leone, A. (2002).Visual cortex excitability increases during visual mental imagery—A TMS study in healthy human subjects. *Brain Research, 938*, 92–97.

Spearman, C. (1904). "General intelligence" objectively determined and measured. *American Journal of Psychology, 15*, 201–293.

Speca, M., Carlson, L. E, Goodey, E., & Angen, E. (2000). A randomized wait-list controlled clinical trial: The effects of a mindfulness meditation-based stress reduction program on mood and symptoms of stress in cancer outpatients. *Psychosomatic Medicine, 6*, 2613–2622.

Sperling, G. (1960). The information available in brief visual presentations. *Psychological Monographs, 74*(11), 1–29.

Speroff, L., Glass, R. H., & Kase, N. G. (1999). Recurrent early pregnancy loss. In *Clinical Gynecologic endocrinology and infertility* (pp. 1042–1055). Philadelphia: Lippincott Williams & Wilkins.

Sperry, R. W. (1968). Mental unity following surgical disconnection of the cerebral hemispheres. *The Harvey Lectures.* Series 62, 293–323. New York: Academic Press.

Spiegel, D., Bloom, J. R., & Gottheil, E. (1989). Effects of psychosocial treatment on survival of patients with metastatic breast cancer. *Lancet, 2*, 888–891.

Springer, S. P., & Deutsch, G. (1998). *Left brain, right brain: Perspectives from cognitive neuroscience* (5th ed.). New York: Freeman.

Squire, L., & Kandel, E. (1999). *Memory: From mind to molecule.* New York: Scientific American Library.

Squire, L. R., Knowlton, B., & Musen, G. (1993). The structure and organization of memory. *Annual Review of Psychology, 44*, 453–495.

Squire, L. R., & Slater, P. C. (1978). Anterograde and retrograde memory impairment in chronic amnesia. *Neuropsychologia, 16*, 313–322.

Squire, L. R., Slater, P. C., & Chace, P. M. (1975). Retrograde amnesia: Temporal gradient in very long-term memory following electroconvulsive therapy. *Science, 187*, 77–79.

Standing, L., Conezio, J., & Haber, R. N. (1970). Perception and memory for pictures: Single-trial learning of 2500 visual stimuli. *Psychonomic Science, 19*, 73–74.

Steele, C. M. (1992). Race and the schooling of Black Americans. *The Atlantic Monthly, 269*(4), 68–78.

Steele, C. M. (1997). A threat in the air: How stereotypes shape intellectual identity and performance. *American Psychologist, 52*, 613–629.

Steele, C. M. (1999, August). Thin ice: "stereotype threat" and Black college students. *The Atlantic Monthly, 284*, 44–54.

Steele, C. M., & Aronson J. (1995). Stereotype threat and the intellectual test performance of African Americans. *Journal of Personality and Social Psychology, 69*, 797–811.

Steele, J., James, J. B., & Barnett, R. C. (2002). Learning in a man's world: Examining the perceptions of undergraduate women in male-dominated academic areas. *Psychology of Women Quarterly, 26*, 46–50.

Steen, C. (1996). Synesthesia. *Health Report with Robin Hughes.* ABC Radio National Transcripts. Retrieved June 8, 2008, from http://www.abc.net.au/rn/talks/8.30/helthrpt/hstories/hr080796.htm.

Stein, H. T. (2001). Adlerian overview of birth order characteristics. Alfred Adler Institute of San Francisco. Retrieved June 16, 2004, at http://pws.cablespeed.com/~htstein/birthord.htm

Stein, S. (1984). *Girls and boys: The limits of non-sexist rearing.* London: Chatto & Windus.

Stein-Behrens, B., Mattson, M. P., Chang, I., Yeh, M., & Sapolsky, R. (1994). Stress exacerbates neuron loss and cytoskeletal pathology in the hippocampus. *Journal of Neuroscience, 14*, 5373–5380.

Steinberg, L., & Silverberg, S. B. (1987). Influences on marital satisfaction during the middle stages of the family life cycle. *Journal of Marriage and the Family, 49*, 751–760.

Steriade, M., & McCarley, R. W. (1990). *Brainstem control of wakefulness and sleep.* New York: Plenum.

Stern, W. (1912). *The psychological methods of testing intelligence* (G. M. Whipple, Trans.) (Educational Psychology Monograph No. 13). Baltimore, MD: Warwick & York, Inc.

Sternberg, R. J. (1986). A triangular theory of love. *Psychological Review, 93*, 119–135.

Sternberg, R. J. (1988a). *The triarchic mind: A new theory of human intelligence.* New York: Viking-Penguin.

Sternberg, R. J. (1988b). Triangulating love. In R. Sternberg & M. Barnes (Eds.), *The psychology of love* (pp. 119–138). New Haven, CT: Yale University Press.

Sternberg, R. J. (1996). *Successful intelligence: How practical and creative intelligence determine success in life.* New York: Simon & Schuster.

Sternberg, R. J. (1997a). Construct validation of a triangular love scale. *European Journal of Social Psychology, 27*, 313–335.

Sternberg, R. J. (1997b). The triarchic theory of intelligence. In P. Flannagan, J. L. Genshaft, & P. L. Harrison (Eds.), *Contemporary intellectual assessment: Theories, tests, and issues* (pp. 92–104). New York: Guilford Press.

Sternberg, R. J. (2005). The triarchic theory of successful intelligence. In *Contemporary Intellectual Assessment: Theories, Tests, and Issues.* New York: Guilford Press.

Sternberg, R. J., & Grigorenko, E. L. (2006). Cultural intelligence and successful intelligence. *Group Organization Management, 31*, 27–39.

Sternberg, R. J., & Kaufman, J. C. (1998). Human abilities. *Annual Review of Psychology, 49*, 479–502.

Sternberger, R. R., et al. (1995). Social phobia: An analysis of possible developmental factors. *Journal of Abnormal Psychology, 194*, 526–531.

Stevenson, M. B., Roach, M. A., Leavitt, L. A., Miller, J. F., & Chapman, R. S. (1988). Early receptive and productive language skills in preterm and full-term 8-month-old infants. *Journal of Psycholinguistic Research, 17*(2), 169–183.

Stickgold, R., Hobson, J. A., Fosse, R., & Fosse, M. (2001). Sleep, learning and dreams: Off-line memory reprocessing. *Science, 294*, 1052–1057.

Stiff, J. B., & Mongeau, P. A. (2002). *Persuasive communication* (2nd ed.). New York: Guilford Press.

Stine, C., Xu, J., Koskela, R., McMahon, F. J., Gschwend, M., Friddle, C., Clark, C. D., McInnis, M. G., Simpson, S. G., Breschel, T. S., Vishio, E., Riskin, K., Feilotter, H., Chen, E., Shen, S., Folstein, S., Meyers, D. A., Botstein, D., Marr, T. G., & DePaulo, J. R. (1995). Evidence for linkage of bipolar disorder to chromosome 18 with a parent-of-origin effect. *American Journal of Human Genetics, 57*(6), 1384–1394.

Stitzer, M. L., & De Wit, H. (1998). Abuse liability of nicotine. In N. L. Benowitz (Ed.), *Nicotine safety and toxicity* (pp. 119–131). New York: Oxford University Press.

Stockhorst, U., Gritzmann, E., Klopp, K., Schottenfeld-Naor, Y., Hübinger, A., Berresheim, H., Steingrüber, H., & Gries, F. A. (1999). Classical conditioning of insulin effects in healthy humans. *Psychosomatic Medicine, 61*, 424–435.

Storey, A. E., Walsh, C. J., Quinton, R. L., & Wynne-Edwards, K. E. (2000). Hormonal correlates of paternal responsiveness in new and expectant fathers. *Evolution and Human Behavior 21*, 79–95.

Stowell, J. R., Kiecolt-Glaser, J. K., & Glaser, R. (2001). Perceived stress and cellular immunity: When coping counts. *Journal of Behavioral Medicine, 24*(4), 323–339.

Stratton, K., Gable, A., & McCormick, M. C. (Eds.). (2001a). *Immunization safety review: Thimerosal-containing vaccines and neurodevelopmental disorders*. Washington, DC: National Academies Press.

Stratton, K., Wilson, C. B., & McCormick, M. C. (Eds.). (2001b). *Immunization safety review: Measles-mumps-rubella vaccine and autism*. Washington, DC: National Academies Press.

Straus, M. A. (2000). Corporal punishment of children and adult depression and suicidal ideation. *Beating the devil out of them: Corporal punishment in American families and its effects on children* (pp. 60–77). New York: Lexington Books .

Straus, M. A., & Stewart, J. H. (1999). Corporal punishment by American parents: National data on prevalence, chronicity, severity, and duration, in relation to child, and family characteristics. *Clinical Child and Family Psychology Review, 2*, 55–70.

Straus, M. A., & Yodanis, C. L. (1994). Physical abuse. In M. A. Straus (Ed.), *Beating the devil out of them: Corporal punishment in American families* (pp. 81–98). San Francisco: New Lexington Press.

Strauss, A. S. (2004). The meaning of death in Northern Cheyenne culture. In A. C. G. M. Robben (Ed.), *Death, mourning, and burial: A cross-cultural reader* (pp. 71–76). Malden, MA: Blackwell.

Strawbridge, W. J., Cohen, R. D., Shema, S. J., & Kaplan, G. A. (1997). Frequent attendance at religious services and mortality over 28 years. *American Journal of Public Health, 87*, 957–961.

Strayer, D. L., & Drews, F. A. (2007). Cell-phone-induced driver distraction. *Current Directions in Psychological Science, 16*, 128–131.

Strayer, D. L., & Johnston, W. A. (2001). Driven to distraction: Dual-task studies of simulated driving and conversing on a cellular phone. *Psychological Science, 12*, 462–466.

Strayer, D. L., Drews, F. A., & Crouch, D. J. (2006). A comparison of the cell phone driver and the drunk driver. *Human Factors, 48*, 381–391.

Strober, M., Freeman, R., Lampert, C., Diamond, J., & Kaye, W. (2000). Controlled family study of anorexia nervosa and bulimia nervosa: Evidence of shared liability and transmission of partial syndromes. *American Journal of Psychiatry, 157*, 393–401.

Ströhle, A. (2008). Physical activity, exercise, depression and anxiety disorders. *Journal of Neural Transmission, 116*(6), 777–784.

Stromeyer, C. F., III, & Psotka, J. (1971). The detailed texture of eidetic images. *Nature, 237*, 109–112.

Stroth, S., Hille, K., Spitzer, M., & Reinhardt, R. (2009). Aerobic endurance exercise benefits memory and affect in young adults. *Neuropsychological Rehabilitation, 19*(2), 223–243.

Strunk, D. R., Brotman, M. A., & DeRubeis, R. J. (2010). The process of change in cognitive therapy for depression: Predictors of early inter-session symptom gains. *Behaviour Research and Therapy, 48*(7), 599–606.

Stubbs, R. J., van Wyk, M. C., Johnstone, A. M., & Harbron, C. G. (1996). Breakfasts high in protein, fat or carbohydrate: Effect on within-day appetite and energy balance. *European Journal of Clinical Nutrition, 50(7)*, 409–417.

Stuss, D. T., Binns, M. A., Murphy, K. J., & Alexander, M. P. (2002). Dissociations within the anterior attentional system: Effects of task complexity and irrelevant information on reaction time speed and accuracy. *Neuropsychology, 16*, 500–513.

Sue, D. W., & Sue, D. (2008). *Counseling the culturally diverse*. Hoboken, NJ: John Wiley & Sons.

Sue, S. (1977). Community mental health services to minority groups: Some optimism, some pessimism. *American Psychologist, 32*, 616–624.

Sue, S. (1992). Ethnicity and mental health: Research and policy issues. *Journal of Social Issues, 48*(2), 187–205.

Sue, S., Zane, N., & Young, K. (1994). Research on psychotherapy in culturally diverse populations. In A. Bergin & S. Garfield (Eds.), *Handbook of psychotherapy and behavior change* (pp. 783–817). New York: Wiley.

Sullivan, P. F. (2005). The genetics of schizophrenia. PLoS Med, 2(7), e212. doi: 05-PLME-RIT-0198R1

Sullivan, P. F., Neale, M. C., & Kendler, K. S. (2000). Genetic epidemiology of major depression: Review and meta-analysis, *American Journal of Psychiatry, 157*, 1552–1562.

Sulloway, F. J. (1996). *Born to rebel: Birth order, family dynamics, and creative lives*. New York: Pantheon.

Suryani, L., & Jensen, S. (1993). *Trance and possession in Bali: A window on western multiple personality, possession disorder, and suicide*. New York: Oxford University Press.

Sutcliffe, N., Clarke, A. E., Levinton, C., Frost, C., Gordon, C., & Isenberg, D. A. (1999). Associates of health status in patients with systemic lupus erythematosus. *Journal of Rheumatology, 26*, 2352–2356.

Sutherland, P. (1992). *Cognitive development today: Piaget and his critics*. London: Paul Chapman.

Swann, J. (1998). Talk control: An illustration from the classroom of problems in analyzing male dominance of conversation. In J. Coates (Ed.), *Language and gender: A reader* (pp. 185–196). Oxford, UK: Blackwell.

Swanson, H. (1994). Index of suspicion. Case 3. Diagnosis: Failure to thrive due to psychosocial dwarfism. *Pediatric Review, 15*(1), 39, 41.

Swanson, J. W., Swartz, M. S., & Elbogen, E. B. (2004). Effectiveness of atypical antipsychotic medications in reducing violent behavior among persons with schizophrenia in community-based treatment. *Schizophrenia Bulletin, 30*(1), 3–20.

Swartz, M. (1990). Somatization disorder. In L. N. Robins (Ed.), *Psychiatric disorder in America* (pp. 220–257). New York: Free Press.

Swartz, M., Blazer, D., George, L., & Winfield, I. (1990). Estimating the prevalence of borderline personality disorder in the community. *Journal of Personality Disorders, 4*(3), 257–272.

Swayze, V. W., II. (1995). Frontal leukotomy and related psychosurgical procedures in the era before antipsychotics (1935–1954): A historical overview. *American Journal of Psychiatry, 152*(4), 505–515.

Swenson, D. D., & Marshall, B. (2005, May 14). Flash flood: Hurricane Katrina's inundation of New Orleans, August 29, 2005. *Times-Picayune*, p. 3.

Szalavitz, M. (2009). Popping smart pills: the case for cognitive enhancement. *Time* in partnership with CNN. Retrieved May 5, 2010, from http://www.time.com/time/health/article/0,8599,1869435,00.html

Taglialatela, J. P., Savage-Rumbaugh, E. S., & Baker, L. A. (2003). Vocal production by a language-competent bonobo (*Pan paniscus*). *International Journal of Comparative Psychology, 24*, 1–17.

Tajfel, H., & Turner, J. C. (1986). The social identity theory of intergroup behaviour. In S. Worchel & W. G. Austin (Eds.), *The psychology of intergroup relations* (Vol. 2, pp. 7–24) New York: Nelson Hall.

Takeuchi, T., Ogilvie, R. D., Murphy, T. I., & Ferrelli, A. V. (2003). EEG activities during elicited sleep onset. REM and NREM periods reflect difference mechanisms of dream generation. *Clinical Neurophysiology, 114*(2), 210–220.

Talbott, G. D. & Crosby, L. R. (2001). Recovery contracts: Seven key elements. In R. H. Coombs (Ed.), *Addiction recovery tools* (pp. 127–144). Thousand Oaks, CA: Sage.

Tamminga, C. A. (2002). Partial dopamine agonists in the treatment of psychosis. *Journal of Neural Transmission, 109*, 411–420.

Taylor, B., Miller, E., Farrington, C. P., Petropoulos, M. C., Favot-Mayaud, I., Li, J., & Waight, P. A. (1999). Autism and measles, mumps, and rubella vaccine: No epidemiological evidence for a causal association. *Lancet, 353*, 2026–2029.

Taylor, C., Manganello, J. A., Lee, S. J., & Rice, J. C. (2010). Mothers' spanking of 3-year-old children and subsequent risk of children's aggressive behavior. *Pediatrics, 125*, 1057–1065.

Taylor, D. M., & Moghaddam, F. M. (1994). *Theories of intergroup relations: International social psychological perspectives* (2nd ed.). Westport, CT: Praeger.

Teicher, M. H., Andersen, S. L., Polcari, A., Anderson, C. M., & Navalta, C. P. (2002). Developmental neurobiology of childhood stress and trauma. *Psychiatric Clinics of North America, 25*, 397–426.

Teigen, K. (1994). Yerkes–Dodson: A law for all seasons. *Theory & Psychology, 4*, 525–547.

Temoshok, L., & Dreher, H. (1992). *The Type C connection: The behavioral links to cancer and your health*. New York: Random House.

Terman, L. M. (1916). *The measurement of intelligence.* Boston: Houghton Mifflin.

Terman, L. M. (1925). *Mental and physical traits of a thousand gifted children (I).* Stanford, CA: Stanford University Press.

Terman, L. M., & Oden, M. H. (1947). *The gifted child grows up: 25 years' follow-up of a superior group: Genetic studies of genius (Vol. 4).* Stanford, CA: Stanford University Press.

Terman, L. M., & Oden, M. H. (1959). *The gifted group at mid-life, thirty-five years follow-up of the superior child: Genetic studies of genius (Vol. 3).* Stanford, CA: Stanford University Press.

Terry, A. V., Jr., Hill, W. D., Parikh, V., Evans, D. R., Waller, J. L., & Mahadik, S. P. (2002). Differential effects of chronic haloperidol and olanzapine exposure on brain cholinergic markers and spatial learning in rats. *Psychopharmacology, 164*(4), 360–368.

Terry, A. V., Jr., Hill, W. D., Parikh, V., Waller, J. L., Evans, D. R., & Mahadik, S. P. (2003). Differential effects of haloperidol, risperidone, and clozapine exposure on cholinergic markers and spatial learning performance in rats. *Neuropsychopharmacology, 28*(2), 300–309.

Thase, M. E. (1999). When are psychotherapy and pharmacotherapy combinations the treatment of choice for major depressive disorders? *Psychiatric Quarterly, 70*(4), 333–346.

Thase, M. E., & Sachs, G. S. (2000). Bipolar depression: Pharmacotherapy and related therapeutic strategies. *Biological Psychiatry, 48*(6), 558–572.

Thiedke, C. C. (2001). Sleep disorders and sleep problems in childhood. *American Family Physician, 63*, 277–284.

Thigpen, C. H., & Cleckley, H. M. (1992, Rev.). *The three faces of Eve.* London: Secker & Warburg.

Thomas, A., & Chess, S. (1977). *Temperament and development.* New York: Brunner/Mazel.

Thomas, M., Thorne, D., Sing, H., Redmond, D., Balkin, T., Wesensten, N., Russo, M., Welsh, A., Rowland, L., Johnson, D., Aladdin, R., Cephus, R., Hall, S., & Belenky, G. (1998). The relationship between driving accidents and microsleep during cumulative partial sleep deprivation. *Journal of Sleep Research, 7*(2), 275.

Thomas, N. J. T. (2001). Mental imagery. In E. N. Zalta (Ed.), *The Stanford encyclopedia of philosophy* (Winter 2001). Retrieved January 20, 2008, from http://plato.stanford.edu/entries/mental-imagery/

Thomas, R. K. (1994). Pavlov's rats "dripped saliva at the sound of a bell." *Psycoloquy,* 5(80). Retrieved May 9, 2008, from http://www.cogsci.ecs.soton.ac.uk/cgi/psyc/newpsy?5.80

Thompson, W. W., Price, C., Goodson, B., Shay, D. K., Benson, P., Hinrichsen, V. L., Lewis, E., Eriksen, E., Ray, P., Marcy, S. M., Dunn, J., Jackson, L. A., Lieu, T. A., Black, S., Stewart, G., Weintraub, E. S., Davis, R. L., & DeStefano, F. (2007). Early thimerosal exposure and neuropsychological outcomes at 7 to 10 years. *The New England Journal of Medicine, 357*(13), 1281–1292.

Thoresen, C. E., & Harris, H. S. (2002). Spirituality and health: What's the evidence and what's needed? *Annals of Behavioral Medicine, 24*, 3–13.

Thorndike, E. L. (1911). *Animal Intelligence: Experimental studies.* New York: MacMillan.

Thorndike, E. L. (1920). A constant error on psychological rating. *Journal of Applied Psychology, 5*, 25–29.

Thornton, A., & Hui-Sheng, L. (1994). Continuity and change. In A. Thornton & Hui-Sheng (Eds.), *Social change and the family in Taiwan* (pp. 396–410). Chicago: University of Chicago Press.

Thurstone, L. (1938). *Primary mental abilities.* Chicago: University of Chicago Press.

Tienari, P., Wynne, L. C., Sorri, A., Lahti, I., Läksy, K., Moring, J., Naarala, M., Nieminen, P., & Wahlberg, K-E. (2004). Genotype-environment interaction in schizophrenia-spectrum disorder: Long-term follow-up study of Finnish adoptees. *The British Journal of Psychiatry, 184*, 216–222.

Tobach, E. (2001). Development of sex and gender. In J. Worell (Ed.), *Encyclopedia of women and gender* (pp. 315–332). San Diego, CA: Academic Press.

Toga, A. W., & Thompson, P. M. (2003). Mapping brain asymmetry. *Nature Reviews Neuroscience, 4*, 37–48.

Tohen, M., Vieta, E., Calabrese, J., Ketter, T. A., Sachs, G., Bowden, C., Mitchell, P. B., Centorrino, F., Risser, R., Baker, R. W., Evans, A. R., Beymer, K., Dube, S., Tollefson, G. D., & Breier, A. (2003). Efficacy of olanzapine and olanzapinefluoxetine combination in the treatment of bipolar I depression. *Archives of General Psychiatry, 60*(11), 1079–1088.

Tolman, E. C. (1932). *Purposive behavior in animals and man.* New York: Century.

Tolman, E. C., & Honzik, C. H. (1930). Introduction and removal of reward and maze learning in rats. *University of California Publications in Psychology, 4*, 257–275.

Tomasello, M., Carpenter, M., & Lizskowski, U. (2007). A new look at infant pointing. *Child Development, 78*, 705–722.

Torgersen, S. (2000). Genetics of patients with borderline personality disorder. *Psychiatric Clinics of North America, 23*, 1–9.

Torrance, E. P. (1993). The Beyonders in a thirty-year longitudinal study of creative achievement. *Roeper Review, 15*(3), 131–135.

Torrey, E. F. (1987). Prevalence studies in schizophrenia. *British Journal of Psychiatry, 150*, 598–608.

Tran, M.-T. (2010, June 27). Teenage sailor Abby Sunderland one step closer to home. *Los Angeles Times.* Retrieved June 27, 2010, from http://articles.latimes.com/2010/jun/26/local/la-me-0626-abby-sunderland-arrives-20100626

Trappey, C. (1996). A meta-analysis of consumer choice and subliminal advertising. *Psychology and Marketing, 13*, 517–530.

Treisman A. [M.] (2006). How the deployment of attention determines what we see. *Visual Cognition, 14*, 411–443.

Treisman, A. M., & Gelade, G. (1980). A feature integration theory of attention. *Cognitive Psychology, 12*, 97–136.

Treisman, M. (1977). Motion sickness: An evolutionary hypothesis. *Science, 197*, 493.

Tremblay, A., Doucet, E., & Imbeault, P. (1999). Physical activity and weight maintenance. *International Journal of Obesity, 23*(3), S50–S54.

Tresniowski, A. (1999, July 12). Troubled sleep. *People Weekly*, 56–59.

Triandis, H. (1971). *Attitude and attitude change.* New York: Wiley.

Trocmé, N., MacLaurin, B., Fallon, B., Daciuk, J., Billingsley, D., Tourigny, M., Mayer, M., Wright, J., Barter, K., Furford, G., Hornick, J., Sullivan, R., & McKenzie, B. (2001). *Canadian incidence study of reported child abuse and neglect: Final report* (pp. 30–31). Ottawa, ON: Minister of Public Works and Government Services Canada.

Troisi, A., & McGuire, M. (2002). Darwinian psychiatry and the concept of mental disorder. *Human Ethology & Evolutionary Psychology, 23*(4), 31–38.

Troncoso, X. G., Macknik, S. L., Otero-Millan, J., & Martinez-Conde, S. (2008). Microsaccades drive illusory motion in the enigma illusion. *Proceedings of the National Academy of Sciences, USA, 105*(41), 16033–16038.

Trut, L. M. (1999). Early canid domestication: The Farm-Fox experiment. *Science,* 283.

Tsai, G. E., Condle, D., Wu, M-T., & Chang, I-W. (1999). Functional magnetic resonance imaging of personality switches in a woman with dissociative identity disorder. *Harvard Review of Psychiatry, 7*, 119–122.

Tsai, J. L., Simeonova, D. I., & Watanabe, J. T. (2004). Somatic and social: Chinese Americans talk about emotion. *Personality and Social Psychology Bulletin, 30*(9), 1226–1238.

Tsapogas, J. (2006). *Characteristics of Doctoral Scientists and Engineers in the United States: 2003*, NSF, 06-320. Arlington, VA: National Science Foundation, Division of Science Resources Statistics.

Tsuang, M., Domschke, K., Jerskey, B. A., & Lyons, M. J. (2004). Agoraphobic behavior and panic attack: A study of male twins. *Journal of Anxiety Disorders, 18*(6), 799–807.

Tucker, E. W., & Potocky-Tripodi, M. (2006). Changing heterosexuals' attitudes toward homosexuals: A systematic review of the empirical literature. *Research on Social Work Practice, 16*(2), 176–190.

Tucker, M. A., Hirota, Y., Wamsley, E. J., Lau, H., Chaklader, A., & Fishbein, W. (2006). A daytime nap containing solely non-REM sleep enhances declarative but not procedural memory. *Neurobiology of Learning and Memory, 86*(2), 241–247.

Tugade, M. M., & Fredrickson, B. L. (2004). Resilient individuals use positive emotions to bounce back from negative emotional experiences. *Journal of Personality and Social Psychology, 86*(2), 320–333.

Tukuitonga, C. F., & Bindman, A. B. (2002). Ethnic and gender differences in the use of coronary artery revascularisation procedures in New Zealand. *New Zealand Medical Journal, 115*, 179–182.

Tulving, E., & Thomson, D. M. (1973). Encoding specificity and retrieval processes in episodic memory. *Psychological Review, 80*, 352–373.

Turk, C. L., Heimberg, R. G., & Magee, L. (2008). Social anxiety disorder. In D. H. Barlow (Ed.), *Clinical handbook of psychological disorders* (pp. 123–163). New York: Guilford Press.

Turner, W. J. (1995). Homosexuality, Type 1: An Xq28 phenomenon. *Archives of Sexual Behavior, 24*(2), 109–134.

Tusel, D. J., Piotrowski, N. A., Sees, K., Reilly, P. M., Banys, P., Meek, P., & Hall, S. M. (1994). Contingency contracting for illicit drug use with opioid addicts in methadone treatment. In L. S., Harris (Ed.), *Problems of drug dependence: Proceedings of the 56th Annual Scientific Meeting.* (National Institute on Drug Abuse Research Monograph No. 153, pp. 155–160). Washington, DC: U.S. Goverment Printing Office.

Tversky, A., & Kahneman, D. (1973). Availability: A heuristic for judging frequency and probability. *Cognitive Psychology, 5*(2), 207–232.

Tversky, A., & Shafir, E. (1992). The disjunction effect in choice under uncertainty. *Psychological Science, 3*(5), 305–309.

Ulmer, J. L., Parsons, L., Moseley, M., & Gabrieli, J. (2006). White matter in cognitive neuroscience: Advances in diffusion tensor imaging and its applications. *Annals of the New York Academy of Sciences, 1064*.

UNAIDS (2008), 2008 Report on the global AIDS epidemic. Retrieved June 8, 2010, from http://www.unaids.org/en/KnowledgeCentre/HIVData/GlobalReport/2008/2008_Global_report.asp

UNAIDS (2009) AIDS epidemic update. Retrieved June 8, 2010, from http://data.unaids.org/pub/Report/2009/JC1700_Epi_Update_2009_en.pdf

Unger, R. (1979). Toward a redefinition of sex and gender. *American Psychologist, 34*, 1085–1094.

Upthegrove, T., Roscigno, V., & Charles, C. (1999). Big money collegiate sports: Racial concentration, contradictory pressures, and academic performance. *Social Science Quarterly, 80*, 718–737.

Uretsky, S. D. (2002). Antianxiety drugs. *Gale Encyclopedia of Medicine*. Gale Group. Retrieved July 19, 2010, from http://www.healthline.com/galecontent/antianxiety-drugs

Vaidya, C. J., Zhao, M., Desmond, J. E., & Gabrieli, J. D. E. (2002). Evidence for cortical encoding specificity in episodic memory: Memory-induced re-activation of picture processing areas. *Neuropsychologia, 40*(12), 2136–2143.

Vail, A. (1976). Factors influencing lower class, black patients' remaining in treatment. *Clinical Psychology, 29*, 12–14.

Vaillant, G. E. (2002). Adaptive mental mechanisms: Their role in a positive psychology. *American Psychologist, 55*, 89–98.

Valverde, R., Pozdnyakova, I., Kajander, T., Venkatraman, J., & Regan, L. (2007). Fragile X mental retardation syndrome: Structure of the KH1-KH2 domains of fragile X mental retardation protein. *Structure, 9*, 1090–1098.

Van de Castle, R. (1994). *Our dreaming mind*. New York: Ballantine Books.

van der Merwe, A., & Garuccio, A. (Eds.). (1994). *Waves and particles in light and matter*. New York: Plenum Press.

van der Stelt, O., van der Molen, M., Boudewijn Gunning, W., & Kok, A. (2010). Neuroelectrical signs of selective attention to color in boys with attention-deficit hyperactivity disorder. *Cognitive Brain Research, 12*(2), 245–264.

Van Dongen, H. P. A., Maislin, G., Mullington, J. M., & Dinges, D. F. (2003). The cumulative cost of additional wakefulness: Dose-response effects on neurobehavioral functions and sleep physiology from chronic sleep restriction and total sleep deprivation. *Sleep, 26*, 117–126.

VandenBos, G. R., & Bulatao, E. Q. (Eds.). (1996). *Violence on the job: Identifying risks and developing solutions*. Washington DC: American Psychological Association.

Vartanian, L. R. (2000). Revisiting the imaginary audience and personal fable constructs of adolescent egocentricism: A conceptual review. *Adolescence, 35*(140), 639–661.

Vasey, P. L. & VanderLaan, D. P. (2010). An adaptive cognitive dissociation between willingness to help kin and nonkin in Samoan *Fa'afafine. Psychological Science, 21*(2), 292–297.

Vaughan, S. (2000). *Half empty, half full: The psychological roots of optimism*. New York: Harcourt.

Veasey, S. C. (2003). Serotonin agonists and antagonists in obstructive sleep apnea: Therapeutic potential. *American Journal of Respiratory Medicine, 2*(1), 21–29.

Vecsey, C. G., Baillie, G. S., Jaganath, D., Havekes, R., Daniels, A., Wimmer, M., Huang, T., Brown, K. M., Li, X. Y., Descalzi, G., Kim, S. S., Chen, T., Shang, Y. Z., Zhuo, M., Houslay, M. D., & Abel, T. (2009). Sleep deprivation impairs cAMP signaling in the hippocampus. *Nature, 461* (7267), 1122–1125.

Vernon, S. W., & Roberts, R. E. (1982). Use of RDC in a tri-ethnic community survey. *Archives of General Psychiatry, 39*, 47.

Villafuerte, S., & Burmeister, M. (2003). Untangling genetic networks of panic, phobia, fear and anxiety. *Genome Biology, 4*(8), 224.

Villani, S. (2001). Impact of media on children and adolescents: A 10-year review of the research. *Journal of the American Academy on Child and Adolescent Psychiatry, 40*(4), 392–401.

Vink, T., Hinney, A., Van Elburg, A. A., Van Goozen, S. H., Sandkuijl, L. A., Sinke, R. J., Herpertz-Dahlman, B. M., Henebrand, J., Remschmidt, H., Van Engeland, H., & Adan, R. A. (2001). Association between an agouti-related protein gene polymorphism and anorexia nervosa. *Molecular Psychiatry, 6*(3), 325–328.

Virkkunen, M., & Linnoila, M. (1996). Serotonin and glucose metabolism in impulsively violent alcoholic offenders. In D. M. Stoff, & R. B. Cairns (Eds.), *Aggression and violence* (pp. 87–100). Mahwah, NJ: Lawrence Erlbaum.

Visser, P. S., & Krosnick, J. A. (1998). Development of attitude strength over the life cycle: Surge and decline. *Journal of Personality and Social Psychology, 75*(6), 1389–1410.

Vogel, G. W. (1975). A review of REM sleep deprivation. *Archives of General Psychiatry, 32*, 749–761.

Vogel, G. W. (1993). Selective deprivation, REM sleep. In M. A. Carskadon (Ed.), *The encyclopedia of sleep and dreaming*. New York: Macmillan.

Voineskos, A. N., Lobaugh, N. J., Bouix, S., Rajji, T. K., Miranda, D., Kennedy, J. L., et al. (2010). Diffusion tensor tractography findings in schizophrenia across the adult lifespan. *Brain: A Journal of Neurology, 17*, 17.

Vokey, J. R., & Read J. D. (1985). Subliminal messages: Between the devil and the media. *American Psychologist, 40*, 1231–1239.

Volkow, N. D., Wang, G.-J., Newcorn, J., Telang, F., Solanto, M. V., Fowler, J. S., et al. (2007). Depressed dopamine activity in caudate and preliminary evidence of limbic involvement in adults with Attention-Deficit/Hyperactivity Disorder. *Archives of General Psychiatry, 64*(8), 932–940.

von Helmholtz, H. (1852). On the theory of compound colours. *Philosophical Magazine, 4*, 519–535.

von Helmholtz, H. L. F. (1863). *Die Lehre von den Tonempfindungen als physiologische Grundlage fur die Theorie der Musik* (1954, XX, trans. by Alexander J. Ellis). *On the sensations of tone as a physiological basis for the theory of music*. New York: Dover.

Voss, M. W., Erickson, K. I., Prakash, R. S., Chaddock, L., Malkowski, E., Alves, H., Kim, J. S., Morris, K. S., White, S. M., Wojcicki, T. R., Hu, L., Szabo, A., Klamm, E., McAuley, E., & Kramer, A. F. (2010). Functional connectivity: A source of variance in the association between cardiorespiratory fitness and cognition? *Neuropsychologia, 48*(5), 1394–1406.

Voyer, D., & Rodgers, M. (2002). Reliability of laterality effects in a dichotic listening task with nonverbal material. *Brain & Cognition, 48*, 602–606.

Voyer, D., Voyer, S., & Bryden, M. (1995). Magnitude of sex differences in spatial abilities: A meta-analysis and consideration of critical variables. *Psychological Bulletin, 117*(2), 250–270.

Vygotsky, L. S. (1934/1962). *Thought and language*. Cambridge, MA: MIT Press.

Vygotsky, L. S. (1978). *Mind in society: The development of higher psychological processes*. Cambridge, MA: Harvard University Press.

Vygotsky, L. S. (1987). Thought and word. In R. W. Riebe & A. S. Carton (Eds.), *The collected works of L. S. Vygotsky: Vol. 1. Problems of general psychology* (pp. 243–288). New York: Plenum.

Wahlsten, D. (1997). The malleability of intelligence is not constrained by heritability. In B. Devlin, S. E. Fienberg, & K. Roeder, *Intelligence, genes, and success: Scientists respond to the bell curve* (pp. 71–87). New York: Springer.

Wakefield, A. J., Murch, S. H., Anthony, A., Linnell, J., Casson, D. M., Malik, M., Berelowitz, M., Dhillon, A. P., Thomson, M. A., Harvey, P., Valentine, A., Davies, S. E., & Walker-Smith J., A. (1998). Ileal-lymphoid-nodular hyperplasia, non-specific colitis, and pervasive developmental disorder in children. *The Lancet, 351*, 9103.

Walker, L. J. (1991). Sex differences in moral reasoning. In W. M. Kurtines & J. L. Gewirtz (Eds.), *Handbook of moral behavior and development: Vol. 2. Research* (pp. 333–364). Hillsdale, NJ: Lawrence Erlbaum.

Walker, M. P. (2005). A refined model of sleep and the time course of memory formation. *Behavioral and Brain Sciences, 28*, 51–64.

Walter, C. (2008). Affairs of the lips. *Scientific American Mind, 19*(6), 24.

Wampold, B. E. (1997). Methodological problems in identifying efficacious psychotherapies. *Psychotherapy Research, 7*, 21–43.

Ward, A. S., Li, D. H., Luedtke, R. R., & Emmett-Oglesby, M. W. (1996). Variations in cocaine self-administration by inbred rat strains under a progressive-ratio schedule. *Psychopharmacology, 127*(3), 204–212.

Ward, C., & Rana-Deuba, A. (1999). Acculturation and adaptation revisited. *Journal of Cross-Cultural Psychology, 30*, 422–442.

Ward, I. L. (1992). Sexual behavior: The product of parinatal hormonal and prepubertal social factors. In A. A. Gerall, H. Moltz, & I. L. Ward. (Eds.), *Handbook of behavioral neurobiology: Vol. 11. Sexual differentiation* (pp. 157–178). New York: Plenum Press.

Ward, J., Mattic, K. R. P., & Hall, W. (1999). *Methadone maintenance treatment and other opioid replacement therapies*. Sydney, Australia: Harwood Academic.

Ward, M. M., Lotstein, D. S., Bush, T. M., Lambert, R. E., van Vollenhoven, R., & Neuwelt, C. M. (1999). Psychosocial correlates of morbidity in women with systemic lupus erythematosus. *Journal of Rheumatology, 26*, 2153–2158.

Wartner, U. G., Grossmann, K., Fremmer-Bombik, E., & Suess, G. (1994). Attachment patterns at age six in south Germany: Predictability from infancy and implications for preschool behavior. *Child Development, 65*, 1014–1027.

Washburn, M. F. (1908). *The animal mind: A text-book of comparative psychology*. New York: Macmillan.

Wasserman, E. A., & Miller, R. R. (1997). What's elementary about associative learning? *Annual Review of Psychology, 48*, 573–607.

Waterhouse, L. (2006a). Inadequate evidence for multiple intelligences, Mozart effect, and emotional intelligence theories. *Educational Psychologist, 41*(4), 247–255.

Waterhouse, L. (2006b). Multiple intelligences, the Mozart effect, and emotional intelligence: A critical review. *Educational Psychologist, 41,* 207–225.

Watkins, C. E., Campbell, V. L., Nieberding, R., & Hallmark, R. (1995). Contemporary practice of psychological assessment by clinical psychologists. *Professional Psychology: Research and Practice, 26*, 54–60.

Watkins, C. E., Jr., & Savickas, M. L. (1990). Psychodynamic career counseling. In W. B. Walsh & S. H. Osipow (Eds.), *Career counseling: Contemporary topics in vocational psychology* (pp. 79–116). Hillsdale, NJ: Lawrence Erlbaum.

Watson, D. L., Hagihara, D. K., & Tenney, A. L. (1999). Skill-building exercises and generalizing psychological concepts to daily life. *Teaching of Psychology, 26*, 193–195.

Watson, J. B. (1913). Psychology as the behaviorist views it. *Psychological Review, 20*, 158–177.

Watson, J. B. (1924). *Behaviorism*. New York: W. W. Norton.

Watson, J. B., & Rayner, R. (1920). Conditioned emotional responses. *Journal of Experimental Psychology, 3*, 1–14.

Watson, J. M., & Strayer, D. L. (2010). Supertaskers: Profiles in extraordinary multitasking ability. *Psychonomic Bulletin & Review, 17*(4), 479–485.

Watt, H. M. G. (2000). Measuring attitudinal change in mathematics and English over the 1st year of junior high school: A multi-dimensional analysis. *Journal of Experimental Education, 68*, 331–361.

Weaver, F. M., Follett, K., Stern, M., Hur, K., Harris, C., Marks, W. J., Jr., et al. (2009). Bilateral deep brain stimulation vs. best medical therapy for patients with advanced Parkinson disease: A randomized controlled trial. *Journal of the American Medical Association, 301*(1), 63–73.

Webb, W. B. (1992). *Sleep: The gentle tyrant* (2nd ed.). Bolton, MA: Ander.

Wechsler, D. (1975). *The collected papers of David Wechsler*. New York: Academic Press.

Wechsler, D. (2002). *WPPSI-III* (Weschsler Preschool and Primary Scale of Intelligence—Third Edition) *Administration and scoring manual*. San Antonio, TX: Pearson.

Wechsler, D. (2003). *WISC-IV* (Weschsler Intelligence Scale for Children—Fourth Edition) *Administration and scoring manual*. San Antonio, TX: Pearson.

Wechsler, D. (2008). *WAIS-IV* (Weschsler Adult Intelligence Scale—Fourth Edition) *Administration and scoring manual*. San Antonio, TX: Pearson.

Wedding, D. (2004). Cross-cultural counseling and psychotherapy. In R. J. Corsini & D. Wedding (Eds.), *Current psychotherapies* (7th ed., p. 485). Itasca, IL: Peacock.

Weinberger, D. R. (1987). Implications of normal brain development for the pathogenesis of schizophrenia. *Archives of General Psychiatry, 44*, 660–668.

Weiner, B. (1985). An attributional theory of achievement motivation. *Psychological Review, 92*, 548–573.

Weiner, I. B. (1997). Current status of the Rorschach Inkblot Method. *Journal of Personality Assessment, 68*, 5–19.

Weis, S., Klaver, P., Reul, J., Elger, C. E., & Fernandez, G. (2004). Temporal and cerebellar brain regions that support both declarative memory formation and retrieval. *Cerebral Cortex, 14*, 256–267.

Weisman, A. (1972). *On dying and denying*. New York: Behavioral Publications.

Weiss, J. M. (1972). Psychological factors in stress and disease. *Scientific American, 26*, 104–113.

Weisse, C. S. (1992). Depression and immunocompetence: A review of the literature. *Psychological Bulletin, 111*, 475–489.

Weissman, M. M., & Klerman, G. L. (1977). Sex differences and the epidemiology of depression. *Archives of General Psychiatry, 34*, 98–111.

Weissman, M. M., Bland, R. C., Canino, G. J., Faravelli, C., Greenwald, S., Hwu, H. G., Joyce, P. R., Karam, E. G., Lee, C. K., Lellouch, J., Lepine, J. P., Newman, S. C., Oakley-Browne, M. A., Rubio-Stipec, M., Wells, J. E., Wickramaratne, P. J., Wittchen, H. U., & Yeh, E. K. (1997). The cross-national epidemiology of panic disorder. *Archives of General Psychiatry, 54*, 305–309.

Weissman, M. M., Bland, R., Joyce, P. R., Newman, S., Wells, J. E., & Wittchen, H. U. (1993). Sex differences in rates of depression: Cross-national perspectives. *Journal of Affective Disorders, 29*, 77–84.

Weizenbaum, J. (1976). *Computer power and human reason*. San Francisco, CA: W. H. Freeman.

Wender, P. H., Wolf, L. E., & Wasserstein, J. (2001). Adults with ADHD. An overview. *Annals of the New York Academy of Sciences, 931*, 1–16.

Wenneberg, S. R., Schneider, R. H., Walton, K. G., Maclean, C. R., Levitsky, D. K., Mandarino, J. V., Waziri, R., & Wallace, R. K. (1997). Anger expression correlates with platelet aggregation. *Behavioral Medicine, 22*(4), 174–177.

Werker, J. F., & Lalonde, C. E. (1988). Cross-language speech perceptions: Initial capabilities and developmental change. *Developmental Psychology, 24*, 672–683.

Wertheimer, M. (1982). *Productive thinking*. Chicago: University of Chicago Press.

Westen, D. (2005). Cognitive neuroscience and psychotherapy: Implications for psychotherapy's second century. In G. Gabbard, J. Beck, & J. Holmes (Eds.), *Oxford textbook of psychotherapy*. Oxford, UK: Oxford University Press.

Wetherell, J. L. (2002). Behavior therapy for anxious older adults. *Behavior Therapist, 25*, 16–17.

Wever, E. G. (1949). *Theory of Hearing*. New York: John Wiley & Sons.

Wever, E. G., & Bray, C. W. (1930). The nature of acoustic response: The relation between sound frequency and frequency of impulses in the auditory nerve. *Journal of Experimental Psychology, 13*(5), 373–387.

Weyant, J. M. (1996). Application of compliance techniques to direct-mail requests for charitable donations. *Psychology and Marketing, 13*, 157–170

White, G. L. (1980). Physical attractiveness and courtship progress. *Journal of Personality and Social Psychology, 39*, 660–668.

White, S. (2000). *The transgender debate (the crisis surrounding gender identity)*. Reading, UK: Garnet.

Whorf, B. L. (1956). *Language, thought and reality*. New York: Wiley.

Wicker, A. W. (1971). An examination of the "other variables" explanation of attitude–behavior inconsistency. *Journal of Personality and Social Psychology, 19*, 18–30.

Widiger, T. A., & Trull, T. J. (2007). Plate tectonics in the classification of personality disorder: Shifting to a dimensional model. *American Psychologist, 62*(2), 71–83. doi:10.1037/0003-066X.62.2.71

Widiger, T. A., & Weissman, M. M. (1991). Epidemiology of borderline personality disorder. *Hospital and Community Psychiatry, 42*, 1015–1021.

Wierenga, C. E., Stricker, N. H., McCauley, A., Simmons, A., Jak, A. J., Chang, Y. L., et al. (2010). Increased functional brain response during word retrieval in cognitively intact older adults at genetic risk for Alzheimer's disease. *Neuroimage, 15,* 15.

Williams, J. A., Pascual-Leone, A., & Fregni, F. (2010). Interhemispheric modulation induced by cortical stimulation and motor training. *Physical Therapy, 90*(3), 398–410.

Williams, M. A., & Sachdev, P. S. (2010). Magnetoencephalography in neuropsychiatry: Ready for application? *Current Opinion in Psychiatry, 4*, 4.

Williams, M. E. (1995). *The American Geriatrics Society's complete guide to aging and mental health*. New York: Random House.

Williams, R. B. (1999). A 69-year-old man with anger and angina. *Journal of the American Medical Association, 282*, 763–770.

Williams, R. B. (2001). Hostility: Effects on health and the potential for successful behavioral approaches to prevention and treatment. In A. Baum, T. A. Revenson, & J. E. Singer (Eds.), *Handbook of Health Psychology*. Mahwah, NJ: Erlbaum.

Williams, R. B., Haney, T. L., Lee, K. L., Kong, Y. H., Blumenthal, J. A., & Whalen, R. E. (1980). Type A behavior, hostility, and coronary atherosclerosis. *Psychosomatic Medicine, 42*(6), 539–549.

Willingham D. T. (2005). Do visual, auditory, and kinesthetic learners need visual, auditory, and kinesthetic instruction? *American Educator, 29*(2), 31–35.

Winningham, R. G., Hyman, I. E., Jr., & Dinnel, D. L. (2000). Flashbulb memories? The effects of when the initial memory report was obtained. *Memory, 8*, 209–216.

Winton, W. M. (1987). Do introductory textbooks present the Yerkes-Dodson law correctly? *American Psychologist, 42*(2), 202–203.

Wise, K., Alhabash, S., & Park, H. (2010). Emotional responses during social information seeking on Facebook. *Cyberpsychology, Behavior, and Social Networking*, 13(5), 555–562.

Wiseman, R. (2007). Quirkology: How we discover the big truths in small things (pp. 7–8, 28–29). New York: Basic Books.

Witelson, S. F. (1991). Neural sexual mosaicism: Sexual differentiation of the human temporo-pariatal region for functional asymmetry. *Psychoneuroendocrinology, 16*, 131–153.

Wojcik, B. E., Stein, C. R., Bagg, K., Humphrey, R. J., & Orosco, J. (2010). Traumatic brain injury hospitalizations of U.S. army soldiers deployed to Afghanistan and Iraq. *American Journal of Preventive Medicine, 38*(Suppl. 1), S108–116.

Wolberg, L. R. (1977). *The technique of psychotherapy*. New York: Grune & Stratton.

Wood, J. M., Nezworski, M. T., & Stejskal, W. J. (1996). The comprehensive system for the Rorschach: A critical examination. *Psychological Science, 7*(1), 3–10, 14–17.

Woodhouse, A. (2005). Phantom limb sensation. *Clinical and Experimental Pharmacology and Physiology, 32*(1–2), 132–134.

Wooten, P. (1980). Humor: an antidote for stress. *Holistic Nursing Practice. 10*(2), 49–56.

World Health Organization (WHO) International Consortium in Psychiatric Epidemiology. (2000). Cross-national comparisons of the prevalences and correlates of mental disorders. *Bulletin of the World Health Organization, 78*(4), 413–426.

Wyman, P. A., Moynihan, J., Eberly, S., Cox, C., Cross, W., Jin, X., & Caserta, M. T. (2007). Association of family stress with natural killer cell activity and the frequency of illnesses in children. *Archives of Pediatric and Adolescent Medicine, 161*, 228–234.

Wynne, C. (1999). Do animals think? The case against the animal mind. *Psychology Today, 32*(6), 50–53.

Wu, C-C., Lee, G. C., & Lai, H-K. (2004). Using concept maps to aid analysis of concept presentation in high school computer textbooks. *Journal of Education and Information Technologies, 9*(2), 10.1023/B:EAIT.0000027930.09631.a5

Yaffe, K., Vittinghoff, E., Lindquist, K., Barnes, D., Covinsky K. E., Neylan, T., Kluse, M., & Marmar, C. (2010). Posttraumatic stress disorder and risk of dementia among U.S. veterans. *Archives of General Psychiatry, 67*(6), 608–613.

Yalom, I. (1995). *The theory and practice of group psychotherapy* (4th ed.). New York: Basic Books.

Yamaguchi, S., Isejima, H., Matsuo, T., Okura, R., Yagita, K., Kobayashi, M., & Okamura, H. (2003). Synchronization of cellular clocks in the suprachiasmatic nucleus. *Science, 302*, 1408–1412.

Yerkes, R. M. (Ed.). (1921). Psychological examining in the United States Army. *Memoirs of the National Academy of Sciences, 15,* 1–890.

Yerkes, R. M., & Dodson, J. D. (1908). The relation of strength of stimulus to rapidity of habit formation. *Journal of Comparative Neurology and Psychology, 18*, 459–482.

Yip, Y. L. (2002, Autumn). Pivot–Qi. *The Journal of Traditional Eastern Health and Fitness, 12*(3).

Yopyk, D., & Prentice, D. A. (2005). Am I an athlete or a student? Identify salience and stereotype threat in student-athletes. *Basic and Applied Social Psychology, 27* (4), 29–336.

Young, J. E., Rygh, J. L., Weinberger, A. D., & Beck, A. T. (2008). Cognitive therapy for depression. In D. H. Barlow (Ed.), *Clinical handbook of psychological disorders* (pp. 250–305). New York: Guilford Press.

Young, S. N. (Ed.) (1996). Melatonin, sleep, aging, and the health protection branch. *Journal of Psychiatry Neuroscience, 21*(3), 161–164.

Young, T. (1802). On the theory of light and colors. *Philosophical Transactions of the Royal Society, 91*, 12–49.

Yuan, Q., Lin, F., Zheng, X., & Sehgal, A. (2005). Serotonin modulates circadian entrainment in *Drosophila*. *Neuron, 47*, 115–127.

Yule, G. (1996). *Pragmatics*. Oxford: Oxford University Press.

Zajonc, R. B. (1965). Social facilitation. *Science, 149*, 269–274.

Zajonc, R. B. (1968). Attitudinal effects of mere exposure. *Journal of Personality and Social Psychology Monographs, 9*(2), 1–27.

Zajonc, R. B. (1980). Feeling and thinking: Preferences need no inferences. *American Psychologist, 35*, 151–175.

Zajonc, R. B. (1984). On the primacy of affect. *American Psychologist, 39*, 117–123.

Zajonc, R. B. (1998). Emotions. In D. T. Gilbert & S. T. Fiske (Eds.), *Handbook of social psychology* (4th ed., Vol. 1, pp. 591–632). New York: McGraw-Hill.

Zajonc, R. B., Heingartner, A., & Herman, E. M. (1970). Social enhancement and impairment of performance in the cockroach. *Journal of Social Psychology, 13*(2), 83–92.

Zanarini, M. C. (2000). Childhood experiences associated with the development of borderline personality disorder. *Psychiatric Clinics of North America, 23*(1), 89–101.

Zedler, Beatrice (1995). "Mary Whiton Calkins." In M. E. Waithe (Ed.), *A history of women philosophers: Vol. 4* (pp. 103–123). Netherlands: Kluwer Academic Publishers.

Zeidner, M., & Matthews, G. (2005). Evaluative anxiety. In A. Elliott & C. Dweck (Eds.), *Handbook of competence and motivation* (pp. 141–146). New York: Guilford Press.

Zeki, S. (2001). Localization and globalization in conscious vision. *Annual Review of Neuroscience, 24*, 57–86.

Zentall, T. R. (2000). Animal intelligence. In R. J. Sternberg (Ed.), *Handbook of intelligence*. Cambridge, MA: Cambridge University Press.

Zhang, L. (2006). Does student-teacher thinking style match/mismatch matter in students' achievement? *Educational Psychology, 26*, 395–409.

Zhao, Y., Montoro, R., Igartua, K., & Thombs, B. D. (2010). Suicidal ideation and attempt among adolescents reporting "unsure" sexual identity or heterosexual identity plus same-sex attraction or behavior: Forgotten groups? *Journal of the American Academy of Child & Adolescent Psychiatry, 49*(2), 104–113.

Zhou, J. N., Hofman, M. A., Gooren, L. J. G., & Swaab, D. F. (1995). A sex difference in the human brain and its relation to transsexuality. *Nature, 378*, 68–70.

Zilles, K. (1990). Cortex. In G. Paxinos (Ed.), *The human nervous system* (pp. 757–802). San Diego, CA: Academic.

Zillmann, D., Baron, R., & Tamborini, R. (1981). Social costs of smoking: Effects of tobacco smoke on hostile behavior. *Psychology Journal of Applied Social, 11*, 548–561.

Zimbardo, P. (1971). The pathology of imprisonment. *Society, 9*(4–8), 4.

Zimbardo, P. G. (1970). The human choice: Individuation, reason, and order versus deindividuation, impulse, and chaos. In N. J. Arnold & D. Levine (Eds.), *Nebraska Symposium on Motivation, 1969*. Lincoln: University of Nebraska Press.

Zimbardo, P. G., & Hartley, C. F. (1985). Cults go to high school: A theoretical and empirical analysis of the initial stage in the recruitment process. *Cultic Studies Journal, 2*, 91–148.

Zimbardo, P., Maslach, C., & Haney, C. (2000). Reflections on the Stanford Prison Experiment: Genesis, transformations, consequences. In T. Blass (Ed.), *Obedience to authority: Current perspectives on the Milgram paradigm* (pp. 193–237). London: Lawrence Erlbaum.

Zisapel, N. (2001). Circadian rhythm sleep disorders: Pathophysiology and potential approaches to management. *CNS Drugs, 15*(4), 311–328.

Zorilla, E. P., Luborsky, L., McKay, J. R., Rosenthal, R., Houldin, A., Tax, A., McCorkle, R., Seligman, D. A., & Schmidt, K. (2001). The relationship of depression and stressors to immunological assays: A meta-analytic review. *Brain, Behavior, and Immunity, 15*, 199–226.

Zuckerman, M. (1979). *Sensation seeking: Beyond the optimal level of arousal*. Hillsdale, NJ: Lawrence Erlbaum.

Zuckerman, M. (1994). *Behavioral expression and biosocial bases of sensation seeking*. New York: Cambridge University Press.

Zuckerman, M. (2002). Zuckerman-Kuhlman Personality Questionnaire (ZKPQ): An alternative five-factorial model. In B. De Raad & M. Perugini (Eds.), *Big Five assessment* (pp. 377–396). Seattle, WA: Hogrefe & Huber.

Zuo, L., & Cramond, B. (2001). An examination of Terman's gifted children from the theory of identity. *Gifted Child Quarterly, 45*(4), 251–259.

Zvolensky, M. J., Schmidt, M. B., & Stewart, S. H. (2003). Panic disorder and smoking. *Clinical Psychology: Science and Practice, 10*, 29–51.

credits

PHOTO CREDITS

FM

© Justin Horrocks/istockphoto; David Mager/Pearson Learning Photo Studio.

Psychology in Action

Page I-3 Kitch Bain/Shutterstock; Page I-3 (Top Right) deepspacedave/Shutterstock; Page I-3 (Top Center) Feng Yu/Shutterstock; Page I-3 (Center) © Ryan Balderas/istockphoto; Page I-3 (Center) Vixit/Shutterstock; Page I-3 (Left) Alex Mit/Shutterstock; Page I-3 (Bottom) ifong/Shutterstock; Page I-5 (Top) Corbis/SuperStock/Superstock Royalty Free; Page I-5 (Bottom) © Andrew Holbrooke/CORBIS All Rights Reserved; Page I-7 (Top) FancyVeerSet8/Alamy Images Royalty Free; Page I-7 (Bottom) Lev Olkha/Shutterstock; Page I-8 Andersen Ross/Photodisc/Getty Images; Page I-9 Stefan Kiefer/Alamy Images; Page I-10 Bill Varie/CORBIS-NY; Page I-12 (Top) © James Marshall/CORBIS All Rights Reserved; Page I-12 (Bottom) © Dex Images/CORBIS; Page I-13 Corbis RF; Page I-14 Pulp Photography/Corbis RF.

Chapter 1

Page 3 androfroll/Shutterstock; Page 3 Paul Maguire/Shutterstock; Page 3 Galushko Sergey/Shutterstock; Ralf Juergen Kraft/Shutterstock; Page 3 R-studio/Shutterstock; Page 3 Norph/ Shutterstock; Page 3 Photos.com; Page 3 © Carlos Alvarez/istockphoto; Page 3 Digital Vision/Jupiter Images; Page 5 FancyVeerSet6/Alamy Images; Page 7 (Top) German Information Center; Page 7 (Bottom) Nancy R. Cohen/Getty Images, Inc.-Photodisc./Royalty Free; Page 8 Archives of the History of American Psychology - The University of Akron; Page 9 Clark University Archives; Page 10 Getty Images Inc. - Hulton Archive Photos; Page 11 (Top) CORBIS-NY; Page 11 (Bottom) © Underwood & Underwood/CORBIS All Rights Reserved; Page 12 G. Paul Bishop; Page 14 Nina Leen/Getty Images/Time Life Pictures; Page 16 "Courtesy, Dr. Arthur W. Toga, Laboratory of Neuro Imaging"; Page 17 © Peter Barrett/CORBIS All Rights Reserved; Page 18 Bill Aron/ PhotoEdit Inc.; Page 20 Paula Solloway/Photolibrary.com; Page 22 Cyril Ruoso/Photolibrary/Peter Arnold, Inc.; Page 23 (Top) Jeff Greenberg/The Image Works; Page 23 (Bottom) The Warren Anatomical Museum, Francis A. Countway Library of Medicine, Harvard Medical School; Page 24 ©The New Yorker Collection 1989 George Price from cartoonbank.com. All Rights Reserved; Page 27 ©The New Yorker Collection 1994 Leo Cullum from cartoonbank.com. All Rights Reserved; Page 28 Bill Aron/PhotoEdit Inc.; Page 30 © John Henley/CORBIS All Rights Reserved; Page 32 © Peter M. Fisher/CORBIS All Rights Reserved; Page 33 ©2000 Tom Chalkley from cartoonbank.com. All Rights Reserved; Page 37 © Jack Barker/Alamy.

Chapter 2

Page 44 © androfroll/istockphoto; Page 45 (Left, Right) PASIEKA/SPL; Page 45 (Center) Patrik Giardino/Riser/Getty Images; Page 47 STEVE GSCHMEISSNER/SPL/Alamy Images Royalty Free; Page 52 Secchi-Lecaque/Roussel-UCLAF/CNRI/Science Photo Library/Photo Researchers, Inc.; Page 53 C.ALLAN MORGAN/Photolibrary/Peter Arnold, Inc.; Page 57 Image Source/Jupiter Images Royalty Free; Page 58 Newscom; Page 60 Peter Hvizdak/The Image Works; Page 61 Philippe Millereau/Newscom; Page 63 Paul Collis CC/Alamy Images; Page 66 Richard T. Nowitz/Photo Researchers, Inc.; Page 67 (Top Left) Noland White/Noland White, Ph.D.; Page 67 (Top Right) Noland White/Noland White, Ph.D.; Page 67 (Bottom Left) Professor Noland White; Page 67 (Bottom Right) Professor Noland White; Page 68 (Left) Courtesy of (insert name); Page 68 Mark Herreid/Shutterstock; Page 68 (Center) Mediscan/Alamy Images; Page 68 (Right) Philippe Psaila/Photo Researchers, Inc.; Page 70 © Moodboard/CORBIS All Rights Reserved; Page 72 (Top) Vladislav Sabanov/Shutterstock; Page 72 (Bottom) Noland White, Ph.D.; Page 75 © Bettmann/CORBIS All Rights Reserved; Page 76 © George Simian/CORBIS All Rights Reserved; Page 77 Marcello Santos/Getty Images - Photodisc-Royalty Free.

Chapter 3

Page 89 © Alexander Kosarev/istockphoto; Page 89 © Monika Adamczyk/istockphoto; Page 89 © Le Do/istockphoto; Page 89 © Anja Jerin/istockphoto; Page 89 © androfroll/istockphoto; Page 89 Valentin Agapov/Shutterstock; Page 89 androfroll/Shutterstock; Page 89 (Center) DK Stock/Robert Glenn/Getty Images; Page 91 (Top) eurekaimages.com/Alamy Images; Page 91 (Bottom) © Beth Dixson/Solus-Veer/CORBIS All Rights Reserved; Page 95 (Top) Noland White/Noland White, Ph.D.; Page 95 (Bottom) Photo Researchers, Inc.; Page 97 (Top) Bryan Allen/CORBIS - NY; Page 97 (Bottom) Fritz Goro/Contributor/Getty Images/Time Life Pictures; Page 101 ©The New Yorker Collection 1998 Charles Barsotti from cartoonbank.com. All Rights Reserved; Page 104 CORBIS- NY; Page 106 Omikron/Photo Researcher, Inc.; Page 108 Robin Sachs/PhotoEdit Inc.; Page 109 AP Wide World Photos; Page 110 © Vince Streano/CORBIS All Rights Reserved; Page 115 (Top Left) Grant V. Faint/Image Bank/Getty Images, Inc.; Page 115 (Top Right) Robin Smith/Photolibrary.com; Page 115 (Bottom Left) Shaen Adey © Dorling Kindersley; Page 115 (Bottom Right) Tom Mareschal/Creative Eye/MIRA.com; Page 118 Larry Landolfi/Photo Researchers, Inc.; Page 120 David Wells/The Image Works; Page 122 Chris Connor/Newscom.

Chapter 4

Page 129 (Center) Digital Vision/Jupiter Images; Page 129 (Bottom Left) androfroll/Shutterstock; Page 129 (Bottom Left) Galushko Sergey/Shutterstock; Page 129 (Bottom Left) Paul Maguire/Shutterstock; Page 129 (Center Right) Ralf Juergen Kraft/Shutterstock; Page 129 (Center Right) Binkski/Shutterstock; Page 129 (Bottom Right) R-studio/Shutterstock; Page 129 (Top Center) Norph/Shutterstock; Page 129 (Top) Photos.com; Page 129 (Top Right) © Carlos Alvarez/istockphoto; Page 131 (Top) © Sunny S. Unal/Value RM/CORBIS All Rights Reserved; Page 131 (Bottom) © Tim Pannell/CORBIS All Rights Reserved; Page 133 (Top) SW Productions/Getty Images, Inc.- Photodisc./Royalty Free; Page 133 (Bottom) David Tejada/Tejada Photography, Inc.; Page 134 Stephen Frink/CORBIS- NY; Page 139 (Top) © Charles Gullung/Zefa/CORBIS All Rights Reserved; Page 139 (Bottom) © Mark Seelen/Zefa/CORBIS All Rights Reserved; Page 140 (Top) Pool/Getty Images, Inc.; Page 140 (Bottom) ©The New Yorker Collection J. Dator from cartoonbank.com. All Rights Reserved; Page 141 © Envision/CORBIS All Rights Reserved; Page 142 *www.CartoonStock.com*; Page 144 (Top) © Sven Hagolani/Zefa/CORBIS All Rights Reserved; Page 144 (Bottom) ©The New Yorker Collection 1973 Dana Fradon from cartoonbank.com. All Rights Reserved; Page 148 © Bettmann/CORBIS All Rights Reserved; Page 151 © Firefly Productions/CORBIS All Rights Reserved; Page 152 The Granger Collection, New York; Page 153 Michael Newman/PhotoEdit Inc.; Page 154 (Top) © Thinkstock/CORBIS All Rights Reserved; Page 154 (Bottom) Newscom; Page 155 © Ashley Cooper/CORBIS All Rights Reserved; Page 159 Burke/Tiolo/Brand X/Jupiter Images Royalty Free; Page 160 Lee Powers/Photo Researchers, Inc.; Page 162 Shutterstock.

Chapter 5

Page 169 (Center) Erik Lam/Shutterstock; Page 169 (Left) Frank Gaglione/Getty; Page 169 (Top) © jclegg/istockphoto; Page 169 (Top Right) © jclegg/istockphoto; Page 169 (Top Left) © Jill Fromer/istockphoto; Page 169 (Center) Keith Bell/Shutterstock; Page 169 (Bottom Center) © androfroll/istockphoto; Page 169 (Center) © androfroll/istockphoto; Page 169 (Bottom Right) Erik Lam/Shutterstock; Page 170 NEIGHBORHOOD © KING FEATURES SYNDICATE; Page 171 © CORBIS; Page 172 (Top) Shelley Rotner/Omni-Photo Communications, Inc.; Page 172 (Bottom) Dagmar Ehling/Photo Researchers, Inc.; Page 177 (Top) Professor Ben Harris, University of New Hampshire; Page 177 (Bottom) © Jim West/Alamy Images; Page 178 Frank Greenaway © Dorling Kindersley, Courtesy of the Natural History Museum, London; Page 181 Nena Leen/Getty Images/Time Life Pictures; Page 184 © The New Yorker Collection

2005 Joe Dator from cartoonbank.com. All Rights Reserved; Page 186 Chris Rogers/Twilight Productions; Page 187 Noel Hendrickson/Blend Images/Corbis RF; Page 188 David Young-Wolff/PhotoEdit Inc.; Page 192 © Syracuse Newspapers/David Lassman/The Image Works, Inc.; Page 193 (Top) Nancy Richmond/The Image Works; Page 193 (Bottom) Bonnie Kamin/PhotoEdit Inc.; Page 197 © The New Yorker Collection 2000 Pat Byrnes from cartoonbank.com. All Rights Reserved; Page 199 SuperStock, Inc.; Page 201 Albert Bandura, Stanford University; Page 205 (Top) Karawynn Long; Page 205 (Bottom) Karawynn Long.

Chapter 6

Page 213 PunchStock - Royalty Free; Page 213 Digital Zoo/Getty Images, Inc.; Page 213 Elena Schweitzer/Shutterstock; Page 213 Image copyright NEUMIARZHYTSKI VALERY, 2010. Used under license from Shutterstock.com; Page 213 Image copyright NEUMIARZHYTSKI VALERY, 2010. Used under license from Shutterstock.com; Page 213 Image copyright Amid, 2010. Used under license from Shutterstock.com; Page 215 Eric Williams; Page 218 Gjon Mili/Getty Images, Inc.; Page 219 © Bob Krist/CORBIS All Rights Reserved; Page 220 Norbert von der Groeben/The Image Works; Page 221 Laura Dwight/PhotoEdit Inc.; Page 222 Kathy Ferguson-Johnson/PhotoEdit Inc.; Page 224 © Will & Deni Mcintyre/CORBIS All Rights Reserved; Page 225 Corbis RF; Page 229 (Top) Michael Newman/PhotoEdit Inc.; Page 229 (Bottom) Reprinted with special permission of King Features Syndicate; Page 231 © Rainer Holz/Zefa/CORBIS All Rights Reserved; Page 232 ©The New Yorker Collection 1988 Lee Lorenz from cartoonbank.com. All Rights Reserved; Page 233 Siner Jeff/The Charlotte Observer; Page 234 Newscom; Page 236 Ryan McVay/Photodisc/Getty Images; Page 237 © Ron Chapple/CORBIS All Rights Reserved; Page 240 Richard Lord/The Image Works; Page 243 (Top) Image of Henry Molaison. Copyright © Suzanne Corkin, used with permission of The Wylie Agency LLC.; Page 243 (Bottom) © Lacy Atkins/San Francisco Chronicle/CORBIS All Rights Reserved; Page 246 © Roger Ressmeyer/CORBIS All Rights Reserved.

Chapter 7

Page 253 (Center) Dex Image/Jupiter Images Royalty Free; Page 253 Andrey Burmakin/Shutterstock; Page 253 © foto-ruhrgebiet/istockphoto; Page 253 Andrey Burmakin/Shutterstock; Page 253 EtiAmmos/Shutterstock; Page 253 Erica Truex/Shutterstock; Page 255 J. Noland White, Ph.D; Page 256 © Phil Banko/CORBIS All Rights Reserved; Page 257 Dave Watts/Nature Picture Library; Page 258 Laura Dwight Photography; Page 259 (Top) © Simon Marcus/CORBIS All Rights Reserved; Page 259 (Bottom) Brigette Sullivan/Outer Focus Photos/Alamy Images; Page 263 Hector Mata/AP Wide World Photos; Page 264 © George Steinmetz/CORBIS All Rights Reserved; Page 265 © (Photographer)/CORBIS All Rights Reserved; Page 266 David Grossman/Photo Researchers, Inc.; Page 267 Eastcott-Momatiuk/The Image Works; Page 272 Ian Cumming/The Photo Library; Page 277 Randy Olson/Aurora Photos, Inc.; Page 278 (Top) United Media/United Feature Syndicate, Inc.; Page 278 (Bottom) Courtesy Stanford University Archives; Page 281 Mark Richards/PhotoEdit Inc.; Page 283 © Karen Kasmauski/CORBIS All Rights Reserved; Page 286 © Carson Ganci/Design Pics/Corbis; Page 288 Replace on Revision.

Chapter 8

Page 297 (Center) Trinette Reed/Blend Images/Getty Images; Page 297 (Center) Alexander Vasilyev/Shutterstock; Page 297 (Left) Ron Krisel/Getty; Page 297 (Right) Masterfile; Page 297 (Left-Right) C Squared Studios/Getty Images, Inc.-Photodisc./Royalty Free; Page 297 (Bottom) Dan Ionut Popescu/Shutterstock; Page 300 (Top) © Jim Sugar/CORBIS All Rights Reserved; Page 300 (Bottom) Digital Art/CORBIS- NY; Page 301 ©Thaves. Reprinted by permission; Page 302 CNRI/Science Photo Library/Photo Researchers, Inc.; Page 305 Steve Wewerka; Page 305 (Top Right, Bottom) Courtesy of Abby and Brittany Hensel; Page 306 (Left) Photo Lennart Nilsson/Bonnier Alba AB, A CHILD IS BORN, Dell Publishing Company; Page 306 (Center) Photo Lennart Nilsson/Bonnier Alba AB, A CHILD IS BORN, Dell Publishing Company; Page 306 (Right) Lennart Nilsson/Scanpix Sweden AB; Page 307 Chad Ehlers/Alamy Images; Page 309 (Top Left) Bloomimage/Corbis RF; Page 309 (Top Center) Mimi Forsyth; Page 309 (Top Right) E. Crews/The Image Works; Page 309 (Bottom Left) Laura Dwight/Laura Dwight Photography; Page 309 (Bottom Right) Laura Elliott/Jupiter Images Royalty Free; Page 310 Mark Richards/PHOTOEDIT; Page 311 (Top Left) Dave King © Dorling Kindersley; Page 311 (Top Center) Elizabeth Crews/Elizabeth Crews Photography; Page 311 (Top Right) Geri Engberg/Geri Engberg Photography; Page 311 (Bottom Left) Kathleen Sleys; Page 311 (Bottom Center) Jo Foord © Dorling Kindersley; Page 311 (Bottom Right) Jo Foord © Dorling Kindersley; Page 314 Laura Dwight/Laura Dwight Photography; Page 315 Dennis MacDonald/PhotoEdit Inc.; Page 316 Mike Good © Dorling Kindersley; Page 317 Saturn Still/Science Photo Library/Photo Researchers, Inc.; Page 320 © Kayoco/zefa/CORBIS All Rights Reserved; Page 321 Harry F. Harlow/Harlow Primate Laboratory/University of Wisconsin; Page 325 © King Features Syndicate. Reprinted with special permission of King Features Syndicate; Page 327 Michael Gibson/Paramont Pictures/CORBIS- NY; Page 331 Voisin/Photo Researchers, Inc.; Page 334 Mike Greenlar/The Image Works; Page 335 Yadid Levy/Alamy Images.

Chapter 9

Page 343 (Top Left) androfroll/Shutterstock; Page 343 (Top Right) © Konstantin Yuganov/istockphoto; Page 343 (Center Left) PunchStock - Royalty Free; Page 343 (Center Right) Regine Mahaux/Image Bank/Getty Images; Page 344 ©The New Yorker Collection 1981 Michael Maslin from cartoonbank.com. All Rights Reserved; Page 346 (Left) Dynamic Graphics, Inc; Page 346 (Right) Phil Schermeister/Photolibrary/Peter Arnold, Inc.; Page 347 © Rick Maiman/Corbis Sygma; Page 348 David Roth/Stone/Getty Images; Page 350 (Top) benng/Shutterstock; Page 350 (Bottom) Suzanne Szasz/Photo Researchers, Inc.; Page 353 David Young-Wolff/PhotoEdit Inc.; Page 354 ©The New Yorker Collection 1986 Lee Lorenz from cartoonbank.com. All Rights Reserved; Page 356 Dr. Neal E. Miller, Yale University; Page 357 (Top) Ryan McVay/Getty Images, Inc.; Page 357 (Bottom) Trinette Reed/CORBIS- NY; Page 358 altrendo images/Getty Images; Page 359 Michael Newman/PhotoEdit Inc.; Page 363 (Top Left) Barbara Penoya/Getty Images, Inc.- Photodisc./Royalty Free; Page 363 (Top Center) © Morgan David de Lossy/CORBIS All Rights Reserved; Page 363 (Top Right) © Pixland/CORBIS All Rights Reserved; Page 363 (Bottom Left) © Guido Alberto Rossi/TIPS Images; Page 363 (Bottom Center) Chris Carroll/CORBIS-NY; Page 363 (Bottom Right) Cheryl Casey/Shutterstock; Page 368 Jack Hollingsworth/Getty Images, Inc. - Photodisc./Royalty Free; Page 371 Lourens Smak/Alamy Images.

Chapter 10

Page 376 (Top) © Stefanie Timmermann/istockphoto; Page 376 (Bottom) © Zee/Alamy; Page 377 © itographer/istockphoto; Page 377 Geoff Brightling/Peter Minister - modelmaker © Dorling Kindersley; Page 377 (Top) C Squared Studios/Getty; Page 377 (Top Center) © D. Hurst/Alamy; Page 377 (Top Right) BBS United/Getty; Page 377 (Left) Shutterstock; Page 377 (Right) © Stefanie Timmermann/istockphoto; Page 377 (Center) Image Source/Jupiter Images; Page 379 Mark Richards/PhotoEdit Inc.; Page 381 Photo Response; Page 382 (Top) © The New Yorker Collection 1995 Robert Mankoff from cartoonbank.com. All Rights Reserved; Page 382 (Bottom) Ellen Senisi; Page 385 © Ariel Skelley/CORBIS All Rights Reserved; Page 386 beyond/Oscar Abrahams/Alamy Images Royalty Free; Page 387 (Top) ©The New Yorker Collection 1995 Donald Reilly from cartoonbank.com. All Rights Reserved; Page 387 (Bottom) Pixtal/Superstock Royalty Free; Page 390 Ira Wyman/CORBIS- NY; Page 393 Wallace Kirkland/Getty Images/Time Life Pictures; Page 394 © Kimberly White/Reuters/CORBIS All Rights Reserved; Page 398 Cynthia Johnson/Getty Images/Time Life Pictures; Page 399 ©Sam Sharpe/The Sharpe Image/CORBIS All Rights Reserved; Page 400 Dwayne Newton/PhotoEdit Inc.; Page 401 (Top) Rachel Epstein/PhotoEdit Inc.; Page 401 (Bottom) Bill Aron/PhotoEdit Inc.

Chapter 11

Page 409 (Top) Giantstep Inc./Image Bank/Getty Images; Page 409 (Center) Image Source/Getty Images; Page 409 (Bottom) Ian Sanderson/Photographer's Choice/Getty Images; Page 411 Robert Harbison; Page 415 Chip Simons/Getty Images, Inc.; Page 417 Stockbroker/Alamy Images Royalty Free; Page 418 Corbis RF; Page 419 Kablonk/Purestock/Superstock Royalty Free; Page 427 ©The New Yorker Collection 1983 Mischa Richter from cartoonbank.com. All Rights Reserved; Page 429 ©The New Yorker Collection 1987 Donald Reilly from cartoonbank.com. All Rights Reserved; Page 430 Ronnie Kaufman/CORBIS- NY; Page 433 © Nathan Benn/CORBIS; Page 434 Gary Conner/PhotoEdit Inc.; Page 435 © David Pollack/CORBIS All Rights Reserved; Page 436 [Photographer]/Stone/Getty Images; Page 437 © Solus-Veer/CORBIS All Rights Reserved;

Page 438 Victor Englebert/Photo Researchers, Inc.; Page 440 Getty Images - Stockbyte, Royalty Free.

Chapter 12
Page 447 (Left) BLOOMimage/Getty Images; Page 447 (Right) WIN-Initiative/Getty Images, Inc.; Page 447 (Left-Right) © Tommaso Colia/istock-photo; Page 449 ©The New Yorker Collection 2003 Alex Gregory from cartoonbank.com. All Rights Reserved; Page 450 Ho New/Reuters Limited; Page 454 Archives of the History of American Psychology; Page 456 © Bettmann/-CORBIS All Rights Reserved; Page 459 neal and molly jansen/Alamy Images Royalty Free; Page 460 DR. NORA VOLKOW/Newscom; Page 461 Tim Pannell/Corbis RF; Page 465 © Reuters New Media Inc./CORBIS; Page 469 (Top) CORBIS- NY; Page 469 (Bottom) ©The New Yorker Collection 2002 Charles Barsotti from cartoonbank.com. All Rights Reserved; Page 470 Allan Tannnbaum/ZUMA Press - Gamma; Page 471 Image Source/Superstock Royalty Free; Page 472 Bill Aron/PhotoEdit Inc.; Page 479 Philip G. Zimbardo, Inc.; Page 480 Exclusive to The Washington Post/EPA; Page 484 CORBIS- NY.

Chapter 13
Page 493 (Top Left) Emilio Simion/PhotoDisc/Getty Images; Page 493 (Top Center) Riko Pictures/Digital Vision/Getty Images, Inc.; Page 493 (Top Right) ColorBlind Images/Iconica/Getty Images, Inc.; Page 493 (Bottom Left) Reggie Casagrande/Digital Vision/Getty Images; Page 493 (Bottom Center) Margo Silver/Riser/Getty Images; Page 493 (Bottom Right) Hill Creek Pictures/UpperCut Images/Getty Images; Page 495 Bjanka Kadic/Alamy Images; Page 499 © Brigitte Sporrer/CORBIS All Rights Reserved; Page 502 Clearviewstock/Alamy Images; Page 507 (Top) Andresr/Shutterstock; Page 507 (Bottom) ©The New Yorker Collection 1990 Peter Steiner from cartoonbank.com. All Rights Reserved; Page 509 Photographer/Alamy Images; Page 510 ©The New Yorker Collection 1994 Lee Lorenz from cartoonbank.com. All Rights Reserved; Page 514 Bob Sacha Photography; Page 519 Noland White, Ph.D.

Chapter 14
Page 531 (Center Top) GoodMood Photo/Shutterstock; Page 531 (Center) Photodisc/Getty Images; Page 531 (Center Bottom) StudioSmart/Shutterstock; Page 533 (Top) American Museum of Natural History; Page 533 (Bottom) Enigma/Alamy Images; Page 534 David R. Frazier Photolibrary, Inc./Alamy Images; Page 535 Getty Images, Inc.; Page 539 © Alan Schein Photography/CORBIS All Rights Reserved; Page 542 (Top) © Janet Street/Images.com/CORBIS All Rights Reserved; Page 542 (Bottom) © Owen Franken/CORBIS All Rights Reserved; Page 543 *www.CartoonStock.com*; Page 544 © (Photographer)/CORBIS All Rights Reserved; Page 545 © B. Bird/Zefa/CORBIS All Rights Reserved; Page 548 © M. Deutsch/Zefa/CORBIS All Rights Reserved; Page 550 © Charles Platiau/Reuters/CORBIS All Rights Reserved; Page 554 Elaine Thompson/AP Wide World Photos; Page 557 Joerg Carstensen/Newscom; Page 558 Larry Brownstein/Ambient Images/Newscom.

Chapter 15
Page 573 (Top) Pling/Shutterstock; Page 573 (Top Center) Erica Truex/ Shutterstock; Page 573 (Left) Marc Dietrich/Shutterstock; Page 573 (Center) Image Source/Getty Images; Page 573 (Bottom Right) Norph/Shutterstock; Page 575 Charles Ciccione/Photo Researchers, Inc.; Page 576 ©The New Yorker Collection 1990. Arnie Levin from cartoonbank.com. All Rights Reserved; Page 577 © Tom Stewart/CORBIS All Rights Reserved; Page 578 Zigy Kaluzny/Getty Images Inc. - Stone Allstock; Page 580 Jaqui Farrow/Alamy Images; Page 582 (Top) ScienceCartoonsPlus.com; Page 582 (Bottom) Lester Sloan/Woodfin Camp & Associates, Inc.; Page 584 Bob Daemmrich/The Image Works; Page 587 George Dodson/Pearson Education/PH College; Page 588 Jim Bates/KRT/Newscom; Page 592 © Mike Twohy/The New Yorker Collection/*www.cartoonbank.com*. All Rights Reserved; Page 593 ©The New Yorker Collection 1999 Barbara Smaller from cartoonbank.com. All Rights Reserved; Page 594 Reprinted with special permission of King Features Syndicate; Page 599 P. Berndt/Custom Medical Stock Photo/Custom Medical Stock Photo/Newscom; Page 600 © Bettmann/CORBIS All Rights Reserved; Page 601 Noland White, Ph.D.; Page 603 (Left) Charles Vandermast, Delft University of Technology; Page 601 (Right) Charles Vandermast, Delft University of Technology; Page 573 (Center) Image Source/Getty Images.

Appendix B
Page B-3 Michal Heron/Michal Heron Photography; Page B-4 Peace Corps; Page B-5 David Young-Wolff/PhotoEdit Inc.; Page B-7 Will & Deni McIntyre/Science Source/Photo Researchers, Inc.; Page B-8 (Top) Laura Dwight/PhotoEdit Inc.; Page B-8 (Bottom) Erika Schultz/Seattle Times/MCT/Newscom; Page B-10 Brian Smith/Brian Smith, Photographer; Page B-11 (Top) Courtesy of AT&T Archives and History Center, Warren, NJ; Page B-11 (Bottom) Journal Inquirer, Jim Michaud/AP Wide World Photos; Page B-13 Dan McCoy/Rainbow Image Library.

TEXT CREDITS

Chapter 1
Page 17, Fig. 1-2a From Tsapogas, J. Project Officer. 2006. Characteristics of Doctoral Scientists and Engineers in the United States: 2003, NSF 06320. Arlington, VA: National Science Foundation, Division of Science Resources Statistics. *http://www.nsf.gov/statistics/nsf06320/*.

Chapter 3
Page 119, Fig. 3-21 Courtesy of Dr. Akiyoshi Kitaoka, Ritsumeikan University; Page 120, Fig. 3-22 Courtesy of Jorge Otero Millan, Barrow Neurological Institute.

Chapter 4
Page 134, Fig. 4-1 Figure 1, "Sleep Patterns of Infants and Adults" from "Ontogenetic Development of the Human Sleep Dream Cycle" by H. P. Roffwarg, J. N. Muzio, and W. C. Dement, Science, (1966), 152, pp. 604 619 Copyright © 1966 by American Association for the Advancement of Science. Reprinted by permission; Page 135, Fig. 4-2 "EEG Results of Brain Activity During both Waking and Sleeping". Courtesy of Dr. Leslie Sherlin; Page 137, Fig. 4-3 From PSYCHOLOGY 4th edition by Saul M. Kassin. (Prentice Hall, 2004). Reprinted by permission of the author; Page 147, Table 4-2 Reprinted from HYPNOTIC SUSCEPTIBILITY by E. Hilgard (Harcourt, Brace & World, 1965). Courtesy of Henry Hilgard; Page 154, Table 4-4 Barone and Roberts (1996); Page 156, Table 4-5 Adapted from MODERATE DRINKING SKILLS STUDY GUIDE published in 2004 by University of Wisconsin Eau Claire Counseling Services. Reprinted by permission.

Chapter 5
Page 174, Fig. 5-2 From Hovland, C.I. "The Generalization of Conditioned Responses: IV. The Effects of Varying Amounts of Reinforcement upon the Degree of Generalization of Conditioned Responses" in Journal of Experimental Psychology, (1937), 21, 261 276; Page 199, Fig. 5-10 "Introduction and Removal of Reward and Maze Learning in Rats" by E. C. Tolman and C. H. Honzik, University of California Publications in Psychology (1930), 4, 257 275.

Chapter 6
Page 230, Fig. 6-7 "Context Dependent Memory in Two Natural Environments: On Land and Underwater" by D. R. Godden and A. D. Baddeley, British Journal of Psychology (1975), 66, 325 331. copyright © 1975. Reprinted by permission of The British Psychological Society; Page 240, Fig. 6-10 From "Long Term Memory for a Common Object" by R. S. Nickerson & J. J. Adams, Cognitive Psychology, (1979), 11, 287 307. Copyright © 1979. Reprinted by permission of Elsevier.

Chapter 7
Page 255, Fig. 7-1 From "Visual Images Preserve Metric Spatial Information: Evidence from Studies of Image Scanning" by S. M. Kosslyn, T. M. Ball, and B. J. Reiser, Journal of Experimental Psychology: Human Perception and Performance (1978) 4, 47 60. Published by American Psychological Association; Page 257, Table 7-1 Adapted from p. 575 in "Family Resemblances: Studies in the Internal Structures of Categories" by E. Rosch and C. Mervis, Cognitive Psychology, (1975) 7, 573 605. Published by Elsevier; Page 269, Table 7-5 From WECHSLER ADULT INTELLIGENCE SCALE Third Edition (WAIS III) by David Wechsler. Copyright © 1997 by NCS Pearson, Inc. Page 272, Table 7-6 Table, "Sample of the Dove Counterbalance General Intelligence Test" in PSYCHOLOGICAL TESTING AND ASSESSMENT 10th edition by Lewis R. Aiken. Copyright © 2000 by Allyn & Bacon. Reprinted by permission of Pearson Education, Inc. Page 277, Table 7-7 Reprinted with permission from the Diagnostic

and Statistical Manual of Mental Disorders, Fourth Edition, Text Revision, (Copyright 2000). American Psychiatric Association.

Chapter 8

Page 306, Table 8-2 From CATALOG OF TERATOGENIC AGENTS 10th edition by Thomas H. Shepard, M.D. Copyright © by The Johns Hopkins University Press. Adapted with permission of The Johns Hopkins University Press.

Chapter 9

Page 350, Table 9-1 AZuckerman Kuhlman Personality Questionaire (ZKQPP: An Alternative Five Factorial Model) in B. De Raad and M. Perugini, eds. BIG FIVE ASSESSMENT (Cambridge: Hogrefe & Huber, 2002). Reprinted by permission of Hogrefe Publishing; Page 352, Table 9-3 From MOTIVATION AND PERSONALITY 3rd edition by Abraham H. Maslow, edited by Robert D. Frager & James Fadiman. Copyright © 1987. Printed and electronically reproduced by permission of Pearson Education, Inc., Upper Saddle River, NJ 07458.

Chapter 10

Page 392, Table 10-1 Use of "The Heterosexual/Homosexual Rating Scale" from SEXUAL BEHAVIOR IN THE HUMAN MALE (W. B. Saunders, 1948). Table of statements from SEXUAL BEHAVIOR IN THE HUMAN FEMALE and THE KINSEY DATA (W. B. Saunders, 1979). Reprinted by permission of The Kinsey Institute for Research in Sex, Gender, and Reproduction, Inc. Page 393, Table 10-2 Reported in THE KINSEY DATA: Marginal Tabulations of 1938 1963 Interviews Conducted by the Institute for Sex Research by P. H. Gebhard & A. B. Johnson. Copyright © 1979, 1998. W. B. Saunders. Page 395, Table 10-3 From THE PRINCETON REVIEW'S SEX ON CAMPUS by Leland Elliott and Cynthia Brantley. Copyright © 1997 by The Princeton Review Publishing, L.L.C. Used by permission of Random House, Inc.

Chapter 11

Page 413, Table 11-1 Holmes, T. H. & Rahe, R. H. (1967). The Social Readjustment Scale. Journal of Psychosomatic Research 11, 213 218. Copyright © 1967 by American Psychological Association; Page 414, Table 11-2 From Renner, M. J. & Mackin, R. S. (1998). A life stress instrument for classroom use. Teaching of Psychology, 25, 47. Copyright © 1998. Reprinted by permission of Copyright Clearance Center on behalf of Taylor & Francis Ltd.

Chapter 12

Page 451, Table 12-1 Adaptation of Table 10.1, "Symptoms of Groupthink" from GROUPTHINK: Psychological Studies of Policy Decisions and Fiascoes 2nd edition by Janis. Copyright © 1982 by Wadsworth, a part of Cengage Learning, Inc. Reproduced by permission. *www.cengage.com/permissions*; Page 454, Table 12-2 Derived from Stanley (1964a/1974); Page 476, Table 12-5 Figure, "Sternberg's Triangular Theory of Love" from "Triangulating Love" by Robert Sternberg in THE PSYCHOLOGY OF LOVE ed. by M. Barnes. Copyright © 1987. Reprinted by permission of Yale University Press; Page 482, Table 12-6 Darley, J. M., & Latané, B. (1968). Bystander intervention in emergencies: Diffusion of responsibility. Journal of Personality and Social Psychology, 8, 377–383. Copyright © 1968 by the American Psychological Association.

Chapter 13

Page 506, Table 13-2 "Reciprocal Determinism" from SELF EFFICACY: The Exercise of Control by Albert Bandura. Copyright © 1997 by W. H. Freeman and Company. Used with permission; Page 511, Table 13-3 From PERSONALITY IN ADULTHOOD 2nd edition by Robert R. MacCrae and Paul T. Costa. Copyright © 1990 by Guilford Publications. Reprinted in format of Textbook by permission of Copyright Clearance Center on behalf of Guilford Publications. Page 511, Table 13-4 Figure depicting data relating to personality profiles for source traits for writers and airline pilots as developed by Cattell, Eber and Tatsuoka, HANDBOOK FOR THE SIXTEEN PERSONALITY FACTOR QUESTIONAIRE (16PF (R), Copyright © 1970, 1988, 1992 by the Institute for Personality and Ability Testing, IPAT Inc, Champaign, IL USA).

Chapter 14

Page 538, Table 14-1 Reprinted with permission from the Diagnostic and Statistical Manual of Mental Disorders, Fourth Edition, Text Revision, (Copyright 2000). American Psychiatric Association. Page 539, Table 14-2 Adapted from National Institutes of Health; Page 542, Table 14-3 Culbertson, F. (2003). The Phobia List. *www.phobialist.com*; Page 559, Fig. 14-3 Graph from "Genetics and Schizophrenia Incidence of Schizophrenia among Related and Unrelated Individuals" in SCHIZOPHRENIA GENESIS: The Origins of Madness edited by Irving I. Gottesman. Copyright © 1990 by Irving I. Gottesman. Reprinted by arrangement with Henry Holt and Company, LLC. Page 561, Table 14-5 Reprinted with permission from the Diagnostic and Statistical Manual of Mental Disorders, Fourth Edition, Text Revision, (Copyright 2000). American Psychiatric Association.

name index

C

E

F

G

H

T

U

V

W

subject index

D

E